# EMERGING FINANCIAL CENTERS

## Legal and Institutional Framework

Edited by
Robert C. Effros

Bahamas • Hong Kong • Ivory Coast
Kenya • Kuwait • Panama • Singapore

International Monetary Fund
Washington, D.C. 1982

# PREFACE

The nineteenth and early twentieth centuries saw the rise of great financial centers. It was a general rule that the countries in which these arose were characterized by powerful and growing economies. In the second half of the twentieth century a new phenomenon has made its appearance. Among the newly developing countries, a certain number are emerging as financial centers. However, unlike the experience of the older financial centers, these are not necessarily situated in the midst of great national economies. In a world characterized by instant communication and increasing mobility of funds, some of the emerging centers are, in fact, geographically distant from the principal sources and destinations of their funds.

This volume contains the chief financial legislation of seven developing financial centers. The legislation is, in each case, introduced by an essay analyzing the individual legal and institutional framework, as well as the particular experiences of the center. The volume will be of interest, not only to central bankers and those directly charged with charting the financial courses of their countries but to legislators, lawyers, economists, and others concerned with the mechanisms of financial service and growth.

The contents of this volume have been selected, assembled, and edited by Mr. Robert C. Effros, Assistant General Counsel for Legislation in the Fund's Legal Department, who has been closely associated with legislative drafting and legal advice on financial matters provided by the Fund to many of its member countries.

December 1982

J. DE LAROSIÈRE

*Managing Director*
*International Monetary Fund*

# FOREWORD

As provided in Article I of its Articles of Agreement, an important purpose of the International Monetary Fund is "To promote international monetary cooperation through a permanent institution which provides the machinery for consultation and collaboration in international monetary problems." In addition, Article VIII of these Articles provides that the Fund "shall act as a centre for the collection and exchange of information on monetary and financial problems, thus facilitating the preparation of studies designed to assist members in developing policies which further the purposes of the Fund."

The present volume is published by the Fund in line with these objectives. The editor of the volume, Mr. Robert C. Effros, is eminently qualified for this task. He has brought to the work the unique expertise that he has acquired since he joined the Fund's staff in 1963 and during the many years that he has been the member of the Legal Department responsible for central banking, commercial banking, and related legislation. It is hoped that the volume will be useful to government officials, bankers, lawyers, and others concerned with this subject.

December 1982

GEORGE P. NICOLETOPOULOS

*Director, Legal Department*
*International Monetary Fund*

# CONTENTS

Page

IVORY COAST (*continued*)

Page

# INTRODUCTION

The subject of this volume is the legal and institutional framework of the financial systems of seven developing societies. The entries have been selected with certain criteria in mind. Each is a burgeoning financial center. Countries from a number of different geographical areas, embodying distinct legal and social traditions, have been included for purposes of comparison.

While each is a success in its own right as a developing financial center, not every one is at the same stage of development. Nor is each invested with the same degree of international or regional significance. Some, like Hong Kong, Singapore, and Panama, have an effect well beyond their boundaries, while the importance of others, such as Kenya, is, as yet, largely national. The common feature of each, which sets it apart from neighboring countries in the area, is the sophistication and development of its financial institutions. In each, banks, insurance companies, specialized financial institutions, securities brokers, and the like, both local and foreign, offer a wide range of services to residents, and often to nonresidents as well.

The format for each entry commences with an essay to provide background and explanation concerning the financial system. This is followed by the monetary, central bank, and general banking laws. The entry concludes with selected laws of the main specialized financial institutions and any securities regulation laws that have been enacted.

An examination of the history and development of each financial center reveals numerous accidental circumstances and diverse causation. It would be astonishing if it were otherwise. The centers are scattered geographically, derive from dissimilar cultures, depend on different economic bases, and are politically heterogeneous.

Despite their obvious differences, these centers have had to confront certain common problems. Their evident success in dealing with similar challenges suggests that there may be some degree of commonality in their legislation and their experience. In searching for general principles, one must be careful not to expect identical solutions but rather to explore for similar treatment. The similarity, moreover, is likely to be greatest among those financial centers that have evolved furthest. To the extent that the centers have acquired international significance, it is likely that they will reflect more uniformity. This tendency may be expected insofar as such centers, in competition with one another and judged against more established international financial centers, must satisfy more rigorous criteria than those that reflect only the needs of the local banking system. In the final analysis, however, the laws and experience of each of the centers must be read on their own. Moreover, they must be read in the context of rapidly changing circumstances.

I should like to express my thanks to the writers of the introductory essays that provide indispensable background and explanation for the legislation of each of the financial centers included in this volume. My gratitude is also due to Miss O. Mary Price whose expert editorial assistance has been invaluable; to Mr. Norman Humphreys and Mr. Augustus Hooke whose patience and encouragement have been notable; to Mr. A. Touami for his able research assistance; and to Mrs. Alice Penalosa, my secretary, for her unfailing enthusiasm and technical competence in the preparation of this volume. I am also indebted to Mr. George Nicoletopoulos and Sir Joseph Gold, present and past Directors of the Legal Department, for the opportunity they have given me to undertake this work. I am beholden to correspondents in each of the financial centers and to the relevant financial authorities, each of whom has generously cooperated in this effort. Thanks are also due to the translators in the Bureau of Language Services who have faithfully rendered a number of pieces of complex legislation into English. The Graphics Section helped in many ways with the production process; the covers were designed by Mr. Hördur Karlsson. Finally, I am indebted to my wife and family for the support that they have given to me during the course of the work.

December 1982

ROBERT C. EFFROS

# Bahamas

Downtown Nassau from water tower
Courtesy Bahamas Tourist Office

# THE BAHAMAS

*Page*

# Financial System of the Bahamas

by

*Samuel J. Stephens* *

## Introduction

The Bahámas emerged as an international financial center during the 1960s, as foreign financial institutions established branches and subsidiaries in Nassau to handle transactions in the growing Eurodollar market. A number of factors have contributed to the success of the Bahamas in this field. These include (1) its tax-haven status (no income, capital gains, succession taxes, or associated withholding); (2) the commitment to secrecy which has been effectively enforced by the financial institutions and the Bahamian authorities; (3) preservation of an open economy and financial and political stability; (4) a well-developed communications system; and (5) the Bahamas' location in the same time zone as New York.

The evolution of the financial system has, to a large extent, been paralleled by legislation designed to give the authorities a greater degree of control over money and credit developments affecting the Bahamas. This is particularly evident in the three major legislative changes culminating in the 1974 law establishing the Central Bank of the Bahamas.

## The Currency Board

As in many former British colonies, the issuance of notes and coins was made the sole prerogative of a currency board, established under the Currency Board Act of 1919. The main principle underlying the operations of such boards was the requirement that the local currency be exchanged on demand for sterling in London, and vice versa, at a fixed rate of exchange between the two currencies that was embodied in the enabling legislation.

The Bahamas Currency Board began its operations in 1921, issuing and redeeming notes against sterling. To ensure convertibility on demand, the Board maintained a sterling asset cover for the note issue

---

* Mr. Stephens is an Assistant Division Chief in the Western Hemisphere Department of the International Monetary Fund and is a graduate of McGill University (Montreal, Canada).

Acknowledgement is made to Mr. Brian C. Stuart, who also contributed to the introduction to the Bahamas.

in a Currency Note Fund consisting of about one third in gold and silver coins and two thirds in sterling-denominated obligations of the United Kingdom and other sterling area countries, principally those in Africa. The Currency Note Fund could not fall below 100 per cent of the note issue, as any depreciation in the value of its assets, which could not include local assets, had by law to be met from the General Revenue of the Bahamas. The expenses of the Board were met from the Currency Note Income Account, while any surplus in this Account at the end of the year was transferred to the General Revenue, subject to the decision of the U.K. Secretary of State for Foreign and Commonwealth Affairs.

The Currency Board Act of 1919 was superseded by the Currency Board Act of 1965, which maintained all the essential features of currency boards. However, a significant new clause that had important monetary implications provided that the external backing of the local currency issue could be reduced from 100 per cent to 50 per cent. The remaining 50 per cent could be held in securities issued by the Government of the Bahamas. This provision for a fiduciary issue, coming as it did in 1965, was several years behind the analogous development in some other British colonies.

The Currency Board Act of 1965 provided for the decimalization of the Bahamian currency as well as for a change in its designation from the Bahamian pound to the Bahamian dollar. The currency retained its statutory link to sterling at a parity of 1 Bahamian dollar to 7 shillings sterling. Inasmuch as the par values of sterling and the U.S. dollar were based on gold under the Articles of Agreement of the International Monetary Fund, the Bahamian dollar also had a fixed relationship with the dollar (as well as with the currencies of other members of the Fund that maintained a par value). Exchange rates fluctuated within permissible margins.

Because of the statutory link to sterling, the Bahamian dollar was devalued automatically and to the same extent when the pound sterling was devalued on November 18, 1967. However, the Bahamian Government decided on November 25, by the Currency (Amendment) Act of 1967, to express the par value of the Bahamian dollar directly in terms of gold and to restore the former relationship between the Bahamian dollar and the U.S. dollar with retroactive effect from the moment of the devaluation of the pound sterling. In December 1971, when it was agreed that the U.S. dollar would be devalued by

7.89 per cent in relation to gold under the Smithsonian Agreement, the Bahamian dollar was devalued by a lesser percentage so that B$0.97 was equivalent to US$1. Experience with a premium of about 3 per cent of the Bahamian dollar against the U.S. dollar indicated that such a differential had many commercial and psychological disadvantages. When, therefore, the U.S. dollar was again devalued by 10 per cent in relation to gold in 1973, the Bahamian Government re-established the former relationship of B$1.00 = US$1.00.

At present the Bahamian dollar is pegged to the U.S. dollar, the intervention currency, at B$1 per US$1.00. The official buying and selling rates for the U.S. dollar are B$1.0025 and B$1.004, respectively, per US$1.00. Buying and selling rates for the pound sterling are also officially quoted, with the buying rate for the pound sterling based on the New York market mid-rate, and the selling rate 0.5 per cent above the buying rate. A stamp tax of 7 cents is applied to all outward remittances where the amount is B$30 or under. A further tax of 7 cents is levied on every additional B$30 or fraction thereof.

There is also a market in which "investment currency" may be negotiated between residents through the intermediacy of an investment currency dealer at freely determined rates, usually attracting a premium over the official market rate.

## Bahamas Monetary Authority

The realization that sterling and the dollar were not inextricably linked came at a time when somewhat more than 50 per cent of the Bahamian dollar deposit liabilities were covered by assets held abroad, mostly in sterling. This proved a costly way to emphasize the need for additional Bahamian dollar assets and, as far as the banks were concerned, the development of additional local assets was perhaps the most practical contribution that a monetary authority could make. Although the Currency Act of 1965 provided for a fiduciary issue, little use was made of that authority. It became increasingly evident that closer control over the financial system was essential. Accordingly, the Bahamas Monetary Authority was established under the Monetary Authority Act of 1968 and started operations in November of that year.

In addition to the issue and redemption of currency, the Monetary Authority was empowered to supervise banks and trust companies operating within the country and to administer exchange controls on behalf of the Government. The Authority was also enjoined to foster close relations between the banks themselves and between the banks and the Government, to advise the Government on banking and monetary matters and, in general, to perform such activities as might be necessary to fulfill these objectives. The Authority was fully owned by the Government with general administration and the formulation of policy the responsibility of a Board of Directors.

In both timing and objectives, the Monetary Authority was a way station between the Currency Board and a central bank. The traditional central bank's tools of monetary policy were outside its scope. However, its powers in respect of transactions in treasury bills removed it from a purely passive status.

The Monetary Authority was empowered to sell and rediscount domestic treasury bills, foreign bills of exchange, and treasury bills. It could also grant loans and advances to banks for fixed periods not exceeding six months on the security of specified assets. Nevertheless, the volume of its rediscounting remained small and no loans against treasury bills were ever made.

Although the Monetary Authority was not authorized to impose reserve requirements, it was able to enter into an agreement with the commercial banks on June 1, 1971 under which they undertook to maintain on average in the form of till cash or balances with the Authority the equivalent of not less than 5½ per cent of their Bahamian dollar deposit liabilities. At least 1 percentage point of this was to be held as deposit balances with the Authority. This pool of balances formed the basis of the new clearing system.

## Central Bank of the Bahamas

The third stage of monetary development began with the establishment of the Central Bank of the Bahamas. The enabling legislation, the Central Bank of the Bahamas Act, was passed on February 6, 1974, approved by the Senate on February 15, and agreed by the Governor-General on April 2, 1974. On June 1, 1974 the Central Bank commenced operation.

The Central Bank of the Bahamas Act, 1974 benefited not only from the experiences of older central banks but also from that of the Bahamas Monetary Authority which it superseded. The Act itself contains the usual provisions regarding the establishment and functions of the Bank, capital and reserves, the issuance and redemption of currency, and foreign exchange and external reserves. The major policy tools available to the Central Bank, covered in secs. 19–22 and secs. 24–27, are summarized below.

### *Reserve requirements*

As has already been noted, the commercial banks were not initially required to maintain any given ratio of cash or balances with the Monetary Authority, but, starting in June 1971, the seven clearing banks agreed to maintain on average in the form of cash or in balances with the Monetary Authority the equivalent of at least 5½ per cent of their total Bahamian dollar deposits and, within this percentage, to hold the equivalent of at least 1 per cent of total Bahamian dollar deposits in their accounts with the Authority.

By way of comparison, the Central Bank is empowered to fix and alter the percentage of deposit liabilities in Bahamian dollars that commercial banks must hold in cash or deposits (statutory reserve requirement) and in specified liquid assets (liquid asset reserve requirement). The Bank is authorized to vary the statutory reserve ratio between 5 per cent and 20 per cent, and to vary the liquid asset ratio between 10 per cent and 30 per cent; increases in these ratios may not exceed 5 percentage points in any period of 30 days. There is no express provision for marginal reserve requirements. The Central Bank also has the authority to establish the ratio of liquid assets held by commercial banks to their deposit liability in Bahamian dollars. This ratio may be varied within a range of 10 to 30 per cent. As in the case of the cash reserve ratio, any increase may not exceed 5 percentage points in any 30-day period. Liquid assets are defined to include, inter alia, money at call and demand balances held domestically, or abroad if in freely convertible currency. The provision is drafted to prevent the circumvention of the liquid asset requirements through the maintenance of reciprocal balances in the Bahamas. The penalty for a cash reserve deficiency is a fine not exceeding $^{1}/_{10}$ of 1 per cent of the amount of the deficiency for each day of noncompliance. Moreover, any commercial bank that does not keep with the Central Bank the required proportion of the statutory reserve or that fails to comply with the liquid reserve requirement is liable to a fine not exceeding B$1,500 for every day of noncompliance.

As of July 1, 1974 commercial banks were also instructed to maintain a liquid assets ratio of 20 per cent against demand deposits and 15 per cent against time and savings deposits. Liquid assets were defined as Bahamian notes and coins, balances with the Central Bank, net call and demand balances with other financial institutions in the Bahamas, treasury bills and other government securities, and net foreign assets (including foreign currency). The sum of these liquid assets held by the banks on March 31, 1974 was about 15 per cent above the ratio prescribed subsequent to that date.

The Bank issued a directive establishing as of July 1, 1974 a statutory reserve ratio of 5 per cent and limiting the amount of cash in till that may serve to fulfill the statutory reserve requirement to the equivalent of 1 per cent of deposit liabilities.

### *Credit control*

While the Monetary Authority had no powers in the area of credit control, the Central Bank may prescribe the maximum amounts of loans or advances that commercial banks may have outstanding, their purpose and maturity, and the security on which they are granted. The coverage of these requirements may be general or applicable to individual banks or specific types of loans and advances. However, the regulations in question may not go into effect earlier than 30 days after the date of their public announcement. The Bank has not yet issued any directives to the commercial banks in this respect.

### *Rediscounts, loans, and advances*

The Monetary Authority indicated its readiness from April 1971 to sell treasury bills from its portfolio, to rediscount bills for banks before maturity, and to lend for a minimum of several days against the collateral of treasury bills. Rediscounting operations took place at a rate ½ percentage point higher than the discount rate on the treasury bill issue of the particular month, except when the resulting rediscount rate was lower than the interbank lending rate. However, as previously noted, the volume of rediscounting was generally small and no loans were made against treasury bills. The Central Bank is authorized to sell and rediscount treasury bills and bills of exchange, promissory notes, or other credit instruments maturing within 180 days from the date of their acquisition by the Bank. It may also make loans and advances to any commercial bank with a maturity not to exceed 93 days on the security of a wide variety of documents.

### *Transactions with Government*

The Central Bank, unlike the Monetary Authority may make temporary advances to the Government. However, the total outstanding amount of advances may not exceed 10 per cent of either an historic annual average of ordinary revenue of the Government or that percentage of the ordinary revenue laid before Parliament in the estimates for the current fiscal year, whichever of the two is lower. For this purpose the historic annual average applies to the last 3 fiscal years for which the Government's accounts have been published, and ordinary revenue means all receipts other than loan proceeds, capital grants, and other receipts on capital account. The Central Bank may also purchase, hold, and sell treasury bills and publicly issued government and government-guaranteed securities maturing within 20 years from the date of their acquisition. However, the total amount of these longer-term securities (including those held as security for any loans and advances) should not exceed the equivalent of 20 per cent of the demand liabilities of the Bank.

## Financial Intermediaries

The rapid expansion in the number of commercial banks and trust companies during the early 1960s prompted the Bahamian Government to enact the Banks and Trust Companies Regulation Act in 1965. Prior to that law, commercial banks were required to obtain licenses under the Banks Act of 1909, while there were no license requirements for trust companies.

Under the Banks and Trust Companies Regulation Act, 1965, all commercial banks and trust companies must be licensed. Prescribed information and references must be submitted with applications for a license to the Minister of Finance. As a revenue measure, the law was amended in 1969 (Banks and Trust Companies (Amendment) Regulation) to provide for a licensing fee, the amount of which varies with the nature of the license. Provision is made for the issuance of several types of licenses.

There are no express statutory capital requirements. It is understood that in considering an application for a license the external affiliation of the applicant, to a large extent, determines the capitalization deemed necessary by the authorities.

The number of banks and trust companies licensed in the Bahamas rose from 37 in 1963 to 323 in 1973, and subsequently increased to 331 by December 1981. A majority of the financial institutions are licensed to deal with the general public although they must abide by special limitations concerning transactions with residents of the Bahamas. Some institutions are licensed to carry out activities limited to certain parties or are restricted to specific types of transactions. Others, registered as nonactive, are in liquidation or serve to prevent the use of a trade name by competitors. Of the 331 institutions licensed under the Banks and Trust Companies Regulation Act of 1965, 94 are nonactive or restricted to transactions with persons specified in the license.

Included among the 237 institutions licensed to deal with the general public are 124 branches of foreign banks operating as accounting centers for Euromarket operations initiated by their head offices or other branches. All these branches are nonresident for the purpose of exchange control. They are believed to account for a substantial amount of the offshore financial transactions channeled through the Bahamas. In this connection, it should be noted that while a substantial volume of transactions is recorded as occurring in the Bahamas, many of the offshore banks and trust companies have a very limited staff. Some even share a manager—whose responsibility is often limited to bookkeeping. Tax and other advantages are said to provide the main incentive for booking transactions through the Bahamas.

The remaining 113 banks and trust companies are incorporated in the Bahamas. Only 11 of these are allowed to operate in both domestic and foreign currencies. As authorized dealers in gold and foreign exchange, their transactions with residents are still subject to the limitations established by the exchange control regulations. Of the 11 authorized dealers, 7 are clearing banks. There are also 7 trust companies licensed as authorized agents that can act as custodians and dealers in foreign securities. In addition to providing regular domestic banking services, the authorized dealers and agents (which are all branches or subsidiaries of foreign banks) also operate in the Euromarket.

Of the 95 institutions that are not authorized dealers, 66 are subsidiaries of banks based outside the Bahamas and the rest are Bahamian-based banks and trust companies. Many of these institutions also operate in the Euromarket, but the volume of their operations is not known.

The Banks and Trust Companies Regulation Act, 1965 provides for an inspector (formerly the Permanent Secretary in the Ministry of Finance but, since 1974, the Central Bank) to carry out inspections of banks and trust companies when deemed expedient. The extent to which such inspections can be effected is circumscribed by a secrecy provision that has been regarded as one of the important contributory factors in the status of the Bahamas as an international financial center.

In recent years there have been a number of bank failures in the Bahamas. These failures fortunately have been limited to relatively small banks. Consideration has been given to tightening the requirements for licensing and to increasing the rigor of inspection. The dilemma which the authorities face, however, is that steps along these lines may be regarded as infringements upon the freedom of activities and the well-publicized attendant secrecy of transactions that have led to the successful proliferation of banking business in the Bahamas.

# The Central Bank of the Bahamas Act, 1974 [1]

An Act to provide for the establishment of a Central Bank; to repeal The Bahamas Monetary Authority Act, 1968; and for connected purposes.

[Assented to 2nd April, 1974]

BE it enacted by The Queen's Most Excellent Majesty, by and with the advice and consent of the Senate and the House of Assembly of the Commonwealth of The Bahamas, and by the authority of the same, as follows: —

## PART I. PRELIMINARY

**Short title and commencement.**

1.—(1) This Act may be cited as The Central Bank of The Bahamas Act, 1974, and, subject to subsection (2), the provisions thereof shall come into operation on such date or dates as the Governor-General may by notice published in the *Gazette* appoint for those provisions or any of them, and different dates may be so appointed for different purposes of those provisions.

(2) This section, section 2 and section 41 shall come into operation on the pass of this Act.

**Interpretation.**

2.—(1) In this Act unless the context otherwise requires—

"Authority" means the Bahamas Monetary Authority established by The Bahamas Monetary Authority Act, 1968;

"Bank" means the Central Bank of The Bahamas established by section 3:

"bank" means a financial institution lawfully carrying on banking business including the accepting of deposits of money withdrawable by cheque;

"banking business" means the business of accepting deposits of money which may be withdrawn or repaid on demand or after a fixed period or after notice, and employing those deposits in whole or in part by lending or otherwise investing them for the account and at the risk of the person accepting them; and "banker" shall be construed accordingly;

"Board" means the Board of Directors of the Bank provided for by subsection (4) of section 3;

[1] The original law, No. 3 of 1974, was assented to on April 2, 1974.

"coins" means coins of the currency of The Bahamas;

"commercial bank" means a bank licensed to carry on business in The Bahamas;

"company" means a company incorporated under any law in force whether in The Bahamas or elsewhere;

"director" means a member of the Board;

"financial institution" means an institution carrying on banking business;

"Financial Secretary" means the Financial Secretary of The Bahamas;

"Government" means the Government of The Bahamas;

"Minister" means the Minister of Finance;

"notes" means notes of the currency of The Bahamas;

"public corporation" means a body corporate established directly by statute for public purposes;

"securities" means shares, stocks, bonds, debentures or debenture stock;

"trust business" means the business of acting as trustee or executor and administrator;

"trust company" means a company carrying on trust business;

"year" means financial year of the Bank.

(2) Unless the contrary intention appears, references in this Act to a section are references to a section of this Act, and references in a section to a subsection are references to a subsection of that section.

## PART II. ESTABLISHMENT AND FUNCTIONS OF THE BANK

The Central Bank of The Bahamas

3.—(1) There shall be a bank, to be called "the Central Bank of The Bahamas" (in this Act referred to as "the Bank"), having the functions assigned to it by the following provisions of this Act.

(2) The Bank shall be a body corporate having perpetual succession and a common seal and, subject to the provisions of this Act, with power to acquire, hold and dispose of movable and immovable property of whatever kind and to enter into contracts and to do all things necessary for the purpose of its functions.

(3) The Bank may sue and be sued in its corporate name and may for all purposes be described by that name.

(4) There shall be a Board of Directors of the Bank, who, subject to the provisions of this Act, shall be responsible for the policy of the Bank and shall manage its affairs and business.

First Schedule.

(5) The provisions of the First Schedule shall have effect as to the Board of Directors and otherwise in relation to the Bank.

Places of business, etc.

4. The Bank shall have its principal place of business in the City of Nassau, and may in The Bahamas or elsewhere—

(*a*) establish and maintain such branch offices; and
(*b*) appoint such agents and correspondents,

as the Bank thinks fit.

The Bank's functions.

5.—(1) It shall be the duty of the Bank, subject to the provisions of this Act—

(*a*) to promote and maintain monetary stability and credit and balance of payments conditions conducive to the orderly development of the economy;
(*b*) in collaboration with the financial institutions, to promote and maintain adequate banking services and high standards of conduct and management therein;
(*c*) to advise the Minister on any matter of a financial or monetary nature referred by him to the Bank for its advice.

(2) The Bank shall, subject as aforesaid, have power to do anything, whether in The Bahamas or elsewhere, which is calculated to facilitate, or is incidental or conducive to, the discharge of its duty under subsection (1).

## PART III. CAPITAL AND RESERVES

Capital of the Bank.

6.—(1) The authorised capital of the Bank shall be three million dollars.

(2) Upon the establishment of the Bank there shall be transferred to the Bank from the Authority, in accordance with subsection (1) of section 40, the capital of the Authority as part of the capital of the Bank.

(3) Any capital required to make up the authorised capital of the Bank after taking into account the transfer provided for by subsection (2) shall be paid from the Consolidated Fund at such times and in such amounts as the Board, with the approval of the Minister, may determine.

General Reserve.

7.—(1) The Bank shall establish and maintain a General Reserve, to which, subject to the provisions of this section, at the end of each year the net profit of the Bank shall be credited (after the making of such deductions and allowances for other reserves and contingencies as the Bank may think fit) or the net loss incurred by the Bank debited, as the case may require.

(2) Whenever at the end of any year the amount in the General Reserve exceeds—

(*a*) twice the authorised capital of the Bank; or

(*b*) fifteen *per centum* of the demand liabilities of the Bank,

whichever is greater, then the amount of any such excess shall be paid over to the Consolidated Fund, unless the Minister otherwise determines.

## PART IV. CURRENCY

Currency of The Bahamas.

8.—(1) The currency of The Bahamas shall be the notes and coins issued by the Bank under the provisions of this Act.

(2) The unit of the said currency shall be the dollar, which shall be divided into one hundred cents.

Parity of the dollar.

9. The parity of the dollar shall be equivalent to 0.736662 grams of fine gold, so, however, that the Minister may, after consultation with the Bank, by order alter the said parity whether in terms of gold or any other standard.

Contracts, etc., deemed to be in Bahamian currency.

10. Every contract, sale, payment, bill, note or security for money and every transaction, dealing, proceeding, matter or thing whatever relating to money or involving the payment of, or the liability to pay, money shall be deemed to be made, executed or entered into in or in relation to the currency of The Bahamas unless it is expressly made, executed or entered into in or in relation to the currency of some other country.

Sole right of Bank to issue notes and coins.

11.—(1) The Bank shall have the sole right and authority to issue notes and coins throughout The Bahamas.

(2) No person other than the Bank shall issue in The Bahamas notes or coins or any documents or tokens having the appearance of notes or coins.

(3) Any person who contravenes the provisions of subsection (2) shall be guilty of an offence against this Act and shall be liable on conviction thereof to a fine not exceeding one thousand dollars or to imprisonment for a term not exceeding twelve months.

**Issue, etc., of notes and coins.**

12. The Bank shall from time to time as circumstances may require—

(*a*) arrange for the printing of notes and the minting of coins; and

(*b*) issue, re-issue and redeem notes and coins.

**Denominations and form of notes and coins.**

13. The Minister may, after consultation with the Bank, by order prescribe—

(*a*) the denominations (being multiples or fractions of a dollar), forms and designs of the notes and coins; and

(*b*) the standard weight and composition of such coins, and the amount of tolerance and the variation which shall be allowed therein.

**Legal tender.**

14.—(1) Subject to the provisions of this section—

(*a*) notes issued by the Bank shall be legal tender in The Bahamas at their face value for the payment of any amount;

(*b*) coins issued by the Bank shall be legal tender in The Bahamas at their face value up to an amount not exceeding one hundred dollars in the case of coins of a denomination of not less than one dollar, and up to an amount not exceeding five dollars in the case of coins of a lesser denomination.

(2) All notes and coins lawfully in circulation immediately before the commencement of this section shall be deemed for all purposes to be notes and coins issued by the Bank under this Act and to be legal tender until withdrawn from circulation under the provisions of subsection (3).

(3) The Bank may, on giving not less than one month's notice in the *Gazette,* call in any notes or coins on payment of the face value thereof, and any such notes or coins shall, on the expiration of the notice, cease to be legal tender but, subject to the provisions of section 15, shall be redeemable by the Bank on demand.

(4) A coin which has been impaired, diminished in size or lightened otherwise than by fair wear and tear, or which has been defaced by stamping, engraving or piercing shall not be legal tender.

**Damaged currency, etc.**

15. No person shall be entitled as of right to recover from the Bank the value of any lost, stolen, mutilated or imperfect note or coin; but the Bank may in its discretion as an act of grace refund to any person the value of any mutilated or imperfect note or coin.

**Exemption from stamp duty.**

16. Notes and coins issued by the Bank shall be exempt from the payment of stamp duty.

## PART V. GOLD, FOREIGN EXCHANGE, EXTERNAL RESERVE, ETC.

Power of Bank in relation to foreign exchange, etc.

17. Subject to the provisions of this Act, the Bank may—

(*a*) buy and sell gold, foreign exchange, foreign bills of exchange and securities of foreign governments;

(*b*) maintain deposits in any foreign financial institution and utilize any such deposit in such manner as the Bank may think expedient for the due performance of the functions of the Bank;

(*c*) make arrangements with any foreign financial institution to borrow, on such terms and conditions as the Bank may think fit, any foreign currency.

External reserve.

18.—(1) The Bank shall at all times maintain a reserve of external assets consisting of all or any of the following—

(*a*) gold (whether coins or bullion);

(*b*) notes and coins (other than gold coins);

(*c*) balances payable on demand held with financial institutions or agents;

(*d*) money at call;

(*e*) bills in the nature of Treasury Bills maturing within one hundred and eighty-four days issued by any foreign government;

(*f*) marketable securities issued or guaranteed by any foreign government;

(*g*) any reserve asset deemed by the Board to be an internationally recognised reserve asset:

Provided that at no time shall any securities held by the Bank pursuant to paragraph (*f*) of this subsection which mature beyond five years constitute more than thirty *per centum* in value of the whole of the assets in the reserve of external assets.

(2) The value of the said reserve shall not at any time be less than fifty *per centum* of the value of the aggregate of the notes and coins in circulation and the demand liabilities of the Bank.

## PART VI. RELATIONS WITH THE COMMERCIAL BANKS

Statutory Reserve.

19.—(1) Subject to the provisions of this section, every commercial bank shall establish and maintain a reserve to be called "the Statutory Reserve" of not less than that percentage of the amount of its deposit liabilities in Bahamian dollars that is at any time fixed by the Bank under this section.

(2) The Bank may by order fix and from time to time vary the percentage required by subsection (1):

Provided that—

*(a)* the percentage fixed as aforesaid shall not at any time be less than five nor more than twenty *per centum;*

*(b)* different percentages may be so fixed for different classes of commercial banks;

*(c)* any such order may require a proportion of the said reserve (which shall be specified in the order) to be lodged with the Bank; and

*(d)* no such order shall be made increasing any percentage at the time in force by more than five *per centum* in any period of thirty days.

(3) If any commercial bank contravenes or fails to comply with any provision of an order made under this section it shall be guilty of an offence against this Act and liable—

*(a)* in the case of a contravention of, or failure to comply with, a requirement under paragraph *(c)* of the proviso to subsection (2), to a fine not exceeding one thousand five hundred dollars; and

*(b)* in the case of a deficiency in the reserve, to a fine not exceeding one tenth of one *per centum* of the amount of the deficiency,

for each day during which the contravention or failure to comply, or, as the case may be, the deficiency, occurred or continued.

Liquid assets.

20.—(1) Every commercial bank shall so conduct its business as to ensure, taking one month with another, that its liquid assets are on average not less than that percentage of the amount of its deposit liabilities in Bahamian dollars that is at any time fixed by the Bank under this section.

(2) The Bank may by order fix and from time to time vary the percentage required by subsection (1):

Provided that—

*(a)* the percentage fixed as aforesaid shall not at any time be less than ten nor more than thirty *per centum;* and

*(b)* different percentages may be so fixed for different classes of commercial banks; and

*(c)* no such order shall be made increasing any percentage at the time in force by more than five *per centum* in any period of thirty days.

(3) In this section "liquid assets" means—

*(a)* notes and coins;

*(b)* any cash balance held at the Bank;
*(c)* money at call and demand balances at any financial institution carrying on business in The Bahamas;
*(d)* Treasury Bills;
*(e)* stock of the Government;
*(f)* any instrument or security of a kind referred to in subparagraph (ii) of paragraph *(f)* of section 27;
*(g)* any freely convertible foreign currency;
*(h)* money at call and demand balances at any financial institution abroad being money at call or demand balances held in freely convertible foreign currency;
*(i)* any other asset designated for the purposes of this subsection by the Bank.

(4) In subsection (3)—

"freely convertible foreign currency" means any foreign currency which at the time in question is in the opinion of the Bank a currency that is freely negotiable and transferable in international exchange markets at exchange rate margins consistent with the Articles of Agreement of the International Monetary Fund; [2]

"money at call and demand balances at any financial institution" means money at call and demand balances held by any commercial bank at any financial institution less money at call and demand balances held at that bank by any financial institution."

(5) If any commercial bank contravenes or fails to comply with any provision of an order made under this section it shall be guilty of an offence against this Act and shall be liable on conviction thereof to a fine not exceeding one thousand five hundred dollars for every day during which the offence continues.

21.—(1) Subject to subsection (2), the Bank may by regulations prescribe— Credit controls.

*(a)* the maximum amounts of loans or advances which commercial banks may have outstanding at any time or during such period or periods as may be specified in the regulations; and
*(b)* the purposes for which, the maturities for which and the security

[2] Following the Second Amendment to the Articles of Agreement of the International Monetary Fund, effective April 1, 1978, a member has been free to choose the exchange arrangements that it wishes to apply in accordance with Article IV, Section 2*(b)*. It may, therefore, maintain the value of its currency in terms of the special drawing right or some other denominator excluding gold. Alternatively, it may allow its currency to float. The Bahamas maintains its exchange rate within relatively narrow margins in terms of the U.S. dollar.

on which loans or advances may or may not be made by commercial banks.

(2) Any such regulations—

(*a*) may be made applicable to all the loans and advances of any specified commercial bank or to any specified class or classes of loans or advances of any specified class or classes of such banks;

(*b*) shall not have effect so as to impose in respect of any loan or advance any limit or restriction that is more rigorous than applies to that loan or advance at the date of the coming into force of the regulations;

(*c*) shall fix a date for the coming into force of the regulations, which shall not be earlier than thirty days after the date of their publication in the *Gazette.*

**Bank as banker to commercial banks.**

22. The Bank may act as banker to any commercial bank in The Bahamas and as banker, agent or correspondent to any bank abroad.

**Clearing house.**

23. The Bank may promote the establishment of a bank clearing system and provide facilities therefor.

## PART VII. RELATIONS WITH THE GOVERNMENT

**Bank as banker to Government, etc.**

24. The Bank may act as banker to the Government or any public corporation.

**Bank as agent for the Government.**

25. The Bank may act generally as agent for the Government on such terms and conditions as may be agreed between the Government and the Bank where the Bank can so act consistently with its functions under this Act and, in particular, the Bank may act as the agent of the Government in the management of the public debt.

**Advances to the Government.**

26.—(1) Subject to the provisions of this section, the Bank may make temporary advances to the Government on such terms and conditions as may be agreed between the Minister and the Bank.

(2) Every such advance made by the Bank to the Government shall be repaid by the Government as soon as possible.

(3) The amount of any such advances by the Bank to the Government which may be outstanding at any one time shall not exceed ten *per centum* of the average ordinary revenue of the Government or ten *per centum* of the estimated ordinary revenue of the Government, whichever is the less.

(4) In subsection (3)—

"ordinary revenue" means all income or contributions to Government revenue not being loans, capital grants or other receipts of a capital nature;

"average ordinary revenue" means the annual average of the ordinary revenue of the Government over the three years (for which accounts have been laid before Parliament) next before the year in which any question under the subsection is raised;

"estimated ordinary revenue" means the ordinary revenue, as estimated in the estimates of the Government as laid before Parliament, for that year.

## PART VIII. GENERAL POWERS OF THE BANK

**Powers of the Bank.**

27. Subject to the provisions of this Act, the Bank may, in the discharge of its functions—

*(a)* open accounts for, accept deposits from, and collect money for or on account of, the Government or any commercial bank or any public corporation;

*(b)* buy, hold, sell, discount or re-discount—

(i) bills of exchange, promissory notes or other credit instruments maturing within one hundred and eighty days from the date of their acquisition by the Bank;

(ii) Treasury Bills;

*(c)* buy, hold and sell securities issued or guaranteed by the Government, being securities issued to the public and maturing within twenty years from the date of their acquisition by the Bank but so that the total amount of any such securities at any time held by the Bank which mature beyond five years after their date of issue (including any such securities held by the Bank as security for any loans or advances) shall not exceed twenty *per centum* of the demand liabilities of the Bank;

*(d)* for the purpose of promoting the development of a securities market, buy, hold and sell fixed term and fixed interest securities of any company, but so that the total amount of any such securities at any time held by the Bank (including any such securities held by the Bank as security for any loans or advances) shall not exceed five *per centum* of the total liabilities of the Bank;

*(e)* with the approval of the Minister, buy, hold and sell securities of any public corporation or any company, being a public corporation or company established for the purpose of developing a

securities market, or financing economic development, in The Bahamas;

*(f)* make to any commercial bank or any public corporation, on such terms and conditions as may be determined by the Bank, loans or advances on the security of any of the following, that is to say—

(i) gold coins or gold bullion;

(ii) bills of exchange, promissory notes, other credit instruments, Treasury Bills or securities, being bills of exchange, promissory notes, credit instruments, Treasury Bills or securities of any kind mentioned in paragraph *(b)* or *(c)* of this section;

(iii) warehouse warrants or other documents to goods duly insured and secured by a letter of hypothecation from the owner; or

(iv) securities of any kind mentioned in paragraph *(d)* or *(e)* of this section:

Provided that where any loan or advance is made on the security of any instrument mentioned in subparagraph (ii) of this paragraph—

*(aa)* the loan or advance shall not extend beyond the maturity date of the instrument itself or ninety-three days, whichever is the longer; and

*(bb)* the amount of any such loan or advance shall not exceed eighty-five *per centum* of the market value of the instrument at the date of its acquisition by the Bank; or

*(g)* do any other banking business incidental to or consequential upon the functions of the Bank.

Prohibited activities.

**28.** Except as expressly authorised by this Act, the Bank shall not—

*(a)* engage in trade or otherwise have a direct interest in any business undertaking, except such as the Bank may acquire in the course of the satisfaction of debts due to the Bank, but so that it shall be the duty of the Bank to dispose as soon as may be of any such interest so acquired; or

*(b)* grant unsecured loans or advances to any person; or

*(c)* acquire any interest in real property except in so far as the Bank may consider necessary or expedient for the provision, or the future provision, of premises for the conduct of its business or for any purpose (including use of, or residence in, any such premises by directors, officers or servants of the Bank) incidental to the performance of its functions.

## PART IX. ACCOUNTANTS AND STATEMENTS AND AUDIT

29. The financial year of the Bank shall end on the thirty-first day of December. Financial year.

30.—(1) The Bank shall, within four months after the end of each financial year, cause to be made and transmit to the Minister— Publication of Accounts and report annually.

*(a)* a report of the operations of the Bank during that year; and

*(b)* a statement of the accounts of the Bank in respect of that year certified by the auditors appointed under subsection (1) of section 32.

(2) The Bank—

*(a)* shall, in the preparation of the said accounts, exclude from its calculations any profit or loss arising from any revaluation of any assets or liabilities of the Bank occasioned by any change in the value of the currency of The Bahamas, or any foreign currency;

*(b)* shall credit or debit, as the case may require, any such profit or loss to an account (to be established and maintained by the Bank and called "the Exchange Equalisation Account"); and

*(c)* may from time to time transfer to the General Reserve provided for by section 7 any balance at any time in the said Account, or any part thereof, as the Bank thinks fit.

(3) The Minister shall as soon as possible after their receipt—

*(a)* cause a copy of the said report and statement of accounts to be laid before each House of Parliament; and

*(b)* cause a copy of the said statement of accounts to be published in the *Gazette.*

31. The Bank shall on or before the end of every month prepare and transmit to the Minister and publish in the *Gazette* a statement of the assets and liabilities of the Bank as at the last working day of the preceding month. Publication of statements monthly.

32.—(1) The accounts of the Bank shall be audited annually by auditors appointed by the Board with the approval of the Minister. Audit.

(2) Without prejudice to the provisions of subsection (1), the Minister may at any time require the Auditor-General to examine and report on the accounts of the Bank as a whole or any aspect of the operations of the Bank, and the Bank shall provide the Auditor-General with all necessary and proper facilities for such an examination.

## PART X. MISCELLANEOUS

**Information may be required from financial institutions.**

33.—(1) The Bank may require any financial institution or trust company, or any director, officer or servant of such an institution or company, to supply to the Bank in such form and within such time as the Bank may determine such information as the Bank considers necessary to enable the Bank to carry out its functions under this Act:

Provided that information regarding any deposit made by any individual customer with any such institution or company may not be required by the Bank by virtue of the provisions of this section.

(2) Any person who fails to comply with any requirement lawfully made by the Bank under subsection (1) shall be guilty of an offence against this Act and shall be liable on conviction thereof to a fine not exceeding one thousand five hundred dollars for every day during which the offence continues.

**Supplying false statement.**

34. Any person who supplies or is concerned in supplying to the Minister or the Bank or any other person any statement, account, report or other information pursuant to this Act or any purpose for which any such statement, account, report or information is lawfully required thereunder, knowing the same to be false in a material particular, shall be guilty of an offence against this Act and shall be liable on conviction thereof to a fine not exceeding five thousand dollars or to imprisonment for a term not exceeding two years.

**Secrecy.**

35.—(1) Every director, officer or servant of the Bank shall preserve and aid in preserving secrecy with regard to any matter relating to the affairs of any financial institution or trust company, or of any customer of any such institution or company, coming to his knowledge in the course of the performance of his duties as such a director, officer or servant.

(2) No director, officer or servant of the Bank shall be required to produce in any court any book or document in his custody as such a director, officer or servant or to divulge or communicate to any court any matter mentioned in subsection (1) except on the direction of the court.

(3) Any director, officer, or servant of the Bank who divulges any such matter as aforesaid to any person other than a person to whom he is authorised by the Bank or a court to divulge it, or who allows access to any book or document relating to the affairs of any financial institution or trust company, or of any customer of any such institution or company, by any person not authorised by the Bank or a court for the purpose shall be guilty of an offence against this Act and shall be

liable on conviction thereof to a fine not exceeding two thousand five hundred dollars or to imprisonment for a term not exceeding two years.

36. Every offence against this Act shall be tried summarily. Offences.

37. Where an offence under this Act which has been committed by a body corporate is proved to have been committed with the consent or connivance of, or to be attributable to any neglect on the part of, a director, manager, secretary or other similar officer of the body corporate, or any person who was purporting to act in any such capacity he, as well as the body corporate, shall be guilty of that offence and be liable to be proceeded against accordingly. Offences by corporations.

38. The Bank shall be exempt from tax under The Real Property Tax Act, 1969. Exemption from real property tax.

PART XI. REPEAL, TRANSITIONAL, ETC.

39. The Bahamas Monetary Authority Act, 1968, is hereby repealed, but so that the proviso to subsection (1) of section 38 of that Act shall continue to have effect on and after the commencement of this section as if that subsection had not been repealed.[3] Repeal.

40.—(1) On the date of commencement of this section the property, rights and liabilities which immediately before that date were property, rights and liabilities of the Authority shall, by virtue of this section, vest in the Bank; and on or after that date any legal proceedings in respect of any such property rights or liabilities as aforesaid may be commenced or continued by or against the Bank as they could have been commenced or continued by or against the Authority if this Act had not been passed. Transitional and saving.

(2) The Minister may by order, made at any time within six months after the aforesaid date, make provision for any matter for which it appears to him requisite or expedient to do so in connexion with, or in consequence of, the vesting by virtue of this section of property, rights or liabilities falling within subsection (1).

[3] Subsection 1 of section 38 of the Bahamas Monetary Authority Act, No. 27 of 1968, provides:

"The Currency Act, 1965, is hereby repealed:

"Provided that no contract, document, sale, payment, bill, note, instrument or security for money and no transaction, dealing, proceeding, matter or thing whatsoever related to money or involving the payment of or liability to pay any money, made, executed, signed, entered into, done or had in or in relation to sterling before the coming into force of the said Currency Act, 1965, shall be affected in any way by such repeal."

Minister may take preliminary action for the Bank.

41. On and after the passing of this Act the Minister shall have power, if it appears to him necessary or expedient to do so in connexion with the establishment of the Bank, to do any act or thing, or incur any expense, which the Bank could have done or incurred by virtue of any provision of this Act if that provision (hereafter in this section referred to as "the relevant provision") had then been in force; and any act or thing done by the Minister under this section shall on and after the commencement of the relevant provision have the same force and validity as if it had been done by the Bank and any expense so incurred shall be deemed to have been incurred by the Bank, notwithstanding that the relevant provision was not at the time in force.

Consequential amendments. Second Schedule.

42. The enactments specified in the first column of the Second Schedule [4] shall have effect subject to the amendments specified in the second column of that Schedule being amendments consequential upon the provisions of this Act.

## FIRST SCHEDULE

(Section 3(5))

### THE BANK

#### THE BOARD OF DIRECTORS

The Board of Directors.

1. The Board of Directors shall consist of—

(a) the following persons, to be appointed by the Governor-General, that is to say, a Governor, a Deputy Governor and four other directors, being persons appearing to the Governor-General to have wide experience in, and to have shown capacity in, financial or commercial matters, industry, law or administration; and

(b) the Financial Secretary *ex officio*,

and paragraphs 2 to 10 (inclusive) of this Schedule shall have effect in relation to the Board, but subject, in the case of the Financial Secretary, to the special provisions of paragraph 11 thereof.

Tenure of office.

2.—(1) Each director shall, subject to the provisions of this paragraph, hold and vacate his office in accordance with the terms of his appointment and shall, on ceasing to hold office, be eligible for reappointment.

(2) The Governor and the Deputy Governor shall not be appointed or re-appointed for a period exceeding five years.

(3) A director other than the Governor or the Deputy Governor shall not be appointed or re-appointed for a period exceeding four years.

---

[4] The Second Schedule, which comprises consequential amendments to other Statutes, is omitted from this volume.

3.—(1) The Governor and the Deputy Governor shall not while holding office as such hold any other office or employment, whether remunerated or not, without the prior approval of the Governor-General. **Disqualifications.**

(2) Subject to sub-paragraph (1) of this paragraph, a person may not be appointed or remain a director who—

*(a)* is a member of either House of Parliament; or
*(b)* is a public officer; or
*(c)* is a director, officer or servant of, or is a shareholder of, or has a controlling interest in, any financial institution.

4. The Governor-General may appoint any person eligible to be appointed a director to act temporarily in the place of any director who is absent or unable to act. **Temporary appointments.**

5. Any director may at any time by notice in writing to the Governor-General resign his office. **Resignations.**

6. If the Governor-General is satisfied that a director— **Dismissal.**

*(a)* has been absent from meetings longer than three consecutive months without the permission of the Board; or
*(b)* has become bankrupt or made arrangements with his creditors; or
*(c)* is incapacitated by physical or mental illness; or
*(d)* is otherwise unable or unfit to discharge the functions of a director,

the Governor-General may declare his office as a director to be vacant and shall notify the fact in such manner as the Governor-General thinks fit, and thereupon that office shall become vacant.

7. The names of all the directors and every change therein shall be published in the *Gazette*. **Publication of membership.**

8. The Bank shall pay to the directors such remuneration (if any), whether by way of salary, honorarium or fees, as the Governor-General may determine and, if a person ceases to be a director and it appears to the Governor-General that there are special circumstances which make it right that that person should receive compensation, the Governor-General may require the Bank to pay to that person a sum of such amount as the Governor-General may determine. **Remuneration.**

9.—(1) The Governor shall, subject to the powers of the Board as set forth in subsection (4) of section 3, be the chief executive of the Bank and have charge of the day-to-day management and operation of the Bank. **Governor and Deputy Governor.**

(2) The Deputy Governor shall perform such functions in relation to the Bank as are assigned to him by the Governor and, in the event of the inability to act of, or a vacancy in the office of, [the] [5] Governor, the Deputy Governor shall have and may exercise the functions of the Governor.

10.—(1) The Board shall meet as often as may be required for the due performance of its functions, and in any case at least once in every month. **Procedure and meetings.**

(2) A meeting of the Board—

[5] Editor's insertion.

(*a*) may be convened by the Governor or, in his absence, the Deputy Governor;

(*b*) shall be convened on the written requisition of two directors or the Financial Secretary, specifying the reasons for which the meeting is required.

(3) Meetings of the Board shall be presided over by the Governor or, in the event of his inability to act, by the Deputy Governor.

(4) Three directors (of whom one shall be either the Governor or the Deputy Governor) shall form a quorum at any meeting.

(5) A decision shall be adopted by a simple majority of the directors present and in the case of an equality of votes the person presiding at the meeting shall have and exercise a casting vote.

(6) A director who is directly or indirectly interested otherwise than as a director or in common with other directors in a contract or other transaction made or proposed to be made by the Bank shall disclose the nature of his interest at the first meeting of the Board at which he is present after the relevant facts have come to his knowledge; and any such disclosure shall be recorded in the minutes of the Board and, after the disclosure, that director shall not take any part in any deliberation or decision of the Board with respect to that contract or transaction.

(7) Minutes of each meeting of the Board shall be kept in such form as the Board may determine.

(8) No act or proceeding of the Board shall be invalidated merely by reason of any vacancy in the Board or of any defect in the appointment of a director.

(9) No action, suit, prosecution or other proceeding shall be brought or instituted personally against any director in respect of any act done *bona fide* in pursuance or execution or intended execution of this Act.

(10) Where any director is exempt from liability by reason only of the provisions of sub-paragraph (9) of this paragraph the Bank shall be liable to the extent than [6] it would be if that member were an employee or agent of the Bank.

**Special provisions regarding the Financial Secretary.**

11. The following provisions of this Schedule shall not apply to or in relation to the Financial Secretary, that is to say, sub-paragraphs (1) and (3) of paragraph 2; sub-paragraph 2*(b)* of paragraph 3; paragraph 4; paragraph 5; paragraph 6.

## STAFF

**Power to employ staff.**

12.—(1) Subject to sub-paragraph (2) of this paragraph, the Bank may appoint and employ at such remuneration and on such terms and conditions as it thinks fit such officers, servants and agents as the Board considers necessary for the due discharge of the functions of the Bank.

(2) An annual salary exceeding twelve thousand dollars shall not be assigned to any post, nor shall an appointment be made to any post to which such a salary is assigned, without the Minister's prior approval.

[6] Editor's query: "that."

13. The Bank shall have power— **Pensions and gratuities for staff.**

*(a)* to pay to or in respect of officers or servants of the Bank such pensions or gratuities; or

*(b)* to make such payments towards the provision for them of pensions or gratuities; or

*(c)* to maintain for them such pension schemes (whether contributory or not),

as the Bank may determine.

AUTHENTICATION OF DOCUMENTS

14.—(1) The seal of the Bank shall be kept under the control of the Governor or the Deputy Governor, and the affixing thereof shall be authenticated by the signature of the Governor or the Deputy Governor and one other director authorised by the Board to act in that behalf.

(2) Any document purporting to be a document duly executed under the seal of the Bank shall be received in evidence and shall, unless the contrary is proved, be deemed to be a document so executed.

*{The Second Schedule is omitted from this volume.}*

# The Banks Act[1]

An Act relating to Banks and Banking.

[23rd August, 1909]

1. This Act may be cited as The Banks Act. **Short title.**

2. In this Act, unless the context otherwise requires— **Interpretation.**

"bank" means any person carrying on banking business;

"banking business" means the business of receiving on current, savings, deposit or other similar account money which is repayable by cheque or order and which may be invested by way of advances to customers or otherwise.

"cashier" includes the cashier of any branch or agency of a bank;

"court" means the Supreme Court;

"manager" includes the manager of any branch or agency of a bank;

[1] The original law, No. 4 of 109, has been amended by No. 10 of 1944; No. 43 of 1964; No. 65 of 1965; and the Second Schedule to The Central Bank of The Bahamas Act, 1974 (No. 3 of 1973).

"Minister" means the Minister responsible for banks;
"Registrar" means the Registrar General;
"Registry" means the Registry of Records.

Application of Act.

3. The provisions of this Act shall apply to every bank in the Colony.[2]

Certified copies of Acts, charters or certificates of incorporation to be recorded.

4.—(1) Every bank commencing to carry on business in the Colony after the coming into operation of this Act, shall, within three days after commencing to carry on such business, cause to be filed in the Registry a copy of the Act, charter or certificate of incorporation of such bank.

(2) Every such bank shall, in like manner, cause to be filed in the Registry copies of any further Act, charter or certificate of incorporation of such bank within three months from the date when such Act, charter or certificate of incorporation shall come into operation.

(3) The correctness of all copies filed under this section shall be authenticated in such manner as the Minister may from time to time direct, and every such copy so filed shall be open to the inspection of all persons desiring to peruse the same without payment of any fee.

Trusts.

5. A bank shall not be bound to see to the execution of any trust, whether expressed, implied or constructive, to which any share of its stock is subject.

Banks may hold real property.

6. A bank may acquire and hold real property within the Colony for its actual use and occupation and the management, transaction and carrying on of its business, and may sell or dispose of such real property and acquire other real property in its stead.

Dividends to be paid out of profits only.

7. All dividends of the shareholders of a bank shall be paid out of the profits and not out of the subscribed capital of the bank.

Yearly statements to be published.

8.—(1) Every bank shall, within four months of the end of its financial year, publish in the *Gazette* a true and full yearly statement of its accounts, and the auditor of the bank shall certify that such statement is properly drawn up so as to exhibit a true and correct view of the state of the bank's affairs as shown by the books of the bank, and the auditor of the bank shall have the right of access at all times to the

[2] Paragraph 3 of The Existing Laws Amendment Order, 1974, provides:
"A reference in an existing law to the Colony meaning thereby the former Colony of the Commonwealth of The Bahama Islands shall be read and construed as a reference to the Commonwealth of The Bahamas."

books, accounts and vouchers of the bank: provided that the Minister may, if he sees fit, exempt any bank from the provisions of this section.

(2) Such statement shall be signed by the cashier or manager or by such other person or officer of the bank as may from time to time be authorised by the bank to sign such statement on behalf of the bank; and the correctness thereof shall be declared to in such manner and by such persons as the Minister may direct.

(3) Such statements shall be in such form and contain such particulars as the Minister may from time to time direct so far as such directions shall not be contrary to the provisions of any law of the United Kingdom or any other country of the Commonwealth under the authority of which a bank is carrying on business within the Colony.

**Minister may call for further information.**

9. A bank shall from time to time, if required by the Minister, furnish to the Minister a special return and such further information as the Minister may reasonably see fit to call for.

**Failure to comply with the requirements of sections 8 and 9.**

10. If any bank or person fails to comply with the requirements of section 8 or 9 of this Act within a period of four months of the end of its financial year in the case of section 8 or for forty-two days after the date appointed by the Minister under section 9 for so doing, as the case may be, the bank or person so in default shall be liable to a penalty of twenty pounds for every day of such default:

Provided that the Minister may extend the time for sending such returns for such further period, not exceeding sixty days as he thinks expedient.

**Injunction to restrain persons, companies, etc., acting contrary to this Act.**

11. The Government of the Colony in the name of the Attorney General may, in addition to recovering any penalty or forfeiture in any action to recover the same, apply to the court for an injunction to restrain any company, corporation, society, partnership, person or bank, acting contrary to or in defiance of the provisions of this Act, from so acting.

**Service of process.**

12. A bank may sue and be sued and may proceed and be proceeded against in its corporate name and whenever it shall be necessary to serve any summons, writ, process, notice or other document on the bank, it shall be sufficient to deliver the same to the cashier or manager or other officer of the bank in the Colony, or to leave the same for him at the principal office of the bank in the Colony; and if service cannot be effected in the manner hereinbefore prescribed it shall be lawful to effect the same by delivering such summons, writ, process, notice or other document to the president or vice-president of the bank, or by leaving the

same for him as aforesaid; and if service cannot be effected in either of the modes hereinbefore prescribed it shall be lawful to effect the same in such manner as the court in which the suit, action or proceeding is being prosecuted, or any judge thereof, shall prescribe.

Notices.

13. In all cases where it may be necessary for a bank to serve or give any summons, demand or notice of any kind whatsoever to any person such summons, demand or notice may be served or given in writing signed by the cashier, manager, attorney or solicitor for the time being of the bank within the Colony without it being required to be under the common seal of the bank.

Byelaws.

14. Such persons or body of persons as may be authorised by the Act, charter or certificate of incorporation of any bank or by this Act, or by any Imperial statute in force in the Colony, or by any statute of any other country of the Commonwealth controlling such bank, may from time to time elect or otherwise provide for the appointment of office-bearers and directors, and also make, ordain and prescribe byelaws, rules and orders for the government of the bank, and the regulation and management of its concerns, and such byelaws, rules and regulations from time to time alter and amend, as to them may seem expedient:

Provided that no such byelaw, rule or order shall be repugnant to the Act, charter or certificate of incorporation or of this Act, or of any Imperial statute in force in the Colony relating to a bank doing business in the Colony or of any statute of any other country of the Commonwealth controlling such bank and until otherwise prescribed by byelaws, rules, regulations and orders made under this section, the byelaws, rules, regulations and orders made by a bank and in force on the coming into operation of this Act, shall remain in full force and effect so far as the same are not repugnant as aforesaid.

Suspension of specie payments for 60 days.

15. In case of the suspension of specie payments on demand by a bank for the space of sixty days in any year, either consecutively or at intervals, or of the breach of any of the conditions upon which a bank is empowered to carry on a banking business, the privileges conferred on such bank within the Colony by the Act, charter or certificate of incorporation of such bank or by this Act shall cease and determine as if the period of time limited therefor by such Act, charter or certificate of incorporation had expired.

Recovery of penalties.

16. All penalties and forfeitures under this Act shall be sued for in the court, in the name of the Attorney General, and the proceeds thereof, when recovered, shall be paid into the Treasury in aid of the general revenue.

17.—(1) Notwithstanding the provisions of any Act or law to the contrary, the manager or assistant manager of a bank may, without the production of probate or letters of administration, pay any sum not exceeding one hundred pounds[3] standing to the credit of a deceased person to any person (in this section referred to as the claimant) who upon producing satisfactory proof of the death of such deceased person and upon producing such evidence as may be required by the manager or assistant manager, appears to such manager or assistant manager to be entitled by law to the said sum standing to the credit of such deceased person:

**Deposits to credit of deceased persons, how dealt with.**

Provided—

*(a)* before any payment is made to any person under this section the claimant shall make and deliver to the bank a declaration in the form prescribed by section 8 of The Oaths Act (in this section referred to as a statutory declaration) to the effect that the deceased person has no real estate and his total personal estate does not exceed one hundred pounds;

*(b)* the claimant shall deliver to the bank evidence that at least two months' notice has been given by advertisement in three issues of the *Gazette* by the claimant calling on all persons having any claims to the estate of the deceased person to notify the bank in writing of such claims;

*(c)* that no other claims to the estate of the deceased person have been received by the bank; and

*(d)* the bank shall forward the statutory declaration and the evidence of the advertisement to the Registrar General.

(2) The bank shall not be liable in respect of any claim by any person in connection with a payment made in accordance with this section but any person may nevertheless recover any sum lawfully due to him from the person receiving any payment so made.

---

[3] As a consequence of the Second Schedule to The Central Bank of The Bahamas Act, 1974 (No. 3 of 1974), the Interpretation Act (Ch. 1) was amended to provide in section 11A as follows:

"11A—(1) In any Act or other instrument having the force of law in The Bahamas a reference to pounds, shillings and pence or fractions of a penny shall be construed as a reference to the equivalent sum in the currency of The Bahamas and for the purposes of this subsection seven shillings shall be deemed to be equivalent to one dollar.

"(2) Where any conversion into currency of The Bahamas under the provisions of this section could result in a fraction of a cent, then—

"*(a)* if that fraction amounts to half a cent or more, it shall be regarded as one cent; and

"*(b)* if that fraction amounts to less than half a cent, it shall be ignored."

Offence of issuing false certificate etc.

**18.** Whoever, being an officer, clerk, or servant of any bank, with intent to cause or enable any person to be defrauded or deceived, or with intent to commit or to facilitate the commission by himself or by any other person of any offence, issues or publishes any certificate or statement purporting to relate to the affairs of the bank or to the account or to the affairs of any customer thereof which he knows to be false in any material particular shall be guilty of an indictable offence against this Act and shall be liable on conviction to a fine not exceeding two thousand pounds[4] or to imprisonment for a term not exceeding two years or to both such fine and imprisonment.

Preservation of secrecy.

**19.**—(1) Except for the purpose of the performance of his duties or the exercise of his functions under this Act or when lawfully required to do so by any court of competent jurisdiction within the Colony or under the provisions of any law, no person shall disclose any information relating to the affairs of a bank or of the customer of a bank which he has acquired in the performance of his duties or the exercise of his functions under this Act.

(2) Every person who contravenes the provisions of subsection (1) of this section shall be guilty of an offence against this Act and shall be liable on summary conviction to a fine not exceeding one thousand pounds[4] or to a term of imprisonment not exceeding one year or to both such fine and imprisonment.

---

[4] See footnote 3 on page 35.

# The Banks and Trust Companies Regulation Act, 1965[1]

An Act to regulate Banking Business and Trust Companies within the Colony[2] and other matters related thereto.

[Assented to 28th October, 1965]
[Commencement 28th October, 1965]

---

[1] Act No. 64 of 1965, as amended by Acts Nos. 20 of 1969 and 15 of 1971, the Second Schedule to The Central Bank of The Bahamas Act, 1974 (No. 3 of 1974), and the Schedule to The Existing Laws Amendment Order, 1974.

[2] The Existing Laws Amendment Order, 1974, provides in section 3:

"A reference in an existing law to the Colony meaning thereby the former Colony of the Commonwealth of The Bahama Islands shall be read and construed as a reference to the Commonwealth of The Bahamas."

BE it enacted by the Governor and Commander-in-Chief in and over the Bahama Islands, by and with the advice and consent of the Senate and the House of Assembly of the said Islands, and by the authority of the same as follows:—

Short title.

1. This Act may be cited as The Banks and Trust Companies Regulation Act 1965.

Interpretation.

2. In this Act unless the context otherwise requires:—

"authorized agent" means a person designated by a bank or trust company under the provisions of section 4 of this Act;

"bank" means any person carrying on banking business;

"banking business" means the business of receiving on current, savings, deposit or other similar account money which is repayable by cheque or order or other instructions and which may be invested by way of advances to customers or otherwise;

"company" means a company incorporated either under the laws of the Colony or under the laws of any other country or place;

"licence" means a licence granted under section 4 of this Act or deemed to be so granted in accordance with that section;

"licensee" means any person holding a licence under the provisions of this Act;

"Minister" means the Minister for Finance;

"person" includes any body of persons corporate or unincorporate;

"prescribed" means prescribed by regulations made under this Act;

"trust business" means the business of acting as trustee, executor or administrator;

"trust company" means any company carrying on trust business.

Licence required to carry on banking business or to operate a trust company.

3.—(1) No banking business shall be carried on from within the Colony whether or not such business is carried on in the Colony except by a person who is in possession of a valid licence granted by the Minister authorizing him to carry on such business:

Provided that any bank in the Colony carrying on banking business at the commencement of this Act shall be deemed to have been granted a licence under section 4 of this Act for a period of six months from the commencement of this Act.

(2) No trust company shall carry on trust business from within the Colony whether or not such business is carried on in the Colony unless it is in possession of a valid licence granted by the Minister authorizing it to carry on such business:

Provided that any trust company in the Colony carrying on trust business at the commencement of this Act shall be deemed to have been granted a licence under section 4 of this Act for a period of six months from the commencement of this Act:

Provided further that anything lawfully done within the provisions of The Securities Act, 1971, by or on behalf of a company which within the meaning of that Act—

(*a*) is a corporation participating in a registered investment company scheme; or

(*b*) is the manager of a registered unit trust scheme,

shall be deemed, in so far as done in relation to such respective scheme, not to be in contravention of this subsection, notwithstanding that such company may not be in possession of a licence granted by the Minister as mentioned in this subsection.

(3) Every person who contravenes the provisions of this section shall be guilty of an offence against this Act and shall be liable on summary conviction to a fine not exceeding one thousand pounds or to imprisonment for a term not exceeding one year or to both such fine and imprisonment and in the case of a continuing offence to a fine not exceeding one hundred pounds for each day during which the offence continues.

Application shall be made to the Minister.

4.—(1) Any person desirous of carrying on banking business and any company desirous of carrying on trust business from within the Colony shall make application to the Minister for the grant of a licence. Every such application shall be in writing and shall contain such information and particulars and shall be accompanied by such references as may be prescribed and the Minister may, if satisfied that the carrying on of such business will not be against the public interest, grant a licence to such person or company subject to such terms and conditions, if any, as the Minister may deem necessary.

(2) Every bank and every trust company in the Colony at the commencement of this Act which proposes to carry on, or continue in, banking business or trust business, as the case may be, shall within six months of that date apply to the Minister for a licence in accordance with the provisions of subsection (1) of this section.

(3) Whenever he considers it to be in the public interest, the Minister may refuse to grant a licence.

(4) A licence shall not be granted to any bank or trust company having its head office or its registered office outside the Colony unless such bank or trust company designates and notifies to the Minister—

(*a*) a principal office in the Colony;

(*b*) by name one of its officers who is to be the bank's or trust company's authorized agent in the Colony; and

(*c*) by name another of its officers who in the absence or inability to act of the officer named under paragraph (*b*) of this subsection is to be the bank's or trust company's authorized agent in the Colony.

(5) It shall be a condition of every licence granted to a bank or trust company to which subsection (4) of this section applies, that the bank or trust company shall forthwith notify the Minister in writing of any change of—

(*a*) its principal office in the Colony; or

(*b*) either or both of the officers designated pursuant to paragraph (*b*) or (*c*) of subsection (4) of this section.

(6) The Minister may by Order revoke any licence—

(*a*) if the licensee has ceased to carry on banking business or trust business; or

(*b*) if the licensee becomes bankrupt or goes into liquidation or is wound up or otherwise dissolved; or

(*c*) in the circumstances and in the manner provided for in section 9 of this Act.

Shares etc. not to be issued or transferred without approval of the Minister.

5. No shares in a company or certificates of deposit or any other securities of such company which is a licensee under this Act shall be issued and no issued shares shall be transferred or disposed of in any manner without the prior approval of the Minister:

Provided that—

(*a*) this section shall not apply to the several banks and trust companies specified in the First Schedule[3] hereto; and

(*b*) the Minister may exempt any other licensee from the provisions of this section subject to such terms and conditions, if any, as the Minister may deem necessary.

Use of the word "bank" etc.

6.—(1) Except with the approval of the Minister no person, other than a licensee shall—

(*a*) use or continue to use the words "bank", "trust", "trust company", "trust corporation", "savings" or "savings and loan" or any of their derivatives either in English or in any other language, in the description or title under which such person is carrying on business from within the Colony whether or not such business is carried on in the Colony;

[3] The First Schedule is omitted from this volume.

(*b*) make or continue to make any representation in any billhead, letter, letterhead, circular, paper, notice, advertisement or in any other manner whatsoever that such person is carrying on banking business or trust business or is authorised by the law of the Bahama Islands to carry on;

(*c*) in any manner whatsoever solicit or receive deposits from the public.

(2) Except with the approval of the Minister, no company shall be registered or continue to be registered, by a name which contains the words "bank", "trust", "trust company", "trust corporation", "savings" or "savings and loan" or any of their derivatives either in English or in any other language, in the description or title under which such company is carrying on business from within the Colony whether or not such business is carried on in the Colony:

Provided that any company in the Colony carrying on banking business or trust business at the date of commencement of this Act shall be deemed to have been granted the approval of the Minister for the continued use of any name used by such company immediately before that date for a period of six months from that date.

(3) Before giving his approval under subsection (1) or subsection (2) of this section the Minister may require of any person such references and such other information and particulars as may be prescribed.

(4) Whenever he considers it to be in the public interest the Minister may withdraw any approval given under subsection (1) of this section.

(5) The Minister may refuse to grant a licence to a bank or a trust company, or if such bank or trust company is already in possession of a licence, he may revoke such licence, if in his opinion such bank or trust company is carrying on or intending to carry on banking or trust business, as the case may be, under a name which—

(*a*) is identical with that of any company, firm or business house whether within the Colony or not or which so nearly resembles that name as to be calculated to deceive; or

(*b*) is calculated to suggest, falsely, the patronage of or connection with some person or authority whether within the Colony or not.

(6) Every person who contravenes the provisions of this section shall be guilty of an offence against this Act and shall be liable on summary conviction to a fine not exceeding one thousand pounds or to a term of imprisonment not exceeding one year or to both such fine

and imprisonment and in the case of a continuing offence to a fine not exceeding one hundred pounds for each day during which the offence continues.

7. The Minister, in relation to a licensee which is or appears likely to become unable to meet its obligations or which in the opinion of the Minister is carrying on business in a manner detrimental to the public interest or to the interest of creditors or depositors of such licensee, may by instrument in writing require the manager or authorized agent of such licensee to supply within such reasonable time as may be specified in the instrument—

The Minister may require financial statement etc. of licensee.

*(a)* the financial statement of that licensee as at a date within the previous fifteen months audited by an auditor who shall be a chartered accountant or a certified public accountant approved of by the Minister; and

*(b)* such other information relating to the licensee as may be so specified;

and any person who contravenes the requirements of such an instrument or who in response to such an instrument knowingly or wilfully supplies false information to the Minister shall be guilty of an offence against this Act and shall be liable on summary conviction to a fine not exceeding five hundred pounds or to a term of imprisonment not exceeding six months or to both such fine and imprisonment.

8.—(1) There is hereby established the office of Inspector of Banks and Trust Companies (in this Act referred to as "the Inspector"), and the functions of that office shall on and after the commencement of Part II of The Central Bank of The Bahamas Act, 1974, vest in the Central Bank of The Bahamas established by section 3 of that Act.

Powers and duties of the Inspector.

(2) It shall be the duty of the Inspector—

*(a)* to maintain a general review of banking practice in the Colony;

*(b)* whenever he thinks fit or when required by the Minister to examine in such manner as he thinks necessary the affairs or business of every licensee carrying on business from within the Colony for the purpose of satisfying himself that the provisions of this Act are being complied with and that the licensee is in a sound financial position, and to report to the Minister the results of every such examination;

*(c)* to examine and to report on the several returns delivered to the Minister pursuant to section 7 of this Act; and

*(d)* to examine and make recommendations to the Minister with respect to applications for licences.

(3) In the performance of his functions under this Act and subject to the provisions of section 10 hereof, the Inspector shall be entitled at all reasonable times—

*(a)* to have access to such books, records, vouchers, documents, cash and securities of any licensee;

*(b)* to call upon the manager or any officer designated by the manager of any licensee for such information or explanation,

as the Inspector may reasonably require for the purpose of enabling him to perform his functions under this Act:

Provided always that the Inspector shall only have access to the account of a depositor of a licensee or to any information, matter or thing relating to or concerning the affairs of any customer of a licensee under the authority of an order of a Judge of the Supreme Court made on the ground that there are no other means of obtaining the information required by him.

(4) The Inspector with the approval of the Minister may in writing authorize any other person to assist the Inspector in the performance of his functions under this Act.

(5) Any person who fails to comply with any requirement made pursuant to subsection (3) of this section by the Inspector or any person authorized under subsection (4) of this section shall be guilty of an offence against this Act and shall be liable on summary conviction to a fine not exceeding five hundred pounds or to a term of imprisonment not exceeding six months or to both such fine and imprisonment.

Powers of the Minister.

**9.** If in the opinion of the Minister a licensee is carrying on its business in a manner detrimental to the public interest or to the interests of its depositors or other creditors or is either in the Colony or elsewhere contravening the provisions of this or any other Act or of any Order or Regulations made under this Act, the Minister may from time to time as may to him seem necessary, require that licensee forthwith to take such steps as he may consider necessary to rectify the matter or may make an order revoking the licence of such licensee and requiring its business in the Colony to be wound up.

Preservation of secrecy.

**10.**—(1) Except for the purpose of the performance of his duties or the exercise of his functions under this Act or when lawfully required to do so by any court of competent jurisdiction within the Colony or under the provisions of any law of the Colony, no person shall disclose any information relating to any application by any person under the provisions of this Act or to the affairs of a licensee or of any customer of a licensee which he has acquired in the performance of his duties or the exercise of his functions under this Act.

(2) Every person who contravenes the provisions of subsection (1) of this section shall be guilty of an offence against this Act and shall be liable on summary conviction to a fine not exceeding one thousand pounds or to a term of imprisonment not exceeding one year or to both such fine and imprisonment.

The Minister may suspend licence.

11.—(1) Whenever the Minister is of the opinion that any action under section 4(6), section 6 or section 9 of this Act should be taken against a licensee, he may forthwith suspend the licence of such licensee and before taking such action the Minister shall give that licensee notice in writing of his intention so to do setting out in such notice the grounds on which he proposes to act and shall afford the licensee within such time as may be specified therein not being less than seven days an opportunity of submitting to him a written statement of objections to such action, and thereafter the Minister shall advise the licensee of his decision.

(2) Whenever the Minister shall suspend a licence under subsection (1) of this section he may cause notice of such suspension to be published in the *Gazette.*

(3) Any suspension of a licence under subsection (1) of this section shall be for a period of ninety days, or until the Minister takes action under section 4(6), section 6 or section 9 of this Act or until the Minister notifies the licensee that the suspension is removed, whichever period is the shorter.

Power of search.

12.—(1) If a justice of the peace is satisfied by information on oath given by the Inspector or by a person authorized under section 8(4) of this Act to assist the Inspector either:—

(*a*) that a licence has been suspended; or

(*b*) that there is reasonable ground for suspecting that an offence against this Act or The Banks Act has been or is being committed and that evidence of the commission of the offence is to be found at any premises specified in the information, or in any vehicle, vessel or aircraft so specified; or

(*c*) that any books, records, vouchers, documents, cash or securities which ought to have been produced under section 8(3) of this Act and have not been produced are to be found at any such premises or in any such vehicle, vessel or aircraft,

he may grant a search warrant authorizing the Inspector or such person authorized under section 8(4) of this Act or any peace officer together with any other person named in the warrant and any other peace officers, to enter the premises specified in the information or, as the case may be, any premises upon which the vehicle, vessel or aircraft so specified may be, at any time within one month from the date of the warrant, and to search the premises or, as the case may be, the vehicle, vessel or aircraft.

(2) The person authorized by any such warrant as aforesaid to search any premises or any vehicle, vessel or aircraft may search every person who is found in or whom he has reasonable ground to believe to have recently left or to be about to enter those premises or that vehicle, vessel or aircraft, as the case may be, and may seize any books, records, vouchers, documents, cash or securities found in the premises or in the vehicle, vessel or aircraft which he has reasonable ground for believing to be evidence of the commission of any offence against this Act or The Banks Act or any such books, records, vouchers, documents, cash or securities found in the premises or in the vehicle, vessel or aircraft which he has reasonable ground for believing ought to have been produced under section 8(3) of this Act:

Provided that no female shall, in pursuance of any warrant issued under this subsection be searched except by a female.

(3) Where by virtue of this section a person has any power to enter any premises he may use such force as is reasonably necessary for the purpose of exercising that power.

(4) Every person who shall obstruct the Inspector or any other person in the exercise of any powers conferred on him by virtue of this section shall be guilty of an offence against this Act and shall be liable on summary conviction to a fine not exceeding one hundred pounds or to imprisonment for a term not exceeding three months or to both such fine and imprisonment.

Attorney General's fiat.

13. No prosecution in respect of any offence committed under this Act shall be instituted except by or with the consent of the Attorney General.

Regulations.

14. The Minister may make regulations for all or any of the following purposes:—

*(a)* to prescribe the information, particulars and references which may be prescribed under section 4(1) and section 6(3) of this Act;

*(b)* generally for carrying the purposes or provisions of this Act into effect.

15.—(1) The provisions of this Act shall have effect in addition to and not in derogation of any other provisions having the force of law in the Colony. Saving.

(2) This Act shall not apply to the Post Office Savings Bank.

16.—(1) An appeal shall lie to the Supreme Court from any decision of the Minister— Appeal.

*(a)* revoking a licence under section 4(6), section 6(5) or section 9 of this Act;
*(b)* withdrawing any approval under section 6(4) of this Act; or
*(c)* requiring a licensee to take certain steps which the Minister may specify under section 9 of this Act.

(2) An appeal against the decision of the Minister shall be on motion. The appellant within twenty-one days after the day on which the Minister has given his decision shall serve on the Attorney General a notice in writing signed by the appellant or his counsel or Attorney of his intention to appeal and of the general ground of his appeal:

Provided that any person aggrieved by the decision of the Minister may upon notice to the Attorney General apply to the Supreme Court for leave to extend the time within which the notice of appeal prescribed by this section may be served, and the Supreme Court upon the hearing of such application may extend the time prescribed by this section as it deems fit.

(3) The Attorney General shall upon receiving the notice of appeal transmit to the Registrar of the Supreme Court without delay a copy of the Minister's decision and all papers relating to the appeal:

Provided that the Attorney General shall not be compelled to disclose any information if he considers that the public interest would suffer by such disclosure.

(4) The Registrar shall set the appeal down for argument on such day, and shall cause notice of the same to be published in such manner, as the Supreme Court may direct.

(5) At the hearing of the appeal the appellant shall, before going into the case, state all the grounds of appeal on which he intends to rely and shall not, unless by leave of the Supreme Court, go into any matters not raised by such statement.

(6) The Supreme Court may adjourn the hearing of the appeal and may upon hearing thereof confirm, reverse, vary or modify the decision of the Minister or remit the matter with the opinion of the Supreme Court thereon to the Minister.

(7) An appeal against a decision of the Minister shall not have the effect of suspending the execution of such decision.

Fees. Second Schedule.

17.—(1) The provisions of the Second Schedule[4] shall have effect for the payment of fees in respect of the matters mentioned in that Schedule, and all such fees shall be payable to the Treasurer.

(2) All fees paid pursuant to subsection (1) of this section and the said Second Schedule shall be placed in the Consolidated Fund.

(3) The Minister may by regulations vary the fees prescribed in the said Second Schedule, so, however, that any such regulations which increase the amount of any fees payable under this Act shall be exempt from the provisions of The Statutory Instruments Act but instead be subject to affirmative resolution of both chambers of the Legislature.[5]

(4) In subsection (3) of this section the expression "affirmative resolution of both chambers of the Legislature" in relation to regulations means that the regulations are not to come into operation unless and until affirmed by a resolution of each of those chambers.

Second Schedule.

(5) If any person fails to comply with any requirement of subsection (1) of this section and the Second Schedule, he, or, where such person is a company, the company and every director, manager, secretary or other officer of the company who knowingly and wilfully authorizes or permits the default, shall on summary conviction be liable, for every day during which the default continues, to a fine not exceeding fifteen dollars.

*{The First and Second Schedules are omitted from this volume.}*

---

[4] The Second Schedule is omitted from this volume.

[5] The Existing Laws Amendment Order, 1974, provides in section 5:

"Except as provided in this Order, a reference in any existing law to the Legislature or to either Houses thereof shall be read and construed as a reference to Parliament or to the corresponding House thereof established by the Constitution."

# The Rate of Interest Act [1]

An Act to regulate the rate of interest which may be charged on loans and for purposes connected therewith.

[17th August, 1948]

1. This Act may be cited as The Rate of Interest Act. Short title.

2. In this Act, unless the context otherwise requires— Interpretation.

"court" means the Supreme Court, or a magistrate's court to the extent to which it has civil jurisdiction under any Act.

3. The rate of interest which may be charged by any person on any loan of money made after the commencement of this Act shall not directly or indirectly exceed twenty per centum per annum simple interest on loans of more than twenty-five pounds,[2] or thirty per centum per annum simple interest on loans of twenty-five pounds or any less amount irrespective of the date fixed for repayment of the said loan. Rates of interest on loans.

4. Any contract, promissory note, bill of exchange, cheque, receipt or any other document entered into after the commencement of this Act, whereby a rate of interest higher than that authorised by section 3 of this Act purports to be payable either expressly or by implication in respect of any loan, shall be absolutely null and void, and no proceedings shall be entertained in any court either for the recovery of the loan or of any interest thereon. Contracts to pay unauthorised rates void.

---

[1] Act No. 25 of 1948, as amended by the Rate of Interest (Amendment) Act, 1980 and the Second Schedule to The Central Bank of The Bahamas Act, 1974 (No. 3 of 1974).

[2] As a consequence of the Second Schedule to The Central Bank of The Bahamas Act, 1974 (No. 3 of 1974), the Interpretation Act (Ch. 1) was amended to provide in section 11A as follows:

"11A—(1) In any Act or other instrument having the force of law in The Bahamas a reference to pounds, shillings and pence or fractions of a penny shall be construed as a reference to the equivalent sum in the currency of The Bahamas and for the purposes of this subsection seven shillings shall be deemed to be equivalent to one dollar.

"(2) Where any conversion into currency of The Bahamas under the provisions of this section could result in a fraction of a cent, then—

"*(a)* if that fraction amounts to half a cent or more, it shall be regarded as one cent; and

"*(b)* if that fraction amounts to less than half a cent, it shall be ignored."

Transaction harsh and unconscionable if rates exceeded on loans made prior to this Act.

5. For the purposes of The Money Lending Act, and the granting of relief thereunder, the fact that interest has been charged on any loan made prior to the commencement of this Act at a rate higher than that authorised by section 3 of this Act shall be conclusive evidence that the rate of interest charged was excessive, and that the transaction was harsh and unconscionable.

When loan deemed to be made.

6. Where any loan made before the commencement of this Act is renewed after the commencement of this Act, or where any note or other document is executed after the commencement of this Act in respect of a loan made prior thereto, such loan shall be deemed to have been made, and such note or other document to have been executed, in respect of a loan made after the commencement of this Act.

Penalties.

7. Any person who contravenes or attempts to contravene any of the provisions of this Act shall be guilty of an offence, and shall be liable on summary conviction to a fine of one hundred pounds [3] or six months imprisonment or to both.

Application of this Act.

8. Notwithstanding anything to the contrary, this Act shall not apply to any loan made—

*(a)* in a currency other than the currency of The Bahamas;

*(b)* in the currency of The Bahamas by any institution licensed under the Banks and Trust Companies Regulation Act, 1965.

[3] See footnote 2 on page 47.

## The Money Lending Act [1]

An Act relating to money lending.

[7th July, 1913]

Short title.

1. This Act may be cited as The Money Lending Act.

Interpretation.

2. In this Act, unless the context otherwise requires—

"court" means the Supreme Court or any magisterial court to the extent to which it has civil jurisdiction under any Act.

[1] Act No. 20 of 1913.

Powers of the court.

3.—(1) If proceedings are taken in any court by any person for the recovery of any money lent after the commencement of this Act or for the enforcement of any agreement or security made or taken after the commencement of this Act in respect of money lent, and if there is evidence which satisfies the court that the interest charged in respect of the sum actually lent is excessive, or that the amounts charged for expenses, inquiries, fines, bonus, premiums, renewals or any other charges, are excessive, and that, in either case, the transaction is harsh and unconscionable, or is otherwise such that a court of equity would give relief, the court may—

*(a)* re-open the transaction and take an account between the lender and the person sued;

*(b)* notwithstanding any statement or settlement of account or any agreement purporting to close previous dealings and create a new obligation re-open any account, already taken between them, and relieve the person sued from payment of any sum in excess of the sum adjudged by the court to be fairly due in respect of such principal, interest and charges, as the court, having regard to the risk and all the circumstances, may adjudge to be reasonable;

*(c)* if any such excess has been paid, or allowed in account, by the debtor, order the creditor to repay it;

*(d)* set aside, either wholly or in part, or revise, or alter, any security given or agreement made in respect of money lent;

*(e)* if the lender has parted with the security, order him to indemnify the borrower or other person sued.

Proceedings by borrower against lender.

(2) Any court in which proceedings might be taken for the recovery of money lent by any person shall have and may, at the instance of the borrower or surety or other person liable, exercise the like powers as may be exercised under this section, where proceedings are taken for the recovery of money lent, and the court shall have power, notwithstanding any provision or agreement to the contrary, to entertain any application under this Act by the borrower or surety, or other person liable, notwithstanding that the time for repayment of the loan, or any instalment thereof, may not have arrived.

Bankruptcy.

(3) On any application relating to the admission or amount of a proof by a person who has lent money in any bankruptcy proceedings, the court may exercise the like powers as may be exercised under this section when proceedings are taken for the recovery of money.

Application to all money lending.

(4) The foregoing provisions of this section shall apply to any transaction which, whatever its form may be, is substantially one of money lending.

*Bona fide* assignee.

(5) Nothing in the foregoing provisions of this section shall affect the rights of any *bona fide* assignee or holder for value without notice.

Existing powers of court.

(6) Nothing in this section shall be construed as derogating from the existing powers or jurisdiction of any court.

# The Bahamas Development Bank Act, 1974 [1]

An Act to provide for the establishment of a financial institution to be known as the Bahamas Development Bank, for the functions of the Institution and for matters connected therewith or incidental thereto.

[Assented to 18th October, 1974]

BE it enacted by The Queen's Most Excellent Majesty, by and with the advice and consent of the Senate and the House of Assembly of the Commonwealth of The Bahamas, and by the authority of the same, as follows:—

## PART I. PRELIMINARY

Short title and commencement.

1. This Act may be cited as The Bahamas Development Bank Act, 1974 and shall come into operation on such date as the Minister may appoint by notice published in the *Gazette*.

Interpretation.

2.—(1) In this Act, unless the context otherwise requires—

"agriculture" includes fisheries, forestry, horticulture, and use of land for any purpose of husbandry including the keeping or breeding of livestock, poultry and bees and the growing of vegetables or fruits and the like;

"agricultural enterprise" means an enterprise in The Bahamas in which is carried on the business of agriculture;

"approved enterprise" means an agricultural enterprise, an industrial enterprise, a tourist industry enterprise or any other enterprise that may from time to time be approved by the Minister by order;

"Bank" means the Bahamas Development Bank established by section 3;

[1] Act No. 18 of 1974.

"Board" means the Board of Directors of the Bank as constituted under section 7;

"Chairman" means the Chairman of the Board;

"debenture" includes debenture stock;

"financial year" in relation to the Bank means the period of twelve months beginning on the first day of January in any year:

Provided that the period beginning on the date of the commencement of this Act and ending on the 31st day of December next following shall be deemed to be a financial year;

"functions" includes powers and duties;

"Government" means the Government of The Bahamas;

"industrial enterprise" means an enterprise in The Bahamas in which is carried on the business of—

(*a*) manufacturing, processing, transforming, assembling, installing, overhauling, reconditioning, altering, repairing, cleaning, packaging, transporting or warehousing of goods;

(*b*) drilling, construction, engineering, technical surveys or scientific research;

(*c*) exploiting natural resources;

(*d*) operating a mine or quarry;

(*e*) generating, supplying or distributing electricity;

(*f*) operating a commercial transport service;

(*g*) supplying premises, machinery or equipment, for any business mentioned in paragraph *(a)*, *(b)*, *(c)*, *(d)*, *(e)* or *(f)* of this definition under a lease, contract or other arrangement whereby title to the premises, machinery or equipment is retained by the supplier;

"managing director" means the managing director of the Bank;

"Minister" means the Minister of Finance;

"securities" include any stock, equity holding, debenture, instrument of indebtedness, warrant or similar document;

"subsidiary" means any body corporate in which the Bank owns or controls more than fifty per centum of the voting rights;

"tourist industry enterprise" means an enterprise in The Bahamas in which is carried on the business of—

(*a*) supplying hotel accommodation or other facilities principally intended for visitors to The Bahamas; or

(*b*) supplying premises or equipment for any business referred to in paragraph *(a)* of this definition under a lease, contract or other arrangement whereby title to the premises or equipment is retained by the supplier.

(2) Unless the contrary intention appears, references in this Act to a Part or section or Schedule are references to a Part or section of, or a Schedule to, this Act and reference in a section to a subsection are references to a subsection of that section.

## PART II. ESTABLISHMENT, GENERAL FUNCTIONS AND RESPONSIBILITIES OF THE BANK

Establishment of Bahamas Development Bank.

3.—(1) There is hereby established for the purposes of this Act a Bank to be known as the Bahamas Development Bank.

(2) The Bank shall be a body corporate having perpetual succession and a common seal and, subject to the provisions of this Act, with power to acquire, hold and dispose of movable and immovable property of whatever kind and to enter into contracts and to do all things necessary for the purposes of its functions.

(3) The Bank may sue and be sued in its corporate name.

(4) The seal of the Bank shall be authenticated by the signature of the Chairman and one other director authorised to act in that behalf and shall be judicially and officially noticed.

(5) All documents, other than those required by law to be under seal, made by, and all decisions of, the Board may be signified under the hand of the Chairman or any director or officer authorised to act in that behalf.

Principal functions of Bank.

4. Subject to the provisions of this Act, the principal functions of the Bank shall be—

(*a*) to promote industrial, agricultural and commercial development in The Bahamas through the financing of, or the investing in approved enterprises;

(*b*) to encourage the participation in approved enterprises by citizens of The Bahamas; and

(*c*) generally to promote and enhance the economic development of The Bahamas.

General powers of Bank.

5. Subject to the provisions of this Act, the Bank shall have power to do anything or to enter into any transaction whether or not involving expenditure, making or guaranteeing of loans or investing of money, the acquisition of any property or rights, which in its opinion

is calculated to facilitate the proper discharge of its functions or is incidental or conducive thereto, and, in particular, but without limiting the generality of the foregoing, may—

(*a*) provide finance in the form of loans, long, medium or short term, or by the purchase of securities or by participating in any share issue of any approved enterprise;

(*b*) obtain funds from international agencies, financial agencies of the governments of countries outside The Bahamas, banks, other financial institutions or the public for the purpose of re-lending such funds within The Bahamas;

(*c*) invest moneys standing to the credit of the Bank by ways of loans, the purchase of securities, participation in any share issue of any approved enterprise or in such other manner as the Bank may from time to time think proper;

(*d*) guarantee loans from other investment sources to persons wishing to establish or modernise any approved enterprise;

(*e*) act as agents for the sale and purchase of any shares or securities or for any other monetary or mercantile transaction;

(*f*) negotiate or pay in advance coupons and interests on public loans or securities;

(*g*) contract for public and private loans and negotiate and issue the same;

(*h*) act as agents for any Government or other authority and for public and private bodies and persons;

(*i*) promote, effect, induce, guarantee, underwrite, participate in, manage, or carry out any issue of Government or other loans or of shares or securities of any company, corporation or association, and lend money for the purposes of any such issue;

(*j*) issue common or preferred stock and other equity securities;

(*k*) accumulate reserves, pay dividends, issue warrants or otherwise distribute profits.

6. The Bank shall have its principal place of business in the City of Nassau and may establish such branch offices elsewhere within The Bahamas and may appoint such agents and correspondents as may be required. Place of business.

7.—(1) There shall be a Board of Directors of the Bank who, subject to the provisions of this Act, shall be responsible for the policy of the Bank and the general administration of its affairs and business. Board of Directors.

(2) The Board shall consist of a Chairman, who shall be a person having in the opinion of the Minister considerable knowledge and

experience of banking and financial matters, and not less than six other directors of whom—

(*a*) one shall be the managing director;
(*b*) five shall be persons having, in the opinion of the Minister, knowledge and experience of the economy of The Bahamas.

(3) The Chairman and every director shall be appointed by the Minister by instrument in writing.

(4) The managing director shall be the chief executive of the Bank and shall be responsible to the Board for—

(*a*) the day to day administration of the Bank's affairs; and
(*b*) the provision of technical advice and guidance in matters of policy.

(5) No action, suit, prosecution or other proceeding shall be brought or instituted personally against the Chairman or any other director in respect of any act done *bona fide* in pursuance or execution or intended execution of the provisions of this Act.

(6) Where any director is exempt from liability by reason only of the provisions of subsection (5), the Bank shall be liable to the extent that it would be if that director were a servant or agent of the Bank.

Schedule.

(7) The provisions of the Schedule shall have effect as to the tenure of office of the directors and the operations of the Board and otherwise in relation thereto.

Appointment of officers, servants and agents.

8. The Board may, subject to the approval of the Minister, appoint and employ at such remuneration and on such terms and conditions as it thinks fit such officers, servants and agents as it thinks necessary for the proper performance of its functions under this Act.

Minister may give policy directions.

9.—(1) The Minister may, after consultation with the Chairman, give to the Bank such directions in writing as to the policy to be followed by the Bank in performance of its functions as appear to the Minister to be requisite in the public interest, and the Bank shall give effect to any such directions.

(2) The Bank shall furnish the Minister with such returns, accounts and other information as he may require with respect to the property and activities of the Bank, and shall afford to him facilities for verifying such information in such manner and at such times as he may reasonably require.

## PART III. SPECIAL FUNCTIONS AND POWERS OF BANK IN RELATION TO SMALL BUSINESS

**10.** For the purposes of this Part, "small business" or "business" means an enterprise of an industrial, commercial, agricultural, manufacturing or servicing character. Interpretation.

11.—(1) Subject to the provisions of this Part, it shall be the duty of the Bank to assist persons who are citizens of The Bahamas in establishing, carrying on or expanding small businesses by granting loans and other forms of financial assistance and generally by giving advice and technical assistance to such persons. Functions of Bank in relation to small businesses.

(2) For the purpose of the discharge of its duty under subsection (1) the Bank shall have power to—

*(a)* grant loans on such terms as to security, rate of interest, repayment of principal and other similar matters as the Bank may think fit;
*(b)* guarantee loans where the purpose of a loan is one for which the Bank would have power to make a loan under this Part;
*(c)* purchase, for the purpose of reselling or letting on hire or hire-purchase to persons establishing or carrying on business to which this Part applies, equipment, plant, tools and other articles necessary for establishing or carrying on such business;
*(d)* make loans to or make investments in registered cooperative societies for the purpose of enabling such societies to perform the same functions in regard to the business [to] [2] which this Part applies as the Bank is required by this Part to perform.

(3) In addition to any powers possessed by the Bank under this or any other Act, the Bank shall have power, subject to the provisions of this Act and of any regulations made thereunder, to do anything and to enter into any transaction which, in the opinion of the Bank, is necessary to ensure the proper discharge of its functions under this Part.

12.—(1) There shall be a standing committee of the Board to be known as the "Small Business Advisory Committee" (hereafter in this Part referred to as "the Committee") which shall consist of— Small Business Advisory Committee.

*(a)* the Chairman or Acting Chairman of the Board;
*(b)* one other Director appointed by the Board; and
*(c)* the managing director.

(2) The Committee shall have power—

[2] Editor's insertion.

(*a*) to co-opt as members of the Committee not more than two persons who are not directors or officers of the Bank;

(*b*) to invite persons who are not members of the Committee to attend meetings thereof and to advise the Committee on any particular matter;

(*c*) to regulate its own procedure.

(3) It shall be the duty of the Committee to advise and make recommendations to the Bank on all matters relating to the functions of the Bank under this Part.

Limitation on operations of Bank under this Part.

13.—(1) No loan or other financial assistance may be granted by the Bank under this Part unless the application for the loan or other financial assistance has first been referred to the Committee and received a favourable recommendation from the Committee.

(2) In granting a loan or other financial assistance under this Part, the Bank shall have regard to the availability of finance from other sources and shall not, as a general rule, itself grant a loan or other financial assistance under this Part if such assistance is available from other sources on terms and conditions which are not less favourable than the Bank itself would impose.

(3) No loan or other financial assistance shall be granted by the Bank under this Part for the sole purpose of enabling goods to be purchased in order that they may be resold in the same condition as that in which they were purchased but, notwithstanding the foregoing provisions of this subsection, the Bank may grant a loan to a person engaged in the retail trade if the purpose of the loan is to enable such a trader to acquire premises in which to establish a business or to enable such a trader to acquire or improve equipment or plant necessary for the purpose of establishing or carrying on his business.

## PART IV. FINANCIAL PROVISIONS

### A—GENERAL

Authorised capital.

14.—(1) The authorised capital of the Bank shall be five million dollars divided into one million shares of the par value of five dollars each.

(2) The Government may subscribe for the said one million five dollars shares such other amount as the Minister may from time to time determine at par.

(3) Subject to the approval signified by resolution of the House of Assembly the authorised capital of the Bank may from time to time be increased by resolution of the Board.

Borrowing powers.

15.—(1) Subject to the provisions of this Act and with the prior approval of the Minister, the Bank may borrow money required by it for meeting any of its obligations or performing any of its functions.

(2) The aggregate of the liabilities of the Bank outstanding at any one time, including direct liabilities such as bonds and debentures issued by the Bank and the contingent liabilities of the Bank in the form of guarantees given or underwriting agreements entered into by it, shall not at any time exceed seven times the aggregate amount of the paid up capital and the reserve fund for which provision is made in section 19.

Guarantee of borrowings by Government.

16.—(1) With the prior approval signified by resolution of the House of Assembly, the Minister may guarantee, in such manner and on such conditions as he may think fit, the payment of the principal and of interest on any authorised borrowings of the Bank.

(2) Where the Minister is satisfied that there has been default in the repayment of any principal moneys or interest guaranteed under the provisions of this section he shall direct the repayment from the Consolidated Fund of the amount in respect of which there has been such default.

Repayment of and interest on advances and sums issued to meet guarantee.

17. The Bank shall make to the Treasurer at such times and in such manner as the Minister may direct payments of such amounts as may be so directed in or towards repayment of advances made to the Bank by Government and of any sums issued at such rate as the Minister may direct and different rates of interest may be directed as respects different advances and sums and as respects interest for different periods.

Securities.

18. The Bank—

*(a)* may issue debentures or bonds for the purpose of exercising its borrowing powers under section 15;

*(b)* shall establish a sinking fund for the redemption of debentures so created;

*(c)* may postpone sinking fund contributions for such period or periods of time as may be approved by the Minister.

Reserve fund.

19. The Bank shall set aside in each year out of the net profits (if any) of the Bank a minimum of twenty-five per centum of such profits

towards a reserve fund to meet contingencies and for such other purposes as the Bank may think fit until the total amount standing to the credit of such reserve fund shall amount to a sum equal to its paid up capital.

Accounts and audit.

20.—(1) The Bank shall keep proper accounts and other records in relation to the business of the Bank and shall prepare annually a statement of accounts in a form satisfactory to the Minister, being a form which shall conform with the best commercial standards.

(2) The accounts of the Bank shall be audited by an auditor or auditors appointed annually by the Bank and approved by the Minister.

(3) So soon as the accounts of the Bank have been audited, the Bank shall send the statement of the accounts referred to in subsection (1) to the Minister together with a copy of any report made by the auditors on that statement or on the accounts of the Bank.

(4) The auditor's fees and expenses of the audit shall be paid by the Bank.

(5) The auditor shall be entitled, on the direction of the Minister, at all reasonable times to examine the accounts and other records in relation to the business of the Bank and the Bank shall provide the auditor with all necessary and proper facilities for such an examination.

(6) The members of the Board, officers and servants of the Bank, shall grant to an auditor appointed under subsection (2) to audit the accounts or to the auditor in the exercise of his functions under subsection (5) access to all books, documents, cash and securities of the Bank and shall give to him on request all such information as may be within their knowledge in relation to the operations of the Bank.

(7) Any person who fails without reasonable excuse to comply with the provisions of subsection (6) shall be guilty of an offence and shall be liable on summary conviction to a fine not exceeding three hundred dollars or to a term of imprisonment not exceeding six months.

Annual Report.

21.—(1) The Bank shall, not later than four months after the end of each financial year, cause to be made and transmitted to the Minister a report dealing with the activities of the Bank during the preceding financial year, and containing such information relating to the proceedings and policy of the Bank as can be made public without detriment to the interests of the Bank.

(2) The Minister shall cause a copy of the report together with the annual statements of accounts and the auditor's report thereon to be laid on the table of both Houses of Parliament.

(3) Copies of the Bank's report together with the annual statement of accounts and the auditor's report on that statement or on the accounts of the Bank shall be published in such manner as the Minister may direct and shall be made available to the public by the Bank at a reasonable price.

Prohibited activities.

22.—(1) Except as expressly authorised by this Act the Bank may not—

*(a)* without the approval signified by resolution of the House of Assembly in each case, sell, pledge, distribute or otherwise dispose of more than twenty-five per centum of its ordinary shares or common stock of any subsidiary of the Bank;

*(b)* except as it becomes necessary through bankruptcies, defaults in performance of agreements or covenants, or other similar events, engage directly in manufacturing, agriculture or any similar business activity.

(2) In computing the percentage of the ordinary shares or common stock specified in paragraph *(a)* of subsection (1) account shall not be taken of any such shares or stock held by other agencies of the Government.

B—OPERATIONAL POWERS

Repayment of loans made by the Bank.

23.—(1) Subject to the provisions of this section, every loan made by the Bank shall be repaid to the Bank in accordance with the terms and conditions under which such loan was made.

(2) The Bank may at any time accept payment of the whole or part of the amount representing the principal of a loan and interest thereon, before the time when such payment is due, upon such terms and conditions as it thinks fit.

Examination of application of moneys lent.

24.—(1) Where the Bank has made or guaranteed a loan of money under the provisions of this Act, it shall—

*(a)* from time to time make or cause to be made such examination as may be necessary to ensure that the loan is being applied to the purposes for which it is made;

*(b)* require the person to whom the loan was made to give either immediately or periodically such information to the Bank as the Bank may require, and such person shall comply with the requirements of the Bank.

(2) The Bank may authorise in writing any of its officers or any other person to make such examination, and any officer or person so

authorised shall be entitled to demand production of all such books, documents and other matters and things as he considers necessary for the purpose of making such examination.

(3) Any person who fails without reasonable cause to give any information as required in accordance with paragraph *(b)* of subsection (1), or to produce a book, document or other matter or thing as demanded in accordance with subsection (2) shall be guilty of an offence and shall be liable on summary conviction to a fine not exceeding three hundred dollars or to a term of imprisonment not exceeding six months.

Order of Bank upon such examination.

25. Where on any examination made under section 24 it appears to the Bank that any sum, being the whole or any part of the loan made or guaranteed by the Bank, has not been applied to the purposes for which the loan was made, it may order that any such sum be, within the time mentioned in the order, applied to such purposes or, if the loan was made by the Bank, that such sum, together with any interest due thereon on the date of the order, be repaid to the Bank within the time mentioned on the order, and any sum with the interest thereon so ordered to be repaid to the Bank shall thereupon become a debt due to the Bank.

Misapplication of loan secured by mortgage or otherwise.

26.—(1) If any loan made under the provisions of this Act or any part of such loan has been misapplied the Bank may—

*(a)* where the loan has been secured by mortgage, by notice in writing addressed to the mortgagor, recall the said loan or any part thereof and may require the loan or that part together with any interest due on the loan or part thereof on the date of the notice, to be repaid on a date to be specified in the notice and in default of payment on such specified date any security given for the purpose of the loan may thereupon be realised;

*(b)* where the loan has been secured otherwise than by way of mortgage, by notice addressed to the borrower, require the loan, or any part thereof, together with any interest due on the loan or part thereof on the date of the notice to be repaid on a date to be specified in the notice, and in default of payment on such specified date any security given for the purpose of the loan may thereupon be realised.

(2) The provisions of subsection (1) shall be in addition to any other proceedings which may be taken by the Bank under any other Act.

27. Where any property mortgaged as security for a loan under the provisions of this Act is sold for the purpose of the enforcement of the security, the Bank may buy such property and may either manage and hold such property or carry on any business with such property or sell or otherwise dispose of it as the Bank thinks fit.

Enforcement of securities.

28.—(1) Notwithstanding that a loan granted by the Bank may not have been secured by a mortgage within the meaning of The Conveyancing and Law of Property Act, the Bank may, if a borrower defaults in respect of a loan made by the Bank, appoint a receiver in respect of the business in connection with which the loan was made, and a receiver so appointed shall have the same powers *mutatis mutandis* as a receiver appointed pursuant to the power conferred on a mortgagee by section 21 of The Conveyancing and Law of Property Act.

Power to appoint a receiver, etc.

(2) A person appointed by the Bank to be a receiver pursuant either to the power conferred on a mortgagee by section 21 of The Conveyancing and Law of Property Act or to the power conferred on the Bank by subsection (1), shall, if the Bank so appoint, be also the manager of the business in respect of which the loan was made and the effect of such an appointment shall be the same as if the person so appointed had been appointed by the Supreme Court to be the receiver and manager of such business.

(3) No person appointed by the Bank to be a receiver or a receiver and manager under this section shall be deemed to be an officer of the Court.

29. Any person who—

Offences in respect of loans.

*(a)* obtains a loan or other financial assistance from the Bank by means of any false representation;

*(b)* wilfully applies any loan made to him by the Bank or guaranteed by the Bank under the provisions of this Act to any purpose other than the purpose for which the loan was made;

*(c)* having obtained a loan from the Bank or the guarantee by the Bank of a loan under the provisions of this Act, wilfully destroys any security given in relation to any such loan or guarantee,

shall be guilty of an offence and shall be liable on summary conviction to a fine not exceeding one thousand five hundred dollars, or to imprisonment for a term not exceeding twelve months or to both such fine and imprisonment.

## PART V. MISCELLANEOUS

Power to delegate.

**30.** Subject to the provisions of this Act, the Bank may—

(*a*) delegate to any director or to the managing director or any other officer of the Bank the power to carry out on behalf of the Bank such duties as the Bank may determine;

(*b*) delegate to the management of any subsidiary such of the Bank's powers in relation to that subsidiary as are consistent with the provisions of the legislation under which the subsidiary is established; and

any such delegation—

(i) shall be made subject to such restrictions and conditions as the Bank thinks fit;

(ii) while in force shall not prevent the exercise by the Bank of the power thereby delegated;

(iii) may at any time be revoked by the Bank.

Minutes receivable in evidence.

**31.** Minutes made of meetings of the Board shall, if duly signed by the Chairman or other director presiding at the meeting, be receivable in evidence in all legal proceedings without further proof and every meeting of the Board in respect of which minutes have been so signed shall be deemed to have been duly convened and held and all the directors present thereat to have been duly qualified to act.

Secrecy.

**32.**—(1) Except in so far as may be necessary for the due performance of his functions under this Act, or as may be required by the provisions of any agreement into which the Bank has entered, every director, officer and employee of the Bank shall preserve and aid in preserving secrecy with regard to all matters relating to the affairs of the Bank or any customer of the Bank or of any person who has any dealings with the Bank, that may come to his knowledge in the course of his duties.

(2) Any director, officer or employee of the Bank who—

(*a*) communicates any matter referred to in subsection (1) to any person other than the Board, a director, an officer or employee of the Bank authorised in that behalf by the managing director of the Bank or a person to whom any such matter is required to be communicated under the provisions of any agreement into which the Bank has entered; or

(*b*) suffers or permits any unauthorised person to have access to any books, papers or other records relating to the Bank or any customer of the Bank or other person having dealings with the Bank,

shall be guilty of an offence and shall be liable on summary conviction to a fine not exceeding two thousand five hundred dollars or to imprisonment for a term not exceeding one year.

(3) No officer or employee of the Bank shall be required to produce in any court any book or document or to divulge or communicate to any court any matter or thing coming under his notice in the performance of his duties under this Act, except on the direction of the court or in so far as may be necessary for the purpose of carrying into effect the provisions of this Act.

Verifying false statements.

33. Any director, officer, employee or auditor of the Bank who verifies any statement, account or report required to be furnished to the Minister pursuant to this Act, or who is concerned with delivering or transmitting the same to the Minister, knowing the same to be false in a material particular, shall be guilty of an offence and shall be liable on summary conviction to a fine not exceeding five thousand dollars or to imprisonment for a term not exceeding two years.

Regulations.

34. The Minister may make regulations—

*(a)* prescribing the maximum amount of any loan which may be made or guaranteed in respect of any one business under Part III; and

*(b)* prescribing any other thing which may be or is required to be prescribed under this Act.

## SCHEDULE

(Section 7(7))

Tenure of office.

1. The term of office of every director shall be specified in the instrument appointing him and—

*(a)* for the Chairman shall not exceed five years; and

*(b)* for every other director shall not exceed three years,

but any director retiring on the expiration of his term of office shall, subject to paragraph 2 of this Schedule, be eligible for reappointment.

Disqualification of directors.

2. A person may not be appointed or remain a director who is a member of Parliament.

Temporary appointment.

3. The Minister may appoint any person who might be appointed a director to act temporarily in the place of any director who is absent or unable to act.

Resignation.

4.—(1) Any director other than the Chairman may at any time resign his office by instrument in writing addressed to the Minister and transmitted through the Chairman, and from the date of the receipt by the Minister of such instrument such director shall cease to be a director of the Bank.

(2) The Chairman may at any time resign his office by instrument in writing addressed to the Minister and such resignation shall take effect on the date of the receipt of such instrument by the Minister.

Revocation of appointments.

5. The Minister may at any time by instrument in writing revoke the appointment of any director if he thinks it expedient so to do.

Filling of vacancies.

6. If any vacancy occurs in the membership of the Board, such vacancy shall be filled by the appointment of another member who shall, subject to the provisions of this Schedule, hold office for the remainder of the period for which the previous member was appointed.

Publication of membership.

7. The names of all members of the Board as first constituted and every change in the membership thereof shall be published in the *Gazette.*

Procedure at meetings.

8.—(1) The Board shall meet as often as it deems necessary or expedient for the due performance of its functions and of the functions of the Bank (but not less frequently than ten times in each year) and such meetings shall be held at such places, on such days and at such times as the Chairman determines.

(2) The Chairman, or, in the event of the absence or inability to act of the Chairman, a director elected by the directors present to act in that behalf, shall preside at a meeting of the Board and the Chairman or director so presiding shall, where the voting is equal, have a casting vote.

(3) The quorum of the Board shall be such number as the Board may fix from time to time being not less than one-half of the total number of members of the Board.

(4) The validity of any proceeding of the Board shall not be affected by any vacancy amongst the directors or by any defect in the appointment of a director.

(5) Subject to the provisions of this Schedule the Board may regulate its own proceedings.

Remuneration.

9. There shall be paid to the Chairman and the other directors such remuneration, if any, as the Minister may determine.

Prevention of conflict of interest.

10. The Bank shall not make an investment in or otherwise transact business with any enterprise in which a director of the Bank is a partner, director or shareholder or is in any other way directly or indirectly interested.

# The Savings Bank Act[1]

An Act relating to the Bahamas Post Office Savings Bank.

[1st June, 1936]

Short title.

1. This Act may be cited as The Savings Bank Act.

[1] Act No. 7 of 1936, as amended by Act No. 43 of 1964 and The Existing Laws Amendment Order, 1974.

2. In this Act, unless the context otherwise requires— Interpretation.

"Minister" means the Minister responsible for the Post Office Savings Bank;

"prescribed" means prescribed by rules under this Act;

"revenue" of the Savings Bank does not include moneys received on deposit;

"Savings Bank" means The Post Office Savings Bank established under The Post Office Act and continued under this Act as the Post Office Savings Bank of the Colony.[2]

3. The Savings Bank (and all offices thereof) subsisting at the time when this Act comes into operation shall be deemed to be constituted and appointed under this Act. Constitution of Savings Bank.

4. Subject to the provisions of section 11 of this Act the Savings Bank shall be under the management and control of the Postmaster who may, subject to the provisions of this Act and any rules made thereunder, take such steps as may be desirable for the encouragement of thrift, for the proper management of the Savings Bank, and otherwise for the promotion of the objects and purposes of this Act. Management under Postmaster.

5. The Postmaster may, with the approval of the Minister, open branch savings banks at any post office in the Colony and may, with like approval, close any branch savings bank. Establishment and closure of branch savings banks.

6. The Governor-General, acting in accordance with the advice of the Public Service Commission, may appoint such persons as may be necessary for the execution of this Act. Appointment of Officers.

7. Deposits of money to be paid into the Savings Bank shall be received and repaid under such conditions as may be prescribed. Deposits and repayments.

8. The repayment of all moneys deposited in the Savings Bank together with interest thereon is guaranteed by the Government of the Colony, and accordingly if at any time or times the assets of the Savings Bank shall be insufficient to pay the lawful claims of every depositor, the Minister of Finance shall cause such deficiency to be met out of the Consolidated Fund, which is hereby appropriated to that purpose. Security of Government.

[2] The Existing Laws Amendment Order, 1974, provides in section 3:

"A reference in an existing law to the Colony meaning thereby the former Colony of the Commonwealth of The Bahama Islands shall be read and construed as a reference to the Commonwealth of The Bahamas."

Interest.

9.—(1) Interest shall be payable on deposits at the rate of two per per centum per annum, or at such other rate as may be fixed from time to time by the Minister:

Provided that not less than three months' notice of any notice of any change of rate shall be given in the *Gazette.*

(2) Such interest shall not be payable on any amount less than one pound or on any fraction of one pound and shall not commence to accrue until the first day of the month next following the day of deposit, and shall cease on the last day of the month preceding that in which such deposit shall be withdrawn.

(3) Interest on deposits shall, subject to the provisions of subsection (2) of this section, be calculated to the thirtieth day of June in every year and shall then be added to and become part of any principal money remaining on deposit.

Salaries and expenses.

10.—(1) All expenses incurred in the execution of this Act shall be met from revenue derived from the investment of moneys deposited in the Savings Bank.

(2) For the purposes of this Act expenses shall mean the cost of any work or service done by or in connection with the Savings Bank, including such sum on account of administrative and other overhead expenses as may, with the approval of the Minister, be reasonably assigned to that work or service.

Disposal of moneys.

11.—(1) Subject to the provisions of this Act moneys in the Savings Bank shall not be applied in any way to the purposes of the Colony, but, except so far as any sums may be prescribed to be kept in hand for the general purposes of the Savings Bank, shall be deposited in the Treasury and shall, as far as practicable, be invested on behalf of the Savings Bank, under the direction of the Treasurer, in such securities or be employed at interest in such manner as shall be approved from time to time by the Minister, and any such investment may at any time be changed into other like securities:

Provided that not more than one-third of such moneys shall at any time be or remain invested in securities of the Government of the Colony.

(2) Any sums of money that may from time to time be required for the repayment of any deposit or deposits under the authority of this Act, or for the payment of interest thereon or expenses incurred in the execution of this Act, may be raised by the sale of the whole or part of such securities:

Provided that any sums of money which may be required for the purposes aforesaid, may, with the approval of the Minister, be advanced to the Savings Bank by the Treasurer out of the general revenues of the Colony until they can be raised by the sale of such securities and such advances shall bear interest at the rate from time to time payable to depositors.

12. Annual accounts of the revenue and expenditure of the Savings Bank and of deposits received and repaid and interest credited to depositors during the year ended on the thirtieth day of June together with a statement of the assets and liabilities of the Savings Bank, shall, after being audited and certified by the Auditor, be laid upon the table of the two Houses of the Legislature not later than the thirty-first day of December ensuing in every year and shall as soon as practicable thereafter be published in the *Gazette.* Accounts.

13.—(1) If in any year the revenue of the Savings Bank shall be insufficient to defray the interest due to depositors and all expenses under this Act, such deficiency shall be met out of the Consolidated Fund which is hereby appropriated to that purpose. Surpluses and deficits.

(2) If in any year the revenue of the Savings Bank shall be more than sufficient to defray the interest due to depositors and all expenses under this Act, then the Minister may direct the transfer of the surplus or any portion thereof to the Consolidated Fund:

Provided that no such transfer shall be made unless the assets of the Savings Bank will thereafter exceed the liabilities by not less than fifteen per centum of the liabilities to depositors.

(3) If on the thirtieth day of June in any year the assets of the Savings Bank exceed the liabilities by more than fifteen per centum of the liabilities to depositors then the Minister may direct that the surplus over fifteen per centum or any portion thereof shall be transferred to the Consolidated Fund.

14.—(1) The Minister may make rules for the management and regulation of the Savings Bank. Powers to make rules.

(2) In particular and without prejudice to the generality of the foregoing powers such rules may—

*(a)* prescribe limits of deposits;
*(b)* prescribe the modes of making deposits;
*(c)* prescribe the modes of withdrawing deposits and interest;
*(d)* prescribe the times at which deposit books shall be returned to the Savings Bank by depositors;

(e) regulate deposits by minors, guardians, trustees, married women, Friendly Societies and other charitable bodies;

(f) prescribe conditions for the withdrawal of moneys by minors, guardians, trustees, married women, Friendly Societies and other charitable bodies;

(g) prescribe the modes of dealing with the deposits of deceased or insane persons;

(h) prescribe penalties not exceeding a fine of twenty-five pounds for the breach of any such rule;

(i) provide for the forfeiture of deposits made in wilful contravention of this Act;

(j) authorise the Postmaster to enter into an arrangement with the Post Office Savings Bank of the United Kingdom of Great Britain and Northern Ireland or with the Government Savings Bank of any other country of the Commonwealth, or any foreign country, for the transfer of any sum standing to the credit of depositors from such Savings Bank to the Colony Savings Bank, and vice-versa, and prescribe conditions for such transfers.

Names of depositors, etc., not to be disclosed.

15.—(1) No person appointed to carry this Act into effect shall disclose the name of any depositor or the amount which may have been deposited or withdrawn by any depositor except in due course of law, or to such person or persons as may be appointed to assist in carrying this Act into operation.

(2) Any person contravening the provisions of this section shall on summary conviction be liable to a fine of one hundred pounds.

Settlement of disputes.

16. If any dispute shall arise between the Postmaster or the officer managing and controlling any branch savings bank and any individual depositor therein, or any executor, administrator, next-of-kin of a depositor, or any creditor or assignee of a depositor who may become bankrupt or insolvent, or any person claiming to be such executor, administrator, next-of-kin, creditor or assignee, or to be entitled to any money deposited in such Savings Bank, then, and in every such case, the matter in dispute shall be referred to an arbitrator to be appointed by the Minister, and if the parties be dissatisfied with the decision given by the single arbitrator so appointed the matter may be referred to arbitration under the provisions of The Arbitration Act.

Non-liability of Government.

17. When any payment is made or act done by the Postmaster or any person acting under his authority in accordance with this Act and the rules for the time being made thereunder, the Government, the Postmaster and such person shall not be liable in respect of any claim

on the part of any person in connection with such payment or act, but any person may nevertheless recover any sum lawfully due to him from the person to whom the Postmaster has paid the same.

# The Securities Act, 1971 [1]

An Act to regulate the business of dealings in securities; to control the issue of prospectuses by companies; to make provision for preventing fraud in connexion with dealings in investments; and for related purposes.

[Assented to 8th June, 1971]

BE it enacted by The Queen's Most Excellent Majesty, by and with the advice and consent of the Senate and the House of Assembly of the Commonwealth of the Bahama Islands, and by the authority of the same, as follows:—

## PART I. PRELIMINARY

Short title and commencement.

1. This Act may be cited as The Securities Act, 1971, and shall come into operation on such day as the Minister may appoint by notice published in the *Gazette.*

Interpretation.

2.—(1) In this Act, unless the context otherwise requires—

"authorised dealer" has the meaning assigned thereto in paragraph (1) of regulation 44 of The Exchange Control Regulations;

"authorised agent" means a person appointed as authorised agent for a beneficial owner of investment currency or foreign currency securities pursuant to The Exchange Control Regulations and licensed under The Banks and Trust Companies Regulation Act, 1965, to carry on trust business;

"Bahamian-based mutual fund scheme" means a mutual fund scheme of a kind specified in the Schedule; Schedule.

"corporation" means any body corporate, incorporated or registered whether in the Bahama Islands or elsewhere;

[1] Act No. 10 of 1971, as amended by the Schedule to The Existing Laws Amendment Order, 1974.

"dealing in securities" means doing any of the following things (whether as a principal or as an agent), that is to say, making or offering to make with any person, or inducing or attempting to induce any person to enter into or offer to enter into—

(*a*) any agreement for, or with a view to, acquiring, disposing of, subscribing for or underwriting securities; or

(*b*) any agreement the purpose or pretended purpose of which is to secure a profit to any of the parties from the yield of securities or by reference to fluctuations in the value of securities,

and "deal in securities" shall be construed accordingly;

"debentures" means any debentures, debenture stock or bonds of a corporation, whether constituting a charge on the assets of the corporation or not;

"investment company scheme" means a scheme consisting of any arrangements made for the purpose, or having the effect, of providing facilities for the participation by persons in profits or income arising from the operation of a corporation engaging primarily, or purporting to engage primarily, in the business of acquiring, holding, managing or disposing of securities or any other property whatsoever;

"licence" means a licence under section 5;

"Minister" means the Minister of Finance;

"mutual fund scheme" means any investment company scheme or unit trust scheme but does not include any such scheme where, under the provisions of the scheme—

(*a*) the persons participating in profits or income in the scheme may not exceed twenty-four; and

(*b*) none of such persons as aforesaid may be a corporation or firm;

"private corporation" means a corporation which, by the charter, statutes or memorandum and articles of the corporation or other instrument constituting or defining the constitution of the corporation—

(*a*) limits the number of its members to twenty-four;

(*b*) prohibits any other corporation or any firm from membership of the corporation or holding any of its securities; and

(*c*) prohibits any person other than the holder from having any interest in any of its securities;

"registered", in relation to a mutual fund scheme, means registered, or deemed to be registered, under section 8; and "unregistered" in relation to such a scheme shall be construed accordingly;

"section" means section of this Act;

"securities" means—

*(a)* shares or debentures, or rights or interests (described whether as units or otherwise) in any shares or debentures; or

*(b)* securities of the Government of the Bahama Islands or of the Government of any country outside the Bahama Islands,

and includes rights or interest (described whether as units or otherwise) which may be acquired under any mutual fund scheme;

"shares" means shares in the share capital of a corporation or stock of a corporation;

"unit trust scheme" means a scheme consisting of any arrangements made for the purpose, or having the effect, of providing facilities for the participation by persons, as beneficiaries under a trust, in profits or income arising from the acquisition, holding, management or disposal of securities or any other property whatsoever.

(2) Any reference in this Act to a licence holder or to the holder of a licence shall be construed as a reference to the person named in the licence as being thereby authorised to carry on the business of dealing in securities.

(3) Any reference in this Act to the manager of a mutual fund scheme or to the trustee of such a scheme shall be construed as a reference to the person in whom are vested the powers of management relating to property for the time being the subject of the scheme or, as the case may be, the person in whom such property is or may be vested in trust in accordance with the terms of the scheme.

(4) Any reference in this Act to a servant of, or to a person employed by, any person shall, in relation to a corporation, be construed as including a reference to any director or officer of the corporation.

(5) For the purposes of this Act, a person shall be deemed to be a director of a corporation if he occupies in relation thereto the position of a director, by whatever name called, or is a person in accordance with whose directions or instructions the directors of a corporation or any of them act:

Provided that a person shall not by reason only that the directors of a corporation act on advice given by him in a professional capacity be taken to be a person in accordance with whose directions or instructions those directors or any of them act.

## PART II. DEALING IN SECURITIES

Dealing in securities prohibited.

3.—(1) Save as expressly allowed under this Act, no person shall engage in, carry on or purport to carry on the business of dealing in securities or, in the capacity of a servant or agent of any person engaged in, carrying on or purporting to carry on that business, deal or purport to deal in securities.

(2) Any person who contravenes this section shall be guilty of an offence and, subject to section 24, liable, on conviction on information, to imprisonment for a term not exceeding two years or to a fine not exceeding one thousand five hundred dollars or to both such imprisonment and fine or, on summary conviction, to imprisonment for a term not exceeding six months or to a fine not exceeding five hundred dollars or to both such imprisonment and fine.

When and by whom dealing in securities permitted.

4. The restrictions imposed by section 3 in relation to dealing in securities shall not apply—

*(a)* to the doing of anything by or on behalf of—

(i) the holder of a licence in respect of any securities or class of securities specified in such licence; or

(ii) an authorised dealer or an authorised agent in respect of any securities other than securities of an unregistered mutual fund scheme; or

(iii) a private corporation in respect of any dealing in securities by such corporation on behalf of the members of such corporation; or

(iv) the manager or trustee of a registered mutual fund scheme in respect of any securities of the scheme; or

*(b)* for the period of two months commencing on the date of commencement of this Act, to any dealing in securities by or on behalf of any person who immediately before that date was engaged in, or carried on, the business of dealing in securities and if, but only if, any such person makes application in writing for the purpose to the Minister before the expiry of that period, for a further period of four months immediately following that period.

5.—(1) Subject to the provisions of this Act, the Minister, upon an application in that behalf made by any person in the prescribed manner and upon payment of the prescribed fee, may grant to that person a licence to deal in securities or in any particular securities or in any such class or classes of securities as the Minister may think fit. Licences to deal in securities.

(2) The Minister shall not grant an application for a licence if it appears to him that—

*(a)* by reason of the applicant or any person employed by or associated with the applicant for the purposes of his business—

(i) having been convicted whether within or without the Bahama Islands of an offence his conviction for which necessarily involved a finding that the applicant or, as the case may be, such person acted fraudulently or dishonestly; or

(ii) having committed any breach of any rules made under this Act for the regulation of the conduct of business by holders of licences; or

*(b)* by reason of any circumstances whatsoever which either are likely to lead to the improper conduct of business by, or reflect discredit on the method of conducting business of the applicant or any person so employed by or associated with him as aforesaid; or

*(c)* by reason of the applicant's lack of experience or financial resources,

the applicant is not a fit and proper person to hold a licence.

(3) A licence shall, unless in the meantime it is revoked, be valid for the period of one year beginning with the day specified in the licence as the day on which it takes effect, so, however, that, upon application made for the purpose in the prescribed manner and upon payment of the prescribed fee, such licence may be renewed by the Minister by endorsement on the licence for a further period of one year, and thereafter for further periods of one year, upon application made, and after payment of the prescribed fee, as aforesaid, successively from year to year if the Minister approves.

(4) A licence shall specify the securities or class or classes of securities in which the holder is thereby authorised to deal.

(5) A licence shall be subject to such conditions as the Minister may deem it expedient to impose.

(6) A licence shall specify the name of the person thereby authorised to carry on the business of dealing in the securities or class or

classes of securities therein mentioned and shall not authorise him to carry on the business under any name other than that specified as his name in the licence:

Provided that, if the Minister thinks fit, such a licence may, at the request of the applicant for the licence, be framed so as to authorise the holder thereof to carry on the said business, either alone or jointly with any other person, being the holder of a licence, under such name or style as the applicant may specify in his application.

(7) A copy of the licence shall be exhibited and kept exhibited at every place in the Bahama Islands where the holder carries on the business authorised thereunder.

Revocation of licences.

6.—(1) Subject to subsection (2) of this section, a licence may be revoked at any time by the Minister in any case where the Minister is satisfied that circumstances exist in which a licence could not be granted to the holder by virtue of the provisions of subsection (2) of section 5.

(2) Any holder of a licence aggrieved by the decision of the Minister to revoke his licence under the provisions of subsection (1) of this section may, within thirty days from the date on which notice of such decision is served upon him, appeal, in accordance with rules of court made under section 41 of The Supreme Court Act, to the Supreme Court, who may, with effect from the date of the making of the order of the Court, reverse the decision of the Minister or confirm it.

Rules with respect to the conduct of business.

7.—(1) The Minister may make rules for regulating the conduct of their business relating to dealing in securities by authorised dealers, authorised agents and holders of licences and, in particular, but without prejudice to the generality of the preceding provisions of this subsection, such rules may make provision for all or any of the following matters, that is to say—

*(a)* for prescribing forms of contracts which may be used in making contracts under the authority of any of the provisions of this Act, and directing that, where any contract is made under the authority of a licence by any person otherwise than in the appropriate form prescribed by the rules, such person shall, for the purposes of the preceding provisions of this Act relating to the refusal and revocation of licences, be deemed to have committed a breach of the rules;

*(b)* for prescribing the books, accounts and other documents which must be kept by any authorised dealer, authorised agent or holder of a licence in relation to any dealing in securities; and

(c) for requiring any such person as aforesaid to produce, for inspection by, or by an agent of, the person with whom he has made any agreement by way of dealing in securities under the authority of any of the provisions of this Act, such contract notes and vouchers as may be prescribed by the rules, and to furnish to that person, on demand and on payment of the prescribed fee, copies of entries in books kept by him which relate to the transaction.

(2) A person shall not be guilty of an offence by reason only of a breach of rules made under this section.

Mutual fund schemes.

**8.**—(1) No person shall, except with the written permission of the Minister, perform or purport to perform within or from within the Bahama Islands, in any capacity whatever, any function relating to—

(a) the management or administration of; or

(b) the custody or distribution or insurance of any securities or other property of; or

(c) the keeping or auditing of the accounts of,

any mutual fund scheme, unless such mutual fund scheme has first been registered by the Minister.

(2) The provisions of subsection (1) of this section shall have effect in relation to a mutual fund scheme notwithstanding that such scheme is organized or established outside the Bahama Islands.

(3) Any person who contravenes the provisions of subsection (1) of this section shall be guilty of an offence and, subject to section 24, liable, on conviction on information, to imprisonment for a term not exceeding two years or to a fine not exceeding one thousand five hundred dollars or to both such imprisonment and fine or, on summary conviction, to imprisonment for a term not exceeding six months or to a fine not exceeding five hundred dollars or to both such imprisonment and fine.

(4) The Minister, upon—

(a) an application in that behalf made in the prescribed manner;

(b) payment of the prescribed fee; and

(c) the production of all such documents and information (verified, if the Minister so thinks fit, by statutory declaration) as the Minister may require,

may register a mutual fund scheme for an initial period not exceeding one year beginning on such day as the Minister may determine, so, however, that, upon application made for the purpose in the prescribed manner and upon payment of the prescribed fee, such registration may be renewed by the Minister for a further period of one year, and thereafter for further periods of one year, upon application made, and after payment of the prescribed fee, as aforesaid, successively from year to year if the Minister approves.

(5) Subject to section 10, the Minister may at any time cancel the registration of a mutual fund scheme.

(6) A register of mutual fund schemes registered under this section shall be kept in such manner and in such place as the Minister may approve and shall be open to inspection by members of the public free of charge during office hours.

(7) Every mutual fund scheme in being immediately before the date of commencement of this Act shall be deemed to be a mutual fund scheme registered by the Minister for a period of two months commencing on that date and if, but only if, application for the purpose is made in writing to the Minister before the expiry of that period on behalf of any such scheme as aforesaid, then such scheme shall be deemed to be a mutual fund scheme registered by the Minister until the expiry of a further period of four months immediately following that period or until the prior cancellation of such registration (which prior cancellation the Minister may effect by order made under this subsection, if he is satisfied that the public interest so requires).

(8) Sections 10 and 11 shall not apply in relation to the cancellation of the registration of a mutual fund scheme effected by an order made under subsection (7) of this section.

Certain overseas mutual fund schemes exempt from registration.

9.—(1) The Minister may by order declare any mutual fund scheme organized or established outside the Bahama Islands to be an exempt mutual fund scheme, and any mutual fund scheme so declared shall, for so long as such declaration continues in force, be deemed to be a mutual fund scheme registered by the Minister in accordance with section 8.

(2) Any order made by the Minister under subsection (1) of this section may be expressed so as to declare to be an exempt mutual fund scheme or to be exempt mutual fund schemes any mutual fund scheme or any class or classes of mutual fund schemes approved, registered or otherwise however to the satisfaction of the Minister sanctioned by the Government of any country outside the Bahama Islands or of any state or province of such a country, or by any agency of such a Government, state or province.

(3) The Minister may, subject to section 10, at any time by order revoke a declaration made under subsection (1) of this section if he is satisfied that the public interest so requires.

Representations concerning cancellation of registration of mutual fund schemes.

10.—(1) Before exercising in any case his power to cancel the registration of a mutual fund scheme under subsection (5) of section 8 or to revoke the declaration of such a scheme under subsection (3) of section 9 the Minister shall serve on the manager of the scheme a written notice (at the same time sending a copy thereof to the trustee, if any, of the scheme) that he is considering such cancellation or revocation, setting out, in such manner as the Minister may think fit, the grounds of such proposed cancellation or revocation, and inviting the manager and the trustee, if any, to make to the Minister, within the period of one month from the date of the service of the notice upon the manager, any representations which he or they may desire to make with respect to such proposed cancellation or revocation.

(2) A notice served under subsection (1) of this section may require that such of the functions mentioned in subsection (1) of section 8 as may be specified in the notice shall not be performed in relation to the scheme or shall be performed in such manner, or subject to such conditions or restrictions, as may be so specified; and if the manager or the trustee, if any, of the scheme or any other person performs any function so specified contrary to any such requirement he shall be guilty of an offence and punishable as if found guilty of an offence against the said subsection (1) of section 8.

(3) Any requirement included under subsection (2) of this section in a notice served under subsection (1) thereof shall take effect immediately upon such service and shall continue in force until the expiration of three months from the date of such service or until cancellation of the registration or revocation of the declaration by the Minister or until the Minister in writing notifies the manager that the requirement is cancelled, whichever event shall first occur.

(4) At any time after the expiration of the period of one month allowed by subsection (1) of this section but before the expiration of three months from the date of service of a notice under the said subsection (1) the Minister may by instrument in writing cancel the registration or revoke the declaration, but, before deciding whether or not to effect such cancellation or revocation, he shall take into account any representations made by the manager or trustee as mentioned in the said subsection (1) and, if either of them so requests, afford him an opportunity of being heard by the Minister.

Appeals against cancellation of registration of mutual fund schemes.

11. Any manager or trustee of a mutual fund scheme the registration of which is cancelled by the Minister under subsection (5) of section 8, or the declaration of which to be an exempt mutual fund scheme is revoked by an order made by him under subsection (3) of section 9, may, if aggrieved by such cancellation or revocation, within one month from the date on which notice of such cancellation or revocation is served upon him, appeal in accordance with rules of court made under section 41 of The Supreme Court Act, to the Supreme Court, who may, with effect from the date of the making of the order of the Court, reverse the decision of the Minister or confirm it.

Striking off of companies connected with unregistered mutual fund schemes.

12.—(1) Except with the approval of the Minister—

*(a)* the Registrar General shall not register a company under The Companies Act or The Foreign Companies Act; and

*(b)* no company if already registered under either of the aforesaid Acts shall be entitled to remain so registered,

with a name which in the opinion of the Registrar General suggests that such company is a participant in a mutual fund scheme that is not registered under section 8 of this Act.

(2) Where it is represented to the Minister by the Registrar General that a company is disentitled to remain registered as aforesaid by reason of being in breach of paragraph *(b)* of subsection (1) of this section, the Minister may direct the Registrar General to serve a notice on the company specifying the breach complained of and requiring the company to show cause within one month why it should not be struck off the register of companies.

(3) If any company fails within one month from the service of a notice under the provisions of subsection (2) of this section to show cause why it should not be struck off the register or to satisfy the Minister that the breach complained of has been discontinued and will not be repeated, then the Minister may in writing direct the Registrar General to strike the company off the register; and the Registrar General shall act accordingly, and thereupon the company shall be dissolved.

(4) Upon the striking off of a company pursuant to this section the provisions of sections 5 to 8 (inclusive) of The Removal of Defunct Companies Act shall have effect in relation to such company as they have effect in relation to a company struck off the register pursuant to that Act, but so that in the application by virtue of this subsection to such a company—

*(a)* of the said section 5, the words "the company was at the time of the striking off thereof carrying on business or in operation, or otherwise" shall be deleted;

(*b*) of the said section 8, the word "Any" shall be deleted and there shall be substituted thereof the words "Subject to the provisions of any order made by the Supreme Court under section 5 of this Act, any".

13. The Minister shall cause to be published in the *Gazette,* at such times as he thinks proper— Publication of particulars of licence-holders and of mutual fund schemes.

(*a*) the names and addresses of all holders of licences and also—

(i) in relation to any such holder of a licence who is not a corporation, his nationality or the fact that he has no nationality; and

(ii) in relation to any such holder of a licence that is a corporation, the country under the law of which the corporation is incorporated; and

(*b*) the name and principal place of business in the Bahama Islands of any mutual fund scheme registered by the Minister under section 8,

so, however, that the said information shall be published not less often than once a year.

## PART III. COMPANY PROSPECTUSES

14.—(1) A prospectus shall not be issued in or from within the Bahama Islands by or on behalf of a company or in relation to an intended company unless before the date of its issue— Approval of prospectuses.

(*a*) there has been delivered to the Minister for the purpose of securing approval of the prospectus a copy thereof signed by every director or proposed director of the company or by his agent authorised in writing; and

(*b*) approval thereof has been obtained,

nor shall a prospectus offering for subscription securities of a company incorporated or to be incorporated outside the Bahama Islands (whether the company has or has not established, or when formed will or will not establish, a place of business in the said Islands) be issued, circulated or distributed in the said Islands unless before the date of such issue, circulation or distribution the conditions specified at paragraphs (*a*) and (*b*) of this subsection have been satisfied.

(2) Every prospectus shall state on the face of it that the prospectus has been approved by the Minister as required by subsection (1) of this section.

(3) It shall not be lawful for any person to issue, circulate or distribute in the Bahama Islands any form of application for, or otherwise to offer to sell to any person in the said Islands, securities of such a company or intended company as is mentioned in subsection (1) of this section unless the form is issued, circulated or distributed with, or the offer is supported by, a prospectus which complies with the requirements of the said subsection (1):

Provided that this subsection shall not apply if it is shown that the form of application was issued, circulated or distributed or the offer was made either—

(a) in connexion with a *bona fide* invitation to a person to enter into an underwriting agreement with respect to the securities; or
(b) in relation to securities which were not offered to the public.

If any person acts in contravention of the provisions of this subsection, he shall be guilty of an offence and, subject to section 24, liable, on summary conviction, to imprisonment for a term not exceeding six months or to a fine not exceeding one thousand dollars.

(4) Nothing in this section shall apply to the issue, circulation or distribution to existing members or debenture holders of a company of a prospectus or form of application relating to, or to an offer made to such members or debenture holders to sell, securities of the company, whether an applicant for or an offeree of securities will or will not have the right to renounce in favour of other persons, but, subject as aforesaid, this section shall apply to a prospectus or form of application or offer whether issued, circulated or distributed or, as the case may be, made on or with reference to the formation of a company or subsequently.

(5) Nothing in this section shall limit or diminish any liability which any person may incur under the general law or this Act apart from this section.

(6) If a prospectus is issued, circulated or distributed without having being approved as required by subsection (1) of this section, every person who is knowingly a party to the issue, circulation or distribution of the prospectus shall be guilty of an offence and, subject to section 24, liable, on summary conviction, to imprisonment for a term not exceeding six months or to a fine not exceeding five hundred dollars for every day from the date of the issue, circulation or distribution of the prospectus until it is withdrawn in a manner which either is reasonable having regard to all the circumstances of the case or accords with the reasonable directions of the Minister.

Minister may approve prospectuses.

15.—(1) The Minister, upon—

*(a)* an application in that behalf made in the prescribed manner;

*(b)* payment of the prescribed fee;

*(c)* the production of all such documents and information as the Minister may require,

may, if in his opinion the public interest so requires, approve a prospectus or refuse to approve it, and the decision of the Minister in every such case shall be final.

(2) Whenever the Minister has approved a prospectus under this section he shall in writing inform the representative of the company in respect of which the application for approval was made of the fact of approval and the date thereof, and every prospectus issued by or on behalf of a company shall show on its face the date of such approval.

Interpretation of this Part.

16.—(1) In this Part, unless the context otherwise requires the expression—

"company" means a company either formed and registered under The Companies Act or incorporated outside the Bahama Islands;

"prospectus" means any prospectus, notice, circular, advertisement or other invitation offering to the public for subscription or purchase any securities of a company.

(2) Where a company (whether formed and registered under The Companies Act or incorporated outside the Bahama Islands) allots or agrees to allot any securities of the company with a view to all or any of those securities being offered for sale to the public, any document by which the offer for sale to the public is made shall for all purposes be deemed to be a prospectus issued by the company, and all enactments and rules of law as to the contents of prospectuses and to liability in respect of statements in and omissions from prospectuses, or otherwise relating to prospectuses, shall apply and have effect accordingly as if the securities had been offered to the public for subscription and as if persons accepting the offer in respect of any securities were subscribers for those securities, but without prejudice to the liability, if any, of the persons by whom the offer is made in respect of misstatements contained in the document or otherwise in respect thereof.

(3) For the purposes of subsection (2) of this section, it shall, unless the contrary is proved, be evidence that an allotment of, or an agreement to allot, securities was made with a view to the securities being offered for sale to the public if it is shown—

*(a)* that an offer of the securities or of any of them for sale to the

public was made within six months after the allotment or agreement to allot; or

*(b)* that at the date when the offer was made the whole consideration to be received by the company in respect of the securities had not been so received.

(4) Where a person making an offer to which subsections (2) and (3) of this section relate is a company or a firm, it shall be sufficient if the document aforesaid is signed on behalf of the company or firm by two directors of the company or not less than half of the partners, as the case may be, and any such director or partner may sign by his agent authorised in writing.

Construction of references to offering securities to the public.

17.—(1) Any reference in this Part to offering securities to the public shall, subject to any provision to the contrary contained therein, be construed as including a reference to offering them to any section of the public, whether selected as members or debenture holders of the company concerned or as clients of the person issuing the prospectus or in any other manner.

(2) Subsection (1) of this section shall not be taken as requiring any offer or invitation to be treated as made to the public if it can properly be regarded, in all the circumstances, as not being calculated to result, directly or indirectly, in the securities becoming available for subscription or purchase by persons other than those receiving the offer or invitation not exceeding twenty-four in number, or otherwise as being a domestic concern of the persons making and receiving it.

## Part IV. General Provisions for the Prevention of Fraud

Penalty for fraudulently inducing persons to invest money.

18. Any person who, by any statement, promise or forecast which he knows to be misleading, false or deceptive, or by any dishonest concealment of material facts, or by the reckless making of any statement, promise or forecast which is misleading, false or deceptive, induces or attempts to induce another person—

*(a)* to enter into or offer to enter into—

(i) any agreement for, or with a view to, acquiring, disposing of, subscribing for or underwriting securities; or

(ii) any agreement the purpose or pretended purpose of which is to secure a profit to any of the parties from the yield of securities or by reference to fluctuations in the value of securities; or (*b*) to acquire or offer to acquire any right or interest under any arrangements the purpose or effect, or pretended purpose or effect, of which is to provide facilities for the participation by persons in profits or income alleged to arise or to be likely to arise from the acquisition, holding, management or disposal of any property other than securities; or

(*c*) to enter into or offer to enter into any agreement the purpose or pretended purpose of which is to secure a profit to any of the parties by reference to fluctuations in the value of any property other than securities,

shall be guilty of an offence and, subject to section 24, liable, on conviction on information, to imprisonment for a term not exceeding seven years.

Restriction on distribution of circulars relating to investments.

19.—(1) Subject to the provisions of this section no person shall—

(*a*) distribute or cause to be distributed any documents, which, to his knowledge, are circulars containing any invitation to persons—

(i) to enter into or to offer to enter into any agreement for, or with a view to, acquiring, disposing of, subscribing for or underwriting securities or any agreement the purpose or pretended purpose of which is to secure a profit to any of the parties from the yield of securities or by reference to fluctuations in the value of securities; or

(ii) to acquire or offer to acquire any right or interest under any arrangements the purpose or effect, or pretended purpose or effect, of which is to provide facilities for the participation by persons in profits or income alleged to arise or to be likely to arise from the acquisition, holding, management or disposal of any property other than securities; or

(iii) to enter into or to offer to enter into any agreement the purpose or pretended purpose of which is to secure a profit to any of the parties by reference to fluctuations in the value of any property other than securities; or

(iv) containing any information calculated to lead directly or indirectly to the doing by the recipient of the information of any of the acts mentioned in sub-paragraphs (i) to (iii) of this paragraph; or

(*b*) have in his possession for the purpose of distribution any documents which to his knowledge are such circulars as aforesaid, being documents of such a nature as to show that the object or principal object of distributing them would be to communicate such an invitation or such information as aforesaid; or

*(c)* permit his name or his address in the Bahama Islands (including a postal box address which he has permission to use) to appear in any document (not being a document the distribution of which is permitted by virtue of the provisions of subsection (2) of this section) which to his knowledge is such a circular as aforesaid, whether or not any such circular is being distributed in the Bahama Islands.

(2) Paragraphs *(a)* and *(b)* of subsection (1) of this section shall not apply in relation to—

*(a)* any distribution of a prospectus or any issue of a form of application for securities which complies with the requirements of section 14; or

*(b)* any distribution of documents which is required or authorised by or under any Act other than this Act; or

*(c)* any distribution of documents which has been approved in writing by the Minister.

(3) This section shall not prohibit the distribution or possession of any document by reason only—

*(a)* that it contains an invitation—

(i) made or given by or on behalf of an authorised dealer or an authorised agent or the holder of a licence with respect to any securities dealing in which by such authorised dealer, authorised agent or licence holder is by virtue of the provisions of section 4 not prohibited by section 3; or

(ii) made or given by or on behalf of a corporation licensed under The Banks and Trust Companies Regulation Act, 1965, to carry on trust business with a view solely to interesting prospective clients in the services provided by that corporation; or

(iii) made or given by or on behalf of the Government of the Bahama Islands or the Minister or the Bahamas Monetary Authority with respect to any securities of that Government; or

(iv) of a kind described in subsection (2) of section 17 as not being made to the public; or

(v) made or given by or on behalf of the manager or trustee of a mutual fund scheme with respect to any securities of that scheme; or

(vi) made or given to beneficiaries under a trust by or on behalf of a person acting in the capacity of a trustee of that trust; or

(vii) made or given with respect to any securities in connexion only with a sale or proposed sale of those securities by auction; or

*(b)* that it contains an invitation or information which a person whose ordinary business or part of whose ordinary business it is to buy and sell any property other than securities (whether as a principal or as an agent) may make or give in the course of buying and selling such property:

Provided that nothing in paragraph *(a)* of this subsection shall authorise the doing of anything in respect of securities of any mutual fund scheme which is not a registered mutual fund scheme; and nothing in paragraph *(b)* of this subsection shall authorise any person to do anything in pursuance of, or for the purposes of, any arrangements the purpose or effect, or the pretended purpose or effect, of which is to provide facilities for the participation by persons in profits or income alleged to arise or to be likely to arise from the acquisition, holding, management or disposal of any property other than securities.

(4) Documents shall not for the purposes of this section be deemed not to be circulars by reason only that they are in the form of, or are contained in, a newspaper, journal, magazine or other periodical publication; but a person shall not be taken to contravene this section by reason only that he distributes, or causes to be distributed, to purchasers thereof, or has in his possession for the purpose of distribution to purchasers thereof, copies of any newspaper, magazine, journal or other periodical publication.

(5) A person shall not be taken to contravene this section by reason only that he distributes documents to persons whose business involves the acquisition and disposal, or the holding, of securities (whether as principal or as agent) or causes documents to be distributed to such persons, or has documents in his possession for the purpose of distribution to such persons.

(6) Any person who contravenes this section shall be guilty of an offence and, subject to section 24, liable, on conviction on information, to imprisonment for a term not exceeding two years or to a fine not exceeding one thousand five hundred dollars or to both such imprisonment and fine or, on summary conviction, to imprisonment for a term not exceeding six months or to a fine not exceeding five hundred dollars or to both such imprisonment and fine.

(7) If a magistrate is satisfied by information on oath that there is reasonable ground for suspecting that, at any such premises as may be specified in the information, a person has any documents in his possession in contravention of this section, the magistrate may grant a warrant under his hand empowering any police officer to enter the premises, if necessary by force, at any time or times within one month from the date of the warrant, and to search for, and seize and remove, any documents found therein which he has reasonable ground for believing to be in the possession of a person in contravention of this section.

(8) Any document seized under this section may be retained for a period of one month or, if within that period there are commenced any proceedings for an offence under this section to which the document is relevant, until the conclusion of those proceedings.

(9) Where any person is convicted of an offence under this section, the court dealing with the case may make an order authorising the destruction, or the disposal in any other specified manner, of any documents produced to the court which are shown to its satisfaction to be documents in respect of which the offence was committed:

Provided that an order under this subsection shall not authorise the destruction of a document, or the disposal of a document in any other manner, until the conclusion of the proceedings in the matter of which the order is made.

## PART V. MISCELLANEOUS

Delegation to Bahamas Monetary Authority of powers under ss. 5 and 15.

20.—(1) The Minister may by instrument in writing delegate to the Bahamas Monetary Authority established under The Bahamas Monetary Authority Act, 1968, the exercise of any power to which this section applies, and any such delegation—

(*a*) may be made subject to such restrictions and conditions as the Minister thinks proper;

(*b*) while in force shall not prevent the exercise by the Minister of the power thereby delegated;

(*c*) may at any time be revoked by the Minister.

(2) Where a delegation is made of a power pursuant to this section—

(*a*) any reference in relation to the exercise of the power by the Minister in this Act or any regulation made thereunder shall be construed accordingly; and

(*b*) any person aggrieved by a decision of the Authority in the exercise of that power may in writing appeal, within fourteen days after receipt of notice of the decision of the Authority, to the Minister, whose decision on such appeal shall be final.

(3) The powers to which this section applies are the power to grant or refuse to grant a licence under section 5 and the power to approve or refuse to approve a prospectus under section 15.

Access by the Minister to premises, information, etc.

21.—(1) Any authorised officer shall be entitled, on behalf of the Minister, at all reasonable times upon demand—

*(a)* to have access to any business premises of any authorised dealer, authorised agent, licence holder or any person performing any function relating to the management or administration of, or to the custody or distribution or insurance of any securities or other property of, a registered Bahamian-based mutual fund scheme and to any such securities, property, cash, books, records, vouchers and any other document therein of any such person as aforesaid; and

*(b)* to require any such person, or any employee of any such person, as aforesaid to supply any such information or explanation,

as the Minister may reasonably require for the purpose of satisfying himself, in the public interest, that the provisions of this Act or of any rules or regulations made thereunder are being complied with by that person in the conduct of any part of his business regulated by this Act or by any such rules or regulations.

(2) With the approval of the Minister an authorised officer may in writing authorise any other person to assist an authorised officer in the exercise of his powers under subsection (1) of this section.

(3) An authorised officer or any person authorised under subsection (2) of this section shall not disclose any information obtained by him in the exercise of his functions under this section except in accordance with the directions of the Minister.

(4) Any person who—

*(a)* fails, without reasonable excuse, to comply with any requirement made in the exercise of the powers conferred by subsection (1) or (2) of this section by an authorised officer or any person authorised under the said subsection (2); or

*(b)* being such an officer or such a person authorised as aforesaid, contravenes the provisions of subsection (3) of this section,

will be guilty of an offence and, subject to section 24, liable, on summary conviction, to imprisonment for a term not exceeding six months or to a fine not exceeding one thousand five hundred dollars or to both such imprisonment and fine.

(5) In this section "authorised officer" means any public officer, or any officer of the Bahamas Monetary Authority, authorised by the Minister in writing to exercise the powers conferred by subsection (1) of this section.

False statements.

22. Any person who, in furnishing any information for any of the purposes of this Act or of any rules or regulations made thereunder, makes any statement which, to his knowledge, is false in a material particular shall be guilty of an offence and liable, on conviction on information, to imprisonment for a term not exceeding two years or to a fine not exceeding five hundred dollars or to both such imprisonment and fine or, on summary conviction, to imprisonment for a term not exceeding three months or to a fine not exceeding two hundred and fifty dollars or to both such imprisonment and fine.

Offences committed by corporations.

23. Where any offence under this Act committed by a corporation is proved to have been committed with the consent or connivance of any director, manager, secretary or other officer of the corporation, he, as well as the corporation, shall be deemed to be guilty of that offence and shall be liable to be proceeded against and punished accordingly.

Limitation on institution of proceedings.

24. Proceedings for an offence under section 3, 8, 14, 18, 19 or 21 shall not be instituted except by, or with the consent of, the Attorney-General:

Provided that this section shall not prevent the arrest, or the issue or execution of a warrant for the arrest, of any person in respect of such an offence, or the remanding, in custody or on bail, of any person charged with such an offence, notwithstanding that the necessary consent to the institution of proceedings for the offence has not been obtained.

Power of Minister to petition for winding up of certain companies.

25.—(1) Notwithstanding the provisions of section 82 of The Companies Act, the Minister shall have power, unless a company to which this section applies is already being wound up by the Court under that Act, to present a petition to the Court for the company to be so wound up if the Court thinks it just and equitable that it should be wound up.

(2) In subsection (1) of this section the expression—

"company to which this section applies" means a corporation incorporated under The Companies Act participating in an investment company scheme;

"Court" has the same meaning as in section 81 of that Act.

26.—(1) The Minister may make regulations generally for the proper carrying out of the purposes and provisions of this Act and may in such regulations make such different provision in respect of different categories of persons, matters or things as he may think fit. Regulations.

(2) In particular, and without prejudice to the generality of the power conferred by subsection (1) of this section, regulations made under this section may—

*(a)* prescribe forms of application for—

(i) the grant and renewal of licences;

(ii) the registration of mutual fund schemes and the renewal of such registration; and

(iii) the grant of approval of prospectuses under section 15,

and the information and documents to be supplied in connexion with such applications;

*(b)* prescribe the fees to be paid in connexion with the making of any such application and on the grant thereof;

*(c)* require the supply by any person, in respect of any licence or any registered mutual fund scheme, of particulars of changes in any information mentioned or referred to in an application for the grant or renewal of such licence or for the registration, or the renewal of the registration, of such scheme;

*(d)* require the supply by any person (whether or not on a periodical basis) of information concerning the accounts of a mutual fund scheme or of the business to which a licence relates;

*(e)* require the notification, by or on behalf of any registered mutual fund scheme, of any disciplinary measure taken against any such category of person connected with such a scheme as may be prescribed by the Government of any overseas country or any agency of such a country having power to regulate dealings in securities in that country;

*(f)* prescribe anything which by this Act (excepting section 7 thereof) is required or authorised to be prescribed.

(3) Regulations made under this section may, notwithstanding the provisions of section 23 of The Interpretation Act, prescribe greater penalties than those specified in the said section 23, so, however, that the maximum penalty that may be imposed by any such regulation shall be a fine of three thousand dollars or imprisonment for a term of twelve months.

27. Any notice to be served under this Act on any person may be served by post, and a letter containing the notice shall be deemed to be properly addressed to that person at his last-known residence or last-known place of business in the Bahama Islands. Service of notices.

SCHEDULE (Sections 2(1), 21(1)*(a)*)

BAHAMIAN-BASED MUTUAL FUND SCHEMES

1. Any unit trust scheme—

*(a)* of which the trustee is either—

(i) a corporation incorporated or registered in the Bahama Islands; or

(ii) an individual who has a place of business in the Bahama Islands or maintains, or has permission to use, a postal box address therein; or

*(b)* the trust instrument of which was created according to the laws of the Bahama Islands; or

*(c)* of which the manager is either—

(i) a corporation incorporated or registered in the Bahama Islands; or

(ii) an individual who has a place of business in the Bahama Islands or maintains, or has permission to use, a postal box address therein.

2. Any investment company scheme—

*(a)* any profits or income of which arise from the operation of a corporation incorporated or registered in the Bahama Islands; or

*(b)* of which the manager is either—

(i) a corporation incorporated or registered in the Bahama Islands; or

(ii) a corporation incorporated outside the said Islands but having a place of business therein; or

(iii) an individual who has a place of business in the Bahama Islands or maintains, or has permission to use, a postal box address therein.

# Hong Kong

Central business district, Hong Kong
Courtesy British Embassy, Hong Kong Office

# HONG KONG

# Financial System of Hong Kong[1]

by

*Ian S. McCarthy* *

## Introduction

Hong Kong Island was ceded by China to Britain in 1842 under the Treaty of Nanking, with the addition of Kowloon in 1860. In 1898 the New Territories were leased from China for 99 years. The Colony was set up as an entrepôt for trade with the Chinese mainland and for most of its history such trade was the main economic activity. However, following the Korean conflict, Hong Kong diversified its economic activity. Export-oriented industries grew rapidly during the 1950s and 1960s until they assumed a dominant position.

The banking system is considerably less rigidly controlled than most. Entry of new banks was for many years virtually unrestricted and the several stock exchanges and the gold market were largely unregulated. However, there have been a number of legislative changes within the last two decades designed to introduce somewhat more control over the financial system.

The financial system comprises the Government of Hong Kong in its role as financial authority; the Financial Secretary as controller of the Exchange Fund (which is used for regulating the exchange value of the currency of Hong Kong); 115 commercial banks; 302 registered deposit-taking companies; 107 representative offices; the gold market, the 4 stock exchanges and assorted nonbank financial intermediaries, such as insurance companies, the commodity exchange, and money brokers. There is no development bank or central bank.

## Financial Institutions

### Government

As there is no central monetary authority the Government has, perforce, assumed some of the responsibilities of a central bank. The Finan-

* Mr. McCarthy, formerly an economist in the Central Banking Service and now in the African Department of the International Monetary Fund, holds degrees from the London School of Economics. He has previously written on offshore banking and deposit insurance.

[1] Much of the data in this introduction has been derived from various issues of *Hong Kong,* a publication of the Government Publications Centre, Hong Kong.

cial Secretary and the Monetary Affairs Branch, which includes the office of the Commissioner of Banking, carry out functions which elsewhere might be the responsibility of a central bank. The issuance of banknotes is handled by two commercial banks. There is no official lender of last resort and the Government's banking is handled, for the most part, by the Hongkong and Shanghai Banking Corporation.

Ultimate responsibility for financial affairs is vested in the Legislative Council, which consists of the Governor, 4 ex officio members (the Chief Secretary, the Attorney-General, the Secretary for Home Affairs, and the Financial Secretary), 17 official members, and 26 unofficial members. While this Council is responsible for financial affairs in Hong Kong, the U.K. Secretary of State for Foreign and Commonwealth Affairs retains a veto power when major decisions are involved. For practical purposes the Financial Secretary is the most important member of the Council when financial matters are concerned, and it is unlikely that the U.K. Secretary of State would overrule decisions of the Council.

A Banking Advisory Committee advises the Governor upon any matter connected with the Banking Ordinance or relating to banking or the carrying on of banking business. The Committee consists of the Financial Secretary, as Chairman, the Secretary for Monetary Affairs, the Commissioner of Banking, and between 4 and 12 other members appointed by the Governor.

The Governor appoints the Commissioner of Banking and can issue directives to both the Financial Secretary and the Commissioner. The Commissioner is responsible for the prudential supervision of the banking system and advising the Governor in Council on the licensing of banks. Under the Banking Ordinance the powers of the Commissioner and the Governor are widely drawn and the banks' rights of appeal are limited.

### Currency

Prior to 1935 Hong Kong was on a silver standard, as was China. When China left the silver standard in November 1935, Hong Kong soon followed suit. At that time Currency Ordinance No. 54 established what is now known as the Exchange Fund.

***Exchange Fund Ordinance.***—The key to understanding the procedure of currency note issuance in Hong Kong is the Exchange Fund Ordinance. The Exchange Fund is used for the purpose of regulating the exchange value of the Hong Kong currency and for the management of the official reserves. The Exchange Fund is managed by the Monetary Affairs Branch of the Government Secretariat under the Financial Secretary. Assets of the Exchange Fund may be held in domestic or foreign currency, gold or silver, and may be invested in securities. The Financial Secretary may borrow amounts for the account of the Exchange Fund up to such limit as may be established by the Legislative Council.[2]

The basic procedure of note issuance is set forth in sec. 4 of the Ordinance. In accordance with this provision, the Financial Secretary may issue to any note-issuing bank noninterest-bearing certificates of indebtedness in return for which the note-issuing bank must transfer to the Financial Secretary collateral equal to the face value of banknotes that the bank may then issue to the public. The collateral that has been transferred by the note-issuing bank to the Financial Secretary must be held by the Exchange Fund for the purpose of redeeming the banknotes issued to the public. However, the Financial Secretary may employ the funds paid to him as collateral by the note-issuing banks for the purpose of purchasing foreign exchange or gold. In order to obtain funds for redemption of the currency, the Financial Secretary may sell the foreign exchange or gold thus purchased.

Funds paid to the Financial Secretary to back the note issue are sold for foreign currencies when this can be done without disturbing the exchange rate. In practice, the note and coin issues are backed almost entirely by assets denominated in foreign currencies. The Exchange Fund's assets do not arise only from the note issue as the Exchange Fund has now taken over the bulk of the assets, which represent the Government's accumulated fiscal surpluses. In exchange for these assets, Exchange Fund debt certificates, which are denominated in Hong Kong dollars, have been issued. In 1979, the Exchange Fund Ordinance was amended so as to require banks which hold short-term deposits from the Exchange Fund to maintain an equivalent holding in specified liquid assets within the meaning of the Banking Ordinance.

The Exchange Fund Ordinance authorizes the Financial Secretary to make transfers to the general revenue fund of Hong Kong whenever the funds in his possession are in excess of 105 per cent of the sum of (a) total borrowings made by him under the Ordinance plus (b) the face value of the outstanding certificates of indebtedness that he has issued.

---

[2] In 1972, the Legislative Council established the limit of HK$7 billion. This was increased in 1981 to HK$30 billion.

***Hongkong and Shanghai Banking Ordinance.***—Until 1978, there were two ordinances each of which applied to one of the note-issuing banks. The third note-issuing bank received its power in respect of note issue from its charter of incorporation (the Chartered Bank). Of the two ordinances, one specifically authorized the Mercantile Bank to issue banknotes. This was called the Mercantile Bank Note Issue Ordinance. It was repealed in 1978. Comparable, although not identical, provisions appear in the Hongkong and Shanghai Banking Corporation Ordinance, which is a general ordinance that applies to note issue as well as to the other activities of the Hongkong and Shanghai Banking Corporation. Mercantile Bank notes still in circulation are now the obligation of the Hongkong and Shanghai Banking Corporation.

Secs. 10 and 11 of the Hongkong and Shanghai Banking Corporation Ordinance provide the authority for that bank to issue banknotes. Sec. 11(1 and 2) authorizes a relatively small original issue not to exceed HK$30 million. As a cover for this issue, the Hongkong and Shanghai Banking Corporation must keep deposited with the Crown Agents, or with trustees appointed by the Secretary of State, approved securities not less in value than HK$30 million. Sec. 11(3) of this Ordinance authorizes the Hongkong and Shanghai Banking Corporation to issue banknotes in excess of the HK$30 million permitted under sec. 11(1 and 2) in accordance with the procedure contemplated by the Exchange Fund Ordinance.

***Related ordinances.***—Three other ordinances are relevant. The Foreign Notes (Prohibition of Circulation) Ordinance provides that the circulation of all bearer banknotes other than those issued by the named note-issuing banks is prohibited. The Bank Notes Issue Ordinance provides that all banknotes lawfully issued shall be legal tender and shall be deemed to be the currency of Hong Kong. A fine is provided for the unauthorized issue of banknotes payable to bearer. Finally, the Dollar and Subsidiary Currency Notes Ordinance authorizes the Financial Secretary to issue a small amount of low-denomination currency notes.

From 1935 to 1967 the currency was linked to sterling. After the sterling devaluation of November 1967 Hong Kong devalued by a smaller amount, breaking the informal link to sterling. (There was never a statutory link.) When the pound was floated in June 1972 the Hong Kong Government briefly switched to fixing the intervention rate in terms of the U.S. dollar, but when the U.S. dollar was devalued in February 1973 this link weakened and in November 1974 the Hong Kong dollar was allowed to float freely.

Before 1971 almost all of Hong Kong's official foreign reserves were denominated in sterling. Since then diversification has taken place and in 1980 the Exchange Fund held less than 15 per cent of its reserves in sterling.

The Government of Hong Kong has the right to vary the currency issuance and, subject to formal approval by the U.K. Secretary of State for Foreign and Commonwealth Affairs, the external value of the dollar.

### Commercial banks

Although nonbank financial intermediaries play an important role in the economy, the commercial banks are the dominant group of financial institutions in Hong Kong. Moreover, because of close links of some of the banks with the great trading companies and the willingness and ability of the banks to take equity stakes, even controlling interests, in industry and commerce, their influence upon the real economy is substantial.

The first bank in Hong Kong opened in 1859 (the Chartered Bank). It was quickly followed by several others, the most notable of which was the Hongkong and Shanghai Banking Corporation (established in 1865). By 1866, 11 banks were operating, but the banking crisis of the same year forced 6 of these to suspend payments. This pattern of "boom and bust" was to be repeated in future years.

For most of its history Hong Kong permitted the ready establishment of new banks. Entry into the banking business, as well as the opening of branches, continued to be relatively unrestricted until 1965. By the end of 1965 there were 91 banks with 94 branches, or a bank for every 28,000 people and a branch for every 27,000. After the 1965 banking crisis involving the failure of Canton Trust, the authorities declared a moratorium on the entry of new banks but not on the establishment of new branches by those banks already licensed. This moratorium applied until 1978, with the exception that a license was granted to Barclays Bank.[3] Although the authorities refused to allow new banks to be established, the setting up of representative offices of foreign banks was not restricted. Between 1970 and 1975 the number of representative offices increased from 32 to 80 and, by the end of 1980, to 107. While these offices are not permitted to accept deposits in Hong Kong, they are able to facilitate offshore business.

[3] Barclays was restricted to one branch until 1976. The exception was granted in order to introduce a London clearing bank.

The permission of the Governor in Council is required in order to transact banking business in Hong Kong and the authorities are able to impose conditions before granting a license to operate. Conceivably, the authorities might have been able to license new banks to carry out exclusively offshore banking or wholesale banking, as their counterparts have done in some other international financial centers. While some consideration was given to this in 1975, different ideas prevailed: from 1965 to 1978 foreign banks wishing to operate out of Hong Kong were forced either to rely upon representative offices or to establish or acquire finance companies. In a few instances, foreign banks, with the prior approval of the authorities, purchased substantial interests in the smaller local banks in order to gain entry. Since 1978 the authorities again began to license foreign banks albeit subject to certain conditions that are described subsequently. At the end of 1980, there were 115 banks in Hong Kong with over 1,200 branches.

Branching within Hong Kong is regulated by the Commissioner of Banking (with appeals permitted to the Governor in Council). While permission to branch has readily been given to indigenous banks, a policy of reciprocity has been applied to foreign banks in accordance with which they have had to show that Hong Kong banks would be able to open branches in their own jurisdictions. Branching abroad by banks incorporated in Hong Kong is legally subject to control.

Noteworthy among the provisions of the Banking Ordinance are the following:

(a) Each bank incorporated in Hong Kong is required to maintain a minimum capital of HK$100 million (secs. 8 and 20).

(b) All banks are required to report to the Commissioner of Banking. They must provide a monthly report on their assets and liabilities, a quarterly statistical return, and such further information as may be required by the Commissioner (sec. 38). In addition, powers of inspection and control are granted to the Commissioner (secs. 15 and 39).

(c) In accordance with sec. 27, acquisition of the share capital of other companies by a bank is allowed but it is not permitted to exceed, in aggregate, 25 per cent of the paid-up capital and reserves of the bank (although an exception is made for an affiliate engaged in a business related to banking). The aggregate of advances to directors, shareholdings, and investments in land is restricted by sec. 29 to 55 per cent of the paid-up capital and reserves (by including real estate adjudged by the Commissioner necessary to the conduct of the business of the bank and for providing housing and amenities for its staff, this percentage may equal 80 per cent).

(d) Although there are no minimum reserve requirements, banks are required by sec. 18 to satisfy a liquid assets ratio. The minimum holding of specified liquid assets was set at 25 per cent of deposit liabilities, with a subsidiary provision that primary liquidity (comprising cash, gold, call money, and demand deposits at other banks and deposit-taking companies, as well as specified treasury bills) should not fall below 15 per cent of deposit liabilities.

(e) A bank incorporated in Hong Kong must appropriate to its published reserve out of the published profit of each year a sum equal to at least one third of such profit before declaring a dividend. Alternatively, it may appropriate a lesser sum so that the aggregate of its paid-up share capital and published reserve is not less than HK$200,000,000 (sec. 19). An additional restriction on distributions is found in sec. 21.

Maximum deposit rates are determined by a Committee of the Hong Kong Association of Banks. The Association was established in January 1981 and replaced the Exchange Banks' Association. The prior association had been in existence since 1897 and from 1964 onward had administered a voluntary interest rates agreement. Membership in the new association is compulsory and its rules bind all of the commercial banks.

In 1980 the authorities enacted the Monetary Statistics Ordinance empowering the Government to collect detailed statistics from all banks and deposit-taking companies. Subsequently, the Commissioner of Banking was given further powers to inspect the operations of banks operating in Hong Kong. Moreover, under the Banking (Amendment) Ordinance 1982, he was empowered under Section 39A to allow examination by foreign banking supervisory authorities of Hong Kong branches, subsidiaries and representative offices of banks incorporated in their countries, as well as to provide information, at his discretion, to such authorities under sec. 53A. Disclosure of information relating to the affairs of individual customers is expressly prohibited.

The growth of banking business has more than matched the proliferation of banks and branches. Unfortunately, data are not available before 1954, but the figures for deposits and amounts due to banks have shown a substantial increase, especially during the 1970s, from HK$1 billion in 1954 to HK$6.5 billion in 1964, to HK$53 billion in 1974, and to HK$235 billion in 1980. Within this decade much of the impetus to the growth in deposits has come from offshore funds. In 1970 balances due to banks abroad equaled HK$2 billion (9 per cent of total liabilities); by 1980 this had increased to HK$118 billion (44 per cent of total liabilities).

The commercial banks may be divided into three categories:

***Hongkong and Shanghai Banking Corporation and its subsidiaries.***—This group is by far the most important single financial institution in Hong Kong: its deposits (including those of its subsidiary banks) make up a substantial proportion of total deposits; its currency issuance is about three fourths of the total; it operates the clearinghouse; it acts as banker to the Government; it has, on occasion, functioned as lender of last resort to both the banking system and to the domestic economy; it is the most important principal in the money market; and it plays a major role in determining interest rates.

The group in the thirty-third largest bank in the world. The Hongkong and Shanghai Banking Corporation had total worldwide assets at the end of 1980 amounting to some HK$239 billion,[4] while the total assets of the Hong Kong offices of the licensed banks amounted to HK$268 billion. The Bank has substantial equity investments. Unlike the U.K. or U.S. banks, it has always been ready to acquire direct interests, even controlling ones.

The Bank owns several subsidiary banks in Hong Kong and elsewhere. It owned a controlling interest in one of the major trading companies, which it rescued, in much the same way as it acquired one of the local banks in 1965, and a substantial interest in the local airline. In 1980 the group purchased a major U.S. bank.

Although the Bank is still the most important commercial bank in Hong Kong, its relative importance has diminished partly as a result of intensified competition from foreign banks. At the same time, its international activities have expanded. While the Bank is in the last analysis a commercial undertaking, it has on occasion provided some of the functions usually carried out by a central bank. Thus, during the 1965 banking crisis—which saw runs on a number of the smaller Chinese banks—the Bank offered support to several of them.

***Other domestic banks.***—Besides the Hongkong and Shanghai Bank group, 40 other banks are organized under Hong Kong law. Of this

[4] "The Top 500 in World Banking: Annual Review," *The Banker,* June 1981. (This figure included subsidiaries besides the two banks in Hong Kong and, therefore, may somewhat overstate the importance of the Hongkong and Shanghai Bank group within Hong Kong.)

number 13 are associated with the People's Republic of China. The main business of the latter banks is servicing trade with and handling remittances to China and they account for about 40 per cent of domestic deposits.

***Foreign banks.***—There are 71 other banks that are foreign owned. They are a heterogeneous group, including the Chartered Bank (the second largest bank in terms of the number of offices which is registered in London), Malaysian and Bengali state banks, and the large international banks.

The major international banks are the most aggressive of the various foreign-owned banks. They have challenged the dominance of the Hongkong and Shanghai Banking Corporation. Generally "takers" on the interbank money market, they were the first to introduce certificates of deposit.

In contrast to the rest of the banks, many of the foreign banks are unused to taking equity positions as opposed to making advances, and, with the exception of the Chartered Bank, they lack a firm base of domestic deposits (partly because of their limited number of branches). Their interest lies more in Hong Kong's position as a regional and offshore center than in the domestic economy alone.

### Deposit-taking companies

Following the 1965 banking crisis a moratorium on the licensing of new banks was introduced which applied, with one exception, for the next 13 years. During this period the Hong Kong economy was buoyant and the Pacific area as a whole became a major growth area. Not surprisingly, therefore, pressures to circumvent the restriction upon entry became great. As mentioned before, some banks were satisfied to set up representative offices but for those that wished to handle onshore business there was another avenue available, namely, the formation of a finance company.

According to sec. 2 of the Banking Ordinance, "banking business" was defined as either:

*(a)* (i) receiving money on current, deposit or other similar account from the general public, and
(ii) paying and collecting cheques drawn by or paid in by customers, and
(iii) making advances to customers; or

(*b*) receiving money on savings account from the general public repayable on demand or within 3 months or at 3 months' notice or less

or both.[5]

One interpretation of this definition was that financial institutions that limited their acceptance of deposits to those having more than three months' maturity were not deemed to be carrying out banking business, and were not, therefore, subject to the Banking Ordinance.

The result of this interpretation, together with the moratorium on the licensing of new banks, was that a multitude of finance companies carrying out a multifarious business was soon established. Merchant banks, in particular, found the establishment of a finance company an attractive way of entering the Hong Kong market as they were then free of the constraints of the Banking Ordinance (such as the limitations upon equity investments). Even some of the commercial banks already located in Hong Kong found it expedient to establish subsidiary finance companies in order to pursue such activities as consumer finance and merchant banking.

The Ordinance required deposit-taking companies to register with the Commissioner of Banking (who was also designated the Commissioner of Deposit-Taking Companies). The business of deposit-taking companies was distinguished from the definition of banking business as that term was defined in sec. 2 of the Banking Ordinance. Deposit-taking companies were not allowed to take deposits of less than a specified sum unless the depositor was a licensed bank or the depositor was an employee of the deposit-taking company, or where the amount standing to the credit of the depositor was not less than the sum stipulated when the deposit was made. Deposit-taking companies were not permitted to operate checking or savings accounts. The purpose of these prohibitions was to confine the small depositor to the commercial banks, whose activities were more closely regulated under the Banking Ordinance. By ensuring that only large and presumably sophisticated depositors would deal with the deposit-taking companies, the authorities reasoned that they would simultaneously fulfill their responsibility to protect the small depositor while sanctioning a more flexible type of operation for the

---

[5] The provision now reads:

" 'banking business' means the business of either—

"(*a*) receiving from the general public money on current, deposit, savings or other similar account repayable on demand or within less than 3 months or at call or notice of less than 3 months; or

"(*b*) paying or collecting cheques drawn by or paid in by customers,

or both."

deposit-taking companies. The latter might then be expected to contribute to the growth of Hong Kong as an important international financial center.

In line with this philosophy, the minimum paid-up capital required of deposit-taking companies was initially set at only HK$2.5 million and, in contrast to the treatment accorded banks, no liquid assets ratio was required; neither was a limitation placed on their owning equity investments. While the companies were required to register with the Commissioner of Banking and to submit to him an annual report, they were not subjected to the system of prudential supervision that mandated monthly reports from the banks and made the latter subject to periodic inspection by the Commissioner.

As previously noted, the idea of promoting deposit-taking companies supplanted a proposal to issue restricted licenses to new banks in order to limit their activities to spheres not involving retail banking. The idea of differentiating commercial banks from other financial institutions caught on and in 1981 there were 302 companies registered under the Deposit-Taking Companies Ordinance. These companies comprise a heterogeneous group. While many of them are fully functioning merchant banks carrying on loan syndication and underwriting business both within and outside Hong Kong, others are involved in small-scale hire-purchase and consumer finance business.

Faced with a moratorium on the granting of licenses under the Banking Ordinance, a number of the major international banks established a presence in Hong Kong by registering under the new Ordinance. An anomaly soon became apparent. Only companies that carry on banking business and hold a valid banking license can use the word "bank" in their titles. The effect of this was that those major international banks whose titles did not include the prohibited word could and did merely register and operate branches under the Ordinance. In contrast, those foreign banks whose titles did include the word "bank" were forced to open subsidiaries under the Ordinance with titles similar to those of the parent but without the offending word. In a number of ways, the former method of operation accorded advantages over the latter. Aside from tax and other advantages that might derive from the law of the country in which the parent was incorporated, the Deposit-Taking Companies Ordinance, itself, created disparities. Thus, its limit on the size of a loan that can be made to an individual borrower is predicated on the amount of the deposit-taking company's paid-up capital and reserves. Since the size of a Hong Kong subsidiary is unlikely to exceed that of the parent, larger loans may, as a rule, be made through a branch than through a subsidiary. Accordingly, an international bank that had registered a branch under the Ordinance would be in a position to undertake loans of a greater amount than would a similar bank that had been required to establish a Hong Kong subsidiary.

It was not long before pressure began to build for a review of the situation. Of course, it did not proceed merely from those who perceived inequity in the disparities that had developed among the deposit-taking companies. The commercial banks, noting the impressive growth of the companies and facing the resulting competition from them in various areas in which their activities overlapped, argued that certain requirements of the Banking Ordinance should be extended to the companies. In particular, the commercial banks felt that the application of the liquidity requirements to their own activities required them to keep a substantial proportion of their assets in relatively unprofitable assets while the exemption of the deposit-taking companies from this requirement allowed the latter a competitive edge.

The authorities also began to have second thoughts concerning the system. Several factors entered into their thinking. In the first place, they had come to view the debate over subsidiaries and branches of foreign banks in a different perspective. Many depositors appeared to act on the belief that, other things being equal, it would be safer to place deposits with the branch of a foreign bank than with a local subsidiary. These depositors reasoned that in the event they encountered difficulties in withdrawing their deposits from the branch in Hong Kong, they would be able to set up their claims against the home office abroad. The responsibility of a parent for the debts of its Hong Kong subsidiary might be less clear. If this line of reasoning proved correct, then the provisions of the Deposit-Taking Companies Ordinance that required many foreign banks to establish subsidiaries rather than branches in Hong Kong did a disservice to the interests of depositors.

In the second place, finding that deposit-taking companies were to a substantial degree dependent on the commercial banks for their sources of funds, the authorities began to be persuaded that their duties to bank depositors required an extension of the system of prudential supervision to deposit-taking companies. This concern was borne out when, after a precipitous decline in the stock market, a run developed on an important finance company and the company required increased financial support from the Hongkong and Shanghai Banking Corporation.

Finally, the authorities had become convinced that the deficiencies of the banking system that had become apparent in 1965 had largely been overcome during the intervening years. They attributed the changes in the atmosphere basically to two causes. Not only had the requirements of prudential supervision worked to ensure banking safety, but there had been an impressive growth of the total assets of licensed banks. These assets had grown from HK$12 billion to HK$100 billion during the period of the moratorium.

In the end, the authorities decided (1) to repeal the moratorium on banking licenses, (2) to extend the system of prudential supervision to the deposit-taking companies, and (3) to make a liquidity requirement applicable to these companies.

Foreign banks, once again, were allowed to open full branches in Hong Kong. The authorities, however, imposed three general criteria. First, applicant banks had to be incorporated in countries whose monetary authorities exercise effective supervision and have, if necessary, approved the establishment by the applicant of a branch in Hong Kong. Second, the applicant bank had to have assets in excess of the equivalent of US$3 billion. Third, the Hong Kong authorities had to be satisfied that some form of reciprocity was available in the applicant's country of incorporation to Hong Kong banks seeking entry there. If these criteria were met and a license was granted, the successful applicant was limited to the establishment of a single office in Hong Kong. The matter is currently governed by Section 12A of the Banking Ordinance which requires the approval of the Commissioner of Banking for the establishment of a branch, while Section 12C governs the establishment of a representative office by a bank incorporated outside Hong Kong.

Following a series of amendments culminating in the Deposit-Taking Companies (Amendment) Ordinance 1982, the law governing these companies has changed substantially. A distinction is now made between a registered and a licensed deposit-taking company. The former may not take a short-term deposit from any person other than a bank or another deposit-taking company. By contrast, a licensed deposit-taking company may accept short-term deposits. A short-term deposit is one with an original maturity (or period of call or notice) of less than three months. Only a registered deposit-taking company can become licensed and thereafter it ceases to be a registered company. The two have different capital requirements and pay different fees to the authorities. All deposit-taking companies must submit monthly reports on their financial condition, must open their books for regular inspection and are now subject to a liquidity ratio. They are required to build a reserve position before declaring dividends, are limited in the amount of credit that they may extend to any single borrower, and are subject to a limitation on the acquisition of share capital in another company. The 1982 amendments to the law introduce provisions for the prudential supervision of activities carried on outside Hong Kong by deposit-taking companies incorporated in Hong Kong. Moreover, they permit the Commissioner, if he considers that it would be in the interest of the depositors, to disclose to a recognized banking supervisory authority outside Hong Kong information relating to the affairs of a deposit-taking company incorporated in the jurisdiction of that authority and of a deposit-taking company incorporated in Hong Kong which has or is proposing to establish in that jurisdiction a foreign branch, representative office, subsidiary or associate. Moreover, the law permits, with the approval of the Commissioner, the examination by such an authority outside Hong Kong of the books, accounts and transactions of a deposit-taking business in Hong Kong and of a subsidiary in Hong Kong of a bank or other deposit-taking institution which is incorporated in the jurisdiction of the foreign authority.

Deposit-taking companies have grown apace. At the end of 1978 their deposits from the public accounted for HK$11 billion of the broad money supply (14 per cent of the total), while by the end of 1980 their deposits had grown to HK$43 million (31 per cent of the total). In terms of total assets/liabilities the growth was equally striking. Between the end of 1978 and 1980 their total assets/liabilities grew by 148 per cent to HK$130 billion, which compares favorably with HK$268 million for the commercial banks. Much of the growth may be ascribed to the flexibility of the deposit-taking companies concerning interest rates. Unlike the commercial banks they have never been subject to an interest rates agreement. Moreover, for much of their existence they have not been subject to liquidity requirements. They were, therefore, able to compete effectively with the banks. This, in turn, led many of the banks to open their own subsidiary deposit-taking companies.

### *Other financial institutions*

Besides the institutions already mentioned, there are a number of other nonbank financial institutions serving both the domestic economy and offshore business.

(a) The Commodities Exchange started operations in May 1977. It is international in scope and is closely regulated (under the Commodities Trading Ordinance of 1976).

(b) There are a large number of life insurance companies, as well as a multitude of general insurance companies. Many of the insurance companies are branches of major international firms; however, there are also a number of small locally incorporated companies. There is little regulation of insurance operations, apart from a minimum security deposit of HK$50,000. The Government plans to introduce legislation to regulate more closely the insurance industry in Hong Kong.

(c) There is a limited number of mutual funds and unit trusts. As of December 1979, 59 such companies were registered with the Securities Commission. However, most of these specialize in foreign shares rather than in Hong Kong shares and their assets are not substantial.

(d) While there is no development bank, there are several quasi-governmental entities whose activities impinge upon financial markets. The most important of these is the Mass Transit Railway Authority. The Authority was established in 1975 with an authorized capital of HK$2 billion (HK$800 million for subscription by the Government). Additional funds were provided by the domestic and international capital markets and the impact upon the domestic securities market was substantial.

It might appear that there is a dearth of certain specialized financial institutions, such as discount houses and development banks. From a functional standpoint, however, the banks and many of the finance companies perform services ordinarily associated with such institutions. They carry out universal rather than specialized banking, thus obviating much of the need for narrowly specialized financial institutions.

As the Government has followed a minimalist philosophy where its own actions are concerned, there has not been a proliferation of government-owned financial institutions.

## Markets

### *Money and capital markets*

Unfortunately there is a lack of published data concerning monetary flows within the Hong Kong financial system. Data has traditionally been gathered from the banks alone, with little attempt to trace flows of funds to other financial institutions. Moreover, the reports of the banks are less than revealing, particularly where the division between foreign and domestic business is concerned. For example, until recently there was no breakdown between deposits of residents and nonresidents or between foreign currency and Hong Kong dollar assets and liabilities. Despite this paucity of data, a few points may be made.

*Money market.*—There is a marked lack of money market instruments in Hong Kong and for the most part the market has been an interbank one. However, with the growth in importance of the deposit-taking companies, transactions between banks and these companies have become increasingly important.

The main characteristics of the money market are the increasing internationalization of the market and, as has previously been noted, the rapid increase in transactions between the licensed deposit-taking companies and the banks.

In 1964 balances due by Hong Kong banks to banks abroad amounted to a half a billion Hong Kong dollars (6 per cent of total liabilities). By 1974 these balances had grown to HK$16 billion (25 per cent of total liabilities) and at the end of 1980 they amounted to HK$118 billion (44 per cent of total liabilities). A similar breakdown for assets is only available from 1978. Foreign assets, largely in the form of claims on banks abroad, accounted at the end of 1980 for HK$130 billion (48 per cent of total assets).

Data on the banks' positions vis-à-vis the deposit-taking companies have also only been available since 1978. In 1978 banks held HK$7 million of balances with deposit-taking companies but had a net liability position of a half a billion Hong Kong dollars. By the end of 1980 balances of banks with deposit-taking companies had grown to HK$21 billion (8 per cent of total assets of banks) but balances of deposit-taking companies with banks had grown even more rapidly to HK$29 billion (11 per cent of the banks' total liabilities). The deposit-taking companies have thus been a net supplier of funds to the commercial banking system, while the banks, in turn, channel funds to and from abroad. The flows to and from abroad reflect both the international character of many of the banks and the process of maturity transformation of funds by the banks, while the flow of funds from the deposit-taking companies reflects their ability to tap local deposit sources.

*Capital market.*—In its broadest sense the capital market is the complex of institutions and channels whereby surplus and deficit financial units are brought together, rather than simply the market for stocks and bonds. In Hong Kong, although the latter market appears to be relatively unimportant as a means of domestic finance, a high rate of investment has nevertheless occurred.

The stock exchanges have seen a great deal of speculation. In 1972 alone HK$2.8 billion of new issues were launched, an amount equal to almost half of gross capital formation. However, the market fluctuated erratically and many of the new issues do not appear to have contributed to productive investment.

Similarly, the bond market has for many years been almost moribund, partly because of the reluctance of both companies and the Government to raise funds via this avenue. Although the bond market remains small, some major companies have issued convertible debentures and the Government and the Mass Transit Railway have floated issues, although the Government has not retired its bond issues.

An additional factor militating against the issuance of bonds on the domestic market has been an interest withholding tax. Because of this tax it has been more attractive to fund projects offshore. However, several borrowers have taken advantage of a loophole in the taxation system and have issued "offshore bonds" denominated in Hong Kong dollars. Over HK$750 million was raised in this manner in 1977. To the extent that the final borrowers are not located in Hong Kong—the Canadian province of Manitoba raised HK$150 million—there might be some "crowding out," as the absorptive capacity of the market is limited. Moreover, the authorities have evinced some wariness where internationalization of the Hong Kong dollar is concerned.

For the most part, the domestic capital market is still dominated by the banking system perhaps because the banks have traditionally been willing to provide longer-term investment financing as well as shorter-term trade financing.

### *Stock exchanges*

The Hong Kong Stock Exchange was established in 1891 and for most of the subsequent 70 years enjoyed a monopoly. In 1969, the Far East Exchange was set up, and in 1971 and 1972, respectively, the Kam Ngan and Kowloon Stock Exchanges began trading. The authorities have viewed the dispersal of stock exchange business among four markets as undesirable. On August 7, 1980 the Stock Exchanges Unification Ordinance was promulgated. It provides that the Stock Exchange of Hong Kong Limited (which was incorporated on July 7, 1980) will become the sole stock exchange upon a date to be prescribed by the Financial Secretary within three years from the commencement of the Ordinance.

Until 1973 the stock market was essentially unregulated and speculative surges swept share prices to excessive heights. For example, by March of 1973 the Hang Seng index of share prices had reached 1,775; in the subsequent collapse of the market the index fell to 150. Later prices rose again, the average for September 1977 being 417. Turnover paralleled price developments to some extent. In 1973 the total turnover of the four stock exchanges reached HK$48 billion, but in subsequent years fell to less than a fourth of that amount, and in 1977 was even more depressed, decreasing to HK$285 million in August. However, by 1980 the turnover had risen to HK$96 billion.

The collapse of the speculative boom led to demands for closer regulation of the stock market. The Securities Ordinance and the Protection of Investors Ordinance were introduced and both became effective in 1974. The Securities Ordinance set up a Securities Commission with a Commissioner to regulate dealings in securities. The Protection of Investors Ordinance provides for regulation of prospectuses and advertisements. As the two ordinances were viewed as a useful first step, there has been continuing review of related matters.

Although its turnover makes the Hong Kong stock market the second largest in the Pacific area after Tokyo, its contribution to domestic investment financing is less clear. The number of new issues has been limited and, as a source of major financing, the market has diminished in importance relative to bond issues and direct loans. However, the internationalization of the market has increased substantially. A number of foreign stockbroking firms are represented in Hong Kong and it is possible that the major contribution of the stock market may be to Hong Kong's position as a regional financial center rather than to the domestic economy.

### Gold markets

The Hong Kong gold market has been an important regional market often acting as a conduit for flight capital. In effect, there are two markets: the Gold and Silver Exchange Society, which is limited in its membership and deals exclusively in "tael" bars that are not accepted as "good delivery" by western gold markets; and a standard bullion market, with complete freedom since 1974 for residents and nonresidents to deal in gold. The latter has expanded rapidly and because of Hong Kong's favorable time zone, it has played an important price-setting role. While turnover has fluctuated widely, it is among the four largest in the world.

## Offshore Finance

In a sense, Hong Kong's offshore and onshore financial markets are indivisible. Until recently statistics of Hong Kong financial institutions did not differentiate between Hong Kong dollar assets and liabilities and those denominated in foreign currency; neither did they identify assets and liabilities relating to residents and nonresidents. This lack of data partially may be the result of the lack of exchange controls, as well as the laissez-faire attitude of the authorities. In analyzing the system, however, it is useful to differentiate between offshore and onshore financial markets.

Until the late 1960s Hong Kong was the major regional financial center for southeast Asia. Since then Singapore has emerged as its major challenger, while Manila is taking measures designed to attract international business. Tokyo—potentially the most important competitor of all—has maintained a relatively closed market.

Hong Kong has not, unlike some other centers, offered special inducement to financial institutions to engage in offshore business. Nonetheless, it has managed to maintain a high rate of growth in foreign business. Between 1968 and 1980 the liabilities of Hong Kong banks to foreign banks grew from US$234 million to US$22.96 billion.

Offshore banking is at present virtually unregulated in Hong Kong. Banks that transact offshore business are subject to the Banking Ordinance and merchant banks have been, since 1977, subject to the Deposit-Taking Companies Ordinance, but these two ordinances, as discussed earlier, are not restrictive. Indeed, there is little or no distinction drawn between onshore and offshore business since there is no exchange control and the authorities have never tried to compartmentalize the market.

In 1978 a change in the fiscal regime was made in Hong Kong that, arguably, may influence the course of some of its offshore business. Hong Kong had traditionally applied a 15 per cent interest withholding tax on interest paid to residents and nonresidents but had not imposed a profits tax on offshore business, as such. Accordingly, in the past, it had sometimes been found expedient to book transactions in financial centers other than Hong Kong even if the transactions, in fact, had originated and were managed in Hong Kong. In this way, the interest withholding tax was bypassed.

As a consequence of a change made in 1978 to the Inland Revenue Ordinance offshore interest income of banks and deposit-taking companies is now subject to taxation in Hong Kong. Before the change, the profits tax charge had been limited to profits satisfying a double test. The first test was that the profits had to have arisen from the carrying on of a trade, profession, or business in Hong Kong. The second test was that the profits themselves had to have arisen in or been derived from Hong Kong. No particular way of determining where interest arose or whence it was derived was provided in the Ordinance, and the Commissioner for Inland Revenue had traditionally applied a test based on the place where the credit was made available to the borrower. It was thus possible for banks and deposit-taking institutions to carry out all necessary operations in Hong Kong and yet escape the profits tax by making the credit available outside Hong Kong. The Ordinance was amended to close this loophole, so that profits derived from interest are subject to the profits tax when it arises through, or from, the carrying on by a bank or deposit-taking company of business in Hong Kong, regardless of whether the credit is made available elsewhere. The rate is currently chargeable at 17 per cent.

Much controversy was generated in the financial community as to whether this change in the tax law was likely to lead to a flight of offshore business from Hong Kong to other financial centers. It was the view of the authorities that this was not likely to occur.

# Bank Notes Issue Ordinance[1]

## To regulate the issue of bank notes and to provide for certain notes being legal tender and for purposes ancillary thereto.

[20th March, 1895]

Short title.

1. This Ordinance may be cited as the Bank Notes Issue Ordinance.

Interpretation.

2. In this Ordinance, unless the context otherwise requires—

"bank" includes any person, partnership, or company carrying on the business of banking within the Colony;

"bank notes lawfully issued" means notes issued in the Colony by any of the note-issuing banks in accordance with the provisions of The Hongkong and Shanghai Banking Corporation Ordinance and the charter of incorporation of The Chartered Bank, or any supplemental charter of that bank, or issued in accordance with the above-mentioned provisions as modified by the Exchange Fund Ordinance, or by this Ordinance;

"note-issuing bank" means The Chartered Bank, and The Hongkong and Shanghai Banking Corporation.

Notes to be legal tender and the currency of the Colony.

3. As from the 6th December 1935, all bank notes lawfully issued shall be legal tender in the Colony to any amount and any liability to pay silver currency may be discharged in such notes and in particular every bank note lawfully issued shall be deemed to be the currency of the Colony for the purpose of any promise to pay printed on such note.

Issue of bank notes.

4. (1) It shall not be lawful for any bank to make, issue, or circulate within the Colony bank notes payable to bearer on demand, except with the sanction of the Secretary of State signified through the Governor.

(2) This section shall not affect any right or privilege possessed by any bank under Royal Charter or Ordinance of issuing or reissuing within the Colony bills or notes payable to bearer on demand.

[1] *Laws of Hong Kong,* Cap. 65 (1978). Originally Nos. 2 of 1895; 54 of 1935; and 21 of 1939 (Cap. 65, 1950). Relevant citations: Nos. 50 of 1911; 51 of 1911; 1 of 1912; 2 of 1912; 43 of 1912; 5 of 1924; 21 of 1939; 2 of 1946; 20 of 1948; 22 of 1950; 54 of 1956; 14 of 1958; 21 of 1969; 7 of 1978; and 21 of 1978.

(3) If any bank makes, issues or circulates within the Colony any bank notes payable to bearer on demand in contravention of the provisions of this section, it and its principal manager or agent in the Colony and each of the partners (if any) therein shall be liable on summary conviction to a fine of $5,000, and in the case of a second or subsequent conviction to imprisonment for 3 months and to a fine of $5,000:

Provided that if the offender be a body corporate it shall be liable on a second or subsequent conviction to a fine of $10,000.

(4) For the purposes of this section "bank note payable to bearer on demand" means a bill of exchange or promissory note, issued by any bank, payable to bearer on demand.

5. [*Replaced, 21 of 1978, s. 2*]

Saving.

6. Nothing in this Ordinance shall affect or be deemed to affect the rights of Her Majesty the Queen, Her Heirs or Successors, or the rights of any body politic or corporate or of any other persons except such as are mentioned in this Ordinance and those claiming by, from or under them.

## Foreign Notes (Prohibition of Circulation) Ordinance[1]

To prohibit the circulation of foreign notes.

[1st August, 1913]

Short title.

1. This Ordinance may be cited as the Foreign Notes (Prohibition of Circulation) Ordinance.

Interpretation.

2. In this Ordinance, unless the context otherwise requires—

"note" includes all promissory notes made by a banker, payable to bearer on demand, and intended to circulate as money, and also all deeds, papers or parchments, written or printed, or partly written and partly printed, by whomsoever issued, purporting to be or to represent money and intended to circulate as money.

[1] *Laws of Hong Kong,* Cap. 68 (1978). Originally No. 13 of 1913 (Cap. 68, 1950). Relevant citations: Nos. 5 of 1924; 33 of 1939; 54 of 1956; and 14 of 1958.

3. The circulation of all kinds of notes other than those of The Hongkong and Shanghai Banking Corporation, the Chartered Bank and Mercantile Bank Limited is prohibited.

Circulation of notes prohibited save in certain authorized cases.

4. (1) Any person who circulates or attempts to circulate any note or notes the circulation of which is prohibited by this Ordinance shall be liable on summary conviction to a fine of twenty-five dollars, and the note or notes so circulated or attempted to be circulated shall be forfeited.

Penalty for unlawful circulation of notes;

(2) For the purposes of this section, a person shall be deemed to circulate notes if he tenders, utters, buys, sells, receives or pays them, or puts them off: Provided that—

circulation defined.

*(a)* a person shall not be deemed to circulate notes if he gives or receives such notes to or from a *bona fide* banker or licensed money-changer in exchange for other notes or coin or for any other purpose;

*(b)* this section shall not be construed so as to prevent or restrict the legitimate business of a *bona fide* exchange banker or licensed money-changer.

5. Whenever a notification appears in the *Gazette* under the hand of the Colonial Secretary to the effect that the issue of notes other than those specified in section 3 has been sanctioned by Royal Charter or Ordinance, then such notes shall be exempted from the provisions of this Ordinance in the same manner as those specified in the said section.

Provisions for addition to authorized exemptions from Ordinance.

## Exchange Fund Ordinance[1]

To make provision for the establishment and management of an exchange fund and as to the employment of its assets in Hong Kong.

[6th December, 1935]

1. This Ordinance may be cited as the Exchange Fund Ordinance.

Short title.

[1] *Laws of Hong Kong,* Cap. 66 (1979). Originally No. 54 of 1935 (Cap. 66, 1950). Relevant citations: Nos. 44 of 1936; 57 of 1936; 9 of 1937; 21 of 1939; 12 of 1946; 20 of 1948; 4 of 1951; 54 of 1956; 14 of 1958; 6 of 1964; 31 of 1968; 47 of 1968; 57 of 1970; 90 of 1970; 25 of 1971; L.N. 150/71; L.N. 125/72; Nos. 8 of 1975; 7 of 1978; 17 of 1979; and L.N. 388/81.

**Interpretation.**

2. In this Ordinance, unless the context otherwise requires—

"bank notes lawfully issued" means notes issued in the Colony by any of the note-issuing banks in accordance with the provisions of The Hongkong and Shanghai Banking Corporation Ordinance and the charter of incorporation of The Chartered Bank or any supplemental charter of that bank, or issued in accordance with the above-mentioned provisions as modified by this Ordinance, or the Bank Notes Issue Ordinance;

"foreign exchange" means all currencies other than Hong Kong currency and includes sterling and other Commonwealth currencies;

"note-issuing bank" means The Chartered Bank, and The Hongkong and Shanghai Banking Corporation.

**Establishment control and management of Exchange Fund.**

3. (1) There shall be established a fund to be called "*the Exchange Fund*" which shall be under the control of the Financial Secretary and shall be used for the purpose of regulating the exchange value of the currency of Hong Kong. The control of the Financial Secretary shall be exercised in consultation with an Exchange Fund Advisory Committee of which the Financial Secretary shall be *ex officio* chairman and of which the other members shall be appointed by the Governor.

(2) The Fund, or any part of it, may be held in Hong Kong currency or in any other currency or in gold or silver or may be invested by the Financial Secretary in securities approved by the Secretary of State; and the Financial Secretary may for the account of the Fund buy or sell such currency or gold or silver or securities accordingly.

(3) Subject to subsection (4), the Financial Secretary may borrow for the account of the Fund either in Hong Kong or elsewhere on the security of any asset held by the Fund or on the general revenue of the Colony.

(4) The aggregate amount of borrowing under subsection (3), other than on certificates of indebtedness issued under section 4, outstanding at any one time shall, subject to subsection (5), not exceed thirty thousand million dollars, or, if held in foreign exchange, the equivalent at the current rate of exchange.

(5) The Legislative Council may from time to time, by resolution proposed by the Governor with the approval of the Secretary of State, determine some other amount to be the amount which the aggregate amount of such borrowings outstanding at any one time shall not exceed.

4. (1) The Financial Secretary is authorized to issue to any note-issuing bank, to be held as cover for bank notes lawfully issued in the Colony, certificates of indebtedness in the form in the Schedule and to require such bank to pay to him for the account of the Fund the face value of such certificates to be held by the Fund exclusively for the redemption of such notes.

Certificates of indebtedness.

Schedule.

(2) The Financial Secretary may employ the funds paid to him in accordance with subsection (1), for the purchase of foreign exchange or gold or otherwise in accordance with the provisions of section 3(2).

(3) The Financial Secretary may apply the proceeds of the sale of foreign exchange or gold for Hong Kong currency in accordance with section 3(2) to the redemption of certificates issued under subsection (1).

4A. (1) Subsection (2A) of section 18 of the Banking Ordinance shall apply to funds held by a bank in Hong Kong for the account of the Fund—

Section 18(2A) of Banking Ordinance applied to short term bank deposits of Fund.

*(a)* on demand; or
*(b)* as money at call; or
*(c)* as money at short notice,

as if they were respectively balances payable on demand, money at call and money at short notice due by that bank to another bank in Hong Kong, and subsection (3) of the said section 18 shall also have effect accordingly.

(2) Notwithstanding subsection (5)*(a)* of the said section 18, funds of a kind mentioned in subsection (1) which are held by a bank in Hong Kong for the account of the Fund shall not be treated as deposit liabilities of that bank for the purposes of subsection (2) of that section.

(3) In this section, "bank", "money at call" and "money at short notice" have the respective meanings assigned to them by section 2 of the Banking Ordinance.

5. Nothing in this Ordinance shall empower any note-issuing bank to issue notes in excess of any maximum limit laid down in any Ordinance or charter governing the issue of such notes, and in issuing certificates under this section the Financial Secretary shall take into account such maximum limits.

Preservation of limits on note issue.

Charges on Fund.

6. There shall be charged to the Fund—

(*a*) expenses incidental to the remuneration, cost of passages and superannuation in respect of officers employed in connexion with the management of the fund including any appropriate share of such expenses in respect of the services of officers of the Government so employed as part of their duties:

Provided that the number of the appointments and the rates of emoluments of such staff have been approved by the Governor and the Secretary of State; and

(*b*) any incidental expenditure which the Governor may approve as necessary for the due performance of the duties laid upon the Financial Secretary and the Advisory Committee in connexion with the operation of the fund.

Audit of Fund.

7. The accounts of all transactions of the Fund shall be audited at such times and in such manner as the Secretary of State may from time to time direct.

Transfer from the Fund.

8. The Financial Secretary may from time to time, after consultation with the Exchange Fund Advisory Committee and with the approval of the Secretary of State, transfer from the Fund to the general revenue of the Colony or to such other funds of the Colony as may be authorized by the Secretary of State any sum, or any part of any sum, in excess of the amount required to maintain the assets of the Fund at 105 *per cent* of the total of—

(*a*) the aggregate of the borrowings made under section 3 and for the time being outstanding; and

(*b*) the aggregate of the face value of the certificates of indebtedness issued under section 4 and for the time being outstanding,

and may for such purpose realize any of the assets of the Fund.

SCHEDULE [s. 4(1).]

EXCHANGE FUND ORDINANCE

*Certificate of Indebtedness for $*......................

This certificate issued under the Exchange Fund Ordinance (Chapter 66) represents indebtedness of the Hong Kong Government without interest to ................................ Bank for the amount of ................................ dollars and is redeemable at any time at the option of the Financial Secretary.

This certificate may be held up to the above-mentioned amount as cover for bank notes lawfully issued in the Colony.

..............................................................

*Financial Secretary.*

HONG KONG,

, 19

# Dollar and Subsidiary Currency Notes Ordinance [1]

To provide for the demonetization of five cent, ten cent and one dollar currency notes and for the consolidation of the law in respect of the issue of limited legal tender currency notes.

[1st September, 1969]

1. This Ordinance may be cited as the Dollar and Subsidiary Currency Notes Ordinance. Short title.

2. (1) All five cents and ten cents currency notes issued by the Financial Secretary under section 2 of the repealed Subsidiary Currency Notes Ordinance 1941 shall cease to be legal tender in Hong Kong from the commencement of this Ordinance. Five cents, ten cents and one dollar currency notes cease to be legal tender.

(2) All one dollar currency notes issued by the Financial Secretary under section 2 of the repealed Dollar Currency Notes Ordinance 1935 shall cease to be legal tender in Hong Kong from the commencement of this Ordinance.

3. (1) All assets of the Subsidiary Note Security Fund established by the Financial Secretary under section 3 of the repealed Subsidiary Currency Notes Ordinance 1941 shall be transferred to the general revenue of Hong Kong. Assets of the note security funds to be transferred to the general revenue.

(2) All assets of the note security fund established by the Financial Secretary under section 4 of the repealed Dollar Currency Notes Ordinance 1935 shall be transferred to the general revenue of Hong Kong.

[1] *Laws of Hong Kong,* Cap. 67 (1969). Originally No. 11 of 1969. Relevant citation: L.N. 16/77.

Financial Secretary may issue one cent, five cents and ten cents currency notes.

4. (1) The Financial Secretary may issue in Hong Kong one cent, five cents and ten cents currency notes, which shall be legal tender for the payment of any amount not exceeding—

(*a*) one dollar in the case of one cent notes; and

(*b*) two dollars in the case of the five cents notes and the ten cents notes:

Provided that the total amount of the currency notes issued under this section which are in circulation shall not exceed ten million dollars.

(2) All one cent currency notes issued under section 2 of the repealed Subsidiary Currency Notes Ordinance 1941 shall be deemed to have been issued under subsection (1) of this section.

Revenue from the issue of notes to be credited to general revenue and expenses in connexion with such issue to be met from general revenue.

5. (1) All moneys which are received as a result of the issue of any currency notes under section 4 shall be credited to the general revenue of Hong Kong.

(2) All expenses which are incurred in connexion with the issue of any currency notes under section 4 shall be paid from the general revenue of Hong Kong.

Five cents, ten cents and one dollar currency notes may be redeemed at face value from general revenue.

6. The holder of any five cents currency note, ten cents currency note or one dollar currency note which, under section 2, has ceased to be legal tender in Hong Kong shall, on surrendering the currency note to the Director of Accounting Services after the commencement of this Ordinance, be paid from the general revenue of Hong Kong an amount in legal tender equal to the face value of the surrendered currency note.

Demonetization of currency notes issued under section 4.

7. (1) The Financial Secretary may from time to time demonetize any currency note issued under section 4.

(2) Notice of the demonetization of any currency note by the Financial Secretary under subsection (1) shall be published in the *Gazette* and the currency note shall cease to be legal tender in Hong Kong from the date specified in the notice.

(3) The holder of any currency note demonetized by the Financial Secretary under subsection (1) shall, on surrendering the currency note to the Director of Accounting Services after the date specified in a notice published under subsection (2), be paid from the general revenue of Hong Kong an amount in legal tender equal to the face value of the demonetized currency note.

8. The total face value of all one cent, five cents and ten cents currency notes which—

Annual publication of total face value of currency notes issued and in circulation.

(*a*) are issued under this Ordinance; and

(*b*) are currency in circulation,

shall be published annually in the *Gazette.*

## The Hongkong and Shanghai Banking Corporation Ordinance[1]

To amend the constitution of The Hongkong and Shanghai Banking Corporation.

[17th May, 1929]

1. This Ordinance may be cited as The Hongkong and Shanghai Banking Corporation Ordinance.

Short title.

2. In this Ordinance, unless the context otherwise requires—

Interpretation.

"auditor" means auditor of the bank;

"bank" means "The Hongkong and Shanghai Banking Corporation" created by virtue of the provisions of the Hongkong and Shanghai Bank Ordinance 1866, and continued by this Ordinance;

"board" means board of directors and (if the context so requires) means the directors assembled at a meeting of the board;

"capital" means the share capital for the time being of the bank;

"chairman" means the chairman or his deputy presiding at any meeting of shareholders or of the board;

"chief accountant" means the person for the time being performing the duties of chief accountant of the bank at the head office;

"chief manager" means the person for the time being performing the duties of chief manager, and "acting chief manager" means the person for the time being performing the duties of acting chief manager of the bank;

[1] *Laws of Hong Kong,* Cap. 70 (1974). Originally No. 6 of 1929 (Cap. 70, 1950). Relevant citations: Nos. 33 of 1939; 8 of 1946; 20 of 1948; 37 of 1950; 27 of 1953; 36 of 1957; 25 of 1961; G.N. 761/65; L.N. 60/69; L.N. 127/73; Nos. 6 of 1978; and 21 of 1978.

"court" means the Supreme Court of the Colony and includes any judge or judges thereof, sitting either together or separately, in court or in chambers;

"directors" means the directors for the time being of the bank or (if the context so requires) directors present and voting at a meeting of the board;

"dividend" includes any interim dividend, bonus or profits on any share;

"dollar" means dollar in Hong Kong currency;

"general meeting" means a general meeting of shareholders;

"head office" means the principal place of business in the Colony for the time being of the bank;

"incapacitated shareholder" means a shareholder being an infant, or an idiot or lunatic, or *non compos mentis,* or a bankrupt or one whose estate has, by the operation of law, become vested in any other person or persons in trust for or for the benefit of his creditors;

"Ordinance" or "the Ordinance" means this Ordinance;

"ordinary resolution" means a resolution of a simple majority of shareholders at a general meeting;

"person" includes a firm, company or corporation;

"regulations" means the regulations of the bank for the time being in force;

"share" means share in the share capital of the bank;

"shareholder" or "holder of a share" or "holder of any share" means every person whose name is entered in any register of shareholders of the bank as a holder of any share or shares.

Incorporation.

3. Notwithstanding the repeal of the Hongkong and Shanghai Bank Ordinance 1866, the bank shall continue to be incorporated by the name of *"The Hongkong and Shanghai Banking Corporation"*, and by that name shall and may sue and be sued in all courts, and in that name shall continue to have perpetual succession, with a common seal which it may vary and change at its pleasure:

Provided that there shall be no limit whatever to the period of incorporation.

Regulations of the bank;

ordinance and regulations binding on all persons;

4. (1) The regulations are hereby substituted for and shall replace the deed of settlement dated the 20th July 1867, and all the articles contained therein and any amendments thereof, and shall be for all purposes the regulations of the bank, and this Ordinance and the regulations shall be binding in all respects upon the bank and upon all persons whatsoever, whether shareholders or not, and shall regulate the

rights and liabilities of all the above persons *inter se,* their heirs, executors, administrators, assigns or successors.

(2) At any time and from time to time it shall be lawful for the shareholders by special resolution to amend the provisions of the regulations or any of them: power to amend regulations;

Provided that no such amendment shall be valid or have any force or effect until it has been approved by the Governor and published in the *Gazette.* Any such power to amend as aforesaid includes the power to amend, vary, rescind, revoke or suspend any regulation or any part thereof and the power to make any new regulation.

(3) A copy of the regulations and of any such special resolution to amend, purporting to be certified by the Colonial Secretary to be a correct copy, shall be received in all courts of justice, and for all purposes, as valid and sufficient evidence of the contents of the regulations and of the fact that such regulations have been duly approved and published in the *Gazette.* proof of regulations.

5. (1) The objects of the bank shall be the carrying on the business of banking and as ancillary thereto the other businesses and objects set forth and contained in regulation 3 of the regulations, and the bank shall be at liberty to continue, commence, carry on and effect all or any of its objects at any of its establishments, that is to say, at its head office and also at its present branches, agencies and sub-agencies and also at any additional branches, agencies and sub-agencies whether in the Colony or elsewhere which may hereafter be established: Objects of the bank and conduct of its business;

Provided that the business of the bank's branches, agencies and sub-agencies shall conform to the laws relating to banking whether passed before or after the date of this Ordinance in any of the territories in which the powers hereby conferred are exercised.

(2) The bank shall have power to close any of its establishments. power to close establishments.

6. It shall be lawful for the bank to sell, dispose of and convert into money any real or personal property of whatever description, mortgaged, charged, pledged or hypothecated to the bank or taken by it in satisfaction, liquidation or payment of any debt or liability. Power to sell and convert property taken as security.

7. (1) The capital of the bank is seven hundred and fifty million dollars divided into three hundred million shares of two dollars and fifty cents each effective from 2nd July 1973. Capital and increase thereof.

(2) The capital of the bank may from time to time be increased by ordinary resolution.

Alteration of capital.

**8.** The shareholders in general meeting shall, in addition to the power hereinbefore conferred of increasing the capital of the bank, have power by ordinary resolution—

(*a*) to consolidate and divide all or any of the capital of the bank into shares of larger nominal amount than its existing shares;

(*b*) to subdivide its shares or any of them into shares of smaller amount than is fixed by this Ordinance or by the regulations, so however that in the subdivision the proportion between the amount paid and the amount, if any, unpaid on each reduced share shall be the same as it was in the case of the share from which the reduced share is derived;

(*c*) to convert any paid-up shares into stock and re-convert that stock into paid-up shares of any amount; and

(*d*) to cancel shares which at the date of the passing of the resolution in that behalf have not been taken or agreed to be taken by any person, and to diminish the amount of its capital by the amount of the shares so cancelled, and a cancellation of shares in pursuance of this section shall not be deemed to be a reduction of capital.

Reorganization of capital.

**9.** (1) The shareholders may by special resolution reorganize the capital, whether by the consolidation of shares of different classes or by the division of the shares into shares of different classes:

Provided that no preference or special privilege attached to or belonging to any class of shares shall be interfered with except by a resolution passed by a majority in number of shareholders of that class holding three-fourths of the share capital of that class and confirmed at a meeting of shareholders of that class in the same manner as a special resolution of the bank is required to be confirmed, and every resolution so passed shall bind all shareholders of the class.

(2) A copy of any such resolution shall be filed with the Colonial Secretary within seven days after the passing of the same or within such further time as the Governor may allow, and the resolution shall not take effect until such copy has been so filed.

Power to issue bearer notes.

**10.** (1) Subject to the provisions of subsection (2) and of the Bank Notes Issue Ordinance, the bank may, in the Colony, but not elsewhere, issue, re-issue and circulate notes of the bank payable to bearer on demand.

(2) The bank shall not issue such notes of a denomination lower than five dollars in excess of such number as may, from time to time, be authorized by the Secretary of State.

11. (1) The total amount of the notes of the bank payable to bearer on demand actually in circulation shall subject to the provisions of subsection (3) not at any time exceed the equivalent of the sum of sixty million dollars.

Amount of and security for note issue.

(2) The bank shall at all times keep deposited with the Crown Agents or with trustees appointed by the Secretary of State or partly with the Crown Agents and partly with such trustees securities, approved by the Secretary of State, not less in value than the said sum of sixty million dollars.

(3) Notwithstanding the provisions of subsection (1), notes of the bank payable to bearer on demand may be issued and be in actual circulation to an amount in excess of the equivalent of the said sum of sixty million dollars, if there has been paid in accordance with section 4(1) of the Exchange Fund Ordinance to the Financial Secretary of the Hong Kong Government for the account of the Exchange Fund referred to in such Ordinance and against the issue to the bank of certificates of indebtedness as provided in such Ordinance an amount equal to the face value of such excess issue for the time being actually in circulation.

(4) The securities deposited in accordance with subsection (2), and, as provided in section 4 of the Exchange Fund Ordinance, the whole of the amount paid in accordance with subsection (3) for the account of the Exchange Fund, shall be held as special funds exclusively available for the redemption of the said notes and in the event of the bank being wound up shall be applied accordingly so far as may be necessary, but without prejudice to the rights of the holders of such notes to rank with other creditors of the bank against the assets of the bank.

12. In the event of the bank being wound up every shareholder shall be liable to contribute to the assets of the bank, in respect of any debts and liabilities of the bank, an amount not exceeding the amount, if any, unpaid on the shares held by him.

Liability of shareholders.

13. (1) Contracts on behalf of the bank may be made as follows—

Form of contracts.

*(a)* any contract, which if made between private persons would be by law required to be in writing under seal, may be made on behalf of the bank in writing under seal and may in the same manner be varied or discharged;

*(b)* any contract, which if made between private persons would be by law required to be in writing signed by the parties to be charged therewith, may be made on behalf of the bank in writ-

ing, signed by any person acting under its authority, express or implied, and may in the same manner be varied or discharged;

(*c*) any contract, which if made between private persons would by law be valid although made by parol only and not reduced into writing, may be made by parol on behalf of the bank by any person acting under its authority, express or implied, and may in the same manner be varied or discharged.

(2) All contracts made according to this section shall be effectual in law and shall bind the bank and its successors and all other parties thereto, their heirs, executors, administrators or assigns or successors, as the case may be.

Bills of exchange and promissory notes.

14. A bill of exchange or promissory note shall be deemed to have been made, accepted or indorsed on behalf of the bank if made, accepted or indorsed in the name of or by or on behalf or on account of the bank by any person acting under its authority.

Limit of accommodation to directors and officers.

15. The bank shall not discount, or in any manner advance money upon, bills of exchange, promissory notes or other negotiable paper in or upon which the name of any director or officer of the bank appears as drawer or acceptor, either on his individual or separate account, or jointly with any partner, or otherwise than as a director or officer of the bank to an amount exceeding one-tenth of the amount of the sum for the time being under discount or advanced by the bank, nor shall any director be allowed to obtain credit on his own personal guarantee.

Limit of debts and liabilities.

16. The total amount of the debts and liabilities of the bank of what nature or kind soever shall not at any time exceed the aggregate amount of the then existing *bona fide* assets and property of the bank.

Winding-up and application.

17. (1) Subject as hereinafter mentioned, the bank may be wound up by the Court, and all the provisions of the Companies Ordinance, with respect to the winding-up of companies registered thereunder shall apply to the bank as if expressly re-enacted in this Ordinance, save and except in such respects as the same may be altered or modified as hereafter mentioned or provided for.

(2) The circumstances under which the bank may be wound up are as follows—

(*a*) in the event of the bank being dissolved or ceasing to carry on business or carrying on business only for the purpose of winding-up its affairs; or

(*b*) whenever the bank is unable to pay its debts; or

(*c*) whenever the court is of opinion that it is just and equitable that the bank should be wound up.

18. Nothing in this Ordinance shall affect or be deemed to affect the rights of Her Majesty the Queen, Her Heirs or Successors, or the rights of any body politic or corporate or of any other persons except such as are mentioned in this Ordinance and those claiming by, from or under them. Saving.

## The Hong Kong Association of Banks Ordinance [1]

To provide for the incorporation of The Hong Kong Association of Banks, for the corporation to assume the functions and to take over the assets and liabilities of The Exchange Banks' Association, Hong Kong and for matters incidental thereto and connected therewith.

[12th January, 1981]

### PART I. PRELIMINARY

1. This Ordinance may be cited as The Hong Kong Association of Banks Ordinance. Short title.

2. In this Ordinance, unless the context otherwise requires— Interpretation.

"Association" means The Hong Kong Association of Banks incorporated by section 3;

"business of banking" means any of the activities or functions of a licensed bank;

"Committee" means the Committee established by section 8;

"Consultative Council" means the Consultative Council established by section 9;

"continuing members" means the continuing members under section 8(1) (*a*);

"deposit" means a loan of money at interest or repayable at a premium or repayable with any consideration in money or money's worth;

"Disciplinary Committee" means the Disciplinary Committee appointed under section 16;

[1] *Laws of Hong Kong,* Cap. 364 (1980). Originally No. 76 of 1980. Relevant citation: L.N. 9/81.

"Exchange Banks' Association" means the unincorporated body known as The Exchange Banks' Association, Hong Kong existing immediately before the commencement of this Ordinance;

"licensed bank" means a bank licensed under section 7 or section 42 of the Banking Ordinance;

"member" means a member of the Association;

"Secretary" means the secretary of the Association appointed pursuant to section 13.

## PART II. INCORPORATION, OBJECTS AND POWERS

Incorporation of Association.

3. (1) There is hereby established a body corporate to be known as The Hong Kong Association of Banks.

(2) The Association shall have perpetual succession and shall be capable of suing and being sued and of doing and suffering all such other acts or things as bodies corporate may lawfully do and suffer.

(3) The Association shall have a common seal which shall not be affixed except pursuant to a resolution of the Committee (or of a sealing subcommittee appointed by the Committee for that purpose) and in the presence of two members of the Committee and of the Secretary, or some other person appointed in his place by the Committee, each of whom shall sign his name.

(4) Any document purporting to be a document duly executed under the seal of the Association authenticated in accordance with subsection (3) shall be received in evidence and shall, until the contrary is proved, be deemed to be a document so executed.

Objects of the Association.

4. The objects of the Association shall be—

*(a)* to further the interests of licensed banks;

*(b)* to make rules from time to time for the conduct of the business of banking;

*(c)* to consider, investigate and inquire into all matters and questions connected with or relating to the business of banking;

*(d)* to promote, consider, support, oppose, make representations as to and generally deal with any law affecting or likely to affect the business of banking;

*(e)* to collect, circulate and disseminate information relating to the business of banking or otherwise likely to be of interest to members and others;

*(f)* to represent its members at and appear before any public body, committee or inquiry or before any court of tribunal;

(*g*) to act as an advisory body to its members and to cooperate and maintain relations with other bodies and organizations in all matters touching or concerning the business of banking;

(*h*) to provide a meeting place or places for its members and to adopt such means of publicizing or making known its activities and information and opinions on matters touching or concerning the business of banking as may be thought fit;

(*i*) to provide or procure, by means of a management agreement or otherwise, facilities for the clearing of cheques and other instruments, and for the processing of banking transactions presented by members;

(*j*) to establish, subsidize, support, co-operate with or otherwise assist any person engaged in any artistic, cultural, benevolent, charitable, welfare or similar activity and to contribute money for and to take part in any such activities as the Committee may think fit;

(*k*) to do or cause to be done all such other acts and things as may conduce to the progress, prosperity and advancement of the general body of members.

**Powers of the Association.**

5. The Association shall have power to do all such things as are necessary for, or incidental to or conducive to, the carrying out of the objects of the Association and may in particular, but without prejudice to the generality of the foregoing—

(*a*) acquire, take on lease, purchase, hold and enjoy any property, and sell, let or otherwise dispose of the same;

(*b*) enter into any contract;

(*c*) invest funds in securities, place funds on deposit and otherwise deal with its funds in such manner as it may think fit, and realize the same at such times as it may consider necessary;

(*d*) borrow or otherwise raise money on such security as may be necessary, and for that purpose charge all or any part of the property of the Association;

(*e*) act as trustee in relation to pension and retirement schemes for its employees and funds for scholarships and prizes;

(*f*) institute, conduct, defend, compound or abandon any legal proceedings by or against it or otherwise concerning its affairs;

(*g*) refer any claim or demand by or against it to arbitration;

(*h*) make and give receipts, releases and other discharges for money payable to and for claims and demands of the Association;

(*i*) publish periodicals, booklets or other written material and produce or sponsor the production of documentary films or audiovisual material, and distribute the same by sale, loan, hire or otherwise, with or without charge, as it shall think fit;

(*j*) accept gifts, donations or testamentary dispositions upon such conditions as it shall determine.

By-laws.

6. (1) The Association may, under its common seal, make such by-laws not inconsistent with this Ordinance as are necessary for, or incidental to or conducive to, the carrying out of the objects of the Association and may in particular, but without prejudice to the generality of the foregoing, make by-laws for—

(*a*) meetings of the Association and the procedure at and the conduct of such meetings;

(*b*) meetings of the Committee and its subcommittees and the procedure at and conduct of such meetings;

(*c*) the procedure for election of members of the Committee as provided in section 8(1)(*b*);

(*d*) the procedure for election of members of the Consultative Council as provided in section 9(1)(*b*);

(*e*) entrance fees and subscriptions for membership of the Association;

(*f*) control of funds of the Association;

(*g*) the keeping of proper accounts of the Association and records in relation thereto and the preparation of annual accounts;

(*h*) the appointment of auditors and the audit of the accounts of the Association;

(*i*) the enforcement of the provisions of section 21(4) or of any by-laws made hereunder.

(2) (*a*) A by-law under subsection (1) may be made only by an affirmative vote of not less than two-thirds of the members present and voting at a meeting of the Association convened for that purpose and notified in accordance with paragraph (*b*).

(*b*) Notice of such meeting and of the resolutions to be proposed thereat shall be delivered, or sent by registered post or recorded delivery, to every member at its registered office or principal place of business in Hong Kong not less than 21 days before the date fixed for the meeting, but the non-receipt of such a notice by any member shall not invalidate the proceedings thereat.

(3) By-laws made under subsection (1)—

(*a*) shall be subject to, and shall not derogate from, any other law;

(*b*) shall be subject to the approval of the Governor in Council.

## PART III. MEMBERSHIP OF THE ASSOCIATION, COMMITTEE AND CONSULTATIVE COUNCIL

Membership of Association.

**7.** (1) Every licensed bank which is so required by a condition attached to its license shall become a member of the Association and shall, subject to this section, remain a member of the Association unless expelled under section 21(1) *(d)*; and membership of the Association shall be restricted to licensed banks.

(2) A member which ceases to be a licensed bank shall *ipso facto* cease to be a member of the Association.

(3) A member shall not be expelled from membership of the Association without the prior approval of the Governor in Council.

Committee.

**8.** (1) There shall be a Committee of the Association which shall comprise—

*(a)* 3 continuing members which shall be—

- (i) the Bank of China;
- (ii) The Chartered Bank;
- (iii) The Hongkong and Shanghai Banking Corporation;

*(b)* 9 elected members which shall be elected in accordance with the by-laws of the Association and which shall be, and be elected,—

- (i) as to 4 members, by those members whose place if incorporation is Hong Kong or which are licensed under section 42 of the Banking Ordinance;
- (ii) as to 5 members, by those members whose place of incorporation is outside Hong Kong.

(2) The 3 continuing members referred to in subsection (1)*(a)* shall, subject to subsection (3), hold office in perpetuity.

(3) Any member of the Committee which ceases for any reason to be a member of the Association shall *ipso facto* cease to be a member of the Committee.

(4) There shall be a Chairman and Vice-Chairman of the Committee and these offices shall be held alternately by The Chartered Bank and The Hongkong and Shanghai Banking Corporation.

(5) The periods of office for the Chairman and the Vice-Chairman shall in each case be two years:

Provided that The Chartered Bank shall hold office as Chairman and The Hongkong and Shanghai Banking Corporation shall hold office as Vice-Chairman until 31 December 1980 and with effect from 1 January

1981 The Hongkong and Shanghai Banking Corporation and The Chartered Bank shall hold office as Chairman and Vice-Chairman respectively.

Consultative Council.

9. (1) There shall be a Consultative Council of the Association which shall comprise—

(*a*) the 3 continuing members; and

Schedule.

(*b*) the number of elected members provided for in the Schedule which members shall be elected in accordance with the by-laws of the Association and which shall be, and be elected by, members incorporated or, in the case of unincorporated members, having their principal place of business, in various regions of the world as provided in the Schedule.

(2) The Chairman and the Vice-Chairman for the time being of the Committee pursuant to section 8(4) and (5) shall *ex officio* be the Chairman and the Vice-Chairman respectively of the Consultative Council.

Schedule.

(3) The Governor in Council may, by order published in the *Gazette,* amend the Schedule.

Schedule.

(4) Where the Schedule is amended pursuant to subsection (3) any variation in the number of elected members required, or the regions from which such members are to be elected, shall take effect from the date of the next following meeting to elect members of the Consultative Council.

Designated representatives of members.

10. (1) Every member of the Association shall designate in writing in a manner acceptable to the Committee a full time employee of that member holding a managerial post who shall as representative of that member—

(*a*) attend and vote at meetings;
(*b*) hold office;
(*c*) execute documents,

and otherwise act for and on behalf of the member for the purposes of this Ordinance and by-laws made hereunder.

(2) If the designated representative is for any reason unable to attend any meeting or otherwise act the member may designate in like manner an alternate representative who shall have the powers and functions of the designated representative.

(3) Every designation may be withdrawn and replaced by a new designation in writing at any time.

## PART IV. GENERAL

Functions of the Committee.

**11.** (1) The management of the Association shall be vested in the Committee and all the powers of the Association shall be vested in and exercisable by the Committee except so far as this Ordinance or any by-laws made hereunder otherwise authorize.

(2) The Committee may appoint subcommittees for the better discharge of its functions under this Ordinance and may delegate to any subcommittee any of its powers and functions:

Provided that the Committee shall not delegate to any subcommittee the power to impose penalties for breach of any rule made by the Committee pursuant to section 12.

(3) The Committee may in its discretion co-opt any member of the Association to be a member of any subcommittee other than the Disciplinary Committee.

Rules as to conduct of business of banking.

**12.** (1) The Committee may, after such consultation with the Financial Secretary as he shall consider appropriate, from time to time make such rules relating to the conduct of the business of banking as do not derogate from any law and may in particular, but without prejudice to the generality of the foregoing, make rules—

(*a*) as to the maximum rates of interest, return, discount or other benefit which may be paid or granted by members, or by any specified category of members, in respect of—

(i) specified Hong Kong dollar deposits of their customers;

(ii) specified instruments;

(*b*) as to the conduct of foreign exchange business and the minimum commissions and charges to be applied therefor;

(*c*) as to the conduct of securities and safe custody business and the minimum commissions and charges to be applied therefor;

(*d*) as to the minimum charges to be applied by members for the issuance of guarantees or other documents;

(*e*) as to any other charges relating to the provision of any banking service, not being charges by way of interest or return payable on loans or advances granted by members;

(*f*) prohibiting members from transacting any specified type of business or using any particular type of instrument.

(2) Rules made by the Committee pursuant to subsection (1)—

(*a*) may be amended by the Committee at any time;

*(b)* shall be binding on each member upon being served on the member as provided in subsection (3);

*(c)* shall not be subsidiary legislation, rules, regulations or by-laws within the meaning of those words in the Interpretation and General Clauses Ordinance including sections 20 and 34 thereof.

(3) Rules made under subsection (1) or amended under subsection (2) shall be delivered, or sent by registered post or recorded delivery, to every member at its registered office or principal place of business in Hong Kong and service shall be deemed to have been effected upon delivery or 48 hours after the time of posting as the case may be.

Appointment of staff.

13. (1) The Committee shall appoint a Secretary and may appoint other officers, servants and agents at such remuneration and upon such terms and conditions of appointment as it thinks fit.

(2) The Committee may grant, or make provision for the grant of pensions, gratuities and retirement or other benefits to employees of the Association.

Function of the Consultative Council.

14. The function of the Consultative Council shall be to advise the Committee on any matter relating to the business of banking which—

*(a)* is referred to it by the Committee;

*(b)* it chooses to consider;

*(c)* it is requested, by a notice in writing signed by not less than 50 members, to consider with a view to advising the Committee.

Meetings of the Consultative Council.

15. (1) Meetings of the Consultative Council shall be held at such times and places as the Consultative Council or the Chairman thereof may from time to time appoint.

(2) The following procedural provisions shall apply to every meeting of the Consultative Council—

*(a)* 15 members shall form a quorum;

*(b)* the Chairman, or in his absence the Vice-Chairman, shall preside or if both are absent the members shall appoint one of their number to preside.

(3) Subject to subsection (2), the Consultative Council shall regulate its own procedure relating to its meeting and the conduct thereof.

(4) The Governor in Council may, by order published in the *Gazette*, amend the number provided for in subsection (2)*(a)*.

## PART V. DISCIPLINARY PROCEEDINGS

16. The Committee shall— Disciplinary Committee.

*(a)* appoint from amongst its members a Disciplinary Committee of 4 members comprising the following—

(i) two continuing members;

(ii) one member whose place of incorporation is Hong Kong or which is licensed under section 42 of the Banking Ordinance;

(iii) one member whose place of incorporation is outside Hong Kong; and

*(b)* designate one of the members of the Disciplinary Committee to be chairman thereof.

17. (1) A complaint that a member has acted in breach of any rule relating to the conduct of the business of banking made under section 12(1) shall be made in writing to the Chairman of the Committee who shall submit the complaint to the Committee which may, in its discretion, refer the complaint to the Disciplinary Committee. Disciplinary provisions.

(2) The Committee may act on its own information in referring a complaint to the Disciplinary Committee.

(3) The Disciplinary Committee shall notify the member in respect of which a complaint is made of the nature of the complaint and of the date, time and place fixed for a hearing of the complaint.

(4) The member in respect of which a complaint is made shall be entitled to appear at the hearing and present its case.

18. (1) For the purposes of the hearing of a complaint the Disciplinary Committee shall have the following powers— Powers of Disciplinary Committee with regard to obtaining evidence.

*(a)* to take evidence on oath;

*(b)* to summon any employee of any member to attend the hearing to give evidence or produce any document or other thing in his possession and to examine him as a witness;

*(c)* to award to a witness such expenses as, in the opinion of the Disciplinary Committee, he has incurred by reason of his attendance.

(2) A summons to a witness shall be signed by the Chairman of the Disciplinary Committee.

Legal representation.

19. At the hearing of a complaint—

(*a*) a member selected for the purpose by the Disciplinary Committee or a solicitor or counsel on its behalf shall present the case against the member in respect of which the complaint is made;

(*b*) the member in respect of which the complaint is made shall be entitled to be represented by a solicitor or counsel.

Powers of Disciplinary Committee.

20. If, after due inquiry, the Disciplinary Committee is satisfied that a complaint under section 17 is proved, the Disciplinary Committee may recommend to the Committee that it should impose or procure to be imposed on the member in respect of which a complaint is made any of the penalties referred to in section 21:

Provided that no such recommendation shall be made by the Disciplinary Committee unless the decision to make the recommendation is by an affirmative vote of not less than three quarters of the members of the Disciplinary Committee present and voting at the inquiry at which such recommendation is made.

Disciplinary powers of the Committee.

21. (1) The Committee may, following a recommendation by the Disciplinary Committee, in its discretion impose or procure to be imposed on a member any of the following penalties for breach of any rule made pursuant to section 12(1)—

(*a*) a reprimand;

(*b*) after consultation with the Financial Secretary, the suspension of membership for any period not exceeding 3 months;

(*c*) after consultation with the Financial Secretary, the suspension of facilities for the clearing of cheques and other instruments of a member for any period not exceeding 3 months;

(*d*) with the approval of the Governor in Council, the expulsion of a member from membership of the Association:

Provided that any decision to impose or procure the imposition of any penalty shall be made by an affirmative vote of not less than three quarters of the members of the Committee present and voting at the meeting at which such decision is taken.

(2) No appeal shall lie against the decision of the Committee to impose or procure to be imposed any penalty pursuant to subsection (1).

(3) Where a penalty is imposed pursuant to subsection (1), the Committee—

(*a*) may cause notice of the imposition of such penalty to be published in the *Gazette;*

(*b*) shall give written notice to the Financial Secretary of such action and the reasons therefor.

(4) Where the Committee, after consultation with the Financial Secretary, suspends or procures the suspension of clearing facilities pursuant to subsection (1)(*c*) then whilst such suspension is in force no member shall act as sub-clearer for the member whose clearing facilities have been so suspended.

## PART VI. TRANSITIONAL

Transfer of assets and liabilities.

22. (1) All property of whatever kind and whether movable or immovable vested in or belonging to the Exchange Banks' Association immediately before the commencement of this Ordinance is as from such commencement transferred to and vested in the same interest in the Association without any further assurance and the Association shall have all powers necessary to take possession of, recover and obtain the benefit of such property.

(2) All rights, obligations and liabilities of the Exchange Banks' Association immediately before the commencement of this Ordinance are as from such commencement the rights, obligations and liabilities of the Association and the Association shall have all necessary powers to exercise or discharge the same.

Other transitional provisions.

23. (1) Every licensed bank which immediately before the commencement of this Ordinance holds office as a member of the general committee of the Exchange Banks' Association shall, as from the commencement of this Ordinance, be a member of the Committee of the Association for the purposes of this Ordinance until the conclusion of the first annual general meeting of members which shall be convened as soon as practicable after the coming into force of by-laws made under section 6(1) relating to the convening of meetings of the Association.

(2) Where anything has been commenced by or under the authority of the Exchange Banks' Association before the commencement of this Ordinance such thing may be carried on and completed by, or under the authority of, the Association.

Consequential amendment of other enactments.

24. In any enactment containing reference to the Exchange Banks' Association or the Hong Kong Exchange Banks' Association or words to the like effect, there shall be substituted for such reference a reference to The Hong Kong Association of Banks.

SCHEDULE [s. 9.]

| *Place of incorporation or principal place of business of member* | *Number of members of the Consultative Council to be elected by members incorporated in or, in the case of unincorporated members, having their principal place of business in, that region* |
|---|---|
| Belgium<br>Italy<br>Netherlands, the<br>Switzerland | 1 |
| Canada | 1 |
| China, The People's Republic of | 2 |
| France | 1 |
| Germany, The Federal Republic of | 1 |
| Hong Kong | 5 |
| Indonesia<br>Malaysia<br>Philippines, the<br>Thailand | 1 |
| Japan | 1 |
| Singapore | 1 |
| United Kingdom | 2 |
| United States of America | 3 |
| Other countries | 1 |
| Total number of elected members | 20 |

# Banking Ordinance[1]

To make better provision for the licensing and control of banks and banking business, to regulate such business for monetary policy purposes, and to make provision for matters connected therewith.

[1st December, 1964]

[1] The original law, No. 30 of 1964, has been amended on a number of occasions. This version, Cap. 155, is based on the version in *Laws of Hong Kong* (Government Printer), reprinted October 1, 1981. Relevant citations: Nos. 26 of 1967; 36 of 1967; 27 of 1969; 65 of 1971; 72 of 1973; L.N. 167/74; No. 80 of 1974; L.N. 86/75; L.N. 94/75; Nos. 30 of 1975; 84 of 1975; 92 of 1975; L.N. 223/76; L.N. 16/77; Nos. 75 of 1978; 18 of 1979; 74 of 1979; 4 of 1980; 25 of 1981; 27 of 1981; L.S. No. 3 of 1982; and No. 8 of 1982. Additional citation: L.N. 168/74.

## PART I. PRELIMINARY

1. This Ordinance may be cited as the Banking Ordinance. **Short title.**

2. (1) In this Ordinance, unless the context otherwise requires— **Interpretation.**

"accounts" means all methods of keeping accounts whether in writing, print or by any machine or device;

"auditor" means a professional accountant holding a practising certificate as provided in the Professional Accountants Ordinance;

"automated teller machine" means a terminal device, whether installed by a bank or by some other person, which is linked directly or indirectly to a computer system used by a bank and which provides facilities to customers of the bank;

"bank" means a company which carries on banking business and holds a valid license granted under section 7;

"bank incorporated in Hong Kong" means a bank incorporated in Hong Kong under the Companies Ordinance or by any other Ordinance;

"bank incorporated outside Hong Kong" means a bank incorporated by or under the law or other authority in any country, state or place outside Hong Kong, and in this respect "incorporated" includes established;

"Banking Advisory Committee" means the committee established by section 3;

"banking business" means the business of either—

(*a*) receiving from the general public money on current, deposit, savings or other similar account repayable on demand or within less than 3 months or at call or notice of less than 3 months; or

(*b*) paying or collecting cheques drawn by or paid in by customers,

or both;

"certificate of deposit" means a document relating to money, in any currency, which has been deposited with the issuer or some other person, being a document which recognizes an obligation to pay a stated amount to bearer or to order, with or without interest, and being a document by the delivery of which, with or without endorsement, the right to receive that stated amount, with or without interest, is transferable;

"Commissioner" means the Commissioner of Banking;

"company" means a company—

(*a*) incorporated under the Companies Ordinance; or

(*b*) incorporated by any other Ordinance; or

(*c*) which is incorporated outside Hong Kong and has complied with the provisions of section 333 of the Companies Ordinance;

"depositor" means a person who has an account at a bank, whether the account is a current account, a deposit account, a savings account or any other account;

"deposit-taking company" means a registered deposit-taking company and a licensed deposit-taking company;

"licence" means a licence granted under section 7 or 42;

"licensed deposit-taking company" means a deposit-taking company licensed under section 16B of the Deposit-Taking Companies Ordinance;

"local branch" means—

*(a)* in the case of a bank incorporated in Hong Kong, a place of business thereof in Hong Kong, other than its principal place of business in Hong Kong, at which it transacts banking business; and

*(b)* in the case of a bank incorporated outside Hong Kong, a place of business thereof in Hong Kong, other than its principal place of business in Hong Kong or a local representative office thereof, at which it transacts banking business,

but in either case does not mean an automated teller machine;

"local representative office" means an office in Hong Kong of a bank incorporated outside Hong Kong which is not—

*(a)* licensed under Section 7,

*(b)* a deposit-taking company, and

*(c)* recognised as the central bank of the country or place in which it is incorporated;

"money at call" means money payable within not more than 24 hours of a demand therefor, but does not include money payable on demand;

"money at short notice" means money, other than money at call, payable within not more than 7 days of a demand therefor;

"overseas branch" means a branch outside Hong Kong of a bank incorporated in Hong Kong, whether or not the business of the branch is limited by the laws or regulations of the country, state or place in which the branch is situated and whether or not the branch is referred to as an agency in such country, state or place, but does not mean an overseas representative office thereof;

"overseas representative office" means an office outside Hong Kong, other than an overseas branch, of a bank incorporated in Hong Kong;

"registered deposit-taking company" means a company registered as a deposit-taking company under the Deposit-Taking Companies Ordinance;

"share" means share in the share capital of a company, and includes stock except where a distinction between stock or shares is expressed or implied; and the expression "shareholder" includes a stockholder;

"specified liquid assets" means all or any of the assets specified in section 18(6);

"unincorporated bank" means an unincorporated person or body of persons to whom or to which a licence to transact banking business in Hong Kong has been granted under section 42.

(1A) Without prejudice to any other meaning which "insolvent" may have, a bank shall, for the purposes of this Ordinance, be deemed to be insolvent if either it has ceased to pay its debts in the ordinary course of business or it cannot pay its debts as they become due.

(2) Powers vested in the Financial Secretary by virtue of the provisions of this Ordinance shall not be exercised by any person other than the Financial Secretary or, in his absence or if he is unable to act, the person for the time being exercising his functions.

## PART II. APPOINTMENTS, GENERAL DUTIES OF COMMISSIONER AND POWER OF GOVERNOR TO GIVE DIRECTIONS

**Banking Advisory Committee.**

3. (1) There is hereby established a Banking Advisory Committee for the purpose of advising the Governor upon any matter connected with this Ordinance or relating to banking and the carrying on of banking business and of advising the Governor in Council in any case where the advice of the Committee is sought under section 14(2).

(2) The Banking Advisory Committee shall consist of a chairman, who shall be the Financial Secretary, the Secretary for Monetary Affairs, the Commissioner, and such other persons, not being less than 4 nor more than 12, as the Governor may from time to time appoint.

(3) The members of the Banking Advisory Committee appointed by the Governor shall hold office for such period and upon such terms as the Governor may specify in their appointments.

(4) In the absence of the chairman at any meeting of the Banking Advisory Committee, the Secretary for Monetary Affairs shall act as the chairman.

**Appointment of a Commissioner of Banking.**

4. The Governor may appoint a Commissioner of Banking who shall be a public officer.

**Commissioner may employ assistants.**

4A. The Commissioner may authorize or employ any person to assist him in the exercise of his functions and duties under this Ordinance, either generally or in any particular case.

Power of Governor to give directions.

**4B.** (1) The Governor may give to the Financial Secretary and the Commissioner such directions as he thinks fit with respect to the exercise or performance of their respective powers, functions and duties under this Ordinance, either generally or in any particular case.

(2) The Financial Secretary and the Commissioner shall, in the exercise or performance of their respective powers, functions and duties under this Ordinance, comply with any directions given by the Governor under subsection (1).

## PART III. LICENSING OF BANKS

Banking business restricted to licensed banks.

5. Except as may be otherwise provided in this Ordinance, no banking business shall be transacted in Hong Kong except by a company which is in possession of a valid licence issued by the Governor in Council authorizing it to transact banking business in Hong Kong.

Receiving of deposits by deposit-taking companies.

**5A.** (1) Notwithstanding section 5 and subject to subsection (2) and to the Deposit-Taking Companies Ordinance—

(*a*) a licensed deposit-taking company may receive money on deposit account repayable within less than 3 months or at call or notice of less than 3 months;

(*b*) a registered deposit-taking company may continue to receive money on deposit account repayable within less than 3 months or at call or notice of less than 3 months as provided in section 6(1B) of the Deposit-Taking Companies Ordinance.

(2) No licensed deposit-taking company or registered deposit-taking company shall receive money on savings account.

Application for licence.

6. (1) A company which wishes to transact, or a body of persons proposing to form a company for the purpose of transacting, banking business in Hong Kong shall apply to the Governor in Council, through the Commissioner, for a licence or, in the case of a body of persons proposing to form a company, for an intimation that a licence will be granted to the company upon the incorporation thereof.

(2) An application for a licence or for an intimation that a licence will be granted shall be accompanied by—

(*a*) a copy of the charter, Ordinance (other than the Companies Ordinance), statutes, memorandum of association and articles of association, or other instrument, under which the company is or is to be incorporated, which shall—

(i) be verified in such manner as the Commissioner or the Governor in Council may require; and

(ii) if it is not written in the English language, be accompanied by a translation thereof certified to the satisfaction of the Commissioner as a true and correct translation; and

*(b)* such other documents and information as may be required by the Commissioner or the Governor in Council.

(3) After receiving an application for a licence, the Commissioner shall forward to the Governor in Council the application and his advice as to whether or not the applicant should be granted a licence or, in the case of a proposed company, whether or not the company upon incorporation should be granted a licence.

**Grant or refusal of licence.**

7. (1)[2] After receiving the application and the advice of the Commissioner pursuant to the provisions of section 6, the Governor in Council may—

*(a)* grant a licence or, in the case of a proposed company, intimate his intention to grant a licence upon receipt of notice of the incorporation thereof;

*(b)* grant a licence subject to such conditions as he may think proper to attach thereto in any particular case or, in the case of a proposed company, intimate his intention, upon receipt of notice of the incorporation thereof, to grant a licence subject to the attachment of such conditions;

*(c)* without assigning any reason therefor, refuse to grant a licence or, in the case of a proposed company, intimate his intention to refuse to grant a licence upon receipt of notice of the incorporation thereof.

**Amendment of conditions of licence.**

**7A.** Without prejudice to section 7(1)*(b)*, the Governor in Council may at any time, by notice in writing served upon a bank, attach to the licence held by that bank such conditions, or amend or cancel any conditions attached to the licence, as he may think proper.

**Minimum paid up share capital for grant of licence.**

**8.** No company which is incorporated in Hong Kong shall be granted a licence unless its share capital issued and paid up is not less than $100,000,000, deduction having been made in respect of a debit balance, if any, appearing in the profit and loss account of the company.

**Revocation of licence.**

9. The Governor in Council may revoke a licence—

*(a)* if he is satisfied that the holder of the licence—

---

[2] Editor's note: subsecs. 2 and 3 have been deleted by sec. 3 of The Banking (Amendment) Ordinance, 1982.

(i) has ceased to transact banking business in Hong Kong; or

(ii) proposes to make, or has made, any composition or arrangement with its creditors or has gone into liquidation or has been wound up or otherwise dissolved; or

*(b)* if the Commissioner has made a report to him under section 13(1)(iv) and the Governor in Council considers that it is in the public interest to revoke the licence.

10. *{Repealed, 26 of 1967, s. 11}*

Effect of revocation of licence.

11. (1) Where a licence is revoked under section 9—

*(a)* notice of such revocation shall be published in the *Gazette;*

*(b)* the bank shall, as from the date of such notice, cease to transact any banking business in Hong Kong.

(2) The provisions of subsection (1)*(b)* shall not prejudice the enforcement by any person of any right or claim against the bank or by the bank of any right or claim against any person.

Licence fee.

12. (1) Every bank shall pay an annual licence fee of $200,000 or such other amount as may from time to time be specified by the Governor in Council and notified in the *Gazette.*

(2) The fee payable under this section shall be paid upon the grant of the licence and thereafter upon the anniversary of the date of the grant thereof.

(3) The Director of Accounting Services shall cause to be published in the *Gazette* each year in the month of April the name of every bank which has within the preceding financial year paid the fees payable under this section.

## PART IIIA. LOCAL BRANCHES, LOCAL REPRESENTATIVE OFFICES AND FEES

Control of establishment of branches of bank.

12A. (1) A bank shall not establish or maintain any local branch thereof without the approval of the Commissioner.

(2) Subsection (1) applies to every bank whether the bank was licensed before, on or after 28 April 1967, and subsections (4) and (5) apply to an approval granted under subsection (1) whether the approval was granted on or after such date.

(3) Approval under subsection (1) shall be deemed to have been granted in respect of any local branch established prior to 28 April 1967.

(4) The Commissioner may at any time, by notice in writing served upon a bank, attach to an approval granted under subsection (1), or deemed to have been granted under subsection (3), in respect of any local branch thereof such conditions, or amend or cancel any conditions so attached, as he may think proper.

(5) The Commissioner may at any time revoke, in such case as he thinks fit, an approval granted under subsection (1), or deemed to have been granted under subsection (3), in respect of any local branch.

(6) Where the Commissioner refuses to grant approval under subsection (1) or revokes an approval under subsection (5), he shall notify the bank concerned in writing of the refusal or revocation.

(7) Any bank aggrieved by the refusal to grant approval under subsection (1) or by the revocation of an approval under subsection (5) may appeal to the Governor in Council against the refusal or revocation.

**Fees in respect of branches of banks.**

**12B.** (1) Whenever the Commissioner gives his approval of the establishment by a bank of a local branch, the bank shall pay to the Director of Accounting Services a fee of $10,000 in relation to that branch and thereafter, so long as the branch continues to be maintained by the bank, the bank shall pay to the Director of Accounting Services a fee of $10,000 on the anniversary in each year of the date of the grant of the bank's licence.

(2) A bank that is maintaining a local branch at the commencement of the Banking (Amendment) Ordinance 1967 shall, so long as the branch continues to be maintained by the bank, pay to the Director of Accounting Services a fee of $10,000 on the anniversary in each year of the date of the grant of the bank's licence.

(3) The Governor in Council may by order amend this section so as to vary the fees payable thereunder.

Control of establishment, etc. of local representative offices.

12C. (1) A bank incorporated outside Hong Kong which is not licensed under section 7 and is not recognized as the central bank of the country or place in which it is incorporated shall not establish or maintain any local representative office thereof without the approval of the Commissioner.

(2) Approval under subsection (1) shall be deemed to have been granted in respect of any local representative office established prior to the commencement of the Banking (Amendment) Ordinance 1982 and in respect of which the Commissioner has granted consent under section 67(1) for the use of the word "bank" or any derivative thereof in the description or title of the local representative office.

(3) Approval under subsection (1) shall not be granted unless the Commissioner is satisfied that the bank is adequately supervised by a recognized banking supervisory authority of the country, state or place in which the bank is incorporated.

(4) The Commissioner may at any time, by notice in writing served upon a bank, attach to an approval granted under subsection (1), or deemed to have been granted under subsection (2), in respect of any local representative office thereof such conditions, or amend or cancel any conditions so attached, as he may think proper.

(5) The Commissioner may at any time revoke, in such case as he thinks fit, an approval granted under subsection (1), or deemed to have been granted under subsection (2), in respect of any local representative office.

(6) Where the Commissioner refuses to grant approval under subsection (1) or revokes an approval under subsection (5), he shall notify the bank concerned in writing of the refusal or revocation.

(7) Any bank aggrieved by the refusal to grant approval under subsection (1) or by the revocation of an approval under subsection (5) may appeal to the Governor in Council against the refusal or revocation.

Supply of information and examination of local representative offices.

**12D.** A bank incorporated outside Hong Kong which maintains a local representative office thereof pursuant to section 12C shall—

*(a)* submit to the Commissioner such information as he may require regarding the functions and activities of the representative office;

*(b)* if the Commissioner wishes to examine the functions and activities of the representative office, for that purpose afford to the person carrying out the examination access to the documents maintained by the representative office and to such information and facilities as may be required to conduct the examination, and shall produce to the person carrying out the examination such documents or other information as he may require.

Fees in respect of local representative offices.

**12E.** (1) Whenever the establishment by a bank incorporated outside Hong Kong of a local representative office is approved under section 12C(1), the bank shall pay to the Director of Accounting Services the fee specified in subsection (3)*(a)* in relation to that representative office and thereafter, so long as the representative office continues to be maintained by the bank, the bank shall pay to the Director of Accounting Services the fee specified in subsection (3)*(b)* on the anniversary in each year of the date of the grant of the approval under section 12C(1).

(2) A bank incorporated outside Hong Kong that is maintaining, at the commencement of the Banking (Amendment) Ordinance 1982, a local representative office to which section 12C(2) applies, shall pay to the Director of Accounting Services the fee specified in subsection (3)*(b)* in relation to that representative office within 14 days after such commencement and thereafter, so long as the representative office continues to be maintained by the bank, the bank shall pay to the Director of Accounting Services the fee specified in subsection (3)*(b)* on the anniversary in each year of such commencement.

(3) *(a)* The fee for the establishment of a local representative office shall be $10,000.

*(b)* The annual fee for maintaining a local representative office shall be $10,000.

(4) The Governor in Council may by order amend subsection (3) so as to vary the fees specified therein.

## PART IIIB. OVERSEAS BRANCHES, OVERSEAS REPRESENTATIVE OFFICES AND FEES

Control of establishment, etc. of overseas branches and overseas reprsentative offices.

**12F.** (1) Without prejudice to section 12A, there shall be deemed to be attached to the licence held by a bank incorporated in Hong Kong a condition that the bank shall not establish or maintain any overseas branch or overseas representative office thereof without the approval of the Commissioner.

(2) Subsection (1) applies to every licence whether the licence was granted before, on or after 28 April 1967, and subsections (4) and (5) apply to an approval granted under subsection (1) whether the approval was granted on or after such date.

(3) Approval under subsection (1) shall be deemed to have been granted in respect of—

*(a)* any overseas branch established prior to 28 April 1967; and

*(b)* any overseas representative office established prior to the commencement of the Banking (Amendment) Ordinance 1982.

(4) The Commissioner may at any time, by notice in writing served upon a bank, attach to an approval granted under subsection (1), or deemed to have been granted under subsection (3), in respect of any overseas branch or overseas representative office thereof such conditions, or amend or cancel any conditions so attached, as he may think proper.

(5) The Commissioner may at any time revoke, in such case as he thinks fit, an approval granted under subsection (1), or deemed to have

been granted under subsection (3), in respect of any overseas branch or overseas representative office.

(6) Where the Commissioner refuses to grant approval under subsection (1) or revokes an approval under subsection (5), he shall notify the bank concerned in writing of the refusal or revocation.

(7) Any bank aggrieved by the refusal to grant approval under subsection (1) or by the revocation of an approval under subsection (5) may appeal to the Governor in Council against the refusal or revocation.

Conditions regarding overseas branches and overseas representative offices.

**12G.** (1) There shall be deemed to be attached to the licence held by a bank incorporated in Hong Kong which maintains an overseas branch thereof a condition that—

*(a)* the bank shall submit to the Commissioner a return in such form, and at such intervals, as he may specify showing the assets and liabilities of the overseas branch;

*(b)* the bank shall submit to the Commissioner such further information as he may consider necessary for the proper understanding of the functions and activities of the overseas branch, and that such information shall be submitted within such period and in such manner as the Commissioner may require;

*(c)* if the Commissioner requires any return submitted to him pursuant to paragraph *(a)*, or any information submitted to him pursuant to a requirement under paragraph *(b)*, to be accompanied by a certificate of an auditor, the bank shall submit a certificate of the auditor appointed under section 36(1) or of the auditors appointed under section 36(1) and (2), as the case may be, as to whether or not, in the opinion of the auditor or auditors, the return or information is correctly compiled from the books and records of the overseas branch;

*(d)* if the Commissioner wishes to examine the books, accounts and transactions of the overseas branch, the bank shall for that purpose afford the person carrying out the examination at the place where the branch is maintained access to the books and accounts of the branch, to documents of title to the assets and other documents and to all securities held by the branch in respect of its customers' transactions and its cash and to such information and facilities as may be required to conduct the examination, and that the bank shall produce to the person carrying out the examination such books, accounts, documents, securities, cash or other information as he may require:

Provided that, so far as is consistent with the conduct of the examination, such books, accounts, documents, securities and cash shall not be required to be produced at such times and such places as shall interfere with the proper conduct of the normal daily business of the branch.

(2) There shall be deemed to be attached to the licence held by a bank incorporated in Hong Kong which maintains an overseas representative office thereof a condition that—

*(a)* the bank shall submit to the Commissioner such information as he may require regarding the functions and activities of the overseas representative office;

*(b)* if the Commissioner wishes to examine the functions and activities of the overseas representative office, the bank shall for that purpose afford the person carrying out the examination at the place where the representative office is maintained access to the documents maintained by the representative office and to such information and facilities as may be required to conduct the examination, and that the bank shall produce to the person carrying out the examination such documents or other information as he may require.

(3) This section applies to every licence whether the licence was granted before, on or after the commencement of the Banking (Amendment) Ordinance 1982.

Fees in respect of overseas branches and overseas representative offices.

**12H.** (1) Whenever the establishment by a bank incorporated in Hong Kong of an overseas branch or overseas representative office is approved under section 12F(1), the bank shall pay to the Director of Accounting Services the fee specified in subsection (3)*(a)* or *(b)*, as the case may be, in relation to that branch or representative office and thereafter, so long as the branch or representative office continues to be maintained by the bank, the bank shall pay to the Director of Accounting Services the fee specified in subsection (3)*(c)* or *(d)*, as the case may be, on the anniversary in each year of the date of the grant of the bank's licence.

(2) A bank incorporated in Hong Kong that is maintaining, at the commencement of the Banking (Amendment) Ordinance 1982, an overseas branch or overseas representative office to which section 12F(3) applies, shall, so long as the branch or representative office continues to be maintained by the bank, pay to the Director of Accounting Services the fee specified in subsection (3)*(c)* or *(d)*, as the case may be, on the anniversary in each year of the date of the grant of the bank's licence.

(3) *(a)* The fee for the establishment of an overseas branch shall be $20,000.

(*b*) The fee for the establishment of an overseas representative office shall be $5,000.

(*c*) The annual fee for maintaining an overseas branch shall be $20,000.

(*d*) The annual fee for maintaining an overseas representative office shall be $5,000.

(4) The Governor in Council may by order amend subsection (3) so as to vary the fees specified therein.

## PART IV. POWERS OF CONTROL OVER BANKS

Powers of Commissioner.

13. (1) Where—

(*a*) a bank informs the Commissioner—

(i) that it is likely to become unable to meet its obligations; or

(ii) that it is insolvent or about to suspend payment;

(*b*) a bank becomes unable to meet its obligations or suspends payment;

(*c*) after an inspection or investigation is made under section 15, the Commissioner is of the opinion that a bank—

(i) is carrying on its business in a manner detrimental to the interests of its depositors or of its creditors;

(ii) is insolvent or is likely to become unable to meet its obligations or is about to suspend payment;

(iii) has contravened or failed to comply with any of the provisions of this Ordinance; or

(iv) has contravened or failed to comply with any condition attached or deemed to be attached to its licence; or

(*d*) the Financial Secretary advises the Commissioner that he considers it in the public interest to do so,

the Commissioner, after consultation with the Financial Secretary, may exercise such one or more of the following powers as may from time to time appear to him to be necessary—

(i) to require the bank forthwith to take any action or to do any act or thing whatsoever in relation to its business as he may consider necessary;

(ii) to appoint a person to advise the bank in the proper conduct of its business;

(iii) to assume control of and carry on the business of the bank, or direct some other person to assume control of and carry on the business of the bank;

(iv) to report the circumstances to the Governor in Council.

(2) Save in the circumstances specified in subsection (1)*(a)*, the Commissioner shall not exercise the power conferred by subsection (1) (iv) unless he has given to the bank not less than 7 days' notice in writing of his intention to exercise such power and a statement in writing of his reasons for the exercise thereof, and has afforded the bank an opportunity to submit to him representations in writing thereon.

(3) Any person aggrieved by the exercise by the Commissioner of any of the powers conferred on him by paragraphs (i), (ii) and (iii) of subsection (1) may appeal to the Governor in Council.

(4) The making of an appeal under subsection (3) shall not stay the exercise of the power pending the determination of the appeal.

Powers of Governor in Council.

14. (1) Where—

*(a)* the Commissioner makes a report to the Governor in Council under section 13(1)(iv); or

*(b)* any person appeals to the Governor in Council under section 13(3),

the Governor in Council may, without prejudice to the powers conferred by section 9*(b)*, exercise one or more of the following powers—

(i) to confirm, vary or reverse any requirement, appointment or direction made by the Commissioner;

(ii) to make such order as he may think fit in relation to the affairs of the bank and exercise any power which the Commissioner may exercise under section 13(1);

(iii) to direct the Financial Secretary to present a petition to the High Court for the winding up of the bank by the High Court.

(2) The Governor in Council may, before considering any report or appeal under subsection (1), seek the advice of the Banking Advisory Committee, but shall not be bound to follow any such advice.

Remuneration and expenses of Commissioner and others in certain cases.

14A. (1) The Commissioner, after consultation with the Financial Secretary, may at any time, whether or not the appointment of such person has terminated, fix the remuneration and expenses to be paid by a bank to any person appointed by the Commissioner under section 13(1) or by the Governor in Council under section 14(1) to advise the bank in the proper conduct of its business.

(2) Where the Commissioner has assumed control of the business of a bank under section 13(1)(iii) or pursuant to an order of the Governor

in Council under section 14(1)(ii) or some other person has assumed control of the business of a bank pursuant to a direction under section 13(1)(iii) or an order of the Governor in Council under section 14(1)(ii), the Commissioner, after consultation with the Financial Secretary, may at any time, whether or not he or such other person has ceased to be in control of the business of the bank, fix the remuneration and expenses to be paid by the bank to him, and to any person employed or authorized by him under section 4A to assist him in the control of and the carrying on of the business of the bank, or to such other person, as the case may be.

(3) Any bank aggrieved by a decision of the Commissioner under subsection (1) or (2) may appeal to the Governor in Council.

**Examination and investigation of banks.**

15. (1) Without prejudice to the provisions of section 13, the Commissioner may at any time, with or without prior notice to the bank, examine the books, accounts and transactions of any bank.

(2) Without prejudice to the provisions of section 13, the Commissioner shall investigate the books, accounts and transactions of a bank—

*(a)* if shareholders of the bank holding not less than one-third of the total number of issued shares in the bank, or depositors holding not less than one-tenth of the gross amount of the total deposit liabilities in Hong Kong of the bank or a sum equal to the aggregate of the paid up share capital of the bank and its published reserve, whichever is the greater, apply to him to make such an investigation and submit to him such evidence as he considers necessary to justify the investigation and furnish such security for the payment of the costs of the investigation as he may require; or

*(b)* if the bank suspends payment or informs him of its intention to suspend payment.

(3) Where an investigation is made by the Commissioner pursuant to subsection (2), the Financial Secretary may order that all expenses incurred in such investigation shall be defrayed—

*(a)* by the bank; or

*(b)* if the investigation was made pursuant to subsection (2)*(a)*, either wholly by the persons who applied for the making of the investigation or partly by such persons and partly by the bank in such proportions as he considers to be just.

16. *[Repealed, 26 of 1967, s. 19]*

17. (1) Where the Commissioner has assumed control of the business of a bank under section 13(1)(iii) or pursuant to an order of the Governor in Council under section 14(1)(ii) or some other person has assumed control of the business of a bank pursuant to a direction under section 13(1)(iii) or an order of the Governor in Council under section 14(1)(ii), then, subject to subsection (2), the Commissioner or such other person, as the case may be, shall remain in control and continue to carry on the business of that bank in the name and on behalf of the bank until it is no longer necessary, in the opinion of the Financial Secretary, for the Commissioner or such other person to remain in control of the bank.

Control of licensed bank by the Commissioner.

(2) Where the Commissioner has assumed control of the business of a bank under section 13(1)(iii) or pursuant to an order of the Governor in Council under section 14(1)(ii) or some other person has assumed control of the business of a bank pursuant to a direction under section 13(1)(iii) or an order of the Governor in Council under section 14(1)(ii), the Governor in Council, upon the application of the bank, may, if he is satisfied that it is no longer necessary for the protection of the depositors of the bank that the Commissioner or such other person should remain in control of the business of the bank, order that the Commissioner or such other person shall cease to control the business of the bank as from a date specified in the order.

(3) Where the Commissioner has assumed control of the business of a bank under section 13(1)(iii) or pursuant to an order of the Governor in Council under section 14(1)(ii) or some other person has assumed control of the business of a bank pursuant to a direction under section 13(1)(iii) or an order of the Governor in Council under section 14(1)(ii) or any such control has been relinquished pursuant to any of the provisions of this section, the Financial Secretary shall cause to be published in the *Gazette* a notification of the fact of the assumption or cessation of such control, as the case may be.

## PART V. DUTIES OF BANKS

18. (1) A bank shall maintain at all times a minimum holding of specified liquid assets, free from encumbrances, in accordance with the provisions of this section.

Minimum holding of specified liquid assets.

(2) The minimum holding of specified liquid assets to be maintained by a bank in any calendar month shall be not less than 25 *per cent* of the deposit liabilities of the bank during that month.

(2A) For the purpose of subsection (2), the specified liquid assets of a bank shall be the specified liquid assets of that bank within the meaning of subsection (6) reduced by an amount equivalent to such bank's total liabilities in respect of—

*(a)* balances payable on demand;
*(b)* money at call; and
*(c)* money at short notice,

owing to other banks or any deposit-taking company in Hong Kong.

(2B) Where the liabilities of a bank during any month do not include any deposit liabilities, the minimum holding of specified liquid assets to be maintained in that month by the bank shall be not less than an amount equivalent to the bank's liabilities during that month in respect of—

*(a)* balances payable on demand;
*(b)* money at call; and
*(c)* money at short notice,

owing to other banks or any deposit-taking company in Hong Kong; and in respect of amounts referred to in paragraphs *(a)* and *(b)*, such specified liquid assets shall be held in any form set out in paragraphs *(a)*, *(aa)*, *(b)*, *(c)*, *(d)*, *(da)*, *(db)* and *(e)* of subsection (6).

(3) The minimum holding of specified liquid assets required by subsection (2) shall include not less than the equivalent of 15 *per cent* of the deposit liabilities of the bank in the form of such specified liquid assets as are set out in paragraphs *(a)*, *(aa)*, *(b)*, *(c)*, *(d)*, *(da)*, *(db)* and *(e)* of subsection (6), and in determining whether the minimum holding includes not less than the equivalent of 15 *per cent* of the deposit liabilities of the bank in the form aforesaid any reduction made pursuant to subsection (2A) in respect of balances payable on demand and money at call shall be deemed to have been made in such specified liquid assets of the bank as are set out in paragraphs *(a)*, *(aa)*, *(b)*, *(c)*, *(d)*, *(da)*, *(db)* and *(e)* of subsection (6).

(4) For the purposes of subsections (2), (2A), (2B) and (3), the assets and liabilities of a bank shall be the arithmetical means of, respectively, the amounts of the assets held by, and the liabilities of, the bank according to the bank's books at the close of business on every such weekday during the month as the Commissioner may specify:

Provided that if any such specified weekday is a public holiday the assets and liabilities as at the close of business on the last working day preceding that specified weekday shall be taken for the purposes of such calculation.

(5) For the purposes of computing the minimum holding of specified liquid assets to be held by a bank—

*(a)* the deposit liabilities of a bank shall be deemed to be its gross demand, time, and savings account liabilities, excluding amounts owing to other banks or any deposit-taking company;

*(b)* in the case of a bank operating in Hong Kong and also elsewhere, the principal place of business in Hong Kong and local branches of the bank shall be deemed collectively to be a separate bank carrying on business in Hong Kong;

*(c)* all the deposit liabilities of a bank owed through the principal place of business in Hong Kong or any local branch of a bank operating in Hong Kong and also elsewhere shall be regarded as if they constituted liabilities of that separate bank, and all the assets held by or to the credit of the principal place of business in Hong Kong or any local branch shall be regarded as if they were assets of that separate bank.

(6) For the purposes of this section, "specified liquid assets" means all or any of the following—

*(a)* notes and coins which are legal tender in Hong Kong;

*(aa)* notes and coins in any currency which is freely remittable to the bank in Hong Kong;

*(b)* refined gold in the form of coin or bars situated in Hong Kong, and refined gold in the form of coin or bars situated outside Hong Kong if the gold, or money into which it can be converted, is freely remittable to the bank in Hong Kong from the place where such gold is situated;

*(c)* the total balance of money payable on demand at, and money at call with, other banks or any deposit-taking company in Hong Kong;

*(d)* balances of money payable on demand at any bank outside Hong Kong and money at call with any bank outside Hong Kong, which are or is freely remittable to the bank in Hong Kong and held in a form approved by the Commissioner;

*(da)* certificates of deposit which are—

(i) issued outside Hong Kong by any bank approved by the Commissioner for the purposes of this section in any foreign currency freely remittable to the bank in Hong Kong; and

(ii) marketable in a manner satisfactory to the Commissioner;

*(db)* such money market instruments, either totally or to such limited extent, as the Financial Secretary may specify by notice in the *Gazette;*

(*e*) treasury bills, maturing within 93 days, issued by the Government or by the Government of the United Kingdom or by the Government of any other country if such treasury bills issued by the Government of any other country are specified by the Financial Secretary and published in the *Gazette;*

(*ea*) money at short notice at other banks or any deposit-taking company in Hong Kong;

(*eb*) money at short notice at any bank outside Hong Kong, which is freely remittable to the bank in Hong Kong and held in a form approved by the Commissioner;

(*ec*) such money market instruments, either totally or to such limited extent, other than an instrument specified under paragraph (*db*), as the Financial Secretary may specify by notice in the *Gazette;*

(*f*) bills of exchange payable at usance outside Hong Kong and discountable in a currency which is freely remittable to the bank in Hong Kong;

(*g*) bills of exchange payable after sight outside Hong Kong in a currency freely remittable to the bank in Hong Kong;

(*h*) such securities (other than securities specified in paragraph (*i*)) issued or guaranteed by the Government, or the Government of any other country, as may be specified by the Financial Secretary and published in the *Gazette;*

(*i*) securities with less than 5 years to maturity issued or guaranteed by the Government or the Government of the United Kingdom, if—

(i) they are quoted on a Stock Exchange in London, Hong Kong or New York;

(ii) they have been dealt in during the preceding 6 months; and

(iii) payment of interest thereon is not in arrear.

(7) The Financial Secretary may, from time to time, in exceptional circumstances, by notice raise or reduce for such period as he may think necessary and to such percentages as he may think fit the minimum percentages specified in subsection (2) or subsection (3) of specified liquid assets in the case of any particular bank or all banks.

(8) *{Deleted, 26 of 1967, s. 21}*

(9) Liabilities in respect of notes issued and assets held as cover for notes issued shall, in the case of a bank which is a note-issuing bank under the Bank Notes Issue Ordinance, be disregarded for the purposes of this section.

(10) For the purposes of this section, the value of any specified liquid asset shall be not more than the market value of such asset.

Variation of minimum holding of specified liquid assets for monetary policy purposes.

**18A.** The Financial Secretary may from time to time, in pursuance of the monetary policy of the Government, by order, which shall be published in the *Gazette,* raise or reduce the minimum percentage of deposit liabilities by reference to which every bank is required to maintain a holding—

*(a)* in specified liquid assets pursuant to section 18(2); or

*(b)* in specified liquid assets in the form mentioned in section 18(3).

Maintenance of reserve.

**19.** Every bank incorporated in Hong Kong shall, before any dividend is declared, appropriate to its published reserve out of the published profit of each year, after due provision has been made for taxation—

*(a)* a sum equal to not less than one-third of such published profits; or

*(b)* such lesser sum, if any, as may be necessary so that the aggregate of the bank's paid up share capital and its published reserve is not less than $200,000,000.

**Maintenance of adequate provision for bad and doubtful debts.**

**19A.** Every bank shall—

*(a)* maintain a provision for its bad and doubtful debts, if any; and

*(b)* before any profit or loss is declared, ensure that such provision is adequate.

Minimum paid up share capital of licensed banks.

**20.** (1) Subject to subsection (2), a bank incorporated in Hong Kong shall not transact banking business in Hong Kong unless its share capital issued and paid up is not less than $100,000,000, deduction having been made in respect of a debit balance, if any, appearing in the profit and loss account of the bank.

(2) A bank which is carrying on banking business at the commencement of the Banking (Amendment) (No. 2) Ordinance 1981 may continue to transact banking business for a period of 24 months after such commencement, or for such further period as the Governor in Council may allow in any particular case, if its share capital issued and paid up is less than $100,000,000 but not less than $10,000,000, deduction having been made in respect of a debit balance, if any, appearing in the profit and loss account of the bank.

Restriction on payment of dividends.

21. A bank incorporated in Hong Kong shall not pay any dividend on its shares or distribute any extraordinary profits unless—

(*a*) all items of expenditure not represented by tangible assets have been completely written off; and

(*b*) in the case of a distribution of extraordinary profits, the aggregate of its paid up share capital and published reserve after such distribution will not be less than $200,000,000.

Advance against security of own shares.

22. A bank shall not grant any advance, loan or credit facility against the security of its own shares.

Limitation on total of advances to one person, firm, etc.

23. (1) A bank shall not grant or permit to be outstanding to any one person, firm, corporation or company, or to any group of companies or persons which such person, firm, corporation or company is able to control or influence, any advances, loans or credit facilities, including irrevocable documentary letters of credit to the extent to which they are not covered by marginal cash deposits, or give any financial guarantees or incur any other liabilities on their behalf to an aggregate amount of such advances, loans, facilities, guarantees or liabilities in excess of 25 *per cent* of the paid up capital and reserves of the bank:

Provided that the provisions of this section shall not apply to—

(*a*) transactions between banks or between the branches of a bank;

(*aa*) transactions to the extent to which they are covered by a form of guarantee acceptable to the Commissioner;

(*ab*) transactions between a bank and a deposit-taking company;

(*b*) the purchase of telegraphic transfers;

(*c*) the purchase of bills of exchange or documents of title to goods where the holder of such bills or documents is entitled to payment outside Hong Kong for exports from Hong Kong; or

(*d*) advances or loans made against telegraphic transfers or against such bills or documents.

(2) For the purposes of subsection (1)—

(*a*) any advances, loans or credit facilities granted or permitted to be outstanding to, and any financial guarantees given and any other liabilities incurred on behalf of, a business or undertaking of which any one person is the sole proprietor shall be deemed to be granted or permitted to be outstanding to or given or incurred on behalf of, as the case may be, that one person;

(*b*) a person shall not be deemed to be able to control or influence a group of companies by reason only that he is a director of any other company in the group.

**Limitation on advances to directors, etc.**

24. (1) A bank shall not grant any facility specified in subsection (3) to or on behalf of any person or body specified in subsection (4) if the aggregate amount of such facilities for the time being granted by that bank to or on behalf of any one or more such persons or bodies would thereby exceed *10 per cent* of the paid up capital and reserves of the bank.

(2) Subject to and notwithstanding the provisions of subsection (1), a bank shall not grant any facility specified in subsection (3) to or on behalf of any person specified in paragraph *(a)*, *(b)* or *(ba)* of subsection (4) if the aggregate amount of such facilities for the time being granted by that bank to or on behalf of that person or any of his relatives would thereby exceed $250,000.

(3) For the purposes of subsections (1) and (2), the following facilities are specified—

*(a)* the granting, or permitting to be outstanding, of unsecured advances, unsecured loans or unsecured credit facilities including unsecured irrevocable documentary letters of credit;
*(b)* the giving of unsecured financial guarantees; and
*(c)* the incurring of any other unsecured liability.

(4) For the purposes of subsections (1) and (2), the following persons and bodies are specified—

*(a)* any director of the bank;
*(b)* any relative of any such director;
*(ba)* any employee of the bank who is responsible, either individually or as a member of a committee, for determining loan applications;
*(c)* any firm, partnership or private company in which the bank or any of its directors or any relative of any of its directors is interested as director, partner, manager or agent; and
*(d)* any individual, firm, partnership or private company of which any director of the bank or any relative of any such director is a guarantor.

(5) The provisions of this section shall apply to a facility granted to or on behalf of a person or body jointly with another person or body as they apply to a facility granted to or on behalf of a person or body severally.

(6) The provisions of this section shall not apply to the purchase of telegraphic transfers.

(7) For the purposes of subsections (2) and (4), a facility granted to or on behalf of any firm, partnership or private company which a director of a bank or a relative of a director of a bank is able to control,

or to or on behalf of a business or undertaking of which a director of a bank or a relative of a director of a bank is the sole proprietor, shall be deemed to be granted to or on behalf of such director or relative of a director.

Limitation on advances to employees.

25. A bank shall not grant or permit to be outstanding to any one of its employees unsecured advances, unsecured loans or unsecured credit facilities to an aggregate amount of such advances, loans or facilities in excess of one year's salary for any such employee.

Bank not to engage in trade or have interest in commercial or industrial concern.

26. (1) A bank shall not—

*(a)* engage, whether on its own account or as agent for another person, in any wholesale, retail, import or export trade; or

*(b)* save as permitted by section 27 or 28 and save to the extent of such interest as a bank may acquire in the course of the satisfaction of debts due to it, have a direct interest in any commercial, agricultural, industrial or other undertaking.

(2) Any interest in any commercial, agricultural, industrial or other undertaking acquired by a bank in the course of the satisfaction of a debt due to it shall be disposed of at the earliest suitable opportunity and in any event not later than 18 months after it was acquired or within such longer period as the Commissioner may allow in any particular case.

Limitation on shareholding by bank.

27. (1) Subject to the provisions of subsection (2), a bank shall not acquire or hold any part of the share capital of any other company or companies to an aggregate value in excess of 25 *per cent* of the paid up capital and reserves of the bank, except such shareholdings as a bank may acquire in the course of the satisfaction of debts due to it:

Provided that all shareholdings acquired in the course of the satisfaction of debts due to it shall be disposed of at the earliest suitable opportunity, and in any event not later than 18 months after the acquisition thereof or within such longer period as the Commissioner may allow in any particular case.

(2) This section shall not apply in respect of any shareholding approved in writing by the Commissioner in another bank or in a subsidiary company formed by the bank concerned for the carrying out of nominee, executor or trustee functions or other functions incidental to banking business.

Limitations on holding of interest in land.

28. (1) A bank shall not purchase or hold any interest or interests in land of a value or to an aggregate value, as the case may be, in excess of 25 *per cent* of the paid up capital and reserves of the bank.

(2) Subject to the provisions of section 29(1)*(b)*, in addition to the value of any land permitted to be purchased or held under subsection (1), a bank may purchase or hold interests in land to any value, where the occupation of such land is, in the opinion of the Commissioner, necessary for conducting the business of the bank or for providing housing or amenities for the staff of the bank.

(3) For the purposes of subsection (2), but without prejudice to the generality thereof, the Commissioner may in his discretion regard as necessary for conducting the business of a bank the whole of any premises in which an office of a bank is situated.

(4) There shall not be taken into account in the assessment of the value of interests in land for the purposes of this section the value of any interest in land mortgaged to the bank to secure a debt due to the bank nor the value of any interest in land acquired pursuant to entry into possession of land so mortgaged, provided that the interest acquired is disposed of at the earliest suitable opportunity, and in any event not later than 18 months after its acquisition or within such longer period as the Commissioner may allow in any particular case.

**Limitations on aggregate holdings under sections 24, 27 and 28.**

29. (1) Notwithstanding anything contained in sections 24, 27 and 28—

*(a)* the aggregate total of—

(i) the amount outstanding of all facilities specified in section 24(3) granted to or on behalf of persons or bodies specified in subsection (4) of that section;

(ii) the value of all holdings of share capital specified in section 27; and

(iii) the value of all holdings of interests in land specified in section 28(1),

shall not at any time exceed 55 *per cent* of the paid up capital and reserves of the bank; and

*(b)* the aggregate total of—

(i) the amount outstanding of all facilities specified in section 24(3) granted to or on behalf of persons or bodies specified in subsection (4) of that section;

(ii) the value of all holdings of share capital specified in section 27; and

(iii) the value of all holdings of interests in land specified in section 28(1) and (2),

shall not at any time exceed 80 *per cent* of the paid up capital and reserves of the bank.

(2) In assessing the aggregate total which is permissible under subsection (1) there shall not be taken into account any matter which is excluded from the operation of section 24, 27 or 28 by virtue of any of the provisions thereof or of section 30.

**Deductions for purposes of sections 23, 24, 27, 28 and 29.**

30. For the purposes of sections 23, 24, 27, 28 and 29 there shall be deducted from the paid up capital and reserves of the bank any debit balance appearing in the profit and loss account of the bank.

**Proof of reserves.**

31. Any bank, if at any time called upon in writing by the Commissioner so to do, shall satisfy him by the production of such evidence or information as he may require, that the bank is not in contravention of any of the provisions of section 23, 24, 27, 28 or 29.

**Definitions.**

32. (1) For the purposes of sections 24 and 25, the expression "unsecured" means granted without security, or, in respect of any advance, loan or credit facility granted or financial guarantee or other liability incurred with security, any part thereof which at any time exceeds the market value of assets constituting that security and the expression "security" shall mean such security as would, in the opinion of the Commissioner, be acceptable to a prudent banker.

(2) For the purposes of sections 27, 28 and 29, "value" means—

*(a)* in the case of shares in a company other than a trust company registered under Part VIII of the Trustee Ordinance, the total of the current book value and the amount for the time being remaining unpaid on the shares; and

*(b)* in any other case, the current book value.

(3) For the purposes of sections 23, 24, 27, 28, 29, 30 and 31, the expression "reserves" means reserves which appear in the accounts of the bank, and does not include any reserves which are represented by the writing down of the value of assets or by provision for the depreciation of fixed assets.

**Alteration in constitution and amalgamation.**

33. (1) A bank, within 3 months after the making of any alteration to the memorandum of association, articles of association or other instrument under which it is incorporated, shall furnish to the Commissioner particulars of such alteration in writing, verified by a director of the bank.

(2) A bank incorporated in Hong Kong shall not, without the prior approval of the Financial Secretary,—

(*a*) make any arrangement or enter into any agreement for the sale or disposal of its business by amalgamation or otherwise;
(*b*) make any reconstruction of its capital; or
(*c*) make any arrangement or enter into any agreement for the purchase or acquisition of the business of any other bank.

(3) A bank aggrieved by a decision of the Financial Secretary refusing his approval for the purposes of subsection (2) may appeal to the Governor in Council.

**Duty to report inability to meet obligations.**

34. If any bank is likely to become unable to meet its obligations or if it is about to suspend payment it shall forthwith report all relevant facts, circumstances and information to the Commissioner.

**Use of English language.**

35. (1) All entries in books and accounts kept by banks shall be recorded in the English language and the Arabic system of numerals shall be employed.

(2) All forms and information required to be sent and all returns required to be made to the Commissioner pursuant to any of the provisions of this Ordinance shall be compiled in the English language and the Arabic system of numerals.

**Audit.**

36. (1) Every bank which is a company, and its auditors, shall comply with the provisions of the Companies Ordinance with respect to the audit of a company's accounts, whether or not the bank is incorporated under that Ordinance.

(2) The Commissioner may appoint another auditor to act with the auditor appointed by a bank in accordance with the Companies Ordinance or, in the case of an unincorporated bank, section 44A.

**Publication and exhibition of audited balance sheet.**

37. (1) Every bank shall, not later than 6 months after the close of each financial year, publish in one English daily newspaper and one Chinese daily newspaper, each of which shall be a newspaper circulating in Hong Kong, and exhibit thereafter throughout the year in a conspicuous position in the principal place of business thereof in Hong Kong and in each local branch thereof—

(*a*) a copy of its latest audited annual balance sheet, and any notes thereon, a copy of the profit and loss account and a copy of the report of the auditor made pursuant to section 141 of the Companies Ordinance or section 44A of this Ordinance;
(*b*) the full and correct names of all persons who are directors or managers for the time being of the bank; and
(*c*) the names of all subsidiary companies, for the time being, of the bank.

(2) A copy of each of the documents referred to in subsection (1) shall be sent to the Commissioner by a bank, prior to first publication thereof under subsection (1) with a list of the names of all companies of which, for the time being, its directors are also directors.

(3) The documents sent to the Commissioner pursuant to subsection (2) shall be accompanied, in the case of a bank which is a company limited by shares or limited by guarantee and having a share capital, by a copy of the report of the directors laid before the company in general meeting in accordance with section 129D(1) of the Companies Ordinance.

(4) If, in the case of a bank incorporated outside Hong Kong, the Commissioner is satisfied that a report has been duly made by an auditor, or any person exercising a similar function in accordance with the law of the country, state or place in which such bank is incorporated, upon the annual balance sheet and accounts of the bank and a copy of such report and the report of the directors of such bank is sent to the Commissioner, he may by notice in writing exempt any such bank from the provisions of this section and of section 36.

(5) The Commissioner may require any bank to submit such further information as he may deem necessary for the proper understanding of the balance sheet and profit and loss accounts sent by that bank under subsection (2); and such information shall be submitted within such period and in such manner as the Commissioner may require.

(6) The annual balance sheet of a bank, copies of which are required by subsection (1) to be published and exhibited, shall be in such form as the Commissioner may approve.

**Returns and information to be submitted to the Commissioner.**

38. (1) Every bank shall submit to the Commissioner—

*(a)* not later than 14 days after the last day of each calendar month a return, in such form as the Commissioner may specify, showing the assets and liabilities of its principal place of business in Hong Kong and all local branches thereof at the close of business on the last business day of that month; and

*(b)* not later than 14 days after the last day of each quarter ending on 31 March, 30 June, 30 September and 31 December respectively, or upon any other day which may be approved by the Commissioner, a return, in such form as he may specify, relating to its principal place of business in Hong Kong and all local branches thereof as at the close of business on the last business day of the preceding quarter:

Provided that the Commissioner may by permission in writing allow the returns referred to in paragraphs *(a)* and *(b)* to be submitted at less frequent intervals.

(2) The Commissioner may require a bank to submit such further information as he may consider necessary for the proper understanding of the financial position of the bank and such information shall be submitted within such period and in such manner as the Commissioner may require.

(2A) The Commissioner may require any return submitted to him pursuant to subsection (1), or any information submitted to him pursuant to a requirement under subsection (2), to be accompanied by a certificate—

*(a)* of the auditor appointed under section 36(1) or of the auditors appointed under section 36(1) and (2), as the case may be;

*(b)* in the case of a bank which has been exempted under section 37(4) from the provisions of section 36, of an auditor approved by the Commissioner for the purposes of this paragraph,

as to whether or not, in the opinion of the auditor or auditors, the return or information is correctly compiled from the books and records of the bank.

(3) Notwithstanding anything in sections 53 and 60, the Commissioner may prepare and publish consolidated returns aggregating the figures in the returns furnished under subsection (1).

Information on shareholding.

**38A.** (1) Every bank incorporated in Hong Kong shall, if so required by the Commissioner, inform him of the name and address of, and the nature of the business carried on by, every company (whether incorporated in or outside Hong Kong and whether or not the company is carrying on business in Hong Kong or has complied with the provisions of section 333 of the Companies Ordinance) in which the bank holds the beneficial ownership, directly or indirectly, of an aggregate of 20 *per cent* or more of the share capital.

(2) The Commissioner may require any bank which has submitted to him information pursuant to subsection (1) to submit to him such further information as he may consider necessary to obtain, in the interests of the depositors of the bank, about the assets, liabilities and transactions of any such company.

(3) Information that is required to be submitted under this section shall be submitted within such period and in such manner as the Commissioner may require.

Production of bank's books, etc.

39. For the purpose of an examination or investigation under section 15, a bank shall afford the person carrying out thet examination or investigation access to its books and accounts, to documents of title to its assets and other documents, to all securities held by it in respect of its customers' transactions and its cash and to such information and facilities as may be required to conduct the examination or investigation, and shall produce to the person carrying out the examination or investigation such books, accounts, documents, securities, cash or other information as he may require:

Provided that, so far as is consistent with the conduct of the examination or investigation, such books, accounts, documents, securities and cash shall not be required to be produced at such times and such places as shall interfere with the proper conduct of the normal daily business of the bank.

Examination by authorities from outside Hong Kong.

39A. The appropriate recognized banking supervisory authority of a country, state or place outside Hong Kong may, with the approval of the Commissioner, examine the books, accounts and transactions of the principal place of business in Hong Kong or any local branch, or the documents of any local representative office,—

(*a*) of a bank which is incorporated in that country, state or place; or
(*b*) of a bank which is incorporated in or outside Hong Kong and is a subsidiary of a bank which is incorporated in that country, state or place.

Licensed bank under control of Commissioner to co-operate with Commissioner.

40. (1) Where the Commissioner has assumed control of the business of a bank under section 13(1)(iii) or pursuant to an order of the Governor in Council under section 14(1)(ii), or some other person has assumed control of the business of a bank pursuant to a direction under section 13(1)(iii) or an order of the Governor in Council under section 14(1)(ii), the bank shall submit its business to the control of the Commissioner or such other person and shall provide him with the services of such members of its staff and such other facilities as he may consider necessary for carrying on the business of the bank and in connexion therewith the directors and managers shall comply with and carry out any directions which the Commissioner or such other person may give to them.

(2) Without prejudice to the provisions of subsection (1), where by reason of the absence of directors or for any reason whatsoever the seal of a bank whose business is—

(*a*) in the control of the Commissioner under section 13(1)(iii) or pursuant to an order of the Governor in Council under section 14(1)(ii), or

(*b*) in the control of some other person pursuant to a direction under section 13(1)(iii) or an order of the Governor in Council under section 14(1)(ii),

cannot be affixed to an instrument in accordance with the bank's articles of association or regulations, the seal may be affixed in the presence of, and its affixing may be attested by, the Commissioner or such other person or a person authorized for the purpose by the Commissioner or such other person.

(3) Where the seal of a bank has been affixed to an instrument, and the affixing thereof has been attested, in accordance with subsection (2), no person shall be concerned to see that the seal could not be affixed in accordance with the bank's articles of association or regulations.

**Disqualification of directors and employees of banks.**

41. Notwithstanding the provisions of any other enactment, no person—

(*a*) who is or who becomes bankrupt, suspends payment or compounds with his creditors; or

(*b*) who is or who has been convicted in any country of an offence involving dishonesty or fraud and has not received a full pardon for the offence of which he was convicted; or

(*c*) who has been a director of, or directly concerned in the management of, a bank licensed under this Ordinance or which was licensed under the Banking Ordinance 1948, now repealed, which is being or has been wound up by a court or the licence of which has been revoked,

shall, without the consent in writing of the Commissioner, act or continue to act as a director, manager, secretary or other employee of any bank.

**Execution of instruments under seal.**

41A. Notwithstanding anything contained in the articles of association or regulations of any bank incorporated in Hong Kong with respect to the execution of instruments under its seal, but without prejudice to anything in such articles or regulations not inconsistent herewith, the seal of the bank shall not be affixed to any instrument except in the presence of a director of the bank and of one other person being either a director or an officer of the bank duly authorized in that behalf, and that director and such other person shall sign every instrument to which the seal of the company is so affixed in their presence.

## PART VI. UNINCORPORATED BANKS

Grant of licences to unincorporated banks.

42. (1) Notwithstanding the provisions of section 5, the Governor in Council may issue a licence to carry on banking business in Hong Kong to any unincorporated person or body of persons who or which, at the commencement of this Ordinance, held a valid licence issued under the Banking Ordinance 1948, now repealed.

(2) A licence may be granted under subsection (1), notwithstanding that the unincorporated person or body of persons does not comply and does not propose to comply with the provision of section 8, 18, 19 or 20.

Application for licence under section 42.

43. (1) An application for a licence under section 42 shall be made to the Governor in Council through the Commissioner.

(2) An application for a licence under section 42 shall be accompanied by such documents and information as the Commissioner or the Governor in Council may require.

Licence fee for unincorporated bank.

44. (1) An unincorporated bank shall pay an annual licence fee of $5,000 or such other sum as may be specified by the Governor in Council and notified in the *Gazette.*

(2) The fees payable under this section shall be paid upon the grant of a licence and thereafter upon the anniversary of the date of the grant of such licence.

(3) The Director of Accounting Services shall cause to be published in the *Gazette* each year in the month of April the name of every unincorporated bank which has within the preceding financial year paid the fees payable under this section.

Auditor.

44A. (1) Every unincorporated bank shall appoint annually an auditor.

(2) The duties of the auditor so appointed shall be—

(*a*) to carry out for the year in respect of which he is appointed an audit of the accounts of the bank;

(*b*) to make a report to the directors of the bank on the audited accounts, the balance sheet and the profit and loss account of the bank; and

(*c*) in every such report to state—

(i) whether or not all the information and explanations which were in the opinion of the auditor necessary for the purposes of the audit have been obtained;

(ii) whether or not, according to the best of the information and explanations given to him, the balance sheet and profit and loss account referred to in the report give in his opinion a true and fair view of the state of the affairs of the bank at the date of the balance sheet, and of the profit or loss for its financial year, regard being had, *inter alia,* to the provisions of this Ordinance;

(iii) whether or not in his opinion proper books of account have been kept by the bank so far as appears from the audit of the accounts; and

(iv) whether or not in his opinion proper returns, adequate for the purposes of the audit, have been received by him from branches of the bank not visited.

**General application of Ordinance to unincorporated banks and members.**

45. (1) An unincorporated bank shall, subject to the provisions of this Part, be deemed to be a bank for the purposes of this Ordinance.

(2) Any person to whom, and any member or partner of any unincorporated body of persons to which, a licence is granted under section 42 shall be deemed for the purposes of this Ordinance to be a director of a bank.

**Application of sections of Ordinance to unincorporated banks.**

46. An unincorporated bank shall, subject to the provisions of this Part, be subject to all the provisions of this Ordinance, *mutatis mutandis,* except—

*(a)* section 15 (2)*(a)*;

*(b)* sections 18, 19, 19A, 20, 21, 22, 23, 24, 25, 26, 27, 28, 29, 30, 31 and 32;

*(c)* section 33(1);

*(d)* section 37 (1)*(c)*; and

*(e)* any other provision of this Ordinance which is inconsistent with the provisions of this Part or which is inapplicable in the case of an unincorporated bank.

**Prohibition on use of word "bank".**

47. An unincorporated bank shall not use the word "bank" or any of its derivatives in English, a translation thereof in any language or the Chinese expression *"ngan hong"* ( 銀行 ) in the description or title under which it carries on business in Hong Kong.

**Prohibition on total of deposits.**

48. An unincorporated bank shall not accept or hold deposits in excess, at any one time, of $2,000,000 or such other sum as the Governor in Council may from time to time specify either generally or in any particular case.

Death of member of unincorporated bank.

49. (1) Upon the death of a member or partner of an unincorporated bank, the licence issued to the unincorporated bank shall become void and of no effect upon a date 6 calendar months after the date of the death except for the purpose of winding up the banking business of the unincorporated bank.

(2) Notwithstanding the provisions of subsection (1), the Governor in Council may issue a new licence under section 42 to the remaining members or partners of that body of persons or to a body of persons consisting of the remaining members of that body of persons and other members or partners who have acquired their interest in the business and assets of the unincorporated bank of which the deceased was a member under the will or upon the intestacy of the deceased.

(3) The remaining members or partners of an unincorporated bank shall notify the Commissioner of the death of a member or partner of the unincorporated bank within 1 month after the death.

## PART VII. MISCELLANEOUS

Governor in Council to decide whether or not banking business is being conducted.

50. (1) In the event of any dispute as to whether a person is carrying on a banking business, the matter, except in the case of a prosecution for any offence against this Ordinance, shall be submitted to the Governor in Council for his determination; and the decision of the Governor in Council shall be final and conclusive for all purposes of this Ordinance.

(2) A submission under subsection (1) may be made by the Financial Secretary or by any bank or person which or who is interested in the determination of the matter.

Power of entry, search, detention and arrest.

51. Whenever it appears to a magistrate, upon the oath of any person, that there is reasonable cause to suspect that a contravention of this Ordinance has been or is being committed in any building or place, such magistrate may by warrant directed to any police officer of or above the rank of inspector empower him with such assistance as may be necessary by day or night—

*(a)* to enter, and, if necessary, to break into such building or place;

*(b)* to search for, detain and take away or remove any machinery, type, appliance, paper, books, documents, accounts, or any thing whatsoever which appears to afford evidence of the commission of such contravention.

Indemnity.

52. No liability shall be incurred by—

*(a)* any public officer;

(*b*) any person authorized or employed by the Commissioner under section 4A;

(*c*) any person appointed under section 13(1)(ii), or by order of the Governor in Council under section 14(1)(ii), to advise a bank in the proper conduct of its business; or

(*d*) any person who has assumed control of the business of a bank pursuant to a direction under section 13(1)(iii) or an order of the Governor in Council under section 14(1)(ii),

as a result of anything done by him *bona fide* in the exercise of any power, or the performance of any function or duty, conferred or imposed by or under this Ordinance.

53. (1) Every person to whom this subsection applies— Secrecy.

(*a*) shall preserve and aid in preserving secrecy with regard to all matters relating to the affairs of any person that may come to his knowledge in the exercise or performance of any function or duty under this Ordinance;

(*b*) shall not communicate any such matter to any person other than the person to whom such matter relates; and

(*c*) shall not suffer or permit any person to have access to any records in the possession, custody or control of any person to whom this subsection applies,

except as may be necessary for the exercise or performance of such function or duty or for carrying into effect the provisions of this Ordinance.

(1A) Subsection (1) shall apply to—

(*a*) any public officer;

(*b*) any person authorized or employed by the Commissioner under section 4A;

(*c*) any person appointed under section 13(1)(ii), or by order of the Governor in Council under section 14(1)(ii), to advise a bank in the proper conduct of its business;

(*d*) any person who has assumed control of the business of a bank pursuant to a direction under section 13(1)(iii) or an order of the Governor in Council under section 14(1)(ii); and

(*e*) any person employed by or assisting a person to whom this subsection applies by virtue of paragraph *(b)*, *(c) or (d)*,

who exercises or performs any function or duty under this Ordinance.

(1B) Where under section 13(1)(iii) or under section 14(1)(ii) the Commissoner assumes control of and carries on the business of a bank or any other person is directed so to do, subsection (1) shall not apply if the Commissioner or such other person is required to comply with a notice to furnish returns and information under section 51 of the Inland Revenue Ordinance.

(2) No person who exercises any function or performs any duty in the course of an examination or investigation under section 12D, 12G or 15 or who receives reports, returns or information submitted under section 12D, 12G, 15, 38, 38A or 39 shall be required to produce in any court any book, account or other document whatsoever or to divulge or communicate to any court any matter or thing coming under his notice in the performance of his functions or duties under this Ordinance, except as may be necessary in the course of a prosecution for any offence or of a winding-up by the High Court under section 55.

Disclosure of information relating to banks.

53A. (1) Subject to subsection (3) and notwithstanding anything in sections 53 and 60, the Commissioner may, if he considers that it is in the interests of the depositors of the bank, provide to the appropriate recognized banking supervisory authority of a country, state or place outside Hong Kong which is, in his opinion, subject to adequate secrecy provisions in that country, state or place information on matters relating to the affairs of a bank—

*(a)* which is incorporated in that country, state or place;
*(b)* which is incorporated in or outside Hong Kong and is a subsidiary or associate of a bank incorporated in that country, state or place; or
*(c)* which is incorporated in Hong Kong and which has, or is proposing to establish, in that country, state or place an overseas branch, overseas representative office, subsidiary or associate of that bank, and where, in the case of a subsidiary or associate, such subsidiary or associate is or would be subject to supervision by that recognized banking supervisory authority.

(2) Subject to subsection (3) and notwithstanding anything in sections 53 and 60, the Commissioner may, if he considers that it is in the interests of customers of the representative office, provide to the appropriate recognized banking supervisory authority of a country, state or place outside Hong Kong which is, in his opinion, subject to adequate secrecy provisions in that country, state or place information on matters relating to the affairs of a local representative office which is maintained by a bank incorporated in that country, state or place.

(3) Under no circumstances shall the Commissioner provide any information under this section relating to the affairs of any individual customer of a bank or local representative office.

**Recovery of fees, expenses, etc.**

54. (1) There shall be recoverable at the suit of the Attorney General as a civil debt due to the Crown from the bank concerned, or in the case of an unincorporated bank, from the directors jointly and severally thereof—

*(a)* the amount of any fees payable under section 12, 12B, 12E, 12H or 44;

*(b)* any remuneration and expenses payable by the bank to any person appointed under section 13(1)(ii), or by order of the Governor in Council under section 14(1)(ii), to advise the bank in the proper conduct of its business;

*(c)* any remuneration and expenses payable by the bank to the Commissioner or to any person employed or authorized by the Commissioner under section 4A to assist him in the control and carrying on of the business of the bank or to any other person who has assumed control of the business of the bank pursuant to a direction under section 13(1)(iii) or an order of the Governor in Council under section 14(1)(ii);

*(d)* any expenses ordered by the Financial Secretary to be defrayed by the bank under section 15(3); and

*(e)* any remuneration payable by the bank to an auditor appointed under section 36(2).

(2) There shall be recoverable, at the suit of the Attorney General, as a civil debt due from the applicants, jointly and severally, to the Crown, any expenses ordered by the Financial Secretary to be defrayed by the applicants under section 15(3).

(3) Any sum recoverable under this section at the suit of the Attorney General shall be a debt due to the Crown within the meaning of section 265(1)*(a)* of the Companies Ordinance and section 38(1)*(a)* of the Bankruptcy Ordinance.

**Winding-up of banks.**

55. (1) The provisions of the Companies Ordinance with regard to a creditors' voluntary winding-up shall not apply to banking companies.

(2) On a petition by the Financial Secretary, acting in accordance with a direction of the Governor in Council under section 14(1)(iii), the High Court may—

*(a)* on any ground specified in section 177 of the Companies Ordinance; or

*(b)* if it is satisfied that it is in the public interest that the bank should be wound up,

order the winding up of a bank in accordance with the provisions of the Companies Ordinance relating to the winding up of companies.

(3) Where before the presentation of a petition for the winding up of a bank by the court, whether or not the petition is presented by the Financial Secretary, the Commissioner has assumed control of the business of the bank under section 13(1)(iii) or pursuant to an order of the Governor in Council under section 14(1)(ii) or some other person has assumed control of the business of the bank pursuant to a direction of the Commissioner under section 13(1)(iii) or an order of the Governor in Council under section 14(1)(ii) and such control has continued at all times until the presentation of the petition, and a winding-up order is made thereon, then, notwithstanding the provisions of section 184(2) of the Companies Ordinance, the winding up of the bank by the court shall, for the purposes of sections 170, 179, 182, 183, 266, 267, 269 and 274, and paragraphs *(d), (e), (h), (i), (j), (k), (l), (m), (n)* and *(o)* of section 271(1), of the Companies Ordinance, be deemed to have commenced at the time the Commissioner or such other person assumed control of the business of the bank.

(4) Where the Commissioner has assumed control of the business of a bank under section 13(1)(iii) or pursuant to an order of the Governor in Council under section 14(1)(ii) or some other person has assumed control of the business of a bank pursuant to a direction of the Commissioner under section 13(1)(iii) or an order of the Governor in Council under section 14(1)(ii), nothing in section 182 of the Companies Ordinance shall invalidate any disposition of the property of the bank made by it under the direction of the Commissioner or such person acting *bona fide* in the course of the carrying on of the business of the bank.

**Bankruptcy of unincorporated banks.**

55A. Where—

*(a)* the Commissioner has assumed control of the business of an unincorporated bank under section 13(1)(iii) or pursuant to an order of the Governor in Council under section 14(1)(ii) or some other person has assumed control of the business of such a bank pursuant to a direction of the Commissioner under section 13(1)(iii) or an order of the Governor in Council under section 14(1)(ii); and

*(b)* within 3 months thereafter, whilst the Commissioner or such other person continues to be in control of the business of such bank, a bankruptcy petition is presented against the bank under the Bankruptcy Ordinance, and on that petition a receiving order is at any time made under the said Ordinance against the bank,

then—

(i) if the date on which the Commissioner or such other person as is referred to in paragraph *(a)* assumed control of the business of such bank preceded the time of the first of the acts of bankruptcy (within the meaning of the Bankruptcy Ordinance) proved to have been committed by such bank within the 3 months next preceding the date of the presentation of the bankruptcy petition, the bankruptcy of the bank shall, for the purposes of sections 40, 43, 47(2) and (3), and 48, of the Bankruptcy Ordinance, be deemed, notwithstanding the provisions of section 42 of the Bankruptcy Ordinance, to have relation back to and to commence at the time the Commissioner or such other person assumed control of the business of such bank;

(ii) section 45(1) of the Bankruptcy Ordinance shall apply as if it included, as an alternative to the reference to notice of the presentation of any bankruptcy petition by or against the debtor or notice of the commission of any available act of bankruptcy by the debtor, a reference, in the case of a debtor which is an unincorporated bank, to notice that the Commissioner or such other person as is referred to in paragraph *(a)* has so assumed control of the business of the debtor;

(iii) section 49(1) of the Bankruptcy Ordinance shall apply as if it included, as an alternative to the reference to the person first referred to therein being adjudged bankrupt on a bankruptcy petition presented within 3 months after the date specified therein, a reference, in a case where such person is an unincorporated bank, to the assumption as aforesaid by the Commissioner or such other person as is referred to in paragraph *(a)* of control of the business of such person within 3 months after such date;

(iv) section 50(1) of the Bankruptcy Ordinance shall apply as if it included, as an alternative to the reference in paragraph *(b)* of the proviso thereto to notice of any available act of bankruptcy committed by the bankrupt before the time referred to therein, a reference, in the case of a bankrupt which is an unincorporated bank, to notice that, before the said time, the Commissioner or such other person as is referred to in paragraph *(a)* has so assumed control of the business of the bankrupt;

(v) section 51 of the Bankruptcy Ordinance shall apply as if it included, as an alternative to the reference to notice of the presentation of a bankruptcy petition, a reference, in a case where the person referred to therein is an unincorporated bank, to notice that the Commissioner or such other person as is referred to in paragraph *(a)* has so assumed control of the business of such person; and

(vi) sections 129, 133, 134, 135 and 136 of the Bankruptcy Ordinance shall apply as if, in a case where the person referred to therein is an unincorporated bank, the reference or references therein to the presentation of a bankruptcy petition included in each case a reference to the assumption as aforesaid by the Commissioner or such other person as is referred to in paragraph *(a)* of control of the business of such person.

**Power of Commissioner to specify forms.**

56. The Commissioner may specify the form of any notice or other document required for the purposes of this Ordinance.

**Application of other Ordinances.**

57. (1) Notwithstanding anything in the Hongkong and Shanghai Banking Corporation Ordinance, all the provisions of this Ordinance shall apply to The Hongkong and Shanghai Banking Corporation.

(2) Where there is any conflict or inconsistency between the provisions of this Ordinance and the provisions of the Hongkong and Shanghai Banking Corporation Ordinance the provisions of this Ordinance shall prevail.

(3) A bank which is incorporated or registered under the Companies Ordinance shall be subject to the provisions of that Ordinance as well as to the provisions of this Ordinance, save that where there is any conflict or inconsistency between the provisions of this Ordinance and the provisions of the Companies Ordinance the provisions of this Ordinance shall prevail.

## PART VIII. OFFENCES

**Defence where director or manager prosecuted.**

58. Any person who is prosecuted in respect of any offence under section 61, 63, 65 or 66 shall have a good defence if he proves that the offence was committed without his consent or connivance and that he exercised all such diligence to prevent the commission of the offence as he ought to have exercised having regard to his position in the bank in respect of which the offence was committed.

**59.** Any director, manager, trustee, employee or agent of any bank who, with intent to deceive—

Offences by directors, employees and agents.

*(a)* wilfully makes, or causes to be made, a false entry in any book of record or in any report, slip, document or statement of the business, affairs, transactions, condition, assets or accounts of such bank; or

*(b)* wilfully omits to make an entry in any book of record or in any report, slip, document or statement of the business, affairs, transactions, condition, assets or accounts of such bank, or wilfully causes any such entry to be omitted; or

*(c)* wilfully alters, abstracts, conceals or destroys an entry in any book of record, or in any report, slip, document or statement of the business, affairs, transactions, condition, assets or accounts of such bank, or wilfully causes any such entry to be altered, abstracted, concealed or destroyed,

shall be liable—

(i) on conviction on indictment to a fine of $500,000 and to imprisonment for 5 years; or

(ii) on summary conviction to a fine of $50,000 and to imprisonment for 2 years.

**60.** Any person who—

Breach of secrecy.

*(a)* contravenes section 53(1); or

*(b)* aids, abets, counsels or procures any person to contravene section 53(1),

shall be guilty of an offence and shall be liable—

(i) on conviction on indictment to a fine of $100,000 and to imprisonment for 2 years; or

(ii) on summary conviction to a fine of $50,000 and to imprisonment for 6 months.

**61.** (1) Any person who and every director and every manager of a company which contravenes section 5 shall be guilty of an offence and shall be liable—

Penalty in event of contravention of section 5 or 47.

*(a)* on conviction on indictment to a fine of $500,000 and to imprisonment for 5 years; or

*(b)* on summary conviction to a fine of $50,000 and to imprisonment for 6 months.

(2) Every director and every manager of an unincorporated bank which contravenes section 47 shall be guilty of an offence and shall be liable—

(a) on conviction on indictment to a fine of $100,000 and to imprisonment for 2 years; or

(b) on summary conviction to a fine of $50,000 and to imprisonment for 6 months.

**Prohibition on receipt of commission by staff.**

62. Any director or employee (other than a compradore) of a bank, who asks for or receives, consents or agrees to receive any gift, commission, emolument, service, gratuity, money, property or thing of value for his own personal benefit or advantage or for that of any of his relatives, for procuring or endeavouring to procure for any person any advance, loan, financial guarantee or credit facility from that bank or the purchase or discount of any draft, note, cheque, bill of exchange or other obligation by that bank, or for permitting any person to overdraw any account with that bank, shall be guilty of an offence and shall be liable—

(a) on conviction on indictment to a fine of $100,000 and to imprisonment for 5 years; or

(b) on summary conviction to a fine of $50,000 and to imprisonment for 2 years.

Criminal liability of directors and managers.

63. (1) Every director and every manager of a bank which contravenes section 18 shall be guilty of an offence and shall be liable on conviction on indictment to a fine of $500,000 and to imprisonment for 5 years and, in the case of a continuing offence, to a further fine of $5,000 for every day during which the offence continues.

(2) Every director and every manager of a bank which contravenes section 20 shall be guilty of an offence and shall be liable on conviction on indictment to a fine of $500,000 and to imprisonment for 5 years and, in the case of a continuing offence, to a further fine of $25,000 for every day during which the offence continues.

(3) Every director and every manager of a bank which contravenes section 23, 24(1) or (2), 27(1), 28, 29 or 34 shall be guilty of an offence and shall be liable—

(a) on conviction on indictment to a fine of $200,000 and to imprisonment for 2 years and, in the case of a continuing offence, to a further fine of $10,000 for every day during which the offence continues; or

(b) on summary conviction to a fine of $50,000 and to imprisonment for 6 months and, in the case of a continuing offence, to a further fine of $5,000 for every day during which the offence continues.

(4) Every director and every manager of a bank which contravenes section 19, 19A, 21, 33(2), 36(1) or 44A(1) shall be guilty of an offence and shall be liable—

(*a*) on conviction on indictment to a fine of $200,000 and to imprisonment for 2 years; or

(*b*) on summary conviction to a fine of $50,000 and to imprisonment for 6 months.

(5) Every director and every manager of a bank which contravenes any condition attached under section 7(1)(*b*) or 7A, or deemed to be attached under section 12F(1) or 12(G), to the licence held by the bank or any condition attached under section 12A(4) or 12F(4), or which contravenes section 12A(1) or 37(1), (2), (3) or (6) shall be guilty of an offence and shall be liable—

(*a*) on conviction on indictment to a fine of $200,000; or

(*b*) on summary conviction to a fine of $50,000,

and, in the case of a continuing offence, to a further fine of $5,000 for every day during which the offence continues.

(6) Every director and every manager of a bank which contravenes section 25, 26, 39 or 48 shall be guilty of an offence and shall be liable—

(*a*) on conviction on indictment to a fine of $100,000 and to imprisonment for 12 months; or

(*b*) on summary conviction to a fine of $50,000 and to imprisonment for 6 months,

and, in the case of a continuing offence, to a further fine of $5,000 for every day during which the offence continues.

(7) Every director and every manager of a bank which contravenes section 22 shall be guilty of an offence and shall be liable—

(*a*) on conviction on indictment to a fine of $100,000 and to imprisonment for 12 months; or

(*b*) on summary conviction to a fine of $50,000 and to imprisonment for 6 months.

(8) Every director and every manager of a bank which contravenes section 33(1), 35, 38(1) or 49(3) shall be guilty of an offence and shall be liable on conviction on indictment or on summary conviction to a fine of $50,000 and, in the case of a continuing offence, to a further fine of $5,000 for every day during which the offence continues.

64. *[Repealed, 27 of 1981, s. 23]*

Offence and penalty for failure to comply with orders, requirements, etc.

65. (1) Every director and every manager of a bank which fails to comply with an order of the Governor in Council under section 14(1)(ii) shall be guilty of an offence and shall be liable—

(*a*) on conviction on indictment to a fine of $1,000,000 and to imprisonment for 5 years and, in the case of a continuing offence, to a further fine of $50,000 for every day during which the offence continues; or

*(b)* on summary conviction to a fine of $50,000 and to imprisonment for 2 years and, in the case of a continuing offence, to a further fine of $5,000 for every day during which the offence continues.

(2) Every director and every manager—

*(a)* of a bank which fails to comply with any requirement of the Commissioner under section 13(1)(i);

*(b)* of a bank which contravenes section 40(1); or

*(c)* who fails to comply with or to carry out any direction given by the Commissioner or some other person under section 40(1),

shall be guilty of an offence and shall be liable—

(i) on conviction on indictment to a fine of $1,000,000 and to imprisonment for 5 years and, in the case of a continuing offence, to a further fine of $50,000 for every day during which the offence continues; or

(ii) on summary conviction to a fine of $50,000 and to imprisonment for 2 years and, in the case of a continuing offence, to a further fine of $5,000 for every day during which the offence continues.

(3) Every director and every manager of a bank which fails to comply with any requirement of the Commissioner under section 31, 38(2) or 38A shall be guilty of an offence and shall be liable—

*(a)* on conviction on indictment to a fine of $200,000 and to imprisonment for 2 years and, in the case of a continuing offence, to a further fine of $10,000 for every day during which the offence continues; or

*(b)* on summary conviction to a fine of $50,000 and to imprisonment for 6 months and, in the case of a continuing offence, to a further fine of $5,000 for every day during which the offence continues.

(4) Every director and every manager of a bank which fails to comply with any requirement of the Commissioner under section 37(5) or 38(2A) shall be guility of an offence and shall be liable on conviction on indictment or on summary conviction to a fine of $50,000 and to imprisonment for 6 months and, in the case of a continuing offence, to a further fine of $2,500 for every day during which the offence continues.

Offence and penalty for production of false books, etc.

66. If a bank produces any book, account, document, security or information whatsoever under section 12D, 12G, 38A or 39 which is false in a material particular, every director and every manager of such bank shall be guilty of an offence and shall be liable—

(*a*) on conviction on indictment to a fine of $500,000 and to imprisonment for 2 years; or
(*b*) on summary conviction to a fine of $50,000 and to imprisonment for 6 months.

**Offence and penalty for false certificates.**

**66A.** Any person who signs any document for the purposes of section 12D, 12G or 38A which he knows or reasonably ought to know to be false in a material particular shall be guilty of an offence and shall be liable—

(*a*) on conviction on indictment to a fine of $500,000 and to imprisonment for 2 years; or
(*b*) on summary conviction to a fine of $50,000 and to imprisonment for 6 months.

**Offences against sections 12C and 12D.**

**66B.** Any person in charge, or who appears to be in charge, of a local representative office established or maintained in contravention of section 12C(1) or in respect of which any condition attached under section 12C(4) is contravened, or any person who fails to comply with any requirement of the Commissioner under section 12D, shall be guilty of an offence and shall be liable—

(*a*) on conviction on indictment to a fine of $200,000; or
(*b*) on summary conviction to a fine of $50,000,

and, in the case of a continuing offence, to a further fine of $5,000 for every day during which the offence continues.

**Restriction on use of title "bank".**

67. (1) Any person, other than a bank licensed under this Ordinance, a bank incorporated outside Hong Kong which is recognized as the central bank of the country or place in which it is incorporated, or a local representative office maintained in accordance with this Ordinance, who, without the written consent of the Commissioner,—

(*a*) uses the word "bank" or any of its derivatives in English, or any translation thereof in any language or uses the Chinese expression *"ngan hong"* ( 银 行 ), or uses the letters "b", "a", "n", "k" in that order, in the description or title under which such person is carrying on business in Hong Kong; or
(*b*) makes any representation in any bill head, letter paper, notice, advertisement or in any other manner whatsoever that such person is a bank or is carrying on banking business in Hong Kong,

shall be liable—

(i) on conviction on indictment to a fine of $200,000 and to imprisonment for 12 months; or
(ii) on summary conviction to a fine of $50,000 and to imprisonment for 6 months.

(2) Nothing in this section shall apply to any association of banks formed for the protection or promotion of their mutual interests or to any association of employees of banks formed for the protection or promotion of the mutual interests of such employees.

Offence against section 41.

68. Any person who contravenes any of the provisions of section 41 shall be guilty of an offence and shall be liable—

*(a)* on conviction on indictment to a fine of $100,000 and to imprisonment for 12 months; or

*(b)* on summary conviction to a fine of $50,000 and to imprisonment for 6 months.

Consent of Attorney General.

69. No prosecution in respect of any offence under this Ordinance shall be instituted without the consent in writing of the Attorney General.

## PART IX. TRANSITIONAL

70–73. *{Repealed, 26 of 1967, s. 62}*

Keeping of books.

74. Notwithstanding the provisions of section 35, any bank which, at the commencement of this Ordinance, held a valid licence issued under the Banking Ordinance 1948, now repealed, and kept its books and accounts in some other language or in some other system of numerals than what is required by that section may continue to do so but shall provide on demand to its auditor or to the Commissioner such translations into the English language and the Arabic system of numerals as either may require, and the cost of so doing shall be borne by the bank concerned.

75–76. *{Repealed, 27 of 1981, s. 28}*

Transitional provisions consequent upon Banking (Amendment) Ordinance 1967.

76A. (1) Any licence granted by the Financial Secretary under section 7 which is in force at the commencement of the Banking (Amendment) Ordinance 1967, whether the same was granted thereunder pursuant to the repealed section 73 or otherwise, shall be deemed to have been granted under section 7 by the Governor in Council.

(2) Any licence granted by the Financial Secretary under section 42 which is in force at the commencement of the Banking (Amendment) Ordinance 1967 shall be deemed to have been granted under section 42 by the Governor in Council.

(3) *{Deleted, 27 of 1981, s. 29}*

(4) Any approval given by the Financial Secretary under section 27(2) and any consent given by the Financial Secretary under section 41 or 67(1) which is in force at the commencement of the Banking (Amendment) Ordinance 1967 shall be deemed to have been given under the same provision by the Commissioner.

# Deposit-Taking Companies Ordinance[1]

To regulate the taking of money on deposit and to make provision for the protection of persons who deposit money and for the regulation of deposit-taking business for monetary policy purposes.

[1st April, 1976]

## PART I. PRELIMINARY

1. This Ordinance may be cited as the Deposit-Taking Companies Ordinance. Short title.

2. (1) In this Ordinance, unless the context otherwise requires— Interpretation.

"accounts" means all methods of keeping accounts whether in writing, print or by any machine or device;

"advertisement" includes every form of advertising, whether notified or published—

*(a)* in a newspaper, magazine, journal or other periodical publication;
*(b)* by the display of posters or notices;
*(c)* by means of circulars, brochures, pamphlets or handbills;
*(d)* by an exhibition of photographs or cinematograph films; or
*(e)* by way of sound broadcasting or television,

and references to the issue of an advertisement shall be construed accordingly;

[1] *Laws of Hong Kong,* Cap. 328. Originally No. 3 of 1976. Relevant citations: L.N. 16/77; No. 74 of 1978; L.N. 272/78; L.N. 289/78; Nos. 19 of 1979; 75 of 1979; 17 of 1981; 26 of 1981; 28 of 1981; and 9 of 1982. Additional citation: L.N. 54/76.

"auditor" means a professional accountant holding a practising certificate as provided in the Professional Accountants Ordinance;

"certificate of deposit" means a document relating to money, in any currency, which has been deposited with the issuer or some other person, being a document which recognizes an obligation to pay a stated amount to bearer or to order, with or without interest, and being a document by the delivery of which, with or without endorsement, the right to receive that stated amount, with or without interest, is transferable;

"Commissioner" means the Commissioner of Deposit-Taking Companies appointed by section 3A;

"Committee" means the Deposit-Taking Companies Advisory Committee established under section 4;

"company" means a company which is—

- *(a)* registered under Part I of the Companies Ordinance;
- *(b)* registered under Part IX of the Companies Ordinance; or
- *(c)* incorporated outside Hong Kong and which has complied with Part XI of the Companies Ordinance;

"deposit" means a loan of money at interest or repayable at a premium or repayable with any consideration in money or money's worth, but does not include a loan of money upon terms involving the issue of debentures or other securities in respect of which a prospectus has been registered under the Companies Ordinance; and references to the taking of a deposit shall be construed accordingly;

"depositor" means a person entitled, or prospectively entitled, to repayment of a deposit, whether made by him or not;

"deposit-taking company" means a registered deposit-taking company and a licensed deposit-taking company;

"document" includes a circular, brochure, pamphlet, poster, handbill, prospectus and any other document which is directed at or likely to be read by members of the public; and also includes any newspaper, magazine, journal or other periodical publication;

"issue", in relation to an advertisement or document, includes publish, circulate, distribute or disseminate the advertisement or document; and also includes causing the advertisement or document to be issued;

"licence" means a licence granted under section 16B;

"licensed bank" means a bank licensed under section 7 or section 42 of the Banking Ordinance;

"licensed deposit-taking company" means a deposit-taking company licensed under section 16B;

"local branch" means a place of business in Hong Kong of a

deposit-taking company, other than its principal place of business in Hong Kong, at which it carries on the business of taking deposits;

"money at call" means money payable within not more than 24 hours of a demand therefor, but does not include money payable on demand;

"money at short notice" means money, other than money at call, payable within not more than 7 days of a demand therefor;

"overseas branch" means a branch outside Hong Kong of a deposit-taking company incorporated in Hong Kong, whether or not the business of the branch is limited by the laws or regulations of the country, state or place in which the branch is situated and whether or not the branch is referred to as an agency in such country, state or place, but does not mean an overseas representative office thereof;

"overseas representative office" means an office outside Hong Kong, other than an overseas branch, of a deposit-taking company incorporated in Hong Kong;

"register" means the register maintained under section 12;

"registered deposit-taking company" means a deposit-taking company registered under section 10 other than a licensed deposit-taking company; and "registered", in relation to a deposit-taking company, means registered under section 10;

"share" means share in the share capital of a company, and includes stock except where a distinction between stock or shares is expressed or implied; and the expression "shareholder" includes a stockholder;

"short-term deposit" means a deposit with an original term to maturity of less than 3 months or with a period of call or notice of less than 3 months;

"specified liquid assets" means all or any of the assets specified in section 24A.

"specified sum"—

*(a)* in relation to a registered deposit-taking company, means the sum referred to in section 8(1)*(a)*; and

*(b)* in relation to a licensed deposit-taking company, means the sum referred to in section 8(1)*(b)*.

(2) For the purposes of this Ordinance—

*(a)* the taking of deposits includes holding out as being prepared to take deposits;

*(b)* an advertisement issued by any person by way of display or exhibition in a public place shall be treated as being issued by

him on every day on which he causes or authorizes it to be displayed or exhibited;

*(c)* an advertisement or document which consists of or contains information likely to lead, directly or indirectly, members of the public to—

(i) deposit money; or

(ii) enter into, or offer to enter into, any agreement to deposit money,

shall be treated as being an advertisement or document which is or contains an advertisement to members of the public to do that act;

*(d)* an advertisement or document issued by one person on behalf of or to the order of another shall be treated as an advertisement or document, as the case may be, by that other person;

*(e)* a reference to a bank incorporated in a country, state or place, or a deposit-taking company incorporated outside Hong Kong, means a bank or company, as the case may be, incorporated by or under the law or other authority in any country, state or place outside Hong Kong, and in this respect "incorporated" includes established.

Application.

3. (1) This Ordinance shall not apply to the taking of any deposit by—

*(a)* a licensed bank;

*(b)* a trust company registered under Part VIII of the Trustee Ordinance;

*(c)* a credit union registered under the Credit Unions Ordinance;

*(d)* a company, where such deposit is secured by a charge registered or to be registered under the Companies Ordinance;

*(e)* a person *bona fide* carrying on insurance business where such deposit is taken in the ordinary course of such business;

*(f)* a person *bona fide* operating a superannuation or provident fund where such deposit is taken for the purposes of such fund;

*(g)* a public utility company specified in the Third Schedule to the Inland Revenue Ordinance where such deposit is taken from a consumer;

*(h)* an employer where such deposit is taken from a *bona fide* employee;

*(i)* a solicitor or professional accountant (within the meaning of the Professional Accountants Ordinance), where such deposit is taken from a client in the ordinary course of his practice;

*(j)* the Urban Council;

*(k)* a person who is a dealer within the meaning of the Securities Ordinance where section 84 of that Ordinance applies to such deposit;

*(l)* a person or class of persons exempted by the Financial Secretary under section 35.

(2) This Ordinance shall not apply to the taking of any deposit from—

*(a)* a licensed bank;

*(b)* a registered deposit-taking company:

Provided that section 8(1)*(a)* shall apply where a deposit is taken by a registered deposit-taking company from another registered deposit-taking company or from a licensed deposit-taking company;

*(ba)* a licensed deposit-taking company:

Provided that section 8(1)*(b)* shall apply where a deposit is taken by a licensed deposit-taking company from another licensed deposit-taking company or from a registered deposit-taking company;

*(c)* a money lender licensed under the Money Lenders Ordinance;

*(d)* a pawnbroker licensed under the Pawnbrokers Ordinance.

Appointment of Commissioner.

**3A.** The Commissioner of Banking appointed under section 4 of the Banking Ordinance shall also be the Commissioner of Deposit-Taking Companies.

Power of Governor to give directions.

**3B.** (1) The Governor may give to the Financial Secretary and the Commissioner such directions as he thinks fit with respect to the exercise or performance of their respective powers, functions and duties under this Ordinance, either generally or in any particular case.

(2) Notwithstanding section 10 and without prejudice to the generality of subsection (1), the Governor may give a direction to the Commissioner—

*(a)* to suspend the further registration of companies as deposit-taking companies; or

*(b)* to refuse to register as a deposit-taking company, either generally or in any particular case, any company by reference to any class or description or otherwise howsoever.

(3) The Financial Secretary and the Commissioner shall, in the exercise or performance of their respective powers, functions and duties under this Ordinance, comply with any directions given by the Governor under this section.

## PART II. DEPOSIT-TAKING COMPANIES ADVISORY COMMITTEE

Establishment and functions of Deposit-Taking Companies Advisory Committee.

4. (1) There is hereby established a committee to be known as the Deposit-Taking Companies Advisory Committee.

(2) The functions of the Committee shall be to advise the Governor on matters relating to this Ordinance.

Constitution of the Committee.

5. (1) The Committee shall consist of—

*(a)* the Financial Secretary, who shall be the chairman;
*(aa)* the Secretary for Monetary Affairs;
*(b)* the Commissioner; and
*(c)* such other persons, being not less than 4 or more than 10, as the Governor may appoint.

(2) The members of the Committee appointed under subsection (1)*(c)* shall hold office for such period, and subject to such terms, as the Governor may specify in their appointment.

(3) In the absence of the chairman at any meeting of the Committee, the Secretary for Monetary Affairs shall act as the chairman.

## PART III. TAKING OF DEPOSITS

Restriction on taking of deposits.

6. (1) No business of taking deposits shall be carried on except by a company which is—

*(a)* a registered deposit-taking company; or
*(b)* a licensed deposit-taking company.

(1A) Subject to subsection (1B), a registered deposit-taking company shall not take any short-term deposit from any person other than a bank or deposit-taking company.

(1B) Subject to subsection (1C) and section 8, a registered deposit-taking company which is registered prior to the commencement of the Deposit-Taking Companies (Amendment) (No. 2) Ordinance 1981 may—

*(a)* during the period of 12 months after such commencement, continue to hold and to take short-term deposits; and
*(b)* during the period beginning from the expiry of 12 months after such commencement and ending on the expiry of 24 months after such commencement, continue to hold and to take short-term deposits amounting at any time in total to not more than 50 *per cent* of the total value of such deposits held by the registered deposit-taking company at such commencement.

(1C) A registered deposit-taking company referred to in subsection (1B) shall not hold or take any short-term deposits on or after the expiry of 24 months after the commencement of the Deposit-Taking Companies (Amendment) (No. 2) Ordinance 1981.

(1D) A registered deposit-taking company shall not, without the written permission of the Commissioner, repay any deposit within a period of less than 3 months from the date on which the deposit was taken by the company:

Provided that this subsection shall not apply to—

*(a)* deposits taken from banks and deposit-taking companies;
*(b)* deposits taken prior to the commencement of the Deposit-Taking Companies (Amendment) (No. 2) Ordinance 1981; and
*(c)* deposits taken under subsection (1B).

(1E) Subject to section 8, a licensed deposit-taking company may take or hold short-term deposits.

(2) Any person who contravenes subsection (1), or any registered deposit-taking company that contravenes subsection (1A), (1B)*(b)*, (1C) or (1D), shall be guilty of an offence and shall be liable—

*(a)* on conviction upon indictment to a fine of $500,000 and to imprisonment for 5 years; or
*(b)* on summary conviction to a fine of $50,000 and to imprisonment for 6 months.

(3) For the purposes of any proceedings for an offence under this section if it is proved that a person took deposits on at least 5 occasions within any period of 30 days, that person shall, until the contrary is proved, be deemed to have been carrying on a business of taking deposits.

7. *{Repealed, 26 of 1981, s. 5}*

**Deposit-taking company not to take deposits less than the specified sum.**

**First Schedule.**

8. (1) Subject to subsection (2)—

*(a)* a registered deposit-taking company shall not take any deposit from a depositor of a sum less than the sum specified in item 1 of the First Schedule;
*(b)* a licensed deposit-taking company shall not take any deposit from a depositor of a sum less than the sum specified in item 2 of the First Schedule.

(2) A deposit-taking company may take a deposit from a depositor of a sum less than the specified sum if—

(*a*) the depositor is a bank;
(*b*) the depositor is a *bona fide* employee of the company; or
(*c*) the amount standing to the credit of the depositor with the company at the time any such deposit is taken is not less than the specified sum.

(3) Except where a depositor withdraws the whole amount standing to his credit with a deposit-taking company, the company shall not at the time of the withdrawal of any sum permit the amount of the balance standing to the credit of the depositor, other than a depositor who is a bank or *bona fide* employee of the company, to be less than the specified sum.

(4) Any deposit-taking company that contravenes subsection (1) or (3) shall be guilty of an offence and shall be liable—

(*a*) on conviction upon indictment to a fine of $500,000 and to imprisonment for 2 years; or
(*b*) on summary conviction to a fine of $50,000 and to imprisonment for 6 months.

(5) Any person who holds himself out, whether as a broker or agent of a deposit-taking company or otherwise, as being prepared to take from any person, other than a person who is a bank or *bona fide* employee of the company, any sum less than the specified sum for the purpose of depositing that sum, or that sum and other sums, with the company shall be guilty of an offence and shall be liable—

(*a*) on conviction upon indictment to a fine of $500,000 and to imprisonment for 2 years; or
(*b*) on summary conviction to a fine $50,000 and to imprisonment for 6 months.

## PART IV. REGISTRATION OF DEPOSIT-TAKING COMPANIES

Application for registration.

9. (1) Every company shall, before it commences a business of taking deposits, apply for registration in accordance with this section.

(2) An application for registration shall be in such form as the Commissioner may specify and, subject to subsection (3), shall be accompanied by—

(*a*) a copy of the memorandum and articles of association or other document constituting the company; and
(*b*) such other documents and information as may be required by the Commissioner for the purposes of registration.

(3) Where an application for registration is made by a company that has been carrying on business for more than 18 months immediately preceding the date of the application and that has completed a financial year ending earlier than 6 months before the date of the application, the application shall also be accompanied by duly signed copies of—

*(a)* in the case of a company (other than a private company) registered under Part I of the Companies Ordinance—

(i) the profit and loss account of the company for that financial year;

(ii) the balance sheet as at the date to which such profit and loss account is made up;

(iii) the auditors' report attached to such balance sheet; and

(iv) the report by the directors (with respect to the state of the company's affairs) attached to such balance sheet,

which are required to be laid before the company in general meeting in accordance with the Companies Ordinance;

*(b)* in the case of a private company registered under Part I of the Companies Ordinance, or a company registered under Part IX of the Companies Ordinance, the documents specified in paragraph *(a)* as if the company were a company to which paragraph *(a)* applies; and

*(c)* in the case of a company incorporated outside Hong Kong and which has complied with Part XI of the Companies Ordinance, the documents specified in paragraph *(a)* which are required to be delivered to the Registrar of Companies in accordance with section 336 of the Companies Ordinance.

(4) For the purposes of paragraph *(c)* of subsection (3), a company to which that paragraph applies shall be treated as if it were required to comply with section 336 of the Companies Ordinance notwithstanding that that section would not, by virtue of subsection (6) of that section, otherwise apply to it.

(5) If any document referred to in subsection (2) or (3) is not written in the English language, there shall be annexed to the document a translation of it in English, certified by a director or the secretary of the company as a true and correct translation of that document.

**Registration of deposit-taking companies.**

**10.** (1) Subject to subsection (2), the Commissioner shall, on receipt of an application in accordance with section 9, register a company as a registered deposit-taking company.

(2) Subject to any direction given under section 3B(2), the Commissioner shall refuse to register a company under subsection (1) if—

(*a*) *{Deleted, 28 of 1981, s. 5}*

(*b*) the paid-up share capital of the company, as determined under subsection (3), is less than $10,000,000, or an equivalent amount in any other currency;

(*c*) the objects of the company as stated in its memorandum or constitution do not include a business of taking deposits;

(*d*) the name of the company, or the name under which the company is carrying on or intends to carry on business in Hong Kong, contains—

(i) any word which by virtue of any Ordinance may not be contained in the name of any company; or

(ii) any word which by virtue of any Ordinance may not without consent be contained in the name of any company, unless such consent has been given;

(*e*) it appears to the Commissioner that, by reason of any circumstances whatsoever, the company is not a fit and proper body to be registered.

(3) For the purposes of determining the paid-up share capital of a company there shall be deducted from it—

(*a*) in the case of an application for registration, any loss disclosed in the balance sheet lodged by the company with the application; and

(*b*) in any other case, any loss disclosed in the most recent balance sheet lodged by the company under section 17.

(4) *{Deleted 9 of 1982, s. 3(b)}*

(5) *{Deleted 9 of 1982, s. 3(b)}*

(6) The registration of a company under subsection (1) as a registered deposit-taking company shall be effected by entering in the register the particulars specified in section 12 and the Commissioner shall notify the company in writing of the registration and date of registration.

(7) Where the Commissioner refuses to register a company under subsection (2), he shall notify the company in writing of the refusal.

(8) *{Deleted, 28 of 1981, s. 5}*

Payment of fees.

11. (1) A registered deposit-taking company shall, within 14 days after the receipt of a notice of registration under section 10(6), pay to the Director of Accounting Services the registration fee specified in the Second Schedule.[2]

Second Schedule.

[2] The Second Schedule is omitted from this volume.

(2) Every registered deposit-taking company shall pay to the Director of Accounting Services annually the renewal or registration fee specified in the Second Schedule—

*(a)* in the case of a company which was carrying on a business of taking deposits at 1 April 1976, within 14 days after the anniversary of the date; and

*(b)* in the case of any other company, within 14 days after the anniversary of the date of registration of such company.

(3) Any fee not paid in accordance with subsection (1) or (2) may, without prejudice to the power to revoke the registration of the company contained in section 14(1)*(f)*, be recovered as a civil debt.

**Register of deposit-taking companies.**

12. (1) The Commissioner shall maintain a register of deposit-taking companies, in such form as he thinks fit, which shall contain—

*(a)* the name and business address of every such company which he decides to register; and

*(b)* such other particulars of such companies as the Commissioner thinks fit.

(2) The register shall be kept at the office of the Commissioner or at such other place as may be notified by the Commissioner in the *Gazette.*

(3) Any member of the public may, with effect from such date and during such hours as shall be notified by the Commissioner in the *Gazette,* on payment of the fee specified in the Second Schedule— Second Schedule.

*(a)* inspect; or

*(b)* obtain a copy or extract of,

the register and any document lodged with the Commissioner under section 9 (other than any document or information referred to in paragraph *(b)* of subsection (2) of that section) and section 17.

(4) A document purporting to be a copy of any extract from or entry in the register, or of any document lodged with the Commissioner by a company under this Ordinance, and purporting to be certified by the Commissioner shall be admitted in evidence in criminal or civil proceedings before any court on its production without further proof, and—

*(a)* until the contrary is proved, the court before which such document is produced shall presume—

(i) that the document is certified by the Commissioner; and

(ii) that the document is a true copy of the extract from or entry in the register, or of the document lodged with the Commissioner, to which it refers; and (*b*) such document shall be *prima facie* evidence of all matters contained therein.

Publication of names of deposit-taking companies.

13. (1) Subject to subsection (2), the Commissioner shall cause to be published in the *Gazette*, at such times and in such manner as he thinks fit, the names of all registered deposit-taking companies.

(2) The publication required by subsection (1) shall be made at least once each year.

(3) Where the name of a registered deposit-taking company is entered in the register, the Commissioner shall publish in the *Gazette* a notice of such entry.

Revocation of registration.

14. (1) Subject to subsection (3) and section 15, the Commissioner may revoke the registration of a registered deposit-taking company if—

(*a*) the company—

(i) has ceased to carry on a business of taking deposits; or

(ii) proposes to make, or has made, a composition or an arrangement with its creditors or is being wound up;

(*b*) the paid-up share capital of the company is, subject to sections 10(3) and 14A, less than that specified in section 10(2)(*b*);

(*c*) the objects of the company as stated in its memorandum of association or constitution no longer include the carrying on of a business of taking deposits;

(*d*) it appears to him that—

(i) the company is not a fit and proper body to remain registered; or

(ii) the company has not provided him, whether before or after being registered, with such information relating to it, and to any circumstances likely to affect its method of business, as is required by or under this Ordinance;

(*e*) the company has been convicted of an offence under section 8(4);

(*f*) the company has failed to pay the registration fee or renewal of registration fee in accordance with section 11;

(*g*) the company has failed to comply with section 17, 17A(1) or 24A.

(2) Without prejudice to subsection (1), the Commissioner may revoke the registration of a registered deposit-taking company on being requested in writing by the company to do so, if he is satisfied that the interests of depositors of that company are adequately safeguarded.

(3) The Commissioner shall not revoke the registration of a registered deposit-taking company for any reason specified in subsection (1) without giving it an opportunity of being heard within such time limit as the Commissioner may specify in writing.

(4) Where the registration of a registered deposit-taking company is revoked under subsection (1) or (2), the Commissioner shall—

*(a)* notify the company in writing of such revocation;
*(b)* publish in the *Gazette* notice of such revocation; and
*(c)* remove from the register the name of the company.

Transitional provision regarding paid-up share capital.

**14A.** (1) A registered deposit-taking company which is registered prior to the commencement of the Deposit-Taking Companies (Amendment) (No. 3) Ordinance 1981 may continue to carry on the business of taking deposits—

*(a)* during the period of 12 months after such commencement, if the paid-up share capital of the company as determined under section 10(3) is less than $5,000,000 but not less than $2,500,000, or an equivalent amount in any other currency; and
*(b)* during the period beginning from the expiry of 12 months after such commencement and ending on the expiry of 24 months after such commencement, if the paid-up share capital of the company as determined under section 10(3) is less than $10,000,000 but not less than $5,000,000, or an equivalent amount in any other currency.

(2) The Governor in Council may, in any particular case, extend any period specified in subsection (1).

Suspension of registration.

**15.** (1) Without prejudice to subsection (1) of section 14, where paragraph *(b)*, *(d)*(ii), *(f)* or *(g)* of that subsection applies, the Commissioner may by notice in writing served on the registered deposit-taking company suspend the registration of the company for a period not exceeding 6 months.

(2) Where the registration of a company is suspended under subsection (1), section 11 and Part V shall apply to the company during the period of the suspension.

Effect of revocation or suspension of registration.

**16.** (1) Without prejudice to any other provision of this Ordinance, where the registration of a company is revoked under section 14 or suspended under section 15, the company shall cease to take deposits with effect from the date of receipt of the notice under section 14(4)*(a)* or 15, as the case may be.

(2) Without prejudice to any other provision of this Ordinance, a company whose registration is revoked or suspended may continue to hold any deposit taken prior to the date referred to in subsection (1).

## PART IVA. LICENSING OF REGISTERED DEPOSIT-TAKING COMPANIES

Application for licence.

**16A.** (1) Every company shall, before it commences a business of taking deposits as a licensed deposit-taking company, apply for a licence in accordance with this section.

(2) An application for a licence shall be made to the Financial Secretary in such form as he may specify and shall be accompanied by such documents and information as may be required by him for the purposes of licensing.

(3) An application for a licence may be made only by a registered deposit-taking company which has—

*(a)* an issued share capital of not less than $100,000,000 or an equivalent amount in any other currency; and

*(b)* a paid-up share capital of not less than $75,000,000 or an equivalent amount in any other currency.

(4) For the purposes of determining the issued share capital or paid-up share capital of a deposit-taking company there shall be deducted from it—

*(a)* in the case of an application for a licence, any loss disclosed in the balance sheet lodged by the company under this Ordinance immediately preceding the application; and

*(b)* in any other case, any loss disclosed in the most recent balance sheet lodged by the company under section 17.

(5) The Governor in Council may, by notice in the *Gazette,* amend the amount of issued share capital or paid-up share capital specified in subsection (3).

Issue of licence.

**16B.** (1) After receiving an application for a licence under section 16A, the Financial Secretary may—

*(a)* grant a licence to a registered deposit-taking company subject to such conditions as he may think proper to attach thereto in any particular case; or

*(b)* without assigning any reason therefor, refuse to grant a licence.

(2) On the grant of a licence to a registered deposit-taking company, the company shall cease to be a registered deposit-taking company.

(3) Without prejudice to the power to attach conditions under subsection (1)*(a)* and to section 16J, the Financial Secretary may at any time, by notice in writing served upon a licensed deposit-taking company, attach to the licence held by that company such conditions, or amend or cancel any conditions attached to the licence, as he may think proper.

(4) Where the Financial Secretary refuses to grant a licence under subsection (1), he shall notify the registered deposit-taking company in writing of the refusal.

(5) Any licensed deposit-taking company that contravenes any condition attached under subsection (1)*(a)* or (3) shall be guilty of an offence and shall be liable—

*(a)* on conviction upon indictment to a fine of $200,000; or
*(b)* on summary conviction to a fine of $50,000,

and, in the case of a continuing offence, to a further fine of $5,000 for every day during which the offence continues.

**16C.** (1) A licensed deposit-taking company shall, within 14 days after the grant of a licence, pay to the Director of Accounting Services the licence fee specified in the Second Schedule. Payment of fees. Second Schedule.

(2) Every licensed deposit-taking company shall pay to the Director of Accounting Services annually the renewal of licence fee specified in the Second Schedule within 14 days after the anniversary of the date of grant of the licence.

(3) Any fee not paid in accordance with subsection (1) or (2) may, without prejudice to the power to revoke a licence under section 16F(1)*(f)*, be recovered as a civil debt.

**16D.** The Commissioner shall enter in a separate part of the register— Register of licensed deposit-taking companies.

*(a)* the name and business address of every licensed deposit-taking company; and
*(b)* such other particulars of such companies as the Commissioner thinks fit.

**16E.** (1) Subject to subsection (2), the Commissioner shall cause to be published in the *Gazette,* at such times and in such manner as he thinks fit, the names of all licensed deposit-taking companies. Publication of names of licensed deposit-taking companies.

(2) The publication required by subsection (1) shall be made at least once a year.

(3) Where the name of a licensed deposit-taking company is entered in the register, the Commissioner shall publish in the *Gazette* a notice of such entry.

Revocation of licence.

**16F.** (1) Subject to subsection (3), the Financial Secretary may revoke the licence of a licensed deposit-taking company if—

(*a*) the company—

(i) has ceased to carry on a business of taking deposits; or

(ii) proposes to make, or has made, a composition or an arrangement with its creditors or is being wound up;

(*b*) the issued share capital or paid-up share capital of the company is, subject to section 16A(4), less than that specified in section 16A(3);

(*c*) the objects of the company as stated in its memorandum of association or constitution no longer include the carrying on of a business of taking deposits;

(*d*) it appears to him that—

(i) the company is not a fit and proper body to remain licensed; or

(ii) the company has not provided him, whether before or after being licensed, with such information relating to it, and to any circumstances likely to affect its method of business, as is required by or under this Ordinance;

(*e*) the company has been convicted of an offence under section 8(4);

(*f*) the company has failed to pay the licence fee or renewal of licence fee in accordance with section 16C;

(*g*) the company has failed to comply with section 17, 17A(1) or 24A.

(2) Without prejudice to subsection (1), the Financial Secretary may revoke the licence of a licenced deposit-taking company on being requested in writing by the company to do so, if he is satisfied that the interests of depositors of that company are adequately safeguarded.

(3) The Financial Secretary shall not revoke the licence of a licensed deposit-taking company for any reason specified in subsection (1) without giving it an opportunity of being heard within such time limit as the Financial Secretary may specify in writing.

(4) Where the licence of a licensed deposit-taking company is revoked under subsection (1) or (2), the Financial Secretary shall—

(*a*) notify the company in writing of such revocation; and

(*b*) direct the Commissioner—

(i) to publish in the *Gazette* notice of such revocation; and
(ii) to remove from the register the name of the company.

Effect of revocation of licence.

**16G.** (1) Without prejudice to any other provision of this Ordinance, where the licence of a licensed deposit-taking company is revoked under section 16F, the company shall cease to take deposits with effect from the date of receipt of the notice under section 16F(4)*(a)*.

(2) Without prejudice to any other provision of this Ordinance, a licensed deposit-taking company whose licence is revoked may continue to hold any deposit taken prior to the date referred to in subsection (1).

## PART IVB. LOCAL BRANCHES AND FEES

Control of establishment, etc. of local branches.

**16H.** (1) A deposit-taking company shall not establish or maintain any local branch thereof without the approval of the Commissioner.

(2) Subsection (1) applies to every deposit-taking company whether the company was registered or licensed before, on or after the commencement of the Deposit-Taking Companies (Amendment) Ordinance 1982, and subsections (4) and (5) apply to an approval granted under subsection (1) whether the approval was granted before, on or after such commencement.

(3) Approval under subsection (1) shall be deemed to have been granted in respect of any local branch established prior to 1 July 1981.

(4) The Commissioner may at any time, by notice in writing served upon a deposit-taking company, attach to an approval granted under subsection (1), or deemed to have been granted under subsection (3), in respect of any local branch thereof such conditions, or amend or cancel any conditions so attached, as he may think proper.

(5) The Commissioner may at any time revoke, in such case as he thinks fit, an approval granted under subsection (1), or deemed to have been granted under subsection (3), in respect of any local branch.

(6) Where the Commissioner refuses to grant approval under subsection (1) or revokes an approval under subsection (5), he shall notify the deposit-taking company concerned in writing of the refusal or revocation.

(7) Any deposit-taking company that contravenes subsection (1) or any condition attached under subsection (4) shall be guilty of an offence and shall be liable—

(*a*) on conviction upon indictment to a fine of $200,000; or
(*b*) on summary conviction to a fine of $50,000,

and, in the case of a continuing offence, to a further fine of $5,000 for every day during which the offence continues.

Fees in respect of branches.

Second Schedule.

**16I.** (1) Whenever the establishment by a deposit-taking company of a local branch is approved under section 16H, the deposit-taking company shall pay to the Director of Accounting Services the fee specified in the Second Schedule[3] in relation to that branch and thereafter, so long as the branch continues to be maintained by the deposit-taking company, it shall pay to the Director of Accounting Services the fee specified in the Second Schedule on the anniversary in each year of the date on which the deposit-taking company was registered or licensed, as the case may be.

(2) A deposit-taking company that is maintaining a local branch at the commencement of the Deposit-Taking Companies (Amendment) (No. 3) Ordinance 1981 shall, so long as the branch continues to be maintained by the deposit-taking company, pay to the Director of Accounting Services the fee specified in the Second Schedule on the anniversary in each year of the date on which the deposit-taking company was registered or licensed, as the case may be.

(3) Any fee not paid in accordance with subsection (1) or (2) may be recovered as a civil debt.

## PART IVC. OVERSEAS BRANCHES, OVERSEAS REPRESENTATIVE OFFICES AND FEES

Control of establishment, etc. of overseas branches and overseas representative offices.

**16J.** (1) Without prejudice to section 16H, a deposit-taking company which is incorporated in Hong Kong shall be subject to a condition that the company shall not establish or maintain any overseas branch or overseas representative office thereof without the approval of the Commissioner.

(2) Subsection (1) applies to every deposit-taking company incorporated in Hong Kong whether the company was registered or licensed before, on or after the commencement of the Deposit-Taking Companies (Amendment) Ordinance 1982, and subsections (4) and (5)

[3] The Second Schedule is omitted from this volume.

apply to an approval granted under subsection (1) whether the approval was granted before, on or after such commencement.

(3) Approval under subsection (1) shall be deemed to have been granted in respect of—

*(a)* any overseas branch established prior to 1 July 1981; and
*(b)* any overseas representative office established prior to the commencement of the Deposit-Taking Companies (Amendment) Ordinance 1982.

(4) The Commissioner may at any time, by notice in writing served upon a deposit-taking company, attach to an approval granted under subsection (1), or deemed to have been granted under subsection (3), in respect of any overseas branch or overseas representative office thereof such conditions, or amend or cancel any conditions so attached, as he may think proper.

(5) The Commissioner may at any time revoke, in such case as he thinks fit, an approval granted under subsection (1), or deemed to have been granted under subsection (3), in respect of any overseas branch or overseas representative office.

(6) Where the Commissioner refuses to grant approval under subsection (1) or revokes an approval under subsection (5), he shall notify the company concerned in writing of the refusal or revocation.

(7) Any deposit-taking company that contravenes the condition in subsection (1) or any condition attached under subsection (4) shall be guilty of an offence and shall be liable—

*(a)* on conviction upon indictment to a fine of $200,000; or
*(b)* on summary conviction to a fine of $50,000,

and, in the case of a continuing offence, to a further fine of $5,000 for every day during which the offence continues.

Conditions regarding overseas branches and overseas representative offices.

**16K.** (1) Every deposit-taking company incorporated in Hong Kong which maintains an overseas branch thereof shall be subject to a condition that—

*(a)* the deposit-taking company shall submit to the Commissioner a return in such form, and at such intervals, as he may specify showing the assets and liabilities of the overseas branch;
*(b)* the deposit-taking company shall submit to the Commissioner such further information as he may consider necessary for the proper understanding of the functions and activities of the over-

seas branch, and that such information shall be submitted within such period and in such manner as the Commissioner may require;

(*c*) if the Commissioner requires any return submitted to him pursuant to paragraph (*a*), or any information submitted to him pursuant to a requirement under paragraph (*b*), to be accompanied by a certificate of an auditor, the deposit-taking company shall submit a certificate of its auditors as to whether or not, in the opinion of the auditors, the return or information is correctly compiled from the books and records of the overseas branch;

(*d*) if the Commissioner wishes to examine the books, accounts and transactions of the overseas branch, the deposit-taking company shall for that purpose afford the person carrying out the examination at the place where the branch is maintained access to the books and accounts of the branch, to documents of title to the assets and other documents and to all securities held by the branch in respect of its customers' transactions and its cash and to such information and facilities as may be required to conduct the examination, and that the company shall produce to the person carrying out the examination such books, accounts, documents, securities, cash or other information as he may require:

Provided that, so far as is consistent with the conduct of the examination, such books, accounts, documents, securities and cash shall not be required to be produced at such times and such places as shall interfere with the proper conduct of the normal daily business of the overseas branch.

(2) Every deposit-taking company incorporated in Hong Kong which maintains an overseas representative office thereof shall be subject to a condition that—

(*a*) the deposit-taking company shall submit to the Commissioner such information as he may require regarding the functions and activities of the overseas representative office;

(*b*) if the Commissioner wishes to examine the functions and activities of the overseas representative office, the deposit-taking company shall for that purpose afford the person carrying out the examination at the place where the representative office is maintained access to the documents maintained by the representative office and to such information and facilities as may be required to conduct the examination, and that the company shall produce to the person carrying out the examination such documents or other information as he may require.

(3) This section applies to every deposit-taking company incorporated in Hong Kong whether the company was registered or licensed before, on or after the commencement of the Deposit-Taking Companies (Amendment) Ordinance 1982.

(4) Any deposit-taking company that contravenes any condition in subsection (1) or (2), or fails to comply with any requirement under those subsections, shall be guilty of an offence and shall be liable—

*(a)* on conviction upon indictment to a fine of $200,000 and to imprisonment for 12 months; or

*(b)* on summary conviction to a fine of $50,000 and to imprisonment for 6 months,

and, in the case of a continuing offence, to a further fine of $5,000 for every day during which the offence continues.

(5) Any deposit-taking company that produces any book, account, document, security or information whatsoever under this section, which is false in a material particular shall be guilty of an offence and shall be liable—

*(a)* on conviction upon indictment to a fine of $500,000 and to imprisonment for 2 years; or

*(b)* on summary conviction to a fine of $50,000 and to imprisonment for 6 months.

(6) Any person who signs any document for the purposes of this section which he knows or reasonably ought to know to be false in a material particular shall be guilty of an offence and shall be liable—

*(a)* on conviction upon indictment to a fine of $500,000 and to imprisonment for 2 years; or

*(b)* on summary conviction to a fine of $50,000 and to imprisonment for 6 months.

Fees in respect of overseas branches and overseas representative offices.

Second Schedule.

**16L.** (1) Whenever the establishment by a deposit-taking company incorporated in Hong Kong of an overseas branch or overseas representative office is approved under section 16J(1), the deposit-taking company shall pay to the Director of Accounting Services the fee specified in the Second Schedule [4] in relation to that branch or representative office and thereafter, so long as the branch or representative office continues to be maintained by the deposit-taking company, it shall pay to the Director of Accounting Services the fee specified in the Second Schedule on the anniversary in each year of the date on which the deposit-taking company was registered or licensed, as the case may be.

[4] The Second Schedule is omitted from this volume.

(2) A deposit-taking company that is maintaining, at the commencement of the Deposit-Taking Companies (Amendment) Ordinance 1982, an overseas branch or overseas representative office to which section 16J(3) applies, shall, so long as the branch or representative office continues to be maintained by the deposit-taking company, pay to the Director of Accounting Services the fee specified in the Second Schedule on the anniversary in each year of the date on which the deposit-taking company was registered or licensed, as the case may be.

(3) Any fee not paid in accordance with subsection (1) or (2) may be recovered as a civil debt.

## PART V. OBLIGATIONS OF DEPOSIT-TAKING COMPANIES

Accounts, etc., to be lodged with the Commissioner annually.

17. (1) Without prejudice to the provisions of Parts IV, IX and XI of the Companies Ordinance relating to company accounts, every deposit-taking company shall, in accordance with this section, in each year lodge with the Commissioner duly signed copies of—

*(a)* in the case of a company (other than a private company) registered under Part I of the Companies Ordinance—

(i) the profit and loss account of the company;

(ii) the balance sheet as at the date to which such profit and loss account is made up;

(iii) the auditor's report attached to such profit and loss account and balance sheet; and

(iv) the report by the directors (with respect to the state of the company's affairs) attached to such balance sheet,

which are required to be laid before the company in general meeting in accordance with the Companies Ordinance;

*(b)* in the case of a private company registered under Part I of the Companies Ordinance, or a company registered under Part IX of the Companies Ordinance, the documents specified in paragraph *(a)* as if the company were a company to which paragraph *(a)* applies; and

*(c)* in the case of a company incorporated outside Hong Kong and which has complied with Part XI of the Companies Ordinance, the documents specified in paragraph *(a)* which are required to be delivered to the Registrar of Companies in accordance with section 336 of the Companies Ordinance.

(2) The documents specified in subsection (1)*(a)* shall—

*(a)* on the first occasion, be the documents in respect of the first financial year which ends on a date not earlier than 6 months

immediately preceding the date of application for registration or licence, as the case may be; and

(*b*) on subsequent occasions, be the documents in respect of each subsequent financial year of the company.

(3) The documents specified in subsection (1) shall be lodged within 6 months after the end of the financial year to which such documents relate.

(4) For the purposes of paragraph (*c*) of subsection (1), a company to which that paragraph applies shall be treated as if it were required to comply with section 336 of the Companies Ordinance notwithstanding that that section would not, by virtue of subsection (6) of that section, otherwise apply to it.

(5) If any document referred to in subsection (1) is not written in the English language, there shall be annexed to the document a translation of it in English, certified by a director or the secretary of the company as a true and correct translation of that document.

(6) Any deposit-taking company that fails to comply with this section shall be guilty of an offence and shall be liable on conviction to a fine of $20,000 and to imprisonment for 6 months and, in the case of a continuing offence, to a further fine of $2,500 for every day during which the offence continues.

(7) Any person who signs any document for the purposes of this section which he knows or reasonably ought to know to be false in a material particular shall be guilty of an offence and shall be liable—

(*a*) on conviction upon indictment to a fine of $500,000 and to imprisonment for 2 years; or

(*b*) on summary conviction to a fine of $50,000 and to imprisonment for 6 months.

Place of business in Hong Kong.

**17A.** (1) Subject to subsection (2), every deposit-taking company which is registered or licensed on or after the commencement of the Deposit-Taking Companies (Amendment) (No. 3) Ordinance 1981 shall, within the period of 3 months after it is registered or licensed, as the case may be, establish and thereafter maintain at all times a place of business in Hong Kong.

(2) Every deposit-taking company which is registered or licensed at the commencement of the Deposit-Taking Companies (Amendment) (No. 3) Ordinance 1981 and which does not have a place of business in Hong Kong shall, within 3 months after such commencement, establish and thereafter maintain at all times a place of business in Hong Kong.

(3) Any deposit-taking company that contravenes this section shall be guilty of an offence and shall be liable on conviction to a fine of $50,000 and, in the case of a continuing offence, to a further fine of $5,000 for every day during which the offence continues.

Appointment of chief executive.

**17B.** (1) Every deposit-taking company shall appoint a chief executive of the deposit-taking company who shall be—

*(a)* an individual; and
*(b)* normally resident in Hong Kong.

(2) Any deposit-taking company that contravenes this section shall be guilty of an offence and shall be liable on conviction to a fine of $50,000 and, in the case of a continuing offence, to a further fine of $5,000 for every day during which the offence continues.

Deposit-taking companies to exhibit accounts, etc. at places of business.

**18.** (1) Every deposit-taking company shall cause to be exhibited in accordance with subsection (2) at each place where it carries on a business of taking deposits copies of the documents which it is required to lodge with the Commissioner under section 9 (other than any document of information referred to in paragraph *(b)* of subsection (2) of that section) and section 17.

(2) The copies of such documents shall be exhibited in a place in which they may be easily inspected by members of the public and shall remain so exhibited—

*(a)* in the case of documents lodged under section 9, from the date on which the company receives a notification of registration under section 10(6) until the date on which documents are lodged under section 17 with the Commissioner for the first time; and
*(b)* in the case of documents lodged under section 17, from the date on which they are lodged with the Commissioner under that section until such documents for the next following financial year are lodged with the Commissioner under that section.

(3) Any deposit-taking company that fails to comply with this section shall be guilty of an offence and shall be liable—

*(a)* on conviction upon indictment to a fine of $200,000; or
*(b)* on summary conviction to a fine of $50,000,

and, in the case of a continuing offence, to a further fine of $5,000 for every day during which the offence continues.

**19.** (1) Where any change occurs in any of the particulars of a deposit-taking company which are specified by the Commissioner under section 36(2), the company shall forthwith notify the Commissioner in writing of such change.

Deposit-taking companies to notify certain changes to the Commissioner.

(2) A deposit-taking company which ceases to carry on a business of taking deposits shall forthwith notify the Commissioner in writing of such cessation.

(3) Any deposit-taking company that fails without reasonable excuse to comply with this section shall be guilty of an offence and shall be liable on conviction to a fine of $10,000.

**19A.** (1) If any deposit-taking company is likely to become unable to meet its obligations or if it is about to suspend payment it shall forthwith report all relevant facts, circumstances and information to the Commissioner.

Duty to report inability to meet obligations.

(2) Any deposit-taking company that fails without reasonable excuse to comply with this section shall be guilty of an offence and shall be liable—

*(a)* on conviction upon indictment to a fine of $200,000 and to imprisonment for 2 years and, in the case of a continuing offence, to a further fine of $10,000 for every day during which the offence continues; or

*(b)* on summary conviction to a fine of $50,000 and to imprisonment for 6 months and, in the case of a continuing offence, to a further fine of $5,000 for every day during which the offence continues.

**20.** (1) Without prejudice to sections 17 and 19, every deposit-taking company shall submit to the Commissioner—

Returns and information to be submitted to the Commissioner.

*(a)* not later than 14 days after the last day of each calendar month a return, in such form as the Commissioner may specify, showing the assets and liabilities of its principal place of business in Hong Kong and all local branches thereof at the close of business on the last business day of that month; and

*(b)* not later that 14 days after the last day of each quarter ending on 31 March, 30 June, 30 September and 31 December respectively, or upon any other day which may be approved by the Commissioner, a return, in such form as he may specify, relating to its principal place of business in Hong Kong and all local branches thereof as at the close of business on the last business day of the preceding quarter:

Provided that the Commissioner may by permission in writing allow the returns referred to in paragraphs *(a)* and *(b)* to be submitted at less frequent intervals.

(2) The Commissioner may require a deposit-taking company to submit such further information as he may consider necessary for the proper understanding of the financial position of the company and such information shall be submitted within such period and in such manner as the Commissioner may require.

(3) The Commissioner may require any return submitted to him pursuant to subsection (1), or any information submitted to him pursuant to a requirement under subsection (2), to be accompanied by a certificate of the auditors of the company as to whether or not, in the opinion of the auditors, the return or information is correctly compiled from the books and records of the company.

(4) Notwithstanding anything in section 25, the Commissioner may prepare and publish consolidated statements aggregating the figures in the returns furnished under subsection (1).

(5) Any deposit-taking company that fails to comply with subsection (1), or with any requirement under subsection (3), shall be guilty of an offence and shall be liable on conviction upon indictment or on summary conviction to a fine of $50,000 and, in the case of a continuing offence, to a further fine of $5,000 for every day during which the offence continues.

(5A) Any deposit-taking company that fails to comply with any requirement under subsection (2) shall be guilty of an offence and shall be liable—

*(a)* on conviction upon indictment to a fine of $200,000 and to imprisonment for 2 years and, in the case of a continuing offence, to a further fine of $10,000 for every day during which the offence continues; or
*(b)* on summary conviction to a fine of $50,000 and to imprisonment for 6 months and, in the case of a continuing offence, to a further fine of $5,000 for every day during which the offence continues.

(6) Any person who signs any document for the purposes of this section which he knows or reasonably ought to know to be false in a material particular shall be guilty of an offence and shall be liable—

*(a)* on conviction upon indictment to a fine of $500,000 and to imprisonment for 2 years; or
*(b)* on summary conviction to a fine of $50,000 and to imprisonment for 6 months.

**20A.** (1) Every deposit-taking company incorporated in Hong Kong shall, if so required by the Commissioner, inform him of the name and address of, and the nature of the business carried on by, every company (whether incorporated in or outside Hong Kong and whether or not the company is carrying on business in Hong Kong or has complied with Part XI of the Companies Ordinance) in which the deposit-taking company holds the beneficial ownership, directly or indirectly, of an aggregate of 20 *per cent* or more of the share capital.

**Information on shareholding.**

(2) The Commissioner may require any deposit-taking company which has submitted to him information pursuant to subsection (1) to submit to him such further information as he may consider necessary to obtain, in the interests of depositors of the deposit-taking company, about the assets, liabilities and transactions of any such company.

(3) Information that is required to be submitted under this section shall be submitted within such period and in such manner as the Commissioner may require.

(4) Any deposit-taking company that fails to comply with any requirement under this section shall be guilty of an offence and shall be liable—

*(a)* on conviction upon indictment to a fine of $200,000 and to imprisonment for 2 years and, in the case of a continuing offence, to a further fine of $10,000 for every day during which the offence continues; or

*(b)* on summary conviction to a fine of $50,000 and to imprisonment for 6 months and, in the case of a continuing offence, to a further fine of $5,000 for every day during which the offence continues.

(5) Any person who signs any document for the purposes of this section which he knows or reasonably ought to know to be false in a material particular shall be guilty of an offence and shall be liable—

*(a)* on conviction upon indictment to a fine of $500,000 and to imprisonment for 2 years; or

*(b)* on summary conviction to a fine of $50,000 and to imprisonment for 6 months.

**21.** (1) A deposit-taking company shall not in any communication, whether written or oral, represent or imply, or permit to be represented or implied, in any manner to any person that the company has in any respect been approved by the Government, the Financial Secretary or the Commissioner.

**Certain representations prohibited.**

(2) Subsection (1) is not contravened by reason only that a statement is made to the effect that a company is registered or licensed under this Ordinance.

(3) Any deposit-taking company that contravenes subsection (1) without reasonable excuse shall be guilty of an offence and shall be liable—

*(a)* on conviction upon indictment to a fine of $500,000 and to imprisonment for 2 years; or

*(b)* on summary conviction to a fine of $100,000 and to imprisonment for 12 months.

Maintenance of reserve.

**21A.** (1) Every deposit-taking company which is incorporated in Hong Kong shall, before any dividend is declared, appropriate to reserve out of the profit of each year, after due provision has been made for taxation—

*(a)* a sum equal to not less than one-third of such profit; or

*(b)* such lesser sum, if any, as may be necessary so that—

(i) in the case of a registered deposit-taking company, the aggregate of the company's paid-up share capital and its reserve is not less than $20,000,000; and

(ii) in the case of a licensed deposit-taking company, the aggregate of the company's paid-up share capital and its reserve is not less than $150,000,000.

(2) Any deposit-taking company that contravenes this section shall be guilty of an offence and shall be liable—

*(a)* on conviction upon indictment to a fine of $200,000 and to imprisonment for 2 years; or

*(b)* on summary conviction to a fine of $50,000 and to imprisonment for 6 months.

Restriction on payment of dividends.

**21B.** (1) A deposit-taking company which is incorporated in Hong Kong shall not pay any dividend on its shares or distribute any extraordinary profits unless—

*(a)* all items of expenditure not represented by tangible assets have been completely written off; and

*(b)* in the case of a distribution of extraordinary profits, the aggregate of its paid-up share capital and reserve after such distribution will not be less than—

(i) $20,000,000, in the case of a registered deposit-taking company; and

(ii) $150,000,000, in the case of a licensed deposit-taking company.

(2) Any deposit-taking company that contravenes this section shall be guilty of an offence and shall be liable—

*(a)* on conviction upon indictment to a fine of $200,000 and to imprisonment for 2 years; or

*(b)* on summary conviction to a fine of $50,000 and to imprisonment for 6 months.

**21C.** (1) A deposit-taking company shall not grant any advance, loan or credit facility against the security of its own shares.

Advance against security of own shares.

(2) Any deposit-taking company that contravenes this section shall be guilty of an offence and shall be liable—

*(a)* on conviction upon indictment to a fine of $100,000 and to imprisonment for 12 months; or

*(b)* on summary conviction to a fine of $50,000 and to imprisonment for 6 months.

**22.** (1) A deposit-taking company shall not grant or permit to be outstanding to any one person, firm, corporation or company, or to any group of companies or persons which such person, firm, corporation or company is able to control or influence, any advances, loans or credit facilities, including irrevocable documentary letters of credit to the extent to which they are not covered by marginal cash deposits, or give any financial guarantees or incur any other liabilities on their behalf to an aggregate amount of such advances, loans, facilities, guarantees or liabilities in excess of 25 *per cent* of the paid-up capital and reserves of the deposit-taking company:

Limitation on advances by deposit-taking companies.

Provided that this subsection shall not apply to—

*(a)* transactions with a bank or another deposit-taking company;

*(b)* transactions to the extent to which they are covered by a form of guarantee acceptable to the Commissioner;

*(c)* the purchase of telegraphic transfers;

*(d)* the purchase of bills of exchange or documents of title to goods where the holder of such bills or documents is entitled to payment outside Hong Kong for goods exported from Hong Kong;

*(e)* any advances or loans made against telegraphic transfers or against any bills or documents referred to in paragraph *(d)*; or

*(f)* transactions entered into before the commencement of this Ordinance.

(2) For the purposes of subsection (1)—

*(a)* any advances, loans or credit facilities granted or permitted to be outstanding to, and any financial guarantees given and any other liabilities incurred on behalf of, a business or undertaking of which any one person is the sole proprietor shall be deemed

to be granted or permitted to be outstanding to or given or incurred on behalf of, as the case may be, that one person;

*(b)* a person shall not be deemed to be able to control or influence a group of companies by reason only that he is a director of any other company in the group.

(3) Any deposit-taking company that contravenes subsection (1) shall be guilty of an offence and shall be liable—

*(a)* on conviction upon indictment to a fine of $200,000 and to imprisonment for 2 years and, in the case of a continuing offence, to a further fine of $10,000 for every day during which the offence continues; or

*(b)* on summary conviction to a fine of $50,000 and to imprisonment for 6 months and, in the case of a continuing offence, to a further fine of $5,000 for every day during which the offence continues.

Limitation on advances to directors, etc.

23. (1) A deposit-taking company shall not grant any facility specified in subsection (3) to or on behalf of any person or body specified in subsection (4)*(c)* or *(d)* if the aggregate amount of such facilities for the time being granted by the deposit-taking company to or on behalf of any one or more such persons or bodies would thereby exceed 10 *per cent* of the paid-up capital and reserves of the deposit-taking company.

(2) A deposit-taking company shall not grant any facility specified in subsection (3) to or on behalf of any person specified in subsection (4)*(a)*, *(b)* or *(ba)*.

(3) For the purposes of subsections (1) and (2), the following facilities are specified—

*(a)* the granting, or permitting to be outstanding, of unsecured advances, unsecured loans or unsecured credit facilities including unsecured irrevocable documentary letters of credit;

*(b)* the giving of unsecured financial guarantees; and

*(c)* the incurring of any other unsecured liability.

(4) For the purposes of subsections (1) and (2), the following persons and bodies are specified—

*(a)* any director of the deposit-taking company;

*(b)* any relative of any such director;

*(ba)* any employee of the deposit-taking company who is responsible, either individually or as a member of a committee, for determining loan applications;

*(c)* any firm, partnership or private company in which the deposit-taking company or any of its directors or any relative of any of

its directors is interested as director, partner, manager, or agent; and

*(d)* any individual, firm, partnership or private company of which any director of the deposit-taking company or any relative of any such director is a guarantor.

(5) The provisions of this section shall apply to a facility granted to or on behalf of a person or body jointly with another person or body as they apply to a facility granted to or on behalf of a person or body severally.

(6) This section shall not apply to—

*(a)* the purchase of telegraphic transfers;

*(aa)* transactions with a licensed bank or with a bank outside Hong Kong or another deposit-taking company; or

*(b)* transactions entered into before the commencement of this Ordinance.

(7) For the purposes of subsections (2) and (4), a facility granted to or on behalf of any firm, partnership or private company which a director of a deposit-taking company or a relative of such director is able to control, or to or on behalf of a business or undertaking of which a director of a deposit-taking company or a relative of such director is the sole proprietor, shall be deemed to be granted to or on behalf of such director or relative of such director.

(8) Any deposit-taking company that contravenes subsection (1) or (2) shall be guilty of an offence and shall be liable—

*(a)* on conviction upon indictment to a fine of $200,000 and to imprisonment for 2 years and, in the case of a continuing offence, to a further fine of $10,000 for every day during which the offence continues; or

*(b)* on summary conviction to a fine of $50,000 and to imprisonment for 6 months and, in the case of a continuing offence, to a further fine of $5,000 for every day during which the offence continues.

**Limitation on advances to employees.**

23A. (1) A deposit-taking company shall not grant or permit to be outstanding to any one of its employees unsecured advances, unsecured loans or unsecured credit facilities to an aggregate amount of such advances, loans or facilities in excess of one year's salary for any such employee.

(2) Any deposit-taking company that contravenes this section shall be guilty of an offence and shall be liable—

*(a)* on conviction upon indictment to a fine of $100,000 and to imprisonment for 12 months; or

(*b*) on summary conviction to a fine of $50,000 and to imprisonment for 6 months,

and, in the case of a continuing offence, to a further fine of $5,000 for every day during which the offence continues.

Limitation on shareholding.

**23B.** (1) Subject to subsections (2), (3) and (4), a deposit-taking company shall not acquire or hold any part of the share capital of any other company or companies to an aggregate value in excess of 25 *per cent* of the paid-up capital and reserves of the deposit-taking company, except such shareholdings as the deposit-taking company may acquire in the course of the satisfaction of debts due to it.

(2) Subsection (1) shall not apply where a deposit-taking company acquires or holds any part of the share capital of any other company or companies under an underwriting or sub-underwriting contract for a period not exceeding 3 months or such further period or periods as the Commissioner may allow in any particular case.

(3) All shareholdings acquired in the course of the satisfaction of debts referred to in subsection (1) shall be disposed of at the earliest suitable opportunity, and in any event not later than 18 months after the acquisition thereof or within such longer period as the Commissioner may allow in any particular case.

(4) Where the value of the shares held or contracted for by a deposit-taking company at the commencement of the Deposit-Taking Companies (Amendment) (No. 3) Ordinance 1981 is in excess of the limit specified in subsection (1), then, during the period of 24 months after such commencement or such longer period as the Governor in Council may allow in any particular case, an amount equal to such excess shall not be taken into account for the purposes of that subsection.

(5) Any deposit-taking company that contravenes this section shall be guilty of an offence and shall be liable—

(*a*) on conviction upon indictment to a fine of $200,000 and to imprisonment for 2 years and, in the case of a continuing offence, to a further fine of $10,000 for every day during which the offence continues; or

(*b*) on summary conviction to a fine of $50,000 and to imprisonment for 6 months and, in the case of a continuing offence, to a further fine of $5,000 for every day during which the offence continues.

Limitation on holding of interest in land.

**23C.** (1) A deposit-taking company shall not purchase or hold any interest or interests in land situated in or outside Hong Kong of a value or to an aggregate value, as the case may be, in excess of 25 *per cent* of the paid-up capital and reserves of the deposit-taking company.

(2) In addition to the value of any land purchased or held under subsection (1), a deposit-taking company may purchase or hold interests in land situated in or outside Hong Kong to any value, where the occupation of such land is, in the opinion of the Commissioner, necessary for conducting the business of the deposit-taking company or for providing housing or amenities for the staff of the deposit-taking company.

(2A) The aggregate value of interests in land purchased or held under subsections (1) and (2) shall not exceed the aggregate amount of the paid-up capital and reserves of the deposit-taking company.

(3) For the purposes of subsection (2), but without prejudice to the generality thereof, the Commissioner may in his discretion regard as necessary for conducting the business of a deposit-taking company the whole of any premises in which an office of a deposit-taking company is situated.

(4) There shall not be taken into account in the assessment of the value of interests in land for the purposes of this section the value of any interest in land mortgaged to the deposit-taking company to secure a debt due to the deposit-taking company nor the value of any interest in land acquired pursuant to entry into possession of land so mortgaged, provided that the interest acquired is disposed of at the earliest possible opportunity, and in any event not later than 18 months after its acquisition or within such longer period as the Commissioner may allow in any particular case.

(5) Where any interest in land held by a deposit-taking company at the commencement of the Deposit-Taking Companies (Amendment) (No. 3) Ordinance 1981 is in excess of the limit specified in subsection (1), then, during the period of 24 months after such commencement or such longer period as the Governor in Council may allow in any particular case, an amount equal to such excess shall not be taken into account for the purposes of that subsection.

(5A) Where the aggregate value of interests in land held by a deposit-taking company at the commencement of the Deposit-Taking Companies (Amendment) Ordinance 1982 is in excess of the limit specified in subsection (2A), then, during the period of 24 months after such date or such longer period as the Governor in Council may allow in any particular case, an amount equal to such excess shall not be taken into account for the purposes of that subsection.

(6) Any deposit-taking company that contravenes this section shall be guilty of an offence and shall be liable—

*(a)* on conviction upon indictment to a fine of $200,000 and to

imprisonment for 2 years and, in the case of a continuing offence, to a further fine of $10,000 for every day during which the offence continues; or

(*b*) on summary conviction to a fine of $50,000 and to imprisonment for 6 months and, in the case of a continuing offence, to a further fine of $5,000 for every day during which the offence continues.

Definitions.

23D. (1) For the purposes of sections 23 and 23A, "unsecured" means granted without security, or, in respect of any advance, loan or credit facility granted or financial guarantee or other liability incurred with security, any part thereof which at any time exceeds the market value of assets constituting that security; and "security" means such security as would, in the opinion of the Commissioner, be acceptable to a prudent deposit-taking company.

(2) For the purposes of section 23B and 23C, "value" means—

(*a*) in the case of shares in a company other than a trust company registered under Part VIII of the Trustee Ordinance, the total of the current book value and the amount for the time being remaining unpaid on the shares; and

(*b*) in any other case, the current book value.

Deductions for the purposes of sections 22, 23, 23B and 23C.

24. For the purposes of sections 22, 23, 23B and 23C there shall be deducted from the paid-up capital and reserves of the deposit-taking company any loss disclosed in the balance sheet of the deposit-taking company lodged with the Commissioner under this Ordinance.

Minimum holding of specified liquid assets.

24A. (1) A deposit-taking company shall maintain at all times a minimum holding of specified liquid assets, free from encumbrances, in accordance with the provisions of this section.

(2) The minimum holding of specified liquid assets to be maintained by a deposit-taking company in any calendar month shall be not less than an amount equivalent to the aggregate of the following—

(*a*) such percentage as the Financial Secretary may specify by notice in the *Gazette* of the deposit liabilities of the company during that month in respect of deposits repayable within 7 days or at 7 days' notice or less, and time deposits in respect of which the depositor may, whether by virtue of any written or oral agreement or by custom, obtain repayment before maturity; and

(*b*) such percentage as the Financial Secretary may so specify of its deposit liabilities during that month in respect of time deposits other than those referred to in paragraph (*a*).

(3) For the purpose of subsection (2), the specified liquid assets of a deposit-taking company shall be the specified liquid assets of that company within the meaning of subsection (7) reduced by an amount equivalent to such company's total liabilities in respect of—

*(a)* balances of money payable on demand;
*(b)* money at call; and
*(c)* money at short notice,

owing to any licensed bank or other deposit-taking company in Hong Kong.

(3A) Where the liabilities of a deposit-taking company during any month do not include any deposit liabilities, the minimum holding of specified liquid assets to be maintained in that month by the company shall be not less than an amount equivalent to the company's liabilities during that month in respect of—

*(a)* balances payable on demand;
*(b)* money at call; and
*(c)* money at short notice,

owing to any licensed bank or other deposit-taking company in Hong Kong; and in respect of amounts referred to in paragraphs *(a)* and *(b)*, such specified liquid assets shall be held in any form set out in paragraphs *(a)*, *(b)*, *(c)*, *(d)*, *(e)*, *(ea)*, *(eb)* and *(f)* of subsection (7).

(4) The minimum holding of specified liquid assets required in pursuance of subsection (2) shall include not less than the equivalent of such percentage of such holding as shall be specified by the Financial Secretary and notified in the *Gazette* in the form of such specified liquid assets as are set out in paragraphs *(a)*, *(b)*, *(c)*, *(d)*, *(e)*, *(ea)*, *(eb)* and *(f)* of subsection (7), and in determining whether the minimum holding includes not less than the equivalent of the specified percentage figure of such holding in the form aforesaid any reduction made pursuant to subsection (3) in respect of balances of money payable on demand and money at call shall be deemed to have been made in such specified liquid assets of the company as are set out in paragraphs *(a)*, *(b)*, *(c)*, *(d)*, *(e)*, *(ea)*, *(eb)* and *(f)* of subsection (7).

(5) For the purposes of subsections (2), (3), (3A) and (4), the assets and liabilities of a deposit-taking company shall be the arithmetical means of, respectively, the amounts of the assets held by, and the liabilities of, the company according to the company's books at the close of business on every such weekday during the month as the Commissioner may specify:

Provided that if any such specified weekday is a public holiday the assets and liabilities as at the close of business on the last working day preceding that specified weekday shall be taken for the purposes of such calculation.

(6) For the purposes of computing the minimum holding of specified liquid assets to be held by a deposit-taking company—

*(a)* the deposit liabilities of a deposit-taking company shall be deemed to be its gross demand and time liabilities, excluding amounts owing to any bank or other deposit-taking company;
*(b)* in the case of a deposit-taking company operating in Hong Kong and also elsewhere, the principal place of business in Hong Kong and local branches of the company shall be deemed collectively to be a separate deposit-taking company carrying on business in Hong Kong;
*(c)* all the deposit liabilities of a deposit-taking company owed through the principal place of business in Hong Kong or any local branch of the company operating in Hong Kong and also elsewhere shall be regarded as if they constituted liabilities of that separate deposit-taking company, and all the assets held by or to the credit of the principal place of business or any local branch shall be regarded as if they were assets of that separate deposit-taking company.

(7) For the purposes of this section, "specified liquid assets" means all or any of the following—

*(a)* notes and coins which are legal tender in Hong Kong;
*(b)* notes and coins in any currency which is freely remittable to the deposit-taking company in Hong Kong;
*(c)* refined gold in the form of coin or bars situated in Hong Kong, and refined gold in the form of coin or bars situated outside Hong Kong if the gold, or money into which it can be converted, is freely remittable to the deposit-taking company in Hong Kong from the place where such gold is situated;
*(d)* the total balance of money payable on demand at any licensed bank or other deposit-taking company in Hong Kong and money at call with any licensed bank or other deposit-taking company in Hong Kong;
*(e)* balances of money payable on demand at any bank outside Hong Kong and money at call with any bank outside Hong Kong, which are or is freely remittable to the deposit-taking company in Hong Kong and held in a form approved by the Commissioner;
*(ea)* certificates of deposit which are—
    (i) issued outside Hong Kong by any bank approved by the Commissioner for the purposes of this section in any for-

eign currency freely remittable to the deposit-taking company in Hong Kong; and

(ii) marketable in a manner satisfactory to the Commissioner;

*(eb)* such money market instruments, either totally or to such limited extent, as the Financial Secretary may specify under section 18(6)*(db)* of the Banking Ordinance;

*(f)* treasury bills, maturing within 93 days, issued by the Government or by the Government of the United Kingdom or by the Government of any other country if such treasury bills issued by the Government of any other country are specified by the Financial Secretary under section 18(6)*(e)* of the Banking Ordinance;

*(g)* money at short notice at any licensed bank or other deposit-taking company in Hong Kong;

*(h)* money at short notice at any bank outside Hong Kong, which is freely remittable to the deposit-taking company in Hong Kong and held in a form approved by the Commissioner;

*(ha)* such money market instruments, either totally or to such limited extent, as the Financial Secretary may specify under section 18(6)*(ec)* of the Banking Ordinance;

*(i)* bills of exchange payable at usance outside Hong Kong and discountable in a currency which is freely remittable to the deposit-taking company in Hong Kong;

*(j)* bills of exchange payable after sight outside Hong Kong in a currency freely remittable to the deposit-taking company in Hong Kong;

*(k)* such securities (other than securities specified in paragraph *(l)*) issued or guaranteed by the Government, or the Government of any other country, as may be specified by the Financial Secretary under section 18(6)*(h)* of the Banking Ordinance;

*(l)* securities with less than 5 years to maturity issued or guaranteed by the Government or the Government of the United Kingdom if—

(i) they are quoted on a Stock Exchange in London, Hong Kong or New York;

(ii) they have been dealt in during the preceding 6 months; and

(iii) payment of interest thereon is not in arrear.

(8) The Financial Secretary may, from time to time, in exceptional circumstances, by notice raise or reduce for such period as he may think necessary and to such percentages as he may think fit the minimum percentages specified in pursuance of subsection (2) or subsection (4)

of specified liquid assets in the case of any particular deposit-taking company.

(9) For the purposes of this section, the value of any specified liquid asset shall be not more than the market value of such asset.

(10) Any deposit-taking company that fails to comply with this section shall be guilty of an offence and shall be liable on conviction upon indictment to a fine of $500,000 and to imprisonment for 5 years and, in the case of a continuing offence, to a further fine of $5,000 for every day during which the offence continues.

Variation of minimum holding of specified liquid assets for monetary policy purposes.

**24B.** The Financial Secretary may from time to time, in pursuance of the monetary policy of the Government, by order, which shall be published in the *Gazette,* raise or reduce the minimum percentage of deposit liabilities by reference to which every deposit-taking company is required to maintain a holding—

(*a*) in specified liquid assets pursuant to section 24A(2); or
(*b*) in specified liquid assets in the form mentioned in section 24A(4).

## PART VI. MISCELLANEOUS

Official secrecy.

**25.** (1) Except as may be necessary for the exercise or performance of any function or duty under this Ordinance or for carrying into effect the provisions of this Ordinance, every person who has been appointed under or who is or has been employed in carrying out or in assisting any person to carry out the provisions of this Ordinance—

(*a*) shall preserve and aid in preserving secrecy with regard to all matters relating to the affairs of any company that may come to his knowledge in the exercise or performance of any function or duty under this Ordinance;
(*b*) shall not communicate any such matter to any person other than the person to whom such matter relates; and
(*c*) shall not suffer or permit any person to have access to any records in the possession, custody or control of any person to whom this subsection applies.

(2) Subsection (1) does not apply—

(*a*) to the disclosure of information in the form of a summary of similar information provided by a number of deposit-taking companies if the summary is so framed as to prevent particulars relating to the business of any particular deposit-taking company being ascertained from it; or (*b*) to the disclosure of information for the purpose of any legal proceedings brought under this Ordinance, or for the purpose of any report of any such proceedings.

(3) Any person who—

(*a*) contravenes subsection (1); or

(*b*) aids, abets, counsels or procures any person to contravene subsection (1),

shall be liable—

(i) on conviction upon indictment to a fine of $100,000 and to imprisonment for 2 years; or

(ii) on summary conviction to a fine of $50,00 and to imprisonment for 6 months.

**Disclosure of information relating to deposit-taking companies.**

**25A.** (1) Subject to subsection (2) and notwithstanding anything in section 25, the Commissioner may, if he considers that it is in the interests of the depositors of the deposit-taking company, provide to the appropriate recognized banking supervisory authority of a country, state or place outside Hong Kong which is, in his opinion, subject to adequate secrecy provisions in that country, state or place information on matters relating to the affairs of a deposit-taking company—

(*a*) which is incorporated in that country, state or place;

(*b*) which is incorporated in or outside Hong Kong and is a subsidiary or associate of a bank incorporated in that country, state or place; or

(*c*) which is incorporated in Hong Kong and which has, or is proposing to establish, in that country, state or place an overseas branch, overseas representative office, subsidiary or associate of that deposit-taking company, and where, in the case of a subsidiary or associate, such subsidiary or associate is or would be subject to supervision by that recognized banking supervisory authority.

(2) Under no circumstances shall the Commissioner provide any information under this section relating to the affairs of any individual customer or a deposit-taking company.

**Offence to avoid the provisions of section 6 or 8.**

**26.** Any person who enters into a contract or arrangement, or uses any device or scheme, which has the effect of, or is designed to have the effect of, avoiding the provisions of section 6(1), (1A), (1B)(*b*), (1C) or (1D) or section 8(1) or (3) shall be guilty of an offence and shall be liable—

(*a*) on conviction upon indictment to a fine of $500,000 and to imprisonment for 5 years; or (*b*) on summary conviction to a fine of $50,000 and to imprisonment for 6 months.

Offence to issue advertisements and documents relating to deposits.

27. (1) Subject to subsection (5), no person shall—

(*a*) issue, or have in his possession for the purposes of issue, any advertisement which to his knowledge is or contains an invitation to members of the public—

(i) to deposit money; or

(ii) to enter into, or offer to enter into, any agreement to deposit money;

(*b*) issue, or have in his possession for the purposes of issue, any document which to his knowledge contains such an advertisement; or

(*c*) in any other manner issue or make an invitation to members of the public to do any of the acts referred to in paragraph (*a*).

(2) Any person who contravenes subsection (1) shall be guilty of an offence and shall be liable on conviction upon indictment to a fine of $10,000.

(3) For the purposes of any proceedings under this section, an advertisement or document in which a person named in the advertisement or document holds himself out as being prepared to take in Hong Kong any deposit shall, subject to subsection (4), be presumed, unless such named person proves to the contrary, to have been issued by him.

(4) A person shall not be taken to contravene this section by reason only that he issues, or has in his possession for the purposes of issue, to purchasers copies of any newspaper, magazine, journal or other periodical publication of general and regular circulation, which contain an advertisement to which this section applies.

(5) This section shall not apply to any advertisement to deposit money or to enter into, or offer to enter into, any agreement to deposit money with a deposit-taking company or a licensed bank.

Fraudulent inducement to deposit money.

28. (1) Any person who, by any fraudulent or reckless misrepresentation, induces another person—

(*a*) to deposit money with him or any other person; or

(*b*) to enter into or to offer to enter into any agreement to deposit money with him or any other person,

shall be guilty of an offence and shall be liable on conviction upon indictment to a fine of $1,000,000 and to imprisonment for 7 years.

(2) For the purposes of subsection (1) "fraudulent or reckless misrepresentation" means—

*(a)* any statement—

(i) which, to the knowledge of the maker of the statement, was false, misleading or deceptive; or

(ii) which was false, misleading or deceptive and was made recklessly;

*(b)* any promise—

(i) which the maker of the promise had no intention of fulfilling;

(ii) which, to the knowledge of the maker of the promise, was not capable of being fulfilled; or

(iii) which was made recklessly;

*(c)* any forecast—

(i) which, to the knowledge of the maker of the forecast, was not justified on the basis of facts known to him at the time when he made it; or

(ii) which was not justified on the facts known to the maker of the forecast at the time when he made it and was made recklessly; or

*(d)* any statement or forecast from which the maker intentionally or recklessly omitted a material fact with the result that the statement or forecast was thereby rendered false, misleading or deceptive.

**Liability in tort for inducing persons to deposit money in certain cases.**

29. (1) Any person who, by any fraudulent, reckless or negligent misrepresentation, induces another person to deposit money with him or any other person shall be liable to pay compensation to the person so induced for any pecuniary loss that such person has sustained by reason of his reliance on that misrepresentation.

(2) For the purposes of subsection (1) "fraudulent, reckless or negligent misrepresentation" means—

*(a)* any statement—

(i) which, to the knowledge of the maker of the statement, was false, misleading or deceptive;

(ii) which was false, misleading or deceptive and was made recklessly; or

(iii) which was false, misleading or deceptive and was made without reasonable care having been taken to ensure its accuracy;

(*b*) any promise—

(i) which the maker of the promise had no intention of fulfilling;

(ii) which, to the knowledge of the maker of the promise, was not capable of being fulfilled; or

(iii) which was made recklessly or without reasonable care having been taken to ensure that it could be fulfilled;

(*c*) any forecast—

(i) which, to the knowledge of the maker of the forecast, was not justified on the basis of facts known to him at the time when he made it; or

(ii) which was not justified on the facts known to the maker of the forecast at the time when he made it and was made recklessly or without reasonable care having been taken to ascertain the accuracy of those facts; or

(*d*) any statement or forecast from which the maker intentionally, recklessly or negligently omitted a material fact with the result that the statement or forecast was thereby rendered false, misleading or deceptive.

(3) For the purposes of this section—

(*a*) where any statement, promise or forecast to which this section relates was made by a company, every person who was a director of the company at the time when the statement, promise or forecast was made shall, until the contrary is proved, be deemed to have caused or permitted it to be made; and

(*b*) a person is deemed to be a director of a company if he occupies the position of a director, whatever the title of his office, or he is a person in accordance with whose directions or instructions the directors of the company or any of them act; but a person shall not, by reason only that the directors of a company act on advice given by him in a professional capacity, be taken to be a person in accordance with whose directions or instructions those directors act.

(4) This section does not affect any liability of any person at common law.

(5) An action may be brought under this section notwithstanding that the evidence on which the action is or will be based, if substantiated, discloses the commission of an offence and no person has been charged with or convicted of the offence.

(6) For the purposes of this section "company" means, in addition

to a company as defined in section 2, any other body of persons, corporate or unincorporate.

Action for recovery of deposits, etc.

**30.** (1) Notwithstanding any rule of law, any deposit taken in contravention of section 6 or 8, and any interest accrued thereon, may be recovered by the depositor as money had and received.

(2) Where the registration of a registered deposit-taking company is revoked under section 14 or suspended under section 15, or where the licence of a licensed deposit-taking company is revoked under section 16F, such revocation or suspension shall not affect any right—

*(a)* of any person against such company; or
*(b)* of such company against any person.

Liability of directors, etc.

**31.** (1) Where an offence under this Ordinance committed by a company is proved to have been committed with the consent or connivance of, or to be attributable to any neglect on the part of, any director, manager, chief executive, secretary or other officer of the company or any person who was purporting to act in any such capacity, he as well as the company, shall be guilty of the offence and shall be liable to be proceeded against and punished accordingly.

(2) For the purposes of this section, a person is deemed to be a director of a company if he occupies the position of a director, whatever the title of his office, or is a person in accordance with whose directions or instructions the directors of the company or any of them act; but a person shall not, by reason only that the directors of a company act on advice given by him in a professional capacity, be taken to be a person in accordance with whose directions or instructions those directors act.

(3) For the purposes of this section "company" means, in addition to a company as defined in section 2, any other body of persons, corporate or unincorporate.

Examination of deposit-taking companies.

**31A.** Without prejudice to the provisions of sections 14, 15 and 16F, the Commissioner may at any time, with or without prior notice to a deposit-taking company, examine the books, accounts and transactions of the company.

Production of company's books, etc.

**31B.** (1) For the purpose of an examination under section 31A, a deposit-taking company shall afford the person carrying out the examination access to its books and accounts, to documents of title to its assets and other documents, to all securities held by it in respect of its customers' transactions and its cash and to such information and facilities as may be required to conduct the examination, and shall produce to the person carrying out the examination such books, accounts, documents, securities, cash or other information as he may require:

Provided that, so far as is consistent with the conduct of the examination, such books, accounts, documents, securities and cash shall not be required to be produced at such times and such places as shall interfere with the proper conduct of the normal daily business of the company.

(2) Any deposit-taking company that fails to comply with subsection (1), or with any requirement under that subsection, shall be guilty of an offence and shall be liable—

*(a)* on conviction upon indictment to a fine of $100,000 and to imprisonment for 12 months; or

*(b)* on summary conviction to a fine of $50,000 and to imprisonment for 6 months,

and, in the case of a continuing offence, to a further fine of $5,000 for every day during which the offence continues.

(3) Any deposit-taking company that produces any book, account, document, security or information whatsoever under subsection (1) which is false in a material particular shall be guilty of an offence and shall be liable—

*(a)* on conviction upon indictment to a fine of $500,000 and to imprisonment for 2 years; or

*(b)* on summary conviction to a fine of $50,000 and to imprisonment for 6 months.

Examination by authorities from outside Hong Kong.

31C. The appropriate recognized banking supervisory authority of a country, state or place outside Hong Kong may, with the approval of the Commissioner, examine the books, accounts and transactions of the principal place of business in Hong Kong or any local branch—

*(a)* of a deposit-taking company which is incorporated in that country, state or place; or

*(b)* of a deposit-taking company which is incorporated in or outside Hong Kong and is a subsidiary of a bank which is incorporated in that country, state or place.

Search warrants and seizure.

32. (1) If a magistrate is satisfied by information on oath that there is reasonable ground for suspecting that an offence under this Ordinance has been committed, the magistrate may issue a warrant empowering any police officer to enter and search any premises specified in the warrant.

(2) A police officer to whom a warrant is issued under subsection (1) may—

*(a)* break open any outer or inner door of or in any premises which he is empowered by the warrant to enter and search;
*(b)* inspect, seize and remove any thing which the police officer has reasonable grounds for believing to be or to contain evidence of an offence under this Ordinance; and
*(c)* remove by force any person who obstructs any entry, search, inspection, seizure or removal which he is empowered by this subsection to make.

(3) A person from whom any books, accounts or other documents have been seized and removed under subsection (2) shall, pending any proceedings for an offence under this Ordinance, be entitled to take copies of or extracts from such books, accounts or other documents.

(4) Any person who obstructs a police officer in the exercise of any power conferred on him by subsection (2) shall be guilty of an offence and shall be liable on conviction to a fine of $50,000 and to imprisonment for 6 months.

Certain persons prohibited from acting as officers or employees of deposit-taking companies except with consent of Commissioner.

33. (1) No person who—

*(a)* is bankrupt or has entered into a composition with his creditors;
*(b)* has been convicted in any country or territory of an offence involving fraud or dishonesty; or
*(c)* has been a director, or otherwise concerned in the management, of any bank or deposit-taking company which has been wound up by a court or whose licence or registration, as the case may be, has been revoked,

shall, without the consent in writing of the Commissioner, be a director, manager or secretary of a deposit-taking company or an employee of such a company in any other capacity.

(2) Any person who contravenes subsection (1) shall be guilty of an offence and shall be liable—

*(a)* on conviction upon indictment to a fine of $100,000 and to imprisonment for 12 months; or
*(b)* on summary conviction to a fine of $50,000 and to imprisonment for 6 months.

Appeals.

34. (1) Where the Commissioner has—

*(a)* refused to register a company under section 10(2);
*(b)* revoked the registration of a company under section 14(1);

(*c*) suspended the registration of a company under section 15;
(*d*) refused to approve the establishment of a branch under section 16H(1) or 16J(1);
(*e*) refused to approve the establishment of an overseas representative office under section 16J(1);
(*f*) revoked an approval for the establishment of a branch under section 16H(5) or 16J(5); or
(*g*) revoked an approval for the establishment of an overseas representative office under section 16J(5),

the company concerned may appeal to the Governor in Council against the refusal, revocation or suspension.

(2) Where the Financial Secretary has—

(*a*) refused to license a company under section 16B(1); or
(*b*) revoked the licence of a company under section 16F(1),

the company concerned may appeal to the Governor in Council against the refusal or revocation.

(3) Where—

(*a*) registration is refused under section 10(2) or revoked under section 14(1) or suspended under section 15; or
(*b*) a licence is refused under section 16B(1) or revoked under section 16F(1),

that refusal, revocation or suspension shall take effect immediately, notwithstanding that an appeal has been or may be made under this section.

Power to grant exemptions.

35. (1) The Financial Secretary may, by notice in the *Gazette,* exempt any person or class of persons from section 6.

(2) An exemption under this section shall be subject to such conditions as are specified in the notice.

(3) The Financial Secretary may at any time by notice in the *Gazette*—

(*a*) revoke an exemption under this section; or
(*b*) revoke, vary, or add to, any condition subject to which such exemption is granted.

Power to specify forms, etc.

36. (1) The Commissioner may specify the form of application for registration and of any notice, certificate or other document required for the purposes of this Ordinance.

(2) The Commissioner shall, by notice in the *Gazette,* specify the class of particulars in respect of a deposit-taking company to which section 19(1) applies.

37. The Governor in Council may, by notice in the *Gazette*, amend any Schedule. Power to amend Schedules.

FIRST SCHEDULE [ss. 8 & 37.]

SPECIFIED SUM

1. The sum for the purposes of section 8(1)*(a)* is $50,000 or an equivalent amount in any other currency.
2. The sum for the purposes of section 8(1)*(b)* is $500,000 or an equivalent amount in any other currency.

*(The Second Schedule is omitted from this volume.)*

# Money Lenders Ordinance[1]

To provide for the control and regulation of money lenders and money-lending transactions, the appointment of a Registrar of Money Lenders and the licensing of persons carrying on business as money lenders; to provide protection and relief against excessive interest rates and extortionate stipulations in respect of loans; to provide for offences and for matters connected with or incidental to the foregoing; and to repeal the Money-lenders Ordinance 1911.

[12th December, 1980]

PART I. PRELIMINARY

1. (1) This Ordinance may be cited as the Money Lenders Ordinance. Short title and application.

(2) This Ordinance shall have effect notwithstanding any agreement to the contrary.

2. (1) In this Ordinance, unless the context otherwise requires— Interpretation.

"disqualified person" means a person in respect of whom there is in force an order made by a court under section 32(2);

"effective rate", in relation to interest, means the true annual percentage rate of interest calculated in accordance with the Second Schedule; Second Schedule.

"firm" means an unincorporate body of 2 or more individuals, or 1 or more individuals and 1 or more bodies corporate, or

[1] *Laws of Hong Kong*, Cap. 163 (1980). Originally No. 29 of 1980. Relevant citations: L.N. 347/80; and L.N. 231/81.

2 or more bodies corporate, who have entered into partnership with one another with a view to carrying on business for profit;

"interest" does not include any sum lawfully agreed to be paid in accordance with this Ordinance on account of stamp duty or other similar duty, but save as aforesaid includes any amount (by whatever name called) in excess of the principal, which amount has been or is to be paid or payable in consideration of or otherwise in respect of a loan;

"licence" means a money lender's licence issued under section 8 or 13, and "licensed" and "licensee" have corresponding meanings;

"licensing court" has the meaning assigned to it by section 10;

"loan" includes advance, discount, money paid for or on account of or on behalf of or at the request of any person, or the forbearance to require payment of money owing on any account whatsoever, and every agreement (whatever its terms or form may be) which is in substance or effect a loan of money, and also an agreement to secure the repayment of any such loan, and "lend" and "lender" shall be construed accordingly;

"money lender" means every person whose business (whether or not he carries on any other business) is that of making loans or who advertises or announces himself or holds himself out in any way as carrying on that business, but does not include a person specified in Part 1 of the First Schedule;

First Schedule.

"prescribed" means prescribed by regulations made under section 34;

"principal", in relation to a loan, means the amount actually lent;

"register" means the register kept by the Registrar under section 4;

"Registrar" means the Registrar of Money Lenders appointed under section 4.

(2) For the purposes of this Ordinance, where by an agreement for the loan of money the interest charged on the loan is not expressed in terms of a rate, any amount paid or payable to the lender under the agreement (other than simple interest charged in accordance with the proviso to section 22) shall be appropriated to principal and interest in the proportion that the total amount of principal bears to the total amount of the interest, and the rate *per cent per annum* represented by the interest charged as calculated in accordance with the Second Schedule shall be deemed to be the rate of interest charged on the loan.

Second Schedule.

(3) For the purpose of determining the amount of the principal of a loan, any amount thereof which is not shown to have been lent except for the purpose of treating it as an instalment paid by the borrower in repayment of the loan and which is so treated by the lender shall be disregarded.

**3.** (1) Parts II and III shall not apply to— Exemption.

*(a)* any person specified in Part 1 of the First Schedule; or First Schedule.

*(b)* as respects a loan specified in Part 2 of the First Schedule, any person who makes such loan.

(2) The Legislative Council may by resolution amend the First Schedule.

**4.** (1) The Governor shall appoint a public officer to be the Registrar of Money Lenders.

Registrar of Money Lenders and supervisory functions of Registrar.

(2) The Registrar shall establish and maintain a register in which he shall cause to be kept particulars, other than specified particulars, of—

*(a)* applications for the issue or renewal of licences;

*(b)* licences which are in force or have been revoked or suspended;

*(c)* such other matters, if any, as he thinks fit.

(3) In this section "specified particulars" mean particulars furnished under section 8 which are specified in regulations made under section 34 as particulars which shall not be entered in the register.

**5.** (1) Except as may be necessary for the exercise or performance of any function or duty under this Ordinance or for carrying into effect the provisions of this Ordinance, the Registrar and every person employed in carrying out or in assisting any person to carry out the provisions of this Ordinance— Official secrecy.

*(a)* shall preserve and aid in preserving secrecy with regard to all matters relating to the affairs of any person that may come to his knowledge in the exercise or performance of any function or duty under this Ordinance;

*(b)* shall not communicate any such matter to any person other than the person to whom such matter relates; and

*(c)* shall not suffer or permit any person to have access to any records in the possession, custody or control of any person to whom this subsection applies.

(2) Subsection (1) does not apply—

*(a)* to the disclosure of information in the form of a summary of similar information provided by a number of persons if the summary is so framed as to prevent particulars relating to the business of any particular person being ascertained from it; or

*(b)* to the disclosure of information for the purpose of any legal proceedings in respect of an offence, or for the purpose of any report of any such proceedings.

(3) Any person who—

(*a*) contravenes subsection (1); or

(*b*) aids, abets, counsels or procures any person to contravene subsection (1),

commits an offence and shall be liable to a fine of $100,000 and to imprisonment for 2 years.

Inspection of register.

6. (1) Any person shall be entitled on payment of the prescribed fee—

(*a*) to inspect the register during ordinary office hours and take copies of any entry; or

(*b*) to obtain from the Registrar a copy, certified by or under the authority of the Registrar to be correct, of any entry in the register.

(2) The Registrar shall give public notice, in such manner as he may deem fit, of the place where and the times when the register may be inspected.

## PART II. LICENSING OF MONEY LENDERS

Restriction on carrying on of business of money lender.

7. (1) No person shall carry on business as a money lender—

(*a*) without a licence;

(*b*) at any place other than the premises specified in such licence; or

(*c*) otherwise than in accordance with the conditions of a licence.

(2) A licence shall be in the prescribed form.

Application for licence and public notification of application.

8. (1) An application for a licence shall be made to the Registrar in the prescribed form and in the prescribed manner, and shall be accompanied by the prescribed fee and a statement in writing containing the prescribed particulars in respect of the application.

(2) An application made under this section in respect of a body corporate may be made by any person authorized in that behalf by such body corporate.

(3) An application made under this section in respect of partners in a firm may be made by any such partner.

(4) The Registrar shall, in such manner as may be prescribed, give public notice of every application made under this section.

Investigation and lodgement of applications.

9. (1) Where an application is made under section 8, the applicant shall at the same time send a copy of the application to the Commissioner of Police, and the Commissioner of Police may cause an investi-

gation to be carried out in respect of the application for the purpose of determining whether, in the opinion of the Commissioner of Police, there are grounds for objecting to the application under section 11.

(2) For the purpose of carrying out an investigation under this section, the Commissioner of Police may in writing require the applicant to produce for inspection such books, records or documents or to furnish such information relating to the application or any business carried on or intended to be carried on by him as the Commissioner of Police may specify.

(3) In respect of an application made under section 8, no step other than the registration of such application shall be taken by the Registrar prior to—

*(a)* the date on which a period of 60 days after the date on which the application is made expires; or

*(b)* the date on which the Commissioner of Police notifies the Registrar that any investigation carried out under this section in respect of the application has been completed,

whichever is the earlier (in this section referred to as "the material date").

(4) Where the Registrar or the Commissioner of Police intends to object under section 11 to any application for a licence, he shall, not later than 7 days after the material date, serve notice on the applicant of his intention to object and of the grounds of such objection; and where such notice is served by the Commissioner of Police, he shall send a copy thereof to the Registrar.

(5) Upon the expiration of a period of 7 days after the material date in respect of any application made under section 8, the Registrar shall lodge the application in the office of a magistrate ordinarily sitting in or nearest to the area where the premises used or intended to be used by the applicant as his principal place of business as a money lender are situated, together with a copy of any notice served on the applicant under subsection (4).

(6) The Registrar shall give notice to the Commissioner of Police of any lodgement made under subsection (5).

**10.** (1) Where an application is lodged in the office of a magistrate under section 9(5), that magistrate sitting with 2 assessors (in this Ordinance referred to as "the licensing court") shall hear and determine the application in accordance with section 11. Licensing court.

(2) The magistrate shall be the presiding member of the licensing court.

(3) In determining any application lodged under section 9(5), the magistrate and each of the assessors shall have a vote but the decision of the licensing court shall be given as a single decision and shall be recorded in writing:

Provided that in the event of a difference between the members in deciding the application, the decision of the licensing court shall be that of the majority of the members.

(4) The Registrar shall be entitled, on request made at the office of the magistrate, to a copy of the decision of the licensing court.

(5) References in this section to an assessor are references to a person appointed to a panel of assessors under section 7A of the Magistrates Ordinance; and with respect to the selection and attendance of any such person as assessor at any sitting of a licensing court, sections 7A and 7B of that Ordinance shall apply *mutatis mutandis* for the purposes of this section as they apply in relation to proceedings heard with an assessor under that Ordinance.

Determination of application for licence.

11. (1) The licensing court shall fix a date for the hearing of an application lodged under section 9(5) and shall give 14 clear days' notice of such date to the applicant, the Registrar and the Commissioner of Police; and the licensing court may adjourn the hearing to another date and from time to time as the licensing court may deem fit.

(2) Subject to subsection (3), the licensing court shall grant a licence upon the hearing of an application lodged under section 9(5) except where—

*(a)* the Registrar or the Commissioner of Police has served notice under section 9 of his intention to object to the application and, at the hearing of the application, objection to the application is made by or on behalf of the Registrar or, as the case may be, the Commissioner of Police; or

*(b)* objection to the application is made by any other person appearing at the hearing in person or by counsel who—

(i) has served notice of his intention to object and the grounds of such objection on the applicant, the Registrar and the Commissioner of Police and lodged a copy of such notice in the office of the licensing court, prior to the date fixed for the hearing under subsection (1); or

(ii) is granted leave by the licensing court to make such objection, and for the purposes of this section "counsel" means a person qualified to practise as a barrister or solicitor under the Legal Practitioners Ordinance.

(3) The licensing court shall not grant a licence to a person who is a disqualified person.

(4) The licensing court shall, in considering an application to which subsection (2)*(a)* or *(b)* applies, hear any evidence given by the applicant or any witnesses called on his behalf and any evidence adduced by or on behalf of the Registrar or the Commissioner of Police or any other person who appears at the hearing under subsection (2)*(b)*.

(5) Subject to subsection (3), the licensing court shall not grant a licence upon an application to which subsection (2)*(a)* or *(b)* applies unless the court is satisfied—

*(a)* that the applicant, or in the case of a firm every partner thereof, is a fit and proper person to carry on business as a money lender;
*(b)* in the case of a body corporate, that any person who controls such body corporate or in accordance with whose directions or instructions the directors thereof are accustomed to act is a fit and proper person to be associated with the business of money-lending;
*(c)* that as respects the carrying on of business as a money lender, any person responsible or proposed to be responsible for the management of the business or any part thereof, or in the case of a body corporate any director or secretary or other officer thereof, is a fit and proper person to be associated with the business of money-lending;
*(d)* that the name under which the applicant applies to be licensed is not misleading or otherwise undesirable;
*(e)* that as respects any of the premises to which the application relates, such premises and the situation thereof are suitable for the carrying on of the business of money-lending;
*(f)* that the applicant has complied with the provisions of this Part and any regulations relating to the application; and
*(g)* that in all the circumstances the grant of such licence is not contrary to the public interest.

(6) A licence granted under this section shall be subject to such conditions as the licensing court may impose.

(7) A licence granted under this section shall not be issued and shall not enter into force except on payment to the licensing court of the prescribed fee.

Effect and duration of licence.

12. Every licence shall authorize the person named therein to carry on business as a money lender at any premises specified therein for a period of 12 months from the date on which it is granted.

Renewal.

13. (1) A licensee may apply for the renewal of his licence within a period of 3 months prior to the expiration thereof.

(2) This section does not apply to a licensee whose licence is revoked.

(3) An application for renewal made under this section shall be made in the prescribed manner and shall be accompanied by the prescribed fee.

(4) Sections 8, 9 ,10 and 11 shall apply to an application for renewal made under this section as they apply to an application made under section 8.

(5) Any licence in respect of which an application for renewal is made under this section and which expires prior to the determination of such application shall, unless such application is withdrawn, or the licence is revoked or suspended under section 14, be deemed to continue in force until the determination of such application.

Revocation and suspension.

14. (1) On the application of the Registrar or the Commissioner of Police, a licensing court may make an order revoking or suspending any licence granted by the licensing court if, in the opinion of the licensing court—

*(a)* the licensee has ceased to be a fit and proper person to carry on business as a money lender; or
*(b)* the premises specified in the licence or any of such premises have, or the situation thereof has, ceased to be suitable for the carrying on of the business of money-lending; or
*(c)* the licensee has been in serious breach of any condition of the licence or has ceased to satisfy any other condition relating to his business as a money lender in respect of which the licensing court is required to be satisfied under section 11(5); or
*(d)* the business of the licensee has been carried on at any time or on any occasion since the date on which the licence was granted by recourse to the use of any methods, or in any manner, contrary to the public interest.

(2) The licensing court shall fix a date for the hearing of an application under this section, and shall give 14 clear days' notice of such date to the Registrar and the Commissioner of Police and the licensee; such notice shall call on the licensee to show cause as to why such application

ought not to be granted and an order for the revocation or suspension of his licence ought not to be made.

(3) In this section "licence" includes a licence deemed to continue in force under section 13(5).

15. (1) Except as provided in this section, a licence shall not be transferable.

Transfer of licence and addition or substitution of new premises.

(2) Where a licensed money lender dies, the widow or widower or any member of the family of the deceased money lender of the age of 21 years or upwards, or any person on behalf of the family, may apply to the licensing court which granted the licence to have his or her name endorsed on the licence.

(3) Where a licensee intends to carry on business as a money lender at any premises in addition to the premises specified in his licence, he may apply to the licensing court which granted the licence to have such additional premises endorsed on his licence.

(4) Where a licensed money lender intends to transfer his business as a money lender from any premises specified in his licence to any premises not so specified, he may apply to the licensing court which granted the licence to have the premises to which he intends to transfer such business endorsed on his licence in substitution for such first-mentioned premises.

(5) Every application under this section shall be made in the prescribed manner and shall be accompanied by the prescribed fee and notice of the application shall be given to the Registrar and the Commissioner of Police.

(6) The Registrar and the Commissioner of Police shall be entitled to appear and be heard at the hearing of any application under this section and to object to the granting of any such application.

(7) The licensing court shall not grant an application under this section unless the court is satisfied that—

*(a)* notice of the application has been given to the Registrar and the Commissioner of Police;
*(b)* in the case of an application under subsection (2), the applicant is a fit and proper person to carry on the business of the deceased money lender;
*(c)* in the case of an application under subsection (3), the additional premises and the situation thereof are suitable for the carrying on of the business of money-lending;

(*d*) in the case of an application under subsection (4), the premises to which the money lender intends to transfer his business and the situation thereof are suitable for the carrying on of the business of money-lender;

(*e*) in the case of an application in respect of any premises under subsection (3) or (4), any person responsible or proposed to be responsible for the management of the business carried on at such premises is a fit and proper person to be associated with the business of money-lending.

(8) Where the licensing court grants an application for an endorsement under this section, the endorsement shall be made in the office of the licensing court upon payment of the prescribed fee.

(9) A licence endorsed under subsection (2) shall have effect in all respects as if the licence had been issued to the person whose name is endorsed thereon and this Ordinance shall apply accordingly to such person as it applies to a licensee.

Appeals.

**16.** Any person aggrieved by a decision of a licensing court under section 11, 13, 14 or 15 may appeal to the High Court and the decision of the High Court shall be final.

Duty to notify changes of particulars.

**17.** (1) Where any change takes place in any particulars entered in the register in respect of any licensee, or a change takes place—

(*a*) in the case of a firm, in the membership thereof whether by reason of an amalgamation or the reduction of the number of partners or otherwise;

(*b*) in the case of a body corporate—

(i) in the officers thereof;

(ii) in the control thereof by any person;

(iii) in the number of shares, or shares of a prescribed class, therein held by any person whereby the nominal value of any such shares held by that person exceeds such proportion of the nominal value of the share capital thereof or of the issued shares of that class, as the case may be, as may be prescribed;

(*c*) in the persons responsible for the management of his business as a money lender at any premises where the business is carried on,

the licensee shall give notice in writing of such change to the Registrar within 21 days after the change takes place.

(2) Where notice of any change is given to the Registrar under subsection (1), the Registrar may by notice in writing require the

licensee to furnish him with such information, verified in such manner, as the Registrar may specify with respect to such change.

## PART III. MONEY LENDERS' TRANSACTIONS

**18.** (1) No agreement for the repayment of money lent by a money lender or for the payment of interest on money so lent, and no security given to any money lender in respect of any such agreement or loan, shall be enforceable unless— Form of agreement.

*(a)* within 7 days after the making of the agreement, a note or memorandum in writing of the agreement is made in accordance with subsection (2) and signed personally by the borrower, and a copy of such note or memorandum is given to the borrower at the time of signing; and

*(b)* there is included in or attached to such copy a summary, in such form as may be prescribed, of such provisions of this Part and Part IV as may be prescribed,

and no such agreement or security shall be enforceable if it is proved that the note or memorandum was not signed by the borrower before the money was lent or the security was given.

(2) The note or memorandum shall contain all the terms of the agreement and in particular shall set out—

*(a)* the name and address of the money lender;
*(b)* the name and address of the borrower;
*(c)* the name and address of the surety, if any;
*(d)* the amount of the principal of the loan in words and figures;
*(e)* the date of the making of the agreement;
*(f)* the date of the making of the loan;
*(g)* the terms of repayment of the loan;
*(h)* the form of security for the loan, if any;
*(i)* the rate of interest charged on the loan expressed as a rate *per cent per annum,* or the rate *per cent per annum* represented by the interest charged as calculated in accordance with the Second Schedule; and Second Schedule.
*(j)* a declaration as to the place of negotiation and completion of the agreement for the loan.

(3) Notwithstanding subsection (1), if the court before which the enforceability of any agreement or security comes in question is satisfied that in all the circumstances it would be inequitable that any such agreement or security which does not comply with this section should be held not to be enforceable, the court may declare that such agreement or

security is enforceable to such extent and subject to such modifications or exceptions as the court may order.

Duty of money lender to give information to borrower.

**19.** (1) In respect of every agreement, whether made before or after the commencement of this Ordinance, for the repayment of money lent by a money lender, the money lender shall, on demand in writing being made by the borrower at any time during the continuance of the agreement and on tender by the borrower of $10 for expenses, supply to the borrower or, if the borrower so requires, to any person specified in that behalf in the demand, a statement signed by the money lender or his agent showing—

(*a*) the date on which the loan was made, the amount of the principal of the loan and the rate *per cent per annum* of interest charged;

(*b*) the amount of any payment already received by the money lender in respect of the loan and the date on which it was made;

(*c*) the amount of every sum due to the money lender but unpaid, and the date on which it became due, and the amount of interest accrued due and unpaid in respect of every such sum; and

(*d*) the amount of every sum not yet due which remains outstanding, and the date on which it will become due.

(2) A money lender shall, on demand in writing by the borrower, supply a copy of any document relating to a loan made by him or any security therefor to the borrower or, if the borrower so requires and on payment by the borrower to the lender of $10, to any person specified in that behalf in the demand.

(3) Subsection (1) or (2) does not apply to a request made by a borrower less than 1 month after a previous request thereunder relating to the same agreement was complied with.

(4) If a money lender to whom a demand has been made under this section fails without reasonable excuse to comply therewith within 1 month after the demand has been made, he shall not, so long as the default continues, be entitled to sue for or recover any sum due under the agreement on account either of principal or interest, and interest shall not be chargeable in respect of the period of default.

Duty of money lender to give information to surety.

**20.** (1) A money lender who makes any agreement for the loan of money in relation to which security is provided shall within 7 days after the making of the agreement give to the surety (if a different person from the borrower)—

(*a*) a copy of the note or memorandum in writing made under section 18(1);

*(b)* a copy of the security instrument, if any; and

*(c)* a statement in writing signed by or on behalf of the money lender showing—

(i) the total sum payable under the agreement by the borrower;

(ii) the various amounts comprised in that total sum with the date, or the mode of determining the date, when each becomes due.

(2) Without prejudice to subsection (1), a surety may at any time during the continuance of an agreement (whether made before or after the commencement of this Ordinance) in relation to which the security is provided require the money lender by notice in writing to furnish him with a statement in writing signed by or on behalf of the money lender showing—

*(a)* the total sum paid under the agreement by the borrower;

*(b)* the total sum which has become payable under the agreement by the borrower but remains unpaid, and the various amounts comprised in that total sum, with the date when each became due; and

*(c)* the total sum which is to become payable under the agreement by the borrower, and the various amounts comprised in that total sum, with the date, or the mode of determining the date, when each becomes due.

(3) Subsection (2) does not apply to a request made by a surety less than 1 month after a previous request under that subsection relating to the same agreement was complied with.

(4) If a money lender fails to comply with subsection (1) or a request to which subsection (2) applies he shall not be entitled, while the default continues, to enforce the security so far as provided in relation to the agreement.

Early payment by borrower.

**21.** (1) Subject to subsection (2), a borrower under any agreement for the loan of money by a money lender shall be entitled at any time by notice in writing to the money lender and the payment to the money lender of all amounts payable as principal by the borrower which are outstanding under the agreement, together with interest computed up to the date of such payment, to discharge his indebtedness under the agreement:

Provided that the effective rate of such interest shall not exceed the effective rate at which interest would have been payable under the agreement if the borrower had not exercised his right under this section to discharge his indebtedness.

(2) Subsection (1) shall not apply in relation to any loan made by a money lender (whether an individual, a firm or a company registered under the Companies Ordinance) who, at the time the agreement for the loan is made and throughout the continuance of the agreement, is recognized by the Financial Secretary by notice in the *Gazette* for the purposes of this subsection or is a member of an association so recognized.

Illegal agreements.

22. Any agreement made for the loan of money by a money lender shall be illegal if it provides directly or indirectly for—

(*a*) the payment of compound interest;

(*b*) prohibiting the repayment of the loan by instalments; or

(*c*) the rate or amount of interest being increased by reason of any default in the payment of sums due under the agreement:

Provided that provision may be made by any such agreement that if default is made in the payment upon the due date of any sum payable to the money lender under the agreement, whether in respect of principal or interest, the money lender shall be entitled, subject to Part IV, to charge simple interest on that sum from the date of the default until the sum is paid at an effective rate not exceeding the effective rate payable in respect of the principal apart from any default, and any interest so charged shall not be reckoned for the purposes of this Ordinance as part of the interest charged in respect of the loan.

Loan etc. not recoverable unless money lender licensed.

23. No money lender shall be entitled to recover in any court any money lent by him or any interest in respect thereof or to enforce any agreement made or security taken in respect of any loan made by him unless he satisfies the court by the production of his licence or otherwise that at the date of the loan or the making of the agreement or the taking of the security (as the case may be) he was licensed.

## PART IV. EXCESSIVE INTEREST RATES

Prohibition of excessive interest rates.

24. (1) Any person (whether a money lender or not) who lends or offers to lend money at an effective rate of interests which exceeds 60 *per cent per annum* commits an offence

(2) No agreement for the repayment of any loan or for the payment of interest on any loan and no security given in respect of any such agreement or loan shall be enforceable in any case in which the effective rate of interest exceeds the rate specified in subsection (1).

(3) The Legislative Council may by resolution alter the rate specified in subsection (1):

Provided that in relation to any agreement for the repayment of any loan or for the payment of interest on any loan which is in force at the date when such rate is so altered, the rate so specified as at the coming into force of such agreement shall continue to apply.

(4) Any person who commits an offence under this section shall be liable to a fine of $100,000 and to imprisonment for 2 years.

**25.** (1) Subject to section 24(2), where— Reopening of certain transactions.

*(a)* proceedings are taken in any court by any person (whether a money lender or not) for the recovery of any money lent or the enforcement of any agreement or security in respect of any loan; and

*(b)* subject to subsection (3), there is evidence which satisfies the court that the transaction is extortionate,

the court may reopen the transaction so as to do justice between the parties having regard to all the circumstances, and, for that purpose, make such orders and give such directions in respect of the terms of the transaction or the rights of the parties thereunder as the court may think fit.

(2) For the purposes of this section, a transaction is extortionate if—

*(a)* it requires the debtor or a relative of his to make payments (whether unconditionally or on certain contingencies) which are grossly exorbitant; or

*(b)* it otherwise grossly contravenes ordinary principles of fair-dealing.

(3) Any agreement for the repayment of a loan or for the payment of interest on a loan in respect of which the effective rate of interest exceeds 48 *per cent per annum* shall, having regard to that fact alone, be presumed for the purposes of this section to be a transaction which is extortionate; but except where such rate exceeds the rate specified in section 24(1), the court may declare that any such agreement is not extortionate for the purposes of this section if, having regard to all the circumstances relating to the agreement, the court is satisfied that such rate is not unreasonable or unfair.

(4) In determining whether a transaction is extortionate for the purposes of this section, regard shall be had to such evidence as is adduced concerning—

*(a)* interest rate prevailing at the time it was made;

*(b)* the factors mentioned in subsections (5) and (6); and

*(c)* any other relevant considerations.

(5) Factors applicable under subsection (4)*(b)* in relation to the debtor include—

*(a)* his age, experience, business capacity and state of health; and

*(b)* the degree to which, at the time of entering into the transaction, he was under financial pressure, and the nature of that pressure.

(6) Factors applicable under subsection (4)*(b)* in relation to the lender or other person by whom the proceedings are taken include—

*(a)* the degree of risk accepted by the lender, having regard to the nature and value of any security provided;

*(b)* his relationship to the debtor;

*(c)* whether or not a specious cash price was quoted for any goods or services included in the transaction; and

*(d)* where one or more other transactions are to be taken into account, the question how far any such other transaction was reasonably required for the protection of the debtor or the lender, or was in the interest of the debtor.

(7) Any court in which proceedings might be taken for the recovery of any loan or security in respect of a loan shall have and may at the instance of the debtor or any surety exercise the like powers as may be exercised under this section where proceedings are taken for the recovery of a loan; and the court may entertain any application under this subsection by the debtor or surety notwithstanding that the time for repayment of the loan or any instalment thereof has not arrived.

(8) On any application relating to the admission or amount of a proof by a money lender in any bankruptcy proceedings, the court may exercise the like powers as may be exercised under this section where proceedings are taken for the recovery of money.

(9) The Legislative Council may by resolution alter the rate specified in subsection (3) but, in relation to any agreement referred to in that subsection which is in force at the date when such rate is so altered, the rate so specified as at the coming into force of such agreement shall continue to apply.

(10) In this section "debtor" means any person primarily liable for the repayment of a loan or for the payment of interest in respect of a loan.

## PART V. GENERAL

Restriction on money-lending advertisements.

**26.** (1) A money lender shall not for the purpose of his business as such issue or publish or cause to be issued or published any advertisement, circular, business letter or other similar document which does not show the name of the money lender as specified in his licence in such manner as to be not less conspicuous than any other name.

(2) Where any advertisement, circular, business letter or other similar document issued or published by or on behalf of a money lender purports to indicate the terms of interest on which he is willing to make loans or any particular loan, such advertisement, circular, business letter or other document shall show the interest proposed to be charged—

*(a)* subject to section 24(1), as a rate *per cent per annum;* and
*(b)* in such manner as to be not less conspicuous than any other matter mentioned therein.

(3) A money lender shall not for the purposes of his business as such issue or publish or cause to be issued or published any advertisement, circular, business letter or other similar document containing a name or description or expression which might reasonably be held to imply that he carries on banking business.

**27.** (1) Subject to subsection (2), any agreement entered into between a money lender and a borrower or intending borrower for the payment by the borrower or intending borrower to the money lender of any sum for or on account of costs, charges or expenses (other than stamp duties or similar duties) incidental to or relating to the negotiations for or the granting of the loan or proposed loan or the guaranteeing or securing of the repayment thereof shall be illegal.

Charges for expenses etc. not recoverable.

(2) Subsection (1) shall not apply in relation to any agreement for the payment of any sum for or on account of costs, charges or expenses in respect of a loan if—

*(a)* except where paragraph *(b)* applies,—
   (i) the money lender (whether an individual, a firm or a company registered under the Companies Ordinance) is approved for the purposes of this paragraph by the Registrar, after consultation with the Financial Secretary, by notice in the *Gazette* or is a member of an association so approved; and
   (ii) the terms of the agreement relating to such costs, charges or expenses comply with such restrictions or conditions, if any, in respect of costs, charges or expenses of that kind as may be specially approved for the purposes of this paragraph by the Registrar, after consultation with the Financial Secretary, by notice in the *Gazette;* or
*(b)* the terms of the agreement relating to such costs, charges or expenses comply with such restrictions or conditions, if any, in

respect of costs, charges or expenses of that kind as may be generally approved for the purposes of this paragraph by the Registrar, after consultation with the Financial Secretary, by notice in the *Gazette*.

(3) It shall not be lawful for any money lender or his partner, employer, employee, principal or agent or any person acting for or in collusion with any money lender to charge, recover or receive any sum as for or on account of any such costs, charges or expenses (other than stamp duties or similar charges) or to demand or receive any remuneration or reward whatsoever from a borrower or intending borrower for or in connexion with or preliminary to procuring, negotiating or obtaining any loan made or guaranteeing or securing the repayment thereof.

(4) If any money or money's worth is directly or indirectly paid or allowed to or received by any person in contravention of this section, the amount or value thereof, to the extent of such contravention and notwithstanding any agreement to the contrary, may be recovered by the borrower from such person or, if such person is the money lender or a partner, employer, employee, principal or agent of the money lender or is in any way acting for or in collusion with him, may be set off against the amount actually lent (and that amount shall be deemed to be reduced accordingly) or may be recovered by the borrower from such person or from the money lender.

Power of Registrar to enter premises and inspect books etc.

**28.** For the purpose of ascertaining whether the provisions of this Ordinance are being or have been complied with by any money lender, the Registrar or any other person authorized by the Registrar in writing in that behalf may enter any premises where the business of such money lender is being carried on and may demand the production of and inspect the money lender's licence or any books, accounts, documents or writings relating to any loan made by the money lender or relating to his business as a money lender, and may take notes, copies or extracts thereof or therefrom.

Offences by money lenders.

**29.** (1) Any person who carries on business as a money lender—

*(a)* without a licence; or

*(b)* at any place other than the premises specified in his licence; or

*(c)* otherwise than in accordance with the conditions of his licence; or

*(d)* during any period when his licence is suspended,

commits an offence.

(2) Any person who makes any false or misleading statement or furnishes any false or misleading information in connexion with any application for a licence or the renewal of a licence commits an offence.

(3) Any person who, being a licensee, fails to give notice under section 17(1) of any change in respect of such licensee, or who, having been required by the Registrar under section 17(2) to furnish any information in respect of such change, fails to furnish such information or furnishes any false or misleading information, commits an offence.

(4) Any money lender who—

*(a)* fails to make a note or memorandum in writing of an agreement in compliance with section 18;

*(b)* fails to give a copy of such note or memorandum to the borrower in compliance with section 18(1)*(a)*; or

*(c)* fails to include in or attach to such copy a summary in writing in compliance with section 18(1)*(b)*,

commits an offence.

(5) Any money lender who demands or accepts security for a loan in any form prohibited by regulations made under section 34 commits an offence.

(6) Any money lender who fails to comply with any demand in writing made by a borrower under section 19 to supply any statement or copy of any document to the borrower or any person specified in the demand commits an offence.

(7) Any money lender who fails to give a surety any information to which the surety is entitled under section 20(1) or in respect of which the surety has made a request by notice in writing under section 20(2) commits an offence.

(8) Any money lender who issues or publishes, or causes to be issued or published, any advertisement, circular, business letter or other similar document which contravenes any of the provisions of section 26 commits an offence.

(9) Any money lender who for any of the purposes of his business uses any name other than the name specified in his licence, or a name or description or expression which might reasonably be held to imply that he carries on banking business commits an offence.

Offences of fraudulent inducement and obstruction.

**30.** (1) Any person who by any false, misleading or deceptive statement, representation or promise, or by any dishonest concealment of material facts, fraudulently induces or attempts to induce—

*(a)* any money lender to lend money to any person or to agree to the terms on which money is or is to be borrowed;

(*b*) any person to borrow money from a money lender or to agree to the terms on which money is or is to be lent,

commits an offence.

(2) Any person who—

(*a*) wilfully obstructs the Registrar or any person authorized by him in writing in the performance of his functions under section 28;

(*b*) without reasonable cause fails to give the Registrar or any such person authorized by him such assistance or information as he may require in the performance of such functions,

commits an offence.

Liability for offences by bodies corporate.

31. Where at any time a body corporate commits an offence under this Ordinance with the consent or connivance of, or because of neglect by, any individual, the individual commits the like offence if at that time—

(*a*) he is a director, manager, secretary or similar officer of the body corporate; or

(*b*) he is purporting to act as such officer; or

(*c*) the body corporate is managed by its members, of whom he is one.

Penalties and disqualification.

32. (1) Any person who commits an offence under this Ordinance shall be liable—

(*a*) in the case of an offence under section 29, to a fine of $100,000 and to imprisonment for 2 years;

(*b*) in the case of any other offence for which no penalty is provided, to a fine of $10,000 and to imprisonment for 6 months.

(2) Where any person is convicted of an offence under this Ordinance, the magistrate may order that such person shall be disqualified from holding a licence for such period not exceeding 5 years from the date of such conviction as may be specified in the order.

(3) A licence held by any person against whom an order is made under subsection (2) shall, as from the date of the order, cease to have effect for the purposes of this Ordinance.

Burden of proof.

33. (1) When in any proceedings under this Ordinance against any person it is alleged that such person is not the holder of a licence, it shall in the absence of proof to the contrary be presumed that such person is not licensed.

(2) When in any proceedings under this Ordinance against any person it is alleged that—

*(a)* such person is not a person specified in Part 1 of the First Schedule; or First Schedule.

*(b)* that a loan alleged to have been made by such person is not a loan specified in Part 2 of the First Schedule,

the fact so alleged shall in the absence of proof to the contrary be presumed.

34. The Governor in Council may make regulations— Regulations.

*(a)* prescribing anything required or permitted to be prescribed under this Ordinance;

*(b)* specifying any particulars furnished under section 8 as particulars which shall not be entered in the register under section 4;

*(c)* imposing restrictions in relation to the form in which security for any loan may be demanded or accepted by a money lender;

*(d)* for the better carrying into effect of this Ordinance.

35. (1) The Money-lenders Ordinance 1911 is repealed. Repeal and saving.

(2) Any money lender who, at the commencement of this Ordinance, is registered under the Money-lenders Ordinance 1911 shall be deemed to be licensed as a money lender under this Ordinance until—

*(a)* the date on which such registration would, if this Ordinance had not been enacted, have expired by virtue of section 4(2) of that Ordinance; or

*(b)* if such money lender makes an application for a licence under this Ordinance within a period of 2 months after the commencement of this Ordinance, the date on which such application is finally disposed of under this Ordinance.

(3) An application for a licence made by a money lender to whom subsection (2) applies shall be made under section 13 and shall be treated as an application for the renewal of a licence.

(4) The Registrar shall take possession of the register and any documents relating thereto kept at the office of the Registrar of Companies under the Money-lenders Ordinance 1911, and such register and other documents shall be deemed to form part of the records kept by the Registrar under this Ordinance and shall be available for inspection in the same manner as the register kept under this Ordinance.

36. (1) This section applies to any agreement made before the commencement of this Ordinance for the payment of any loan or for the payment of interest on any loan, and to any security given (whether Existing loans.

given before or after the commencement of this Ordinance) in respect of any such agreement or loan

(2) Nothing in this Ordinance shall render any agreement or security to which this section applies void or unenforceable, but no such agreement or security shall be enforceable as against the borrower or surety or any other person except to the extent that—

*(a)* any benefit accruing to the lender by virtue thereof is not more favourable; and

*(b)* any obligation or liability incurred by the borrower or surety or other person by virtue thereof is not more onerous,

that [2] it would have been if such agreement had been made or, as the case may be, such security had been given on terms consistent with the requirements of this Ordinance.

(3) Where proceedings are taken in any court for the enforcement of any agreement or security to which this section applies, the court may make such orders and give such directions in respect of the terms thereof or the rights and obligations of the parties in respect thereof as the court may deem necessary or desirable having regard to the requirements of this Ordinance relating to an agreement or security of the kind in question.

## FIRST SCHEDULE [ss. 2, 3 & 33.]

### PART 1—EXEMPTED PERSONS

1. A bank licensed under the Banking Ordinance and any subsidiary thereof.
2. A deposit-taking company registered or licensed under the Deposit-Taking Companies Ordinance and any subsidiary thereof.
3. A co-operative society registered under the Co-operative Societies Ordinance.
4. A credit union registered under the Credit Unions Ordinance and the Credit Union League of Hong Kong incorporated under Part XI of that Ordinance.
5. A trade union registered under the Trade Unions Ordinance.
6. A life insurance company registered as a company under the Companies Ordinance.
7. The Hong Kong Building and Loan Agency Limited.
8. The University and Polytechnic Grants Committee.

### PART 2—EXEMPTED LOANS

1. A loan made by an employer to a *bona fide* employee.
2. A loan made to a registered company secured by the issue of a debenture or similar instrument.
3. A loan made by a company registered under the Companies Ordinance (other than a bank or a deposit-taking company) under a *bona fide* credit-

[2] Editor's query: "than."

card scheme operated by the company to any holder of a credit-card issued under that scheme.

4. A loan made *bona fide* for the purchase of immovable property on the security of a mortgage of that property.

5. A loan made by a company registered under the Companies Ordinance or a firm or individual whose ordinary business does not primarily or mainly involve the lending of money, in the ordinary course of that business.

6. A loan made by a licensed pawnbroker under the Pawnbrokers Ordinance, being a loan to which that Ordinance applies.

7. A loan regulated by any Ordinance relating to hire-purchase transactions.

8. A loan made by any statutory body under any power conferred by law in that behalf.

9. A loan made from—

   (*a*) a fund established by resolution of the Legislative Council or by or under an Ordinance;

   (*b*) any superannuation or provident fund.

10. A loan made from any chit-fund operated under the Chit-Fund Business (Prohibition) Ordinance.

---

## SECOND SCHEDULE [ss. 2 & 18.]

### CALCULATION OF TRUE ANNUAL PERCENTAGE RATE OF INTEREST

1. Any amount paid or payable to the lender under the agreement (other than simple interest charged in accordance with the proviso to section 22) shall be appropriated to principal and interest in the proportion that the total amount of principal bears to the total amount of the interest.

2. The amount of principal outstanding at any time shall be taken to be the balance remaining after deducting from the principal the total of the portions of any payments appropriated to principal in accordance with paragraph 1.

3. The several amounts taken to be outstanding by way of principal during the several periods ending on the dates on which payments are made shall be multiplied in each case by the number of calendar months during which those amounts are taken to be respectively outstanding, and there shall be ascertained the aggregate amount of the sum so produced.

4. The total amount of the interest shall be divided by one-twelfth part of the aggregate amount mentioned in paragraph 3 and the quotient, multiplied by one hundred, shall be taken to be the rate of interest *per cent per annum*.

5. If having regard to the intervals between successive payments it is desired so to do, the calculation of interest may be made by reference to weeks instead of months, and in such a case the foregoing paragraphs shall have effect as though in paragraph 3 the word "weeks" were substituted for the words "calendar months", and in paragraph 4 the words "one-fifty-second" were substituted for the words "one-twelfth".

6. Where any interval between successive payments is not a number of complete weeks or complete months, the foregoing paragraphs shall have effect as though 1 day were one-seventh part of a week or one-thirtieth part of a month (as the case may be).

# Pawnbrokers Ordinance[1]

To amend the law relating to pawnbrokers.

[17th October, 1930]

Short title.

1. This Ordinance may be cited as the Pawnbrokers Ordinance.

Interpretation.

2. In this Ordinance, unless the context otherwise requires—

"identity document" means—

*(a)* an identity card issued in accordance with the provisions of the Registration of Persons Ordinance;

*(b)* a passport issued by a competent authority within or outside the Colony;

*(c)* any document which establishes the identity of the holder and is accepted by the Director of Immigration in lieu of a passport; and

*(d)* in the case of a member of the police force, the warrant card issued to him under section 18 of the Police Force Ordinance;

"licence" means a pawnbroker's licence in force under section 8;

"month" means a Chinese lunar month;

"pawnbroker" includes every person who carries on the business of taking goods and chattels in pawn, or who purchases, receives or takes in any goods or chattels, and pays money for or advances money upon the same, with or under any undertaking, agreement or condition, express, implied or reasonably to be inferred from the nature or character of the dealing or the usage in respect thereof, that the said goods or chattels in whole or in part may be afterwards redeemed or repurchased upon any terms whatsoever.

Regulations.

3. The Governor in Council may by regulation provide for—

*(a)* conditions under which pawnbrokers' licences shall be granted or renewed or revoked;

*(b)* the periods referred to in section 17;

*(c)* fees to be paid for such licences and for the renewal of such licences;

[1] *Laws of Hong Kong,* Cap. 166 (1970). Originally No. 16 of 1930 (Cap 166, 1950). Relevant citations: Nos. 33 of 1939; 23 of 1946; 23 of 1947; G.N. 733/47; Nos. 57 of 1948; 22 of 1950; 24 of 1950; 1 of 1963; 13 of 1966; 2 of 1970; 21 of 1970; and 51 of 1970.

(*d*) the forms of such licences;

(*e*) books and documents to be kept by pawnbrokers and the particulars to be noted therein;

(*f*) maximum rates of interest to be charged by pawnbrokers;

(*g*) limiting the number of pawnbrokers' shops that may be allowed in any area;

(*h*) the form of the pawn ticket and the particulars to be stated therein;

(*i*) forms to be used under this Ordinance;

(*j*) hours during which the business of pawnbroking may be carried on;

(*k*) the storage and safe keeping of pledges;

(*l*) offences in the case of contravention of any regulations made hereunder and prescribing penalties therefor:

Provided that no penalty so prescribed shall exceed a fine of five hundred dollars; and

(*m*) generally more effectively carrying out the provisions of this Ordinance.

4. For the purposes of this Ordinance anything done or omitted by the servant or agent of a pawnbroker in the course of or in relation to the business of the pawnbroker shall be deemed to be done or omitted (as the case may be) by the pawnbroker; and anything by this Ordinance authorized to be done by a pawnbroker may be done by his servant or agent. Servant, agent, etc., of pawnbrokers.

5. The rights, powers and benefits by this Ordinance reserved to and conferred on pawners shall extend to and be deemed to be reserved to and conferred on the assigns of pawners and to and on the executors or administrators of deceased pawners; but any person representing himself to a pawnbroker to be the assign, executor or administrator of a pawner shall, if required by the pawnbroker, produce to the pawnbroker the assignment, probate, letters of administration or other instrument under which he claims. Assigns, executors, etc., of pawners.

6. Nothing in this Ordinance shall apply to a loan by a pawnbroker of above five thousand dollars, or to the pledge on which the loan is made, or to the pawnbroker or pawner in relation to the loan or pledge; and notwithstanding anything in this Ordinance a person shall not be deemed a pawnbroker by reason only of his paying, advancing or lending on any terms any sum or sums of above five thousand dollars. Non-application to loans above $5,000.

7. No person shall carry on the trade or business of a pawnbroker in any premises except under and in accordance with a valid pawn- Licence.

broker's licence in respect thereof on which any fees then due have been paid.

Grant and renewal of licences.

8. (1) The Commissioner of Police may grant to any person a pawnbroker's licence.

(2) A pawnbroker's licence shall be valid for one year from the date on which it is issued and may be renewed from year to year.

(3) Subject to subsection (4), the fee for a pawnbroker's licence shall be paid in advance.

(4) A licensee may pay the licence fee in quarterly instalments in advance on finding security for such instalments to the satisfaction of the Secretary for Home Affairs.

(5) If the Commissioner of Police refuses to grant or renew a licence under subsection (1) or (2) the applicant for, or the holder of, the licence, as the case may be, may, within fourteen days of being notified of the refusal, appeal by way of petition to the Governor who may confirm, reverse or vary the decision of the Commissioner.

Suspension and cancellation of licences.

9. (1) Where a person holding a pawnbroker's licence is convicted of any offence punishable by imprisonment for not less than twelve months, the court by which he is convicted may, in addition to imposing a penalty for such offence, order—

(*a*) that the licence shall be suspended for such period as may be specified in the order or that the licence shall be cancelled; and

(*b*) that the convicted licensee shall be disqualified from holding a licence for such period as the court determines.

(2) Upon making an order under subsection (1) the court shall cause particulars thereof to be endorsed on the licence and to be transmitted to the Commissioner of Police.

(3) A licensee shall in such manner and within such time as the court directs produce his licence for the purpose of an endorsement under subsection (2).

(4) No order of suspension, cancellation or disqualification under subsection (1) shall affect any contract of pawn or other contract made by the pawnbroker as such, nor shall he by reason only of the order lose his lien on, or right to, any pledge or to the loan and profit thereon, but he shall be allowed to pursue and wind up his business in respect of pledges which he has received before the making of the order.

**10.** No pawnbroker shall during the continuance of his licence carry on any trade or occupation in his place of business as such pawnbroker except that of pawnbroking and the sale of pledges forfeited under the provisions of this Ordinance.

Restriction of trade to pawnbroking.

**11.** Every pawnbroker shall cause to be painted and kept painted in large and legible English letters and Chinese characters, over the door of his said place of business, his or his firm's name at length, with the addition of the word *"Pawnbroker"* after the English name and the character "押" after the Chinese name.

Notification of name and nature of business.

**12.** Every pawnbroker shall, whenever required by the Commissioner of Police or by any police officer not below the rank of sergeant, or by any police officer authorized thereto in writing by the Commissioner either generally or for a particular occasion or for particular premises, produce for the inspection of the person so requiring him all or any goods pawned or deposited with him and all books and papers relating to the same.

Inspection of goods, books, etc.

**13.** (1) Every pawnbroker may demand, receive and take simple interest, over and above the principal paid or advanced by him upon any goods pawned with him, from the person applying to redeem the said goods, before redelivering the same, at the following rates or at such other rates as may from time to time be prescribed by the Governor in Council—

Interest on loans.

| | *First month.* | *Succeeding months.* |
|---|---|---|
| On any sum— | | |
| not exceeding $3 .................. | 10% | 3 % |
| exceeding— | | |
| $ 3 and not exceeding $ 14 ....... | 8% | 3 % |
| $ 14 " " " $ 28 ....... | 5% | 3 % |
| $ 28 " " " $ 84 ....... | 3% | 2 % |
| $ 84 " " " $280 ....... | 2% | 2 % |
| $280 .......................... | 2% | 1½%: |

Provided that, in the case of the special classes of goods set forth in the regulations the special rates of interest there set forth may subject to alteration by the Governor in Council be charged by the pawnbroker in lieu of the foregoing rates.

Regulations.

(2) The first month's interest shall be deemed to be due on the first day of the first month of the loan and shall be deducted from the amount of the loan.

(3) The principal and interest shall be accepted by the pawnbroker in full satisfaction of all charges for or incidental to the loan to which the same relate, and no pawnbroker shall demand interest in excess of the authorized rate or shall charge compound interest.

List of rates to be exposed in the shop.

(4) Every pawnbroker shall expose in a conspicuous place in his shop a clearly legible list, in English and Chinese, to be furnished by the Secretary for Home Affairs, of the rates chargeable under this section.

Loans and interest must be in local currency.

(5) No loans shall be made by any pawnbroker, and no interest on loans shall be charged by him, in any currency other than the currency of the Colony.

Book to be kept by pawnbroker. Regulations. Form 1.

14. Every pawnbroker shall before advancing any money on loan enter or cause to be entered in a book to be kept by him for that purpose, and to be called the general book, a legible statement in the prescribed form or its equivalent in Chinese. If a Chinese form is used the rate of interest shall be denoted by a chop.

Ticket to be given to borrower. Regulations. Form 2.

15. Every pawnbroker shall at the time of making any loan deliver to the borrower a ticket containing a true and legible statement in the prescribed form or its equivalent in Chinese. If a Chinese form is used the rate of interest shall be denoted by a chop.

Return of ticket on redelivery of goods.

16. In order to entitle any person to redeem from the pawnbroker the goods pawned, the ticket must be returned to the pawnbroker by the person applying to redeem the goods, except as provided for in section 19.

Delivery of goods on production of ticket and repayment.

17. (1) On the tender of any such ticket together with the full amount then due for principal and simple interest, if made within six months from the day of making the loan in the case of goods pawned in any part of the New Territories (other than New Kowloon), and four months from the day of making the loan in the case of goods pawned elsewhere in the Colony, the pawnbroker shall deliver up the goods described therein to the person so tendering.

(2) The Governor in Council may by regulation prescribe periods in substitution for the periods of six months and of four months specified in subsection (1).

**18.** Section 17 shall not apply to cases where, on or before such tender, the pawnbroker has had from the borrower or the owner of the goods notice not to deliver the same, or has had knowledge or notice that the same have been or are suspected to have been unlawfully obtained from or lost by the owner, or to tickets as to which the borrower has taken such proceedings as are provided by section 19, in all which cases the pawnbroker shall withhold the goods.

Exceptions to duty to deliver goods.

**19.** (1) On the application of any person representing himself to be the borrower or the owner of the goods or ticket, as the case may be, and to have lost or been unlawfully deprived of the same, the pawnbroker shall, if the goods are still unredeemed or unsold, forthwith deliver to such applicant a copy of the entry in the general book, and the said applicant shall immediately thereupon proceed to a magistrate and shall verify such representation by written information on oath before such magistrate.

Protection of owners and of pawners not having pawntickets.

(2) If the said applicant verifies such representation to the satisfaction of the magistrate and obtains a certificate to that effect, endorsed upon the said copy, the pawnbroker shall, on the copy so endorsed being delivered by the said applicant, deliver to him, according to the circumstances of the case and as the magistrate may order, another ticket or the goods, either with or without payment of the principal or interest or both principal and interest, as the magistrate may direct.

**20.** A magistrate shall, upon written information on oath being laid before him that there are probable grounds for believing that any goods have been pawned without the privity of their owner, issue his warrant for searching any place where the goods may appear to him to be; and if any of the goods are discovered upon such search, the person executing the warrant shall take them or cause them to be taken into safe keeping to abide the order of a magistrate.

Issue of search warrant for goods pawned without privity of owner.

**21.** Subject to the provisions of this Ordinance, goods pawned shall, from and after the expiration of the prescribed period specified in section 17, become, if the same are unredeemed, the property of the pawnbroker absolutely:

Unredeemed goods to become the property of pawnbroker.

Provided nevertheless that if before the expiration of any such period the borrower is desirous of continuing the loan for a further period not exceeding the prescribed period applicable, the pawnbroker shall allow him to do so on his paying the interest then due. In any such case a new ticket shall be issued and a new entry shall be made in the general book.

Information to be given by applicant.

22. (1) Every person applying to borrow shall at the time of his application give to the pawnbroker to whom such application is made true information so as to enable him to comply with the requirements of sections 14 and 15.

(2) Every person applying to redeem goods or for a copy of an entry shall at the time of his application give to the person to whom such application is made a full and true account of himself, his name, his place of abode, the name and place of abode of the owner and the circumstances under which his application is made.

Unlawful pawning.

23. No person shall pawn or attempt to pawn the goods of any other person without being duly authorized or employed in that behalf.

Pawnbroker to seize applicant suspected of unlawful conduct.

24. Every pawnbroker to whom any application is made to borrow or redeem, or for a copy of an entry, who has reasonable cause to suspect any unlawful conduct on the part of the applicant in any of the above cases, is hereby required to seize and detain such applicant and is empowered to call in the aid of any other person for that purpose; and every person so seized shall with all reasonable speed be delivered into the custody of a police constable who shall convey him before a magistrate.

Liability of pawnbroker in respect of loss or damage.

25. (1) A pawnbroker shall make good all loss or damage accruing to a borrower in the following cases—

*(a)* where the goods pawned have been stolen, embezzled, lost or otherwise improperly disposed of before the period for the redemption thereof has elapsed; and

*(b)* where the goods before the said period has elapsed have by the default, neglect or misfeasance of the pawnbroker been destroyed, damaged or impaired in value.

(2) In any of the said cases a magistrate shall allow and award an amount in satisfaction of such loss or damage, from which shall be deducted the amount of principal and interest then due in respect of such goods.

(3) A pawnbroker shall not be responsible for damage caused by fire, rats, insects or other causes not attributable to his default.

Pawnbroker not to receive goods in pawn from person under 17.

26. No pawnbroker shall receive any goods in pawn from any person who is apparently under the age of seventeen years.

27. No pawnbroker shall receive any goods in pawn from any person unless he has first inspected the identity document of the borrower.

Pawnbroker not to receive goods in pawn unless identity document produced.

28. It shall not be lawful for any pawnbroker to receive in pawn any goods having upon them any mark or sign denoting them to be or to have been the property of the Crown or of any public department.

Taking in pawn goods with certain marks.

29. Subject to any regulation made under this Ordinance by the Governor in Council, no goods shall be pawned or redeemed before 8 a.m. or after 8 p.m.:

Hours of business.

Provided that goods may be pawned or redeemed on the day preceding Lunar New Year's Day until 12 o'clock midnight.

30. (1) If in any proceedings before a court or magistrate it appears that any goods brought before such court or magistrate have been unlawfully pawned with a pawnbroker, the court or magistrate, on proof of the ownership of the goods, may order either the delivery or the non-delivery thereof to the owner—

Delivery to owner of property unlawfully pawned, with or without compensation to pawnbroker.

*(a)* on payment to the pawnbroker of the amount of the loan advanced by him thereon and the interest due; or

*(b)* on payment of any part of such loan or interest; or

*(c)* without payment of any part of such loan or interest,

as may seem just and fitting to the court or magistrate, according to the conduct of the owner and the pawnbroker and the other circumstances of the case.

(2) No such order shall be made by the court or magistrate unless the pawnbroker and the owner have been given an opportunity of being heard.

(3) Any such order made by the court or magistrate shall bar any civil remedy which the owner would have had for the recovery of the goods, and the owner shall not be entitled to claim the return of the goods from the pawnbroker except in accordance with the terms of such order.

31. (1) Every person who contravenes any of the provisions of section 23 shall be guilty of an offence and shall be liable on conviction to a fine of five hundred dollars and to imprisonment for six calendar months.

Penalties.

(2) Every person who contravenes any of the other provisions of this Ordinance, shall be guilty of an offence and shall be liable on conviction to a fine of five hundred dollars.

## Credit Unions Ordinance[1]

To incorporate and regulate credit unions and the Credit Union League of Hong Kong, and to provide for matters incidental thereto.

[28th February, 1970]

### PART I. PRELIMINARY

Short title and commencement.

1. This Ordinance may be cited as the Credit Unions Ordinance and shall come into operation on a day to be appointed by the Governor by notice in the *Gazette*.

Interpretation.

2. In this Ordinance, unless the context otherwise requires—

"board" means a board of directors of a credit union constituted under section 28;

"by-laws" means the by-laws made in accordance with Part VII and approved by the Registrar under subsection (3) of section 5 or the by-laws (if any) prescribed under section 85;

"credit union" means a credit union registered under this Ordinance;

"director" means a director of a board;

"financial year" means the twelve months ending on the 31st day of March in any year or on such other annual date as may be provided in the by-laws;

"League" means the Credit Union League of Hong Kong incorporated under Part XI;

"officer" and "officer of a credit union" mean any of the persons specified in section 30;

"Registrar" means the Registrar of Credit Unions appointed under section 82;

[1] *Laws of Hong Kong,* Cap. 119 (1968). Originally No. 39 of 1968. Relevant citations: L.N. 30/70; and No. 39 of 1976.

"share" means, in relation to a credit union, each sum of five dollars standing to the credit of a member in the accounts of that credit union;

"share balance" means the total value of all—

(*a*) fully paid up shares; and

(*b*) instalments paid in respect of other shares,

appearing for the time being in the accounts of a credit union;

"treasurer" means the person appointed under section 29 as treasurer or as treasurer and secretary of a board.

## PART II. FORMATION AND POWERS OF CREDIT UNIONS

3. (1) Any fifteen or more persons— Conditions of registration.

(*a*) each of whom is not less than sixteen years of age;

(*b*) at least three of whom are not less than twenty-one years of age;

(*c*) who satisfy the requirements of section 15;

(*d*) who wish to associate themselves together as a credit union for the objects set forth in subsection (2),

may be registered as a credit union.

(2) The objects of a credit union shall be—

(*a*) to promote thrift among its members;

(*b*) to receive the savings of its members either as payment on shares or as deposits; and

(*c*) to make loans to its members, exclusively for provident or productive purposes.

4. (1) The persons referred to in section 3 may apply for the registration of a credit union to the Registrar. Memorandum of association.

(2) Such persons shall sign in duplicate before two witnesses (who shall not be subscribers to the memorandum) a memorandum of association in the prescribed form and cause both copies thereof to be filed in the office of the Registrar.

(3) There shall be attached to the memorandum of association two copies of the by-laws by which it is proposed that the credit union shall be governed.

(4) The persons signing the memorandum of association shall appoint a provisional secretary, who shall hold office until a secretary of the board is appointed under section 29.

Registration.

5. (1) When the memorandum of association is duly filed, the Registrar shall consider whether the application complies with this Ordinance and may make such inquiries as he deems necessary for that purpose.

(2) The Registrar, after making such inquiries, may register the credit union, if he is satisfied—

*(a)* that the proposed by-laws do not conflict with any provision of this Ordinance;
*(b)* that the proposed by-laws are sufficient to enable the credit union to carry out its objects;
*(c)* that the body to which membership is limited is such as to ensure reasonable personal association amongst the members;
*(d)* that the applicants have reasonable prospects of carrying out the objects of a credit union;
*(e)* that the applicants and the application comply with the requirements of this Ordinance.

(3) On such registration the Registrar shall send to the provisional secretary of the credit union—

*(a)* one copy of the memorandum of association;
*(b)* one copy of the by-laws, with his approval endorsed thereon; and
*(c)* a certificate of registration, in the prescribed form.

Incorporation with limited liability; and effect thereof.

6. (1) Upon its registration, a credit union shall be a body corporate with perpetual succession and shall be capable of suing and being sued in its registered name and, subject to this Ordinance, of doing and suffering all such other acts and things as bodies corporate may lawfully do and suffer.

(2) In addition, upon such registration—

*(a)* all the movable property for the time being vested in any person in trust for the credit union shall vest in it;
*(b)* all liabilities incurred by any person as trustee of the credit union shall become its liabilities; and
*(c)* all legal proceedings pending by or against any such trustee may be prosecuted by or against the credit union in its registered name.

(3) The liability of a member of a credit union shall be limited to the amount of the shares held by him.

Restriction on name.

7. No credit union shall be registered under a name identical with that by which any other existing credit union has been registered, or

so nearly resembling the same as to be likely to deceive. and the expression "credit union", or the Chinese expression "儲蓄互助社", shall be the last words of the name of every credit union.

Amendment of memorandum of association.

**8.** (1) Subject to this Ordinance, a credit union may, by resolution passed by two-thirds of the members, present and qualified to vote, at an annual meeting, or at a special meeting called for the purpose, amend its memorandum of association.

(2) No such amendment shall be of any effect until approved by the Registrar and his approval is endorsed by him on the memorandum of association.

Registered office.

**9.** Every credit union shall have a registered office in the Colony to which all communications and notices shall be sent. The credit union shall send to the Registrar written notice of the address of its registered office and of every change of the address thereof.

Powers.

**10.** For the purpose of carrying out its objects, a credit union may—

*(a)* deposit money in any bank in the Colony approved by the Registrar;
*(b)* invest in any stock, debenture stock, funds or securities in which a trustee may invest by virtue of the Trustee Ordinance;
*(c)* become a member of any other credit union;
*(d)* subject to section 43, borrow money;
*(e)* insure its loans, funds and property against loss;
*(f)* subject to this Ordinance, under the hands of its president and treasurer, or vice-president and treasurer, draw, make, accept, endorse, execute and issue promissory notes, bills of exchange, bills of lading, warrants and other negotiable or transferable instruments;
*(g)* hold, purchase, take on lease, sell, exchange, lease or otherwise dispose of any land;
*(h)* do all such other acts and things as are incidental or conducive to or consequential upon the attainment of the objects mentioned in section 3.

## PART III. CAPITAL, SHARES AND MEMBERSHIP

Capital divided into shares.

**11.** The capital of a credit union shall be unlimited in amount and shall be divided into shares of a value of five dollars each.

Allotment and subscription for shares.

12. (1) Subject to this Ordinance, shares in a credit union may be allotted, subscribed and paid for in the manner provided in the by-laws.

(2) Shares in a credit union shall be allotted only to the members thereof.

(3) No share shall be allotted to a member until he has paid for it in cash in full without any premium or discount.

(4) A credit union shall not issue to a member a certificate denoting ownership of a share.

Disposal of shares.

13. (1) Subject to this Ordinance, shares in a credit union may be transferred or withdrawn by the holder thereof in the manner provided in the by-laws.

(2) No transfer or withdrawal of shares in a credit union shall be valid unless approved by the board, which approval shall be withheld if the transfer or withdrawal would reduce the total number of members of the credit union to less than fifteen.

(3) A transfer of shares in a credit union may take place only between the members thereof and no charge in respect of any transfer shall be imposed by the credit union.

(4) A member of a credit union may not transfer or withdraw any shares if the transfer or withdrawal would make the total value of his shares less than his total liability to the credit union, whether as borrower, pledgor, guarantor or otherwise.

Restriction on disposal of shares by officers, etc.

14. (1) No officer or member of a credit union, whilst entrusted with or participating in the management of the affairs of the credit union, shall pledge, transfer, withdraw or otherwise dispose of his shares except in accordance with this Ordinance and the by-laws.

(2) If a credit union is wound up under Part IX, any disposition of shares by way of pledge, transfer, withdrawal or otherwise made by an officer or member thereof within the four months preceding the commencement of the winding-up shall be invalid and the officer or member shall remain liable to the creditors of the credit union to the extent of any shares so disposed of.

Membership limited to persons with common occupation, etc.

15. The membership of a credit union shall be limited to persons having a common bond of occupation, employment, association, or residence within a defined neighbourhood, community, or rural or urban area:

Provided that a member of a credit union who ceases to have the common bond to which membership of the credit union is limited may retain his membership thereof but may not obtain the grant of any loan therefrom exceeding the value of his shares in the credit union.

Admission to and conditions of membership.

16. (1) A person shall not be admitted to membership of a credit union unless—

(a) his application for membership has been approved by the board;

(b) he has paid such entrance fee, not exceeding one dollar, as may be provided in the by-laws; and

(c) he has subscribed to at least one share and has paid an amount thereon not less than such initial instalment as may be provided in the by-laws.

(2) Subject to subsection (1), the conditions of membership of a credit union shall be in accordance with the by-laws.

Minors.

17. (1) A minor may be admitted to membership of a credit union but shall not be qualified to vote at the annual or special meetings thereof until he has attained the age of sixteen years.

(2) The minority of any person duly admitted as a member of any credit union shall not debar that person from executing any document necessary to be executed or given under this Ordinance, and shall not be a ground for invalidating or avoiding any contract entered into by any such person with the credit union; and any such contract entered into by any such person with the credit union, whether as principal or as surety, shall be enforceable at law by or against such person notwithstanding his minority.

Expulsion of member.

18. (1) A member of the credit union who contravenes any provision of this Ordinance or acts in any way detrimental to the interests of the credit union may be expelled therefrom upon a resolution passed by two-thirds of the members present and qualified to vote, at an annual meeting, or at a special meeting called for the purpose.

(2) The grounds on which his expulsion is being considered shall be communicated to the member in writing by the board not less than seven days before the resolution for his expulsion is to be moved and he shall be given the opportunity to answer, either in writing before the meeting or orally thereat.

(3) The by-laws of a credit union may make provision in respect of the expulsion of members therefrom.

Cessation of membership.

19. Subject to this Ordinance, a member of a credit union who transfers or withdraws all his shares therein or who is expelled there-

from shall, from the date of such transfer, withdrawal or expulsion, cease to be a member of the credit union.

Payment on cessation of membership.

20. (1) Subject to this section, any money owed in respect of shares by a credit union to a past member thereof shall, after deduction of any money owed by him to the credit union, be paid to him.

(2) A credit union may, if it thinks fit, postpone the payment of any money owed to a past member for not more than ninety days after his membership ends.

(3) No payment shall be made by a credit union to a past member unless all his liabilities to the credit union, whether as borrower, pledgor, guarantor or otherwise, have been fully discharged or otherwise fully provided for by a person other than the credit union.

Liability on cessation of membership.

21. A past member of a credit union shall have no further rights therein but shall not thereby be released from any remaining liability to the credit union.

Debts owed by members or past members.

22. (1) Any money owed to a credit union by a member or a past member shall be a civil debt and recoverable as such in a court of competent jurisdiction.

(2) A credit union shall have a lien on the shares of a member for any debt owed to it by him, and may set off any sum standing to the credit of such member in the accounts of the credit union towards the payment of such debt.

Payment to nominee or person entitled upon death of member.

23. (1) Subject to this section, any money owed in respect of shares by a credit union to a member thereof who dies shall be paid to the person nominated in accordance with this section, or, if there is no person so nominated, to such person as may appear to the board, on such evidence as it deems satisfactory, to be entitled by law to receive the same, after deducting such amounts as may be owed by the deceased member to the credit union.

(2) A member of a credit union over the age of sixteen years may in writing, signed by him in the presence of two attesting witnesses and deposited during his lifetime with the treasurer of the credit union, nominate any person (hereinafter in this section referred to as a nominee) to receive in the event of his death any money owed to him in respect of shares by the credit union.

(3) A member of a credit union shall be entitled to appoint only one nominee unless he holds more than one share.

(4) If more than one nominee is appointed by a member the exact proportion of the amount available which is to be payable to each nominee shall be specified at the time of nomination.

(5) If any payment is made under this section to a nominee who is a minor, a receipt given either by the minor or by his guardian shall be sufficient discharge to the credit union.

Record of members and shares.

24. A record of members and shares shall be kept by every credit union and shall contain and be *prima facie* evidence of—

*(a)* the name, address and occupation of each member;
*(b)* the number of shares (with the dates of allotment thereof) held by each member;
*(c)* the total number of shares and the amount paid up in respect thereof;
*(d)* the date on which each member was admitted to membership;
*(e)* the date on which a member ceased to be such;
*(f)* every appointment of a nominee under section 23.

## PART IV. MEETINGS AND ELECTION OF BOARD AND COMMITTEES

Annual and special meetings.

25. (1) There shall be an annual meeting of the members of a credit union within sixty days after the end of the financial year within which the first meeting of the credit union is held pursuant to section 27 and thereafter within sixty days after the end of each subsequent financial year.

(2) Subject to this Ordinance, special meetings of the members may be called at the times and in the manner provided in the by-laws.

(3) Where in any case, due to the nature of the common occupation or employment of the persons forming a credit union, it is not practicable for all the members thereof to be present at the same instance at its annual or special meetings, substitute meetings of members may be held on two separate occasions in the manner provided in the by-laws, and meetings so held shall together be deemed to be annual or special meetings, whichever is appropriate.

(4) Subject to section 26, the voting and the procedure at annual and special meetings shall be in accordance with the by-laws.

Voting.

26. (1) No member shall have more than one vote at any annual or special meeting and no voting by proxy shall be allowed thereat.

(2) Voting at an election of members to the board, the supervisory committee or the credit committee of a credit union shall be by secret ballot.

First meeting.

27. (1) The provisional secretary of a credit union shall, within ten days after the receipt by him of the certificate of registration issued in accordance with section 5, notify each of the members of the credit union that he has received it and shall summon the first meeting of the members, which shall be held within fourteen days of the date of his receipt of the certificate.

(2) For the purposes of subsection (1), the body of persons which has been registered as a credit union under section 5 shall be deemed to be the members of the credit union.

Election and tenure of office of board of directors and committees.

28. (1) At its first meeting after registration, a credit union shall elect from among its members—

*(a)* a board consisting of five directors or of such greater number, not exceeding fifteen, as may be provided in the by-laws;
*(b)* a supervisory committee consisting of three members; and
*(c)* a credit committee consisting of three members.

(2) At the annual meeting in every subsequent financial year there shall retire from office the number nearest one-third of the directors, one member of the supervisory committee and one member of the credit committee.

(3) The directors and committee members who shall retire in any year shall be those who have been longest in office since their last election; as between persons who became directors or committee members on the same day, those who shall retire shall (unless they otherwise agree among themselves) be determined by lot.

(4) A retiring director or committee member shall be eligible for re-election.

(5) At the annual meeting at which a director or committee member retires under subsection (2) the credit union shall fill the vacated office by electing a person thereto from among its members.

(6) Any vacancy occurring—

*(a)* on the board or the credit committee, shall be filled by appointment by the board within fourteen days of the occurrence of such vacancy; or
*(b)* on the supervisory committee, shall be filled by appointment by

that committee within fourteen days of the occurrence of such vacancy.

(7) Where an appointment is made under subsection (6) other than for the purpose of filling a temporary vacancy caused through illness, absence from the Colony or any other cause, the person so appointed shall retire at the same time as if he had become a director or committee member, as the case may be, on the day on which the person in whose place he is appointed was last elected.

Meetings of board and committees, and appointment of officers and procedure.

29. (1) Immediately following its election the board shall hold its first meeting and thereat shall appoint from among its members a president, a vice-president, a treasurer and a secretary:

Provided that the board may appoint one person to perform the functions of both treasurer and secretary.

(2) The supervisory committee and the credit committee shall hold their first meetings immediately after election and shall appoint for each committee—

*(a)* a chairman, who shall preside at the meetings of the committee; and

*(b)* a secretary.

(3) Subsequent meetings of the board and of each committee shall be held at least once in every month and at such other times as may be considered necessary by the president, in the case of the board, or by the chairman, in the case of each committee, or as may be provided in the by-laws.

(4) If the president and vice-president are both absent from any meeting of the board, the members present may appoint one of themselves to preside at the meeting.

(5) If the chairman is absent from any meeting of the supervisory committee or the credit committee, the members present may appoint one of themselves to preside at the meeting.

(6) The number of members which shall constitute a quorum at a meeting of the board, the credit committee or the supervisory committee shall be as provided by the by-laws.

Officers of a credit union.

30. The persons for the time being appointed to the offices referred to in section 29 shall be the officers of the credit union concerned.

Composition of the committees.

31. (1) No member of the supervisory committee may be a director of the board or a member of the credit committee.

(2) Neither the president nor the treasurer of the board nor more than one director of a credit union may be a member of the credit committee thereof.

Remuneration.

32. No director or member of either committee of a credit union shall, as such, receive remuneration from that credit union:

Provided that the treasurer may be paid such remuneration as may be determined at an annual meeting of the credit union.

## PART V. MANAGEMENT

### POWERS AND DUTIES OF BOARD

Powers and duties of the board.

33. (1) The board of a credit union shall have the general management of the affairs, funds and records of the credit union and, except where a contrary intention appears, shall exercise and perform all the powers and duties conferred and imposed by this Ordinance and in particular shall—

*(a)* act and make decisions upon all applications for membership of the credit union;

*(b)* determine the maximum number of shares which may be held by any one member, which shall not without the permission of the board exceed twenty *per cent* of the shares of the credit union and which shall apply to all members;

*(c)* determine the length of notice (which shall not exceed ninety days) required from a member of his intention to transfer or withdraw shares;

*(d)* determine the maximum length of time in respect of which loans made by the credit union to its members may remain outstanding, in whole or in part;

*(e)* subject to subsection (2) of section 40, determine the maximum amount of loans which may be made to a member, with security or without security;

*(f)* subject to section 41, determine the rates of interest payable during any specified period on such loans;

*(g)* fix from time to time the amount of any surety bond which shall be required in respect of any officer or member concerned with the receipt, management or expenditure of money for or on behalf of the credit union, and for such purposes may authorize the payment of any premium on such bonds by the credit union;

*(h)* appoint persons to act, under the direction of the board, in the furtherance of the education of persons in the objects and practices of credit unions.

(2) The board shall exercise and perform such other powers and duties as may be conferred or imposed upon it by the by-laws.

POWERS AND DUTIES OF SUPERVISORY COMMITTEE

34. In addition to such powers and duties as may be conferred or imposed by the by-laws, the supervisory committee— Powers and duties of supervisory committee.

(*a*) shall carry out an examination of the affairs and audit the accounts of the credit union and prepare a balance sheet on the accounts at least once in each quarter of every financial year;

(*b*) shall make or provide for an annual audit of the accounts of the credit union and submit a report thereon together with a balance sheet to the annual meeting of the credit union for its approval;

(*c*) may, if it deems it to be necessary in the interests of the credit union, by the unanimous vote of all its members suspend any director of the board or any member of the credit committee from the functions of his office and call a special meeting of the credit union to consider a report of the committee on such suspension;

(*d*) may call a special meeting of the credit union to consider any matter which in the opinion of the committee ought to receive such consideration.

POWERS AND DUTIES OF CREDIT COMMITTEE

35. In addition to such powers and duties as may be conferred or imposed by the by-laws, the credit committee shall have general supervision over all loans made to the members of the credit union and, subject to paragraphs (*d*), (*e*) and (*f*) of subsection (1) of section 33, shall, in respect of every such loan— Powers and duties of credit committee.

(*a*) fix the amount thereof;

(*b*) decide on the security (if any) required therefor; and

(*c*) determine the conditions for repayment thereof.

36. Save as provided in section 38, no loan shall be made to a member of the credit union except with the prior and unanimous approval of the members of the credit committee. Approval of loans.

37. In addition to or in lieu of any other form of security, the credit committee may in its discretion accept an endorsement of a note by a member as guarantor or a pledge of shares by a member as security for a loan. Acceptable security for loans.

Loan officers.

38. (1) The credit committee, with the prior approval of the board, may appoint members of the credit committee as loan officers to act under the committee's supervision.

(2) Notwithstanding anything contained in section 36, a loan officer may make loans to members of the credit union in the manner provided in the by-laws.

## PART VI. LOANS, BORROWING, RESERVE FUND AND DIVIDENDS

### LOANS TO MEMBERS

Purposes of loans.

39. No loan shall be made to a member of a credit union under this Ordinance other than for provident or productive purposes.

Restrictions on loans.

40. (1) Save as is provided in paragraphs (*a*) and (*b*) of section 10, no credit union shall make a loan to any person who is not a member thereof.

(2) A loan shall not be made by a credit union to a member thereof if this would cause the member to owe the credit union more than ten *per cent* of the aggregate amount of the share balance, the reserve fund and any other funds of the credit union.

Rates of interest.

41. (1) The interest rate on any loan made by a credit union to a member thereof shall not exceed one *per cent* per month on the total of the unpaid balance of any such loan plus all charges (if any) made by the credit union in making the loan.

(2) The interest rate determined in respect of loans made to members of a credit union during any specified period shall be the same for all such loans.

Unanimous vote required for loans to directors or committee members.

42. No director or member of the supervisory committee or the credit committee may obtain a loan from the credit union in excess of the value of his shares except upon the unanimous vote of a majority of the board, the supervisory committee and the credit committee, sitting together, such director or member not being present at the taking of the vote.

### BORROWING POWERS

Borrowing powers.

43. (1) Subject to this section, a credit union may borrow money for the carrying out of its objects.

(2) No money shall be borrowed by a credit union save upon a resolution of its board.

(3) A credit union may not borrow money so that its total indebtedness would in consequence exceed fifty *per cent* of its share balance.

(4) A credit union may not borrow money so that its total indebtedness would in consequence exceed twenty-five *per cent* of its share balance, except in addition to the board's resolution, upon a resolution passed by not less than three-fourths of the members, present and qualified to vote, at a special meeting of the credit union called for the purpose or if sanctioned in writing by not less than two-thirds of the total number of the members of the credit union qualified to vote.

44. A credit union may mortgage, charge or pledge any of its property to secure any liability for the repayment of money borrowed in accordance with section 43. Power to mortgage, etc. as security for borrowed money.

RESERVE FUND

45. (1) The board shall set aside a reserve fund, into which shall be paid— Reserve fund.

*(a)* all entrance fees and fines collected from members; and

*(b)* during each financial year, not less than twenty *per cent* of the net earnings for the previous financial year, before the declaration or payment of any dividend in relation to the previous financial year,

until the reserve fund is equal to at least ten *per cent* of the share balance of the credit union, and such further amounts of the net earnings shall be paid into the fund in every year as may be necessary to maintain that percentage.

(2) The reserve fund shall not be used in making loans to members of the credit union.

(3) Any income received from any part of the reserve fund which is deposited or invested shall be paid to the general revenue of the credit union.

(4) The reserve fund shall be kept as a reserve against losses incurred from loans made by the credit union which remain outstanding after the time for their repayment in full has expired and other losses, other than excess expenditure over income, incurred by the credit union, and shall not be used for any other purpose except upon the

winding-up of the credit union or with the prior approval in writing of the Registrar:

Provided that during the twelve months next following the date of its registration, an amount not exceeding the total of the entrance fees collected from members may be drawn from the reserve fund to meet any expenses incurred in the formation and organization of a credit union.

### DIVIDENDS

Declaration, limit and payment of dividend.

46. (1) After provision is made for the reserve fund, in accordance with section 45, and before the holding of the annual meeting of the credit union for that year, the board may by resolution recommend that a dividend, not exceeding six *per cent* per annum, shall be paid from the remainder of the net earnings and shall present any such resolution to that annual meeting.

(2) The annual meeting may declare a dividend for that year, which shall not exceed the amount recommended by the board.

(3) A dividend so declared shall be paid on all shares fully paid up and registered in the name of the same member throughout the previous financial year:

Provided that a member who is registered as owner at the end of a financial year of shares which became fully paid up during that year shall be entitled to the proportional part of such dividend calculated from the fifth day of the month following the date upon which such shares became fully paid up.

(4) Subject to subsection (3), payment of the dividend (if any) so declared may be made in such manner and amounts and at such times as may be provided in the by-laws.

## PART VII. BY-LAWS

By-laws.

47. (1) The by-laws of every credit union shall be in a form approved by the Registrar.

(2) The by-laws of a credit union may, and, if so directed by the Registrar, shall, include provision for all or any of the following—

(*a*) the depositing of all or any specified funds or money of a credit union in a bank in the Colony approved by the Registrar;

(*b*) the imposition of charges on any member whose account remains inactive for a specified period;

*(c)* the imposition of fines upon members for failure to meet their obligations to the credit union;

*(d)* specifying the purposes for which the profits of the credit union may be used.

(3) Any by-laws which are prescribed under paragraph *(a)* of section 85 shall, subject to such modification as may be approved by the Registrar, be deemed to be the by-laws of a credit union.

(4) Notwithstanding anything contained in section 20 of the Interpretation and General Clauses Ordinance, it shall not be necessary to publish the by-laws of a credit union in the *Gazette.*

Amendment of by-laws.

48. (1) By-laws may be amended only by a resolution of two-thirds of the members present and qualified to vote, at the annual meeting of the credit union or at a special meeting thereof called for the purpose.

(2) No such amendment shall be of any effect until the same has been approved in writing by the Registrar.

Binding effect of the by-laws.

49. The by-laws of a credit union shall bind the credit union and the members thereof to the same extent as if each member had subscribed his name and affixed his seal thereto and there were in such by-laws a covenant on the part of himself, his executors, administrators and assigns to conform to such by-laws, subject to the provisions of this Ordinance.

## PART VIII. RETURNS, AUDIT, INFORMATION AND INQUIRY

Return of names of officers.

50. A record of the name, occupation and address of each officer of a credit union shall be furnished to the Registrar not later than ten days after the appointment of the officer.

Return of supervisory annual audit.

51. A copy of the audit report and balance sheet, submitted to the annual meeting in accordance with paragraph *(b)* of section 34 and approved thereat, shall be furnished to the Registrar not later than thirty days after the date of such meeting.

Registrar's annual examination.

52. (1) The accounts of a credit union shall be examined at least once in every year by or under the direction of the Registrar and a credit union undergoing such examination shall produce all cash in hand, books, records and other documents required by the person conducting the examination.

(2) Every such examination shall include an inquiry into overdue debts (if any) and a valuation of the assets and liabilities of the credit union.

(3) A copy of the report of the last examination carried out under this section and a copy of the audit report and balance sheet referred to in section 51 shall be posted in a conspicuous place at the registered office of the credit union for not less than one month.

Information for Registrar and verification thereof.

53. (1) A credit union shall furnish the Registrar with such statements with respect to its business, finances and other affairs and with such other information as he may from time to time require.

(2) Any statement and other information and any record and report required to be furnished by a credit union to the Registrar under this Ordinance or the by-laws shall be certified by the supervisory committee and verified by the president and the treasurer of the credit union.

Inquiry, examination and suspension.

54. (1) The Registrar and any person authorized by him may inquire into the condition and affairs of a credit union and for this purpose shall be given access to all books, records and other documents of the credit union and may make such inquiries as are in his opinion necessary to ascertain its financial condition, its ability to provide for the payment of its liabilities as they become due and whether or not it has complied with this Ordinance.

(2) The Registrar may, if he is satisfied, from an inquiry into the condition and affairs of a credit union, that any of its funds, securities or other property may have been misappropriated or improperly used or that the books, records or other documents do not show its true financial position, appoint an auditor to make such inquiry and audit of the affairs of the credit union as the Registrar considers necessary.

(3) The Registrar may, after an inquiry under this section, if he is satisfied that the continuance in business of such credit union would not be in the interests of its members or of the public, order the credit union to suspend business for such time as he may decide.

## PART IX. WINDING-UP

Winding-up of credit unions.

55. No credit union shall be wound up otherwise than in accordance with this Part.

56. (1) Save as is otherwise provided in this Part, the provisions of the Companies Ordinance relating to the winding-up of a company shall, to the extent that such provisions are applicable in the case, apply to the winding-up of a credit union.

Application of Companies Ordinance.

(2) For the purposes of such winding-up, the term "Registrar" in the Companies Ordinance shall have the meaning assigned to it by this Ordinance.

(3) The Colonial Secretary shall appoint a person to discharge the duties of Official Receiver in any such winding-up.

57. (1) Subject to this section, a credit union may—

Credit union may resolve to be wound up by the court.

*(a)* by instrument in writing signed by three-quarters of its members qualified to vote at its meetings; or

*(b)* by resolution passed by three-quarters of its members qualified to vote and voting at a special meeting called for the purpose,

resolve that it be wound up by the court.

(2) Every credit union shall give at least ten days prior notice in writing to the Registrar of its intention to issue any such instrument for the signature of its members or to hold any such meeting, as the case may be.

(3) Where a credit union resolves under subsection (1) that it be wound up by the court, a copy of the instrument or a record of the resolution, certified by the president and treasurer of the credit union, shall be delivered forthwith to the Registrar who shall, as soon as practicable thereafter, petition the court for an order to wind up the credit union.

58. (1) The Registrar may, if he thinks fit, petition the court for an order to wind up a credit union if he is satisfied that—

Petition by Registrar for winding-up in other cases.

*(a)* the number of members qualified to vote at meetings of the credit union has been reduced to less than fifteen;

*(b)* the registration of the credit union was obtained by fraud or mistake;

*(c)* it is not a *bona fide* credit union;

*(d)* it exists for an illegal purpose;

*(e)* it is not carrying on business or is not in operation; or

*(f)* it has wilfully, after notice from the Registrar, contravened any of the provisions of this Ordinance.

(2) The Registrar may, if he thinks fit, give notice to a credit union of his intention to petition the court under this section, setting out the

grounds therefor and stating that, unless cause is shown to the contrary within a specified period, he will petition the court accordingly.

(3) The Registrar may, if he has given notice under subsection (2), and unless in his opinion sufficient cause to the contrary is shown by the credit union within the specified period, proceed with the petition.

No deposit required on winding-up.

59. Notwithstanding any requirement in any rules made under the Companies Ordinance relating to the winding-up of companies, no deposit with the Official Receiver shall be required in respect of a petition under section 57 or 58.

Winding-up for insolvency or on equitable grounds.

60. Notwithstanding anything contained in section 58, a credit union may be wound up by the court if—

(*a*) the credit union is unable to pay its debts;

(*b*) the court is of opinion that it is just and equitable that the credit union should be wound up.

Qualification as to contribution in winding-up.

61. In its application to the winding-up of a credit union subsection (1) of section 170 of the Companies Ordinance shall be so construed that a person shall be deemed to have ceased to be a member of the credit union, in respect of any share validly withdrawn or transferred before the commencement of the winding-up, with effect from the date of the receipt by the board of the notice of intention to withdraw or transfer such share.

## PART X. APPEALS

Appeal against action of Registrar.

62. (1) If the Registrar—

(*a*) refuses to register a credit union under section 5;

(*b*) fails to register a credit union within thirty days of the receipt of a memorandum of association duly filed for the purpose;

(*c*) refuses or fails to give his approval, within thirty days of the receipt, of any written application therefor, when his approval is required for any purpose under this Ordinance;

(*d*) under section 54, orders a credit union to suspend business,

any person aggrieved thereby may, subject to this section, appeal against such refusal, failure or order to the District Court.

(2) An appeal under this section shall be entered within fourteen days—

(*a*) after the date of any refusal to register or of any suspension order, in the case of an appeal under paragraph *(a)* or *(d)* of subsection (1); or

*(b)* after the date of the expiry of the period of thirty days mentioned therein, in the case of an appeal under paragraph *(b)* or *(c)* of subsection (1).

(3) The decision of the District Court on any such appeal shall be final.

## PART XI. THE CREDIT UNION LEAGUE OF HONG KONG

63. (1) The body known as the Credit Union League of Hong Kong (hereinafter in this Part referred to as the former League) shall, on the date of commencement of this Ordinance, become a body corporate with perpetual succession and shall be capable of suing and being sued in the name of the Credit Union League of Hong Kong and, subject to this Ordinance, of doing and suffering all such other acts and things as bodies corporate may lawfully do and suffer. Incorporation of league of credit unions.

(2) The League shall have and may use a common seal.

64. The objects of the League are— Objects of League.

*(a)* to protect and assist the credit unions which are members of the League;
*(b)* to provide educational and advisory services for credit unions;
*(c)* to encourage and assist in the organization of credit unions;
*(d)* to arrange for bonds and insurance on behalf of credit unions and their employees;
*(e)* to set up a stabilization fund in accordance with section 72;
*(f)* to undertake such other services for credit unions and the credit union movement as shall be consistent with this Ordinance.

65. On the date of commencement of this Ordinance— Vesting.

*(a)* all movable property vested before that date in any person in trust for the former League shall vest in the League;
*(b)* all liabilities lawfully incurred before that date by any person as trustee of the former League shall become liabilities of the League; and
*(c)* all legal proceedings pending by or against any such trustee may be prosecuted by or against the League.

66. (1) There shall be a board of the League consisting of five directors or of such greater number not exceeding fifteen as may be provided by the by-laws of the League. Board of directors and officers.

(2) The first board of directors shall consist of the persons—

Schedule.

(a) whose names appear in the first column of the Schedule [2];

(b) whose residential addresses are specified in the second column of the Schedule; and

(c) each of whom shall hold the office, if any, specified opposite each name in the third column of the Schedule.

(3) The first directors of the board shall hold office until either a board of directors is elected in accordance with the by-laws of the League or the 1st day of July 1970, whichever is the earlier.

(4) The board of the League shall have the general direction and management of the affairs, funds and records of the League.

League by-laws.

67. (1) The League may make by-laws, which shall be subject to the approval of the Registrar, for the carrying out of its objects.

(2) Such by-laws shall be consistent with this Ordinance and shall include provision for membership of the League and for the composition of and elections to the board.

(3) Notwithstanding anything contained in subsection (1), any by-laws which are prescribed under paragraph (a) of section 85 shall, subject to such modification as may be approved by the Registrar, be deemed to be the by-laws of the League.

(4) The by-laws of the League may, subject to the approval of the Registrar, be amended from time to time in the manner provided therein.

(5) Notwithstanding anything contained in section 20 of the Interpretation and General Clauses Ordinance, it shall not be necessary to publish the by-laws of the League in the *Gazette*.

Registration with Registrar.

68. (1) The League shall forward to the Registrar for registration the following—

(a) notice of the address of the principal office of the League and any change thereof;

(b) a copy of the by-laws of the League and any amendment thereto, certified as correct by two members of the board of the League; and

(c) a list of the name, occupation and address of each member of the board and each officer of the League and any change therein, certified as correct by two members of the board of the League.

[2] The Schedule is omitted from this volume.

(2) A document required to be registered under subsection (1) shall be forwarded to the Registrar within twenty-eight days of the commencement of this Ordinance or within twenty-eight days of any change or amendment, as the case may be.

**Sealing and signing of documents.**

69. (1) The common seal of the League shall not be affixed to any instrument except by the authority of a resolution of the board and in the presence of the president of the board and either the treasurer thereof or such other person as the board may appoint for the purpose.

(2) The president and the treasurer, or such other person, shall sign every instrument to which the seal is so affixed.

(3) The board shall be responsible for the safe custody of the common seal of the League.

**Membership.**

70. Subject to this Part, a credit union may become a member of the League.

**Levy.**

71. (1) A credit union which is a member of the League may, for the purpose of financing the League, provide in its by-laws for a yearly levy on each of its members.

(2) The amount of such levy and the time and manner of payment thereof to the League shall be as provided in the by-laws of the League.

**Stabilization fund.**

72. (1) The League may set up a fund, to be known as the stabilization fund, which shall be used in the manner set out in this section and shall not be used in any other manner except with the prior approval in writing of the Registrar.

(2) The stabilization fund may be used in providing interest free loans to a member credit union for the purpose of avoiding a liquidation thereof or for assisting in any matter connected with such liquidation.

(3) No such loan shall be provided except—

*(a)* where the League is satisfied that such provision is in the best interests of the credit union movement; and

*(b)* on a resolution, passed by at least two-thirds of the members of the board of the League, determining the amount of the loan and the conditions under which it is to be provided.

(4) Section 43 shall not apply in respect of any such loan.

**Borrowing powers.**

72A. (1) Subject to this section, the League may borrow money for the carrying out of its objects.

(2) No money shall be borrowed by the League save upon a resolution of its board.

(3) The League may not borrow money so that its total indebtedness would in consequence exceed fifty *per cent* of its total assets.

(4) The League may not borrow money, so that its total indebtedness would in consequence exceed twenty-five *per cent* of its total assets, except in addition to the board's resolution, upon a resolution passed by not less than three-fourths of the members, present and qualified to vote, at a special meeting of the League called for the purpose or if sanctioned in writing by not less than two-thirds of the total number of the members of the League qualified to vote.

(5) In this section "total assets" does not include the stabilization fund set up under section 72.

Power to mortgage etc. as security for borrowed money.

**72B.** The League may mortgage, charge or pledge any of its property to secure any liability for the repayment of money borrowed in accordance with section 72A.

Application of other sections to League.

73. Save in so far as is otherwise provided in this Part, sections 10, 49, 52, 53, 54, 76, 77, 80 and 81 shall, to the extent that they are applicable, apply to the League as though it were a credit union.

Saving.

74. Nothing in this Part shall affect or be deemed to affect the rights of Her Majesty the Queen, Her Heirs or Successors, or the rights of any body politic or corporate or of any other persons except such as are mentioned in this Part and those claiming by, from or under them.

## PART XII. OFFENCES AND PENALTIES

Illegal loans.

75. (1) Save as is provided in paragraphs *(a)* and *(b)* of section 10, any director or any member of the supervisory committee or of the credit committee of a credit union, or any loan officer thereof, who knowingly makes or permits the making of a loan from any fund of the credit union to any person who is not a member of the credit union shall be guilty of an offence and shall be liable on conviction to a fine of three thousand dollars and to imprisonment for one year.

(2) A person who is convicted of an offence under subsection (1) shall be liable to the credit union for the amount so loaned, and the illegality of such a loan shall be no defence in any proceedings by the credit union for the recovery of that amount.

76. Any person who makes any return or furnishes any information, statement, record, or other document required by this Ordinance to be made or furnished to the Registrar knowing the same to be in any respect false or insufficient shall be guilty of an offence.

False returns to Registrar.

77. Any officer of a credit union, or any person entrusted with or participating in the management thereof, who discloses to any person any information regarding a transaction of a member of that credit union therewith, save in so far as may be necessary for the proper conduct of the business of that credit union, shall be guilty of an offence.

Prohibition of disclosure of certain information.

78. Any person who—

(*a*) contravenes the provisions of subsection (2) of section 57; or

(*b*) being a president or treasurer of a credit union, fails to deliver to the Registrar a copy of the instrument or record of the resolution in accordance with subsection (3) of section 57,

shall be guilty of an offence.

Failure to report resolution for winding-up.

79. Any person, other than a credit union or the League, who trades or carries on any business under any name or title of which the expression "credit union", or the Chinese expression "儲蓄互助社", is part shall be guilty of an offence:

Provided that nothing in this section shall apply to the use by any person or his successors in interest of any name or title under which he traded or carried on business at the commencement of this Ordinance.

Restriction on use of expression "credit union" or in Chinese "儲蓄互助社".

80. Any person guilty of an offence against this Ordinance for which no penalty is provided shall be liable on conviction to a fine of two thousand dollars and, in the case of a continuing offence, to an additional daily penalty of fifty dollars.

Penalty.

81. Every offence committed by a credit union shall be deemed to have been also committed by each officer of the credit union who is bound by this Ordinance or the by-laws of the credit union to fulfill the duties whereof such an offence is a breach or, if there is no such officer, then by each of the directors and members of the supervisory committee and credit committee, unless such officer, director or member is proved to have been ignorant of, or to have attempted to prevent, the commission of such offence.

Criminal liability of officers of credit union.

## PART XIII. REGISTRAR

Appointment of Registrar.

82. (1) The Governor may appoint a public officer to be the Registrar of Credit Unions and may appoint other public officers to assist the Registrar.

(2) The Registrar may delegate to any public officer appointed to assist him under subsection (1) all or any of the powers and duties conferred or imposed on him by this Ordinance.

Register of Credit Unions to be kept.

83. (1) The Registrar shall keep at his office a register, to be known as the Register of Credit Unions, in which shall be entered particulars of the registration of every credit union.

(2) The Registrar shall keep such other records relating to credit unions as may be prescribed.

Forms of records, etc.

84. A credit union shall keep accounts, balance sheets, forms, records and books in such form as may be approved by the Registrar.

## PART XIV. REGULATIONS

Regulations.

85. The Governor in Council may make regulations for all or any of the following matters—

*(a)* the adoption by all or some credit unions or the League of such by-laws as may be prescribed hereunder;
*(b)* the procedure to be followed under this Ordinance;
*(c)* the examination of the accounts of credit unions by the Registrar or under his direction;
*(d)* the qualifications required of any person carrying out an audit under subsection (2) of section 54;
*(e)* the fees payable on the registration of a credit union under this Ordinance;
*(f)* the scale of fees payable to the Registrar for services rendered under this Ordinance;
*(g)* the form of a memorandum of association required under subsection (2) of section 4 and of a certificate of registration issued under subsection (3) of section 5;
*(h)* the records relating to credit unions which are to be kept by the Registrar;
*(i)* prescribing anything which is to be or may be prescribed under this Ordinance;

*(j)* any other matter necessary or expedient to carry out effectively the intent and purpose of this Ordinance.

*{The Schedule is omitted from this volume.}*

## Chit-Fund Businesses (Prohibition) Ordinance[1]

To prohibit chit-fund businesses and to make provision for other connected purposes.

[12th May, 1972]

1. This Ordinance may be cited as the Chit-Fund Businesses (Prohibition) Ordinance. Short title.

2. In this Ordinance, unless the context otherwise requires— Interpretation

"chit-fund" means a scheme or arrangement, whether known as chit-fund or *"hwei"* or by any other name, whereby or as part of which the participants subscribe periodically or otherwise to a common fund and that common fund is put up for sale or payment to the participants by auction, tender, bid, ballot or otherwise;

"operate" includes manage, form, conduct, organize, advertise and aid, assist or take part in operating;

"Registrar" means the Registrar of Companies.

3. (1) Subject to section 5 and to subsection (2), any person who operates a chit-fund shall be guilty of an offence and shall be liable on conviction to a fine of 10,000 dollars and to imprisonment for 3 years. Chit-fund business an offence.

(2) Notwithstanding subsection (1), if an offence is committed under this section by reason only of the breach of one or both of paragraphs *(a)* and *(c)* of section 5(2), the offender shall be liable to a fine of 1,000 dollars and to imprisonment for one year.

[1] *Laws of Hong Kong,* Cap. 262 (1972). Originally No. 29 of 1972.

Continuation of chit-funds upon filing of particulars.

4. (1) Subject to subsection (2) a person who was operating a chit-fund on the 1st December 1971, other than a chit-fund operated in accordance with section 5(2), may continue its operation until completion of the chit-fund or until the 31st December 1973, whichever is the earlier, if, within 30 days after the commencement of this Ordinance and upon payment of a fee of 5 dollars, he files with the Registrar in the form set out in the Schedule [2] the particulars required thereby.

Schedule.

(2) Subsection (1) shall not apply in a case where the particulars filed—

(*a*) are in any respect incomplete;
(*b*) are false or misleading;
(*c*) do not adequately identify the chit-fund to which they refer.

(3) Any person who files false or misleading particulars under this section shall be guilty of an offence and shall be liable on conviction to a fine of 10,000 dollars and to imprisonment for 3 years.

(4) A form filed under this section shall be available for inspection by any member of the public upon payment of a fee of 1 dollar.

Application of section 3.

5. (1) Section 3 shall not have effect—

(*a*) in respect of a chit-fund in operation on the 1st December 1971 until 30 days after the commencement of this Ordinance;
(*b*) in respect of a chit-fund continuing to operate by virtue of section 4(1);
(*c*) in respect of a chit-fund operated in accordance with subsection (2).

(2) A chit-fund may be operated if—

(*a*) there are not more than 30 participants;
(*b*) the operator is not at the same time operating another chit-fund;
(*c*) the common fund put up for sale or payment to the participants does not exceed 10,000 dollars; and
(*d*) no benefit accrues to the operator other than a right to receive the first subscription free of interest.

(3) Notwithstanding anything contained in this section any person who advertises a chit-fund, whether in a newspaper or by any other means, shall be guilty of an offence and shall be liable to a fine of 10,000 dollars and to imprisonment for 3 years.

Prohibition on registration of chit-fund companies.

6. A company which has as its object or as one of its objects the operation of chit-funds shall not be registered under the Companies Ordinance after the commencement of this Ordinance.

---

[2] The Schedule is omitted from this volume.

Alternatives open to registered chit-fund companies.

7. (1) Subject to subsection (2), a registered company which has as its object or one of its objects the operation of chit-funds shall within 90 days after the commencement of this Ordinance—

*(a)* amend its memorandum and articles of association in accordance with sections 8(1) and 13(1) of the Companies Ordinance so as to delete all references to the operation of chit-funds, and, if necessary, change its name in accordance with section 22(1) of the Companies Ordinance so as to delete any reference therein to chit-funds; or

*(b)* pass a resolution that it be wound up voluntarily in accordance with section 228(1)*(b)* of the Companies Ordinance; or

*(c)* pass a resolution that it be wound up by the court in accordance with section 177*(a)* of the Companies Ordinance and present a petition to that effect under section 179(1) of that Ordinance.

(2) In the case of a registered company continuing to operate a chit-fund by virtue of section 4(1), the period of 90 days specified in subsection (1) of this section shall run from the last day of operation of the fund.

Striking off of companies failing to comply with section 7.

8. (1) If a registered company—

*(a)* fails to comply with section 7; or

*(b)* having taken action under paragraph *(b)* or *(c)* of section 7(1), fails to proceed expeditiously in the opinion of the Registrar to complete its winding-up,

the company shall be deemed, for the purposes of section 291 of the Companies Ordinance, to have ceased to carry on business.

(2) Where a company is deemed under subsection (1) to have ceased to carry on business, the Registrar may, without complying with section 291(1) and (2) of the Companies Ordinance but after complying with section 291(3) of that Ordinance, strike the name of the company off the register under section 291(6) of that Ordinance.

(3) Save as provided in subsections (1) and (2), nothing in this section shall affect the application of the Companies Ordinance or the procedure prescribed thereby.

Liability of directors, managers, etc., under sections 3 and 4.

9. (1) If an offence under this Ordinance has been committed by a body of persons, whether corporate or unincorporate, any person who was, at the time of the offence, a director, partner, member, manager, secretary or principal officer of or employed by such body, or who was purporting to act in any such capacity, shall be guilty of a like offence.

(2) Where any person referred to in subsection (1) is charged with an offence under this Ordinance, it shall be a defence for him to prove that the offence was committed without his consent or connivance, and that he exercised such diligence to prevent the commission of the offence as he ought to have exercised having regard to the nature of his functions and to all other circumstances.

(3) Where the agent or servant of a person (hereinafter referred to in this section as "the principal") does or omits to do anything which, if done or omitted to be done by the principal, would constitute an offence under this Ordinance, then the agent or servant and the principal shall be deemed to have committed an offence and shall be liable to be proceeded against and punished accordingly.

(4) Where the principal is charged with an offence under this Ordinance, it shall be a defence for him to prove—

*(a)* that he did not ratify the act or omission complained of; and
*(b)* that the act or omission was not within the ordinary scope of the employment of the agent or servant,

but it shall be no defence that he had no knowledge of the act or omission.

Savings of rights and claims.

**10.** Nothing in this Ordinance shall prejudice the enforcement by any person of any right or claim against any person ceasing to carry on business or to operate chit-funds, by virtue of this Ordinance.

*{The Schedule is omitted from this volume.}*

## Securities Ordinance[1]

To establish a Securities Commission and a federation of stock exchanges, to make provision in relation to stock exchanges

[1] *Laws of Hong Kong,* Cap 333 (1978). Originally No. 12 of 1974. Relevant citations: L.N. 56/74; L.N. 140/74; Nos. 62 of 1976; 8 of 1978; and 47 of 1981. Additional citations: L.N. 39/74; L.N. 93/74; L.N. 107/74; L.N. 166/74; L.N. 197/74; L.N. 209/74; L.N. 247/74; L.N. 296/76; L.N. 8/78; and L.N. 92/80.

and dealers in securities, to control trading in securities and the business of advising on making investments, and to provide for the protection of investors and associated matters.

[For dates, see footnote 2, below.]

## PART I. PRELIMINARY MATTERS

1. This Ordinance may be cited as the Securities Ordinance. Short title.

2. (1) In this Ordinance, unless the context otherwise requires— Interpretation.

"auditor" means a professional accountant registered and holding a practising certificate under the Professional Accountants Ordinance;

"banker's books" means—

(*a*) books of a banker;

(*b*) cheques, orders for the payment of money, bills of exchange, and promissory notes in the possession of or under the control of a banker; and

(*c*) securities in the possession or under the control of a banker, whether by way of pledge or otherwise;

"books" includes accounts and deeds;

"business", in relation to a dealer, means the business of dealing in securities;

"certificate of registration" means a certificate of registration issued under Part VI;

"Commission" means the Securities Commission established under Part II;

"Commissioner" means the Commissioner for Securities appointed under section 6;

"committee", in relation to a stock exchange or a company seeking approval as a stock exchange, means the management committee, executive committee, or board of directors, by whatever name

[2] Parts I and II, March 1, 1974; Parts III and IV, June 1, 1974; Part V, October 11, 1974; Parts VI and VII, October 1, 1974; Part VIII, November 29, 1974; Part IX (except sec. 88), January 1, 1977; Part IX, sec. 88, December 30, 1977; Part X, August 19, 1974; Part XI, October 1, 1974; Part XII, secs. 135–139 and 141, March 6, 1974; Part XIIA, February 17, 1978; Part XIII, August 19, 1974.

it may be known, which is responsible for the day to day administration of the exchange or company, as the case may be;

"company" means a company as defined in section 2 of the Companies Ordinance, a company to which Part XI of that Ordinance applies, and any body corporate incorporated in Hong Kong having a share capital;

"constitution", in relation to a company, means the memorandum and articles of association of the company or other instrument providing the constitution of the company;

"corporate member" means a company which carries on a business of dealing in securities and is a member of a stock exchange;

"corporation" means any company or other body corporate formed or incorporated either in Hong Kong or elsewhere; but does not include—

*(a)* any body corporate that is incorporated in Hong Kong and is a public authority or an organ or agency of the Crown;
*(b)* any corporation sole;
*(c)* any credit union registered under the Credit Unions Ordinance;
*(d)* any corporation registered under the Multi-storey Buildings (Owners Incorporation) Ordinance;
*(e)* any corporation which has been exempted by regulations from the provisions of this Ordinance that affect corporations, or any corporation that belongs to a class of corporations that has been so exempted;

"Council" means the Council of the Federation constituted under Part IV;

"Court" means the High Court;

"dealer", subject to section 82(1), means a person who carries on a business of dealing in securities, whether he carries on any other business or not, and, in the case of a corporation which is a dealer, includes any director of the corporation who actively participates in, or is in any way directly responsible for the supervision of, the corporation's business of dealing in securities; but does not include—

*(a)* a solicitor or professional accountant whose carrying on business as a dealer is wholly incidental to the practice of his profession;
*(b)* except where specifically provided in this Ordinance, an exempt dealer;
*(c)* a person who carries on a business of dealing in securities only through a registered or exempt dealer;

"dealer's representative" means a person in the employment of, or acting for or by arrangement with, a dealer, not being an exempt dealer who performs for that dealer any of the functions of a dealer (other than work ordinarily performed by an accountant, clerk, or cashier) whether his remuneration is by way of salary, wages, commission, or otherwise, but, in the case of a corporation which is a dealer, does not include a director of the corporation;

"dealing in securities", in relation to any person (whether acting as principal or agent), subject to section 3, means making or offering to make an agreement with any other person, or inducing or attempting to induce any other person to enter into or offer to enter into any agreement—

*(a)* for or with a view to acquiring, disposing of, subscribing for or underwriting securities;

*(b)* the purpose or pretended purpose of which is to secure a profit to any of the parties from the yield of securities or by reference to fluctuations in the value of securities;

"defalcation" means a misapplication of money, securities, or other property;

"director" has the same meaning as in section 2 of the Companies Ordinance;

"Disciplinary Committee" means the Securities Commission Disciplinary Committee established under section 38;

"document" includes any register, books, record, tape recording, any form of computer input or output, and any other document or similar material (whether produced mechanically, electrically, or manually, or by any other means whatsoever);

"exempt dealer" means a person declared under section 60 to be an exempt dealer for the purposes of this Ordinance;

"exempt investment adviser" means a person declared under section 61 to be an exempt investment adviser for the purposes of this Ordinance;

"Federation" means the Hong Kong Federation of Stock Exchanges constituted under Part IV;

"financial year" means—

*(a)* in the case of a dealer, the period notified by him under section 87A or permitted by the Commissioner under that section;

*(b)* in any other case, a period of 12 months ending on the 31st March in any calendar year;

"foreign stock exchange" means a stock exchange which is permitted to operate in a country or territory outside Hong Kong by the law of that country or territory or, in the case of a country or territory which has no written law relating to stock exchanges, is not prevented from operating by the law of that country or territory;

"individual member" means a natural person who carries on a business of dealing in securities on his own account, and not as a partner of a member firm or as a director of a corporate member, and is a member of a stock exchange;

"investment adviser" means any person who—

*(a)* for direct remuneration carries on a business of advising other persons concerning securities;

*(b)* for direct remuneration as part of a regular business issues analyses or reports concerning securities; or

*(c)* for direct remuneration pursuant to a contract or arrangement with a client, undertakes on behalf of the client the management of a portfolio of securities, including the arranging of purchases, sales, or exchanges of securities through a dealer or exempt dealer,

and, in the case of a corporation which is an investment adviser, includes any director of the corporation who actively participates in, or is in any way directly responsible for the supervision of, the corporation's business as an investment adviser; but does not include—

(i) a licensed bank;

(ii) a solicitor or professional accountant whose carrying on business as an investment adviser is wholly incidental to the practice of his profession;

(iii) the proprietor or publisher of, or any contributor to, a *bona fide* newspaper, magazine, journal, or other periodical publication that is generally available to the public, otherwise than on subscription, who, only in that *bona fide* newspaper, magazine, journal, or periodical publication, advises other persons concerning securities, or issues analyses or reports concerning securities, not being the proprietor or publisher of, or a contributor to, a newspaper, journal, magazine, or other periodical publication whose principal or only object is to advise others concerning securities or to issue analyses or reports concerning securities;

(iv) a dealer or exempt dealer to the extent that his giving of investment advice is incidental to his carrying on business as a dealer or exempt dealer;

(v) a trustee company registered under Part VIII of the Trustee Ordinance;

(vi) an exempt investment adviser;

"investment representative" means a person in the employment of, or acting for or by arrangement with, an investment adviser, not being an exempt investment adviser, who performs for that investment adviser any of the functions of an investment adviser (other than work ordinarily performed by an accountant, clerk or cashier) whether his remuneration is by way of salary, wages, commission, or otherwise, but, in the case of a corporation which is an investment adviser, does not include a director of the corporation;

"issue" includes distribute and circulate;

"licensed bank" means a bank licensed under the Banking Ordinance to carry on banking business in Hong Kong;

"listing", in relation to a security, means the procedure whereby a security is listed on a stock exchange;

"member firm" means a firm which carries on a business of dealing in securities and is a member of a stock exchange;

"mutual fund corporation" means any corporation which is or holds itself out as being engaged primarily, or proposes to engage primarily, in the business of investing, reinvesting or trading in securities and which is offering for sale or has outstanding any redeemable shares of which it is the issuer;

"purchase", in relation to any securities, includes subscribing for those securities;

"registered", in relation to a dealer, dealer's representative, investment adviser, or investment representative, means registered under this Ordinance;

"registered company" means a company formed and registered under the Companies Ordinance;

"representative" means a dealer's representative or an investment representative;

"rules", in relation to a stock exchange, means the rules governing the conduct of the exchange or its members, by whatever name they may be called and wherever contained;

"securities" means any shares, stocks, debentures, loan stocks, funds, bonds, or notes of, or issued by, any body, whether incorporated or unincorporated, or of any government or local government authority; and includes—

*(a)* rights, options, or interests (whether described as units or otherwise) in or in respect of any of the foregoing;

*(b)* certificates of interest or participation in, or temporary or

interim certificates for, receipts for, or warrants to subscribe to or purchase, any of the foregoing; or

*(c)* any instruments commonly known as securities;

but does not include—

(i) any shares or debentures of any company which is a private company within the meaning of section 29 of the Companies Ordinance;

(ii) any interest arising under a partnership agreement or proposed partnership agreement (other than an agreement creating a limited partnership), unless the agreement or proposed agreement relates to an undertaking, scheme, enterprise, or investment contract promoted by or on behalf of a person whose ordinary business is or includes the promotion of similar undertakings, schemes, enterprises, or investment contracts, whether or not that person is, or is to become, a party to the agreement or proposed agreement, or unless the agreement is or would be an agreement, or is or would be within a class of agreements, prescribed by regulations for the purposes of this paragraph;

(iii) any negotiable receipt or other negotiable certificate or document evidencing the deposit of a sum of money, or any rights or interests arising under any such receipt, certificate, or document;

(iv) any bill of exchange within the meaning of section 3 or the Bills of Exchange Ordinance and any promissory note within the meaning of section 89 thereof;

(v) any debenture that specifically provides that it is not negotiable or transferable;

"share" means a share in the capital of a corporation; and includes the stock or any part of the stock of a corporation;

"stockbroker" means a dealer who is a member of a stock exchange, whether as an individual member, partner of a member firm, or director of a corporate member;

"stock exchange" or "exchange" means any company that is for the time being approved or deemed to be approved by the Commission under section 25;

"stock market" means a place where persons regularly meet together to negotiate sales and purchases of securities (including prices), or a place at which facilities are provided for bringing together sellers and purchasers of securities; but does not include the office of a stockbroker, or of a member firm or corporate member of a stock exchange;

"title" includes name or description;

"trust account" means a trust account established under section 84;

"underwriter" means a person who for remuneration undertakes to subscribe for or purchase on specified terms such specified securities as are offered to the public by a person issuing or selling those securities, but are not subscribed for or purchased by the public;

"unit trust" means any arrangement made for the purpose, or having the effect, of providing facilities for the participation by persons, as beneficiaries under a trust, in profits or income arising from the acquisition, holding, management or disposal of securities or any other property whatsoever.

(2) In this Ordinance a reference to securities of a corporation is a reference to securities—

*(a)* issued, made available, or granted by the corporation;

*(b)* proposed to be issued, made available, or granted by the corporation; or

*(c)* proposed to be issued, made available, or granted by the corporation when it is formed.

(3) In this Ordinance a security is regarded as listed on a stock exchange when the stock exchange has on the application of the company which issued the security, or on the application of any holder of the security, agreed to allow, subject to the requirements of this Ordinance, dealings in that security to take place on that exchange.

(4) A person shall not be treated as carrying on a business of dealing in securities by reason only of the fact that he is a member of a partnership which carries on such a business.

**Saving for certain transactions.**

3. (1) For the purpose of determining whether or not a person has dealt in securities or has communicated an offer to acquire or dispose of securities, no account shall be taken of his having (whether as principal or as agent)—

*(a)* effected any dealing through, or made an offer to acquire or dispose of securities to, a registered dealer or a registered dealer's representative, or an exempt dealer or an exempt dealer's representative;

*(b)* issued a prospectus which complies with, or is exempt from compliance with, Part II of the Companies Ordinance, or in the case of a company incorporated outside Hong Kong, complies with or is exempted from compliance with Part XII of that Ordinance;

*(c)* issued any document relating to securities of a corporation incor-

porated in Hong Kong that is not a registered company, being a document which—

(i) would if the corporation were a registered company be a prospectus to which section 38 of the Companies Ordinance applies, or would apply if not excluded by subsection (5)*(b)* of that section or by section 38A of that Ordinance; and

(ii) contains all the matters which, by virtue of Part XII of that Ordinance, it would be required to contain if the corporation were a company incorporated outside Hong Kong and the document were a prospectus issued by that company;

*(d)* issued a form of application for shares or debentures of a company, together with—

(i) a prospectus which complies with, or is exempt from compliance with, Part II of the Companies Ordinance or, in the case of a company incorporated outside Hong Kong, complies with or is exempt from compliance with Part XII of that Ordinance; or

(ii) in the case of a corporation incorporated in Hong Kong which is not a registered company, a document which contains the matters specified in paragraph *(c)*(ii);

*(e)* issued a prospectus which has been approved by the Commissioner in relation to a mutual fund corporation or unit trust authorized by the Commission under section 15;

*(f)* issued a form of application for the shares of a mutual fund corporation or the units of a unit trust, being a mutual fund corporation or unit trust which has been authorized by the Commission under section 15, together with a prospectus approved by the Commissioner;

or of his having as principal, acquired, subscribed for, or underwritten securities, or effected transactions with a person whose business involves the acquisition and disposal, or the holding, of securities (whether as principal or as agent).

(2) The Commissioner may, on application being made to him in that behalf, approve a prospectus for the purposes of subsection (1)*(e)*.

(3) Any approval under subsection (2) may be given subject to such conditions as the Commissioner thinks fit.

Definition of related corporation.

4. (1) Where a corporation—

*(a)* is the holding company of another corporation;

(*b*) is a subsidiary of another corporation; or

(*c*) is a subsidiary of the holding company of another corporation,

that first-mentioned corporation and that other corporation are, for the purposes of this Ordinance, deemed to be related to each other.

(2) For the purposes of subsection (1), a corporation shall, subject to subsection (3), be deemed to be a subsidiary of another corporation if—

(*a*) that other corporation—

(i) controls the composition of the board of directors of the first-mentioned corporation;

(ii) controls more than half of the voting power of the first-mentioned corporation; or

(iii) holds more than half of the issued share capital of the first-mentioned corporation (excluding any part which carries no right to participate beyond a specified amount on a distribution of either profits or capital); or

(*b*) the first-mentioned corporation is a subsidiary of any corporation which is that other corporation's subsidiary.

(3) For the purposes of subsection (2), the composition of a corporation's board of directors shall be deemed to be controlled by another corporation if that other corporation by the exercise, of some power exercisable by it, without the consent or concurrence of any other person, can appoint or remove all or a majority of the directors, and for the purposes of this provision, that other corporation shall be deemed to have power to appoint or remove a director if—

(*a*) a person cannot be appointed as a director without the exercise in his favour by that other corporation of such a power; or

(*b*) a person's appointment as a director follows necessarily from his being a director or other officer of that other corporation.

(4) In determining whether one corporation is a subsidiary of another corporation—

(*a*) any shares held by or power exercisable by that other corporation in a fiduciary capacity shall be treated as not held or exercisable by it;

(*b*) subject to paragraphs (*c*) and (*d*), any shares held or power exercisable—

(i) by any person as a nominee for that other corporation (except where that other corporation is concerned only in a fiduciary capacity); or

(ii) by, or by a nominee for, a subsidiary of that other corporation, not being a subsidiary which is concerned only in a fiduciary capacity,

shall be treated as exercisable by that other corporation;

(*c*) any shares held or power exercisable by any person by virtue of the provisions of any debenture of the first-mentioned corporation or of a trust deed for securing any issue of any such debenture shall be disregarded; and

(*d*) any shares held or power exercisable by, or by a nominee for, that other corporation or its subsidiary (not being held or exercisable as mentioned in paragraph (*c*)) shall be treated as not held or exercisable by that other corporation if the ordinary business of that other corporation or its subsidiary, as the case may be, includes the lending of money and the shares are held or power is exercisable as aforesaid by way of security only for the purposes of a transaction entered into in the ordinary course of that business.

Interests in securities.

5. (1) Subject to this section, a person has an interest in securities for the purposes of sections 19, 67, 79, 135 and 141E(3) if he has authority (whether formal or informal or express or implied) to dispose of, or to exercise control over the disposal of, those securities.

(2) It is immaterial for the purposes of subsection (1) that the authority of a person to dispose of, or to exercise control over the disposal of, particular securities is, or is capable of being made, subject to restraint or restriction.

(3) For the purposes of subsection (1), a person shall not be deemed not to have authority to dispose of, or to exercise control over the disposal of, particular securities by reason only that his authority is exercisable jointly with another person.

(4) For the purposes of subsection (1), where a corporation has authority (whether formal or informal or express or implied) to dispose of, or to exercise control over the disposal of, securities and—

(*a*) the corporation is, or its directors are, accustomed or under an obligation, whether formal or informal, to act in accordance with the directions of a person in relation to those securities; or

(*b*) a person, or an associate of a person, has a controlling interest in the corporation,

that person shall be deemed to have authority to dispose of, or to exercise control over the disposal of, those securities.

(5) For the purposes of subsection (4) of this section, and of sub-

section (4) of section 135, a person is an associate of another person if the first-mentioned person is—

*(a)* a corporation that, by virtue of section 4, is deemed to be related to that other person;

*(b)* a person in accordance with whose directions that other person is accustomed or is under an obligation, whether formal or informal, to act in relation to the securities referred to in those subsections;

*(c)* a person who is accustomed or is under an obligation, whether formal or informal, to act in accordance with the directions of that other person in relation to those securities;

*(d)* a corporation that is, or the directors of which are, accustomed or under an obligation, whether formal or informal, to act in accordance with the directions of that other person in relation to those securities; or

*(e)* a corporation in accordance with the directions of which, or of the directors of which, that other person is accustomed or under an obligation, whether formal or informal, to act in relation to those securities.

(6) Where a person—

*(a)* has entered into a contract to purchase securities;

*(b)* has a right to have securities transferred to him or to his order, whether the right is exercisable presently or in the future and whether on the fulfilment of a condition or not; or

*(c)* has the right to acquire securities, or an interest in securities, under an option, whether the right is exercisable presently or in the future and whether on the fulfilment of a condition or not,

that person shall, to the extent to which he could do so on completing the contract, enforcing the right or exercising the option, be deemed to have authority to dispose of, or to exercise control over the disposal of, those securities.

(7) There shall be disregarded—

*(a)* for the purposes of sections 67 and 141E(3), an interest in securities of a person whose ordinary business includes the lending of money if he holds the interest only by way of security for the purposes of a transaction entered into in the ordinary course of business in connexion with the lending of money;

*(b)* for the purposes of sections 67, 79 and 141E(3), an interest in securities of a person who holds that interest only by virtue of his having control over the securities as a manager, agent, trustee, or nominee for, or as an employee of, another;

(c) where securities referred to in section 135(4) or 141E(3) are subject to a trust, the interest of a trustee in those securities if a person who is not a trustee has an interest in those securities by virtue of subsection (6)(b) of this section; and

(d) for the purposes of any prescribed provision of section 19, section 67, section 79, section 135 or section 141E(3), a prescribed interest in securities, being an interest of such person, or of the persons included in such class of persons, as is prescribed by regulations.

## PART II. COMMISSIONER FOR SECURITIES AND SECURITIES COMMISSION

### COMMISSIONER FOR SECURITIES

Appointment of Commissioner for Securities.

6. The Governor may appoint a Commissioner for Securities.

Powers, functions and duties of Commissioner.

7. The Commissioner shall carry out the directions of the Commission in relation to the exercise of its functions and shall have and may exercise or perform such other powers, duties, and functions as are conferred or imposed upon him by or under this or any other Ordinance.

Commissioner to have seal.

8. (1) The Commissioner shall have an official seal which shall be affixed to all certificates of registration and other documents issued by him pursuant to this Ordinance, and shall be authenticated by his signature.

(2) Any certificate or other document purporting to be a certificate or document duly executed under the seal of the Commissioner shall be admissible in evidence and shall, unless the contrary is proved, be presumed to be a certificate or instrument so executed.

### SECURITIES COMMISSION

Establishment of Securities Commission.

9. There is hereby established a Securities Commission, which shall be a body corporate with perpetual succession and a common seal and in that name may sue and be sued.

Membership of Commission.

10. (1) The Commission shall consist of not less than 7 members of whom—

(a) one shall be the Commissioner;
(b) another shall be the Registrar of Companies; and
(c) the remainder shall be persons appointed by the Governor.

(2) At least one of the members of the Commission appointed under subsection (1)*(c)* shall be a person qualified in law.

(3) Subject to this Part, a member of the Commission appointed under subsection (1)*(c)* shall hold office for a period of 2 years from the date of his appointment.

(4) At the expiry of his period of appointment, every retiring member of the Commission shall, subject to this Part, be eligible for reappointment.

(5) Any member of the Commission may at any time resign by giving notice in writing to the chairman of the Commission or, in the case of the chairman, by giving notice in writing to the Governor.

(6) Where any member of the Commission resigns or the office of any such member otherwise becomes vacant before the expiry of the period of his appointment, the Governor may appoint another person to hold office until the expiry of the period for which such member was originally appointed.

(7) If any member of the Commission—

*(a)* has been absent from the meetings of the Commission without its permission for a period longer than 3 months;
*(b)* becomes bankrupt or makes an arrangement with his creditors;
*(c)* becomes incapacitated by physical or mental illness;
*(d)* is found guilty, whether in Hong Kong or elsewhere, of any offence involving fraud or dishonesty or is sentenced to a term of imprisonment for any offence (whether or not involving fraud or dishonesty);
*(e)* ceases to be ordinarily resident in Hong Kong; or
*(f)* is otherwise unable or unfit to discharge the functions of a member of the Commission,

the Governor may by notice in writing declare his office as a member of the Commission to be vacant.

(8) The powers of the Commission shall not be affected by any vacancy in its membership, including a vacancy in consequence of which the number of members of the Commission is reduced below 7.

Chairman and deputy chairman of Commission.

11. (1) The Governor shall appoint one of the members of the Commission appointed under section 10(1)*(c)* to be the chairman of the Commission and may revoke the appointment at any time.

(2) If the office of chairman is vacant, or the chairman is absent from any meeting of the Commission or is incapacitated by illness or

other cause from performing the duties of his office, the remaining members of the Commission may elect one of their number to act as chairman during the vacancy, absence or incapacity, as the case may be.

(3) A member of the Commission elected under subsection (2) shall, for the period that he acts as chairman, have and may exercise all the powers and functions of the chairman.

Meetings of the Commission.

12. (1) Meetings of the Commission shall be held at such times and places as the Commission or its chairman may appoint.

(2) At all meetings of the Commission 4 members shall form a quorum.

(3) At any meeting of the Commission, the chairman shall have a deliberative vote, and, in the case of an equality of votes, shall also have a casting vote.

(4) All questions before the Commission shall be decided by a majority of the valid votes recorded thereon. A question shall in the first instance be decided by a show of hands, but any member of the Commission may require a ballot to be held to determine the question.

(5) Subject to subsections (1) to (4) the procedure at meetings of the Commission shall be determined by the Commission, and for that purpose the Commission may make standing orders.

Functions of Commission.

13. The Commission shall have the following functions—

*(a)* to advise the Financial Secretary on all matters relating to securities;

*(b)* without prejudice to any duties imposed or powers conferred on any other person in regard to the enforcement of the law relating to securities, to be responsible for ensuring that the provisions of this Ordinance and the Protection of Investors Ordinance, and the provisions of any other Ordinance so far as they relate to securities, are complied with;

*(ba)* to report to the Financial Secretary the occurrence of any dealing in relation to securities which it believes or suspects to be an insider dealing within the meaning of section 141B;

*(c)* to be responsible for supervising the activities of the Federation;

*(d)* to take all reasonable steps to safeguard the interests of persons who invest or propose to invest in securities;

*(e)* to promote and encourage proper conduct amongst members of the Federation;

*(f)* to suppress illegal, dishonourable, and improper practices in rela-

tion to dealings in securities, whether on stock exchanges or otherwise;

*(g)* to promote and maintain the integrity of stockbrokers and other persons dealing in securities, and encourage the promulgation by stockbrokers and other dealers in securities of balanced and informed advice to their clients and to the public generally;

*(h)* to consider and suggest reforms of the law relating to securities.

14. (1) The Commission may, after consultation with the Federation, make rules in respect of all or any of the following matters— Rules.

*(a)* the listing of securities on stock exchanges, and in particular—

(i) prescribing the requirements to be met before securities may be listed on exchanges;

(ii) prescribing the procedure for dealing with applications for the listing of securities at exchanges; and

(iii) providing for the cancellation of the listing of any specified securities at any stock exchange if the Commission's requirements for listing, or the requirements of the undertaking referred to in paragraph *(f)*, are not complied with or the Commission considers that such action is necessary to maintain an orderly market in Hong Kong;

*(b)* the conditions subject to which, and the circumstances in which, any stock exchange shall suspend dealings in securities;

*(c)* the procedure for and the method of allotment of any securities arising out of an offer made to members of the public in respect of those securities;

*(d)* the qualifications for membership of stock exchanges and the maximum number of persons that may be admitted to membership of any stock exchange;

*(e)* the type of business that may be carried on at stock exchanges;

*(f)* requiring companies the securities of which are listed or accepted for listing on a stock exchange to enter into an undertaking in the prescribed form with the exchange to provide such information at such times as may be specified, and to carry out such duties in relation to its securities as may be imposed, in the undertaking;

*(fa)* requiring the chairman of a stock exchange committee who has become aware of any matter which adversely affects, or is likely to adversely affect, the ability of any member of the exchange to meet his obligations as a dealer, to make a report concerning the matter to the Commission as soon as practicable after becoming aware of the matter;

*(fb)* requiring a stock exchange which expels, or suspends the membership of, any of its members, or requests any of its members to resign his membership, to notify the Commission of that fact within 3 trading days after the expulsion, suspension or making of the request, as the case may be, and, in addition, to cause the expulsion, suspension or request to be notified to the public in such manner and within such period as may be prescribed in the rules;

*(g)* anything which is to be or may be prescribed by rules.

(2) No rules made under this section shall have effect until they have been approved by the Governor and published in the *Gazette.*

(3) Nothing in this section prevents the Federation or any stock exchange from making rules on any matter mentioned in subsection (1) if those rules have been approved by the Commission and are not repugnant to any rule made by the Commission under subsection (1).

Powers of Commission.

15. (1) The Commission shall have all such powers as may be necessary to enable it to carry out its functions, and in particular may—

*(a)* refer complaints relating to the activities of stock exchanges to the Disciplinary Committee and, if it considers necessary, hold preliminary investigations into any such complaints;

*(b)* acquire, hold, and dispose of all forms of movable and immovable property;

*(c)* authorize mutual fund corporations and unit trusts for the purposes of this Ordinance.

(2) An authorization under subsection (1)*(c)* may be granted subject to such conditions as the Commission considers fair and reasonable.

Commission may establish committees.

16. (1) The Commission may establish standing or special committees and may refer to any such committee any matters for consideration, inquiry or management.

(2) Subject to sections 38 and 100, the Commission may delegate any of its powers, functions, and duties (other than the powers conferred by this section and the power to make rules conferred by section 14) to any committee established under subsection (1).

(3) The Commission may appoint as a member of any committee established under subsection (1) any person (including a stockbroker) who, in its opinion, appears to be qualified to be a member of the committee, whether that person is a member of the Commission or not.

(4) Every delegation under subsection (2) and every appointment under subsection (3) may be revoked by the Commission at any time, and no such delegation shall prevent the exercise or performance of any power or function or duty by the Commission.

(5) Where any committee established under subsection (1) purports to act pursuant to any delegation made under subsection (2), it shall be presumed, until the contrary is proved, to be acting in accordance with the terms of delegation.

(6) A committee established under subsection (1) may elect any of its members to be chairman and may, subject to any direction of the Commission, regulate its procedure in such manner as it thinks fit.

## MISCELLANEOUS MATTERS RELATING TO COMMISSIONER AND COMMISSION

Power of Governor to give directions to Commissioner and Commission.

**17.** (1) The Governor may give such directions as he thinks fit (either generally or in any particular case) with respect to the exercise or performance by the Commissioner or the Commission of the powers, duties, and functions of the Commissioner or the Commission under this Ordinance.

(2) The Commissioner and the Commission shall, in the exercise or performance of any powers, duties, or functions under this Ordinance, comply with any directions given by the Governor under subsection (1).

(3) The Commission shall, when required by the Financial Secretary, furnish to him reports with respect to the policy that it is pursuing or proposes to pursue in the exercise or performance of any of its powers, duties, and functions under this Ordinance.

Expenditure and income of Commissioner and Commission.

**18.** (1) All expenses incurred by the Commissioner or the Commission or any other person in the administration of this Ordinance shall be met out of money provided by the Legislative Council.

(2) All money, other than deposits made under Part VI or X, received by virtue of this Ordinance by the Commissioner or the Commission (including the Disciplinary Committee) in the exercise or performance of any of their powers, duties, or functions under this Ordinance shall be paid into the general revenue.

Unlawful use of information.

**19.** (1) Except in the performance of his duties under this Ordinance, every person who has been appointed under or who is or has been employed in carrying out or in assisting any persons to carry out the provisions of this Ordinance shall preserve and aid in preserving secrecy with regard to all matters coming to his knowledge in the performance of his duties under this Ordinance, and shall not communicate any such matter to any person nor suffer or permit any person to have access to any records in the possession, custody, or control of the Commissioner.

(2) Nothing in subsection (1) shall preclude a person from producing any document to any court in criminal proceedings or from disclosing to any court in criminal proceedings any matter or thing coming to his notice in the performance of his official duties referred to in that subsection or from producing any document or disclosing any matter or thing as aforesaid to the Tribunal established by section 141G.

(3) Regulations made under this Ordinance may prescribe a public office for the purposes of this section, and it shall not be a contravention of subsection (1) to disclose to the holder of that public office information connected with the duties of that office.

(4) Subject to subsection (5), a member of the Commission and a person employed in the administration of this Ordinance shall not directly or indirectly effect or cause to be effected on his own account or for the benefit of any other person any transaction in securities which he knows to be, or to be of a class which is, subject to investigation or proceedings under this Ordinance or otherwise under consideration by the Commissioner, or in respect of which a prospectus or any take-over document is, to his knowledge, being considered by the Registrar of Companies for registration under the Companies Ordinance.

(5) Subsection (4) does not apply to or in respect of any right of the holder of a security by virtue of being that holder—

*(a)* to exchange the security or convert it to another form of security;
*(b)* to participate in a scheme of arrangement approved by the Court under the Companies Ordinance;
*(c)* to subscribe for other securities or dispose of a right to subscribe for other securities;
*(d)* to charge or pledge the security to secure the repayment of money;
*(e)* to realize the security for the purpose of repaying money referred to in paragraph *(d)*; or
*(f)* to realize the security in the course of performing a duty imposed by law.

(6) Where any member of the Commission or any person employed

in the administration of this Ordinance is, in the course of his duties, required to consider any matter relating to—

*(a)* securities in which he has an interest or any corporation in the securities of which he has an interest;

*(b)* securities of the same class as securities in which he has an interest; or

*(c)* a person—

(i) with whom he is or has been employed or associated;

(ii) of whom he is or has been a client; or

(iii) who is or was a client of a person with whom he is or was employed or associated,

he shall forthwith so inform the Commission or the Commissioner.

(7) Any person who, without lawful authority or reasonable excuse, contravenes subsection (1), subsection (4), or subsection (6) shall be guilty of an offence and shall be liable on conviction to a fine of $10,000 and to imprisonment for 6 months.

## PART III. STOCK EXCHANGES

Restriction on establishment of stock exchanges.

**20.** (1) No person shall—

*(a)* establish or operate a stock market that is not the stock market of a stock exchange; or

*(b)* assist in the operation of a stock market that, to his knowledge, is not the stock market of a stock exchange.

(2) Any person who contravenes subsection (1) shall be guilty of an offence and shall be liable on conviction to a fine of $500,000 and, in the case of a continuing offence, to a further fine of $50,000 for each day during which the offence continues.

Restriction on use of the title "stock exchange".

**21.** (1) No person, other than a stock exchange, shall—

*(a)* take or use the title "stock exchange"; or

*(b)* take or use, or have attached to or exhibited at any place, any title which resembles the title "stock exchange" or so closely resembles that title as to be calculated to deceive.

(2) Any person who contravenes subsection (1) shall be guilty of an offence and shall be liable on conviction to a fine of $100,000 and, in the case of a continuing offence, to a further fine of $5,000 for each day during which the offence continues.

Dealer not to deal in securities in a stock market that is not a stock exchange.

22. Any dealer who transacts a dealing in securities at or through a stock market in Hong Kong which, to his knowledge, is not the stock market of a stock exchange shall be guilty of an offence, and shall be liable on conviction to a fine of $50,000 in respect of each such dealing.

Power of entry and search, etc.

23. (1) Any authorized officer may, with the assistance of such other officers as may be necessary, without warrant—

(*a*) enter and search any premises in which he reasonably suspects that an offence against section 20 or section 22 is being or has been committed; and

(*b*) remove and detain any thing which he has reason to believe is evidence of the commission of the offence.

(2) Any such officer may, in the exercise of the powers conferred on him under subsection (1)—

(*a*) break open any outer or inner door of any premises which he is empowered to enter under that subsection;

(*b*) remove by force any person or thing obstructing him in the exercise of any such powers;

(*c*) detain any person found in the premises until they have been searched.

(3) In this section "authorized officer" means the Commissioner or any police officer not below the rank of superintendent.

(4) The provisions of section 102 of the Criminal Procedure Ordinance (which makes provision for the disposal of property connected with offences) shall apply to any thing which has come into the possession of the Commissioner under this section in the same way as it applies to property which has come into the possession of the police.

Power to order closure.

24. (1) If any person is charged with an offence against section 20, a magistrate may, on application made by or on behalf of the Commissioner, order that any premises in which the stock market is alleged to have been operated be locked and secured until the charge is heard and determined.

(2) Any person aggrieved by the making of an order under subsection (1) and having an interest in the premises in respect of which the order was made may apply to a magistrate to have the order discharged; and on the hearing of the application the magistrate may either confirm the order or direct that it be discharged.

(3) An application under subsection (2) shall not be heard unless

a copy of the application has been served on the Commissioner at least 24 hours before the hearing.

(4) If any person is convicted of an offence against section 20, the court may order the premises in which the stock exchange was operated to be locked and secured for such period not exceeding 3 months as may be specified in the order.

(5) Where any order under subsection (1) or subsection (4) has been made, any authorized officer may take such steps as may be necessary to ensure that the premises to which the order relates are locked and secured.

(6) Any person who enters or attempts to enter any premises in respect of which an order made under subsection (1) or subsection (4) is in force without the authority of the Commissioner shall be guilty of an offence and shall be liable on conviction to a fine of $50,000.

(7) In this section "authorized officer" means the Commissioner or any police officer.

Power of Commission to approve a registered company as a stock exchange.

25. (1) An application may be made to the Commission under this section by or on behalf of a registered company for the approval of the company as a stock exchange.

(2) On receipt of any such application and a copy of the company's memorandum and articles of association, the Commission in its discretion may, by certificate in writing under its seal, approve the company as a stock exchange if it is satisfied that the requirements specified in subsection (3) have been complied with.

(3) The requirements referred to in subsection (2) are as follows—

*(a)* that the objects contained in the company's constitution include a provision giving the company power to operate a stock exchange;

*(b)* that at least 20 members of the company will carry on businesses of dealing in securities independently and in competition with one another;

*(c)* that the constitution of the company makes satisfactory provision for the exclusion from membership of the company of—

(i) a person who is not a registered dealer;

(ii) a person who is a director or employee of a licensed bank;

(iii) a person who is a solicitor or professional accountant holding a current practising certificate;

(iv) a person who performs any occupation, or carries on any business, for the time being prescribed by rules;

(v) a person who was not born in Hong Kong or who has not been ordinarily resident in Hong Kong for 5 out of the 7 years immediately preceding his application for membership of the company, unless he is, in the opinion of the Commission, a person of good reputation experienced in dealing in securities;

(vi) a corporation or firm which does not carry on a business solely as a dealer or as a dealer and investment adviser;

(vii) a corporation of which any director was not born in Hong Kong or has not been ordinarily resident in Hong Kong for 5 out of the 7 years immediately preceding the application of the corporation for membership of the company, unless the director is, in the opinion of the Commission, a person of good reputation experienced in dealing in securities;

(viii) a corporation, unless at least one of its directors or, in the case of a corporation having only one director, that director, actively participates in, or is directly responsible for the supervision of, the corporation's business of dealing in securities, and unless each of the directors of the corporation who actively participates in, or is in any way directly responsible for the supervision of, the corporation's business of dealing in securities is a member of the applicant company or of another company which is approved as a stock exchange under subsection (2);

(ix) a corporation the liability of whose members is limited, unless each director of the corporation who actively participates in the corporation's business of dealing in securities is jointly and severally liable for the debts and obligations of the corporation, whether incurred before or after he became a director of the corporation;

(x) a firm of which any partner, being an individual, was not born in Hong Kong or has not been ordinarily resident in Hong Kong for 5 out of the 7 years immediately preceding the application of the firm for membership of the company, unless that individual is, in the opinion of the Commission, a person of good reputation experienced in dealing in securities;

(xi) a firm of which any partner is a corporation if that corporation is one which would be required to be excluded from membership of the company by virtue of subparagraph (vii);

(xii) a firm, unless at least one of its partners actively participates in, or is directly responsible for the supervision of, the firm's business of dealing in securities, and unless each of the partners of the firm who actively participates in, or is in any way directly responsible for the supervision of, the firm's business of dealing in securities is a member of the applicant company or of another company which is approved as a stock exchange under subsection (2);

(xiii) a limited partnership registered under the Limited Partnerships Ordinance, unless at least one of its partners actively participates in, or is directly responsible for the supervision of, the partnership's business of dealing in securities, and unless each of the partners of the partnership who actively participates in, or is in any way directly responsible for the supervision of, the partnership's business of dealing in securities is a general partner and is a member of the applicant company or of another company which is approved as a stock exchange under subsection (2); and

(xiv) a person who is in partnership with another person who carries on a business of dealing in securities but is not a member of the applicant company or of another company which is approved as a stock exchange under subsection (2);

*(d)* that the constitution of the company makes satisfactory provision—

(i) for the election by ballot at a general meeting of the company of a committee to administer the stock exchange to be operated by the company;

(ii) for all members of the company to have equal rights of voting at its general meetings;

(iii) for at least four-fifths of the membership of the committee referred to in sub-paragraph (i) to be comprised of persons who are members of the stock exchange to be operated by the company;

(iv) for the retirement of all the members of the committee at the first annual meeting of the company after approval under this section and for the retirement of at least one-third of the committee at each succeeding annual general meeting so that no person may be a member of the committee for more than 3 years without standing for re-election;

*(e)* that the rules of the stock exchange to be operated by the company are such as to ensure dealing in securities in such a

manner as to protect purchasers, holders and sellers of securities to be dealt with on the exchange and include, in addition to any other provisions required by or under this Ordinance—

(i) a provision to the effect that, when a dealer who is a member of the company is purchasing and selling securities on his own account, he shall notify that fact to the person with whom he is dealing;

(ii) a provision prohibiting any member of the company who is a director of a corporation from acting as a dealer in the shares of that corporation;

(iii) a provision requiring the company to maintain adequate daily records of all dealings in securities on the stock exchange;

(iv) a provision requiring the company to keep the records maintained under sub-paragraph (iii) available for inspection by members of the public on payment of a fee not exceeding that prescribed by rules;

*(f)* that the company—

(i) has and will maintain to the satisfaction of the Commission an adequate and properly equipped place of business; and

(ii) undertakes to operate its stock market only at a place in Hong Kong approved by the Commission;

*(g)* that the company will make the deposits required to be made to the compensation fund established under Part X;

*(h)* that it is in the public interest to grant approval under this section.

(4) The Commission may, on application being made to it in writing by a company approved or deemed to be approved under this section, authorize the company to admit to membership—

*(a)* an individual who is not eligible for membership of the company by reason of his not being born in Hong Kong or not fulfilling the residential requirement for membership of the company if, in the opinion of the Commission, he is a person of good reputation experienced in dealing in securities;

*(b)* a corporation of which any director was not born in Hong Kong or has not been ordinarily resident in Hong Kong for 5 out of the 7 years immediately preceding the application of the corporation for membership of the company, if, in the opinion of the Commission, the director is a person of good reputation experienced in dealing in securities;

*(c)* a firm of which any partner—

(i) is an individual who was not born in Hong Kong or has not been ordinarily resident in Hong Kong for 5 out of the 7 years immediately preceding the application of the firm for membership of the company; or

(ii) is a corporation of which any director was not born in Hong Kong or has not resided in Hong Kong for 5 out of the 7 years immediately preceding the application of the firm for membership of the company,

if, in the opinion of the Commission, the individual or, as the case may be, the director is a person of good reputation experienced in dealing in securities.

(5) Where, immediately before the commencement of this Part, any company was a recognized stock exchange within the meaning of section 2 of the Stock Exchanges Control Ordinance, that company, subject to subsection (6), shall be deemed to be approved as a stock exchange under subsection (2).

(6) Every company to which subsection (5) relates shall, not later than 6 months after the commencement of this Part, satisfy the Commission that it has complied with the requirements of paragraphs *(b)*, *(c)*, *(d)*, *(e)*, *(f)*, and *(g)* of subsection (3), except that in relation to paragraph *(c)* the company is not required to amend its constitution so to provide for the exclusion from membership of the company of any of those persons mentioned in sub-paragraphs (iii), (v), (vii), (x), and (xi) of that paragraph who were members of the company at the commencement of this Part and who would, but for this exception, be liable under the constitution of the company to be excluded from that membership.

(7) If any company to which subsection (5) relates fails to satisfy the Commission as required by subsection (6), the Commission may, at any time while the requirements of subsection (6) remain unsatisfied, revoke the approval deemed to have been given under subsection (5).

**Revocation of approval and suspension of dealings for misconduct, etc.**

26. (1) The Commission may revoke any approval given or deemed to have been given under section 25 on giving 14 days' notice in writing to the company of its intention to do so on the ground—

*(a)* that the stock exchange operated by the company no longer has at least 20 members;

*(b)* that the constitution of the company no longer complies with the requirements specified in paragraphs *(c)* and *(d)* of section 25(3);

*(c)* that the rules of the stock exchange no longer comply with the requirements of section 25(3)*(e)*;

(*d*) that the stock exchange no longer maintains a place of business which complies with the requirement of section 25(3)(*f*) or that the exchange operates a stock market in Hong Kong at any other place of business;

(*e*) that the stock exchange has failed to make any deposit or payment into the compensation fund as required under Part X; or

(*f*) that the company is being wound up or has ceased to operate a stock market.

(2) The Commission may, instead of revoking the approval given or deemed to have been given under section 25, direct that the premises of the stock exchange be closed forthwith for the transaction of dealings in securities until such time as the stock exchange has, to the satisfaction of the Commission, complied with the requirement in question.

(3) Without prejudice to the exercise of its powers under subsections 1) and (2), the Commission may, where it has received a recommendation from the Disciplinary Committee pursuant to section 39 (2) (*a*) in respect of a stock exchange which the Committee has found guilty of misconduct under that section—

(*a*) revoke the approval given or deemed to have been given under section 25; or

(*b*) direct that the premises of the stock exchange be closed for the transaction of dealings in securities until the Commission revokes the direction.

(4) While a direction under subsection (2) or subsection (3) remains in force, the approval given or deemed to have been given under section 25 to the company in question shall, for the purposes of the application of sections 20 to 22, be deemed to have been revoked.

(5) Where any direction under subsection (2) or subsection (3) is in force, any authorized officer may take such steps as may be necessary to ensure that the premises to which the direction relates are locked and secured.

(6) Any person who enters or attempts to enter any premises in respect of which a direction made under subsection (2) or subsection (3) is in force without the authority of an authorized officer shall be guilty of an offence and shall be liable on conviction to a fine of $50,000.

(7) In this section "authorized officer" means the Commissioner or any police officer.

27. (1) Without prejudice to the powers of the Commission under section 26, the Commissioner may, after consultation with the Federation, order that all stock exchanges be closed for the transaction of dealings in securities for a period not exceeding 5 bank trading days.

Commissioner may order closure of stock exchanges in emergencies, etc.

(2) The Commissioner may make an order under subsection (1) on the ground that, in his opinion, the orderly transaction of business at stock exchanges is being or is likely to be prevented because—

*(a)* an emergency or natural disaster has occurred in Hong Kong; or

*(b)* there exists an economic or financial crisis, whether in Hong Kong or elsewhere, or any other circumstance, which is likely to prevent orderly trading from being carried on at stock exchanges.

(3) Any order made under subsection (1) or under this subsection may be renewed by a further order for a further period of not more than 5 bank trading days.

(4) Any dealer who deals in securities at or through a stock exchange while an order made under subsection (1) is in force in respect of the exchange (being an order which has been notified to the committee of the exchange) shall be guilty of an offence, and shall be liable on conviction to a fine of $50,000.

(5) Where any order under subsection (1) has been made, the Commissioner may take such steps as are necessary to secure compliance with the order and may, in particular, cause the premises of stock exchanges to be locked and secured.

(6) Any person who, without the authority of the Commissioner, enters or attempts to enter the premises of a stock exchange which have been locked and secured under subsection (5) shall be guilty of an offence and shall be liable on conviction to a fine of $20,000.

28. Where the Commission revokes any approval given or deemed to have been given under section 25 or issues any direction under section 26, or the Commissioner makes any order under section 27, notice of the revocation, direction, or order, as the case may be, shall be published in the *Gazette.*

Revocation of approval, etc., to be notified in the *Gazette.*

29. (1) Where—

Appeal against revocation of approval, etc.

*(a)* the Commission has refused to approve a registered company as a stock exchange under section 25, has revoked any approval under section 26, or has given a direction under subsection (2) or (3) of section 26 in relation to a stock exchange; or

(*b*) the Disciplinary Committee has imposed any penalty on any stock exchange, or on any member of the committee of a stock exchange, pursuant to paragraph (*b*) or paragraph (*c*) of section 39(2),

the stock exchange or such member of the committee may, within 14 days—

(i) after notification of the refusal or after the publication in the *Gazette* of notice of the revocation or direction; or

(ii) after being notified of the decision of the Disciplinary Committee imposing the penalty,

appeal to the Governor in Council against the refusal, revocation or direction or against the decision of the Disciplinary Committee.

(2) After considering any appeal under subsection (1) the Governor in Council may confirm, reverse or vary the decision of the Commission or of the Disciplinary Committee, as the case may be; and the decision of the Governor in Council shall be final.

(3) Where approval is refused under section 25, any approval is revoked under section 26, or any direction is made under subsection (2) or subsection (3) of section 26, that refusal, revocation or direction shall take effect immediately, notwithstanding that an appeal has been or may be made under this section.

Commission to be notified of proposed amendments to constitution and rules of stock exchange.

**30.** (1) No amendment to the constitution or rules of a stock exchange, whether by way of rescission, alteration, or addition, shall have effect unless the amendment has been approved by the Commission.

(2) Where it is proposed to amend the constitution or rules of a stock exchange, the committee of the stock exchange shall forward written notice of the amendment to the Commission for its approval.

(3) The Commission may, within 14 days after receipt of a notice under subsection (2), give notice that it disallows the whole or any specified part of the proposed amendment to which the notice relates.

(4) A notice under this section may be served personally or by post.

## PART IV. HONG KONG FEDERATION OF STOCK EXCHANGES

Establishment of Hong Kong Federation of Stock Exchanges.

**31.** (1) There shall be an association of stock exchanges to be known as the Hong Kong Federation of Stock Exchanges.

(2) The Federation shall be a body corporate with perpetual succession and shall have a common seal which shall include the name of the Federation.

(3) Every stock exchange, when approved or deemed to have been approved under section 25, shall be deemed to be a member of the Federation.

(4) Any stock exchange whose approval is revoked under section 26 shall thereupon cease to be a member of the Federation.

Council of Federation.

32. (1) The Federation shall have a council, to be known as the Council of the Hong Kong Federation of Stock Exchanges, which shall have the management of the Federation and shall perform on behalf of the Federation the functions prescribed by section 36.

(2) Two persons shall be appointed by the committee of each stock exchange from among the members of the committee of that exchange to be members of the Council.

(3) Every appointment under subsection (2) shall be made annually, not later than a date specified by the Commission.

(4) Subject to this Ordinance, a member appointed under subsection (2) shall hold office for a period of 12 months.

(5) A retiring member of the Council shall be eligible for reappointment to the Council.

(6) If any member of the Council ceases to be a member, the committee of the stock exchange which appointed him may appoint another person who is a member of the committee of that exchange to be a member of the Council in his place until the expiry of the period for which the first-mentioned person was appointed.

(7) A member of the Council may at any time resign by giving notice to the Council in writing.

(8) Notwithstanding anything to the contrary in this section, no person shall be eligible to be a member of the Council if he—

*(a)* is not ordinarily resident in Hong Kong;
*(b)* is an undischarged bankrupt;
*(c)* has been convicted of an offence, whether in Hong Kong or elsewhere, involving fraud or dishonesty; or
*(d)* is serving a sentence of imprisonment or detained in a mental hospital.

(9) If the Council is satisfied that any of its members—

*(a)* has been absent from meetings of the Council for a period longer than 3 months without its permission;
*(b)* has become bankrupt or made an arrangement with his creditors;

(*ba*) has been convicted of an offence, whether in Hong Kong or elsewhere, involving fraud or dishonesty or has been convicted of any offence in respect of which he is sentenced to a term of imprisonment;

(*c*) is incapacitated from carrying out his duties by reason of physical or mental illness;

(*d*) is no longer ordinarily resident in Hong Kong; or

(*e*) is otherwise unable or unfit to discharge the functions of a member of the Council,

it may declare his office as a member of the Council to be vacant.

(10) The powers of the Council shall not be affected by any vacancy in its membership, or any irregularity in the appointment of any member of the Council.

(11) If any stock exchange for any reason ceases to be a member of the Federation, the membership of the Council of any person appointed by the committee of that exchange shall thereupon cease.

(12) If any stock exchange fails to appoint members of the Council as required by this section, the Commission may, after giving the exchange 14 days' notice in writing of its intention to do so, appoint persons to fill the vacancies.

Chairman and deputy chairman of the Council.

33. (1) The Council shall, at its first meeting and in each year thereafter at the first meeting after the anniversary of the date on which it was constituted, elect one of its members to be chairman of the Council, and the person so elected shall hold office during its pleasure until the election of another chairman.

(2) When a member of the Council ceases to hold office as chairman of the Council, neither he, nor any other member of the Council who is a member of the stock exchange of which he is a member, shall be eligible for election as chairman of the Council until the expiry of at least 4 years from the date on which the first-mentioned member of the Council was elected to be the chairman.

(3) If the office of chairman is vacant for more than one month, the Commission may appoint such person as it thinks fit (including a person who is not a member of the Council) to be chairman for a period not exceeding 12 months.

(4) The Council may, at its first meeting and in each year thereafter after the anniversary of the date on which it was constituted, elect any other of its members to be deputy chairman, and the person so elected

shall hold office as such during its pleasure until the election of another deputy chairman.[3]

(5) If the office of chairman is vacant, or the chairman is absent from any meeting of the Council or is incapacitated by illness or other cause from performing the duties of his office, the deputy chairman shall have and may exercise all the functions and powers of the chairman.

Deputies of members.

34. (1) If any member does not attend a meeting of the Council, the committee of the stock exchange which appointed him may appoint one of the other members of the exchange to attend the meeting as his deputy.

(2) While a person is attending any meeting as a deputy under this section, he shall be deemed for all purposes to be a member of the Council.

(3) No appointment of a deputy and no act done by him as such, and no act done by the Council while any deputy is acting as such, shall in any proceedings be questioned on the ground that the occasion for his appointment has not arisen or had ceased.

Meetings of the Council.

35. (1) Meetings of the Council shall be held not less often than once in every month at such times and places as the Council or its chairman may appoint.

(2) At all meetings of the Council 4 members shall form a quorum.

(3) At any meeting of the Council the chairman shall have a deliberative vote, and, in the case of an equality of votes, shall also have a casting vote.

(4) All questions before the Council shall be decided by a majority of the members present and voting thereon.

(5) A decision taken at a meeting of the Council shall be binding on each of the members of the Federation, whether the representatives of the member were present at the meeting or not.

(6) Subject to subsections (1) to (5) the procedure at meetings of the Council shall be determined by the Council.

Functions of the Federation.

36. The Federation shall have the following functions—

*(a)* to communicate the views of its members to the Commission,

[3] The editor notes a difference in wording between section 33(1) and section 33(4).

and to communicate the decisions of the Commission to its members;

(*b*) to encourage or provide facilities for the training of persons desirous of becoming stockbrokers;

(*c*) to provide or promote facilities for the obtaining by stockbrokers, and persons desirous of becoming stockbrokers, of professional qualifications by means of examinations;

(*d*) to provide means for the amicable settlement of disputes between—

(i) members of the Federation;

(ii) any members of one member of the Federation and any members of another member of the Federation; or

(iii) any member of the Federation and any members of any other member of the Federation;

(*e*) to be the sole representative of members of the Federation in respect of any matter other than one involving the internal administration of the stock exchange of any such member;

(*f*) to promote research into all aspects of investment in securities;

(*g*) to encourage its members to improve the efficiency, methods, and procedures of the stock markets operated by them;

(*h*) to fix the hours of trading on stock exchanges;

(*i*) to determine all matters relating to the levying of brokerage in respect of transactions on stock exchanges, including the fixing of a uniform rate of brokerage in relation to all stock exchanges;

(*j*) to establish a uniform procedure for the transaction of dealings between members of one stock exchange and members of another;

(*k*) to perform any other function in relation to dealings in securities determined by the unanimous decision of the Council and approved by the Commission, not being a function which is inconsistent with this Ordinance.

Powers of Federation and Council.

37. (1) The Federation shall have all such powers as may be necessary to enable it to carry out its functions, and without prejudice to the generality of the foregoing may—

(*a*) acquire, hold, or dispose of movable or immovable property;

(*b*) for the purpose of financing its operations, impose levies on its members of such amounts as may be determined by the Council, with the concurrence of the Commissioner;

(*c*) appoint officers and other staff on such terms and conditions as the Council thinks fit.

(2) The Council may appoint committees of its members and may

delegate to any such committee any of its functions or powers (other than the power of delegation conferred by this subsection) and may authorize such a committee to co-opt as members thereof persons who are not members of the Council.

(3) The Federation may, and if so directed by the Commission shall, make rules on any matter within its functions.

(4) Every rule made under subsection (3) shall be binding on and be enforceable against each stock exchange and against the members of each stock exchange, except to the extent that any such rule purports to exempt any specified stock exchange or any members or class of members of a stock exchange from its operation.

(5) The Federation may cause any rules made under subsection (3) to be promulgated in such manner as it thinks fit.

(6) All rules made under subsection (3) shall, subject to subsection (7), come into operation on the date on which they are made or on such later date as may be specified in the rules.

(7) No rule made under subsection (3) (not being a rule made at the direction of the Commission) shall come into operation unless it has been previously approved by the Commission.

## PART V. SECURITIES COMMISSION DISCIPLINARY COMMITTEE

Constitution of Disciplinary Committee.

**38.** (1) There shall be a committee, to be known as the Securities Commission Disciplinary Committee, appointed in accordance with this section to exercise the powers and perform the functions conferred on it by this Ordinance.

(2) The Disciplinary Committee shall be appointed by the Commission, and shall consist of 5 persons of whom—

*(a)* one shall be the member of the Commission appointed under section 10(1)*(c)* who is qualified in law, or if there is more than one such member, one of those members;
*(b)* two shall be other members of the Commission (other than the Commissioner);
*(c)* two shall be persons nominated by the Federation.

(3) The member of the Disciplinary Committee referred to in subsection (2)*(a)* shall be chairman of the Disciplinary Committee.

(4) A quorum of the Disciplinary Committee shall be 4 persons.

(5) A decision of the majority of the members of the Disciplinary Committee shall be the decision of the Committee. In the event of there being no majority, the decision of the chairman and one other member of the Committee shall be the decision of the Committee.

Powers of Disciplinary Committee.

39. (1) The Disciplinary Committee may inquire into any allegation, whether made by the Commission, the Commissioner or any other person, that any stock exchange, or the committee or any member of the committee of any such exchange, has been guilty of any misconduct.

(2) If, after inquiring into any such allegation, the Disciplinary Committee is of the opinion that the allegation is proved it may, if it thinks fit, subject to the provisions of this Ordinance, do one or more of the following things—

*(a)* recommend to the Commission that it exercise any of the powers conferred on it by section 26;

*(b)* disqualify any member of the committee of the stock exchange from holding office as such either permanently or for such period as the Disciplinary Committee may specify;

*(c)* impose a fine on the stock exchange not exceeding $10,000;

*(d)* reprimand the committee of the stock exchange or any member of the committee of the stock exchange.

(3) The Disciplinary Committee shall not, in respect of any allegation inquired into under subsection (1), impose on any stock exchange, or on the committee or any member of the committee of the exchange, any of the penalties referred to in subsection (2), or make any recommendation under that subsection, without first giving the committee of the exchange or, as the case may be, the member of the committee, an opportunity of being heard.

(4) Any stock exchange, or committee or member of the committee of a stock exchange, against which or whom an allegation of misconduct has been made, and any person appealing to the Disciplinary Committee under section 58, shall have a right to be represented by a solicitor or counsel at the inquiry under subsection (1) or on the hearing of the appeal.

(5) Where a stock exchange has been proceeded against before a court of law in respect of an offence arising out of misconduct, the Disciplinary Committee shall not impose a fine under subsection (2)*(c)* in relation to that misconduct.

(6) For the purposes of this section "misconduct" means—

*(a)* any failure by a stock exchange or the committee of a stock

exchange to comply with the requirements of this Ordinance or any rules, regulations, or directions made or given thereunder;

(*b*) any wilful contravention by a stock exchange or the committee of a stock exchange of the constitution or rules of the exchange;

(*c*) any failure by a stock exchange or by the committee of a stock exchange to ensure that the rules of the exchange are complied with by its members;

(*d*) any act or omission relating to the operation of a stock exchange which, in the opinion of the Disciplinary Committee, is or is likely to be prejudicial to the interests of members of the investing public.

Costs.

40. After the hearing of any inquiry under section 39, or of any appeal under section 58, the Disciplinary Committee may make such order as to the payment of costs as it considers just.

Recovery of penalties, costs, and expenses.

41. Any sum ordered by the Disciplinary Committee to be paid by way of fine or costs in relation to an inquiry under section 39, or in relation to an appeal made under section 58, shall be deemed to be a civil debt due from the person ordered to pay it to the person to whom it is ordered to be paid and shall be recoverable accordingly in any court of competent jurisdiction.

Evidence at hearing, etc.

42. (1) The Disciplinary Committee, by notice in writing signed by the chairman and served on any person to whom it is addressed, may require the person to attend and give evidence before it at the hearing of any inquiry under section 39 or any appeal under section 58, and to produce all books, papers, and documents in that person's custody or under his control relating to the subject-matter of the inquiry or appeal, as the case may be.

(2) At any inquiry under section 39 or at the hearing of any appeal under section 58, the Disciplinary Committee may—

(*a*) receive such evidence as it considers relevant to the inquiry or appeal, whether it would be admissible in a court of law or not; and

(*b*) require evidence to be given on oath, either orally or in writing, and books, papers, or documents to be produced.

(3) For the purpose of subsection (2) the chairman of the Committee may administer an oath.

(4) Any person who, without lawful authority or reasonable excuse, refuses or fails—

(*a*) to attend and give evidence when required to do so by the Disciplinary Committee; or

(*b*) to answer truly and fully questions put to him by a member of the Disciplinary Committee; or

(*c*) to produce any book, paper, or document which he has been required to produce,

shall be guilty of an offence and shall be liable on conviction to a fine of $10,000.

Immunity of Disciplinary Committee, witnesses, solicitors and counsel.

43. The Disciplinary Committee, and witnesses and any solicitor or counsel appearing before the Disciplinary Committee, shall have the same privileges and immunities in inquiries and appeals heard under this Part as they would have if those proceedings were proceedings in a court.

Witnesses' expenses.

44. (1) Every witness giving evidence or attending to give evidence at the hearing of any inquiry under section 39 or any appeal under section 58 shall be entitled in the discretion of the Disciplinary Committee to such sum for his expenses and loss of time as the Disciplinary Committee may determine.

(2) Subject to any order made by the Disciplinary Committee as to the payment of costs or expenses, all such witnesses' expenses shall be paid out of money provided by the Legislative Council.

Rules of procedure.

45. Subject to this Part, the Commission may make rules in respect of the hearing and determination of inquiries under this Part and of appeals made under section 58.

Form and proof of orders of Disciplinary Committee.

46. (1) Every decision of the Disciplinary Committee shall be in writing signed by the chairman of the Committee and shall contain a statement of the reasons for the decision.

(2) Every document purporting to contain a decision of the Disciplinary Committee and to be signed by the Committee's chairman shall, until the contrary is proved, be deemed to be a decision of the Committee duly made.

## Part VI. Registration of Dealers, Investment Advisers, and Representatives

Application of Part VI.

47. (1) Except so far as specifically provided, this Part does not apply to an exempt dealer or to an exempt investment adviser, or to

the representative of an exempt dealer or exempt investment adviser, but—

(*a*) subject to section 61, nothing in this subsection exempts an exempt dealer who carries on a business as an investment adviser from being registered as such under this Part; and

(*b*) subject to section 60, nothing in this subsection exempts an exempt investment adviser who carries on a business of dealing in securities from being registered as a dealer.

(2) Where a person would, but for this subsection, be liable to a penalty for not being registered as a dealer, dealer's representative, investment adviser, or investment representative, he shall not be so liable—

(*a*) until the expiry of a period of 3 months immediately following the commencement of this Part; or

(*b*) where, before the expiry of that period, he applies for registration, until—

(i) he is registered; or

(ii) his application is refused.

Registration as a dealer.

48. (1) A person (whether an individual or a body corporate, or a member of a partnership or director of a body corporate) shall not carry on a business in Hong Kong of dealing in securities, or hold himself out as carrying on such a business, unless he is registered as a dealer under this Part.

(1A) A corporation shall not carry on a business in Hong Kong of dealing in securities, or hold itself out as carrying on such a business, unless at least one of the directors of the corporation, or, in the case of a corporation having only one director, that director, actively participates in, or is directly responsible for the supervision of, the corporation's business of dealing in securities and is registered as a dealer under this Part.

(2) Any person who knowingly acts in contravention of subsection (1) or (1A) shall be guilty of an offence and shall be liable on conviction to a fine of $50,000 and, in the case of a continuing offence, to a further fine of $500 for each day during which the offence continues.

Registration as an investment adviser.

49. (1) A person (whether an individual or a body corporate, or a member of a partnership or director of a body corporate) shall not in Hong Kong act as an investment adviser or hold himself out to be an investment adviser unless he is registered as an investment adviser under this Part.

(1A) A corporation shall not in Hong Kong act as an investment adviser, or hold itself out to be an investment adviser, unless at least one of the directors of the corporation, or, in the case of a corporation having only one director, that director, actively participates in, or is directly responsible for the supervision of, the corporation's business as an investment adviser and is registered as an investment adviser under this Part.

(2) Any person who knowingly acts in contravention of subsection (1) or (1A) shall be guilty of an offence and shall be liable on conviction to a fine of $20,000 and, in the case of a continuing offence, to a further fine of $200 for each day during which the offence continues.

Registration as a representative.

50. (1) No person shall—

*(a)* act as a dealer's representative in Hong Kong unless he is registered as such under this Part; or

*(b)* act as an investment representative in Hong Kong unless he is registered as such under this Part.

(2) Any person who knowingly acts in contravention of subsection (1) shall be guilty of an offence and shall be liable on conviction to a fine of $10,000 and, in the case of a continuing offence, to a further fine of $100 for each day during which the offence continues.

Grant of certificates of registration.

51. (1) Subject to sections 51A, 52 and 53, the Commissioner shall, on application by any person in the prescribed manner and on payment of the prescribed fee, issue to that person—

*(a)* a certificate of registration authorizing him to carry on business as a dealer in securities;

*(b)* a certificate of registration authorizing him to deal in securities as a representative of a registered dealer;

*(c)* a certificate of registration authorizing him to carry on business as an investment adviser; or

*(d)* a certificate of registration authorizing him to act as a representative of a registered investment adviser.

(2) A certificate of registration shall be—

*(a)* valid for a period of 12 months beginning with the day on which it is issued; and

*(b)* subject to such reasonable conditions as the Commissioner considers necessary.

(3) A certificate of registration issued to a dealer or investment adviser shall specify the name of the person thereby authorized to carry

on a business of dealing in securities or as an investment adviser, as the case may be.

(4) The issue of a certificate of registration to a person shall not authorize such a person to carry on that business under any name other than that specified in the certificate.

(5) Notwithstanding subsection (4), if the Commissioner thinks fit, a certificate of registration to which that subsection relates may, at the request of the applicant for registration, authorize the applicant to carry on business as a dealer or investment adviser, either alone or jointly with any other person who is registered as a dealer or investment adviser, as the case may be, under such name or style as the applicant may specify.

Private company to have at least one director.

51A. Where an applicant is a corporation and is a private company within the meaning of the Companies Ordinance, the Commissioner shall not register the applicant as a dealer or as an investment adviser unless the corporation has at least one director thereof.

Deposit required before registration as a dealer.

52. (1) Subject to subsection (6), the Commissioner shall not register an applicant as a dealer unless the applicant has deposited with the Commissioner such amount as is prescribed in regulations.

(1A) Subject to subsection (6), where an applicant is a corporation the Commissioner shall not register the corporation as a dealer unless there has been deposited with the Commissioner in respect of each director of the corporation who actively participates in, or is in any way directly responsible for, the corporation's business of dealing in securities in Hong Kong such amount as is prescribed in regulations.

(2) If—

*(a)* the dealer, being an individual person or member of a partnership of dealers, becomes bankrupt, the Commissioner shall pay the deposit to the dealer's trustee in bankruptcy;

*(b)* the dealer, being a corporation, is ordered to be wound up by or under the supervision of the Court, the Commissioner shall pay the deposit to the liquidator of the corporation; or

*(c)* the certificate of registration of the dealer is revoked, or the dealer or any servant of the dealer, or where the dealer is a partnership or a corporation any member of the partnership or director or officer of the corporation, is convicted of an offence necessarily involving a finding that he or it was guilty of a breach of trust, defalcation, fraud, or misfeasance in respect of any money or securities of a person who is a client of the dealer,

the Commissioner may direct that all or any part of the deposit be forfeited.

(3) In the event of the deposit or any part of the deposit being paid to the dealer's trustee in bankruptcy or liquidator under subsection (2)*(a)* or subsection (2)*(b)*, the amount paid shall be applied by the trustee or liquidator, as the case may be, in accordance with regulations made under this Ordinance for the purposes of this subsection.

(4) In the event of the deposit or any part of the deposit being forfeited under subsection (2)*(c)*, the amount forfeited shall be applied by the Commissioner subject to and in accordance with regulations made under this Ordinance for the purposes of this subsection.

(5) Except as provided in this section or under regulations made under this Ordinance, no person may withdraw or transfer any deposit made under this section.

(6) The following persons are exempt from being required to deposit the amount required under this section—

*(a)* a dealer who carries on a business of dealing in securities only in the capacity of a stockbroker;
*(b)* any corporate member or member firm of a stock exchange;
*(c)* any corporation carrying on a business as a dealer each of whose directors who is engaged in dealing in securities has deposited the amount so required; and
*(d)* any other dealer who belongs to a class of dealers exempted from the provisions of this section by regulations.

(7) The Commissioner shall open one or more accounts at a licensed bank into which he shall pay all sums received from dealers by way of deposit under this section, and shall then ascertain what proportion of those sums ought, in his opinion, to be retained in the accounts to enable liabilities under subsection (2), or such other liabilities as may be prescribed by regulations, to be satisfied.

(8) After ascertaining the amount required to be retained under subsection (7), the Commissioner shall cause the balance of the sums to be invested in such manner as the Financial Secretary may direct.

(8A) Any document relating to the investment of money under subsection (8) may be kept in the office of the Commissioner or deposited by him for safe keeping with a licensed bank.

(9) Where the Financial Secretary has given a direction under subsection (8), he shall, as soon as practicable after the end of each financial year, by notice in the *Gazette*—

(*a*) declare a rate of interest to be paid for that financial year in respect of each sum deposited under this section;
(*b*) specify the manner and time of payment of that interest; and
(*c*) specify an amount to be charged for management expenses incurred by the Commissioner in administering that sum under this section.

(10) As soon as practicable after the publication of the notice referred to in subsection (9), the Commissioner shall, after deducting the appropriate amount chargeable in respect of management expenses, pay to each person who has deposited the prescribed sum under this section, or to that person's duly authorized agent or personal representative, the appropriate amount of interest due in respect of that sum for the financial year in question.

(11) If any person who has made a deposit under this section ceases to be registered as a dealer and the deposit has not been or is not required to be disposed of under subsection (2), that person, or his agent or personal representative, may apply to the Commissioner for the deposit to be released to him.

(12) On making an application under subsection (11), the applicant shall—

(*a*) satisfy the Commissioner by a statutory declaration—
    (i) that he knows of no other person who has made or is entitled to make a claim in respect of the deposit;
    (ii) if he is not the dealer who made the deposit, that he is entitled to give a good discharge for the deposit and stating the circumstances in which he is so entitled; and
(*b*) provide the Commissioner with such information as will satisfy him that an advertisement in a form approved by him has been inserted once in an English language newspaper, and once in a Chinese language newspaper, circulating in Hong Kong.

(13) The Commissioner, on being so satisfied, shall cause the amount of the deposit to be released to the applicant.

**52A.** (1) The Commissioner shall keep proper accounts of all sums deposited under section 52, and shall in respect of the financial year beginning before and ending after the day on which this section commences, and in respect of each subsequent financial year, prepare a revenue and expenditure account, and a balance sheet made up to the last day of that year.

Accounts of sums deposited under section 52.

(2) The Commissioner shall appoint an auditor who shall audit the

accounts kept under subsection (1) and shall audit and prepare an auditor's report in respect of each balance sheet and revenue and expenditure account prepared under subsection (1) and shall submit the report to the Commissioner.

(3) Not later than the 31st July in each year the Commissioner shall cause a copy of the audited balance sheet, revenue and expenditure account and the auditor's report to be sent to the Financial Secretary.

Refusal of registration.

53. (1) The Commissioner may refuse to register an applicant for registration under this Part—

*(a)* in the case of an applicant who is an individual, on the grounds that—

(i) the applicant has not provided the Commissioner with such information relating to him or any person employed by or associated with him, and to any circumstances likely to affect his method of conducting business, as may be prescribed by or under this Ordinance;

(ii) the applicant is detained under the Mental Health Ordinance in a mental hospital or is a patient, as defined in section 2 of that Ordinance;

(iii) the applicant is an undischarged bankrupt;

(iv) it appears to the Commissioner that, by reason of the applicant, or any person employed by or associated with the applicant for the purposes of his business, having been convicted, whether in Hong Kong or elsewhere, of an offence his conviction for which necessarily involved a finding that he acted fraudulently or dishonestly, or having been convicted of an offence against this Ordinance, or having committed a breach of any regulations made under this Ordinance relating to dealers, investment advisers, or representatives, the applicant is not a fit and proper person to be registered under this Part;

(v) it appears to the Commissioner that, by reason of any other circumstances whatsoever which either are likely to lead to improper conduct of business by, or reflect discredit on the method of conducting business of, the applicant or any person employed by or associated with him, the applicant is not a fit and proper person to be registered under this Part; or

(vi) the applicant is under 21 years of age; or

*(b)* in the case of an applicant that is a corporation, on the grounds that—

(i) the applicant has not provided the Commissioner with such information relating to it or any person employed by or associated with it, and to any circumstances likely to affect its method of conducting business as may be prescribed by or under this Ordinance;

(ii) any director of the applicant is detained under the Mental Health Ordinance in a mental hospital or is a patient as defined in section 2 of that Ordinance;

(iii) any director of the applicant is an undischarged bankrupt;

(iii*a*) where the application is for registration as a dealer, no director of the applicant is, or is in the opinion of the Commissioner likely to be, registered as a dealer, or where the application is for registration as an investment adviser, no director of the applicant is, or is in the opinion of the Commissioner likely to be, registered as an investment adviser;

(iv) it appears to the Commissioner that, by reason of the applicant, or any director or secretary of the applicant or any officer concerned in the management of the applicant's business or any employee of the applicant, having been convicted, whether in Hong Kong or elsewhere, of an offence its or his conviction for which necessarily involved a finding that it or he acted fraudulently or dishonestly, or having been convicted of an offence against this Ordinance, or having committed a breach of any regulations made under this Ordinance relating to dealers, investment advisers, or representatives, the applicant is not a fit and proper person to be registered under this Part; or

(v) it appears to the Commissioner that, by reason of any other circumstances whatsoever which either are likely to lead to improper conduct of business by, or reflect discredit on the method of conducting business of, the applicant or any director or secretary of the applicant, or any officer concerned in the management of the applicant's business, or any employee of the applicant, the applicant is not a fit and proper person to be registered under this Part

(2) The Commissioner shall not refuse an application for registration without first giving the applicant an opportunity of being heard.

(3) Where the Commissioner refuses an application for registration,

he shall notify the applicant in writing of that fact and shall include in the notice a statement of the reasons for the refusal.

Renewal of registration.

54. (1) An application for renewal of registration under this Part shall—

(*a*) be made to the Commissioner in the manner prescribed by regulations;
(*b*) be accompanied by the fee prescribed by regulations; and
(*c*) be made not later than one month before the day on which the certificate of registration, if not renewed, would expire.

(2) The Commissioner may require an applicant under this section to supply him with any further information that he considers necessary to deal with the application.

(3) The Commissioner may not refuse an application under this section except—

(*a*) on a ground that would entitle him to revoke the registration of a person under section 55 or section 56; or
(*b*) by reason of the failure of the applicant to comply with subsection (1) or with any requirement of the Commissioner under subsection (2).

(4) An application under this section may be granted subject to such reasonable conditions as the Commissioner thinks necessary.

(5) On granting an application under this section, the Commissioner shall issue the appropriate certificate of registration which shall be valid for a period of 12 months from the expiry of the certificate of registration held by the applicant at the time of his application.

(6) Nothing in this section shall be construed as preventing a certificate of registration that has been renewed from being further renewed for a further period of 12 months.

(7) The Commissioner shall not refuse an application for renewal of registration under this section without first giving the applicant an opportunity of being heard.

(8) Where the Commissioner refuses an application for renewal of registration under this section, he shall notify the applicant in writing of that fact and shall include in the notice a statement of the reasons for the refusal.

**55.** (1) Where any registered person—

Revocation and suspension of certificates of registration in certain cases.

(*a*) being an individual, dies; or

(*b*) being a corporation, is dissolved,

the registration of that person is deemed to be revoked.

(2) The Commissioner may revoke the registration of a registered person or, if he thinks it appropriate to do so, suspend the registration of such a person for such time, or until the happening of such event, as he may determine—

(*a*) in the case of a registered person who is an individual, if that person—

(i) becomes a mentally disordered person or a patient, as defined in section 2 of the Mental Health Ordinance;

(ii) becomes bankrupt, or compounds with his creditors or makes an assignment of his estate for their benefit;

(iii) is convicted, whether in Hong Kong or elsewhere, of an offence the conviction for which necessarily involved a finding that he acted fraudulently or dishonestly;

(iv) is convicted of an offence against this Ordinance;

(v) ceases to carry on business in Hong Kong; or

(vi) is registered as a representative and the registration of the dealer or investment adviser, in relation to whom the certificate of registration of the representative was granted, is revoked or suspended; or

(*b*) in the case of a registered person that is a corporation if—

(i) the corporation goes into liquidation or is ordered to be wound up;

(ii) a receiver or manager of the property of the corporation is appointed;

(iii) the corporation has ceased to carry on business;

(iv) a levy of execution in respect of the corporation has not been satisfied;

(v) the corporation has entered into a compromise or scheme of arrangement with its creditors;

(vi) any director of the corporation is convicted, whether in Hong Kong or elsewhere, of an offence the conviction for which necessarily involved a finding that he acted fraudulently or dishonestly;

(vii) any director of the corporation is convicted of an offence against this Ordinance;

(viii) a director, secretary, or other person concerned in the management of the corporation who is required to be registered under this Part is not so registered or the registration of such a director, secretary, or other person has been revoked or suspended.

(3) The Commissioner may revoke a certificate of registration at the request of its holder.

(4) The Commissioner may at any time remove the suspension of the registration of a registered person if it appears to him desirable to do so.

(5) Every decision of the Commissioner revoking or suspending the registration of a registered person shall be notified to that person in writing and shall include a statement of the reasons on which it is based and take effect from the date on which it is notified to that person or such later date as is specified in the notice.

Powers of Commissioner in relation to misconduct, etc.

56. (1) The Commissioner may inquire into any allegation—

*(a)* that a registered person, whether an individual or corporation—

(i) has not provided the Commissioner, whether before or after becoming registered under this Ordinance, with such information relating to him, and to any circumstances likely to affect his method of conducting business, as may be required by or under this Ordinance;

(ii) is or has been guilty of any misconduct in relation to the conduct of his business; or

(iii) is no longer a fit and proper person to be registered by reason of any other circumstances which have led or are likely to lead to the improper conduct of business by him or to reflect discredit on the method of conducting his business; or

*(b)* that, in the case of a registered person that is a corporation, a director, secretary, or person concerned in the management of the corporation—

(i) is or has been guilty of any misconduct in relation to the conduct of his business; or

(ii) is not or is no longer a fit and proper person to be a director of, or a person concerned with the management of, the corporation.

(2) If after inquiring into any such allegation against a registered person, the Commissioner is of the opinion that the allegation is proved, he may if he thinks fit, subject to the provisions of this Ordinance,

revoke the registration of that person or if he thinks it appropriate to do so—

*(a)* suspend the registration of the person for such time, or until the happening of such event, as he may determine; or

*(b)* reprimand him or, in the case of a registered person that is a corporation, reprimand any director, secretary, or person concerned in the management of the corporation.

(3) The Commissioner shall not impose any penalty under subsection (2) without first giving the registered person, and, in the case of a registered person that is a corporation, any director, secretary, or officer concerned in the management of the corporation against whom an allegation has been made under subsection (1), an opportunity of being heard.

(4) Every decision of the Commissioner imposing a penalty under subsection (2) on a person shall be notified to that person in writing and shall include a statement of the reasons on which it is based and take effect from the date on which it is notified to him, or such later date as is specified in the notice, notwithstanding that an appeal against the decision may be made under section 58 or that the time limited for the making of such an appeal has not expired.

(5) For the purposes of this section "misconduct" means—

*(a)* any failure to comply with the requirements of any regulations made under this Ordinance with respect to dealers, investment advisers, or representatives;

*(b)* any failure to observe the terms and conditions of a certificate of registration;

*(c)* any act or omission relating to the conduct of business of a dealer, investment adviser, or representative, which is or is likely to be prejudicial to the interests of members of the investing public.

**Effect of revoking or suspending registration.**

57. (1) For the purposes of sections 48 to 50 a person whose registration is revoked or suspended shall be deemed not to be registered.

(2) Subsection (1) does not operate so as to—

*(a)* avoid or affect any agreement transaction or arrangement relating to a dealing in securities entered into by a person whose registration has been suspended or revoked, whether the agreement, transaction, or arrangement was entered into before or after the suspension or revocation of the registration; or

(*b*) affect any right, obligation, or liability arising under any such agreement, transaction, or arrangement.

(3) A person whose registration is revoked under section 55 or section 56 may not apply to be registered under this Part, whether as a dealer, investment adviser, or representative, until the expiration of at least 12 months from the revocation.

(4) Where the Commissioner revokes or suspends the registration of any person under section 55 or section 56 or imposes any other penalty under section 56, he shall notify that person in writing of the revocation, suspension, or other penalty, and shall include in the notice a statement of the reasons as to why the registration of the person was revoked or suspended or, as the case may be, the penalty was imposed.

Appeal to the Disciplinary Committee against refusals of application, etc.

58. (1) Where—

(*a*) the application of any person for registration or renewal of registration under this Part is refused; or

(*b*) the application of a person for registration or renewal of registration under this Part is granted subject to conditions with which he is dissatisfied; or

(*c*) the registration of any registered person is revoked or suspended under section 55 or section 56; or

(*d*) the deposit of a registered dealer is forfeited under section 52(2)(*c*),

that person may, within one month of being notified of the decision by the Commissioner, appeal to the Disciplinary Committee in accordance with any rules made under section 45.

(2) After considering the representations submitted and evidence produced by or on behalf of the appellant and the Commissioner, the Disciplinary Committee may confirm, reverse, or vary that decision.

Appeals from decisions of the Disciplinary Committee, etc. in certain cases.

59. (1) An appeal shall lie to the Court against any decision of the Disciplinary Committee in relation to the hearing of an appeal under section 58 by any interested party who is aggrieved by the decision of the Committee; and the Court may confirm, vary, or reverse the decision of the Committee and give such other directions as it thinks just and equitable.

(2) Every such appeal shall be made within such time and in such manner, and shall be heard in accordance with such procedure, as may be prescribed by rules of court made under the Supreme Court Ordinance.

(3) The decision of the Court on an appeal under this section shall be final.

**60.** (1) The Commissioner may declare any person to be an exempt dealer for the purposes of this Ordinance if he is satisfied that the business of that person complies with the following requirement, that is to say— Exempt dealers.

*(a)* the main business of that person consists of one or both of the following activities—

(i) carrying on some business other than the business of dealing in securities;

(ii) dealing in securities in one or more of the ways specified in subsection (2); and

*(b)* the greater part of any business of dealing in securities done by him in Hong Kong, otherwise than in one of the ways specified in subsection (2), is effected with or through the agency of one or more of the following persons—

(i) a registered dealer;

(ii) an exempt dealer; or

(iii) a member of a stock exchange outside Hong Kong.

(2) The ways of dealing in securities referred to in subsection (1) are—

*(a)* issuing any document which is or is to be deemed to be a prospectus within the meaning of the Companies Ordinance or any prospectus approved by the Commissioner that is issued by a mutual fund corporation or unit trust authorized by the Commission;

*(b)* making or offering to make with any person an agreement for or with a view to the underwriting of securities by that person;

*(c)* making any invitation to persons to subscribe for securities or to purchase securities on the first occasion that they are sold;

*(d)* making any invitation to persons to subscribe for or purchase securities of the Government or the government of any country or territory outside Hong Kong;

*(e)* effecting any transaction with a person whose business involves the acquisition and disposal or the holding of securities, being a transaction with that person as a principal.

(3) The Commissioner may revoke a declaration under subsection (1) that a person is an exempt dealer if it appears to him that—

*(a)* the business of that person does not comply with the requirements set out in subsection (1); or

(*b*) the circumstances relevant to the making of the declaration have materially changed since it was made.

(4) Without prejudice to subsection (1), the Commissioner may, by notice in the *Gazette*, declare—

(*a*) any licensed bank;

(*b*) any trustee company registered under Part VIII of the Trustee Ordinance; or

(*c*) any person belonging to[4] class of persons, or carrying on a type of business, prescribed in regulations for the purposes of this paragraph,

to be an exempt dealer for the purposes of this Ordinance.

(5) The Commissioner may at any time revoke a declaration made under subsection (4).

(6) The Commissioner shall cause to be published in the *Gazette* at least once in every year the names and addresses of all persons who are exempt dealers.

Exempt investment advisers.

61. (1) The Commissioner may declare any person to be an exempt investment adviser for the purposes of this Ordinance if he is satisfied that the business of that person complies with the following requirements, that is to say—

(*a*) the investment advice is given mainly to persons whose business involves the acquisition and disposal or the holding of securities; or

(*b*) the investment advice is given only to persons residing outside Hong Kong.

(2) The Commissioner may at any time revoke a declaration under subsection (1).

Offence to make a false representation for the purpose of obtaining a certificate of registration under this Part.

62. (1) Any person who for the purpose of obtaining a certificate of registration under this Part, whether for himself or for any other person, makes any representation, whether in writing, orally or otherwise, which he knows to be false or misleading as to a material particular shall be guilty of an offence, and shall be liable on conviction on indictment, to imprisonment for 5 years.

(2) For the purposes of subsection (1), "representation" means a representation—

(*a*) of a matter of fact, either present or past; or

(*b*) about a future event; or

[4] Editor's query: "a."

*(c)* about an existing intention, opinion, belief, knowledge, or other state of mind.

(3) Proceedings in respect of an offence against this section may be brought at any time within 6 months of the discovery of the offence.

Information to be provided by dealers, etc.

**63.** (1) Every dealer and investment adviser shall forthwith notify the Commissioner in writing of any change which, while his certificate of registration is in force, may occur—

*(a)* in the address in Hong Kong at which he carries on the business of dealing in securities or of investment adviser, as the case may be; or

*(b)* in any information supplied in or in connexion with his application for registration or renewal of registration, being information prescribed by regulations.

(2) Every dealer and investment adviser shall forthwith, on ceasing to carry on business in Hong Kong as a dealer or an investment adviser, notify the Commissioner in writing of that fact.

(3) If, at any time while a corporation is registered as a dealer or investment adviser, any person becomes or ceases to be a director of the corporation, the corporation shall within 7 days after that event notify the Commissioner in writing of the name and address of that person and also his nationality or the fact that he has no nationality.

(4) If, at any time while a person is registered as a dealer's representative or investment representative, that person leaves or enters the service of, or becomes or ceases to be an agent of, any dealer or investment adviser, that person shall within 7 days after that event notify the Commissioner in writing of the fact and of the name and address of the dealer or investment adviser.

(5) Any person who, without reasonable excuse, contravenes any of the provisions of this section shall be guilty of an offence and shall be liable on conviction to a fine of $2,000.

Commissioner to keep a register of dealers, etc.

**64.** (1) The Commissioner shall establish and maintain at his office—

*(a)* a register of dealers in which shall be entered the name of every registered dealer and such other particulars as may be prescribed by regulations in relation to registered dealers;

*(b)* a register of investment advisers in which shall be entered the name of every registered investment adviser and such other

particulars as may be prescribed by regulations in relation to registered investment advisers;

(*c*) a register of dealers' representatives in which shall be entered the name of every registered dealer's representative and such other particulars as may be prescribed by regulations in relation to registered dealers' representatives; and

(*d*) a register of investment representatives in which shall be entered the name of every registered investment representative and such other particulars as may be prescribed by regulations in relation to registered investment representatives.

(2) The registers kept under this section and, after registration or renewal of registration, as the case may be, all applications made for registration or renewal of registration under this Part shall, during such hours as may be prescribed and on payment of any fee prescribed by regulations, be open to inspection by members of the public.

(3) A copy of any extract of or entry in the registers kept under this section, purporting to be certified by the Commissioner, shall be admissible as evidence in any legal proceedings, whether under this Ordinance or otherwise.

Publication of names of registered dealers, etc.

65. (1) The Commissioner shall cause to be published in the *Gazette,* at such times and in such manner as he thinks proper, the names and addresses of all persons who are registered under this Part, and also—

(*a*) in relation to any such person who is not a corporation, his nationality or, as the case may be, that he has no nationality; or

(*b*) in relation to any such person which is a corporation, the country where the corporation is domiciled or under the law of which the corporation is incorporated.

(2) The information required by subsection (1) shall be published at least once each year.

(3) If the Commissioner at any time amends any of the registers kept by him under this Part by adding or removing the name of any person, he shall cause particulars of the amendment to be published in the *Gazette* within one month after making the amendment.

## PART VII. RECORDS

Application of Part VII.

66. (1) This Part applies to and in relation to—

(*a*) a person who is—

(i) a dealer;
(ii) a dealer's representative;
(iii) an investment adviser; or
(iv) an investment representative; and

(*b*) securities listed on a stock exchange and any other securities of a class prescribed in regulations for the purposes of this subsection.

(2) The Governor in Council may, by order, apply any of the provisions of this Part, with such modifications and additions as he thinks fit, to financial journalists.

(3) For the purposes of subsection (2) "financial journalist" means a person who, in the course of his business or employment, contributes advice concerning securities for publication in a newspaper, magazine, journal, or other periodical publication.

Certain persons to maintain registers of securities.

67. (1) A person to whom this Part applies shall maintain a register of the securities in which he has an interest and of the particulars relating to their acquisition and disposal in a manner and form approved by the Commissioner.

(2) Particulars of the securities in which a person to whom this Part applies has an interest and particulars of his interest in those securities shall be entered by that person in the register within 14 days after he becomes aware of the acquisition of the interest or after the commencement of this section, whichever is the later.

(3) Where there is a change (not being a change prescribed by regulations) in the interest or interests in securities of a person to whom this Part applies, he shall, within 14 days after he becomes aware of the change, enter in the register full particulars of the change, including the date when the change occurred and the circumstances by reason of which the change occurred.

(4) For the purposes of this section, where a person acquires or disposes of securities there shall be deemed to be a change in the interest or interests of that person.

(5) A person who contravenes any provision of this section that is applicable to him shall be guilty of an offence and shall be liable on conviction to a fine of $5,000.

Certain notices to be given to the Commissioner.

68. (1) A person to whom this Part applies shall notify in writing to the Commissioner the place at which he keeps or intends to keep the register of his interests in securities.

(2) Notice under subsection (1) shall be given—

*(a)* if the person is a person to whom this Part applies at the commencement of this section, within one month after that date; or

*(b)* in any other case, in or as part of the person's application for registration under this Ordinance.

(3) A notice under paragraph *(a)* of subsection (2) shall be given as provided in that paragraph notwithstanding that the person has ceased to be a person to whom this Part applies before the expiration of the appropriate time referred to in that paragraph.

(4) A person to whom this Part applies shall keep the register of his interests in securities at the place specified in the notice given under subsection (1) unless he gives a subsequent notice to the Commissioner in the form prescribed by regulations to the effect that the register is kept at some other place specified in the subsequent notice, in which case he shall keep the register—

*(a)* where only one such subsequent notice has been given, at the other place specified in that notice, or

*(b)* where more than one such subsequent notice has been given, at the other place specified in the later or latest of those notices.

(5) A person who ceases to be a person to whom this Part applies shall give notice in the form prescribed by regulations to the Commissioner of that fact within 14 days thereafter.

(6) A person who contravenes any provision of this section that is applicable to him shall be guilty of an offence and shall be liable on conviction to a fine of $2,000.

Defences.

**69.** (1) It shall be a defence to a prosecution for contravening any provision of section 67(5) or section 68(6) if the defendant proves that the contravention was due to his not being aware of a fact or occurrence the existence of which was necessary to constitute the offence.

(2) For the purposes of this Part, a person shall, in the absence of proof to the contrary, be presumed to have been aware at a particular time of a fact or occurrence relating to securities of which a servant or agent of the person, being a servant or agent having duties or acting in relation to his employer's or principal's interest in the relevant securities, was aware at that time.

**70.** The Commissioner may require a person to whom this Part applies to produce for inspection the register required to be kept pursuant to section 67, and the Commissioner may make copies of or take extracts from the register.

Power of Commissioner to require certain information to be supplied to him.

**71.** The Commissioner may supply a copy of any such register, or a copy of an extract from it, to the Attorney General, who may, if he has reason to believe that an offence under this Ordinance may have been committed, deliver the copy to any person whom he thinks fit for the purposes of an investigation or a prosecution of the offence.

Power of Commissioner to supply copy of register.

## PART VIII. TRADING IN SECURITIES

72. (1) A dealer shall not in Hong Kong communicate an offer to acquire or dispose of securities of a corporation unless—

Offers by dealers.

*(a)* the offer—

(i) is written in the English or Chinese language; or

(ii) if communicated verbally, is reduced to writing in the English or Chinese language and delivered to the person or persons to whom it was made not later than 24 hours after the verbal communication; and

*(b)* the offer—

(i) specifies the name and address of the offeror and, if any person is making the offer on behalf of the offeror, the name and address of that person;

(ii) contains a description of securities sufficient to identify them;

(iii) specifies the terms of the offer (including where appropriate the amount of consideration proposed to be paid for securities acquired pursuant to the offer);

(iv) where a dividend has been declared or recommended in respect of the securities, or it is anticipated that a dividend will be so declared or recommended before the transfer of the securities, states whether the securities are to be transferred with or without that dividend;

(v) specifies whether, in the event of a person accepting the offer, the offeror will pay any stamp duty which that person will become liable to pay in respect of the contract note as a result of the transaction;

(vi) bears a date which is not more than 3 days before the date on which the offer is communicated;

(vii) if the offer relates to the acquisition of securities, satisfies the requirements of the First Schedule;

First Schedule.

(viii) if the offer relates to the disposal of securities, satisfies the requirements of the Second Schedule;

Second Schedule.

(ix) where a report of an expert in connexion with the offer is included in or annexed to the offer, contains a statement to the effect that the expert has consented to the inclusion or annexure, and has not, before the communication of the offer, withdrawn that consent;

*(c)* the offer includes a translation, as the case requires, in the Chinese or English language of all the particulars required under paragraph *(b)*, except where the Commissioner has previously agreed that the requirements of this paragraph may be dispensed with in any particular case.

(2) A document containing an offer to which subsection (1) relates which includes a statement purporting to be made by an expert shall not be communicated unless the expert has given and has not, before communication of a copy of the offer, withdrawn his written consent to the communication of the offer with the inclusion of the statement in the form and context in which it is included.

(3) Subject to subsection (5), any dealer who communicates an offer for the acquisition or disposal of securities without having complied with subsection (1) and subsection (2) shall be guilty of an offence and shall be liable on conviction to a fine of $10,000.

(4) Where any person has accepted an offer for the disposal or acquisition of securities under this section and the offer has been made without the requirements of subsection (1) and subsection (2) having been complied with in a material particular, that person may, subject to the rights of any *bona fide* purchaser of the securities for value, rescind the acceptance, by notice in writing, within 14 days after the date of the acceptance.

(5) Without prejudice to the provisions of section 3, this section does not apply to—

*(a)* any offer to dispose of securities of a corporation to persons who already hold securities of that corporation;

*(b)* any offer by a dealer if the offer is made to a person with whom, or on whose behalf, the dealer has transacted the sale or purchase of securities on at least 3 occasions during the period of 3 years immediately preceding the offer;

(c) any offer made to—

(i) a person whose business involves the acquisition or disposal or holding of securities; or

(ii) a solicitor or professional accountant; or

(iii) any other person who belongs to a class of persons prescribed in regulations for the purposes of this paragraph; or

(d) any offer made by a stockbroker in the ordinary course of trading on the exchange.

(6) Where a dealer communicates an invitation which invites a person to acquire or dispose of any security held by that person in a corporation, then for the purposes of this section—

(a) that invitation is deemed to be an offer; and

(b) an offer to acquire or dispose of that security made by that person in response to the invitation is deemed to be an acceptance by that person of an offer to acquire or, as the case may be, an offer to dispose of the security,

and references in this section to "acceptance" shall be construed accordingly.

(7) An offer to acquire or dispose of a right to acquire or dispose of a security or an interest in a security is deemed to be an offer to acquire or dispose of a security; and a reference to a person who holds securities includes a reference to a person who holds a right to acquire a security or an interest in a security.

(8) For the purposes of this section "expert" includes an engineer, valuer, professional accountant, and solicitor, and any other person whose profession gives authority to a statement made by him.

(9) For the purposes of this section an offer to acquire or dispose of securities in consideration or part consideration for other securities is deemed to be both an offer to acquire and an offer to dispose of securities.

Calls by registered dealers.

73. (1) Subject to subsection (3), a dealer shall not during, or as a consequence of, a call on any person, whether at his place of residence or his place of employment or otherwise, enter into any contract for the sale of securities unless he—

(a) calls on the person at the invitation of that person; and

(b) before entering into the contract provides the person with a written statement containing all the information which he would have been required to give to that person if the contract had been entered into as a result of an offer made under section 72.

(2) Any dealer who contravenes subsection (1) shall be guilty of an offence and shall be liable on conviction to a fine of $10,000 and to imprisonment for 2 years.

(3) Subsection (1) does not apply to—

*(a)* any contract for the sale of securities of a corporation with a person who already holds securities of that corporation;

*(b)* any contract for the sale of securities by a dealer with a person with whom the dealer has transacted the sale or purchase of securities on at least 3 occasions during the period of 3 years immediately preceding the date of the contract; or

*(c)* any contract for the sale of securities with—

(i) a person whose business involves the acquisition or disposal or holding of securities;

(ii) a solicitor or professional accountant;

(iii) any other person who belongs to a class of persons precribed in regulations for the purpose of this paragraph.

(4) Where any contract for the sale of securities is entered into in contravention of subsection (1), the purchaser may, subject to the rights of any *bona fide* purchaser of the securities for value, rescind the contract by giving notice in writing to the seller within 28 days after the date on whch the contract was entered into.

(5) In this section "call" includes a visit in person and a communication by telephone.

Hawking of securities.

74. (1) Subject to subsections (2) and (3), a person shall not, whether on his own behalf or otherwise and whether by appointment or otherwise, call from place to place—

*(a)* making or offering to make with any person—

(i) an agreement for or with a view to having that other person purchase specific securities; or

(ii) an agreement the purpose or pretended purpose of which is to secure a profit to that other person from the yield of specific securities or by reference to fluctuations in the value of specific securities; or

*(b)* inducing or attempting to induce any other person to enter into an agreement of the type referred to in sub-paragraph (i) or sub-paragraph (ii) of paragraph *(a)*,

whether or not in calling from place to place he does any other act or thing.

(2) Subsection (1) does not apply to—

*(a)* a person in so far as—

(i) he calls at the place of another person who is a banker, solicitor, professional accountant, registered or exempt dealer, registered or exempt investment adviser or registered dealer's representative or registered investment representative; and

(ii) whether as principal or agent, he makes, or offers to make, with that other person an agreement referred to in subsection (1) or induces, or attempts to induce, that other person to enter into such an agreement; or

*(b)* any other person calling from place to place who belongs to a class of persons prescribed in regulations for the purpose of this subsection.

(3) Nothing in this section applies to securities or any class of securities which have been exempted by the Commission for the purposes of this section provided that any conditions subject to which the exemption was granted have been fulfilled.

(4) Any person who contravenes subsection (1) shall be guilty of an offence and shall be liable on conviction to a fine of $50,000 and to imprisonment for 2 years.

(5) If in any proceedings for an offence against subsection (4) it is proved that the accused did any of the acts mentioned in paragraph *(a)* or paragraph *(b)* of subsection (1) on 2 or more occasions within any period of 14 days, he shall, until the contrary is proved, be deemed to have been calling from place to place.

(6) In this section "to call" includes to visit in person and to communicate by telephone.

Issue of contract notes.

75. (1) Every dealer (including an exempt dealer) shall, in respect of every contract for the purchase, sale, or exchange of securities entered into by him in Hong Kong (whether as principal or agent), not later than the end of the next trading day after the contract was entered into, make out a contract note which complies with subsection (2) and—

*(a)* where the contract was entered into as agent, deliver the contract note to the person on whose behalf he entered into the contract; or

(*b*) where the contract was entered into as principal, retain the contract note for himself.

(2) A contract note made out by a dealer under subsection (1) shall include—

(*a*) the name or style under which the dealer carries on his business as a dealer and the address of the principal place at which he so carries on business;
(*b*) where the dealer is acting as principal, a statement that he is so acting;
(*c*) the name of the person (if any) to whom the dealer is required to give the contract note;
(*d*) the date of the contract, and the date on which the contract note is made out;
(*e*) the quantity and description of the securities that are being acquired or disposed of;
(*f*) except in the case of an exchange, the price per unit of the securities;
(*g*) the amount of consideration payable under the contract or, in the case of an exchange, particulars of the securities exchanged sufficient to identify them;
(*h*) the rate or amount of commission (if any) payable in respect of the contract;
(*i*) the amount of stamp duty (if any) payable in connexion with the contract and, where applicable, in respect of the transfer;
(*j*) the date of settlement.

(3) Any dealer (including an exempt dealer) who completes a contract for the purchase, sale, or exchange of securities without having complied with subsection (1) shall be guilty of an offence and shall be liable on conviction to a fine of $5,000.

Dealers not to engage in option or forward trading.

**76.** (1) Except as provided in regulations, a dealer (including an exempt dealer) shall not transact in Hong Kong, or hold himself out as being prepared to transact in Hong Kong—

(*a*) any dealing whereby the dealer confers on any person an option to purchase from or sell to the dealer any securities listed on a stock exchange in Hong Kong; or
(*b*) any dealing in any such securities which is completed later than the end of the next trading day after the dealing was entered into.

(2) Any dealer who contravenes subsection (1) shall, subject to subsection (3), be guilty of an offence and shall be liable on conviction to a fine of $5,000.

(3) It shall be a defence to any criminal proceedings brought under subsection (2) in respect of a dealing mentioned in paragraph *(b)* of subsection (1) for the accused to prove that he took all reasonable and practicable steps to secure completion of the transaction within the period permitted by that paragraph.

(4) A contract entered into in contravention of subsection (1) shall not be enforceable by either the dealer or the other contracting party.

**Dealers to provide certain information, etc. to client.**

**77.** (1) Subject to subsection (2), every dealer (including an exempt dealer) shall, on being requested to do so by any person on whose behalf he has transacted a dealing in securities—

*(a)* provide that person with a copy of the contract note relating to the dealing, and a copy of his account with the dealer; and
*(b)* if the Commissioner on the application of the person so directs, make available for inspection by that person, at all reasonable times during the dealer's ordinary hours of business, the dealer's copy of the contract note and the person's account with the dealer.

(2) Subsection (1) does not require a dealer (including an exempt dealer) to—

*(a)* provide, or keep available for inspection, a copy of any contract note which relates to a dealing transacted more than 2 years before the date of the request; or
*(b)* provide a copy of, or keep available for inspection, any account which relates to a dealing transacted more than 6 years before the date of the request.

(3) Any such dealer may impose a charge not exceeding an amount prescribed by regulations for a copy of a document provided pursuant to subsection (1).

(4) Any dealer who, without reasonable excuse, fails to comply with subsection (1) shall be guilty of an offence and shall be liable on conviction to a fine of $2,000.

**Certain representations prohibited.**

**78.** (1) A registered person shall not in any communication, whether written or oral, represent or imply or knowingly permit to be represented or implied in any manner to a person that the abilities or qualifications of the registered person have in any respect been approved by the Hong Kong Government, the Commission or the Commissioner.

(2) A statement made to the effect that a person is registered

under this Ordinance or is the holder of a certificate of registration is not a contravention of subsection (1).

(3) Any registered person who, without reasonable excuse, contravenes subsection (1) shall be guilty of an offence and shall be liable on conviction to a fine of $2,000.

Disclosure of certain interests.

79. (1) Where, in a circular or other written communication issued in Hong Kong by him to more than one person, a dealer or an investment adviser (including an exempt dealer or exempt investment adviser) makes a recommendation, whether expressly or by implication, with respect to any securities or any class of securities of a corporation, he shall include in the circular or other communication, in type not less bold and not less legible than that used in its text, a statement as to whether or not he has, at the date specified in the circular or communication pursuant to subsection (5), an interest in any of the securities of that corporation.

(2) Subsection (1) does not require in the case of a circular or other written communication issued by a stockbroker the inclusion of a statement in relation to an interest that consists of the right to charge commission as provided by the rules of the stock exchange of which he is a member on the sale or purchase of the securities or class of securities that are being recommended.

(3) For the purposes of subsection (1), a person who has entered into an underwriting agreement in respect of any securities shall be deemed to have a financial interest in the sale or purchase of those securities.

(4) Where an offer to the public of securities is not fully subscribed, a person who has subscribed for or taken up, or is required to subscribe for or take up, any of those securities under an underwriting agreement shall not, during the period of 90 days after the close of the offer, make any offer or recommendation in respect of those securities unless the offer or recommendation contains or is accompanied by a statement to the effect that the offer or recommendation relates to securities that he has acquired, or is or will be required to acquire, under an underwriting agreement as a result of the offer to the public not being fully subscribed.

(5) Every circular or other written communication to which this section relates shall be dated and shall contain on its face the name of the dealer or investment adviser who issued it.

(6) A dealer or investment adviser who issues a circular or communication to which this section relates shall retain a copy of it bearing

his signature in such manner, and for such time or until the happening of such event, as may be prescribed by regulations.

(7) For the purposes of this section, a circular or other written communication shall be deemed to have been issued by the person whose name is contained on its face.

(8) In this section a reference to securities does not include a reference to the stock or debentures of, or bonds made available by, a government or a local government authority, or to securities guaranteed by a government or a local government authority.

(9) Without prejudice to the power to make regulations under section 146, regulations may be made under that section—

*(a)* requiring the lodging with the Commissioner of copies of any circular or other written communication issued by a dealer or investment adviser; and

*(b)* making provision for or with respect to the keeping of records of circulars or other similar written communications issued by a dealer or by an investment adviser.

(10) Any dealer or investment adviser, whether registered or exempted from registration, who—

*(a)* issues a circular or other written communication in contravention of subsection (1) or subsection (5);

*(b)* contravenes subsection (4); or

*(c)* fails to retain a copy of a circular or other written communication as required by subsection (6),

shall be guilty of an offence and shall be liable on conviction to a fine of $5,000.

(11) An offence against subsection (10) is not committed by reason only that a circular or other written communication is issued to a person whose business involves the acquisition, disposal, or holding of securities.

**80.** (1) A person shall not sell securities at or through a stock exchange unless, at the time he sells them— Short selling prohibited.

*(a)* he has or, where he is selling as agent, his principal has; or

*(b)* he reasonably and honestly believes that he has or, where he is selling as agent, that his principal has,

a presently exercisable and unconditional right to vest the securities in the purchaser of them.

(2) Any person who contravenes subsection (1) shall be guilty of

an offence and shall be liable on conviction to a fine of $10,000 and to imprisonment for 6 months.

(3) For the purposes of subsection (1)—

*(a)* a person shall be deemed to be selling securities if he—

(i) purports to sell the securities;

(ii) offers to sell the securities;

(iii) holds himself out as entitled to sell the securities; or

(iv) instructs a dealer to sell the securities;

*(b)* a person who, at a particular time, has a presently exercisable and unconditional right to have securities vested in him or in accordance with his directions shall be deemed to have at that time a presently exercisable and unconditional right to vest the securities in a purchaser of them; and

*(c)* a right of a person to vest securities in a purchaser thereof shall not be deemed not to be unconditional by reason only of the fact that the securities are charged or pledged in favour of some other person to secure the repayment of money.

(4) Subsection (1) does not apply to or in relation to—

*(a)* a person acting in good faith in the reasonable and honest belief that he has a right, title, or interest to or in securities that he purports to sell, offers for sale, or holds himself out as capable of selling;

*(b)* a dealer acting in good faith for or on behalf of some other person in the reasonable and honest belief that such other person has a right, title, or interest to or in securities that he purports to sell, offers for sale, or holds himself out as capable of selling;

*(c)* a sale of securities by a stockbroker acting as principal when he acts as an odd lot specialist in accordance with the rules of the stock exchange of which he is a member, being a sale made solely for the purpose of—

(i) accepting an offer to purchase an odd lot of securities; or

(ii) disposing of a parcel or securities that is less than one board lot of securities, by means of the sale of one board lot of those securities; or

*(d)* a sale of securities falling within a class of transaction prescribed by regulations for the purposes of this paragraph.

Disposition of security documents.

81. (1) Where securities that are not the property of a dealer (including an exempt dealer) and for which the dealer, or any nominee controlled by the dealer, is accountable are held for safe custody in

Hong Kong, the dealer shall, subject to subsection (2), either cause the securities—

*(a)* (not being bearer securities) to be registered as soon as practicable in the name of the person to whom the dealer or nominee is accountable or in the name of the dealer's nominee; or

*(b)* to be deposited in safe custody in a designated account with the dealer's bankers or with any other institution which provides facilities for the safe custody of documents to the satisfaction of the Commissioner.

(2) The Commissioner may, on the application of a dealer in writing, exempt the dealer from the provisions of subsection (1), but in granting the exemption may impose such conditions as he thinks fit.

(3) No dealer shall, without the specific authority in writing of the person to whom he is accountable, deposit any securities of which the dealer is not the owner as security for loans or advances made to the dealer or lend or otherwise part with the possession of any such securities for any purpose.

(4) An authority conferred under subsection (3) shall specify the period for which it is current, but shall not in any event, subject to subsection (5), remain in force for a period of more than 12 months.

(5) An authority conferred under subsection (3) may be renewed in writing for one or more further periods not exceeding 12 months at any one time.

(6) Any dealer who, without lawful authority or reasonable excuse, contravenes subsection (1) or subsection (3) shall be guilty of an offence.

(7) Any person guilty of an offence under subsection (6) shall be liable on conviction—

*(a)* in the case of a contravention of subsection (1), to a fine of $2,000; and

*(b)* in the case of a contravention of subsection (3), to a fine of $20,000 and to imprisonment for 2 years.

## PART IX. ACCOUNTS AND AUDIT

**82.** (1) This Part applies to the business of a registered dealer, other than a registered dealer who is a director of a corporation when acting for or on behalf of the corporation in its business of dealing in

Application and interpretation of Part IX.

securities; and every reference in this Part to the term "dealer" shall be construed accordingly.

(2) In this Part, unless the context otherwise requires, any reference to the books, accounts, records, securities, trust accounts, or business of, or in relation to, a dealer who carries on business in partnership shall be read and construed as a reference to the books, accounts, records, securities, trust accounts, or business (as the case requires) of or in relation to the partnership.

(3) The Governor in Council may, by order published in the *Gazette*, apply all or any of the provisions of this Part, with or without modifications, to registered investment advisers.

Accounts to be kept by dealers.

**83.** (1) A dealer shall—

*(a)* cause to be kept such accounting and other records as will sufficiently explain the transactions, and reflect the financial position, of the business of dealing in securities carried on by him, and will enable true and fair profit and loss accounts and balance sheets to be prepared from time to time; and

*(b)* cause those records to be kept in such a manner as will enable them to be conveniently and properly audited.

(2) The records referred to in subsection (1) shall be kept—

*(a)* in writing in the English language; or

*(b)* in such a manner as to enable them to be readily accessible and readily converted into written form in the English language.

(3) Without affecting the generality of subsection (1), a dealer shall cause records to be kept—

*(a)* in sufficient detail to show particulars of—

(i) all money received and paid by the dealer, including money paid to, and disbursed from, a trust account;

(ii) all purchases and sales of securities made by the dealer, the charges and credits arising from them, and the names of the buyer and seller, respectively, of each of those securities;

(iii) all income received from commissions, interest, and other sources, and all expenses, commissions, and interest paid by the dealer;

(iv) all the assets and liabilities (including contingent liabilities) of the dealer;

(v) all securities that are the property of the dealer, showing by whom the security documents are held and, where they are held by some other person, whether or not they are held as security against loans or advances;

(vi) all securities that are not the property of the dealer and for which the dealer or any nominee controlled by the dealer is accountable, showing by whom, and for whom, the security documents are held distinguishing those which are held for safe custody, and those which are deposited with a third party whether as security for loans or advances made to the dealer or any related corporation or for any other purpose; and

(vii) all underwriting and sub-underwriting transactions entered into by the dealer; and

*(b)* containing copies of acknowledgements of the receipt of securities received by the dealer from or on behalf of clients, clearly identifying in respect of each receipt of securities the client and the securities.

(4) Without prejudice to subsection (3), a dealer shall keep records in sufficient details to show separately particulars of all transactions by the dealer with, or for the account of—

*(a)* clients of the dealer; and

*(b)* the dealer himself.

(5) A dealer shall retain—

*(a)* for a period of not less than 6 years, the records referred to in subsection (1); and

*(b)* for a period of not less than 2 years—

(i) each contract note received by him or made out to himself as principal; and

(ii) a copy of each contract note made out by him as agent.

(6) An entry in the accounting and other records of a dealer kept in accordance with this section shall be deemed to have been made by, or with the authority of, the dealer.

(7) Where matter that is intended to be used in connexion with the keeping of a record referred to in this section is recorded or stored by means of a mechanical device, an electronic device, or any other device in an illegible form, a person who wilfully—

*(a)* records or stores in that device matter that he knows to be false or misleading in a material particular;

*(b)* destroys, removes, or falsifies matter that is recorded or stored in that device; or

*(c)* fails to record or store matter in that device with intent to falsify

any entry made or intended to be complied, wholly or in part, from that matter,

shall be guilty of an offence and shall be liable on conviction to a fine of $10,000 and to imprisonment for 6 months.

(8) For the purposes of this section, a record required to be kept by a dealer may be kept either by making entries in a bound book or by recording the relevant matters in any other manner.

(9) Where a record required by this section to be kept is not kept by making entries in a bound book but by some other means, the dealer shall take reasonable precautions for guarding against falsification and for facilitating discovery of any falsification.

(10) Notwithstanding any other provision of this section, a dealer shall not be deemed to have failed to keep a record referred to in subsection (1) by reason only that the record is kept as a part of, or in conjunction with, the records relating to any business other than dealing in securities that is carried on by him.

Certain money received by dealer to be paid into a trust account.

84. (1) A dealer shall establish and keep at a licensed bank one or more trust accounts designated or evidenced as such into which he shall pay—

*(a)* all amounts (less brokerage and other proper charges) which are received for or on account of any person (other than a stockbroker) from the sale of securities, except those amounts paid to that person or in accordance with his directions within 4 bank trading days after their receipt;
*(b)* all amounts (less any brokerage and other proper charges) which are received from or on account of any person (other than a stockbroker) for the purchase of securities, except those amounts attributable to the purchase of securities which are delivered to the dealer within 4 bank trading days after receipt of the amounts; and
*(c)* subject to any agreement to the contrary, all amounts derived by way of interest from the retention in a trust account of any amount mentioned in paragraph *(a)* or paragraph *(b)*.

(2) All amounts required to be paid into a trust account under subsection (1) shall be retained there by the dealer until they are paid to the person on whose behalf they are being held or in accordance with his directions or, as the case may be, until they are required to complete payment in respect of the purchase of securities on behalf of any such person.

(3) Money required by this section to be paid into a trust account shall be so paid within 4 bank trading days after it is received by the dealer.

(4) All sums derived by way of interest from the payment of money by a dealer into a trust account under this section shall, subject to any agreement to the contrary, belong to the person to whom the dealer is accountable.

(5) No amount other than an amount referred to in paragraph *(a)* or *(b)* of subsection (1) shall be paid into a trust account.

(6) Every dealer shall keep records of—

*(a)* all amounts paid into a trust account kept by him, specifying the persons on whose behalf the amounts are held and the dates on which they were paid into the account;

*(b)* all withdrawals from the trust account, the dates of those withdrawals, and the names of the persons on whose behalf the withdrawals are made; and

*(c)* such other particulars (if any) as may be prescribed by regulations.

(7) A person who—

*(a)* without reasonable excuse, contravenes any provision of this section shall be guilty of an offence and shall be liable on conviction to a fine of $10,000; or

*(b)* with intent to defraud, contravenes any provision of this section shall be guilty of an offence and shall be liable on conviction on indictment to a fine of $50,000 and to imprisonment for 5 years.

Money in trust account not available for payment of debts, etc.

**85.** (1) Except as otherwise provided in this Part, money held in a trust account shall not be available for payment of the debts of a dealer or be liable to be paid or taken in execution under the order or process of any court of competent jurisdiction.

(2) Any payment made in contravention of subsection (1) shall be void *ab initio,* and no person to whom the money is paid shall obtain any title to it.

Claims and liens not affected.

**86.** Nothing in this Part shall be construed as taking away or affecting any lawful claim or lien which any person has in respect of any money held in a trust account or in respect of any money received for the purchase of securities or from the sale of securities before the money is paid into a trust account.

Dealer to appoint auditor.

87. (1) A dealer shall appoint an auditor to audit his accounts (including all trust accounts required to be kept by the dealer under section 84) and, where for any reason the auditor ceases to act for the dealer, the dealer shall, as soon as practicable thereafter, appoint another auditor to replace him.

(2) A person is not eligible for appointment under subsection (1) if—

*(a)* he is a servant of the dealer or is in the employment of any such servant;
*(b)* where the dealer is a partnership, he is a member of the partnership or in the employment of any such member;
*(c)* where the dealer is a corporation, he is an officer of the corporation or is in the employment of any such officer; or
*(d)* he belongs to any other class of persons prescribed in regulations for the purposes of this paragraph.

Dealer's financial year.

87A. (1) A dealer shall—

*(a)* within one month after the date on which this section commences; or
*(b)* if he is not registered at that date, within one month after the issue to him of a certificate of registration under section 51,

notify the Commissioner in writing of the date on which his financial year ends.

(2) On application in writing by a dealer, the Commissioner may, subject to such conditions as he thinks fit, grant permission to the dealer to alter his financial year.

(3) Except with the written permission of the Commissioner, the period of a dealer's financial year shall not exceed 12 months.

(4) Nothing in this section shall prejudice the operation of section 122 of the Companies Ordinance.

Dealer to lodge auditor's report.

88. (1) A dealer shall, in respect of the financial year beginning before and ending after—

*(a)* the day on which this section commences; or
*(b)* the day on which the dealer commences to carry on business as a dealer,

whichever is the later day, and in respect of each subsequent financial year, prepare a true and fair profit and loss account and a balance sheet made up to the last day of the financial year and cause those documents to be lodged with the Commissioner not later than 4 months after the end of the financial year, together with an auditor's report containing the information prescribed by regulations.

(2) Notwithstanding subsection (1), the period within which the documents referred to in subsection (1) are required to be lodged may be extended by the Commissioner for a period not exceeding one month, where an application for the extension is made by the dealer and the Commissioner is satisfied there are special reasons for requiring the extension.

(3) An extension under subsection (2) may be allowed subject to such conditions, if any, as the Commissioner thinks fit to impose.

(4) Any dealer who fails to lodge the documents required by this section with the Commissioner within the time allowed by or under this section shall be guilty of an offence and shall be liable on conviction to a fine of $5,000.

Auditor to send report directly to Commissioner in certain cases.

**89.** If, during the performance of his duties as auditor for a dealer, an auditor—

*(a)* becomes aware of any matter which in his opinion adversely affects the financial position of the dealer to a material extent; or

*(b)* discovers evidence of a contravention by the dealer of section 81, section 83, or section 84,

he shall, as soon as practicable thereafter, send to the Commissioner and to the dealer a report in writing of the matter or, as the case may be, concerning the contravention.

Power of Commissioner to appoint auditor.

**90.** (1) Where—

*(a)* a dealer has failed to lodge an auditor's report under section 88; or

*(b)* the Commissioner has received a report under section 89,

the Commissioner may, if he is satisfied that it is in the interests of the dealer concerned, the dealer's clients, or the general public, to do so, appoint in writing an auditor to examine, audit, and report, either generally or in relation to any matter, on the books, accounts, and records of, and securities held by, the dealer.

(2) Where the Commissioner is of the opinion that the whole or any part of the costs and expenses of an auditor appointed by him under this section should be borne by the dealer concerned or the stock exchange of which he is a member, he may, by order in writing, direct the dealer or stock exchange to pay a specified amount, being the

whole or part of those costs and expenses, within the time and in the manner specified.

(3) Where a dealer or stock exchange has failed to comply with an order of the Commissioner under subsection (2) the amount specified in the order may be sued for and recovered by the Commissioner as a debt in any court of competent jurisdiction.

Power of Commissioner to appoint an auditor on the application of a client.

91. (1) On receipt of an application in writing from a person who alleges that a dealer has failed to account to him in respect of any money or securities held or received by that dealer for him or on his behalf, the Commissioner may, after first giving the dealer an opportunity to give an explanation of the failure, appoint in writing an auditor to examine, audit, and report, either generally or in relation to any particular matter, on the books, accounts, and records of, and securities held by, that dealer.

(2) Every application under subsection (1) shall state—

*(a)* particulars of the circumstances under which the dealer received the money or securities in respect of which he is alleged to have failed to account;

*(b)* particulars of that money or those securities and of the transactions of the applicant and the dealer relating thereto; and

*(c)* such other particulars as may be prescribed by regulations.

(3) Every statement in any such application shall be verified by statutory declaration made by the applicant and shall, if made in good faith and without malice, be privileged.

(4) The Commissioner shall not appoint an auditor under subsection (1) unless he is satisfied—

*(a)* that the applicant has good reason for making the application; and

*(b)* that it is in the interests of the dealer or the applicant or the public generally that the books, accounts, and records of, and securities held by, the dealer should be examined, audited, and reported on.

Auditor to report to Commissioner.

92. An auditor appointed under section 90 or section 91 shall, on the conclusion of the examination and audit in respect of which he was appointed, make a report thereon to the Commissioner.

Powers of auditors.

93. An auditor appointed by the Commissioner to examine and audit the books, accounts, and records of, and securities held by, a dealer may for the purpose of carrying out the examination and audit—

*(a)* examine on oath the dealer concerned and, where the dealer

carries on business in partnership or is a corporation, any of the members of the partnership or, as the case may be, any director of the corporation and any of the dealer's servants and agents and any other auditor appointed under this Ordinance in relation to those books, accounts, records, and securities;

*(b)* employ such persons as he considers necessary; and

*(c)* by instrument in writing under his hand, authorize any person employed by him to do, in relation to the examination and audit, any act or thing that he could do himself as an auditor, except to examine any person on oath or to exercise any other powers conferred by this paragraph.

Right of auditors and employees to communicate certain matters.

94. Except for the purpose of carrying into effect the provisions of this Ordinance or so far as may be required for the purposes of any legal proceedings, whether civil or criminal, an auditor appointed under section 90 or section 91 and an employee of any such auditor shall not divulge any information which may come to his knowledge in the course of performing his duties as an auditor or employee under section 90 or section 91, as the case may be, to any person other than—

*(a)* the Commission;

*(b)* the Commissioner;

*(c)* the Financial Secretary or any person approved or designated by the Financial Secretary; and

*(d)* in the case of an employee, the auditor by whom he is employed.

Books, accounts, and records to be produced on demand.

95. (1) On request by an auditor appointed under this Part or a person who produces a written authority in that behalf under section 93*(c)*—

*(a)* a dealer and, where the dealer is a corporation or carries on business in partnership, the directors of the corporation or the other members of the partnership, and the dealer's servants and agents, shall produce any books, accounts, and records of any securities held by the dealer relating to the dealer's business; and

*(b)* an auditor appointed by a dealer shall produce any books, accounts, and records held by him relating to the business of the dealer.

(2) A dealer and, where the dealer is a corporation or carries on business in partnership, the directors of the corporation or the other members of the partnership, as the case may be, and the dealer's servants and agents and any auditor appointed by the dealer shall answer all questions relevant to an examination and audit which are put to him by an auditor appointed under this Part or a person who produces a written authority in that behalf given under section 93*(c)*.

(3) Any person mentioned in subsection (1) who, without reasonable excuse, fails to comply with any request made to him under that subsection, or any person mentioned in subsection (2) who, without reasonable excuse, refuses or fails to answer any question put to him under that subsection, shall be guilty of an offence and shall be liable on conviction to a fine of $10,000 and to imprisonment for 2 years.

Offence to destroy, conceal, or alter records or send records or other property outside Hong Kong.

96. (1) Any person who, with intent to prevent, delay, or obstruct the carrying out of any examination and audit under this Part—

*(a)* destroys, conceals or alters any book, account, record or document relating to the business of a dealer; or

*(b)* sends or attempts to send, or conspires with any other person to send, out of Hong Kong any such book, account, record, or document, or any property of any description belonging to or in the disposition of or under the control of a dealer,

shall be guilty of an offence and shall be liable on conviction to a fine of $50,000 and to imprisonment for 2 years.

(2) If, in a prosecution for an offence under subsection (1), it is proved that the person charged—

*(a)* destroyed, concealed, or altered any book, account, record, or document mentioned in that subsection; or

*(b)* sent or attempted to send, or conspired to send, out of Hong Kong any such book, account, record, or document or any property mentioned in paragraph *(b)* of that subsection,

the onus of proving that in so doing he did not act with intent to prevent, delay, or obstruct the carrying out of an examination and audit under this Part shall lie on him.

(3) Any person who, with intent to prevent, delay, or obstruct the carrying out of an examination and audit under this Part, leaves, or attempts to leave, Hong Kong shall be guilty of an offence and shall be liable on conviction to a fine of $50,000 and to imprisonment for 2 years.

Right of committee to impose obligations, etc., on members of exchange not affected by this Part.

97. Nothing in this Part shall prevent the committee of a stock exchange from imposing on members of the exchange any further obligations or requirements which the committee thinks necessary with respect to—

*(a)* the audit of accounts;

*(b)* the information to be given in reports by auditors; or

*(c)* the keeping of accounts, books, and records.

## PART X. COMPENSATION FUND

**98.** (1) In this Part, unless the context otherwise requires— Interpretation.

"Committee" means the Securities Commission Compensation Fund Committee established under section 100(1);

"compensation fund" means the fund established under section 99;

"default", in relation to the failure of a stockbroker, or a member firm or corporate member of a stock exchange, to perform a legal obligation, means a default arising from—

*(a)* the bankruptcy or insolvency of the stockbroker or member firm or, as the case may be, the winding up or insolvency of the corporate member;

*(b)* any breach of trust committed by the stockbroker, member firm, or corporate member; or

*(c)* any defalcation, fraud, or misfeasance committed by the stockbroker, member firm, or corporate member or any servant employed by that stockbroker, member firm, or corporate member;

"legal obligation" includes an obligation aising under a contract or quasi-contract or under a trust (including a constructive trust);

"stockbroking business" means—

*(a)* a stockbroker's business of dealing in securities listed or quoted on a stock exchange;

*(b)* the administration of any trust, or the carrying on of the business of any company, in conjunction with, or as an adjunct to, a stockbroking business; and

*(c)* the retention of securities whether for safe-keeping or otherwise, and whether for specific consideration or otherwise.

(2) A reference in this Part to a claimant or person making a claim includes, in the event of his death, insolvency, or other disability, a reference to his personal representative or any other person having authority to administer his estate.

**99.** The Commission shall establish and maintain a compensation fund, to be known as the Stock Exchanges Compensation Fund, for the purposes set out in this Part. Establishment of compensation fund.

**100.** (1) There shall be a committee, to be known as the Securities Commission Compensation Fund Committee, which shall be responsible, subject to this section, for the administration of the compensation fund. Securities Commission Compensation Fund Committee.

(2) The Committee shall consist of five persons appointed by the Commission of whom at least two shall be members of the Commission and two shall be persons nominated by the Council of the Federation.

(3) The Commission shall nominate one of the members of the Committee who is also a member of the Commission to be chairman of the Committee.

(4) The Committee shall exercise on behalf of the Commission such of the powers, duties, and functions of the Commission under this Part as may from time to time be delegated to the Committee by the Commission; but the Commission may not delegate its power of delegation under this section or its powers under section 110.

(5) Any power, duty, or function delegated under this section may be exercised by members forming a majority of the Committee as if by this Part that power, duty, or function had been conferred on a majority of the members of the Committee.

(6) Any delegation under this section may at any time be varied or revoked.

(7) The Commission may at any time remove any member of the Committee appointed by it under this section and may fill any vacancy in the Committee however arising.

(8) Subject to any direction of the Commission, the Committee may regulate its procedure in such manner as it thinks fit.

Money constituting the compensation fund.

101. (1) The compensation fund shall consist of—

*(a)* all money paid to or deposited with the Commission by stock exchanges in accordance with the provisions of this Part;
*(b)* all money recovered under any guarantee entered into under this Part;
*(c)* all money recovered by or on behalf of the Commission by the exercise of any right of action conferred by this Part;
*(d)* all money borrowed under subsection (2);
*(e)* all other money lawfully paid into the fund.

(2) The Commission may from time to time borrow for the purposes of the compensation fund from any lender and may charge any investments acquired under section 105 by way of security for any such loan; but the aggregate sum owing at any one time in respect of any such loans shall not exceed $1,000,000.

**102.** The Commission shall open at one or more licensed banks a separate bank account or separate bank accounts and shall, pending its application in accordance with this Part, pay into or transfer to that account or those accounts all money forming part of the compensation fund.

Money to be kept in bank account.

**103.** (1) The Commission shall keep proper accounts of the compensation fund, and shall in respect of the financial year beginning before and ending after the day on which this section commences, and in respect of each subsequent financial year, prepare a revenue and expenditure account, and a balance sheet made up to the last day of that year.

Accounts of fund.

(2) The Commission shall appoint an auditor to audit the compensation fund.

(3) The auditor so appointed shall annually audit the accounts of the compensation fund and shall audit, and prepare an auditor's report in respect of, each balance sheet and revenue and expenditure account prepared under subsection (1) and shall submit the report to the Commission.

(4) Not later than the 31st day of July in each year the Commission shall cause a copy of the audited balance sheet, revenue and expenditure account, and the auditor's report to be sent to the Council of the Federation and to each stock exchange.

**104.** (1) Every stock exchange shall, subject to the provisions of this Part, deposit with the Commission and keep deposited in respect of each stockbroker belonging to that exchange—

Stock exchanges to make deposits in respect of members.

*(a)* a sum of $25,000 payable in cash; and

*(b)* a guarantee, in such form and complying with such conditions as may be prescribed by rules, given by a licensed bank guaranteeing the payment to the compensation fund, on the demand of the Commission, of the sum of $25,000.

(2) The amount and, subject to subsection (3), the guarantee referred to in subsection (1) shall be deposited—

*(a)* in respect of every stockbroker who is a member of a stock exchange at the date of commencement of this Part, not later than one month after that date; and

*(b)* in respect of every stockbroker who is admitted as a member of a stock exchange after the commencement of this Part, not later than one month after the date on which he is admitted to membership of the exchange.

(3) The Commission may, if it is satisfied that a stock exchange is operating a system whereby the obligations of any stockbroker belonging to the exchange to any other stockbroker belonging to that exchange will be met or substantially met in the event of his failing to fulfil those obligations or any of them, exempt the exchange from compliance with depositing the guarantee required under subsection (1)*(b)*.

(4) Any amount due under this section may be sued for and recovered by the Commission as a debt in any court of competent jurisdiction.

Balance of sums in bank account may be invested.

**105.** (1) The Commission may invest any money which forms part of the compensation fund and is not immediately required for any other purposes provided for by this Part either—

*(a)* on fixed deposit with a licensed bank; or
*(b)* in securities in which trustees are authorized by law to invest trust funds.

(2) As soon as practicable after the end of each financial year, the Commission shall notify the contributing stock exchanges in writing of—

*(a)* the rate of interest to be paid for that financial year in respect of each sum deposited under section 104(1)*(a)*;
*(b)* the manner and time of payment of that interest; and
*(c)* the amount to be charged to meet the expenses incurred or involved in the administration of the compensation fund.

(3) Any fixed deposit receipts or documents relating to the investment of money in securities under subsection (1) may be kept in the office of the Commission or deposited by the Commission for safekeeping with a licensed bank.

Repayment of deposits in certain cases.

**106.** (1) Where a stock exchange has deposited a sum of money or a guarantee with the Commission under section 104 in respect of a stockbroker and that stockbroker dies or otherwise ceases to be a member of the stock exchange, the Commission shall, unless the money or guarantee is required to satisfy any claims or liabilities arising before the stockbroker died or otherwise ceased to be a member of the exchange, within 6 months after the death of the stockbroker or his ceasing to be a member of the exchange, deliver to the exchange the sum or guarantee deposited in respect of the stockbroker.

(2) If—

*(a)* any money or guarantee has been delivered to a stock exchange pursuant to subsection (1); and

(*b*) the exchange obtained the guarantee by means of a direct levy imposed on the stockbroker in respect of whom the money or guarantee was deposited,

the exchange shall, if that stockbroker has satisfied all financial obligations due from him to the exchange and is otherwise in good standing with the exchange and is not bankrupt or insolvent, deliver the money or guarantee to him or, if he has died, to his personal representative.

**Replenishment of fund in certain cases.**

107. (1) Subject to subsection (4), if at any time resort has to be made to any money or guarantee deposited under section 104 in order to satisfy any claim made against the compensation fund in relation to a stockbroker, or to a member firm or corporate member of a stock exchange, the exchange to which the stockbroker, member firm, or corporate member belongs, or belonged at the time of the default giving rise to the claim, shall, on being required to do so by the Commission, replenish the fund by depositing with the Commission an amount that is equal to that paid in connexion with the satisfaction of the claim, including any legal and other expenses paid or incurred in relation to the claim.

(2) Subject to subsections (3) and (4), if any stock exchange, whether because of insolvency or any other reason, is unable to deposit the amount required under subsection (1), each remaining stock exchange shall, if required to do so by the Commission, replenish the compensation fund by depositing in respect of each stockbroker belonging to the exchange a sum equal to that proportion which the amount not deposited in accordance with subsection (1) bears to the total number of stockbrokers belonging to the remaining exchanges.

(3) A stock exchange may not be required, pursuant to subsection (2), to deposit any sum or sums representing an amount exceeding $50,000 in respect of each stockbroker belonging to the exchange; and if on one or more occasions a stock exchange has, pursuant to that subsection, deposited a sum or sums representing that amount, the exchange shall not be liable to deposit further sums under that subsection.

(4) The Commission may not require a stock exchange—

(*a*) to make a deposit under subsection (1) in respect of any payment made to satisfy a claim under this Part unless it has first exhausted all relevant rights of action and other legal remedies, conferred by section 118, against the stockbroker, member firm, or corporate member in relation to whom or to which the claim arose; or

(*b*) to make a deposit under subsection (2) unless it has first exhausted all relevant rights of action and other legal remedies against the stock exchange that is primarily liable by virtue of subsection (1).

(5) Any amount required to be deposited under this section may be sued for and recovered by the Commission as a debt in any court of competent jurisdiction.

Payments out of the fund.

**108.** (1) Subject to this Part, there shall from time to time be paid out of the compensation fund as required and in the following order—

*(a)* all legal and other expenses incurred in investigating or defending claims made under this Part or incurred in relation to the fund or in the exercise by the Council of the Federation or the Commission of the rights, powers, and authorities vested in them by this Part in relation to the fund;

*(b)* the expenses incurred or involved in the administration of the fund;

*(c)* the amounts of all claims, including costs, allowed by the Council of the Federation or established against the Federation under this Part; and

*(d)* all other money payable out of the fund in accordance with this Part.

(2) If at any time the money deposited in the compensation fund is insufficient for any payment under subsection (1), the Commission may require the guarantor under any guarantee deposited with it under section 104(1) to pay to the Commission all or any part of the sum guaranteed, in which event the guarantor shall pay the amount so required.

(3) Any amount required to be paid under subsection (2) may be sued for and recovered by the Commission as a debt in any court of competent jurisdiction.

Claims against the fund.

**109.** (1) Where in consequence of any act done in the course of or in connexion with the stockbroking business of a stockbroker, or a member firm or corporate member of a stock exchange, a person has a cause of action against that stockbroker, member firm or corporate member in relation to any money, securities or other property entrusted to or received by the stockbroker, member firm or corporate member or any person employed by the stockbroker, member firm or corporate member, that person shall be entitled, subject to this Part, to claim compensation from the compensation fund in respect of any pecuniary loss suffered by him.

(2) Subsection (1) does not entitle any stockbroker, or any member firm or corporate member of a stock exchange, to make a claim against the compensation fund.

(3) Except as otherwise provided in this Part, the total amount that may be paid under this Part to all persons who suffer loss through any default mentioned in subsection (1) shall not in any event exceed $1,000,000 in respect of each stockbroker concerned in or connected with the default; but for the purposes of this subsection any amount paid from the compensation fund shall, to the extent that the fund is subsequently reimbursed in respect of any such payment (not being a deposit made under section 107), be disregarded.

(4) A person shall not have a claim against the compensation fund in respect of a default committed before the commencement of this Part.

(5) Subject to this Part, the amount which any claimant is entitled to claim as compensation from the compensation fund is the amount of the actual pecuniary loss suffered by him (including the reasonable costs of and incidental to the making and proving of his claim) less the amount or value of money or other benefits received or receivable by him in reduction of the loss from any source other than the compensation fund.

(6) In addition to any compensation payable under this Part, interest shall be payable out of the compensation fund on the amount of the compensation, less any amount attributable to costs and disbursements, at such rate as may be determined by the Commission from time to time, which shall be calculated from the day on which the default was committed and continue until the day on which the claim is satisfied.

(7) For the purposes of this section—

*(a)* "stockbroker" includes a person who has been, but, at the time of any default mentioned in subsection (1), had ceased to be, a member of a stock exchange if, at the time when the claimant entered into the transaction or course of dealing giving rise to the claim, the claimant had reasonable grounds for believing that person to be a member of the exchange;

*(b)* "member firm" includes a firm which has been, but, at the time of any default mentioned in subsection (1), had ceased to be, a member firm of a stock exchange if, at the time at which the claimant entered into the transaction or course of dealing giving rise to the claim, the person claiming compensation had reasonable grounds for believing that firm to be a member firm of a stock exchange;

*(c)* "corporate member" includes a corporation which has been, but, at the time of any default mentioned in subsection (1), had ceased to be, a corporate member of a stock exchange if, at the time when the claimant entered into the transaction or other course of dealing giving rise to the claim, the claimant had reasonable grounds for believing that corporation to be a corporate member of a stock exchange.

Powers of Commision to increase payments made in respect of claims.

110. (1) If, after consultation with the Council of the Federation and after taking into account all ascertained or contingent liabilities of the compensation fund, the Commission considers that the assets of the fund so permit, it may by notice published in the *Gazette* increase the total amount which may be claimed from the fund under section 109; and from the date of that publication, until the notice is revoked or varied, the amount specified in the notice shall be the maximum amount that may be claimed under that section.

(2) A notice under subsection (1) may be varied or revoked by the Commission by notice published in the *Gazette.*

Rights of innocent partner, etc. in relation to the fund.

111. (1) Notwithstanding anything to the contrary in this Part, where all persons submitting claims under section 109 have been fully compensated in accordance with the provisions of this Part for the loss sustained by them as a result of the failure of a partner of a member firm or a director of a corporate member to perform a legal obligation, any other partner of that firm who has made payment to any person in compensation for loss sustained by him as a result of that failure or, where a corporate member or director of a corporate member has made such a payment, that corporate member, or director, shall be subrogated to the extent of that payment to all the rights and remedies of that person against the compensation fund if the Council of the Federation considers, having regard to all the circumstances, that he—

*(a)* was in no way party to the default which resulted in the failure to perform that obligation; and

*(b)* acted honestly and reasonably in the matter.

(2) If any partner of the firm, or any corporate member or director of a corporate member, is aggrieved by the decision of the Council of the Federation under subsection (1), he or it may, within 28 days after receipt of notice of the decision, appeal to the Commission against the decision.

(3) An appellant shall, on the same day as lodging a notice of appeal with the Commission, lodge a copy of the notice with the Council of the Federation.

(4) The Commission shall inquire into and decide on the appeal and, if the Commission considers having regard to all the circumstances that the appellant—

(*a*) was in no way a party to the default in question; and
(*b*) acted honestly and reasonably in the matter,

it may direct that the appellant shall, to the extent of any payment made by him, be subrogated to all the rights and remedies in relation to the compensation fund of the person to whom he or it has made payment in compensation.

Notice calling for claims against the fund.

112. (1) The Council of the Federation may cause to be published in one or more English language newspapers and one or more Chinese language newspapers, published daily and circulating generally in Hong Kong, a notice specifying a date, not being earlier than 3 months after publication of the notice, on or before which claims for compensation from the compensation funds may be made in relation to the person specified in the notice.

(2) Where any person wishes to claim compensation under this Part, he shall lodge his claim in writing with the Council of the Federation—

(*a*) if a notice under subsection (1) has been published, on or before the date specified in the notice; or
(*b*) if no such notice has been published, within 6 months after the claimant became aware of the default giving rise to the claim.

(3) Any claim which is not made within the time limited by subsection (2) shall, unless the Council of the Federation otherwise determines, be barred.

(4) An action for damages shall not lie against the Federation or against any member or employee of the Federation or against any member of the Council of the Federation by reason of any notice published for the purposes of this section in good faith and without malice.

Power of the Council of Federation in respect of claims.

113. (1) Where the Council of the Federation is satisfied that a claim made under section 109 is a proper claim, it shall, subject to this Part, make a determination allowing the claim.

(2) If the Council is not satisfied as to the propriety of a claim under section 109, it shall make a determination disallowing the claim or, if it is satisfied only as to the propriety of part of such a claim, it shall make a determination allowing the claim as to that part.

(3) Where the Council of the Federation makes a determination

under subsection (1) or subsection (2), it shall forthwith serve notice of its determination in writing on the claimant or on his solicitor and deliver a copy of the notice to the Commission.

(4) If the Council of the Federation disallows or only partially allows a claim against the compensation fund, the determination of the Council shall specify the reasons for the disallowance or, as the case may be, partial allowance.

(5) If, in the case of any particular claim, after taking into account all ascertained and contingent liabilities of the compensation fund, the Council of the Federation considers that the assets of the fund so permit, it may, with the prior approval of the Commission, allow in respect of a claim which is in excess of the total amount limited by or under section 109 such additional sum in or towards the compensation of the claimant as it thinks fit.

(6) The receipt of a copy of a notice under subsection (3) notifying the allowance or partial allowance of a claim is sufficient authority for the Commission to pay to the claimant the amount allowed under this section.

Council of Federation may require production of securities, etc.

114. (1) The Council of the Federation may at any time require any person to produce any securities, documents, or statements of evidence necessary—

*(a)* in order to substantiate any claim made against the compensation fund; or
*(b)* for the purpose either of exercising its rights against a stockbroker, or against a member firm or corporate member of a stock exchange, or against any other person concerned; or
*(c)* for the purpose of enabling criminal proceedings to be brought against any person in respect of a default, being a default which is or involves the commission of a criminal offence.

(2) Where any claimant required to produce any securities, documents, or statements of evidence under subsection (1) fails to produce them the Council of the Federation may, if it is satisfied that securities, documents, or statements are in the possession of, or available to, the claimant, refuse to allow the claimant's claim until such time as he produces them.

Court proceedings to establish a claim against the fund.

115. (1) Subject to subsection (2), a person whose claim has been disallowed, or only partially allowed, under section 113 may, at any time after the service under that section of the notice notifying the disallowance or partial allowance, commence proceedings against the Federation to establish his claim against the compensation fund.

(2) Except with leave of the Court, no proceedings against the Federation in respect of a claim which has been disallowed, or only partially allowed, under section 113 may be commenced after the expiration of 3 months after the service of the notice under subsection (3) of that section.

(3) Any proceedings brought against the Federation to establish a claim against the compensation fund shall be by action as for a debt due from the Federation.

Supplementary provisions relating to proceedings brought under section 115.

116. In any proceedings brought under section 115—

*(a)* all defences that would have been available to the person or persons in relation to whom the claim arose shall be available to the Federation;

*(b)* all questions as to costs shall be in the discretion of the Court; and

*(c)* evidence which would be admissible against the stockbroker or any other person by whom it is alleged a default was committed is admissible to prove the commission of the default, notwithstanding that the stockbroker or other person is not the defendant in or a party to those proceedings.

Form of court order establishing claim.

117. Where, in any proceedings brought against the Federation to establish a claim against the compensation fund, the Court is satisfied that the default on which the claim is founded was actually committed and that the claimant otherwise has a valid claim, the Court shall by order—

*(a)* allow the amount of the claim or such part of the claim as it thinks proper;

*(b)* declare the fact and date of the default and the amount allowed under paragraph *(a)*; and

*(c)* direct the Commission to pay to the claimant the amount declared under paragraph *(b)*.

Subrogation of the Commission to rights, etc., of claimant on payment from fund.

118. On the Commission making any payment out of the compensation fund in respect of any claim under this Part—

*(a)* the Commission shall be subrogated to the extent of that payment to all the rights and remedies of the claimant in relation to the loss sustained by him by reason of the default on which the claim was based; and

*(b)* the claimant shall have no right under bankruptcy or legal proceedings or otherwise to receive in respect of the loss any sum out of the assets of the stockbroker, member firm, or

corporate member concerned, or where the loss was caused by the defalcation, fraud, or misfeasance of a servant of a stockbroker, member firm, or corporate member, the assets of that servant, until the Commission has been reimbursed the full amount of its payment.

Payment of claims only from the fund.

119. No money or other property belonging to the Commission or to the Federation or to a stock exchange, other than the compensation fund, shall be available for the payment of any claim under this Part, whether the claim is allowed by the Council of the Federation or is made the subject of an order of the Court or otherwise.

Provision where fund is insufficient to meet claims or where claims exceed total amount payable.

120. (1) Where the amount at credit in the compensation fund is insufficient to enable the payment of the whole amount of all claims against it which have been allowed or in respect of which orders have been made, then the amount at credit shall, subject to subsection (2), be apportioned between the claimants in such manner as the Council of the Federation or, as the case may be, the Court thinks equitable; and any such claim, so far as it remains unpaid, shall be charged against further receipts of the fund and paid out of the fund when there is again money available in the fund.

(2) Where the aggregate of all claims against the compensation fund which have been allowed, or in respect of which orders of the Court have been made, in relation to the default giving rise to the claims exceeds the total amount which may be paid under this Part in respect of the stockbroker or stockbrokers concerned in the default, that total amount shall be apportioned between the claimants in such manner as the Council of the Federation or, as the case may be, the Court thinks equitable; and, on payment out of the fund of that total amount in accordance with that apportionment—

*(a)* all such claims and any order of the Court relating to them; and

*(b)* all other claims which may subsequently arise or be made in connexion with the default,

shall be absolutely discharged.

Power of Commission to return contributions on winding up stock exchange.

121. In the event of a stock exchange being wound up under the Companies Ordinance, the Commission may, in its absolute discretion, after the satisfaction of all outstanding liabilities against the compensation fund, pay to the liquidator of the exchange the whole or any part of the amounts contributed by the exchange under this Part, together with any income accrued in respect thereof; and on any such payment being made those amounts shall form part of the assets of the exchange

and be available to the liquidator for distribution in accordance with the Companies Ordinance.

## PART XI. INSPECTIONS AND INVESTIGATIONS

### INSPECTIONS

Inspection of books, etc. of registered persons and others.

122. (1) For the purpose of ascertaining whether a person who is, or at any time has been, a registered dealer, an exempt dealer, a registered investment adviser, or a registered representative is complying or has complied with the provisions of this Ordinance that are applicable to him in that capacity, and, in the case of a person who is or was a registered person, the conditions' or restrictions (if any) subject to which his certificate of registration was issued, the Commissioner may inspect and make copies of or take extracts from any—

(*a*) register or document required by this Ordinance, or, in the case of a person who is or was registered under this Ordinance, by the conditions and restrictions to which the certificate is or has been subject, to be kept by that person; and

(*b*) banker's books, and the books of any dealer or exempt dealer, in so far as they relate to the business carried on by the first-mentioned person in his capacity as a registered dealer, an exempt dealer, a registered investment adviser, or a registered representative.

(2) For the purpose of enabling the Commissioner to exercise his powers under subsection (1) the Commissioner may require any person whom he has reason to believe to be in possession of any register, document, or books mentioned in that subsection to produce to him that register or document or, as the case may be, those books.

(3) The Commissioner shall not, except for the purposes of this Ordinance or in the course of criminal proceedings, make a record of, or disclose to another person, any information that he acquires by reason of the making of an inspection under this section.

(4) If the Commissioner contravenes subsection (3), he shall be guilty of an offence and shall be liable on conviction to a fine of $2,000.

(5) It is not a contravention of subsection (3) to communicate information to the holder of a prescribed office.

(6) In this section, "prescribed office" means a public office that is prescribed by regulations for the purposes of this section.

Power of Commissioner to investigate transactions.

123. (1) The Commissioner may require—

(*a*) a registered dealer;

(*b*) an exempt dealer;

(*c*) a person whom the Commissioner reasonably believes to have acquired or disposed of securities through a nominee for him or a trustee on his behalf or to be or have been the real owner of securities held by a nominee or trustee;

(*d*) a nominee or trustee referred to in paragraph (*c*) (including an authorized trustee company registered under Part VIII of the Trustee Ordinance);

(*e*) an agent of a person referred to in paragraphs (*c*) and (*d*),

to disclose to him in relation to any acquisition, disposition or holding of securities the name (including any aliases), address and occupation of the person from or to or through whom or on whose behalf the securities were acquired or disposed of or were or are held, the quantity of securities so acquired, disposed of or held, and the actual instructions given to or by that person in respect thereof.

(2) A person who—

(*a*) without lawful excuse fails to disclose to the Commissioner under subsection (1) all information referred to therein which he has or can obtain; or

(*b*) knowingly furnishes to the Commissioner thereunder information that is false or misleading in a material particular,

commits an offence and is liable on conviction to a fine of $5,000 and to imprisonment for 3 months.

Investigation of certain matters.

124. Where the Commissioner has reason to suspect that a person has contravened a provision of this Ordinance or has been guilty of a breach of trust, defalcation, fraud, or misfeasance or of an offence against any other law with respect to trading or dealing in securities or that insider dealing within the meaning of section 141B has taken place, the Commissioner may make such investigation as he thinks expedient for the due administration of this Ordinance.

Seizure of documents and articles believed to relate to a contravention of Part VIII or Part XII.

125. (1) If a magistrate is satisfied by information on oath that there is reasonable ground for suspecting that, at premises that are specified in the information, a person is in possession of any document or article which relates to an offence alleged to have been committed against Part VIII or Part XII, the magistrate may grant a warrant empowering the Commissioner or any police officer—

(*a*) to enter the premises, if necessary by force, at any time within one month from the date of the warrant; and

(*b*) to search for, seize, and remove any document or article which the Commissioner or police officer has reasonable grounds for believing to be evidence of the alleged offence.

(2) Any document or article seized under subsection (1) may be retained for a period of 6 months from the date of seizure or, if within that period any proceedings in respect of an offence against Part VIII or Part XII are commenced and the document or article is relevant to those proceedings, until the conclusion of those proceedings.

(3) Notwithstanding subsection (2), a document or article seized under subsection (1) may be retained for a period longer than 6 months if the person entitled to it is not in Hong Kong or his whereabouts are unknown; and if that person subsequently returns to Hong Kong or his whereabouts subsequently become known and, within 14 days of that return or the discovery of his whereabouts, any proceedings in respect of an offence against Part VIII or Part XII are commenced against him, and the document or article is relevant to those proceedings, the document or article may be retained until the conclusion of those proceedings.

(4) A person from whom a document has been seized under subsection (1) shall, unless the document is already the subject of an order made under subsection (5), be entitled at all reasonable times to inspect and to take copies of or extracts from the document.

(5) Where any person is convicted of an offence against Part VIII or Part XII, the court may make an order authorizing the destruction, or the disposal in any other specified manner, of any documents or articles produced to the court which are shown to its satisfaction to be connected with the commission of the offence; but an order under this subsection may not authorize the destruction or disposal of a document or article before the conclusion of the proceedings to which the order relates.

(6) Subject to subsections (2) to (5), section 102 of the Criminal Procedure Ordinance (which makes provision for the disposal of property connected with offences) shall apply to property which has come into the possession of the Commissioner under this section in the same way as it applies to property which has come into the possession of the police.

## INVESTIGATIONS

Interpretation for the purposes of sections 127 to 134.

**126.** In sections 127 to 134, unless the context otherwise requires—

"inspector" means an inspector appointed under section 127(1);

"investigation" means an investigation made under section 127 by an inspector;

"prescribed person" means a person suspected or believed by an inspector, on reasonable grounds, to be capable of giving information concerning any matter to be investigated by the inspector.

Investigation by inspector.

127. (1) Where it appears to the Commission that it is desirable for the protection of the public or of the holders of securities to appoint an inspector to investigate—

*(a)* any alleged breach of trust, defalcation, fraud, or misfeasance; or

*(b)* any matter concerning dealing in securities or the giving of investment advice,

the Commission may, by instrument in writing, appoint a person as an inspector to investigate the allegation or matter and to report on it in such manner as the Commission directs.

(2) The Commission shall, in an instrument appointing an inspector, specify full particulars of the appointment including—

*(a)* the matters into which the investigation is to be made; and

*(b)* the terms and conditions of the appointment including terms and conditions relating to remuneration.

(3) An inspector may require a prescribed person by notice in the form prescribed by regulations given in the manner as prescribed—

*(a)* to produce to the inspector such documents relating to a matter with which his investigation is concerned as are in the custody or under the control of that person;

*(b)* to give to the inspector all reasonable assistance in connexion with the investigation; and

*(c)* to appear before the inspector for examination on oath,

and may administer the oath referred to in paragraph (*c*).

(4) Where documents are produced to an inspector under this section the inspector may take possession of them for such period as he considers necessary for the purposes of his investigation, and during that period he shall permit a person who would be entitled to inspect any one or more of those documents if they were not in the possession of the inspector to inspect at all reasonable times such of them as that person would be so entitled to inspect.

(5) A prescribed person—

*(a)* shall comply with a requirement of an inspector under subsection (3);

*(b)* shall not knowingly furnish to the inspector, whether on examination in pursuance of such requirement or otherwise, information that is false or misleading in a material particular; or

*(c)* when appearing before an inspector for examination in pursuance of such a requirement, shall take an oath in accordance with the requirement.

(6) Any person who, without reasonable excuse, contravenes any of the provisions of subsection (5) shall be guilty of an offence and shall be liable on conviction to a fine of $5,000.

(7) A solicitor or counsel acting for a prescribed person—

*(a)* may attend an examination of that person; and
*(b)* may, to the extent that the inspector permits—
 (i) address the inspector; and
 (ii) examine that person,

in relation to matters in respect of which the inspector has questioned that person.

(8) A prescribed person is not excused from answering a question put to him by an inspector on the ground that the answer might tend to incriminate him but, where that person claims, before answering the question, that the answer might tend to incriminate him, neither the question nor the answer is admissible in evidence against him in criminal proceedings other than proceedings under subsection (6) or in relation to a charge of perjury in respect of the answer.

(9) A person who complies with the requirement of an inspector under subsection (3) shall not incur any liability to any person by reason only of that compliance.

(10) A person required to attend for examination under this section is entitled to such allowances and expenses as may be prescribed by regulations.

(11) Where a prescribed person fails to comply with a requirement of an inspector under subsection (3), the inspector may, unless that person proves that he had a lawful authority for his failure, certify the failure by writing under his hand to the Court.

(12) Where an inspector gives a certificate under subsection (11), the Court may inquire into the case and—

*(a)* order the prescribed person to whom the certificate relates to comply with the requirement of the inspector within such period as is fixed by the Court; or
*(b)* if the Court is satisfied that that person failed without lawful authority to comply with the requirement of the inspector, punish him in the same manner as if he had been guilty of contempt of court.

Notes of examination.

**128.** (1) An inspector may cause notes of an examination made by him under this Part to be recorded in writing and be read to or by the person examined and may require that person to sign the notes and, subject to this section, notes signed by that person may be used in evidence in any legal proceedings against that person.

(2) A copy of the notes signed by a person shall be furnished without charge to that person upon request made by him in writing.

(3) Notes made under this section that relate to a question the answer to which a person has claimed might tend to incriminate him shall not be used as evidence in criminal proceedings other than proceedings under section 127(6) or in relation to a charge of perjury in respect of the answer.

(4) Nothing in this section affects or limits the admissibility of other written evidence or of oral evidence.

(5) The Commission may give a copy of notes made under this section to a solicitor or counsel who satisfies the Commission that he is acting for a person who is conducting or is, in good faith, contemplating legal proceedings in respect of matters required to be investigated by the inspector, being affairs investigated by an inspector under this Part.

(6) A solicitor or counsel to whom a copy of notes is given under subsection (5) shall not use the notes except in connexion with the institution or preparation of, and in the course of, legal proceedings and shall not disclose for any other purpose the notes or any part of the contents of them to any person.

(7) Any solicitor or counsel who contravenes subsection (6) shall be guilty of an offence and shall be liable on conviction to a fine of $2,000.

(8) Where a report is made under section 130 any notes recorded under this section relating to that report shall be furnished with the report.

Delegation of powers, etc., by inspector.

**129.** (1) An inspector may by instrument in writing—

*(a)* delegate all or any of his powers or functions under this Part except this power of delegation, the power to administer an oath, and the power to examine on oath; and
*(b)* vary or revoke a delegation given by him.

(2) A power or function delegated by an inspector may be exercised

or performed by the delegate in accordance with the instrument of delegation as in force from time to time.

(3) A delegate shall, at the request of a prescribed person, produce the instrument of delegation for inspection.

(4) A delegation under this section by an inspector of a power or function does not prevent the exercise of the power or the performance of the function by the inspector.

Report of inspector.

**130.** (1) On completion of an investigation under section 127, the inspector shall report his findings to the Commission and shall deliver a copy of the report to the Attorney General.

(2) Subject to subsection (3), the Commission shall give a copy of the inspector's report to the prescribed person whose affairs were investigated by the inspector.

(3) Subject to subsection (4), the Commission shall not give a report to a prescribed person if the Attorney General believes that legal proceedings that have been, or that in its opinion might be, instituted might be prejudiced by the report.

(4) The court before which legal proceedings are brought against a prescribed person for or in respect of matters dealt with in a report under this section may order that a copy of the report be given to that person.

(5) The Commission may, if it is of the opinion that it is in the public interest to do so, cause the whole or any part of a report under this section to be printed and published.

(6) If, from a report under this section, it appears to the Attorney General that an offence may have been committed by a person and that a prosecution ought to be instituted, the Attorney General shall cause a prosecution to be instituted.

(7) Where it appears to the Attorney General that a prosecution ought to be instituted, he may, by notice in writing given before or after the institution of a prosecution in accordance with subsection (6), require a prescribed person to give all assistance in connexion with prosecution that he is reasonably able to give.

(8) If from a report under this section it appears to the Commission or to the Attorney General that proceedings ought in the public interest to be brought by a prescribed person for the recovery of damages in respect of a breach of trust, defalcation, fraud, or misfeasance in connexion with the affairs of the prescribed person or for

the recovery of property of the prescribed person, either the Commission or the Attorney General may cause proceedings to be instituted accordingly in the name of the prescribed person.

Privileged communications.

131. (1) An inspector shall not require disclosure by a solicitor or counsel of any privileged communication, whether oral or written, made to or by him in that capacity, except as regards the name and address of his client.

(2) Nothing in sections 127 to 130 shall be construed as affecting section 4 of the Inland Revenue Ordinance.

Cost of investigation.

132. (1) Subject to this section, the expenses of and incidental to an investigation by an inspector (including the expenses incurred and payable by the Commission in any proceedings brought by it in the name of a prescribed person) shall be paid out of money provided by the Legislative Council.

(2) An application referred to in subsection (3) may be made to a court by or on behalf of—

(*a*) the Commission or the Attorney General in the course of proceedings in that court instituted in the name of a prescribed person under section 130(8); or

(*b*) the Attorney General on, or within 14 days after, a conviction by the court in proceedings certified by the Attorney General, for the purposes of the application, to have been instituted as a result of an investigation by an inspector;

and the court may make such order with respect to the application and its subject matter as it thinks fit.

(3) The application that may be made under subsection (2) is an application for one or more of the following orders—

(*a*) that a specified person pay the whole, or a specified part of, the expenses of and incidental to, the investigation that led to the proceedings;

(*b*) where expenses have been paid under subsection (1), that a specified person reimburse the Commission to the extent of the payment;

(*c*) that a specified person reimburse the Commission in respect of the remuneration of any person employed by the Commission in connexion with the investigation.

(4) If no proceedings under section 130(6) are commenced against a prescribed person, or, where the prescribed person is a corporation, against any director of the corporation, within 6 months after the

completion of an investigation by an inspector, the prescribed person may apply to a court for an order for the payment of costs incurred by him in connexion with the investigation; and the court may, if it finds that the investigation was not warranted, order the Commission to pay to the prescribed person such sum, not exceeding the amount of costs actually incurred by the prescribed person in respect of the investigation, as it thinks just.

(5) A copy of an application made under subsection (4) shall be served on the Commission and the Commission shall be entitled to be heard at the proceedings to determine the application.

Concealing, etc., of books relating to securities.

133. (1) A person who—

*(a)* conceals, destroys, mutilates, or alters a document relating to a matter which is the subject of an investigation by an inspector;

*(b)* sends, causes to be sent, or conspires with another person to send, out of Hong Kong any such document; or

*(c)* being a prescribed person to whom notice has been given under section 127(3), leaves Hong Kong,

shall be guilty of an offence and shall be liable on conviction to a fine of $20,000 and to imprisonment for 2 years.

(2) It shall be a defence to a prosecution under subsection (1) to prove that the person charged did not act with intent to defeat the purposes of section 127 or to delay or obstruct the carrying out of an investigation under that section.

Commission may make certain orders.

134. (1) Where an investigation is being made under section 127 and it appears to the Commission that facts concerning securities to which the investigation relates cannot be ascertained because a prescribed person referred to in that section has failed or refused to comply with a requirement of an inspector under that section, the Commission may, by order published in the *Gazette*, make one or more of the following orders—

*(a)* an order restraining a specified person from disposing of any interest in specified securities;

*(b)* an order restraining a specified person from acquiring specified securities;

*(c)* an order restraining the exercise of any voting or other rights attached to specified securities;

*(d)* an order directing a person who is registered as the holder of securities in respect of which an order under this section is in force to give notice in writing of that order to any person whom

he knows to be entitled to exercise a right to vote attached to those shares;

(e) an order directing a company not to make payment, except in the course of a winding up by the Court, of any sum due from the company in respect of specified securities;

(f) an order directing a company not to register the transfer or transmission of specified securities;

(g) an order directing a company not to issue shares to a person who holds shares in the company by reason of his holding those shares nor in pursuance of an offer made to such a person by reason of his holding those shares.

(2) A copy of an order under subsection (1) and of any order by which it is revoked or altered shall be served—

(a) where it relates to specified securities, on the authority or body that issued them or made them available or, where the securities are rights or options, on the authority or body against whom the right is, or would be enforceable, or which issued or made available the securities to which the option relates; and

(b) where it relates to a corporation, on the corporation.

(3) A person aggrieved by an order under subsection (1) may apply to the Court for revocation of the order and the Court may, if it is satisfied that it is reasonable to do so, revoke the order and any order by which it has been altered or varied.

(4) Any person who contravenes an order under subsection (1) shall be guilty of an offence and shall be liable on conviction to a fine of $5,000.

(5) Without prejudice to the powers of the Attorney General in relation to the prosecution of criminal offences, a prosecution under this section shall not be instituted except with the consent in writing of the Commission.

## Part XII. Prevention of Improper Trading Practices

### OFFENCES

False markets and trading.

135. (1) A person shall not intentionally create or cause to be created, or do anything with the intention of creating—

(a) a false or misleading appearance of active trading in any securities on any stock market in Hong Kong; or

(b) a false market in respect of any securities on any such stock market.

(2) For the purposes of subsection (1)*(b)*, a false market is created in relation to securities when the market price of those securities is raised or depressed or pegged or stabilized by means of—

*(a)* sales and purchases transacted by persons acting in collaboration with each other for the purpose of securing a market price for those securities that is not justified either by the assets of the corporation which issued the securities or by the profits (including anticipated profits) of the corporation;

*(b)* any act which has the effect of preventing or inhibiting the free negotiation of market prices for the purchase or sale of the securities; or

*(c)* the employment of any fictitious transaction or device or any other form of deception or contrivance.

(3) A person shall not with the intention of depressing, raising, or causing fluctuations in the market price of any securities effect any purchase or sale of any such securities which involves no change in the beneficial ownership of those securities.

(4) A purchase or sale of securities involves no change in beneficial ownership within the meaning of subsection (3) if a person who held an interest in the securities before the purchase or sale, or a person associated with him in relation to those securities, holds an interest in the securities after the purchase or sale.

(5) A person shall not circulate or disseminate, or authorize or be concerned in the circulation or dissemination of, any statement or information to the effect that the price of any securities will or is likely to rise or fall because of the market operations of one or more persons which, to his knowledge, are conducted in contravention of subsection (1).

Employment of fraudulent or deceptive devices, etc.

**136.** A person shall not, directly or indirectly, in connexion with any transaction with any other person involving the purchase, sale, or exchange of securities—

*(a)* employ any device, scheme, or artifice to defraud that other person; or

*(b)* engage in any act, practice, or course of business which operates as a fraud or deception, or is likely to operate as a fraud or deception, of that other person.

Restrictions on fixing, etc. prices for securities.

**137.** A person shall not, either alone or with one or more other persons, effect any series of transactions for the purchase or sale of securities, or the purchase and sale, of any securities for the purpose of pegging or stabilizing the price of securities of that class in contravention of any regulations made for the purposes of this section.

False or misleading statements about securities.

138. A person shall not, directly or indirectly, for the purposes of inducing the sale of the securities of any corporation, make with respect to those securities, or with respect to the operations or the past or future performance of the corporation—

(*a*) any statement which is, at the time and in the light of the circumstances in which it is made, false or misleading with respect to any material fact and which he knows or has reasonable ground to believe to be false or misleading; or

(*b*) any statement which is, by reason of the omission of a material fact, rendered false or misleading and which he knows or has reasonable grounds for knowing is rendered false or misleading by reason of the omission of that fact.

Offences and penalty in relation to sections 135 to 138.

139. Any person who contravenes any of the provisions of section 135, section 136, section 137, or section 138 shall be guilty of an offence and shall be liable on conviction on indictment to a fine of $50,000 and to imprisonment for 2 years.

140. *(Repealed, 8 of 1978, s.7)*

ACTION IN TORT

Liability to pay compensation.

141. (1) A person who contravenes section 135, section 136, section 137, or section 138 shall, in addition to any liability under section 139, be liable to pay compensation by way of damages to any person who has sustained pecuniary loss as a result of having purchased or sold securities at a price affected by the act or transaction which comprises or is the subject of the contravention.

(2) An action may be brought under subsection (1) in respect of a contravention referred to in that subsection notwithstanding that no person has been charged or convicted under section 139 in respect of the contravention.

(3) Nothing in this section limits or diminishes any liability which any person may incur under the common law.

PART XIIA. INSIDER DEALING

Application of this Part.

141A. (1) This Part applies to the securities of a corporation only if they are listed on a stock exchange or have been so listed at any time within five years immediately preceding any dealing in relation to those securities within the meaning of section 141B(1).

(2) No transaction shall be void or voidable by reason only that it is an insider dealing within the meaning of this Part.

DEFINITION OF INSIDER DEALING

**141B.** (1) Insider dealing in relation to the securities of a corporation takes place and, pursuant to section 141C, may be culpable for the purposes of this Part— When insider dealing takes place.

*(a)* when a dealing in the securities is made, procured or occasioned by a person connected with that corporation who is in possession of relevant information concerning the securities;

*(b)* when relevant information concerning the securities is disclosed by a person connected with that corporation, directly or indirectly, to another person and the first-mentioned person knows or has reasonable grounds for believing that the other person will make use of the information for the purpose of dealing, or procuring another to deal, in those securities.

(2) A dealing in the securities of a corporation is occasioned by a person connected with that corporation for the purposes of subsection (1)*(a)* when a person who has obtained relevant information in the circumstances described in subsection (1)*(b)* actually makes use of that information for the purpose of dealing, or procuring another to deal, in those securities.

141C. (1) A person who enters into a transaction which is an insider dealing within section 141B(1)*(a)* is not culpable for the purposes of this Part— Culpability of insider dealing.

*(a)* if his sole purpose in entering into the transaction is the acquisition of qualification shares required by him as a director or intending director of any corporation; or

*(b)* if he enters into the transaction—

(i) in the *bona fide* performance of an underwriting agreement with respect to the securities to which the transaction relates; or

(ii) in the *bona fide* exercise of his functions as a personal representative, liquidator, receiver or trustee in bankruptcy.

(2) A corporation which enters into a transaction which is an insider dealing within section 141B(1)*(a)* is not culpable for the purposes of

this Part if, although relevant information concerning the securities is in the possession of a director or employee of the corporation—

(*a*) the decision to enter into the transaction was taken on its behalf by a person other than that director or employee; and

(*b*) arrangements were then in existence for securing that the information was not communicated to that person and that no advice with respect to the transaction was given to him by a person in possession of the information; and

(*c*) the information was not in fact so communicated and advice was not in fact so given.

(3) A person who enters into a transaction which is an insider dealing within section 141B(1)(*a*) may be held not culpable for the purposes of this Part if his purpose is not, or is not primarily, the making of a profit or the avoiding of a loss (whether for himself or another) by the use of relevant information.

(4) A person who, as agent for another, enters into a transaction which is an insider dealing within section 141B(1)(*a*) may be held not culpable for the purposes of this Part if he did not select or advise on the selection of the securities to which the transaction relates.

(5) In arriving at its determination under section 141H(3) as to the culpability of a person in relation to an insider dealing within section 141B, the Tribunal shall have regard, as the case may be—

(*a*) to the fact that such person of his own initiative disclosed the dealing to the Commissioner and, where the disclosure was made after the dealing took place, to the promptness with which the disclosure was made; or

(*b*) to the fact that such person did not of his own initiative disclose the dealing to the Commissioner and to the reasonableness of any explanation offered by such person for the fact that the dealing was not so disclosed.

(6) Subject to this section, the culpability of any person in relation to an insider dealing within section 141B is a matter for the Tribunal to determine under section 141H(3).

Definitions applicable to this Part.

**141D.** (1) For the purposes of this Part—

"related corporation" in relation to a corporation means a corporation which is deemed by section 4 to be related to it;

"relevant information" in relation to securities means information which is not generally available but, if it were, would be likely to bring about a material change in the price of those securities.

(2) Without limiting the meaning of the phrase "dealing in relation to securities" in section 141B(1) and notwithstanding sections 2 and 3, a person deals in securities for the purposes of this Part if (whether as principal or agent) he buys, sells, exchanges or subscribes for, or agrees to buy, sell, exchange or subscribe for, any securities or acquires or disposes of, or agrees to acquire to dispose of, the right to buy, sell, exchange or subscribe for, any securities.

141E. (1) A person is connected with a corporation for the purposes of section 141B if, being an individual—

Definition of person connected with a corporation.

*(a)* he is a director or employee of that corporation or a related corporation; or

*(b)* he is a substantial shareholder in the corporation or a related corporation; or

*(c)* he occupies a position which may reasonably be expected to give him access to relevant information concerning the securities of the corporation by virtue of—

(i) any professional or business relationship existing between himself (or his employer or a corporation of which he is a director or a firm of which he is a partner) and that corporation, a related corporation or a substantial shareholder in either of such corporations; or

(ii) his being a director, employee or partner of a substantial shareholder in the corporation or a related corporation; or

*(d)* he has access to relevant information concerning the securities of the corporation by virtue of his being connected (within the meaning in paragraph *(a)*, *(b)* or *(c)*) with another corporation being information which relates to any transaction (actual or expected) involving both those corporations or involving one of them and the securities of the other; or

*(e)* he was at any time within the 6 months preceding any dealing in relation to securities within the meaning of section 141B(1) a person connected with the corporation within the meaning in paragraph *(a)*, *(b)*, *(c)* or *(d)*.

(2) A corporation is a person connected with a corporation for the purposes of section 141B so long as any of its directors or employees is a person connected with that other corporation within the meaning in subsection (1).

(3) In subsection (1) "substantial shareholder" in relation to a corporation means a person who has an interest in securities comprised in the equity share capital of that corporation being securities which—

(*a*) have a nominal value equal to more than 10 *per cent* of that share capital; or

(*b*) entitle the holder to exercise or control the exercise of more than 10 *per cent* of the voting power at any general meeting of that corporation.

Possession of relevant information by public officers.

141F. (1) A public officer who in his capacity as such obtains relevant information concerning the securities of a corporation shall be deemed to be a person connected with that corporation for the purposes of section 141B.

(2) In subsection (1) "public officer" means a member or employee, whether temporary or permanent or paid or unpaid, of any of the following—

(*a*) the Government;
(*b*) the Executive Council;
(*c*) the Legislative Council;
(*d*) the Urban Council;
(*e*) any board, commission, committee or other body appointed by or on behalf of the Governor or the Governor in Council; and
(*f*) any body corporate that is an organ or agency of the Crown.

INSIDER DEALING TRIBUNAL

Insider Dealing Tribunal established.

141G. (1) There is hereby established a Tribunal to be known as the Insider Dealing Tribunal (in this Part referred to as "the Tribunal").

(2) The Tribunal shall consist of a chairman and 2 other members all of whom shall be appointed by the Governor.

(3) The chairman of the Tribunal shall be a judge of the Supreme Court and the other 2 members shall not be public officers (within the meaning of that term in section 3 of the Interpretation and General Clauses Ordinance).

(4) A member of the Tribunal other than the chairman may be paid, as a fee for his services, such amount as the Financial Secretary thinks fit, and that amount may be paid out of the general revenue of Hong Kong without further appropriation than this subsection.

Third Schedule.

(5) The provisions in the Third Schedule shall have effect in relation to the appointment of members and temporary members of the Tribunal, and the procedural and other matters concerning the Tribunal and its sittings for which provision is made therein.

INQUIRIES BY TRIBUNAL

Inquiries into insider dealings.

**141H.** (1) If it appears to the Financial Secretary, whether following representations by the Commission or otherwise, that insider dealing in relation to the securities of a corporation has taken place or may have taken place, he may in accordance with this section require the Tribunal to inquire into the matter (in this Part referred to as "an inquiry").

(2) An inquiry shall be instituted by notice in writing from the Financial Secretary to the chairman of the Tribunal containing such particulars as are sufficient to define the terms of reference of the inquiry.

(3) The object of an inquiry shall be to determine, within the Tribunal's terms of reference—

*(a)* whether culpable insider dealing in relation to the securities of a corporation has taken place; and
*(b)* the identity of the persons involved therein and the extent of their culpability.

(4) In making a determination under subsection (3)*(b)*, the Tribunal shall not be limited to the identity and culpability of an immediate party to an insider dealing but may, subject to section 141C—

*(a)* include any other person connected with the dealing;
*(b)* in the case of a body corporate, include the individuals who exercised control in the management thereof.

Report of Tribunal following inquiry. Third Schedule.

**141I.** (1) Upon receipt of a notice under section 141H(2) the Tribunal shall conduct an inquiry in accordance with the provisions of this Part and the Third Schedule, and prepare a written report thereon.

(2) No person shall publish any material received by the Tribunal for the purposes of an inquiry and which comes to his knowledge by virtue of being so received.

(3) Any person who contravenes subsection (2) commits an offence and is liable on conviction on indictment to a fine of $10,000 and to imprisonment for 1 year.

(4) The Tribunal shall issue its report in the following manner—

*(a)* by first furnishing a copy to the Financial Secretary; and
*(b)* thereafter, subject to subsection (5), by—

(i) causing the report to be published in such manner that copies thereof are available to the public; and

(ii) furnishing a copy, so far as is reasonably practicable, to any person whose conduct was directly in question in the inquiry.

(5) Where the Tribunal intends to cause a report to be published which contains a finding that a person is not culpable in respect of a dealing which has been the subject of an inquiry, the following provisions shall apply—

*(a)* if that person has supplied to the Tribunal an address for service for the purposes of this subsection, the Tribunal shall cause a copy of the proposed report, so far as it relates to the dealing in question, to be delivered to or left for him at that address;

*(b)* if within 7 days after such delivery the Tribunal has received notice in writing that the person objects to being named in relation to the dealing in question, the Tribunal shall not name the person in the report in respect of that dealing;

*(c)* if the Tribunal has not, within the said 7 days, received notice in accordance with paragraph *(b)*, or if the person has not supplied an address for service under paragraph *(a)*, the Tribunal shall name the person in the report in respect of the said dealing.

(6) No person shall be liable to any civil or criminal proceedings by reason of the publication by him of a true and accurate account or a fair and accurate summary of any report of the Tribunal which has been published under subsection (4)*(b)*.

POWERS OF TRIBUNAL

Application to Tribunal of Commissions of Inquiry Ordinance.

**141J.** (1) Sections 4(1) (other than paragraphs *(i)*, *(j)*, and *(ma)*), 5, 7, 8 (other than subsections (1)*(ca)*, (2)*(d)*, (2)*(e)* and (3)) and 9 to 14 of the Commissions of Inquiry Ordinance shall, subject to this Ordinance, apply for the purposes of an inquiry as if—

*(a)* the inquiry were an inquiry to which that Ordinance applies;

*(b)* references therein to a Commission, the Chairman and a Commissioner were respectively references to the Tribunal, the chairman and a member thereof;

*(c)* paragraph *(h)* of the said section 4(1) authorized payment to a person appearing before the Tribunal of expenses as well as sums for loss of time;

*(d)* the Tribunal were a Commission with full powers to deal with contempts under the said section 9;

*(e)* all necessary changes were made to Form 2 in the Schedule of the said Ordinance.

(2) The Tribunal may order that any document or article which comes into its possession or the possession of the Commissioner for the purposes of an inquiry shall be dealt with in such manner as the justice of the case requires.

Further powers of Tribunal to obtain information.

**141K.** (1) Where it appears to the Tribunal that it would assist the conduct of an inquiry to do so, the Tribunal may in writing authorize the Commissioner to exercise all or any of the powers set out in subsection (2) and to report to the Tribunal the information so obtained which is relevant to the inquiry.

(2) The powers referred to in subsection (1) are—

*(a)* to inspect the books and documents of any person where the Tribunal has reasonable grounds to believe or suspect that those books or documents may contain information relevant to the inquiry;

*(b)* to make copies of and take extracts from books and documents referred to in paragraph *(a)* and, subject to subsection (3), to take possession of the same for such period (not exceeding 2 days) as is necessary for the purpose of doing so;

*(c)* to require any person to give any explanation or particulars concerning books and documents referred to in paragraph *(a)*;

*(d)* in writing to require from any person information as to whether or not there is at any premises any book or document which may contain information relevant to the inquiry, and particulars as to such premises, book or document;

*(e)* to require that any information or particulars furnished pursuant to this section be verified by statutory declaration and to take any such declaration.

(3) Where the Commissioner takes possession of any book or document under subsection (2)*(b)* he shall permit a person who would be entitled to inspect it if it were not in the possession of the Commissioner to inspect it, and to make copies and take extracts, at all reasonable times.

(4) A person shall produce all books and documents in his custody or under his control, the inspection whereof is sought by the Commissioner under the authority of this section.

(5) Any person who is required under this section to disclose any information or particulars or give any explanation shall comply with that requirement so far as lies within his power to do so and shall, if requested, verify the information, particulars or explanation by statutory declaration.

(6) A person commits an offence who—

*(a)* contravenes subsection (4) or (5);

*(b)* in purported compliance with subsection (4) or (5), makes any statement which he knows to be false or misleading or recklessly makes any statement which is false or misleading in a material particular;

*(c)* obstructs the Commissioner in the exercise of his powers under this section;

*(d)* conceals, destroys, mutilates or alters any book or document which contains information which is relevant to an inquiry or sends any such book or document out of Hong Kong or causes the same to be so sent,

and is liable on conviction to a fine of $5,000 and to imprisonment for 3 months.

(7) An offence specified in subsection (6) shall be deemed to be a contempt of the Tribunal and the Tribunal may deal with any such offence in accordance with the powers referred to in section 141J(1)*(d)* to deal with contempts committed otherwise than in the presence of the Tribunal and may impose the punishments provided for by the said subsection (6).

(8) It shall be a defence to a prosecution under subsection (6)*(d)* if the person charged proves that he did not act with intent to defeat the discovery of a dealing in relation to securities within section 141B(1) or to delay or obstruct the carrying out of an inquiry.

(9) In this section "books" includes bankers' books.

No privilege allowed except to legal advisers.

141L. (1) Except as provided in subsection (2), a person shall not be excused on account of privilege from complying with any requirement under section 141K or, on appearing before the Tribunal, from answering any question or disclosing any information or particulars or producing any book or document.

(2) Nothing in this Part shall require the disclosure by a solicitor or counsel of any privileged communication, whether oral or written, made to or by him in that capacity, except as regards the name and address of his client.

(3) Nothing in subsection (1) shall be construed as affecting section 4 of the Inland Revenue Ordinance.

## Part XIII. Miscellaneous Provisions

Restriction on use of title "stockbroker", "underwriter", etc.

142. (1) A person who is not a stockbroker shall not—

*(a)* take or use the title "stockbroker"; or

*(b)* take or use, or have attached to or exhibited at any place, any title that resembles the title "stockbroker" or so closely resembles that title as to be calculated to deceive.

(2) A person who is not an underwriter shall not—

*(a)* take or use the title "underwriter"; or

*(b)* take or use, or have attached to or exhibited at any place, any title that resembles the title "underwriter" or so closely resembles that title as to be calculated to deceive.

(3) Any person who contravenes subsection (1) or subsection (2) shall be guilty of an offence and shall be liable on conviction to a fine of $5,000.

(4) A person who is a member of a stock exchange outside Hong Kong does not contravene subsection (1) by reason only of—

*(a)* taking or using the title "stockbroker"; or

*(b)* taking or using, or having attached to or exhibited at any place in Hong Kong, any title that resembles the title "stockbroker",

if in any such case the name of the stock exchange and the place at which it is located is quoted in conjunction with the title "stockbroker".

(5) A person who carries on a business as an insurance underwriter does not contravene subsection (2) by reason only that he takes or uses the title "underwriter" in circumstances that make it clear that he is not holding himself out as being an underwriter within the meaning of section 2.

Investment advisory contracts.

143. (1) No investment adviser shall enter into an investment advisory contract with any person in Hong Kong (in this section referred to as his client), or extend or renew any such contract, or in any way perform any such investment advisory contract entered into, extended, or renewed after the commencement of this section, if the contract—

*(a)* provides for remuneration to be paid by the client to the investment adviser on the basis of a share of capital gains of the funds or any part of the funds of the client;

*(b)* does not include a provision to the effect that an assignment of the contract by the investment adviser shall be made only with the consent of the client; or

*(c)* does not include a provision to the effect that the investment adviser—

(i) if a firm, will notify the client of any change in the partner of the firm; or

(ii) if a corporation, will notify the client of any change in the directors of the corporation,

within a reasonable time after the change.

(2) Subsection (1)*(a)* does not—

*(a)* prohibit an investment advisory contract which provides for remuneration based on the total value of a fund averaged over a definite period, or on definite dates, or taken on a definite date; or

*(b)* apply to an investment advisory contract with the manager or other representative of a unit trust or mutual fund corporation authorized by the Commission for the purposes of this Ordinance, or a company carrying on business as an investment company and registered under the Companies Ordinance, which contract provides for remuneration based on the asset value of the trust, corporation, or company under management averaged over a specified period and increasing and decreasing proportionately in accordance with the performance of the trust, corporation, or company over a specified period in relation either to—

(i) the investment record of an appropriate index of securities; or

(ii) such other measure of investment performance as the Commission may specify in writing on the application of either party to a contract or intended contract.

(3) For the purposes of subsection (1)*(b)* and *(c)*, "investment advisory contract" means a contract or agreement whereby a person agrees to act as investment adviser or to manage any investment or trading account of a client, not being a unit trust or mutual fund corporation authorized by the Commission for the purposes of this Ordinance, or a company carrying on business as an investment company and registered under the Companies Ordinance.

(4) Any investment adviser who knowingly enters into any contract in contravention of any of the provisions of subsection (1) shall be guilty of an offence and shall be liable on conviction to a fine of $2,000.

(5) Any contract entered into in contravention of any of the provisions-

sions of subsection (1) shall, notwithstanding anything in the contract, be voidable at the option of the client.

Court may make certain orders.

144. (1) Where, on the application of the Commissioner, it appears to the Court that a person has contravened this Ordinance or any conditions of registration thereunder, or is about to do an act with respect to dealing in securities that, if done, would be such a contravention, the Court may, without prejudice to any orders it would be entitled to make otherwise than pursuant to this section, make one or more of the following orders—

*(a)* an order restraining a person from acquiring, disposing of, or otherwise dealing with any securities specified in the order;
*(b)* in relation to a registered dealer, an order appointing a person to administer the property of the dealer;
*(c)* an order declaring a contract relating to securities to be void or voidable;
*(d)* for the purpose of securing compliance with any other order under this section, an order directing a person to do or refrain from doing a specified act; or
*(e)* any ancillary order which it considers necessary in consequence of the making of an order under paragraphs *(a)* to *(d)*.

(2) The Court shall, before making an order under subsection (1), satisfy itself, so far as it can reasonably do so, that the order would not unfairly prejudice any person.

(3) The Court may, before making an order under subsection (1), direct that notice of the application be given to such persons as it thinks fit or direct that notice of the application be published in such manner as it thinks fit, or both.

(4) The Court may reverse, vary, or discharge an order made by it under this section or suspend the operation of such an order.

Miscellaneous offences.

145. Any person who—

*(a)* obstructs the Commissioner or any other public officer or any person in the exercise or performance of any power, authority, duty, or function under this Ordinance; or
*(b)* fails to produce any document that the Commissioner or a person authorized by the Commissioner has, pursuant to any provision of this Ordinance, required that person to produce for inspection by the Commissioner or the person so authorized,

shall be guilty of an offence and shall be liable on conviction to a fine of $5,000 and to imprisonment for 3 months.

Regulations.

**146.** (1) The Governor in Council may, after consultation with the Commission, make regulations for all or any of the following matters—

*(a)* the conduct of business by registered dealers, registered investment advisers, registered dealers' representatives, and registered investment representatives;

*(b)* matters incidental to the registration of dealers, investment advisers, dealers' representatives, and investment representatives under this Ordinance;

*(c)* the class of persons in relation to whom, and the manner and circumstances in which, registered dealers and registered dealers' representatives may deal in securities;

*(d)* the class of persons in relation to whom, and the manner and circumstances in which, registered investment advisers and registered investment representatives may carry on business as investment advisers or as investment representatives, as the case may be;

*(e)* prescribing the amount of deposit required to be made for the purposes of section 52, and providing for the application of deposits under subsections (3) and (4) of that section;

*(f)* requiring dealers and registered investment advisers to exhibit their certificates of registration at their places of business;

*(g)* prescribing the information to be notified for the purposes of section 63(1)*(b)*;

*(h)* prescribing the particulars to be recorded in relation to registered dealers, registered investment advisers, registered dealers' representatives, and registered investment representatives, under section 64;

*(i)* empowering the Commissioner to correct any errors in any register kept under this Ordinance;

*(j)* empowering the Commissioner, on payment of the prescribed fee (if any), to issue duplicate certificates of registration in the event of loss or destruction of the original certificate or of any duplicate certificate;

*(k)* prescribing the manner, time, or circumstances for retaining copies of circulars for the purposes of section 79(5);

*(l)* prescribing the particulars to be recorded in relation to accounts kept under section 84;

*(m)* prescribing the particulars to be recorded in relation to the profit and loss account and balance sheet and the information to be contained in the auditor's report required to be lodged under section 88;

*(n)* *[Deleted, 62 of 1976, s. 34]*

*(o)* prescribing forms for the purposes of this Ordinance, and pre-

scribing the manner in which applications are to be made for registration under Part VI;

*(p)* prescribing fees and charges to be paid in respect of any matter or thing required for the purposes of this Ordinance;

*(q)* prescribing public offices for the purposes of sections 19 and 122;

*(r)* prescribing the procedure for the holding of investigations under Part XI, and providing for the reception of evidence, whether written or oral, and for the summoning and examination of witnesses, during the course of such an investigation;

*(s)* prescribing anything which is to be or may be prescribed by regulations.

(2) Regulations made under this section may provide that a contravention of specified provisions thereof shall be an offence and may provide penalties therefor not exceeding a fine of $2,000 and imprisonment for 3 months.

(3) Except as otherwise provided in this Ordinance, regulations made under this section may be of general or special application.

(4) Regulations made under this section may provide that, subject to such terms and conditions as may be prescribed thereby, the provisions of Parts VI to IX, or such of them as are specified in the regulations—

*(a)* shall not have effect in relation to any specified person or to any person who is a member of a specified class of persons—

(i) who is or may be a dealer or investment adviser by reason only of his doing anything that is incidental to another business;

(ii) who does not deal in securities for or on behalf of any other person; or

(iii) who is a dealer or investment adviser by reason only of his entering into any specified transaction or class of transactions;

*(b)* shall not have effect in relation to a representative of any such person, or a member of any such class of persons, as is referred to in paragraph *(a)*;

*(c)* shall have effect in relation to any such person or member, or a representative of any such person or member, to such extent as is prescribed; or

*(d)* shall not have effect in relation to a specified transaction or class of transactions entered into by a specified person or class of persons.

Liability of directors, etc.

147. (1) Where an offence under this Ordinance committed by a corporation is proved to have been committed with the consent or connivance of, or to be attributable to any neglect on the part of, any director, manager, secretary, or other similar officer of the corporation, or any person who was purporting to act in any such capacity, he, as well as the corporation, shall be guilty of the offence and shall be liable to be proceeded against and punished accordingly.

(2) Subject to subsection (3), for the purposes of this section, a person is deemed to be a director of a corporation if he occupies the position of a director by whatever name he may be called or is a person in accordance with whose directions or instructions the directors of the corporation or any of them act.

(3) A person shall not, by reason only that the directors of a corporation act on advice given by him in a professional capacity, be taken to be a person in accordance with whose directions or instructions those directors act.

Commissioner may prosecute certain offences against this Ordinance.

148. Without prejudice to the provisions of any other enactment relating to the prosecution of criminal offences and without prejudice to the powers of the Attorney General in relation to the prosecution of such offences, the Commissioner may institute proceedings in respect of any offence against this Ordinance that is punishable on summary conviction.

Amendment of Schedules and certain specified amounts.

149. The Governor in Council may, by order published in the *Gazette,* amend—

*(a)* the First and Second Schedules; and
*(b)* any amount or sum specified in Part X.

## FIRST SCHEDULE [ss. 72 & 149.]

### REQUIREMENTS TO BE SATISFIED IN RELATION TO OFFERS TO ACQUIRE SECURITIES

1. If the securities to be acquired are currently listed or quoted on a stock exchange (including a foreign stock exchange), the offer shall, subject to paragraph 2—

*(a)* state this fact and specify the exchange or exchanges on which the securities are currently listed or quoted;
*(b)* specify the last recorded price paid in respect of the securities at a stock exchange where they are listed, or, in the case of a foreign stock exchange, listed or quoted, on the latest practicable date during the period of 3 months immediately preceding the date of the offer;

(*c*) specify the last price paid in respect of the securities on the last trading day of each of the 6 months immediately preceding the date of the offer;

(*d*) specify the highest and the lowest prices paid in respect of the securities during the period of 6 months immediately preceding the date of the offer;

(*e*) where the offer has been the subject of a public announcement, whether in a newspaper or in any other form of news medium or otherwise, specify the last price paid in respect of the securities on the last trading day during the period of 3 months immediately preceding the public announcement, or, if the securities were not dealt in during that period, this should be stated.

2. If the securities proposed to be acquired are not listed or quoted on a stock exchange (including a foreign stock exchange), the offer shall contain—

(*a*) any information that the offeror may have as to the number and nominal value of those securities that have been sold in Hong Kong during the period of 6 months immediately preceding the date of the offer and the prices yielded by those sales, or, where the offeror has no such information, a statement to that effect; and

(*b*) particulars of any restriction in the constitution of the corporation which issued the securities on the right to transfer the securities which has the effect of requiring the offerees, before transferring securities held by them in the corporation, to offer those securities for purchase to members of the corporation or to any other person, and, where there is any such restriction, the arrangements (if any) being made to enable the securities to be transferred in pursuance of the offer.

3. Where the securities proposed to be acquired are those of a corporation incorporated outside Hong Kong and any holders of those securities reside in Hong Kong, and those securities are listed or quoted on a stock exchange of the country or territory in which the corporation is incorporated, the offer shall state this fact and specify the stock exchange on which they are listed or quoted.

4. The offer shall contain, in a prominent position in printing not smaller than eight point Times, a notice in the following form—

"*IMPORTANT*

If you are in doubt as to any aspect of this offer, you should consult a stockbroker or other registered dealer in securities, a bank manager, solicitor, professional accountant, or other professional adviser.".

## SECOND SCHEDULE [ss. 72 & 149.]

### REQUIREMENTS TO BE SATISFIED IN RELATION TO OFFERS TO DISPOSE OF SECURITIES

1. If the securities offered are currently listed or quoted on a stock exchange (including a foreign stock exchange) and will be uniform in all respects with the securities so currently listed or quoted, the offer shall—

(*a*) state that fact and specify the exchange on which those securities, or the securities with which they will be uniform, are currently listed or quoted;

(*b*) specify the last recorded price paid in respect of the securities at a stock exchange where they are listed, or, in the case of a foreign stock exchange, listed or quoted, on the latest practicable date during the period of 3 months immediately preceding the date of the offer;

*(c)* specify the last price paid in respect of the securities on the last trading day of each of the 6 months immediately preceding the date of the offer;

*(d)* specify the highest and the lowest prices paid in respect of the securities during the period of 6 months immediately preceding the date of the offer;

*(e)* where the offer has been the subject of a public announcement, whether in a newspaper or in any other form of news medium or otherwise, specify the last price paid on the last trading day during the period of 3 months immediately preceding the public announcement, or, if the securities were not dealt in during that period, this should be stated.

2. Where the securities offered are those of a corporation incorporated outside Hong Kong and—

*(a)* are listed or quoted on a stock exchange in the country or territory where the corporation was incorporated; or

*(b)* are yet to be issued but will be in all respects uniform with the securities already so listed or quoted,

the offer shall specify that fact and the name of the stock exchange on which those securities, or the securities with which they will be uniform, are so listed or quoted.

3. The offer shall, in the case of securities of a corporation which are not listed or quoted on a stock exchange (including a foreign stock exchange), or which are not uniform in all respects with securities so listed or quoted—

*(a)* give particulars of any restriction in the corporation's constitution which has the effect of requiring a holder of the corporation's securities to offer them for purchase to members of the corporation or any other person before transferring them in pursuance of the offer;

*(b)* except where the offer is accompanied by a document which conforms with Part II or Part XII of the Companies Ordinance in relation to the corporation whose securities are the subject of the offer, contain the particulars specified in paragraph 4 of this Schedule or be accompanied by a statement in writing containing those particulars.

4. (1) The particulars referred to in paragraph 3*(b)* are as follows—

*(a)* (i) the year in which, and the country or territory in which, the issuing corporation was incorporated;

(ii) the address of its registered or principal office in Hong Kong; and

(iii) where the issuing corporation is incorporated outside Hong Kong, the address of its registered or principal office in the country or territory in which it was incorporated or is resident;

*(b)* (i) the authorized capital of the issuing corporation;

(ii) the amount of the authorized capital of the corporation that has been issued and is outstanding at the date specified as being the close of the 5 financial years of the corporation immediately preceding the date of the offer;

(iii) the classes of shares into which that capital is divided;

(iv) the rights of each class of shareholder in respect of capital, dividends and voting; and

(v) the number and total nominal value respectively of shares issued for cash and shares issued as fully or partly paid up for a consideration other than cash;

*(c)* (i) the number and total nominal value of shares issued since the close of the last financial year of the issuing corporation;

(ii) the classes (if any) into which the shares are divided and the rights of each class of shareholder in respect of capital, dividends and voting;

(iii) the number and total nominal value respectively of shares issued as fully or partly paid up for cash or as fully or partly paid up for a consideration other than cash, or both;

(iv) the number of redeemable preference shares (if any) redeemed and the amounts repaid in respect of the shares so redeemed; and

(v) particulars of any reduction of capital lawfully authorized in respect of the corporation;

*(d)* particulars of any reorganization of the capital of the issuing corporation during each of its 2 financial years preceding the date of the offer;

*(e)* (i) the amount of the net profit or loss of the issuing corporation (before taking into account any form of tax calculated by reference to the amount of profits of the corporation);

(ii) the rate *per cent* of dividends paid by the issuing corporation and the amount distributed by way of dividends on each class of shares during each of the 5 financial years immediately preceding the offer; and

(iii) where no dividend has been paid in respect of shares of any particular class during any of those years, a statement to that effect;

*(f)* the total amount of any debentures issued by the issuing corporation and outstanding not more than 28 days before the date of the offer, and the total amount of mortgage debts, loans, or charges due from the corporation not more than 28 days before that date, together with the rate of interest payable in respect of them;

*(g)* the names and addresses of the directors of the issuing corporation;

*(h)* the number, description, and nominal value of the securities of the issuing corporation held by or on behalf of each of its directors or, if a director does not hold any such securities and no securities are held on his behalf, a statement to that effect; and

*(i)* whether or not the securities offered are, or, in the case of securities to be issued, will be, fully paid up, and, if not, to what extent they are or will be paid up, and, if the issuing corporation has fixed a date and amount for payment of outstanding calls, the date and amount of each such call.

(2) If any of the particulars required by sub-paragraph (1) are not available by reason of the issuing corporation not having carried on business for a sufficient length of time, or for any other reason, the offer shall state that fact; and if the issuing corporation is one incorporated in Hong Kong in respect of which those particulars are not available in the returns of the corporation filed with the Registrar of Companies, the offer shall also state that fact.

5. If the securities offered are yet to be issued, the offer shall—

*(a)* state—

(i) whether or not the issue requires the authority of a resolution of the issuing corporation;

(ii) the first dividend in which the securities will participate; and

(iii) whether or not there has been, to the knowledge of the offeror, any material change in the financial position of the issuing corporation since the date of the balance sheet and profit and loss account of the corporation for the financial year preceding the date of the offer and, if so, particulars of the change;

(*b*) be accompanied by copies of the balance sheet and profit and loss account of the corporation (if any) made up to the end of the last financial year of the corporation preceding the date of the offer;

(*c*) be accompanied by copies of the memorandum and articles of association or other document constituting or defining the constitution of the issuing corporation unless the offer specifies—

(i) a place in Hong Kong at which copies of those documents may be inspected by offerees; and

(ii) the times at which they may be inspected;

(*d*) in the case of securities which will be uniform in all respects with previously issued securities of the issuing corporation that are not currently listed on a stock exchange, give any information that the offeror may have as to the number and nominal value of those securities which have been sold during the period of 6 months preceding the date of the offer, and the prices yielded from the sales or, if the offeror has no such information, state that fact;

(*e*) in the case of securities which will not be uniform in all respects with securities previously issued by the issuing corporation, state—

(i) the respects in which the securities will differ from the previously issued securities;

(ii) whether or not any voting rights will attach to the securities and, if so, the limitations (if any) on those rights; and

(iii) whether or not application for permission to have the securities listed or quoted has been or will be made to a stock exchange (including a foreign stock exchange) and, if such an application has been made, the name of the stock exchange applied to.

6. The offer shall contain in a prominent position, in printing not smaller than eight point Times, a notice in the following form—

"*IMPORTANT*

If you are in doubt as to any aspect of this offer, you should consult a stockbroker or other registered dealer in securities, a bank manager, solicitor, professional accountant, or other professional adviser.".

THIRD SCHEDULE [ss. 141G & 141I.]

INSIDER DEALING TRIBUNAL

1. In this Schedule, unless the context otherwise requires—

"chairman" means the chairman of the Tribunal;

"inquiry" means an inquiry under section 141H;

"member" means a member of the Tribunal;

"Tribunal" means the Tribunal established by section 141G.

*Appointment of members*

2. Subject to paragraphs 4 and 5, the chairman shall be appointed for a term of 3 years but may from time to time, so long as he remains qualified under section 141G(3), be reappointed.

3. The other 2 members shall be appointed to act in relation to any specified inquiry or inquiries and any such member may be so appointed more than once.

4. A member may at any time resign his office by notice in writing to the Governor.

5. The chairman shall vacate his office if at any time he ceases to hold office as a judge of the Supreme Court.

6. A member other than the chairman may be removed from office by the Governor for disability, bankruptcy, neglect of duty or misconduct proved to the satisfaction of the Governor.

7. If an inquiry has been commenced by the Tribunal but not completed before the expiry of the chairman's term of office or before the resignation from or vacation of office by a member takes effect, the Governor may authorize the chairman or member to continue as chairman or a member of the Tribunal for the purpose of completing that inquiry.

8. An inquiry may be continued, notwithstanding any change in the membership of the Tribunal, as if the change had not occurred; and in particular evidence taken by the Tribunal need not be taken again on account of the change.

*Temporary members*

9. The Governor may appoint a temporary member of the Tribunal to act in place of any member who is precluded by illness, absence from Hong Kong or any other cause from exercising his functions or who considers it improper or undesirable that he should exercise his functions in relation to any specified matter.

10. A temporary member who is appointed to act in place of the chairman shall be a person who holds office as a judge of the Supreme Court and a temporary member who is appointed to act for an ordinary member shall not be a person who would be disqualified under section 141G(3) from appointment as a member.

11. A temporary member who acts in place of the chairman or other member shall be deemed for all purposes to be the chairman or other member of the Tribunal as the case may be.

*Sittings and representation*

12. The chairman shall convene such sittings of the Tribunal as he thinks necessary for the efficient performance of its functions.

13. The chairman shall preside at all sittings of the Tribunal and no sitting shall be held unless the other 2 members are also present.

14. Every question before the Tribunal shall be determined by the opinion of the majority of the members except a question of law which shall be determined by the chairman.

15. Every sitting of the Tribunal shall be held *in camera* and, subject to paragraph 16, the Tribunal shall determine which persons may be present.

16. A person whose conduct is the subject of an inquiry or who is implicated, or concerned in the subject matter of an inquiry shall be entitled to be present in person at any sitting of the Tribunal relating to that inquiry and to be represented by a barrister or solicitor.

17. For the purposes of paragraph 16 the Tribunal shall determine whether

the conduct of any person is the subject of the inquiry or whether a person is in any way implicated or concerned in the subject matter of the inquiry.

18. The Tribunal may appoint a legal officer nominated by the Attorney General, a barrister or a solicitor to act as counsel for the Tribunal.

19. In paragraph 16 "sitting" does not include any meeting of the Tribunal which is held for the purpose of deliberating on any question before the Tribunal.

# Protection of Investors Ordinance[1]

To provide for the protection of investors in securities and other property.

[29th March, 1974]

Short title.

1. This Ordinance may be cited as the Protection of Investors Ordinance.

Interpretation.

2. (1) In this Ordinance, unless the context otherwise requires—

"Commission" means the Securities Commission established under the Securities Ordinance;

"Commissioner" means the Commissioner for Securities appointed under the Securities Ordinance;

"corporation" has the same meaning as in the Securities Ordinance;

"credit union" means a credit union registered under the Credit Unions Ordinance;

"issue", in relation to an advertisement, invitation, or document, includes publish, circulate, distribute, or disseminate the advertisement, invitation, or document; and also includes causing the advertisement, invitation, or document to be issued;

"investment arrangements", in relation to property other than securities, means arrangements the purpose or effect, or pretended purpose or effect, of which is to enable persons taking part in the arrangements (whether by becoming owners of the property or otherwise) to participate in or receive—

*(a)* profits or income alleged to arise or to be likely to arise from the acquisition, holding, management, or disposal of the property or any part of the property; or

[1] *Laws of Hong Kong,* Cap. 335 (1974). Originally No. 13 of 1974. Relevant citations: L.N. 38/74; and L.N. 56/74. Additional citation: L.N. 72/74.

(*b*) sums to be paid or alleged to be likely to be paid out of any such profits or income;

"invitation" includes an offer, and also includes an invitation made by means of a telephone call or personal visit;

"securities" has the same meaning as in the Securities Ordinance.

(2) For the purposes of this Ordinance—

(*a*) "advertisement" includes every form of advertising, whether notified or published—

(i) in a newspaper, magazine, journal, or other periodical publication;

(ii) by the display of posters or notices;

(iii) by means of circulars, brochures, pamphlets, or handbills;

(iv) by an exhibition of photographs or cinematograph films; or

(v) by way of sound broadcasting or television,

and references to the issue of an advertisement shall be construed accordingly;

(*b*) "document" includes a circular, brochure, pamphlet, poster, handbill, prospectus, and any other document which is directed at or likely to be read by the public; and also includes any newspaper, magazine, journal, or other periodical publication;

(*c*) an advertisement issued by any person by way of display or exhibition in a public place shall be treated as being issued by him on every day on which he causes or authorizes it to be displayed or exhibited;

(*d*) an advertisement, invitation, or document which consists of or contains information likely to lead, directly or indirectly, to the doing by members of the public of any act mentioned in paragraphs (*a*) and (*b*) of section 3(1) shall be treated as being an advertisement, invitation, or document which is or contains an advertisement or invitation to the public to do that act;

(*e*) an advertisement, invitation, or document issued by one person on behalf of another shall be treated as an advertisement, invitation, or a document, as the case may be, issued by that other person.

## OFFENCES

Offence fraudulently or recklessly to induce persons to invest money.

3. (1) Any person who, by any fraudulent or reckless misrepresentation, induces another person—

(*a*) to enter into or offer to enter into any agreement—

(i) for or with a view to acquiring, disposing of, subscribing for or underwriting securities; or

(ii) the purpose or effect, or pretended purpose or effect, of which is to secure to any of the parties to the agreement a profit from the yield of securities or by reference to fluctuations in the value of securities or property other than securities; or

*(b)* to take part in or offer to take part in any investment arrangements in respect of property other than securities,

shall be guilty of an offence.

(2) For the purposes of subsection (1) "fraudulent or reckless misrepresentation" means—

*(a)* any statement—

(i) which to the knowledge of its maker was false, misleading, or deceptive; or

(ii) which is false, misleading, or deceptive and was made recklessly;

*(b)* any promise—

(i) which the maker of the promise had no intention of fulfilling;

(ii) which, to the knowledge of the maker of the promise, was not capable of being fulfilled; or

(iii) which was made recklessly;

*(c)* any forecast—

(i) which, to the knowledge of the maker of the forecast, was not justified on the facts known to him at the time when he made it; or

(ii) which was not justified on the facts known to the maker of the forecast at the time when he made it and was made recklessly; or

*(d)* any statement or forecast from which the maker of the statement intentionally or recklessly omitted a material fact, with the result that the statement was thereby rendered untrue, misleading, or deceptive, or, as the case may be, the forecast was thereby not capable of being justified or was thereby rendered misleading or deceptive.

(3) Any person who is guilty of an offence against this section shall be liable on conviction on indictment to a fine of $1,000,000 and to imprisonment for 7 years.

**4.** (1) Subject to subsections (2) and (3), no person shall—

Offence to issue advertisements and documents relating to investments in certain cases.

*(a)* issue, or have in his possession for the purposes of issue, any advertisement or invitation which to his knowledge is or contains an invitation to the public to do any of the acts referred to in paragraphs *(a)* and *(b)* of section 3(1); or

*(b)* issue, or have in his possession for the purposes of issue, any document which to his knowledge contains an advertisement or invitation to the public to do any of those acts.

(2) Subsection (1) does not apply in relation to—

*(a)* the issue of a prospectus which complies with or is exempt from compliance with Part II of the Companies Ordinance or, in the case of a company incorporated outside Hong Kong, complies with or is exempt from compliance with Part XII of that Ordinance;

*(b)* the issue of a document relating to securities of a body corporate incorporated in Hong Kong that is not a company registered under the Companies Ordinance, being a document which—

(i) would, if the body corporate were a registered company, be a prospectus to which section 38 of the Companies Ordinance applies, or would apply if not excluded by subsection (5)*(b)* of that section or by section 38A of that Ordinance; and

(ii) contains all the matters which, by virtue of Part XII of that Ordinance, it would be required to contain if the body corporate were a company incorporated outside Hong Kong and the document were a prospectus issued by that company;

*(c)* the issue of a form of application for shares or debentures of a company, together with—

(i) a prospectus which complies with or is exempt from compliance with Part II of the Companies Ordinance or, in the case of a company incorporated outside Hong Kong, complies with or is exempt from compliance with Part XII of that Ordinance; or

(ii) in the case of a body corporate incorporated in Hong Kong which is not a registered company, a document containing the matters specified in paragraph *(b)*(ii);

*(d)* the issue of a form of application for the securities of a company in connexion with an invitation made in good faith to a person to enter into an underwriting agreement with respect to those securities;

(e) the issue of a prospectus which has been approved by the Commissioner in relation to a mutual fund corporation or unit trust authorized by the Commission under the Securities Ordinance;

(f) the issue of a form of application for the shares of a mutual fund corporation or the units of a unit trust, being a mutual fund corporation or unit trust which has been authorized by the Commission, together with a prospectus approved by the Commissioner; or

(g) the issue of any advertisements, invitations, or documents (being advertisements, invitations, or documents to which this section relates) which is required or authorized by or under any other Ordinance, or has been authorized by the Commission before issue.

(3) This section does not prohibit the issue or possession of any advertisement, invitation, or document by reason only—

(a) that it is or contains an advertisement or invitation to which this section relates made—

(i) with respect to securities, by or on behalf of a dealer or investment adviser who is registered under the Securities Ordinance or who is a dealer exempted from registration under that Ordinance;

(ii) by or on behalf of a corporation to holders of securities or creditors of, or servants or agents employed by, that corporation, or a corporation which is deemed to be related to that corporation by virtue of section 4 of the Securities Ordinance, in respect of securities of that corporation or that related corporation;

(iii) by or on behalf of the manager or trustee of a unit trust authorized by the Commission pursuant to the Securities Ordinance to holders of units, or creditors, of the trust, or to servants or agents employed by that manager or trustee;

(iv) by or on behalf of the Government in respect of securities issued by it;

(v) by or on behalf of a credit union in respect of shares in the union;

(vi) by or on behalf of a person acting as trustee of a trust (not being a unit trust) to beneficiaries under the trust; or

(vii) with respect to securities intended to be disposed of to persons outside Hong Kong or to be disposed of in Hong Kong only to persons whose business involves the acquisition, disposal, or holding of securities, whether as principal or as agent; or

*(b)* that it is or contains an advertisement or invitation which a person who is engaged in the business of buying and selling property other than securities (either as principal or as agent) may make or give in the ordinary course of that business; but nothing in this paragraph authorizes any person to do anything pursuant to or for the purpose of any investment arrangements in respect of any such property.

(4) Subject to the provisions of this section, any person who contravenes subsection (1) shall be guilty of an offence and shall be liable on conviction on indictment to a fine of $500,000 and to imprisonment for 3 years.

(5) A person shall not be taken to contravene this section by reason only that he—

*(a)* issues, or has in his possession for the purposes of issue, to purchasers copies of any newspaper, journal, magazine, or other periodical publication of general and regular circulation, which contain an invitation to which this section relates; or

*(b)* issues advertisements which are or contain, or issues or has in his possession for the purposes of issue documents which contain, invitations to which this section relates to persons who are dealers or investment advisers registered under the Securities Ordinance or who are exempted from registration under that Ordinance.

(6) For the purposes of any proceedings under this section, an advertisement, invitation, or document which is or contains an advertisement or invitation to enter into or offer to enter into any agreement referred to in section 3(1) with a person specified in the advertisement, invitation, or document shall, subject to subsection (5), be presumed, unless he proves to the contrary, to have been issued by him.

(7) For the purposes of subsection (2)*(g)*, the Commission may in authorizing the issue of any advertisement, invitation, or document impose such conditions as it thinks fit.

Offence to issue advertisement relating to an investment management business unless registered.

5. (1) A person shall not—

*(a)* issue, or have in his possession for the purposes of issue, any advertisement in which to his knowledge a person other than an investment adviser registered under the Securities Ordinance holds himself out as being prepared—

(i) to give investment advice in return for remuneration; or

(ii) to undertake for remuneration the management of investors' portfolios of securities; or

(*b*) issue or have in his possession for the purposes of issue any document which to his knowledge contains such an advertisement.

(2) Any person who contravenes subsection (1) shall be guilty of an offence, and shall be liable on conviction to a fine of $10,000.

(3) A person shall not be taken to contravene this section by reason only that he—

(*a*) issues, or has in his possession for the purposes of issue, to purchasers copies of any newspaper, journal, magazine, or other periodical publication of general and regular circulation, which contain an advertisement to which this section relates; or
(*b*) issues advertisements which are or contain, or issues or has in his possession for the purposes of issue documents which contain, invitations to which this section relates to persons who are dealers or investment advisers registered under the Securities Ordinance or who are exempted from registration under that Ordinance.

(4) For the purposes of any proceedings under this section, an advertisement or document in which a person named in the advertisement or document holds himself out as being prepared—

(*a*) to give investment advice in return for remuneration; or
(*b*) to undertake for remuneration the management of investors' portfolios of securities,

shall, subject to subsection (3), be presumed, unless he proves to the contrary, to have been issued by him.

Seizure etc. of documents.

6. (1) If a magistrate is satisfied by information on oath that there is reasonable ground for suspecting that, at premises that are specified in the information, a person is in possession of any document which relates to an offence alleged to have been committed against this Ordinance, the magistrate may grant a warrant empowering the Commissioner or any police officer—

(*a*) to enter the premises, if necessary by force, at any time within 1 month from the date of the warrant; and
(*b*) to search for, seize and remove, any document found on the premises which the Commissioner or, as the case may be, the police officer has reasonable grounds for believing to have been involved in or connected with the alleged offence.

(2) Any document seized under subsection (1) may be retained for a period of 6 months or, if within that period any proceedings in respect of an offence against this Ordinance are commenced and the document is relevant to those proceedings, until the conclusion of those proceedings.

(3) Notwithstanding subsection (2), a document seized under subsection (1) may be retained for a period longer than 6 months if the person entitled to it is not in Hong Kong or his whereabouts are unknown; and if—

*(a)* that person subsequently returns to Hong Kong or his whereabouts subsequently become known; and

*(b)* within 14 days of his return or the discovery of his whereabouts, any proceedings in respect of an offence against this Ordinance are commenced, and the document is relevant to those proceedings,

the document may be retained until the conclusion of those proceedings.

(4) The person to whom a document seized under subsection (1) belongs shall, unless the document is the subject of an order under subsection (5), be entitled at all reasonable times to take copies of or extracts from it.

(5) Where any person is convicted of an offence against this Ordinance, the court dealing with the case may make an order authorizing the destruction, or the disposal in any other specified manner, of any documents produced to the court which are shown to its satisfaction to be involved in or connected with the commission of the offence; but an order under this subsection may not authorize the destruction or disposal of a document before the conclusion of the proceedings to which the order relates.

(6) Subject to subsections (2), (3), (4), and (5), section 102 of the Criminal Procedure Ordinance (which makes provision for the disposal of property connected with offences) shall apply to property which has come into the possession of the Commissioner or the police under this section in the same way as it applies to property which has come into the possession of the police in the circumstances mentioned in that section.

(7) Any person who—

*(a)* obstructs the exercise of any right of entry or search conferred by virtue of a warrant under this section; or

*(b)* obstructs the exercise of any right so conferred to seize any document,

shall be guilty of an offence and liable on conviction to a fine of $5,000 and to imprisonment for 6 months.

Liability of directors, etc.

7. (1) Where an offence against this Ordinance committed by a company or other body corporate is proved to have been committed with the consent or connivance of, or to be attributable to any neglect on the part of, any director, manager, secretary, or other similar officer of the company or body corporate or any person who was purporting to act in any such capacity, he, as well as the company or body, shall be guilty of the offence and shall be liable to be proceeded against and punished accordingly.

(2) Subject to subsection (3), for the purposes of this section, a person is deemed to be a director of a company or other body corporate if he occupies the position of a director by whatever name called, or is a person in accordance with whose directions or instructions the directors of the company or other body corporate or any of them act.

(3) A person shall not, by reason only that the directors of a company or other body corporate act on advice given by him in a professional capacity, be taken to be a person in accordance with whose directions or instructions those directors act.

## ACTION IN TORT

Liability in tort for inducing persons to invest money in certain cases.

8. (1) Any person who, by any fraudulent, reckless, or negligent misrepresentation, induces another person—

*(a)* to enter into any agreement—

- (i) for or with a view to acquiring, disposing of, subscribing for, or underwriting securities; or
- (ii) the purpose or effect, or pretended purpose or effect, of which is to secure to any of the parties to the agreement a profit from the yield or securities or by reference to fluctuations in the value of securities or property other than securities; or

*(b)* to take part in any investment arrangements in respect of property other than securities,

shall be liable to pay compensation to that other person for any pecuniary loss that he has sustained by reason of his reliance on the misrepresentation.

(2) For the purposes of subsection (1) "fraudulent, reckless, or negligent misrepresentation" means—

*(a)* any statement—

(i) which to the knowledge of its maker was false, misleading, or deceptive;

(ii) which is false, misleading, or deceptive and was made recklessly; or

(iii) which is false, misleading, or deceptive and was made without reasonable care having been taken to ensure its accuracy;

*(b)* any promise—

(i) which the maker of the promise had no intention of fulfilling;

(ii) which, to the knowledge of the maker of the promise, was not capable of being fulfilled; or

(iii) which was made recklessly or without reasonable care having been taken to ensure that it could be fulfilled;

*(c)* any forecast—

(i) which, to the knowledge of the maker of the forecast, was not justified on the facts known to him at the time when he made it; or

(ii) which was not justified on the facts known to the maker of the forecast at the time when he made it and was made recklessly or without reasonable care having been taken to ascertain the accuracy of those facts; or

*(d)* any statement or forecast from which the maker of the statement intentionally, recklessly, or negligently omitted a material fact of which he had knowledge or ought to have had knowledge, with the result that the statement was thereby rendered untrue, misleading, or deceptive, or, as the case may be, the forecast was thereby not capable of being justified or was thereby rendered misleading or deceptive.

(3) For the purposes of this section—

*(a)* where any statement, forecast, or promise to which this section relates was made by a company or other body corporate, every person who was a director of the company or body corporate at the time when the statement, forecast, or promise was made shall, in the absence of evidence to the contrary, be taken to have caused or authorized it to be made; and

*(b)* a person is deemed to be a director of a company or other body corporate if he occupies the position of director by whatever name he may be called, or is a person in accordance with whose directions or instructions the directors of the company or other

body or any of them act; but a person shall not, by reason only that the directors of a company or other body corporate act on advice given by him in a professional capacity, be taken to be a person in accordance with whose directions or instructions those directors act.

(4) Nothing in this section limits or diminishes any liability which any person may incur under the common law.

(5) This section does not confer a right of action in any case to which section 40 of the Companies Ordinance applies.

(6) An action may be brought under this section whether or not a person has been charged with or convicted of an offence under this Ordinance.

# Ivory Coast

Street scene in Abidjan, capital of Ivory Coast
Courtesy Wide World Photos

# IVORY COAST

# Financial System of Ivory Coast

by

*Robert A. Franks**

## Introduction

Formerly part of French West Africa, Ivory Coast gained independence in 1960. The country is a Republic with a presidential system of government, a National Assembly, and an independent judiciary. It is a member of a number of regional organizations, including the West African Monetary Union, described below, the Council of the Entente, the West African Economic Community (CEAO)—as well as the wider-membership Economic Community of West African States (CEDEAO).

At the coast Ivory Coast's climate is equatorial, becoming progressively drier farther inland. This variation enables a relatively wide range of crops to be produced for both local and export markets. The main export products are coffee, cocoa, tropical hardwoods, bananas, pineapples, cotton, palm oil, and rubber. The first three products, in processed and unprocessed form, account for three fourths of Ivory Coast's total exports. The natural resources of the country are primarily agricultural, although oil has been found offshore, and there are small diamond workings. Deposits of iron ore and manganese are at present unexploited.

## The Economy

Since independence, the Ivorian economy has grown very rapidly; in spite of a high rate of population growth, real per capita income has increased by 4 per cent per annum on average and, at SDR 978 in 1980, gross domestic product (GDP) per capita is now the highest in West Africa. While all sectors of the economy have contributed to this expansion in output, the export sector has been the main stimulus to growth. The growth in agricultural exports has been made possible by an abundant supply of labor, particularly of migrant workers, the avail-

---

* Mr. Franks, Senior Economist in the Midwest African Division of the African Department, is a graduate of the University of Cambridge, the European Institute of Business Administration (INSEAD), and the University of Sussex.

Other members of the African Department who collaborated on the introduction to Ivory Coast were Messrs. Jean Philippe Briffaux, Michel Fiator, and Christopher Green (who has since left the Fund) and Ms. Ulrike Wilson.

ability of large areas of suitable, though ecologically fragile, land, and government policies providing high and stable producer prices. Investment has also risen sharply both in absolute terms and as a proportion of GDP, reaching 28 per cent of GDP in 1980, compared with 13 per cent of GDP in 1960. The public sector has invested heavily in diversifying agricultural production with particular emphasis on palm oil, sugar, and rubber. Private investment has been concentrated mainly in manufacturing, construction, and services. Investment has been financed from both a high level of local saving and substantial capital inflows encouraged by liberal exchange policies and tax incentives.

Ivory Coast's success in promoting such a rapid rate of economic development has been achieved in spite of a number of serious problems which typically face economic policymakers in developing countries. The most important problem has been sharp fluctuations in income from year to year reflecting both the impact of the weather on agricultural production and changes in world prices for primary commodities. These fluctuations in income and the terms of trade inevitably have been reflected in Ivory Coast's balance of payments. However, Ivory Coast's membership in a multinational monetary union has helped the country to weather such fluctuations without the need for drastic and disruptive short-term stabilization measures. Ivory Coast's growth has also depended heavily on external factors, both labor and capital. Foreign labor has made its contribution at both ends of the employment scale. Substantial numbers of unskilled migrants are employed, particularly in agriculture, as well as highly skilled expatriate managers and technicians. This dependency on external factors has given rise to a rapid growth in external debt, in debt servicing, and in workers' remittances abroad. The rapid growth in debt servicing has led to pressure on the level of domestic savings available for investment, while high factor-income payments abroad have aggravated balance of payments pressures due to fluctuations in income and the terms of trade.

To alleviate these growing problems, the Ivorian Government introduced some important measures, a number of which were reflected in the objectives of the 1976–80 Development Plan. While development had previously been concentrated in import-substitution industry, emphasis was now placed on developing processing and manufacturing industries geared for export. The objective was to reduce the country's dependence on primary product exports and hence on volatile primary product prices. In order to diversify further the agricultural sector, investment was stepped up in the cotton, cereals, and livestock sectors.

To reduce the dependence of the economy on external factors, steps were taken to accelerate the assumption of managerial responsibility and ownership by nationals in the private sector, and to increase the mobilization of domestic savings. At the same time Ivory Coast's traditional liberal attitude to foreign private investment was maintained.

A major reform of the monetary system in 1975 provided the authorities with the means to increase the mobilization of domestic savings while providing the central bank with more effective instruments of monetary policy to deal with growing inflationary pressures in the economy.

## The Monetary and Financial System

Ivory Coast is a member of the West African Monetary Union (Union Monétaire Ouest Africaine), together with five other countries: Benin, Niger, Senegal, Togo, and Upper Volta. Originally established in 1962, the Monetary Union was substantially reorganized and reformed in a new treaty signed on November 14, 1973, which entered into effect, after ratification by members, in 1975. The Monetary Union provides for centralized foreign currency reserves, a single currency issued by a common central bank, the Central Bank of West African States (Banque Centrale des Etats de l'Afrique de l'Ouest—BCEAO), a common interest rate structure, free transfer of funds within the Union, and common banking legislation.

Under the current treaty, a Conference of Heads of State of member countries has become the supreme decision-making body of the Monetary Union. The Conference meets at least once a year to decide on matters related to membership in the Monetary Union and on all unresolved matters from the next level of authority below the Conference, the Council of Ministers. The Council of Ministers, which, prior to the reform was the highest level of authority, is composed of two ministers from each member country, one of whom is the minister of finance. Both the Conference and Council require a unanimous vote to reach a decision. The Council of Ministers is responsible for the formulation of monetary policy for the Monetary Union as a whole, for supervising its implementation by the BCEAO, and for overseeing the coordination of banking legislation among member countries. Within the guidelines set for the Monetary Union as a whole, a National Credit Committee in each member country, chaired by the minister of finance, is responsible for applying monetary and credit policy within the country and for supervising its implementation by the national branch of the BCEAO.

The statutes regulating the operations of the Monetary Union's joint central bank, the BCEAO, were revised simultaneously with the new Monetary Union Treaty. The BCEAO, with headquarters now located in Dakar, Senegal, is managed by a Governor and a board of directors. The Governor, who is also chairman of the board, is appointed for a six-year term by the Council of Ministers. The board is composed of 14 members, with 2 representatives appointed by each member country and 2 by France. Each country, including France, has an equal vote and board decisions are taken on the basis of a simple majority for most central banking operations, including changes in interest rates and the establishment of credit ceilings. The power to change money market interest rates can be, and has been, delegated to the Governor of the BCEAO. More important decisions require a two-thirds majority, while amendments to the statutes require unanimity. Prior to the reform, most decisions required a two-thirds majority and French representation on the board amounted to one third. The BCEAO has a national branch in each member country headed by a national director; there are also a number of subbranches in secondary centers.

The BCEAO issues the Monetary Union's common currency, the CFA (Communauté Financière Africaine) franc. Notes and coins issued by the BCEAO are legal tender in all member countries and circulate freely within the Monetary Union. CFA notes are marked by a code letter following the serial number to enable the BCEAO to keep separate accounts for each country of both currency in circulation and its corresponding share in the pool of external reserves. The identification of notes has revealed that the movement of currency between Ivory Coast and Upper Volta and Niger is fairly large, reflecting traditional trading patterns as well as movements of migrants. Coins are not identified by country.

Although not a member of the Monetary Union, France was active in its establishment and development. Under a cooperation agreement, also revised in 1973, France has agreed to furnish such assistance as the Monetary Union may require to assure the free convertibility of the CFA franc, in particular by providing overdraft facilities through the Union's Operations Account with the French Treasury. In return, the Monetary Union has agreed to maintain at least 65 per cent of its foreign currency reserves in the Operations Account. Previously, the Monetary Union had to maintain with the French Treasury all its foreign currency reserves apart from working balances, each country's reserve tranche with the International Monetary Fund, holdings of SDRs, and, since 1967, small holdings of World Bank bonds. The present exchange rate of the CFA franc with respect to the French franc, CFAF 50=F 1, has been unchanged since the post-World War II realignment of the metropolitan franc with respect to the franc circulating in French overseas dependencies. However, the parity can be changed by the Monetary Union in consultation with France. All the members of the Monetary Union are also members of the French franc area and align their exchange control policies with those of the area. Transfers within the French franc zone are subject to only minimal statistical controls.

Ivory Coast has a highly developed and rapidly growing banking sector. Besides the BCEAO, there were 20 deposit money banks operating in Ivory Coast at the end of September 1981. There were also 7 representative offices of foreign banks and 12 nonbank financial institutions. Of the 20 banks, 5 were branches of foreign banks, while 15 had their head office in Ivory Coast. The principal banks operated more than 276 counters in the country at the end of September 1981, compared with 35 in 1964 and 95 in 1974.

Of the 20 banks, 5 can be characterized as specialized credit institutions and are mainly publicly owned. Formerly, these banks were classified as development banks by the BCEAO, and the others as commercial banks. However, the BCEAO no longer draws this distinction and now treats all banks as deposit money banks. General provisions concerning banks and financial institutions are set out in Law No. 75-549 of August 1975. All banking rules and regulations are uniformly applied, although the BCEAO does take account of specialization in the application of sectoral credit priorities.

One important specialized institution is the Banking Department of the Autonomous Amortization Fund (Caisse Autonome d'Amortissement), established in 1959. This Fund acts as banker to the public sector and, through a separate department, also manages Ivory Coast's public debt. Most public agencies and institutions are required to deposit their surplus funds with the Fund's Banking Department. Depositors include the Agricultural Price Stabilization Fund and the Autonomous Amortization Fund's own public debt department. The Fund is not authorized to make direct loans to the Treasury, but it can rediscount customs duty bills held by the Treasury.

Two institutions provide medium- and long-term credit for industry: the Ivorian Industrial Development Bank (Banque Ivorienne de Développement Industriel—BIDI), established in 1965, which concentrates mainly on larger industrial loans; and the Credit Bank of Ivory Coast (Crédit de la Côte d'Ivoire—CCI), established in 1955, which extends loans to small industrial and handicraft ventures, as well as for automobiles, housing, and construction.

The functions of the National Fund for Agricultural Credit (Caisse Nationale de Crédit Agricole), formed in 1959 with 100 per cent government equity, were taken over by the National Agricultural Development Bank (Banque Nationale de Développement Agricole—BNDA) in January 1968. In addition to making medium-term loans to farmers, the BNDA extends loans for agricultural projects mainly through the official agencies responsible for the different sectors of agricultural production.

Financing for the housing sector is provided by the National Bank for Savings and Credit (Banque Nationale pour l'Epargne et le Crédit —BNEC), established in 1975. The BNEC accepts savings deposits and makes loans to real estate companies and to finance low-cost housing.

In 1978 the existing Postal Checking System and the National Savings Bank were amalgamated into the Ivorian Bank for Savings and Development of Post and Telecommunications (Banque Ivoirienne d'Epargne et de Développement des Postes et Télécommunications—BIPT). The BIPT collected savings, placed Post Office funds with the Treasury, the Autonomous Amortization Fund, and the banks, and participated in the financing of the Post Office's investment program. In 1981 the BIPT was dissolved and the Postal Checking System and the National Savings Bank were re-established as autonomous entities.

Besides the deposit money banks, Ivory Coast has a diversified and rapidly growing system of nonbank financial institutions. These include companies that finance the purchase of vehicles and other equipment, those that finance building construction, leasing companies, and mutual credit associations. Three publicly owned institutions have played an important role in promoting savings and investment.

The National Investment Fund (Fonds National d'Investissements) was created in 1962 to stimulate private investment activities. Its resources are derived mainly from a 10 per cent surcharge on the profits tax, with a basic exemption of CFAF 80,000 to exclude small taxpayers who would find it difficult to meet the conditions for reimbursement. Taxpayers receive noninterest-bearing certificates with no specific maturity. If a certain multiple of these certificates is invested, the Investment Fund reimburses a proportion that varies according to the priority attached to the investment. If no investment is undertaken, the certificates may be converted into bonds of the National Finance Company, provided that the holder invests an equal amount of cash in such bonds. If not used for these two purposes, the certificates can be converted into 40-year, 2.5 per cent government bonds issued by the Autonomous Amortization Fund.

The National Finance Company (Société Nationale de Financement —SONAFI) was created in November 1963 with the primary objective of mobilizing voluntary domestic savings through long-term bond sales to private individuals and enterprises. It issued bonds maturing in 20 years with 7 per cent interest, tax free. Although in principle the resources of the company may be used for a wide range of investments, in practice they have been utilized mainly for government capital participation in enterprises. The dissolution of SONAFI was announced in 1980.

In 1968 the Ivorian Government established the Fund to Guarantee Credits to Ivorian Enterprises (Fonds de Garantie des Crédits aux Entreprises Ivoiriennes) to provide guarantees for commercial bank credit to small and medium-sized indigenous enterprises, in particular for those that would have difficulties obtaining bank credit without such a guarantee. Short-, medium-, and long-term credits, up to a maximum of CFAF 25 million for each enterprise, may be guaranteed by this fund. The guarantees may cover up to 80 per cent of the amount of credit, while the local entrepreneur must provide equity of at least 10 per cent of the cost of the program for which the credit has been requested.

A substantial number of insurance companies operate in Ivory Coast. As the bulk of their business is non-life, they are not a major generator of savings although legal reserve requirements provide some funds for local placement.

To help in diversifying further the range of financial instruments available to local savers, a stock exchange began operations in Abidjan in 1976. Besides bonds issued by the public sector, the shares of 23 enterprises, with a market capitalization of over CFAF 60 billion, were traded on the stock exchange at the end of October 1981, with a monthly volume of approximately CFAF 50 million. The principal banks act as brokers and jobbers in the market.

Mention should also be made of the African Development Bank, which has its headquarters in Abidjan. This institution, which began operations in 1966, now has 50 member countries.

## Monetary and Financial Policies

The year 1975 was a watershed in the development of Ivory Coast's monetary system. Prior to the reform, monetary policy in the Monetary Union was essentially passive, reacting to events rather than positively shaping them. The main impetus for reform came from a desire to see monetary policy and the banking and financial system play a more dynamic role in development. Up to 1975 the implementation of monetary policy in Ivory Coast depended on two principal instruments, rediscount ceilings and a liquidity ratio. The BCEAO also had authority to establish reserve ratios for the banks but this authority was never used. Rediscount limits were established for each individual borrower by the BCEAO. Those for short-term credit were based mainly on considerations of creditworthiness rather than on the priority of the investment for economic development. Rediscountable medium-term credit, on the other hand, was only granted for projects included in the national plan and approved by the planning authorities. Borrowers could, however, borrow over the limits at higher interest rates, but this nonrediscountable credit could not be refinanced by the banks at the BCEAO. Furthermore, as the banks' rediscounted and rediscountable credit were both included in the numerator of the liquidity ratio, banks were encouraged to extend rediscountable credit. Nevertheless, to the extent that the banks could obtain resources of more than six months' term (which were excluded from the denominator of the liquidity ratio), they could expand credit and, in particular, nonrediscountable credit without any constraint from the monetary authorities. Levels of rediscountable credit on the other hand were subject to control by the ceilings on rediscounts set by the BCEAO for the country as a whole and for each individual bank. However, the seasonal credit needs of each country, to finance the harvest, were always accorded the highest priority and granted virtually without limit while the ceilings on nonseasonal credit were set mainly in relation to the projected needs of the real economy. Furthermore, as most projects of high priority were accorded access to rediscountable credit, any excessive restriction of rediscount ceilings would slow, or increase the cost of, priority projects. In spite of these weaknesses in the instruments and application of credit policy, other aspects of the Monetary Union system made important contributions to Ivory Coast's development. The convertibility arrangements for the CFA franc were and continue to be an essential confidence-building component in Ivory Coast's liberal approach to foreign investment, while the corollary of such arrangements, the absence of exchange controls, has prevented the appearance of distortions in the growing economy that are invariably associated with such controls.

While, under the original provisions of the Monetary Union, it proved difficult to fine tune credit to the private sector, in contrast a firm and very restrictive limit on credit to the Government was maintained. Credit to the Government by the BCEAO, including discounted treasury bills and ways and means advances, and by banks using the BCEAO's rediscount facilities, to the extent of such use, was limited to 10 per cent (increased to 15 per cent in 1968) of the Government's fiscal receipts in the previous year. The term of such credit was originally limited to 240 days in each year but this limit could be and was relaxed by the BCEAO in the light of the Monetary Union's overall reserve position. The limit was an effective bar to excessive deficit financing of government budgets. Such discipline was not only necessary to prevent monetary depreciation and hence a devaluation of the exchange rate, or an unlimited overdraft on the Operations Account with the French Treasury, but also to assure among members equitable treatment in access to the resources of the Monetary Union.

The aims of the monetary reform can be summarized under three main headings. The first objective, as already mentioned, was to increase the role of the monetary system in promoting the economic development of members of the Monetary Union, by increasing and optimizing the use of financial savings and by retaining these savings within the Union. Second, measures were taken to increase the flexibility of monetary policy so as to enable it to be adapted more closely to the particular circumstances of individual members. In other words, the aim was to increase the degree of national control of monetary policy while at the same time preserving the advantages in terms of mutual support furnished by a multinational Monetary Union. Third, the reform accelerated the process of staffing the BCEAO with nationals of members of the Monetary Union, while a complementary decision was taken to relocate the head office of the BCEAO from Paris to Dakar (implemented in June 1978). Measures were also taken to increase credit to small and medium-sized enterprises owned by nationals of member countries in order to promote local entrepreneurship and hence develop and strengthen local participation in the national economies of member states.

One of the most important measures taken to implement these objectives was a major upward revision of interest rates. In 1973 the discount rate, which had been unchanged since the creation of the BCEAO, was increased from 3.5 per cent to 5.5 per cent. In comparison, however, interest rates in France soared to a record 13 per cent in 1974. This differential in interest rates continued to pull funds out of the Monetary Union. In July 1975 the basic discount rate of the BCEAO was increased to 8 per cent. At the same time, to ease the economic impact of such a sharp rise in interest rates, particularly on the economically weaker members of the Monetary Union, a new preferential discount rate of 5.5 per cent was introduced for crop financing, credit to governments, certain housing loans, and credit to small and medium-sized national entrepreneurs. The whole structure of interest rates in the Monetary Union was revised to take account of these new basic rates. In April 1980 both these discount rates were raised by 2.5 percentage points and again in April 1982 by an additional 2 percentage points. The banks' lending and borrowing rates were adjusted accordingly.

A money market was established for interbank funds within each member country and within the Monetary Union as a whole. The objective was to provide the BCEAO with another instrument to influence the cost of funds to banks. Rates in the market, which can be changed by decision of the Governor of the BCEAO, have been set to reflect interest rates abroad, particularly in France. The money market thus enables banks to employ excess funds gainfully within the Monetary Union instead of being obliged to place them abroad. By providing funds either through the money market, or by discounting at the basic discount rate, or at the preferential rate, the BCEAO can increase or reduce the cost of the banks' resources.

Besides establishing a preferential discount rate on bank lending to the Government, the revised statutes of the BCEAO increased the limit on such lending to 20 per cent of the previous year's fiscal revenue. Furthermore, the BCEAO was empowered to discount within this overall ceiling medium-term government paper (up to ten years) in order to provide finance for development projects. To increase further the flow of resources into the development effort in the Monetary Union, a joint development bank, the West African Development Bank (Banque Ouest-Africaine de Développement) was established. Half of this bank's initial capital of CFAF 2.4 billion was provided by the BCEAO, the remainder by the member states of the Monetary Union.

In addition to the incentive provided by the preferential discount rate for increasing credit to certain priority sectors, the new system has provided another tool for influencing the sectoral distribution of credit.

Credits extended by banks to customers with more than CFAF 30 million in credit outstanding (CFAF 100 million in Ivory Coast and CFAF 70 million in Senegal) are now subject to prior approval by the National Credit Committee. For loans of under CFAF 500 million this power has been delegated to the respective National Director of the BCEAO. The granting of prior authorization is governed by guidelines established on the basis of national development objectives.

A further element of the reform was a substantial elaboration of the methodology for establishing monetary targets. Before the beginning of each year detailed forecasts are prepared of the main economic aggregates for each member of the Monetary Union. Targets are established for changes in the gross foreign assets of the BCEAO for the Monetary Union as a whole and for each member. In light of these targets and the expected developments in the real economy, appropriate levels of central bank credit to governments and to banks are established. These targets, after approval by the Council of Ministers, guide the intervention of the central bank in each member's economy.

## Conclusion

The rapid growth and increasing complexity of the Ivorian economy have sharply increased demands on the banking and financial system, whose role in the mobilization and efficient allocation of financial resources is becoming increasingly important for the future development of the economy. The growing number of specialized financial institutions reflects the response of the financial sector to the increasingly sophisticated requirements of borrowers, while the increase in the number of commercial banks reflects both the expanding needs of borrowers and the growing opportunities for lenders. Overall growth of the financial sector has increased competition and hence promoted efficiency, while the expansion of branch networks by the principal banks throughout the country has played an important role in the monetization of the economy and the promotion of personal savings. The 1975 monetary reform provided the authorities with more effective tools to guide the development of the monetary system in the medium term and to improve the formulation, execution, and effectiveness of monetary policy in the short term.

# Treaty Establishing the West African Monetary Union[1]

The Government of the Republic of Ivory Coast,
The Government of the Republic of Dahomey,
The Government of the Republic of Upper Volta,
The Government of the Republic of Niger,
The Government of the Republic of Senegal,
The Government of the Togolese Republic,

Conscious of the profound solidarity of their States;

Convinced that it constitutes one of the essential means for a rapid and, at the same time, coordinated development of their national economies;

Believing that it is in their individual countries' and their common interests to continue as a monetary union and, in order to ensure the operation of that union, to maintain a common central bank;

Anxious, nevertheless, that each should, as far as it is concerned, watch over the proper allocation of national monetary resources for the development of their economies:

Convinced that a definition and strict observance of the rights and obligations of the members of such a monetary union are essential in order to ensure its functioning in the common interests and in the interests of each of its members,

have agreed on the following provisions:

## TITLE I. GENERAL PROVISIONS

**Art. 1.** The West African Monetary Union, established among the States that are signatories to this Treaty, is characterized by the recognition of one and the same monetary unit, the issuance of which is entrusted to a common bank of issue lending its cooperation to the national economies, under the control of the Governments pursuant to the terms set forth hereinafter.

**Art. 2.** Any West African State may, upon applying to the Conference of Heads of State of the Union, be admitted to the West African Monetary Union.

The terms of its membership shall be determined by agreement between its Government and the Governments of the Member States of the

[1] Traité Constituant l'Union Monétaire Ouest Africaine. Signed on November 14, 1973.

Union pursuant to a proposal by the Council of Ministers of the Union established under Title III hereinafter.

**Art. 3.** Any Member State may withdraw from the Union. The Conference of Heads of State of the Union must be notified of the Member State's decision. Such decision shall, *de jure,* take effect 180 days after notification thereof. This period may, however, be shortened by agreement of the parties.

The terms relating to the transfer of the issue service shall be fixed by agreement between the Government of the withdrawing State and the bank of issue of the Union acting on account of and pursuant to the terms laid down by the Council of Ministers of the Union.

That agreement shall likewise specify such portion of the negative positions that may appear in the item "external liquid assets" of the statement of certain other States of the Union as must be taken over by the withdrawing State owing to its joint and several participation in the previous management of the common currency.

**Art. 4.** The signatory States undertake, under penalty of automatic exclusion from the Union, to respect the provisions of this Treaty and of the implementing provisions thereunder, especially as regards:

(1) the rules underlying currency issue,
(2) centralization of monetary reserves,
(3) free circulation of currency and freedom of transfers between States of the Union,
(4) the provisions of the articles hereinafter.

The Conference of Heads of State of the Union shall, subject to the unanimous vote of the Heads of State of the other Members of the Union, note the withdrawal from the Union of any State that has failed to respect the above-mentioned undertakings. The Council of Ministers shall draw such conclusions as might be necessary to safeguard the interests of the Union.

## Title II. Conference of the Heads of State

**Art. 5.** The Heads of the Member States of the Union meeting as a Conference shall constitute the supreme authority of the Union.

The Conference of Heads of State shall rule on the admission of new members, note the withdrawal and the exclusion of members from the Union, and determine the location of its bank of issue.

The Conference of Heads of State shall decide any question that could not be solved unanimously by the Council of Ministers of the Union and which is submitted by the latter for its decision.

Conference decisions, called "Conference Acts," shall be adopted by unanimous vote.

The Conference shall be in session for one calendar year in each of the States of the Union, rotating in the alphabetical order of their names.

It shall meet at least once a year and as often as may be necessary, on the initiative of the incumbent Chairman or at the request of one or more Heads of Member States of the Union.

The chairmanship of the Conference shall be held by the Head of the Member State in which the Conference is in session.

The incumbent Chairman shall determine the dates and places of the meetings and shall draw up their agendas.

In case of emergency, the incumbent Chairman may consult the other Heads of State of the Union at their domiciles by a written procedure.

## TITLE III. COUNCIL OF MINISTERS OF THE UNION

**Art. 6.** The Monetary Union shall be managed by the Council of Ministers of the Monetary Union.

Each of the States shall be represented at the Council by two Ministers and shall have only one vote, cast by its Minister of Finance.

Each of the Ministers who are members of the Council shall designate an alternate who shall assist him at meetings of the Council and shall replace him in case of absence.

**Art. 7.** The Council shall choose one of the Ministers of Finance of the Union to preside over its work.

This election made *ex officio* shall call on the Ministers of Finance of the Union to serve as chairmen of the Council on a rotating basis.

The term of office of the Chairman shall be two years.

The Chairman of the Council of Ministers shall call and preside over the meetings of the Council. He shall see both to the preparation of reports and proposals for decisions that are submitted to him and to the action taken on them.

For purposes of discharging his office, the Chairman of the Council of Ministers may call for information and assistance from the bank of issue of the Union. The bank of issue shall provide for the organization of the meetings of the Council of Ministers and shall furnish its secretariat.

**Art. 8.** The Governor of the bank of issue of the Union shall attend the meetings of the Council of Ministers. He may request to be heard by the latter. He may arrange to be assisted by those of his associates whose cooperation he deems necessary.

**Art. 9.** The Council of Ministers of the Union may invite duly accredited representatives of international institutions or of States with which a cooperation agreement may have been concluded by the Governments of the States of the Union to participate in work or deliberations, with the right to speak in an advisory capacity, pursuant to the terms laid down in such agreement.

**Art. 10.** The Council of Ministers shall meet at least twice a year upon being called by its Chairman, either on the latter's initiative or at the request of the Ministers representing a Member State or on request by the Governor of the Union's bank of issue.

**Art. 11.** The Council of Ministers shall by unanimous vote adopt decisions on matters referred to its jurisdiction by the provisions of this Treaty and the Charter of the joint bank of issue that is attached thereto, as well as on all those which the Governments of the Member States of the Union may agree to submit to it for examination or to refer to it for decision. Such decisions must respect the international commitments contracted by the Member States of the Union.

**Art. 12.** The Council of Ministers of the Union shall determine the monetary and credit policy of the Union in order to ensure that the common currency will be safeguarded and to provide for the financing of the economic development and activity of the States of the Union.

In order to enable the Council of Ministers to carry out its duties, the Governments of the Member States of the Union shall keep it informed of the economic and financial situation, the prospects for development of that situation, and their decisions and plans, knowledge of which would seem necessary to the Council.

**Art. 13.** The Council of Ministers shall approve any agreement or convention, involving an obligation or undertaking of the joint bank of issue, that is to be concluded with foreign governments and banks of issue or international institutions.

It shall approve in particular clearing and payments agreements between the joint bank of issue and foreign banks of issue, designed to facilitate external settlements of the States of the Monetary Union.

It may empower its Chairman or the governor of the bank of issue to sign agreements and conventions in its name.

## Title IV. Common Currency Unit

**Art. 14.** The legal currency unit of the Member States of the Union shall be the franc of the African Financial Community (CFAF).

The definition of the franc of the African Financial Community shall be the one in force at the time this Treaty is signed.

The name and the definition of the currency unit of the Union may be modified by a decision of the Council of Ministers, provided the international commitments contracted by the Member States of the Union are respected.

## Title V. Common Bank of Issue

**Art. 15.** In the territory of the signatory States, the exclusive power of currency issue shall be entrusted to a common bank of issue, the Central Bank of the West African States, hereinafter called the "Central Bank."

**Art. 16.** The Central Bank shall be governed by the Charter attached to this Treaty. The provisions of the Charter may be amended by the Council of Ministers of the Union pursuant to an opinion unanimously expressed by the Board of Directors of the Central Bank.

**Art. 17.** With a view to allowing the Central Bank to carry out the duties entrusted to it, the immunities and privileges usually recognized for international financial institutions shall be granted to it in the territory of each of the Member States of the Union pursuant to the terms laid down in its Charter.

The Central Bank shall not be subject to any obligations or controls other than those specified by this Treaty or by its Charter.

**Art. 18.** Currency issued in each of the States of the Union by the Central Bank shall be legal tender throughout the territory of the States of the Union.

The banknotes issued by the Central Bank shall be identified by a special letter for each State, which shall be included in their serial number.

In each State, the cash offices of the Central Bank, public cash offices, and banks domiciled at the location of an agency or a subagency of the Central Bank may place in circulation only banknotes bearing the identification mark of the State.

**Art. 19.** The Central Bank shall draw up for each State of the Union a separate statement of currency issued and of its counterparts.

**Art. 20.** The Central Bank shall keep a statement:

of the external liquid assets of the Treasuries, public establishments and enterprises, and local governments of the States of the Union,

of that portion of the external liquid assets, corresponding to their business in the Union, of the banks and credit establishments that are established there.

Should its external liquid assets be exhausted, the Central Bank shall require that external liquid assets in French francs or other foreign currencies held by any public or private agencies amenable to the jurisdiction of the States of the Union be surrendered for the benefit of the Central Bank in return for currency issued by it.

In proportion to the foreseeable requirements, it may limit such call to public agencies and to banks and may do so with priority in the States whose statement of currency issue, drawn up in pursuance of Article 19 hereinabove, shows a negative position of the item "external liquid assets."

**Art. 21.** The Central Bank shall keep the Council of Ministers and the Ministers of Finance of the Member States informed of the flow of financial movements and of the development of claims and debts between these States and the outside world.

To this end, it may requisition, either directly or through banks, financial establishments, the Postal Administration, and notaries, any information on the external transactions of public administrative agencies, natural or juridical persons, public or private, having their residence or their registered office in the Union, and persons having their residence or their registered office abroad for their transactions relating to their stay or activity in the Union.

## TITLE VI. HARMONIZATION OF MONETARY AND BANKING LAWS

**Art. 22.** To allow the full application of the principles of monetary union defined above, the Governments of the Member States agree to adopt uniform rules, the provisions of which shall be laid down by the Council of Ministers of the Union, concerning in particular:

implementation of and control over their financial relations with countries that do not belong to the Union;

general organization of credit distribution and control;

general rules governing the exercise of the banking profession and related activities;

negotiable instruments;

curbing the counterfeiting of currency and the use of counterfeit currency.

The Council of Ministers of the Union may, without impairing the underlying principles, authorize such waivers in respect of the provisions agreed to as may seem justified to it by the particular conditions and needs of a Member State of the Union.

## Title VII. Joint Financing and Development Institutions

**Art. 23.** The Council of Ministers of the Union may decide to have the Central Bank create or participate in the setting up of any special fund, organization, or institution designed, in the interest of the coordinated development and integration of the Member States of the Union, in particular:

*(a)* to assist the Member States in the coordination of their development plans with a view to making better use of their resources, achieving greater complementarity of their production, and developing their external trade, especially trade among themselves;
*(b)* to gather available internal funds;
*(c)* to look for external capital;
*(d)* to organize a money market and a financial market;
*(e)* through participation, loans, endorsement guarantees or payment of interest, to grant direct financial cooperation for investments or activities of common interest;
*(f)* to grant complementary financial cooperation through participation, loans, endorsement guarantees, or interest subsidies to the States of the Union or to national development agencies;
*(g)* to teach banking techniques and to train the staff of banks and banking establishments.

The Council of Ministers shall determine the charters and the terms of setting up the capital or appropriation for such joint institutions of the Union as it may decide to create.

## Title VIII. Miscellaneous Provisions

**Art. 24.** The provisions of the Treaty shall, *de jure,* supersede those of the Treaty Establishing the West African Monetary Union, concluded May 12, 1962.

The rights and obligations of the Central Bank of West African States in respect of third parties shall not be affected by this supersession.

**Art. 25.** This Treaty shall become applicable after notification of its ratification by the Signatory States has been conveyed to the Republic of the State in which the headquarters of the Central Bank of West African States will be established, on a date which shall be fixed by joint agreement among the parties by the Signatory Governments.

*{The signatory clause is omitted.}*

## Charter of the Central Bank of West African States[1]

TITLE I. FORMATION—CAPITAL—LEGAL STATUS

**Art. 1.** The Central Bank of West African States, hereinafter called "The Central Bank," is an international public institution, formed by the Member States of the West African Monetary Union.

**Art. 2.** The headquarters of the Central Bank shall be established in one of the Member States of the West African Monetary Union, chosen by the Heads of these States.

The Central Bank shall have an agency in each of the Member States of the West African Monetary Union.

In agreement with the Government concerned, the Board of Directors may decide to open subagencies, banknote depositories, and offices.

It may likewise decide to open offices outside the Union in order to meet the operating requirements of the Central Bank.

**Art. 3.** The capital of the Central Bank shall be fully subscribed by the Member States of the Union and divided among them in equal shares.

It may be increased either by contribution in cash or by incorporation of reserves. It shall also be increased on the accession of new members to the West African Monetary Union.

It may be reduced when one of the participating States withdraws from membership or in order to meet losses.

[1] Statuts de la Banque Centrale des Etats de l'Afrique de l'Ouest. Signed in Dakar on December 4, 1973.

**Art. 4.** In order for the Central Bank to carry out its functions, it shall enjoy in the territory of the States of the Union the status, immunities, and privileges of international financial institutions.

Among other things, the Central Bank shall have full juridical personality and, in particular, the capacity to conclude contracts, to acquire and dispose of property and real estate, and to institute legal proceedings.

For this purpose, it shall, in each of the States of the Union, enjoy the fullest legal capacity accorded juridical persons by the national laws.

In the course of any legal proceedings, the Central Bank shall be exempt from the requirement of furnishing security and an advance in all cases in which the laws of the States provide that this obligation is incumbent upon the parties.

The property and assets of the Central Bank, wherever located and by whomsoever held, shall be immune from all forms of seizure, attachment, or execution until such time as a final judgment is rendered against it.

The property and assets of the Central Bank thus defined shall be immune from search, requisition, confiscation, expropriation, or any other form of seizure ordered by the executive or legislative branches of the Member States.

The records of the Central Bank shall be inviolable.

Its assets shall be immune from any restrictive measures.

Official communications of the Central Bank shall be accorded by each Member State of the Union the same treatment as official communications of the other Member States.

However, when the Central Bank is entrusted by a State with special tasks, these exemptions shall not be applicable to such tasks.

## TITLE II. OPERATIONS OF THE CENTRAL BANK

### SECTION 1. GENERAL PROVISIONS

**Art. 5.** Operations of the Central Bank must relate to the organization and management of the monetary, banking, and financial systems of the West African Monetary Union and of its Member States and be carried out pursuant to this Charter.

### SECTION 2. ISSUE OF CURRENCY

**Art. 6.** The Central Bank shall have the exclusive privilege of issuing the currency units, banknotes, and coins that shall constitute lawful currency and legal tender in the Member States of the West African Monetary Union.

**Art. 7.** Pursuant to a proposal by the Board of Directors of the Central Bank, the Council of Ministers of the Union shall decide on the creation and issuance of banknotes and coins, their withdrawal, and their cancellation.

The Board shall fix their face value. It shall determine the form of their denominations and the signatures they must bear.

It shall decree the features identifying them by State or issuing agency.

**Art. 8.** In the event of withdrawal from circulation of one or more categories of banknotes or coins, such banknotes or coins as have not been presented to the Central Bank within the prescribed time limits shall cease to be legal tender.

The equivalent of the currency units identified by State or issuing agency shall be paid to the State in which they were issued, and that of unidentified currency units shall be earmarked by a decision of the Council of Ministers of the Union.

### SECTION 3. OPERATIONS ENGENDERING CURRENCY ISSUE

**Art. 9.** The Central Bank may for its own account or for account of third parties carry out any operations involving gold, means of payment, and securities denominated in foreign currencies or defined by weight of gold.

It may lend or borrow amounts of currency issued by its vis-à-vis foreign banks and foreign or international monetary institutions or agencies.

In connection with these operations, the Central Bank shall require or grant such guarantees as seem appropriate to it.

**Art. 10.** The Central Bank may discount, acquire, sell, and take as collateral or as security, claims on the States of the Union and on enterprises or individuals in circumstances defined by the Board of Directors.

The Central Bank may buy, sell, or take as collateral, bills or securities listed by the Board of Directors.

**Art. 11.** Under the provisions of Article 10 hereinabove, the Board of Directors shall decide, in particular, the terms and the amount of medium-term central bank assistance that may be granted by the National Credit Committees for the establishment and promotion of national enterprises.

**Art. 12.** The Central Bank may discount, or accept as collateral or as security, customs duty bills and tax bills drawn to the order of the Treasuries of the States of the Union, with not more than four months to maturity, subject to solvency of the drawer and to a bank guarantee.

**Art. 13.** The Central Bank may grant banks advances on government securities created or guaranteed by Member States of the Union to the extent of the amounts fixed by the Board of Directors.

Moreover, the Central Bank may purchase from banks, and resell to them without endorsement, these same securities provided that they have not more than one year to run and that they are not negotiated for the benefit of public Treasuries.

**Art. 14.** The Central Bank may grant to the public Treasuries of the States of the Union, at its discount rate, overdrafts on current account.

The unsettled balance of the Central Bank's postal current account shall be treated, for the purposes of this article and of Article 16 hereinafter, as an overdraft granted to the public Treasury.

**Art. 15.** The Central Bank may discount or rediscount public securities maturing within not more than ten years and created by the States and local governments of the Union, which may be presented to it by the States and local governments, the West African Development Bank, and banks or financial establishments of the Union, to finance the creation or improvement of public facilities, infrastructure, or action designed to improve production conditions, or to subscribe to the capital of enterprises contributing to development.

The appropriations required to service the interest on and repayment of the securities issued must be entered in the budget of the State or of the issuing local government, and operations so financed must have been approved by the Board of Directors of the Central Bank.

**Art. 16.** The total amount of assistance granted by the Central Bank to a State of the Union, pursuant to the provisions of Articles 13, 14, and 15, hereinabove, may not exceed the equivalent of 20 per cent of the national tax revenue recorded in the course of the past fiscal year.

Within this limit, the National Credit Committees of all the States of the Union, in cooperation with the Board of Directors, shall determine a ceiling for each of the operations that may be effected according to the provisions of Articles 13, 14, and 15, hereinabove.

Total assistance actually being used at any time must not exceed the limit fixed in the first paragraph of this article,

minus:

the amount of the balance of the Central Bank's postal current account opened with the Postal Administration of the State concerned;

the amount of public securities of the State concerned, discounted by the Central Bank, and also the amount of these securities accepted by it as collateral for advances for the benefit of banks of the Union having recourse to the Central Bank's assistance;

the amount of loans, advances, and deposits at the public Treasury, in postal current accounts or with public credit or deposit establishments of the States of the Union, made by banks enjoying the Central Bank's assistance, which deduction may be limited to the total amount of the latter assistance when this is less than the said loans, advances, or deposits;

and plus:

the amount of the credit balance of the accounts opened at the public Treasury of the State concerned in the accounting records of the Central Bank.

**Art. 17.** The Central Bank shall be authorized to take shares in the capital of the West African Development Bank and of the other joint financing establishments set up under Article 23 of the Treaty Establishing the West African Monetary Union. Such participation must be authorized by the Board of Directors pursuant to the procedures set forth in Article 51, second paragraph, hereinbelow.

**Art. 18.** The Central Bank may demand that external liquid assets in French francs or other currencies, held by any public or private agencies under the jurisdiction of the States of the Union, be surrendered for its benefit in exchange for currency issued by it.

Depending on the foreseeable requirements, it may restrict such calls to public agencies and banks and may assign priority in making such calls to States whose currency issue statements show a negative position in the item of external liquid assets.

### SECTION 4. OTHER OPERATIONS

**Art. 19.** The Central Bank may open on its books accounts for banks, financial establishments, public establishments, and local governments. Such accounts may not show a debit balance.

**Art. 20.** The Central Bank shall carry out, between its agencies' main offices, such transfers as it may be requested to make by the public Treasuries, banks, and financial establishments, as well as by holders of accounts on its books.

**Art. 21.** The Central Bank may undertake the encashment and collection of securities that are turned over to it.

**Art. 22.** The Central Bank may take shares in the capital of establishments or agencies whose activity is of general interest to one or more States of the Union.

It may also purchase, sell, or exchange real property, and take or transfer shares in real estate companies to meet its operational requirements or to provide housing for its staff.

The purchases and participations authorized hereinabove must be paid for out of its own funds, capital, and reserves and must previously be authorized by its Board of Directors.

### SECTION 5. RELATIONS OF CENTRAL BANK WITH BANKS AND FINANCIAL INSTITUTIONS OF WEST AFRICAN MONETARY UNION

**Art. 23.** The Central Bank may grant assistance only in favor of the West African Development Bank, the other joint financing institutions established under Article 23 of the Treaty establishing the West African Monetary Union, and banks and financial institutions authorized to operate in the States of the Union, under the conditions laid down in the banking legislation and credit regulations determined in accordance with Article 22 of the aforesaid Treaty.

**Art. 24.** The Central Bank shall be empowered to require banking and financial institutions to supply it with any papers and information it needs to fulfill its functions.

It may, moreover, contact enterprises and professional groups with a view to conducting investigations for its own information and that of the Council of Ministers and the States of the Union.

**Art. 25.** The Central Bank may require banks, financial institutions, and postal current account agencies to report payment difficulties.

**Art. 26.** The Central Bank shall organize and manage clearinghouses in localities where it considers this necessary.

**Art. 27.** The Central Bank shall ensure enforcement in each State of the legal and regulatory provisions adopted by the national authorities pursuant to Article 22 of the Treaty establishing the Monetary Union, relating to the exercise of the banking profession and the control of credit.

Applications for authorization to establish or open banking institutions or financial institutions shall be passed on by the Central Bank.

**Art. 28.** The Central Bank shall, insofar as needed, propose to the Council of Ministers of the Union any provisions making it compulsory for banks and financial institutions to set up obligatory reserves deposited with them, the observance of a ratio between the various items of their resources and uses, or the observance of a ceiling or a minimum for the amount of certain of their uses. It shall ensure implementation of the relevant decisions of the Council of Ministers of the Union.

## SECTION 6. ASSISTANCE GIVEN BY CENTRAL BANK TO GOVERNMENTS OF WEST AFRICAN MONETARY UNION

**Art. 29.** At the places where it is established the Central Bank shall maintain the accounts of the Treasuries of the States of the Union.

It shall, without charge:

encash amounts paid into these accounts;

collect local bills and checks drawn on or endorsed to the order of the Treasuries;

pay checks and transfers drawn by the Treasurers on the accounts of the Treasuries;

effect transfers between its offices, made by order of the Treasuries.

At the end of each period of ten days the Central Bank shall clear any balances on current accounts held by it with the postal agencies or offices by transferring them to the accounts of the Treasuries on its books.

The accounts opened for the Treasuries of the States of the Union may not show a debit balance beyond the overdraft granted in pursuance of the provisions of Article 16 hereinabove.

**Art. 30.** At the request of the Government of a State of the Union, the Central Bank shall, without charge:

administer the portfolio of bills made out to the order of public accountable officers by parties owing taxes, levies, and duties;

provide safe custody for the cash assets belonging to the Treasuries of the States of the Union;

issue or sell for account of the States of the Union short-term bills made out by holders of an account on the books of the Central Bank;

pay bearer coupons and redeem securities of the States of the Union that are presented at its counters by holders of an account on its books;

make any investment of funds requested by the Treasuries of the States of the Union.

**Art. 31.** The Central Bank shall lend assistance in connection with the execution of external financial operations of the Governments of the Union.

Art. 32. The Central Bank may, upon the request of any Government of the Union, administer its external and internal public debt.

It may also, upon request, assist any Government of the Union in negotiating its external borrowing and in studying the conditions for issue and redemption of its domestic loans.

Art. 33. The Central Bank shall, upon request by them, assist the Governments of the States of the Union in their relations with international financial and monetary institutions and in negotiations entered into by them with a view to concluding international financial arrangements.

It may be entrusted with the execution of these arrangements pursuant to terms laid down in agreements approved by the Board of Directors.

In any event, it shall be kept informed of arrangements entered into and of their execution.

Pursuant to conditions spelled out by the Council of Ministers, it shall pay their quotas in the International Monetary Fund, carry out their operations and transactions with the latter, and keep account of the special drawing rights allocated to them.

Art. 34. The Central Bank shall propose to the Governments any measure designed to ensure or maintain harmonization of the laws and regulations concerning the currency and operation of the West African Monetary Union, pursuant to the provisions of Article 22 of the Treaty Establishing the West African Monetary Union.

Art. 35. Upon request by the Governments of the States of the Union, the Central Bank may assist in implementing the regulations of their external financial relations and on foreign exchange, or certain provisions of those regulations.

Art. 36. The Central Bank shall be empowered to require the public Treasuries, postal administrations, and all public agencies to provide it with the information and data needed to carry out the provisions of this Charter and for it and the Council of Ministers of the Union to be informed about the overall monetary and financial position of the Union and its development prospects.

It shall ensure the gathering of information and data provided for in Article 21 of the Treaty Establishing the Monetary Union, by means and for purposes determined thereunder.

## TITLE III. ADMINISTRATION OF CENTRAL BANK

**Art. 37.** Under the ultimate direction and supervision of the Council of Ministers of the Union, the Central Bank shall be administered by:

a Governor;

a Board of Directors;

National Credit Committees, one in each of the States of the Union.

The Governor, the members of the Board of Directors and those of the National Credit Committees must, under their respective charters, be in possession of their civil and political rights and shall not have been convicted of any offense involving imprisonment or loss of civil rights.

The members of the Board of Directors and of the National Credit Committees may not be chosen from among the directors, managers, or representatives of banks, financial institutions, and private enterprises unless they assume those duties on behalf of the State.

### SECTION 1. COUNCIL OF MINISTERS

**Art. 38.** The Council of Ministers instituted by and organized under the Treaty of November 14, 1973 Establishing the West African Monetary Union shall, pursuant to the conditions laid down by the Treaty, consider matters devolving upon its jurisdiction. It shall be incumbent upon the Council of Ministers in particular:

to decide any change in the denomination of the monetary unit of the Union and to fix that of its divisions;

to modify the definition of this currency unit, subject to observance of international commitments contracted by the Member States of the Union, and consequently to determine the declaration of parity of the currency of the Union that is to be made to the International Monetary Fund;

to approve any arrangement or agreement involving an obligation or commitment of the Central Bank that is to be concluded with foreign governments and banks of issue or international institutions, and in particular clearing or payment arrangements to be concluded with foreign banks of issue pursuant to the terms laid down in Article 13 of the Treaty;

to decide on the creation by the Central Bank or on the latter's participation in the creation of any organizations or institutions aimed at the development of the States of the Union in the areas and for the purposes set forth in Article 23 of the Treaty;

to decree plans and regulations, prepared on its initiative or on that of the Central Bank, concerning the matters enumerated in Article 22 of the Treaty and to consent to waivers deemed necessary so as to adapt them to the specific conditions of the States of the Union;

to draw up draft agreements to be concluded with the Governments of the West African States that have applied for membership in the Monetary Union pursuant to the provisions of Article 2 of the Treaty;

to draw up draft agreements to be concluded with the Government of a Member State of the Union that has given notice of its decision to withdraw from the Union pursuant to the provisions of Article 3 of the Treaty;

to state for the record that a Member State having failed to meet its commitments set forth in Article 4 of the Treaty has left the Union and to draw pertinent inferences for the purpose of safeguarding the interests of the Union.

**Art. 39.** The Council of Ministers may amend the provisions of this Charter of the Central Bank pursuant to the terms set forth in Article 16 of the Treaty of November 14, 1973 Establishing the West African Monetary Union.

**Art. 40.** For the purpose of implementing this Charter, the Council of Ministers of the Union shall:

appoint the Governor and the Auditor-Examiner provided for in Article 64 of this Charter;

fix the expenses to be repaid and the attendance fees to be granted to the members of the Council of Ministers of the Union, of the Board of Directors, of the National Credit Committees, and also the fees of Auditor-Examiner and of the national Examiners;

fix the remuneration, the compensation, and the benefits in kind to be granted to the Governor of the Central Bank;

decree the characteristics of the banknotes and coins to be issued by the Central Bank, and the conditions for their being placed into circulation, withdrawn, and canceled;

decide the use, provided for by Article 67 of this Charter, of the statutory royalty and of the balance of profits after earmarking for reserves provided for by the same article.

### SECTION 2. GOVERNOR AND OFFICIALS OF CENTRAL BANK

**Art. 41.** The Governor of the Central Bank shall be appointed by the Council of Ministers for a nonrenewable term of six years.

He must be so chosen that a national of each of the Member States of the Union will be called upon in turn to discharge that office.

He shall swear before the Chairman of the Council of Ministers that he will duly and faithfully direct the Central Bank, in accordance with the terms of the Treaty establishing the Monetary Union, and with the international commitments contracted by it and wtih the Charter of the Central Bank.

**Art. 42.** The Governor shall be assisted in the discharge of his duties by a Deputy Governor appointed by the Board of Directors for a non-renewable term of five years.

The Deputy Governor must be so chosen that a national of each of the Member States of the Union will be called upon in turn to discharge that office.

**Art. 43.** The duties of Governor and Deputy Governor shall preclude all assistance, whether or not against remuneration, in the activity of a private or public enterprise, except international governmental institutions, if any.

**Art. 44.** The Governor shall assure observance of the provisions of treaties, arrangements, international agreements, and this Charter, as well as of legislative and regulatory provisions relating to the Central Bank, and shall enforce the relevant provisions.

He shall call meetings of the Board of Directors, determine the agenda for its work, and conduct its deliberations.

He may request the Chairman of the Council of Ministers of the Union to call a meeting of the Council and may ask to be heard by the Council, whose meetings he shall attend with the right to speak in an advisory capacity.

He shall cause the decisions of the Council of Ministers and of the Board of Directors to be carried out.

He shall represent the Central Bank vis-à-vis third parties; he alone shall sign all arrangements and agreements by which the Central Bank is committed, except instruments in respect of which authority to sign has been delegated expressly to the Chairman of the Council of Ministers of the Union.

He shall manage the Central Bank's external liquid assets.

He shall personally or by proxy represent the Central Bank at meetings of international institutions in which the Central Bank is invited to participate.

He shall present to the Board of Directors the accounts of the Central Bank and the Annual Report on its activities; he shall submit that Report to the Council of Ministers of the Union.

**Art. 45.** The Governor shall be responsible for the organization of the departments of the Central Bank and for their work.

He may delegate part of his powers to the Deputy Governor or to officials of the Central Bank.

**Art. 46.** The Governor:

shall hire and appoint the staff of the Central Bank, subject to receipt of approval, for the appointment of the director of an agency, from the Government of the State in which such agency has its head office;

shall assign all officials of the Central Bank to posts, cause their retirement rights to be respected, and discharge them;

shall fix their remunerations, retirement pensions, and benefits in kind that are granted to them.

**Art. 47.** The Governor, the Deputy Governor, and all the officials of the Central Bank shall be bound by professional secrecy, subject to the penalties provided for by penal legislation.

**Art. 48.** Officials of the Central Bank may not take or receive any share or any interest or remuneration whatever, through work or advice, in any industrial, commercial, or financial enterprise, public or private, except pursuant to waivers granted by the Governor.

The provisions of this article shall not be applicable to the production of scientific, literary, or artistic works.

### SECTION 3. BOARD OF DIRECTORS

**Art. 49.** The Board of Directors shall be composed of Directors appointed by the Governments of the States participating in the management of the Bank, each of which shall designate two Directors.

In case he is unable to discharge his duties, any Director may commission, to represent him, either another Director or an alternate designated on a temporary basis by the Government he represents; the Governor of the Central Bank shall be notified of such commission and of the designation of alternates.

Directors may receive attendance fees, the amount of which shall be determined by the Council of Ministers of the Union.

**Art. 50.** The chairmanship of the Board of Directors shall be carried out by the Governor and, should he be prevented from discharging his duties, by the Deputy Governor.

The Board of Directors shall meet as often as necessary, but at least four times a year, upon being called by its Chairman either on its initiative or in pursuance of the provisions of Article 51, fourth paragraph, or upon request by one third of the Directors, or upon request by the Chairman of the Council of Ministers or by an Auditor.

**Art. 51.** For the deliberations of the Board of Directors to be valid, at least two thirds of its members shall be present or represented. The Governor, or his representative serving as chairman of the meeting, shall not take part in the voting.

Decisions shall be passed by a simple majority, except those adopted in pursuance of Article 52 (1), (3), and (8) hereinafter, which require six sevenths of the votes, and those amending this Charter, which require a unanimous vote.

When the ratio of the average amount of external holdings of the Bank and the average amount of its sight liabilities in the course of three consecutive months has remained equal to or less than 20 per cent, the Governor, after having advised the Chairman of the Council of Ministers of the Union accordingly, shall immediately call a meeting of the Board of Directors in order to examine the situation and to take all appropriate measures, especially for the purpose of re-examining those of the decisions adopted previously that may have affected the monetary situation of the Union.

As long as the ratio specified hereinabove remains equal to or less than 20 per cent, supplementary decisions of the Board in matters referred to in Article 52 (3) and (8) must be adopted by unanimous vote.

**Art. 52.** The Board of Directors shall, within the framework of the directives of the Council of Ministers of the Union:

(1) specify the general conditions pursuant to which the Central Bank shall carry out operations authorized by Articles 10 to 15 of this Charter;

(2) fix the amounts of advances which the Central Bank may grant to banks on public securities issued or guaranteed by the Member States of the Union;

(3) specify the operations of discounting or rediscounting public securities maturing within not more than ten years as provided for by Article 15 of this Charter;

(4) fix the discount rate and the rates and conditions for all operations handled by the Central Bank;

(5) issue the rules applicable to the National Credit Committees in the exercise of their powers;

(6) revise such decisions of the National Credit Committees as

would be contrary to the provisions of this Charter and to the general rules relating to the exercise of their powers as determined by the Board of Directors;

(7) determine, according to a regular schedule fixed by it, the overall amount of assistance that was to be granted by the Central Bank for financing the economic activity and the development of each of the States of the Union;

(8) authorize the Central Bank to take shares in the capital of joint financial development institutions, within the scope of the provisions of Article 17 of this Charter;

(9) authorize the Central Bank to require that external liquid assets be surrendered for its benefit in exchange for currency issued by it, pursuant to the terms provided in Article 18 of this Charter;

(10) authorize acquisitions and transfers of title to real property and participations allowed by Article 22 of this Charter;

(11) close the annual accounts of the Central Bank pursuant to the terms laid down in Article 63 hereinbelow;

(12) determine the value at which claims held in suspense may remain included in the accounts on the assets side, and proceed with any write-off and the setting up of any reserves that may be deemed necessary;

(13) decide on the establishment, by the Central Bank, of subagencies, banknote depositories, and offices;

(14) draw up amendments to this Charter that must be submitted to the Council of Ministers of the Union for ratification.

## SECTION 4. NATIONAL CREDIT COMMITTEES

Art. 53. A National Credit Committee shall have its headquarters at the Central Bank's agency established in each of the States of the Union in pursuance of the second paragraph of Article 2 of this Charter.

That Committee shall be composed of the Minister of Finance, of two State representatives on the Board of Directors, and of four other members appointed by the Government of the State concerned from among the persons meeting the requirements laid down in Article 37 hereinabove.

Art. 54. The National Credit Committee shall ensure implementation in the Member State of such assistance as may be granted for the financing of its economic activity and development by the Central Bank according to the provisions of its Charter, the directives of the Council of Ministers of the Union, and the general rules laid down by the Board of Directors of the Central Bank.

**Art. 55.** The Committee shall be chaired by the Minister of Finance.

Meetings of the Committee shall be called by its Chairman, who shall prescribe the agenda upon recommendation by the Director of the agency.

Committee members who are unable to attend a meeting may empower another member of the Committee to represent them. No member of the Committee may have more than one vote in addition to his own.

The Director of the agency shall examine and report to the Committee on matters included in the agenda.

Committee decisions shall be adopted by a majority of its members present or represented. In case of a tie, the Chairman shall have the casting vote.

The Governor or the Deputy Governor of the Central Bank and the Directors on mission duty shall attend the Committee's meetings with the right to speak in an advisory capacity.

**Art. 56.** The Committee shall estimate the amount needed to finance the activity and the development of the State and the resources available to meet these needs, as well as such assistance as may be contributed by the Central Bank, according to the provisions of its Charter, the directives of the Council of Ministers of the Union, and the general rules laid down by the Board of Directors.

He shall report accordingly to the Board of Directors and shall propose to it the overall amount of assistance to be granted by the Central Bank.

**Art. 57.** Within the limits of the overall amount decided on by the Board of Directors, the Committee shall determine the amounts of assistance that can be granted by the Central Bank:

to the banks and financial institutions in pursuance of the provisions of Articles 10 and 11 hereinabove, as regards short-term and medium-term assistance, respectively;

to the public Treasury by rediscounting customs duty bills issued to its order in pursuance of the provisions of Article 12 hereinabove;

to a central government and to local governments in pursuance of the provisions of Article 16 of this Charter.

**Art. 58.** Within the scope of the general rules laid down by the Board of Executive Directors, the National Credit Committee shall be empowered, in particular:

(1) to fix the minimum amount of credits the granting of which

by a bank or a financial institution to one and the same enterprise shall be subject to its approval;

(2) to agree to, submit conditionally, or reject credit proposals that are thus presented to it;

(3) to set the individual limit on the various credits granted to one and the same enterprise that may be mobilized at the Central Bank;

(4) to fix the minimum amount or proportion of the various types of financing that may be employed by banks and financial institutions;

(5) to spell out the procedures for applying any other measures concerning the control and management of credits to the economy.

Art. 59. The Committee may delegate the exercise of its powers, in respect of the matters, limits, and conditions that it establishes, to the Director of the agency, who must report to it on the use made by him of such delegation of powers.

Art. 60. Decisions of the Committee shall be communicated by the Director of the agency to the Governor of the Central Bank.

The latter may propose to the Board of Directors that it revise such decisions of the Committee as would be inconsistent with the provisions of this Charter, the general rules for special decisions of the Board of Directors, or the directives of the Council of Ministers of the Union.

## Title IV. Miscellaneous Provisions

### Section 1. Accounting

Art. 61. Operations of the Central Bank shall be carried out and accounted for according to commercial and banking rules and usage.

### Section 2. Tax Exemptions

Art. 62. By reason of its international character and with a view to ensuring a fair distribution of its business profits, the Central Bank, its holdings, its property, its income, as well as the operations and transactions which it is authorized to carry out under this Charter, shall be exempt from all taxes, duties, and imposts levied by the States of the Union or local governments under them.

### SECTION 3. AUDIT AND APPROVAL OF ACCOUNTS

**Art. 63.** The accounts of the Central Bank shall be closed at least once a year at a date set by the Board; within the six months following the close of the financial year they shall be submitted to the Board of Directors for approval pursuant to a report of the Auditors.

**Art. 64.** The audit of the Central Bank's accounts shall be carried out by National Auditors entrusted with the task of auditing the individual accounts of the agencies and an Auditor-Examiner entrusted with the task of centralizing the comments of the National Auditors and checking the centralized accounting of the Central Bank.

The National Auditors shall be designated, at the rate of one for each State, by the Minister of Finance of each Member State of the Union.

The Auditor-Examiner provided for in the first paragraph hereinabove shall be appointed by the Council of Ministers of the Union.

### SECTION 4. DETERMINATION AND DISTRIBUTION OF EARNINGS

**Art. 65.** For purposes of drawing up the profit and loss account, revenues shall be so applied as to give priority to covering the operating expenses of the headquarters and the agencies.

**Art. 66.** The Board of Directors shall determine the value at which claims held in suspense may remain included in the accounts on the assets side and shall proceed with any write-off and the setting up of any reserves that may be deemed necessary.

**Art. 67.** After discharging deficits of previous financial years and setting up reserves and appropriations for write-offs, the available excess revenues shall constitute earnings.

Earnings so defined shall be applied on a priority basis:

(1) To the financing of fixed assets and acquisitions of capital shares.

(2) To the payment of a statutory royalty in an amount equal to 12 per cent of the gross proceeds from the Central Bank's operations in the course of the past financial year; the amount of this royalty is, however, limited to the amount of the earnings remaining for distribution if the latter amount is lower. The royalty so calculated shall be earmarked as will be indicated by the Council of Ministers of the Union.

From the remaining earnings, 15 per cent shall be taken to set up a statutory reserve. Setting aside such percentage shall cease to be compulsory as soon as this reserve amounts to one half of the capital; it shall be resumed if this ratio is no longer attained.

After allocations to any optional reserves, general or special, the balance shall be earmarked in pursuance of a decision of the Council of Ministers of the Union.

The reserves may be allotted to increases in capital.

**Art. 68.** Financial losses resulting from failure to recover credits shall be chargeable to the State concerned, which shall make payment within the month following approval, by the Council of Ministers of the Union, of the accounts of the financial year in the course of which such losses have been ascertained.

Deduction may be made, from the royalty or earnings paid to a State, of an amount equivalent to that of the result of multiplying the average negative position of the section of the liquid external assets account reflecting the operations of the State concerned by the average rate of interest applicable to the liquid assets of the Central Bank invested abroad or of any borrowings it might have effected to remedy an insufficiency of its external holdings.

Should the product as calculated above exceed the amount of royalty or earnings to which the State concerned is entitled, the difference would have to be paid by such State to the Central Bank within the month following approval of the accounts of the fiscal year.

### SECTION 5. MONTHLY STATEMENTS AND ANNUAL REPORT

**Art. 69.** Each month the Central Bank shall draw up a statement of its accounts, which shall be published in the *Journal officiel* of each of the States participating in its management.

Each month it shall likewise prepare a statement, by agency, of currency issued and of its counterparts.

**Art. 70.** A report on the development of the monetary situation of the Union and on the operations of the Central Bank in the course of each financial year shall be made to the Board of Directors by the Governor of the Central Bank for presentation to the Council of Ministers of the Union and to the Heads of State participating in the management of the Bank.

# Agreement on Cooperation Between the French Republic and the Member Republics of the West African Monetary Union[1]

The Government of the Republic of Ivory Coast,
The Government of the Republic of Dahomey,
The Government of the Republic of Upper Volta,
The Government of the Republic of Niger,
The Government of the Republic of Senegal,
The Government of the Togolese Republic,
The Government of the French Republic,

Determined to continue their relationship in a spirit of mutual understanding, reciprocal trust and cooperation, especially in the economic, monetary and financial areas;

Considering the resolution of the West African States that are parties to this Agreement to remain within a monetary union with a common central bank;

Desirous of having these common monetary institutions, supported by assistance from the French Republic, make the greatest possible contribution to the financing of the development of the States of the West African Monetary Union,

have agreed on the following provisions:

**Art. 1.** The French Republic shall lend assistance to the West African Monetary Union in order to enable it to ensure free convertibility of its currency.

The terms of that assistance shall be defined by an operations account Convention concluded between the Minister of Economy and Finance of the French Republic and the Chairman of the Council of Ministers of the Union acting on behalf of the Central Bank of the West African States.

**Art. 2.** Transactions between the French franc and the currency of the Union shall be effected at a fixed rate, on the basis of the parity in force.

Transactions between the currency of the Union and currencies other than the French franc shall be carried out at the exchange market rate according to the provisions agreed under Article 6 hereinafter.

[1] Accord de Coopération entre la République Française et les Républiques Membres de l'Union Monétaire Ouest Africaine. Signed at Dakar on December 4, 1973.

Art. 3. The Member States of the Union agree to centralize their holdings in foreign currencies and other international means of payment under the terms set forth in the Convention referred to in Article 1.

Art. 4. The credit balance of the account referred to in Article 3 of this Agreement shall be guaranteed by reference to a unit of account agreed to by the parties.

Art. 5. The signatory States shall consult with each other, as far as at all possible, on the matter of changes they will propose to make in the definition of their currency and in the terms for trading that currency in the exchange markets.

The French Republic shall keep the Council of Ministers of the Union informed of the development of the condition of the French franc in the exchange markets and on any monetary matter of special interest to the Union.

Art. 6. The uniform regulations governing the external financial relations of the States of the Union, as laid down in pursuance of the provisions of Article 22 of the Treaty of November 14, 1973 Establishing the West African Monetary Union, shall be kept consistent with those of the French Republic.

This harmonization, agreed by the Board of Executive Directors of the Central Bank shall ensure, in particular, freedom of financial relations between France and the States of the Union.

If needs or circumstances should cause one of the Signatory Governments of this Agreement to find it necessary to depart from the harmonization agreed to in the preceding paragraphs, it would, before taking any relevant measure, so advise the other Signatory Governments with a view to reaching a concerted decision, according to the provisions of Article 13 of this Agreement.

Art. 7. The authorities of the French Republic and those of the Member States of the Union shall cooperate on bringing to light and curbing violations of the exchange regulations pursuant to terms to be set forth in a special protocol.

Art. 8. Pursuant to conditions to be agreed by them, the Bank of France and the Central Bank of the West African States shall exchange statistical data gathered by them on the payments and movements of claims and debts between France and the States of the West African Monetary Union.

**Art. 9.** The French Republic shall lend assistance in connection with the establishment and the financing of joint financial development institutions which the Council of Ministers of the Union would decide to create in pursuance of Article 23 of the Treaty of November 14, 1973 Establishing the West African Monetary Union.

These joint financing institutions shall be authorized to float loans in the French financial market and to borrow from French banks and credit institutions. Such loans may be guaranteed by the French Republic.

The terms of assistance lent by the French Republic for the purpose of implementing this article shall be the subject of appropriate agreements between the Minister of Economy and Finance of the French Republic, on behalf of the French Republic, and the Chairman of the Council of Ministers of the Union, on behalf of the joint institutions of the Union.

**Art. 10.** Two Executive Directors appointed by the French Government shall be members of the Board of Executive Directors of the Central Bank of West African States on the same terms and with the same rights and duties as the Executive Directors appointed by the Member States of the Union.

**Art. 11.** The French Republic acknowledges that the Central Bank of West African States shall, for its institutions and operations in its territory, enjoy the immunities, privileges and tax exemptions the enjoyment of which is acknowledged for it by the Member States of the Monetary Union and spelled out by Articles 4 and 62 of the Charter of the Central Bank.

**Art. 12.** In case any of the Member States of the Monetary Union should unilaterally fail to observe the commitments stipulated in this Agreement and in the Treaty of November 14, 1973, Establishing the West African Monetary Union, implementation of the Convention referred to in Article 1 hereinabove would *de jure* be suspended insofar as such State is concerned.

The same would apply in case of exclusion from the Monetary Union of one of its members, in pursuance of Article 4 of the Treaty of November 14, 1973, Establishing the West African Monetary Union.

**Art. 13.** At the request of any Signatory State to this Agreement that would consider that the regime defined by this Agreement compromises or may compromise its interests substantially, the Signatory States would without delay take counsel together in order to decide on appropriate measures. If no decision could be adopted jointly, this Agreement could be denounced by any signatory.

If denounced by any Member State of the Union, this Agreement shall remain in force among the other Signatory States.

Should this Agreement be denounced, the Signatory States shall act in concert without delay in order to decide on new grounds for their cooperation in monetary matters and, possibly, on the terms of a transitional regime.

**Art. 14.** The provisions of this Agreement shall supersede any contrary provisions of the agreements and conventions listed hereinafter:

Agreement on Cooperation between the French Republic and the Member Republics of the West African Monetary Union, concluded on May 12, 1962 and supplemented by the Convention of November 27, 1963 among the same parties;

Agreement on Cooperation in Economic, Monetary and Financial Matters between the French Republic and the Republic of Ivory Coast, signed on April 24, 1961;

Agreement on Cooperation in Economic, Monetary and Financial Matters between the French Republic and the Republic of Dahomey, signed on April 24, 1961;

Agreement on Cooperation in Economic, Monetary and Financial Matters between the French Republic and the Republic of Upper Volta, signed on April 24, 1961;

Agreement on Cooperation in Economic, Monetary and Financial Matters between the French Republic and the Republic of Niger, signed on April 24, 1961;

Agreement concluded between the French Republic and the Federation of Mali, on June 22, 1960, the rights and obligations of which the Republic of Senegal agreed to assume by an exchange of letters dated September 16 and 19, 1961;

Agreement on Cooperation in Economic, Monetary and Financial Matters between the French Republic and the Togolese Republic, concluded on July 10, 1963.

**Art. 15.** Subject to the necessary ratifications, this Agreement shall become applicable as of the effective date of the Treaty Establishing the West African Monetary Union, concluded on November 14, 1973 among the Member States of that Union.

*[The signatory clause is omitted.]*

# Convention on the Operations Account[1]

Between the undersigned,

Mr. Valéry Giscard d'Estaing, Minister of Economy and Finance, acting in the name of the French Republic,
on the one hand, and

Mr. Edouard Kodjo, Chairman of the Council of Ministers of the West African Monetary Union, acting in the name of the Central Bank of West African States and empowered to this end by decision of the Council of Ministers of the West African Monetary Union dated December 4, 1973, on the other hand,
the following has been agreed for purposes of applying the provisions of Article 1 of the Agreement on Cooperation between the French Republic and the Member Republics of the West African Monetary Union, concluded November 14, 1973:

**Art. 1.** A current account called "Operations Account" shall be opened in the accounting records of the French Treasury, in the name of the Central Bank of West African States, hereinafter called "Central Bank."

**Art. 2** The Central Bank shall pay into the Operations Account liquid assets that it may set up for itself outside its issue area, except:

(1) sums needed to meet current cash requirements;

(2) sums needed to meet liabilities incurred by the States of the Monetary Union vis-à-vis the International Monetary Fund and which it may have undertaken to meet pursuant to terms laid down in agreements concluded with these States and approved by the Council of Ministers of the Union;

(3) such sums as the Board of Directors of the Central Bank may decide to deposit in current accounts, denominated in foreign currencies, with the Bank for International Settlements or foreign banks of issue, or to use for subscription of negotiable notes, with a maturity not exceeding two years, expressed in convertible currencies, issued by international financial institutions whose purpose goes beyond the geographic scope of the West African Monetary Union and whose membership includes the Member States of this Union; the cumulative amount of the sums so deposited in foreign currencies or used for the subscription of notes denominated in foreign currencies other than the French franc may not exceed 35 per cent of the net external holdings of the Central

[1] Convention de Compte d'Opérations. Done at Dakar on December 4, 1973.

Bank, exclusive of the gold tranche position [2] in the International Monetary Fund of the Member States of the Monetary Union and of the special drawing rights held by them which it would be authorized to count among its external holdings in pursuance of the agreements provided for in paragraph (2) of this article.

**Art. 3.** The Central Bank shall maintain the regular current account of the French Treasury in the towns where it has its own facilities.

The Operations Account shall be debited or credited, as the case may be, with the amount of transfers resulting from the leveling off or funding of this account.

**Art. 4.** In case of a change in the parity of the French franc in relation to the unit of account referred to in Article 4 of the Agreement on Cooperation, the guarantee shall be determined by taking into consideration:

on the one hand, the ratio existing on the day of the signing of this Convention between the official value of the French franc and that of the unit of account, and,

on the other hand, the ratio between these two values resulting from the change in the parity of the French franc.

If the second ratio is lower than the first, the increase coefficient obtained by dividing the ratio existing on the day of the signing of this Convention by that second ratio shall be applied to the credit balance of the Operations Account.

**Art. 5.** When developments in the liquid assets of the Central Bank in the Operations Account make it possible to anticipate that they will not suffice to meet the payments to be made against the debit thereof, the Central Bank:

shall supply it by drawing on such liquid assets as it may have set up for itself in foreign currencies;

shall invite the Member States of the Union to use their drawing rights at the International Monetary Fund or to exchange special drawing rights held by them for foreign currencies;

shall make use of its rights under the last two paragraphs of Article 20 of the Treaty of November 14, 1973 Establishing the West African Monetary Union.

**Art. 6.** If the measures taken in pursuance of Article 5 hereinabove do not allow the Central Bank to be sure that it will have available the

[2] Reserve tranche purchase is defined in Article XXX*(c)* of the Articles of Agreement of the International Monetary Fund.

liquid funds needed to cover the transfers outside the West African Monetary Union which it should effect, these means of payments shall be granted to it as an overdraft from its Operations Account.

**Art.** 7. When the Operations Account shows a debit balance, the Central Bank shall pay interest on such balance at a rate which shall be fixed as follows:

on the tranche comprising of between 0 and 5 million francs: 1 per cent

on the tranche comprising of between 5 and 10 million francs: 2 per cent

above 10 million francs: a rate equal to that fixed in the following paragraph.

When there is a credit balance, the average amount of funds on deposit in the course of each quarter shall bear interest at a rate equal to the arithmetic mean of the Bank of France's intervention rates on the shortest term government securities during the quarter under consideration.

**Art.** 8. An Examiner designated by the Government of the French Republic and the Auditor-Examiner provided for by Article 64 of the Charter of the Central Bank shall supervise the implementation of the provisions of this Convention.

Upon request addressed to the Central Bank, they shall be given access to all records, statements or supporting documents that will enable them to carry out their mission.

**Art.** 9. Implementation of this Convention shall by right be suspended as provided in Article 12 of the Agreement on Cooperation between the French Republic and the Member States of the West African Monetary Union, concluded December 4, 1973.

The same shall be true in case notice of termination of the said Agreement is given in pursuance of the conditions provided for in Article 13.

**Art.** 10. Upon expiration or notice of termination of this Convention:

the debit balance of the Operations Account shall be subject to demand by the French Republic only in the territory of the States in which the Central Bank exercises the issue privilege and shall be settled in CFA francs; the credit balance shall be subject to demand by the Central Bank of West African States only in Paris, in French francs which shall be freely convertible.

Art. 11. The Convention on the Operations Account of March 20, 1963 between the French Republic and the Central Bank of West African States, as amended by supplementary agreements of June 2, 1967 and December 4, 1969, is abrogated as from the effective date of the Agreement on Cooperation between the French Republic and the Member Republics of the West African Monetary Union, concluded on December 4, 1973.

*[The signatory clause is omitted.]*

## Agreement Establishing a West African Development Bank[1]

The Government of the Republic of Ivory Coast,
The Government of the Republic of Dahomey,
The Government of the Republic of Upper Volta,
The Government of the Republic of Niger,
The Government of the Republic of Senegal,
The Government of the Togolese Republic,

Aware that membership in the West African Monetary Union and the management of their common currency by a single bank of issue, the Central Bank of West African States, assure them of the monetary institutions best suited to the progress of their national economies, the development of their mutual relations, their integration and their relations with other countries;

Considering, however, that currency unity alone cannot ensure equitable distribution among the member States of the means afforded them by membership in the Union to develop their economies;

Anxious to use the financing potential resulting from their unity in monetary matters to equip their economies, transform agricultural production, promote new activities, transfer ownership of the means of production to juridical persons, public or private, or to individuals who are nationals, especially in those areas most likely to promote integration of their economies;

[1] Accord Instituant une Banque Ouest Africaine de Développement. Signed on November 14, 1973.

Considering this objective could best be attained, without jeopardizing the position of their common currency, through a joint financing institution set up and administered in close cooperation with their joint bank of issue;

Recognizing the willingness of West African States to increase economic cooperation and promote economic integration together with equitable geographic distribution of development potential;

Considering the desire expressed by certain countries outside the Union to contribute to the development of the States of the West African Monetary Union;

have agreed to the following provisions:

**Art. 1.** A West African Development Bank shall be established. Its organization, management, and operations shall be defined by a Charter to be approved by the Council of Ministers of the West African Monetary Union under the provisions of Article 23 of the Treaty of November 14, 1973 establishing the Union.

**Art. 2.** This Agreement shall take effect when the State in which the Bank's headquarters are to be located, at a date determined by agreement among the signatory Governments, has been notified of the ratification of the Agreement by the signatories.

*[The signatory clause is omitted.]*

## Charter of the West African Development Bank[1]

**Art. 1.** The West African Development Bank, hereinafter called the "Bank," shall be incorporated, and shall carry out its functions and business in accordance with the provisions of Article 23 of the Treaty Establishing the West African Monetary Union, hereinafter called the "Union," and this Charter.

**Art. 2.** The purpose of the Bank shall be to promote the balanced

[1] Statuts de la Banque Ouest Africaine de Développement. Signed in Abidjan on January 5, 1967.

development of member States and achieve the economic integration of West Africa.

The Bank shall, directly, through subsidiaries, special funds set up by it, or national financial institutions, contribute towards:

1. mobilizing funds available domestically in accordance with national legislation;
2. obtaining foreign capital through loans or grants;
3. financing investments or activities by acquiring capital holdings, extending loans, guaranteeing endorsements, or granting interest subsidies for the purpose of:
   building or improving the infrastructure required for development;
   improving conditions for, and means of, production;
   establishing new businesses;
   transferring title to means of production and distribution of goods and services to public or private juridical persons under the jurisdiction of the Union or of one of its Members, or to individuals who are nationals of the member States of the Union;
4. preparing and evaluating development projects technically and financially, and establishing and operating the agencies entrusted with their implementation.

In selecting projects for assistance, it shall give priority to those most likely to:

facilitate the development of those member States of the Union least endowed with material resources;
promote the economic integration of the States of the Union.

## TITLE I. LEGAL STATUS

### SECTION 1.1—LEGAL STATUS

**Art. 3.** The Bank shall have the status of a juridical person with full enjoyment of the legal rights pertaining thereto, including in particular the capacity to contract, to acquire and dispose of real estate and assets, to receive gifts, bequests and endowments, and to appear in court.

It shall enjoy the fullest legal privileges accorded to juridical persons by each of the States of the Union under their national laws.

### SECTION 1.2—JUDICIAL PROCEEDINGS

**Art. 4.** Litigation between the Bank, and its lenders, borrowers, or third parties shall be settled by the competent national courts, subject to the provisions of Article 5 hereinafter.

### SECTION 1.3—PRIVILEGES AND IMMUNITIES

**Art. 5.** In order for the Bank to carry out its functions, it shall enjoy the immunities and privileges of international financial institutions in the territory of the States of the Union. However, when a State entrusts the Bank with an assignment under the terms of a special agreement, such immunities and privileges shall not apply if the agreement so stipulates.

1. No proceedings may be initiated against the Bank by the member States of the Union, or by persons representing them or acting on their behalf.
2. The Bank shall be exempt from the obligation of furnishing bond and advance payment in the course of judicial proceedings, whenever the laws of the States provide that this requirement shall be met.
3. The Bank's property and assets, wherever located and by whomsoever held, shall be exempt from any kind of attachment, claim, or enforcement until a final ruling has been made.
4. The Bank's property and assets, as defined above, shall be exempt from search, requisition, confiscation, expropriation, or any other form of seizure ordered by the executive or legislative authority of any member State.
5. Its assets shall be safeguarded from any restrictive measures.
6. The Bank's records shall be inviolable.
7. The Bank's official communications shall enjoy the same treatment as official communications in all of the member States.
8. The Bank's assets and operations shall benefit from the tax exemptions under Article 38 below.

## TITLE II. PARTICIPATION, CAPITAL, AND HEADQUARTERS

### SECTION 2.1—MEMBERSHIP OF THE BANK

**Art. 6.** The members of the Bank participating in its capital and management are:

The member States of the West African Monetary Union;

The Central Bank of West African States, bank of issue of the Union, hereinafter called the "Central Bank"; and

Those States who, although not members, wish to provide assistance for its development and are approved by the Council of Ministers of the Union.

SECTION 2.2—CAPITAL

**Art. 7.** The initial capital of the Bank shall be two billion four hundred million CFA francs, subscribed at the rate of:

one billion two hundred million CFA francs by the member States of the Union;

one billion two hundred million CFA francs by the Central Bank out of its own funds.

**Art. 8.** The capital of the Bank may be increased by cash contributions or incorporation of reserves.

It shall be increased with the admission of new members into the Union.

It shall be increased likewise by subscription of nonmember States of the Union, but their share of subscribed capital may not exceed one third of the total amount.

It may be reduced with the withdrawal of a member State or to cancel losses.

**Art. 9.** Upon ceasing to be a member of the Union, any member State shall cease to participate in the Bank.

Conditions for withdrawal shall be fixed by an agreement approved by the Council of Ministers of the Union, and the representatives of the withdrawing State shall not participate in the deliberations in this connection.

If the statement of debts and claims vis-à-vis the withdrawing State shows a credit balance for the Bank, such balance shall be taken from the external holdings to be surrendered by the Central Bank in connection with the transfer of currency to the State withdrawing from the Union.

SECTION 2.3—HEADQUARTERS

**Art. 10.** The Bank's headquarters shall be established in one of the member States of the Union, by common agreement of the Heads of these States.

The Bank may establish an agency in each of the member States of the West African Monetary Union.

It may likewise, for its operating requirements, establish offices within or outside the Union.

## TITLE III. MANAGEMENT

**Art. 11.** Under the direction and supervision of the Council of Ministers of the Union, the Bank shall be managed and administered by:

a President;
a Managing Board;

whose appointment and qualifications are set forth hereinafter.

**Art. 12.** The members of the Managing Board and the President must have full civil and political rights and must never have been sentenced to the loss of their freedom or civil rights.

Members of the Managing Board must not be selected from among executive directors, directors, or representatives, of banks, financial establishments or private enterprises unless they undertake such office on behalf of the State.

### SECTION 3.1—MANAGING BOARD

**Art. 13.** The Managing Board shall be composed of:

the President of the Bank, who shall act as Chairman;
one representative, and one alternate, appointed by each of the member States of the Union;
the Governor of the Central Bank, or his representative;
representatives of nonmember States of the Union, in proportion to the amount of capital subscribed by them, but not exceeding three, each having an alternate designated by him.

Any Board member unable to attend a meeting shall be represented by his alternate.

**Art. 14.** Meetings of the Board shall be convened by its Chairman, when necessary, and at least four times a year, either at his initiative, at the request of two thirds of the representatives of member States, or at the request of the Governor of the Central Bank.

**Art. 15.** The Board's deliberations shall be considered valid when at least two thirds of the member States and the Central Bank are represented.

Decisions of the Board shall be adopted by a majority of votes.

The representatives of the Union's member States on the Board shall have a total of six votes, the Governor of the Central Bank three votes, the representatives of the States that are not members of the Union shall have a number of votes to be determined on the basis of the capital subscribed by them, but which may not exceed three.

The President of the Bank shall not take part in the voting.

**Art. 16.** Within the framework of the guidelines it receives from the Council of Ministers of the Union, the Managing Board shall:

1. decide increases or reductions in the capital of the Bank pursuant to the provisions of Articles 8 and 9 of this Charter;
2. approve the Bank's acquisition of capital holdings in enterprises or institutions;
3. determine the rules governing loans and guarantees granted by the Bank;
4. decide what financial assistance may be provided by the Bank under the provisions of Articles 26 to 29 of this Charter;
5. decide on the loans to be contracted by the Bank;
6. draw up the rules governing the use of the Bank's available funds, subject to the provisions of Article 36 hereinafter;
7. approve agreements to be concluded by the Bank for the purpose of accepting grants, setting up special funds, and managing and operating such funds;
8. draw up the annual accounts of the Bank and the Annual Report on its activities.

**Art. 17.** The States' representatives on the Managing Board may receive attendance fees, the amount of which shall be determined by the Council of Ministers of the Union.

SECTION 3.2—THE PRESIDENT AND OFFICERS OF THE BANK

**Art. 18.** The President of the Bank shall be appointed by the Council of Ministers of the Union for a nonrenewable six-year term.

He must be chosen so as to ensure that a national of each of the member States of the Union shall hold office in succession.

The President shall be assisted in the discharge of his duties by a Vice President, appointed by the Managing Board for a nonrenewable five-year term.

**Art. 19.** The President and Vice President of the Bank may not be chosen from among the incumbent or alternate representatives of the States of the Union on the Council of Ministers, on the Board of Directors of the Central Bank, on the National Credit Committees, or on the Managing Board of the Bank.

Their functions shall preclude them from work, whether remunerated or not, for any private or public enterprise, except international governmental institutions, were the occasion to arise.

The remuneration of the President shall be determined by the Council of Ministers of the Union, and that of the Vice President by the Managing Board.

**Art. 20.** The President of the Bank shall be responsible for the implementation of the provisions of this Charter and of the agreements concluded by the Bank.

He shall serve as Chairman of the Bank's Managing Board and shall convene its meetings, draw up its agenda, and conduct its deliberations.

He shall be responsible for the implementation of the Managing Board's decisions.

He shall submit the accounts of the Bank and the Annual Report on its activities to the Board.

**Art. 21.** The President shall represent the Bank vis-à-vis third parties.

He alone shall sign all instruments committing the Bank except agreements and conventions with governments, international institutions, and foreign institutions, where power to sign has been expressly delegated to the Chairman of the Council of Ministers of the Union.

He shall represent the Bank personally, or through persons delegated by him, at meetings of international institutions in which the Bank is invited to participate.

**Art. 22.** The President shall determine the organization of the Bank's departments and the number of their staff. He shall direct their activities.

He shall hire, assign and discharge all officers of the Bank. He shall fix their remuneration as well as their pensions and all benefits in kind granted to them.

**Art. 23.** The President and the officers of the Bank shall be bound by professional secrecy and shall be subject to the penalties provided for under the penal code.

**Art. 24.** Officers of the Bank may neither take nor receive any share, interest or remuneration for work for, or advice to, any public or private industrial, commercial or financial institution, unless a waiver is exceptionally granted by the President of the Bank.

The provisions of this article do not apply to the production of scientific, literary or artistic works.

## Title IV. Operations of the Bank

**Art. 25.** All the Bank's operations must relate to its purpose as defined in Article 2 of this Charter.

### SECTION 4.1—BANK ASSISTANCE IN FINANCING ECONOMIC DEVELOPMENT

**Art. 26.** The Bank may provide all or part of the capital of institutions and enterprises.

Such participation must be subscribed out of the Bank's own funds.

**Art. 27.** The Bank may contribute, through an interest subsidy, in the payment of interest on loans taken up by the Union's common agencies, by the States, by local governments and public institutions of the Union, and by agencies involved in promoting the development of their economies through the establishment or improvement of the basic infrastructure, the conversion of means of production, and the launching of new activities.

Such contributions must be made out of the Bank's own funds or out of funds from grants placed at its disposal.

**Art. 28.** The Bank may grant loans to the Union's common agencies, to the member States, to their local governments and public institutions and to agencies and enterprises involved in promoting the development or integration of the economies of the Union.

**Art. 29.** The Bank may by endorsement guarantee repayment of the principal of, and payment of interest on, loans from international or foreign financial institutions and from foreign governments to the beneficiaries listed in Article 28 hereinabove.

**Art. 30.** The conditions under which the Bank may grant loans and loan guarantees shall be specified in regulations issued by its Managing Board.

### SECTION 4.2—BANK PARTICIPATION IN MOBILIZING FINANCING RESOURCES

**Art. 31.** The Bank may float loans on the internal market of the Union or on external financial markets and may contract loans with international or foreign public or private agencies, with maturities of any length and subject to any repayment conditions, both in currency of the Union and in foreign currencies or in units of account as will be deemed advisable by the Bank's Managing Board.

**Art. 32.** Subject to the conditions set by the Central Bank, the Bank may rediscount paper mobilizing credits it has granted.

**Art. 33.** The Bank may accept grants, whether subject to earmarking and special conditions concerning their use or not, from international or foreign institutions, from States of the Union or from foreign States.

Collection and use of specially earmarked funds shall be recorded by the Bank in accounts opened for this purpose on its books.

### SECTION 4.3—BANK CONTRIBUTIONS TO ORGANIZATION AND FINANCING OF MONEY AND FINANCIAL MARKETS OF THE UNION

**Art. 34.** The Bank may buy and sell shares in national or foreign business firms whose activities are of interest to the Union.

It may likewise buy and sell bonds issued by such firms.

**Art. 35.** The Bank may organize or help organize a financial market of the Union and contribute to its proper operation.

**Art. 36.** The current liquid assets of the Bank are deposited with the Central Bank, which shall be responsible for the Bank's cash operations. These assets may be deposited in special interest-bearing accounts at the Central Bank and be used in the latter's money market activities.

### SECTION 4.4—BANK TECHNICAL ASSISTANCE

**Art. 37.** The Bank, through its own staff, that of its subsidiaries or specially hired consultants, shall assist in drawing up projects it intends to finance.

It may likewise provide technical assistance, on the same terms, for the organization, operation, and supervision of agencies and enterprises entrusted with executing projects financed or likely to be financed by it.

### SECTION 4.5—TAX EXEMPTIONS

**Art. 38.** The Bank, its income, its property and other assets, as well as the transactions and operations it carries out under this Charter, shall be exempt from all direct and indirect taxes.

The States and local governments of the Union shall levy no tax on bonds issued by the Bank or on the interest thereon, irrespective of the holder of these securities.

## TITLE V. THE BANK'S ACCOUNTS AND USE OF ITS PROFITS

**Art. 39.** The Bank's operations shall be carried out and recorded in accordance with commercial and banking rules and practice.

Entries shall be recorded in accordance with an accounting plan approved by the Central Bank.

Every month, the Bank shall draw up a statement of account and shall publish it in the *Journal officiel* of each of the States of the Union.

**Art. 40.** The Bank's accounts shall be verified by an Auditor appointed by the Council of Ministers of the Union, which shall determine the level of his remuneration.

**Art. 41.** The accounts of the Bank shall be drawn up at least once a year on the same date as the accounts of the Central Bank. They shall be drawn up by the Managing Board.

The Managing Board shall determine the value of any overdue credits to be included on the assets side of the balance sheet, and shall constitute any reserves or make such allowances for depreciation it considers necessary.

After covering any deficits in respect of previous financial years, constituting any reserves, and deducting any allowances for depreciation, the outstanding balance shall constitute the revenue of the Bank.

The revenue so defined in its entirety shall be applied to the constitution of reserves.

**Art. 42.** Within the six months following the close of the financial year, the Bank's accounts and the report of the Auditor appointed under Article 40 above shall be submitted to the Council of Ministers of the Union for approval.

These accounts shall be published in the *Journal officiel* of each of the States of the Union.

A report on the activities and operations of the Bank in the course of each financial year shall be submitted to the Managing Board by the President of the Bank, who shall subsequently submit it to the Council of Ministers of the Union. The Chairman of the Council of Ministers shall, in turn, submit this report to the Heads of States of the Union.

## TITLE VI. AMENDMENTS TO THE CHARTER

**Art. 43.** The provisions of the Charter may be amended by unanimous decision of the Council of Ministers of the Union.

# Decree No. 66-330 [1]

## Organizing the National Credit Council [2]

[September 5, 1966]

The President of the Republic,

Considering the Constitution of the Republic of Ivory Coast;

Considering Law No. 65-252 of August 4, 1965, regulating credit and organizing the banking and related professions, particularly in its Article 25;

Considering Decree No. 66-45 of March 8, 1966, determining the powers of the Minister of Economic and Financial Affairs;

The Council of Ministers having been heard,

DECREES:

Art. 1. The National Credit Council, provided for in Article 25 of Law No. 65-252 of August 4, 1965,[3] is placed under the chairmanship of the Minister of Economic and Financial Affairs, Chairman of the National Monetary Committee.

It is composed of the following members:

the Minister of Economic and Financial Affairs;

two representatives of the National Assembly;

two representatives of the Economic and Social Council;

two members of the National Monetary Committee, appointed by its chairman;

three representatives of the Professional Association of Banks, two of them representing deposit money banks and financial institutions, and one representing commercial banks;

the Chief Treasurer and Paymaster;

---

[1] The decree was signed at Abidjan on September 5, 1966 and was published in the *Journal officiel de la République de Côte d'Ivoire* (hereinafter referred to as *Journal officiel*), September 15, 1966.

[2] Conseil national du Crédit.

[3] Article 25 of Law No. 65-252 of August 4, 1965 states:

"There shall be created a National Credit Council and a Bank Control Commission, the composition and powers of which shall be fixed by decree."

It should be noted that Article 75 of Law No. 75-549 of August 5, 1975 provides that all legal provisions in conflict with that law and particularly those of Law No. 65-252 are rescinded.

the Director of the Abidjan office of the Central Bank of West African States;
the Secretary General of the National Investment Fund;
the Director of Foreign Trade;
the Director of Consumer Affairs;
the Director of the Autonomous Amortization Fund;
an official appointed by the Minister of Posts and Telecommunications;
two experts in financial affairs appointed by the Minister in charge of Economic and Financial Affairs;
a high official appointed by the Minister in charge of Planning;
a representative of the Chamber of Commerce;
a representative of the Chamber of Agriculture;
a representative of the Chamber of Industry;
a representative of the General Labor Union of Ivory Coast.

The National Credit Council may form as many internal committees as necessary. The Director of the Central Bank of West African States shall sit on these committees, which may be supplemented, as necessary, by experts not belonging to the Council.

The Director of External Finance and Credit attends the sessions of the National Credit Council and its internal committees.

The Secretariat of the National Credit Council is provided by the Central Bank of West African States.

**Art.** 2. At the Government's request, the National Credit Council may be asked to carry out any kind of research relating to the direction of credit policy, the distribution of credit, or the organization of the banking profession.

It submits its conclusions to the Minister for Economic and Financial Affairs, who instructs the Commission for the Control of Banks and Financial Establishments to execute the decisions adopted.

**Art.** 3. The National Credit Council meets when convened by its chairman at least twice a year or at the request of two thirds of its members.

At least half of the titular members of the National Credit Council shall constitute a quorum.

**Art.** 4. The National Credit Council shall receive from all ministerial departments, all public or quasi-public agencies, the Central Bank of West African States, and banks and financial establishments all the documents necessary for the fulfillment of its mission.

Art. 5. This decree shall be published in the *Journal officiel* of the Republic of Ivory Coast and communicated wherever necessary.

*{The signatory clause is omitted.}*

# Decree No. 66-331 [1]

## Organizing the Commission for the Control of Banks and Financial Establishments [2]

[September 5, 1966]

The President of the Republic,

Having regard to Law No. 65-252 of August 4, 1965 regulating credit and organizing the banking and related professions, particularly Article 25 of that law; [3]

Having regard to Decree No. 66-45 of March 8, 1966, determining the functions and powers of the Minister in charge of Economic and Financial Affairs;

The Council of Ministers having been heard,

DECREES:

Art. 1. The Commission for the Control of Banks and Financial Establishments shall be composed of the following members:

Chairman: The Director of External Finance and of Credit.

Vice-Chairman: The Director of the Abidjan Office of the Central Bank of West African States.

Members:

The Chief Treasurer and Paymaster;

A counselor of the Chamber of Accounts appointed by the President of the Supreme Court;

---

[1] The decree was signed at Abidjan on September 5, 1966 and was published in the *Journal officiel*, September 15, 1966.

[2] Commission de contrôle des banques et des établissements financiers.

[3] See footnote 3 to Decree No. 66-330 on page 477.

A member of the National Monetary Committee appointed by its chairman.

**Art. 2.** The Commission for the Control of Banks and Financial Establishments shall meet when convened by its chairman or at the request of at least three of its members.

Not less than three of its members shall constitute a quorum.

**Art. 3.** The Commission for the Control of Banks and Financial Establishments shall give its opinion on the creation of new banks or financial establishments and on the opening of additional counters. It shall be responsible for executing the decisions of the Minister for Economic and Financial Affairs and for supervising implementation of the regulation of the banking profession. It shall have power of initiative for control of documents and on-premises inspection, shall make rulings in response to any requests that may be addressed to it by the Minister for Economic and Financial Affairs, the Central Bank of West African States, or the Professional Association of Banks, and, in accordance with Article 7 of this decree, shall penalize violations noted.

**Art. 4.** The Commission for the Control of Banks and Financial Establishments may appoint a liquidator to the banks or financial establishments which have been removed from the registration list and which have received notice that they must cease their operations within a fixed period.

When the administration, management, or directorate of a bank or financial establishment can no longer, whatever the reason for the deficiency, be exercised by persons properly empowered to do so, the Commission may designate to such bank or financial establishment an interim administrator, upon whom it shall confer the necessary powers for the administration, management, or directorate.

**Art. 5.** The Commission for the Control of Banks and Financial Establishments shall exercise its authority on the basis of balance sheets and periodic statements which shall be submitted to it, and by means of data, clarifications, and supporting documents which it may ask for in accordance with Article 24 of Law No. 65-252 of August 4, 1965.[4]

---

[4] Article 24 of Law No. 65-252 of August 4, 1965, states:

"Banks shall be required to furnish, whenever the Control Commission or the Central Bank so requests, any information, clarification, and supporting evidence deemed useful in carrying out their mission.

"The Bank Control Commission may entrust the departments of the Central Bank with any such tasks as verifying or checking on the strength of documentary records and on the spot, if necessary, operations and accounts of banks and credit establishments as will allow it to make sure that such establishments

Moreover, it may cause all necessary checks to be effected on the spot, by the officers it appoints.

Art. 6. The Commission for the Control of Banks and Financial Establishments shall draw up, prior to March 31 of each year, a report in which it shall summarize its findings and formulate any suggestions which it considers necessary with regard to the structure and general organization of banking and financial establishments.

This report shall be sent to the Minister for Economic and Financial Affairs who shall communicate it to the National Credit Council.

Art. 7. If the control exercised by the Commission for the Control of Banks and Financial Establishments shows that an establishment has violated the rules established by the above-mentioned law or by the regulations laid down in application of this law, the Commission for the Control of Banks and Financial Establishments shall levy disciplinary sanctions, without prejudice to the applicable penal sanctions, which are, by order of severity:

a warning;
a reprimand;
prohibition of certain operations and any limitations in the exercise of the profession;
suspension of the officials responsible, with or without the appointment of an interim administrator;
proposal to the competent monetary authorities for the limitation or discontinuance of any facilities from the Central Bank of West African States;
proposal that the institution be struck off the list of banks or the list of financial establishments.

The decision of the Commission for the Control of Banks and Financial Establishments must be handed down with a statement of reasons: they must also specify, if applicable, the conditions and time limits for their implementation. They may only be appealed before the Supreme Court for action *ultra vires*. This appeal operates as a stay, unless the Control Commission decides on urgent measures.

---

have complied with the provisions of this law and with general or special provisions adopted for the implementation thereof.

"Any bank refusing to meet requests for information from the Control Commission or from the Central Bank shall be liable to a fine of up to 10,000 francs for each day of delay, which shall accrue to the Treasury."

It should be noted that Article 75 of Law No. 75-549 of August 5, 1975 provides that all legal provisions in conflict with that law and particularly those of Law No. 65-252 are rescinded.

**Art. 8.** The sanctions pronounced by the Control Commission are valid only if the interested parties or their representatives have been convened and heard.

When they have been called upon to appear before the Control Commission, the parties concerned may be represented or counseled by a lawyer called to a bar, by a member of the Professional Association of Banks or by the manager of an establishment which is an individual or joint member of said association.

The other procedural rules shall be determined by order of the Minister for Economic and Financial Affairs.

**Art. 9.** All decisions of the Commission for the Control of Banks and Financial Establishments shall be communicated to the National Credit Council.

**Art. 10.** The present decree shall be published in the *Journal officiel* of the Republic of Ivory Coast and communicated wherever necessary.

*[The signatory clause is omitted.]*

## Order No. 23[1]

Determining the conditions in which the Commission for the Control of Banks and Financial Establishments may ensure its operating costs

[January 5, 1967]

**Art. 1.** The expenditures incurred by the Commission for the Control of Banks and Financial Establishments shall be borne by the Professional Association of Banks which shall divide them every six months among its members.

[1] The order was signed at Abidjan on January 5, 1967 and was published in the *Journal officiel*, January 19, 1967.

**Art. 2.** The Professional Association may, at the beginning of each six-month period, request the banks and financial establishments to make a provisional payment calculated on the basis of the estimates of the expenditures of the Commission for the Control of Banks and Financial Establishments.

**Art. 3.** The payments provided for in Articles 1 and 2 hereinabove shall, for each bank or financial establishment, be calculated in proportion to the amount of its balance sheet made up as at September 30 of each year plus its rediscount commitment as of that date.

**Art. 4.** Each bank or financial establishment shall be debited for the entire six-month period, even if incomplete, in which it has appeared on the official lists.

**Art. 5.** The receipt and expenditure accounts of the Commission for the Control of Banks and Financial Establishments shall be kept by the Central Bank, to which the secretariat of that body shall be entrusted. They must be communicated annually to the Minister of Economic and Financial Affairs.

**Art. 6.** This Order shall be published in the *Journal officiel* of the Republic of Ivory Coast.

*{The signatory clause is omitted.}*

## Decree No. 66-172 [1]

Making it obligatory for banks and financial establishments to form a Professional Association of Banks and Financial Establishments [2]

[April 26, 1966]

[1] The decree was signed at Abidjan on April 26, 1966 and was published in the *Journal officiel,* May 19, 1966.

[2] Association professionnelle des banques et établissements financiers.

The President of the Republic,

Having regard to Law No. 65-252 of August 4, 1965, regulating credit and organizing the banking and related professions;

Having regard to Decree No. 66-45 of March 8, 1966, determining the functions and powers of the Minister in charge of Economic and Financial Affairs;

The Council of Ministers having been heard,

DECREES:

**Art. 1.** In accordance with the provisions of Article 26 of Law No. 65-252 of August 4, 1965,[3] the authorized banks in Ivory Coast are to set up a Professional Association of Banks and Financial Establishments and to become members of it.

**Art. 2.** The approved financial establishments in Ivory Coast are to belong to this association.

**Art. 3.** The Professional Association of Banks and Financial Establishments shall be governed by the provisions of Law No. 60-315 of September 21, 1960; it is placed under the control of the Minister for Economic and Financial Affairs. Its by-laws shall be approved by the Minister for Economic and Financial Affairs and published in the *Journal officiel.*

**Art. 4.** No other professional association, and no other trade union grouping of banking or financial establishments, may, from promulgation of this decree, represent such establishments vis-à-vis the public authorities.

**Art. 5.** An order from the Minister for Economic and Financial Affairs shall determine the circumstances in which the Professional Association of Banks and Financial Establishments shall take over the operating expenses of the Commission for the Control of Banks and Financial Establishments.

---

[3] Article 26 of Law No. 65-252 of August 4, 1965 states:

"All banks that have been approved and registered shall be required to join the Professional Association of Banks organized under the provisions of the law of September 21, 1960."

It should be noted that Article 75 of Law No. 75-549 of August 5, 1975 provides that all legal provisions in conflict with that law and particularly those of Law No. 65-252 are rescinded.

**Art. 6.** This decree shall be published in the *Journal officiel* of the Republic of Ivory Coast.

*[The signatory clause is omitted.]*

# Law No. 75-549

## On regulation of banks[1]

[August 5, 1975]

The National Assembly has adopted,
The President of the Republic promulgates the law worded as follows:

### TITLE I. SCOPE OF APPLICATION OF THE BANKING REGULATIONS

**Art. 1.** This law shall apply to banks and financial institutions conducting business in the territory of Ivory Coast, regardless of their legal status, the location of their registered or main office, and the nationality of the owners of their capital or the nationality of their officers.

**Art. 2.** This law shall not apply, however:

to the Central Bank of West African States, hereinafter called the Central Bank;

to international financial institutions or to official foreign aid and cooperation institutions whose operations in the territory of Ivory Coast are authorized by treaties, agreements, or conventions to which Ivory Coast is a party;

to the Office of Posts and Telecommunications, except for the provisions of Article 47.

---

[1] *Loi N° 75-549 du 5 août 1975, portant réglementation bancaire,* signed in Abidjan on August 5, 1975 and published in *Journal officiel,* No. 43, September 4, 1975 (p. 1564), incorporating the amendments made to Law No. 75-549 by the Corrigendum published in the *Journal officiel,* No. 20, May 6, 1976 and appended to the French text of that law.

Articles 20–31 of this law shall not apply to the special-status banks and public financial institutions included on the list to be drawn up by the Council of Ministers of the West African Monetary Union. In addition, the Council of Ministers of the West African Monetary Union may exclude these banks and financial institutions in whole or in part from the scope of application of this law, except for Articles 43–46 and Article 60.

**Art. 3.** Enterprises whose normal business is to receive funds which may be drawn by check or transfer and which they employ, for their own account or for the account of others, in credit or investment operations shall be deemed to be banks.

**Art. 4.** Natural or juridical persons, other than banks, whose normal business is to conduct for their own account credit operations, operations involving sales on credit or the financing of sales on credit, or exchange operations, or which normally receive funds they employ for their own account in investment operations, or which normally serve as agents or brokers or other intermediaries in the aforementioned operations, shall be deemed to be financial institutions.

**Art. 5.** Loans, discounts, temporary advances against collateral, acquisition of claims, guarantees, financing of credit sales, and leases shall be deemed to be credit operations.

All acquisitions of equity in existing enterprises or in enterprises in the process of formation, and any acquisition of securities issued by government or nongovernment entities, shall be deemed to be investment operations.

**Art. 6.** The following shall not be deemed to be banks or financial institutions:

(*a*) Insurance companies and retirement funds;
(*b*) Notaries and ministry officials in the exercise of their duties;
(*c*) Stock and commercial brokers.

However, all enterprises, funds, and persons specified in this article shall be subject to the provisions of Article 69.

## Title II. Authorization of Banks and Financial Institutions

### Chapter I. Authorization of Banks

**Art. 7.** No entity may engage in the activities defined in Article 3, or describe itself as a bank or a banker, or cause the terms "bank," "banker," or "banking" to appear in any language in its appellation, trade name, or publicity, or make any use of them whatsoever in its activities, unless and until it has been authorized and registered on the list of banks.

**Art. 8.** The conditions and procedures governing the authorization of banks and the withdrawal of such authorization shall be set by decree.

**Art. 9.** All requests for authorization shall be presented through the Central Bank. The Minister of Economy and Finance shall be responsible for issuing and withdrawing authorization.

Authorization shall be formalized by registration on the list of banks, and withdrawn by striking from that list.

The list of banks shall be drawn up and kept current by the Central Bank. Each Bank shall be assigned a registration number.

The initial list of banks, and all amendments to it, including the striking of entries, shall be published in the *Journal officiel.*

**Art. 10.** Banks must show their bank registration numbers in the same circumstances, on the same documents, and under penalty of the same sanctions as applicable with regard to the commercial register.

**Art. 11.** Banks struck from the list of banks shall cease operations within the time period set in the decision to withdraw authorization.

## CHAPTER II. AUTHORIZATION AND CLASSIFICATION OF FINANCIAL INSTITUTIONS

**Art. 12.** No entity may engage in any of the activities defined in Article 4 unless and until it has been authorized and registered on the list of financial institutions.

The conditions and procedures governing authorization of financial institutions and the withdrawal of such authorization shall be set by decree.

The provisions of Articles 9 through 11 shall apply to financial institutions.

**Art. 13.** Financial institutions may be classified by decree into different categories on the basis of their activities.

No financial institution in any given category shall engage in the activities of other categories without prior approval granted in the same way as the authorization.

## Title III. Directors and Personnel of Banks and Financial Institutions

**Art. 14.** No one may direct, administer, or manage a bank, a financial institution, or an agency thereof who is not a national of Ivory Coast or a member country of the West African Monetary Union, unless he is granted the status of an Ivorian national for this purpose under the terms of the founding agreement.

The Minister of Economy and Finance may grant individual exemptions from the provisions of this article.

**Art. 15.** Anyone convicted of a common crime, of forgery or the use thereof in private, commercial, or bank accounting, of theft, of fraud or offenses punishable as fraud, of breach of trust, of bankruptcy, of embezzlement of public funds, of withdrawal by a public depository, of extortion of monies or securities, of issuing checks without cover, of undermining the Government's credit standing, or of concealing anything obtained through these infractions, shall be disqualified from all of the following:

directing, administering, or managing any bank or financial institution, or any agency thereof;

engaging in any of the activities defined in Article 4; and

proposing to the public the establishment of any bank or financial institution.

Any person who has been convicted of an attempt to commit any of the aforementioned infractions, or of complicity in them, shall also be so disqualified.

Persons whose bankruptcy has not been repealed, ministerial officials who have been removed from office, and executives suspended under the terms of Article 53 shall be similarly disqualified.

Any person who has been convicted, declared bankrupt, or removed from office in a foreign country shall also be so disqualified. In such an event, the government ministry or the person concerned may apply to the criminal court for a finding as to whether or not the conditions entailing disqualification have been fulfilled.

The court shall rule after weighing the propriety and the legality of the foreign decision and after duly granting a hearing to the person concerned.

In the event a decision resulting in disqualification as provided for in this article is subsequently repealed or invalidated, the disqualification shall terminate automatically unless the new decision can be appealed.

**Art. 16.** Any person who contravenes any of the proscriptions imposed by Article 14 or 15 shall be punished by imprisonment for a term of six months to two years or a fine of CFAF 1,000,000 to CFAF 2,000,000, or both.

**Art. 17.** No person convicted of any of the deeds specified in the first two paragraphs of Article 15 or in Article 16 may be employed in any capacity by a bank or a financial institution. The provisions of Article 15, paragraphs 4 and 5, shall apply to this prohibition.

In the event the prohibition is contravened, the infractor shall be subject to the punishments provided for in Article 16, and the employer to a fine of CFAF 1,000,000 to CFAF 2,000,000.

**Art. 18.** Every bank and every financial institution must deposit, with the Central Bank and the court officer maintaining the commercial register, a full list of the persons directing, administering, and managing the bank or financial institution and its agencies, and must keep said list up to date.

The court officer shall furnish the district attorney, within a week, with a copy of the list on unstamped paper.

**Art. 19.** All persons involved in the direction, administration, management, audit, and operation of any bank or financial institution shall be bound by professional confidentiality.

## TITLE IV. REGULATIONS GOVERNING BANKS AND FINANCIAL INSTITUTIONS

### CHAPTER I. LEGAL STATUS

**Art. 20.** Banks shall be constituted as companies or other juridical persons.

Banks domiciled in Ivory Coast shall take the form of joint-stock companies with fixed capital.

**Art. 21.** Financial institutions domiciled in Ivory Coast shall take the form of joint-stock companies with fixed capital, limited liability companies, or cooperative companies with variable capital.

Natural persons may be forbidden by decree to engage in all or part of the activities defined in Article 4.

The legal form to be adopted by the various categories of financial institutions may be prescribed by decree.

**Art. 22.** All shares issued by banks or financial institutions domiciled in Ivory Coast shall be registered shares.

## CHAPTER II. CAPITAL AND SPECIAL RESERVE

**Art. 23.** The registered capital of banks and financial institutions domiciled in Ivory Coast shall not be less than a minimum to be set by decree. This minimum need not be the same for banks and for the various categories of financial institutions.

The registered capital shall be fully paid up, up to the minimum amount provided for above, at the time the bank or financial institution is established.

**Art. 24.** Banks and financial establishments that will need to increase their registered capital in order to meet the prescribed requirement shall have six months to do so.

**Art. 25.** Banks and financial institutions domiciled abroad may be required to prove at any time that they have appropriated for their transactions in Ivory Coast resources at least equal to the minimum amount provided for in Article 23.

**Art. 26.** Subject to the provisions of Article 28, the paid-in proprietary capital of any bank or financial institution must at all times be at least equal to the minimum amount referred to in Article 23, and may not be less than the minimum amount of paid-in proprietary capital that may be prescribed pursuant to Article 48, paragraph 2.

A directive to be issued by the Central Bank shall define what constitutes paid-in proprietary capital for the purposes of this article and of Article 48.

**Art. 27.** Banks and financial institutions with the status of juridical persons shall be required to constitute a special reserve, including any legal reserve that may be required by the laws and regulations in force. Fifteen per cent of accrued net profits shall be set aside annually for maintenance of this special reserve.

The special reserve of the banks and financial institutions specified in Article 25 shall be over and above the appropriation required under the terms of that article.

**Art. 28.** Financial institutions not endowed with the status of juridical persons shall be required to hold a bank guarantee furnished by an authorized bank in a member State of the West African Monetary Union, in an amount equal to the minimum provided for in Article 23.

## CHAPTER III. MISCELLANEOUS AUTHORIZATIONS

**Art. 29.** The following shall require prior authorization from the Minister of Economy and Finance:

Any merger, by takeover or by the creation of a new company, and any split involving a bank or financial institution domiciled in Ivory Coast;

The early winding-up of any bank or financial institution domiciled in Ivory Coast; and

Any acquisition of equity in a bank or financial institution domiciled in Ivory Coast that would result in raising, directly or through an intermediary, the holdings of any single natural or juridical person, first above 20 per cent and then above 50 per cent of the registered capital of that bank or financial institution.

All banks and financial institutions domiciled abroad shall inform the Minister of Economy and Finance of any merger, early winding-up, or acquisition of equity under the terms of the preceding paragraph, in which they may be involved.

The following, in particular, shall be deemed to be intermediaries of a single natural or juridical person:

Juridical persons more than 50 per cent of whose registered capital is held by that person;

Subsidiary companies, namely, companies more than 50 per cent of whose registered capital is held by the corporations referred to in the preceding subparagraph, or by the corporations referred to in the preceding subparagraph and by the natural or juridical person concerned, taken together; and

Subsidiaries of subsidiary companies within the meaning of the preceding subparagraph.

**Art. 30.** The following shall also require prior authorization from the Minister of Economy and Finance:

Any assignment by a bank or financial institution of more than 20 per cent of those assets earmarked for its operations in Ivory Coast;

Any management contracting all its operations in Ivory Coast; and

Any opening, closing, conversion, transfer, assignment, or management contracting of an office or agency in Ivory Coast.

**Art. 31.** Prior authorizations under the terms of this chapter shall be granted as in the case of bank authorization. However, authorizations under the terms of the last subparagraph of Article 30 may be granted by the Central Bank under the delegated authority of the Ministry of Economy and Finance.

## CHAPTER IV. OPERATIONS

### Section I: Bank Operations

**Art. 32.** The equity held by a bank in any single enterprise may not exceed 25 per cent of the enterprise's capital, or 15 per cent of the bank's paid-in proprietary capital, unencumbered by contractual obligations, as defined by a directive from the Central Bank.

The provisions of the preceding subparagraph shall not apply to the following acquisitions of equity:

in other banks or financial institutions;

in real estate companies, subject to the provisions of Articles 33 and 34.

**Art. 33.** Banks may not hold equity in real estate companies or own real estate in excess of an aggregate amount of 15 per cent of their paid-in proprietary capital unencumbered by contractual obligations.

Without prejudice to the provisions of Article 34, the terms of the preceding subparagraph shall not apply to transactions relating to such real estate as is required for the banks' operation or for the housing and welfare of their personnel.

**Art. 34.** The total equity and fixed capital held by a single bank in other enterprises, excluding any operations financed with funds other than its own, may not exceed the total of the bank's paid-in proprietary capital unencumbered by contractual obligations.

**Art. 35.** The provisions of Articles 32 through 34 shall not apply to assets acquired by the banks in the process of claims conversion, provided such assets are disposed of within one year.

**Art. 36.** Banks shall be prohibited from engaging in commercial, industrial, agricultural, or service activities, on their own behalf or on another's, except insofar as such operations are required for, or accessory to, the pursuit of their banking activity, or necessitated by claims conversion.

**Art. 37.** The credit granted by any bank to a single natural or juridical person, or to any group of natural or juridical persons whose interests are closely bound, may not exceed the total amount of the bank's paid-in proprietary capital as defined by a Central Bank directive.

The following, in particular, shall be deemed to be groups of persons whose interests are closely bound:

Juridical persons and their executives, where credits granted to the latter are intended to be used for activities of the juridical person;

Natural or juridical persons jointly pursuing an activity for which the credits are intended; and

Groups consisting of a natural or juridical person and of persons considered intermediaries within the meaning of Article 29.

The provisions of this article shall not apply to the following:

Agricultural credits granted to institutions under direct or indirect government control;

Credits secured by government contracts or by export products whose market value is generally agreed or has been checked by the Central Bank, provided such credits do not exceed an amount fixed by Central Bank directive;

Credits granted to the Treasury or guaranteed by it; and

Credits to other banks.

A Central Bank directive shall define agricultural credits for the purposes of this law.

**Art. 38.** Banks are prohibited from purchasing their own shares or accepting them as collateral for their loans.

**Art. 39.** Banks are prohibited from directly or indirectly granting credits in excess of an aggregate amount equal to 20 per cent of their paid-in proprietary capital to any persons performing executive, administrative, managerial, audit, or operational duties for them.

The same prohibition shall apply to credits granted to private enterprises headed, administered, or managed by aforementioned persons or in which such persons hold more than one fourth of the registered capital.

The provisions of this decree shall not apply to credits secured by government contracts or by export products whose market value is generally recognized or has been verified by the Central Bank, provided that such credits do not exceed an amount fixed by the latter's directive.

**Art. 40.** The Minister of Economy and Finance may, after consultation with the Central Bank, grant individual exemptions from the provisions of this section.

## Section II: Operations of Financial Institutions

**Art. 41.** The operations of the various categories of institutions shall be regulated by decree in accordance with the nature of their activities.

Art. 42. Financial institutions shall accept deposits of funds from the public only if they are authorized to do so by decree and insofar as such acceptance is consistent with their activities and with the terms of the authorizing decree.

## CHAPTER V. ACCOUNTS AND REPORTING TO THE CENTRAL BANK

Art. 43. Banks and financial institutions shall close their financial year on September 30 of each year.

They shall maintain at their head office, their main establishment, or their main agency in Ivory Coast, specific accounting records of their transactions on the Republic's territory.

Art. 44. Banks and financial institutions shall forward to the Central Bank by December 31 of each year, in accordance with the rules and forms prescribed by the Central Bank, the following:

their balance sheet;

their operating account; and

their profit and loss account.

The validity and accuracy of these documents shall be certified by an auditor selected from the list of auditors approved by the Court of Appeals.

The annual balance sheet shall be published in the *Journal officiel.* The cost of publication shall be borne by the Bank.

Art. 45. Banks and financial institutions shall draw up statements of their assets and liabilities in the course of the financial year, at intervals set by the Central Bank and in the form prescribed by it. The Central Bank shall collect and examine all these documents and forward them, with its assessment, to the Commission for the Control of Banks and Financial Establishments to be established under the terms of Article 50.

Art. 46. All banks and financial institutions shall be required to provide the Central Bank, at its request, with any information, explanations, evidence, and documents deemed useful to assess their position and risks, to draw up a list of unpaid checks and commercial bills, and, generally, to enable the Central Bank to perform its duties.

Art. 47. The terms of Article 46 shall apply to the Office of Posts and Telecommunications as regards its financial and postal checking operations.

## Title V. Rules of the West African Monetary Union

**Art. 48.** Pursuant to Article 11 of the Treaty Establishing the West African Monetary Union, the Council of Ministers of the West African Monetary Union may take any decisions that would:

Require banks and financial institutions to establish obligatory reserves and to deposit them with the Central Bank, to maintain ratios between the various components of their resources and uses, or to impose maximum or minimum amounts for certain uses;

Set the rates and terms of any transactions of the banks and financial institutions with their customers.

Among others, such decisions could set the minimum paid-in proprietary capital ratio and the minimum cash ratio to be maintained by the banks and the various categories of financial institutions, without prejudice to the terms of Article 26.

The Central Bank shall notify the banks and financial institutions of any decisions under the terms of this article.

The implementation of these decisions shall be governed by directives to be issued by the Central Bank.

**Art. 49.** Banks and financial institutions shall comply with any Central Bank decisions taken in the exercise of the powers vested in it by the aforementioned treaty and by its charter annexed to the treaty.

## Title VI. Control and Sanctions

### Chapter I. Control

**Art. 50.** A Commission for the Control of Banks and Financial Establishments, hereafter referred to as the Control Commission, shall be established. Its composition and operations shall be prescribed by decree.

The Control Commission shall determine whether banking regulations have been violated and shall determine what disciplinary action is to be taken against the violators.

The members of the Control Commission and any persons participating in its activities shall be bound by professional secrecy. The members of the Commission, except those representing the Government, shall hold no position, paid or unpaid, in a bank or financial institution, nor shall they receive any remuneration, direct or indirect, from any bank or financial institution.

The Central Bank shall act as secretariat to the Control Commission.

**Art. 51.** It shall be the task of the Central Bank to satisfy itself that banking regulations are respected. To this end, the Bank may, on its own initiative or at the request of the Control Commission, undertake any audit of the documents or inspection.

**Art. 52.** The Central Bank shall inform the Control Commission of any violations of banking regulations known to it.

## CHAPTER II. DISCIPLINARY SANCTIONS

**Art. 53.** In the event the Control Commission, acting on a report from the Central Bank or a request from the Minister of Economy and Finance, should find that a bank or a financial institution has violated the banking regulations, it shall apply the following disciplinary sanctions, without prejudice to other applicable penalties or other sanctions:

warning;

censure;

suspension or prohibition of certain operations, or any other limitations on the conduct of business;

suspension of the executives responsible, with or without the appointment of a temporary administrator;

striking from the list of banks or financial institutions.

**Art. 54.** No disciplinary sanction may be taken by the Control Commission unless the party concerned or its representative has been duly heard or summoned.

**Art. 55.** The Control Commission's decisions must be based on the evidence of reason. Their implementation shall require prior approval by the Minister of Economy and Finance.

## CHAPTER III. PUNITIVE SANCTIONS

**Art. 56.** Any person contravening, on his own behalf or on another's, the terms of Article 7, Article 12, or Article 13, subparagraph 2, shall be punished by imprisonment for a term of one month to two years, by a fine of CFAF 2,000,000 to CFAF 20,000,000, or both.

For second offenders, the maximum penalty shall be raised to five years' imprisonment and a fine of CFAF 50,000,000.

**Art. 57.** Any person who, acting on his own behalf or on another's, knowingly provides the Central Bank with inaccurate documents or information, or offers opposition to any audit or inspection effected by the Central Bank under the terms of Article 51, shall be punished by imprisonment for a term of one month to one year, by a fine of CFAF 1,000,000 to CFAF 10,000,000, or both.

For second offenders, the maximum penalty shall be raised to two years' imprisonment and a fine of CFAF 20,000,000.

**Art. 58.** Any bank or financial institution that contravenes the terms of Articles 18, 27, 30, last subparagraph, 44, 45, or 46, or decisions under the terms of Article 48 or 49, shall be punished by a fine of CFAF 1,000,000 to CFAF 10,000,000, without prejudice to the sanctions provided for in Chapter IV of this title.

The same penalty may be imposed on the executives who were responsible for the violation.

Persons acquiring equity in a bank or financial institution in contravention of the terms of Article 29 shall be subject to the same penalty.

## CHAPTER IV. OTHER SANCTIONS

**Art. 59.** Any bank or financial institution that fails to establish any obligatory reserve instituted under the terms of Article 48 with the Central Bank, or fails to sell its foreign exchange holdings to the Central Bank if required to do so pursuant to Article 18 of the Bank's charter, shall be charged interest by the Central Bank on overdue payments at a rate not to exceed 1 per cent each day of delay.

**Art. 60.** Any bank or financial institution that fails to provide the Central Bank with documents or information as provided for in Articles 44, 45, or 46, may be charged the following penalties each day of delay:

CFAF 10,000 during the first 15 days;

CFAF 20,000 during the following 15 days;

CFAF 50,000 thereafter.

The penalties shall be collected by the Central Bank for the account of the Treasury.

**Art. 61.** Any bank or financial institution that contravenes West African Monetary Union regulations requiring it to maintain ratios between the various components of its resources and uses, or to maintain maximum or minimum amounts for certain uses, may be required by the Central Bank to make a noninterest-bearing deposit with it in an amount not to exceed 200 per cent of such irregularities as have been found for a period not to exceed the period of the violation.

In the event of delay in making such a deposit, the provisions of Article 59 relating to interest on overdue payments shall apply.

**Art. 62.** Any bank or financial institution that contravenes West African Monetary Union regulations setting the rates and terms of its transactions with customers or requiring prior authorization for the grant to any single enterprise of credits in excess of a specified amount, may be required by the Central Bank to make a noninterest-bearing deposit with it in an amount not to exceed 200 per cent of such irregularities as have been found for a period not to exceed one month, or, in the event of remuneration improperly collected or paid, in an amount not to exceed 500 per cent of such remuneration.

In the event of delay in making such a deposit, the provisions of Article 59 relating to interest on overdue payments shall apply.

**Art. 63.** Penalties for delays, and interest on overdue payments, pursuant to Articles 60, 61, 62, shall not begin to accrue before ten clear days have elapsed since the receipt, by the bank or financial institution concerned, of a formal notice delivered by the Central Bank.

**Art. 64.** Decisions taken by the Central Bank pursuant to the provisions of this chapter can be appealed only to the Council of Ministers of the Monetary Union. The Council shall prescribe the conditions governing such appeals.

## TITLE VI. MISCELLANEOUS PROVISIONS

### CHAPTER I. PROVISIONS COMMON TO BANKS AND FINANCIAL INSTITUTIONS

**Art. 65.** Every bank or financial institution must, within one month of its registration on the list of banks or financial institutions, join the Professional Association of Banks and Financial Establishments.

The charter of the Association shall be subject to the approval of the Minister of Economy and Finance.

**Art. 66.** The Minister of Economy and Finance may, after consultation with the Central Bank, suspend all, or part of, the operations of any bank and financial institution. Such a suspension may not exceed six working days. It may be extended by another six working days in the same manner.

**Art. 67.** In the event the persons legally empowered to direct, administer, or manage a bank or a financial institution should for any reason no longer be able to do so, or in the event the manner in which a bank or financial institution is managed should endanger the funds deposited there, the Minister of Economy and Finance may, after consultation with the Control Commission and the Central Bank, designate a temporary administrator whom he shall vest with the powers required to direct, administer, or manage the bank or financial institution concerned.

**Art. 68.** The Minister of Economy and Finance may, after consultation with the Control Commission, appoint a liquidator for banks and financial institutions that have been struck from the list of banks and financial institutions, or that were not registered on the list and have been notified they must cease operations.

## CHAPTER II. OTHER PROVISIONS

**Art. 69.** The enterprises, funds, and persons specified in Article 6 shall, under penalty of the sanctions provided for in Article 58, provide the Central Bank, at its request, with the information and documents it requires in order to discharge its duties as defined in the Treaty Establishing the West African Monetary Union, in its charter, and in the laws and regulations in effect.

The provisions of Article 57 shall apply in the event the documents or information provided are inaccurate.

**Art. 70.** No natural or juridical person, other than a bank or financial institution, whose business it is, as his principal or accessory activity, to create business for banks or financial institutions or to do business on their behalf, shall engage in such activity without prior authorization from the Minister of Economy and Finance. Requests for such authorizations shall be examined by the Central Bank.

The provisions of this article shall not apply to the directors or personnel of banks or financial institutions.

Any person who, acting on his own behalf or on another's, contravenes the provisions of this article, shall be punished by a fine of CFAF 500,000 to CFAF 5,000,000.

Second offenders shall be punished by imprisonment for a term of two months to two years, by a fine of CFAF 1,000,000 to CFAF 10,000,000, or both.

**Art. 71.** Subject to the provisions of Article 42 and the laws and regulations governing certain natural or juridical persons, no natural or juridical person other than a bank shall solicit or accept deposits of funds from the public for any period of time.

Any person who, acting on his own behalf or on another's, contravenes the provisions of the preceding subparagraph, shall be punished by imprisonment for a term of one month to two years, a fine of CFAF 2,000,000 to CFAF 10,000,000, or both.

For second offenders, the maximum penalty shall be raised to five years' imprisonment and a fine of CFAF 50,000,000.

The following shall not be regarded as having been received from the public:

Funds constituting the enterprise's capital;

Funds received from the enterprise's directors or from partners or company members holding 10 per cent or more of the registered capital;

Funds received from banks or financial institutions in connection with credit operations;

Funds received from the enterprise's personnel, provided they aggregate less than 10 per cent of the enterprise's paid-in proprietary capital.

Funds originating from issues of cash vouchers shall in every case be regarded as deposits of funds received from the public.

Art. 72. The Attorney General of the Republic shall inform the Central Bank of any action at law instituted against any person pursuant to the provisions of this law.

## Title VIII. Transitional Arrangements and Implementing Regulations

Art. 73. All banks and financial institutions at present registered on the list of banks or financial institutions shall be automatically authorized and registered on the lists provided for in Articles 7 and 12. They must comply with the provisions of this law within a year from the date of its entry into force.

Art. 74. The Central Bank shall be consulted before implementing regulations for this law are issued.

Art. 75. All legal provisions conflicting with this law, and particularly those of Law No. 65-252 of August 4, 1965, are hereby rescinded.

Art. 76. This law shall be enforced as a law of the State and published in the *Journal officiel* of the Republic of Ivory Coast.

*{The signatory clause is omitted.}*

# Decree No. 66-167[1]

## Fixing the minimum amount of capital for banks and financial establishments as well as the terms for setting up reserve funds

[April 26, 1966]

The President of the Republic,

Having regard to Law No. 65-252 of August 4, 1965 regulating credit and organizing the banking profession and related professions,

Having regard to Decree No. 66-45 of March 8, 1966 determining the powers of the Minister for Economic and Financial Affairs,

Having heard the Council of Ministers,

DECREES:

Art. 1. Any registered bank operating in the territory of the Republic of Ivory Coast shall be required at any time to furnish proof of having a capital the amount of which, without ever being allowed to be less than CFAF 300 million, must be equal to or greater than:

8 per cent of the risks appearing in its balance sheet or outside its balance sheet as of the closing date of its most recent fiscal year, for a commercial and deposit bank;

12 per cent of the risks appearing in its balance sheet or outside its balance sheet as of the closing date of its most recent fiscal year, for an investment or development bank.

The same ratios must exist between risks and allocated capital of which, in accordance with Article 19 of Law No. 65-252 of August 4, 1965,[2] foreign banks authorized to carry on their business in the territory of Ivory Coast are required to furnish proof.

---

[1] The decree was signed at Abidjan on April 26, 1966 and was published in the *Journal officiel,* May 19, 1966.

[2] Article 19 of Law No. 65-252 of August 4, 1965 states:

"Foreign banks must be registered pursuant to the conditions provided in Article 11 and must, in order to carry on their activities in Ivory Coast:

"Maintain, at the office established in Ivory Coast, special accounting records of the operations they conduct in the territory of the Republic;

"Furnish, for all these operations and their investments in Ivory Coast, proof of capital resources equal to the minimum capital provided for in the Article hereinabove."

It should be noted that Article 75 of Law No. 75-549 of August 5, 1975 provides that all legal provisions in conflict with that law and particularly those of Law No. 65-252 are rescinded.

**Art. 2.** Every registered financial establishment must at all times furnish evidence of its having a capital the amount of which may not be less than 10 per cent of its risks recorded in the balance sheet and outside the balance sheet as of the date of its last fiscal year, but this capital may not be less than CFAF 60 million.

**Art. 3.** For purposes of implementing this Decree,

"capital" should be held to mean the own funds available to the bank or the financial establishment consisting of the total of the authorized capital, reserves, allocations, nonearmarked provisions and profits carried forward subject to deduction of losses; insofar as investment and development banks are concerned, the capital so determined shall be increased by loans granted by the State against a prior claim assignment;

"risks" should be held to mean all credits granted by the bank or the financial establishment irrespective of the length of time of such credits, whether or not they have been rediscounted or pawned, guarantees and endorsements excluding guarantees for public contracts, counterguarantees given to local or external banks, confirmed credit opened but not yet used; from the total so determined shall be deducted counterguarantees received from local or external banks, guarantees furnished by the State, and provisions for risks that have been earmarked.

**Art. 4.** The provisions of Article 1 hereinabove shall go into effect, on the basis of the balance sheet and accounting statement as of September 30, 1965, on a date which shall be fixed by an order of the Minister for Economic and Financial Affairs. However, in the case of commercial and deposit banks, the ratio provided for in Article 1 applied to their balance sheet as of September 30, 1965 may not exceed 4 per cent, provided that advances on blocked accounts of the external registered offices or parent firms, being added to the capital as defined in Article 3, establish the ratio prescribed in Article 1 permanently at 8 per cent.

The minimum ratio of 4 per cent so authorized as at September 30, 1965 shall be raised, according to a progressive scale subsequently determined by an order of the Minister for Economic and Financial Affairs, adopted pursuant to advice from the Central Bank of West African States, so as to reach on September 30, 1969 the rate of 8 per cent fixed in Article 1 of this Decree.

**Art. 5.** The reserve funds which banks and financial establishments are required to set up in pursuance of Article 21 of Law No. 65-252 of August 4, 1965 [3] shall be augmented by taking 4 per cent from the combined charges and commission charges collected in the course of the year.

**Art. 6.** Special instructions shall set forth the terms for computing the ratios provided for in the articles hereinabove as well as the terms for providing advances in blocked accounts.

**Art. 7.** This Decree shall be published in the *Journal officiel* of the Republic of Ivory Coast.

*[The signatory clause is omitted.]*

---

[3] Article 21 of Law No. 65-252 of August 4, 1965 states:

"Banks and financial establishments shall be required to set up a reserve fund supplied by a percentage of all premiums and charges collected during the course of the year. This percentage shall be fixed by decree."

It should be noted that Article 75 of Law No. 75-549 of August 5, 1975 provides that all legal provisions in conflict with that law and particularly those of Law No. 65-252 are rescinded.

# Order No. 2976 [1]

## Raising from 5 per cent to at least 6 per cent the share of own resources in the minimum capital of commercial banks and deposit banks as defined by Article 3 of Decree No. 66-167 of April 26, 1966

[October 3, 1967]

The Minister for Economic and Financial Affairs,

Having regard for Law No. 65-252 of August 4, 1965, regulating credit and organizing the banking profession and related professions;

---

[1] The order was signed at Abidjan on October 3, 1967 and was published in the *Journal officiel,* October 12, 1967.

Having regard to Decree No. 66-167 of April 26, 1966, fixing the minimum amount of capital for banks and financial establishments and the terms for setting up reserve funds, and especially to its Article 4;
Having regard to Decree No. 66-45 of March 8, 1966 determining the powers of the Minister for Economic and Financial Affairs,

ORDERS:

Art. 1. According to the provisions of Article 1 of Decree No. 66-167 of April 26, 1966, commercial and deposit banks established in the territory of the Republic of Ivory Coast shall be required during the fiscal year 1967/68, and at all times, to furnish proof of having a capital the amount of which, without being allowed to be less than CFAF 300 million, must be equal to or greater than 8 per cent of the risks shown in their balance sheet or outside the balance sheet on September 30, 1967.

Art. 2. However, the ratio provided for in Article 1, applied to the balance sheets of the commercial and deposit banks, made up to September 30, 1967, may not exceed 6 per cent, provided that advances on blocked accounts of the partners or external offices being added to the capital, as defined in Article 3 of Decree No. 66-167 of April 26, 1966, permanently establish at 8 per cent the ratio prescribed in Article 1.

Art. 3. This Order shall be published in the *Journal officiel* of the Republic of Ivory Coast.

*[The signatory clause is omitted.]*

## Decree No. 66-168 [1]

Regulating the opening and closing of banks and financial establishments in the territory of the Republic of Ivory Coast and the opening and closing of their offices and counters

---

[1] The decree was signed at Abidjan on April 26, 1966 and was published in the *Journal officiel*, May 19, 1966.

[April 26, 1966]

The President of the Republic,

Having regard to Law No. 65-252 of August 4, 1965, regulating credit and organizing the banking and related professions;

Having regard to Decree No. 66-45 of March 8, 1966, determining the functions and powers of the Minister in charge of Economic and Financial Affairs;

The Council of Ministers having been heard,

DECREES:

**Art. 1.** The banks and financial establishments defined in Articles 1 and 7 of Law No. 65-252 of August 4, 1965 [2] and which wish to do business in the territory of the Republic must apply for authorization to the Minister for Economic and Financial Affairs. This application must be accompanied by the following documents:

*(a)* charter of the bank or financial establishment;
*(b)* list of members of the governing board and of the directors;
*(c)* list of the principal shareholders;
*(d)* nationality of the capital pledged;
*(e)* receipt for an application for registration on the Commercial Register.

**Art. 2.** The Minister for Economic and Financial Affairs is made responsible for arranging for examination of these applications, obtaining the opinion of the Commission for Control of Banks and Financial Establishments, the Central Bank of West African States, and the Professional Association of Banks.

---

[2] Articles 1 and 7 of Law No. 65-252 of August 4, 1965 state:

"*Art. 1.* As banks, pursuant to the terms of this law, shall be considered only enterprises or establishments under public or private law that make it their regular business to receive from the public or from the Administration or from State establishments, in the form of deposits or otherwise, funds which they use either for their own account or for account of their customers in discount operations, in credit operations or in financial operations."

"*Art. 7.* Financial establishments shall be considered as enterprises regularly engaging in credit operations, regardless of the relevant term, in the form of advances with pledges or guarantees, participation, acceptance in pawn or for discount, includng real-property operations comprising credit operations in any form whatever."

It should be noted that Article 75 of Law No. 75-549 of August 5, 1975 provides that all legal provisions in conflict with that law and particularly those of Law No. 65-252 are rescinded.

**Art. 3.** Before making his decision, the Minister for Economic and Financial Affairs shall obtain the results of the inquiry set up by the Public Prosecutor, for which provision is made in Article 16, paragraph 9 of the above-mentioned law.[3]

**Art. 4.** In the event of a favorable decision the Minister for Economic and Financial Affairs shall give, by order, full instructions to the Central Bank of West African States, Abidjan Office, for assignment of a registration number on the list of banks or financial establishments, as such instructions are provided for in Article 11 and Article 15 of said law.[4]

**Art. 5.** Striking-off from the list of banks may be ordered by the Minister for Economic and Financial Affairs either at the request of the institution concerned, or on the opinion of the National Credit Council, or at the request of the Commission for the Control of Banks and Financial Establishments.

**Art. 6.** Banks and financial establishments authorized to do business in the territory of the Republic of Ivory Coast may not open, reopen, cede, or transfer a permanent, periodic, or seasonal office or counter without prior authorization from the Minister for Economic and Financial Affairs.

The Minister for Economic and Financial Affairs is made responsible for arranging the examination of these applications, obtaining the opinion of the Commission for the Control of Banks and Financial Establish-

---

[3] Article 16, paragraph 9 of Law No. 65-252 of August 4, 1965 states:

"The Public Prosecutor of the Republic shall immediately request the court record or any equivalent documents of Ivorian or foreign persons referred to in this Article."

It should be noted that Article 75 of Law No. 75-549 of August 5, 1975 provides that all legal provisions in conflict with that law and particularly those of Law No. 65-252 are rescinded.

[4] Articles 11 and 15 of Law No. 65-252 of August 4, 1965 state:

"*Art. 11.* No enterprise or establishment considered as a bank pursuant to the provisions of Article 1 hereinabove may carry on its business without having previously been authorized in pursuance of the conditions laid down by decree and registered on the list of banks. Applications for opening additional offices shall be subject to the same formalities."

"*Art. 15.* No enterprise may, without having previously been registered in the list of financial establishments, carry on the activities defined in Article 7.

"The rules for and procedures of registration or cancellation shall be the same as those defined for banks."

It should be noted that Article 75 of Law No. 75-549 of August 5, 1975 provides that all legal provisions in conflict with that law and particularly those of Law No. 65-252 are rescinded.

ments, the Central Bank of West African States, and the Professional Association of Banks.

**Art. 7.** The closing of any office or counter formerly opened in due form must, before any commencement of execution, be brought to the notice of the Commission for the Control of Banks and Financial Establishments, which shall inform the Minister for Economic and Financial Affairs of the matter. Without authorization from the minister, the operations of an office or counter may not be discontinued until three months after announcement of the intention to close it.

**Art. 8.** A bank or financial establishment shall be regarded as having an office or counter in a given location if, in that location, it carries out operations with its customers in premises accessible to the public, by means of staff whom it remunerates.

An office or counter is regarded as permanent if its access is open to the public more than twice a week, however long the daily opening may be.

An office or counter is regarded as periodic if its access is open not more than two days a week, however long the daily opening may be.

An office or counter is regarded as seasonal if its access is open to the public for a single annual period of less than four consecutive months.

The prior authorization required under Article 1 above is also necessary for changing the classification of an office or counter.

**Art. 9.** The assignment, transfer, or merger of banks and financial establishments or their offices, and also any transfer of a substantial portion of their assets, is also subject to prior authorization from the Minister for Economic and Financial Affairs.

**Art. 10.** This decree shall be published in the *Journal officiel* of the Republic of Ivory Coast.

*{The signatory clause is omitted.}*

# Decree No. 66-169[1]

Organizing the legal prosecution of infractions of the banking regulations

[April 26, 1966]

The President of the Republic,

Having regard to Law No. 65-252 of August 4, 1965, regulating credit and organizing the banking and related professions, particularly its Article 33;

Having regard to Decree No. 66-45 of March 8, 1966, determining the functions and powers of the Minister in charge of Economic and Financial Affairs;

The Council of Ministers having been heard,

DECREES:

Art. 1. Legal action against the infractions referred to in Articles 29 to 32 of Law No. 65-252 of August 4, 1965[2] may be brought only on a complaint by the Minister for Economic and Financial Affairs or one of his representatives empowered for this purpose.

---

[1] The decree was signed at Abidjan on April 26, 1966 and was published in the *Journal officiel,* May 19, 1966.

[2] Articles 29 to 32 of Law No. 65-252 of August 4, 1965 state:

"*Art. 29.* All members of the various advisory and control bodies that are in existence or may be created with a view to intervening, directly or indirectly, as regards organization, banking regulations, and credit management and persons called upon even exceptionally to perform any relevant work shall be strictly required to maintain professional secrecy in respect of all matters they have to deal with, for any reason whatever, subject to the penalties provided for by Article 378 of the Penal Code.

"*Art. 30.* Violations of this law, especially of the provisions of Article 2, shall make any persons committing them liable to disciplinary sanction, imposed by the Commission for Control of Banks and Financial Establishments; if warranted, to punitive sanction pronounced by the criminal courts pursuant to the terms laid down in Articles 31 to 33 hereinafter.

"*Art. 31.* Any person who, acting either for his own account without being registered in the List of Banks or the List of Financial Establishments or for account of a company not recorded in these same lists, engages in the activities specified in Articles 1 and 7 of this law or makes use of the terms 'banks' or 'banker,' in the conditions provided for in Article 11 above, shall be liable to imprisonment for from one month to two years and to a fine of from CFAF 500,000 to CFAF 5,000,000 or to only one of these two penalties.

"*Art. 32.* Anyone who, acting as a representative of a bank, knowingly gives

Art. 2. If infractions referred to in the law mentioned in the foregoing article are prejudicial to credit or the currency, the Minister for Economic and Financial Affairs may institute a civil action on behalf of the State in conjunction with the penal action brought against the persons committing those infractions.

Art. 3. The Minister for Economic and Financial Affairs and the Minister of Justice are responsible for implementation of this decree, which shall be published in the *Journal officiel* of the Republic of Ivory Coast.

*[The signatory clause is omitted.]*

---

inaccurate information to the Central Bank or to the Control Commission shall be liable to a fine of from CFAF 500,000 to CFAF 2,500,000.

"In case the same violation is repeated, the offender shall be punished by a fine of from CFAF 1,000,000 to CFAF 5,000,000 and with imprisonment of from one to six months, or by only one of these two penalties."

It should be noted that Article 75 of Law No. 75-549 of August 5, 1975 provides that all legal provisions in conflict with that law and particularly those of Law No. 65-252 are rescinded.

## Law No. 62-54[1]

### Establishing a National Investment Fund[2]

[February 12, 1962]

The National Assembly has adopted,
The President of the Republic promulgates the following law:

Art. 1. A National Investment Fund, financed by an additional levy on direct taxes in the manner described below, is hereby established.

---

[1] The law was signed at Abidjan on February 12, 1962. It was amended by Art. 8 of Law No. 65-424 of December 20, 1965, published in *Journal officiel,* 1966, p. 1.

[2] Fonds National d'Investissement.

**Art. 2.** This levy is payable by those subject to:

taxes on industrial and commercial profits, profits from farming, and profits from noncommercial occupations, at the rate of 10 per cent of realized profits;

the real estate tax on buildings, at the rate of 10 per cent of net income.

The exemptions provided for in Law No. 59-134 of September 3, 1959 do not apply to the aforementioned levy.

Levies, which shall be rounded down to the next lower thousand-franc figure, shall not be collected if they amount to 10,000 francs or less.

Buildings or parts of buildings used exclusively as residences and inhabited mainly by their owners shall not be subject to the additional real estate tax levy.

**Art. 3.** In exchange for their payments, payers shall receive shares in the Fund's capital in an amount equal to their payments.

These shares may be redeemed when their holders submit evidence of having invested an amount equal to at least double the value of their shares in projects recognized as useful to economic, cultural, or social development.

**Art. 4.** The National Investment Fund shall possess legal personality and financial autonomy. It shall be managed by a Board of Directors and a Management Committee.

Of the amounts paid into the Fund:

a maximum of 10 per cent shall be used for studies and research required for the establishment of economic, cultural, and social development programs;

the remaining 90 per cent shall be used for investment operations and share redemption.

**Art. 5.** Decrees adopted by the Council of Ministers shall set forth the procedures by which this law shall be implemented, specifically with respect to:

the membership of the Board of Directors and the Management Committee;

the timetable of the share redemption procedure;

the nature and type of investments required for share redemption, the procedure for approving these investments, and, pursuant to Art. 3 above, the ratio between the amount redeemed and the amount of the approved investments.

**Art. 6.** This law shall be published in the *Journal officiel* of the Republic of Ivory Coast and executed as a law of the State.

*[The signatory clause is omitted.]*

# Decree No. 62-113

## Setting forth the membership and functions of the administrative and management bodies of the National Investment Fund

[April 18, 1962]

The President of the Republic,

On the basis of the report of the Minister of Finance, Economic Affairs, and Planning;

In light of Law No. 62-54 of February 12, 1962 creating a National Investment Fund;

Having heard the Council of Ministers,

DECREES:

Art. 1. The Board of Directors of the National Investment Fund shall consist of:

the Minister of Finance, Economic Affairs, and Planning (chairman);

a representative of the Minister of the Interior;

a representative of the Minister of Defense;

a representative of the Minister of Public Works, Transportation, and Post and Telecommunications;

a representative of the Minister of Agriculture and Cooperation;

a representative of the Minister of Livestock Production;

a representative of the Minister of Labor and Social Affairs;

a representative of the Minister of Construction and Town Planning;

five representatives of the contributors to the Fund, selected by their trade associations and approved by the Minister of Finance, Economic Affairs, and Planning;

three prominent persons selected by the Minister of Finance, Economic Affairs, and Planning on the basis of their positions or competence in the financial, economic, cultural, or social field.

The Board of Directors shall be assisted by a Secretary General of the National Investment Fund, appointed by the Management Committee, who attends meetings in an advisory capacity and examines investment proposals.

**Art. 2.** The Board of Directors shall define the general policies of the Fund and offer suggestions concerning:

the shares in the Fund's capital referred to in Article 2 of the Law of February 12, 1962;

the timetable and procedure of share redemption;

the nature and type of investments required for share redemption;

the procedure for approving these investments;

the ratio, pursuant to Article 3 of the aforementioned law, between the amount redeemed and the amount of approved investments.

**Art. 3.** The Management Committee of the National Investment Fund shall consist of:

the Minister of Finance, Economic Affairs, and Planning (chairman);

six members of the Board of Directors, three of whom shall be representatives of the Ministers referred to in Article 1 above;

two representatives of contributors to the Fund;

one prominent person.

The Secretary General shall also attend meetings of the Management Committee in an advisory capacity.

**Art. 4.** The Minister of Finance, Economic Affairs, and Planning shall be responsible for execution of this decree, which shall be published in the *Journal officiel.*

*{The signatory clause is omitted.}*

# Decree No. 62-134

Setting forth rules for implementing Law No. 62-54 of February 12, 1962 creating a National Investment Fund

[April 28, 1962]

The President of the Republic,

On the basis of the report of the Minister of Finance, Economic Affairs, and Planning;

In light of Law No. 62-54 of February 12, 1962 creating a National Investment Fund, and of Decree No. 62-113 of April 18, 1962 setting forth the membership and functions of the Board of Directors and Management Committee of the Fund;

In light of the minutes of the meeting of the Board of Directors of April 24, 1961;

Having heard the Council of Ministers,

DECREES:

**Art. 1.** The additional levies provided for in Article 2 of the law referred to above, No. 62-54 of February 12, 1962, shall be calculated as follows:

With respect to the profits of those subject to taxes on industrial and commercial profits, profits from farming, and profits from noncommercial occupations: on the taxable profits on which calculation of these taxes is based, notwithstanding the exemptions granted by current laws, especially Law No. 59-134 of September 3, 1959, and before any deductions, especially those provided for in Article 84 of the General Tax Code;

With respect to those subject to the real estate tax on buildings: on net income, notwithstanding the exemptions granted by Law No. 59-134 of September 3, 1959 or by the General Tax Code, especially in Article 4.

**Art. 2.** Investments in the normal development of an existing enterprise, especially those entailing the deduction from profits provided for in Article 84 of the General Tax Code, shall not satisfy the requirements for the redemption referred to in Article 3, second paragraph, of the aforementioned Law No. 62-54 of February 12, 1962.

**Art. 3.** The shares referred to in that Article 3, first paragraph, which shall be given to levy-payers in exchange for their payments and in an amount equal to those payments, shall be in the form of registered stock. They shall not be assignable or transferable, except as may be stipulated in the future by order of the Minister of Finance, Economic Affairs, and Planning after hearing the opinion of the Board of Directors of the National Investment Fund.

There shall be Series A shares and Series B shares. Series A certificates shall be issued in exchange for payments by those subject to taxes on industrial and commercial profits, profits from farming, and profits from noncommercial occupations. Series B certificates shall be issued in exchange for payments made by those subject to the real estate tax on buildings.

Series A certificates may be used for all investment categories referred to in Article 4 below; Series B certificates may be used only for Categories II and III investments.[1]

**Art. 4.** Investments satisfying the requirements for redemption of the shares in the capital of the Fund shall be classified in three categories:

*Category I:* Investments in commercial, industrial, or agricultural enterprises belonging to shareholders; subscriptions to increases in the capital of those enterprises; participation in the creation of new enterprises of the same type;

*Category II:* Investments in housing construction;

*Category III:* Subscription of bonds in approved national investment companies.

Categories I and II investments must be approved in advance by the Management Committee. Category III investments may be made on the basis of a simple declaration, observing the conditions set forth in Articles 5 and 6 below.

**Art. 5.** Investment proposals for Categories I and II investments must be submitted within 15 months.

Subscription of bonds issued by national investment companies (Category III) must take place within 12 months.

---

[1] The following is provided in 108 Finance, Economic Affairs, and Planning of January 24, 1963:

"In implementation of the provisions of Art. 3 of Decree No. 62-134 of April 28, 1962:

"*(a)* On the death of a contributor, the initial stock certificate may be replaced by certificates of equal total value issued in the names of the heirs;

"*(b)* In case of fund transfers or company mergers, the transferor's certificate may be transferred to the acquirer's name;

"*(c)* In case of liquidation of a company, the certificate held by the company may be replaced by certificates issued in the name of each partner in proportion to their respective interests, as indicated by the liquidation account."

Stock certificates not used within two years shall automatically be used to subscribe long-term government loans on terms to be set forth by decree, taking account of the provisions of the laws authorizing such loans.

**Art. 6.** The ratio between the amount invested and the amount of shares redeemed shall be set as follows:

*Category I.* Three times the face value of the certificate, with individual deviations of up to one point;

*Category II.* Four times the face value of the certificate, with individual deviations of up to one point;

*Category III.* Twice the face value of the certificate.

The deviations referred to above may be granted only by the Board of Directors.

Categories I and II investment projects may not be in amounts of less than CFAF 15,000,000.

**Art. 7.** In connection with Categories I and II investments, shareholders may form a group, on the terms set forth in Article 4 above, to submit a joint project proposal. They must support their application with documents:

identifying the certificates they hold and the value of the individual investments they are committed to making;

giving a complete, detailed subscription [2] of the project;

giving a precise estimate of planned expenditures and, if appropriate, showing the relevant plans;

indicating the time required for completion, which shall not exceed two years except where specifically authorized;

indicating the number and category of new jobs to be created;

containing a provisional balance sheet and a provisional trading account for the first three years of the operation.

A decision on approval must be handed down within three months; thereafter, if notification of approval has not been given, approval shall be assumed.

**Art. 8.** Share redemption for approved projects or for subscription of bonds issued by national investment companies, in accordance with the ratios specified in Article 6 above, shall be effected upon presentation to the Secretary General of the Fund of documents attesting to payment of the expenditures.

---

[2] While the original French word is "*souscription,*" the editor queries whether this should be understood as "description" in English.

Art. 9. The Minister of Finance, Economic Affairs, and Planning shall be responsible for execution of this decree, which shall be published in the *Journal officiel.*

*{The signatory clause is omitted.}*

## Law No. 68-346 [1]

### Creating a Guarantee Fund for Credits to Ivorian Enterprises [2]

[July 29, 1968]

The National Assembly has adopted,
The President of the Republic promulgates the law the wording of which follows:

Art. 1. There is created a Guarantee Fund for Credits to Ivorian Enterprises in the form of a public establishment endowed with the status of a juridical person and with financial autonomy.

Art. 2. The purpose of the Fund is to promote Ivorian enterprise by guaranteeing short-, medium-, and long-term bank credits needed for development thereof.

Art. 3. The Fund shall derive from State budget appropriations such subsidies and grants as may be accorded to it, income from its investments and proceeds from the collection of its claims.

Art. 4. Operations of the Fund shall be guaranteed by the State.

Art. 5. The organization and the terms of operation and intervention

[1] The law was signed at Abidjan on July 29, 1968 and was published in the *Journal officiel* on August 8, 1968.
[2] Fonds de Garantie des Crédits aux Entreprises Ivoiriennes.

of the Fund shall be the subject of a decree adopted by the Council of Ministers.

**Art. 6.** This law shall be executed as a law of the State and shall be published in the *Journal officiel* of the Republic of Ivory Coast.

*[The signatory clause is omitted.]*

## Decree No. 68-508 [1]

Providing for the organization of the Guarantee Fund for Credits to Ivorian Enterprises

[October 26, 1968]

The President of the Republic,

Pursuant to the report of the Minister of Economic and Financial Affairs,

Having regard to Law No. 68-346 of July 29, 1968, creating the Guarantee Fund for Credits to Ivorian Enterprises, and especially to Article 5 thereof,

Having heard the Council of Ministers,

DECREES:

**Art. 1.** The purpose of this Decree is to define the organization, the terms of intervention, and the operating conditions of the Guarantee Fund for Credits to Ivorian Enterprises, a public establishment endowed with the status of a juridical person and with financial autonomy, created by Law No. 68-346 of July 29, 1968.

**Art. 2.** The Fund is designed to guarantee credits granted by the banking establishments to Ivorian nationals or to Ivorian companies the

[1] The decree was signed at Abidjan on October 26, 1968 and was published in the *Journal officiel,* on November 21, 1968, amended by Decree No. 69-206 of May 22, 1969, published in the *Journal officiel* on June 5, 1969.

capital of which is held to the extent of more than 50 per cent by Ivorian nationals. It also intervenes by giving a guarantee for signed commitments made by banking establishments in favor of Ivorian enterprises.

Borrowers must show a sound financial position. When applying for medium-term credits, they must finance out of their own resources a portion of the planned investments, providing that such self-financed portion may not in any event be less than 10 per cent.

**Art. 3.** The resources of the Fund shall be deposited with the Autonomous Amortization Fund; such deposits shall bear interest.

**Art. 4.** Interventions by the Fund shall be decided by a Management Committee composed of:

a representative of the Minister of Economic and Financial Affairs,
a representative of the Minister of Planning,
a representative of the National Assembly,
a representative of the Economic and Social Council,
the Director of Public Accounting and of the Treasury,
the Director of the Central Bank of West African States,
the Director of the Autonomous Amortization Fund,
the Director of the National Office for the Promotion of Ivorian Enterprise,
a person designated by the Minister of Economic and Financial Affairs by reason of his competence in economic and financial matters.

The Chairman of the Management Committee shall be elected by the latter pursuant to a proposal by the Minister of Economic and Financial Affairs.

The Management Committee shall meet upon being convened by its Chairman as often as required by the operations of the Fund.

The Management Committee shall constitute a quorum when two thirds of its members are present. If a member is absent or unable to attend to his duties, he may arrange to be represented by a person from the agency or organization that designated him.

Only the Management Committee shall be qualified to grant the Fund guarantee for operations that are submitted to it.

The Management Committee shall, moreover, decide all matters concerning the Fund, especially:

the annual estimates of receipts and expenditures
the accounts at the end of the fiscal year.

**Art. 5.** The administrative and accounting part of the Fund's activity shall be entrusted to a Secretary General designated by the Minister of Economic and Financial Affairs.

**Art. 6.** The Secretary General shall be responsible for:

preparing the draft operating budget and for submitting it to the Management Committee,

presenting to the Management Committee, within at most five months following the end of each fiscal year ended on September 30, the annual balance sheet and for preparing a report on the activities of the Fund in the course of such fiscal year,

examining the records presented to him by lending bankers and for submitting them to the Management Committee together with a memorandum of presentation,

ensuring and supervising the due execution of the decisions of the Management Committee,

following at the accounting level the development of risks assumed by the Fund,

representing the Fund vis-à-vis third parties and, especially, banks.

**Art. 7.** Control of the Fund's operations shall be ensured by a State Comptroller designated by the Minister of Economic and Financial Affairs.

The State Comptroller may demand to be given discovery of any documents needed to accomplish his mission.

The State Comptroller shall report to the Minister of Economic and Financial Affairs on the execution of his assignment within not more than five months following the end of each fiscal year.

The Fund's accounts shall become definitive only after having been approved by the Minister of Economic and Financial Affairs.

**Art. 8.** The combined guarantees granted by the Fund may not exceed 5 times the amount of its available resources. In order to determine this ceiling, the sum total of the guarantees given minus amortization payments made shall be taken into consideration.

**Art. 9.** The Fund's guarantee, whether given as a direct guarantee or as a counterguarantee for commitments assumed by signature, may not exceed 80 per cent of the amount of loans granted and related interest accruals. During the entire duration of the credits, this guaranteed part shall proportionately remain the same and shall be the subject of amortization payments identical with those of the part not covered by the guarantee.

**Art. 10.** Projects submitted to the Management Committee for examination must be supported by technical and financial studies made, if necessary, by specialized agencies, such as the National Office for the Promotion of Ivorian Enterprise. These specialized agencies may also carry out any missions of control and supervision that might prove necessary after the credits have been granted.

Implementation of credits shall be subject to the borrowers expressly agreeing to this control.

**Art. 11.** The lending bankers must make sure that credits are implemented according to the conditions laid down by the Management Committee.

**Art. 12.** Borrowers must formally undertake to have only one bank account in one local commercial bank and to cause all operations relating to their activities to be channeled through that account.

**Art. 13.** The Fund's guarantee may be used only after recourse to the usual legal channels and realization of other guarantees that might be applicable to the credits. The lending banker may, however, succeed in having the Fund's guarantee used six months after verification of default of the debtor.

**Art. 14.** Following realization on the guarantee, the Fund shall, to the extent due, be subrogated to all the rights of the lending banker.

**Art. 15.** Should the Fund be dissolved, its liquid resources shall be transferred back to the Treasury.

**Art. 16.** The Minister of Economic and Financial Affairs shall be charged with the implementation of this Decree, which shall be published in the *Journal officiel* of the Republic of Ivory Coast.

*[The signatory clause is omitted.]*

# 15 AE PL 1 [1]

## Order establishing the public company known as the Credit Bank of Ivory Coast [2]

The Minister of French Overseas Departments and Territories,

Having regard to the law of April 30, 1946 on the establishment, financing, and implementation of the services and development plans in the territories under the jurisdiction of the Minister of French Overseas Departments and Territories, and particularly to Article 2 thereof;

Having regard to Decree No. 46-2356 of October 24, 1946, determining the terms under which the French Central Overseas Fund [3] shall carry out the operations authorized by the law of April 30, 1946;

Having regard to the decree of December 20, 1951, organizing the supervision of public and semipublic enterprises set up pursuant to the law of April 30, 1946;

Having regard to the deliberation on November 22, 1954, of the Territorial Assembly of Ivory Coast;

Having regard to the resolution adopted on January 4, 1955 by the management committee of FIDES; [4]

Having regard to the resolution adopted on January 6, 1955 by the supervisory council of the French Central Overseas Fund,

ORDERS:

**Art. 1.** A public company which shall be a multipurpose credit institution known as the Credit Bank of Ivory Coast and governed by the following charter is hereby established:

## Charter of the Credit Bank of Ivory Coast [5]

*Art. 1.* A company to be governed by this charter is hereby established under the name of the Credit Bank of Ivory Coast. Said company

---

[1] Executed in Paris on February 4, 1955. Promulgated by General Order No. 1502 S.ET of March 2, 1955; published in *Journal officiel* No. 8 of April 1, 1955.

[2] Crédit de la Côte d'Ivoire.

[3] Caisse Centrale de la France d'Outre-Mer.

[4] Fonds d'Investissement pour le Développement Economique et Social.

[5] This version of the Charter was registered in Abidjan on July 8, 1963 and subsequently modified and approved by the Board of Directors on April 4, 1968 and on December 22, 1970. It replaces the original Charter of 1955.

shall be a financially autonomous juridical person with the status of a business and shall be listed in the Ivory Coast Commercial Register.

*Art. 2.* The Credit Bank of Ivory Coast is authorized to provide technical or financial assistance for any project promoting the economic and social development of Ivory Coast.

In particular, it is authorized to:

*(a)* Carry out on its own authority any financially sound operation and which contributes to:

the development of trade, industry and fisheries;

the improvement of housing conditions and family living standards;

providing the supplies and equipment used by members of the liberal professions.

To this end, the Credit Bank may:

mobilize domestic resources either in the form of deposits or by borrowing;

borrow abroad;

lend, discount, and extend guarantees;

take up equity capital in private companies, regional development corporations, supply and equipment companies or any other entity;

engage in construction activities for rental or lease-purchase purposes.

*(b)* Provide the assistance of its technical organization to the Republic of Ivory Coast or its agencies, under terms mutually agreed upon by the parties, for purposes of examining any problem or proposal having an economic or financial impact as well as to study, conduct, and provide accounting services for operations which, regardless of whether they fall into the categories referred to in paragraph *(a)* above, are to be carried out by the Credit Bank of Ivory Coast using resources other than its own and for which it is not at risk.

The agreements under which the Credit Bank of Ivory Coast is entrusted with management of such resources may specify, as appropriate, special authorization conditions applicable to the operations financed therewith. Said agreements may, inter alia, provide for a management committee whose membership differs from that of the Board of Directors. Such agreements shall have the prior approval of the Board of Directors.

*Art. 3.* The ceilings applicable to amounts lent to individual borrowers, and to the overall volume and term of the operations of the Credit

Bank of Ivory Coast, as well as the rules relating to the nature and origin of the deposits which the Credit Bank is authorized to receive, shall be specified in the internal by-laws of the Credit Bank, approved by a three-fourths majority of the Board of Directors.

*Art. 4.* The Credit Bank of Ivory Coast shall conduct its business in accordance with the laws and practices governing private enterprises. With respect to advertising, it shall observe the same formalities as joint-stock companies.

*Art. 5.* The head office of the Credit Bank of Ivory Coast shall be located in Abidjan at a site to be selected by the Board of Directors. It may be transferred to any other location in Ivory Coast by simple decision of the Board of Directors.

*Art. 6.* Corporate capital shall be fixed at CFAF 4.8 billion, subscribed by:

the Republic of Ivory Coast: CFAF 2.8 billion;
the Caisse Centrale de Coopération Economique: CFAF 1.6 billion;
the Central Bank of West African States: CFAF 400 million.

Said capital may be increased by a three fourths majority decision of the Board of Directors.

*Art. 7.* The Credit Bank of Ivory Coast shall be administered by a Board of Directors made up of 12 members. Shareholders shall be represented on the Board in proportion to their participation in the capital and may organize themselves in order to exercise this right. Each shareholder or group of shareholders shall thus have one seat on the Board for every 1/12 of the capital it holds. Seats which cannot be allocated in accordance with this procedure shall go to those shareholders or groups thereof with the largest unrepresented balances.

Directors' terms of office shall end upon their resignation or death, and upon notification sent to the company by the appointing authority or agency.

The office of the Director shall be unremunerated. However, the Chairman of the Board may receive an administrative allowance.

*Art. 8.* The Chairman of the Board of Directors shall be appointed by the Board from among its members by a three-fourths majority. If the voting is tied, the Chairman shall have the casting vote. In his absence, he shall be replaced by the Vice-Chairman, the representative of the Caisse Centrale de Coopération Economique.

The functions of Chairman of the Credit Bank of Ivory Coast shall be inconsistent with the holding of any political office.

*Art. 9.* Board decisions shall be valid if at least six of its members are in attendance or are represented. Any Director may be represented by another Director for a particular meeting. A Director may repesent no more than one of his colleagues. Board decisions shall be reached by simple majority vote except as otherwise provided by this Charter or by the internal by-laws.

The Board shall meet when convened by its Chairman, who may delegate his authority to the General Manager. It shall also meet at the request of any five of its members.

*Art. 10.* The Board of Directors is vested with the broadest possible powers with respect to taking action on behalf of the company and authorizing any activities relating to its purpose.

In particular, its powers include those listed below for reference purposes; the list is nonrestrictive except insofar as this Charter expressly delimits their terms or extent. The Board shall:

appoint the Chairman and General Manager,

conclude all purchases, sales and rentals of real property,

contract all loans with or without mortgage or lien on the property of the Credit Bank of Ivory Coast, approve all arbitration agreements, acceptances of judgments, waivers of legal action, cancellations of distraint order registrations, or objection procedures before or after payment; it shall initiate and pursue any and all legal actions or proceedings in any jurisdiction, either as defendant or plaintiff; it shall carry out all purchases, conveyances and asset transfers; and it shall decide, upon a proposal by the General Manager, which loans to extend and may not delegate this power except under the conditions and in the amounts set forth in the internal by-laws.

*Art. 11.* Management of the company shall be provided by and under the responsibility of the General Manager, who shall be appointed by the Board of Directors by a three-fourths majority.

The post of General Manager shall be inconsistent with the holding of any political office. The General Manager may not engage in any business or have any interest in a commercial enterprise. He shall represent the company vis-à-vis third parties. He shall appoint and dismiss staff. He may delegate his power for a specific purpose and toward a given objective.

*Art. 12.* All acts and operations of the company decided upon by the Board of Directors, as well as withdrawals of funds or securities, payment orders against bankers, debtors, or depositors and subscription endorsements, acceptance or receipt of commercial paper, must, in order for the company to be committed, be signed by the General Manager or his authorized delegate.

*Art. 13.* The exclusionary clauses and clauses relating to conflicts of interest set forth by the laws and decrees in force with respect to exercising the functions of Chairman, Director, General Manager, or Auditor in joint-stock companies shall be applicable to the individuals holding the corresponding positions at the Credit Bank of Ivory Coast.

*Art. 14.* No agreement between the Credit Bank of Ivory Coast and its General Manager, whether concluded directly or indirectly, shall be valid if it has not previously been authorized by the Board of Directors.

The same shall hold true for agreements between the Credit Bank and any enterprise of which the General Manager of the Credit Bank or any of the Directors is an owner, an associate by name or by the holding of shares, director, or general manager.

*Art. 15.* The source of the resources to be used in the company's own operations shall be:

*(a)* its capital;
*(b)* its private or public deposits;
*(c)* grants and advances, whether of domestic or foreign origin, extended in order to promote the development of credit in Ivory Coast;
*(d)* credits extended by the Central Bank of West African States.

*Art. 16.* The accounting operations of the Credit Bank of Ivory Coast shall be carried out and written up in accordance with customary practice in industrial and commercial enterprises.

The fiscal year shall begin on October 1 and end on September 30 of each year.

At the end of each fiscal year, the General Manager shall draw up an annual report and prepare a balance sheet and profit and loss account for approval by the Board. The latter shall then determine the amount of net profits by subtracting the following from the proceeds:

*(a)* all overhead and welfare expenditure, including inter alia interest and amortization on all loans, remuneration of management and staff, and all administrative and control costs;

(*b*) all amounts earmarked for various amortization payments and provisions for possible amortization or commercial risks which the Board deems it appropriate to establish for the property and securities of the Credit Bank of Ivory Coast.

Net profit shall be earmarked for the accumulation of reserves.

*Art. 17.* The Credit Bank of Ivory Coast shall have two auditors appointed by the Board of Directors by a three-fourths majority upon a proposal made severally or by the two largest shareholders together.

The auditors shall perform their duties as prescribed by law.

Their report shall be addressed to the Board of Directors.

*Art. 18.* The accounts of the Credit Bank shall not be deemed final until they have been approved by a three-fourths majority of the Board of Directors.

*Art. 19.* In the event of liquidation of the Credit Bank, assets shall be realized and liabilities paid off in accordance with the law applicable to commercial companies.

*Art. 20.* This Charter may be amended only in the manner in which it was approved.

Art. 2. Officials at present in service who may be made available to the company shall be placed on secondment as prescribed by the regulations in effect. Their emoluments shall be fixed by the Board of Directors under the terms provided for by the regulations in effect.

Art. 3. This order shall be published in the *Journal officiel* of the French Republic and the *Journal officiel* of the A.O.F., and included in the *Bulletin officiel* of the Ministry of French Overseas Departments and Territories.

*{The signatory clause is omitted.}*

# Decree No. 75-445[1]

Establishing a corporation called National Bank for Savings and Credit[2] and laying down rules for the management and control of said corporation

[June 23, 1975]

The President of the Republic,

Pursuant to the report of the Minister of Economy and Finance,

Having regard to Law No. 65-252 of August 4, 1965, regulating credit and organizing the banking profession and related professions,

Having regard to Law No. 70-633 of November 5, 1970, laying down the rules governing companies in which the Government holds equity,

Having regard to Law No. 70-486 of August 3, 1970, establishing the list of high-level government positions,

Having regard to Decree No. 66-48 of March 8, 1966, as amended by Decree No. 66-339 of September 5, 1966, determining the powers of the Minister in charge of Economic and Financial Affairs and organizing the Ministry,

Having regard to Decree No. 75-148 of March 11, 1975, organizing the supervision of companies in which the Government holds equity,

Having regard to Decree No. 75-149 of March 11, 1975, laying down the rules for management and control of companies in which the Government holds equity,

Having heard the Council of Ministers,

DECREES:

**Art. 1.** There is hereby created under the name of National Bank for Savings and Credit (BNEC), a public corporation governed by the laws and regulations pertaining to companies in which the Government holds equity, the texts regulating the banking profession and related professions, the texts governing joint-stock companies in Ivory Coast, and the by-laws annexed hereto.

**Art. 2.** The BNEC shall be under the supervision of an Interminis-
the Minister of Planning.
terial Committee made up of the Minister of Economy and Finance and

[1] The decree was signed at Abidjan on June 23, 1975.

[2] Banque Nationale pour l'Epargne et le Crédit (BNEC).

**Art. 3.** The purpose of the BNEC shall be:

1. To finance site development for the construction of low-cost housing;
2. To seek and set up the financing needed by governmental housing enterprises for carrying out low-cost housing projects that come within the objectives of the Plan and whose technical features meet the norms laid down in joint orders of the Minister of Economy and Finance and the Minister of Construction and Urban Development;
3. To collect and receive the savings deposits of natural or juridical persons with a view to facilitating access to real property, and to grant short-, medium-, and long-term loans for the construction, purchase, completion or remodeling of low-cost and medium-cost housing, and, more generally, to carry out all financial, banking, or commercial operations, concerning personal property or real estate, that directly or indirectly relate to the above purpose.

**Art. 4.** The capital shall be fixed at CFAF 1,000,000,000. The capital may be increased.

**Art. 5.** To achieve its purpose the BNEC may:

(*a*) Receive deposits from savers;
(*b*) Issue on any financial market, or contract, by negotiation, any loans after authorization by the Minister of Economy and Finance and the Select Committee referred to in Article 9.
(*c*) Receive tax revenue allocated.

**Art. 6.** Tax revenue allocated may be used only for site development, improvement, and consolidation of loans contracted by housing enterprises for the financing of low-cost housing.

**Art. 7.** The repayment of loans contracted by the BNEC shall be guaranteed by the public treasury.

Furthermore, the BNEC is empowered to pay interest on deposits entrusted to it at a rate slightly higher than that applied by commercial banks.

**Art. 8.** The BNEC shall be administered by a Board made up of at least 10 (ten) but not more than 12 (twelve) members.

It must include:

one representative of the National Assembly;
one representative of the Economic and Social Council;

two representatives of the Minister of Economy and Finance;
one representative of the Minister of Construction and Urban Development;
one representative of the Minister of Planning;
one representative of the Minister of Labor and Social Affairs;
one representative of the Agricultural Price Stabilization Fund;
one representative of the Central Bank of West African States;
one representative of the National Savings Bank.

The Directors shall be appointed by joint order of the Minister of Economy and Finance and the Minister of Planning. Upon the proposal of the Board, any person whose presence is deemed useful by reason of his qualifications may be appointed a Director.

**Art. 9.** A Select Committee shall be established, made up of the following Directors:

one representative of the Minister of Economy and Finance,
the representative of the Minister of Planning.

The task of the Committee is set out in Section IV of Decree No. 75-149 of March 11, 1975 laying down the rules for management and control of companies in which the Government holds equity, and in Article 13 of the by-laws.[3]

**Art. 10.** The BNEC shall be managed by a General Manager, appointed by decree on the basis of a report of the supervising Ministries.

**Art. 11.** In addition to the control exercised by the Select Committee, the BNEC shall be subject to the control of two auditors, chosen from the list of experts accredited by the Appellate Court and by the Equity Holdings Department of the Ministry of Economy and Finance.

**Art. 12.** The by-laws attached to this Decree are hereby approved.

**Art. 13.** The Minister of Economy and Finance and the Minister of Planning shall be responsible, each insofar as he is concerned, for the implementation of this Decree, which shall be published in the *Journal officiel* of the Republic of Ivory Coast.

*{The signatory clause is omitted.}*

[3] This decree and the by-laws are not published in this volume.

# Law No. 68-08[1]

## Establishing the National Bank for Agricultural Development[2]

[January 6, 1968]

**Art. 1.** With a view to promoting the agricultural development of Ivory Coast, a banking establishment of national scope, known as the National Bank for Agricultural Development and governed by the body of common laws applicable to joint-stock companies and the by-laws below, is hereby established.

**Art. 2.** The procedures to implement this law and the attached by-laws shall be established by decree.

**Art. 3.** Government supervision of the National Bank for Agricultural Development shall be exercised in conformity with the laws in force.

**Art. 4.** Any legislative or regulatory provisions inconsistent with the provisions of this law are hereby revoked.

---

[1] Published in the *Journal officiel,* 1968, p. 107. Amended by Decree No. 68-306.

[2] La Banque Nationale pour le Développement Agricole.

# By-Laws of the National Bank for Agricultural Development

**Art. 1.** The National Bank for Agricultural Development, a banking establishment serving the national interest, shall be governed by the body of common laws applicable to joint-stock companies, except as otherwise specified in these by-laws.

It shall also be subject to the provisions of the law regulating credit and organizing the banking profession and related professions.

### HEAD OFFICE

**Art. 2.** The head office of the National Bank for Agricultural Development shall be in Abidjan. It may be transferred to any other location by simple decision of the Board of Directors. The National Bank for Agricultural Development shall be authorized to open branches in accordance with the relevant provisions laid down by the banking regulations.

PURPOSE

**Art. 3.** Under the supervision of the competent administrative authority, the National Bank for Agricultural Development shall be empowered to lend its technical or financial support to any project promoting rural development in Ivory Coast, in particular, in the areas of agricultural, livestock or forest production, fisheries, or rural handicrafts.

To this end it may intervene either on its own behalf or on behalf of the Government or government agencies.

(*a*) *Operations on its own behalf*

It shall have the authority to carry out, on its own responsibility, any operations offering sufficient guarantees of financial soundness and, in particular:

to mobilize local resources, either in the form of demand or time deposits or by the issuance of short-, medium- or long-term loans;

to rediscount its credits and contract any loans required to fulfill its mission;

to lend at short, medium or long term, to discount and to provide guarantees;

to carry out, in general, any financial operations or operations with personal or real property which relate directly or indirectly to the social purpose referred to above.

(*b*) *Operations carried out on behalf of the Government or government agencies*

In particular, the Bank shall have the authority to lend its technical capability to the examination of any agricultural problem having financial implications, as well as to the study, execution and accounting of operations to be carried out using resources which do not belong to the Bank and which it does not use at its own risk. Specifically, it may receive on deposit and use earmarked funds of public origin under the terms and conditions laid down in agreements to be reached with the agencies concerned.

DURATION

**Art. 4.** Barring extensions or early dissolution, the duration of the National Bank for Agricultural Development shall be ninety-nine years from the date of its establishment.

CAPITAL

Art. 5. The initial capital shall be CFAF 700,000,000 subscribed by the Republic of Ivory Coast, by juridical persons under Ivorian public or private law, and, if appropriate, by non-Ivorian public or private agencies able to make a worthwhile contribution to the rural development of Ivory Coast.

Apportionment of the capital will be determined by decree; the same procedure will be used to approve capital increases, whether they come about through subscriptions from the original associates or from new participants.

RESOURCES

Art. 6. The resources intended for use in the corporation's own operations shall come from:

its capital;

annual appropriations to it made by legislation or regulation;

reserves and funds that it is required to set aside or that are called for by the Board of Directors;

grants, bequests, or gifts of any kind;

subsidies which may be granted to it by public authorities and income from funds managed by it;

the net proceeds from any liquidation of agricultural organizations decided on by the competent authorities;

loans it is authorized to float and domestic or international advances which may be granted to it;

proceeds from discounting or pledging its portfolio and securities;

funds entrusted to it on deposit;

proceeds from all of its operations.

Under terms and conditions to be laid down by decree, the grants or subsidies made to the corporation may be earmarked in whole or in part to the financing of short-, medium- and long-term credit operations, be they of individuals or of groups.

INTERVENTION ARRANGEMENTS

Art. 7. The rules applicable to the operations of the National Bank for Agricultural Development shall be contained in the rules of procedure, which must be approved by a three-fourths majority of the Board of Directors.

## ADMINISTRATION

**Art. 8.** The National Bank for Agricultural Development shall be administered by a twelve-member Board of Directors whose composition shall be determined by decree. Each subscriber shall have at least one seat on the Board.

The Directors' term of office shall be three years. Their appointment shall be renewable.

The duties of Directors shall end upon expiry of their term, upon resignation, at death, or following notification to the corporation by the authority or agency which appointed them.

The office of Directors shall be unremunerated; only the Chairman may receive compensation for his work.

However, Directors meeting in regular session may claim a lump-sum allowance determined by the Board of Directors, as well as the reimbursement of their round-trip transportation costs.

## CHAIRMAN OF THE BOARD OF DIRECTORS

**Art. 9.** Upon a proposal from the supervisory ministry, the Board of Directors shall elect a Chairman from among its members by a three-fourths majority of the appointed Directors.

## MEETINGS OF THE BOARD OF DIRECTORS

**Art. 10.** The Board of Directors shall meet at least four times a year, when called by its Chairman (who may delegate his authority in this respect) at least one week prior to the scheduled date of the meeting. Two thirds of its members must be present or represented for a quorum to exist, and one proxy only may be conferred on each Director.

Decisions shall be taken by simple majority, except as otherwise provided by these by-laws or by the rules of procedure.

In the event of a tie, the Chairman shall cast the deciding vote.

## POWERS OF THE BOARD OF DIRECTORS

**Art. 11.** The Board of Directors shall have the broadest powers to act on behalf of the corporation and to authorize all acts relating to it.

Among its powers, which are listed by way of indication and are not limitative except to the extent that these by-laws expressly restrict the condition or scope of their exercise, shall be the following.

The Board shall:

appoint the Chairman of the Board of Directors and the General

Manager under the terms and conditions set forth in Articles 10 and 13 of the by-laws;

draw up the rules of procedure of the corporation;

establish, install or close branches;

conclude all purchases, sales and rentals of real estate and sign and authorize all agreements or contracts;

contract all loans, with or without mortgages or pledges, on the assets of the corporation. Borrowing, however, which requires government approval or guarantee shall be subject to the regulations pertaining to the supervision of government finance;

authorize all arrangements, consents, waivers, removals of encumbrances, distraints or attachments before or after payment;

institute or engage in legal actions or proceedings in all courts, either as plaintiff or as defendant;

effect all acquisitions, assignments and transfers involving value;

on a proposal from the General Manager, it shall decide which operations are to be carried out under Article 3 of these by-laws and, in particular, on the allocation of loans.

To this end, it may delegate a portion of its powers both to a select committee known as the "Loan Committee" and to the General Manager, subject to the condition that it be informed at its next meeting of any decisions reached.

Within a maximum of four months following the closing date for the corporate financial year, the Board of Directors shall close out the balance sheet, the operating account, the profit and loss account, and take cognizance of the auditors' report; it shall then forward these documents, together with an activities report, to the supervisory authority for approval.

If the Board receives no objections from the supervisory authority within three months of the date of dispatch of said documents, the accounts shall be considered approved and the Directors fully discharged from the management thereof.

### ADMINISTRATION

**Art. 12.** Responsibility for the administration of the corporation shall be entrusted to a General Manager appointed by a three-fourths majority of the Board of Directors upon a proposal from the supervisory authority.

The General Manager shall ensure that the staff of the National Bank for Agricultural Development performs its duties and that the decisions of the Board of Directors and the Loan Committee are implemented.

To enable him to carry out this mission, the Board of Directors may decide by three-fourths majority to delegate some of its powers to him and, inter alia, authorize him to:

sign all documents, notifications and agreements which commit the corporation;

pay and collect all amounts and issue receipts for the same;

open all current accounts;

grant and accept all guarantees, and contract for, authorize, grant or withdraw all sureties and guarantees, whether cash, securities or otherwise;

represent the corporation before the courts and engage in legal actions of any kind as either plaintiff or defendant;

buy, sell or exchange all shares of stock and securities and accept, guarantee, endorse and rediscount all bills, drafts, letters of exchange and commercial paper, and rediscount the portfolio; and

conclude all rental and lease agreements for real estate, and authorize all arrangements, consents, waivers and removals of encumbrances, distraints or attachments before or after payment.

The General Manager shall prepare and submit to the Board of Directors the annual report on the corporation's financial position and activities, the balance sheet, the profit and loss account, and all other financial documents.

He shall represent the National Bank for Agricultural Development vis-à-vis all third parties; in order for the corporation to be committed, all the acts and operations of the corporation decided on by the Board of Directors or by its authority must be signed by the General Manager or by the person to whom he has delegated the power to do so.

He shall hire and dismiss all staff members, determine the amount of their wages and assign the duties of each employee subject to the conditions imposed by labor law.

He may delegate his authority for a given purpose and toward a given objective to one or more representatives of the corporation. During his periods of leave, said delegations of authority must be confirmed by the Board of Directors.

The remuneration of the General Manager shall be determined by the Board of Directors and approved by the supervisory authority.

## INCOMPATIBILITIES

**Art. 13.** The duties of General Manager shall be incompatible with holding a political office. The exclusion clauses and incompatibilities laid down by the laws and decrees in force with respect to carrying out the duties of President, Director, General Manager and Auditor in joint-stock companies shall be applicable to the individuals carrying out the corresponding duties at the National Bank for Agricultural Development.

Art. 14. Any agreement between the National Bank for Agricultural Development and its General Manager, whether concluded directly or indirectly, shall be null and void unless authorized in advance by its Board of Directors.

The same shall hold true for agreements between the National Bank for Agricultural Development and any enterprises of which the General Manager of the National Bank for Agricultural Development or one of its Directors is an owner, partner or investor, manager, director or general manager.

### LOAN COMMITTEE

Art. 15. The membership of the Loan Committee, provided for by Article 12 of these by-laws, shall be specified by decree.

### ACCOUNTING

Art. 16. The accounting operations of the National Bank for Agricultural Development shall be carried out and defined in conformity with the prevailing rules of the banking profession.

The corporate financial year shall begin on October 1 and end on September 30 of each year.

### AUDITORS

Art. 17. Two auditors, at least one of whom is from the private sector, shall jointly draw up an annual report on the operations of the National Bank for Agricultural Development.

They shall carry out their mission under the terms and conditions prescribed by law.

### SURVEILLANCE

Art. 18. The National Bank for Agricultural Development shall engage in ongoing surveillance of all individuals or juridical persons receiving advances or loans from it.

### RESERVE FUND

Art. 19. After completing the accounting of administrative costs and expenses and after providing for amortizations and reserves, all net profits for each fiscal year shall be transferred to a Reserve Fund to be used as the Board of Directors determines. Nevertheless, the decisions of the Board in this regard shall be effective only if the supervisory authority raises no objection to them within one month of its receipt of the minutes of the Board of Directors meeting during which the relevant decisions were reached.

STAMP DUTIES AND REGISTRATION FEES

**Art. 20.** All documents, contracts and loans and, in general, all papers drawn up by the National Bank for Agricultural Development in implementation of these by-laws shall be exempt from stamp duties and registration fees. This exemption shall be noted in writing on the above documents.

**Art. 21.** In the event of dissolution, the assets shall be realized and liabilities paid off in accordance with the law pertaining to commercial corporations.

Nevertheless, any grants, bequests and other gifts which may have been provided under special earmark shall devolve upon those government agencies or institutions acknowledged to serve the public interest which are capable of carrying out the wishes of the donors.

# Decree No. 68-305[1]

## Concerning the National Bank for Agricultural Development

[June 24, 1968]

**Art. 1.** The initial capital of the National Bank for Agricultural Development, fixed at 700 million francs, is subscribed as follows:

| | |
|---|---|
| Republic of Ivory Coast | 466.7 M |
| Agricultural Products Price Stabilization and Support Fund | 116.7 M |
| Central Bank of West African States | 58.3 M |
| Central Fund for Economic Cooperation | 58.3 M |
| | 700 M |

[1] Published in the *Journal officiel,* 1968, p. 1106. Amended by Decree No. 69-305, July 4, 1969, published in the *Journal officiel,* 1969, p. 1040.

**Art.** 2. The National Bank for Agricultural Development shall be administered by a governing board of 12 members, including:

The Minister for Agriculture or his representative;
The Minister of Livestock Production or his representative;
The Minister for Economic and Financial Affairs or his representative;
The Minister for Planning or his representative;
A representative of the National Assembly;
A representative of the Economic and Social Council;
A representative of the Central Bank of West African States;
A representative of the Central Fund for Economic Cooperation;
Two representatives of the Agricultural Products Price Stabilization and Support Fund;
A technician from the Ministry of Agriculture; and
A representative of the private sector.

**Art.** 3. In addition to reviewing credit applications, the Loan Committee shall oversee the proper functioning of the National Bank for Agricultural Development in general.

It shall be composed of Directors of the Bank and be presided over by the Chairman of the Board of Directors.

It shall include the following members:

The Minister of Agriculture or his representative or the technician from his Ministry;
The Minister for Economic and Financial Affairs or his representative;
The Minister of Planning or his representative;
The representative of the Agricultural Products Price Stabilization and Support Fund;
The representative of the Central Bank of West African States; and
The representative of the Central Fund for Economic Cooperation.

To these ex officio members shall be added the Minister of Livestock Production or his representative whenever matters technically coming within his purview are studied.

The Director-General shall attend the meetings and arrange for the relevant administrative services.

**Art.** 4. On proposals from the ministries or agencies concerned, the members of the Board of Directors and of the Loan Committee shall be appointed by decree of the Minister for Economic and Financial Affairs.

# Decree No. 68-306[1]

## Establishing supervision of the National Bank for Agricultural Development

[June 24, 1968]

**Art. 1.** The National Bank for Agricultural Development is hereby placed under the supervision of the Minister for Economic and Financial Affairs and of the Minister for Agriculture.

**Art. 2.** The Minister for Economic and Financial Affairs shall ensure that the National Bank for Agricultural Development complies with the provisions of the law of August 4, 1965[2] organizing the banking profession and with its implementing decrees.

Furthermore, the National Bank for Agricultural Development shall be subject to the provisions of Law No. 62-255 of July 31, 1962[3] on the equity holdings of the Government in joint-stock companies, its representation on the boards of directors of such enterprises, and the supervisory powers of government commissioners.

**Art. 3.** The Minister for Agriculture shall have supervisory powers with respect to the definition and implementation of agricultural credit policy.

---

[1] Published in the *Journal officiel,* 1968, p. 1106.
[2] Law No. 65-252 has been abrogated by Law No. 75-549 of August 5, 1975.
[3] This law has been abrogated by Law No. 70-633 of November 5, 1970.

# Kenya

Overview of Nairobi, capital of Kenya
Courtesy World Bank, Kay Chernush

# KENYA

# KENYA

# Financial System of Kenya

by

*Edward A. Arowolo* *

## Introduction

The rapid development of the economy of Kenya has been accompanied by a marked expansion in the number, size, and operations of financial institutions. The growth of the economy has involved a sharply expanded volume of investment requiring a substantial mobilization of domestic savings, which has been facilitated by the increase in the number of financial institutions and the enlargement of their operations. In addition to the legal environment and the public sector's role in fostering the growth of financial institutions, the nature of economic enterprise in Kenya (that of mixed enterprise with a distinct private sector dominance) has provided the underpinning for the development of both the financial institutions and capital and money markets.

The growth of the capital and money markets in Kenya was characterized at the outset by the need for funds in the private sector rather than by the Government's need to borrow locally. Prior to Kenya's independence in late 1963, public investment was rather modest and its financing was mainly through foreign borrowing and grants; hence, the minor role of the Government in spearheading the development of the capital and money markets as a borrower in those markets. For example, it was not until early 1969 that the Government began to issue treasury bills, both in a deliberate attempt to foster the growth of a money market and, increasingly, to meet the needs for short-term funds in financing the budget. However, the Government of Kenya has for many years provided the legal framework within which such a market could reasonably operate and through legislation has created a number of agencies, particularly nonbank financial institutions whose impact on the operations of the capital and money markets has been especially significant.

---

* Mr. Arowolo, who prepared the original manuscript, was a Division Chief in the African Department of the International Monetary Fund at the time of his death. He was a graduate of London University, had done postgraduate work at the University of Saskatchewan and McGill University (Canada), and had been an Inspector of Taxes in Western Nigeria's Treasury.

Acknowledgments are made to Ms. Naheed Kirmani and Messrs. J. D. Simpson and R. T. Stillson, who also contributed to the introduction to Kenya.

This introduction to Kenya's banking legislation is aimed at providing the background to the scope of, and the limitations on, the controls exercised by the Central Bank of Kenya over the commercial banks and other financial institutions. After examining the structure and operations of the existing financial institutions, and the steps taken in the development of the capital and money markets, the statutory regulation and central bank control of the financial institutions are described.

## Structure of Financial Institutions

Kenya's complex of financial institutions can be grouped into three broad categories, namely, the banking system, the public nonbank financial institutions, and the private nonbank financial institutions.

The banking system comprises the Central Bank of Kenya and the commercial banks. There are, besides, both public and private nonbank financial institutions with an assortment of functions. In addition, there are several insurance companies (life and nonlife) engaged in the mobilization of liquid resources and participating in investment activities, a post office savings bank, and a development bank (the East African Development Bank) jointly established by the three partner states (Kenya, Tanzania, and Uganda) of the now defunct East African Community.

### *History* [1]

The East African Currency Board, established in 1919, was authorized to issue currency in the territories of Kenya, Uganda, and what was then Tanganyika. The currency initially issued was the East African florin, but this was replaced in 1922 by the East African shilling. The silver rupees that had circulated earlier in East Africa were redeemed by the Board at a substantial loss owing to a redemption rate well in excess of their exchange value and the fact of their continuing depreciation over the redemption period. As a consequence of this, it was not until 1950 that the Board achieved the 100 per cent sterling currency cover that had been contemplated for the shilling. For many years, the Board was without any real influence on monetary conditions in the economy. Its function was limited to issuing and redeeming the East African shilling in exchange for sterling at par, subject only to commission charges.

[1] See *Money and Banking in Kenya,* published by the Central Bank of Kenya (Nairobi) [1972].

Beginning in 1955, however, the Board's powers were increased in successive steps that permitted it first to subscribe to local securities, then to discount and rediscount certain negotiable instruments, and finally to influence interest rates. As Kenya, Uganda, and Tanzania approached independence, the concept of a common central bank which would succeed the Board generated some interest but ultimately failed to materialize.

### *Central Bank*

The Central Bank of Kenya was established in March 1966 as a successor to the East African Currency Board and began operations on September 14, 1966. The main objectives of the Bank are broadly "to regulate the issue of notes and coins, to assist in the development and maintenance of a sound monetary, credit and banking system in Kenya conducive to the orderly and balanced economic development of the country and the external stability of the currency, and to serve as banker and financial adviser to the Government."[2]

### *Commercial banks*

There are 18 commercial banks operating in Kenya. Of these, several are local, of which the largest was established in late 1970 through the acquisition by the Government of a majority share holding in an existing expatriate bank, the National and Grindlays Bank, Ltd., to form Kenya Commercial Bank now wholly owned by the Government. The largest banks (including two local banks) are engaged in general banking business and have branches outside Nairobi (the capital city) and Mombasa. The smaller banks are more specialized. For example, Grindlays Bank International is engaged exclusively in international banking and extends credit primarily to exporters and importers, while the Cooperative Bank of Kenya, Ltd., accepts deposits from and extends credit to only rural cooperative societies.

### *Public nonbank financial institutions*

In line with the Government's active promotion of development, a number of public nonbank financial institutions have been established primarily to provide finance to the private sector, especially where exist-

[2] *Laws of Kenya,* The Central Bank of Kenya Act, cap. 491 (rev. 1967), sec. 4.

ing institutions have failed to meet such needs. These institutions tend to have special areas to which they cater, e.g., agriculture, housing, and industrial development.

There are three institutions for the agricultural sector, reflecting the dominance of agriculture in the economy of Kenya and the special problems of providing agricultural finance. Because of the inadequacy of bank finance for agriculture, the Government established the Agricultural Finance Corporation, which absorbed the existing Land and Agricultural Bank of Kenya in 1963, to provide credit for farmers from public sources. In order to facilitate the capacity of farmers to borrow, the Government has embarked on changing the land tenure in the traditional African areas so that farmers are provided with title deeds to their land. Where necessary, it has also attempted to consolidate scattered holdings. The modernization of land tenure began in 1956, and by 1965 about 18 per cent of all registrable land had been registered.[3] In addition, a land settlement program involving the purchase of land formerly owned by expatriate farmers facilitated the extension of credit to the agricultural sector. Of note is the One-Million Acre Settlement Scheme, which by the end of 1972 had settled farmers on 1.2 million acres. Other institutions engaged in extending credit to the agricultural sector include the Cereals and Sugar Finance Corporation, which provides funds to the Kenya Farmers' Association (Cooperative), Ltd., for the financing of the cooperatives and to the National Cereals and Produce Board for the purchase of maize, which is Kenya's main staple food, and the Agricultural Development Corporation.[4]

Of the remaining five institutions, the Housing Finance Company of Kenya, Ltd., functions in the field of housing, having taken over two other smaller institutions, while the Industrial and Commercial Development Corporation (ICDC) provides funds for industrial development. The ICDC, the most important public sector financial institution, was set up in 1954 with the objective of promoting industrialization by assisting in or initiating the establishment of industrial and commercial ventures and of facilitating participation by the public in commerce and industry.

The East African Development Bank was jointly established by Kenya, Tanzania, and Uganda to provide industrial development finance in all three countries. The Post Office Savings Bank collects deposits

[3] Kenya, *Development Plan, 1979–83*, p. 53.

[4] The Kenya Tea Development Authority also extends credit to farmers but is not licensed as a financial institution.

from small savers and is administered by the Kenya Posts and Telecommunications Corporation.

### *Private nonbank financial institutions*

Most nonbank private financial institutions are licensed under the Banking Act, although two, the East African Building Society, Ltd., and Pioneer Building Society were licensed under the Societies Act. A number of them have been designated as "specified financial institutions," in accordance with sec. 2 of the Central Bank of Kenya Act, so as to come within the ambit of the regulatory powers of the Central Bank. A notable aspect of these institutions is their ownership by, or strong links with, the commercial banks. These institutions provide medium- and long-term financing for a variety of activities. Broadly speaking, their activities fall within the fields of mortgage lending, hire purchase, and merchant banking, and the institutions tend to specialize. Their operations have increased substantially and they play a significant role in Kenya's financial system through the collection of deposits and the extension of credit.

### *Insurance companies*

Several insurance companies, mainly subsidiaries of foreign companies, operate in Kenya. After years of relative stability, their operations have expanded noticeably, particularly those of the life insurance companies. The total assets of the life insurance companies grew from K Sh 948,020,000 in 1974 to about K Sh 1,260,760,000 in 1978.[5] The Government has encouraged the investment of these funds locally.

## Development of Capital and Money Markets

### *Demand for capital*

As indicated above, the Government's role in fostering the expansion of capital and money markets in Kenya has been limited, primarily because current budget savings were for many years largely sufficient to meet the need for development financing not covered by external loans and grants.[6] However, with more vigorous implementation of development plans, the need for greater domestic mobilization of savings arose, and increased use was made of the sale of debt instruments.

---

[5] Kenya, Ministry of Economic Planning and Development, *Statistical Abstract, 1980,* p. 173; hereinafter referred to as *Statistical Abstract, 1980.*

[6] For details see Edward A. Arowolo, "The Development of Capital Markets in Africa, with Particular Reference to Kenya and Nigeria," International Monetary Fund, *Staff Papers,* Vol. 18 (July 1971), pp. 420–72.

The extent to which the Government has contributed to the growth of the capital market is illustrated by the substantial expansion in its issuance of funded debt, which rose from K Sh 1,284,220,000 at the end of June 1971 to K Sh 8,065,190,000 at the end of June 1981. This debt is held by a number of institutions, of which the National Social Security Fund (NSSF), commercial banks, and insurance companies are major holders. The NSSF marks an aspect of the Government's endeavor to mobilize domestic savings; the National Social Security Law was enacted in 1966, and in but a few years the fund established by it accounted for a substantial proportion of the public funded debt on the local register.

### *Supply of capital funds*

With respect to the supply of capital to the economy, it is instructive to examine both the nature of the capital market and the structure of companies, having regard also to their ability to generate internal resources for expansion. In financing the Government's capital formation in the period 1958–69, domestic borrowing accounted for only 11.3 per cent, while current budget savings provided 31.7 per cent and the remainder was in the form of external loans and grants. Private sector capital formation during the same period (1958–69) was financed largely by funds internally generated by business firms and by the raising of new capital on the domestic market. For example, between 1958 and 1965 new capital issues amounted to K Sh 2,640 million, somewhat in excess of depreciation funds, the two together financing 68.8 per cent of private sector capital formation. Indications are that the contribution of these sources of financing continued to increase in later years. Net foreign capital inflow has been of small importance in financing private sector investment in Kenya. The mobilization of domestic capital in the required magnitude stimulated the development of a capital market, as the capital of companies had to be structured in a manner that would enable them to raise public funds and facilities had to be provided for purchases and sales of securities.

The structure of companies and corporations registered in Kenya shows a preponderance of private companies.[7] In practice, such private companies are largely family business and subsidiary firms. Of 11,443

[7] A private company is one with fewer than 50 shareholders and one whose shares are not available for purchase by the public at large. A public company, on the other hand, is widely owned, can offer its shares for sale to the public, and, among other things, must publish its accounts as required by law.

local companies that were registered as of the end of 1975, only a fraction were public companies.[8] The preponderance of private companies has not encouraged the expansion of the capital market, for in financing their operations such companies have usually relied on sources other than the public for funds, notably the individual resources of those launching the businesses and private placement of loans. In contrast, in some other countries the expansion of the capital market on a broad front has been attributable to the group of public companies that issues shares and debentures to investors. Although adequate data are not available for analysis with regard to the capital structure and the new capital funds raised, a gradual increase in the annual registration of new local public companies from 4 in 1962 to 157 in 1979 suggests the basis for an expanding capital market.

### Financial intermediaries

Financial intermediaries such as private nonbank financial institutions, insurance companies, and building societies have contributed to the breadth of the capital market, playing a prominent role in the issuance of long-term and medium-term loans for capital expansion and in the mobilization of savings. Government action has also been of importance in this field. The extension of exchange control regulations to sterling area countries in mid-1965 facilitated the accumulation of domestic savings. Also, the Government's policy of encouraging the investment of insurance funds locally to the point where local liabilities are covered by local assets has helped to increase the role of insurance companies in the process of mobilizing and allocating financial resources. In addition, the Government is responsible for the establishment of certain financial institutions.

### Stock exchange

The establishment of a stock exchange and the flotation of shares and bonds on it has contributed to the development of the capital market. Through the initiative of the private sector, the Nairobi Stock Exchange was established in July 1954 to replace the earlier links with external markets in Rhodesia, South Africa, and the United Kingdom. Initially, the members of the exchange were the few stockbrokers who had earlier formed a stockbrokers' association, and business continued to be transacted between these brokers from their respective offices, there being

[8] *Statistical Abstract, 1980,* p. 96.

no "floor" trading of shares. From a system involving a weekly "call-over" in order to complete deals, there is now a daily "call-over," reflecting the expansion in the volume of business.

The operations of the stock exchange remain limited compared with those of the exchanges in Europe or the United States of America. Institutions such as insurance companies, investment trusts, and semiofficial bodies comprise the bulk of traders on the Nairobi Stock Exchange. However, the number and activity of individual traders have increased as a result of larger flotation of company shares. Moreover, the volume of transactions on the exchange is believed to be rising. A significant increase has also occurred in the number of industrial shares and government stocks listed.

The Nairobi Stock Exchange operated for many years as a "regional" exchange serving the three countries (Kenya, Tanzania, and Uganda) that formed the East African Community. This was made possible by the establishment of companies on an East African basis, the maintenance of common market arrangements and common exchange regulations regarding capital movements to countries outside East Africa, and the virtually free movement of capital among the three countries. However, nationalization measures in Kenya's partner states, the introduction of currency and exchange measures, and the breakup of the Community reduced the effectiveness of the regional aspect of the exchange.

### Money market

Despite the existence of a wide network of financial institutions on a relatively well-developed scale, the emergence of an organized and effective money market in Kenya was retarded. Both the lending practices of commercial banks and the apparent inadequacy of short-term investment opportunities and instruments help to explain this delay. An additional factor was the early lack of a systematic approach to the raising of short-term funds to meet government needs. For example, the Kenya Government did not make any major use of the facility to place treasury bills with the East African Currency Board (EACB) as part of its fiduciary issue.[9]

Until March 1969 the Government of Kenya met its short-term borrowing needs through direct advances from commercial banks or through the machinery of the Cereals and Sugar Finance Corporation. Treasury bills were not issued except on one occasion (during the last quarter

[9] East African Currency Board, *Annual Report for the Year Ended 30th June, 1966.*

of 1965), when the Government issued an amount of K Sh 20 million to meet a temporary shortage of funds. The bills were quickly redeemed. However, in order to promote a money market in Kenya, a decision was made early in 1969 to borrow actively through the issuance of treasury bills. The Appropriations Act, 1968, which authorized short-term borrowing by the Government up to K Sh 200 million, provided the legal basis for issuing treasury bills. The first issue of treasury bills was made on March 24, 1969, and further issues followed at regular intervals.

Beginning in December 1969 the Government began to reduce the amount of bills outstanding, and by the end of April 1970 the total amount outstanding had been repaid. No new issues were made between February and December 1970, when the issuance of treasury bills resumed. The purpose of suspending new issues was to reduce the amount of short-term asset instruments available in the fledgling money market as the bills outstanding were retired. The relatively high liquidity of the commercial banks during the period 1969–70 played a significant part in the success of the earlier treasury bill issues.

Since treasury bills are included as eligible liquid assets for purposes of meeting the liquidity ratio requirement, commercial bank holdings of them have increased. However, bank lending through the discount of commercial bills remains modest in Kenya and accordingly has not aided the expansion of the money market. The preference of commercial banks for direct financing rather than use of commercial bills and other short-term lending instruments, and the initial prohibition of interbank lending, inhibited their participation in the development of a money market. However, interbank lending has been permitted since early 1973 and since that time has assisted in the development of the money market.

While the capital market has expanded rapidly, neither the needs of monetary management nor the mobilization of liquid resources initially activated or expanded the money market beyond the establishment of a network of financial institutions and the sale of a small volume of short-term asset instruments. Progress in the development of the money market had to occur slowly. That it has occurred may be appreciated from an examination of the growth of the market in treasury bills. As of June 30, 1971 the amount of treasury bills outstanding was K Sh 200 million, while as of June 30, 1981 this figure had increased to K Sh 1,940 million.[10]

[10] Central Bank of Kenya, *Annual Report,* June 1981, p. 67.

## Financial Mobilization and Allocation

Deposits with all financial institutions, public as well as private, including the commercial banks but excluding the Central Bank, have increased rapidly. This rapid increase reflects both the growth of the economy and its increased monetization. By way of illustration, total deposits in the commercial banks grew from K Sh 4,954,600,000 at the end of 1974 to K Sh 14,002,140,000 at the end of 1980.[11] While commercial bank deposits substantially exceed those made with other financial institutions, deposits with the private nonbank financial institutions have increased more rapidly. Public nonbank financial institutions have also succeeded in increasing their rate of savings mobilization. In quantitative terms, deposits with nonbank financial institutions, taken as a group, have been estimated to have risen on average by 82 per cent a year, compared with an average annual rate of increase of 30 per cent in commercial banks' deposit resources over the period December 1974 through December 1980. Accordingly, deposits in these institutions as a proportion of commercial bank deposits rose from 16 per cent in 1973 to 35 per cent by December 1980. This comparison in favor of the nonbank financial institutions may reflect the higher interest rates on deposits paid by these institutions (insofar as they are not subject to the interest rate controls applicable to commercial banks) and the fact that in certain respects they are more suited to the needs of small savers.

An important aspect of the role of money and capital markets is the machinery provided for the allocation of funds among possible users, i.e., credit and capital allocation. The commercial banks predominate in the provision of credit to the economy. However, commercial bank credit has been mainly short term and traditionally has been concentrated in the export-import, commercial, and manufacturing fields. While lending by private nonbank financial institutions is comparatively of lesser magnitude, it has been largely in the areas neglected by the banks, and to meet medium- and long-term needs. By way of example, in terms of amounts loaned, the sectors receiving the most financing from these institutions in 1979 were housing, personal, business, trades, and manufacturing.[12] Public nonbank financial institutions have generally lent in agricultural and industrial activities. The lending operations of the private nonbank financial intermediaries have increased especially rapidly. As a general rule, the allocation of resources by financial institu-

[11] *Ibid.*, p. 42.
[12] *Statistical Abstract, 1980,* p. 178.

tions consists of direct lending to borrowers in the various sectors, and only a small part takes the form of purchases of securities from them or holdings of negotiable instruments.

In considering the network of financial institutions, the role of insurance companies in mobilizing financial resources needs to be mentioned. The total assets of these companies amounted to K Sh 2,116,600,000 at the end of 1978.[13] A rapid increase in insurance premiums collected is evidence of the savings generated through this medium.

## Central Bank and Financial System

At the apex of Kenya's financial system is the Central Bank of Kenya, which is vested with certain statutory functions, including the control and inspection of commercial banks and other financial institutions. The Central Bank Act of 1967 spells out the role of the Central Bank and its regulatory duties vis-à-vis other financial institutions. The Banking Act of 1968 specifies the conditions governing the establishment and operation of commercial banks and specified financial institutions and their relationship with the Central Bank.

The Central Bank of Kenya has endeavored to develop and maintain sound monetary and credit policies and to carry out the functions vested in it by the enabling Act. In addition, the Central Bank has, since its inception, developed and implemented a system for regulating the banks and other financial institutions. Notable in this regard, is its ability to designate a nonbank financial institution as a "specified financial institution" so as to subject it to appropriate regulation and supervision. The Central Bank has taken over the foreign assets of the country, a policy that involved the surrender by the commercial banks and other institutions of their foreign asset holdings.

In the field of credit controls, the Central Bank, through the power conferred by the Banking Act of 1968, has gradually assumed regulatory functions over the lending practices (volume of credit), interest rate policy, and manner of operations, particularly through an inspection and reporting system, of commercial banks and nonbank financial institutions. This development arose as an aspect of monetary management as well as to safeguard the deposits with these institutions.

Two points concerning the power conferred by the Banking Act should be mentioned. First, the Act has enabled the Central Bank to

[13] *Ibid.*, pp. 173 and 174.

impose a liquid assets ratio on the commercial banks.[14] This is, of course, different from the power conferred by the Central Bank of Kenya Act, which enables it to require the commercial banks to keep on deposit with the Central Bank reserves of up to 20 per cent of their deposits and other liabilities. The second is the power of inspection.[15] Through regular inspection the Central Bank can safeguard the soundness of banking and financial institutions' operations. The purpose of such inspection is to ensure compliance with the law as well as to provide information as to the state of affairs of individual banks and other financial institutions. In addition, the Banking Act provides for minimum capital requirements (sec. 7) for all commercial banks (assigned capital in the case of banks not locally incorporated) and institutions licensed under the Act.

Under the Banking Act, commercial banks and licensed financial institutions are prohibited from specified activities. Of significance is the limitation on lending to any one customer; such lending must not exceed 5 per cent of deposit liabilities or 100 per cent of the lending institution's capital plus unimpaired reserves, whichever is greater. Ordinary trading activities are prohibited, and a limit is put on the amount of real estate loans that can be made by a bank.[16] In licensing new banks and financial institutions, opening new places of business, and changing the location of an existing place of business, the Central Bank acts in an advisory capacity to the Ministry of Finance which is vested with the power to grant licenses.[17] Two kinds of licenses are prescribed: to transact banking business, which authorizes the holder to engage in any kind of banking business including acceptance of deposits subject to transfer by checks, and to engage in the business of a financial institution, with ability to accept deposits which are not subject to transfer through checks.

The Central Bank initially used its credit control powers sparingly, relying more on moral suasion. However, in late 1971 the Bank introduced a 5 per cent cash reserve requirement in addition to the 12½ per cent liquidity ratio requirement already in effect. Although early in 1972 the 5 per cent additional cash reserve requirement was rescinded, the liquidity ratio requirement was raised to 15 per cent. In 1976 quantitative limits on credit expansion were introduced and the liquidity ratio

[14] *Laws of Kenya,* The Banking Act, cap. 488 (rev. 1970), sec. 18.
[15] *Ibid.,* sec. 19.
[16] *Ibid.,* secs. 11 and 12.
[17] *Ibid.,* sec. 24.

requirement was raised to 18 per cent, to which point it returned in 1978 after reaching 20 per cent the year before. In 1978 a cash ratio was reintroduced in the amount of 3 per cent dropped in April 1981. In June of the following year the liquidity ratio requirement was once again lowered, to 16 per cent and again to 15 per cent in March 1981. Interest rate policy has been used on occasion, while the Central Bank has attempted to influence the allocation of credit through sectoral credit targets and preferential interest rates.

Apart from its role of surveillance over Kenya's financial system, the Central Bank plays an active role in fostering the development of capital and money markets in Kenya. With respect to money market operations, the Central Bank offers rediscount facilities to the commercial banks. In addition, it assumes the management of treasury bill issues and stands ready to discount these bills to ensure marketability. In other ways, for example, through the provision of rediscount facilities and the administration of the exchange control regulations, the influence of the Central Bank on the expansion of the capital market is quite important.

## Summary and Prospects

The growth of financial institutions and their financial operations in Kenya has been rapid. This has been aided by the marked expansion in economic activities and the promotional efforts of the authorities. The capital and money markets have consequently grown to meet the needs of the rapidly expanding economy for the mobilization of savings.

Despite the existence of a wide network of financial institutions on a relatively well-developed scale, the emergence of an organized and effective money market was retarded due to the apparent dearth of short-term investment opportunities and the lack, at least initially, of a systematic approach to the raising of short-term funds to meet government needs. However, an increasing volume of treasury bill issues and the granting of permission for interbank lending have contributed to the growth of the money market. With respect to the capital market, the increasing volume of government bonds and industrial securities, the growth of the network of financial institutions, and the functioning of the Nairobi Stock Exchange have established a firm basis for sustained expansion. These developments are likely to foster mobilization of the large amount of capital required by the country for sustained economic growth.

# The Central Bank of Kenya Act[1]

*Commencement:*
*Parts I to IV: 23rd May 1966*
*Parts V to X: 14th September 1966*

An Act of Parliament to establish the Central Bank of Kenya and to provide for the operation thereof; to establish the currency of Kenya and for matters connected therewith and related thereto

## PART I—PRELIMINARY

Short title.

1. This Act may be cited as the Central Bank of Kenya Act.

Interpretation.

2. In this Act, except where the context otherwise requires—

"the Bank" means the Central Bank of Kenya (or the Banki Kuu ya Kenya) established by section 3 of this Act;

"Board" means the Board of Directors of the Bank appointed under Part IV of this Act;

"convertible", in relation to any exchange, means exchange which is freely negotiable and transferable in international exchange markets at exchange rate margins consistent with the Articles of Agreement of the International Monetary Fund; [2]

"Minister" means the Minister for the time being responsible for finance;

"public entity" means the Government, the Organization, the Authority, any local authority, or any public body specified by the Minister, on the recommendation of the Bank, as a public entity for the purposes of this Act;

"shilling" means a Kenya shilling as provided in section 19 of this Act, or a shilling issued by the East African Currency Board for so long

[1] The original Act, No. 15 of 1966, was revised in 1967 and published as cap. 491 in *Laws of Kenya* (Government Printer, Nairobi), rev. ed. 1967 and amended by The Finance Act, 1980, No. 10 of 1980, assented to August 12, 1980 and commenced August 15, 1980. The Subsidiary Legislation to this Act has not been reproduced in this volume.

[2] Following the Second Amendment to the Articles of Agreement of the International Monetary Fund, effective April 1, 1978, a member has been free to choose the exchange arrangements that it wishes to apply in accordance with Article IV, Section 2*(b)*. It may therefore maintain the value of its currency in terms of the special drawing right or some other denominator excluding gold. Alternatively, it may allow its currency to float. Kenya maintains its exchange rate within relatively narrow margins in terms of the special drawing right.

as it is legal tender in Kenya in accordance with this Act;

"specified bank" means any licensed bank within the meaning of the Banking Act which is specified by the Bank for the purposes of this Act;

"specified financial institution" means any financial institution specified by the Bank for the purposes of this Act.

## PART II—ESTABLISHMENT, CONSTITUTION AND OBJECTS

Establishment of Bank and legal status.

3. (1) There is hereby established a bank which shall be known as the Central Bank of Kenya and which shall also be known by the alternative corporate name of the Banki Kuu ya Kenya.

(2) The Bank shall be a body corporate with perpetual succession and a common seal, with power to acquire, own, possess and dispose of property, to contract, and to sue and to be sued in its own name.

(3) The Bank shall exercise any type of central banking function unless specifically excluded under this Act, and shall enjoy all the prerogatives of a central bank.

(4) The Bank may make its own rules of conduct or procedure, not inconsistent with the provisions of this Act, for the good order and proper management of the Bank.

(5) The Bank shall not be subject to the Companies Act or the Banking Act.

Objects of Bank.

4. The principal objects of the Bank shall be to regulate the issue of notes and coins, to assist in the development and maintenance of a sound monetary, credit and banking system in Kenya conducive to the orderly and balanced economic development of the country and the external stability of the currency, and to serve as banker and financial adviser to the Government.

Head office and branches.

5. (1) The Bank shall have its head office in Nairobi:

Provided that during a time of national emergency the Bank may, unless the President otherwise directs, establish its head office temporarily or permanently in any other place within Kenya or elsewhere.

(2) *(a)* The Bank may establish or close branches in any place within Kenya.

*(b)* The Bank may, with the prior approval of the Minister, open or close branches outside Kenya.

Agents.

6. The Bank may, with the prior approval of the Minister, appoint, on such terms as it considers appropriate, or cancel the appointment of, agents, both within and outside Kenya.

Exemption from tax.

7. (1) The Bank shall not be liable to any taxation imposed by any law in respect of income or profits.

(2) No duty shall be chargeable under the Stamp Duty Act in respect of any instrument executed by or on behalf of or in favour of the Bank in any case where, but for this exemption, the Bank would be liable to pay such duty.

(3) The Minister may, whether for the purpose of removing any doubt as to the extent of the foregoing provisions of this section or for the purpose of extending the immunities of the Bank, by order published in the Gazette specify any tax, duty, fee, rate, levy, cess or other impost as one to which the Bank shall not be liable, and the law relating thereto shall have effect accordingly.

(4) This section shall have effect notwithstanding anything contained in any Act of the Organization.

## PART III—CAPITAL AND RESERVES

Authorized capital of Bank.

8. (1) The authorized capital of the Bank shall be twenty-six million shillings, which shall be paid up as a charge on and issued out of the consolidated fund as the Minister shall, at the request of the Bank, from time to time direct.

(2) The ownership of the entire paid up capital of the Bank shall be vested in the Permanent Secretary to the Treasury.

General Reserve Fund.

9. (1) The Bank shall establish and maintain a fund designated as the General Reserve Fund, to which shall be transferred at the end of each financial year, if the sums standing to the credit of the General Reserve Fund at the end of that year are less than the authorized capital of the Bank, one quarter of the net annual profits of the Bank after allowing for the expenses of operation and after provision has been made for bad and doubtful debts, depreciation in assets, contributions to staff benefit funds, and such other contingencies and accounting provisions as the Bank deems appropriate.

(2) Subject to subsection (1) of this section, the net annual profits of the Bank, calculated in accordance with that subsection, shall be paid into the consolidated fund.

(3) The amount of any net losses of the Bank in any financial year which is in excess of the sums standing to the credit of the general reserve fund of the Bank shall be charged upon and paid out of the consolidated fund without further appropriation than this Act.

## PART IV—MANAGEMENT

Board of Directors.

**10.** There shall be a Board of Directors of the Bank, constituted as provided in section 11 of this Act, which shall, subject to the provisions of this Act, be responsible for determining the policy of the Bank.

Constitution of Board.

**11.** (1) The Board shall consist of—

*(a)* a Governor;

*(b)* a Deputy Governor;

*(c)* the Permanent Secretary to the Treasury, or, in his absence an official of the Treasury nominated by the Minister (hereinafter referred to as the representative of the Treasury); and

*(d)* four Directors.

(2) The Governor and the Deputy Governor shall be the Chairman and Deputy Chairman of the Board respectively, and shall be appointed by the President for terms of four years each and shall be eligible for reappointment:

Provided that in the case of a person who is not a citizen of Kenya any such appointment shall be at the pleasure of the President.

(3) The Directors shall be appointed by the President for terms of four years and shall be eligible for reappointment:

Provided that—

(i) for the four Directors first appointed, the appointments shall be for one, two, three and four years, respectively; and

(ii) if a Director's appointment on the Board is terminated before his term of office has expired the President shall appoint a new Director to serve for the remainder of that term of office.

(4) Where the Governor, the Deputy Governor or a Director is unable to perform the functions of his office due to any temporary incapacity which is likely to be prolonged, the President may appoint a substitute for that member of the Board to act with the full powers of that member until such time as the President determines that the incapacity of that member has ceased.

Meetings of Board.

**12.** (1) The Governor, as Chairman of the Board, shall convene meetings of the Board not less than once in every two months, or whenever the business of the Bank so requires, or whenever he is so requested by at least two Directors, or by the representative of the Treasury.

(2) A quorum for any meeting of the Board shall be the Governor or the Deputy Governor, the representative of the Treasury and two Directors.

(3) Decisions of the Board shall be adopted by a majority of the votes of those present at that meeting, and in case of an equality of votes the Chairman or Deputy Chairman presiding at the meeting shall have a second or casting vote.

(4) The validity of any proceedings of the Board shall not be affected by any vacancy in the membership of the Board, or by any defect in the appointment or disqualification of any member which is discovered subsequent to those proceedings.

(5) Where the Governor and the representative of the Treasury consider that, because of exceptional circumstances, a decision is necessary before a full meeting of the Board can be convened, then that decision may be taken by the Governor with the concurrence of the representative of the Treasury and such decision shall be valid and binding on the Bank; and the Governor shall immediately convene a meeting of the Board and report any such decision to it.

(6) The Governor and the representative of the Treasury shall each have the right to suspend a vote by the Board and refer the matter to the Minister for a decision, and the decision of the Minister as to whether the vote shall stand or shall not stand shall be binding on the Board.

Governor.

13. (1) The Governor shall be the chief executive officer of the Bank and, subject to the general policy decisions of the Board, shall be responsible for the management of the Bank, including the organization, appointment and dismissal of the staff in accordance with the general terms and conditions of service established by the Board, and the Governor shall have authority to incur expenditure for the Bank within the administrative budget approved by the Board.

(2) The Governor shall be the principal representative of the Bank and shall, in that capacity, have authority—

*(a)* to represent the Bank in its relations with other public entities, persons or bodies;

*(b)* to represent the Bank, either personally or through counsel, in any legal proceedings to which the Bank is a party;

*(c)* to sign individually or jointly with other persons contracts concluded by the Bank, notes and securities issued by the Bank, reports, balance sheets, and other financial statements, correspondence and other documents of the Bank.

(3) The Deputy Governor shall act for the Governor and shall exercise all the powers and shall perform all of the functions conferred on the Governor under this Act whenever the Governor is temporarily absent, and shall perform such other functions as the Governor may from time to time assign to him.

(4) The Governor may delegate any of his powers provided for in this section to other officers of the Bank.

General disqualifications for all Board members.

14. (1) No person shall be appointed as Governor, Deputy Governor or a Director who is—

*(a)* a member of the National Assembly;
*(b)* a salaried employee of any public entity (except on a secondment basis);
*(c)* a director, officer, employee, partner in or shareholder of any specified bank or specified financial institution:

Provided that—

(i) paragraph *(b)* above shall not apply in the case of the representative of the Treasury; and
(ii) the President may in exceptional cases waive any of the above provisions with respect to any Director (other than the Governor or Deputy Governor) if such waiver is in the interests of the Bank and likely to promote the objects of the Bank under section 4 of this Act.

(2) The President shall terminate the appointment of a Governor, Deputy Governor or a Director who—

*(a)* becomes subject to any of the disqualifications described in subsection (1) of this section;
*(b)* is adjudged bankrupt or enters into a composition or scheme of arrangement with his creditors;
*(c)* is convicted of an offence involving dishonesty or fraud or moral turpitude; or
*(d)* becomes for any reason incapable of properly performing the functions of his office.

(3) The President shall terminate the appointment of any Director who absents himself from three consecutive meetings of the Board without leave of the Board.

Special disqualifications for Governor and Deputy Governor.

15. (1) The Governor and the Deputy Governor shall owe their allegiance entirely to the Bank and shall not engage in any paid employment or business or professional activity outside the duties of their respective offices:

Provided that nothing in this subsection shall prevent the Governor or Deputy Governor from accepting or holding any academic office or position in an institution of higher learning or any advisory position or membership in any committee or commission with public responsibility, or from serving in any international financial institution of which Kenya is a member or with which Kenya is associated, or any specialized financial institution established by the Government.

(2) If the Governor or the Deputy Governor engages in any paid employment or business or professional activity outside the duties of his office contrary to subsection (1) of this section, the President shall terminate his appointment.

(3) The President may specifically exempt any transactions or activities from the restrictions of this section.

Remuneration.

16. (1) The Governor, the Deputy Governor, and any substitute appointed under section 11 (4) of this Act shall be paid by the Bank such salaries and allowances as may be determined from time to time by the President, but such salaries and allowances shall not be altered to the detriment of any person during his term of office.

(2) The Directors and any substitute appointed under section 11 (4) of this Act shall be paid by the Bank such allowances as may from time to time be determined by the President.

Preservation of secrecy.

17. (1) Except for the purpose of the performance of his duties or the exercise of his powers, the Governor, the Deputy Governor, any Director or any other officer or employee of the Bank shall not disclose any information which he has acquired in the performance of his duties or the exercise of his powers.

(2) Any person who contravenes subsection (1) of this section shall be guilty of an offence and liable to a fine not exceeding two thousand shillings or to imprisonment for a term not exceeding one year, or to both such fine and such imprisonment, in addition to any disciplinary action which may be taken by the Board.

Declaration of interest.

18. The Governor, the Deputy Governor and any Director shall declare his interest in any specific proposal being considered or to be considered by the Board.

## Part V—Currency

Currency of Kenya.

19. (1) The unit of currency of Kenya shall be the Kenya shilling, which shall be divided into one hundred cents.

(2) Twenty shillings shall equal one Kenya pound.

20. The par value of the Kenya shilling in terms of gold shall be determined by the President, acting on the advice of the Bank and in accordance with any international agreement in that behalf to which Kenya is a party or with which it is associated, and shall be notified by notice in the Gazette.[3]

Par value.

21. All monetary obligations or transactions entered into or made in Kenya shall be deemed to be expressed and recorded, and shall be settled, in Kenya currency unless otherwise provided for by law or agreed upon between the parties.

Use of Kenya shilling.

22. (1) The Bank shall have the sole right to issue notes and coins in Kenya and, subject to subsection (4) of this section, only such notes and coins shall be legal tender in Kenya:

Issue of notes and coins, legal tender, and withdrawal.

Provided that coins of a denomination of fifty cents shall be legal tender only for payments up to twenty shillings, and coins of a denomination of less than fifty cents shall be legal tender only for payments up to five shillings.

(2) The denominations, inscriptions, form, material and other characteristics of the notes and coins issued by the Bank shall be determined by the Minister, acting on the recommendations of the Bank, and shall be notified in the Gazette and in other media of public information likely to bring them to the attention of the public.

(3) The Bank shall have power to withdraw any notes or coins issued by the Bank, and the procedure for and effect of any such withdrawal shall be as follows—

*(a)* a notice published in the Gazette, and in such other manner as the Bank considers likely to bring that notice to the attention of the public, shall specify the issues, and the denominations forming part of such issues, of notes or coins that are to be withdrawn, the places where those notes or coins may be taken for exchange, and the date on which those notes or coins shall cease to be legal tender;

*(b)* the notice given under the foregoing paragraph may provide

[3] The Second Amendment to the Articles of Agreement of the International Monetary Fund, effective April 1, 1978, abrogated par values under the Articles. Provision is made for a new par value system if the Fund decides in its favor by 85 per cent of the total voting power. Should such a decision be taken, each member would be able to decide whether to propose a par value for its currency. Under such a regime the margins around parity within which exchange transactions involving currencies with par values would have to be confined would be wider than those consistent with the original Articles of Agreement.

that, after such period as may be specified in the notice, the notes or coins to which the notice applies shall only be exchanged at the head office of the Bank;

*(c)* the notes or coins specified in a notice given under paragraph *(a)* of this subsection shall be exchanged at their face value for legal tender at the places and for the periods (which shall be of reasonable duration) specified in relation to those places in the notice, and shall cease to be legal tender on the date specified in the notice;

*(d)* the Bank may, by notice published in the same manner as notice given under paragraph *(a)* of this subsection, specify a period during which notes or coins which have ceased to be legal tender may nevertheless be exchanged at the head office of the bank, and after which such notes or coins shall no longer be exchanged.

(4) Notwithstanding subsection (1) of this section, the notes and coins of any issue or denomination issued by the East African Currency Board shall continue to be legal tender in Kenya for such time as the Minister may, on the recommendation of the Bank, determine.

Exchange of East African Currency Board notes and coins.

23. For so long as the East African Currency Board notes and coins continue to be legal tender in Kenya under section 22 (4) of this Act, such notes and coins shall be exchanged at par for Kenya currency notes and coins at all offices of the Bank, and thereafter the Bank shall continue to exchange East African Currency Board notes and coins at par for such further periods as the Bank shall, with the approval of the Minister, determine and publish in the Gazette and other media of public information.

Exchange of mutilated notes and coins.

24. The Bank shall not be obliged to exchange any note or coin which is mutilated, defaced, soiled or otherwise defective, and the conditions subject to which the Bank may as a matter of grace exchange any such note or coin shall be within the absolute discretion of the Bank.

Bills of exchange, promissory notes, etc.

25. (1) The Minister may, if the Bank so recommends, by regulations published in the Gazette prohibit the issue by any person other than the Bank of any bill of exchange, promissory note or similar instrument for the payment of money to the bearer on demand, and any such regulations may make different provision for different cases or classes of case, and may impose penalties for any offence under the regulations of a fine not exceeding ten thousand shillings or of imprisonment for a term not exceeding two years, or of both such fine and such imprisonment.

(2) Subject to any regulations made under this section the issue of any such bill, note or instrument as is referred to in the foregoing subsection shall not be deemed to contravene the sole right of the Bank to issue notes in Kenya.

## PART VI—EXTERNAL RELATIONS

Reserve of external assets.

26. (1) The Bank shall at all times use its best endeavours to maintain a reserve of external assets at an aggregate amount of not less than the value of four months imports as recorded and averaged for the last three preceding years; and subject to subsection (3) of this section such reserve shall consist of any or all of the following—

*(a)* gold;

*(b)* convertible foreign exchange in the form of—

(i) demand or time deposits with foreign central banks or with the Bank's agents or correspondents outside Kenya;

(ii) documents and instruments customarily used for the making of payments or transfers in international transactions;

(iii) notes or coins;

*(c)* convertible and marketable securities of, or guaranteed by, foreign governments or international financial institutions.

(2) The Bank shall from time to time determine the type and form of convertible foreign exchange and the kinds of securities which may be held in the reserve of external assets pursuant to subsection (1) of this section.

(3) The Bank may include in its reserve of external assets any liquid external asset not included in subsection (1) of this section, or any readily available international drawing facility, which the Bank, after consultation with the International Monetary Fund and with the approval of the Minister, considers suitable for inclusion in such reserve.

Dealings in gold and foreign exchange.

27. (1) The Bank may buy, sell, import, export, hold or otherwise deal in gold or foreign exchange under such terms and conditions as it shall determine:

Provided that the buying and selling rates involved in such transactions shall be in accordance with international agreements to which Kenya is a party, or with which Kenya is associated.

(2) The Bank may hold balances, denominated in foreign currencies, with foreign central banks or with the Bank's agents of correspondents abroad and, in its discretion, may invest such balances in

marketable short-term foreign securities denominated in convertible currencies.

Institutions with which Bank may deal in foreign exchange.

28. The Bank may engage in foreign exchange transactions only with—

(*a*) specified banks;
(*b*) public entities;
(*c*) foreign central banks, foreign banks, or foreign financial institutions;
(*d*) foreign governments or agencies of foreign governments;
(*e*) international financial institutions;
(*f*) any other person or body of persons whom the Minister, on the recommendation of the Bank, may, by notice in the Gazette, prescribe for the purposes of this section.

Relations with foreign central banks, foreign banks and foreign financial institutions.

29. The Bank may open accounts for and accept deposits from, collect money and other monetary claims for and on account of, foreign central banks, foreign banks and foreign financial institutions, and may generally act as banker to such banks or institutions.

Exchange control.

30. The Bank shall administer any law relating to exchange control that may be in force at any time in Kenya.

Payments agreements.

31. The Bank shall administer any payments agreement entered into by Kenya, and the Bank shall be consulted by the Government in negotiating any payments agreement.

Fiscal agent for Government's transactions with international financial institutions.

32. The Bank shall be the fiscal agent for all of the Government's transactions with international financial institutions of which Kenya is a member or with which Kenya is associated.

Depository.

33. The Bank shall act as depository for Kenya currency holdings owned by international financial institutions of which Kenya is a member or with which Kenya is associated.

## Part VII—Relations with Specified Banks

Banker to specified banks.

34. (1) The Bank shall open accounts for and accept deposits from, collect money and other monetary claims for and on account of, specified banks, and generally act as banker to specified banks.

(2) The Bank may provide any additional services or facilities that it considers desirable including inter-bank clearings to specified banks operating in Kenya.

35. The Bank may purchase from, sell to and rediscount on behalf of specified banks, bills of exchange, promissory notes and other credit instruments, bearing at least two good signatures, the last being the endorsement of a specified bank, maturing within one hundred and eighty days from the date of rediscount or acquisition by the Bank, and issued or made for the purpose of financing— Rediscounts.

*(a)* the importation or exportation of goods, or the transportation of goods within Kenya;

*(b)* the storage of non-perishable goods and products which are duly insured or deposited under conditions assuring their preservation in authorized warehouses or in other places approved by the Bank;

*(c)* industrial or agricultural production:

Provided that—

(i) if the Bank finds it to be in the interest of the national economy, the Bank may from time to time declare acceptable for the purposes of this paragraph instruments relating to industrial or agricultural production maturing within two hundred and seventy days; and

(ii) the Bank may require the credit instruments accepted by it under this paragraph to be secured by a pledge, hypothecation or assignment of the related products or crops.

36. The Bank may grant loans or advances for fixed periods not exceeding six months to specified banks which pledge the following as security for such loans or advances— Loans.

*(a)* the credit instruments referred to in section 35 of this Act; or

*(b)* negotiable securities issued or guaranteed by the Government, subject to the specifications and limitations provided for in sections 47, 48 and 49 of this Act.

37. Subject to the provisions of sections 35 and 36 of this Act, the Bank may determine the general terms and conditions under which it extends credit to specified banks, and in particular, the Bank shall determine and announce the rates of interest it will charge for rediscounting instruments, in accordance with section 35 of this Act, and granting loans or advances to specified banks in accordance with section 36 of this Act; and the Bank may determine different rates for different classes of transactions or maturities. Conditions for credit transactions.

38. (1) The Bank may, from time to time, require specified banks to maintain minimum cash balances on deposit with the Bank as reserves against their deposit and other liabilities: Reserve requirements.

Provided that such balances shall not exceed twenty per cent of each specified bank's total liabilities.

(2) Subject to the limit specified in subsection (1) of this section, the Bank may specify different ratios for different types of liabilities and may further specify the method of computing the amount of the total liabilities of a specified bank:

Provided that the ratios specified shall be the same for all specified banks.

(3) Any specification of, or increase in, the minimum reserve requirements under subsection (1) or subsection (2) of this section shall take effect only after the expiration of thirty days' notice to the specified banks of the Bank's intention to take such action.

(4) The Bank may impose on any specified bank which fails to maintain sufficient minimum cash balances required under subsection (1) or subsection (2) of this section a penalty interest charge not exceeding one per cent per day on the amount of the deficiency for each day for which the deficiency continues.

(5) The Bank may, if in its opinion circumstances of an unusual nature render it desirable so to do, pay interest at such rates and subject to such qualifications as it may determine on minimum cash balances deposited with the Bank in accordance with this section.

Regulation of interest rates of specified banks or specified financial institutions.

39. The Bank may, from time to time, acting in consultation with the Minister, determine and publish the maximum and minimum rates of interest which specified banks or specified financial institutions may pay on deposits and charge for loans or advances:

Provided that the Bank may in consultation with the Minister determine different rates of interest—

(i) for different types of deposits and loans; and

(ii) for different types of specified banks and financial institutions.

Credit controls over specified banks.

40. (1) The Bank may issue instructions specifying in respect of any loans, advances or investments made by specified banks—

*(a)* the purposes for which they may or may not be granted;

*(b)* the maximum maturities or, in the case of loans and advances, the type and minimum amount of security which shall be required, and in the case of letters of credit, the minimum amount of margin deposit; or

*(c)* the limits for any particular categories of loans, advances or investments or for their total amount outstanding.

(2) Instructions issued under this section shall not have retrospective effect, shall apply uniformly to all specified banks engaging in the credit transactions covered by the instructions, and shall, together with their effective dates, be published in the Gazette.

Credit controls over specified financial institutions.

41. (1) The Bank may issue instructions designed to control the volume, terms and conditions of credit, including instalment facilities, in the form of loans, advances or investments, extended by specified financial institutions.

(2) Instructions issued under this section shall not have retrospective effect, shall apply uniformly to all specified financial institutions engaged in any credit transactions covered by the instructions and shall, together with their effective dates, be published in the Gazette.

Bank to be consulted in licensing, etc., of banking businesses.

42. Whenever under any law relating to banking for the time being in force, an application for a licence to transact banking business is to be granted or refused, the power to issue licences or to exempt from the necessity to obtain a licence shall only be exercised with the concurrence of the Bank.[4]

Information to be furnished by specified banks, etc.

43. (1) Every specified bank and specified financial institution shall furnish to the Bank, at such time and in such manner as the Bank may prescribe, all such information and data as the Bank may reasonably require for the proper discharge of its functions under this Act.

(2) The Bank may publish in whole or in part, at such times and in such manner as it may decide, any information or data furnished under this section:

Provided that no such information shall be published which would disclose the financial affairs of any person or undertaking unless the prior consent in writing of such person or undertaking has first been obtained by the Bank.

## PART VIII—RELATIONS WITH PUBLIC ENTITIES

Fiscal agent and banker to public entities.

44. (1) The Bank shall act as fiscal agent of and banker to the Government.

(2) The Bank may also perform the functions of fiscal agent and banker for any other public entity in accordance with, and within the scope determined by, any special arrangements made between the Bank and the public entity concerned.

---

[4] Sec. 33 of The Banking Act, 1968 provides as follows:
"Section 42 of The Central Bank of Kenya Act is repealed."

Functions as fiscal agent.

45. The Bank in its capacity as fiscal agent and banker to any public entity shall, subject to the instructions of that public entity, have power—

(*a*) to be the official depository of the public entity concerned and accept deposits and effect payments for the account of that public entity:

Provided that the Bank may, after consultation with the Minister, select any specified bank to act in its name and for its account as the official depository of that public entity in places where the Bank has no office or branch;

(*b*) to maintain and operate special official accounts in accordance with arrangements made between the Bank and the public entity concerned;

(*c*) as an agent of the Government, to administer the public debt including the issuance of, payment of interest on, and redemption of, bonds and other securities of the Government;

(*d*) to pay, remit, collect or accept for deposit or custody funds in Kenya or abroad;

(*e*) to purchase, sell, transfer or accept for custody cheques, bills of exchange and securities;

(*f*) to collect the proceeds, whether principal or interest, resulting from the sale for, or accruing to the interest of, a public entity of securities or other property;

(*g*) to purchase, sell, transfer or accept for custody gold or foreign exchange.

Direct advances to Government.

46. (1) The Bank may make direct advances to the Government.

(2) Advances made under this section shall bear interest at such rate as may be determined by the Bank with the consent of the Minister, but in no event shall such rate be less than three per cent per annum.

Credit operations with Government securities.

47. The Bank may purchase, hold or sell negotiable securities of any maturity issued by the Government, or issued by any other public entity and guaranteed by the Government.

Limit on lending to Government.

48. The aggregate of—

(*a*) the Bank's direct advances to the Government under the authority of section 46 of this Act;

(*b*) the value of securities owned by the Bank in accordance with section 47 of this Act; and

(*c*) the value of securities held by the Bank as security in accordance with section 36(*b*) of this Act, shall not at any one time exceed two hundred and forty million shillings:

Provided that of this amount the value of securities which mature later than twelve months from the date of acquisition or acceptance as security by the Bank shall not at any one time exceed sixty million shillings.

49. Except as provided in accordance with sections 36*(b)*, 46, 47 and 48 of this Act, the Bank shall not extend any credit directly or indirectly to any public entity.

Prohibition of other credit to public entities.

50. (1) It shall be the duty of the Bank to advise the Minister on any matter which in its opinion is likely to affect the achievement of the principal objects of the Bank as specified in section 4 of this Act.

Adviser to Government.

(2) The Bank may tender advice to the Minister on any matter in which the Bank is concerned.

(3) The Minister may request the Bank to give its advice on any particular measures, situations or transactions, or on monetary, banking and credit conditions in or outside Kenya, and the Bank shall give its advice accordingly.

## PART IX—MISCELLANEOUS PROVISIONS

51. (1) Profits or losses which are attributable to any revaluation of the Bank's net assets or liabilities in gold, foreign exchange or foreign securities made as a result of any change in the par value of any currency unit shall be excluded from the computation of the annual profits and losses of the Bank.

Revaluation profits.

(2) All profits or losses so excluded shall be transferred to a special account to be called the Revaluation Account.

52. The Bank shall not—

Prohibited operations.

*(a)* save as expressly authorized by this Act, engage in trade, or own or acquire any direct interest in any commercial, agricultural, industrial or similar undertaking, except in the course of obtaining satisfaction for any debt due to the Bank, provided that any such interest shall be disposed of at the earliest suitable opportunity;

*(b)* purchase, acquire or lease immovable property for commercial purposes or as an investment except for its own business requirements or for the use of its employees;

(*c*) draw or accept bills payable otherwise than on demand; or
(*d*) guarantee any loan, advance or investment.

Financial year.

53. The financial year of the Bank shall be the same as the Government's financial year and the accounts of the Bank shall be closed at the end of each financial year.

Annual reports.

54. Within three months after the close of each financial year the Bank shall submit to the Minister a report on the Bank's operations throughout that year, together with the balance sheet and the profit and loss account as certified by auditors appointed by the Bank and approved by the Minister.

Publication of reports, etc.

55. (1) After submission to the Minister the Bank shall publish the annual report referred to in section 54 of this Act.

(2) The Bank may also issue such other publications as it considers to be in the public interest.

Audit by Controller and Auditor-General.

56. The Minister may, in addition to the audit carried out under section 54 of this Act, if he thinks fit, require the Controller and Auditor-General to audit the accounts of the Bank.

[57. *Spent.*]

## PART X—TRANSITIONAL PROVISIONS

Repeal. O.I.C., Group 17.

58. The East African Currency Board Regulations 1955, in so far as they apply to Kenya, may be repealed by the Minister, by notice in the Gazette, in whole or in part, as and when he considers necessary.

Taking over assets of East African Currency Board.

59. Kenya's share of the assets of the East African Currency Board shall be transferred to the Bank as and when those assets become available and the Bank shall have the sole right to receive those assets.

Exclusion of fiduciary issue from the limits on Government credit.

60. Any Kenya securities or their equivalent on conversion received by the Bank as part of Kenya's share of the assets of the East African Currency Board shall not be deemed to be credits to the Government for the purposes of computing the limits on credit specified in section 48 of this Act.

[61. *Spent.*]

[SCHEDULE. *Spent.*]

*{The Subsidiary Legislation is omitted from this volume.}*

# Treaty Amending and Re-Enacting the Charter of the East African Development Bank

WHEREAS the Governments of the United Republic of Tanzania, the Republic of Uganda, and the Republic of Kenya (hereinafter referred to as the Parties) did in Article 21 of the Treaty for East African Co-operation of 6 June 1967 (hereinafter referred to as the Treaty of 1967), agree to establish a development bank, known as the East African Development Bank (hereinafter referred to as the Bank), the Charter therefor (hereinafter referred to as the Charter) being set out in Annex VI of said Treaty of 1967;

WHEREAS the said Treaty of 1967 is no longer operative;

WHEREAS the Parties wish to adopt certain amendments to the Charter and to re-enact the Charter as thus amended;

NOW THEREFORE the Parties, being all the States members of the Bank, agree as follows:

## Art. 1. AMENDMENTS TO THE BANK CHARTER

1. The Parties adopt as amendments to the Charter all the modifications thereto incorporated in the text of the Charter in the Annex to this Treaty.

2. The Parties agree that the Charter, as amended in pursuance of the provisions of the preceding paragraph, shall henceforth derive its legal force from and be applied on the basis of this Treaty, and by operation of its provisions, without regard to the Treaty of 1967. The Charter shall therefore continue in force notwithstanding any termination, denunciation, suspension, amendment, modification, or any other event or occurrence affecting the validity or effectiveness of the Treaty of 1967 in whole or in part.

Art. 2. ENTRY INTO FORCE

This Treaty and the amendments to the Charter shall come into force when the last signature has been affixed to this Treaty.

Art. 3. DEPOSITARY

This Treaty shall be deposited with the Secretary of the Bank who, as Depositary, shall register it with the Secretary-General of the United Nations, and shall send certified true copies to all the Parties and to the bodies corporate, enterprises or institutions members of the Bank. The aforementioned bodies corporate, enterprises or institutions members of the Bank may thereupon signify their acceptance of the amendments by transmitting Letters of Acceptance to the Depositary. The Depositary shall notify all members of the Bank of Letters of Acceptance as they are received.

IN WITNESS WHEREOF the Parties have signed this Treaty in the English language on the dates and at the places indicated beneath their respective signatures.

For the Government of the United Republic of Tanzania:
Minister of Finance
7th January 1980
Dar-es-Salaam

For the Government of the Republic of Uganda:
Minister of Regional Cooperation
13th September 1979
Kampala

For the Government of the Republic of Kenya:
Minister of Planning and Economic Development
23rd July 1980
Nairobi

## The Charter of the East African Development Bank

WHEREAS the Governments of the United Republic of Tanzania, the Sovereign State of Uganda and the Republic of Kenya have in Article 21 of the Treaty for East African Co-operation, of 6 June 1967 agreed to establish a Development Bank to be known as the East African Development Bank:

WHEREAS the said Governments have agreed in Article 22 of the Treaty that the Charter of the East African Development Bank shall be set out in an Annex to the Treaty:

WHEREAS the said Governments, by virtue of a Treaty amending and re-enacting the Charter of the East African Development Bank signed by them on 23.7.1980, have decided to confer legal force and existence on the Charter independent of the Treaty for East African Co-operation and to amend the Charter to make possible a wider membership of the Bank, to emphasize its consulting and promotion functions, and for other purposes:

AND WHEREAS the said Governments share a common desire to promote the equitable distribution of benefits available from the East African Development Bank among Member States:

NOW THEREFORE it is agreed that the East African Development Bank (hereinafter referred to as "the Bank") be established and operate in accordance with the following provisions:

## CHAPTER I. OBJECTIVES AND MEMBERSHIP

### Art. 1. OBJECTIVES OF THE BANK

The objectives of the Bank shall be—

*(a)* to provide financial assistance to promote the development of the Member States;

*(b)* to provide consulting, promotion, agency and other similar services for the region;

*(c)* to give attention, in accordance with the operating principles contained in this Charter, to economic development in the Member States, in such fields as industry, tourism, agriculture, infrastructure such as transport and telecommunications and similar or related fields of development;

*(d)* to generally promote the development of the region;

*(e)* to supplement the activities of the national development agencies of the Member States by joint financing operations, technical assistance and by the use of such agencies as channels for financing specific projects;

*(f)* to co-operate, within the terms of this Charter, with other institutions and organizations, public or private, national or international, which are interested in the development of the Member States; and

*(g)* to undertake such other activities and provide such other services as may advance the objectives of the Bank.

**Art. 2.** MEMBERSHIP IN THE BANK

1. The original members of the Bank shall be the Member States and such bodies corporate, enterprises or institutions who remain members of the Bank on the date of entry into force of the amendments to this Charter adopted by the Member States in the Treaty of 23.7.1980 amending and re-enacting this Charter.

2. Upon an affirmative decision of the Governing Council, any state in the region, body corporate, enterprise or institution, which has not become a member under paragraph 1 of this Article, may be admitted to membership of the Bank under such terms and conditions consistent with this Charter, as the Bank may determine.

## CHAPTER II. CAPITAL

**Art. 3.** AUTHORIZED CAPITAL

1. The authorized capital stock of the Bank shall be 400,000,000 units of account and the value of the unit of account shall be 0.124414 grams of fine gold.

2. The authorized capital stock of the Bank shall be divided into 4,000 shares having a par value of 100,000 units of account each which shall be available for subscription only by members in accordance with Article 4 of this Charter.

3. The original authorized capital stock of the Bank shall be divided equally into paid-in shares and callable shares.

4. The authorized capital stock of the Bank may, after consultation with the Board of Directors, be increased by the Governing Council.

**Art. 4.** SUBSCRIPTION OF SHARES

1. Each member of the Bank shall subscribe to shares of the capital stock of the Bank.

2. Each subscription to the original authorized capital stock of the Bank shall be for paid-in shares and callable shares in equal parts.

3. The initial subscription of each of the Member States to the original authorized capital stock of the Bank shall be 800 shares and the initial subscriptions of other original members to the original authorized capital stock of the Bank shall be as determined by the Governments of the Member States.

4. The initial subscriptions of members, other than original members, to the authorized capital stock of the Bank shall be determined by

the Bank but no subscription shall be authorized which would have the effect of reducing the percentage of capital stock held by the Member States below 51 per cent of the total subscribed capital stock.

5. If the authorized capital stock of the Bank is increased, the following provisions shall apply—

   *(a)* subject to this Article, subscriptions to any increase of the authorized capital stock shall be subject to such terms and conditions as the Bank shall determine;

   *(b)* the Member States shall subscribe to equal parts only of the increased capital stock; and

   *(c)* each member, other than a Member State, shall be given a reasonable opportunity to subscribe to a proportion of the increase of stock equivalent to the proportion which its stock theretofore subscribed bears to the total subscribed capital stock immediately prior to such increase:

   Provided that no such member shall be obligated to subscribe to any part of an increase of capital stock;

   Provided that the foregoing provisions of sub-paragraphs *(b)* and *(c)* of this paragraph 5 shall not apply in respect of any increase or portion of an increase in the authorized capital stock which is intended solely to give effect to determinations of the Bank under paragraph 4; and

   Provided further that subscriptions shall be restricted proportionately to the extent necessary to ensure that the percentage of capital stock held by the Member States remains not less than 51 per cent of the total subscribed capital stock.

6. Shares of stock initially subscribed for by the original members shall be issued at par. Other shares shall be issued at par unless the Bank, by a vote representing a majority of the total voting power of members, decides in special circumstances to issue them on other terms.

7. Shares of stock shall not be pledged or encumbered in any manner whatsoever and they shall not be transferable except to the Bank;

   Provided that if any shares of stock which are transferred to the Bank are subsequently subscribed for by or otherwise transferred to the Member States, they shall take up such shares in equal parts only.

8. The liability of the members on shares shall be limited to the unpaid portion of the issue price of the shares.

9. No member shall be liable, by reason of its membership in the Bank, for obligations of the Bank.

Art. 5. PAYMENT OF SUBSCRIPTIONS

1. Payment of the amount initially subscribed by the original members to the paid-in capital stock of the Bank shall be made in four instalments the first of which shall be 10 per cent of such amount and the remaining instalments shall each be 30 per cent of such amount. The first instalment payable by each Member State shall be paid within 30 days after the coming into force of the Treaty to which this Charter is annexed and in the case of original members other than Member States, the first instalment shall be paid within 30 days of their becoming a member. The second instalment shall be paid six calendar months after the date on which the Treaty comes into force. The remaining two instalments shall each be paid successively six calendar months from the date on which the preceding instalment becomes due under this paragraph.

2. Notwithstanding the provisions of paragraph 1 of this Article, in respect of any instalment, other than the first instalment of the initial subscriptions to the original paid-in capital stock, the Bank shall, if the funds are not immediately required, either defer the due date for payment of such instalment or require that part only of such instalment be payable on the due date and at the same time prescribe a due date for the remainder of such instalment.

3. Of each instalment for the payment of subscriptions by each of the Member States to the original paid-in capital stock—

   *(a)* 50 per cent shall be paid in convertible currency;
   *(b)* 50 per cent shall be paid in the currency of the Member State concerned.

4. Each payment of a Member State in its own currency under sub-paragraph *(b)* of paragraph 3 of this Article shall be in such amount as the Bank, after such consultation with the International Monetary Fund as the Bank may consider necessary, determines to be equivalent to the full value in terms of the unit of account as expressed in paragraph 1 of Article 3 of this Charter of the portion of the subscription being paid.

5. This initial payment of a Member State under sub-paragraph *(b)* of paragraph 3 of this Article shall be in such amount as the member considers appropriate but shall be subject to such adjustment, to be effected within 90 days of the date on which such payment was made, as the Bank shall determine to be necessary to constitute the full value of such payment in terms of the unit of account as expressed in paragraph 1 of Article 3 of this Charter.

6. Each instalment for the payment of subscriptions by members other than Member States to the original paid-in capital stock shall be paid in convertible currency.

7. Payment of the amount subscribed for callable shares in the capital stock of the Bank shall be subject to call by the Board of Directors from time to time but such calls shall only be made as and when the amount thereof shall be required by the Bank—

   *(a)* To repay moneys raised by the Bank in capital markets borrowed or otherwise acquired by the Bank for the purpose of making or participating in direct loans;
   *(b)* to pay or repay any loans or loans guaranteed in whole or in part by the Bank in furtherance of its objectives.

8. In the event of a call being made in terms of paragraph 7 of this Article, payment may be made at the option of the member in convertible currency or in the currency required to discharge the obligations of the Bank for the purposes for which the call is made. Calls on unpaid subscriptions shall be uniform in percentage on all callable shares.

9. The Bank shall determine the place for any payment of subscriptions, provided that, until the first meeting of its Board of Directors, the payment of the first instalment referred to in paragraph 1 of this Article shall be made to the Bank of Uganda as Trustee for the Bank.

## CHAPTER III. ORDINARY CAPITAL RESOURCES AND SPECIAL FUNDS

### Art. 6. ORDINARY CAPITAL RESOURCES

In the context of this Charter, the term "ordinary capital resources" of the Bank shall include—

*(a)* the authorized capital stock of the Bank including both paid-in and callable shares subscribed pursuant to Article 4 of this Charter;
*(b)* funds raised by borrowings of the Bank by virtue of powers conferred by Article 19 of this Charter to which the commitment to calls provided for in paragraph 7 of Article 5 of this Charter is applicable;
*(c)* funds received in repayment of loans or guarantees made with the resources specified in paragraphs *(a)* and *(b)* of this Article;
*(d)* income derived from loans made from the above-mentioned funds or from guarantees to which the commitment to calls pro-

vided for in paragraph 7 of Article 5 of this Charter is applicable; and

(*e*) any other funds or income received by the Bank which do not form part of its Special Funds referred to in Article 7 of this Charter.

**Art. 7.** SPECIAL FUNDS

1. The Bank may accept for administration, from such sources as it considers appropriate, Special Funds which are designed to promote the objectives of the Bank.
2. Special Funds accepted by the Bank under paragraph 1 of this Article shall be used in such manner and on such terms and conditions as are not inconsistent with the objectives of the Bank and the agreement under which such funds are accepted by the Bank for administration.
3. The Board of Directors shall make such regulations as may be necessary for the administration and use of each Special Fund. Such regulations shall be consistent with the provisions of this Charter, other than those provisions which expressly relate only to the ordinary operations of the Bank.
4. The term "Special Funds" as used in this Charter shall refer to the resources of any Special Fund and shall include—

   (*a*) funds accepted by the Bank in any Special Fund;

   (*b*) funds repaid in respect of loans or guarantees financed from any Special Fund which, under the regulations of the Bank covering that Special Fund, are received by such Special Fund; and

   (*c*) income derived from operations of the Bank in which any of the above-mentioned resources or funds are used or committed if, under the regulations of the Bank covering the Special Fund concerned, that income accrues to such Special Fund.

## CHAPTER IV. OPERATIONS OF THE BANK

**Art. 8.** USE OF RESOURCES

The resources and facilities of the Bank shall be used exclusively to implement the objectives of the Bank as set forth in Article 1 of this Charter.

**Art. 9.** ORDINARY AND SPECIAL OPERATIONS

1. The operations of the Bank shall consist of ordinary operations and special operations. Ordinary operations shall be those financed from

the ordinary capital resources of the Bank and special operations shall be those financed from the Special Funds referred to in Article 7 of this Charter.

2. The ordinary capital resources and the Special Funds of the Bank shall at all times and in all respects be held, used, committed, invested or otherwise disposed of entirely separately from each other.

3. The ordinary capital resources of the Bank shall not be charged with, or used to discharge, losses or liabilities arising out of special operations for which Special Funds were originally used or committed.

4. Expenses relating directly to ordinary operations shall be charged to ordinary capital resources of the Bank and those relating to special operations shall be charged to the Special Funds. Any other expenses shall be charged as the Bank shall determine.

### Art. 10. METHODS OF OPERATION

Subject to the conditions set forth in this Charter, the Bank may provide finances or facilitate financing in any of the following ways to any agency, entity or enterprise operating in the territories of the Member States—

*(a)* by making or participating in direct loans with its unimpaired paid-in capital and, except in the case of its Special Reserve as defined in Article 17 of this Charter, with its reserves and undistributed surplus or with the unimpaired Special Funds;
*(b)* by making or participating in direct loans with funds raised by the Bank in capital markets or borrowed or otherwise acquired by the Bank for inclusion in its ordinary capital resources;
*(c)* by investment of funds referred to in paragraphs *(a)* and *(b)* of this Article in the equity capital of an institution or enterprise; or
*(d)* by guaranteeing, in whole or in part, loans made by others for industrial development.

### Art. 11. LIMITATIONS ON OPERATIONS

1. The total amount outstanding of loans, equity investments and guarantees made by the Bank in its ordinary operations shall not at any time exceed one and a half times the total amount of its unimpaired subscribed capital, reserves and surplus included in its ordinary capital resources, excluding the Special Reserve and any other reserves not available for ordinary operations.

2. The total amount outstanding in respect of the special operations of the Bank relating to any Special Fund shall not at any time exceed

the total amount of the unimpaired special resources appertaining to that Special Fund.

3. In the case of loans made with funds borrowed by the Bank to which the commitment to calls provided for in paragraph 7 of Article 5 of this Charter is applicable, the total amount of principal outstanding and payable to the Bank in a specific currency shall not at any time exceed the total amount of the principal of outstanding borrowings by the Bank that are payable in the same currency.

4. In the case of funds invested in equity capital out of the ordinary capital resources of the Bank, the total amount invested shall not exceed 10 per cent of the aggregate amount of the unimpaired paid-in capital stock of the Bank actually paid up at any given time together with the reserves and surplus included in its ordinary capital resources, excluding the Special Reserve.

5. The amount of any equity investment in any entity or enterprise shall not exceed such percentage of the equity capital of that entity or enterprise as the Board of Directors shall in each specific case determine to be appropriate. The Bank shall not seek to obtain by such investment a controlling interest in the entity or enterprise concerned, except where necessary to safeguard the investment of the Bank.

6. In the case of guarantees given by the Bank in the course of its ordinary operations, the total amount guaranteed shall not exceed 10 per cent of the aggregate amount of the unimpaired paid-in capital stock of the Bank actually paid up at any given time together with the reserves and surplus included in its ordinary capital resources excluding the Special Reserve.

### Art. 12. PROVISION OF CURRENCIES FOR DIRECT LOANS

In making direct loans or participating in them, the Bank may provide finance in the following ways—

*(a)* by furnishing the borrower with currencies other than the currency of the Member State in whose territory the project is located, which are needed by the borrower to meet the foreign exchange costs of the project; or

*(b)* by providing, when local currency required for the purposes of the loan cannot be raised by the borrower on reasonable terms, local currency but not exceeding a reasonable portion of the total local expenditure to be incurred by the borrower.

**Art. 13.** OPERATING PRINCIPLES

The operations of the Bank shall be conducted in accordance with the following principles—

*(a)* the Bank shall be guided by sound banking principles in its operations and shall finance only economically sound and technically feasible projects, and shall not make loans or undertake any responsibility for the discharge or re-financing of earlier commitments by borrowers;

*(b)* in selecting projects, the Bank shall always be guided by the need to pursue the objectives set forth in Article 1 of this Charter, and shall also always adhere to the principle of equitable distribution of benefits of the Bank;

*(c)* the Bank shall so conduct its operations as to earn a reasonable return on its capital;

*(d)* the operations of the Bank shall provide principally for the financing directly of specific projects within the Member States but may include loans to or guarantees of loans made to the national development agencies of the Member States so long as such loans or guarantees are in respect of and used for specific projects which are agreed to by the Bank;

*(e)* the Bank shall seek to maintain a reasonable diversification in its investments;

*(f)* the Bank shall seek to revolve its funds by selling its investments in equity capital to other investors wherever it can appropriately do so on satisfactory terms;

*(g)* the Bank shall not undertake any operation in the territory of any State if that State objects to such operation;

*(h)* before a loan is granted or guaranteed or an investment made, the applicant shall have submitted an adequate proposal to the Bank, and the Director-General of the Bank shall have presented to the Board of Directors a written report regarding the proposal, together with his recommendations;

*(i)* in considering an application for a loan or guarantee, the Bank shall pay due regard to the ability of the borrower to obtain finance or facilities elsewhere on terms and conditions that the Bank considers reasonable for the recipient, taking into account all pertinent factors;

*(j)* in making or guaranteeing a loan, the Bank shall pay due regard to the prospects that the borrower and its guarantor, if any, will be able to meet their obligations under the loan contract;

*(k)* in making or guaranteeing a loan, the rate of interest, other charges and the schedule for repayment of principal shall be

such as are, in the opinion of the Bank, appropriate for the loan concerned;

(*l*) in guaranteeing a loan made by other investors, the Bank shall charge a suitable fee or commission for its risk;

(*m*) in the case of a direct loan made by the Bank, the borrower shall be permitted by the Bank to draw the loan funds only to meet payments in connection with the project as they fall due;

(*n*) the Bank shall take all necessary measures to ensure that the proceeds of any loan made, guaranteed or participated in by the Bank are used only for the purposes for which the loan was granted and with due attention to considerations of economy and efficiency; and

(*o*) the Bank shall ensure that every loan contract entered into by it shall enable the Bank to exercise all necessary powers of entry, inspection and supervision of operations in connection with the project and shall further enable the Bank to require the borrower to provide information and to allow inspection of its books and records during such time as any part of the loan remains outstanding.

## Art. 14. PROHIBITION OF POLITICAL ACTIVITY

1. The Bank shall not accept loans, Special Funds or assistance that may in any way prejudice, limit, deflect or otherwise alter its objectives or functions.
2. The Bank, its Director-General and officers and staff shall not interfere in the political affairs of any state, nor shall they be influenced in their decisions by the political character of a State. Only economic considerations shall be relevant to their decisions and such considerations shall be weighed impartially to achieve and carry out the objectives and functions of the Bank.

## Art. 15. TERMS AND CONDITIONS FOR DIRECT LOANS AND GUARANTEES

1. In the case of direct loans made or participated in or loans guaranteed by the Bank, the contract shall establish, in conformity with the operating principles set out above and subject to the other provisions of this Charter, the terms and conditions for the loan or the guarantee concerned, including payment of principal, interest, commitment fee and other charges, maturities and dates of payment in respect of the loan, or the fees and other charges in respect of the guarantee, respectively.
2. The contract shall provide that all payments to the Bank under the contract shall be made in the currency loaned, unless, in the case of

a loan made or guaranteed as part of special operations, the regulations of the Bank provide otherwise.

3. Guarantees by the Bank shall also provide that the Bank may terminate its liability with respect to interest if, upon default by the borrower or any other guarantor, the Bank offers to purchase, at par and interest accrued to a date designated in the offer, the bonds or other obligations guaranteed.

4. Whenever it considers it appropriate, the Bank may require as a condition of granting or participating in a loan that the Member State in whose territory a project is to be carried out, or a public agency or instrumentality of that Member State acceptable to the Bank, guarantee the repayment of the principal and the payment of interest and other charges on the loan in accordance with the terms thereof.

5. The loan or guarantee contract shall specifically state the currency in which all payments to the Bank thereunder shall be made.

### Art. 16. COMMISSION AND FEES

1. In addition to interest, the Bank shall charge a commission on direct loans made or participated in as part of its ordinary operations at a rate to be determined by the Board of Directors and computed on the amount outstanding on each loan or participation.

2. In guaranteeing a loan as part of its ordinary operations, the Bank shall charge a guarantee fee at a rate determined by the Board of Directors payable periodically on the amount of the loan outstanding.

3. Other charges, including commitment fee, of the Bank in its ordinary operations and any commission, fees or other charges in relation to its special operations shall be determined by the Board of Directors. Such charges shall be set at such a level that said charges, together with interest and other expected earnings, shall enable the Bank to earn a reasonable return on its capital.

### Art. 17. SPECIAL RESERVE

The amount of commissions and guarantee fees received by the Bank under the provisions of Article 16 of this Charter shall be set aside as a Special Reserve which shall be kept for meeting liabilities of the Bank in accordance with Article 18 of this Charter. The Special Reserve shall be held in such liquid form as the Board of Directors may decide but the Board of Directors shall ensure that any part of the Special Reserve which it may decide to invest in the territories of the Member States shall be invested, as nearly as possible, in equal proportions in each Member State.

Art. 18. DEFAULTS ON LOANS AND METHODS OF MEETING LIABILITIES OF THE BANK

1. In cases of default on loans made, participated in or guaranteed by the Bank in its ordinary operations, the Bank shall take such action as it considers appropriate to conserve its investment including modification of the terms of the loan, other than any term as to the currency of repayment.
2. Payments in discharge of the Bank's liabilities on borrowings or guarantees chargeable to the ordinary capital resources shall be charged firstly against the Special Reserve and then, to the extent necessary and at the discretion of the Bank, against other reserves, surplus and capital available to the Bank.
3. Whenever necessary to meet contractual payments of interest, other charges or amortization on borrowings of the Bank in its ordinary operations, or to meet its liabilities with respect to similar payments in relation to loans guaranteed by it, chargeable to its ordinary capital resources, the Bank may call an appropriate amount of the uncalled subscribed callable capital in accordance with paragraphs 7 and 8 of Article 5 of this Charter.

## CHAPTER V. MISCELLANEOUS POWERS AND DUTIES OF THE BANK

Art. 19. MISCELLANEOUS POWERS

In addition to the powers specified elsewhere in this Charter, the Bank shall be empowered—

*(a)* to borrow funds in the territories of the Member States, or elsewhere, and in this connection to furnish such collateral or other security therefore as the Bank shall determine:
Provided that—
(i) before selling its obligations or otherwise borrowing in the territory of a country, the Bank shall obtain the approval of the Government of that country to the sale; and
(ii) before deciding to sell its obligations or otherwise borrowing in a particular country, the Bank shall consider the amount of previous borrowing, if any, in that country with

a view to diversifying its borrowing to the maximum extent possible;

(*b*) to buy and sell securities which the Bank has issued or guaranteed or in which it has invested;

(*c*) to guarantee securities in which it has invested in order to facilitate their sale;

(*d*) to invest funds not immediately needed in its operations in such obligations as it may determine and invest funds held by the Bank for pensions or similar purposes in marketable securities, but the Bank shall ensure that any funds which it may decide to invest in the territories of the Member States shall be invested, as nearly as possible, in equal proportions in each Member State;

(*e*) to charge for such technical advice and assistance as it may provide; and

(*f*) to study and promote the investment opportunities within the Member States.

## Art. 20. ALLOCATION OF NET INCOME

1. The Board of Directors shall determine annually what part of the net income of the Bank, including the net income accruing to the Special Funds, shall be allocated, after making provision for reserves to surplus and what part, if any, shall be distributed to the members.

2. Any distributions to members made pursuant to paragraph 1 of this Article shall be in proportion to the number of shares held by each member and payments shall be made in such manner and in such currency as the Board of Directors shall determine.

## Art. 21. POWER TO MAKE REGULATIONS

The Board of Directors may make such regulations, including financial regulations, being consistent with the provisions of this Charter as it considers necessary or appropriate to further the objectives and functions of the Bank.

## Art. 22. NOTICE TO BE PLACED ON SECURITIES

Every security issued or guaranteed by the Bank shall bear on its face a conspicuous statement to the effect that it is not an obligation of any Government, unless it is in fact the obligation of a particular Government, in which case it shall so state.

## CHAPTER VI. CURRENCIES

### Art. 23. DETERMINATION OF CONVERTIBILITY

Whenever it shall become necessary under this Charter to determine whether any currency is convertible, such determination shall be made by the Bank after consultation with the International Monetary Fund.

### Art. 24. USE OF CURRENCIES

1. The Member States may not maintain or impose any restriction on the holding or use by the Bank or by any recipient from the Bank for payments in any country of the following—
   *(a)* currencies received by the Bank in payment of subscriptions to its capital stock;
   *(b)* currencies purchased with the currencies referred to in sub-paragraph *(a)* of this paragraph;
   *(c)* currencies obtained by the Bank by borrowing for inclusion in its ordinary capital resources;
   *(d)* currencies received by the Bank in payment of principal, interest, dividends or other charges in respect of loans or investments made out of any of the funds referred to in sub-paragraphs *(a)*, *(b)* and *(c)* of this paragraph or in payment of fees in respect of guarantees made by the Bank; and
   *(e)* currencies received from the Bank in distribution of the net income of the Bank in accordance with Article 20 of this Charter.

2. The Member States may not maintain or impose any restriction on the holding or use by the Bank or by any recipient from the Bank, for payments in any country, of currency received by the Bank which does not come within the provisions of paragraph 1 of this Article unless such currency forms part of the Special Funds of the Bank and its use is subject to special regulations.

3. The Member States may not maintain or impose any restriction on the holding or use by the Bank, for making amortization payments or for repurchasing in whole or in part the Bank's own obligations, of currencies received by the Bank in repayment of direct loans made out of its ordinary capital resources.

4. Each Member State shall ensure, in respect of projects within its territories, that the currencies necessary to enable payments to be made to the Bank in accordance with the provisions of the contracts referred to in Article 15 of this Charter shall be made available in exchange for currency of the Member State concerned.

**Art. 25.** MAINTENANCE OF VALUE OF CURRENCY HOLDINGS

1. Whenever the par value[1] of the International Monetary Fund of the currency of a Member State is reduced or the foreign exchange value of the currency of a Member State has, in the opinion of the Bank, depreciated to a significant extent within the territory of that Member State, such Member State shall pay to the Bank within a reasonable time an additional amount of its own currency sufficient to maintain the value, as of the time of subscription, of the amount of the currency of such Member State paid in to the Bank by that Member State under sub-paragraph *(b)* of paragraph 3 of Article 5 of this Charter, and currency furnished under the provisions of this paragraph, provided, however, that the foregoing shall apply only so long as and to the extent that such currency shall not have been initially disbursed or exchanged for another currency.

2. Whenever the par value[1] of the International Monetary Fund of the currency of a Member State is increased, or the foreign exchange value of the currency of a State has, in the opinion of the Bank, appreciated to a significant extent within the territory of that Member State, the Bank shall return to such Member State within a reasonable time an amount of the currency of that Member State equal to the increase in the value of the amount of such currency to which the provisions of paragraph 1 of this Article are applicable.

## CHAPTER VII. ORGANIZATION AND MANAGEMENT OF THE BANK

**Art. 26.** STRUCTURE

The Bank shall have a Governing Council, a Board of Directors, a Director-General and such other officers and staff as it may consider necessary.

**Art. 27.** GOVERNING COUNCIL

1. The Governing Council shall have the following functions and powers:
   *(a)* to discuss and give guidance to the Board of Directors as appropriate with respect to:
      (i) the operations of the Bank;
      (ii) the Annual Report of the Bank; and
      (iii) any matters which the Board of Directors may refer to it;
   *(b)* to approve the annual accounts of the Bank;

[1] See footnote 3 on page 565.

(*c*) to approve any distribution or other allocation of net income by the Board of Directors; and

(*d*) to approve the appointment of external auditors or such other experts as may be necessary to examine and report on the general management of the Bank.

2. The Governing Council shall also take decisions, in pursuance of other provisions of this Charter, on:

(*a*) the admission of new members, under Article 2, paragraph 2;

(*b*) any increases in the authorized capital stock, under Article 3, paragraph 4;

(*c*) the election of the Chairman and Vice-Chairman of the Board of Directors, under Article 29, paragraph 2;

(*d*) the appointment, or cessation in office, of the Director-General, under Article 31;

(*e*) the termination of the operations of the Bank, under Article 40; and

(*f*) any amendment to the Charter, under Article 53.

3. The Governing Council shall consist of Ministers so designated by the Member States. It shall determine its own procedure, including that for convening its meetings, for the conduct of business thereat and at other times, and for the rotation of the office of Chairman among the Members.

4. Where a specific rule of voting is not established by another provision of this Charter, any member of the Governing Council may record his objection to a proposal submitted for the decision of the Governing Council and, if any such objection is recorded, the Governing Council shall not proceed with the proposal unless the objection is withdrawn.

**Art. 28.** BOARD OF DIRECTORS

1. All the powers of the Bank shall, subject to this Charter, be vested in the Board of Directors.

2. The Board of Directors shall consist of as many members as may result from the operation of the following provisions:

(*a*) each Member State shall be represented by, and shall appoint a director;

(*b*) up to two shall be elected by members other than Member States, unless the Governing Council decides otherwise:

Provided that no single member shall be represented by more than one director.

3. All directors shall be persons possessing high competence and wide experience in economic, financial and banking affairs.

4. Directors shall hold office for a term of three years and shall be eligible for reappointment or re-election:
Provided that—
   *(a)* of the first directors of the Bank two, who shall be chosen by the directors by lot, shall hold office for two years;
   *(b)* a director shall remain in office until his successor has been appointed or elected;
   *(c)* a director appointed or elected in place of one whose office has become vacant before the end of his term shall hold office only for the remainder of that term;
   *(d)* a director appointed by a Member State may be required at any time by that Member State to vacate his office.

5. There shall be appointed or elected, as the case may be, an alternate director in respect of each substantive director and an alternate director shall be appointed or elected in the same manner and for the same term of office as the director to whom he is an alternate; and an alternate director shall remain in office until his successor has been appointed or elected.

6. An alternate director may participate in meetings but may vote only when he is acting in place of and in the absence of the director to whom he is an alternate.

7. While the office of a director is vacant the alternate of the former director shall exercise the powers of that director.

## Art. 29. PROCEDURE OF THE BOARD OF DIRECTORS

1. The Board of Directors shall normally meet at the principal office of the Bank and shall meet at least once every three months or more frequently if the business of the Bank so requires.

2. The Governing Council shall elect from among the members of the Board of Directors a Chairman and a Vice-Chairman of the Board. The Chairman, or in his absence, the Vice-Chairman, shall act as presiding officer of the Board. Meetings of the Board shall be convened by the Chairman, or in his absence, by the Vice-Chairman. Meetings other than regular meetings shall be so convened:
   *(a)* whenever the Chairman or, in his absence, the Vice-Chairman deems it necessary or desirable; or
   *(b)* whenever the Director-General so requests; or

(*c*) whenever a majority of the members of the Board or of the members of the Bank so requests.

3. A quorum for any meeting of the Board of Directors shall be either: (i) four directors, including three directors appointed by the Member States, or, if there is no member other than the Member States, then three directors; or (ii) if there be six or more Member States, a majority of the total number of directors including a majority of the directors appointed by the Member States.

   Provided that if within two hours of the time appointed for the holding of a meeting of the Board of Directors a quorum is not present the meeting shall automatically stand adjourned to the next day, at the same time and place, or if that day is a public holiday, to the next succeeding day which is not a public holiday at the same time and place, and if at such adjourned meeting a quorum is not present within two hours from the time appointed for the meeting, the directors present shall constitute a quorum and may transact the business for which the meeting was called.

4. The Board of Directors may, by regulation, establish a procedure whereby a decision in writing signed by all the Directors of the Bank shall be as valid and effectual as if it had been made at a meeting of the Board of Directors.

## Art. 30. VOTING

1. The voting power of each member of the Bank shall be equal to the number of shares of the capital stock of the Bank held by that member.

2. In voting in the Board of Directors—

   (*a*) an appointed director shall be entitled to cast the number of votes of the Member State which appointed him;

   (*b*) each elected director shall be entitled to cast the number of votes of those members of the Bank whom he represents, which votes need not be cast as a unit; for the purposes of this provision, each member (not being a Member State) shall notify the Bank which elected director represents that member; and

   (*c*) except as otherwise expressly provided in this Charter, all matters before the Board of Directors shall be decided by a majority of the total voting power of the members of the Bank.

## Art. 31. DIRECTOR-GENERAL OF THE BANK

1. There shall be a Director-General of the Bank who shall be appointed by the Governing Council, and who, while he remains Director-

General, may not hold office as a director or an alternate to a director, or any other directorship. Nor shall he perform any function outside the Bank which in the opinion of the Board is incompatible with his office in the Bank.

2. Subject to paragraph 3 of this Article, the Director-General shall hold office for a term of five years and may be re-appointed.
3. The Director-General shall vacate his office if the Governing Council so decides.
4. If the office of Director-General becomes vacant for any reason, a successor shall be appointed for a new term of five years.
5. The Director-General shall be the legal representative of the Bank.
6. The Director-General shall be chief of the staff of the Bank and shall conduct under the direction of the Board of Directors the current business of the Bank. He shall be responsible for the organization, appointment and dismissal of the officers and staff in accordance with regulations adopted by the Board of Directors.
7. In appointing officers and staff the Director-General shall, subject to the paramount importance of securing the highest standards of efficiency and technical competence, pay due regard to the recruitment of citizens of the Member States.
8. The Board shall make arrangements for another officer of the Bank to perform the duties and exercise the powers of the Director-General in the event of the temporary absence or incapacity of the Director-General.
9. Decisions of the Governing Council concerning the appointment or cessation in office of the Director-General shall be taken by a vote representing not less than 75 per cent of the total voting power of the members of the Bank.

**Art. 32.** LOYALTIES OF DIRECTOR-GENERAL AND OFFICERS AND STAFF

The Director-General and officers and staff of the Bank, in the discharge of their offices, owe their duty entirely to the Bank and to no other authority. Each member of the Bank shall respect the international character of this duty and shall refrain from all attempts to influence the Director-General or any of the officers and staff in the discharge of their duties.

**Art. 33.** OFFICES OF THE BANK

The principal office of the Bank shall be located at Kampala in Uganda and the Bank may establish offices or agencies elsewhere.

**Art. 34.** CHANNEL OF COMMUNICATIONS AND DEPOSITORIES

1. Each member of the Bank shall designate an appropriate official, entity or person with whom the Bank may communicate in connection with any matter arising under this Charter.

2. Each Member State shall designate its central bank, or such other agency as may be agreed upon with the Bank, as a depository with which the Bank may keep its holdings of currency and other assets.

**Art. 35.** WORKING LANGUAGE

The working language of the Bank shall be English.

**Art. 36.** ACCOUNTS AND REPORTS

1. The Board of Directors shall ensure that proper accounts and proper records are kept in relation to the operations of the Bank and such accounts shall be audited in respect of each financial year by auditors of high repute selected by the Board of Directors.

2. The Bank shall prepare and transmit to the Governing Council and to the members of the Bank, and shall also publish, an annual report containing an audited statement of its accounts.

3. The Bank shall prepare and transmit to its members quarterly a summary statement of its financial position, and a profit and loss statement showing the results of its operations.

4. All financial statements of the Bank shall show ordinary operations and the operations of each Special Fund separately.

5. The Bank may also publish such other reports as it considers desirable in carrying out its objectives and functions, and such reports shall be transmitted to members of the Bank.

## CHAPTER VIII. WITHDRAWAL AND SUSPENSION OF MEMBERS

**Art. 37.** WITHDRAWAL OF MEMBERS

1. A Member State may not withdraw from the Bank.

2. Any member, other than a Member State, may withdraw from the Bank at any time by delivering a notice in writing to the Bank at its principal office.

3. Withdrawal by a member under paragraph 2 of this Article shall become effective, and its membership shall cease, on the date

specified in its notice but in no event less than six months after the date that notice has been received by the Bank. However, at any time before the withdrawal becomes finally effective, the member may notify the Bank in writing of the cancellation of its notice of intention to withdraw.

**Art. 38.** SUSPENSION OF MEMBERSHIP

1. If a member of the Bank, other than a Member State, fails to fulfil any of its obligations to the Bank, the Board of Directors may suspend such member by a majority vote of the total number of Directors representing not less than 75 per cent of the total voting power of the members including the affirmative votes of each of the Member States.
2. The member so suspended shall automatically cease to be a member of the Bank six months from the date of its suspension unless the Board of Directors decides, within that period and by the same majority necessary for suspension, to restore the member to good standing.
3. While under suspension, a member shall not be entitled to exercise any rights under this Charter but shall remain subject to all its obligations.

**Art. 39.** SETTLEMENT OF ACCOUNTS

1. *(a)* For the purposes of this paragraph the words "the relevant date" shall mean in respect to any member either the date on which that member delivered a withdrawal notice in accordance with Article 37 hereof (if such member ceased to be a member as a result of such notice) or, as the case may be, the date on which that member ceased to be a member in accordance with Article 38 hereof;

   *(b)* after the relevant date, a member shall remain liable for any balance required by the Bank to be paid by the member on account of the amount originally subscribed for its shares and for any calls made by the Bank pursuant to Article 5(7) hereof in respect of the member's shares on or before the relevant date and also for the contingent liability of that member for any calls made by the Bank in respect of that member's shares after the relevant date to meet obligations of the Bank resulting from any loans or guarantees contracted by the Bank before the relevant date; but such member shall not incur liability with respect to loans and guarantees entered into by the Bank after

the relevant date nor shall it share either in the income or the expense of the Bank after the relevant date.

2. At the time a member ceases to be a member, the Bank may arrange for the repurchase of its shares as a part of the settlement of accounts with such member in accordance with the provisions of paragraphs 3 and 4 of this Article. For this purpose, the repurchase price of the shares shall be the amount certified by auditors of high repute selected by the Board of Directors on the date the member ceases to be a member.

3. The payment for shares repurchased by the Bank under this Article shall be governed by the following conditions—

   *(a)* any amount due to the member concerned for its shares shall be withheld so long as that member remains liable immediately, in the future or contingently as a borrower or guarantor, to the Bank and such amount may, at the option of the Bank, be applied on any such liability as it matures. No amount shall be withheld on account of the contingent liability of the member for future calls on its subscription for shares in accordance with paragraph 7 of Article 5 of this Charter. In any event, no amount due to a member for its shares shall be paid six months after the date on which the member ceases to be a member;

   *(b)* payments for shares may be made from time to time, upon their surrender by the member concerned, to the extent by which the amount due as the repurchase price in accordance with paragraph 2 of this Article exceeds the aggregate amount due immediately, in the future or contingently from such member as a borrower from or a guarantor to the Bank as referred to in sub-paragraph *(a)* in this paragraph, until the former member has received the full repurchase price;

   *(c)* payments shall be made in such available currencies as the Bank determines, taking into account its financial position;

   *(d)* if losses are sustained by the Bank on any guarantees or loans which were outstanding on the date when a member ceased to be a member and the amount of such losses exceeds the amount of any reserve specifically provided against such losses on that date, the member concerned shall repay, upon demand, the amount by which the repurchase price of its shares would have been reduced if the losses had been taken into account when the repurchase price was determined. In addition, the former member shall remain liable on any call for unpaid subscriptions in accordance with paragraph 7 of Article 5 of this Charter, to the same extent that it would have been required to respond if

the impairment of capital had occurred and the call had been made at the time the repurchase price of its shares was determined; and

(*e*) nothing herein contained shall render any member, whether or not he shall cease to be a member, liable in his capacity as a member or former member of the Bank for any sum or sums in excess of the portion of the issue price of his shares for the time being unpaid.

4. If the Bank terminates its operations pursuant to Article 40 of this Charter within six months of the date upon which any member ceases to be a member, all rights of the member concerned shall be determined in accordance with the provisions of Articles 40 to 42 of this Charter. Such member shall be considered as still a member for the purposes of such Articles but shall have no voting rights.

## Chapter IX. Termination of Operations

### Art. 40. TERMINATION OF OPERATIONS

1. The Bank may terminate its operations by resolution of the Governing Council approved by a vote representing not less than 85 per cent of the total voting power of the members.

2. After such termination, the Bank shall forthwith cease all activities, except those incidental to the orderly realization, conservation and preservation of its assets and the settlement of its obligations.

### Art. 41. LIABILITY OF MEMBERS AND PAYMENT OF CLAIMS

1. In the event of termination of the operations of the Bank, the liability of all members for uncalled subscriptions to the capital stock of the Bank shall continue until all claims of creditors, including all contingent claims, shall have been discharged.

2. All creditors holding direct claims shall first be paid out of the assets of the Bank and then out of payments to the Bank on unpaid or callable subscriptions. Before making any payments to creditors holding direct claims, the Board of Directors shall make such arrangements as are necessary, in its judgment, to ensure a *pro rata* distribution among holders of direct and contingent claims.

### Art. 42. DISTRIBUTION OF ASSETS

1. No distribution of assets shall be made to members on account of their subscriptions to the capital stock of the Bank until all liabilities

to creditors shall have been discharged or provided for and any such distribution shall be approved by the Board of Directors by a vote representing not less than 85 per cent of the total voting power of the members.

2. Any distribution of the assets of the Bank to the members shall be in proportion to the capital stock held by each member and shall be effected at such times and under such conditions as the Bank shall consider fair and equitable. The shares of assets distributed need not be uniform as to type of asset. No member shall be entitled to receive its share in such a distribution of assets until it has settled all of its obligations to the Bank.

3. Any member receiving assets distributed pursuant to this Article shall enjoy the same rights with respect to such assets as the Bank enjoyed prior to their distribution.

## Chapter X. Status, Immunities and Privileges

### Art. 43. PURPOSE OF CHAPTER

To enable the Bank effectively to fulfil its objectives and carry out the functions with which it is entrusted, the status immunities, exemptions and privileges set forth in this Chapter shall be accorded to the Bank in the territories of each of the Member States.

### Art. 44. LEGAL STATUS

The Bank shall possess full juridical personality and, in particular, full capacity—

*(a)* to contract;
*(b)* to acquire, and dispose of, immovable and movable property; and
*(c)* to institute legal proceedings.

### Art. 45. JUDICIAL PROCEEDINGS

1. Actions may be brought against the Bank in the territories of the Member States only in a court of competent jurisdiction in a Member State in which the Bank has an office, has appointed an agent for the purpose of accepting service or notice of process, or has issued or guaranteed securities.

2. No action shall be brought against the Bank by members or persons acting for or deriving claims from members. However members shall have recourse to such special procedures for the settlement of controversies between the Bank and its members as may be prescribed

in this Charter, in the regulations of the Bank or in contracts entered into with the Bank.

**Art. 46.** IMMUNITY OF ASSETS

1. Property and other assets of the Bank, wheresoever located and by whomsoever held, shall be immune from requisition, confiscation, expropriation or any other form of taking or foreclosure by executive or legislative action and premises used for the business of the Bank shall be immune from search.

2. The Bank shall prevent its premises from becoming refuges for fugitives from justice, or for persons subject to extradition, or persons avoiding service of legal process or a judicial proceeding.

**Art. 47.** IMMUNITY OF ARCHIVES

The archives of the Bank and all documents belonging to it, or held by it, shall be inviolable wherever located.

**Art. 48.** FREEDOM OF ASSETS FROM RESTRICTION

To the extent necessary to carry out the objectives and functions of the Bank and subject to the provisions of this Charter, all property and other assets of the Bank shall be free from restrictions, regulations, controls and moratoria of any nature.

**Art. 49.** PERSONAL IMMUNITIES AND PRIVILEGES

1. All directors, alternates, officers and employees of the Bank—
   *(a)* shall be immune from civil process with respect to acts performed by them in their official capacity; and
   *(b)* shall be accorded such immunities from immigration restrictions or alien registration, and where they are not citizens of a Member State, such facilities in relation to exchange regulations as are accorded by Member States to the representatives, officials and employees of comparable rank of other Member States.

2. Experts or consultants rendering services to the Bank shall be accorded the same immunities and privileges as in paragraph 1 above, unless the Member State concerned determines otherwise.

**Art. 50.** EXEMPTION FROM TAXATION

1. The Bank shall be enabled to import free of customs duty any goods required for the purpose of its operations except such goods as are intended for sale, or are sold, to the public.

2. The Bank shall be exempted from income tax and stamp duty.

**Art. 51.** IMPLEMENTATION

Each Member State shall promptly take such action as is necessary to make effective within that Member State the provisions set forth in this Chapter and shall inform the Bank of the action which it has taken on the matter.

**Art. 52.** WAIVER OF IMMUNITIES

1. The Bank at its discretion may waive any of the privileges immunities and exemptions conferred under this Chapter in any case or instance, in such manner and upon such conditions as it may determine to be appropriate in the best interests of the Bank.
2. The Bank shall take every measure to ensure that the privileges, immunities, exemptions and facilities conferred by this Charter are not abused and for this purpose shall establish such regulations as it may consider necessary and expedient.

## Chapter XI. Amendment, Interpretation and Arbitration

**Art. 53.** AMENDMENT OF THE CHARTER

1. This Charter may be amended only by a resolution of the Governing Council approved by a vote representing not less than 85 per cent of the total voting power of the members.
2. When an amendment has been adopted the Bank shall certify it in a formal communication addressed to all members. Amendments shall enter into force for all members three calendar months after the month in which such communication is issued, unless the resolution referred to in paragraph 1 of this Article specifies therein a different period.
3. Notwithstanding the provisions of paragraph 1 of this Article, the unanimous agreement of the Governing Council shall be required for the approval of any amendment of the Charter modifying—
   *(a)* the right of a member, other than a Member State, to withdraw from the Bank as provided in Article 37 of this Charter;
   *(b)* the right to subscribe to capital stock of the Bank as provided in paragraph 5 of Article 4 of this Charter; and
   *(c)* the limitation on liability as provided in paragraphs 8 and 9 of Article 4 of this Charter.

### Art. 54. INTERPRETATION OR APPLICATION

Any question of interpretation or application of the provisions of this Charter arising between any member and the Bank or between two or more members of the Bank shall be submitted to the Board of Directors for decision.

### Art. 55. ARBITRATION

1. If a disagreement shall arise between the Bank and a member or between the Bank and a former member of the Bank including a disagreement in respect of a decision of the Board of Directors under Article 54 of this Charter, such disagreement shall be submitted to arbitration by a tribunal of three arbitrators. One of the arbitrators shall be appointed by the Bank, another by the member or former member concerned and the third, unless the parties otherwise agree, by the Executive Secretary of the Economic Commission for Africa or such other authority as may have been prescribed by regulations made by the Board of Directors.

2. A majority vote of the arbitrators shall be sufficient to reach a decision which shall be final and binding on the parties and a decision of the arbitrators may include an order as to payment of costs and expenses.

3. The third arbitrator shall be empowered to settle all questions of procedure in any case where the parties are in disagreement with respect thereto.

## CHAPTER XII. FINAL PROVISIONS

### Art. 56. ACQUISITION OF MEMBERSHIP: DEPOSITARY

1. States which the Governing Council decides to admit to membership of the Bank in pursuance of Article 2, paragraph 2 of this Charter, may become members by accession thereto. The Government of any such State shall deposit, on or before the date appointed by the Council, an Instrument of Accession with the Secretary of the Bank who, as Depositary, shall notify such deposit and the date thereof to the Bank and to its members. Upon such deposit, the State shall become a member of the Bank on the appointed date.

2. Any body corporate, enterprise or institution which the Governing Council decides to admit to membership of the Bank in pursuance of Article 2, paragraph 2 of this Charter may become a member by accepting its provisions. It shall deposit, on or before the date

appointed by the Board, a Letter of Acceptance of the provisions of this Charter, with the Secretary of the Bank who shall notify such deposit and the date thereof to the members. Upon such deposit, the body corporate, enterprise or institution concerned shall become a member of the Bank on the appointed date.

**Art. 57.** ENTRY INTO FORCE

This Charter shall enter into force at the same time as does the Treaty to which it is annexed.

**Art. 58.** COMMENCEMENT OF OPERATIONS

1. As soon as this Charter enters into force, the directors shall be appointed or elected in accordance with the provisions of Article 28 of this Charter and the Director-General of the Bank shall call the first meeting of the Board of Directors.[2]

[2] Editor notes that, although this is designated as paragraph 1 of Article 58, there appears to be no succeeding paragraph.

# The Banking Act[1]

*Commencement: 3rd June, 1969*

An Act of Parliament to regulate the business of banking, and for matters incidental thereto and matters connected therewith

## PART I—PRELIMINARY

Short title.

1. This Act may be cited as the Banking Act.

Interpretation.

2. In this Act, except where the context otherwise requires—

"the appointed day" means such day as the Minister may, by notice in

[1] Act No. 56 of 1968—The Banking Act 1968—published in a Special Issue of the *Kenya Gazette Supplement,* No. 96 (Acts No. 17) (Government Printer, Nairobi), November 25, 1968. Amended by The Banking Act, cap. 488, *Laws of Kenya,* rev. ed., 1981, with June 3, 1969 commencement in Legal Notice 115/1969; Nos. 13 of 1979; 10 of 1980; and 12 of 1980. The Schedule and Subsidiary Legislation are omitted from this volume.

the Gazette, appoint to be the appointed day for the purposes of section 3(1) of this Act;

"bank" means any company carrying on banking business in Kenya and includes the Co-operative Bank of Kenya Limited; all branches and offices in Kenya of a bank incorporated outside Kenya shall be deemed to be one bank for the purpose of this Act;

"banking business" means any business which includes the accepting of deposits of money from the public repayable on demand or after a fixed period or after notice, the employing of those deposits in whole or in part by lending or any other means for the account and at the risk of the person accepting the deposits and the paying and collecting of cheques;

"branch" means the second and each subsequent premises at which a bank or financial institution transacts banking business;

"the Central Bank" means the Central Bank of Kenya established by the Central Bank of Kenya Act;

"company" means—

*(a)* a company within the meaning of the Companies Act; or

*(b)* a foreign company within the meaning of Part X of the Companies Act which has complied with the requirements of that Part;

"convertible", in relation to any exchange, means that the exchange is freely negotiable and transferable in international exchange markets at exchange rate margins consistent with the Articles of Agreement of the International Monetary Fund; [2]

"financial institution" means a company, other than a bank, which in Kenya accepts deposits of money from the public repayable on demand or after a fixed period or after notice and employs those deposits in whole or in part by lending or any other means for the account and at the risk of the person accepting the deposits, and any other company carrying on financial business which the Minister may by notice in the Gazette, declare to be a financial institution for the purposes of this Act;

"licence" means a licence granted under section 4;

"municipality", "town council" and "urban council" have the meanings assigned to them in the Local Government Act;

"officer", in relation to a bank or financial institution, means any person by whatever name he may be called who carries out or is empow-

[2] Following the Second Amendment to the Articles of Agreement of the International Monetary Fund, effective April 1, 1978, a member has been free to choose the exchange arrangements that it wishes to apply in accordance with Article IV, Section 2*(b)*. It may therefore maintain the value of its currency in terms of the special drawing right or some other denominator excluding gold. Alternatively, it may allow its currency to float. Kenya maintains its exchange rate within relatively narrow margins in terms of the special drawing right.

ered to carry out functions relating to the overall direction in Kenya of that Bank or financial institution or takes part in its general management in Kenya;

"public entity" means the Government, a local authority, or a public body declared by the Minister to be a public entity for the purposes of this Act;

"total deposit liabilities" means the total deposits in Kenya in any bank or financial institution which are repayable on demand or after a fixed period or after notice.

## PART II—LICENSING OF BANKS AND FINANCIAL INSTITUTIONS

Restriction on carrying banking business.

3. (1) No person other than a licensed bank shall after the appointed day—

(*a*) transact banking business in Kenya;

(*b*) without the consent of the Minister, use the word "bank" or any of its derivatives or any other word indicating the transaction of banking business, or the equivalent of the foregoing in any other language, in the name, description or title under which that person transacts business in Kenya, or makes any representation that it transacted banking business, in any bill head, letter paper, notice, advertisement or in any other manner whatsoever.

(2) Any person who contravenes subsection (1) shall be guilty of an offence and liable to a fine not exceeding ten thousand shillings or to imprisonment for a term not exceeding one year, or to both such fine and imprisonment.

Licensing of banks and financial institutions.

4. The Minister may grant a licence to a bank or financial institution to carry on business as such.

Licence application.

5. (1) Every bank and financial institution proposing to transact banking business in Kenya shall, before commencing business, apply in writing to the Minister for a licence.

(2) In considering an application for a licence, the Minister may require to be satisfied as to the financial condition and history of the bank or financial institution, the character of its management, the adequacy of its capital structure and earning prospects and the convenience and needs of the community to be served, and that the public interest will be served by the granting of the licence.

(3) The fees set out in the Schedule[3] shall be payable on the granting of a licence and on each anniversary of the granting of a licence, for so long as the licence is in force, in respect of each bank or financial institution licensed.

Revocation of licence.

6. The Minister may, by notice in writing to the licensee, revoke a licence if the licensee—

*(a)* ceases to carry on business in Kenya or goes into liquidation or is wound up or otherwise dissolved; or

*(b)* fails to comply with this Act, the Central Bank of Kenya Act or the Exchange Control Act, or any rules, regulations, orders or directions issued under any of those Acts:

Provided that—

(i) the Minister, before revoking a licence, shall give to the licensee not less than twenty-eight days' notice in writing of his intention, and shall consider any representations made to him in writing by the licensee within that period before revoking the licence;

(ii) a bank or financial institution may, notwithstanding that its licence has been revoked under this subsection, continue to carry on for the purpose of winding up its affairs for such period as the Minister may determine so long as it does not accept new deposits or make fresh loans.

Minimum capital requirements.

7. (1) Subject to this Act, a licence shall not be granted to a bank, and a bank may not carry on banking business, unless—

*(a)* in the case of a bank incorporated in Kenya, its paid-up capital is at least two hundred and fifty thousand Kenya pounds and its paid-up capital and unimpaired reserves are not less than five per cent of its total deposit liabilities;

*(b)* in the case of a bank incorporated outside Kenya, its paid-up capital is not less than two million, five hundred thousand Kenya pounds, and in addition the board of management or other controlling authority has given an undertaking satisfactory to the Minister to keep within Kenya at all times during the currency of its licence, out of its own funds, a capital assigned to its Kenya branches (in this Act referred to as assigned capital) amounting to not less than five per cent of its total deposit liabilities in Kenya with a minimum of five hundred thousand Kenya pounds.

(2) Subject to this Act, a licence shall not be granted to a financial institution, and a financial institution shall not carry on business, unless—

[3] The Schedule is omitted from this volume.

(*a*) in the case of a financial institution incorporated in Kenya, its paid-up capital is at least fifty thousand Kenya pounds;

(*b*) in the case of a financial institution incorporated outside Kenya, its paid-up capital is at least two hundred and fifty thousand Kenya pounds, and in addition the board of management or other controlling authority gives an undertaking satisfactory to the Minister to keep within Kenya at all times during the currency of its licence, out of its own funds, assigned capital amounting to not less than five per cent of its total deposit liabilities in Kenya with a minimum of fifty thousand Kenya pounds.

Location of places of business.

8. (1) No licensed bank or licensed financial institution shall open in Kenya a new place of business, or change the location of an existing place of business, in Kenya (otherwise than to another place of business within the same town), without the approval of the Minister.

(2) Before granting approval under subsection (1) the Minister may require to be satisfied as to the history and financial condition of the bank or financial institution, the general character of its management, the adequacy of its capital structure and earning prospects and the convenience and needs of the community to be served, and that the public interest will be served by the opening or, as the case may be, change of location of the place of business.

(3) No licensed bank or licensed financial institution shall close any of its places of business in Kenya without first giving to the Minister six months' written notice of its intention to do so, or such shorter period of notice as the Minister may allow.

Merger.

9. (1) No bank or financial institution operating in Kenya shall be merged or consolidated with any other bank or financial institution in Kenya and no bank or financial institution incorporated in Kenya shall be merged or consolidated with any other bank or financial institution, without the approval of the Minister.

(2) To enable him to consider whether to give his approval under subsection (1), the Minister shall have power to call for such information as he may require.

## PART III—PROHIBITED BUSINESS

Advances, credits and guarantees.

10. (1) A licensed bank or licensed financial institution shall not in Kenya—

(*a*) grant to any person any advance or credit facility or give any financial guarantee or incur any other liability on behalf of any person, so that the total value of the advances, credit facilities, financial guarantees and other liabilities in respect of that person at any time exceed five per cent of the total deposit liabilities of that bank or financial institution or more than one hundred per cent of its paid-up capital or assigned capital and unimpaired reserves, whichever is the greater:

Provided that this paragraph does not apply to transactions with a public entity, or to transactions between banks or between branches of a bank, or to the purchase of or advances made against clean or documentary bills of exchange or documents of title to goods entitling some person to payment outside Kenya for exports; or

*(b)* grant any advance or credit facility against the security of its own shares; or

*(c)* grant or permit to be outstanding any unsecured advances in respect of any of its officers or employees, or members of their families, or any company of which the officer or employee or member of their families is a shareholder, director or employee.

(2) A licensed financial institution shall not grant or permit to be outstanding any advance or credit facilities or give any financial guarantee or incur any other liability to, or in favour of, or on behalf of, any company in which the financial institution has an equity interest, whether directly or indirectly, exceeding twenty-five per cent of the share capital of that company.

Restrictions on trading and investment by licensed banks.

11. A licensed bank shall not in Kenya—

*(a)* engage on its account, alone or with others, in wholesale or retail trade, including the import or export trade, except in the course of the satisfaction of debts due to it; and any trading interest carried on by a licensed bank at the commencement of this Act shall be disposed of by the bank within such time as the Central Bank may allow;

*(b)* acquire, or hold any part of the share capital of, or otherwise have a direct interest in, any financial, commercial, agricultural, industrial or other undertaking where the value of the bank's interest would exceed in the aggregate twenty-five per cent of the sum of the paid-up capital and published reserves of that bank (or, in the case of a bank incorporated outside Kenya, the assigned capital and unimpaired reserves in Kenya of the bank):

Provided that—

(i) a bank may take an interest in such an undertaking in satisfaction of a debt due to it, but if it does so it shall dispose of the interest within such time as the Central Bank may allow;

(ii) a shareholding in any corporation established for the purpose of promoting development in Kenya and approved by the Minister shall not be included in the said percentage;

*(c)* purchase or acquire any immovable property or any interest or right therein, except as may be reasonably necessary for the purpose of conducting its business or of housing or providing amenities for its staff:

Provided that this paragraph does not prevent a bank—

(i) letting part of any building which is used for the purpose of conducting its business;

(ii) securing a debt on immovable property and, in the event of default in payment of the debt, holding such property for so long as in the opinion of the Central Bank is needed for its realization;

(iii) acquiring land for the purpose of its own development.

Restrictions on licensed banks making loans on security of immovable property.

**12.** (1) No licensed bank shall make loans or advances on the security of immovable property for the purpose of purchasing, improving or altering the property, so that the aggregate amount of those loans or advances exceeds fifteen per cent (or with the approval of the Central Bank, thirty per cent) of the amount of its total deposit liabilities.

(2) For the purposes of subsection (1), a loan or advance secured solely by a mortgage, deed of trust or other instrument upon immovable property, or by notes or other obligations which are so secured, is a loan or advance secured by immovable property, and a loan or advance secured in part by mortgage, deed of trust, or other instrument upon immovable property, or by notes or other obligations which are so secured, and by any other form of security is a loan or advance secured by immovable property, to the extent only of the value of the immovable property security as determined by the Central Bank.

(3) Subsection (1) does not prevent a licensed bank accepting as security for a loan or advance made in good faith without security or upon security since found to be inadequate a mortgage, deed of trust, or other instrument upon immovable property, or notes or other obligations which are so secured.

13. *[Spent.]*

## PART IV—DIVIDENDS AND ACCOUNTS

14. No licensed bank or licensed financial institution which is incorporated in Kenya shall pay any dividend on its shares until all its capitalized expenditure (including preliminary expenses, organization expenses, share-selling commission, brokerage, amount of losses incurred and items of expenditure not represented by tangible assets) has been written off. Dividends.

15. All entries in any books and all accounts kept by a licensed bank or licensed financial institution shall be recorded and kept in the English language, using the system of numerals employed in Government accounts. Books and accounts to be kept in English.

16. A licensed bank or licensed financial institution shall exhibit throughout the year in a conspicuous position in every office and branch in Kenya a copy of its last audited balance sheet together with the full and correct names of all persons who are officers of the bank or financial institution in Kenya, and shall cause a copy of the balance sheet to be published in a national newspaper. Balance sheet.

17. (1) A licensed bank or licensed financial institution shall, not later than six months after the end of its financial year, submit to the Central Bank an audited balance sheet showing its assets and liabilities in Kenya, and an audited profit and loss account covering its activities in Kenya, in the prescribed form. Furnishing of information.

(2) A licensed bank or licensed financial institution which is incorporated outside Kenya, and a licensed bank or licensed financial institution which is incorporated in Kenya and maintains branches outside Kenya, shall submit to the Central Bank, at least once in every year beginning on the 1st January and not more than fifteen months after the submission of the last ones, an audited balance sheet and an audited profit and loss account of the bank or institution as a whole.

(3) The Central Bank may require a licensed bank or licensed financial institution to furnish to it, at such time and in such manner as it may direct, such information as the Central Bank may reasonably require for the proper discharge of its functions.

(4) The Central Bank may publish in whole or in part, at such times and in such manner as it thinks fit, any information furnished to it under subsection (3):

Provided that information so furnished shall not be published if it would disclose the financial affairs of any person, unless the consent in writing of that person has first been given.

(5) The Minister may require the Central Bank, a licensed bank or a licensed financial institution to furnish to him, at such time and in such manner as he may direct, such information as the Minister may reasonably require.

(6) Where the Central Bank, a licensed bank or a licensed financial institution is required to furnish information under subsection (3) or subsection (5), it shall furnish that information and any supplemental material that may be required as a result of that information within the period specified in the direction or within such reasonable period thereafter as may be agreed.

## PART V—MINIMUM LIQUID ASSETS

Minimum holdings of liquid assets.

**18.** (1) A licensed bank or licensed financial institution shall maintain such minimum holding of liquid assets as the Central Bank may from time to time determine.

(2) The Central Bank shall determine the method of computing the amounts of liquid assets to be held by banks and financial institutions.

(3) For the purposes of this section, "liquid assets" means all or any of the following—

*(a)* notes and coins which are legal tender in Kenya;

*(b)* balances held at the Central Bank;

*(c)* balances at other banks in Kenya after deducting therefrom balances owed to those other banks;

*(d)* balances at banks abroad withdrawable on demand, and money at call abroad after deducting therefrom balances owed to banks abroad, as may be determined by the Central Bank, where the balances and money at call and short notice are denominated in convertible currencies; and in this paragraph "bank abroad" means a bank outside Kenya or an office outside Kenya of any bank;

*(e)* Kenya treasury bills of a maturity not exceeding ninety-one days which are freely marketable and rediscountable at the Central Bank;

*(f)* such other assets as the Minister may specify.

(4) Any licensed bank or licensed financial institution which fails to comply, within such reasonable time as the Central Bank may fix, with any requirement of subsection (1) shall be liable to pay, on being called

upon to do so by the Central Bank, a penalty interest charge not exceeding one tenth of one per cent of the amount of the deficiency for every day on which the offence continues.

## PART VI—INSPECTION OF BANKS AND FINANCIAL INSTITUTIONS

Inspection of banks and financial institutions.

**19.** (1) The Central Bank or any person authorized by the Central Bank in writing may, and if so directed by the Minister shall, cause an inspection to be made of any licensed bank or licensed financial institution and of its books and accounts, and where it does so it shall supply to that bank or financial institution a report of the inspection.

(2) Where an inspection is made under subsection (1), the bank or financial institution concerned shall produce to the officer or authorized person making the inspection all such books, accounts and other documents in his custody or power and to furnish the officer or authorized person with such statements or information relating to the affairs in Kenya of the bank or financial institution, as the officer or authorized person may require of him, within such reasonable time as the officer or authorized person may specify:

Provided that—

(i) books, accounts and other documents may be required to be produced only at the premises of the bank or financial institution concerned; and

(ii) all information obtained in the course of inspection shall be treated as confidential and used solely for the purposes of this Act and the Central Bank of Kenya Act.

Central Bank may issue orders after inspection.

**20.** (1) If it is found upon an inspection under section 19 that the affairs of the bank or financial institution concerned are being conducted in a manner detrimental to the interests of the depositors or to the interests of the bank or financial institution, the Central Bank may issue directions to the bank or financial institution requiring it to take such corrective action as the Central Bank considers to be necessary or to discontinue the harmful practices or procedures.

(2) No directions shall be issued under subsection (1) unless the bank or financial institution has been given an opportunity to present its views.

(3) A bank or financial institution which receives directions under subsection (1) shall, within the period specified in the directions, comply with the directions and show to the Central Bank that it has done so.

(4) The Minister may, upon representations made to him or on his own initiative, modify or cancel any directions issued under subsection (1), and in so modifying or cancelling them he may impose such conditions as he thinks fit subject to which the modification or cancellation shall have effect.

## Part VII—Audit

Appointment of auditor.

21. (1) Every licensed bank and every licensed financial institution shall appoint annually an auditor qualified under section 161 of the Companies Act and approved by the Central Bank, whose duty it shall be to audit and make a report upon the annual balance sheet and profit and loss account which are to be submitted to the Central Bank under section 17(1) of this Act.

(2) The bank or financial institution shall send a copy of the auditor's report to the Central Bank.

Appointment of auditor by Central Bank.

22. If a licensed bank or licensed financial institution fails to appoint an approved auditor under section 21(1), or to fill any vacancy for auditor which may arise, the Central Bank may appoint an auditor and fix the remuneration to be paid by the bank or financial institution to him.

## Part VIII—Miscellaneous

Restriction on increase in bank charges.

23. No licensed bank or licensed financial institution shall increase its rate of banking or other charges except with the prior agreement of the Minister.

Minister to consult with Central Bank.

24. The Minister shall consult with the Central Bank in the exercise of his functions under this Act.

Bank holidays.

25. Where the Minister considers that it is in the public interest that banks, or a particular bank, or a particular branch of a bank, should remain closed on a day which is not a public holiday, he may, by notice in the Gazette, declare that day to be a bank holiday for all banks, or for that particular bank, or for that particular branch, as the case may be, and every licensed bank, or that particular bank, or that particular branch, as the case may be, shall remain closed on that day.

Order by High Court.

26. (1) The High Court, on application made *ex parte* by the Minister may, if it considers it to be in the interests of the depositors of a licensed bank or licensed financial institution, make an order—

(*a*) prohibiting the bank or financial institution from carrying on business; and

(*b*) staying the commencement or continuance of any actions or proceedings against the bank or financial institution in regard to any business for a specified period of time on such terms and conditions as it considers reasonable,

and may from time to time extend the specified period up to a total of six months from the beginning of the stay.

(2) So long as an order under subsection (1) remains in force, the licence granted to the bank or financial institution under this Act shall be deemed to be suspended.

Disqualification of officers.

27. (1) A person who is an officer of a licensed bank or licensed financial institution shall cease to hold office if he—

(*a*) becomes bankrupt or suspends payment or compounds with his creditors; or

(*b*) is convicted of an offence involving dishonesty or fraud; or

(*c*) is directly or indirectly concerned with the management of a bank or financial institution which has been compulsorily wound up.

(2) Any person who continues to act as an officer of a licensed bank or licensed financial institution after he has been disqualified by virtue of this section shall be guilty of an offence and liable to a fine not exceeding five thousand shillings or to imprisonment for a term not exceeding six months, or to both such fine and imprisonment.

Penalties for contraventions by banks and financial institutions.

28. Where any licensed bank or licensed financial institution contravenes any of sections 8, 9, 16, 19, 20 and 21

(*a*) it shall be guilty of an offence and liable to a fine not exceeding twenty thousand shillings; and

(*b*) every officer of the bank or financial institution shall be guilty of the offence and liable to a fine not exceeding five thousand shillings or to imprisonment for a term not exceeding six months, or to both such fine and imprisonment, unless he proves that, through no act or omission on his part, he was not aware that the contravention was taking place or was intended or about to take place, or that he took all reasonable steps to prevent it taking place.

Penalties for default by officers.

29. (1) Any officer of a licensed bank or licensed financial institution who—

(*a*) fails to take all reasonable steps to secure the compliance of the bank or financial institution with this Act; or (*b*) fails to take all reasonable steps to secure the accuracy and correctness of any statement submitted under this Act or any other written law applicable to banks,

shall be guilty of an offence and liable to imprisonment for a term not exceeding one year or to a fine not exceeding ten thousand shillings or to both such imprisonment and fine.

(2) It shall be a defence to a charge under subsection (1) for an officer to show that he reasonably thought that another competent person had been charged with the responsibility or duty in respect of which the default arose.

Exemption.

**30.** The Minister may, by notice in the Gazette, exempt any corporation from all or any of the provisions of this Act.

Exceptions.

**31.** This Act does not apply in respect of—

(*a*) the Kenya Post Office Savings Bank established under the Kenya Post Office Savings Bank Act;

(*b*) the Agricultural Finance Corporation established under the Agricultural Finance Corporation Act;

(*c*) a society registered as a co-operative society under the Co-operative Societies Act, other than the Co-operative Bank of Kenya Limited; or

(*d*) a society registered as a building society under the Building Societies Act.

Regulations.

**32.** The Minister may make regulations generally for carrying out the purposes and provisions of this Act.

*[The Schedule and the Subsidiary Legislation are omitted from this volume.]*

# The Money-Lenders Act [1]

*Commencement: 1st January, 1933*

An Act to make provision with respect to persons carrying on business as money-lenders

1. This Act may be cited as the Money-lenders Act. Short title.

2. (1) In this Act, except where the context otherwise requires— Interpretation.

"authorized name" and "authorized address" mean respectively the name under which and the address at which a money-lender is authorized by a certificate granted under this Act to carry on business as a money-lender;

"business name" means the name or style under which any business is carried on whether in partnership or otherwise;

"company" means any body corporate being a money-lender;

"firm" means an unincorporate body of two or more individuals, or one or more individuals and one or more corporations, or two or more corporations, who have entered into partnership with one another with a view to carrying on business for profit;

"interest" does not include any sum lawfully charged in accordance with the provisions of this Act by a money-lender for or on account of costs, charges or expenses, but, save as aforesaid, includes any amount, by whatsoever name called, in excess of the principal, paid or payable to a money-lender in consideration of or otherwise in respect of a loan;

"money-lender" includes every person whose business is that of money-lending, or who advertises or announces himself or holds himself out in any way as carrying on that business, but does not include—

(*a*) a pawnbroker licensed under the Pawnbrokers Act, in respect of business carried on by him in accordance with that Act; or

(*b*) a building society registered under the Building Societies Act, or lawfully carrying on the business of a building society before the commencement of that Act; or

---

[1] *Laws of Kenya,* Cap. 528 (1962). Originally Cap. 307 (1948). Relevant citations: Nos. 36 of 1959; 21 of 1966; L.N. 462/1963; L.N. 2/1964; and No. 10 of 1980.

(c) a company licensed under the Banking Act, or lawfully and bona fide carrying on the business of banking before the commencement of that Act; or

(d) a person bona fide carrying on the business of insurance; or

(e) a person bona fide carrying on a business not having for its primary object the lending of money, in the course of which and for the purposes whereof he lends money; or

(f) a person for the time being exempted from the provisions of this Act, or from any of them, by order of the Minister;

"principal" means in relation to a loan the amount actually lent to the borrower.

(2) Where by a contract for the loan of money by a money-lender the interest charged on the loan is not expressed in terms of a rate, any amount paid or payable to the money-lender under the contract (other than simple interest charged in accordance with the proviso to section 12 of this Act) shall be appropriated to principal and interest in the proportion that the principal bears to the total amount of the interest, and the rate per cent per annum represented by the interest charged as calculated in accordance with the provisions of the Schedule [2] to this Act shall be deemed to be the rate of interest charged on the loan.

Transactions to which the Act does not apply.

3. (1) The provisions of this Act shall not apply—

(a) to any money-lending transaction where the security for repayment of the loan or of interest thereon is effected by execution of a chattels transfer in which the interest provided for is not in excess of nine per centum per annum;

(b) to any money-lending transaction where the security for repayment of the loan or of interest thereon is effected by execution of a legal or equitable mortgage upon immovable property or of a charge upon immovable property or of any bona fide transaction of money-lending upon such mortgage or charge.

(2) The exemption provided for in this section shall apply whether the transactions referred to are effected by a money-lender or not.

Reopening of transactions of money-lenders.

4. (1) Where proceedings are taken in any court by a money-lender for the recovery of any money lent after the commencement of this Act, or the enforcement of any agreement or security made or taken after the commencement of this Act, in respect of money lent either before or after the commencement of this Act, and there is evidence which satisfies the court that the interest charged in respect of the sum actually lent is excessive, or that the amounts charged for expenses, inquiries, fines,

[2] The Schedule is omitted from this volume.

bonus, premium, renewals or any other charges, are excessive, and that, in either case, the transaction is harsh and unconscionable, or is otherwise such that a court of equity would give relief, the court may reopen the transaction, and take an account between the money-lender and the person sued, and may, notwithstanding any statement or settlement of account or any agreement purporting to close previous dealings, and create a new obligation, reopen any account already taken between them, and relieve the person sued from payment of any sum in excess of the sum adjudged by the court to be fairly due in respect of such principal, interest and charges, as the court, having regard to the risk and all the circumstances, may adjudge to be reasonable; and if any such excess has been paid, or allowed in account, by the debtor, may order the creditor to repay it; and may set aside, either wholly or in part, or revise or alter any security given or agreement made, in respect of money lent by the money-lender, and if the money-lender has parted with the security may order him to indemnify the borrower or other person sued.

(2) Any court in which proceedings might be taken for the recovery of money lent by a money-lender shall have and may, at the instance of the borrower or surety or other person liable, exercise the like powers as may be exercised under this section, where proceedings are taken for the recovery of the money lent, and the court shall have power, notwithstanding any provision or agreement to the contrary, to entertain any application under this Act by the borrower or surety, or other person liable, notwithstanding that the time for repayment of the loan, or any instalment thereof, may not have arrived.

(3) On any application relating to the admission or amount of a proof by a money-lender in any bankruptcy proceedings, the court may exercise the like powers as may be exercised under this section when proceedings are taken for the recovery of money.

(4) The foregoing provisions of this section shall apply to any transaction which, whatever its form may be, is substantially one of money-lending by a money-lender.

(5) Nothing in the foregoing provisions of this section shall affect the rights of any bona fide assignee or holder for value without notice.

(6) Nothing in this section shall be construed as derogating from the existing powers or jurisdiction of any court.

Penalty for false statements and representations.

5. If any money-lender, or any manager, agent or clerk of a money-lender, or if any person being a director, manager or other officer of any corporation carrying on the business of a money-lender, by any false, misleading or deceptive statement, representation or promise, or by any

dishonest concealment of material facts, fraudulently induces or attempts to induce any person to borrow money or to agree to the terms on which money is or is to be borrowed, he shall be guilty of an offence and liable to imprisonment for a term not exceeding two years, or to a fine not exceeding ten thousand shillings, or to both.

Licences to be taken out by money-lenders.

6. (1) Except as hereinafter provided, every money-lender and every company carrying on business as a money-lender shall take out annually in respect of every address at which he or it carries on his or its business as such, a licence (in this Act referred to as a money-lender's licence) which shall expire on the 31st December in every year, and there shall be charged on every money-lender's licence the fee prescribed in pursuance of the provisions of subsection (2) of this section:

Provided that if one partner in a firm of money-lenders has duly taken out a money-lender's licence, every other partner in the firm shall, subject to the provisions of section 7 of this Act, be issued with a money-lender's licence free of charge for the business of the firm for such time as he shall remain a member of the firm.

(2) Subject to the provisions of this Act, money-lenders' licences shall be in such form as the Minister may direct, and shall be granted on payment of the licence fee by any officer authorized by the Minister to grant them, and regulations made by the Minister may make provision as to the procedure to be followed in making application for money-lenders' licences and as to the fee or fees payable therefor:

Provided that a money-lender's licence shall be taken out by a money-lender in his true name, and shall be void if it be taken out in any other name, but every money-lender's licence shall also show the money-lender's authorized name and authorized address.

(3) If any person—

*(a)* takes out a money-lender's licence in any name other than his true name; or

*(b)* carries on business as a money-lender without having in force a proper money-lender's licence authorizing him so to do, or being licensed as a money-lender, carries on business as such in any name other than his authorized name, or at any other place than his authorized address or addresses; or

*(c)* enters into any agreement in the course of his business as a money-lender with respect to the advance or repayment of money, or takes any security for money in the course of his business as a money-lender, otherwise than in his authorized name,

he shall be guilty of an offence and liable to a penalty of two thousand shillings:

Provided that, on a second or subsequent conviction of any person (other than a company) for an offence under this subsection, the court may, in lieu of or in addition to ordering the offender to pay the penalty aforesaid, order him to be imprisoned for a term not exceeding three months, and an offender being a company shall on a second or subsequent conviction be liable to a penalty of ten thousand shillings.

Certificate required for grant of money-lender's licence.

7. (1) A money-lender's licence shall not be granted except to a person who holds a certificate granted in accordance with the provisions of this section authorizing the grant of the licence to that person, and a separate certificate shall be required in respect of every separate licence; and any money-lender's licence granted in contravention of this subsection shall be void.

(2) Certificates under this section (in this Act referred to as certificates) shall be granted by the subordinate court of the first or second class having jurisdiction in the district in which the money-lender's business is to be carried on.

(3) Every certificate granted to a money-lender shall show his true name and the name under which, and the address at which, he is authorized by the certificate to carry on business as such, and a certificate shall not authorize a money-lender to carry on business at more than one address, or under more than one name, or under any name which includes the word "bank", or otherwise implies that he carries on banking business, and no certificate shall authorize a money-lender to carry on business under any name except—

- *(a)* his true name; or
- *(b)* the name of a firm in which he is a partner, not being a firm required by the Registration of Business Names Act to be registered; or
- *(c)* a business name, whether of an individual or of a firm in which he is a partner, under which he or the firm has, at the commencement of this Act, been registered for not less than three years under the Registration of Business Names Act.

(4) A certificate shall come into force on the date specified therein, and shall expire on the next following 31st December.

(5) The Minister may make rules with respect to the procedure to be followed in making applications for certificates (including the notices to be given of intention to make such an application), and certificates shall be in such form as may be prescribed by rules so made.

(6) A certificate shall not be refused except on some one or more of the following grounds—

(a) that satisfactory evidence has not been produced of the good character of the applicant, and in the case of a company of the persons responsible for the management thereof;

(b) that satisfactory evidence has been produced that the applicant, or any person responsible or proposed to be responsible for the management of his business as a money-lender, is not a fit and proper person to hold a certificate;

(c) that the applicant, or any person responsible or proposed to be responsible for the management of his business as a money-lender, is by order of a court disqualified for holding a certificate;

(d) that the applicant has not complied with the provisions of any rules made under this section with respect to applications for certificates.

(7) Any person aggrieved by the refusal of a subordinate court of the first or second class to grant a certificate may appeal to the High Court.

Suspension and forfeiture of money-lenders' certificates.

**8.** (1) Where any person, being the holder of a certificate, is convicted of any offence under this Act, the court—

(a) may order that any certificate held by that person, and in the case of a partner in a firm by any other partner in the firm, shall either be suspended for such time as the court thinks fit, or shall be forfeited, and may also, if the court thinks fit, declare any such person, or any person responsible for the management of the money-lending business carried on by the person convicted, to be disqualified for obtaining a certificate for such time as the court thinks fit; and

(b) shall cause particulars of the conviction and of any order made by the court under this subsection to be endorsed on every certificate held by the person convicted or by any other person affected by the order, and shall cause copies of those particulars to be sent to the authority by whom any certificate so endorsed was granted:

Provided that, where by order of a court a certificate held by any person is suspended or forfeited, or any person is disqualified for obtaining a certificate, he may, whether or not he is the person convicted, appeal against the order in the same manner as any person convicted may appeal against his conviction, and the court may, if it thinks fit, pending the appeal, defer the operation of the order.

(2) Any certificate required by a court for endorsement in accordance with the foregoing provisions of this section shall be produced, in such manner and within such time as may be directed by the court, by the person by whom it is held, and any person who, without reason-

able cause, makes default in producing any certificate so required shall, in respect of each offence, be liable on conviction by a subordinate court of the first or second class to a penalty not exceeding one hundred shillings for each day during which the default continues.

(3) Where a certificate held by any person is ordered to be suspended or to be forfeited under the foregoing provisions of this section, any money-lender's licences granted to that person, whether in pursuance of that or any other certificate, shall be suspended during the period for which the certificate is ordered to be suspended or become void, as the case may be.

Names to be stated on documents issued by money-lenders.

9. (1) Without prejudice to the provisions of the last foregoing section and of section 23 of the Registration of Business Names Act, a money-lender shall not, for the purposes of his business as such, issue or publish, or cause to be issued or published, any advertisement, circular, business letter or other similar document which does not show in such manner as to be not less conspicuous than any other name, the authorized name of the money-lender, and any money-lender who acts in contravention of this subsection shall be guilty of an offence and liable on conviction by a subordinate court of the first or second class to a fine not exceeding four hundred shillings in respect of each offence.

(2) If a money-lender, for the purposes of his business as such, issues or publishes, or causes to be issued or published, any advertisement, circular or document of any kind whatsoever containing expressions which might reasonably be held to imply that he carries on banking business, he shall be guilty of an offence and, on conviction by a subordinate court of the first or second class, liable to a fine not exceeding two thousand shillings, and on a second or subsequent conviction, in lieu of or in addition to such a fine as aforesaid, to imprisonment for a term not exceeding three months, or, in the case of a second or subsequent conviction of an offender being a company, to a fine not exceeding ten thousand shillings.

Restrictions on money-lending advertisements.

10. (1) No person shall knowingly send or deliver or cause to be sent or delivered to any person except in response to his written request any circular or other document advertising the name, address or telephone number of a money-lender, or containing an invitation—

*(a)* to borrow money from a money-lender;
*(b)* to enter into any transaction involving the borrowing of money from a money-lender;
*(c)* to apply to any place with a view to obtaining information or advice as to borrowing any money from a money-lender.

(2) Subject as hereinafter provided, no person shall publish or cause to be published in any newspaper or other printed paper issued periodically for public circulation, or by means of any poster or placard, an advertisement advertising any such particulars, or containing any such invitation, as aforesaid:

Provided that an advertisement in conformity with the requirements of this Act relating to the use of names on money-lenders' documents may be published by or on behalf of a money-lender in any newspaper or in any such paper as aforesaid or by means of a poster or placard exhibited at any authorized address of the money-lender, if it contains no addition to the particulars necessary to comply with the said requirements, except any of the following particulars, that is to say, any authorized address at which he carries on business as a money-lender, and the telegraphic address and telephone number thereof, any address at which he formerly carried on business, a statement that he lends money with or without security, and of the highest and lowest sums that he is prepared to lend, and a statement of the date on which the business carried on by him was first established.

(3) No money-lender or any person on his behalf shall employ any agent or canvasser for the purpose of inviting any person to borrow money or to enter into any transaction involving the borrowing of money from a money-lender, and no person shall act as such agent or canvasser, or demand or receive, directly or indirectly, any sum or other valuable consideration by way of commission or otherwise for introducing or undertaking to introduce to a money-lender any person desiring to borrow money.

(4) Where any document issued or published by or on behalf of a money-lender purports to indicate the terms of interest upon which he is willing to make loans or any particular loan, the document shall either express the interest proposed to be charged in terms of a rate per centum per annum or show the rate per centum per annum represented by the interest proposed to be charged as calculated in accordance with the provisions of the Schedule to this Act.

(5) Any person who contravenes any of the provisions of this section shall be guilty of an offence and liable to imprisonment for a term not exceeding three months or a fine not exceeding two thousand shillings, or to both such imprisonment and fine.

(6) Where it is shown that a money-lending transaction was brought about by a contravention of any of the provisions of this section, the transaction shall, notwithstanding that the money-lender was duly licensed under this Act, be illegal unless the money-lender proves that the contravention occurred without his consent or connivance.

Form of money-lenders' contracts.

11. (1) No contract for the repayment by a borrower of money lent to him or to any agent on his behalf by a money-lender after the commencement of this Act or for the payment by him of interest on money so lent, and no security given by the borrower or by any such agent as aforesaid in respect of any such contract shall be enforceable, unless a note or memorandum in writing of the contract be made and signed personally by the borrower, and unless a copy thereof be delivered or sent to the borrower within seven days of the making of the contract; and no such contract or security shall be enforceable if it is proved that the note or memorandum aforesaid was not signed by the borrower before the money was lent or before the security was given, as the case may be.

(2) The note or memorandum aforesaid shall contain all the terms of the contract, and in particular shall show the date on which the loan is made, the amount of the principal of the loan, and either the interest charged on the loan expressed in terms of a rate per centum per annum, or the rate per centum per annum represented by the interest charged as calculated in accordance with the provisions of the Schedule to this Act.

Prohibition of compound interest and provision as to defaults.

12. Subject as hereinafter provided, any contract made after the commencement of this Act for the loan of money by a money-lender shall be illegal in so far as it provides directly or indirectly for the payment of compound interest or for the rate or amount of interest being increased by reason of any default in the payment of sums due under the contract:

Provided that provision may be made by any such contract that if default is made in the payment upon the due date of any sum payable to the money-lender under the contract, whether in respect of principal or interest, the money-lender shall be entitled to charge simple interest on that sum from the date of the default until the sum is paid, at a rate not exceeding the rate payable in respect of the principal apart from any default, and any interest so charged shall not be reckoned for the purposes of this Act as part of the interest charged in respect of the loan.

Obligation of money-lender to supply information as to state of loan and copies of documents relating thereto.

13. (1) In respect of every contract for the repayment of money lent by a money-lender, whether made before or after the commencement of this Act, the money-lender shall, on any reasonable demand in writing being made by the borrower at any time during the continuance of the contract and on tender by the borrower of the sum of one shilling for expenses, supply to the borrower or, if the borrower so requires, to any person specified in that behalf in the demand, a statement signed by the money-lender or his agent showing—

(*a*) the date on which the loan was made, the amount of the principal of the loan and the rate per centum per annum of interest charged; and

(*b*) the amount of any payment already received by the money-lender in respect of the loan and the date on which it was made; and

(*c*) the amount of every sum due to the money-lender, but unpaid, and the date upon which it became due, and the amount of interest accrued due and unpaid in respect of every such sum; and

(*d*) the amount of every sum not yet due which remains outstanding, and the date upon which it will become due.

(2) A money-lender shall, on any reasonable demand in writing by the borrower, and on tender of a reasonable sum for expenses, supply a copy of any document relating to a loan made by him or any security therefor, to the borrower, or, if the borrower so requires, to any person specified in that behalf in the demand.

(3) If a money-lender to whom a demand has been made under this section fails without reasonable excuse to comply therewith within one month after the demand has been made, he shall not, so long as the default continues, be entitled to sue for or recover any sum due under the contract on account either of principal or interest, and interest shall not be chargeable in respect of the period of the default, and if such default is made or continued after proceedings have ceased to lie in respect of the loan, the money-lender shall be guilty of an offence and liable on conviction by a subordinate court of the first or second class to a fine not exceeding one hundred shillings for every day on which the default continues.

Provisions as to bankruptcy proceedings for money-lenders' loans.

14. (1) (*a*) Where a debt due to a money-lender in respect of a loan made by him after the commencement of this Act includes interest, that interest shall, for the purposes of the provisions of the Bankruptcy Act relating to the presentation of a bankruptcy petition, voting at meetings, compositions and schemes of arrangement and dividend, be calculated at a rate not exceeding five per centum per annum, but nothing in the foregoing provision shall prejudice the right of the creditor to receive out of the estate, after all the debts proved in the estate have been paid in full, any higher rate of interest to which he may be entitled.

(*b*) The provisions of this subsection shall, in relation to such a debt as aforesaid, have effect in substitution for the provisions of subsection (1) of section 70 of the Bankruptcy Act.

(2) No proof of a debt due to a money-lender in respect of a loan made by him shall be admitted for any of the purposes of the Bankruptcy Act unless the affidavit verifying the debt is accompanied by a statement showing in detail—

*(a)* the amount of the sums actually lent to the debtor and the dates on which they were lent, and the amount of every payment already received by the money-lender in respect of the loan and the date on which every such payment was made; and

*(b)* the amount of the balance which remains unpaid, distinguishing the amount of the principal from the amount of interest included therein, the appropriation between principal and interest being made in accordance with the provisions of this Act where the interest is not expressed by the contract for the loan in terms of a rate; and

*(c)* where the amount of interest included in the unpaid balance represents a rate per centum per annum exceeding five per centum, the amount of interest which would be so included if it were calculated at the rate of five per centum per annum.

(3) Rules may be made under section 122 of the Bankruptcy Act for the purpose of carrying into effect the objects of this section.

Interest at a rate exceeding 24 per cent to be deemed harsh and unconscionable.

**15.** (1) Where, in any proceedings in respect of any money lent by a money-lender after the commencement of this Act or in respect of any agreement or security made or taken after the commencement of this Act in respect of money lent either before or after the commencement of this Act, it is found that the interest charged exceeds the rate of twenty-four per centum per annum, or the corresponding rate in respect of any other period, the court shall presume, for the purposes of section 4 of this Act, that the interest charged is excessive and that the transaction is harsh and unconscionable, but this provision shall be without prejudice to the powers of the court under that section where the court is satisfied that the interest charged, although not exceeding forty-eight per centum per annum, is excessive.

(2) Where a court reopens a transaction of a money-lender under section 4 of this Act, the court may require the money-lender to produce any certificate granted to him in accordance with the provisions of this Act, and may cause such particulars as the court thinks desirable to be endorsed on any such certificate, and a copy of the particulars to be sent to the authority by whom the certificate was granted.

(3) The powers of a court under section 4 of this Act with respect to the reopening of the transactions of money-lenders shall extend to any

transaction effected under a special contract made in accordance with the provisions of section 20 of the Pawnbrokers Act, and accordingly, for the purposes of the first-mentioned section, the provisions of paragraph *(a)* of the definition of the term "money-lender" in section 2 of this Act shall not apply with respect to any such transaction.

(4) The powers of a court under subsection (2) of section 4 of this Act may, in the event of the bankruptcy of the borrower, be exercised at the instance of the trustee in bankruptcy, notwithstanding that he may not be a person liable in respect of the transaction.

(5) The powers of a court under subsection (2) of section 4 of this Act may be exercised notwithstanding that the money-lender's right of action for the recovery of the money lent is barred.

Courts for proceedings on money-lending transactions.

16. Subject as hereinafter provided, no action by a money-lender for the recovery of money lent by him or for enforcing any agreement or security relating to any such money shall be brought in any subordinate court other than a subordinate court of the first class:

Provided that the Chief Justice may by order direct that any subordinate court specified in the order shall have the same jurisdiction as respects such actions as aforesaid as it would have had but for the provisions of this section, and any such order may contain such provisions as appear to the Chief Justice expedient with respect to the making of rules for regulating the procedure to be followed in the case of any such action.

Prohibition of charge for expenses on loans by money-lenders.

17. Any agreement between a money-lender and a borrower or intending borrower for the payment by the borrower or intending borrower to the money-lender of any sum on account of costs, charges or expenses incidental to or relating to the negotiations for or the granting of the loan or proposed loan shall be illegal, and if any sum is paid to a money-lender by a borrower or intending borrower as for or on account of any such costs, charges or expenses, that sum shall be recoverable as a debt due to the borrower or intending borrower, or, in the event of the loan being completed, shall, if not so recovered, be set off against the amount actually lent and that amount shall be deemed to be reduced accordingly.

Limitation of time for proceedings.

18. (1) No proceedings shall lie for the recovery by a money-lender of any money lent by him after the commencement of this Act or of any interest in respect thereof, or for the enforcement of any agreement made or security taken after the commencement of this Act in respect of any loan made by him, unless the proceedings are commenced before

the expiration of twelve months from the date on which the cause of action accrued:

Provided that—

(i) if, during the period of twelve months aforesaid or at any time within any subsequent period during which proceedings may by virtue of this proviso be brought, the debtor acknowledges in writing the amount due and gives a written undertaking to the money-lender to pay that amount, proceedings for the recovery of the amount due may be brought at any time within a period of twelve months from the date of the acknowledgment and undertaking;

(ii) the time limited by the foregoing provisions of this section for the commencement of proceedings shall not begin to run in respect of any payments from time to time becoming due to a money-lender under a contract for the loan of money until a cause of action accrues in respect of the last payment becoming due under the contract;

(iii) if, at the date on which the cause of action accrues or on which any such acknowledgment and undertaking as aforesaid is given by the debtor, the person entitled to take the proceedings is *non compos mentis,* the time limited by the foregoing provisions of this section for the commencement of proceedings shall not begin to run until that person ceases to be *non compos mentis* or dies, whichever first occurs; and

(iv) if, at the date on which the cause of action accrues or on which any such acknowledgment and undertaking as aforesaid is given by the debtor, the debtor is out of Kenya, the time limited by the foregoing provisions of this section for the commencement of proceedings shall not begin to run until he returns to Kenya.

(2) Without prejudice to the powers of a court under section 4 of this Act, if, at the time when proceedings are taken by a money-lender in respect of a default in the payment of any sum due to him under a contract for the loan of money, any further amount is outstanding under the contract but not yet due, the court may determine the contract and order the principal outstanding to be paid to the money-lender with such interest thereon, if any, as the court may allow up to the date of payment.

Special provisions as to pawnbrokers' loans.

19. (1) The provisions of sections 11, 17 and 18 of this Act shall not apply in relation to any loan by a pawnbroker on a pledge, or in relation to any debt in respect of such a loan, or any interest thereon, notwithstanding that the loan is not made in the course of the business

carried on by the pawnbroker in accordance with any law for the time being in force in relation to pawnbrokers, so long as the following conditions are complied with in respect of the loan—

*(a)* the pawnbroker shall deliver or send to the pawner within seven days a note or memorandum containing all the terms of contract, and in particular showing the date on which the loan is made, the amount of the principal of the loan, the interest charged on the loan expressed in terms of a rate per centum per annum, and any other charges payable by the pawner under the contract, and the rate of interest charged shall not exceed the rate of twenty per centum per annum;

*(b)* subject as hereinafter provided, the pawner shall not be charged any sum on account of costs, charges or expenses incidental to or relating to the negotiations for or the granting of the loan or proposed loan, except a charge for the preparation of documents relating to the loan not exceeding the sum of one shilling, and a charge equal to the actual amount of any stamp duty paid by the pawnbroker upon any such document:

Provided that a pawnbroker shall not be deemed to have failed to comply with the foregoing conditions by reason of his having made in good faith and in accordance with the terms of the contract for the loan—

(i) a reasonable charge in respect of the storage or care of any pledge which is not physically delivered to him or which, although so delivered, is of such weight or size that it would not under the East African Postal Regulations for the time being in force be received for transmission by parcel post; or

(ii) a charge for interest at a rate not exceeding twenty per centum per annum upon any sum reasonably expended by the pawnbroker in respect of the storage or care of the pledge; or

(iii) a charge not exceeding one shilling for rendering any account of the sale of any pledge; or

(iv) a charge not exceeding one shilling in respect of any inspection of the pawnbroker's books.

(2) Any charge authorized by this section for the preparation of documents relating to a loan, or in respect of stamp duty upon any such document, may be deducted by the pawnbroker from the amount of the loan, and, if so deducted, shall be deemed for the purposes of this Act to be included in the principal.

Notice and information to be given on assignment of money-lenders' debts.

**20.** (1) Where any debt in respect of money lent by a money-lender whether before or after the commencement of this Act or in respect of interest on any such debt or the benefit of any agreement made or security taken in respect of any such debt or interest is assigned to any assignee, the assignor (whether he is the money-lender by whom the money was lent or any person to whom the debt has been previously assigned) shall, before the assignment is made—

(*a*) give to the assignee notice in writing that the debt, agreement or security is affected by the operation of this Act; and

(*b*) supply to the assignee all information necessary to enable him to comply with the provisions of this Act relating to the obligation to supply information as to the state of loans and copies of documents relating thereto,

and any person contravening any of the provisions of this section shall be liable to indemnify any other person who is prejudiced by the contravention, and shall also be guilty of an offence and liable to imprisonment for a term not exceeding two years, or to a fine not exceeding ten thousand shillings, or to both such imprisonment and fine.

(2) In this section the expression "assigned" means assigned by any assignment *inter vivos* other than an assignment by operation of law, and the expressions "assignor" and "assignee" have corresponding meanings.

Application of Act as respects assignees.

**21.** (1) Subject as hereinafter provided, the provisions of this Act shall continue to apply as respects any debt to a money-lender in respect of money lent by him after the commencement of this Act or in respect of interest on money so lent or of the benefit of any agreement made or security taken in respect of any such debt or interest, notwithstanding that the debt or the benefit of the agreement or security may have been assigned to any assignee, and, except where the context otherwise requires, references in this Act to a money-lender shall accordingly be construed as including any such assignee as aforesaid:

Provided that notwithstanding anything in this Act—

(i) any agreement with, or security taken by, a money-lender in respect of money lent by him after the commencement of this Act shall be valid in favour of any bona fide assignee or holder for value without notice of any defect due to the operation of this Act and of any person deriving title under him; and

(ii) any payment or transfer of money or property made bona fide by any person, whether acting in a fiduciary capacity or otherwise, on the faith of the validity of any such agreement or security, without notice of any such defect shall, in favour of that person, be as valid as it would have been if the agreement or security had been valid; and

(iii) the provisions of this Act limiting the time for proceedings in respect of money lent shall not apply to any proceedings in respect of any such agreement or security commenced by a bona fide assignee or holder for value without notice that the agreement or security was affected by the operation of this Act, or by any person deriving title under him.

but in every such case the money-lender shall be liable to indemnify the borrower or any other person who is prejudiced by virtue of this section, and nothing in this proviso shall render valid an agreement or security in favour of, or apply to proceedings commenced by, an assignee or holder for value who is himself a money-lender.

(2) Nothing in this section shall render valid for any purpose any agreement, security or other transaction which would, apart from the provisions of this Act, have been void or unenforceable.

*{The Schedule is omitted from this volume.}*

## The Pawnbrokers Act[1]

*Commencement: 13th October, 1913*

An Act to regulate the business of pawnbroking

Short title.

1. This Act may be cited as the Pawnbrokers Act.

Interpretation.

2. In this Act—

"pawnbroker" includes every person who carries on the business of taking goods and chattels in pawn;

"pawner" means a person delivering an article for pawn to a pawnbroker;

[1] *Laws of Kenya,* Cap. 529 (1962). Relevant citations: No. 28 of 1961; L.N. 462 of 1963; and No. 21 of 1966.

"pledge" means an article pawned with a pawnbroker;

"shop" includes dwelling-house and warehouse, or other place of business or place where business is transacted;

"unfinished goods or materials" includes any goods of any manufacturer or of any part or branch of any manufacture either mixed or separate or any material whatever plainly intended for the composing or manufacturing of any goods, after such goods or materials are put into a state or course of manufacture or into a state for any process or operation to be performed thereupon or therewith and before the same are completed or finished for the purpose of wear or consumption.

Application of Act to keepers of certain shops.

3. In order to prevent evasion of the provisions of this Act, the following persons shall be deemed to be persons carrying on the business of taking goods and chattels in pawn; that is to say, every person who keeps a shop for the purchase or sale of goods or chattels, or for taking in goods or chattels by way of security for money advanced thereon, and who purchases or receives or takes in goods or chattels and pays or advances or lends thereon any sum of money not exceeding three hundred shillings with or under an agreement or understanding expressed or implied, or to be from the nature and character of the dealing reasonably inferred, that those goods or chattels may be afterwards redeemed or repurchased on any terms; and every such transaction, article, payment, advance and loan shall be deemed a pawning, pledge and loan respectively within this Act.

Executors of pawnbrokers.

4. The provisions of this Act relating to pawnbrokers shall extend to and include the executors or administrators of deceased pawnbrokers, except that an executor or administrator shall not be answerable for any penalty or forfeiture personally or out of his own estate, unless the same is incurred by his own act or neglect.

Servants, apprentices and agents of pawnbrokers.

5. For the purposes of this Act, anything done or omitted by the servant, apprentice or agent of a pawnbroker in the course of or in relation to the business of the pawnbroker shall be deemed to be done or omitted (as the case may be) by the pawnbroker; and anything by this Act authorized to be done by a pawnbroker may be done by his servant, apprentice or agent.

Assigns and executors of pawners.

6. The rights, powers and benefits by this Act reserved to and conferred on pawners shall extend to the assigns of pawners, and to the executors or administrators of deceased pawners; but any person representing himself to a pawnbroker to be the assign, executor or administrator of a pawner shall, if required by the pawnbroker, produce to the

pawnbroker the assignment, probate, letters of administration or other instrument under which he claims.

Application of Act according to amount of loan.

7. (1) This Act shall apply—

(*a*) to every loan by a pawnbroker of sixty shillings or under;

(*b*) to every loan by a pawnbroker of above sixty shillings and not above three hundred shillings, except as in this Act otherwise provided in relation to cases where a special contract respecting the terms of the loan (as authorized by this Act) is made between the pawner and the pawnbroker at the time of the pawning.

(2) Notwithstanding anything in this Act, a person shall not be deemed a pawnbroker by reason only of his paying, advancing or lending on any terms any sum or sums of above three hundred shillings.

Pawnbrokers to keep books, as in First Schedule.

8. (1) A pawnbroker shall keep and use in his business such books and documents as are specified in the First Schedule [2] to this Act in the forms therein specified, or to the like effect, and shall from time to time as occasion requires enter therein in English and in a fair and legible manner the particulars indicated in and in accordance with the directions of that Schedule, and shall make all inquiries necessary for that purpose.

(2) If a pawnbroker fails in any respect to comply with the requisitions of this section he shall be guilty of an offence.

Pawnbrokers to exhibit name, table of rates, etc., and to permit police to enter premises.

9. (1) A pawnbroker shall always keep exhibited in large characters over the outer door of his shop his name or names with the word "pawnbroker".

(2) A pawnbroker shall always keep placed in a conspicuous part of his shop (so as to be legible by every person pawning or redeeming pledges standing in any box or part of the shop provided for persons pawning or redeeming pledges) the same information as is by the First Schedule to this Act required to be printed on pawntickets.

(3) A pawnbroker shall allow the police at any time to enter and inspect his premises and any article or thing taken in pawn and his books and papers relating to his business, on production of an order from a magistrate or a Superintendent or Assistant Superintendent of Police.

[2] The First Schedule is omitted from this volume.

(4) If a pawnbroker fails in any respect to comply with the requisitions of this section he shall be guilty of an offence.

## Pawning, Redemption, Sale

Pawntickets.

10. A pawnbroker shall on taking a pledge in pawn give to the pawner a pawnticket in the prescribed form, and shall not take a pledge in pawn unless the pawner takes the pawnticket.

Profits and charges allowed to pawnbrokers.

11. (1) A pawnbroker may take profit on a loan on a pledge at a rate not exceeding that specified in the Second Schedule[3] to this Act.

(2) A pawnbroker may demand and take the charges specified in the said Schedule, in the cases and according to the rules therein stated and prescribed.

(3) A pawnbroker shall not, in respect of a loan on a pledge, take any profit or demand or take any charge or sum whatever other than those specified in the said Schedule.

(4) A pawnbroker shall, if required at the time of redemption, give a receipt for the amount of loan and profit paid to him.

Period for redemption.

12. (1) Every pledge pawned for fifteen shillings or under shall be redeemable within six months from the day of pawning, exclusive of that day; and there shall be added to that six months of redemption seven days of grace within which every such pledge (if not redeemed within the six months of redemption) shall continue to be redeemable.

(2) Every pledge pawned for above fifteen shillings shall be redeemable within twelve months from the date of pawning, exclusive of that day; and there shall be added to that twelve months of redemption seven days of grace within which every such pledge (if not redeemed within the year of redemption) shall continue redeemable.

Pledges for Sh. 15 or under forfeited if not redeemed in time.

13. A pledge pawned for fifteen shillings or under, if not redeemed within the six months and days of grace, shall at the end of the days of grace become and be the pawnbroker's absolute property.

Pledges above Sh. 15 redeemable until sale.

14. A pledge pawned for above fifteen shillings shall further continue redeemable until it is disposed of as in this Act provided, although the year of redemption and days of grace are expired.

---

[3] The Second Schedule is omitted from this volume.

Pledge above Sh. 15 to be sold by auction.

15. (1) A pledge pawned for more than fifteen shillings shall, when disposed of by the pawnbroker, be disposed of by public auction, and not otherwise; and the regulations in the Third Schedule[4] to this Act shall be observed with reference to the sale.

(2) A pawnbroker may bid for and purchase at a sale by auction, made or purporting to be made under this Act, a pledge pawned with him; and on such purchase he shall be deemed the absolute owner of the pledge purchased.

Offences by auctioneers.

16. If an auctioneer does anything in contravention of the provisions of this Act relating to auctioneers, or fails to do anything which he is required by this Act to do, he shall be guilty of an offence.

Power to inspect sale book.

17. At any time within three years after the auction at which a pledge pawned for above fifteen shillings is sold, the holder of the pawnticket may inspect the entry of the sale in the pawnbroker's book, and in the filled-up catalogue of the auction (authenticated by the signature of the auctioneer), or in either of them.

Pawnbroker to account for surplus within three years, subject to set-off.

18. (1) Where a pledge pawned for above fifteen shillings is sold and appears from the pawnbroker's book to have been sold for more than the amount of the loan and profit due at the time of sale, the pawnbroker shall on demand pay the surplus to the holder of the pawnticket, in case the demand is made within three years after the sale, the necessary costs and charges of the sale being first deducted.

(2) If on any such demand it appears from the pawnbroker's book that the sale of a pledge or pledges has resulted in a surplus, and that within twelve months before or after that sale the sale of another pledge or other pledges of the same person has resulted in a deficit, the pawnbroker may set off the deficit against the surplus, and shall be liable to pay the balance only after such set-off.

Offences as to pledges above Sh.15.

19. If, with respect to pledges for loans of above fifteen shillings, a pawnbroker—

(*a*) does not bona fide according to the directions of this Act sell a pledge pawned with him;

(*b*) enters in his book a pledge as sold for less than the sum for which it was sold or fails duly to enter the same;

(*c*) refuses to permit any person entitled under this Act to inspection of an entry of sale in the pawnbroker's book, or of a

[4] The Third Schedule is omitted from this volume.

filled-up catalogue of the auction authenticated by the auctioneer's signature, to inspect the same;

(*d*) fails without lawful excuse (proof whereof shall lie on him) to produce such a catalogue on lawful demand;

(*e*) refuses to pay on demand the surplus to the person entitled to receive the same;

he shall in every such case be guilty of an offence and liable to forfeit to the person aggrieved a sum not exceeding three hundred shillings.

## Special Contracts

Power to make special contract for pledge above Sh. 60.

**20.** (1) Notwithstanding anything in this Act, a pawnbroker may make a special contract with the pawner in respect of a pledge on which the pawnbroker makes a loan of above sixty shillings:

Provided that—

(i) the pawnbroker at the time of the pawning shall deliver to the pawner a special contract pawnticket signed by the pawnbroker;

(ii) a duplicate of the special contract pawnticket shall be signed by the pawner.

(2) The provisions of this Act, save as far as the application thereof is excluded by the terms of the special contract, shall apply thereto.

(3) A special contract pawnticket or the duplicate thereof shall not be subject to stamp duty.

## Delivery Up of Pledge

Holder of pawnticket entitled to redeem.

**21.** The holder for the time being of a pawnticket shall be presumed to be the person entitled to redeem the pledge, and, subject to the provisions of this Act, the pawnbroker shall accordingly (on payment of the loan and profit) deliver the pledge to the person producing the pawnticket, and he is hereby indemnified for so doing.

Production of pawnticket on redemption.

**22.** A pawnbroker shall not (except as in this Act provided) be bound to deliver back a pledge unless the pawnticket for it is delivered to him.

Liability of pawnbroker in case of fire.

**23.** (1) Where a pledge is destroyed or damaged by or in consequence of fire, the pawnbroker shall nevertheless be liable on application within the period during which the pledge would have been redeemable to pay the value of the pledge after deducting the amount of the loan and profit, such value to be the amount of the loan and profit and twenty-five per centum on the amount of the loan.

(2) A pawnbroker shall be entitled to insure to the extent of the value so estimated.

Compensation for depreciation of pledge.

24. If a person entitled and offering to redeem a pledge shows to the satisfaction of a magistrate that the pledge has become or has been rendered of less value than it was at the time of the pawning thereof by or through the default or neglect or wilful misbehaviour of the pawnbroker, the magistrate may if he thinks fit award a reasonable satisfaction to the owner of the pledge in respect of the damage, and the amount awarded shall be deducted from the amount payable to the pawnbroker, or shall be paid by the pawnbroker (as the case requires) in such manner as the magistrate directs.

Protection of owners and of pawners not having pawntickets.

25. (1) The following provisions shall have effect for protection of owners of articles pawned, and of pawners not having their pawntickets to produce—

(*a*) any person claiming to be the owner of a pledge but not holding the pawnticket, or any person claiming to be entitled to hold a pawnticket but alleging that the same has been lost, mislaid, destroyed or stolen or fraudulently obtained from him, may apply to the pawnbroker for a printed form of declaration, which the pawnbroker shall deliver to him;

(*b*) if the applicant delivers back to the pawnbroker the declaration duly made before a magistrate or justice of the peace by the applicant and a person identifying him, the applicant shall thereupon have as between him and the pawnbroker all the same rights and remedies as if he had produced the pawnticket:

Provided that such a declaration shall not be effectual for that purpose unless it is duly made and delivered back to the pawnbroker within five days after the day on which the form is delivered to the applicant by the pawnbroker;

(*c*) the pawnbroker is hereby indemnified for not delivering the pledge to any person until the expiration of the period aforesaid;

(*d*) the pawnbroker is further hereby indemnified for delivering the pledge or otherwise acting in conformity with the declaration, unless he has actual or constructive notice that the declaration is fraudulent or is false in any material particular.

(2) If a person makes a declaration under this Act, either as an applicant or as identifying an applicant, which is false, and which he either knows or believes to be false or does not believe to be true, he shall be guilty of an offence and liable to imprisonment for a term not exceeding three years or to a fine not exceeding three thousand shillings, or to both such imprisonment and such fine.

**26.** In each of the following cases—

Delivery to owner of property unlawfully pawned.

(*a*) if any person is convicted under this Act before a court of knowingly and designedly pawning with a pawnbroker anything being the property of another person, the pawner not being employed or authorized by the owner thereof to pawn the same; or

(*b*) if any person is convicted before a court of dishonestly taking or misappropriating fraudulently or dishonestly obtaining any goods or chattels, and it appears to the court that the same have been pawned with a pawnbroker; or

(*c*) if in any proceedings before a court it appears to it that any goods and chattels brought before it have been unlawfully pawned with a pawnbroker;

the court may, if it thinks fit, on proof of the ownership of the goods and chattels, order the delivery thereof to the owner either on payment to the pawnbroker of the amount of the loan or of any part thereof or without payment thereof or of any part thereof, as it thinks fit.

Summary order for delivery of pledge to person entitled.

**27.** If a pawnbroker without reasonable excuse (proof whereof shall lie on him) neglects or refuses to deliver a pledge to the person entitled to delivery thereof under this Act, he shall be guilty of an offence, and a magistrate may, if he thinks fit, with or without imposing a penalty, order the delivery of the pledge on payment of the amount of the loan and profit.

## General Restrictions on Pawnbrokers

Prohibition of taking pledges from children and other restrictions.

**28.** If a pawnbroker does any of the following things—

(*a*) takes an article in pawn from any person appearing to be under the age of fourteen years, or to be intoxicated;

(*b*) purchases or takes in pawn or exchange a pawnticket issued by another pawnbroker;

(*c*) employs any person under fourteen years of age to take pledges in pawn;

(*d*) under any pretence purchases, except at public auction, any pledge while in pawn with him;

(*e*) suffers any pledge while in pawn with him to be redeemed with a view to his purchasing it;

(*f*) makes any contract or agreement with any person pawning or offering to pawn any article, or with the owner thereof, for the purchase, sale or disposition thereof within the time of redemption;

(*g*) sells or otherwise disposes of any pledge pawned with him except at such times and in such manner as authorized by this Act,

he shall be guilty of an offence.

## UNLAWFUL PAWNING AND TAKING IN PAWN

Unlawful pawning of goods not property of pawner.

29. If any person does any of the following things—

(*a*) knowingly and designedly pawns with a pawnbroker anything being the property of any other person, the pawner not being employed or authorized by the owner thereof to pawn the same;

(*b*) offers to a pawnbroker an article by way of pawn, being unable or refusing to give a satisfactory account of the means by which he became possessed of the article;

(*c*) wilfully gives false information to a pawnbroker as to whether an article offered by him in pawn to the pawnbroker is his own property or not, or as to his name or address, or as to the name and address of the owner of the article;

(*d*) not being entitled, and not having any colour of title by law, to redeem a pledge, attempts or endeavours to redeem the same,

he shall be guilty of an offence.

Prohibition of taking in pawn linen, apparel or unfinished goods or materials.

30. If a pawnbroker knowingly takes in pawn any linen or apparel or unfinished goods or materials entrusted to any person to wash, scour, iron, mend, manufacture, work up, finish or make up, he shall be guilty of an offence and liable on conviction to forfeit a sum not exceeding double the amount of the loan, and shall also be liable to restore the pledge to the owner thereof in the presence of the magistrate, or as he shall direct.

## LICENCES

Yearly licence.

31. (1) Every pawnbroker shall take out from the District Commissioner of the district in which he is carrying on his business a yearly licence for carrying on his business, on which licence there shall be charged and paid a fee of forty shillings.

(2) Every licence shall be dated on the day on which it is issued, and shall expire on the 31st December following.

(3) A separate licence shall be taken out and paid for by the pawnbroker for each pawnbroker's shop kept by him.

(4) Every licence shall specify the premises on which the licensee may conduct his business, and the licensee shall not carry on his business

except on the premises specified without the sanction in writing of the District Commissioner.

(5) If a person acts as a pawnbroker without having in force a proper licence, he shall be guilty of an offence and liable to a fine not exceeding one thousand five hundred shillings.

32. If a pawnbroker is convicted of any fraud in his business or of receiving stolen goods knowing them to be stolen, the court by which he is convicted may, if it thinks fit, direct that his licence shall cease to have effect, and the same shall so cease accordingly. Cesser of licence on conviction.

33. A person intending to apply for the first time for a licence under this Act shall, twenty-one days at least before the application, give notice in writing to the officer in charge of the police in the district in which he intends to carry on business, and shall in the notice set forth his name and address. Notice of first application.

34. A licence shall not be refused except on one of the following grounds— Grounds of refusal of licence.

(*a*) that the applicant has failed to produce satisfactory evidence of good character;

(*b*) that the shop in which he intends to carry on the business of pawnbroker, or any adjacent house or place owned or occupied by him, is frequented by thieves or persons of bad character;

(*c*) that he has not complied with section 33 of this Act.

## Penalties and Legal Proceedings

35. If a pawnbroker or other person is guilty of an offence under this Act in respect whereof a specific forfeiture or penalty is not prescribed by this Act, he shall be liable to a fine not exceeding six hundred shillings, and in default of payment to six months' imprisonment. General penalty.

36. Penalties recovered under this Act, not directed to be otherwise applied, may be applied under direction of the court in which they are recovered, as follows— Application of penalties.

(*a*) where the complainant is the party aggrieved, one moiety of the penalty may be paid to him;

(*b*) where the complainant is not the party aggrieved, there shall be paid to him no part or such part only of the penalty as the court thinks fit.

Detention of persons offering forged pawntickets.

**37.** If any person utters, produces, shows or offers to a pawnbroker a pawnticket which the pawnbroker reasonably suspects to have been counterfeited, forged or altered, the pawnbroker may seize and detain the person and the ticket, or either of them, and shall deliver the person and the ticket, or either of them (as the case may be) as soon as may be into the custody of a police officer, who shall, as soon as may be, convey the person if so detained before a magistrate to be dealt with according to law.

Production of books before magistrate.

**38.** (1) A pawnbroker shall at any time, when ordered or summoned by a court, attend before the court and produce all books and papers relating to his business which he is required by the court to produce.

(2) If he fails to do so, he shall be guilty of an offence.

Contracts not void on account of offences.

**39.** Where a pawnbroker is guilty of an offence under this Act (not being an offence under any provision of this Act relating to licences), any contract of pawn or other contract made by him in relation to his business of pawnbroker shall nevertheless not be void by reason only of that offence, nor shall he by reason only of that offence lose his lien on or right to the pledge or to the loan and profit; but nothing in this section shall restrict the operation of any provision of this Act providing for the delivery of any goods and chattels, or the restoration of any linen, apparel, goods, materials or article to the owner, under the order of any court.

Rules.

**40.** The Minister may make rules for the better carrying out of this Act.

*{The First, Second, and Third Schedules are omitted from this volume.}*

# The Building Societies Act[1]

*Commencement: 6th July, 1956*

An Act to provide for the formation and registration of building societies; and for matters incidental thereto and connected therewith

## PART I—PRELIMINARY

1. This Act may be cited as the Building Societies Act. Short title.

2. In this Act, except where the context otherwise requires— Interpretation.

"basic advance", in relation to any advance made or to be made by a building society for the purpose of its being used in defraying the purchase price of land, means the maximum amount which the society would consider proper to advance upon the security of that land if no other security were taken by the society;

"board of directors", in relation to any building society, means the managing body thereof by whatever name called;

"building society" means a society formed for the purpose of raising by the subscription of members a stock or fund from which to make advances to members and registered in accordance with the provisions of this Act;

"continuing arrangement" means any arrangement made between a building society and another person whereby, in contemplation of a series of advances comprising excess advances being made by the society to members for the purpose of their being used in defraying the purchase price of land, that person undertakes to give to the society a series of guarantees, each of which is to secure sums payable to the society in respect of such an advance;

"director" means a member of a board of directors;

"dispute" means a dispute between a building society and a member, or any representative of a member in his capacity as a member of the society, unless by the rules of any society for the time being it is otherwise expressly provided; and, in the absence of such express provision, shall not apply to any dispute

[1] *Laws of Kenya,* Cap. 489 (1962). Originally No. 29 of 1956. Relevant citations: Nos. 28 of 1959; 27 of 1961; 9 of 1967; 29 of 1967; 34 of 1967; L.N. 589/1960; L.N. 142/1961; L.N. 147/1961; L.N. 457/1963; L.N. 462/1963; L.N. 2/1964; L.N. 374/1964; Nos. 21 of 1966; and 9 of 1967.

between any such society and any member thereof, or other person whatever, as to the construction or effect of any instrument of mortgage or any contract contained in any document, other than the rules of the society, and shall not prevent any society, or any member thereof, or any person claiming through or under him, from obtaining in the ordinary course of law any remedy in respect of any such mortgage or other contract to which he or the society would otherwise be by law entitled;

"excess advance" means, in relation to any advance, the amount by which the advance exceeds the basic advance;

"existing society" means any society, association, partnership or company, whether incorporated or registered in or outside Kenya, which was carrying on business as a building society in Kenya immediately before the commencement of this Act;

"land" includes freehold or leasehold land and all buildings thereon, whether the same were erected before, or are erected during, the period for which any mortgage on such land in favour of a building society subsists;

"mortgage" includes a legal charge, and "mortgagor" and "mortgagee" shall be construed accordingly;

"register" means the register of building societies to be kept by the Registrar under section 7 of this Act;

"Registrar" means the Registrar of Building Societies appointed under section 3 of this Act, and includes a Deputy Registrar and an Assistant Registrar;

"special resolution" means a resolution passed by not less than three-fourths of the members of a building society present and entitled to vote at any general meeting of which notice specifying the intention to propose that resolution has been duly given according to the rules of the society.

Appointment of Registrar.

3. The Minister shall appoint a Registrar of Building Societies to perform the duties and exercise the powers imposed and conferred by this Act, and may appoint a Deputy Registrar and any number of Assistant Registrars, who shall be subject to the directions of the Registrar.

Certificates, etc., to be evidence.

4. (1) A certificate of registration of a society issued by the Registrar shall, upon its mere production, in the absence of proof of fraud, be conclusive evidence that all the requirements of this Act in respect of registration and of matters precedent and incidental thereto have been complied with and that the society is duly registered.

(2) Any other document relating to a building society and purporting to be signed by the Registrar shall, in the absence of any evidence

to the contrary, be admissible as evidence in any court without proof of the signature.

Indemnity of the Registrar and other persons.

5. The Registrar shall not, nor shall any person acting under the authority of the Registrar or under any regulation made under this Act, be personally liable for or in respect of any act or matter done in good faith in the exercise or supposed exercise of the powers conferred by this Act or by any regulation made under this Act.

## PART II—FORMATION AND REGISTRATION

Formation of building societies.

6. (1) Any ten or more persons may form a building society by subscribing their names and addresses to rules agreed by them for the government of such society and by obtaining registration under this Act.

(2) Subject to the provisions of this section, persons intending to establish a building society may apply to the Registrar for registration in the prescribed form, accompanied by two copies of such rules.

(3) If the Registrar is satisfied that the application and the rules are in compliance with the provisions of this Act and any regulations made thereunder, he shall enter the prescribed particulars relating thereto in the register.

(4) The Registrar shall issue a certificate of registration in the prescribed form to every building society registered under this section.

Maintenance of register.

7. The Registrar shall keep a register of building societies in which he shall record, in respect of all building societies registered under section 6 or section 75 of this Act, the following particulars, that is to say—

(*a*) the name of the society;
(*b*) the situation and postal address of the head office in Kenya of the society;
(*c*) such other information as may be prescribed.

Effect of registration.

8. From the date of registration of a society under this Act, such society shall be a body corporate by its registered name with perpetual succession, and may in such name sue and be sued, and, subject to the provisions of this Act and of its rules, shall be capable of doing all such acts as a body corporate may by law perform.

Names of building societies.

9. (1) No building society shall be registered by a name which is identical with that of any other building society previously incorporated or registered, or by a name which so nearly resembles the same as to be

likely to deceive, unless such other society is in course of being terminated or dissolved and consents to such registration.

(2) The name of every building society shall end with the words "Building Society".

(3) A building society shall not use any name or title other than its registered name.

(4) The Registrar may, unless otherwise ordered by the Minister, refuse to register a building society by a name which in his opinion is calculated to mislead the public or to cause offence to any person or class of persons.

Contents of rules of building societies.

**10.** The rules of every building society shall set forth—

*(a)* the name of the society and the situation and postal address of the chief office of the society;

*(b)* the principal objects of the society;

*(c)* the manner in which a person may become a member, and may cease to be a member, of the society;

*(d)* the manner in which the funds of the society are to be raised, the purposes to which they are to be applied and the manner in which surplus funds are to be invested;

*(e)* the classes of shares to be issued, the conditions of redemption or repayment of shares and the preferential and other special rights attaching to each class of shares;

*(f)* the terms upon which shares are to be issued and withdrawn and the manner in which contributions are to be paid to the society;

*(g)* the conditions upon which the society will accept and repay deposits;

*(h)* the manner in which and the conditions upon which advances upon the security of a mortgage or otherwise are to be made and repaid and the conditions upon which a borrower can redeem the amount due from him before the expiration of the period for which the advance was made, with tables, where applicable in the opinion of the Registrar, showing the amounts due from the borrower after each stipulated payment;

*(i)* the manner in which profits or losses are to be ascertained and dealt with or provided for;

*(j)* whether the society intends to borrow money and, if so, within what limits not exceeding those prescribed by this Act;

*(k)* the limits of loans to or deposits by any one person;

*(l)* the manner of altering and rescinding the rules of the society and of making additional rules;

(*m*) the manner of appointing, remunerating and removing the board of directors, their qualifications, powers and duties, and the manner of appointing, remunerating and removing members of local boards or committees and of auditors and other officers of the society;

(*n*) the manner of calling general and special meetings of the members, the quorum necessary for the transaction of business at such meetings and the right to and manner of voting thereat;

(*o*) provision for an annual or more frequent audit of the accounts and inspection by the auditors of the mortgages and other securities belonging to the society;

(*p*) whether disputes between the society and any of its members, or any person claiming by or through any member, or under the rules, shall be settled by reference to the Supreme Court, to the Registrar or to arbitration;

(*q*) provision for the device, custody and use of the common seal of the society;

(*r*) provision for the custody of the instruments of mortgage and of other securities belonging to the society;

(*s*) the charges, fees, fines and forfeitures which may be demanded from or imposed on members of the society and borrowers;

(*t*) the manner in which the society shall be dissolved;

(*u*) the financial year of the society; and

(*v*) such other matters as may be prescribed from time to time.

Common seal.

11. (1) Every building society shall have a common seal which shall bear the registered name of the society.

(2) A building society which is by its rules permitted to carry on its business outside Kenya may, if authorized by its rules, have for use in any place not situate in Kenya an official seal, which shall be a facsimile of the common seal of the society with the addition on its face of the name of the place where it is to be used.

(3) A deed or other document to which an official seal of a foreign building society registered under section 75 of this Act is duly affixed shall bind the society as if it had been sealed with the common seal of the society.

Head office and postal address.

12. Every building society shall have a head office and postal address in Kenya to which all communications and notices may be addressed.

## PART III—MANAGEMENT OF BUILDING SOCIETIES

Directors.

13. (1) Every building society shall have a board of directors consisting of three or more persons, of whom the secretary may, but need not, be one.

(2) The duties of every director of a building society shall include the duty of satisfying himself that the arrangements made for assessing the adequacy of any security to be taken in respect of any advance to be made by the society are such as may be reasonably expected to ensure that the adequacy of any security to be so taken will be assessed by a competent and prudent person experienced in the matters relevant to the determination of the value of that security:

Provided that nothing in this subsection shall preclude a director of a building society from approving such arrangements as aforesaid by reason only that the arrangements provide for the assessment of the adequacy of such security by himself or any other director of the society.

Secretary.

14. (1) Every building society shall have a secretary.

(2) Anything required or authorized to be done by or to the secretary may, if the office is vacant or there is for any other reason no secretary capable of acting, be done by or to any assistant or deputy secretary, or, if there is no assistant or deputy secretary capable of acting, by or to an officer of the society authorized generally or specially in that behalf by the board of directors.

Auditors.

15. Every building society shall have one or more auditors, who shall be a person or persons approved for that purpose by the Registrar, and one at least of whom shall be a person who publicly carries on the business of an accountant in Kenya.

Officers to give security.

16. Every officer of a building society having the receipt or charge of any money belonging to the society shall before taking upon himself the execution of his office become bound with one sufficient surety at the least in a bond in the prescribed form, or give such other security as the society may direct, in such sum as the society may require, conditioned for rendering a just and true account of all moneys received and paid by him on account of the society, and for payment of all sums of money due from him to the society at such times as its rules appoint or as the society may require.

Officers to account.

17. Every officer of a building society and his executors or administrators shall, upon demand made or notice in writing given or left at his

last or usual place of residence, render an account of all moneys received or paid by him on account of the society and for all moneys remaining in his hands and shall deliver all securities and effects, books, papers and property of the society in his hands or custody to such person as the society may appoint.

Officers not to accept gifts.

**18.** (1) No director, secretary, surveyor, advocate or other officer of a building society shall, in addition to the remuneration prescribed or authorized by the rules of the society, receive from any other person any gift, bonus, commission or benefit for or in connexion with any transaction whatsoever relating to the business of the society.

(2) Any person who pays or accepts any such gift, bonus, commission or benefit shall be guilty of an offence and liable to a fine not exceeding ten thousand shillings and in default of payment to imprisonment for a term not exceeding six months, and the person accepting any such gift, bonus, commission or benefit shall, as and when instructed by the court by whom he is convicted, pay over to the society the amount or value of such gift, bonus, commission or benefit, and in default of such payments shall be liable to imprisonment for a term not exceeding six months.

Restriction of payment of commissions.

19. (1) It shall not be lawful—

(*a*) for a person having a financial interest in the disposition of any land to receive or to agree to receive any commission or gift from a building society or from any officer, servant or agent of a building society, in consideration of the introduction of mortgage business to the society in connexion with the disposition of the land or in consideration of a promise to introduce such business to the society; or

(*b*) for a building society, or any officer, servant or agent of a building society, to offer to give or agree to give any commission or gift to any person known to the society, officer, servant or agent, as the case may be, to have a financial interest in the disposition of any land or to be a servant of a person having such an interest, for any such consideration as is mentioned in paragraph (*a*) of this subsection.

(2) For the purposes of this section, a person who is employed, otherwise than in pursuance of a contract of service, in connexion with the disposition of any land by a person who has a financial interest in the said disposition shall be treated, so far as relates to the disposition of that land, as a servant of the person having the said interest, unless he carries on, independently of that person, the business of an advocate, estate agent, surveyor or auctioneer.

(3) Where a building society has a financial interest in the disposition of any land, nothing in this section shall prohibit—

*(a)* the society, or any officer, servant or agent of the society, from offering or giving or agreeing to give, in relation to the disposition of that land, any commission or gift to a servant of the society (not being a person who, to the knowledge of the society, officer, servant or agent, as the case may be, either himself has a financial interest in the disposition of the land or is, in addition to being a servant of the society, also the servant of any person other than the society who has such an interest) for any such consideration as is mentioned in subsection (1) of this section; or

*(b)* a servant of the society (not being a person who himself has a financial interest in the disposition of that land, or who is, in addition to being the servant of the society, also the servant of any person other than the society who has such an interest) from receiving or agreeing to receive, in relation to the disposition of that land, any commission or gift from the society, or from any officer, servant or agent of the society, for any such consideration as aforesaid.

(4) Any person who contravenes the provisions of this section shall be guilty of an offence and liable to a fine not exceeding ten thousand shillings or to imprisonment for a term not exceeding six months, or to both such fine and such imprisonment.

Provisions excluding liability of officers forbidden.

**20.** Any provision, whether contained in the rules of a building society or in any contract with a building society or otherwise, for exempting any director, manager or officer of a building society, or any person (whether an officer of the society or not) employed by the society as auditor, from, or indemnifying him against, any liability which by virtue of any rule of law would otherwise attach to him in respect of any negligence, default, breach of duty or breach of trust of which he may be guilty in relation to the society, shall be void:

Provided that a building society may, in pursuance of any such provision as aforesaid, indemnify any such director, manager, officer or auditor against any liability incurred by him in defending any proceedings, whether civil or criminal, in which judgment is given in his favour or in which he is acquitted or in connexion with any application under section 21 of this Act in which relief is granted to him by the court.

Powers of court to grant relief in certain cases.

**21.** (1) If, in any proceedings for negligence, default, breach of duty or breach of trust against any person to whom this section applies, it appears to the court hearing the case that that person is or may be liable in respect of the negligence, default, breach of duty or breach of trust, but that he has acted honestly and reasonably, and that having regard to all the circumstances of the case, including those connected with his appointment, he ought fairly to be excused for the negligence, default, breach of duty or breach of trust, that court may relieve him either wholly or partly from his liability on such terms as the court may think fit.

(2) Where any person to whom this section applies has reason to apprehend that any claim will or might be made against him in respect of any negligence, default, breach of duty or breach of trust, he may apply to the Supreme Court for relief, and the Supreme Court on any such application shall have the same power to relieve him as under this section it would have had if it had been a court before which proceedings against that person for negligence, default, breach of duty or breach of trust had been brought.

(3) The persons to whom this section applies are the directors, the members and officers of a building society, and any person employed by a building society as an auditor, whether he is or is not an officer of the society.

## PART IV—POWERS OF BUILDING SOCIETIES

22. (1) Subject to the provisions of the Act, a building society may receive deposits or loans at interest from its members or from other persons to be applied to the purposes of the society. Power to borrow.

(2) The total amount so received on deposit or loan and not repaid by the society shall not at any time exceed two-thirds of the amount for the time being secured to the society by mortgages from its members.

(3) The amount of such deposits or loans from any one person shall be within any limits prescribed by the rules of the society.

(4) In calculating the amount for the time being secured to a building society by mortgages from its members for the purposes of subsection (2) of this section, there shall be disregarded—

*(a)* the amount secured on properties the payments in respect of which, whether of principal, interest or otherwise, were upwards of twelve months in arrear at the date of the society's last preceding annual account and statement; and

*(b)* the amount secured on properties of which the society had been twelve months in possession at the date of such account and statement.

(5) Money deposited with a building society as security for an advance made by the building society to a member, or as security for any guarantee given in respect of such an advance, shall be deemed to be money borrowed by the society.

(6) A building society shall not accept any deposit or loan except on the terms that not less than one month's notice may be required by the society before repayment or withdrawal.

(7) Every deposit book or acknowledgment or security of any kind given for a deposit or loan by a building society shall have printed or written therein or thereon the whole of this section.

(8) If a building society contravenes this section, the society and every director, secretary or other officer of the society who is a party to the contravention shall be guilty of an offence and liable to a fine not exceeding two thousand shillings.

(9) If any building society receives loans or deposits in excess of the limits prescribed by this Act, the directors of the society shall be personally liable for the amount so received in excess.

Power to hold land.

23. (1) Subject to the provisions of the Crown Lands Act, the Trust Land Act, and the Land Control Act, it shall be lawful for a building society—

(*a*) to acquire and hold any land which the society requires for its business premises or for the housing of its staff; and

(*b*) to acquire by foreclosure or surrender any land mortgaged to the society:

Provided that any land acquired by a building society under paragraph *(b)* of this subsection shall be sold and converted into money within a period of two years or such longer period as the Registrar may authorize in writing.

(2) A building society may let any part of its business premises which is not required for the immediate use of the society.

Power to make advances to members.

24. (1) A building society may, subject to the provisions of this section, make advances to its members out of its funds upon the security of land:

Provided that no building society shall advance money on the security of any land which is subject to a prior mortgage, unless such prior mortgage is in favour of the society making the advance; and if any advance is made in contravention of this proviso, the directors of the society who authorized the advance shall be jointly and severally liable for any loss on the advance occasioned to the society.

(2) No building society shall make an advance in excess of such amount as may be prescribed without the consent in writing of the Registrar.

(3) In determining the amount of any advance made by a building society to one of its members upon the security of any land, the society shall not take into account the value of any additional security taken by the society for the advance, other than a security of a class specified in the Schedule to this Act.

(4) Where a charge upon a policy of life assurance is taken as additional security for an advance, the value of the policy shall be assessed at an amount not exceeding the surrender value thereof at the time when the advance is made.

(5) Where a guarantee given in pursuance of a continuing arrangement is taken as additional security for such an advance as aforesaid, the advance shall not exceed such amount as may be prescribed or ninety per centum of the amount of the purchase price for the defraying of which the advance is made, whichever is the less, without the consent in writing of the Registrar; and in any such case the basic advance shall not exceed sixty-five per centum of that amount and the excess advance shall not exceed twenty-five per centum of that amount.

(6) Where a building society takes as additional security for an advance to a member a guarantee given in pursuance of a continuing arrangement, the terms of the advance shall not provide for the payment of any sums to the society in respect of the advance after the expiration of a period of twenty years (or such other period, being either longer or shorter, as the Registrar may authorize in writing) from the date on which the advance is made, nor, after any such advance as aforesaid has been made by the society, shall the society make any agreement which has the effect of rendering any sums payable to the society in respect of the advance after the expiration of the said period:

Provided that nothing in this subsection shall affect the power of a society to make any such agreement as aforesaid in relation to any advance which has been made by the society not less than one year before the making of the agreement if, in the opinion of the directors, it is desirable so to do in order to avoid hardship to a member of the society.

Power to invest.

25. (1) A building society may, from time to time as its rules permit, invest any portion of its funds not immediately required for its purposes in or upon any stock, shares or securities for the time being authorized by law for the investment of trust moneys or in any other

class or classes of investment authorized by the Minister by notice in the Gazette.

(2) A building society shall have power to keep money on current account and deposit account at one or more banks or with the Post Office Savings Bank.

Power to make further advances.

26. (1) For the purposes of facilitating repayment to a building society of an advance made or to be made by the society to a member upon the security of land, a society shall have power to make to the member, by way of addition to the advance aforesaid, a further advance of the whole or part of such sum as may be necessary to enable payment to be made of a single premium payable in respect of a policy of life assurance upon the life of the member or the spouse or son or daughter of the member, being a policy which provides for payment, in the event of the death of the person upon whose life the policy is effected before the advance has been repaid, of any sum not exceeding such sum as is sufficient to defray the sums which are, at and after the time of the death, payable to the society in respect of the advance as increased by the additional advance made by the society under the power conferred by this subsection.

(2) Where, in pursuance of the power conferred by subsection (1) of this section, a society has added any sum to an advance made by the society upon the security of land, the sum so added to the advance shall not be deemed to form part thereof for the purpose of determining whether the advance is beyond the power of the society by reason—

*(a)* of the amount of the advance being excessive, or
*(b)* of the amount of any excess advance included in the advance being greater than that which is authorized by this Act.

(3) Where a society has made an advance to a member upon the security of land, and the advance is an advance to which the provisions of subsection (6) of section 24 of this Act apply, then, if the society subsequently adds to the advance a further advance under the power conferred by this section, the said provisions shall also apply in relation to that further advance; and, for the purpose of the application thereto of those provisions, the further advance shall be deemed to have been made at the time when the original advance was made.

Notice to be given where security for advance to member is taken from third party.

27. (1) Where a building society makes to a member an advance for the purpose of its being used in defraying the purchase price of land and takes any security for the advance from another person, then, unless before any contract requiring the member to repay the advance is entered into the society gives to the member a notice in writing, in the prescribed form—

(*a*) stating, if the land is mortgaged or is to be mortgaged to the society as security for the advance, the maximum amount which the society would consider proper to advance upon the security of that land if no other security were taken by the society for the advance, and the amount, if any, by which the advance exceeds the said maximum amount; and

(*b*) containing such particulars as may be prescribed relating to any security for the advance which is taken or is to be taken from any person other than the member,

no sums shall be recoverable, either by the society or by any other person, in respect of the advance or of any security given therefor (whether by the member or otherwise), nor shall any rights be exercisable by virtue of any such security, except by leave of the court.

(2) Where a society makes such an advance and takes such security as aforesaid without giving notice to the member in accordance with the foregoing provisions of this section, the court may, either upon an application for such leave as aforesaid, or upon an application made by the member, reopen the transaction, and may make such orders as to the sums which may be recovered in respect of the advance and of any security given therefor, as to the exercise of any rights conferred by any such security and otherwise as the court considers just.

Power to carry on business abroad.

**28.** A building society shall have power, provided that its rules so allow, to carry on business in any place outside Kenya and to invest any portion of its funds not immediately required for its purposes in advances upon the security of land in any such place:

Provided that—

(i) no building society, other than an existing society, shall make any such investment within five years of its registration under this Act;

(ii) the amount which a building society may invest outside Kenya shall not, without the consent of the Minister, exceed one-fifth of its capital assets for the time being in Kenya.

Additional powers of building societies.

**29.** Subject to the provisions of this Act, and to its rules, a building society shall have the following powers in addition to the powers hereinbefore conferred—

(*a*) to borrow money at interest, other than in the form of deposit, from a bank, or, if the terms are approved in writing by the Registrar, from any person other than a banker, and to arrange overdraft facilities with a bank;

(*b*) to act as the agent of insurance companies in effecting insurances in respect of property mortgaged or to be mortgaged to the society and any other insurances designed to secure a debt to the society, and to collect on behalf of such companies the premiums in respect of any insurance so effected and of the insurances pledged to the society;

(*c*) to pay pensions or gratuities to its employees, or to establish a pension fund or to adopt a pension scheme for providing pensions or gratuities for its employees, or to join with other societies in establishing or adopting any such fund or pension scheme.

Dividends payable only out of profits.

**30.** Notwithstanding anything to the contrary contained in its rules, no building society shall pay any dividend or interest on any of its shares otherwise than out of profits earned by the society.

## PART V—MEETINGS AND PERIODICAL RETURNS

Annual general meeting.

**31.** Every building society shall within five months of the end of its financial year hold a general meeting as its annual general meeting in addition to any other meetings in that year, and shall specify the meeting as such in the notices calling it.

Other meetings.

**32.** The board of directors of a building society shall call such other general or special meetings as may be required by the rules of the society or they may consider desirable, and shall, notwithstanding anything contained in the rules of the society, call a general or special meeting on the application of not less than one-tenth of the whole number of members or of not less than fifty members, whichever is the lesser.

Annual accounts and statement.

**33.** (1) (*a*) Every building society shall, as soon as is practicable and not more than four months after the expiration of its financial year, cause to be prepared an account of all the income and expenditure of the society during such financial year and a general statement of its funds and effects, liabilities and assets.

(*b*) Every such account and statement shall be attested by the auditors of the society and shall be countersigned by at least two directors thereof.

(2) Every such account and statement shall be in such form and shall contain such particulars as may be prescribed, and, without prejudice to the generality of the foregoing, shall show—

(*a*) the amounts due to the holders of the various classes of shares respectively;
(*b*) the amounts due to depositors and creditors for loans;
(*c*) the balance due or outstanding on the security of mortgages (not including prospective interest); and
(*d*) the amount invested by the society in other securities, showing separately investments in and investments outside Kenya.

(3) Every auditor in attesting any such annual account or statement shall either certify that it is correct, duly vouched and in accordance with the law or specially report to the society in what respect he finds it incorrect, unvouched or not in accordance with the law, and shall also certify that he has at that audit actually inspected the securities belonging to the society, and shall state the number of properties with respect to which evidence of title has been produced to and actually inspected by him.

(4) Every member of a building society shall be entitled to receive on demand a copy of such account and statement, and copies thereof shall also be available at the offices of the building society not less than fourteen days before the meeting at which they are to be presented.

(5) A copy of every such annual account and statement, certified in such manner as may be prescribed, shall be sent to the Registrar within fourteen days after the annual or other general meeting at which it is presented or within five months after the expiration of the financial year to which it relates, whichever period expires first.

(6) If any building society fails to comply with the provisions of this section, the society and every director, secretary or other officer of the society shall be guilty of an offence and liable to a fine not exceeding five thousand shillings.

34. Every building society shall, in respect of each financial year, cause to be prepared and sent to the Registrar at the same time as its annual account and statement is sent a return in such form as may be prescribed containing such particulars as may be prescribed with respect to— Returns of sales and transfers.

(*a*) every property which has, during the period to which the return relates, been sold by the society in the exercise of its powers as mortgagee thereof;
(*b*) every mortgage which, during the said period, has been transferred by the society.

## PART VI—MISCELLANEOUS PROVISIONS

Books and records to be kept by building societies.

35. (1) Every building society shall keep the following books, that is to say—

(a) a minute book recording all proceedings of general meetings;
(b) a minute book recording all proceedings of the board of directors;
(c) a register of directors, showing the full names of every director, his postal and residential address, his nationality and, if that nationality is not his nationality of origin, his nationality of origin, the date of his appointment and the date of his ceasing to hold office as such director; and
(d) such books of account as may be necessary to show the receipts and expenditure of the society, the amounts due to the holders of the various classes of shares respectively and to depositors and creditors for loans, the balance due or outstanding on the security of mortgages and the amount invested by the society.

(2) Every building society shall cause to be kept records showing with respect to every advance made by the society on the security of any land—

(a) the amount at which the land was assessed and the name of the person by whom the assessment was made; and
(b) particulars of any additional security taken by the society, including the amount at which it was assessed and the name of the person by whom the assessment was made.

(3) Every building society registered under section 6 of this Act shall keep all registers, minute books, books of account and other records, which it is required by this Act to keep, in English.

(4) If any building society fails to comply with the provisions of this section, the society and every director, secretary or other officer of the society shall be guilty of an offence and liable to a fine not exceeding one thousand shillings.

Rules to be binding on members and others.

36. The rules of a building society as for the time being registered under this Act shall be binding on the several members and officers of the society and on all persons claiming on account of a member or under the rules, all of whom shall be deemed and taken to have full notice thereof.

Duty to supply copies of rules.

37. Every building society shall supply to any person requiring the same a complete printed copy of its rules, with a copy of the certificate of registration appended thereto, and shall be entitled to charge for the same a sum not exceeding five shillings.

38. A copy of the rules of a building society, certified by the secretary or other officer of the society to be a true copy of its registered rules, shall, in the absence of any evidence to the contrary, be admissible as evidence of the rules. Evidence of rules.

39. (1) Any person who is under the age of twenty-one years may be admitted as a member of any building society the rules of which do not prohibit such admission. Persons under twenty-one.

(2) A member of a building society while under the age of twenty-one years may—

(*a*) give all necessary acquittances;
(*b*) consent to the dissolution of the society; and
(*c*) by his next friend, present a petition for winding-up;

but may not—

(i) vote at any meeting of the society;
(ii) hold any office in the society;
(iii) transfer any share standing in his name; or
(iv) execute a mortgage to secure advances made to him by the society.

40. Two or more persons may jointly hold a share or shares in a building society: Shares may be held jointly.

Provided that the right to vote at any meeting of the society shall be limited to one of such shareholders.

41. No building society shall cause or permit applicants for advances to ballot for precedence or in any way make the granting of an advance depend on any chance or lot. Prohibition of balloting.

42. Where a building society makes to a member an advance for the purpose of its being used in defraying the purchase price of land, the society shall be deemed to warrant to the member that the purchase price is reasonable unless, before any contract requiring the member to repay the advance is entered into, the society gives to the member a notice in writing in such form as may be prescribed stating that the making of the advance implies no such warranty. Implied warranty.

43. (1) A building society exercising its power of sale of any land mortgaged to it shall take reasonable care to ensure that in the exercise Exercise of power of sale.

of the power the price at which the land is sold is the best price which can reasonably be obtained; and any agreement if and so far as it relieves or may have the effect of relieving a society from the obligations imposed by this section shall be void.

(2) Where a building society has exercised its power of sale of any land mortgaged to it, it shall, within twenty-eight days from the completion of the sale, send by registered post to the person who immediately before the sale was the owner of the land at his last known address a notice containing such particulars relating to the sale as may be prescribed.

(3) Nothing in subsection (2) of this section shall affect the operation of any rule of law relating to the duty of a mortgagee to account to a mortgagor.

(4) If a building society contravenes the provisions of subsection (2) of this section, the society and every director, secretary or other officer of the society shall be guilty of an offence and liable to a fine not exceeding one thousand shillings.

Lost or destroyed share certificates, etc.

44. (1) If any share certificate, savings deposit pass book, subscription share pass book, deposit receipt or fixed deposit receipt, or any statement or other record of payment, issued by a society is lost or destroyed, the society, upon such evidence and subject to such terms and conditions as the directors think fit, and after the loss or destruction thereof has been duly advertised once in the Gazette and once in a newspaper circulating in the town or district in which the member or depositor, as the case may be, resides, may issue a certified copy of such certificate, pass book, receipt, statement or record:

Provided that the directors may in their discretion authorize the issue of such a certified copy without requiring the loss to be advertised.

(2) Such certified copy shall thereafter for all purposes take the place of the certificate, pass book, receipt, statement or record so lost or destroyed and be the sole evidence thereof.

Inspection of documents by public.

45. On payment of the prescribed fees, any person may inspect at the office of the Registrar the documents relating to any society and required to be lodged with the Registrar in terms of this Act or obtain from the Registrar a certificate of the registration of any society or a copy or extract of any such document or part of any such document kept by the Registrar.

## PART VII—CHANGE OF NAME, ADDRESS, OFFICERS AND CONSTITUTION

46. (1) A building society may, by special resolution, change its name. Change of name.

(2) A society which changes its name in accordance with the provisions of subsection (1) of this section shall, within fourteen days from the date of the meeting at which the resolution was adopted, send to the Registrar two copies of the resolution certified in such manner as may be prescribed.

(3) Subject to the provisions of section 9 of this Act, the Registrar shall register one copy of the resolution and return the other to the society endorsed with a certificate of registration.

(4) A change of name by a building society in accordance with the provisions of this section shall not affect any right or obligation of the society or any member thereof, or other person concerned, or render defective any legal proceedings by or against the society, and any legal proceedings that may have been continued or commenced against it by its former name may be continued or commenced against it by its new name.

47. Every building society which changes the situation of its registered office or its postal address shall, within fourteen days after such change, send to the Registrar notice thereof in the prescribed form, and the Registrar shall register the same. Change of address.

48. Whenever any person is appointed a director of a building society or ceases for any reason to be a director of a building society, the society shall within fourteen days after such happening send to the Registrar notice thereof in the prescribed form. Change of directors.

49. (1) A building society may, by special resolution, alter or rescind any of its rules or make any additional rule: Alteration of rules.

Provided that no such special resolution shall have any validity until registered under subsection (3) of this section.

(2) Where a building society has altered or rescinded any of its rules or made any additional rule, it shall, within fourteen days from the date of the meeting at which the resolution was adopted, send to the Registrar two copies of the resolution, certified in such manner as may be prescribed.

(3) If the Registrar is satisfied that the alteration, addition or rescission is in conformity with this Act, he shall register one copy of the resolution and return the other to the society endorsed with a certificate of registration.

Penalties.

**50.** If any building society fails to comply with the provisions of subsection (2) of section 46, section 47, section 48 or subsection (2) of section 49 of this Act, the society and every director, secretary and other officers of the society shall be guilty of an offence and liable to a fine not exceeding five thousand shillings.

## Part VIII—Amalgamation of Societies and Transfer of Engagements

Amalgamation of building societies.

**51.** (1) Subject to the provisions of section 53 of this Act, two or more building societies may unite and become one society, with or without any dissolution or division of the funds of such societies or either of them, upon such terms as are agreed by special resolution of each of such societies.

(2) Notice of any such union shall be sent to the Registrar in the prescribed form.

(3) Upon completion of the union in terms of this section, the building societies so united shall be deemed to be dissolved and, their registrations having been cancelled, the Registrar shall register the new society in terms of this Act.

Transfer of engagements.

**52.** (1) Subject to the provisions of section 53 of this Act, a building society may by a special resolution transfer its engagements to any other building society which may undertake to fulfil those engagements, and a building society may undertake to fulfil the engagements of any other building society by a special resolution.

(2) Notice of any such transfer shall be sent to the Registrar in the prescribed form and shall be registered by him.

Special provisions relating to amalgamations and transfers of engagements.

**35.** (1) Save as is hereinafter provided, no union of building societies and no transfer of engagements shall take effect unless or until the consent thereto in writing of holders of not less than two-thirds of the whole number of shares of each society party thereto has been obtained.

(2) A building society desiring to unite with one or more other building societies, or to transfer its engagements to another building

society, or to undertake to fulfil the engagements of another building society, may make an application in that behalf to the Registrar in the prescribed manner, and shall publish notice of the application in the Gazette and, if the Registrar so requires, in one or more newspapers, and the Registrar, after hearing the society and any other person whom he considers entitled to be heard, may confirm the union, transfer or undertaking notwithstanding that the consent of the holders of two-thirds of the whole number of shares of the society has not been obtained in the manner required by this section.

Registration of amalgamation or transfer of engagements to operate as conveyance.

54. Upon the registration by the Registrar of the notice of union of any building societies under section 51, or of the transfer of the engagements of any building society to another building society under section 52, or upon the confirmation by the Registrar of any such union or transfer under section 53, of this Act, there shall vest in the united society or in the society to which another society has transferred its engagements, as the case may be, by virtue of this section and without further or other assurance, all the funds, assets and movable or immovable property vested or held in the name of the societies so uniting or of the society so transferring its engagements.

Amalgamation or transfer of engagements not to prejudice creditors.

55. No union of building societies and no transfer of engagements from one building society to another shall affect the rights of any creditor of either or any of the societies concerned.

## PART IX—DETERMINATION OF DISPUTES

Determination of disputes by arbitrators or the Registrar.

56. (1) Where the rules of a building society direct that any disputes shall be referred to arbitration by arbitrators, arbitrators shall be nominated in the manner provided by the rules, or, if there is no such provision, may be elected at a general meeting of the society, none of the said arbitrators being beneficially interested, directly or indirectly, in the funds of the society.

(2) Not less than three such arbitrators shall be chosen by ballot in each case of dispute, the number of the arbitrators and mode of ballot being determined by the rules of the society.

(3) In the case of the death or refusal or neglect of any of the said arbitrators to act, the society shall nominate, or elect in general meeting, as the case may require, an arbitrator to act in the place of the arbitrator dying, or refusing or neglecting to act.

(4) The names of all arbitrators nominated or elected to act under the provisions of this section shall be entered in the minute book of the society.

(5) Any award made by arbitrators or the major part of them shall determine the dispute.

(6) Where the parties to any dispute arising in a building society agree to refer the dispute to the Registrar, or where the rules of the society direct disputes to be referred to the Registrar, the award of the Registrar shall have the same effect as that of arbitrators.

(7) The arbitrators or the Registrar shall, at the request of any party to the arbitration or any person claiming under him, and upon payment of the costs and charges of filing the award, cause the award, or a signed copy of it, to be filed in the High Court; and notice of the filing shall be given to the parties by the arbitrators or the Registrar.

(8) An award in an arbitration under this section, on being filed in the High Court in accordance with subsection (7) of this section, shall be enforceable as if it were a decree of the Court.

Determination of disputes by the Supreme Court.

57. The High Court may hear and determine any dispute—

*(a)* if it appears to the Court, upon the petition of any person concerned, that application has been made by either party to the dispute to the other party for the purpose of having the dispute settled by arbitration under the rules of the society and that such application has not within forty days been complied with or that the arbitrators have refused or for a period of twenty-one days have neglected to make any award; or

*(b)* where the rules of the society direct that any dispute shall be referred to the High Court.

Determination of disputes by arbitrators or the Registrar to be final.

58. Every determination by arbitrators or by the Registrar under this Act of a dispute shall be binding and conclusive on all parties and shall be final to all intents and purposes, and shall not be subject to appeal and shall not be removed or removable into any court or restrained or restrainable by the injunction of any court:

Provided always that the arbitrators or the Registrar, as the case may be, may, at the request of either party, state a case for the opinion of the High Court on any question of law (but shall not be compelled to do so), and shall have power to grant to either party in the dispute such discovery as to documents and otherwise as might be granted by the High Court, such discovery to be made on behalf of the society by such officer of the society as the arbitrators or the Registrar may determine.

## PART X—POWERS OF THE REGISTRAR

Power to require production of books, etc.

59. (1) The Registrar may at any time, by notice in writing served on a building society or on any person who is or has been an officer of such a society, require the society or person to produce to the Registrar such books, accounts, deeds and other documents relating to the business of the society and to furnish to him such other information relating to that business as he considers necessary for the exercise of the powers given him by this Act, and any such notice may contain a requirement that any information to be furnished in accordance with the notice shall be verified by a statutory declaration.

(2) If any building society or other person fails to comply with the requirements of a notice under this section, the society, and every director, secretary or other officer of the society or such other person, as the case may be, shall be guilty of an offence and liable to a fine not exceeding five thousand shillings.

Power to cause inspection of books.

60. (1) The Registrar may, if he thinks fit, on the application of one-tenth of the whole number of members of a building society or of fifty members, whichever is the lesser, each such applicant having been a member of the society for not less than twelve months immediately preceding the date of the application, appoint an accountant or actuary to inspect the books of the society and to report thereon.

(2) Any person applying under subsection (1) of this section for inspection shall deposit with the Registrar such sum as a security for the costs of the proposed inspection as the Registrar may require.

(3) All expenses of or incidental to any such inspection shall be defrayed by the applicants, or out of the funds of the society, or by the members or officers, or former members or officers, of the society in such proportions as the Registrar may direct.

(4) A person appointed under this section shall have power to make copies of any books of the society and to take extracts therefrom at all reasonable hours at the registered office of the society or at any place where the books are kept.

(5) The Registrar shall communicate the results of any such inspection to the applicants and to the society.

Power to appoint inspector.

**61.** (1) The Registrar may, with the consent of the Minister, on the application of one-tenth of the whole number of members of a building society or of fifty members, whichever is the lesser, either—

(*a*) appoint an inspector to examine into and report on the affairs of the society; or

(*b*) call a special meeting of the society.

(2) Any application under this section shall be supported by such evidence as the Registrar may direct for the purpose of showing that the applicants have good reason for requiring the inspection to be made or the meeting to be called and that they are not actuated by malicious motives in their application.

(3) Such notice of the application shall be given to the society as the Registrar may direct.

(4) The Registrar shall require the applicants to give security for the costs of the proposed inspection or meeting before the inspector is appointed or the meeting is called.

(5) All expenses of and incidental to such inspection or meeting shall be defrayed by the applicants or out of the funds of the society, or by the members or officers, or former members or officers, of the society in such proportions as the Registrar may direct.

(6) An inspector appointed under this section may require the production of all or any of the books, accounts, securities and documents of the society, and may examine on oath its officers, members, agents and servants in relation to its business, and may administer an oath accordingly.

(7) The Registrar may direct at what time and place a special meeting under this section is to be held, and what matters are to be discussed and determined at the meeting, and the meeting shall have all the powers of a meeting called according to the rules of the society, and shall in all cases have power to appoint its own chairman, any rule of the society to the contrary notwithstanding.

(8) The Registrar may, without any application by members, but with the consent of the Minister given on each occasion, exercise the powers given by this section—

(*a*) where a building society has, for two months, after notice, failed to make any return required by this Act;

(*b*) where a building society has, for two months, after notice, failed to correct or complete any such return;

(c) where evidence is furnished by statutory declaration of not less than three members of a building society of facts which, in the opinion of the Registrar, calls for investigation:

Provided that the Registrar shall forthwith, on receipt of such declaration, send a copy thereof to the society, and such society shall, within fourteen days from the sending of such copy, be entitled to give the Registrar an explanatory statement in writing by way of reply thereto.

Power to forbid invitations for subscriptions, etc.

62. (1) If, with respect to any building society, the Registrar considers it expedient to do so in the interest of persons who have invested or deposited or may invest or deposit money with the society, he may by order direct that, unless and until the order is revoked, no invitation to subscribe for, or to acquire or offer to acquire, securities or to lend or deposit money shall be made by or on behalf of the society:

Provided that, before making any order under this section, the Registrar shall serve on the society a written notice stating his intention to make the order, and shall consider any representations with respect to the proposed order made to him by the society within the period of thirty days from the date of the service of the notice and, if the society so requests, afford it an opportunity of being heard by him within that period.

(2) Any order made under subsection (1) of this section may be revoked by a subsequent order of the Registrar.

(3) If any invitation is made in contravention of an order made under subsection (1) of this section, the person by whom the invitation is so made shall be guilty of an offence and liable to imprisonment for a term not exceeding two years or to a fine not exceeding ten thousand shillings, or to both such imprisonment and such fine.

Power to suspend or cancel registration.

63. (1) Where the Registrar is satisfied that a certificate of registration has been obtained for a building society by fraud or mistake, or that any such society exists for an illegal purpose, or has wilfully and after notice from the Registrar violated any of the provisions of this Act, or has ceased to exist, the Registrar may by notice in writing cancel the registration of the society or suspend the registration thereof for any term not exceeding three months, and may renew such suspension from time to time for the like period.

(2) The Registrar shall, before cancelling or suspending the registration of a building society under powers conferred by subsection (1) of this section, give to the society not less than two months' previous notice in writing, specifying briefly the ground of the proposed cancel-

lation or suspension, and shall, as soon as practicable after the cancellation or suspension takes place, cause notice thereof to be published in the Gazette and in such one or more newspapers (if any) as he may determine.

(3) A building society may appeal to the High Court against the cancellation or suspension of its registration, and thereupon the Court may, if it thinks it just so to do, set aside the cancellation or suspension.

(4) The Registrar may also, if he thinks fit, at the request of any building society, evidenced in such manner as he may direct, cancel the registration of the society.

(5) A building society whose registration has been cancelled or suspended shall from the time of such cancellation or suspension (but in the case of suspension only while the suspension lasts, and in any case subject to the right of appeal given by this section) cease absolutely to enjoy the privileges conferred by this Act, but without prejudice to any liability incurred by the society, and any such liability may be enforced against the society as if the cancellation or suspension had not taken place.

## PART XI—DISSOLUTION AND WINDING UP

Dissolution.

64. (1) A building society may be dissolved—

*(a)* by dissolution in the manner prescribed by its rules;
*(b)* by dissolution with the consent of three-fourths of the whole number of members, holding not less than two-thirds of the whole number of shares of the society, testified by their signatures to an instrument of dissolution; or
*(c)* by winding up either voluntarily, under the supervision of the High Court, or by the High Court.

(2) Notice of the commencement and completion of any dissolution or winding up shall be sent to the Registrar and registered by him.

Instruments of dissolution.

65. (1) Every instrument of dissolution of a building society shall set forth—

*(a)* the liabilities and assets of the society in detail;
*(b)* the number of members, and the amount standing to the credit in the books of the society;
*(c)* the claims of depositors and other creditors, and the provision to be made for their payment;
*(d)* the intended appropriation or division of the funds and property of the society; and

(*e*) the names of one or more persons to be appointed trustees for the purpose of the dissolution, and their remuneration.

(2) The provisions of an instrument of dissolution may be varied with the like consent, testified in the same manner, as is required for an instrument of dissolution.

(3) Every instrument of dissolution, and every instrument varying the provisions of an instrument of dissolution, shall be made and signed in duplicate and sent to the Registrar within fourteen days of signature, whereupon the Registrar shall register one copy of the instrument and return the other to the society endorsed with a certificate of registration.

(4) An instrument of dissolution, and any instrument varying the provisions of an instrument of dissolution, shall, when registered, be binding upon all the members of the society.

Winding up.

66. (1) The High Court may, on the petition of—

(*a*) any member authorized to present the same on behalf of the society by three-fourths of the members present at a general meeting of the society specially called for the purpose; or

(*b*) any judgment-creditor for not less than one thousand shillings,

but not otherwise, order that a building society be wound up, either voluntarily under the supervision of the Court or by the Court.

(2) The provisions of the Companies Act relating to the winding up of companies voluntarily, under the supervision of the Court, or by the Court, shall apply, *mutatis mutandis,* to the winding up of a building society.

Obligations of liquidators and trustees in case of dissolution.

67. When a building society is being dissolved in accordance with paragraph (*a*) or paragraph (*b*) of subsection (1) of section 64 of this Act, the provisions of this Act shall continue to apply as if the liquidators or other persons conducting the dissolution of the society, or the trustees appointed under the instrument of dissolution, were the board of directors of the society.

Liability of members in the event of dissolution.

68. (1) When a building society is being dissolved or wound up, the liability of any member of such society in respect of any share upon which no advance has been made shall be limited to the amount actually paid, or in arrear on such share, and in respect of any share upon which an advance has been made shall be limited to the amount payable thereon under any mortgage or other security or under the rules of the society.

(2) When a building society is being dissolved or wound up, a member to whom an advance has been made under any mortgage or other security, or under the rules of the society, shall not be liable to pay the amount payable under the mortgage or other security, or under the rules, except at the time or times and subject to the conditions therein expressed.

Account and balance sheet on dissolution.

69. If a building society is dissolved in accordance with paragraph *(a)* or paragraph *(b)* of subsection (1) of section 64 of this Act, the liquidators, trustees and other persons having the conduct of the dissolution shall, within twenty-eight days from the termination of the dissolution, send to the Registrar an account and balance sheet, signed and certified by them as correct and showing the assets and liabilities of the society at the commencement of the dissolution and the way in which those assets and liabilities have been applied and discharged.

Dissolution by order of Registrar.

70. (1) On the application in writing of one-tenth of the whole number of members of any building society or of fifty members, whichever is the lesser, setting forth that the society is unable to meet the claims of its members, and that it would be for their benefit that it should be dissolved, and requesting an investigation into the affairs of the society with a view to the dissolution thereof, the Registrar may investigate the affairs of the society, but shall before doing so give not less than two months' previous notice in writing to the society at its registered office.

(2) If on such investigation it appears that the society is unable to meet the claims of its members, and that it would be for their benefit that it should be dissolved, the Registrar may, if he considers it expedient so to do, order that the society be dissolved, and shall direct in what manner the affairs of the society are to be wound up:

Provided that the Registrar may suspend his order for such period as he may deem necessary to enable the society to make such alterations of its rules as will, in his judgment, prevent the necessity of the order being made.

(3) The Registrar shall, within twenty-one days after the making of any order for dissolution under this section, cause notice thereof to be advertised in the Gazette and in such one or more newspapers (if any) as he may determine.

(4) The Registrar of his own motion, if he has reason to believe that the society is unable to meet the claims of its members, and that it would be for their benefit that it should be dissolved, may investigate the affairs of the society.

## PART XII—OFFENCES

71. (1) No society, association, partnership or company shall commence or carry on business in Kenya as a building society unless it is registered in terms of this Act.

Prohibition of unregistered building societies.

(2) No society, association, partnership or company shall commence or carry on business in Kenya under or by any name which includes the words "Building Society" unless it is registered in terms of this Act.

(3) The Registrar may at any time make an inspection or cause an inspection to be made of the books, accounts and records of any society, association, partnership or company for the purpose of determining whether the same is carrying on the business of a building society or not.

(4) Any society, association, partnership or company which contravenes the provisions of subsection (1) or subsection (2) of this section shall be guilty of an offence and liable to a fine not exceeding ten thousand shillings.

72. (1) If any person by false representation or imposition obtains possession of any moneys, securities, books, papers or other effects of a building society, or having the same in possession withholds or misapplies the same or wilfully applies any part thereof to purposes other than those expressed or directed in the rules of the society and authorized by this Act, he shall be guilty of an offence and liable to a fine not exceeding five thousand shillings and to be ordered to deliver up to the society all such moneys, securities, books, papers or other effects and to repay the amount of money applied improperly, and in default of such delivery of effects or repayment of such amount of money shall be liable to imprisonment for a term not exceeding six months.

Withholding or misapplying property of a building society an offence.

(2) Proceedings under subsection (1) of this section may be taken at the instance of—

(*a*) the society; or
(*b*) any member authorized by the society or by the board of directors or by the Registrar; or
(*c*) the Registrar.

73. If any person makes any false statement or orders or allows any false statement to be made in any document which is required by this Act or any regulations thereunder to be sent to the Registrar, or which such person expects will be published, knowing such statement to be false, or by addition, alteration, erasure or omission falsifies any such

False statements.

document, knowing that the addition, alteration, erasure or omission will cause a falsification of the document, he shall be guilty of an offence and liable to imprisonment for a term not exceeding six months.

Offences.

74. If any building society neglects or refuses—

(a) to give any notice, send any return or document or do or allow to be done anything which the society is by this Act or any regulations thereunder required to give, send, do or allow to be done; or

(b) to do any act or furnish any information required for the purposes of this Act by the Registrar or by an inspector,

the society, and every officer thereof bound by the rules of the society to fulfil the duty whereof a breach has been so committed, and, if there is no such officer, then every director, unless it appears that he was ignorant of or attempted to prevent the breach, shall be guilty of an offence and, unless a special penalty is provided by this Act, liable to a fine not exceeding two thousand shillings.

## PART XIII—FOREIGN BUILDING SOCIETIES

Registration of foreign building societies.

75. (1) A building society registered or incorporated outside Kenya, the rules of which—

(a) contain substantially the like matters which in the case of building societies to be registered in Kenya are required by section 10 of this Act to be set forth; and

(b) contain no provision which is incompatible with any provision of this Act; and

(c) expressly authorize the society to carry on business outside the country in which it is registered or incorporated,

may apply for registration under this Act.

(2) Every such application shall be in the prescribed form and shall be accompanied by—

(a) a copy of its rules and a copy of the certificate of registration or incorporation, each certified in such manner as may be prescribed, and, if the same are not written in the English language, certified translations of the same; and

(b) a statement of the situation and the postal address of its registered or chief office in the country of its registration or incorporation; and

(c) a statement of the situation and of the postal address of its head office in Kenya; and (*d*) a copy of its latest annual statement and account; and

(*e*) a statement of the names and addresses of the directors.

(3) The Registrar may in his discretion, and subject to the provisions of section 9 of this Act, allow or refuse an application for registration made under subsection (1) of this section:

Provided that any person aggrieved by the refusal of the Registrar to register a building society under this section may within one month, or such extended period as the Minister may allow, from the date of such refusal appeal against such refusal to the Minister, whose decision shall be final.

(4) Where the Registrar allows an application, he shall enter the prescribed particulars relating to the society in the register, and thereupon the society shall, subject to the provisions of section 23 of this Act, become entitled to hold land and to take mortgages of land in Kenya.

(5) The Registrar shall issue a certificate of registration to every building society registered under this section.

(6) No building society registered or incorporated outside Kenya shall commence business in Kenya as a building society unless it is registered under this Act.

**76.** The provisions of this Act relating to building societies registered under section 6 of this Act shall apply to building societies registered under section 75 of this Act, and in addition thereto the following special provisions shall apply to every building society registered under the said section 75—

Provisions of Act generally to apply to foreign building societies.

(*a*) the society shall maintain an office and a postal address in Kenya; and

(*b*) the society shall keep in English separate records and books of account in respect of its business in Kenya, which records and books shall be kept at the society's principal place of business in Kenya; and

(*c*) the society shall prepare in English a separate account and statements in respect of its business in Kenya, which shall be in the form required in the case of a building society registered in Kenya with such modifications as the Registrar may allow, as well as a consolidated account and statement; and

(*d*) the society shall not, save with the prior approval of the Minister, invest outside Kenya any moneys raised in Kenya in excess of one-fifth of the capital assets for the time being of the society in Kenya; and (*e*) the society shall show in all advertisements and announcements and on all documents issued by it the place where it was originally registered or incorporated:

Provided that the Minister may, by order, either generally or in any particular case, exempt any society registered under the said section 75 from all or any of the provisions of this Act, or direct that such provisions of this Act as are specified in such order shall, in their application to any such society, be modified in such manner as may be provided therein.

## PART XIV—ORDERS, RULES AND REGULATIONS

**Orders, rules and regulations.**

77. (1) The Minister may by order—

(*a*) fix the maximum rate of interest which may be paid or charged by building societies in respect of the borrowing or advancing of money;

(*b*) require building societies to hold such amount in cash or on deposit or in investments in accordance with section 25 of this Act as may be specified in such order as security for the prompt repayment of shares, deposits, loans and overdrafts and for the payment of interest accrued thereon.

(2) The Chief Justice may make rules of court for regulating proceedings before the High Court, and applications and appeals thereto, under the provisions of this Act, and for the fees to be paid in respect thereof.

(3) Subject to the provisions of subsections (1) and (2) of this section, the Minister may make regulations prescribing anything required to be prescribed under this Act, and, for the better carrying into effect of the provisions of this Act, and without prejudice to the generality of the foregoing, such regulations may provide for the procedure in the registry of building societies, the hours in which the registry is to be open for business, the forms to be used and the fees to be paid in respect of any matter under this Act required, permitted or entitled to be done.

## SCHEDULE (s. 24)

### CLASSES OF ADDITIONAL SECURITY WHICH MAY BE TAKEN INTO ACCOUNT IN DETERMINING THE AMOUNT OF ADVANCES TO MEMBERS

1. A charge upon a policy of life assurance.

2. A guarantee given, whether in pursuance of a continuing arrangement or not, by the Government, a local authority or an insurance company, or any other person approved by the Minister.

3. A charge given by the member upon money deposited with the society or upon any stocks, shares or securities for the time being authorized by law for the investment of trust moneys.

4. A guarantee, not being a guarantee given in pursuance of a continuing arrangement, accepted by the society with the written consent of the member and supported by a charge upon money deposited with the society or upon any such stocks, shares or securities as aforesaid.

5. A charge upon money deposited with the society, being a charge which is given in accordance with arrangements which are approved by the Registrar and which provide that the society shall also take, as further security for each advance in respect of which such a charge is given to the society, a guarantee given by an insurance company.

# The Industrial and Commercial Development Act[1]

*Commencement: 15th February, 1955*

An Act to establish a corporation to be known as the Industrial and Commercial Development Corporation for facilitating the industrial and economic development of Kenya

1. This Act may be cited as the Industrial and Commercial Development Act. Short title.

2. In this Act, except where the context otherwise requires— Interpretation.

"Corporation" means the Industrial and Commercial Development Corporation established by section 3 of this Act;

"director" means a person appointed as a director under section 4 of this Act;

"Minister" means the Minister for the time being responsible for commerce and industry;

"Minister for Finance" means the Minister for the time being responsible for finance.

[1] *Laws of Kenya,* Cap. 517 (1972). Originally No. 63 of 1954. Relevant citations: L.N. 2/1964; L.N. 374/1964; and No. 7 of 1967.

Establishment and functions of Corporation.

3. (1) There is hereby established a corporation to be known as the Industrial and Commercial Development Corporation, for the purposes of facilitating the industrial and economic development of Kenya by the initiation, assistance or expansion or by aiding in the initiation, assistance or expansion of industrial, commercial or other undertakings or enterprises in Kenya or elsewhere.

(2) In the exercise of its functions under this Act, the Corporation shall have regard generally to the desirability of—

*(a)* acting principally as an auxiliary finance organization and not as the sole source of the provision of finance in respect of any particular undertaking or enterprise as aforesaid;

*(b)* exercising its powers of affording financial assistance, so far as possible and except where the Minister for Finance otherwise directs, by way of guarantee, loan or investment and not by way of grant or subsidy;

*(c)* requiring early liquidation or repayment of any guarantee, loan or investment made by the Corporation, in order to ensure so far as possible that the liquid resources of the Corporation may be available for other purposes within the scope of the functions of the Corporation under this Act,

and, in particular, to the desirability of ensuring that any such undertaking or enterprise as aforesaid will be of long-term value in relation to the development of Kenya, whether or not it is likely to prove self-supporting or to furnish direct profits either immediately or in the future.

(3) The Corporation shall be a body corporate with perpetual succession and a common seal, with power to hold land and to sue and be sued in its corporate name.

(4) The application of the seal of the Corporation shall be authenticated by the signatures of the chairman of the Corporation (or some other director authorized by the Corporation to authenticate the application of the seal thereof) and of another director.

(5) Every document purporting to be an instrument issued by the Corporation and to be sealed as aforesaid or to be signed on behalf of the Corporation shall be received in evidence and be deemed to be such an instrument without further proof unless the contrary is shown.

Constitution of Corporation.

4. (1) The Corporation shall consist of a chairman and not less than five nor more than nine other directors, all of whom shall be appointed by the Minister from among persons appearing to him to

have had experience and shown capacity in industry, trade or administration.

(2) Every director of the Corporation shall hold and vacate his office in accordance with the terms of his appointment and shall, on ceasing to be a director, be eligible for reappointment:

Provided that any director may at any time by notice in writing to the Minister resign his office.

(3) All appointments under this section shall be made by the Minister after consultation with the Corporation.

(4) The validity of any proceedings of the Corporation shall not be affected by any vacancy amongst the directors or by any defect in the appointment of a director.

(5) If the chairman of the Corporation ceases to be a director he shall also cease to be chairman.

(6) If the Minister is satisfied that any director—

*(a)* has become bankrupt or has made an arrangement with his creditors; or

*(b)* is incapacitated by physical or mental illness; or

*(c)* has been absent from meetings of the Corporation for a period longer than three consecutive months without the permission of the Corporation; or

*(d)* is otherwise unable or unfit to discharge the functions of a director, or is unsuitable to continue as a director,

the Minister may remove him from his office as a director.

5. (1) Subject to the approval of the Minister, each director shall have power to appoint either another director or any person approved by the other directors, or by a majority of them, to act as an alternate director in his place during his absence or his inability to attend any meeting, and may at his discretion remove such alternate director: Alternate directors.

Provided that no director or person shall at one and the same time act as alternate director in place of more than one director.

(2) An alternate director shall, whilst so acting (except as regards remuneration and the power to appoint an alternate director), be subject in all respects to the provisions of this Act relating to directors, and each alternate director shall, whilst so acting, exercise and discharge all the functions, powers and duties of his appointor in his appointor's absence.

(3) A director acting as alternate director shall have an additional vote for the director for whom he so acts.

(4) An alternate director shall cease to be an alternate director whenever his appointor ceases for any reason to be a director.

Remuneration.

6. (1) The Corporation shall pay to the chairman and each director such remuneration and allowances as may from time to time be determined by the Corporation with the approval of the Minister.

(2) If any director or person is employed about the affairs of the Corporation otherwise than as a director, the Corporation may pay him such remuneration and allowances (in addition to the remuneration or allowances, if any, to which he may be entitled as a director), as the Corporation, with the approval of the Minister, may determine.

Management.

7. The Corporation may appoint a general manager, and such managers, accountants, secretaries, managing agents and such other servants or agents as the Corporation may consider necessary for the proper discharge of its functions, on such terms and conditions as the Corporation may determine.

Powers of Corporation.

8. Without prejudice to the generality of the provisions of section 3 of this Act the Corporation shall, subject to the approval, generally or specially, of the Minister and subject to such terms and conditions as he may impose in giving any such approval, have power—

*(a)* to provide credit and finance by means of loans or the subscription of loan or share capital or otherwise for industrial, commercial or other undertakings or enterprises in Kenya or elsewhere;

*(b)* to subscribe for, conditionally or unconditionally, to underwrite, issue on commission or otherwise, take, hold, deal in and convert shares, stocks, obligations and securities of all kinds, and to enter into partnership, or into any arrangement for participating in undertakings, sharing profits, union of interest, reciprocal concession or co-operation with any person, partnership or company, and to take or otherwise acquire and hold shares or stocks in or obligations or securities of, and to subsidize, any person, partnership or company, and to sell, hold, reissue, with or without guarantee, or otherwise deal with any such shares, stocks, obligations or securities, and to promote and aid in promoting, constitute, form or organize companies, syndicates, or partnerships of all kinds and to exercise and enforce all rights and powers conferred by or incident to its ownership of any shares, stocks, obligations or securities for the time being held or owned by the Corporation;

*(c)* to advance, deposit or lend money, securities and property to or with such persons, partnerships or companies and on such

terms as may seem expedient; to create, make, draw, accept, endorse, execute, issue, discount, buy, sell, negotiate and deal in bills, notes, bills of lading, warrants, coupons, debentures and other negotiable or transferable instruments;

(*d*) subject to the provisions of section 10 of this Act, to guarantee or become liable by way of suretyship or indemnity for the payment of money, or for the performance of any contracts or obligations, and generally to transact all kinds of guarantee, trust or agency business;

(*e*) to purchase, take on lease, hire or otherwise acquire, and to sell, exchange, surrender, lease, mortgage, charge, convert, turn to account, dispose of and deal with, any movable or immovable property and rights of all kinds;

(*f*) to purchase or otherwise acquire and carry on the whole or any part of the business, property, goodwill and assets of any person, partnership or company carrying on, or proposing to carry on, any business which the Corporation is authorized to carry on, or which can be conveniently carried on in connexion with such business or may seem calculated, directly or indirectly, to benefit the Corporation, or possessed of property suitable for the purposes of the Corporation, and, as part of the consideration for any of the acts or things aforesaid or property acquired, to undertake all or any of the liabilities of such person, partnership or company, or to acquire an interest in, amalgamate with or enter into any arrangement for sharing profits or for co-operation or for limiting competition or for mutual assistance with any such person, partnership or company, and to give, issue or accept cash or any shares, stocks, obligations or securities that may be agreed upon, and to hold and retain or sell, mortgage and deal with any shares, stocks, obligations or securities so received;

(*g*) to sell, exchange, mortgage (with or without power of sale), assign, lease, sublet, improve, manage, develop, dispose of, turn to account, grant rights and privileges in respect of and generally otherwise deal with the whole or any part of the business, estates, property, rights or undertakings of the Corporation, upon any terms, either together or in portions, and as a going concern or otherwise, for such consideration, whether of cash, shares, stocks, obligations or securities, as the Corporation may think fit;

(*h*) to invest and deal with money upon such securities and in such manner as may from time to time be determined, and to place money on deposit or current account with any bank or building society;

(i) subject to the provisions of section 9 of this Act, to raise or borrow money, with or without security, and also to secure the payment of money by the issue of or upon debentures or debenture stock, perpetual, terminable or otherwise, or bonds, or other obligations charged or not charged upon, or by mortgage, charge, hypothecation, lien or pledge of the whole or any part of the undertaking, property, assets and rights of the Corporation, both present and future, and generally in such other manner and on such terms as may seem expedient, and to issue any of the Corporation's obligations or securities for such consideration and on such terms as may be thought fit; and also, by a similar mortgage, charge, hypothecation, lien or pledge, to secure and guarantee the performance by the Corporation of any obligation or liability it may undertake, and to redeem or pay off any such securities;

(j) to act as the manager, agent or secretary of any undertaking and to nominate or appoint any person to act as director of, or in any other capacity in relation to, any undertaking, and to act as the agent or representative of any undertaking, whether carrying on business in Kenya or elsewhere;

(k) to do all or any of the above things as principals, managers, agents, contractors, trustees or otherwise, and either by or through trustees, agents, subcontractors or otherwise, and either alone or in partnership or in conjunction with any other person, partnership or company, and to contract for the carrying on of any operation connected with the Corporation's business by any other person, partnership or company;

(l) to do all such other things whether of an industrial, commercial or other nature as may be deemed to be incidental or conducive to the attainment of the above objects or any of them and to the exercise of the rights, powers and authorities given by this Act.

Power of Minister to give directions.

**8A.** The Industrial and Commercial Development Corporation shall, in the exercise of its powers and in the performance of its duties under this Act or any other written law, act in accordance with any general or special directions that may be given to it by the Minister.

Borrowing powers.

**9.** (1) The borrowing powers of the Corporation shall be exercisable only with the approval of the Minister for Finance as to amount, the sources of the borrowing and the terms and conditions on which the borrowing may be effected.

(2) Any approval given for the purposes of this section may be either general or limited to a particular borrowing or otherwise, and may be either conditional or unconditional.

(3) A person lending money to the Corporation shall not be bound to inquire whether the borrowing of money is within the power of the Corporation or be concerned to see to the application thereof or be answerable for any loss or misapplication thereof.

Powers of guarantee, etc.

10. The power of the Corporation to guarantee, or become liable by way of suretyship or indemnity for, the payment of money, or the performance of any contracts or obligations, shall be limited to the extent that the aggregate amount remaining undischarged under all liabilities by way of guarantee, suretyship or indemnity assumed by the Corporation shall not at any time exceed the value, as determined by the Minister for Finance from time to time, of the assets of the Corporation available for meeting such aggregate amount as aforesaid.

Advances or grants by Government.

11. To enable the Corporation to exercise its powers or to fulfil any of its obligations, the Minister for Finance may, with the consent of the National Assembly, make advances or grants to the Corporation.

Surplus funds.

12. The Minister for Finance may, from time to time, after consultation with the Minister, direct the Corporation to pay into the consolidated fund any money held by the Corporation and deemed by the Minister for Finance to be surplus to its existing or anticipated requirements.

Meetings and proceedings.

13. (1) The quorum necessary for the transaction of business of the Corporation shall, except where regulations made under this Act otherwise provide, be four.

(2) The chairman of a meeting shall in the case of equality of votes have a second or casting vote.

(3) The directors shall cause minutes of all proceedings at their meetings, and of all proceedings at meetings of every committee that may be appointed by them, to be entered in books kept for that purpose.

(4) The books containing the minutes of such proceedings shall remain the property of the Corporation and shall be kept at such place as the directors think fit, and shall at all times be made available to the Minister and to all persons authorized by him in that behalf.

(5) Subject to the provisions of this Act and of any regulations made thereunder, the Corporation shall regulate its own procedure.

Accounts and report.

14. (1) The directors shall cause to be kept proper books of account and such other records as are necessary to give a true and fair view of the state of the Corporation's affairs and to explain its transactions, and such books of account and other records shall be kept at such place as the directors think fit, and shall at all times be made available to the Minister and to all persons authorized by him in that behalf.

(2) The directors shall as soon as practicable after the end of each financial year of the Corporation cause to be prepared a statement of accounts in such form as the Minister may, with the approval of the Minister for Finance, direct.

(3) The accounts of the Corporation shall be audited annually by an auditor or auditors appointed by the Minister.

(4) The directors shall as soon as practicable after the end of each financial year of the Corporation make an annual report to the Minister dealing generally with the operations of the Corporation during that year.

(5) The accounts and annual report shall within six months after completion of each financial year of the Corporation be laid before the National Assembly by the Minister.

Winding up.

15. The Corporation shall not be wound up except by or under the authority of an Act.

Application of the Companies Act.

16. The Minister may from time to time, by order published in the Gazette, apply to the Corporation any provision of the Companies Act not being inconsistent with the provisions of this Act, and where any such order is made such provision shall apply to the Corporation as it applies to a company within the meaning of the Companies Act.

Directors not to be personally liable.

17. No director or officer of the Corporation shall be personally liable for any act or thing done or omitted to be done by him as such in good faith and without negligence in the course of the operations of the Corporation.

Regulations.

18. The Minister may, after consultation with the directors, make such regulations as he may consider necessary or desirable for the proper conduct of the business of the Corporation including, without prejudice to the generality of the foregoing, regulations with regard to any of the following matters—

(*a*) the convening of the meetings of the Corporation, directors and committees, and the procedure to be followed thereat;
(*b*) the appointment or establishment of committees of the directors, and the co-opting of persons other than directors to such committees; and
(*c*) the provision of a common seal and the custody and use thereof.

## The Agricultural Development Corporation Act [1]

*Commencement: 29th October, 1965*

An Act of Parliament to provide for the establishment of the Agricultural Development Corporation and for purposes incidental thereto and connected therewith

Short title.

1. This Act may be cited as the Agricultural Development Corporation Act.

Interpretation.

2. In this Act, except where the context otherwise requires—

"Act" means this Act and any rules made thereunder;

"Corporation" means the Agricultural Development Corporation established by section 3 of this Act;

"General Manager" means the General Manager to the Corporation appointed under section 14 of this Act;

"Minister" means the Minister for the time being responsible for agriculture.

Establishment of Agricultural Development Corporation.

3. There is hereby established a Corporation, to be known as the Agricultural Development Corporation, which shall be a body corporate having perpetual succession and a common seal, with power to sue and be sued, purchase, hold, manage and dispose of land and any other property and to enter into such contracts as it may consider necessary or expedient for the purposes of performing its functions under this Act.

Directions of Minister.

4. In the exercise of its powers and in the performance of its functions under this Act, the Corporation shall comply with such general or special directions as the Minister may from time to time issue.

[1] *Laws of Kenya,* Cap. 346 (1967). Originally No. 7 of 1965.

Membership of Corporation.

5. (1) The Corporation shall consist of—

*(a)* a chairman, appointed by the Minister;

*(b)* not more than ten members appointed by the Minister who, in his opinion, possess qualities likely to be of benefit to the Corporation, of whom—

(i) not less than one shall be a member of one of the professional bodies specified in the Schedule to the Accountants (Designations) Act;

(ii) not less than one shall be appointed by reason of his knowledge of international finance;

(iii) not less than one shall be appointed by reason of his knowledge of the processing and marketing of agricultural produce;

(iv) not less than one shall be appointed to represent the interests of lenders of funds to the Corporation;

*(c)* two members appointed by the Minister from a panel of not less than five names submitted by the Central Agricultural Board established under the Agriculture Act;

*(d)* the Permanent Secretary to the Ministry, or a person deputed by him in writing for the purposes of this Act;

*(e)* the Permanent Secretary to the Ministry for the time being responsible for finance, or a person deputed by him in writing for the purposes of this Act;

*(f)* the Permanent Secretary to the Ministry for the time being responsible for economic planning and development, or a person deputed by him in writing for the purposes of this Act.

(2) The Corporation may co-opt to serve on it for such length of time as it thinks fit any person or persons whose assistance or advice it may require, but a person so co-opted shall not be entitled to vote at any meeting of the Corporation or be counted as a member for the purpose of forming a quorum.

(3) The Corporation shall elect a vice-chairman annually from among its members.

Duration of office of members of Corporation.

6. (1) The chairman shall hold office for three years and shall then retire but shall be eligible for reappointment.

(2) Two of the members appointed under paragraph *(b)* and one of the members appointed under paragraph *(c)* of section 5(1) of this Act shall retire annually but shall be eligible for reappointment; the members to retire shall be those who have been continuously longest in office, and, as between members who have been continuously longest in

office, the order of retirement shall, in default of agreement between them, be determined by lot.

(3) A member of the Corporation shall cease to hold office—

(*a*) if he delivers to the Minister a written resignation of his office; or

(*b*) if the Corporation declares by resolution that he has been absent from three consecutive meetings of the Corporation without the leave of the Corporation; or

(*c*) if, on the advice of the Corporation, the Minister removes him from office on the grounds that he is incapacitated by mental or physical illness or is otherwise unable or unfit to discharge the functions of a member or is unable to continue as a member; or

(*d*) if he is adjudged bankrupt or enters into a composition or scheme of arrangement with his creditors; or

(*e*) if he is sentenced by a court to imprisonment for a term of six months or more.

Remuneration and expenses of members of Corporation.

7. (1) The members of the Corporation (other than public officers in receipt of a salary) shall be paid out of the funds of the Corporation such remuneration as the Minister, after consultation with the Corporation, may from time to time determine.

(2) The Corporation may, at its discretion, pay such travelling and other expenses as may reasonably have been incurred by its members by reason of their office.

Meetings of Corporation.

**8.** (1) A general meeting of the Corporation shall be convened by the chairman at least four times every year.

(2) The chairman may at any time convene a special meeting of the Corporation and shall do so within one month of the receipt by him of a written request signed by at least two members.

(3) In the absence of the chairman from any Corporation meeting, the vice-chairman shall preside, and in the absence of both chairman and vice-chairman, the members present shall elect one of their number to preside, and such member shall, as concerns that meeting, have all the powers and attributes of the chairman under this Act.

(4) At every meeting of the Corporation the member presiding shall have a casting as well as a deliberative vote.

(5) The quorum of the Corporation shall be five.

Declaration of interest.

9. Every member of the Corporation who is or is likely to be concerned in, or who participates in the profits of, any contract with or work done for the Corporation, otherwise than in his capacity as a member of the Corporation, shall, on the matter coming before the Corporation for consideration, immediately declare his interest therein, and shall, unless the Corporation otherwise agrees, retire from the meeting, and shall in any case abstain from voting on the matter:

Provided that this section shall not apply to a member who has been appointed under section 5(1)(*b*)(iv) of this Act, in respect of the interests he was appointed to represent.

Authentication of documents.

10. (1) The common seal of the Corporation shall be authenticated by the signature of the chairman or such other member of the Corporation as may be authorized by the Corporation to act in that behalf, together with the signature of some other member or officer authorized by the Corporation to act in that behalf.

(2) All documents made by the Corporation, other than those required by law to be under seal, shall be executed, and all decisions of the Corporation shall be signified, under the hand of the chairman or of any member, officer or servant of the Corporation authorized in that behalf.

Committees of Corporation.

11. The Corporation may appoint committees, whether of its own members or otherwise, to carry out such general or special functions as may be specified by the Corporation, and may delegate to any such committee such of its powers as the Corporation may deem fit.

Functions of Corporation.

12. (1) The functions of the Corporation shall be to promote and execute schemes for agricultural development and reconstruction in Kenya by the initiation, assistance or expansion of agricultural undertakings or enterprises.

(2) In the performance of its functions under this Act the Corporation shall have proper regard to the economic and commercial merits of any undertaking it plans to initiate, assist or expand.

(3) If the Minister, after consultation with the Minister for the time being responsible for finance, instructs the Corporation to initiate, assist or expand any undertaking which it considers economically or otherwise unsound, the Corporation shall not be required to proceed with such initiation, assistance or expansion until the Government has undertaken to reimburse the Corporation with any losses incurred thereby.

Powers of Corporation.

13. (1) The Corporation shall, subject to the provisions of this Act, have power to do all such things and to enter into all such transactions

as to the Corporation appear to be necessary for, or conducive or incidental to, the performance of its functions under this Act.

(2) Without prejudice to the generality of subsection (1) of this section, the Corporation shall have power—

*(a)* to provide credit and finance by means of loans or the subscription of loan or share capital or otherwise for agricultural undertakings in Kenya;

*(b)* to advance, deposit or lend money, securities and property to or with such persons and on such terms as may seem expedient; to create, make, draw, accept, endorse, execute, issue, discount, buy, sell, negotiate and deal in bills, notes, bills of lading, warrants, coupons, debentures and other negotiable or transferable instruments;

*(c)* to borrow money in support of the Corporation on such terms and for such purposes as may be approved by the Minister after consultation with the Minister for the time being responsible for finance;

*(d)* to purchase, take on lease or otherwise acquire, and to sell, exchange, surrender, lease, mortgage, charge, convert, turn to account, dispose of and deal with, any movable or immovable property and rights of all kinds;

*(e)* to appoint such agents as the Corporation may consider necessary for the proper discharge of its functions as the Corporation may determine;

*(f)* to do all such other things, whether of an agricultural or other nature, as may be deemed to be incidental or conducive to the proper discharge of the functions of the Corporation.

General Manager.

14. (1) The Minister shall, with the agreement of the Corporation, appoint a General Manager of the Corporation, who shall be the chief executive officer of the Corporation, and shall be present at all meetings of the Corporation unless he has obtained leave of absence from the Corporation or is incapacitated by sickness or other cause.

(2) The Corporation shall delegate to the General Manager such of its functions under this Act as are necessary to enable him to transact effectively the day-to-day business of the Corporation of every kind whatsoever.

(3) In the event of the General Manager being absent on leave or on account of incapacitation, the Corporation, with the approval of the Minister, may appoint a person to act as General Manager during such period of absence or incapacitation, and the person so acting may exer-

cise all the powers and discharge all the duties by this Act exercisable or to be performed by the General Manager.

Staff of Corporation.

15. (1) The Corporation may employ such officers and servants as may be necessary for the efficient conduct and operation of the Corporation.

(2) The Corporation may with the consent of the Minister provide for its General Manager, officers and servants by means of insurance, pension, superannuation or provident funds or otherwise, pecuniary benefits upon leave, retirement, death or termination of service, or in the event of sickness or injury, and may require the General Manager or any such officer or servant to contribute thereto.

Protection of Corporation, etc., from liability.

16. No act or thing done by any member of the Corporation, the General Manager or any officer or servant of the Corporation shall, if the act or thing be done in good faith and without negligence for the purposes of this Act, render that member, the General Manager, officer or employee, or any person acting by his directions, personally liable to any action, proceeding, claim or demand whatsoever.

Accounts and audit.

17. (1) The Corporation shall cause to be kept proper books of account and other books in relation thereto and to all its undertakings, funds, activities and property, and shall prepare such other accounts as the Minister may require and, in addition, yearly balance sheets made up to the end of its financial year, showing in detail the assets and liabilities of the Corporation.

(2) The Corporation shall appoint one or more members of the professional bodies specified in the Schedule to the Accountants (Designations) Act (hereinafter referred to in this Act as the auditors) who shall annually examine, audit and report on the accounts of the Corporation.

(3) The Corporation shall produce and lay before the auditors all books and accounts of the Corporation, with all vouchers in support thereof, and all books, papers and writings in its possession or control relating thereto, and the auditors shall be entitled to require from all members, officers, agents and employees of the Corporation such information and explanation as may be necessary for the performance of their duties as auditors.

(4) The expenses of and incidental to the audit shall be paid by the Corporation.

Annual report.

**18.** (1) The Corporation shall, within a period of six months after the end of its financial year or within such longer period as the Minister may approve, submit to the Minister a report of its operations during such year, and the auditor's report, together with the yearly balance sheets and such other statements of account as the Minister shall require; and the Corporation shall, if the Minister so requires, publish them in such manner as the Minister may specify.

(2) The Minister shall lay the Corporation's report and the auditor's report, together with the balance sheet and such other statements of account as he may have required, before the National Assembly as soon as practicable.

Reserve Fund and surplus moneys.

**19.** (1) The Corporation may establish and maintain a Reserve Fund and shall pay into such fund such part of the surplus moneys earned by the Corporation in the course of its operations in any one year as the Board may determine.

(2) The Reserve Fund shall be applied by the Corporation in making good any loss or deficiency which may occur in the course of the business of the Corporation.

(3) Any surplus moneys after deducting therefrom such sums as are required for the purpose specified in subsection (2) of this section shall be disposed of in such manner as the Corporation, subject to the approval of the Minister and the Minister for the time being responsible for finance, may direct, but a prudent balance shall remain in the Reserve Fund.

Rules.

**20.** The Minister may, after consultation with the Corporation, make rules generally for better carrying out the purposes and provisions of this Act and, in particular and without prejudice to the foregoing generality, may make rules for—

(*a*) raising such loans and making investments, on such terms as the Minister may, after consultation with the Minister for the time being responsible for finance, approve;
(*b*) regulating and controlling the Corporation or any of its agencies;
(*c*) prescribing the procedure to be followed in the appointment of members to the Corporation and its agencies;
(*d*) controlling and regulating the purchase and sale of land for agricultural development;
(*e*) regulating and prescribing the powers, duties, functions, responsibilities and remunerations of officers, employees and agents of the Corporation;

(*f*) prescribing, controlling and regulating schemes for agricultural development.

Exemption from stamp duty.

21. No duty shall be chargeable under the Stamp Duty Act in respect of any instrument executed by or on behalf of or in favour of the Agricultural Development Corporation in cases where, but for this exemption, the Corporation would be liable to pay such duty.

## The Agricultural Finance Corporation Act [1]

*Commencement: 21st March, 1969*

An Act of Parliament to establish an Agricultural Finance Corporation and to prescribe its powers and duties

### PART I—PRELIMINARY

Short title.

1. This Act may be cited as the Agricultural Finance Corporation Act.

Interpretation.

2. In this Act, except where the context otherwise requires—

"this Act" includes any rules or regulations made under this Act;

"agricultural industry" means any industry connected with agriculture or with the processing of agricultural produce;

"agricultural produce" includes anything (whether live or dead) produced in the course of agriculture;

"agriculture" means agriculture as defined in section 2 (1) of the Agriculture Act, and also forestry and the establishment, maintenance and exploitation of fisheries in private ownership;

"appraiser" means a person appointed as an appraiser under section 38 of this Act;

"the Board" means the Board of Directors of the Corporation established by section 4 of this Act;

"the Central Agricultural Board" means the Central Agricultural Board established by section 35 of the Agriculture Act;

[1] *Laws of Kenya,* Cap. 323 (1970). Originally No. 1 of 1969. Relevant citation: L.N. 163 of October 28, 1975.

"co-operative society" means a co-operative society registered under the Co-operative Societies Act;

"the Corporation" means the Agricultural Finance Corporation established by section 3 of this Act;

"Director" means a person who is a member of the Board by virtue of section 4 of this Act or of an appointment made thereunder;

"farmer" means a person who engages in agriculture in Kenya;

"fishery" means a privately-conducted establishment directed to fish culture in farm ponds and fish farming;

"the General Manager" means the General Manager of the Corporation appointed under section 9 of this Act;

"land" includes anything attached to the land;

"the land registrar" means the person charged with the registration of documents of title to land under the written law under which the land is registered;

"loan" means a loan made under this Act;

"mortgage" includes a charge, lien or other security or encumbrance;

"mortgagor" means a person who has mortgaged any land to the Corporation or to whom a loan has been made under this Act, or his personal representative;

"net profit" means the excess of income over expenditure after making adequate provision for depreciation, amortization, and bad and doubtful debts;

"staff" means the officers and servants of the Corporation appointed under section 10 of this Act.

## PART II—THE AGRICULTURAL FINANCE CORPORATION

3. (1) There is hereby established a Corporation, to be known as the Agricultural Finance Corporation. Establishment of Corporation.

(2) The functions of the Corporation shall be to assist in the development of agriculture and agricultural industries by making loans to farmers, co-operative societies, incorporated group representatives, private companies, public bodies, local authorities and other persons engaging in agriculture or agricultural industries.

(3) The Corporation shall be a body corporate with perpetual succession and a common seal, and shall have power to acquire, own, possess and dispose of property, and to contract, and to sue and be sued in its own name.

(4) The Corporation is not subject to the Companies Act or the Banking Act.

Board of Directors.

4. (1) There shall be a Board of Directors of the Corporation, which shall, subject to this Act, be responsible for determining the policy of the Corporation and for controlling its operations.

(2) The Board shall consist of—

(*a*) not less than four and not more than six persons appointed by the Minister of whom at least two shall be appointed by reason of their knowledge of banking or financial matters;

(*b*) the Permanent Secretary of the Ministry, or a person deputed by him in writing to take his place as a Director of the Board; and

(*c*) the Permanent Secretary of the Ministry for the time being responsible for finance, or a person deputed by him in writing to take his place as a Director of the Board.

(3) A chairman and a deputy chairman shall be appointed by the Minister, after consultation with the Minister for the time being responsible for finance, from among the Directors, and the deputy chairman may, in the absence of the chairman, exercise all the powers and discharge all the duties which are conferred and imposed by this Act upon the chairman.

(4) A Director appointed under paragraph *(a)* of subsection (2) of this section shall hold office for such period not exceeding three years from the date of his appointment as may be specified in the instrument appointing him and shall then retire but shall be eligible for reappointment, and in default of any other person having been appointed by the Minister to succeed him within one month of the date of his retirement shall be deemed to have been reappointed.

(5) In the exercise of its powers and in the performance of its functions under this Act, the Board shall act in accordance with any general or special directions that the Minister may give it:

Provided that, if the Minister gives the Board directions which in the Board's opinion will involve the Corporation in financial loss, the Board is not required to act in accordance with those directions unless the Government has undertaken to reimburse the Corporation the amount of any losses incurred in so acting.

Disqualification of Director.

5. (1) No person shall be appointed a Director if—

(*a*) he is insolvent or has conveyed or assigned his property for the benefit of his creditors generally or has made a composition or arrangement with his creditors; or

(*b*) he is of unsound mind or has been convicted within the preceding five years of an offence and sentenced to imprisonment without the option of a fine.

(2) If the Minister is satisfied that the chairman, the deputy chairman or any other Director appointed under paragraph *(a)* of subsection (2) of section 4 of this Act—

*(a)* is incapacitated by physical or mental illness; or

*(b)* has become subject to any of the disqualifications specified in subsection (1) of this section; or

*(c)* has been absent from two consecutive meetings of the Board without the leave of the Board; or

*(d)* is otherwise unable or unfitted to discharge the functions of his office,

the Minister may declare his office as chairman, deputy chairman or Director, as the case may be, to be vacant, and shall notify the fact in such manner as the Minister thinks fit; and thereupon the office shall become vacant.

(3) If the chairman, the deputy chairman and any other Director to whom subsection (2) of this section applies—

*(a)* at any time, by notice in writing under his hand addressed to the Minister, resigns his office as such;

*(b)* dies; or

*(c)* is declared under that subsection to have vacated his office,

the Minister shall appoint a new Director to discharge the functions of that office:

Provided that where the vacancy to be filled is in the office of chairman or deputy chairman the Minister shall consult the Minister for the time being responsible for finance before exercising such power of appointment.

Meetings of Board.

6. (1) Meetings of the Board shall be convened by the chairman, or in his absence by the deputy chairman, at such times and places as he determines but not less than four times a year.

(2) The chairman, or in his absence the deputy chairman, may at any time, and shall at the request in writing of at least three Directors, convene a special meeting of the Board.

(3) A notice convening a special meeting of the Board shall state the purposes for which the special meeting is convened.

Procedure of Board.

7. (1) If the chairman is absent from a meeting of the Board, the deputy chairman shall act as chairman at that meeting.

(2) Three Directors who include the chairman or the deputy chairman shall constitute a quorum at any meeting of the Board, and all acts,

matters or things authorized or required to be done by the Board shall be effected by resolution passed by a majority of the Directors present and voting at a meeting at which a quorum is present.

(3) At every meeting of the Board, the chairman, or in his absence the deputy chairman, shall have a casting vote in addition to his deliberative vote as a Director.

(4) All orders, directions and decisions of the Board shall be made, given and notified under the hand of the chairman or deputy chairman, or of the General Manager if he is so authorized by the Board.

(5) Minutes of the proceedings of every meeting of the Board shall be regularly entered in a minute book, and the book shall be kept so as to show proper tabulated details of the business conducted or transacted at each meeting.

(6) The minutes of the proceedings of each meeting shall be placed before the next ensuing meeting and, if then passed as correct, shall be confirmed by the signature of the person who presided at that meeting, and when so confirmed shall be *prima facie* evidence in all proceedings of the matter recorded in the minutes.

(7) Subject to this Act and to any general or specific directions of the Minister, the Board shall regulate the procedure at its meetings as it considers proper.

Matters on which Director may not vote.

**8.** (1) A Director shall not at a meeting of the Board take part in the discussion of nor vote upon an application for a loan made by a person who is—

(*a*) related to that Director within the third degree of affinity or consanguinity; or
(*b*) a debtor, creditor, partner or employee of that Director; or
(*c*) a debtor under a mortgage of a body of persons, whether incorporated or not, of which that Director is a director or under which he holds any office or position other than that of auditor.

(2) A Director who is in any way whether directly or indirectly, interested in a proposed loan or in a loan then subsisting shall declare the nature of his interest at the first meeting at which he is present when the question of that loan is taken into consideration, if his interest then exists, or, in any other case, at the first meeting at which he is present after he becomes so interested, and shall take all reasonable steps to ensure that such declaration shall be recorded in the minutes of the meeting:

Provided that a general notice given by a Director to the effect that he is a member of a specified body of persons, company or firm and is to be regarded as interested in all transactions connected therewith shall be a sufficient declaration under this subsection.

(3) Subject to subsection (1) of this section a Director who shall have declared his interest in accordance with subsection (2) of this section may attend and be counted in the quorum of, but shall not vote in relation to that matter, at any meeting which may consider or pass any application or other resolution in respect of such a loan.

(4) Any person who contravenes subsection (1) or subsection (2) of this section shall be guilty of an offence and liable to imprisonment for a term not exceeding three years or to a fine not exceeding five thousand shillings, or to both such imprisonment and such fine.

9. (1) The Board, with the approval of the Minister given after consultation with the Minister for the time being responsible for finance, shall appoint a General Manager of the Corporation, who shall as far as possible be present at all meetings of the Board and shall at such meetings be entitled to speak but not to vote. Appointment and duties of General Manager.

(2) It shall be the duty of the General Manager to undertake executive responsibility for the functions of the Corporation and to perform the other functions conferred upon him by this Act.

(3) The General Manager shall act in accordance with any special or general directions which the Board may give him.

(4) The General Manager is hereby empowered to administer oaths and take statutory declarations in matters where statements upon oath and statutory declarations are required by this Act.

(5) In the event of the General Manager being unable to exercise his functions as such through illness, leave, absence from Kenya or other cause, a person shall be appointed in the manner specified in subsection (1) of this section to act as General Manager, and the person so appointed may exercise all the power and discharge all the duties which are conferred and imposed by this Act upon the General Manager until such time as the Board considers that the General Manager is again able to exercise his functions as such.

10. (1) The Board may appoint, upon such terms and conditions as it thinks proper, such other officers and servants as it considers necessary or desirable for the efficient conduct and operation of the Corporation. Appointment of staff.

(2) Every member of the staff shall, subject to this Act, exercise the powers and functions and perform the duties assigned to him from time to time by the General Manager.

Remuneration.

11. The Directors (other than public officers in receipt of salary), the General Manager and the staff shall be paid out of the funds of the Corporation such salaries and allowances as the Corporation, with the approval of the Treasury, may from time to time determine, and such travelling and other expenses as they may incur in the performance of their duties as such.

Pension and provident funds.

12. (1) The Board may, subject to the approval of the Minister and the Treasury, establish, control, manage, maintain and contribute to pension or provident funds for the benefit of the General Manager and the staff, and may grant pensions and gratuities from any such fund to them on their retirement from the service of the Corporation and to their dependants on their death.

(2) If neither a pension nor a provident fund is established under subsection (1) of this section, or if a fund is established but in the opinion of the Board it provides insufficient benefits, the Board may, with the approval of the Minister and the Treasury, grant from the funds of the Corporation pensions and gratuities, or additional pensions and gratuities, as the case may be, to the General Manager and the staff on their retirement from the service of the Corporation and to their dependants on their death.

Execution of documents.

13. (1) The common seal of the Corporation shall be authenticated by the signature of the chairman or deputy chairman of the Board and by the signature of the General Manager or some other person so authorized by the Board.

(2) All documents, other than those required by law to be under seal, made by, and all decisions of, the Corporation may be signified under the hand of the chairman or deputy chairman of the Board, or of the General Manager if he is so authorized by the Board.

Powers of Corporation.

14. (1) The Corporation shall, subject to this Act, have power to do all such things and to enter into all such transactions as it considers necessary for, or conducive or incidental to, the proper discharge of the functions described in section 3(2) of this Act, including, without prejudice to the generality of the foregoing, power—

(*a*) to make loans of money in accordance with Part III of this Act;

(*b*) with the concurrence of, and subject to such limitations as may be imposed by, the Treasury, to borrow money or obtain credit either in Kenya or abroad;

(*c*) to furnish managerial, technical and administrative advice, or to assist in obtaining such advice, for agricultural industries;

(*d*) after consultation with the Treasury, to invest money which is not for the time being needed for discharging the functions of the Corporation in investments for the time being authorized by law for the investment of trust moneys, or to place any such money on deposit at interest with any public body;

(*e*) to create, make, draw, accept, endorse, execute, issue, discount, buy, sell, negotiate and deal in bills, notes, warrants, coupons, stock, debentures and other negotiable or transferable instruments;

(*f*) subject to this Act, to mortgage the property of the Corporation to secure the repayment of money borrowed by the Corporation.

(2) Notwithstanding subsection (1) of this section, the Corporation shall not borrow any money where the result would be that the total indebtedness (whether present or contingent) of the Corporation would exceed the sum of fifteen million pounds, or such larger amount as the Treasury may, by notice in the Gazette, determine.[2]

(3) The Corporation may delegate to the General Manager its power to grant loans under this Act.

(4) No loan shall be made out of the funds of the Corporation to any Director or to any member of the staff unless—

(*a*) it is for the purchase of housing accommodation or a motor vehicle; or

(*b*) it is for agricultural purposes,

and the interest of the applicant has been disclosed and recorded in the minutes of the meeting recommending approval of the application and the consent of the Minister to the proposal has been obtained.

15. (1) The funds of the Corporation shall consist of— Funds of Corporation.

(*a*) all moneys, funds and securities vested in the Corporation by section 48 of this Act;

---

[2] By Legal Notice No. 163 of October 28, 1975, published as Legislative Supplement No. 45 in *Kenya Gazette Supplement* No. 62 of November 7, 1975, the Minister for Finance and Planning made the following determination:

"In pursuance of subsection (2) of section 14 of the Agricultural Finance Corporation Act, the Treasury hereby determines that the sum of fifty million pounds shall be the amount of the total indebtedness (whether present or contingent) of the Corporation which shall not be exceeded as the result of the borrowing of any money."

(*b*) any money provided by Parliament;

(*c*) any money borrowed under section 14(1)(*b*) of this Act;

(*d*) any money received by way of interest on, or in repayment of, or otherwise in connexion with, loans made by or vested in the Corporation;

(*e*) such moneys as the Minister may from time to time approve as funds of the Corporation.

(2) The Corporation shall pay to the Government interest, at such rate as the Treasury, after consultation with the Minister and with the Board, may from time to time determine upon any money provided by Parliament and upon any money which, by virtue of subsection (1)(*a*) of this section, forms part of its funds and was provided by Parliament; and any interest payable under this subsection shall be paid upon such dates as the Permanent Secretary to the Treasury may direct.

Reserve fund.

16. (1) The Board shall create a reserve fund which shall be credited from time to time with any net profit earned by the Corporation.

(2) The reserve fund shall be applied by the Board in making good any loss or deficiency which may occur in any of the transactions of the Corporation.

(3) Whenever any balance remains in the reserve fund after providing for any loss or deficiency as aforesaid, it may be devoted to any of the purposes to which any other fund of the Corporation may by this Act be devoted.

(4) The reserve fund created in accordance with subsection (1) of this section shall be credited with any net profit earned by the Corporation until such time as the balance remaining after providing for any loss or deficiency as aforesaid shall exceed ten per centum of the funds of the Corporation as defined in section 15 of this Act, and shall thereafter not be reduced below that level.

(5) Subject to subsection (4) of this section, as soon as the reserve fund and other funds of the Corporation total such amount as in the Board's opinion is adequate to enable the Corporation fully to carry out its objects, there shall as soon as possible after the accounts have been duly audited and certified in accordance with section 40 (1) of this Act be paid to the Permanent Secretary to the Treasury such amount as the Board shall direct out of—

(*a*) the profits of the Corporation; and

(*b*) the reserve funds of the Corporation.

(6) All amounts paid to the Permanent Secretary to the Treasury under subsection (5) of this section shall be applied towards the re-

demption of any loans made by the Government to the Corporation, and interest upon the amount repaid shall cease to be payable as from the date of repayment.

**17.** Any moneys borrowed by the Corporation under section 14(1)*(b)* of this Act are by this section charged upon the assets of the Corporation, and shall be repayable primarily out of the revenues of the Corporation.

Moneys borrowed by Corporation charged on assets.

## PART III—LOANS

**18.** In this Part, "farmer" includes the duly authorized attorney of a farmer, the personal representative of a deceased farmer, a trustee of a farmer appointed by deed or will and a receiver appointed by an order of the court or by a mortgagee, even though that person may not have been specifically authorized to mortgage land.

Interpretation of Part.

**19.** (1) The Corporation may, in accordance with rules made under this Act and subject to the provisions of subsection (3) of section 14 of this Act but otherwise upon such terms and conditions as to interest, repayment, security or otherwise and in such manner as the Board may think fit, make a loan to a farmer to enable him to engage more effectively in agriculture—

Loans to farmers.

*(a)* upon his applying for a loan in writing in such form as the Board from time to time approves; and

*(b)* upon the authority of a resolution of a meeting of the Board at which the application is properly considered and approved.

(2) A loan under this section may be made for the purpose of reducing or discharging an existing first mortgage if in the opinion of the Board the terms of the mortgage are onerous:

Provided that a loan shall not be made for the purpose of reducing an existing mortgage unless the mortgagee executes a waiver of priority in favour of the Corporation under section 28 of this Act.

(3) A loan under this section shall be made for such period, not exceeding thirty years, and on such terms, as the Board may determine.

**20.** (1) Where the Board so directs a farmer who is the registered owner of land which is not encumbered with any mortgage (other than one in respect of which the mortgagee has executed a waiver of priority in favour of the Corporation under section 28 of this Act) shall execute a first mortgage of the land in favour of the Corporation.

Charge on the land.

(2) Where the conditions of the loan are such that the Board is satisfied that the execution of a formal first mortgage is not necessary, or where the Board otherwise directs, the borrower shall not be required to execute such a document, and instead the General Manager shall—

(*a*) deliver a written notification of the loan in the prescribed form to the land registrar, who shall register it against the title to the borrower's land and, where appropriate, endorse a memorandum of the loan on the grant or certificate of title, and thereupon the land shall stand charged with the repayment of the loan and the interest thereon subject to any prior registered charge; and

(*b*) upon repayment of the loan and all interest due on it, give written notice of the repayment to the land registrar, who shall register it against the title to the borrower's land and cancel any memorandum of the loan which is endorsed on the grant or certificate of title, and thereupon the charge created in respect of the loan shall be extinguished,

and a written notification delivered under this subsection shall for all the purposes of this Act be deemed to be a mortgage of the land comprised therein executed by the borrower to secure the loan.

(3) In addition to the action prescribed by subsection (2) of this section, the General Manager shall—

(*a*) deliver a written notification of the loan in the prescribed form to the Registrar-General, who shall register it as an instrument under the Chattels Transfer Act, and it shall be deemed to be an instrument within the meaning of that Act assigning and transferring to the Corporation, by way of mortgage to secure the loan and the interest on it, all the movable property for the time being of the borrower (other than his household and personal effects); and

(*b*) upon repayment of the loan and all interest due on it, give written notice of the repayment to the Registrar-General, who shall register it as a memorandum of satisfaction under the Chattels Transfer Act, and it shall be deemed to be a memorandum of satisfaction within the meaning of that Act in respect of the whole of the loan.

Extension of time.

21. The Board may in its discretion postpone the repayment or extend the time for the repayment of a loan or for the payment of any interest payable thereon, but so that the maximum period for repayment in respect of any loan shall not exceed thirty years.

22. If a trustee consents to his security being postponed to enable a loan to be made, his consent shall not itself be deemed improper or a breach of trust so as to render the trustee liable in respect of any loss resulting from the loan having been made.

Consent by trustee to short-term loan.

23. (1) The Corporation may make a loan to any co-operative society primarily engaged in agriculture to enable the society to erect buildings, install equipment or buy land or otherwise to promote any one or more of the objects of the society—

Loan to co-operative society.

(*a*) upon the society applying for a loan in writing in such form as the Board from time to time approves signed by the chairman and the secretary of the society; and

(*b*) upon the Board being satisfied that the chairman and secretary of the society have been authorized, by a resolution of a meeting of the society passed by a majority of two-thirds of the members of the society and which does not offend any by-laws of the society, to apply for a loan; and

(*c*) upon the society lodging with its application a list of the persons who were members of the society at the time of the resolution; and

(*d*) upon the Board being satisfied that the accounts, books, papers and documents of the society are in order; and

(*e*) upon such security (if any) as the Board may require; and

(*f*) upon the authority of a resolution of a meeting of the Board at which the application is properly considered and approved.

(2) The Commissioner for Co-operative Development shall, at the request of the Board, furnish such lists and other information as the Board may require regarding any co-operative society.

24. The Board shall at all times have full access to all accounts, books, papers and documents of any co-operative society to which a loan has been made or from which an application for a loan has been received, and may cause all such accounts, documents, papers or books to be examined by a member of the staff or by such other person as the Board may appoint.

Examination of books of co-operative society.

25. (1) Where a loan is made to a co-operative society, all persons who were members of the society at the time of the application for the loan and are named in the list referred to in section 23(1)(*c*) of this Act shall be jointly and severally liable to repay the loan and to pay the interest payable on the loan.

Liability of members of co-operative society.

(2) If a person who was a member of a co-operative society at the time of the application for a loan and is named in the list referred to in section 23(1)*(c)* of this Act ceases to be a member of that society, he shall nevertheless remain liable under subsection (1) of this section in respect of any part of a loan and any interest which was outstanding at the time he ceased to be a member, and on ceasing to be a member he shall provide security to the satisfaction of the Board for the due discharge of that liability.

(3) Where a co-operative society is a company registered under the Companies Act, the liability of the shareholders of the company is limited to the amount (if any) of the share capital not called up, and subsection (2) of this section shall not apply to a person who has ceased to be a shareholder in the company.

## PART IV—GENERAL PROVISIONS AS TO LOANS

Rate of interest, and form of security.

**26.** (1) A loan shall bear such rate of interest as the Board, with the approval of the Minister for the time being responsible for finance given after consultation with the Minister, may prescribe, either generally or for any particular class of loan.

(2) A mortgage given under this Act shall be in such form as is prescribed under any written law relating to that mortgage or, where no such form is prescribed, in such form as the Board may determine.

Appraisal of land offered as security.

**27.** The Board, if it considers it desirable, shall cause land offered as security for a loan to be appraised by an appraiser, and in such case the appraiser shall render to the Corporation an appraisal of the land in a form approved by the Board.

Waiver of priority.

**28.** Any mortgagee may, by waiver endorsed upon or incorporated in the mortgage, agree that a mortgage in favour of the Corporation shall have priority, either for the purposes of this Part or for any of the other purposes of this Act, over his mortgage, and such agreement when registered in the same manner as the mortgage held by him shall for all purposes be binding upon him and as from the date of registration upon his successors in title.

Loan to be taken up within three months.

**29.** If a loan has been authorized by the Board and the applicant does not, within a period to be fixed by the Corporation (but not exceeding three months after the applicant has been notified of the authorization), execute such documents as the Board may consider necessary to complete the security and lodge them with the Corporation together with the title deeds of and other documents relative to the applicant's title to the property (if it is to be mortgaged), the Board may withdraw its authorization of the loan, and in that event the loan shall not be made and no part of the fees paid in connexion with the application shall be refunded.

Covenants and conditions to be implied in mortgages.

**30.** (1) In every mortgage or other security document executed to secure a loan, there shall be implied on the part of the farmer and in favour of the Corporation the covenants and conditions set out in the Schedule to this Act.

(2) All such covenants and conditions shall extend to and bind the successor in title of the mortgagor.

Corporation may withhold loan where debtor in default.

**31.** If a loan is made, and—

*(a)* at any time any sum of money, whether principal or interest, due in respect of the loan is unpaid; or
*(b)* the Board considers that the loan has not been applied to the purposes for which it was made or has not been carefully and economically expended; or
*(c)* the debtor becomes insolvent, or is sentenced to imprisonment without the option of a fine, or conveys or assigns his property for the benefit of his creditors generally, or makes a composition or arrangement with his creditors, or (the debtor having died) his estate is or is about to be administered in bankruptcy; or
*(d)* there has been a breach of any other condition of the loan; or
*(e)* the loan is not applied within such time as the Corporation may consider reasonable to the purpose for which it was made,

the Corporation may in addition to any other remedies refuse to pay any portion of the loan which has been approved but not yet paid.

Application of money repaid prematurely.

**32.** (1) If a person to whom a loan has been made under this Act (in this section referred to as a borrower) at any time pays to the Corporation an amount in excess of the instalment then due under the mortgage, the Corporation may, if it thinks fit, on the date when the next instalment falls due, apply such amount in payment of the capital portion of one or more of the instalments which would otherwise thereafter fall due, and the instalments may then be recalculated on the basis of balance of capital owing by the borrower over the remainder of the period for which the loan was originally made.

(2) Such an excess payment, and its application by the Corporation as provided in subsection (1) of this section, shall not exempt the bor-

rower from paying his next instalment when it is due, reduced or recalculated where appropriate.

(3) The Corporation may allow a borrower a rebate of interest, in respect of money paid prematurely, and the rebate shall be in the form of a reduction of the rate of interest charged on that money by one per cent per annum from the date of the payment up to the date when the next instalment falls due.

(4) If the total amount owing to the Corporation is paid off before the due date for payment, the Corporation may claim interest only up to the date of payment:

Provided that, in the case of repayment on a date before the due date for repayment, three months' notice of intention to repay shall be given to the Corporation, and if no such notice is given the Corporation may claim interest in respect of such amount for the period by which the notice actually given falls short of three months.

Procedure for recovery on default by occupation or sale of property.

33. (1) In any of the circumstances or events mentioned in section 31 of this Act, the Corporation may, by notice served on the person to whom the loan has been made or his personal representative (in this section referred to as the debtor) personally or by post, demand repayment of the loan and, after due notice of such demand has been served in similar manner on all subsequent mortgagees of the land on the security of which the loan was made, the Corporation may, without recourse to any court, enter upon the land and either take possession of or sell by public auction the whole or (where subdivision is not prohibited under section 34 of the Government Lands Act) any part of the land upon such terms and conditions as the Board may in all the circumstances consider proper.

(2) At a public auction held in pursuance of subsection (1) of this section, the Corporation, by its agent duly authorized in writing, may bid for and purchase the whole or any part of the land offered for sale.

(3) The Corporation, as agent of the debtor, may transfer the land to itself or any other purchaser and give a good and unencumbered title to it, and may execute all such documents and do all such other acts as may be necessary to complete the transfer.

(4) A sale under subsection (1) of this section shall not be held until—

(*a*) a notice of the sale has been published in the Gazette, or in a newspaper circulating in the area in which the land is situated, stating the date, time and place of the sale, and the terms and conditions of the sale; and (*b*) twenty-one days have elapsed since the date of publication of the notice; and

(*c*) all reasonable steps have been taken by the Corporation to notify in writing the persons having a registered interest (or any unregistered interest of which the Corporation knows) in the land of the intended sale.

Inspection of land.

34. For the purpose of ascertaining whether a loan has been or is being properly applied, any member of the staff, or any person deputed by the Corporation to inspect land under this Act, may enter upon any land in respect of which the loan was made and make such inspections thereon as he considers proper.

Protection against liability.

35. Where a loan is made in good faith, and it is afterwards discovered that—

(*a*) the land comprised in any mortgage or other security document in respect of the development of which a loan was granted was not used, or was not to be used, as the case may be, for agricultural purposes; or

(*b*) the loan was not applied for the purpose for which it was made within the time specified by the Board, or the loan was applied for purposes other than that for which it was made,

no Director and no member of the staff shall be personally liable therefor, but—

(i) the Board or the General Manager may refuse to pay any part of the loan which has not already been paid; and

(ii) the Board may at once proceed to call in and recover the money already lent.

## PART V—POWERS OF CORPORATION

Power of Corporation to inspect valuation rolls.

36. The Corporation may inspect without fee or charge the valuation roll of any local authority which now exists or hereafter exists, and it shall be the duty of officers of a local authority, upon application, to supply to the Corporation without fee or charge, particulars as to any valuation of rateable property in respect of which the local authority has the power to levy rates.

Power of Corporation to hold land.

37. (1) The Corporation may hold land which is—

(*a*) required for its business premises; or

(*b*) required for the provision of housing accommodation for the staff; or (*c*) acquired as the result of foreclosure or otherwise on account of indebtedness to the Corporation,

but not otherwise.

(2) All developed land acquired in accordance with subsection (1)(*c*) of this section shall be sold at the earliest favourable opportunity upon such special terms and conditions as the Corporation may determine, but the Directors, the General Manager and members of the staff shall not buy directly or indirectly any land sold in pursuance of this subsection.

Power of Corporation to appoint appraisers.

**38.** (1) The Corporation may appoint appraisers to inspect and appraise land for the purposes of this Act.

(2) Fees and travelling expenses of appraisers shall be paid in accordance with rates specified by the Corporation with the approval of the Treasury, and shall be payable by the applicants.

(3) Every administrative officer, Government surveyor, police officer or other public officer shall, without additional emolument, when required by the Corporation to do so, report on any cases submitted to him and generally act as agent or inspector of the Corporation.

Power of Corporation to act as agent.

**39.** The Corporation may be appointed and may act as agent of the Government in the making, administration and recovery on behalf of the Government of any loans to farmers or others:

Provided that no expenses of such agency shall fall to be paid from the funds of the Corporation, and the Corporation shall be indemnified by the Government against any losses, costs and expenses which may be sustained or incurred by the Corporation in the performance of such agency.

## PART VI—ACCOUNTS OF CORPORATION

Publication of accounts.

**40.** (1) The General Manager shall, within four months after the 31st March in each year, deliver to the Minister a statement of accounts duly audited and certified showing—

(*a*) the assets and liabilities of the Corporation on that date; and

(*b*) a profit and loss account of the Corporation for the year.

(2) Every such statement shall be signed as correct by the General Manager and at least two Directors.

(3) The Minister shall cause every statement delivered to him under subsection (1) of this section to be laid before the National Assembly.

(4) In addition, the General Manager shall render to the Minister promptly such other accounts, reports and statements as the Minister may from time to time require.

Inspection and audit of accounts.

41. (1) The Treasury shall have full access to all accounts, documents, papers and books of the Corporation, and the General Manager shall at all times furnish to the Treasury all such information as it may require.

(2) The accounts of the Corporation shall be examined, audited and reported on annually by the Controller and Auditor-General or by such other person as the Minister may appoint, being a person who is a member of one or more of the bodies specified in the Schedule to the Accountants (Designations) Act.

## PART VII—MISCELLANEOUS

False statements.

42. Any applicant for a loan who wilfully fails to disclose any material information within his knowledge, or who wilfully makes any statement which he knows to be false or does not believe to be true, shall be guilty of an offence and liable to imprisonment for a term not exceeding three years or to a fine not exceeding five thousand shillings, or to both such imprisonment and such fine, and shall further be liable to have any loan made to him cancelled forthwith and to repay to the Corporation forthwith all sums lent to him together with interest thereon.

Corrupt acts.

43. (1) If a Director, the General Manager or a member of the staff, or any appraiser, inspector or agent appointed by the Corporation, directly or indirectly receives any fee or reward (other than as authorized by or under this Act) from any person in respect of or in connexion with a loan or an application for a loan, he shall be guilty of an offence and liable to imprisonment for a term not exceeding five years or to a fine not exceeding ten thousand shillings, or to both such imprisonment and such fine.

(2) If any person in respect of or in connexion with a loan or an application for a loan, bribes or corruptly influences a Director, the General Manager or a member of the staff, or any appraiser, inspector or agent appointed by the Corporation, he shall be guilty of an offence and liable to imprisonment for a term not exceeding five years or to a fine not exceeding ten thousand shillings, or to both such imprisonment and such fine.

(3) Any person who—

(a) having a pecuniary interest in any land offered as security for a loan; or

(b) being a debtor, creditor, partner or employee of an applicant for a loan or being related to such an applicant within the third degree of affinity or consanguinity,

acts as appraiser in connexion with the land offered as security for such loan shall be guilty of an offence and liable to imprisonment for a term not exceeding three years or to a fine not exceeding five thousand shillings, or to both such imprisonment and such fine.

Secrecy.

44. (1) Any person who is on official duty under, or is employed in the administration of, this Act shall treat all documents, information, returns and forms relating to an application for a loan or the making of a loan as secret.

(2) Any person who has possession of or control over any document, information, return or form relating to an application for a loan or the making of a loan, and who communicates any such information or anything contained in any such document, return or form to any person—

(a) other than a person to whom he is authorized by proper authority to communicate it; or

(b) otherwise than for the purposes of this Act,

shall be guilty of an offence and liable to imprisonment for a term not exceeding twelve months or to a fine not exceeding three thousand shillings, or to both such imprisonment and such fine.

Rules.

45. The Minister, on the advice of the Board, may make rules as to all or any of the following matters, namely—

(a) the meeting and proceedings of the Board;

(b) the procedure for applying for loans, and the conditions which may be imposed on the making of a loan;

(c) the recovery of any costs resulting from examination of application for advances;

(d) the appointment of agents and the establishment of agencies, and their respective powers;

(e) the management of the Board and its agencies;

(f) the cases in which property given as security shall be insured;

(g) the forms to be used, and the books, accounts and records to be kept;

(h) the rights and privileges and the duties of the staff and the manner of the performance of their duties;

(*i*) generally for fully and effectually carrying out and giving effect to the provisions and purposes of this Act, and for guarding against violations of this Act.

46. The Board, with the consent of the Minister, may make regulations prescribing the fees, costs and expenses to be charged and payable in respect of loans and applications for loans, and any such regulations may provide for— Regulations.

(*a*) scales of application fees and appraisal fees based on the amount of the loan for which application is made;

(*b*) reduced scales of application fees and appraisal fees where the application is for a short-term loan;

(*c*) the basis upon which travelling expenses incurred by appraisers on appraisals are to be calculated;

(*d*) the refund or partial refund of the application fee where an application for a loan is refused;

(*e*) the reduction of the application fee where an amount less than that applied for is lent;

(*f*) a scale of conveyancing costs and fees for the preparation and completion of mortgages and other securities and discharges thereof;

(*g*) charging the borrower with any expenses, including copying charges, actually incurred by the Corporation at any time during the continuance of the loan in connexion with such loan;

(*h*) the time and mode of payment of fees, costs and expenses;

(*i*) the remission of fees, costs and expenses by the Board.

47. Subject to section 48 of this Act, the Agricultural Credit Act is repealed.

48. (1) On the commencement of this Act— Transfer of property and liabilities of former Corporation and Land and Agricultural Bank.

(*a*) all the property of every kind of the former Corporation, and all the property of every kind of the Land Bank, shall be transferred to and vest in the Corporation by virtue of this section and without further assurance;

(*b*) all the liabilities and contractual obligations of the former Corporation, and all the liabilities and contractual obligations of the Land Bank, shall become those of the Corporation;

(*c*) all directions, orders, rules, appointments, requirements, authorizations, registrations and other things given, made or done by the former Corporation or the Land Bank under the former Act or any subsidiary legislation thereunder, and subsisting immediately before such commencement, shall be deemed to have been given, made or done by the Corporation;

(*d*) every appointment of the former Corporation or of the Land Bank to do anything, and every reference to the former Corporation or to the Land Bank in any written law or instrument, shall be deemed to be an appointment of or reference to the Corporation;

(*e*) any reference to the former Corporation or to the Land Bank in any contract shall be deemed to be a reference to the Corporation; and

(*f*) every person who, immediately before such commencement, was an officer or servant of the former Corporation or of the Land Bank (not being then under notice of dismissal or resignation) shall become a servant of the Corporation:

Provided that such a person who gives to the Corporation within two weeks after such commencement notice in writing that he does not wish to become an officer or servant of the Corporation shall be deemed not to have become an officer or servant of the Corporation on such commencement but to have retired from the service of the Corporation or the Land Bank, as the case may be, on the day but one preceding such commencement.

(2) In subsection (1) of this section—

"the former Corporation" means the Agricultural Finance Corporation established by section 3 of the former Act;

"the former Act" means the Agricultural Credit Act (hereby repealed);

"the Land Bank" means the Land and Agricultural Bank established by section 19 of the former Act.

## SCHEDULE (s. 30)

### COVENANTS AND CONDITIONS IMPLIED IN EVERY MORTGAGE

1. That the mortgagor will from time to time, so long as money remains owing on this security, pay the rent after it becomes due under any agreement, lease or licence under which he holds the land, and will well and substantially repair and keep in good and substantial repair and condition all buildings and other improvements erected and made upon the land; and that the Corporation shall at all times be at liberty by itself, its agents or its servants to enter upon the land to view and inspect the said buildings and improvements.

2. That the mortgagor will not at any time alienate his interest in the said security, or any part thereof, by way of sale or gift or in any other manner whatsoever, without the prior consent in writing of the Corporation, which consent shall not be unreasonably withheld.

3. That if the mortgagor fails or neglects to pay the rent as aforesaid, to repair the said buildings and improvements or keep them in good and substantial repair and condition as aforesaid, it shall be lawful for, but not obligatory upon, the Corporation, at the cost and expense in all things of the mortgagor, to pay the rent, to repair the buildings and improvements or to keep them in good and substantial repair and condition, as the case may be.

4. That all moneys expended by the Corporation in paying rent as aforesaid, or in repairing or keeping in repair any of the buildings and improvements as aforesaid, or in the insurance thereof or in attempting to exercise any power, right or remedy herein contained or implied in favour of the Corporation, shall be a charge on the land, together with interest at the rate of not more than the rate per centum charged in the mortgage computed from the date or dates of such moneys being expended.

5. That insurance shall be effected as may be prescribed or directed by the Board in the joint names of the applicant and the Corporation; and that every policy of insurance so effected and every renewal receipt shall be deposited with the Corporation.

6. That if the mortgagor makes default in the full and punctual payment of any instalment of interest or principal, or if the mortgagor makes default in the faithful observance and performance of any covenant or condition contained in or implied by the mortgage, the Corporation shall be at liberty to call up and compel payment of all principal, interest and other moneys for the time being owing under this security, notwithstanding that the time or times appointed for their payment thereof respectively may not have arrived.

7. That the mortgagor will at all times cultivate and manage the land in a skilful and proper manner, either personally or by proxy, according to the rules of good husbandry, and particularly will fulfil all conditions of development and occupation to which in any grant from the Government such lands are subject (failure in the performance of this condition entailing the immediate recovery of the loan should the Corporation so desire), and that the conditions of any grant from the Government in respect of land used exclusively for stock farming shall in all respects be punctually fulfilled.

# The Kenya Post Office Savings Bank Act, 1977 [1]

*Date of Assent: 30th December, 1977*

*Date of Commencement: By Notice*

## An Act of Parliament to establish the Kenya Post Office Savings Bank and to encourage and facilitate personal saving

ENACTED by the Parliament of Kenya as follows—

[1] *Laws of Kenya,* Cap. 493B (1980). Originally No. 23 of 1977. Relevant citation: No. 8 of 1978.

Short title and commencement.

1. This Act may be cited as the Kenya Post Office Savings Bank Act, 1977, and shall come into operation on such date as the Minister may, by notice in the Gazette, appoint.

Interpretation.

2. In this Act—

"Bank" means the Kenya Post Office Savings Bank established under section 3;

"Board" means the Board of Directors appointed under section 5;

"Corporation" means the Kenya Posts and Telecommunications Corporation established under the Kenya Posts and Telecommunications Corporation Act, 1977;

"expenses" has the meaning assigned to it in section 10;

"former Bank" means the Post Office Savings Bank established under the Post Office Savings Bank Act (now repealed);

"revenue" means income of the Bank but does not include moneys received on deposit.

Establishment of the Bank and vesting of assets and liabilities.

3. (1) There is hereby established a savings bank to be known as the Kenya Post Office Savings Bank which shall replace the former Bank and which shall be a body corporate with perpetual succession and a common seal and shall have power to sue and be sued in its corporate name and to acquire, hold and dispose of movable and immovable property for the purposes of the Bank.

(2) The assets and liabilities of the former Bank subsisting at the commencement of this Act shall on that day be vested in the Bank.

(3) Savings accounts vested in the Bank under subsection (2) shall be maintained by the Bank subject to any rules made under section 15.

Functions of the Bank.

4. It shall be the responsibility of the Bank—

(*a*) to encourage thrift and provide the means and opportunities for the people of Kenya to save;

(*b*) to open, maintain or close branches at such places, including at any office of the Corporation, as the Board deems appropriate;

(*c*) to provide facilities for savings accounts including the accounts vested in the Bank on the commencement of this Act;

(*d*) to issue such other instruments or facilities for personal saving in such form as it may from time to time deem to be appropriate and desirable in furtherance of the objects of this Act;

(*e*) to invest any surplus funds in accordance with section 11;

(*f*) to cover the expenses of its operation with revenue earned from its investments taking one year with another.

**Appointment of Board of Directors.**

5. (1) The Bank shall be under the control of a Board of Directors which shall, subject to the direction of the Minister, take such steps as may be necessary and desirable for the proper management of the Bank and for the promotion of the objects and purposes of this Act.

(2) The Board shall consist of—

*(a)* the Permanent Secretary to the Treasury who shall be the chairman;

*(b)* the Managing Director of the Corporation;

*(c)* a public officer employed by the Treasury appointed by the Minister;

*(d)* three other members appointed by the Minister who shall not be employees of the Government.

(3) A quorum for any meeting of the Board shall be three:

Provided that no meeting of the Board shall be held or continued notwithstanding that there is a quorum unless either the Permanent Secretary to the Treasury or the public officer appointed under paragraph *(c)* of subsection (2) is present.

**Appointment of General Manager.**

6. (1) The Board shall appoint a General Manager who shall be responsible for the implementation of the policy and savings programmes of the Bank as laid down by the Board from time to time.

(2) The General Manager shall attend meetings of the Board.

(3) The General Manager may with the consent of the Board employ such persons as may be necessary for the execution of this Act.

(4) Employees of the Bank shall be engaged on such terms of service as the Board and the Treasury may approve:

Provided that the Bank may arrange with the Corporation that employees of the Corporation shall undertake duties on behalf of the Bank and that the Corporation shall be reimbursed in accordance with section 10.

**Deposits and repayments.**

7. Deposits of money to be paid into the Bank whether paid into a savings account or in respect of any other savings facility issued by the Bank from time to time shall be received and repaid under such conditions as may be prescribed in accordance with rules made by the Board under section 15.

**Security of moneys deposited.**

8. (1) The repayment of all moneys deposited in the Bank together with interest thereon is hereby guaranteed by the Government and accordingly if at any time the assets of the Bank are insufficient to pay

the outstanding lawful claim of any depositor, the deficiency shall be charged upon and paid out of the Consolidated Fund.

(2) The deficit in the reserve account of the former Bank as at the 31st December, 1975, shall be charged upon and paid out of the Consolidated Fund within six months of the commencement of this Act.

Interest payable.

9. Interest shall be payable on savings deposits and on such other savings instruments as may be issued by the Bank from time to time in accordance with rules made by the Board under section 15.

Exemption from lottery licences.

9A. Nothing in the Betting, Lotteries and Gaming Act shall be taken to apply to any instrument issued under this Act by reason of any use or proposed use of chance to select particular instruments for special benefits, if the terms of the issue provide that the amount subscribed is to be repayable in full in the case of all the instruments.

Expenses.

10. (1) All expenses incurred in the execution of this Act shall be met from the revenue of the Bank.

(2) For the purposes of this Act, "expenses" means the cost of any work or service done by or in connection with the Bank, including such sum on account of administrative and other overhead expenses incurred by the Corporation as may, with the approval of the Permanent Secretary to the Treasury, be reasonably assigned to that work or service.

Investment of funds.

11. (1) Except in so far as any sums may be prescribed by the Board to be kept in hand for the general purposes of the Bank, the Board shall ensure that any surplus of cash in the Bank shall be invested in interest-bearing securities or be employed at interest as the Board may direct.

(2) Any sums of money that may from time to time be required for the repayment of any deposits or for the payment of interest thereon or expenses incurred in the execution of this Act may be raised by the sale of the whole or a part of such securities:

Provided that any sums of money which may be required for such purposes may, with the approval of the Minister, be advanced to the Bank by the Treasury until they can be raised by the sale of such securities and such advances shall bear interest at the rate of interest from time to time payable to depositors.

(3) Any advances made in pursuance of the proviso to subsection (2) shall be charged upon and paid out of the Consolidated Fund

and every sum repaid on account of such advance shall be forthwith paid into the exchequer account.

**Accounts.**

12. (1) Annual accounts of the revenue and expenditure of the Bank for each year ending on the 31st December, together with a statement of the assets and liabilities of the Bank, shall, after being audited and certified by the Controller and Auditor-General, be laid by the Minister before the National Assembly as soon as possible after the close of each year and shall thereafter without delay be published in the Gazette.

(2) The annual accounts shall include a statement of moneys received and repaid by the Bank separately for each savings facility, including a statement of the amount of interest credited to each facility.

**Surplus and deficits.**

13. (1) Without prejudice to paragraph *(f)* of section 4, if in any year the revenue of the Bank is insufficient to defray the interest due to depositors and all expenses under this Act, such deficiency shall be charged upon and paid out of the Consolidated Fund.

(2) If in any year the revenue of the Bank shall be more than sufficient to defray the interest due to depositors and all expenses under this Act, then the Minister may direct the transfer of the surplus or any portion thereof to the Consolidated Fund:

Provided that no such transfer shall be made unless the assets of the Bank will thereafter exceed the liabilities by not less than fifteen per centum of the liabilities to depositors.

Settlement of disputes.

14. If any dispute shall arise between the Bank and any individual depositor therein, or any executor, administrator or next-of-kin of a depositor, or any creditor or assignee of a depositor who may become bankrupt or insolvent, or any person claiming to be such an executor, administrator, next-of-kin, creditor or assignee, or to be entitled to any money deposited in the Bank, then the matter in dispute shall be referred to an arbitrator to be appointed by the Minister, and any award, order or determination of or by such arbitrator shall be final and binding on all parties to the arbitration.

**Rules.**

15. (1) The Board may make rules for the management and regulation of the Bank.

(2) In particular and without prejudice to the generality of the foregoing, such rules may—

*(a)* prescribe the terms under which deposits will be accepted;

(*b*) prescribe the limits of deposits acceptable under various terms;

(*c*) prescribe the rates of interest payable on deposits accepted under various terms and how such interest will be payable;

(*d*) prescribe procedures for making and withdrawing deposits together with any interest thereon;

(*e*) prescribe the times at which deposit books shall be returned to the Bank by depositors;

(*f*) regulate deposits and withdrawals by minors, guardians, trustees, friendly societies, charitable bodies or any other bodies of persons of whatsoever description;

(*g*) prescribe procedures for dealing with deposits of deceased, insane or otherwise incapacitated persons.

Secrecy.

16. (1) No person appointed to carry this Act into effect shall disclose the name of any depositor or the amount which may have been deposited or withdrawn by any depositor except in due course of law or to such person or persons as may be appointed to assist in carrying this Act into operation.

(2) Any person who contravenes the provisions of this section shall be guilty of an offence and liable to a fine not exceeding five thousand shillings.

Repeal of Cap. 501.

17. The Post Office Savings Bank Act is hereby repealed.

# Kuwait

Overview of Kuwait City, capital of Kuwait
Courtesy World Wide Photos

# KUWAIT

*Page*

# Financial System of Kuwait

by

*Abdulhay Kayoumy**

## Introduction

Kuwait has been engaged in commercial oil production for about three decades and is now a major producer and exporter of crude petroleum. Oil income, which dominates Kuwait's economy, enabled the Government to modernize the country and improve the standard of living. The physical and social infrastructure was substantially completed during the 1960s. In the 1970s, concurrently with a sharp increase in oil income, the country began to realize a high rate of growth in public and private savings. This development gave an impetus to the development of the financial institutions in the country.

Kuwait's financial system comprises a central bank, six commercial banks (all locally owned), a branch of the Bank of Bahrain and Kuwait, a number of investment companies, a credit and savings bank, an industrial bank, and a real estate bank. In addition, there are a number of insurance companies, exchange dealers, stockbrokers, the Public Institution for Social Security, and an economic development fund.

The currency of Kuwait is the Kuwaiti dinar (KD). The value of the KD is determined on the basis of a weighted basket of currencies of Kuwait's major trading partners.

## Structure of Banking System

### *Kuwait Currency Board*

The Kuwait Currency Board was established as a separate legal entity attached to the Ministry of Finance and Economy. Its governing members consisted of a chairman, as the head of the Board, and six directors, all appointed by an Amiri Decree for a three-year period. The Board was the sole authority for the issuance of notes and coin, and had to maintain

---

* Mr. Kayoumy is Senior Economist in the Middle Eastern Department of the International Monetary Fund. Prior to his career with the Fund, he taught comparative economics systems and macroeconomics at the University of Washington, Seattle (U.S.A.). A number of his articles on exchange rates and demand elasticities have been published in economic journals. He received his PhD and Master's degrees from the University of Washington.

a gold currency cover of at least 50 per cent. The balance could consist of convertible foreign exchange, government paper, and prime commercial paper. The Currency Board's revenue from its holdings of bills and paper was to accrue to a reserve fund until this fund totaled 10 per cent of the currency in circulation; additional revenue had to revert directly to the Government.

Over the period of its existence, 1960–69, the Currency Board carried out its designated functions successfully. Nevertheless, with the substantial expansion in banking and financial activities in the latter part of the 1960s, the Currency Board's powers were considered to be too limited to deal with the growing needs of the financial sector. Accordingly, the Kuwaiti authorities decided to replace the Currency Board by a central bank.

### Central Bank of Kuwait

The Central Bank was established on April 1, 1969 under the Law Concerning Currency the Central Bank of Kuwait and the Organization of Banking Business.[1] In addition to being endowed with a paid-up capital of KD 2 million (which was subsequently increased to KD 5 million) it took over the assets and liabilities of the Currency Board. The law represented the first comprehensive set of rules governing Kuwait's money and banking system. It was amended in a number of particulars in 1977.[2] As implied by its title, the law is divided into three major chapters: the first deals with the national currency, the second with the Central Bank of Kuwait, and the third with the regulation of the banking system. The first chapter restates the main provisions of the previous currency board law, i.e., it defines the national currency, its issuance, its circulation and withdrawal, and the currency cover requirements. While initially it was mandated that 50 per cent of the value of currency in circulation be covered by gold, this requirement was deleted by an amendment in 1977.

The second chapter of the law focuses on the Central Bank's objectives and the rules for its capitalization, management, and operations. The Central Bank's main objectives are to safeguard the internal and external value of the national currency, to maintain the currency's international convertibility, and to promote appropriate monetary conditions for strengthening the country's financial system and economy. In order

[1] Law No. 32 of 1968.
[2] Decree Law No. 130 of 1977.

to achieve these objectives, the Central Bank of Kuwait is empowered to issue currency, administer the country's international reserves, regulate the banking system, function as the Government's fiscal agent and financial advisor, engage in open market operations, and trade in coins, bullion, or other precious metals, and foreign exchange. Moreover, the Central Bank of Kuwait may, subject to the approval of the Minister of Finance, trade in the securities of Kuwaiti joint stock companies, concessionary companies in Kuwait, or public agencies. Against the collateral of such securities, the Central Bank of Kuwait may make loans to banks or to public financial or credit establishments, provided that the amounts allocated for the acquisition of such securities, or for making loans, shall not exceed the value of the Bank's reserves. Direct advances to the Government may not exceed 10 per cent of the previous year's general government revenues. While according to the law the Central Bank is the fiscal agent of the Government, in fact it holds a relatively small part of the Government's assets. The Central Bank holds dinar-denominated deposits of the Government arising from the Government's domestic operations and also receives a part of foreign exchange receipts of the Government for conversion to dinar deposits for the account of the Government. The Government normally converts a small part of its foreign exchange receipts to dinars, maintaining the remaining large part with the Ministry of Finance which invests it abroad for the account of the Government. Besides the general budget account, the Ministry of Finance maintains two other accounts: one is the Reserve Account which functions as a conduit for all extrabudgetary operations, and the other is the Reserve Fund for Future Generations which received 50 per cent of total funds of the Reserve Account upon its establishment in 1976 and is credited annually with 10 per cent of total government revenues, 10 per cent of investment income accruing to the Reserve Account, and all the income accruing from the investments of the Reserve Fund for Future Generations. The Reserve Fund for Future Generations was established in order to provide a source of income when the oil reserves of the country are depleted and the income derived from them ceases. The total foreign asset holdings of the country are estimated to have amounted to about US$68 billion at the end of 1981.

The Central Bank of Kuwait is managed by a board of directors consisting of a Governor, a Deputy Governor, a representative of the Ministry of Finance, a representative of the Ministry of Commerce and Industry, and four other members. The Governor, appointed by a decree for a renewable period of five years on the recommendation of the

Minister of Finance, is the Central Bank's chief executive with full powers to manage the Bank's operations. The board of directors performs such functions as formulating the Central Bank's policies regarding reserve requirements, discount rates, commission charges (on loans, advances, and discounted commercial paper), and credit ceilings for loans and advances by the commercial banks operating in Kuwait. The representative of the Ministry of Finance to the board of directors may delay any resolution relating to monetary and credit policy by referring the resolutions to the Minister of Finance; if the Minister fails to decide on the matter within seven days, the resolution becomes effective.

The third chapter of the law deals with the organization and supervision of the commercial banking system. Public credit institutions, investment banks, and companies financing the acquisition and development of real estate are exempt from the provisions of this chapter, although a procedure exists to subject them to its provisions if necessary. All commercial banks operating in Kuwait must have a minimum capital of KD 3 million. Commercial banks must be registered with the Central Bank and any cessation of operations or merger must receive the approval of the Minister of Finance on the recommendation of the Central Bank. The Central Bank may delete the registration of a bank in the case of bankruptcy, merger, liquidity or solvency problems, cessation of its operations, or for violation of the law. Commercial banks are not allowed to engage (as a line of regular business) in trade, industry, real estate, nor are they allowed to deal in their own shares. Commercial banks may, without prior approval of the Central Bank, purchase for their own account, up to an amount not exceeding 50 per cent of their own funds, shares of commercial companies. The Central Bank is authorized to issue instructions to the commercial banks to give effect to its credit and monetary policy. Various financial ratios and limits may be established by the Central Bank. These relate to liquidity and solvency requirements, credit ceilings to individual borrowers, documentary credit deposits, legal reserve requirements, local asset ratios, composition of portfolios, and maximum rates of interest on loans and deposits. All commercial banks must submit regular reports to the Central Bank. Special rules are applicable to specialized banks. Banks, financial companies, and investment institutions are subject to inspection by the Central Bank.

The Central Bank used its powers sparingly during its early years and only thereafter did it take significant measures to influence credit and monetary conditions. During 1973 the Central Bank used moral suasion to persuade commercial banks to curtail credit expansion for purchases of stocks which had been experiencing a rapid and speculative rise in value. Late in 1973 the Central Bank imposed, for the first time, a liquidity ratio and instituted payment of interest on deposits of commercial banks with it. It set the liquidity ratio at 25 per cent of all deposit liabilities of commercial banks, with 7½ percentage points of this ratio to be maintained in domestic currency. It set the interest rate on commercial bank deposits with the Central Bank at ½ per cent above the prevailing savings deposit rate of 4 per cent. In late 1974 and early 1975, with the acceleration of economic activity and the accompanying sharp increase in demand for credit, commercial banks had begun to experience some pressure on their liquidity in Kuwaiti dinars because they could not convert foreign assets without incurring a loss. To remedy the situation, the Central Bank took a number of measures, effective February 1, 1975. It opened a discount window for commercial paper of three months' maturity; the discount rate for this paper was set at 5½ per cent. The Central Bank established a second line of credit for commercial banks with interest rates to be determined case by case. To further assist the commercial banks in meeting their immediate needs, the Central Bank placed part of the government deposits with these banks. Also, to prevent weakening of the Kuwaiti dinar's exchange rate vis-à-vis the currencies of Kuwait's trading partners, the authorities unpegged the dinar from the U.S. dollar as of March 18, 1975. Since then, the exchange rate for the Kuwaiti dinar has been maintained on the basis of its value in terms of a weighted average of currencies of Kuwait's main trading partners. During the subsequent three years monetary expansion accelerated. To check this acceleration the central bank authorities took a number of measures as summarized below.

Prior to 1977, interest rates in Kuwait were subject to a legal ceiling of 7 per cent, and within this ceiling the Central Bank was empowered to determine interest rates offered and charged by commercial banks.[3] During most of the 1968–76 period the effective market interest rate was near or at the 7 per cent ceiling and this ceiling was seldom exceeded. In November 1976 the law setting this legal ceiling was amended and the Central Bank was authorized to determine the interest rate ceilings with the approval of the Ministry of Finance. Consequently, effective February 20, 1977, the Central Bank increased the ceiling rate to 10 per cent on Kuwaiti dinar borrowing and lending

[3] In accordance with Art. 166 of the Law of Commerce of 1961 and the Central Bank Law of 1968. The relevant provision of the Law of Commerce now appears in Art. 111.

operations by the domestic financial system, including the investment companies. However, a maximum rate of 7 per cent was maintained for loans to the productive sectors (defined to include trade, manufacturing, and construction) secured by approved collateral and with a maturity of one year or less. For all other loans of one-year maturity or less, the ceiling rate was raised to 8.5 per cent, while loans of over one-year maturity were subject to a 10 per cent legal ceiling. At the same time, the minimum interest rate payable on savings deposits was increased from 4 per cent to 4.5 per cent; the determination of time deposit rates was left to market forces subject to the legal 10 per cent ceiling. Interest rates on loans and deposits denominated in foreign currency were not subject to any limits. Also in February 1977 the Central Bank increased the interest rate payable on commercial bank time deposits at the Central Bank from 4.5 per cent (effective since late 1973) to 5 per cent. Considering the openness of the Kuwaiti economy and the free movement of capital, the rigidity of the interest rate structure had at times led to flows of funds in response to large differentials between rates in the domestic market and those prevailing in international money markets. Moreover, reliance on fixed interest rate ceilings had prevented their use as an important instrument of monetary and credit policy.

With regard to discount policy, as mentioned before, the Central Bank began discounting commercial paper in February 1975, but limited acceptable notes and bills to a maturity of three months or less from the date of acquisition by the Bank. In October 1977 some flexibility was added to the Central Bank's discount policy. An amendment to the Central Bank Law authorized the Central Bank to discount commercial papers with maturities of up to one year at rates ranging between 5.5 and 6.5 per cent.

A number of other important amendments to the Central Bank Law became effective as of 1977 under Decree Law No. 130. These authorized the Central Bank to issue negotiable money market instruments to be used to approximate open market operations, and to extend the maturity period of the Bank's emergency credit for commercial banks from three to six months. The amendments also permitted the Government to deposit long-term Kuwaiti dinar funds with financial institutions other than the Central Bank after seeking the opinion of the Central Bank and in a manner not conflicting with the monetary policy in force. In addition, the Central Bank was authorized to recommend the final decision with respect to the opening of new banks and the closing of banks violating the banking laws, to inspect all banks and restrict their dealings if these were considered harmful to the banking system, and to issue directives (rather than recommendations as previously) to the banks in order to achieve monetary and credit objectives. The paid-up capital of the Central Bank was set at KD 5 million and the General Reserve Fund of the Bank was allowed to be increased by KD 3 million to KD 25 million through the allocation of net profits. At the same time, the Central Bank was authorized to undertake the sale and management of securities issued (or guaranteed) by the Government or issued by any other Kuwaiti public institution. Amendments also canceled the provisions fixing a gold parity for the Kuwaiti dinar and a minimum gold currency cover.

As a result of the amendments, the Central Bank was able to initiate a number of additional monetary measures including the revision of the liquidity requirements that became effective April 1, 1978. The new liquidity requirements were applied to both the commercial and specialized banks, but the investment companies were excluded. For demand deposits the liquidity ratio was increased to 35 per cent, and liquid assets were defined to include free demand or time deposits with the Central Bank or current deposits with other banks. For savings deposits, the liquidity ratio was set at 30 per cent, while for time deposits and certificates of deposit, the ratio was allowed to vary according to the term of the deposit or certificate from 30 per cent for maturities of one month or less to 5 per cent for maturities of six months to one year; no liquidity ratio was applied to deposits or certificates of more than one-year maturity. For savings and time deposits, the definition of liquid assets was expanded to include time deposits with and certificates of deposit and bankers' acceptances by other banks, all with a maturity of one month or less. Of the total liquid assets held against all types of deposits, at least one third was to be held in Kuwaiti dinar-denominated assets.

In April 1978 the monetary authorities initiated Kuwaiti dinar/U.S. dollar swap arrangements with the commercial banks in order to enhance the Central Bank's control over bank liquidity. The practice thus far has been for the Bank to buy U.S. dollars spot from the commercial banks and sell them forward, although it can also use the arrangement in the opposite direction. The swap rates quoted by the Central Bank are based on the difference between interest rates in the Eurodollar market and the Kuwaiti dinar interbank market. In order to introduce flexibility into its control of commercial bank liquidity, the Central Bank initiated the issuance of short-term marketable bills. At the same time it discontinued a central bank time deposit facility which had been provided to the banks.

### Commercial banks

Until 1952 a branch of the British Bank of the Middle East was the only commercial bank operating in Kuwait, and other foreign banks were precluded from opening branches. In 1952 a group of Kuwaiti merchants formed the National Bank of Kuwait, which has since risen rapidly in prominence. Another Kuwaiti-owned bank, the Commercial Bank of Kuwait, began operations in April 1961, and in the same year a third local bank, the Gulf Bank, opened for business. Since then three additional commercial banks have been opened. The commercial banks have over 100 branches in Kuwait.

Commercial banks in Kuwait act mainly as intermediaries or clearinghouses for Kuwaiti funds that are to be invested abroad. A substantial proportion of their total resources is invested in foreign assets which have risen sharply, increasing from KD 487 million at the end of March 1973 to KD 1.9 billion at the end of December 1980. The main reason for this investment pattern is the scarcity of domestic investment opportunities. (Nevertheless, as a result of a recent rapid growth of domestic economic and financial activities, there has been a decline in the ratio of foreign to total commercial banks' assets from 63 per cent at the end of 1973 to 39 per cent at the end of December 1980.) Commercial banks maintain a substantial proportion of their foreign assets in short-term deposits with foreign banks abroad. At the same time commercial banks are active in short-term borrowing and investing in European money markets. Although very little is known about the nature of these operations, their existence is evidenced by the erratic movements in banks' foreign liabilities. Movements in commercial banks' net foreign assets tend to reflect developments in international financial markets, especially interest rate changes and the uncertainties associated with the exchange rates of major currencies.

An impediment to the domestic operations of commercial banks was the relative lack of breadth in the local money market. However, in more recent years there has been a substantial expansion in the operations of this market, and this impediment has been removed. Active money market operations take place not only in the interbank deposit and the foreign exchange markets but also in primary and secondary commercial paper, certificates of deposit, and bank acceptances. The interbank money market among Kuwait's commercial and specialized banks has expanded rapidly under the encouragement of the Central Bank. The availability of debt instruments has expanded as a number of international institutions have marketed in Kuwaiti bonds denominated in Kuwaiti dinars since 1973 and domestic financial institutions have initiated since late 1975 the floating of their own bonds. The leading domestic institutions in this respect have been the Industrial Bank of Kuwait and the Kuwait Real Estate Bank, which have floated a number of issues of their own bonds with maturities of from three to ten years. Beginning in October 1977 all commercial and specialized banks were allowed to issue certificates of deposit. Under current regulations, a certificate's term may range up to three years, but most of the KD 54 million of certificates outstanding at the end of October 1979 (and issued by three commercial and two specialized banks) have one year's maturity. The scope of monetary instruments has expanded further with the issuance of short-term bills by the Central Bank.

The sectoral distribution of commercial bank credit in Kuwait has undergone a gradual shift. In 1973/74 commercial bank credit was primarily accounted for by the trade sector (31 per cent), the construction sector (26 per cent), and by personal loans (22 per cent). During the 1975/76 economic boom and the speculative surge in the equity and real estate markets, the sharpest increases in credit were recorded by short-term lending for financial and other services (200 per cent), for the construction sector (55 per cent), and for the trade sector and personal loans (50 per cent each); from a very limited base, credit classified as "other," but which includes borrowing by the specialized banks, expanded by over 400 per cent. In 1976/77 the impact of central bank measures directed at tightening credit policy in order to curb speculative financing was reflected in a sharp decline in the growth of lending for financial and other services, while the rate of growth of credit for personal loans has risen steeply despite the Bank's moral suasion policy. The category of loans extended to the trade and construction sectors has remained in the range of 50–55 per cent, while credit in the "other" category has risen rapidly.

During 1980 and 1981 the Central Bank adopted a number of monetary policy measures. These were designed to help maintain price stability, to encourage growth of the productive sectors, and to restrain speculative activities. In order to rationalize credit operations, banks were asked, for the first time, in January 1980 to scale down the ratio of their overdrafts from the then prevailing ratio of 80 per cent to 55 per cent of their total credit by the end of 1980; this ratio was required to be further reduced to 45 per cent by the end of 1981.

In order to facilitate the holding by banks of bills issued by the Central Bank of Kuwait, an automatic Repurchase Agreement Scheme was introduced during 1981. Under this scheme an emergency overdraft in a bank's current account with the Central Bank could be covered by a part of the bank's bills held in safe custody with the Central Bank, pending the restoration of normal conditions in its balances. The scheme was designed not so much as a source of central bank credit as a device to cover overdrawn accounts through the use of Central Bank of Kuwait bills. It was expected to help extend the ownership base of Central Bank of Kuwait bills to more banks and thereby, in the course of time, to contribute to the flexible operation of the market for them. In addition, financial and investment companies were authorized to hold these bills.

In 1981 the Central Bank permitted the reopening of the primary market for Kuwaiti dinar bond issues. This market had been suspended in 1979 in view of the then severe strain on domestic liquidity. The reopening of the market was accompanied by a number of other measures aimed at reorganizing the management of new issues so as to avoid detrimental effects on domestic liquidity in the future and to ensure the solvency of the borrowers.

Liquidity ratios have been continued as before and a complementary measure of reserve requirements was introduced in the middle of 1980. At the same time, the Central Bank continued its policy of providing liquidity to banks, as and when needed, through swap and rediscount facilities. All these policies were supplemented by the use of moral suasion and close supervision of bank operations.

The Central Bank's policy of stipulating a ceiling on all lending rates for Kuwaiti dinar transactions was continued during the year. This policy is not, however, as rigid in practice as it might otherwise appear. Banks in Kuwait, faced with demand for credit and competition from the international markets, have adopted certain indirect devices to raise the effective cost of credit to their borrowers. Moreover, the ceilings on interest rates have not remained unchanged. Prior to 1977, the overall ceiling on interest rates on loans in Kuwaiti dinars was 7 per cent. This was subsequently raised to 10 per cent. It should be noted that the Central Bank is empowered not only to vary the ceilings but also to introduce multiple ceilings—higher on medium- and long-term loans, and lower on shorter-term commercial loans.

The structure of interest rates in Kuwait may also be considered from the deposit standpoint. The rate on time deposits of banks was about 10–11 per cent in 1980 and 1981, while that on certificates of deposit was about 11 per cent. These rates were highly sensitive, varying with the rates in the interbank market, which, in turn, responded to changes in rates in the international markets. Since deposit rates are allowed to move freely while the maximum on lending rates is fixed, banks' profit margins have narrowed. At the end of 1980, the weighted average cost of Kuwaiti dinar bank time deposits and the weighted average cost of bank loans was 9.3 per cent and 9.2 per cent, respectively. These figures compare with the corresponding figures of 7.9 per cent and 8.5 per cent at the end of 1979. The negative spread late in 1980 did not necessarily imply that the banks incurred losses. This was because a large proportion of their deposits—about one fifth—was in interest-free demand deposits and the maximum rate on savings deposits was much below the rate on time deposits. Furthermore, the banks were generally in a position to cushion their costs by borrowing from the Central Bank at a rate much lower than the interbank rate or the rate they paid on time deposits.

### Other financial institutions

Established financial institutions other than commercial banks are numerous; the major ones are the Kuwait Fund for Arab Economic Development, the Kuwait Investment Company, the Kuwait Foreign Trading Contracting and Investment Company, the Kuwait International Investment Company, the Industrial Bank of Kuwait, the Savings and Credit Bank, and the Kuwait Real Estate Bank. This sector also includes insurance companies, exchange dealers, and stockbrokers.

The role of the publicly owned investment banks such as the Kuwait Fund for Arab Economic Development, the Investment Company, and the Foreign Trading Contracting and Investment Company has been mainly to act as intermediaries in placing abroad part of government surplus funds. The Kuwait Fund for Arab Economic Development has been the vehicle for soft-loan finance, while the other two institutions have concentrated on commercial development finance by underwriting stocks and bonds. The Government has been the most important single source of funds for these institutions. The Government has also participated in their Eurobond transactions and it has on occasion purchased their unsold bonds. With inducements from the Government, these institutions have increased their investment in Arab and non-Arab developing countries. They have done this by providing various lines of credit as well as by establishing direct branch networks and associated companies. Another publicly supported financial institution, the Savings and Credit Bank of Kuwait, provides (only for domestic customers) largely medium-term loans at low interest rates for construction, agriculture, and social purposes. The bank is allowed to accept deposits, fixed and current, on which it pays interest. Its liabilities are fully guaranteed by the Government.

The institutions with private ownership, such as the Industrial Bank of Kuwait, the Kuwait International Investment Company, and the Kuwait Real Estate Bank, extend credit from their own capital and from proceeds of bonds sold to private investors and institutions. They also engage in heavy underwriting of stocks for local and foreign companies. During 1977 and 1978 two new financial institutions were established. The Arab Company for Trading Shares was established in mid-1977 for the purpose of promoting a secondary market in Kuwaiti dinar-denominated money market instruments as well as Eurocurrency-denominated bonds involving Arab management or underwriting. The Kuwait Finance House was established in September 1978 with the objective of conducting interest-free banking in accordance with Islamic law. Holders of time deposits along with the shareholders would receive a proportion of the company's profits. The company does not undertake interest-bearing investments, but instead limits its undertakings to real estate and equities.

Mention should also be made of a regional financial institution, located in Kuwait, in which Kuwait is an active participant. This is the Arab Fund for Economic and Social Development.

## Capital Market

During the last two decades, Kuwait has made substantial progress in expanding its financial system. From only two banks in the 1950s, the system has grown to seven commercial banks, three specialized banks, and several investment and insurance companies, exchange dealers, and stockbrokers. Nevertheless, the capital market in Kuwait is underdeveloped compared with the older, more established markets abroad (even though it is relatively advanced compared with many markets in the region). The Kuwaiti capital market is composed of several isolated markets with different instruments. In the absence of a central securities clearing market, there is no unity among these markets and it is difficult to compare the relative advantages of the instruments. The foreign securities market has less activity than the domestic shares market. The poor performance of the securities markets abroad and exchange rate uncertainties have been the main causes for the sluggishness of the foreign securities market in Kuwait during the last several years. In contrast, the domestic share market is quite active with a relatively large volume of new issues and several secondary markets. Intense activity in the new issues market is a recent development, while activity in the secondary market has been substantial for a number of years. In order to provide a broad base for the domestic market by increasing the number of potential share subscribers, the nominal price of new shares was reduced in 1978 to one Kuwaiti dinar. Among the reasons for the increased activity in the Kuwaiti shares market are the previously noted shift of interest away from foreign securities, a genuine optimism about prospects for Kuwait and the Arab region, a growing belief that the Government will not allow any Kuwaiti enterprise to fail, and the relative ease with which credit can be obtained from the banks which share this belief.

Financial legislation pertaining to the issuance of new shares was enacted so as to forbid trading in shares of new companies before the companies have actually begun operations. Its purpose was to prevent the establishment of companies merely for speculative purposes. Nevertheless, the law was not adequate to cope with the vast expansion in the shares market. One harmful outcome has been speculation. Accordingly, late in 1976 the Ministry of Commerce established a special securities committee to provide guidelines and requirements for the improvement of regulation.

# Law No. 32 of the Year 1968[1]

## Concerning Currency, the Central Bank of Kuwait and the Organization of Banking Business

WE, Sabah al-Salim al-Sabah, Amir of Kuwait,

Having regard to the Constitution, particularly Articles 20, 23, 65, 77, 148 and 154 thereof,

And the Kuwait Currency Law issued under Amiri Decree No. 41 of 1960.

And Law No. 23 of 1962 concerning the accession of the State of Kuwait to the Agreements of the International Monetary Fund and the International Bank for Reconstruction and Development,

And Amiri Decree issued on 12th November 1964 concerning Exchange Control,

And the approval by the National Assembly of the following Law,

Have sanctioned and do hereby promulgate it:

### CHAPTER I. CURRENCY

#### SECTION I. UNIT OF CURRENCY AND PAR VALUE

**Art. 1.** The unit of currency shall be the Kuwaiti dinar and shall be divided into one thousand Fils.

**Art. 2.** The basis for fixing the exchange rate for the Kuwaiti dinar shall be specified by a decree after the opinion of the Governor of the Central Bank has been sought.

**Art. 3.** (1) Every transaction or agreement relating to money or involving the payment of money shall, in the absence of express agreement to the contrary, be deemed to have been made and agreed to be executed on the basis of the Kuwaiti dinar.

(2) The Central Bank shall, whenever necessary and for all legal purposes it defines including the collection of duties, declare the exchange rates for the most important foreign currencies, either on the

[1] Law No. 32 of 1968 (issued on 4 Rabi-ul-Thani, 1388 A. H., corresponding to June 30, 1968) has been amended under Decree Law No. 130 of 1977, issued on October 25, 1977 and published in Arabic in the Official Gazette *Al-Kuwait Al-Yawm,* No. 1164, dated October 30, 1977. This version is based on a translation prepared by the Central Bank of Kuwait. The only legal version is the Arabic text.

basis of the par value declared by the IMF or on any other basis which the Bank may decide.[2]

## SECTION II. ISSUE OF CURRENCY NOTES AND COINS

**Art. 4.** (1) The issue of currency shall be the exclusive privilege of the State. This privilege shall be exercised solely and exclusively by the Central Bank.

(2) No party other than the Central Bank may issue or circulate any notes or coins or any instrument or document payable to bearer on demand and apt to be circulated as legal tender, for the purpose of using them as means of payment in place of the currency issued in accordance with the provisions of this Law.

(3) Any person who violates the provisions of this Article shall be subject to the penalties laid down in the Penal Code for forgery of currency notes or coins.

**Art. 5.** (1) The Central Bank may issue currency notes in the following denominations: one dinar, five dinars and ten dinars, or in such higher denominations as may be specified by a decree issued upon a recommendation of the Minister of Finance and a proposal by the Board of Directors of the Bank.

(2) The above notes shall bear the signatures of the Minister of Finance and the Governor of the Central Bank.

(3) The currency notes referred to in this Article shall be legal tender in the State of Kuwait for the payment of any amount.

**Art. 6.** (1) The Central Bank may issue currency notes of a value less than the unit of currency in denominations of half a dinar and a quarter dinar.

(2) The above currency notes shall bear the signatures of the Minister of Finance and the Governor of the Central Bank.

(3) The currency notes referred to in this Article shall be legal tender in the State of Kuwait for the payment of amounts up to the following limits:

---

[2] The Second Amendment to the Articles of Agreement of the International Monetary Fund, effective April 1, 1978, abrogated par values under the Articles. Provision is made for a new par value system if the Fund decides in its favor by 85 per cent of the total voting power. Should such a decision be taken, each member would be able to decide whether to propose a par value for its currency. Under such a regime the margins around parity within which exchange transactions involving currencies with par values would have to be confined would be wider than those consistent with the original Articles of Agreement.

*(a)* twenty Kuwaiti dinars for half-dinar notes;
*(b)* ten Kuwaiti dinars for quarter-dinar notes.

(4) The Central Bank and the cash-offices of the State and banks operating in the State of Kuwait shall accept currency notes of small denominations without any quantitative limitation.

**Art. 7.** (1) The Central Bank may issue coins.

(2) Non-gold coins shall be legal tender in the State of Kuwait for the payment of any amount up to two dinars, but the Central Bank shall accept them without any quantitative limitation.

(3) The Central Bank may specify the conditions for selling and buying gold coins by its cash-offices.

(4) The Central Bank may issue gold and non-gold commemorative coins, and the Bank shall determine the terms and conditions for the sale and purchase of such coins.

(5) Any person who refuses to accept the Kuwaiti currency provided for in this Article and in the preceding two Articles, as per their traded value and within their relative legal tender, shall be liable to the payment of a fine not exceeding one hundred dinars.

**Art. 8.** The Council of Ministers shall decide the following on the recommendation of the Central Bank:

(1) The wording to be borne by currency notes for indicating their value, as well as the form, design and other characteristics of the notes.

(2) The denominations of coins to be issued by the Central Bank, their designs, forms, standard weights and permitted variations in weight, composition, and other specifications.

## SECTION III. CIRCULATION AND WITHDRAWAL OF NOTES AND COINS

### First: Currency Notes

**Art. 9.** Various denominations of new currency notes shall be put into circulation by a decision of the Board of Directors of the Central Bank, setting out their descriptions and denominations. Such decision shall be published in the Official Gazette and announced to the public by various suitable means of publicity.

**Art. 10.** (1) The Board of the Central Bank may, upon approval of the Minister of Finance, decide to withdraw any denomination of currency notes from circulation against payment of their face value.

Such decision shall be published in the Official Gazette and announced to the public by various suitable means of publicity.

The decision to withdraw shall fix the period for the exchange of withdrawn currency notes, provided that that period shall not be less than 90 days in normal circumstances and 15 days in cases of emergency.

Upon the end of the exchange period specified in the decision of withdrawal the withdrawn currency notes shall cease to be legal tender, but the bearer shall have the right to exchange them in the cash-offices of the Central Bank within ten years from the date of enforcement of the decision to withdraw. Currency notes which are not exchanged during this period shall be deducted from the currency in circulation, and their value shall be added to the account provided for in Article 48 of this Law.

(2) The Central Bank shall be under no obligation to refund the value of any lost or stolen currency notes, or to accept or pay for forged notes.

(3) The Central Bank shall pay the value of mutilated or imperfect currency notes in accordance with the instructions issued by the Bank. Currency notes which do not meet the requirements set out in the instructions shall be withdrawn from circulation without refund.

(4) The Central Bank shall destroy the currency notes withdrawn from circulation in accordance with the instructions issued by the Bank in this connection.

## Second: Non-Gold Coins

Art. 11. (1) Various denominations of non-gold coins shall be put into circulation by a decision of the Board of Directors of the Central Bank, setting out the descriptions of such coins. Such decision shall be published in the Official Gazette and announced to the public by various suitable means of publicity.

(2) Coins of any denomination may be withdrawn against payment of their face value. The decision to withdraw shall be taken by the Board of the Central Bank, published in the Official Gazette and announced to the public by various suitable means of publicity.

(3) The decision to withdraw shall specify the period for exchange which shall not be less than six months.

(4) Coins not presented for exchange within the above-mentioned period shall cease to be legal tender and their value shall be deducted from currency in circulation and added to the Special Account provided for in Article 48 of this Law.

(5) Coins which have been impaired, diminished, lightened or defaced by any cause other than fair wear and tear shall be withdrawn from circulation without refund.

### SECTION IV. CURRENCY COVER

**Art.** 12. Currency in circulation and demand deposits held with the Central Bank shall have a cover consisting, at all times, of the following:

*(a)* gold coins or bullion;
*(b)* demand or time deposits in freely convertible currencies, placed with local banks or placed abroad with central banks, state treasuries, the Bank for International Settlements, the International Monetary Fund or with commercial banks;
*(c)* foreign securities, instruments, bills or certificates issued or guaranteed by foreign governments or by international financial or monetary institutions, provided that they are expressed in freely convertible currencies and easily negotiable in financial markets;
*(d)* foreign securities or bills other than those issued or guaranteed by foreign governments or international financial or monetary institutions, provided that they are expressed in freely convertible currencies and easily negotiable in financial markets;
*(e)* commercial papers expressed in freely convertible foreign currencies and acceptable to foreign commercial banks;
*(f)* treasury bills and bonds issued or guaranteed by the Government of Kuwait, and advances granted by the Central Bank to the Treasury of the Government of Kuwait;
*(g)* domestic commercial papers discounted in the Central Bank, and loans and advances granted to local banks against adequate guarantees.

## CHAPTER II. CENTRAL BANK OF KUWAIT

### SECTION I. ESTABLISHMENT OF THE CENTRAL BANK

**Art.** 13. There shall be established a public institution, having an independent juridical personality, to be called "Central Bank of Kuwait." It shall be referred to in this Law as the Central Bank.

The City of Kuwait shall be the seat of the Bank, and the Bank may open branches in the State of Kuwait and appoint agents and correspondents abroad.

**Art. 14.** The Central Bank shall have a special budget which shall be prepared in a commercial pattern.

The Bank shall be considered as a merchant in its relations with other parties, and its operations and accounts shall be conducted and organised in accordance with commercial banking rules.

Apart from Constitutional provisions in force with regard to the operations, budget and closing account of the Bank, the Board of Directors shall, with the approval of the Minister of Finance, lay down all rules and regulations concerning the administrative and financial affairs of the Bank, including staff and accounting matters, without being limited in all this by the provisions of the Public Tenders and Civil Service Laws.

The provisions concerning advance control in Law No. 30 of 1964 establishing the Audit Bureau shall not apply to the operations of the Central Bank. The functions of the Audit Bureau shall be limited to auditing the accounts and assets of the Bank, and the Bureau shall not, in any manner, interfere in the operations of the Bank or question its policy. The technical officer of the Audit Bureau, assigned to audit the operations of the Bank, shall have adequate technical qualifications and special experience in banking business.

## SECTION II. OBJECTS OF THE CENTRAL BANK

**Art. 15.** The objects of the Central Bank shall be:

(*a*) to exercise the privilege of the issue of currency on behalf of the State;
(*b*) to endeavour to secure the stability of the Kuwaiti currency and its free convertibility into foreign currencies;
(*c*) to endeavour to direct credit policy in such a manner as to assist the social and economic progress and the growth of national income;
(*d*) to control the banking system in the State of Kuwait;
(*e*) to serve as Banker to the Government;
(*f*) to render financial advice to the Government.

## SECTION III. CAPITAL AND RESERVES OF THE CENTRAL BANK

**Art. 16.** The capital of the Central Bank shall be five million Kuwaiti dinars and shall be fully paid by the Government. The capital of the Bank may be increased by decree, and such increase shall be taken from the General Reserve of the Bank.

**Art. 17.** (1) The Central Bank shall establish a General Reserve Fund.

(2) At the end of each financial year net profit shall be the profits realised by the Bank, after deducting the expenses of operations and making the provisions necessary to meet bad or doubtful debts, depreciation in assets, contributions to the Pension Fund and such other contingency expenses usually provided for by banks.

(3) The net profit of the Bank shall be dealt with as follows:

*(a)* The net profit of the Bank shall be paid into the General Reserve Fund until the balance of the Fund amounts to twenty-five million Kuwaiti dinars. The General Reserve Fund may be increased by a decision of the Board of Directors of the Bank with the approval of the Minister of Finance.

*(b)* When the balance of the General Reserve Fund reaches the specified maximum limit the net profit shall be fully paid to the Government.

*(c)* If the General Reserve Fund, in any year, is insufficient to meet the losses of the Bank, or if it cannot be used to meet the losses, the Government shall cover the deficit.

## SECTION IV. MANAGEMENT

**Art. 18.** The management of the Central Bank shall be carried out by a Board of Directors composed of:

*(a)* the Governor, who shall be the Chairman of the Board;
*(b)* the Deputy Governor;
*(c)* a representative of the Ministry of Finance;
*(d)* a representative of the Ministry of Commerce and Industry;
*(e)* four other members;

provided that all members of the Board shall be Kuwaitis.

**Art. 19.** The Governor and the Deputy Governor shall be appointed by decree for a renewable period of five years on the recommendation of the Minister of Finance, provided that they have experience in banking business.

The salaries, allowances and emoluments of the Governor and Deputy Governor shall be fixed by a decision of the Council of Ministers on the recommendation of the Minister of Finance.

**Art. 20.** (1) The Council of Ministers shall, on the recommendation of the Ministers concerned, appoint the representatives of the Ministry of Finance and the Ministry of Commerce and Industry and fix their remunerations, and shall name the alternates to take their place in their absence.

(2) The other members shall be appointed by decree on the recommendation of the Minister of Finance for a renewable period of three years, provided that they shall have experience in economic and financial or banking affairs. Their remunerations shall be fixed by a decision of the Council of Ministers, on the recommendation of the Minister of Finance.

(3) The members referred to in the preceding two paragraphs may not be directors, managers or officials of any bank operating in the State of Kuwait.

**Art. 21.** (1) The Governor shall have the full powers necessary to manage the operations of the Central Bank and to issue the regulations and instructions relevant thereto. He shall be responsible for the implementation of this Law and the regulations of the Bank as well as for the execution of the resolutions of the Board of Directors. He shall be the legal representative of the Bank and shall have the power to sign on its behalf. The Governor may, upon approval of the Board of Directors, delegate some of his powers to the Deputy Governor or to any other official of the Bank.

(2) The Deputy Governor shall temporarily replace the Governor in his absence or if his office becomes vacant.

(3) The Governor and the Deputy Governor shall devote the whole of their professional time to their work in the Bank and, while holding office, neither of them may occupy any other office, or work for any party other than the Bank, whether with or without remuneration, or have an interest in obligations entered into by the Government or public establishments or combine his office with membership in the board of directors of any company.

Exceptions to this shall be the activities related to committees, establishments or organisations formed by the Government, or by public institutions and organisations, and the activities related to international conferences.

**Art. 22.** (1) No person shall be appointed member of the Board of Directors of the Central Bank who:

*(a)* has been convicted of an offence involving dishonesty or misconduct;

*(b)* has been declared bankrupt, or has suspended payment.

(2) Apart from the cases provided for in the preceding paragraph the services of any member of the Board of Directors may be terminated by decree or by a decision of the Council of Ministers, whichever is the relevant means of appointment, in the following two cases:

*(a)* if he gravely violates his duties or commits serious mistakes in the administration of the Bank;

*(b)* if he is absent from all meetings of the Board of Directors during three consecutive months without the approval of the Board, unless such absence is due to his being on official assignment, annual leave or sick leave.

**Art. 23.** The Board of Directors shall convene at the request of the Governor, and the Governor shall summon the Board to convene if the meeting is requested by the Minister of Finance or by three members at least. The meetings of the Board may not be less than eight times a year.

**Art. 24.** At meetings of the Board the quorum shall consist of five members at least, including the Governor or his Deputy and the representative of the Ministry of Finance or his alternate.

Resolutions shall be adopted by a majority of the votes of the members present, and in case of an equality of votes, the Chairman's side shall prevail.

**Art. 25.** The Board of Directors may seek the assistance of experts, and may invite to its meetings any persons whose advice on any particular subject it wishes to listen to.

**Art. 26.** Within the provisions of this Law, the Board of Directors shall exercise the full powers necessary to perform its duties, and shall do the following in particular:

*(a)* draw up the monetary and credit policy of the Bank;

*(b)* decide on matters relating to the issue, circulation and withdrawal of currency;

*(c)* determine the system of discounting and rediscounting commercial papers, granting of loans and advances, and specify the collaterals required;

*(d)* fix the rates of discount, rediscount, interest and commission to be charged by the Bank on loans, advances and discount of commercial papers;

*(e)* decide on matters relating to the organisation and control of the banking business;

*(f)* consider applications received from the Government for advances;

(*g*) fix the maximum limit for advances and loans which may be given to banks operating in Kuwait;
(*h*) fix the amounts allocated for the purchase and discount of public securities or government treasury bills;
(*i*) establish clearing centres;
(*j*) establish Staff and Employees Pension Fund and decide on contributions by the Bank to the said Fund;
(*k*) approve the estimates of the annual revenues and expenditures;
(*l*) review periodically the position of the Bank and the progress of its operations;
(*m*) approve the annual balance sheet, the profit and loss account and the closing account of the Bank. The Board's approval of the estimates of revenues and expenditures, the balance sheet, the profit and loss account and the closing account shall be sanctioned by the Minister of Finance;
(*n*) approve the Bank's annual report to be submitted by the Governor to the Minister of Finance in accordance with the provisions of Article 50 of this Law;
(*o*) issue the internal regulations relating to the financial and administrative affairs, as well as any other regulations it deems necessary for the proper management of the Bank;
(*p*) deal with all matters which under this Law, or any other law, are within the competence of the Board of Directors.

**Art. 27.** The representative of the Ministry of Finance in the Board of Directors may request the suspension of any resolution issued by the Board relating to monetary and credit policy for referral to the Minister of Finance. If the Minister of Finance does not give a decision on the issue within seven days from the date of suspension, such resolution shall become effective.

**Art. 28.** Unless otherwise permitted by law, no member of the Board of Directors, manager, official or employee of the Central Bank shall disclose any information which relates to the affairs of the Bank or its customers or the affairs of other banks subject to the control of the Central Bank and to which he has access by reason of the duties of his office.

Information which shall not be disclosed will be determined by a decision of the Minister of Finance after having obtained the opinion of the Board of Directors of the Central Bank.

Without prejudice to the application of any severer punishment under any other law, anyone who violates the prohibition provided for in the preceding two paragraphs shall be liable to imprisonment for a term not exceeding three months and to the payment of a fine not exceeding two hundred and twenty-five dinars, or to either one of the said punishments plus dismissal from service in all cases.

**Art. 29.** No salary, wages, fees, allowance, remuneration or bonus may be paid by the Central Bank to or for the benefit of those working for it on the basis of the profits realised by the Bank.

### SECTION V. OPERATIONS OF THE CENTRAL BANK

#### First: Relations with the Government

**Art. 30.** The Central Bank will offer advice to the Government in order to facilitate the realisation of its objectives and functions, and the Government will consult the Bank in matters relating to monetary and credit policy.

**Art. 31.** The Central Bank shall act as banker and fiscal agent for the Government. On this basis:

(*a*) government funds in Kuwaiti dinars on current accounts shall be held solely with the Bank. No interest shall be paid by the Bank on such deposits;

(*b*) the Bank shall in general carry out, free of charge, banking transactions and services relating to the Government inside and outside the country;

(*c*) the Government may place funds in Kuwaiti dinars with local banks, after seeking the opinion of the Central Bank and in a manner not conflicting with the monetary policy in force;

(*d*) the Minister of Finance may entrust the Central Bank with the administration of any other Government funds in accordance with the conditions agreed upon at the time;

(*e*) the Ministry of Finance shall transfer to the Central Bank such amounts as may be necessary for the implementation of any particular monetary policy, after the Minister of Finance has approved such policy.

**Art. 32.** (1) The provisions of paragraphs *(a)* and *(b)* of the preceding Article may be applied to municipalities and public establishments by a decision of the Council of Ministers.

(2) As an exception, interest may be paid to these bodies on their deposits, but in this case they shall not be exempt from charges on banking transactions and services.

**Art. 33.** The Central Bank shall enforce the laws and regulations pertaining to exchange control.

**Art. 34.** The Central Bank shall, either directly or through banks and other financial institutions, undertake the operations relating to the sale and management of securities issued or guaranteed by the Government.

The Bank may also undertake operations relating to the sale and management of securities issued in Kuwaiti dinars by any public institution in Kuwait.

**Art.** 35. In accordance with the provisions of Article 26 *(b)* of this Law, the Central Bank may:

*(a)* purchase, sell, discount or rediscount government treasury bills;

*(b)* purchase and sell public debt securities issued and offered for sale by the Government.

**Art.** 36. The Central Bank may not give any loans to the Government, municipalities or public establishments or bodies except in the following case:

The Bank may give temporary advances to the Government to cover deficit in Budget revenues. Such interest as may be determined by the Board of Directors of the Bank in agreement with the Minister of Finance shall be paid by the Government on these advances.

The total of such advances may not, at any time, exceed 10 per cent of the public revenues of the State Budget for the preceding fiscal year.

Such advances shall be repaid as soon as possible. If they are not repaid by the end of the fiscal year following the one during which they were given, the Bank shall not grant any new advances until those outstanding have been repaid.

**Art.** 37. For the purpose of financing development projects or strengthening the financial market, the Central Bank may upon approval of the Minister of Finance:

*(a)* own or sell shares or stocks of any Kuwaiti joint-stock company or concessionary company or public establishment in Kuwait;

*(b)* give loans to banks, public financial or credit establishments, against mortgage of their holdings of such shares or stock;

provided that the total amounts allocated for the acquisition of the aforementioned shares or stocks, or for loans against their mortgage, shall not exceed the value of the reserves of the Bank;

*(c)* issue negotiable bills.

**Art.** 38. (1) The Governor shall keep the Minister of Finance continuously informed of the monetary and credit policy pursued or intended to be pursued by the Bank.

(2) If the Minister of Finance has a different view he may issue general directives to be followed by the Bank, and such directives shall become binding on the Bank.

(3) If the Board of Directors has any objections to these directives, it may submit such objections, together with the reasons for them, in writing to the Minister. The Minister shall then submit the directives, together with the objections, to the Council of Ministers to decide on the matter. The decision of the Council of Ministers on the matter shall be final.

**Art.** 39. Government departments, public institutions and organisations, and companies operating in the State of Kuwait shall submit to the Governor of the Central Bank all information and statistics which the Bank may require for its studies.

**Second: Relations with Local Banks**

**Art.** 40. The Central Bank may:

*(a)* open deposit accounts for banks and financial institutions operating in the State of Kuwait, and for public credit institutions;

*(b)* open deposit accounts for other institutions, upon approval of the Minister of Finance;

No interest shall be paid on the accounts referred to in the preceding two paragraphs except in such special cases as may be decided by the Board of Directors of the Central Bank and approved by the Minister of Finance.

*(c)* open accounts in Kuwaiti dinars with banks;

*(d)* participate with banks in any scheme relating to the insurance of deposits.

**Art.** 41. The Central Bank may carry out the following operations with banks only, and not otherwise:

*(a)* sell, purchase, discount or rediscount commercial papers provided that these shall mature within one year from the date of acquisition, discount or rediscount by the Bank;

*(b)* give loans or advances, in emergency cases, through current account for a period not exceeding six months against such collateral as the Bank may consider adequate.

**Art.** 42. The Central Bank must not:

*(a)* extend the term of loans given under paragraph *(b)* of the preceding Article for more than six months;

*(b)* accept, for discount or as mortgage, commercial papers signed by any member of the Board of Directors or by any one of the Bank's officials or employees.

## Third: Gold and Foreign Exchange Operations Inside and Outside the Country

Art. 43. The Central Bank may:

*(a)* purchase, sell, import and export gold and silver coins and bullion;
*(b)* carry out foreign exchange operations and transfers of all kinds;
*(c)* open accounts with foreign central banks or other banks and with international financial or monetary institutions;
*(d)* open accounts for central banks, or other foreign banks and for international financial or monetary institutions, and act as correspondent for such banks and institutions;
*(e)* grant advances or credits to central banks, other foreign banks or international financial or monetary institutions, and obtain credits, advances or loans from them, provided that such operations are within the scope of its functions as central bank;
*(f)* purchase, sell, discount or rediscount bills or securities or certificates issued or guaranteed by foreign governments or international financial or monetary institutions, provided that they are expressed in freely convertible currencies and are easily negotiable in financial markets;
*(g)* purchase and sell foreign bonds or bills other than those issued or guaranteed by foreign governments or international financial or monetary institutions, provided that they are expressed in convertible foreign currencies and are easily negotiable in financial markets;
*(h)* purchase and sell commercial papers acceptable to foreign banks.

Art. 44. The Central Bank may:

*(a)* invest the Pension Fund set up for the benefit of the officials and employees of the Bank, and grant loans to such officials and employees in accordance with the regulations decided by the Board of Directors;
*(b)* own only such immovable property as assigned for running the business of the Bank;
*(c)* in general, carry out all operations customarily carried out by central banks and not inconsistent with the exercise of its powers or the discharge of its duties under this Law, and undertake such duties as may be assigned to it under any other law.

## Fourth: Prohibited Operations

Art. 45. The Central Bank must not:

*(a)* engage in trade operations outside the scope of its functions

specified in this Law, or have a direct interest in any commercial, agricultural or industrial or any other undertaking except as provided in Article 37;

(*b*) buy or sell immovable property except as provided in paragraph 2 of Article 44. However, the Bank may purchase or acquire, by accord or by forced-sale, movable or immovable property in the way of collecting any of its claims, provided that the Bank shall re-sell such property within the shortest possible time unless it is used for running its business.

(*c*) purchase shares or stocks of companies or public establishments, except as provided in Article 37.

## SECTION VI. ACCOUNTS AND STATEMENTS

**Art. 46.** The financial year of the Central Bank shall be the same as the financial year of the State.

**Art. 47.** The bases for evaluation of the assets of the Central Bank shall be specified by decree.

**Art. 48.** The Central Bank shall enter in a Special Account the profits realized and the losses incurred as a result of altering the exchange rate of the Kuwaiti currency or any foreign currency, or altering the value of gold in terms of the Kuwaiti currency, as well as the profits resulting from the withdrawal of currency notes and coins under the provisions of Articles 10 and 11 of this Law.

Credit balances on this account shall not be entered in the Profit and Loss Account of the Bank. Debit balances shall be met by the Government unless the Board of Directors decides otherwise.

**Art. 49.** The accounts of the Central Bank shall be audited by one auditor or more. The Council of Ministers shall, on the proposal of the Minister of Finance, select the auditor or auditors and fix their fees.

**Art. 50.** The Governor of the Central Bank shall submit to the Minister of Finance:

(*a*) A monthly statement showing the assets and liabilities of the Bank. Such statement shall be published in the Official Gazette.

(*b*) An annual report on the Bank's operations, including the Balance Sheet and the Profit and Loss Account for the ending financial year, and a general review of the monetary, banking, financial and economic affairs. This report shall be submitted not later than four months after the end of the financial year.

(*c*) A report on the events affecting the monetary or financial position, including the causes and outcome of such events and recommendations for handling them.

### GENERAL PROVISIONS

**Art. 51.** The Central Bank shall be exempt from all taxes, duties, and financial dues whatsoever, whether they be for the Treasury, municipalities or any other public institution or body.

The Bank shall also be exempt from the advance payment of judicial fees, deposits and guarantees, and settlement thereof shall be deferred until the case under litigation has been decided.

**Art. 52.** Debts due to the Central Bank shall be treated in the same way as debts due to the Government, and shall take priority over debts due to other creditors. Such debts shall be collected by the same procedures provided for the collection of debts due to the State.

**Art. 53.** The Central Bank may only be liquidated by a law specifying the liquidation procedures and their dates.

## CHAPTER III. ORGANISATION OF BANKING BUSINESS

### SECTION I. ESTABLISHMENT OF BANKS

**Art. 54.** Banks are those institutions whose basic and usual functions involve the receipt of deposits for use in banking operations such as the discount, purchase and sale of commercial papers, granting of loans and advances, issuing and collecting cheques, placing public and private loans, dealing in foreign exchange and precious metals, and any other credit operations or operations considered by the Law of Commerce or by custom as banking operations. For the purposes of implementation of the provisions of this Law, and unless provided otherwise, the branches of any bank operating in the State of Kuwait shall be considered as one bank.

**Art. 55.** The provisions of this chapter shall not apply to:

(*a*) Public credit institutions set up by law.

(*b*) Financial and investment institutions and companies even if they are permitted by their articles of association to receive deposits and execute investment operations and some banking operations.

(*c*) Real-estate companies which undertake the partition of land or the construction of buildings and the sale thereof on credit.

The Board of Directors of the Central Bank may—upon approval of the Minister of Finance—subject all or some of the institutions and companies referred to in this Article to all or some of the provisions of this chapter, or to any rules which the Board of Directors may draw up for purposes of supervision and which are in harmony with the nature of the activities of such institutions and companies.

The opinion of the Central Bank shall be sought in respect of the articles of association and memorandums of agreement relating to financial and investment companies, or amendments thereto, in order to ascertain the economic viability of such companies.

**Art. 56.** (1) Without prejudice to the provisions of the Law of Commerce, wherever they are not in conflict with the provisions of this Law, banking business may only be practised by institutions set up in the form of joint-stock companies the shares of which are placed for public subscription.

(2) Joint-stock companies in which the Government is a cofounder, and branches of foreign banks in which the Government of Kuwait or Kuwaiti banking or financial institutions are shareholders, may be excepted from the provisions of the preceding paragraph by a decision of the Council of Ministers when such banks are permitted to open branches in Kuwait.

(3) Before the formalities of incorporation are processed, the applications for setting up banks should be presented to the Board of Directors of the Central Bank to issue the recommendations necessary.

**Art. 57.** The paid-up capital of any bank shall not be less than three million dinars.

Branches of any foreign bank shall prove that they have allocated an amount equal to this sum for their operations in Kuwait.

**Art. 58.** If the capital of a bank falls below the minimum limit referred to in the preceding Article the bank shall cover the deficit within such period as may be fixed by the Central Bank, provided that the period shall not exceed one year from the date the bank concerned is notified.

The Central Bank shall solely have the right to assess the amount of the deficit in the capital.

## SECTION II. REGISTRATION OF BANKS

**Art. 59.** Without prejudice to the provisions of the Law of Commerce and the Law of Commercial Companies, wherever they are not in conflict with the provisions of this Law, no banking institution is allowed to start operation until it has been registered in the Register of Banks at the Central Bank.

No institutions other than those registered in the Register of Banks are allowed to practice banking business or use in their business addresses, publications or advertisements the terms: "bank," "banker," "bank owner" or any other wording the usage of which may mislead the public as to the nature of the institution.

The Central Bank may—where necessary—ascertain by any means it deems fit that no particular company or individual firm violates the provisions of the preceding paragraph.

Without prejudice to any severer punishment under any other law, anyone who violates the provisions of the preceding two paragraphs shall be liable to imprisonment for a term not exceeding three months and the payment of a fine not less than one hundred dinars but not exceeding two hundred and twenty-five dinars, or to either one of these two punishments. Where the violation is repeated the place of business shall be closed down.

**Art. 60.** Registration or refusal of registration of banks shall be effected by a decision of the Minister of Finance on the recommendation of the Board of Directors of the Central Bank.

The Minister of Finance shall, on the recommendation of the Board of Directors of the Central Bank, issue regulations for the registration of banks, including the rules, procedures and dates for registration, amendments and publication of registration.

**Art. 61.** (1) Registered banks shall notify the Central Bank of any amendment they intend to make to their Memorandum of Agreement or Articles of Association. If such amendment is approved in principle by the Central Bank, the formalities necessary for processing them may then be accomplished in accordance with the provisions of the Law of Commercial Companies. Such amendments shall not be effective until they have been entered in the Register of Banks.

(2) Amendment of entries related to other data which are subject to registration in the Register but not involving amendment of the Articles of Association or Memorandum of Agreement may be effected upon approval thereof by the Governor of the Central Bank.

## SECTION III. DELETION FROM REGISTER AND LIQUIDATION OF BANKS

**Art. 62.** Without prejudice to the provisions of the Law of Commercial Companies, no bank may cease its operations or merge with any other bank unless it is given an advance permission by the Minister of Finance on the recommendation of the Board of Directors of the Central Bank.

The Board of Directors of the Central Bank shall, in such a case, ascertain that the bank has discharged all its obligations toward its customers and creditors in accordance with the general provisions laid down in this respect.

**Art. 63.** (1) A bank may be deleted from the Register of Banks:

(*a*) at its own request;
(*b*) if it does not start business within one year from the date it is notified of the decision regarding its registration in the Register of Banks;
(*c*) if it is declared bankrupt;
(*d*) if it merges with another bank;
(*e*) if it ceases its operations or if its liquidity or solvency are endangered;
(*f*) if it commits any act in violation of the provisions of this Law.

(2) The deletion of any bank under *(e)* and *(f)* above shall not be proposed until the bank concerned has been notified of the proposal and given an opportunity to express its views.

(3) The Minister of Finance shall, on the proposal of the Board of Directors of the Central Bank, issue a decision regarding the deletion. The decision shall be effective from the date of its publication in the Official Gazette.

**Art. 64.** Before proposing the deletion from the Register of any bank the liquidity or solvency of which is endangered, the Board of Directors of the Central Bank may take any or all of the following measures:

(*a*) forbid the bank from undertaking certain operations, or set limits on the business of the bank;
(*b*) appoint a temporary controller to supervise the progress of the bank's business;
(*c*) assign the Central Bank to manage the bank for a certain period of time, and thereafter decide whether the bank can carry on by itself or should be deleted from the Register and liquidated. Expenses incurred for management purposes shall be borne by the bank involved.

In all cases, the Central Bank may—if it deems it in the interest of depositors—ask the appropriate court to issue a decision prohibiting measures against the bank involved and staying all lawsuits filed against it. Such a decision shall be valid for one year.

**Art. 65.** Every bank which it has been decided to delete from the Register of Banks shall be liquidated. The Board of Directors of the Central Bank shall specify the rules for liquidating the transactions outstanding at the time the decision is issued.

## SECTION IV. ACTIVITIES NOT TO BE UNDERTAKEN BY BANKS

**Art. 66.** Banks must not:

(*a*) engage in trade or industry, or own any goods unless such goods have been acquired in settlement of debts due to them. Such goods shall be sold by the bank within one year from the date of acquisition;

(*b*) purchase any real estate other than that required for conducting their business or accommodating their staff, unless such property has been acquired in settlement of debts. In the latter case, the bank shall sell the real estate within a period not exceeding three years. The said period, however, may be extended by a decision of the Board of Directors of the Central Bank;

(*c*) own or deal in their own shares unless such shares have been acquired in settlement of debts due to them, and provided that they sell them within two years from the date of acquisition.

**Art. 67.** Banks may:

(*a*) purchase, for their own account, shares of other commercial companies within a limit of 50 per cent of the bank's own funds. This limit may not be exceeded without prior approval by the Central Bank;

(*b*) own shares or other assets held with them in settlement of debts due to them. In such cases the bank shall dispose of these assets within two years from the date of acquisition.

**Art. 68.** No person who has been convicted of an offence involving dishonourable conduct or dishonesty, or who has been declared bankrupt or has suspended payment, may be a member of the board of directors or a manager of any bank.

**Art. 69.** Banks must not, in any form, give loans or overdrafts through current account, or issue guarantees in favour of the members of their boards of directors without prior permission from the General Assembly. Such loans, advances and guarantees shall be subject to the rules applied by the bank to other customers.

This prohibition shall not include the opening of documentary credits.

**Art. 70.** No bank may issue "travellers' cheques" without prior permission from the Central Bank.

## SECTION V. PROVISIONS RELATING TO SUPERVISION

**Art. 71.** The Central Bank may issue to the banks such instructions as it deems necessary to realize its credit or monetary policy or to ensure the sound progress of banking business.

**Art. 72.** The Board of Directors of the Central Bank may—whenever necessary—draw up rules and regulations to which all banks shall adhere in order to ensure their liquidity and solvency, particularly with regard to the ratios which must be maintained between the following items:

*(a)* the bank's own funds on the one hand and the amount of its liabilities on the other;
*(b)* the bank's liquid funds on the one hand and the aggregate of its term and demand liabilities on the other;
*(c)* the amount of the bank's own funds on the one hand and the amount of its liabilities in the form of acceptances and guarantees on the other.

In the instructions issued and notified by the Central Bank to the banks the Central Bank shall define the meaning of the terms: "bank's own funds," "liquid funds," "liabilities" and such other items.

**Art. 73.** The Board of Directors of the Central Bank may, upon approval of the Minister of Finance:

(1) Fix for banks the maximum amount for discount or loan operations, or for other banking operations which they may carry out with effect from a certain date.

(2) Fix for banks:

*(a)* the minimum amount which customers must pay in cash to cover the opening of documentary credits;
*(b)* the maximum amount which may be lent to any single person—whether natural or juridical—in proportion to the bank's own funds;
*(c)* the proportion of the bank's funds which must be deposited in cash with the Central Bank;

(*d*) the proportion of the bank's funds which must be invested in the local market;

(*e*) the rate of interest which the banks shall pay on deposits, and the maximum rates of interest and commission which they may charge their customers.[3]

**Art. 74.** Decisions issued by the Central Bank in application of the provisions of the preceding two Articles shall have no retroactive effect and shall not hinder the execution of agreements concluded between banks and their customers prior to the issue of such decisions.

**Art. 75.** In the event exceptional circumstances rise and threaten the regularity of banking business, the Governor of the Central Bank may —upon approval of the Minister of Finance—order the banks to close temporarily and to stop all their operations. The banks shall, then, resume their operations by a decision to be issued by the Governor of the Central Bank and approved by the Minister of Finance.

## SECTION VI. SPECIALIZED BANKS

**Art. 76.** Specialized banks are meant to be those banks the main function of which is to finance certain economic sectors, such as the real-estate, industrial or agricultural sectors, and which do not basically receive demand deposits.

**Art. 77.** Specialized banks shall be subject to the provisions relating to the organisation of banking business, wherever such provisions are not in conflict with the nature of the activities of these banks.

The Board of Directors of the Central Bank may lay down special

---

[3] Secs. 110 and 111 of the Law of Commerce provide:

"*Sec. 110.* When the object of an obligation is the payment of a sum of money of which the amount is known at the time the obligation arises, the debtor shall be bound, in case of delay in payment, to pay to the creditor, as damages for the delay, statutory interest at the rate of seven per cent.

"*Sec. 111.* 1. The parties may agree upon another rate of interest, provided that this rate does not exceed the rate of interest published by the Central Bank as determined by the Bank's Board of Directors and approved by the Minister of Finance. If the parties agreed to a higher rate of interest, it shall be reduced to the published rate in effect at the time the contract was concluded, and any surplus paid shall be refunded.

"2. Any commission or other consideration of whatsoever nature stipulated by the creditor which, together with the agreed interest, exceeds the maximum limits of interest set out above, will be considered as disguised interest and will be subject to reduction, if it is not established that this commission or this consideration is in respect of a service actually rendered by the creditor or of a lawful expense."

rules for the supervision of each type of the specialized banks. Such rules shall, in particular, cover the following:

(*a*) terms for receipt of deposits;
(*b*) the maximum limit for the value of bonds specialized banks may issue, as well as the terms for such issue;
(*c*) the terms relating to loans and other credit facilities given by specialized banks;
(*d*) the rules relating to participation in other companies, or the purchase of their shares.

## SECTION VII. INSPECTION OF BANKS AND INSTITUTIONS SUBJECT TO SUPERVISION BY THE CENTRAL BANK

**Art. 78**

(1) The Central Bank shall, at any time, inspect banks and financial companies and institutions subjected to supervision by the Central Bank under the provisions of this Law.
(2) Central Bank staff authorized to conduct inspection shall have the right to see the accounts, books, records, instruments and all documents they deem necessary for inspection. They may ask any member of the board of directors, or any official of the bank or institution to submit and give such data and information they deem necessary for the purposes of inspection. Review of books, records and instruments shall be carried out within the premises of the bank or institution inspected.
(3) The Central Bank shall make a comprehensive report on the findings of inspection made in any bank or institution. The report shall incorporate recommendations on the measures the Central Bank deems useful for rectifying any unsound position discovered through inspection. The Governor of the Central Bank shall send a copy of the report to the chairman of the board of directors or to the manager of the bank or institution inspected. The Governor of the Central Bank may fix a period of grace for the bank or institution to eliminate violations or correct unsound positions discovered through inspection. Periodic dates and rules relating to inspection shall be set by the Board of Directors of the Central Bank.

**Art. 79.** Without prejudice to any severer penalty under any other law, every member of the board of directors, manager, or official of the bank or institution inspected, who refuses to submit information and data or to present books, records, and instruments required by the inspector for inspection purposes, or who gives information or data while knowing that it is untrue, shall be liable to imprisonment for a term not exceeding three months and to the payment of a fine not less than one hundred but not exceeding two hundred twenty-five dinars, or to either of these two punishments.

**Art. 80.** Central Bank officials authorized to conduct inspection shall —during the term of their service and after quitting their jobs—maintain the secrecy of accounts, books, and instruments they review by virtue of their duty. They shall not disclose any information relating to the affairs of banks or institutions inspected, or to the affairs of their customers, except in such cases where it is permissible to do so by law.

Without prejudice to any severe punishment under any other law, every person who violates the prohibition provided for in the preceding paragraph shall be liable to imprisonment for a period not exceeding three months and to the payment of a fine not exceeding two hundred twenty-five dinars, or to either of these two punishments plus discharge from service.

## SECTION VIII. ACCOUNTS AND STATEMENTS

**Art. 81.** Banks shall do the following:

(*a*) end their financial year on the thirty-first of December every year;

(*b*) submit to the Central Bank, within three months from the end of their financial year, their balance-sheet and profit and loss account.

Foreign bank branches permitted to be opened under the provisions of Article 56 of this Law shall maintain independent accounts for all their operations in Kuwait, including balance-sheets and profit and loss accounts.

**Art. 82.** (1) The Central Bank may ask the banks to submit such statements, information and statistical data as the Bank considers necessary to carry out its functions. The Central Bank may also establish a system for the collection of statistics of banking credit on periodical basis.

(2) The nature of such statements, information and statistical data, as well as their forms and the periods during which they should be submitted, shall be specified by the Board of Directors of the Central Bank.

(3) Banks must submit to the Central Bank all the statements, information and statistical data it requests in accordance with the system the Bank lays down for this purpose.

All such information shall remain confidential, but statistical data may be published in consolidated form.

**Art. 83.** The Central Bank may establish a System of Risks for the purpose of assisting banks to evaluate the financial positions of persons applying to them for credit, and for enabling the Central Bank to be constantly aware of the trends of banking credit and to assist in the application of the system of discount and rediscount at the Central Bank.

The Board of Directors of the Central Bank shall lay down the rules and procedures for the System, and shall fix the data and returns relating to its enforcement.

Data and information acquired through the System of Risks shall only be disclosed to persons who should be advised thereof under the rules laid for the implementation of the System.

Without prejudice to any severer punishment under any other law, anyone who violates this prohibition shall be liable to imprisonment for a term not exceeding three months and to the payment of a fine not exceeding two hundred twenty-five dinars, or to either one of these two punishments plus discharge from service in all cases.

**Art. 84**

(1) The auditor shall indicate in his annual report the means and practices whereby he ascertained the assets and evaluated them, and how the valuation of outstanding liabilities was effected by him.

(2) The auditor shall clarify in his report whether the operations audited were contrary to any rules or provisions of the "Law Concerning the Central Bank and the Organization of Banking Business", or to the regulations and decisions issued in pursuance of the said Law. A copy of the report shall be forwarded to the Governor of the Central Bank.

(3) The auditor shall—on request of the Central Bank—sign any statements or accounting data forwarded to the Central Bank by the bank the accounts of which have been checked by the auditor. Such signature shall testify to the correctness of the statements and data.

(4) The auditor may not receive any loans—whether with or without collateral—or guarantees from the bank the accounts of which he audits.

## SECTION IX. ADMINISTRATIVE PENALTIES

**Art. 85.** (1) If a bank violates the provisions of its Articles of Association or the provisions of this Law or the arrangements imposed by the Central Bank in pursuance of the provisions of this Law, or if it fails to submit the documents, statements or information required from it, or submits statements in variance with facts, the following penalties may be imposed on it:

(*a*) warning;
(*b*) reduction or suspension of credit facilities granted to it;
(*c*) prohibition from carrying out certain operations, or the imposition of any other limitations on its business;
(*d*) appointment of a temporary controller to supervise the progress of its business;
(*e*) deletion from the Register of Banks.

(2) The penalties provided for in paragraphs *(a)* and *(b)* shall be imposed by a decision of the Governor. The other penalties shall be imposed by a decision of the Board of Directors of the Central Bank. All this shall be after hearing the explanation of the bank concerned, and the implementation of penalties provided for in paragraphs *(c)*, *(d)* and *(e)* shall require the approval of the Minister of Finance.

## Chapter IV. General and Transitional Provisions

### Art. 86

(1) With effect from the date of coming into operation of the provisions of Chapters I and II of this Law, currency notes and coins issued by the Kuwait Currency Board shall be deemed to be the liabilities of the Central Bank, and such notes and coins shall, for all purposes, be regarded as notes and coins issued by the Central Bank.
(2) The Central Bank shall take over from the Kuwait Currency Board all stocks of unissued currency notes and coins.
(3) The Central Bank may put the notes and coins of Kuwait Currency Board into circulation as notes and coins of the Bank.

### Art. 87

(1) With effect from the date of coming into operation of Chapters I and II of this Law, the Kuwait Currency Board shall transfer to the Central Bank gold and foreign exchange assets equal in value to the currency liabilities taken over by the Bank. Should the assets of the Kuwait Currency Board be insufficient for this purpose, the deficiency shall be made good by the Government.
(2) Any surplus held by the Kuwait Currency Board, after settling

all outstanding commitments, shall be transferred to the General Reserve Fund provided for in Article 17 of this Law.

(3) Gold and foreign exchange assets transferred under the terms of this Article shall be valued in the manner laid down in Article 47 of this Law.

**Art. 88.** As an exception to the provisions of Article 46 of this Law, the first financial year of the Central Bank shall begin as from the date of coming into operation of the provisions of Chapters I and II of this Law, and shall end when the financial year ends. If this period is less than six months, the annual reports which the Governor is required to submit under the provisions of Article 50 shall be submitted at the end of the following financial year.

**Art. 89.** Amiri Decree No. 41 of the year 1960 concerning the Kuwait Currency Law, and the Decrees amending it, shall be repealed as from the date of coming into operation of Chapters I and II of this Law, and the Kuwait Currency Board shall be liquidated after it has submitted its Statement of Accounts and Report for the last accounting period, and after it has settled all its previous commitments.

**Art. 90.** The Minister of Finance shall issue the decisions required for the implementation of this Law.

**Art. 91.** The Ministers—each in so far as he is concerned—shall put this Law into force, and it shall be published in the Official Gazette. An Amiri Decree shall be issued fixing the date of enforcement of this Law in whole or in part.

## Decree Law No. 72 of the Year 1977[1]

### Licensing Establishment of a Kuwaiti Shareholding Company named "Kuwait Finance House"

We, Sabah al-Salim al-Sabah, Amir of the State of Kuwait,

Having regard to Amiri Order issued on the 4th of Ramadan 1396

[1] Issued at Al-Seef Palace on 3 Rabi-ul-Thani, 1397 A.H. [March 23, 1977].

AH, corresponding to 29th August 1976 AD, concerning the revision of the Constitution,

Articles 2, 20, and 13 of the Constitution,

Law No. 15 of the year 1960, promulgating Commercial Companies Law and its amending Laws,

Law No. 2 of the year 1961, promulgating the Commercial Law, as amended by Law No. 7 of the year 1962 and Law No. 102 of the year 1976,

Law No. 32 of the year 1968 concerning Currency, the Central Bank of Kuwait and the Organization of Banking Business,

And upon recommendation of the Minister of Awkaf & Islamic Affairs, the Minister of Commerce & Industry, the Minister of Justice and the Minister of Finance,

And upon approval of the Council of Ministers,

Have sanctioned and do hereby promulgate the following law:

**Art. 1.** The Ministry of Awkaf & Islamic Affairs, the Ministry of Justice (Department of Minors' Affairs) and the Ministry of Finance are hereby authorized to set up a Kuwaiti shareholding company under the name of "Kuwait Finance House," with a capital of KD 10,000,000/- (Kuwaiti dinars ten million).

**Art. 2.** The founders shall, within their legal capacity, abide by the provisions of the Memorandum of Agreement [2] and Articles of Association of the Company, of which official copies are attached hereto.

**Art. 3.** This Licence shall not confer any monopoly or concession on the Company, nor shall it result in any liability on the part of the Government.

**Art. 4.** The Ministers—each insofar as he is concerned—shall enforce this Decree which shall be effective as of the date of its publication in the Official Gazette.

*{The promulgation clause is omitted here.}*

[2] The Memorandum of Agreement is omitted from this volume.

# Articles of Association

## Chapter One. Establishment of the Company

### I. FUNDAMENTALS OF INCORPORATION

**Art. 1.** In accordance with the provisions of law and these Articles of Association, a Kuwaiti shareholding company is hereby established under the name: "Kuwait Finance House," by and between the shareholders, as per the rules of ownership set hereinafter and without prejudice to such rules which exempt the Company from laws in force, as explained in these Articles, and which are confirmed by the law issued with respect to the establishment of the said Company.

**Art. 2.** The head office and legal domicile of the Company shall be in the City of Kuwait, and the Board of Directors may institute branches, offices or agencies for the Company inside and outside Kuwait.

**Art. 3.** The duration of the Company shall be unlimited.

**Art. 4.** The objectives of the Company shall be as follows:

1. To conduct all banking operations and services, whether for its own account or for the account of third parties, without practicing usury in any form whatsoever.

2. To carry out direct investments, or purchase or finance projects or activities owned by others, on a basis that is not usurious.

The Company may cooperate with other organizations which engage in activities similar to its own, or which may assist it to achieve its own objectives. The Company may further participate in such organizations, or associate with them in one way or another, through agency or procuration or integration and may join any consortium recognized by law or by custom, covering holding, subsidiary or associated companies and corporations.

**Art. 5.** With respect to banking services and operations, the Company may for example:

1. Receive various types of cash deposits, either for safe-custody or for conditional or unconditional reinvestment, provided that this shall not be on a usurious basis.

2. Purchase and sell gold bullion, acquire foreign exchange, and sell or purchase drafts in such exchange.

3. Provide short-term financing, against collateral in the form of commercial papers and at an agreed commercial yield not involving usury.

4. Open letters of credit and provide banking credit facilities, with or without security.

5. Issue guarantees in favour of third parties, with or without security.

6. Collect the value of drafts, promissory notes, cheques, bills of lading and all other instruments against commission for the account of permanent customers and other parties.

7. Receive subscription payments related to the establishment of new shareholding companies or capital increases.

8. Purchase and sell shares, certificates of investment and similar financial papers either for the account of the Company or for the account of other parties (not on a usurious basis).

9. Safe-keep all kinds of currencies, precious metals, jewellery, documents, packages and parcels, and rent safes for private use.

10. Act as depository and agent, accept agencies and appoint agents with or without fee.

In general, the Company may carry out all banking operations and services as well as other operations permissible by law, regulations and statutes observed by banks, on condition that such operations shall not be usurious.

**Art. 6.** With regard to investment operations, the Company may, for example:

1. Establish new companies, and participate in or provide financing to companies in existence.

2. Provide individuals, organizations and governments with studies, expertise, research, and advice on capital placements, including the provision of all services concerning such operations.

3. Open documentary credits, and provide all banking facilities with or without security, in return for participation in commercial yields.

4. Engage in various activities related to overland transport and marine and air navigation, or finance such activities for fleet construction or operation.

5. Engage in all kinds of activities related to import and export of crops and various commodities.

6. Finance trade in commodities and movables intended to be offered for sale or rent.

7. Store all kinds of commodities and crops by traditional methods or in modern cold storage facilities or installations.

8. Purchase land and other real estate either for the purpose of selling them in their original condition or after parcellation, or for renting them as open land or including installations, buildings, and equipment added thereto.

9. Establish mutual relief associations subject to Islamic Shari'ah provisions, to insure the Company's own funds, cash deposits and all other fixed and movable assets, as well as mutual insurance organizations for the benefit of other parties.

10. Invest funds in construction activities and related engineering industries, as well as in electrical, mechanical, electronic and related activities.

11. Invest funds in activities related to metal and oil extraction, quarries, fertilizer production and other natural resources.

12. Invest funds in all agricultural enterprises related to production of natural crops, fruits and forests, or to animal husbandry or dairy or wool production.

13. Invest funds for the construction, expansion and replanning of towns, and related infrastructure and housing.

14. Invest funds in fisheries, sponge dredging, pearling and other marine or riverine resources.

15. Invest funds for building ships, tankers and boats of all kinds and sizes, and for construction of dry docks, floating docks, and shipping maintenance and repair yards.

16. Invest funds for digging, widening, dredging and maintaining canals.

17. Invest funds in public information media, such as newspapers, magazines, radio, television and cinemas, and in projects for verification, publication and dissemination of human heritage, as well as in activities related to archeological excavations and exhibits.

In general, the Company may carry out all such activities as may assist it realize its banking and investment objectives whether directly or through cooperation with other organizations, companies and governments, provided that it shall not do so on a usurious basis.

## II. CAPITAL OF THE COMPANY

**Art. 7.** The capital of the Company shall be KD 10,000,000/- (Kuwaiti dinars ten million) divided into ten million shares of one dinar each. All shares shall be paid for in cash.

**Art. 8.** The founders shall subscribe to 4,900,000 shares (four million nine hundred thousand shares) in the capital of the Company, and undertake to pay twenty-five per cent of the nominal value amounting to four million nine hundred thousand dinars by deposit with one of the registered banks in Kuwait.

The remaining shares, amounting to five million one hundred thousand, shall be placed for public subscription in Kuwait, and the founders shall specify the procedures and conditions for subscription.

**Art. 9.** The shares of the Company shall be nominal and shall not be owned by non-Kuwaitis.

**Art. 10.** Each subscriber shall pay twenty-five per cent of the share's value at the time of subscription. The remaining value must be paid within the maximum of five years from the date of issue of the establishment Decree, on such dates and in such manner as may be determined by the Board of Directors. In case of default by any subscriber, the Board of Directors shall have the right to sell the shares for the account of such shareholder, on his own responsibility and without need for any advance official notification provided that such sale shall be by auction. The Board shall then have priority to collect from the proceeds of the sale the value of installments due on the shares plus all relative charges, and refund the balance to the defaulting shareholder. In case the proceeds of the sale are insufficient to cover the amount due, the Company shall have the right to set claim against the shareholder's private funds.

**Art. 11.** No person may subscribe to more than fifty shares, or at any time own more than 4,000 shares (four thousand shares) except through inheritance or will.

**Art. 12.** The Board of Directors shall issue each shareholder a provisional certificate representing the shares he owns, within three months from the date the incorporation of the Company is declared final.

Final delivery of shares shall be effected by the Board within three months from the date of payment of the last installment.

**Art. 13.** Ownership of shares shall *ipso facto* purport acceptance of the Articles of Association of the Company and the resolutions of the General Assembly.

**Art. 14.** Each share shall entitle its holder to such unprivileged and equal right as that of other shareholders in both ownership of the assets of the Company and in dividends distributable in the manner indicated hereinafter. As the Company's shares are nominal, the last owner whose name is registered in the Company's records shall solely have the right to receive the share earnings whether in the form of dividends or equity in the Company's assets.

**Art. 15.** The capital of the Company may not be increased unless the value of the original shares has been paid in full. New shares may not be issued at less than their face value but where such shares are issued at more than that value, the difference outstanding after paying off the expenses of the issue shall be added to the statutory reserves. The General Assembly shall have the right either to determine priorities related to subscription to new share issues or forgo such priorities or restrict them.

## Chapter Two. Management of the Company

### I. BOARD OF DIRECTORS

**Art. 16.** The Company shall be managed by a Board of Directors consisting of ten members of whom five shall be appointed by the founders and the other five elected by the General Assembly in secret ballot.

Members of the Board of Directors shall serve for a term of three years, and may be re-elected.

**Art. 17.** An elected member of the Board of Directors should be the owner of not less than five hundred shares—either through his personal capacity, or through representation of a juristic entity. If at the time of election a member did not own this number of shares, he shall have to acquire such number within one month, otherwise his membership shall drop. This number of shares shall be retained as membership commitment guarantee, and shall be deposited with the Company within one month from the date of appointment, to be held therewith—without being negotiable—until the term of membership ends, and the balance sheet for the last fiscal year during which the member performed his duties has been approved. If a member, however, fails to submit the guarantee in the above-prescribed manner, his membership shall be considered void.

With respect to the first Board of Directors, however, a member of the Board shall deposit the membership guarantee shares within three months from the date the first Company balance sheet is published for a period of at least twelve months.

**Art. 18.** A member of the Board of Directors may not be a member of the Board of Directors of any similar or competitory company, nor may he be a merchant engaged in business similar to or competitory with that of the Company, or have any direct or indirect interest in contracts and transactions concluded with the Company, or for its own account, or have an interest conflicting with the Company's unless he is given special authorization by the General Assembly, and under such conditions as the Company may apply to deals with third parties.

Neither the Chairman nor any member of the Board of Directors—even where he represents a juristic entity—may use any information acquired by virtue of his position, for his own benefit or for the benefit of others, nor may he sell or buy the Company shares during the term of his service as a member of the Board of Directors.

**Art. 19.** In the event the post of an elected member of the Board of Directors becomes vacant it shall be occupied by the unsuccessful candidate who had obtained the highest number of votes in the latest ballot.

In the event the vacant posts are equal to one quarter of the original number of posts, or no qualified candidates are available, the Board of Directors must convene the General Assembly within two months from the date on which the last post became vacant for election of members to fill the vacant posts. In all such cases, the new member shall only serve up to the end of the term of his predecessor.

**Art. 20.** The Board of Directors shall elect its Chairman and Deputy Chairman by secret ballot for a three-year term.

**Art. 21.** The Chairman shall represent the Company before judicial authorities and shall be responsible for the execution of resolutions passed by the Board.

The Deputy Chairman shall replace the Chairman in his absence as well as in case he is incapacitated.

The Board of Directors may appoint one or more of its members as Managing Director, and may also appoint a General Manager for the Company and determine his duties.

**Art. 22.** Authority to sign solely on behalf of the Company shall be given to the Chairman of the Board of Directors, or to his Deputy in his absence, or to any other member assigned for the purpose by the Board.

**Art. 23.** The Board of Directors shall convene at the request of the Chairman at least once every three months. It shall also convene if requested to do so by at least three Board members. At meetings of the Board, a quorum shall consist of the majority of members, but attendance by proxy shall not be held valid.

**Art. 24.** Resolutions of the Board of Directors shall pass by majority of the votes of the members present, and in case of a tie, the Chairman shall have a casting vote. Minutes of the Board meeting shall be recorded in a special register to be signed by the Chairman, and any dissenting member may request that his opinion be recorded therein.

**Art. 25.** A member of the Board of Directors shall lose his post in any of the following cases:

1. If he fails to attend four consecutive meetings without valid justification upon a resolution by the Board of Directors.
2. If he submits his resignation in writing.
3. If he becomes incapacitated.
4. If he is declared bankrupt.
5. If he occupies any salaried position in the Company, other than the post of Chairman, Managing Director or General Manager.
6. If he is convicted of an offence involving dishonesty or misconduct.

**Art. 26.** Without prejudice to the provisions of the Law of Commercial Companies, the Ordinary General Assembly shall fix the remunerations of the Board of Directors, and the Board of Directors shall fix the remunerations of the Managing Directors and the salary of the General Manager.

**Art. 27.** The Board of Directors shall have full authority to manage the Company and to conduct all such activities as may be required to realize the objectives of the Company. The Board's authority shall only be limited by restrictions provided for by Law, by these Articles, or by such resolutions as may be issued by the General Assembly.

The Board of Directors may, in particular, pay all initial fees and expenses required for the establishment of the Company, including fees and expenses related to registration, publication and implementation of requirements embodied in the Memorandum of Agreement. It may also carry out all legal procedures required for these purposes, fix the general expenses for the Management, draw up Company by-laws and work procedures and appoint managers, supervisors, officers, deputies and assistants of all administrative levels. Furthermore, the Board may draw up job descriptions, specify staff authorities and responsibilities, and fix their salaries and bonuses.

**Art. 28.** The Board of Directors shall have full power to purchase and sell movables and immovables, and to dispose of the Company's assets in whole or in part by sale or otherwise, against such price as it may deem profitable, or in exchange for shares, stocks or other financial papers issued by any other company. The Board shall also have power to borrow or acquire money in such manner as it may deem suitable, inside or outside Kuwait, and to conclude lease agreements or any and all transactions it deems suitable and within the Company's objectives. The Board of Directors may further sell or mortgage the Company's property, or issue guarantees or conclude loans against security of the Company's real estate; provided that all this shall not be effected on a usurious basis. Moreover, the Board may give permission for filing lawsuits or defending the interests of the Company before courts, whether the Company is plaintiff or defendant. It may also endorse reconciliation and arbitration, quash entries, waive rights—with or without recompense—and decide how the Company's assets including reserves should be used. In general, the Board shall manage the Company in the most appropriate way.

**Art. 29.** The members of the Board of Directors shall not be personally held liable for Company undertakings by reason of performing their duties within the limits of their competence.

**Art. 30.** The Chairman and members of the Board of Directors shall account to the Company, the shareholders and third parties for any fraudulent act, misuse of authority, violation of the Law or of the Articles of Association or mismanagement.

No vote by the General Assembly shall absolve the Board of Directors from responsibility, or prevent the filing of lawsuits against it for liability.

## II. GENERAL ASSEMBLY

**Art. 31.** Invitations for meetings of the General Assembly, of whatever nature, shall be addressed to the shareholders by registered mail and shall include the agenda. The agenda for meetings of the Constituent General Assembly shall be prepared by the founders but the agenda for meetings of the Ordinary or Extraordinary General Assembly shall be prepared by the Board of Directors.

Where it is permissible to convene the General Assembly at the request of the shareholders, or the auditors, or the Ministry of Commerce and Industry, the agenda shall be prepared by the party requesting the meeting, but items not listed on the agenda may not be discussed at such meetings.

**Art. 32.** Each shareholder shall be entitled to a number of votes equal to the number of shares he owns. Attendance of meetings by proxy shall be allowed, and minors and interdicted persons shall be represented by their legal conservators.

No shareholder or representative by proxy may vote on his own behalf or on behalf of the person he represents on matters connected with his personal interest or on disputes between him and the Company.

**Art. 33.** Shareholders shall register their names in a special record to be prepared for this purpose at the Head Office of the Company, at least twenty-four hours prior to the date set for the meeting of the General Assembly. Each shareholder shall be provided with an admission card indicating the number of votes he is entitled to.

**Art. 34.** The quorum for meetings of the General Assembly, and for the majority of votes necessary to pass resolutions, shall be subject to the provisions of the Law of Commercial Companies.

**Art. 35.** Voting in General Assembly meetings shall be carried out in such manner as may be prescribed by the Chairman unless the General Assembly decides otherwise. The election and discharge of the members of the Board of Directors shall be conducted by secret ballot.

**Art. 36.** The founders shall—within thirty days from the date of closing subscription—invite the shareholders to meet as a Constituent General Assembly, and shall submit a report on the formalities of incorporation of the Company, together with the relevant supporting documents. The General Assembly shall ascertain the correctness of such documents and their conformity with the provisions of the law, the Memorandum of Agreement and the Articles of Association. The Assembly shall also look into reports which may be submitted by the Ministry of Commerce and Industry in this connection, and elect the members of the Board of Directors, appoint the auditors, and announce the final incorporation of the Company.

**Art. 37.** The Ordinary General Assembly shall convene upon invitation of the Board of Directors at least once a year, but within three months from the end of the fiscal year of the Company. The Board of Directors may call this General Assembly whenever it deems necessary, and shall also convene it whenever requested to do so by a number of shareholders owning not less than one tenth of the capital. The General Assembly shall also convene if so requested by the Ministry of Commerce and Industry.

**Art. 38.** The Ordinary General Assembly shall have power to consider all matters related to the Company's activities, except for those matters which by Law and/or the Articles of Association are to be considered by an Extraordinary Assembly or by the Constituent Assembly.

**Art. 39.** The Board of Directors shall submit to the Ordinary General Assembly a full report on the operations of the Company and its financial and economic position, including the Balance Sheet, Profit and Loss Account, the Board of Directors' remunerations, the auditor's fees, and a proposal for distribution of dividends.

**Art. 40.** The Ordinary General Assembly shall consider and decide on the report of the Board of Directors, and shall review the auditor's report, and the report of the Ministry of Commerce and Industry, if any. It shall also elect the members of the Board of Directors and determine their remunerations and appoint the auditors for the next year and fix their fees.

**Art. 41.** The Extraordinary General Assembly shall convene either upon invitation by the Board of Directors or upon a written request from a number of shareholders holding not less than one quarter of the Company's shares. In the latter case, the Board of Directors shall convene the General Assembly within one month from the date on which the Board receives the request.

**Art. 42.** The following matters shall be considered only by an Extraordinary General Assembly:

1. Amendments to the Memorandum of Agreement or the Articles of Association of the Company.

2. Sale or disposal of the Company's entire project.

3. Dissolution of the Company, or its merger or affiliation with any other company or entity.

4. Increase or decrease of the Company's capital.

However such amendments, disposal, merger, affiliation or any other action aimed at bolstering the Company's financing capability shall not under any circumstances infringe on the concept of not dealing with usury in any form whatsoever.

Moreover, no amendment to the Articles of Association of the Company shall be considered effective except after the Ministry of Commerce and Industry has approved it, and all requirements in the Law concerning Currency, the Central Bank of Kuwait and the Organization of Banking Business, and the Law of Commercial Companies have been satisfied. Furthermore, no amendment involving the name of the Company, or its objectives or capital (excluding increase of the capital through issue of shares against profits realized by the Company, or as a result of adding nonblocked reserves to the capital), shall be considered effective unless a Decree is issued in connection therewith.

## III. OPERATIONS OF THE COMPANY

### A. DEPOSITS

**Art. 43.** The Company shall receive two kinds of deposits:

1. Deposits not committed for investment, which shall take the form of current accounts, saving accounts and ordinary deposits at call.

2. Deposits committed for conditional or unconditional investment.

**Art. 44.** Deposits not committed for investment may be withdrawn from the Company in whole or in part at any time.

**Art. 45.** Deposits committed for investment shall be included within funds assigned for investment in projects carried out by the Company itself, or for financing third-party projects. Commitment of deposits may either be limited to investment in any one particular project, e.g., real-estate, industrial, financial or any other type of Company projects, or made absolute and unconditional.

The deposit agreement shall specify whether the deposit is for limited or unlimited term.

Where a deposit is intended for an unlimited term the agreement shall specify the period of notice to be served to the Company in advance of withdrawal and settlement of the deposit investment account.

Deposits made for limited periods shall, in essence, not be withdrawable before the date specified in the deposit agreement. As an exception to this rule, they may be withdrawn before such date under special circumstances upon request of the depositor, and with the approval of the Board of Directors, provided the depositor shall relinquish his profits either for the whole fiscal year during which withdrawal took place or for part thereof as may be decided by the Board of Directors.

**Art. 46.** Profits on deposits committed for investment shall be calculated on a pro rata basis with the capital of the Company. If the rate of profit distribution exceeds 20 per cent, an extra rate of profit not exceeding 10 per cent may be assigned to the capital and any surplus shall be added to the reserves.

### B. ROUTINE BANKING OPERATIONS

**Art. 47.** The Board of Directors shall lay down special by-laws for the Company's banking services, specifying, in particular, the rates of fees and commissions which the Company shall charge for such services, provided that such rates shall not be usurious in any manner whatsoever.

### C. FINANCING

**Art. 48.** The Board of Directors shall lay down a plan for investment of the Company's own funds as well as the funds of deposits in different economic sectors on short, medium and long terms and in such way as to achieve the Company's objectives within the framework of public interest.

**Art. 49.** The Board of Directors shall form a permanent ad hoc committee to assist it in implementing the plan referred to in Article 48.

**Art. 50.** The Board of Directors shall specify the percentage of the working capital to be used for financing any new or existing project, provided that such percentage shall not exceed 5 per cent for any one project or 30 per cent for all short-, medium- and long-term projects.

**Art. 51.** The Board of Directors shall decide the percentage for Company participation in any new project or for financing any existing project, provided that such percentage shall be within the limit permissible by the financial position of the Company and the technical considerations required by law or custom.

### IV. ACCOUNTS OF THE COMPANY

**Art. 52.** The Company shall have one or more certified auditors whose appointment and fees shall be decided by the General Assembly, and who shall be responsible for auditing the accounts for the fiscal year for which he is appointed.

**Art. 53.** The fiscal year of the Company shall commence on the 1st of January and end on the 31st of December each year, with the exception of the first fiscal year which shall commence from the date of final incorporation of the Company and end on the 31st of December the following year.

**Art. 54.** The auditor shall have such power and carry out such obligations as stated in the Law of Commercial Companies. In particular, he shall have access to all books, records and documents of the Company at all times, and may request any information he may deem necessary. He shall also have the right to ascertain the assets and liabilities of the Company, and in the event he is obstructed or unable to exercise these powers he shall report the fact in writing to the Board of Directors and to the General Assembly. He may also invite the General Assembly to convene for this purpose.

**Art. 55.** The auditor shall submit to the General Assembly a report stating whether the Balance Sheet and Profit and Loss Account reflect fairly the actual financial position of the Company; whether the Company keeps proper books of account; whenever inventories were conducted in accordance with established practices; whether the information given in the report of the Board of Directors is in agreement with the books of the Company; whether any violations of the law or the Company Articles of Association were committed during the fiscal year in such a way as to materially affect the Company's activities or financial position; and in his capacity as agent for all shareholders, the auditor shall be responsible for the accuracy of the information contained in his report, and any shareholder may, during the General Assembly meeting, discuss and request clarification on the contents of the auditor's report.

**Art. 56.** A percentage of the gross profits shall be fixed and allocated by the Board of Directors for formation of special reserves such as debt reserves, currency fluctuation reserves, depreciation reserves and any other reserves and allocations required by law or custom or under the provisions of these Articles.

**Art. 57.** A percentage of the gross profits shall be fixed and allocated by the Board of Directors for amortization or depreciation of the Company's assets. Such deduction shall be used for purchase of materials, machines and replacements for repair. Moreover, a portion of the gross profits shall also be recommended by the Board of Directors and approved by the Ordinary General Assembly, for discharge of the Company's obligations under labor laws.

**Art. 58.** The net profits shall be disposed of as follows:

1. Ten per cent to be allocated to the Statutory Reserve Account.

2. Ten per cent to be allocated to the Voluntary Reserve Account. This allocation shall be stopped by a decision of the Ordinary General Assembly on the recommendation of the Board of Directors.

3. A five per cent deduction shall be set aside as first portion of the profits to be distributed among shareholders and investment depositors for the paid value of their shares.

4. An amount not exceeding 10 per cent of the net profits shall then be set aside as remunerations for the Board of Directors, pending approval of the Ordinary General Assembly.

5. The remaining portion of profits shall either be distributed among shareholders and investment depositors as an extra profit, or carried forward to the following year on the recommendation of the Board of Directors or allocated for formation of a reserve for settlement of profits in such years where the net profit is inadequate, or for formation of extraordinary allocations.

**Art. 59.** Dividends shall be paid to shareholders at such place and time as may be specified by the Board of Directors.

**Art. 60.** The reserve funds shall be utilized upon decision of the Board of Directors to the best interest of the Company. The statutory reserve shall not be distributed among shareholders, but may be used to secure distribution, among shareholders, of dividends amounting to 5 per cent in such years where the profits of the Company do not facilitate distribution up to such percentage.

If the statutory reserve exceeds half the capital of the Company, the General Assembly may decide to discontinue deductions or to use the excess amount in such manner as it deems appropriate and in the interest of the Company and its shareholders.

**Art. 61.** Cash funds of the Company shall be deposited with such bank or banks as may be specified by the Board of Directors. The Board of Directors shall fix the maximum limit for cash which the treasurer may hold in the Company's safe. All such arrangements shall be made with full regard to legal provisions concerning deposits with the Central Bank of Kuwait.

## Chapter Three. Consultative Bodies

**Art. 62.** The Company shall retain consultative bodies specialized in economic, financial and legal studies. Such specialized body—or bodies—may be composed of a number of experts of international repute. For certain specialties, the Company may retain only one expert or counselor, but appointment of all such experts and counselors shall be effected by decision of the Board of Directors. The relationship between such appointees and the Company shall be limited to such studies as may be assigned to them, and their research and recommendations shall be submitted either to the Chairman of the Board of Directors or to such Board members as may be delegated by the Board for the purpose.

**Art. 63.** Consultative bodies, experts and individual consultants shall basically execute their assignments in Kuwait. However, consultation sessions may in special cases be held outside Kuwait, under a decision to be issued by the Board of Directors covering each and every case per se on the recommendation of the Chairman or the Managing Director. In this respect, the Board's decision shall specify the person who should represent the Board of Directors at such session or sessions outside Kuwait.

**Art. 64.** The Board of Directors shall, upon recommendation of the Chairman or the Managing Director, determine the terms of reference for the consultative bodies, experts and individual consultants, regardless whether their relationship with the Company is permanent or occasional. Moreover, the Board of Directors shall lay down rules within the Company's by-laws concerning such activities and assignments.

## Dissolution and Liquidation of the Company

**Art. 65.** The Company shall, *ipso jure,* be dissolved and liquidated for any of the reasons provided for in the Law of Commercial Companies.

Art. 66. On dissolution, the Company's holdings shall be liquidated in accordance with the relevant provisions of the Law of Commercial Companies, and the Law concerning Currency, the Central Bank of Kuwait and the Organization of Banking Business.

## Law No. 30 of the Year 1965[1]

### Establishing the Credit and Savings Bank

We, Abdallah al-Salim al-Sabah, Amir of Kuwait,

After perusing Articles 20, 23, 65, 136, and 137 of the Constitution, and Law No. 40 for the year 1965 for the establishment of the Credit Bank, amended by Laws Nos. 8, 12, 18, and 33 for the year 1961, the National Assembly has approved the law whose text follows:

We have ratified it and enacted the same.

Art. 1. A Bank by the name of "Credit and Savings Bank" is to be established as a public corporation which shall have an autonomous legal personality under the supervision of the Minister of Finance and Industry.

The headquarters of the Bank shall be situated in the city of Kuwait. The Bank can open branch offices in Kuwait and can appoint agents and intermediaries abroad. The Bank shall be allowed to designate individuals and other legal entities to act on its behalf, by proxy, with respect to some of its operations and in compliance with its by-laws.

The Bank shall have a president and a vice-president to be appointed by a decree from the Minister of Finance and Industry.

The Bank shall be managed by a board of directors whose structure and competence are specified in its by-laws.

The president shall represent the Bank in its relations with others and before the court.

Art. 2. The Bank shall have an independent budget which shows its receipts and expenditures and which is drafted and implemented in accordance with the regulations contained in its by-laws.

---

[1] The law was issued on 10 Rabi-ul-Awwal, 1385 [July 8, 1965].

**Art. 3.** The by-laws of the Bank are issued by a resolution from the Minister of Finance and Industry. The regulations and by-laws followed heretofore by the Credit Bank shall remain in effect—as long as they do not contradict the terms of this law—until another set of by-laws is issued.

**Art. 4.** The Bank—in accordance with the terms and conditions specified in its by-laws—shall attempt to achieve the following objectives:

First, providing credits for real estate, industrial, and agricultural purposes, in the State of Kuwait, for Kuwaiti citizens and Kuwaiti legal entities. Priority shall be given to the following loans:

(*a*) *Real Estate Credits*

1. Providing individuals with loans—guaranteed by mortgage—to construct private dwellings, to repair the existing ones, or to render them more useful.

2. Giving loans to cooperatives and institutions authorized by law —guaranteed by mortgage—for the purpose of building dwellings for their members.

3. Granting loans guaranteed by the Government to citizens whose income is limited and who do not, as yet, possess title deeds. The loans are to be used for building dwellings or enlarging the existing ones. However, the title deeds will not be issued to the beneficiaries until they have paid all the necessary payments to the Bank.

(*b*) *Industrial Credits*

Providing loans to the owners of factories and industrial projects guaranteed by mortgage or the fixed assets of the plant. The loans are to be used for setting up factories, enlarging or improving the existing ones, or constructing housing units for their workers.

(*c*) *Agricultural Credits*

Providing loans to farmers guaranteed by mortgage or their agricultural produce, so that they can purchase seeds, fertilizers, farming machines, cattle or for breeding poultry, constructing water pipelines, digging wells, or other related agricultural activities.

Second, providing social credits to citizens guaranteed by mortgage, shares of Kuwaiti companies which are legally recognized, personal pledge from a co-signer of solid financial status, pledge from the employer, the salaries, remunerations, or the accrued pensions of the officials, employees, or workers, in compliance with the prevailing laws.

Third, mobilizing the savings, investing them, and paying the investment returns to the savers. The Government guarantees the savings and their returns.

**Art. 5.** The Bank, in order to achieve the objectives specified in the preceding Article, is entitled to own and dispose of real estate and transfers.

The Bank is also allowed to establish or to participate in establishing firms which engage in activities that have bearing on its objectives and help to achieve them. The Bank may subscribe to the capital of such firms, may contribute to the implementation of the construction projects, and may invest its surplus funds in any type of secured investments.

**Art. 6.** The capital of the Bank is 20,000,000 dinars, to be drawn from the general reserve fund of the State. The Minister of Finance and Industry is authorized to do this in one or more payments. Some of the payments can be in the form of a transfer to the Bank of government financial claims on others.

Also considered part of the capital are the funds which had already been paid to the Credit Bank, which was established by Law No. 40 for the year 1960.

**Art. 7.** The Bank can borrow funds from the Government or from others, with the Government acting as a guarantor, within limits that do not exceed its paid-in capital.

The Bank can also borrow by issuing bonds. The terms which determine the issuing and maturity of such bonds must be established by a decree.

**Art. 8.** The assets and liabilities of the Credit Bank, which was established by Law No. 40 for the year 1960, and amended by Laws Nos. 8, 12, 18, and 33 for the year 1961, are to be transferred to the Credit and Savings Bank.

**Art. 9.** With the exception of the provisions of Article 118 of the Law of Commerce, discerning minors are allowed to deposit their savings in the Bank. The terms of depositing and withdrawing of such savings are subject to the provisions and conditions set by the Board of Directors in this regard.

**Art. 10.** The officials, employees, and workers of the Bank are subject to the provisions of the Public Civil Employment Law.

**Art. 11.** Law No. 40, for the year 1960, which established the Credit Bank, together with its amendments, Laws Nos. 8, 12, 18, and 33 for the year 1961, are to be abolished.

Art. 12. The Minister of Finance and Industry, and all other Ministers of the Cabinet—each within his own jurisdiction—are to implement this law and put it into effect on the date it is published in the official journal.

*[The promulgation clause is omitted here.]*

## Law No. 25 of the Year 1974 [1]

### For the Reorganization of the Kuwait Fund for Arab Economic Development

We, Jaber al-Ahmed al-Jaber al-Sabah, Deputy Amir and Crown Prince of the State of Kuwait,

Having considered Article 61 and Article 65 of the Constitution,

And Law No. 35 (1961) for the Establishment of the Kuwait Fund for Arab Economic Development, as amended by Law No. 9 (1963) and Law No. 64 (1966),

Hereby assent to and enact the law passed by the National Assembly and set forth herein below:

Art. 1. The Kuwait Fund for Arab Economic Development, hereinafter called the Fund, shall be a public corporation with an independent legal personality under the supervision of the Prime Minister who shall be the Chairman of its Board of Directors.

Art. 2. The purpose of the Fund is to assist Arab States and Developing States in developing their economies and, in particular, to provide such States with loans for the implementation of their development programs, in accordance with the provisions of a Charter to be made by Order of the Prime Minister.

Art. 3

(*a*) The capital of the Fund shall be one thousand million Kuwaiti dinars.

[1] Given at Al-Sif Palace on 27 Jumada-al-Thani, 1394 A.H. [July 17, 1974].

(*b*) An amount of four hundred million Kuwaiti dinars of the said capital shall be paid out of government reserves by transfers made from time to time according to the needs of the Fund.

(*c*) The remaining part of the Fund's capital amounting to six hundred million Kuwaiti dinars shall be paid out of the public revenues of the State by the appropriation of a percentage of the said revenues annually.

The law enacting the State Budget shall determine in each year the percentage of public revenues to be appropriated for payment of the aforesaid part of the capital.

**Art. 4.** The Fund may borrow and issue bonds subject to the limit of twice the amount of its capital and reserves in accordance with such terms and conditions as may be determined by the Prime Minister upon the recommendation of the Board of Directors.

**Art. 5.** The Fund shall be administered by a Board of Directors in accordance with the Charter.

**Art. 6.** The Prime Minister shall lay down the Charter of the Fund, which shall, in particular, provide for the composition of the Board of Directors and its functions, regulate the technical and administrative work of the Fund and the manner of preparing its budget; and prescribe such other procedures as may be necessary for the proper conduct of the affairs of the Fund.

**Art. 7.** The Prime Minister may delegate all or part of his powers under this law to the Minister of Finance and Oil.[2]

**Art. 8.** Law No. 35 (1961) for the Establishment of the Kuwait Fund for Arab Economic Development is hereby repealed. However, all Orders made for its implementation not in conflict with the provisions of this law shall remain in force until superseded by new orders.

**Art. 9.** The Prime Minister and the Minister of Finance and Oil shall implement this Law which shall take effect from the date of its publication in the Official Gazette.

*{The promulgation clause is omitted here.}*

---

[2] Wherever reference is made to "the Minister of Finance and Oil" in the Kuwait Fund's Law or Charter, it should read now "the Minister of Finance."

# Order of the Prime Minister for the Implementation of Law No. 25 (1974) for the Reorganization of the Kuwait Fund for Arab Economic Development[1]

The Prime Minister,

Having considered Law No. 25 (1975) for the Reorganization of the Kuwait Fund for Arab Economic Development,

Hereby makes the following Order:

Art. 1. The Kuwait Fund for Arab Economic Development shall operate in accordance with the provisions of the Charter attached hereto.

Art. 2. The Order of the Minister of Finance and Oil laying down the Charter for the Kuwait Fund for Arab Economic Development and published in the Official Gazette No. 423 dated April 14, 1963 is hereby repealed.

Art. 3. The Board of Directors of the Kuwait Fund for Arab Economic Development shall implement this Order which shall take effect from the date of its publication in the Official Gazette.

*{The promulgation clause is omitted here.}*

# Charter of the Kuwait Fund for Arab Economic Development

## Chapter One

### GENERAL PROVISIONS

Art. 1. The Kuwait Fund for Arab Economic Development, hereinafter called the Fund, is a Kuwaiti Public Corporation with an independent legal personality as well as financial and administrative autonomy under the supervision of the Prime Minister who shall be the Chairman of its Board of Directors.

[1] Given on 2 Zul Hijjah, 1394 A.H. [December 22, 1974].

**Art. 2.** The purpose of the Fund is to assist Arab and other developing States in developing their economies and, in particular, to provide such States with loans for the implementation of their development programs, in accordance with the provisions of this Charter.

**Art. 3.** The capital of the Fund is one thousand million Kuwaiti dinars.

**Art. 4.** The principal office of the Fund shall be located in the City of Kuwait.

## Chapter Two

### THE ADMINISTRATION OF THE FUND

**Art. 5.** The Fund shall be administered by a Board of Directors composed of the Prime Minister, as Chairman, and eight other Kuwaiti members of recognized competence appointed by the Prime Minister for a term of two years subject to renewal.

In the event that the office of a member shall become vacant, a new member shall be appointed to hold office for the remainder of the term of his predecessor.

The Director-General of the Fund shall attend the meetings of the Board of Directors and participate in its deliberations but shall not be entitled to vote.

The Chairman may designate a member of the Board of Directors to preside over a meeting of the Board of Directors in his absence.

**Art. 6.** The Chairman of the Board of Directors shall have the authority to sign agreements whereby the Fund lends or borrows money, as well as any bonds issued by the Fund. The Chairman may delegate such authority to the Director-General.

**Art. 7.** The Board of Directors shall be the highest authority of the Fund. It shall have the power to determine the general policy of the Fund for the achievement of its objectives and shall, in particular, have the power to:

*(a)* consider the recommendations submitted by the Director-General concerning proposed loans and other forms of assistance to Arab and other developing States and make the appropriate decisions;

*(b)* determine, subject to the provisions of this Charter, the form

and terms for the participation of the Fund in the development project and programs of Arab and other developing States;

*(c)* approve the amounts of loans and other types of assistance;

*(d)* determine the general policy of investments by the Fund and the forms of such investments. The Board of Directors may delegate its powers in this respect to the Director-General;

*(e)* authorize the borrowings of the Fund and determine the amounts and terms of such borrowings;

*(f)* lay down administrative and financial regulations for the Fund and supervise their implementation;

*(g)* approve the proposed administrative budget and the closing account of the Fund;

*(h)* appoint the Fund auditors and determine their remuneration.

**Art. 8.** The Board of Directors shall hold at least four meetings annually. Meetings shall be held at the invitation of the Chairman or the Director-General. A quorum for any meeting of the Board of Directors shall be a majority of the members. Unless otherwise provided in this Charter, resolutions of the Board of Directors shall be adopted by a simple majority of the votes of members present. In the event of an equal division of votes, the vote of the Chairman shall be deemed a casting vote.

**Art. 9.** The Board of Directors may from time to time appoint subcommittees from among its members to study such matters as may be referred to them and submit their recommendations to the Board. Each subcommittee shall elect a Chairman from among its members.

**Art. 10.** The resolutions of the Board of Directors approving loans and grants, as well as the administrative budget and the closing account, shall be subject to confirmation by the Chairman.

**Art. 11.** The Chairman of the Board of Directors shall appoint the Director-General of the Fund and one or more Deputies upon the recommendation of the Board of Directors. The appointment of other staff of the Fund shall be made in accordance with the staff regulations to be laid down by the Board of Directors.

**Art. 12.** The Director-General shall have the direct responsibility for all administrative, financial and technical matters in the Fund. He shall represent the Fund before the Courts of Law and in relation to third parties. His functions shall, in particular, include the following:

*(a)* implementation of the resolutions of the Board of Directors;
*(b)* preparation and submission to the Board of Directors of the proposed administrative budget and the closing account;
*(c)* authorization of expenditures within the limits of the administrative budget;
*(d)* submission of an annual report to the Board of Directors on the progress of work in the Fund; such report shall include financial statements certified by auditors and a detailed account of the activities of the Fund during the preceding financial year;
*(e)* receipt of applications for loans and financial and technical assistance; appraising such applications and submitting appropriate recommendations thereon to the Board of Directors;
*(f)* implementation of loan and other agreements for the provision of assistance; and
*(g)* undertaking such other tasks as may be entrusted to him by the Board of Directors in conformity with the provisions of this Charter.

The Director-General shall be assisted by one or more Deputies in carrying out his duties. The senior Deputy present shall act for the Director-General in his absence.

## Chapter Three

### OPERATIONS OF THE FUND

Art. 13. The Fund may assist Arab and other developing States in implementing development projects and programs by making loans to such states or to corporate entities which are under the control of such states or which are subjects of, or constitute joint ventures among such states, provided that the objectives of such corporate entities are not purely limited to the making of profit. The Fund may also provide assistance by issuing guarantees for the obligations of such states or corporate entities, or through any other means which the Board of Directors may consider appropriate.

Art. 14. The Fund may not finance by means of a loan more than 50 per cent of the total costs of any project or program. Notwithstanding this provision, the Board of Directors may, by a majority of two thirds of the members present, approve loans in amounts exceeding the aforesaid limit in exceptional cases when the necessary financing for a vital project or program cannot otherwise be obtained on reasonable terms.

**Art. 15.** The loans made by the Fund shall be for the purpose of financing, exclusively, all or part of the foreign exchange costs of projects or programs. However, in exceptional cases where sufficient justification exists, the Fund may, pursuant to a decision of the Board of Directors by a majority of two-thirds of the members present, participate in financing the local component of the cost of such projects or programs.

**Art. 16.** The Kuwaiti dinar shall be the unit of account in all operations of the Fund. All loans and other forms of financial assistance made by the Fund shall be paid and repaid, as the case may be, in Kuwaiti dinars on the basis of the gold parity of the dinar as specified in the Special Agreement with the International Monetary Fund at the time of signing the agreement for the loan or other type of financial assistance.

**Art. 17.** Each loan agreement shall provide for the payment to the Fund, in addition to the interest charged, if any, of a service charge of one-half of one per cent (0.5%) annually on the amounts withdrawn from the loan and outstanding, to cover administrative expenses and other costs incurred in the execution of the loan agreement.

**Art. 18.** All loan agreements between the Fund and the borrowers shall include the following:

(*a*) financial clauses specifying the duration allowed and conditions for withdrawal of proceeds of the loan, and the dates and conditions for the repayment of the principal thereof and payment of interest, if any, and other charges on the loan;

(*b*) an undertaking by the borrower to furnish sufficient information to the Fund on the progress of work on the project financed, starting from the date of signature of the loan agreement until the loan is fully repaid;

(*c*) an undertaking by the borrower to afford all the necessary facilities to representatives of the Fund to enable them to follow up the progress of the project financed;

(*d*) provisions setting out arrangements for ensuring that the amounts withdrawn from the loan shall be used exclusively for financing expenditures on the project financed and only as such expenditures are actually incurred;

(*e*) an undertaking that no other external debt shall have priority over the loan of the Fund or the interest or other charges thereon by way of a lien on the assets of the borrower, except within such limits as the Fund may accept;

*(f)* an undertaking to exempt all transactions, assets and income of the Fund in the recipient state from all taxes, dues and other impositions;

*(g)* an undertaking from the monetary or any other competent authority in the recipient state to facilitate all the financial operations of the Fund and, in particular, to lift all foreign exchange restrictions on direct and indirect transfers arising out of the loan agreement;

*(h)* an undertaking to consider all Fund documents, records, correspondence and similar material, as confidential, and to accord the Fund full immunity from censorship and inspection of printed matters; and

*(i)* an undertaking to exempt all the assets and income of the Fund from nationalization, confiscation and seizure.

Where the loan is made to an entity other than the recipient state, the undertakings set out in paragraphs *(f)*, *(g)*, *(h)* and *(i)* of this Article shall be incorporated in a Guarantee Agreement to be concluded between the Fund and the Government of the State guaranteeing the loan.

**Art. 19.** The Fund may require, depending on the nature of each transaction, additional guarantees other than those provided for in the preceding Article, and may accept guarantees made by third parties including those of national, regional and international financial institutions.

**Art. 20.** In considering loan applications the Fund shall be guided by the recognized principles of development finance including, in particular, the following:

*(a)* the degree of importance of the project or program for which the loan is requested and its priority rating in relation to other projects or programs;

*(b)* the completeness and accuracy of the cost estimates for the project or program;

*(c)* the adequacy of the economic and technical evaluation of the project;

*(d)* ascertainment of the availability of the funds necessary, in addition to the financing to be provided by the Fund, for the execution and completion of the project or program;

*(e)* the solvency of the applicant and the guarantor, if any.

**Art. 21.** All loan agreements between the Fund and the borrowers shall be made in the Arabic language.

**Art. 22.** The Fund shall not make grants to any beneficiaries except against its accumulated net profits.

**Art. 23.** The Fund may borrow money, issue bonds and give guarantees within the limit of twice the amount of its capital and reserves, in accordance with such terms and conditions as may be determined by the Prime Minister upon the recommendation of the Board of Directors.

## CHAPTER FOUR

### FINANCIAL PROVISIONS

**Art. 24.** The financial year of the Fund shall begin on the first day of April and end on the last day of March of the following year.

**Art. 25.** The Fund shall have an administrative budget comprising its income and current expenditures and shall prepare a closing account in respect of such income and expenditures. The Director-General shall submit the draft administrative budget to the Board of Directors not later than two months before the end of each financial year.

**Art. 26.** The Fund shall prepare a Balance Sheet, an Income and Expenditure Statement and a Reserve Account. The said financial statements shall be certified by auditors and submitted to the Board of Directors, together with the Closing Account and the Annual Report on the activities of the Fund, not later than June 30 of each year.

**Art. 27.** The Fund shall keep proper books of accounts to show a true and fair view of the state of affairs of the Fund and explain its transactions. The Auditors' report shall be submitted to the Board of Directors for consideration and approval.

**Art. 28.** Without prejudice to the provisions of Article 22 of this Charter, net profits of the Fund shall be credited to a reserve account until reserves shall become equal to twenty per cent (20%) of the capital of the Fund. Thereafter, net profits shall be added to the capital of the Fund provided, however, that the reserves shall always remain equal to twenty per cent of the capital.

## Chapter Five

### MISCELLANEOUS PROVISIONS

**Art. 29.** The Prime Minister may delegate all or part of his powers under this Charter to the Minister of Finance and Oil.

**Art. 30.** This Charter may be amended by a decision of the Prime Minister upon the recommendation of the Board of Directors.

# Law No. 32 of the Year 1970 [1]

## Concerning the Organization of Stock Market Operations for Companies

We, Sabah al-Salim al-Sabah, Amir of Kuwait,

After perusing the Constitution, Commercial Law No. 2 for the year 1961 and its amendments, Law No. 15 for the year 1960 concerning commercial firms and its amendments, and Law No. 27 for the year 1962 concerning the organization of stock market operations for companies established abroad, the National Assembly has approved the text of the following law,

We hereby ratify and enact the same.

**Art. 1.** It is not permitted for the stocks and bonds of companies established inside or outside the State of Kuwait to be issued for public subscription nor can they be sold in any way, and no investment can be made in any investment funds unless permission is obtained from the Ministry of Commerce and Industry.

**Art. 2.** The permit mentioned above in Article 1 can only be granted to a bank in Kuwait if the stocks and bonds are issued for public subscription and for a Kuwaiti joint-stock company in accordance with Article 77 of Law No. 15 for the year 1960 regarding commercial firms. If the permit is required to conduct stock market operations for com-

[1] The law was issued at Sayf Palace on 28 Ramadan, 1391 A.H. [November 26, 1970].

panies established inside and outside Kuwait and if the stocks are not issued for public subscription, the permit may be granted to a bank in Kuwait, or a licensed company in Kuwait, or an authorized Kuwaiti commercial agent.

Art. 3. Until a law for establishing a stock market is decreed, the Minister of Commerce and Industry can issue the regulations necessary for organizing the stock market operations for Kuwaiti companies. He will do that after consulting with the Financial Counseling Committee as provided in Article 11 of this law.

Art. 4. If the requested permit is for stocks that are already in circulation in foreign stock markets, the applicant has to submit the following documents:

1. Proof of the fact that the capital paid is not less than 50,000 dinars if he plans to conduct investment operations for himself and others.

2. Proof of the fact that he has legally registered with one of the brokers authorized to work in any of the foreign stock markets or any of the investment firms.

3. A copy of the regulations of the foreign stock market.

4. A certificate signed by the administration of the stock market proving that the aforementioned broker is registered with the stock market and licensed to buy and sell stocks.

5. A pledge from both the applicant and the broker that they will not deal in the stocks of companies that are not listed in the aforementioned stock market unless they have obtained written permission from the client in advance.

6. A written pledge from both the applicant and the broker that they will not deal in stocks which are for Israeli companies or any other companies with whom it is forbidden to deal in accordance with the decisions of the Israel Boycott Office.

7. A written pledge from both the foreign broker and company, certified by the stock market, to pay all of the financial obligations incurred because of their operations in Kuwait, however large they may be; the pledge should also mention that the broker or company enjoy the privileges of insurance as specified in the by-laws of the company.

8. A certified copy of the insurance document for the company or the broker.

9. A pledge from the broker or the foreign company, certified by the stock market, that it will be bound by the regulations in force at the principal headquarters, regarding its operations in Kuwait, and that it will make sure that its branch in Kuwait will abide by such regulations.

10. A pledge that the company will submit periodic statements for which the Minister of Commerce and Industry will issue a resolution; the pledge should also state that the main office has no objection to providing these statements or any other statements at any time.

11. A pledge that the company will keep records and account books in accordance with the resolution issued by the Minister of Commerce and Industry.

12. A bank guarantee in the name of the applicant and to the order of the Minister of Commerce and Industry in the amount of 250,000 dinars. The Kuwaiti joint-stock companies, whose paid capital is not less than one million dinars, are exempt from having to submit such guarantees.

13. A pledge that the applicant will give his customers a periodic report in which he mentions their net liquid balances plus or minus the market value of long- or short-term investments.

14. A pledge from the company that it will take the measures necessary to pay the interest and profits of stocks and bonds in Kuwait.

15. A pledge to submit any documents or other reports which the Minister of Commerce and Industry may deem necessary.

When stocks are bought and sold, the company or the broker must submit to the purchaser the stock certificate within a period not to exceed fifteen days after the buying and selling operation is completed.

**Art. 5.** Foreign companies, which are licensed to operate in Kuwait, must have their accounts audited by an accountant registered with the Ministry of Commerce and Industry. The accountant should submit a report to the Ministry every six months at least. Reports are submitted to the Counseling Committee if necessary. The Ministry of Commerce and Industry may appoint a certified accountant from the Ministry to audit the accounts of any of these companies in Kuwait at the expense of the company itself, if necessary.

**Art. 6.** The Ministry of Commerce and Industry must send inspectors to review the documents, books, and records of the companies which deal in stocks, once every six months at the main office of the company in Kuwait, whenever that is required for valid reasons or for matters related to the common interest.

The inspector is appointed by a resolution from the Minister of Commerce and Industry. As soon as he is appointed, he will work in the capacity of a legal inspector, and he will prepare a confidential report about his inspection activities, which may be submitted to the Counseling Committee if necessary.

**Art. 7.** The companies which deal in stocks must submit monthly reports to the Ministry of Commerce and Industry in the first half of the month, including information about its activities in Kuwait and especially the following:

A. the volume of monthly production;
B. the names of companies with whom they have conducted stock operations during the month;
C. the lowest and the highest buying and selling prices.

**Art. 8.** It is not permitted to sell foreign stocks or to deal in them in any way, except through the offices set up for that purpose or through licensed brokers who are registered with the Ministry of Commerce and Industry.

**Art. 9.** Dealing in stock operations on a credit basis is prohibited except within the boundaries set by the Ministry of Commerce and Industry and decreed by the Minister himself.

**Art. 10.** Dealing in consolidated accounts is forbidden. It is also forbidden to conclude commodity contracts except for parties who trade in such commodities. These persons have to sign the purchase and selling orders.

**Art. 11.** A Counseling Committee will be formed to take charge of the regulations concerning stock market operations under the chairmanship of the Minister of Commerce and Industry and with the following membership:

—representatives from the Ministry of Commerce and Industry,
—a representative from the Ministry of Finance and Oil,
—a representative from the Central Bank,
—five citizens who have expertise and who are specialized.

Those members are appointed by a decree from the Council of Ministers in accordance with the proposal of the Minister of Commerce and Industry. The term of membership is two years and is renewable.

The remuneration of the members is fixed by a resolution from the Council of Ministers. The Minister of Commerce and Industry will issue a resolution on the regulations that guide the Committee's work. The Committee studies the issues that are presented to it by the Minister of Commerce and Industry and particularly the following:

A. proposing legislative texts and regulatory procedures concerning the stock market and foreign currencies;
B. safeguarding the implementation of the laws and regulations related to stock market operations;
C. drawing up proposals concerning the establishment of a stock market;
D. proposing measures necessary to safeguard the economic and financial interests of the country when there is an abrupt change in stock market values;
E. reviewing the reports submitted by accountants and inspectors as specified in both Articles 5 and 6 of this law;
F. reviewing the requests of any foreign company which desires to issue its stocks in Kuwait.

**Art. 12.** Whoever violates the provisions of Articles 1, 5, and 10 of this law will be punished by imprisonment for a period not to exceed six months and a fine not less than 100 dinars nor more than 200 dinars. However, if there exists a stronger penalty contained in another law, he may be punished by either of the two penalties.

If he commits the same violation, the term of imprisonment and the aforementioned fine will be doubled. However, the maximum fine should not exceed 225 dinars.

If this violation is committed by a bank or organization, the penalty will fall on those in charge of its management. The court may order that the funds and documents, which give evidence to the violation, be confiscated.

**Art. 13.** The director of the company, or the one in charge of managing it, will be punished by a fine not less than 100 dinars and not exceeding 200 if he refuses to hand over the reports mentioned in Article 7 or prevents the inspectors from performing their duties as specified in Article 6 when such an attitude is not justified.

**Art. 14.** The Minister of Commerce and Industry, after consulting with the Financial Counseling Committee, will issue a resolution to regulate the circulation of the investment shares of the foreign investment funds.

**Art. 15.** Law No. 27 for the year 1962 is abolished and replaced by this law.

**Art. 16.** The Prime Minister and the Minister—each within his own jurisdiction—are to implement this law, and it comes into effect on the date when it is published in the official journal.

*{The promulgation clause is omitted here.}*

# Panama

Panorama of modern Panama
Courtesy Photo Library of Organization of American States

# PANAMA

# Financial System of Panama

by

*Mario T. Hernandez* *

## Introduction

The milestones in Panama's financial legislation are (i) the Monetary Convention of 1904,[1] (ii) the enactment in 1904 of a law to establish the National Bank, (iii) two laws aimed at establishing a central bank (1913 and 1941), and (iv) two laws regulating the financial system (1941 and 1970).

Once a country elects a particular monetary system, this choice limits the list of financial policies available to the authorities as well as influencing the operations of its financial institutions. In Panama the choice of currency decisively influenced the nature of its financial system and set the parameters for the financial legislation that followed.

With the establishment of the Republic of Panama in 1903, one priority of the authorities was to furnish the country with a national currency. This meant substituting a new currency for the Colombian peso circulating at that time. Accordingly, the commissioners of the new Panamanian Government met with W. H. Taft, then U.S. Secretary of War and acting supervisor and director of the Isthmian Canal Commission, to discuss the matter. In a note addressed to the Special Fiscal Commissioners of the Republic of Panama, dated June 20, 1904, which was to give rise to the Monetary Convention of 1904, Mr. Taft said that:

> The Isthmian Canal Commission . . . is vitally interested in the maintenance in the Canal Zone of a stable currency, based upon the gold standard.
>
> I conceive it to be of common benefit to the Republic and to the Isthmian Canal Commission that the currency used in the Republic and in the Canal Zone should be the same. . . .

The note went on to specify, among other things, that:

> Assuming that legislation will be enacted substantially to the foregoing effect, I agree on behalf of the Isthmian Canal Commission and by direction of the President of the United States:

---

* Mr. Hernandez, at present an economist with the Central American Division in the Western Hemisphere Department of the International Monetary Fund, was at the time this introduction was written with the Grand Columbian Division. He holds degrees in economics from the Universidad Nacional de Buenos Aires (Argentina) and the University of Chicago (U.S.A.).

[1] This Convention may be found in *Treaties and Other International Agreements of the United States of America, 1776–1949,* Vol. 10 (Washington, 1972), at pp. 681–683.

First. That the Isthmian Canal Commission will make the gold and silver coins of the Republic of Panama legal tender within the Canal Zone, by appropriate legislation.

Second. That it will employ such gold and silver coin of the Republic in its disbursements in the Canal Zone and in the Republic, as the Canal Commission shall find practicable and convenient.

A week later, by Law No. 84 of June 28, 1904, Panama's National Convention authorized the legal circulation of the gold U.S. dollar in the Republic and established for the new balboa a one to one parity with the U.S. gold dollar. In addition, this law provided for conditions to guide the issuance of silver coins and their gold guarantee. It also provided for the conversion of Colombian silver coins in circulation. Finally, it allowed the Executive to approve a monetary convention with the U.S. Government on the basis of this law and the stipulations of the Washington agreement of June 20. On December 6, 1904, the President of the Republic signed Decree No. 74 approving the Washington agreement. This decree set out limits on the issuance of silver coins and provided for a gold guarantee of them.

On the basis of the background just described, economic analysis leads to the conclusion that the U.S. dollar would inevitably take the place of Panamanian currency. Indeed, as the Panamanian authorities could only issue gold or silver currency, and the issuance of silver coinage had to be guaranteed by gold to be deposited in the United States, and as all coins had to be minted in the United States before they could be transported to Panama, the cost of issuing an independent Panamanian currency would have been substantial. It was more economical to use U.S. currency instead. As a result, while over the years several denominations of silver balboas were minted, U.S. dollar notes and coins have consistently furnished most of Panama's circulating medium.

It can be argued, at least from a theoretical point of view, that this outcome may have been beneficial for the country. Indeed, the theory of optimum currency areas, in one of its versions, suggests that for a small open economy changes in exchange rates will operate only inefficiently, at best, to bring about external equilibrium. Panama, lacking a national currency, could not resort to this "suboptimal" adjustment policy.

In summary, the Monetary Convention may have had distinct advantages from an economic standpoint. Balanced against these considerations, however, is the corollary that the arrangements entered into afforded the monetary authorities little scope to pursue an independent monetary policy.

## Structure of Banking System, 1903–40

With the matter of a national currency thus settled,[2] for many years the authorities saw no need for a general law to regulate banking activities.[3] Since, during most of the period under consideration, the banking system consisted of only two government-owned banks and two foreign-owned banks, there was some justification for this view. Given the existing monetary system there was little the authorities could regulate effectively. As a result, they limited themselves to establishing a maximum interest rate policy (Law No. 4 of 1935) and to assuring the economic soundness of the government banks by requiring security for their loans and establishing quantitative limits on the amounts that they might lend to any one person or firm. In order to attract funds into the economy, the authorities facilitated the foreign operations of the banks by exempting foreign deposits from the legal reserve requirements applicable to local deposits.

### *National Bank of Panama*

The first national financial institution in the country was established by the Government in June 1904. This was the Mortgage and Secured Loans Bank of the Republic (Banco Hipotecario y Prendario de la República). Since, at the time of its establishment, the country had not yet decided on the monetary system to follow, a mortgage bank was considered to be the safest type of institution to create, having in mind the possibility of default during a period of uncertainty and the consequential overriding need for good collateral. The bank was funded with local capital. Its operations were restricted by ceilings on interest rates that it could charge on its loans, as well as by a limit on the amount of credit that it could make available to any single borrower.

By Law No. 6 of 1911, the National Assembly renamed the Mortgage and Secured Loans Bank of the Republic the National Bank (Banco Nacional). It also doubled the bank's capital to B 250,000 and increased the range of its operations. Now it was allowed to make loans for

[2] The Constitution of Panama 1972 provides:

"*Article 230.* The power of issuing currency belongs to the State, which may transfer it to official banks of issue, in the manner prescribed by law.

"*Article 231.* There shall be no paper money of compulsory tender in the Republic."

[3] But see Article 232 of the Constitution of Panama 1972. This may be found in *Constitutions of the Countries of the World,* eds. Blaustein and Flanz, Vol 11 (New York, 1979).

commercial and agricultural purposes. More important still, it was authorized to receive checking and savings deposits. Today the bank performs both public and private banking functions and also acts as a development bank. On the one hand, it is the depository of a portion of the legal reserves required of the commercial banks. On the other hand, it operates as a commercial bank itself. Despite the general growth of the banking sector, or perhaps because of it, the National Bank's liabilities to the private sector have declined relatively. As a proportion of the banking system's liabilities to the private sector, the National Bank's liabilities declined from 38 per cent in 1950 to 15 per cent in 1970, and to only 10 per cent in 1980.[4]

### Other financial institutions

The National Bank was not alone in the country. The International Banking Corporation (which would become the Citibank of New York) had been operating in Panama since 1904. Accordingly, when Law No. 45 of 1911 followed shortly after the enactment of Law No. 6 of 1911, its provisions, while dealing in the main with the National Bank, also went beyond in order to provide the authority for the Executive to audit and control other credit institutions as well.

Law No. 19 of 1913 authorized the establishment of the Bank of Panama (Banco de Panama). While some believe that the bank might eventually have evolved into a central bank, in the form in which it was proposed it could only have performed as a bank of issue carrying out few of the tasks generally assigned to a central bank. As envisaged in the law, the bank would have been a private company authorized to accept deposits from the public and to make commercial and mortgage loans. It would also have become the financial agent of the Government and would have been authorized to issue currency notes.

The Bank of Panama never opened its doors for business, which is not surprising given the manner in which its activities were to be hampered by restrictions and obligations imposed by Law No. 19. First, currency issued by the bank would not have been legal tender for all purposes. It would have carried this status only when given in payment of taxes or for the purchase of government property. Second, the bank would have been required to extend a permanent line of credit to the Government at a fixed interest rate. Third, the bank would have enjoyed

[4] International Monetary Fund, *International Financial Statistics Yearbook*, 1981.

no assurance of a monopoly on the issuance of currency. The Executive served notice that it had reserved the right to grant to other banks the same privileges that had been made available to the Bank of Panama.

Law No. 37 of 1917 enabled the Government to achieve some degree of control over the volume of credit. For the first time banks were required to hold reserve requirements against deposits. However, the law was promptly amended to exempt foreign deposits. The exemption may be interpreted as an effort by the authorities not to tax the foreign financing of the banks in order that they might attract foreign savings to finance domestic economic activity.

Several financial institutions catering to the needs of particular sectors of the economy were established in the 1920s. Thus, the National Bank for Agricultural Credit (Banco Nacional de Crédito Agrícola) was intended to service the agricultural sector, while the National Pawnshop (Monte de Piedad) was intended to make loans to low-income families. In the face of mounting liquidity problems, however, these financial institutions did not survive for very long.

### Savings Bank

The national Savings Bank (Caja de Ahorros) was established in June 1934, when the world economy was still struggling to emerge from the Great Depression. Its operations were restricted to receiving savings deposits, and to making loans secured by first mortgages or other suitable forms of collateral. The maximum rate of interest it could charge was 6 per cent. Legal reserve requirements equivalent to 15 per cent of its deposits, as well as any cash that it required for its operations, would be deposited with the National Bank. As noted previously, these deposits reflect a practice that continues to this day, the effect of which is to bolster the liquidity position of the National Bank.

Subsequently, the Savings Bank's law was modified, enabling it to hold up to 25 per cent of its deposits outside the National Bank, either in domestic or foreign banks, as long as such funds are related to lines of credit for its program of financing mortgage and construction credit.

Recognition of tightness in the credit market resulted in legislation that provided the banks with authority to raise their interest rates. Law No. 4 of 1935 not only increased the maximum rates that the banks might charge, but established differential ceilings: 7 per cent for commercial loans and 9 per cent for civil obligations. Refinement of regulation was not limited to loans. By Law No. 44 of 1938, a differential was introduced into the legal reserve requirements: 20 per cent for demand deposits and 10 per cent for time deposits.

With the improvement in the economy's overall liquidity, it was decided to reduce the maximum interest rates that banks could charge on loans. Accordingly, Law No. 77 of 1941, which restructured both the National Bank and the Savings Bank, reduced the maximum interest rates on bank loans to 6 per cent thus eliminating the differentials that had been established in 1935. This law also reduced the reserve requirements that the Savings Bank had to hold with the National Bank.

The advent of World War II provided a boon to the Panamanian economy. Expenditures arising from mounting traffic through the Panama Canal and from the stationing of additional military personnel in the Canal Zone increased sharply. The resulting flow of funds into the Panamanian economy led both to an upturn in general economic activity and to a substantial increase in the liquidity of the banking system. This development in the monetary field was promptly reflected in new financial legislation.

## First General Banking Law

Law No. 101 of 1941 was the first wide-ranging banking law introduced in Panama. In it the authorities sought to define banking operations and the nature of different types of banks that would be allowed to operate in the system. Accordingly, the law (a) enumerated which institutions would be considered banks; (b) established differential minimum capital requirements for the different types of banks—B 250,000 for commercial and savings banks and B 100,000 for mortgage banks; (c) provided a detailed list of operations allowed each type of bank; and (d) mandated that the banking system would be supervised by the Comptroller General's office, whose duty would be to request specified information from the banks at least four times a year. The law did not provide for a panoply of monetary and credit policy instruments. Two instruments that did find inclusion in the law were differential reserve requirements and a local asset ratio. The latter required investment in local assets of a minimum proportion of a bank's domestic deposit liabilities. Its purpose was to lock funds into the domestic economy. Since it was recognized that both the reserve requirement and the local asset ratio in effect operate so as to tax banking activity, provision was made for limiting their application.

If the success of a banking law were to be measured by the entry of new private banks in response to it, Law No. 101 could not be judged an unqualified success: the next two entries of banks into the system occurred in 1948 and 1955.

A second attempt was made to establish a rudimentary central bank. Decree Law No. 6 of 1941 authorized the creation of the Central Bank of Issue of the Republic of Panama (Banco Central de Emisión de la República de Panama). It was primarily intended to serve as a bank of issue. Several improvements over the earlier attempt were incorporated in the law. Thus, the currency would have unlimited legal tender, the costs of its issuance (as well as the administrative costs of the bank) would be borne by the Government and implicitly it would have a monopoly of the currency issue in Panama. Nevertheless, the strict cover requirements on currency issued were such as to eliminate the seigniorage, i.e., the profitability of issuing currency. In the end, this attempt proved no more successful than its forerunner.

## Post-World War II Period: Emphasis on Economic Development

In the aftermath of World War II, the developed as well as the developing countries' economic policies focused on economic growth. In Panama this was reflected in the establishment of a number of institutions to further the development of the economy. This drive reached its climax in 1953, with Law No. 3 establishing the Institute for Economic Development (Instituto de Fomento Económico). This institution, a sort of development bank, was funded with the assets of three banks: the Agricultural and Industrial Bank (established 1941), the Urbanization and Rehabilitation Bank (established 1946), and the Bank of the Central Provinces (established 1946). A subsidy from the Government was forthcoming.

The Institute was divided into three departments: the Commercial Banking Department, the Development Department, and the Rehabilitation Department. Its stated objective was to plan, increase, diversify and rationalize production and the national economy. To this end, it would devote its energies to all sectors of the economy and would provide banking services where its authorities found them unsatisfactory. Interest on its loans was made subject to a 6 per cent ceiling.

The broad range of duties assigned to the Institute burdened its administrative capability. Accordingly, when the National Bank was reorganized in 1956, jurisdiction over the Bank of the Central Provinces was transferred from the Institute to the National Bank. Subsequently, those functions deriving from the Urbanization and Rehabilitation Bank were transferred to the Institute for Housing and Urban Development (Instituto de Vivienda y Urbanismo) and the industrial promotional functions were transferred to the Ministry of Agriculture, Commerce, and Industry. The remaining agricultural functions were split between the Bank for Agricultural Development (Banco de Desarrollo Agropecuario) and the Institute for Agricultural Marketing (Instituto de Mercadeo Agropecuario).

## Expansion and Diversification of Financial System: 1960–69

The decade that began in 1960 was characterized by acceleration in the growth rate of the economy sustained in part by increasing inflows of foreign capital. These flows originated mainly from the international financial institutions. The Inter-American Development Bank was the pioneering institution and others soon followed. The surge in financial activity brought in its wake a substantial increase in the number of banks. The entry of 12 banks, representing an increase of 200 per cent in this period, gave a clear indication of the rapid development of the financial sector.

Rapid expansion of the economy, in turn, produced an increase in the demand for credit that exceeded the supply of funds. The excess demand for credit found recognition in two different ways: (i) through an adjustment in the interest rate structure as well as (ii) in the establishment of new institutions specially designed to handle the credit problems of particular sectors of the economy.

In order to increase the flow of funds into the banking system, interest rates were allowed to rise on deposits as well as on loans. Banks made both savings and time deposits more attractive by offering preferential interest rates and, for the first time, began to tap a different class of savings by offering a new instrument, the certificate of deposit. The National Bank was authorized, in 1962, to increase to 9 per cent the interest rate on its loans.

The demand for credit originated principally in two different sectors of the economy. One sector was composed of low-income recipients; the other, the burgeoning construction industry. New legislation was the response to the needs of both sectors.

By Law No. 88 of 1960 the Bank for Popular Credit (Banco de Crédito Popular) was established to make loans to low-income families. This group had perhaps suffered most by the general nonobservance of the maximum interest rates that had been mandated by the usury law (Law No. 4 of 1935). Henceforth, they would have an independent source of funds until the absorption of this bank by the National Bank.

The period under consideration was marked by an impressive boom in construction. The construction industry had traditionally been financed by government institutions such as the Savings Bank, the Social Security Fund (Caja de Seguro Social), and the Institute for Housing and Urban Development. Meanwhile private purchasers of homes started to utilize the newly established savings and loan associations to finance their acquisitions. In order to deal with the problems associated with the financing of new construction, it was now thought propitious to introduce legislation that would facilitate the granting and holding of mortgages while simultaneously extending a measure of government supervision to the activities of the savings and loan associations.

Law No. 50 of 1963 established the Institute for the Promotion of Insured Mortgages (Instituto de Fomento de Hipotecas Aseguradas). To encourage mortgage lending and to widen the market for mortgages, the Institute was authorized to insure loans secured by eligible mortgages. In addition, the Institute was authorized to grant loans to savings and loan associations, to request information on their activities, and to levy a 10 per cent legal reserve requirement on their liabilities to the private sector. When the Institute was reorganized in 1965 by Decree Law No. 14, the interest rate ceiling on its loans to savings and loan associations was raised from 7 to 9 per cent in recognition of the general increase in interest rates. Subsequently it became the National Mortgage Bank (Banco Hipotecario Nacional).

It is convenient for purposes of analysis to study the growth in the banking system by dividing the decade into two periods. The first period, from 1960 through 1963, saw the entry into the system of only one new bank. In contrast, the remaining period between 1964 and 1970 registered the entry of 11 new banks, representing a large increase when it is recalled that in the preceding 60 years only 7 banks in all had been established.

It may be significant that the second period of growth in the banking system occurred after the resolution of a political crisis in 1964, which, among other things, had resulted in a run on the banking system. Once the differences between Panama and the United States over the Canal

Zone had subsided, the U.S. Agency for International Development (AID) announced plans to establish a private development bank. The Industrial Development Company (Desarrollo Industrial S.A.) was inaugurated with capital of B 11.6 million, of which B 9.6 million was provided by the AID, while the remainder was raised through the issuance of shares on the domestic market. As a symbol of understanding between the two countries, the creation of this institution may well have contributed to a climate of confidence that ushered in the ensuing expansion of the banking system.

The rapid expansion of the banking system impressed upon the authorities the need to establish an appropriate legal framework and the requisite institutions to guarantee the smooth functioning of the system. One step in this direction was for the authorities to assume responsibility for providing the clearinghouse services which had previously been supplied by the banks themselves. This step was taken in 1967 by Decree Law No. 157. Of greater importance were the consultations carried out by the authorities in the late 1960s centering on the reform and improvement of the existing banking legislation. Those consulted included not only the private banks but also banking experts provided by the International Monetary Fund. These efforts were crowned in July 1970 by the issuance of Cabinet Decree No. 238, which reformed the banking system and established the National Banking Commission.[5]

## Cabinet Decree No. 238 of 1970

The National Banking Commission was initially established as an agency of the Ministry of Finance and Treasury, but subsequently became an adjunct of the Ministry of Planning and Economic Policy. Its objectives are twofold: (a) to ensure the soundness and efficiency of the banking system so as to promote conditions conducive to stability and growth in the national economy, and (b) to foster conditions favorable to the development of Panama as an international financial center. The Commission is composed of seven members. Three members are from the official sector, namely, the Minister of Finance and Treasury (chairman), the General Manager of the National Bank, and

[5] It should be noted that in the same year two other significant financial loans were enacted: Cabinet Decree No. 247 of July 16, 1970 establishing the National Securities Commission and Cabinet Decree No. 248 of July 16, 1970 concerning mutual funds.

the Director General of the Planning and Administration Department. Four members are appointed by the Executive Branch from the private sector. Of these, three must be bank representatives of Panamanian nationality selected from among candidates proposed by the Banking Association, while the fourth must not be a bank official. The importance of this composition of the Commission cannot be underestimated in underscoring the cooperation with the private banking sector upon which the system is premised. A quorum comprises five commissioners. While it is provided that most decisions are to be adopted by simple majority, the law specifies a number of important occasions when a higher majority is required. The tenure of the commissioners is secure insofar as they can be removed only for the specific causes stated in the law and, then, only at the request of five of their colleagues.

The Commission is empowered to consider and grant applications for licenses to engage in banking business. It must act on an application within 90 days of its receipt and, in the event of refusal, must state its reasons therefor. It has power to cancel licenses, to rule on mergers and consolidations, and to take possession of a bank in certain stated circumstances. The latter power, which must be exercised only with the affirmative vote of five commissioners, may be invoked in respect of a bank that is in unsound condition or whose business is being conducted unlawfully, or that has refused to submit the required accounting records or has obstructed inspection by the Commission. The law provides that, generally, the only appeal that may be taken against resolutions of the Commission must be one for reconsideration by the Commission itself.

Three classes of licenses are issued by the Commission. The first type is a general license which may be issued to banks organized abroad that wish to do banking business in Panama and to banks organized in Panama that wish to do banking business there and abroad. The second type of license is issued to banks organized in Panama that confine their activities to transactions abroad. Finally, a third type of license is granted to banks organized under foreign law that permits them to establish representative offices in Panama. Once licensed, a bank may open a new branch without prior authorization from the Commission but such authorization is required before it closes one or changes its location.

The class of license that a bank is granted determines which of the provisions of the law are applicable to it. In this way a division is made between banks that carry on banking business in Panama, to which strict provisions apply, and those that confine their activities to transactions abroad, which are largely exempt from the substantive provisions of the Decree. Another basic distinction that runs through the law for the same reason is that between local deposits and foreign deposits, the former being the subject of a number of monetary instruments which, by their terms, exempt the latter. It is clear from these divisions, that the authorities sought to bifurcate the law in order to promote both objectives of the Commission. On the one hand, the development of Panama as an international financial center would be fostered by permitting wide latitude of operation for banks that confined their activities to external transactions. On the other hand, the Commission would strive to promote the inherent soundness of the domestic banking system. It should be noted that the two goals do not necessarily conflict. In view of Panama's dependence on a foreign currency, promotion of the first objective operates to attract funds needed from abroad which may then find their way into the domestic economy, thereby ensuring the availability of a source of currency and credit.

One example of the division between domestic and international regulations may be seen in the capital requirements. While banks engaging in banking business in Panama (general license) must have paid-up capital of B 1 million, those banks organized under Panamanian law that engage exclusively in banking business abroad (international license) are required to have a much smaller capital of only B 250,000. It should be noted that the law does not require a foreign banking applicant to organize a subsidiary corporation under Panamanian law. That applicant may, if it prefers, choose to conduct its business in Panama through a branch of its home office. However, if the latter option is selected, the applicant will not find a financial saving in the amount of initial funds that it will have to bring into the country. The law postulates a concept of "assigned capital" for the branch that is required to be kept equal in amount to the capital stock that would be required of a subsidiary. It should be further noted in this connection that, in addition to the initial capital required on the occasion of the establishment of a new bank, the law also mandates the maintenance of a capital reserve fund which, together with the amount of the capital, must not fall below 5 per cent of earning assets. The capital cushion is thus expected to grow in proportion to the growth of the bank.

The difference between domestic and foreign operations finds expression in the provisions governing the collection and payment of interest. The law first exempts banks from the rigid and outdated ceiling of the usury law (Law No. 4 of 1935). It then, by implication, distinguishes between local loans and credit facilities, on the one hand, which cover funds used or invested within the country, and those that are used or invested abroad. The latter are freely allowed to mirror the rates prevailing on the international markets so as not to work a competitive disadvantage on banks established in Panama that operate abroad, compared with banks operating in the same markets from bases outside Panama. As for local loans and credit facilities, in practice, these too are allowed to reflect the international rates so that funds may be attracted for use in Panama from abroad. Nevertheless, the interest rate that may be charged on local loans and funds may be regulated, but only if five members of the National Banking Commission vote in favor of such regulation.

Even as the law distinguishes between interest chargeable by banks on local, as opposed to foreign, loans and credit, it sets up an analogous distinction in respect of deposits. While the law expressly permits banks to pay interest at such rates as they may elect on both foreign deposits and on local time deposits, it expressly forbids the payment of interest on local sight deposits. Provision is made with the affirmative vote of five members of the National Banking Commission to permit the establishment of ceilings on interest payable in respect of savings deposits, and these ceilings shall establish a differential of not less than 1 percentage point in favor of rates payable by mortgage banks in order to assure such banks of an adequate source of funds.

A requirement that banks maintain a legal reserve may be justified on two grounds. On the one hand, if flexible, it provides the monetary authorities with an instrument to regulate credit. On the other hand, it may operate as a security for depositors. An undesirable consequence of such a requirement is that assets complying with the requirement are unlikely to earn as high a yield as they would if employed in the ordinary credit operations of the banks. Under the law, the National Banking Commission is authorized to vary the requirements between 5 and 25 per cent of total local deposits, differentiating, if it chooses to do so, between different categories of these deposits. Foreign deposits are not subject to the requirement. Inasmuch as they are thus exempt from the "economic tax" that is required of local deposits, their free flow into Panama is encouraged. Not less than 30 per cent of the legal reserve must consist of vault cash in the tills of the banks. This requirement attempts to assure that each bank has on hand the requisite cash in the absence of a central bank issuing its own currency that might otherwise serve as a lender of last resort. The remainder of the legal reserve requirement must be held as sight deposits with the National Bank or in the form of short-term treasury bills. A different composition for the remainder may be prescribed on the affirmative vote of five members of the National Banking Commission.

One way of ensuring that domestic savings will be employed in the domestic economy is to set up a local assets ratio. This instrument has been incorporated into the law, its application being limited only to local deposits. In accordance with the appropriate provision, the National Banking Commission is authorized to prescribe the percentage of local deposits that must be held by banks in the form of assets in Panama.

As previously indicated, the National Banking Commission is authorized to set differentials in the interest rates that may be paid on savings deposits in order to encourage the flow of these funds into the mortgage banks. Another instrument that the authorities have at their command to ensure the availability of funds for mortgages is that of directed credit. The law mandates that banks operating in Panama that receive savings deposits, other than the mortgage banks themselves, must invest at least 50 per cent of these deposits in mortgage loans on real estate situated in Panama.

As has been noted, a number of provisions in the law have been designed to assure a flow of funds from abroad. The authorities were not content, however, to rely on removing handicaps on and obstacles to that flow. What if, despite the incentives offered, the flow did not materialize or even, in the event of a financial crisis, reversed itself? To guard against the latter danger, a new instrument was devised: the stand-by credit. This instrument has, of course, analogies in the world of commercial banking and international finance. In the context of banking law, however, at the time of its introduction it was virtually unique. The applicable provisions require every bank engaged in banking business in Panama, as a condition of remaining licensed, to be the beneficiary of a stand-by credit in U.S. dollars from a foreign bank or, in the case of a branch, from its main office abroad. The stand-by must be of an amount not less than 10 per cent of the bank's total earning assets, determined semiannually. (In comparison with the minimum required capital of a bank, it is therefore likely to be quite substantial.) The National Banking Commission is authorized to negotiate, on behalf of any bank that is unable to obtain or renew a stand-by credit, with the other banks in Panama in order to put together a short-term credit to that bank from the pro rata contributions of the others.

The stand-by credits are to be invoked in the event that withdrawals occur during a six-month period that exceed 10 per cent of total deposits used or invested in Panama. In this event, the National Banking Commission is authorized to require banks to draw on their credits and hold the proceeds for use in Panama.

A series of prohibitions and limitations is set out in the law. A bank may not transfer profits or declare a dividend unless it has amortized or provided reserves sufficient for the amortization of all deferred expenses, losses incurred, and deficiency in capital. Subject to certain exceptions, a bank is forbidden to make loans to any single borrower in excess of an amount related to its deposits, capital, and reserves. A bank may not grant or obtain loans secured by its own shares. It may not grant unsecured loans in excess of 15 per cent of the sum of the capital and the capital reserve to its directors, or in excess of certain other amounts to its employees. A bank's power to acquire or lease real estate is restricted. Finally, subject to certain exceptions, a bank may not acquire shares or participations in any other enterprise in excess of 25 per cent of the sum of its capital and capital reserves.

All banks must appoint certified public accountants to act as external auditors and report to their principals, as well as to the National Banking Commission, on the state of the accounts and whether they accurately reflect operations. In addition to balance sheets and profit and loss statements, which must be made available to the National Banking Commission annually, banks are required to provide the Commission with more frequent statements and analyses of their credit facilities and other assets. The National Banking Commission, in turn, is required to inspect each bank at least every two years. If the inspection reveals that the bank's operations are being conducted in an unlawful or negligent manner, the National Banking Commission may require the bank to assist and oversee the remedial action.

One matter that required careful consideration was the scope of bank examination. The problem here is the delicate line that must be drawn between the need of the authorities to supervise the operations of the banks (in part for the protection of the depositors) as opposed to the need to preserve the confidentiality of the relations between the banks and their customers. In the end, the authorities decided to impose strict limits on the examinations, which may be overcome only by court order. The law provides, moreover, that the National Banking Commission is prohibited from investigating the personal affairs of any bank client. Information obtained by the National Banking Commission may not be revealed to any person or authority unless so required by court order and reports submitted to it containing confidential data may be published only in the form of consolidated data.

A word should be said about coded bank accounts. These are permitted by Law No. 18 of 1959, which authorizes banks and other credit institutions to operate such accounts in cash or securities. Coded checking accounts may be operated on the basis of a previously furnished signature and an assigned number. Secrecy must be observed in respect of coded accounts concerning their existence, amount, and the identity of their owners. Information concerning these matters is to be furnished only in connection with criminal proceedings. Interest paid on the accounts is reported on a global basis to the fiscal authorities without specifying the amount paid to each depositor. Unauthorized disclosure is subject to fine, imprisonment, or both.

A banking law is not complete unless it contains provisions that prescribe the circumstances and manner in which a failing or fraudulent bank may be seized and thereafter either restored to its owners, reorganized, or liquidated, as may be appropriate. The Panamanian law contains detailed provisions on this complicated subject that have been employed efficiently and with dispatch to weed out such institutions and protect the public from the calamities of unregulated bank failure. In this connection, a schedule of preferences is set out to determine an equitable priority between competing claimants to a bank's assets in the event that these prove insufficient to satisfy all. It is of interest to note that in this eventuality, local deposits are to be repaid first.

## Evaluation

Since the enactment of Cabinet Decree No. 238 of 1970, there has been a remarkable growth in the Panamanian banking system. Foreign deposits increased at a phenomenal average annual rate of 65 per cent in 1970–80, from US$218.0 million to US$19.5 billion. (This compares with an annual average rate of growth of 12 per cent in the period 1950–69.) The net impact of this on the domestic economy was a substantial increase in the domestic exposure in Panama of the commercial banks. This exposure, as measured by the increase in the banks' net foreign short-term liabilities (which had been limited in the period 1950–60 to US$28.0 million and in 1961–70 to US$66.0 million), jumped in 1971–80 to US$933.0 million. The resulting net capital inflow enabled the Panamanian banking system to expand credit to both the private and public sectors at a faster rate.

Indeed, the Central Government, which in the period 1949–68 had been a net creditor of the banking system, was able to increase its borrowing from the banking system from US$10 million in 1970 to US$291.0 million in 1980. Likewise, the banking system was able to increase credit to the private sector in the period 1970–80 at an annual average rate of 22 per cent from US$282 million in 1970 to US$2.1 billion at the end of 1980. This represented a substantial acceleration in the banking system's expansion of credit to the private sector, which in the period 1951–70 had increased at an average annual rate of 14 per cent.

A correlation of the growth in the banking system with the enactment of the new banking law has been noted by a number of observers. While other factors, such as the simultaneous growth in world liquidity coupled with political instability in other countries in the area, cannot be ruled out as having in some measure contributed to this growth, the statistics presented above appear to lend some support to the correlation.

# Decree No. 74 [1]

[December 6, 1904]

The President of the Republic, exercising the powers conferred on him by Article 13 of Law No. 84 of 1904 on currency,

DECREES:

Art. 1. The Convention concluded in Washington on June 20 of this year between the Secretary of War of the United States of America and the Fiscal Commissioners of the Republic of Panama, contained in the two following communications, is approved in all its parts:

June 20, 1904

To Messrs.
RICARDO ARIAS and
EUSEBIO A. MORALES
*Special Fiscal Commissioners of the Republic of Panama*

GENTLEMEN:

I understand that there is now pending in the Convention of the Republic of Panama, exercising legislative power for the Republic, a Bill to establish a monetary standard and to provide for the coinage necessary in the Republic. The Isthmian Canal Commission, whose action, by direction of the President of the United States, I am authorized to supervise and direct, is vitally interested in the maintenance in the Canal Zone of a stable currency, based upon the gold standard.

I conceive it to be of common benefit to the Republic and to the Isthmian Canal Commission that the currency used in the Republic and in the Canal Zone should be the same. I am informed that the Convention of the Republic has under consideration a measure which in substance provides:

I. That the monetary unit of the Republic shall be a gold peso of the weight of one gram, 672 milligrams, and of nine hundred one-thousandths fineness, divisible into one hundred cents, to be issued as and when considered by the Republic necessary or convenient for its requirements.

II. That the present gold dollar of the United States of America, and its multiples, shall also be legal tender in the Republic of Panama for its nominal value, as equivalent to one gold peso of the Republic.

III. That fractional silver coins shall be issued by the Republic, of various denominations, all to be of an alloy composed of nine hundred one-thousandths of pure silver and one hundred one-thousandths of copper, the declared value of the same bearing a ratio to the same weight of gold of approximately one to

[1] Done at Panama City, December 6, 1904 and published in *Gazeta Oficial*, No. 67 of 1904.

thirty-two, and that such fractional silver currency shall be legal tender in all transactions.

IV. That the silver to be coined shall be in fractional denominations of the gold peso or dollar, and, except as hereinafter specifically provided, shall be coined only in exchange or conversion of the Colombian silver peso and fractional currency now legally in circulation in the Republic, and that the amount thus converted shall not exceed $3,000,000 of such Colombian silver pesos.

V. That after July 1st, 1905, there shall be coined and issued by the Republic such additional amount of fractional silver currency to the limit in the aggregate in value of one million, five hundred thousand pesos or gold dollars, equivalent to three million half-dollar pieces, as may be deemed by the Secretary of War of the United States necessary or advisable in the construction of the Isthmian Canal and as may be requested by him of the Executive Power of the Republic.

VI. The Republic of Panama, in order to secure the legal parity and equivalence with the gold standard of such fractional silver coins, shall create a Reserve Fund by deposit with a responsible banking institution in the United States, of a sum in lawful currency of the United States equivalent to fifteen per centum of the nominal value of the silver fractional currency issued by the Republic, and as the same is issued, together with an amount equal to the seigniorage on the silver coins issued at the request of the Secretary of War as aforesaid, less all necessary costs of coinage and transportation.

VII. That after conference with the Isthmian Canal Commission or its representatives or fiscal agents, the Republic of Panama will take such steps with respect to exchange by drafts upon its reserve fund as will tend to prevent the disturbance of the legal parity of the silver fractional currency of the Republic of Panama with the gold standard.

VIII. That the Republic of Panama shall cause its coinage to be executed at the mints of the United States.

Assuming that legislation will be enacted substantially to the foregoing effect, I agree on behalf of the Isthmian Canal Commission and by direction of the President of the United States:

First. That the Isthmian Canal Commission will make the gold and silver coin of the Republic of Panama legal tender within the Canal Zone, by appropriate legislation.

Second. That it will employ such gold and silver coin of the Republic in its disbursements in the Canal Zone and in the Republic, as the Canal Commission shall find practicable and convenient.

Third. The Isthmian Canal Commission shall cooperate with the Republic of Panama to maintain the parity of the fractional silver coinage of the Republic of Panama with the gold standard by sale of drafts upon its funds at reasonable rates and on terms which will tend to prevent the disturbance of such parity.

Fourth. It is mutually agreed that nothing herein contained shall be construed to restrict the right of the Republic to reduce its silver currency after the opening of the canal to commerce, to such an amount as it may deem advisable and thereupon to reduce and withdraw, pro rata, the reserve fund corresponding to the reduction of the amount of silver coinage outstanding.

Will you please confirm your accord with the foregoing?

Very respectfully,

WM. H. TAFT
*Secretary of War*

June 20, 1904

Hon. WM. H. TAFT,
*Secretary of War,*
*Washington, D.C.*

SIR:

Pursuant to the powers conferred upon us by the general directions of the Government of the Republic of Panama, and subject to the enactment by the Republic of the necessary legislation, we hereby declare our complete accord with the Convention embodied in your communication of this date and agree to the same as therein set forth.

We are, dear sir,
Very truly yours,

RICARDO ARIAS EUSEBIO A. MORALES

*Special Fiscal Commissioners of the Republic of Panama*

Art. 2. The minting of the fractional silver coinage of the Republic shall be restricted: (1) to the amount necessary for effecting the conversion of Colombian silver currency pursuant to Law No. 84 of this year; however, this minting may not exceed three million pesos ($3,000,000); (2) from next June 1 further mintings and issues shall be effected up to three million pesos ($3,000,000) in Panamanian currency, equivalent to one million, five hundred thousand balboas (B 1,500,000.00) at the request of the Secretary of War of the United States, in such time and amounts as he may stipulate.

Art. 3. To guarantee parity between the new gold and silver coins having legal tender in the Republic, there shall be deposited in a banking institution of the United States 15 per cent of the nominal value of each minting, with a further amount equal to the seigniorage produced by the second minting, less costs of coinage and transportation of the money to this Republic. These deposits shall be made as and when the minted coins are issued.

*{The signatory clause is omitted.}*

# Cabinet Decree No. 238[1]

[July 2, 1970]

## Reorganizing the banking system and establishing the National Banking Commission

The Provisional Junta of Government

DECREES:

### PRELIMINARY TITLE

#### CHAPTER I. SCOPE OF APPLICATION AND DEFINITIONS

**Art. 1.** This cabinet decree shall apply to banks which are established in accordance with the laws of Panama and which engage in banking business in Panama or abroad, and to banks established abroad engaging in banking business in Panama.

*Paragraph:* Only juridical persons may engage in the banking business.[2]

**Art. 2.** For the purposes of this cabinet decree, the terms listed below shall be understood in the following sense:

*(a)* "Bank": any juridical person engaging in banking business, except savings and loan associations, authorized in accordance with the law;

*(b)* "Banking business": principally, the operation of obtaining financial resources from the public by the acceptance on deposit of money demandable with or without notice, or by any other means authorized by the applicable law, and the use of such resources, for the account and at the risk of the bank, for loans, investments, or any other operation authorized by law or by banking practice;

*(c)* "Establishment": any office, branch, or agency of a bank carrying out any or all of the activities or business of banking;

[1] This law, *Reformase el régimen bancario y crease la Comisión Bancaria Nacional,* effective July 2, 1970, was published in *Gaceta Oficial,* Vol. LXVI, No. 16.640 of July 6, 1970. The version published incorporates amendments made by Law No. 20 of February 28, 1973, and Law No. 104 of October 4, 1973.

[2] The preceding paragraph was declared unconstitutional by a Supreme Court decision of December 28, 1977.

(*d*) "Commission": the National Banking Commission;

(*e*) "Commissioners": the members of the National Banking Commission;

(*f*) "Demand deposits": all deposits that must be paid upon request;

(*g*) "Time deposits": all deposits that are not payable upon demand. These fall into two categories: fixed time deposits and savings deposits;

(*h*) "Local deposits" are:

(1) deposits payable to natural persons residing in Panama;

(2) deposits payable to juridical persons organized in accordance with Panamanian law and earning taxable income in Panama, with the sole exception of juridical persons whose income is derived from areas outside Panamanian territory; and

(3) deposits payable to foreign juridical persons with branches authorized to operate in Panama under the effective control of the Panamanian branch;

(*i*) "Foreign deposits": all deposits other than "local deposits;"

(*j*) "Unsecured credit facilities": credit facilities granted without real guarantee, or credit facilities secured by real guarantee, the value of which is less than the amount owed;

(*k*) "Assigned capital": the part of the paid-up capital stock that any bank established abroad will appropriate, channel, or use, through its establishments, in its banking business in Panama;

(*l*) "Earning assets": loans and investments which are located in the economy within the Republic of Panama;

(*m*) "Capital reserve": the reserve constituted with funds from profits earned or from other sources, which are accumulated for the purpose of strengthening the Bank's financial position;

(*n*) "Representatives' offices": offices which are established for the purpose of acting as banks' representatives and which do not effect banking business in their own behalf;

(*o*) "Mortgage banks": banks with loan portfolios not less than seventy-five per cent (75%) of which is composed of mortgage loans with maturities of not less than five (5) years;

(*p*) "Stand-by credit": credit granted to banks engaged in the banking business in Panama by another bank located abroad, or, in the case of branches or agencies of foreign banks, by its main branch. The terms and conditions established by the Commission shall be stipulated in such credit;

(*q*) "Interest"; the amount(s) which in any form or under any name are collected or paid with money.

## TITLE I. THE NATIONAL BANKING COMMISSION

### CHAPTER I. GENERAL PROVISIONS

**Art. 3.** The National Banking Commission is hereby created as an agency of the Ministry of Planning and Economic Policy.

**Art. 4.** The objectives of the Commission, in addition to the others assigned to it by this cabinet decree, shall be:

(*a*) To ensure that the soundness and efficiency of the banking system are maintained, in order to promote monetary and credit conditions suitable to the permanent stability and growth of the national economy.

(*b*) To strengthen and foster conditions favorable to the development of Panama as an international financial center.

### CHAPTER II. ITS ORGANIZATION

**Art. 5.** The Commission shall be composed of seven (7) members with voting and speaking rights, namely:

(*a*) The Minister of Planning and Economic Policy, who shall preside;

(*b*) The Minister of Finance and the Treasury;

(*c*) The General Manager of the National Bank of Panama;

(*d*) Three (3) bank representatives, who shall be Panamanian citizens, residents of the Republic, and bank officials. They shall be appointed by the Executive Branch from three (3) lists each of which contains the names of three persons. These lists shall be submitted by the Banking Association of Panama;

(*e*) One member, appointed by the Executive Branch, who may not be a bank director, official, or staff member.

**Art. 6.** The Commission shall have a Technical Secretariat headed by a Secretary and staffed as necessary in order to fulfill its duties. The Secretary shall attend the meetings of the Commission, with the right to speak only.

The staff, accounts, files, and property of the Technical Secretariat of the Commission shall be transferred to the Ministry of Planning and Economic Policy.

**Art. 7.** The alternates for the Minister of Planning and Economic Policy, the Minister of Finance and the Treasury, and the General Manager of the National Bank shall be, respectively, the Deputy Minister of Planning and Economic Policy, the Deputy Minister of Finance and the Treasury, and the General Manager of the Savings Bank.

**Art. 8.** Each bank representative shall have an alternate, who shall be chosen in the same manner as his principal.

**Art. 9.** The commissioner chosen in accordance with Article 5*(e)* shall have an alternate, who shall be chosen in the same manner as his principal.

**Art. 10.** The commissioners and their alternates shall be appointed *ad honorem* by the Executive Branch for a period of three (3) years.

*Transitional paragraph.* The periods of office of the first commissioners proposed by the Banking Association of Panama, and of their alternates, shall be one, two, and three years, respectively, so that the term of one of the commissioners and of his alternate expires each year. The term to be assigned to each of them shall be decided by lot at the Commission's first meeting.

**Art. 11.** The commissioners may only be removed by the Executive Branch at the request of five (5) commissioners, if:

*(a)* They are permanently incapacitated for the performance of their duties;

*(b)* They are declared bankrupt or are in a manifest state of insolvency;

*(c)* They are convicted of a crime against morality or the public faith; or

*(d)* They no longer fulfill the requirements established for their election. In case of removal of any of the commissioners, the vacancy shall be filled by his alternate until such time as a new principal is elected and appointed for the rest of the term of office of the removed commissioner.

**Art. 12.** During their temporary absences, and during their permanent absences until a new appointment is made, commissioners shall be replaced by their alternates.

**Art. 13.** The commissioners mentioned in Article 5*(d)* shall not be competent in matters considered by the Commission and concerning the bank of which they are officials.

**Art. 14.** The duties of the Commission, in addition to those conferred upon it by this cabinet decree, are the following:

*(a)* To meet at least every two months and, also, whenever convened by the Chairman of the Commission or upon the request of not less than three commissioners;

*(b)* To resolve matters submitted to it by the Chairman, the Secretary, or any of its members;

*(c)* To issue the resolutions to which this cabinet decree refers;

*(d)* To cooperate with the Executive Branch in preparing regulations for implementation of the provisions of this cabinet decree, and to issue its own by-laws, subject to the approval of the Executive Branch;

*(e)* To recommend to the Executive Branch the appointment of subordinate personnel required by the Commission for due fulfillment of its duties; and

*(f)* To make administrative decisions regarding the interpretation and scope of the banking laws.

**Art. 15.** The decisions of the Commission shall be adopted by simple majority, except in the special cases mentioned in this cabinet decree.

At least five (5) commissioners must be present in order to form a quorum.

## Title II. The Banking System

### CHAPTER I. AUTHORIZATIONS

**Art. 16.** With the exception of official banks, no person may engage in banking business before obtaining due authorization from the Commission, which shall issue the appropriate license.

Three (3) kinds of licenses shall be issued, namely:

(1) A license to be granted to banks established in accordance with foreign law, to operate in Panama, and to banks established in accordance with Panamanian law, to engage in the banking business, whether in Panama or abroad;

(2) A license to be granted to banks established in accordance with Panamanian law which, from an office established in Panama, engage exclusively in transactions that are completed or consummated, or that produce their effects, abroad.

(3) A license to be granted to banks established in accordance with foreign law that wish exclusively to establish representatives' offices in Panama.

**Art. 17.** Upon entry into effect of this cabinet decree, current licenses to engage in the banking business shall be considered valid for a one (1) year period, which may be extended, when the Commission deems justified, for not more than one additional year. Within this period, holders of such licenses must comply with the provisions of Articles 30 and 31 in order to be eligible to receive a license in accordance with this cabinet decree. The above notwithstanding, banks established in accordance with Panamanian legislation, in which at least 75 per cent of the shares or equity capital is owned by natural persons of Panamanian nationality or by foreigners with at least five (5) years' residence in Panama, shall have five (5) years to comply with the provisions of the aforementioned Articles 30 and 31 of this cabinet decree.

**Art. 18.** With the exception of national institutions or groups engaging exclusively in philanthropic or charitable activities, no person other than an authorized bank may, without the Commission's license, use the word "bank," or any of that word's derivates in any language, in its firm or trade name, description or title on billheads, stationery, notices, advertisements, or in any other manner to indicate that it engages in banking business.

*Paragraph.* Notaries are forbidden to authorize legal papers or copies thereof, documents, declarations or instruments peculiar to their office, and authentications of firms that contravene this article. The same prohibition applies to the Public Register with regard to their registration. Upon entry into effect of this cabinet decree, companies already registered, which were established in conformity with the laws of Panama or authorized to engage in business in the Republic, the trade or firm name of which contravenes the provisions of this article, shall have a period of 90 days in which to dissolve voluntarily, obtain a license from the Commission to engage in banking business, or amend their charter in order to change their trade or firm name. Upon expiry of this period, the Commission shall instruct the Director General of the Public Register to make a marginal note beside the registration of any company that has not complied with the aforesaid provisions, indicating that that company is automatically dissolved or that its authorization to do business in Panama is canceled, according to whether it is a Panamanian or a foreign company.

**Art. 19.** Whenever it is known, or there is justified reason for believing, that a natural or juridical person is engaging in the banking business in violation of the provisions of this cabinet decree, the Commission shall be empowered to examine that person's books, accounts, and documents in order to determine whether or not it has infringed or is infringing upon any provision of this cabinet decree. Any refusal to produce such books, accounts, or documents shall be considered presumption of fact of engaging in banking business without a license, in which case the Commission shall be authorized to instruct the Public Register to make the marginal note mentioned in the preceding article, and to impose the appropriate penalties.

**Art. 20.** As regards new banks to be established in accordance with the laws of Panama, the Commission shall issue a temporary permit for a ninety (90) day period, in order that, pending receipt of the proper license, the organizational structure of the company using the word "bank" or any of its derivatives may be entered in the Public Register. Upon expiry of this period, if all requirements for issuance of the license have not been fulfilled, the Commission shall instruct the Director General of the Public Register to make the marginal note mentioned in Article 18.

**Art. 21.** Applications for the license to engage in banking business must be made to the Commission in writing, enclosing:

(*a*) An authenticated copy of the enterprise's charter and by-laws, with the amendments to these, if any. If these documents were drawn up in a foreign language, the corresponding translations, done by legally authorized persons, must also be included.
(*b*) A copy of the balance sheet, with closing date not more than ninety (90) days prior to the date of the application, duly certified by a firm of certified public accountants.
(*c*) A certified check in favor of the National Treasury in the amount of B 500, in the case of a bank established under the laws of Panama, and of B 1,000 in the case of a bank established abroad, in order to defray the costs of the investigation mentioned in Article 23 of this cabinet decree.
(*d*) Any other requirement that may be established by law or by the Commission.

**Art. 22.** Whenever the Commission instructs the Director General of the Public Register to make the marginal note mentioned in Articles 18, 19, and 20, the Commission shall publish such instruction for three (3) consecutive days in a daily newspaper widely circulated throughout the Republic and once in the *Gazeta Oficial.*

**Art. 23.** When considering an application for a license, the Commission shall make, or order to be made, such investigations as it may deem necessary to verify the authenticity of the documents submitted, the financial situation and antecedents of the applicant, the reputation and experience of its officials, the adequacy of its capital, and any other information necessary for proper implementation of this cabinet decree.

**Art. 24.** Within ninety (90) days of receipt of the application, the Commission must issue or refuse the license, by resolution with statement of reasons, and shall personally advise the applicant of its decision.

**Art. 25.** Banks established abroad must appoint at least two (2) General Agents, both natural persons residing in Panama, one of whom, at least, must be a Panamanian citizen, so that at no time shall representation be lacking.

**Art. 26.** The Commission shall cancel the license of any bank that:

(1) Ceases to engage in banking business, or

(2) Does not initiate operations within six (6) months following issuance of the license. The Commission may also, by resolution adopted with the majority vote of five (5) Commissioners, cancel the license of any bank failing to comply with any of the provisions of this Cabinet Decree. Before canceling the license, the Commission shall personally inform the bank of its intention to cancel, with statement of the reasons therefor, and the bank shall have a period of twenty-one (21) calendar days, counting from the date of notification, to show cause why its license should not be canceled, submitting such evidence previously existing as it considers relevant. Upon expiry of this period, the Commission, by resoluton with statement of reasons, shall decide the appropriate measures.

**Art. 27.** Once the resolution canceling the license has been executed, the Commission shall immediately proceed to:

(1) Inform the Director General of the Public Register of the measure, so that he may make the necessary marginal note; and

(2) Publish the resolution in a newspaper of general circulation for three (3) consecutive days and once in the *Gazeta Oficial.*

**Art. 28.** No bank may open a new establishment without notifying the Commission. If a bank considers it necessary to close, or change the location of, an existing establishment, it must obtain the prior authorization of the Commission, for the sole purpose of enabling the Commission to verify that the closing is carried out in an orderly fashion, and in a way that protects the interests of the depositors of that establishment.

**Art. 29.** Without the prior authorization of the Commission no bank engaging in the banking business in Panama may merge or consolidate, nor may it sell all or part of its assets in Panama when such action would be equivalent to a merger or consolidation.

## CHAPTER II. CAPITAL

**Art. 30.** All banks engaging in the banking business in Panama must have a paid-up capital stock, or assigned capital, as the case may be, of not less than one million balboas (B 1,000,000).

The paid-up or assigned capital must consist of unencumbered assets maintained at all times within the Republic of Panama.

*Paragraph 1.* All banks established in accordance with the laws of Panama and engaging exclusively in the banking business abroad must at all times maintain in Panama, in unencumbered assets of such kinds as the Commission may authorize, a sum of not less than two hundred fifty thousand balboas (B 250,000), in order to guarantee due fulfillment of their obligations.

*Paragraph 2.* All banks established in accordance with the laws of Panama, in which at least 75 per cent of the shares are owned by natural persons of Panamanian nationality or by foreigners with more than five years' continuous residence in Panama, may initiate operations with a paid-up capital of two hundred fifty thousand balboas (B 250,000). This capital must be periodically augmented, until the minimum capital mentioned in this article has been attained, within a maximum period of ten (10) years.

The capital increases shall be no less than:

*(a)* Forty thousand balboas (B 40,000) a year during the first five (5) years; and

*(b)* Seventy-five thousand balboas (B 75,000) a year during the last five years.

Any shortfall shall be made up before expiry of the period stipulated above.

**Art. 31.** All banks engaging in the banking business in Panama must maintain a capital reserve fund to ensure that their total paid-up or assigned capital, as the case may be, plus the said capital reserve, is at no time less than five (5) per cent of their earning assets.

No bank shall declare, credit, or pay dividends, or distribute or transfer any part of its profits, before it has formed the reserve mentioned in this article.

**Art. 32.** All banks shall hold assets in Panama equivalent to a percentage of their local deposits. This percentage shall be fixed by the Commission in accordance with the national economic or financial situation. It shall be equal for all banks and shall not exceed one hundred per cent (100%) of the said deposits.

*Paragraph:* Upon entry into effect of this cabinet decree, and until the Commission decides otherwise, the percentage referred to in this article shall be eighty-five per cent (85%).

**Art. 33.** Banks other than mortgage banks, which operate in Panama and receive local savings deposits, shall be obliged to invest at least fifty per cent (50%) of these deposits in mortgage loans on real property situated in the Republic of Panama, at terms of not less than ten years, or in interest-bearing certificates, securities, or bonds issued by the National Mortgage Bank.

In consultation with the Ministry of Housing, the Commission shall periodically determine what proportion of the aforementioned 50 per cent shall be used for loans for government-subsidized housing or for interest-bearing certificates, securities, or bonds issued by the National Mortgage Bank.

The Commission shall determine the terms and conditions under which banks other than mortgage banks shall adapt their operations to the provisions of this article.

*Paragraph:* Banks are prohibited from investing their savings deposits in their own certificates, securities, or bonds.

## CHAPTER III. STAND-BY CREDITS

**Art. 34.** To be able to keep its license, every bank must be the beneficiary of a stand-by credit in U.S. dollars, granted it by a foreign bank or, in the case of a foreign bank's branch office (approved by the Commission), by its own main office abroad, in an amount of no less than ten per cent (10%) of the bank's total earning assets as at the preceding December 31 or June 30, as the case may be. Nevertheless, the Commission may require review thereof on any other date. The terms and conditions of this credit shall be laid down by the Commission.

If for any reason any bank of the system is unable to obtain or renew the stand-by credit discussed in Articles 34 and 35, the Commission shall be authorized to negotiate with the bank concerned and the other banks in the national banking system to have the latter grant the former a special short-term credit to which all the other banks of the system shall contribute in proportion to the minimum amount of the stand-by credit to which each is committed. Before being entitled to receive this special credit, the bank in question must prove that it was unable to obtain or renew the above-mentioned stand-by credit.

**Art. 35.** The stand-by credit shall be used by the beneficiary bank if sums are withdrawn from the national banking system in excess of ten per cent (10%) of its total deposits used or invested in Panama within a period of six (6) months. The Commission may in this case require the banks to use these credits in whole or in part and to hold the proceeds thereof in Panama. Each bank, at its own discretion, shall decide upon the use of the funds thus obtained.

If any bank in the system encounters difficulties with respect to liquidity as a result of decreasing deposits, the Commission shall be authorized to negotiate with the bank concerned and the other banks in the national banking system, to have the latter grant the former a special short-term credit to which all the other banks of the system shall contribute in proportion to the minimum amount of the stand-by credit to which each is committed.

Before being entitled to receive this special credit, the bank in question must exhaust its own stand-by credit.

## CHAPTER IV. LEGAL RESERVE

**Art. 36.** Each bank must maintain a legal reserve consisting of cash assets of no less than five (5), and no more than twenty-five (25), per cent of the sum total of its local deposits. The Commission shall periodically fix the legal reserve requirement within these minimum and maximum limits and shall advise each bank in writing of the amount required.

**Art. 37.** Not less than 30 per cent of the legal reserve must consist of currency having legal tender in Panama, held by each bank.

The remainder may consist of sight deposits at the National Bank of Panama or of National Treasury bills bearing interest at an annual rate not exceeding three (3) per cent, and with maturities not exceeding ninety (90) days. The Commission must be able to verify such deposits.

*Paragraph 1.* Upon entry into force of this cabinet decree and until such time as the Commission decides otherwise, the legal reserve shall be twelve per cent (12%) for sight deposits and six per cent (6%) for time deposits, and the minimum percentage of this reserve which must consist of currency having legal tender in Panama shall be thirty per cent (30%).

*Paragraph 2.* The banks shall have a period of thirty (30) days, counting from the date of entry into force of this cabinet decree, to comply with the provisions of this article.

*Paragraph 3.* The Commission may authorize that the remainder, up to seventy per cent (70%), consist of other assets, provided that this authorization is adopted with the affirmative vote of five (5) of the Commission members. There must be sufficient liquidity in respect of these assets to meet the legal reserve requirements.

**Art. 38.** The legal reserve requirements shall be uniform for all banks, but the Commission may prescribe different reserves for the various categories of deposits.

**Art. 39.** Banks must submit a report to the Commission, within the period, in the form, and with such frequency as the latter may specify, for the purpose of ensuring due fulfillment of the provisions of this chapter.

**Art. 40.** The Commission shall give all banks failing to comply with the provisions of this chapter three (3) working days' notice to correct such noncompliance. Upon expiry of this time limit, if the fault has not been corrected, the Commission shall impose upon the bank a fine equivalent to two (2) per cent of the amount of the reserve's deficiency, and shall allow the bank fifteen (15) calendar days to correct such deficiency.

**Art. 41.** If a bank repeatedly violates or fails to comply with the provisions of this chapter upon expiry of the fifteen (15) days mentioned in the preceding article, the Commission shall be empowered to cancel that bank's license or to follow, where applicable, the procedure provided for in Chapter XI.

## CHAPTER V. BANK LIQUIDITY

**Art. 42.** All banks engaging in the banking business in Panama must at all times maintain a minimum balance of liquid assets equivalent to the percentage, fixed periodically by the Commission, of the gross amount of their deposits. This percentage shall not exceed thirty-five per cent (35%), except in respect of mortgage banks, for which this percentage shall not exceed twelve per cent (12%). Other than this exception, the percentage shall be equal for all banks.

*Paragraph.* If a bank operating in Panama receives loans or deposits from its main office, branch, subsidiary, or affiliate abroad, such loans or deposits shall not be included when the gross total of its deposits is calculated to determine the percentage of liquidity.

**Art. 43.** Changes in the liquidity percentage requirement must be complied with within such time as the Commission may specify, which shall not be less than thirty (30) calendar days. Upon entry into effect of this cabinet decree, and until such time as the Commission decides otherwise, the applicable liquidity percentage requirement shall be ten per cent (10%) for mortgage banks and thirty per cent (30%) for all other banks. Banks currently authorized to operate shall have a period of ninety (90) days, counting from the effective date of this cabinet decree, to comply with these liquidity percentage requirements.

**Art. 44.** For purposes of the preceding articles, "liquid assets" shall be held to mean such assets as are described below, provided they are freely transferable and unencumbered by any charge or lien whatsoever:

*(a)* Gold or currency having legal tender in Panama;

*(b)* Net balances held at the Clearing House in the Republic of Panama;

*(c)* Net balances at any bank in Panama, withdrawable on demand or at notice not exceeding 186 days, and liabilities payable in Panama upon demand or at not more than 186 days' notice;

*(d)* Treasury bills and other paper issued by the State with maturities of not more than one year;

*(e)* Net balances—up to a maximum of 30 per cent of the liquidity percentage requirement—in any foreign bank approved by the Commission, payable upon demand or at notice not exceeding 186 days in currencies which, in the opinion of the Commission, are freely convertible and transferable;

*(f)* Unmatured bills of exchange bearing the signatures of at least two solvent persons as drawer and drawee, and payable within 186 days in any location and any currency approved by the Commission in accordance with the criteria set forth under item *(e)* above;

*(g)* Treasury notes issued by a foreign government or by international financial organizations in accordance with the criteria set forth under item *(e)* of this article, up to a maximum of 5 per cent of the liquidity percentage requirement;

*(h)* Such other assets as the Commission may authorize by the majority vote of five (5) of its members.

*Paragraph.* Subject to the above-mentioned percentage limitations and any other requirements laid down in this cabinet decree, the distribution of the various kinds of liquid assets discussed in this article shall be at the discretion of each bank.

**Art. 45.** The Commission shall penalize violations of the provisions of this chapter with a fine of not less than B 1,000 nor more than B 10,000.

**Art. 46.** A bank shall be presumed to have infringed the provisions of this chapter and of the preceding chapter if it fails to submit, within the required time limit, such documents and reports as the Commission may periodically request for the purpose of verifying whether the bank is complying with the provisions of Articles 36, 37, 42, and 43.

## CHAPTER VI. BANK INTEREST

**Art. 47.** The provisions of Law No. 4 of 1935 shall not be applicable to banks authorized in accordance with this cabinet decree.[3]

When necessary for the achievement of the objectives referred to in Article 4, the Commission, by resolution adopted with five (5) of its members voting in favor, may fix the maximum interest rate that banks may collect directly or indirectly on the local loans or credit facilities which they grant, that is to say, which are invested or used in the economy within the Republic of Panama. Interest shall be calculated on balances owing.

**Art. 48.** All banks may pay such interest as they deem fit on their foreign deposits and on their time local deposits. However, in order to establish a differential between the interest rate mortgage banks may pay on local "savings deposits" and that payable by the other banks, the Commission must hand down a resolution, adopted with the affirmative vote of five (5) of its members, fixing the maximum interest rate payable by both types of bank on such "local savings deposits," with a minimum difference which at no time may be less than one per cent (1%) in favor of the mortgage banks. Interest may not be paid on local sight deposits.

*Paragraph.* For the purposes of this article, the Commission shall determine the maximum amount under which a time deposit shall be considered a "savings deposit."

**Art. 49.** The Commission shall penalize violations of the provisions of this chapter with a fine of not less than B 1,000 nor more than B 10,000, without prejudice to the obligation of refunding excess interest collected.

---

[3] Law No. 4 of January 2, 1935, provides in Article 2:

"Seven per cent per annum (7%) is fixed as maximum interest for commercial obligations and nine per cent (9%) for civil obligations.

"A higher rate of interest shall be regarded as usurious and the court shall reduce it even though the debtor does not plead the exception of usury. A waiver of this right shall not be valid, nor shall any agreement preventing the debtor from exercising it."

## CHAPTER VII. DOCUMENTS AND REPORTS

**Art. 50.** Within the three (3) months following the close of each fiscal year, banks established in Panama, in respect of all their operations, and banks established abroad, in respect of operations effected by their establishments in Panama, must submit to the Commission the corresponding balance sheets and profit and loss accounts, which shall bear the signature of the bank's Legal Representative or General Agent. The financial statements referred to in this article shall be submitted and audited in such form as the Commission may prescribe.

**Art. 51.** Banks shall exhibit throughout the year, in a conspicuous place in each of their establishments in Panama, a copy of their latest audited balance sheet, and shall publish it in a newspaper of general circulation in the Republic within three (3) months of the close of each fiscal year.

## CHAPTER VIII. PROHIBITIONS AND LIMITATIONS

**Art. 52.** No bank shall declare, credit, or pay any dividend, or distribute or transfer all or part of its profits, until amortization, or the establishment of reserves sufficient for total amortization, of all its deferred expenses, including initial expenses, organization expenses, share selling commissions, brokerage, losses incurred, and any other expenditure item not represented by tangible assets of the bank, or as long as there is a shortage in its capital.

**Art. 53.** Banks are forbidden to grant loans or credit facilities to any individual natural or juridical person, or to issue any guarantee, or contract any other liability in respect of such person, in a total amount that at any time exceeds five (5) per cent of the bank's deposits, capital, and reserves.

The limitation provided in this article shall not apply to transactions which:

(1) Consist of the negotiation of *(a)* bills of exchange made out or notes issued in good faith against real guarantee or upon bank acceptances, or *(b)* other commercial paper authorized by the Commission and owned by the person discounting them at the bank with endorsement in blank without recourse.

(2) Are secured either by bankers' avals or collateral deposits, or by real guarantees duly ensured in their total value and having an ascertainable value on the market or otherwise having a value as security, as

determined in good faith by an official of the bank, in an amount exceeding the amount of the liabilities they guarantee by at least fifteen (15) per cent.

(3) Represent loans to the State, to its autonomous or semiautonomous agencies, or to municipalities, or are guaranteed by the Government or any foreign nation approved by the Commission.

**Art. 54.** Banks are forbidden to:

(1) Grant or obtain loans or credit facilities secured by their own shares.

(2) Grant unsecured loans or credit facilities in an amount exceeding fifteen (15) per cent of their capital and capital reserve to:

*(a)* One or more of their directors, whether granted jointly or severally;
*(b)* Any juridical person of which one or more of the directors is a director or official or a guarantor of the loan or credit facility;
*(c)* Any juridical person or association of persons in which the bank concerned, or one or more of its directors or officials, jointly or severally holds a controlling interest.

(3) Grant loans or credit facilities without guarantee or independent surety, to any of their employees in a total amount which exceeds the annual wages, salaries, or other emoluments of the employees concerned.

**Art. 55.** In the application of the prohibitions laid down in Articles 53 and 54, the Commission may determine whether the interests of a group of natural or juridical persons are so interrelated that they should be regarded as a single person. However, a bank shall not be deemed to have violated the provisions of those articles merely because the group's indebtedness exceeds the applicable limits at the time it is computed, provided the bank takes the necessary steps to wipe out any part of such indebtedness that exceeds the limit within such time as the Commission may indicate.

**Art. 56.** Banks are forbidden to acquire or hold shares or participations in any other kind of enterprise, unless such holdings are in trust, in excess of twenty-five (25) per cent of the bank's paid-up or assigned capital plus its capital reserves, except such participations or shares as the bank may acquire in collecting amounts due it, in which case such participations or shares must be liquidated at the earliest opportunity in keeping with the bank's economic interests, as determined by the Commission, which may stipulate a deadline for this purpose.

**Art. 57.** The provisions of the preceding article shall not prevent the purchase or sale of shares upon the order and in behalf of a customer.

Nor shall they prevent, subject to the Commission's authorization, the purchase or sale of shares of any corporation established for the purpose of insuring bank deposits, fostering the development of a money or securities market in Panama, or improving the system for financing economic development.

**Art. 58.** Banks are forbidden to purchase, acquire, or lease real estate for themselves, except:

(*a*) When necessary for carrying out their operations or for the housing or recreation of their personnel;

(*b*) When they acquire land in order to construct any kind of housing, or real estate development with the intention of selling it, provided that the sale is effected within the period of time mentioned in Article 56;

(*c*) Under exceptional circumstances, with the Commission's prior authorization.

*Paragraph.* However, banks that have accepted real estate as guarantee for their loans may, in case of nonpayment, acquire such real estate with the intention of selling it at the earliest opportunity in keeping with the bank's economic interests, as determined by the Commission.

**Art. 59.** Any bank that has participated in any transaction incompatible with the provisions of this chapter, prior to entry into effect of this cabinet decree, must submit a statement of such transactions to the Commission within three (3) months of entry into effect of the same, and must finally liquidate all such transactions within the following three (3) years, unless the Commission grants extensions in view of exceptional circumstances.

**Art. 60.** While in a state of insolvency, banks are forbidden to receive deposits, nor may they receive any other resources from anyone not having been previously informed by the bank of such state of insolvency. No officer, director, or official who has or should have knowledge of such insolvency shall accept or authorize the receipt of deposits or resources in violation of the provisions of this article.

**Art. 61.** The Commission shall impose a fine of not less than one thousand balboas (B 1,000) nor more than ten thousand balboas (B 10,000) for violations of the provisions of this chapter.

## CHAPTER IX. INSPECTION OF BANKS

**Art. 62.** All banks must send the Commission, in such form as the latter may prescribe:

(1) Not later than the twentieth (20th) day of each month, a statement showing the assets and liabilities of their establishments in Panama at the close of business on the last working day of the preceding month; and,

(2) Before the last working day of the month following the quarterly periods ending on March 31, June 30, September 30, and December 31, a statement containing an analysis of the credit facilities and other assets held by their establishments in Panama at the close of business of each quarter.

*Paragraph.* Without prejudice to the foregoing, the Commission is empowered to ask any bank, or any firm operating in Panama in which the bank has a majority participation or effective control, for the documents and reports concerning the operations and activities of its establishments.

**Art. 63.** If the reports submitted to it under the preceding article are of a confidential nature in accordance with the provisions of Article 74, the Commission may only publish consolidated data with aggregate figures.

**Art. 64.** The Commission must inspect each bank at least once every two (2) years, in order to determine whether the bank's financial condition is solvent and whether in the course of its operations it has complied with the provisions of this cabinet decree. These inspections shall include establishments and firms in Panama in which the banks have majority participation or effective control. The total cost of the inspection and related expenses shall be paid by the bank being inspected.

**Art. 65.** When requested in writing, every bank shall be required to submit, to any inspector authorized by the Commission to examine the bank's operations, all books, minutes, cash, securities owned by the bank, documents and vouchers, and the reports and documents concerning its operations. However, in order to protect the interests of the bank's customers and to ensure the discretion required for their operations, the examination on the part of the Commission's inspectors may not include deposit accounts of any kind, or securities held in safekeeping, or safe-deposit boxes, or documents connected with credit operations between customers and the bank, except by court order, in accordance with Article 89 of the Commercial Code.

**Art. 66.** Any refusal on the part of the bank to submit to the inspection as provided for in the preceding article shall be penalized by the Commission with a fine that shall not exceed B 1,000, without prejudice to application of the provisions of Article 26 of this cabinet decree. If any document or report submitted should prove to be in any way false, the Commission shall impose upon the bank a fine of not less than one thousand balboas (B 1,000) nor more than ten thousand balboas (B 10,000), without prejudice to other applicable penalties.

**Art. 67.** If, in the opinion of the Commission, the inspection reveals that the bank's operations are being conducted in an unlawful or negligent manner, or that its capital has been impaired, or that it is in an insolvent condition, the Commission shall require the bank immediately to take such necessary steps to rectify the deficiencies as the former may specify for this purpose, and may appoint a person with the proper training and experience to advise the bank on the steps it must take in order to rectify the deficiency. The Commission shall fix his remuneration, which shall be paid by the bank.

**Art. 68.** Every bank must at its own expense annually appoint certified public accountants whom the Commission considers to be professionally qualified and whose duty it shall be to make a report on the fiscal year, to the shareholders or partners of each bank established in Panama, and to the head office in the case of a bank established abroad. In this report these auditors shall state whether, in their judgment, the balance sheet and the profit and loss account are complete and accurate, and whether they are a true and correct reflection of the bank's operations.

The report of the certified public accountants shall be read, together with the report of the bank's Board, at the annual meeting of shareholders or partners of each bank established in Panama, and shall be transmitted to the head office of each bank established abroad. A copy of the report shall be sent to the Commission.

**Art. 69.** If a bank fails to make the appointment as provided in the preceding article, the Commission shall make the appointment in question, and shall fix the remuneration to be paid to the certified public accountants thus appointed. This remuneration shall be paid for by the bank.

**Art. 70.** No certified public accountant or firm of certified public accountants in which any of the partners or employees is or has been an employee, director, or official of a bank, or is or becomes a shareholder or partner of a bank, may act as an auditor of that bank.

**Art. 71.** Without prejudice to the provisions of the Commercial Code and other laws in effect, any person who holds the office of director or official of a bank, and all other persons responsible for the administration of a bank, shall cease to hold office:

(1) If declared bankrupt or insolvent; or

(2) If convicted of any offense against public property or trust.

Such persons may not again hold such offices or positions in any bank without the Commission's express authorization.

**Art. 72.** No person who has been a director or official, or taken part in the management, of a bank that has been in forced liquidation may act as a director of official or take part in the management of another bank without the Commission's express authorization.

**Art. 73.** The Commission shall be immediately informed of any civil or criminal proceedings initiated in respect of the violation of any provision of this cabinet decree committed by a bank or other person.

**Art. 74.** The Commission is prohibited from investigating, or ordering an investigation of, the personal affairs of any bank client. The information obtained by the Commission in the exercise of its duties may not be revealed to any person or authority unless courts require it to do so in accordance with the laws in effect, or unless such information consists of consolidated data with aggregate figures. Violation of this rule shall be penalized in accordance with the provisions of Article 101 of this cabinet decree.

*Paragraph.* The Commission may not publish any information furnished it under this cabinet decree, unless it has obtained the written consent of the bank or client concerned prior to such publication.

**Art. 75.** Official banks are in all cases subject to the inspection and supervision of the Office of the Comptroller General of the Republic in the terms of the Constitution and the Law. Therefore, the provisions of Articles 64 and 68 of this cabinet decree shall not apply to official banks.

## CHAPTER X. VOLUNTARY LIQUIDATION

**Art. 76.** Before proceeding to liquidate or dissolve, all banks must obtain the authorization of the Commission, which shall grant such authorization if the bank is solvent, that is, if it has sufficient liquid assets to reimburse its depositors and repay its creditors.

**Art. 77.** Once the authorization has been granted, the bank shall forthwith cease to do business, and shall have only the powers necessary to effect the liquidation, collect its claims, reimburse its depositors, pay its creditors, and wind up its affairs.

**Art. 78.** Within thirty (30) days after the authorization has been granted, the bank must mail to each depositor, creditor, person interested in the funds that the bank holds as trustee, lessor of a safe-deposit box, or depositor of assets in safekeeping, a notice of liquidation, which shall contain such information as the Commission may specify. This notice shall also be posted in a visible place on the premises of each of the bank's establishments, and shall be published in such form as the Commission may direct.

**Art. 79.** Authorization for liquidation shall not prejudice the right of a depositor or creditor to payment in full of the amount of his claim, or the right of a holder of funds or other assets to have such assets returned to him. All legitimate claims of creditors and depositors must be paid, and all the funds and other assets held by the bank for any other reason shall be returned to their owners within such time as the Commission may prescribe when authorizing the liquidation.

**Art. 80.** The assets may not be distributed among the shareholders or partners until all claims of depositors and creditors have been satisfied in accordance with the liquidation procedure approved by the Commission.

The bank shall turn over to whomever the Commission designates an amount sufficient to satisfy any disputed claims. This person shall hold the said amount until the courts hand down a decision with respect to the claims.

**Art. 81.** Upon completion of liquidation, the bank shall turn over the amount needed to cover any unclaimed funds or claims to whomever the Commission designates. All unclaimed assets and securities, and a certified inventory thereof, shall also be turned over to whomever the Commission designates. The funds thus deposited shall be transferred to the State at the end of five (5) years and, with the prior approval of the Commission, the assets and securities may be sold by the depositary upon expiry of the first year, and upon expiry of the fifth year the proceeds from such sale shall be transferred to the State if not claimed by the owners.

*Paragraph.* The provisions of this article shall be understood without prejudice to the right granted under Article 103.

**Art. 82.** In the course of voluntary liquidation, the liquidators shall be obliged to:

(1) Submit to the Commission, as often as the latter may specify, such reports as it may request regarding the course of the liquidation; and

(2) Inform the Commission as soon as it is considered that their realizable assets will not be sufficient to reimburse the depositors and to pay the creditors.

## CHAPTER XI. INTERVENTION, REORGANIZATION, AND FORCED LIQUIDATION

**Art. 83.** The Commission, by resolution with statement of reasons approved with five (5) of its members voting in favor, may intervene in a bank, taking possession of its assets and taking over its management as provided in Article 85, in any of the following cases:

*(a)* If its capital or capital reserve falls short or is otherwise in an unsound condition;
*(b)* If its business is being conducted in an unlawful negligent, or fraudulent manner;
*(c)* If it can no longer safely pursue its business;
*(d)* If it has refused, after proper demand, to submit the accounting records of its operations, or has in any way obstructed inspection of the bank;
*(e)* If the bank's assets are not sufficient to meet all its liabilities; or
*(f)* If the Commission deems it advisable, because completion of the voluntary liquidation has been unduly delayed.

**Art. 84.** When effecting the intervention, the Commission shall order that a notice to that effect be fixed on the bank's premises, indicating the time at which it became effective, which shall in no case be prior to posting of the notice.

**Art. 85.** When the Commission decides to intervene in a bank, it shall appoint such supervisor(s) as it deems necessary, exclusively to exercise administration and control of the same, with such powers as the Commission specifies, which shall include the following:

(*a*) To stop or limit payment of the bank's obligations;
(*b*) To employ the necessary auxiliary personnel;
(*c*) To execute any document in behalf of the bank;
(*d*) To initiate, defend, and conduct in the bank's behalf any action or proceedings to which it may be a party.

As soon as intervention has taken place, the supervisor(s) shall prepare an inventory of the bank's assets and liabilities, and send a copy to the Commission, which shall make it available to the interested parties if they so request.

**Art. 86.** The resolution ordering intervention in a bank entails the power to order its reorganization, request its forced liquidation, or desist from intervention, for which the Commission shall have sixty (60) calendar days counting from the date on which the notices mentioned in Article 84 were posted, or, if the appeal provided for in the following article is filed, sixty (60) days from the date on which judgment is handed down.

**Art. 87.** The bank affected shall be entitled to appeal the resolution ordering the intervention only to the executive courts having full jurisdiction. The term for filing such appeal shall be thirty (30) working days, counting from the date on which the notice provided in Article 84 is posted.

The court may in no case temporarily suspend the effects of the decreed intervention, but in order that the Commission may give instructions for the reorganization or request the forced liquidation of the bank concerned, judgment must have been handed down in respect of the pending appeal.

**Art. 88.** When the Commission intervenes in a bank, it shall be understood that the statutory term of any claim or right of action on the part of the bank, and the time limits in any action or proceedings to which the bank may be a party, are suspended for up to six (6) months.

**Art. 89.** If, before expiry of the deadline established in Article 86, the Commission decides that reorganization of the bank is in order, it shall, after hearing the opinion of the bank concerned, prepare the plan for reorganization and publish it for three (3) consecutive days in a newspaper of general circulation in the Republic.

**Art. 90.** No asset of the bank shall be subject to attachment, lien, or withholding while the bank is in the intervention or reorganization process.

**Art. 91.** With the Commission's authorization, the supervisors may obtain loans in behalf of the bank and pledge the bank's assets as security.

**Art. 92.** All necessary expenses occasioned by intervention, reorganization, or liquidation shall be defrayed from the assets of the bank.

**Art. 93.** No reorganization plan shall be drawn up that does not comply with the following requisites:

*(a)* It must be feasible and fair for all the depositors, creditors, shareholders, or partners, as the case may be;

*(b)* It must ensure the dismissal of any director, official, or employee who, because of his negligent, fraudulent, or unlawful action, is responsible for the existence of conditions making reorganization necessary;

*(c)* Any contemplated merger or consolidation must conform to the requirements of this cabinet decree and other legal provisions in force.

**Art. 94.** Whenever, in the course of reorganization, circumstances arise that render the plan unfair or its execution undesirable, the Commission may modify the plan or request liquidation of the bank, as set forth below.

**Art. 95.** If the Commission decides that it is in order to request the liquidation of a bank, it shall notify that bank's legal representative personally, and shall advise its shareholders or partners, depositors, and creditors, by publishing the resolution in which such decision was made for three (3) consecutive days in a newspaper of general circulation, and shall file a request for dissolution and liquidation of the bank with the competent court, in accordance with the legal provisions in effect.

**Art. 96.** Once the liquidation is requested, the Commission shall have notice of such request for liquidation sent by mail, using the address appearing on the bank's books, to each depositor, creditor, lessee of a safe-deposit box, or bailor of property. A copy of the notice shall be posted in a visible place in the bank's establishments. Together with the notice, a statement must be sent indicating the amount shown on the bank's books to be the claim of the depositor or creditor.

**Art. 97.** Safe-deposit boxes, the contents of which have not been removed thirty (30) days subsequent to the date of the court's decision ordering the liquidation, shall be opened by the competent court and the contents and unclaimed assets at the bank shall be subject to the procedure established in Article 81.

## CHAPTER XII. MISCELLANEOUS PROVISIONS

**Art. 98.** The classification of each bank, referred to in Article 1010 of the Tax Code, shall be effected by the Commission in accordance with the criteria it shall establish for this purpose.

**Art. 99.** The Commission, after informing the public, shall declare days on which no bank may effect operations with the public. These days shall not necessarily coincide with national holidays.

**Art. 100.** The Commission shall fix the days of the week and the hours during which the banks shall be open to the public.

The Commission, when it deems justified, may authorize exceptions to the general rule.

**Art. 101.** All persons who submit information in violation of this cabinet decree, or who violate any of the provisions thereof for which no specific sanction has been indicated, shall be held liable for a fine of B 500 to B 1,000, which shall be imposed by the Commission, without prejudice to the other appropriate civil and penal liabilities.

**Art. 102.** All banks must inform the Commission of any assets, funds, or securities in their possession which remain inactive for five (5) years and belong to persons whose whereabouts are unknown. The Commission, after verifying this fact, shall order the net value of the assets to be transferred to the National Treasury.

**Art. 103.** The State shall be obliged to restore the funds mentioned in the preceding article to the owners, provided they are claimed within ten (10) years following the date on which they were transferred, but they shall be restored without interest.

**Art. 104.** Without prejudice to the provisions of the Tax Code, all establishments of a bank in Panama shall be considered a single bank for the purposes of this cabinet decree.

## TITLE III

### FINAL PROVISIONS

**Art. 105.** With the exception of the provisions of Article 87, the only appeal recourse that may be had against the resolutions handed down by the Commission is an appeal for reconsideration, through government channels, to the Commission itself, for which purpose the party concerned shall have a period of five (5) working days counting from the date on which it is notified of such resolution.

**Art. 106.** In all cases of voluntary or forced liquidation of a bank, its liabilities, including deposits, must be paid off in accordance with the order of priorities established by the laws in effect. The foregoing notwithstanding, if the special credit mentioned in Artcle 35 has been delivered to the bank being liquidated, that credit shall have preference over any other of the bank's current liabilities.

As regards deposits, the order of priority shall be the following:

*(a)* Local deposits of natural or juridical persons domiciled within the territory under the jurisdiction of the Panamanian authorities shall be paid first;

*(b)* When the local deposits have been refunded, consideration shall be given to and refund made, as far as possible, of deposits which physically entered the territory of the Republic of Panama and the bank's premises and which belong to persons domiciled abroad; and

*(c)* If any balance remains after these refunds are made, it shall be distributed among the owners of deposits which come from foreign countries and which have not physically entered the territory of Panama.

**Art. 107.** Banks in which an intervention has been made and which are in the process of liquidation when this cabinet decree enters into force shall be governed by Law No. 101 of July 8, 1941 and its amendments or supplements.

**Art. 108.** Banks wishing to adhere to a fiscal period other than that of the calendar year, approval of which has been granted by the Ministry of Finance and Treasury, must notify the Commission of such authorization.

**Art. 109.** Only the provisions of Chapters V, VII, VIII, and IX of Title II shall be applicable to official banks, provided that these provisions do not conflict with the laws governing such banks. The foregoing notwithstanding, Chapters IV and VI, and Articles 99 and 100 of Chapter XII, shall at all times apply to official banks.

**Art. 110.** This cabinet decree revokes Law No. 101 of July 8, 1941 in its entirety, and all other legal provisions that may be contrary to it.

**Art. 111.** This cabinet decree shall enter into force from the date of its publication in the *Gazeta Oficial.*

*{The signatory clause is omitted.}*

## Law No. 18 [1]

[January 28, 1959]

Whereby regulations are enacted on coded bank accounts

The National Assembly of Panama

DECREES:

Art. 1. Banking enterprises and other credit institutions legally established in the territory of the Republic may operate coded current or deposit accounts, which shall be governed by the pertinent provisions of the Code of Commerce, as amended by the within law.

Art. 2. The coded banking account is a contract whereby a person, whether natural or juridical, maintains on deposit with a bank cash or securities or a credit, and such bank agrees to meet the orders of payments of said depositor up to the amounts of cash or delivery of securities that he may have deposited, or of the credit granted to him, and to observe strict secrecy as to the existence of the account, its balance and the identity of the depositor.

The interests which under the provisions of a bank account contract may be earned by the depositor are an integral part of the account for all legal purposes.

[1] Issued in Panama on January 26, 1959.

**Art. 3.** It is not necessary that the name of the drawer appear on the checks and payment orders drawn against coded current bank accounts or on orders for delivery of securities. The bank shall be required to pay such checks and orders of payment provided that the usual signature previously furnished by the customer and the number assigned to the account appear thereon.

**Art. 4.** Managers, officers, officials and other employees of banking institutions, whether national or foreign, who reveal or disclose to persons alien to the institution and to the handling of these accounts any information with reference to the existence, balance or identity of the customer of a coded bank account shall be punished with imprisonment of from thirty (30) days to six (6) months, fines of from one thousand balboas (B 1,000) to ten thousand balboas (B 10,000), or both.

**Art. 5.** The information on coded current bank accounts referred to in the preceding article may be revealed by managers and other employees of banking institutions to investigating officers, judges and magistrates who hear criminal proceedings, and who shall hold the information in strict reserve in the event that such information is not conducive to clarifying the punishable facts under investigation.

In the cases in which public functionaries, whether of a judicial or administrative category, other than those mentioned in this article, request from banking institutions any information or the attachment or embargo of coded bank accounts, including probate proceedings, the bank shall not furnish the information, nor withhold the funds or securities deposited in coded accounts, and shall reply to the request stating that it is not possible to furnish any information, even in the cases where there exist the account or the funds or securities covered by the request.

**Art. 6.** The managers, officers and other functionaries of banking enterprises handling coded current bank accounts shall be subject to the penalties provided for in Article 4 of the within law, even in the cases in which they disclose information on said accounts to officials or employees of the Legislative Organ, the Executive Organ, the Ministry of Finance and Treasury, the Independent Agencies of the State, the Office of the Comptroller General of the Republic, or the Judicial Organ, other than in the exceptions relative to criminal proceedings stipulated in the preceding article.

**Art. 7.** The provisions of Article 17 of Law No. 101 of 1941, as amended by Law No. 47 of 1954, shall not apply to coded bank accounts.

**Art. 8.** Banking institutions which by law are required to report to the Department of Internal Revenue of the Ministry of Finance and

Treasury on the amounts of interest paid to depositors of coded accounts, shall do so globally, that is, without specifying the amount paid to each depositor.

Art. 9. In the event of the demise of one of the persons authorized to draw against a joint account, the survivors may continue drawing against same.

*Proviso:* A joint account is that against which more than one person may draw.

Art. 10. The power to withdraw funds from coded bank accounts does not cease upon the demise of the grantor of such power.

Art. 11. All provisions contrary to this law are hereby repealed.

Art. 12. This law shall become effective upon its publication in the *Gazeta Oficial.*

*{The signatory clause is omitted.}*

# Law No. 20 [1]

[April 22, 1975]

## Reorganizing the National Bank of Panama [2]

The National Legislative Council

DECREES:

### CHAPTER I

#### PURPOSES AND OBJECTIVES

Art. 1. The National Bank of Panama, established by Law No. 74 of 1904, Law No. 27 of 1906, and Law No. 6 of 1911, is an autonomous agency of the State having its own capital. Further, it is an official bank

[1] Published in *Gazeta Oficial* No. 17832 of May 5, 1975. This law superseded Law No. 11 of February 7, 1956 and was, in turn, amended by Law No. 17 of April 9, 1976 and Law No. 76 of September 19, 1978. The amendments are incorporated in the version published here.

[2] Banco Nacional de Panamá.

with independent juridical personality and is autonomous and independent as regards its internal system and administration, subject solely and exclusively to the surveillance of the Executive under the conditions established in this law. It shall be the State's preeminent financial organization and shall have, in addition to the objectives expressly stated in this law, the purpose of engaging, within the official sector, in the business of banking as defined in the law and seeking to obtain the financing necessary to the development of the national economy.

**Art. 2.** The National Bank of Panama is regulated primarily by this law and complementarily by Cabinet Decree No. 238 of July 2, 1970, whereby the banking system is reorganized and the National Banking Commission is established, under the conditions stipulated in Article 109 of said Cabinet Decree.

**Art. 3.** The State is responsible for all liabilities of the National Bank of Panama.[3]

**Art. 4.** The minimum capital stock of the National Bank of Panama shall be ten million balboas (B 10,000,000.00), of which the State initially provided the sum of one million balboas (B 1,000,000.00).

The capital stock of the National Bank of Panama may be changed depending on the institution's reserve funds. Such funds shall be constituted from the profits earned by the National Bank of Panama on its operations.

**Art. 5.** The National Bank of Panama shall not charge the State any amount whatsoever for cash office services or for any other kind of banking service it renders to the State.

Nevertheless, the National Bank of Panama may charge public law juridical persons, State and semipublic enterprises, and municipalities for special services provided them, even if such services are not expressly mentioned in this law.

**Art. 6.** The National Bank of Panama shall at all times be exempt from the payment of any national, municipal or other tax, duty, or assessment, and in any judicial or administrative proceedings to which

[3] The responsibility of the State is referred to in Article 232 of the Constitution. That article provides:

> "The law shall establish and regulate official and semiofficial banks which shall function as autonomous institutions under the supervision of the State, and shall determine its ancillary responsibilities in connection with the liabilities contracted by these institutions. The law shall regulate the banking system."

it may be a party it shall enjoy all the privileges that the laws of procedure accord to the State.

The exemptions and privileges specified in this provision do not extend to the personnel in the Bank's service.

**Art. 7.** All authorities of the Republic shall give effective assistance to the General Manager and other officials of the National Bank of Panama when asked to do so in matters connected with the institution.

**Art. 8.** Public law juridical persons, semipublic or State enterprises, and municipalities shall be required to keep their moneys on deposit with the National Bank of Panama.

**Art. 9.** The General Manager of the National Bank of Panama shall send to the Comptroller General of the Republic a daily cash balance sheet [and,] [4] each month, a cumulative general balance sheet. The General Manager shall submit each year to the Executive a report on the activities of the Bank.

**Art. 10.** The check clearing system and the clearinghouse of the national banking system shall function under the direction and responsibility of the National Bank of Panama. To this end, the National Bank of Panama shall regulate by decision of its Board of Directors the operations and functions of the check clearing system and the clearinghouse, whereupon Executive Decree No. 157 of October 17, 1967 and any other complementary provisions on this subject shall be deemed superseded.

## CHAPTER II

### ADMINISTRATION OF THE BANK

**Art. 11.** The management, direction and administration of the National Bank of Panama shall be the responsibility of a General Manager and a Board of Directors composed of five (5) members, all of whom shall be appointed by the Executive.

The Board of Directors shall have a Secretary, whose functions shall be those stipulated in the law and such others as may be established by the Board.

The General Manager shall place at the disposal of the Board of Directors such administrative personnel and other facilities as may be necessary for it to perform its assigned functions.

---

[4] Editor's addition.

**Art. 12.** To be a member of the Board of Directors or General Manager of the Bank one must have been engaged in commercial or industrial activities, in executive positions, for at least five (5) of the last ten (10) years or be knowledgeable in economics or finance.

**Art. 13.** The Board of Directors shall have the following duties and powers:

(*a*) To meet at least once a month and whenever convened by the General Manager or at the request of at least three (3) directors.

(*b*) To set the salary and representation allowance of the General Manager.

(*c*) To establish guidelines for the proper operation of the Bank in all its aspects, and especially as regards its administrative, economic and legal affairs, in conformity with the economic development policy established by the Executive. To this end, it shall prescribe such by-laws as may be necessary for the proper functioning of the Bank.

(*d*) To approve the Bank's organizational structure and its functions as proposed by the General Manager, which will be revised when deemed necessary in view of the expansion of the Bank.

(*e*) To approve the establishment and closing of branches and agencies as proposed by the General Manager.

(*f*) To approve or disapprove operations proposed to the Bank in an amount exceeding five hundred thousand balboas (B 500,000). Operations not exceeding five hundred thousand balboas (B 500,000) shall be decided upon by Credit Committees, whose functions and procedures shall be regulated by the Board of Directors.
Credit operations requested of the Bank by the State, public law juridical persons, State or semipublic enterprises, or municipalities may be decided upon by the General Manager, subject to authorization by the Executive.

(*g*) To empower the General Manager to contract for the construction or repair of facilities and for the purchase, sale or leasing of property belonging to the Bank on behalf of the Bank and without public competitive bidding, when the Bank's interests so justify in the judgment of the Board.

(*h*) To take cognizance of operations effected in amounts greater than two hundred and fifty thousand balboas (B 250,000) but smaller than five hundred thousand balboas (B 500,000). The General Manager of the Bank shall inform the Board of Directors of such operations in the first meeting following the date of each such operation.

*(i)* To approve the expenditure budget.
*(j)* Such other duties and powers as may be established by law.

**Art. 14.** The members of the Board of Directors shall be paid a fee of fifty balboas (B 50) each for each meeting they attend.

**Art. 15.** Approval of resolutions and decisions by the Board of Directors requires a majority vote of the members of the Board and the favorable opinion of the General Manager of the Bank, except in special cases in which a larger number of directors' votes is required in accordance with this law.

**Art. 16.** The General Manager can be suspended from office only by an unappealable judicial sentence for criminal offenses. He may also be suspended by the Executive at the request of the Board of Directors in the cases mentioned in the following article.

**Art. 17.** In the event that the General Manager acts beyond his legal authority in a manner which may give rise to liability for the Bank, or effects operations without due authorization from the Board of Directors when such authorization is necessary, the Board of Directors shall order the appropriate investigation to be made and may, by vote of at least four (4) of its members, request the Executive to suspend the General Manager. The General Manager shall be temporarily suspended as from the date on which the Board of Directors sends the request for suspension to the Executive.
If the Executive, after studying the case filed by the Board of Directors and making such investigations as it may deem advisable, considers the Board of Directors' request justified, it shall order by Executive Decree the suspension of the General Manager, who shall be permanently removed from office as from the date of the decree.

**Art. 18.** The General Manager is the legal representative of the Bank, and actions he performs and contracts he enters into in the name of the Bank shall be binding on the Bank, without prejudice to the responsibilities specified in this law.

**Art. 19.** In cases of temporary or occasional absence of the General Manager, an official designated by the General Manager with the approval of the Board of Directors shall act in his stead. In case of permanent absence of the General Manager, he shall be replaced temporarily by an official designated by the Board of Directors pending a new appointment by the Executive.

**Art. 20.** The office of General Manager of the National Bank of Panama is incompatible with the exercise of any other remunerated public office or position except those which by virtue of other laws he performs as General Manager of the Bank and that of professor in an establishment of higher education.

**Art. 21.** The General Manager of the National Bank of Panama shall be authorized:

*(a)* To decide on operations proposed to the Bank in amounts not exceeding two hundred and fifty thousand balboas (B 250,000) in the case of collateralized credit facilities and in amounts not exceeding one hundred thousand balboas (B 100,000) in the case of unsecured credit facilities.

*(b)* To determine the size of operations or credit facilities that may be authorized by Bank officials. In no case may these ceilings exceed those established by law for the General Manager.

**Art. 22.** The Bank shall insure the performance of the General Manager and of all its officials and subordinate employees by contracting comprehensive or group insurance, whose premiums shall be covered by the Bank.

**Art. 23.** The National Bank of Panama shall also have an external audit department, which shall be directly responsible to the Office of the Comptroller General of the Republic and whose function shall be to audit, inspect, and verify its operations. This department shall be headed by an auditor appointed by the Comptroller General of the Republic.

**Art. 24.** The National Bank of Panama shall have as many officers and employees as necessary for its proper functioning; they shall be freely appointed, transferred and removed by the General Manager, and their salaries shall be set by the General Manager.

The General Manager may not appoint as a subordinate any relative of his within the fourth degree of consanguinity or within the second degree of affinity, or his spouse.

**Art. 25.** Neither the General Manager of the Bank nor any other officer or employee of the Bank may bind himself as guarantor or joint debtor to the National Bank of Panama while occupying his position.

## CHAPTER III

### OPERATIONS AND FACILITIES OF THE BANK

**Art. 26.** The National Bank of Panama shall be authorized to perform the following operations:

*(a)* Grant secured and unsecured credit facilities.
*(b)* Discount negotiable credit, securities and documents.
*(c)* Purchase and sell drafts and bills of exchange or promissory notes issued or payable in the Republic or abroad.
*(d)* Act on commission and as agent, and accept in deposit all kinds of property capable of being deposited.
*(e)* Accept money for deposit in current accounts, savings accounts, term accounts, numbered accounts, and in any other fashion in which moneys can be accepted in accordance with banking custom and practice.
*(f)* Act as trustee or proxy.
*(g)* Purchase and sell real estate and movable property for the use or benefit of the Bank; receive property as grants, by assignment, or in payment of liabilities incurred toward the Bank, whether or not such property is encumbered in favor of the Bank.
*(h)* Approve overdrafts.
*(i)* Grant all kinds of commercial, personal and other credit.
*(j)* Issue letters of credit.
*(k)* Furnish its bank guarantee.
*(l)* Act as custodian and transporter of moneys and other valuables.
*(m)* Carry out collection operations.
*(n)* Invest moneys in public law or private law juridical persons in an amount not greater than ten per cent (10%) of the Bank's assets.
*(ñ)* Trade in State obligations and foreign currencies, but not speculate in securities.
The Bank shall use prevailing market quotations as the basis for all transactions in currencies or foreign securities.
*(o)* Incur liabilities in the Republic or abroad.
*(p)* In general, conduct all operations permitted to the business of banking in accordance with the law or banking practice.

**Art. 27.** In every document dealing with an operation for which the prior authorization of the Board of Directors is necessary, the date of the meeting at which such operation was authorized shall be recorded.

**Art. 28.** Antichresis must be agreed as an accessory to the mortgage guarantee in all cases of mortgage-guaranteed credit facilities. In every mortgage-guaranteed credit facility it shall also be stipulated that the debtor waives executory process.

**Art. 29.** Mortgage-guaranteed credit facilities may be granted for up to 90 per cent of the commercial value of the property guaranteeing them.

For loans guaranteed by collateral, the amount of the credit facility shall not exceed the commercial value of the property pledged at the time of the operation. Whenever the value of property pledged to the Bank is smaller than the amount lent or owed, the General Manager shall require the debtor, and the debtor shall be obliged, to improve the guarantee, and if he should fail to do so the obligation shall be considered due and steps shall be taken toward its immediate collection.

**Art. 30.** The General Manager shall cause to be inspected, whenever he deems it appropriate, property pledged to the Bank in guarantee of liabilities to the Bank. If at any time the value of such property is found to have decreased to the point that it no longer guarantees the payment of the obligation, the General Manager shall require the debtor, and the debtor shall be obliged, to improve the guarantee or to furnish others, and if he should fail to do so the debt shall be considered due and steps shall be taken toward its immediate collection.

Such inspections may be conducted by Bank officials or by private persons who are expert in the field. In any event, the cost of such inspections shall be borne by the debtor involved.

**Art. 31.** Every mortgage-guaranteed credit facility granted by the National Bank of Panama and involving improved real property shall entail the obligation on the part of the debtor to maintain insurance on such improvements and to assign any indemnification for loss to the Bank. The amount and type of insurance shall be established in each specific instance in the document containing the credit facility.

The Bank shall be entitled to insure the property or renew the policy in the event that the debtor does not do so, but in this case any amount spent by the Bank for the purpose shall be charged to the debtor and shall accrue interest at the same rate as the principal. Such amounts and interest thereon shall be payable upon request.

**Art. 32.** Property acquired by the Bank in payment of obligations to it may be sold in accordance with the Bank's best interest. Such sales shall be made at the commercial market price after an independent appraisal. If there is more than one prospective purchaser, the Bank shall make the sale to the one offering the highest price.

**Art. 33.** At the request of the Executive, the National Bank of Panama shall coordinate the credit policies of State financial and credit institutions to achieve a more effective utilization of their resources and shall take part in the negotiation and contracting of loans and in the placement of bonds in which the State, any other public law juridical person or any State or semipublic enterprise is a party.

**Art. 34.** The administration of the Bank's property and the administration of its debtors' property which it exercises by antichresis, attachment, power of attorney or any other reason, may be handled by the Bank itself or by third parties who are expert in the field.

## CHAPTER IV

### EXECUTORY COLLECTION

**Art. 35.** The General Manager of the Bank is hereby granted summary jurisdiction for collection of liabilities to the Bank that have fallen due. This authority may be delegated to such Bank officials as the General Manager may determine.

**Art. 36.** The General Manager of the Bank may empower any lawyer to collect the Bank's claims, but in such cases the action must be brought before ordinary courts.

**Art. 37.** In collection proceedings instituted by the National Bank of Panama by summary jurisdiction, there shall be such legal costs as the Bank's Board of Directors may determine.

The Bank may acquire property of its debtors at auction for the account of the liabilities to be paid. In such processes the date of the auction shall be publicly announced and may not be less than five (5) days after the date of posting or publication of the notice.

**Art. 38.** Claims of the National Bank of Panama which have been acknowledged by a writ of execution issued by ordinary courts or by executory judges by virtue of summary jurisdiction and which have not been paid may be sent by the National Bank of Panama to the Directorate General of Revenue for collection. The proceeds of the collection of such claims shall be paid to the National Treasury.

In such cases, the Directorate General of Revenue will not issue the Certificate of Compliance referred to in Article 739 of the Tax Code until the debt has been paid in full.

**Art. 39.** If the party involved does not personally prove that he has fully paid the National Bank of Panama in connection with a case of the type referred to in the preceding article, the deeds and contracts mentioned in Article 739 of the Tax Code may not be authorized, permitted or admitted by the relevant public or private officials.

**Art. 40.** For purposes of the preceding article, the parties involved will prove that they have fully paid the National Bank of Panama in connection with a case of the type referred to in Article 39 hereof by means of a certificate to be issued by the Directorate General of Revenue.

**Art. 41.** The provisions of Articles 740, 741, 743, 744, 745, and 746 of the Tax Code shall be applicable for purposes of collection of the claims referred to in Article 39 hereof.

## CHAPTER V

### RETIREMENT

**Art. 42.** Employees and former employees of the National Bank of Panama shall be entitled to retire when this law comes into force, subject to the following conditions:

That the employee has been employed by the Bank for at least twenty-eight (28) years; or that upon the entry into force of this law he be sixty (60) years of age and have been employed by the Bank for at least twenty (20) consecutive years.

**Art. 43.** An employee requesting retirement in accordance with the preceding article shall be paid, for life, seventy-five per cent (75%) of the last salary earned, which in no case may be greater than five hundred balboas (B 500).

**Art. 44.** Employees of the National Bank of Panama who leave the Bank's employ because of total permanent physical disability, fully confirmed by a medical certificate and accepted as factual by the Board of Directors of the Bank, shall also retire on seventy-five per cent (75%) of the last salary earned, which in no case may be greater than five hundred balboas (B 500), provided they have been employed by the institution for at least ten (10) consecutive years.

**Art. 45.** The amount of the retirement pensions allowed in Articles 43 and 44 hereof shall be paid in its entirety by the Social Contributions Complementary Fund created by Law No. 16 of 1975, as provided in Article 31 of Law No. 15 of March 31, 1975.

**Art. 46.** Employees of the National Bank of Panama who request retirement may opt for the benefits granted them by Law No. 20 of April 22, 1975 or for the benefits provided by the Social Contributions Complementary Fund created by Law No. 16 of 1975, provided they meet the conditions and requirements established in the respective law.

**Art. 47.** The employees of institutions incorporated into the National Bank of Panama under this law may avail themselves, taking into account the years of service with said institutions, of the retirement and pension benefits which are the subject of this chapter.

**Art. 48.** This law supersedes Law No. 11 of February 7, 1956.

**Art. 49.** This law shall come into force upon its publication.

*{The signatory clause is omitted.}*

# Law No. 13 [1]

[January 25, 1973]

## Creating the Agricultural Development Bank [2]

The National Legislative Council

DECREES:

### TITLE I

#### PURPOSE AND FUNCTIONS

**Art. 1.** A government enterprise named the Agricultural Development Bank is hereby created. It shall have legal personality, its own

[1] Done at Panama City on January 25, 1973, and amended by Law No. 86, September 20, 1973, and Law No. 19, January 29, 1974.

[2] Banco de Desarrollo Agropecuario.

capital, and autonomy in its internal rules, subject to the guidance of the Executive Branch through the Ministry of Agricultural Development and to supervision by the Comptroller General of the Republic. Its purpose shall be to provide funding for agricultural development programs and agriculturally related industrial projects. The Bank shall arrange credit assistance for producers in the agricultural sector with limited resources and for organized groups of such producers, with emphasis on small and medium-scale producers, as provided in Article 115 of the Political Constitution.

**Art. 2.** The Minister of Agricultural Development shall be the legal representative of the Bank.

**Art. 3.** The nation shall be liable jointly and severally for the liabilities of the Agricultural Development Bank.[3]

**Art. 4.** The Agricultural Development Bank shall be exempt from payment of taxes, levies, and assessments and shall enjoy the same privileges as the nation in legal proceedings to which it is a party.

**Art. 5.** The Agricultural Development Bank shall carry out the credit policies of the Ministry of Agricultural Development and shall have the following functions:

*(a)* To provide financing, duly supervised by officials of the sector, for agricultural and agriculturally related industrial activities to
1. farmer and cooperative organizations;
2. small and medium-scale producers in the agricultural sector;
3. agriculturally related industrial projects encouraged by the Ministry of Agricultural Development;
4. municipalities and local boards conducting agricultural, agriculturally related industrial, or fisheries activities;
5. any other individuals or legal entities engaged in activities compatible with the economic policies of the Ministry of Agricultural Development.

*(b)* To issue securities of any kind and to float them on the domestic or foreign financial market.

---

[3] The responsibility of the State is referred to in Article 232 of the Constitution. That article provides:

"The law shall establish and regulate official and semiofficial banks which shall function as autonomous institutions under the supervision of the State, and shall determine its ancillary responsibilities in connection with the liabilities contracted by these institutions. The law shall regulate the banking system."

*(c)* To borrow from multinational, foreign, or domestic financial institutions for the purposes set forth in this law.

*(d)* To assume the financial liabilities to multinational, international, foreign, or domestic credit institutions of government agencies that have actually transferred all or part of their assets to the Bank.

*(e)* Any other functions set forth in this law and other functions which may be set forth in the future.

*(f)* To contribute to the capital of farm enterprises, cooperatives, local boards, and agriculturally related industrial enterprises, with the right to participate in their management.

*(g)* To receive collections in respect of outstanding borrowing from the Inter-American Development Bank (IDB), for which payment of principal and interest will be assumed by the nation.

*(h)* To effect any other banking operations authorized by Executive Decree.

*(i)* To grant, upon the authorization of the Cabinet Council, guarantees for agricultural, livestock-raising, and agriculturally related industrial activities, to small farmers and to associations and federations of such farmers.

## TITLE II

### ORGANIZATION

**Art. 6.** The Agricultural Development Bank shall be administered by an Executive Committee and a General Manager.

**Art. 7.** The Executive Committee shall be composed of five (5) Commissioners and their Alternates:

*(a)* the Minister of Agricultural Development, who shall be its Chairman;

*(b)* the Minister of Commerce and Industry;

*(c)* the General Manager of the National Bank;

*(d)* a representative of the independent agricultural producers; and

*(e)* a representative of the organized producers.

**Art. 8.** The Alternates of the Minister of Agricultural Development, the Minister of Commerce and Industry, and the General Manager of the National Bank shall be the Vice Minister of Agricultural Development, the Vice Minister of Commerce and Industry, and the Manager of the National Bank of Panama selected by the General Manager of that Bank, respectively. The Representatives of the producers and rural organizations and their Alternates shall be appointed by the Executive Branch.

**Art. 9.** The General Manager of the Agricultural Development Bank shall attend Executive Committee meetings in an advisory capacity and shall be the Committee's Secretary.

**Art. 10.** The Executive Committee shall establish the internal rules of the Agricultural Development Bank, determine its staff structure, and assign the various salaries.

**Art. 11.** The General Manager of the Agricultural Development Bank must be a Panamanian, be at least 25 years of age, be proficient in economics and finance, and be knowledgeable in banking or have held executive positions in agriculture for at least five (5) years.

The General Manager shall be appointed by the President of the Republic.

**Art. 12.** In the temporary or occasional absence of the [General][4] Manager, an official of the Bank selected by the Executive Committee shall serve in his stead. In the permanent absence of the General Manager, the official selected by the Executive Committee shall temporarily act in his stead, pending a new appointment by the President of the Republic.

**Art. 13.** The functions of General Manager are incompatible with those of any other compensated public or private position or office, except for those of university teaching.

**Art. 14.** The Chairman of the Executive Committee may delegate the legal representation of the Bank to the General Manager or to another official.

This delegation of functions may be revoked at any time by the Chairman of the Executive Committee, and in making decisions the delegate shall state that he is doing so by delegation. Delegated functions may in no case be delegated onward.

Failure to comply with the requirements set forth in this article shall cause the acts of the delegate to be invalid.

[4] Editor's addition.

## Title III

### RESOURCES AND OPERATIONS OF THE BANK

**Art. 15.** The Agricultural Development Bank shall have the following resources:

(*a*) the interest on its credit operations;
(*b*) subsidies and allocations granted to it by the National Government;
(*c*) property or claims acquired by it on any basis;
(*d*) proceeds from the securities it issues and from its borrowing;
(*e*) other income from its operations;
(*f*) funds transferred to it by the Ministry of Agricultural Development out of the surpluses referred to in Article 14 of Law No. 12 of January 25, 1973 and from the sale of land; and
(*g*) the property and assets of the Economic Promotion Institute, including those of the Real Estate Department and except for those of its Promotion Office. Immovable property transferred to the Agricultural Development Bank as provided for in the preceding paragraph shall be registered in the Public Registry in the name of the Agricultural Development Bank. This provision shall have retroactive effect as from January 25, 1973.

**Art. 16.** The General Manager of the Agricultural Development Bank shall have summary jurisdiction, the exercise of which he may delegate to any official of the Bank.

**Art. 17.** This law shall take effect upon its approval.

*[The signatory clause is omitted.]*

# Law No. 10 [1]

[January 25, 1973]

## Creating the National Mortgage Bank [2]

### TITLE I

### PURPOSE AND FUNCTIONS

**Art. 1.** A government enterprise called the National Mortgage Bank is hereby created. It shall possess legal personality, its own capital, and autonomy in its internal rules, subject to the guidance of the Executive Branch through the Ministry of Housing and to supervision by the Comptroller General of the Republic, and shall have the purpose of providing financing for national housing programs designed to give effect to the right guaranteed by Article 109 of the Constitution.

**Art. 2.** The Minister of Housing shall be the legal representative of the Bank.

**Art. 3.** The nation is liable jointly and severally for the liabilities of the National Mortgage Bank. [3]

**Art. 4.** The National Mortgage Bank shall be exempt from payment of taxes, levies, and assessments and shall enjoy the same privileges as the nation in legal proceedings to which it is a party.

**Art. 5.** The National Mortgage Bank shall carry out the policies of the Ministry of Housing in the area of housing and shall have the following functions:

(*a*) to grant credit and discount facilities to qualifying institutions pursuant to the criteria established by the Ministry of Housing;
(*b*) to guarantee payment of mortgage loans made by qualified institutions, and to charge a fee for such guarantees;

---

[1] Done at Panama City on January 25, 1973, and amended by Law No. 103, October 4, 1973, and Law No. 69, December 15, 1975.

[2] Banco Hipotecario Nacional.

[3] The responsibility of the State is referred to in Article 232 of the Constitution. That article provides:

"The law shall establish and regulate official and semiofficial banks which shall function as autonomous institutions under the supervision of the State, and shall determine its ancillary responsibilities in connection with the liabilities contracted by these institutions. The law shall regulate the banking system."

*(c)* to issue notes, mortgage bonds, or other types of securities on the basis of its portfolio, and to place those securities on the domestic or foreign financial market;

*(d)* to borrow from multinational, foreign, or domestic financial institutions for the purposes set forth in this law;

*(e)* to assume the financial liabilities to multinational, international, foreign, or domestic credit institutions of government agencies that have actually transferred all or part of their assets to the Bank;

*(f)* to discount, purchase, or commit itself to purchase or discount credits or claims held by public or private juridical persons or individuals, provided such credits are guaranteed by mortgages and antichresis and provided they are based on housing investment plans previously approved by the National Mortgage Bank;

*(g)* to pay or guarantee payment of liabilities contracted by borrowers in connection with loans made for the purchase of housing under investment plans previously approved by the National Mortgage Bank.

*Subitem.* The Executive Committee shall, by resolution, determine the requirements, amounts, periods, terms, and conditions of the investment plan or plans under which the National Mortgage Bank shall contract liabilities pursuant to the powers stipulated in Article 5*(f)* and *(g)*, and shall give prior approval to any contract binding the National Mortgage Bank.

Contracts entered into by the National Mortgage Bank pursuant to the powers stipulated in Article 5*(f)* and *(g)* shall be exempt from the stamp tax, the stamped paper tax, the notary fee tax, and other taxes.

*(h)* any other powers set forth in this law and other powers which may be set forth in the future.

## TITLE II

### ORGANIZATION

**Art. 6.** The National Mortgage Bank shall be administered by an Executive Committee and a General Manager.

**Art. 7.** The Executive Committee shall consist of four Commissioners and their Alternates:

*(a)* the Minister of Housing, who shall be Chairman;

*(b)* the Minister of Planning and Economic Policy;

(*c*) the Minister of Labor and Welfare;
(*d*) the General Manager of the National Bank of Panama.

**Art. 8.** The alternates of the Minister of Housing, the Minister of Planning and Economic Policy, the Minister of Labor and Welfare, and the General Manager of the National Bank shall be the Vice Minister of Housing, the Vice Minister of Planning and Economic Policy, the Vice Minister of Labor and Welfare, and the Manager of the National Bank of Panama selected by the General Manager of that Bank, respectively.

**Art. 9.** The General Manager of the National Mortgage Bank shall attend Executive Committee meetings in an advisory capacity and shall be the Committee's Secretary.

**Art. 10.** The Executive Committee shall establish the internal rules of the National Mortgage Bank, determine its staff structure, and assign the various salaries.

**Art. 11.** The General Manager of the National Mortgage Bank must be a Panamanian, at least 25 years of age, proficient in economics and finance, and knowledgeable in banking or have held executive positions in commerce or industry for at least five (5) years.

The General Manager shall be freely appointed and may be freely removed by the President of the Republic.

**Art. 12.** In the temporary or occasional absence of the General Manager, an official of the Bank selected by the Executive Committee shall serve in his stead.

In the permanent absence of the General Manager, the official selected by the Executive Committee shall temporarily act in his stead, pending a new appointment by the President of the Republic.

**Art. 13.** The functions of General Manager are incompatible with those of any other compensated public or private position or office, except for those of university teaching.

**Art. 14.** The Chairman of the Executive Committee may delegate the legal representation of the Bank to the General Manager or another official.

This delegation of functions may be revoked at any time by the Chairman of the Executive Committee, and in making decisions the delegate shall state that he is doing so by delegation. Delegated functions may in no case be delegated onward.

Failure to comply with the requirements set forth in this article shall cause the acts of the delegate to be invalid.

## TITLE III

### ASSETS AND OPERATIONS OF THE BANK

**Art. 15.** The National Mortgage Bank shall have the following resources:

*(a)* the fees paid for the Bank's guarantees of loans made by qualifying government or private mortgage institutions;

*(b)* subsidies and allocations granted to it by the National Government for the execution of its programs;

*(c)* property acquired by it on any basis;

*(d)* proceeds from notes, mortgage bonds, and other types of securities issued by it on the basis of its portfolio, and from borrowing;

*(e)* the income from its operations and other resources with which it is endowed by the law.

**Art. 16.** The President of the National Mortgage Bank shall have summary jurisdiction, which he may delegate to other officials of the Bank.

**Art. 17.** This law shall take effect upon its approval.

*{The signatory clause is omitted.}*

# Law No. 87 [1]

[November 23, 1960]

## Enacting the Charter of the Savings Bank [2]

The National Assembly of Panama

DECREES:

### CHAPTER I

#### GENERAL PROVISIONS

**Art. 1.** The Savings Bank, established by Executive Decrees Nos. 54 of June 15, 1934 and 27 of February 23, 1939, and reorganized by Law No. 77 of June 20, 1941, shall continue to exist and operate in accordance with the provisions of this law and be known as the Savings Bank.

**Art. 2.** The Savings Bank shall be an autonomous government institution, having its own legal status and being internally self-governing and self-managing, subject only to the supervision and inspection of the Executive under the terms set forth in this law.

**Art. 3.** The nation shall bear secondary liability for all obligations of the Savings Bank.[3]

**Art. 4.** The Savings Bank shall maintain its Head Office in Panama City; it may, however, establish branches or agencies therein or in any other part of the Republic.

**Art. 5.** The existing capital of the Savings Bank is one million eight hundred thousand balboas (B 1,800,000) of which the State

---

[1] Done at Panama City on November 21, 1960, and amended by Cabinet Decree No. 208, July 8, 1969, and Law No. 58, December 13, 1979.

[2] Caja de Ahorros.

[3] The responsibility of the State is referred to in Article 232 of the Constitution. That article provides:

> "The law shall establish and regulate official and semiofficial banks which shall function as autonomous institutions under the supervision of the State, and shall determine its ancillary responsibilities in connection with the liabilities contracted by these institutions. The law shall regulate the banking system."

has provided one hundred fifty thousand balboas (B 150,000) with the remainder being taken in stages from the Reserve Fund of the Savings Bank itself. Whenever said Reserve Fund exceeds three hundred thousand balboas (B 300,000), the capital shall be increased by the Board of Directors in the amount of one hundred fifty thousand balboas (B 150,000), which shall be taken from the Reserve Fund.

**Art. 6.** The Savings Bank shall at all times be exempt from paying any tax, levy, or charge, and all its proceedings shall enjoy all the privileges that the law accords to the government.

The exemptions and privileges established by this provision shall not extend to the personnel of the Savings Bank.

**Art. 7.** All authorities of the Republic shall lend effective support to the General Manager and other officials of the Savings Bank, when they so request, in matters relating to the institution.

**Art. 8.** During the first ten (10) days of each ordinary session of the National Assembly, the General Manager shall submit to that body a detailed report on the transactions and progress of the institution, and shall propose measures which he regards as desirable both with respect to its improved operation and administration and to the development of the national economy.

## CHAPTER II

### ADMINISTRATION

**Art. 9.** The management, direction and administration of the Savings Bank shall be entrusted to a General Manager, who will be appointed by the Executive with the approval of the National Assembly, and to a Board of Directors, comprised of five (5) Principal Directors who together with their Alternates will be appointed by the Executive with the approval of the National Assembly.

**Art. 10.** The General Manager and the Principal and Alternate Directors on the Savings Bank's Board of Directors must be of Panamanian nationality, at least twenty-five (25) years of age, knowledgeable about economics and finance, possess banking expertise, and have been engaged in executive positions in banking, commercial or industrial activities for no less than five (5) years.

**Art. 11.** The General Manager of the Savings Bank or whoever acts in his stead shall be the legal representative of the institution. With the approval of the Board of Directors, the General Manager may both confer powers and delegate responsibilities to the institution's Managers and Assistant Managers.

**Art. 12.** The term of office of the General Manager and of the Directors and Alternate Directors of the Board of Directors shall be four (4) years. They may be re-elected to their offices. Appointments to fill vacancies shall be made for the remainder of the term.

**Art. 13.** Except where otherwise provided for in this law, decisions by the Board of Directors shall be taken by majority vote provided, however, that if the General Manager is opposed the vote of four (4) Directors shall be required.

**Art. 14.** The Board of Directors shall have the following duties and powers:

(*a*) meet at least once a month upon convocation by the General Manager or at the request of three Directors;
(*b*) determine the salary and representation allowance of the General Manager;
(*c*) approve the establishment of branches proposed by the General Manager;
(*d*) decide on all matters submitted to it by the General Manager or any of the Directors;
(*e*) approve the expenditure budget; and
(*f*) such other duties and powers as may be provided for by law.

**Art. 15.** Members of the Board of Directors shall each receive twenty balboas (B 20) as compensation for every meeting they attend.

**Art. 16.** With the approval of the Board of Directors, the General Manager shall prescribe the by-laws of the Savings Bank.

**Art. 17.** The Savings Bank shall insure the performance of the General Manager and his subordinates by taking out a global or group policy for an amount to be determined by the General Manager with the approval of the Board of Directors; premiums shall be paid with Savings Bank funds.

**Art. 18.** The duties of the General Manager are incompatible with those of any other employment or remunerated public office and with engaging in trade or the management or intervention in the administration of any other business or enterprise whatever, with the exception of those which, by virtue of this law, he discharges as General Manager of the Savings Bank.

**Art. 19.** The General Manager may be removed from office solely for mismanagement, incompetence or conduct which brings discredit to the institution. The Board of Directors must petition the Executive for removal of the General Manager, stipulating the reasons for its action.

**Art. 20.** Within the first fifteen (15) days of each month, the General Manager shall submit to the Board of Directors a report setting forth the following:

(*a*) total deposits at the end of the preceding month;
(*b*) interest accrued but not paid;
(*c*) number of depositors;
(*d*) money invested in mortgages;
(*e*) money invested in collateral loans;
(*f*) expenditure for the month;
(*g*) other receipts for the month;
(*h*) number and amount of mortgages with interest arrears;
(*i*) number and amount of mortgages with principal repayment arrears;
(*j*) other information required to enable the Board of Directors to take stock of the movements and operations of the Savings Bank during the preceding month.

**Art. 21.** The Savings Bank shall also have as many Managers, Assistant Managers, and other employees as are required for its smooth operation; they shall be freely appointed and dismissed by the General Manager. The General Manager shall not appoint as a subordinate any of his relatives within the fourth degree of relationship by consanguinity or the second degree of relationship by affinity, or his spouse.

**Art. 22.** If the General Manager is temporarily or occasionally absent, the Board of Directors shall appoint a Manager to act in his stead. If the General Manager is permanently absent, the Manager appointed by the Board of Directors shall provisionally act in his stead until the Executive designates a successor for the remainder of the term.

**Art. 23.** With the approval of the Board of Directors, the General Manager shall draw up the rules and regulations under which the Savings Bank will grant loans.

**Art. 24.** The Savings Bank shall retain an attorney appointed by the General Manager. His remuneration shall be determined by the Board of Directors. The institution's attorney must be of Panamanian nationality, hold a law degree, have had five (5) years of professional experience or have held a certificate of competence for more than twenty (20) years and been professionally active during that time. The attorney shall be Secretary to the Board of Directors and shall have such responsibilities as may be assigned to him by the General Manager with the approval of the Board of Directors.

## CHAPTER III

### OPERATIONS

**Art. 25.** The Savings Bank may perform the following operations:

*(a)* accept savings account deposits in accordance with such categories as may be established by the general management with the approval of the Board of Directors;

*(b)* issue mortgage certificates;

*(c)* issue savings bonds guaranteed by its capital and other assets;

*(d)* administer real estate for natural or juridical persons or the government;

*(e)* administer loans on real estate of natural or juridical persons or the government;

*(f)* grant loans with mortgage and antichretic guarantee on income-producing urban or suburban property located anywhere in the Republic;

*(g)* grant loans with mortgage and antichretic guarantee for the construction of residential housing, including residential buildings owned as apartments or stories (horizontal property);

*(h)* accept deposit accounts with itself as security for up to 90 per cent of the amount of loans granted by itself and as security for obligations contracted with the National Lottery. Obligations secured by these accounts shall receive preferential payment. In the event of a court-ordered or administrative attachment or seizure, the Savings Bank shall deduct the full amount guaranteed, plus interest, from the balance of the account tendered as security, and keep at the disposal of the relevant authority the amount subject to seizure or attachment;

*(i)* acquire movable property and real estate pledged to the Savings Bank as security for obligations contracted with said Bank, for total or partial payment of such obligations;

(*j*) acquire movable property and real estate for its own use;
(*k*) lease safe-deposit boxes;
(*l*) issue savings stamps;
(*ll*) apply for and obtain money on loan domestically and abroad, for which the joint guarantee of the Savings Bank and the government may be given after authorization is obtained from the Executive;
(*m*) finance projects which involve real estate development and the construction of qualified housing;
(*n*) acquire land for development and construction of qualified housing;
(*ñ*) administer trusts;
(*o*) make real estate appraisals and evaluations;
(*p*) sell travelers checks; and
(*q*) effect any operation permitted in the banking industry, pursuant to the law and banking practices.

*Paragraph:* The Savings Bank may issue mortgage certificates up to an amount equal to the value of the collateral and mortgage loans, respectively, which it holds on its own behalf. Such mortgage certificates shall be government securities, exempt from all taxes both as to principal and interest, and may be used by banks, credit institutions and insurance companies as part of the deposits or investments which the law requires them to maintain in the Republic. The Board of Directors of the Savings Bank shall fix the interest to be paid on mortgage certificates, the manner of payment, their denominations, maturities, redemption and all other matters concerning the issue of such securities.

**Art. 26.** Loans against shares and bonds shall be based on the market value of such instruments and only against national securities or those of entities established in the country whose securities have been issued for at least five (5) years and which have not defaulted on dividend payment.

**Art. 27.** No more than eighty (80) per cent of the market value shall be lent on national bonds or sixty (60) per cent on other securities.

**Art. 28.** The Savings Bank shall not lend more than a total of five (5) per cent of the face value of a company's entire issue of bonds or shares.

**Art. 29.** The Savings Bank shall accept savings account deposits for such minimum and maximum amounts as may be determined by the Board of Directors on the recommendation of the General Manager.

**Art. 30.** Any minor may open a savings account for himself in the Savings Bank and make deposits in it. If he is less than fourteen (14) years of age, he may not make withdrawals from the account unless accompanied by a parent or guardian. If he is older than fourteen (14) but less than eighteen (18) years of age, he may make withdrawals on his own, provided the Savings Bank has written authorization from the parent or guardian. If he is over eighteen (18) years of age he may freely make withdrawals, unless the Savings Bank should have written instructions to the contrary from the minor's parent or guardian.

If a savings account is opened by a minor in person, no other individual may make withdrawals from that account against the minor's will, duly notified to the Savings Bank's General Manager.

The above provisions shall apply solely to savings accounts opened by minors in person. If an account is opened by the parent or guardian of a minor or by anyone else in the name of the minor, the person who opens the account shall exclusively be entitled to make withdrawals as long as the minor remains under age, unless said person gives written notification to the contrary.

**Art. 31.** The Board of Directors of the Savings Bank, on the recommendation of the General Manager, shall be empowered to set the rate of interest to be paid on savings account deposits and the ways in which such interest is to be calculated and compounded.

**Art. 32.** A passbook shall be issued to each depositor; his deposits and withdrawals shall be noted in it.

**Art. 33.** In order to withdraw funds deposited with the Savings Bank, thirty (30) days' advance notice must be given in writing. The General Manager may, however, agree to the withdrawal of such funds without requiring this formal notification.

**Art. 34.** In order to withdraw funds which have been deposited with the Savings Bank, the depositor must establish his identity and present the passbook issued to him.

**Art. 35.** If a passbook is lost, a duplicate may be issued to its owner. In it shall be noted the balance of the account in favor of the depositor. The original passbook shall be voided *de facto,* and this shall be noted in the duplicate.

**Art. 36.** The Board of Directors of the Savings Bank, on the recommendation of the General Manager, shall be empowered to establish the percentages of the assessed valuations of properties securing its loans up to which it will make such loans in the case of borrowers' own residences, commercial properties, and qualified dwellings, as well as the criteria identifying the latter dwellings.

**Art. 37.** In order for mortgage-secured loans to be made, collateral property must first be appraised. The appraisal, made at the expense of the interested party, will be carried out by the Savings Bank and must be approved by the General Manager. The General Manager, with the approval of the Board of Directors, shall establish rules governing the appraisal procedure to be followed by the Savings Bank.

**Art. 38.** Credit operations shall be decided on by groups of officials to be known as "Credit Committees," whose membership, organization, and operations shall be determined by a regulation proposed by the General Manager and approved by the Board of Directors.

**Art. 39.** If the transaction involves more than thirty thousand balboas (B 30,000), it must be approved by the General Manager and by unanimous vote of the Board of Directors. In no case may such a transaction exceed seventy-five thousand balboas (B 75,000) for a single individual, company, or spouse, even if separate guarantees are given.

**Art. 40.** The first five thousand balboas (B 5,000) deposited in the Savings Bank may not be seized or attached except for alimony or in connection with the commission of a crime. Any seizure or attachment ordered in violation of the provisions of this article shall be lifted at the request of the party concerned or of the Savings Bank itself.

**Art. 40A.** The first five thousand balboas (B 5,000) of the minimum annual balances of individuals' savings account deposits with the Savings Bank shall be exempt from inheritance tax. These five thousand balboas (B 5,000) or less may be paid directly by the Savings Bank without further formality or legal procedure to the person named by the account holder as beneficiary for such purposes upon proof of identity and of the account holder's demise. Beneficiaries shall be named by the account holder or holders in the presence of Savings Bank officials on forms provided by the institution.

If the principal did not name a beneficiary, payment shall be made to his proven inheritors, either directly or upon court order. It shall be understood that if the sum of the minimum balances of one or more savings accounts belonging to the same person exceeds five thousand balboas (B 5,000), it shall be exempt from inheritance tax up to said amount and shall be paid only up to the equivalent of said amount.

*Paragraph:* The exemption provided for in this article shall supplement the prescription on inheritance taxes contained in the Tax Code.

**Art.** 41. The principal of mortgage-secured loans made by the Savings Bank shall be repaid in monthly installments as determined by the Credit Committees, taking into account the provisions of Article 42. Nonpayment of three (3) monthly installments shall render the obligation immediately due and payable.

**Art.** 42. No mortgage loans shall be made for a period exceeding five (5) years. Nevertheless, extensions for periods of five (5) years each may be granted, up to a maximum of four (4) such extensions, provided the party concerned is up-to-date with his interest and principal payments and the collateral has not deteriorated. Extensions shall be granted by the Credit Committees.

**Art.** 43. Where it deems appropriate, the Savings Bank shall have an inspection made of properties mortgaged to guarantee payment of obligations contracted with said Bank.

If it is found at any time that the value of the mortgaged real estate has dropped for whatever reason to the point of no longer covering on that date the percentage of the amount owing which, pursuant to Article 36, served as the basis for the loan, the General Manager shall request that the debtor increase the security. Should the latter fail to do so, the debt shall be considered due and its immediate collection undertaken.

**Art.** 44. All loan agreements with mortgage security entered into by the Savings Bank shall oblige the debtor to insure the mortgaged property and to endorse the relevant policy or policies to the Savings Bank. The amount and type of insurance, which in no case shall be less than the value of the relevant improvements, shall be determined in the loan agreement; if it is not, it shall be established by the General Manager of the institution.

The Savings Bank shall insure the property or renew the policy or policies should the debtor fail to do so. Any amounts which the Savings Bank has to disburse to this end shall be charged to the debtor and shall earn interest at the same rate as that stipulated in the loan agreement. Such amounts and their interest shall be payable upon notice from the Bank.

In the event of total or partial loss of whatever kind, the Bank shall collect the insurance indemnity and apply it to the debt. The Board of Directors, in concert with the General Manager, may establish rules for collecting insurance on mortgage loans.

**Art. 45.** It shall be stipulated in all mortgage contracts that the Bank has the right to take charge of the administration of the mortgaged property whenever the debtor defaults on the payments he is contractually obliged to make. Nevertheless, an antichresis may be agreed upon as an accessory to the mortgage guarantee, with the Bank, where it deems appropriate, being entitled to leave the debtor responsible for management.

**Art. 46.** All mortgage contracts shall also provide that the debtor renounces executory process.

**Art. 47.** The interest rate on Savings Bank loans shall be set by the Board of Directors and shall not exceed nine (9) per cent per annum. Should, however, a law of the Republic authorize collection of higher interest, the Board of Directors shall be empowered to raise the interest rate in accordance with such new law. Interest shall be payable in monthly installments. Failure to pay three (3) monthly installments shall cause the entire debt to become immediately due and payable. Any borrower from the Savings Bank must pay the costs involved in appraisals, credit investigation and examination of the proposed collateral, drafting of memoranda and for other services in connection with studying his loan application, as determined by the Board of Directors on the recommendation of the General Manager.

**Art. 48.** The Savings Bank shall keep its deposits in current accounts with the National Bank of Panama. Nevertheless, should the Bank deem it advisable, and with prior authorization from the Board of Directors, up to twenty-five (25) per cent of its deposits may be kept in other banks, either domestic or foreign, where such deposits are required in connection with lines of credit extended to the Savings Bank.

**Art. 49.** The Savings Bank shall maintain a cash reserve in order to guarantee its deposits. The amount shall be determined from time to time by the Board of Directors and must in no case be less than ten (10) per cent of total deposits.

**Art. 50.** Business of the Savings Bank in those parts of the country where it does not have offices shall be handled by the National Bank in accordance with arrangements to be worked out between the two institutions.

**Art. 51.** Any loan instrument prepared by the Savings Bank shall specify that the institution may assign the credit at any time without necessarily giving the debtor prior notice.

**Art. 52.** Neither the General Manager nor the employees of the Savings Bank may in any way act as guarantor or surety for third parties.

**Art. 53.** The Savings Bank shall not lend to the General Manager, the Directors, or their spouses.

**Art. 54.** The General Manager shall be granted summary jurisdiction for ensuring settlement of obligations undertaken toward the Bank.

**Art. 55.** Whenever summary jurisdiction is resorted to, the legal proceedings shall be held in the offices of the Savings Bank or the relevant branch.

**Art. 56.** The General Manager of the Savings Bank or the Managers of its branches may empower any attorney to collect the Bank's debts; in such cases, however, proceedings must be held in the courts.

**Art. 57.** Collections under summary jurisdiction shall not entail court costs. Debtors shall pay only the expenses incurred by the Savings Bank in the proceedings.

The provisions of this article shall apply to collections made in accordance with Article 58 of this law.

**Art. 58.** In suits brought against debtors of the Bank, the latter may acquire goods of the debtor at auction and credit them to the debt being claimed.

**Art. 59.** The Savings Bank may only purchase real estate for its own use and for that of official bodies. It shall not speculate in securities; nevertheless, it may deal in government bonds.

**Art. 60.** Those instances in which the Savings Bank acquires property as full or partial payment of obligations entered into in its favor shall not be affected by the provisions of the previous article. Real estate acquired by the Savings Bank in accordance with the provisions of this article shall be sold through competitive bidding announced in three (3) consecutive notices appearing in one of the area's most widely circulating daily newspapers, and in the *Gazeta Oficial,* at least ten (10) days in advance.

The Board of Directors shall establish the terms for the bidding, but in no case may the minimum acceptable bid in the first auction be less than the amount for which the Bank acquired the property. Sale will be made to the highest bidder, provided his bid is not lower than the minimum acceptable bid. Should no bidders come forth, the Board of Directors, acting by a majority and with the General Manager's agreement, may arrange for new auctions to be held using the same public announcement procedure and such terms as it shall determine.

Real estate which the Bank acquires pursuant to the provisions of this article may be sold by the General Manager, with the approval of the Board of Directors, to whomever offers to buy it at a price not below its commercial value on the market. If there are several buyers, it will be sold to whichever offers the highest price.

**Art. 61.** Employees and former employees of the Savings Bank shall be entitled to retire upon entry into force of this law, provided the employee has worked for the Bank for at least twenty-eight (28) years or, upon entry into force of this law, is sixty (60) years old and has worked for the Bank for at least twenty (20) consecutive years.

**Art. 62.** A Savings Bank employee who requests retirement in accordance with the previous article, will be paid for the remainder of his life seventy-five (75) per cent of the last salary earned, which in no case shall exceed five hundred balboas (B 500). This pay will be entirely disbursed by the Bank as long as the employee or former employee has not reached the age where he qualifies for old-age pension from the Social Security Fund. When the employee or former employee qualifies for this pension, the Bank will contribute the amount needed to make up the salary he retired with.

**Art. 63.** Savings Bank employees who retire from service owing to complete and permanent physical disability, fully supported by a medical certificate and confirmed by the Board of Directors, shall also be retired with seventy-five (75) per cent of the last salary earned, which in no case shall exceed five hundred balboas (B 500), provided they have served the institution for at least ten (10) consecutive years.

**Art. 64.** Pay for employees who retire because of the above physical disability shall be comprised of the disability pension paid to them by the Social Security Fund and of the amount needed to make up the salary they retired with, which amount will be contributed by the Savings Bank.

**Art. 65.** After retiring from service and entering the category of retired or pensioned persons, beneficiaries shall continue paying their monthly contribution to the Social Security Fund as insured persons, as will the Savings Bank as employer, in accordance with the law; and any retired or pensioned individual who fails to do this shall lose his pension entitlement.

**Art. 66.** The following are hereby revoked: Executive Decree No. 54 of June 15, 1934; Executive Decree No. 27 of February 23, 1939; Articles 72 through 113 of Law No. 77 of 1941, and Articles 6, 7, 34, 42, 43, 44, 45, and 51 of the same law (these are the only provisions of that law which were still in force); Article 5 of Law No. 132 of 1943; Article 1 of Decree-Law No. 31 of 1942; Article 1 of Decree-Law No. 42 of 1947; Law No. 6 of 1948; Article 82 of Law No. 11 of 1956, and Articles 6, 7, 28, 40, 41, 42, 43, 49, 71, 72, 73, 74, 75, and 76 of that same law, but only as they apply to the Savings Bank, since they will remain in force with respect to the National Bank. All other provisions which conflict with this law are also hereby revoked.

**Art. 67.** This law shall enter into force upon its publication.

*[The signatory clause is omitted.]*

## Cabinet Decree No. 247 [1]

[July 16, 1970]

Whereby the National Securities Commission [2] is established, the sale of stocks in the Republic of Panama is regulated and measures to protect minority stockholders are adopted

[1] Given in Panama City on July 16, 1970, amended by Cabinet Decree No. 30, February 24, 1972.

[2] Comisión Nacional de Valores.

The Provisional Government Council

DECREES:

## TITLE I

## THE NATIONAL SECURITIES COMMISSION

**Art. 1.** The National Securities Commission is hereby established as a unit operating under the Ministry of Commerce and Industry, with its own juridical personality and autonomy in regard to its organization and internal management, subject to the supervision and inspection of the Executive Branch and the Office of the Comptroller General of the Republic, pursuant to the terms stipulated in this cabinet decree.

**Art. 2.** The National Securities Commission will have the following attributes:

*(a)* To verify the accuracy of the information to be furnished by the companies as established in this cabinet decree and in the cabinet decree on mutual funds.

*(b)* To authorize, prohibit or suspend the public sale of stocks or securities in accordance with the provisions of this cabinet decree.

*(c)* To coordinate with the chambers of commerce, industrialist unions and similar organizations the most effective and expeditious means of issuing securities in the area and to promote securities exchange transactions consistent with growth and development of the economy.

*(d)* To rule on applications submitted to it in compliance with the provisions of this cabinet decree and of the cabinet decree on mutual funds.

*(e)* To issue the necessary licenses to sales agents for mutual funds and securities and to revoke such licenses in accordance with the provisions of this cabinet decree.

*(f)* To ensure that the mutual fund companies established or to be established in the country comply with their obligations as stipulated in this cabinet decree and in the cabinet decree on mutual funds.

*(g)* To ensure that the authorized distributors of mutual funds established or to be established in the country comply with all of their obligations as stipulated in this cabinet decree and in the cabinet decree on mutual funds.

(*h*) To examine, at least once a year, the financial statements to be presented by companies selling stocks, securities or mutual funds in accordance with this cabinet decree.

(*i*) To ensure compliance with all current legal provisions by those engaged in the various activities envisaged in this cabinet decree and in the cabinet decree on mutual funds.

**Art. 3.** The National Securities Commission will be composed of the following five (5) members:

(*a*) the Minister of Commerce and Industry, or such public official as he may designate, who will preside;

(*b*) the Manager of the National Bank, or such person as he may designate;

(*c*) one member prominent in banking, who must have at least five (5) years of experience in this activity in the Republic of Panama;

(*d*) one member prominent in industry, who must have at least five (5) years of experience in manufacturing production in the Republic of Panama;

(*e*) one member prominent in commerce, who must have at least five (5) years of experience in this activity in the Republic of Panama.

The members of the National Securities Commission referred to in sections (*c*), (*d*), and (*e*) of this article will be appointed by the Executive Branch for a term of three (3) years.

*Paragraph:* The original appointments of the members of the National Securities Commission referred to in sections (*c*), (*d*), and (*e*) of this article will be made for terms of one (1), two (2) and three (3) years, respectively; as these original terms expire, subsequent appointments will be made for terms of three (3) years.

**Art. 4.** Compliance with the policy established by the National Securities Commission and implementation of any decision made by that Commission shall be the responsibility of an Executive Director appointed by the Executive Branch.

**Art. 5.** The Executive Director must be a Panamanian citizen of legal age with a university degree in a field relating to the matters regulated by this cabinet decree, such as finance, economics, business administration or law, or equivalent experience of not less than five (5) years.

**Art. 6.** Companies subject to the regulations outlined in this cabinet decree are those offering their own stocks, mutual funds or any other securities for sale to the public, within the national territory, by means of the usual advertising media; by mail, cable, telephone or telegraph; through distributors, sales agents, brokers or intermediaries, or by any other means which, in the opinion of the National Securities Commission represents offer, distribution or sale to undetermined persons or potential buyers.

*Paragraph:* The following securities shall remain outside the scope of this cabinet decree:

(1) Direct verbal offers communicated privately or by letter by the issuing company or its promoters to no more than ten (10) persons within a period of one (1) year.

(2) Insurance or endowment policies or compounding certificates issued by companies subject to the supervision of the Insurance Superintendency.

(3) Securities issued by the National Government, its autonomous or semiautonomous governmental agencies, or interministerial bodies.

(4) Commercial paper or negotiable instruments issued for normal business transactions.

(5) Securities issued by nonprofit religious, social, educational, charitable and fraternal bodies which have established that legal personality has been appointed to them.

**Art. 6A.** Any company offering its securities to the public must make its offers in an informative prospectus duly approved by the National Securities Commission and of which the investor must have cognizance before the sale is completed.

Those offers deemed worthy of exemption by the National Securities Commission shall not be subject to this requirement.

**Art. 7.** Companies wishing to offer their own stocks or other securities for sale to the public within the national territory must request authorization for this purpose, through an attorney, from the National Securities Commission, which requests shall be accompanied by the following documents:

*(a)* the power of the attorney who will handle the authorization before the National Securities Commission;

*(b)* a public document containing the partnership agreement or charter of the requesting company and its amendments and proof of the registration of such papers in the Public Registry;

(*c*) a certificate from the Public Registry stating the names of the directors and principal officers of the company, if the latter was constituted in accordance with the laws of the Republic;

(*d*) a copy of the draft informative prospectus to be issued by the company, which shall comply with the rules and regulations of the National Securities Commission on such matters;

(*e*) a resolution of the board of directors or of the competent corporate body, authorizing the sale of the securities, their number and price, including any deductions that may be applicable; the names of the persons empowered to countersign all arrangements implied in the offer; and a specimen of the securities whose sale is proposed;

(*f*) a copy of the most recent financial statements, which may date from more than four (4) months before the date of the application, duly certified by an independent certified public accountant;

(*g*) profit and loss statements for the last fiscal year and the two fiscal years immediately preceding it, duly certified by an independent certified public accountant;

(*h*) depending on the kind of company, business or securities offered, the National Securities Commission shall require such additional information as it may consider necessary or of interest to investors.

*Transitional Paragraph:* Depending on the size of the issue and of the assets of the applicant company, the National Securities Commission may accept, during the next two years, profit and loss statements for the two (2) years preceding the last fiscal year, as required in item (*g*) without the due certification by an independent certified public accountant.

*Paragraph 1:* New companies must comply with the provisions of items (*a*), (*b*), (*c*), (*d*), (*e*), (*f*), and (*h*).

*Paragraph 2:* If the company was constituted in accordance with the laws of a foreign country, the certification referred to in items (*f*) and (*g*) may be issued by an accountant not authorized to exercise his profession in the Republic, in which case it must be accompanied by documents from the competent official authorities in the country where the company operates authenticating the qualifications of the accountant certifying the respective balance sheets.

**Art. 8.** Once the authenticity of the documentation referred to in the preceding article has been established and during the month following submission of the application, the National Securities Commission shall decide on the submitted application. Within that period, the Commission may request from the company additional information to supplement the documentation or require such corrections or changes as may be appropriate, and the company shall have a period of ten (10) days following such request to comply therewith. During this time, the deadline for the Commission's decision shall be regarded as suspended. The resolution approving the sale of the securities shall state that authorization does not imply that the Commission recommends investment in such securities, nor will a favorable or unfavorable opinion be issued on the prospects of the business. Companies which request authorization to offer securities to the public shall, once they have obtained such authorization, be deemed to be registered companies and comply with the provisions in this cabinet decree applying to such companies in addition to fulfilling their obligations as companies offering their securities to the public.

**Art. 8A.** The National Securities Commission may, after giving notice to and hearing the interested parties, deny, suspend or cancel the sale of securities or the registration of any company if it is established that before or after a company is registered with the Commission it has been involved in any of the following deeds or omissions:

(1) if the documents or information submitted to the National Securities Commission or to investors contains untrue or inaccurate statements;

(2) if information or documents were withheld from the National Securities Commission or from the public and the Commission deems said material to be necessary or complementary in order to give a full idea of the business;

(3) if it is established that any of its directors, officials, partners or any other person linked to the company's management has been sentenced for, within the ten (10) years prior to registration with the National Securities Commission, or is indicted or sued for offenses involving fraud, deceitful representations or other offenses against the public trust in his conduct as investor, director or entrepreneur.

In addition to imposing fines, the Commission may bring legal action against the persons directly responsible for the omissions, falsehoods or inaccuracies referred to in this article.

**Art. 9.** Recourse against decisions prohibiting or suspending the sale of stocks will consist of reconsideration or repeal, regular appeal and appeal to the administrative court with plenary jurisdiction.

**Art. 10.** When the National Securities Commission authorizes the sale of stocks, the authorization for such sale will cover a period of not less than one (1) nor more than two (2) years. In the event that the

Commission should fail to resolve the matter within the month referred to in Article 8, the sale may be carried out within a period of one (1) year from the end of that month. Upon expiration of the terms within which the stocks may be sold, the company concerned may not continue their sale without again complying with the requirements of this cabinet decree.

**Art.** 11. Any company which is not required to comply with the rules set forth in Articles 6 and 7 of this cabinet decree may request the National Securities Commission to open a file under its name so that interested parties may obtain information on the business in which the company is engaged and its past record. To this end, the company shall submit the appropriate application to the National Securities Commission, accompanied by the documents mentioned in items *(a)*, *(b)*, *(c)*, *(d)*, *(f)*, *(g)*, and *(h)* of Article 7 of this cabinet decree.

Said company shall be required to comply with the provisions laid down for registered companies in this cabinet decree and shall enjoy the same tax privileges.

## Title II

### SECURITIES SALES AGENTS

**Art.** 12. Securities sales agents are those natural or juridical persons engaged in serving as intermediaries between the companies issuing and offering for public sale their own securities or the securities of other companies and the persons investing their money in such securities. Those classified as juridical persons will operate through the conduct of natural persons holding the proper license.

**Art.** 13. Once this cabinet decree enters into effect, only those natural persons holding the proper license in their own name or in representation of juridical persons and who are duly empowered for the purpose by a company authorized to offer securities for public sale may serve as securities sales agents.

**Art.** 14. The license mentioned in the preceding article will be issued by the National Securities Commission upon receipt of an application that satisfies the following requirements:

*(a)* The applicant must be a Panamanian citizen by birth or naturalization or a foreigner with not less than five (5) years of continuous residence in the country.

(*b*) The applicant must be of legal age and full legal standing; he must not have been convicted of any crime against property or have any infectious or contagious disease.

(*c*) A bond of one thousand balboas (B 1,000) must have been posted and maintained, in favor of the national government, in cash or in bonds of the government or its decentralized agencies or of an insurance company in order to safeguard the government against penalties imposed pursuant to this cabinet decree and against any damage that may be caused to private parties in the exercise of their activities.

(*d*) A certificate issued by the Administrative Secretary of the National Securities Commission must be presented stipulating that the applicant has passed the examination referred to in Article 16 of this cabinet decree.

**Art. 15.** The Administrative Secretary will designate a date or dates for the examination of securities sales agent candidates as he deems advisable, whenever he has received requests for examination from ten (10) or more candidates.

**Art. 16.** The examination referred to in the preceding article will be written and will cover:

(*a*) Basic knowledge of securities and mutual funds.

(*b*) Current legal provisions concerning securities and mutual funds.

(*c*) General concepts with regard to the economic system and securities operations.

**Art. 17.** The Administrative Secretary will issue a certificate to the candidates who pass the examination. An examination fee of ten balboas (B 10) will be charged. The candidate will enclose a certified or manager's check made out to the National Treasury for that amount with the examination request.

**Art. 18.** The certificates will be issued in duplicate, with the original delivered to the candidate and the copy filed in the office of the National Securities Commission.

**Art. 19.** The certificates will be countersigned by the Minister of Commerce and Industry, or the officer of that ministry to whom the minister delegates this function, and registered with the National Securities Commission, which may issue as many copies as are requested. National stamps for a value of ten balboas (B 10) will be affixed to such copies.

**Art. 20.** The National Securities Commission will furnish monthly to the companies offering securities or mutual funds for public sale or to their authorized distributors the names of the securities sales agents qualified to operate as such.

**Art. 21.** At the justified request of an interested party, the National Securities Commission may revoke the license of a securities sales agent. Causes for such action will be improper appropriation, in whole or in part, of installments corresponding to sales contracts for securities or mutual funds or the procurement of business by means of bribery, fraud or fraudulent schemes. The sales agent whose license has been revoked may have recourse to the Ministry of Commerce and Industry through the National Securities Commission, which will issue a reasoned opinion.

## TITLE III

### INSPECTION OF COMPANIES

**Art. 22.** The National Securities Commission shall supervise the management of registered companies, mutual fund companies and companies which sell shares to the public without authorization, and of authorized distributors and sales agents, and shall ensure that they comply with the provisions of this cabinet decree and its respective regulations and with the provisions of the cabinet decree on mutual funds.

**Art. 23.** In order to verify that financial statements comply with the legal provisions of its officers and employees, the National Securities Commission may inspect and examine registered companies and mutual fund companies and their authorized distributors; perform audits; require presentation of accounting books and of the documents, records and correspondence justifying each entry or account; verify portfolio investments; and examine the records of agencies of the company. The right of examination extends to any subsidiary of the company or affiliate in which the company examined has invested more than twenty per cent (20%) of its portfolio.

The National Security Commission may delegate this function to auditors of the Ministry of Finance and the Treasury.

**Art. 24.** The National Securities Commission shall also be empowered to establish standards for the accounting and financial reports of companies offering securities or mutual funds for public sale. It may further require them periodically to present balance sheets and financial statements, statistical sales charts and accounts and reports in general, in order to provide an exact idea of the business of the companies, their investments, and their relationships with affiliate and subsidiary companies.

The National Securities Commission shall further have full power to regulate advertising and advertising standards and any other information connected with the buying and selling of securities by companies and distributors authorized to offer securities to the public and by companies which are not authorized to offer their securities to the public but which wish to use the mass communications media to impart to the public an appraisal, quotation or valuation of their securities.

**Art. 25.** Within the first four (4) months of their financial years, registered companies shall, through their legal representatives, submit to the National Securities Commission and send to all their registered shareholders or investors, their financial statements for the immediately preceding year, duly audited by an independent certified public accountant, together with a detailed statement of investments made and obligations undertaken in the course of said period.

Furthermore, registered companies shall submit to the National Securities Commission and send to their shareholders and investors at intervals to be determined by the National Securities Commission, a report containing a profit and loss statement on transactions to date and a report on investments made and obligations undertaken during the period covered.

Depending on the type of company or business involved, the National Securities Commission may require that the details it considers necessary appear both in annual reports and in periodic reports.

**Art. 26.** Any company which applies for authorization to offer securities or mutual funds for sale to the public, either directly or through authorized distributors, shall publish in two widely read local newspapers, once in each and on two different business days, a copy of the balance sheets and financial statements it submitted to the National Securities Commission within thirty (30) days of such submission to the Commission for authorization.

**Art. 27.** Any decrease in the deposits or bonds referred to in this cabinet decree or in the cabinet decree on mutual funds for whatever reason must be replenished within an absolute term of forty-five (45) calendar days from the date of such decrease. After that time, if the deposit or bond has not been replenished, the National Securities Commission will cancel the corresponding authorization or license.

## Title IV

### PENALTIES

**Art. 28.** A fine equivalent to 100 per cent of sales made shall be imposed jointly on directors or employees of a company who are involved in the offer of securities of said company if the latter is not duly authorized in accordance with this cabinet decree.

If it cannot be established that sales were made although there were public offers, the Commission shall be empowered to impose a fine of one thousand balboas (B 1,000) to ten thousand balboas (B 10,000) in the same manner as provided in the preceding paragraph.

**Art. 29.** Natural or juridical persons acting, in the capacity of distributors or sales agents, to transact or intervene in the sale of securities on behalf of companies not authorized to engage in such business in Panama will be subject to the same penalty as that established in the preceding article. If such person is a sales agent for securities authorized by the Commission, the violation referred to in this article shall also entail revocation of his license.

**Art. 30.** Without prejudice to other lawful penalties, the National Securities Commission shall be empowered to impose fines of one hundred balboas (B 100) to one thousand balboas (B 1,000) for any violation of or noncompliance with the provisions of this cabinet decree, its regulations or instructions it has lawfully issued, for which no special sanction has been provided for in this decree. If the offense is repeated, the fine shall be from one thousand balboas (B 1,000) to five thousand balboas (B 5,000). Resolutions imposing fines may be appealed to the Ministry of Commerce and Industry.

The National Securities Commission shall be empowered to invalidate, upon request by an interested party, such portions of a sales contract for securities as contain clauses that violate legal provisions concerning securities, security regulations, or lawful instructions issued by the Commission.

**Art. 31.** Any employee of the National Securities Commission who improperly divulges information obtained in the performance of his duties with reference to securities or mutual fund companies, their authorized distributors or sales agents will be penalized by a fine of from fifty balboas (B 50) to two hundred balboas (B 200) and immediate dismissal from his post, without prejudice to the penalties established in the Penal Code.

**Art. 32.** Any person may report to the National Securities Commission any violation of the provisions of this cabinet decree. In the event of such report, the person making it will receive fifty per cent (50%) of the monies received from the fine levied on the natural or juridical person penalized.

**Art. 33.** All fines referred to under this title and other penalties provided for in this cabinet decree will, unless otherwise stipulated, be imposed by the National Securities Commission and received by the National Treasury. The pertinent resolutions may be appealed to the Minister of Commerce and Industry.

## TITLE V

### PROTECTION OF MINORITY STOCKHOLDERS

**Art. 34.** In order for any business or contract between a company and one or more of its directors or one or more of its officers or in which one or more of the persons mentioned have a direct or indirect interest to be binding on the company, it must be submitted for approval or disapproval by the Board of Directors of the company. Each resolution of the Board of Directors in such case will be reported to the next Stockholders Meeting, which, if it should disapprove of the action taken by the Board of Directors, will decide whether or not to institute the relevant legal action against the directors or officers of the Board of Directors who voted in favor of the resolution.

*Paragraph:* The content of this article does not imply that the stockholders individually are prohibited from making use of any right or taking any action authorized by law.

**Art. 35.** The stocks of a company that are owned by another company in which the former is the majority stockholder will have no voting rights at any Stockholders Meeting nor will they be considered as stocks issued and in circulation for purposes of constituting a quorum.

**Art. 36.** In order to report a person who represents the company for crimes against property prejudicial to the company, such as improper appropriation, fraud and others, which, according to procedural law, must be reported by the party affected, the holders of at least five per cent (5%) of the stocks in circulation may constitute themselves as representatives of the company for that purpose as follows: they will request the Board of Directors to grant them the status of special representative of the company in order to make the corresponding report. If the Board of Directors should deny the request or fail to reach a decision within the ten (10) calendar days following such request, the stockholders concerned may proceed to make the corresponding report. In this case, they must confirm their status as stockholders by presenting the proper certificates and the fact that they have made the request by presenting a copy of the same and of the certified receipt proving that it was mailed or delivered in person.

**Art.** 37. The provisions of Articles 34, 35, and 36 above shall apply to joint-stock companies registered with the National Securities Commission and to those whose shares are sold on the market, even if such companies do not offer their own shares to the public.

**Art.** 38. Article 418 of the Commercial Code, which was reinstated by Law No. 9 of 1946, will read as follows:

"*Art. 418.* Every stockholder will have the right to protest any resolutions adopted by the General Stockholders Meeting that run counter to the law, to the partnership agreement or charter or to the statutes by filing, within an absolute term of thirty (30) days, a claim for nullity with the competent judge, who, if he considers the matter to be urgent, may suspend implementation of the resolution until such time as the claim has been decided. In no case will such suspension occur if the stockholder files his claim in plenary rather than summary proceedings."

**Art.** 39. Article 420 of the Commercial Code, which was reinstated by Law No. 9 of 1946, will read as follows:

"*Art. 420.* The General Stockholders Meeting will be called by the Board of Directors, by the persons duly authorized for this purpose under the law, the charter or the statutes, or by the competent circuit judge. Judicial convocation will be invoked only when so requested by one or more stockholders whose holdings represent at least one twentieth of the capital stock, provided the charter or the statutes do not concede this right to stockholders with a smaller representation. The request covered by this article will be resolved by plenary judgment."

**Art.** 40. Judicial convocation will be announced by means of a notice to be published on three consecutive days in two widely circulated newspapers in the place of domicile of the company or in Panama City; the Meeting will be held not less than ten nor more than twenty days following the third publication.

**Art. 41.** Article 444 of the Commercial Code, which was reinstated by Law No. 9 of 1946, will read as follows:

"*Art. 444.* The directors will incur no personal responsibility for the obligations of the company but will be accountable individually or jointly, as the case may be, to the company and to third parties for the effective disbursement of payments appearing as made by the partners, for the actual existence of dividends approved, for sound accounting management and in general for the fulfillment or nonfulfillment of the mandate or violation of the laws, charter, statutes or resolutions of the General Stockholders Meeting. Directors who in due course protested the decision of the majority or who were not in attendance for justified cause will not be held responsible. Accountability may be exacted only by decision of the General Stockholders Meeting."

**Art. 42.** Article 531 of the Commercial Code, which was reinstated by Law No. 9 of 1946, will read as follows:

"*Art. 531.* When no decision has been reached by the partners in a partnership or limited copartnership or by the General Meeting in a stock company, the judge may, at the request of any of the partners or stockholders and following confirmation of the existence of cause for dissolution as established by law, declare liquidation and appoint receivers in accordance with the company charter, if it so provides. This article will be applicable only when the company has been dissolved pursuant to law."

**Art. 43.** The Executive Branch will regulate operation of the National Securities Commission in accordance with the provisions of this cabinet decree.

## GENERAL PROVISIONS

**Art. 44.** Capital gains obtained by natural or juridical persons from the sale of bonds, shares and other securities referred to in item *(e)* of Article 701 of the Tax Code as amended by Cabinet Decree No. 33 of February 12, 1970 shall not be considered taxable income if the negotiated shares were issued by a company registered with the National Securities Commission, if at least twenty-five (25) per cent of their assets is invested within the national territory, and if said persons are not intermediaries in securities trading.

If the companies are registered pursuant to Cabinet Decree No. 247 of July 16, 1970, the transactions shall be exempt from said tax provided at least seventy-five (75) per cent of such companies' investments are made within the national territory.

**Art. 44A.** The annual interest paid on bonds, financial paper, mortgage bonds and other debt instruments which are redeemable or mature no less than three (3) years from their date of issue and which are registered with the National Securities Commission shall be subject to a single annual tax of five (5) per cent which shall be withheld by the juridical person who pays it. Once the withholding has been made, the holder of the bonds, mortgage bonds or other debt instruments need not include in his income declaration the interest thus received.

Bonds, securities and other debt instruments registered with the National Securities Commission and convertible into common voting shares of the issuing company or its affiliates shall be taxed in the same way and under the same conditions, even if such securities have a maturity or redemption term of less than three (3) years.

*Paragraph:* Once the tax referred to in this article has been withheld, it shall be paid into the National Treasury, with a sworn statement on forms which will be provided by the General Directorate of Revenue of the Ministry of Finance and the Treasury, within ten (10) days of the date of withholding.

Failure to withhold, payment after the stipulated term, and false declarations shall be penalized in accordance with the Tax Code.

**Art. 45.** All provisions contradicting this cabinet decree are hereby revoked.

**Art. 46.** This cabinet decree will enter into effect upon its proclamation.

**Art. 47.** If an enterprise offers securities or mutual funds for public sale without being duly authorized in accordance with the legal provisions in force, and its domicile and that of its legal representatives are unknown, the National Securities Commission shall be duly empowered to serve it notice by means of a summons, which shall be published on two consecutive days in a local newspaper calling for the party concerned to appear within three (3) business days of the last publication. Publication need not be made in the *Gazeta Oficial.*

**Art. 48.** In the event that the person summoned does not appear before expiration of the period mentioned in the preceding article, the National Securities Commission, without taking further steps, may impose on the enterprise concerned such penalty as it may deem appropriate pursuant to the provisions of Cabinet Decrees No. 247 and No. 248 of July 16, 1970. Notification of the resolution in this case shall take effect in the manner provided for the summons, it being understood that the relevant resolution shall be enforceable forty-eight (48) hours from its last publication.

**Art. 49.** In addition to the other functions set forth in this cabinet decree, the National Securities Commission shall be empowered to determine the administrative interpretation and scope of the legal provisions dealing with securities and mutual funds.

*[The signatory clause is omitted.]*

# Cabinet Decree No. 248 [1]

[July 16, 1970]

## Whereby the operation of companies known as mutual funds, their distributors and sales agents are regulated

The Provisional Government Council

DECREES:

### TITLE I

### MUTUAL FUND COMPANIES

**Art. 1.** The companies subject to the regulations contained in this cabinet decree are those already established or to be established in the future that are engaged in the activity commonly known as mutual funds, that is, which, through the issue of their own stocks, bonds, docu-

[1] Given in Panama City on July 16, 1970.

ments, securities or certificates of participation or investment or by any other means engage in obtaining monies from the general public, within the national territory, in either lump-sum payments or installments, for the purpose of investing them in the acquisition of stocks, bonds or securities of any type or in real property, inside or outside of the Republic.

**Art. 2.** For the effects of this cabinet decree, a company will be understood to be engaged in obtaining monies from the general public when, for the purpose mentioned in Article 1, it

*(a)* publishes or announces through the press, radio or television; or
*(b)* offers its stocks, bonds, documents, securities or certificates of participation or investment by means of mail, cable, telephone or telegraph or any other medium of communication; or
*(c)* circulates printed advertising publicity, descriptive pamphlets or prospectuses on the stocks, bonds, documents, securities or certificates of participation or investment offered or sends communications or requests to prospective purchasers, or
*(d)* makes offers through authorized distributors or sales agents; or
*(e)* employs any other means which, in the opinion of the National Securities Commission, signifies the offer, distribution or sale to undetermined persons or prospective purchasers.

**Art. 3.** The operations described in the preceding article may be undertaken only by the juridical persons constituted or to be constituted for this purpose in accordance with the legislation of the Republic of Panama or of a foreign state, provided they are authorized to that effect by the National Securities Commission.

**Art. 4.** Mutual fund companies will cause to appear on all their publicity their firm or trade designation or name, as the case may be, accompanied by an indication of the fact that they are engaged in the business of mutual funds.

**Art. 5.** Mutual fund companies may not undertake the following operations in the national territory:

*(a)* Purchase of stocks, securities or bonds by payment of only part of their price, securing the unpaid balance of that price by means of a loan guaranteed by pledge of the securities so acquired.
*(b)* Sale of stocks, bonds or securities which they do not own at the time of the sale.

(*c*) Purchase of stocks or securities of companies that are not authorized by the National Securities Commission to sell their stocks or securities.
(*d*) Guarantee to a company of the placement of its securities or stocks in the market.
(*e*) Purchase of more than forty per cent (40%) of the stocks, bonds or securities issued by a single natural or juridical person. This prohibition is not applicable to certificates or bonds of the national government or its decentralized agencies or to the purchase of real property.

## TITLE II

### NATIONAL MUTUAL FUND COMPANIES

**Art. 6.** For the effects of this cabinet decree, national companies will be defined as those constituted in accordance with the laws of the Republic of Panama that maintain their books and accounting records within the national territory.

**Art. 7.** The paid-in corporate capital of a national mutual fund company will be at least two hundred thousand balboas (B 200,000).

**Art. 8.** National mutual fund companies will post annually with the National Securities Commission a bond equivalent to ten per cent (10%) of the stocks, securities or bonds they have sold in the national territory, which bond will in no case amount to less than fifty thousand (B 50,000) and will consist of cash, checks issued or certified by local banks, insurance policies (guarantee bonds) or government bonds. This bond will guarantee the payment of any claims that might be filed against the company by its own stockholders or by third persons and any penalties that might be imposed pursuant to this cabinet decree.

**Art. 9.** Prior to commencing operations, national mutual fund companies will formulate, through an attorney, a request for authorization to the National Securities Commission, accompanied by the following documents:

(*a*) Public document containing the corporate charter and statutes of the requesting company and their amendments and proof of the registration of such papers in the Public Registry.
(*b*) Certificate of the Public Registry stating the names of the directors and principal officers of the company.

(*c*) Sworn notarized statement by the president and treasurer of the requesting company to the effect that, according to the stock ledger and books of account, the company has a paid-in corporate capital of at least two hundred thousand balboas (B 200,000).

(*d*) Proof that the bond described in Article 8 has been posted.

(*e*) The advertising plans, programs and prospectuses, as well as the specimen stocks, bonds, documents, securities or certificates with which the company will initiate its operations.

(*f*) The tables of investments and deductions applicable to programs for acquisition of the stocks, bonds, documents, securities or certificates of participation or investment. It is understood that these tables will contain at least the following information:

1. Amount of the brokerage or any other fee to be charged directly or indirectly by the authorized distributors or their sales agents or any other intermediary of the requesting company.
2. Charges for administrative services and brokerage payable to the persons described in Title IX of this cabinet decree.
3. Any other deductions to be made from the sums received by the requesting company.
4. The net remainder that will actually be credited to the price of the stocks, bonds, documents, securities or certificates, as the case may be.

(*g*) The forms, annexes and contracts to be utilized by the requesting company for the purposes of Title VII of this cabinet decree.

*Paragraph:* A period of four (4) months is granted to national companies established in Panama for obtaining the respective authorization from the National Securities Commission.

**Art. 10.** The National Securities Commission will study the documents presented and, if it finds them to be consistent with this cabinet decree, will issue the authorizing resolution with a statement of its reasons. Otherwise, it will refuse authorization by means of a resolution also including a statement of its reasons.

**Art. 11.** After obtaining the required authorization, the requesting company will apply for the corresponding commercial license, enclosing with the application a true and faithful copy of the resolution issued by the National Securities Commission.

## TITLE III

### FOREIGN MUTUAL FUND COMPANIES

**Art. 12.** For the effects of this cabinet decree, foreign companies will be defined as those constituted in accordance with the laws of foreign states and those constituted in Panama that do not maintain their books and accounting records within the national territory.

**Art. 13.** Foreign mutual fund companies constituted in accordance with the laws of foreign states may not offer for sale their stocks, bonds, documents, securities or certificates of participation or investment either directly or through distributors without having secured authorization for offices or agencies in the Republic, pursuant to the provisions of Section Ten of Law No. 32 of February 26, 1927, on stock companies.

**Art. 14.** The paid-in corporate capital of a foreign mutual fund company offering or proposing to offer its stocks in Panama directly or through authorized distributors will be at least five million balboas (B 5,000,000) or the equivalent in the national currency of the country of origin.

**Art. 15.** Foreign mutual fund companies will post annually with the National Securities Commission a bond equivalent to ten per cent (10%) of the stocks, securities or bonds they have sold in the national territory, which bond will in no case amount to less than two hundred and fifty thousand balboas (B 250,000) and will consist of cash, checks issued or certified by local banks, insurance policies (guarantee bonds) or government bonds. This bond will guarantee the payment of any claims that might be filed against the company by its own stockholders or by third persons and any penalties that might be imposed pursuant to this cabinet decree.

**Art. 16.** Before they can sell their stocks in the national territory, foreign mutual fund companies must formulate, through an attorney, a request for authorization to the National Securities Commission, accompanied by the following documents:

*(a)* Public document containing the corporate charter and statutes of the requesting company and their amendments and proof of the registration of such papers in the Public Registry.

*(b)* Certificate issued by the public agency responsible for the control and supervision of mutual fund companies, where available, in

the place of domicile of the applicant stating that the company has the legal capacity necessary for the conduct of mutual fund operations and that it has the paid-in corporate capital required by Article 14.

(*c*) Copy of the laws, by-laws and all legal provisions governing this type of company in the country of origin, where available, duly authenticated by the Panamanian Consul.

(*d*) Proof that the bond described in Article 15 has been posted.

(*e*) The advertising plans, programs and prospectuses, as well as the specimen stocks, bonds, documents, securities or certificates to be utilized by the company in its operations.

(*f*) The tables, forms, annexes, contracts and other documents described in subsections (*e*) and (*f*) of Article 9 of this cabinet decree.

(*g*) True and faithful copy of the distribution contract signed by the foreign mutual fund company with its authorized distributor for the Republic of Panama, in the event that distribution and sale are not carried out directly by the company itself.

(*h*) Certified and true and faithful copy of the balance sheets of the foreign mutual fund company for the past two (2) years.

(*i*) Declaration of the investment policy followed by the company.

(*j*) Document containing the power of attorney granted to the legal representative of the applicant in the Republic, who will be fully authorized to represent the company in legal, administrative and judicial matters, duly registered in the Public Registry.

*Paragraph:* A period of four (4) months is granted to foreign companies established or to be established in Panama for obtaining the respective authorization from the National Securities Commission.

**Art. 17.** The National Securities Commission will study the documents presented and, if it finds them to be consistent with this cabinet decree, will issue the resolution referred to in Article 10.

## TITLE IV

### OBLIGATION TO INVEST IN PANAMA

**Art. 18.** Both national and foreign companies must invest in Panama part of the monies they collect within the national territory. The National Securities Commission is authorized to stipulate the amount of this national investment, which will not be less than twenty-five per cent (25%), and to alter that amount by sixty (60) days' advance notice to the mutual fund companies, with the understanding that the new percentage will not be applied retroactively.

The investment referred to in this article may be made in:

(*a*) stocks of national companies engaged or proposing to engage, within the territory of the Republic, in industrial, mining, construction, craft, transportation or service activities on a commercial scale;
(*b*) state securities;
(*c*) real property located in the national territory;
(*d*) mortgages or mortgage certificates on real property located in the national territory.

At the request of the mutual fund company, the National Securities Commission may authorize up to one third (⅓) of the investment in fixed-term deposits in the Savings Bank of Panama.

*Transitory Paragraph:* Unless the National Securities Commission stipulates otherwise, the amount of the local investment will be equal to 35% of the monies collected within the national territory.

**Art. 19.** When the bond to be posted by the mutual fund companies consists of cash, state bonds or checks issued or certified by local banks, such bond will be considered as national investment for the purposes of this title.

**Art. 20.** Within the three (3) months following the close of each fiscal year, the mutual fund companies and their distributors, if any, will present to the National Securities Commission a sworn statement setting forth the total amount of monies collected in the national territory during the previous year and the amount of their local investments.

The National Securities Commission will be authorized to request information in addition to that presented by the companies and to make any investigation it deems advisable in order to ensure faithful compliance with this title, which function it may delegate to the Ministry of Finance and the Treasury.

## TITLE V

### AUTHORIZED DISTRIBUTORS OF MUTUAL FUND COMPANIES

**Art. 21.** Only those national or foreign natural or juridical persons authorized by the National Securities Commission to perform such activity in accordance with the provisions of this cabinet decree may engage in the distribution of mutual funds.

A period of four (4) months is granted to natural or juridical persons engaged or proposing to engage in the distribution and sale of mutual funds for obtaining the respective authorization from the National Securities Commission.

**Art. 22.** A single natural or juridical person duly authorized for the purpose may distribute and sell simultaneously stocks or securities of various mutual fund companies, provided that each of those companies has obtained the necessary authorization from the National Securities Commission referred to in this cabinet decree.

Authorized distributors will conduct their distribution operations in the name and on behalf of the mutual fund companies and will act as their agents in sales contracts signed with third parties, as established in Article 30.

**Art. 23.** When the authorized distributor for one or more mutual fund companies is a juridical person, it will, by means of a public document registered in the Public Registry, accredit a permanent agent with full authority to represent the distributor company as plaintiff or defendant in both judicial and extrajudicial proceedings.

**Art. 24.** In order to verify financial statements, the National Securities Commission may, through its officers and employees, inspect and examine authorized distributors of mutual funds, conduct appraisals and audits, require presentation of the accounting books and of the documents and files justifying each entry or account, confirm portfolio investments and examine the records of the company agencies. The right of examination extends to any subsidiary or affiliate in which the company examined has invested more than twenty per cent (20%) of its portfolio.

The National Securities Commission may delegate this function to auditors of the Ministry of Finance and the Treasury.

## Title VI

### MUTUAL FUND SALES AGENTS OR BROKERS

**Art. 25.** Mutual fund sales agents are those natural persons engaged in serving as intermediaries between mutual fund companies or their authorized distributors and persons investing their money in stocks or other securities of these companies.

**Art. 26.** Following the entry into force of this cabinet decree, only those natural persons who hold the proper license, which will be issued by the National Securities Commission in accordance with the provisions of the cabinet decree establishing that Commission, and who are duly authorized by a national mutual fund or by an authorized distributor of a foreign mutual fund company may act as mutual fund sales agents.

**Art. 27.** Mutual fund sales agents may not grant discounts to or share commissions or any other advantages they may derive from the placement of mutual fund stocks with any of the following persons:

*(a)* The investor signing the mutual fund contract.
*(b)* Any person who is not licensed as a mutual fund sales agent.
*(c)* Employees of mutual fund companies.

**Art. 28.** A period of four months from the entry into force of this cabinet decree is granted to mutual fund sales agents currently operating as such for compliance with the requirements established herein.

**Art. 29.** Cause for revocation of the license of a mutual fund sales agent will be improper appropriation, in whole or in part, of the amounts corresponding to stocks or securities sold or the retention of such amounts beyond the time usually required for their receipt by the mutual fund companies or their authorized distributors.

## TITLE VII

### MUTUAL FUND SALES CONTRACT

**Art. 30.** The mutual fund sales contract will be recorded in a private document which will contain:

*(a)* The name of the mutual fund company concerned.
*(b)* The name and domicile of its distributor in the Republic of Panama, if any.
*(c)* The plan to which the contract signed belongs.
*(d)* The amount of the installment selected by the investor and the terms of payment, in the case of periodic payment programs, or the total amount to be invested, in the case of lump-sum payment programs.

(*e*) The place and date of signature of the contract, which will be signed by the legal representative of the mutual fund company or of the authorized distributor of the company, as the case may be, and the investor.

(*f*) A statement to the effect that the investor has received a prospectus describing the obligations of the company, its investment policy, its most recent financial statement and his own liquidation and conversion privileges.

(*g*) A full and detailed account of the procedure for liquidation of stocks of the investor.

(*h*) A table showing any commissions or discounts to be charged to or deducted from the amounts actually paid in by the investor.

## TITLE VIII

### RIGHT OF LIQUIDATION

**Art. 31.** Any person who is the owner of stocks, documents, bonds or other securities issued by a mutual fund company may, in accordance with the procedure established in the sales contract of each company, request the liquidation of all or part of his securities. In such case, the company will pay in cash within a period of not more than thirty (30) days an amount equivalent to the market value of the securities presented for liquidation, after making the discounts referred to in subsection (*h*) of the preceding article.

*Paragraph:* Market value of the securities presented for liquidation will be defined as the market value or stock market quotation prevailing on the day on which the stock certificate is received with the request for liquidation at the main offices of the mutual fund company in the Republic of Panama.

## TITLE IX

### CONSULTING CONTRACTS

**Art. 32.** The mutual fund companies may sign with natural or juridical persons contracts for administration or consulting services in connection with the investment of its funds, with the understanding, however, that in no case may the annual fees of administrator or consulting companies exceed one per cent (1%) of the total investments subject to such administration or consultation. These fees will be paid annually on the basis of the financial statements presented by the companies to the National Securities Commission.

**Art. 33.** A true and faithful copy of each administration or consulting services contract will be presented at the offices of the National Securities Commission upon formulation of the request described in Titles II and III of this cabinet decree, or, if none should then be available, at the time such contract enters into force.

## TITLE X

### PENALTIES

**Art. 34.** Companies which engage in the business of mutual funds without due authorization pursuant to this cabinet decree will be penalized by a fine equivalent to one hundred per cent (100%) of the value of the sale or sales transacted.

**Art. 35.** Natural or juridical persons acting, in the capacity of distributors or sales agents, to transact or intervene in the sale of mutual fund stocks on behalf of companies not authorized to engage in such business in Panama will be subject to the same penalty as that established in the preceding article.

**Art. 36.** Mutual fund companies, distributor companies and sales agents paying commissions, brokerage or fees of any type not mentioned in the reports referred to in Articles 9 and 16 of this cabinet decree that make such payment in any amount to natural or juridical persons not authorized to receive it will be penalized by a fine equivalent to twice the amount of the commission, brokerage or fee so paid. The fine for a second offense will be ten times the amount of such commission, brokerage or fee.

**Art. 37.** Any mutual fund company which refuses to furnish reports to the National Securities Commission or that furnishes false or inaccurate reports will be penalized by a fine of five thousand balboas (B 5,000) to ten thousand balboas (B 10,000), in addition to any other penalty that may be applicable in accordance with this cabinet decree.

**Art. 38.** Any natural or juridical person violating any of the provisions of this cabinet decree will be liable to a fine of one hundred balboas (B 100) to one thousand balboas (B 1,000), unless the decree stipulates a specific penalty for the violation concerned. The fine for a second offense will be one thousand balboas (B 1,000) to five thousand balboas (B 5,000).

**Art. 39.** Any person may report to the National Securities Commission any violation of the provisions of this cabinet decree. In the event of such report, the person making it will receive fifty per cent (50%) of the monies received by the National Treasury from the fine levied on the natural or juridical person penalized.

**Art. 40.** All fines referred to under this title and other penalties provided for in this cabinet decree will, unless otherwise stipulated, be imposed by the National Securities Commission and received by the National Treasury. The pertinent resolutions may be appealed to the Minister of Commerce and Industry.

## TITLE XI

### VOLUNTARY LIQUIDATION

**Art. 41.** In order to effect its liquidation or dissolution, any company selling securities or mutual funds to the public must obtain prior authorization from the National Securities Commission, which will so authorize when the company is solvent, that is, when its liquid assets are sufficient to reimburse its investors and pay its creditors.

**Art. 42.** Once authorization has been granted, the company will immediately cease operations, and its powers will be confined to those needed to carry out the liquidation, collect its credits, reimburse its investors, pay its creditors and settle its business.

**Art. 43.** Within the thirty (30) days following such authorization, the company will remit by mail to each investor, creditor or party interested in the funds held by the company a notice of the liquidation which will contain such information as the National Securities Commission may indicate. This notice will also be posted in a prominent place on the premises of each establishment of the company and published as stipulated by the Commission.

**Art. 44.** The liquidation authorization will not prejudice the right of investors or creditors to receipt in full of the amount of their credits or the right of other owners of record to return of their assets. All legitimate credits of creditors and investors will be paid and all other assets retained by the company for any reason returned to their owners within the term established by the Commission in authorizing the liquidation.

**Art. 45.** No distribution of assets among the stockholders may take place until all credits of investors and creditors have been satisfied pursuant to the plan of liquidation approved by the Commission.

In the case of credits in litigation, the company will deposit an amount sufficient to cover such credits with the National Bank, which will hold this sum until such time as a legal decision is reached.

**Art. 46.** If any unclaimed funds or credits should remain upon completion of its liquidation, the company will deliver to the National Bank the amount necessary to cover this item. The unclaimed assets will be deposited with the National Bank of Panama. The funds so deposited will be transferred to the State at the end of five (5) years. In turn, the assets and securities may be sold by their depositary, with the approval of the Commission, after the end of the first year. The proceeds from their sale will be transferred to the State at the end of the fifth year, unless claimed by the owners.

**Art. 47.** The State is obliged to make restitution to the owner of the funds described in the preceding article, provided they are claimed within the ten (10) years following the date of their transfer; such restitution will not include interest payments.

**Art. 48.** During the course of the voluntary liquidation, the liquidators will be obliged to:

1. furnish to the Commission, on a schedule to be determined by the latter, such reports as it may request on the progress of the liquidation, and
2. report to the Commission as soon as they perceive that their liquid assets will not be sufficient to reimburse the investors and pay the creditors.

## TITLE XII

### INTERVENTION, REORGANIZATION, AND FORCED LIQUIDATION

**Art. 49.** The Commission may, by a reasoned resolution approved by a majority vote of its members, intervene in a company, taking control of its assets and assuming their administration pursuant to the terms stipulated in Article 51, in any of the following cases:

(*a*) If its capital has declined or lacks solidity.

(*b*) If it is conducting its operations illegally, negligently or fraudulently.

(*c*) If its continued operation is uncertain.

(*d*) If it refuses to present the accounting records of its operations as duly requested or has in any way obstructed inspection of the company.

(*e*) If the assets of the company are not sufficient to cover all of its liabilities.

(*f*) If the Commission deems such a step to be advisable because of undue delay in terminating voluntary liquidation.

**Art. 50.** In carrying out the intervention, the Commission will order a notice to be posted on the premises of the company announcing this action and stating the time when it will enter into effect, which will in no case be prior to such posting.

**Art. 51.** When the Commission decides to intervene in a company, it will appoint the receiver or receivers it deems necessary to exercise exclusive administration and control of the company, with such powers as the Commission may authorize, which will include the following:

(*a*) Suspension or limitation of the payment of obligations.

(*b*) Employment of the auxiliary personnel necessary.

(*c*) Execution of any document in the name of the company.

(*d*) Initiation, defense or prosecution in the name of the company of any action or procedure to which it may be a party.

Once the intervention has been effected, the receiver or receivers will take an inventory of assets and liabilities and forward a copy thereof to the Commission, which will make it available to any interested parties that may so request.

**Art. 52.** The resolution ordering intervention of a company entails the authority to order its reorganization, request its forced liquidation or desist from the intervention, for which purpose the Commission will be allowed sixty (60) calendar days from the date of posting of the notices described in Article 50, or, if the appeal described in the following article should have been filed, sixty (60) days from the corresponding ruling.

**Art. 53.** The sole recourse against the resolution authorizing intervention available to the company concerned will consist of appeal to the

Executive Branch, which will be considered without suspension of execution and without prejudice to an appeal to the administrative court with plenary jurisdiction. A period of thirty (30) working days from the date of posting of the notice described in Article 50 will be allowed for filing such appeal.

The Supreme Court may in no case provisionally suspend the effects of the intervention decreed, but the pending appeal must have been ruled on in order for the Commission to order reorganization or request forced liquidation of the company concerned.

**Art. 54.** When the Commission intervenes in a company, the prescribed terms of all rights or actions to which the company is entitled, as well as the terms of lawsuits or procedures to which the company is a party, will be understood to be suspended for up to six (6) months.

**Art. 55.** If, within the period established in Article 52, the Commission should decide to proceed with reorganization of the company, it will, after hearing the opinion of the company concerned, prepare a reorganization plan which will be published for three (3) consecutive days in a widely circulated national newspaper.

**Art. 56.** No asset of the company will be subject to seizure, attachment or retention during the period of intervention or reorganization.

**Art. 57.** With the authorization of the Commission, the receivers may obtain loans in the name of the company and pledge its assets in guarantee.

**Art. 58.** All necessary expenditures incurred by the intervention, reorganization or liquidation will be charged to the assets of the company.

**Art. 59.** No reorganization plan will be prepared that does not meet the following requirements:

*(a)* It is feasible and equitable for all investors, creditors, stockholders or partners, as the case may be.

*(b)* It guarantees the dismissal of any director, officer or employee responsible for the situation leading to the reorganization through his negligent, fraudulent or unlawful acts.

*(c)* Any merger or consolidation proposed is consistent with the requirements of this cabinet decree and other current legal provisions.

**Art. 60.** When, because of situations arising in the course of reorganization, the plan becomes inequitable or inadvisable to implement, the Commission may revise it or request liquidation of the company as stipulated subsequently.

**Art. 61.** If the Commission should deem it desirable to request liquidation of a company, it will so notify the legal representative of the company in person; inform its stockholders or partners, investors and creditors by publication of the authorizing resolution for three (3) consecutive days in a widely circulated newspaper, and request dissolution and liquidation of the company from the competent court in accordance with current legal provisions.

**Art. 62.** Once the liquidation has been requested, the Commission will mail to each investor and creditor of the company at the address appearing in the company books a notice of the liquidation request. A copy of the notice will be posted in a prominent place in the establishments of the company. A statement showing the amount credited to the investor or creditor in the company books will accompany the notice.

**Art. 63.** In every case of voluntary or forced liquidation of a mutual fund company, its obligations to its investors will be settled in accordance with the order of priority established by current legislation.

With regard to credits of investors, payments will be made in the following order:

(*a*) First payment will be made to local investors, that is, to natural or juridicial persons domiciled in territory under the jurisdiction of the Panamanian authorities.

(*b*) Once reimbursement has been made to local investors, investments that entered from outside of the territory of the Republic, belonging to persons domiciled abroad, will be considered and reimbursed to the extent possible.

**Art. 64.** This cabinet decree will enter into effect upon its proclamation.

*{The signatory clause is omitted.}*

# Singapore

Overview of Singapore
Courtesy World Bank

# SINGAPORE

# Financial System of Singapore

by

*Michio Ishihara* and *Hyong Chun Kim* *

## Introduction

Modern Singapore was founded in 1819 with the establishment of a trading station for the British East India Company. This marked the beginning of British rule and gave rise to the development of Singapore's entrepôt trade. In 1959 Singapore was granted full self-government in domestic affairs and in September 1963 it became part of Malaysia. On August 9, 1965, following its separation from Malaysia, Singapore proclaimed itself an independent republic. As a result of its long-standing role as an entrepôt, Singapore has developed a relatively extensive and sophisticated banking system over the years and has become a major financial center of the region.

The financial system in Singapore has undergone significant changes following the establishment of the Asian Currency Market in 1968 and, subsequently, the Monetary Authority of Singapore in 1971. Since then, a number of new financial institutions have been established and their activities have widened with the rapid development of the existing financial markets. These developments, while largely a result of government policy measures, also reflected the expansion of the domestic economy, as well as the rapid growth of the world economy in the early 1970s.

The financial system in Singapore comprises the Currency Board, the Monetary Authority of Singapore, commercial banks, the Central Provident Fund, the Post Office Savings Bank, the Development Bank of Singapore, merchant banks, discount houses, finance companies, and insurance companies. The Monetary Authority of Singapore performs central banking functions, excluding currency issue which is vested in the Board of Commissioners of Currency (the Currency Board). The major financial markets in Singapore are the money market, the capital market, and the Singapore-based Asian Currency Market.

---

* Mr. Ishihara, an economist in the Asian Department of the International Monetary Fund at the time this introduction was written, is a graduate of the Economics Department, Syracuse University (U.S.A.).

Mr. Kim, a senior economist in the Fund's Asian Department, obtained a degree from the University of Oregon and taught economics at a California state college before joining the Asian Department of the International Monetary Fund in February 1967.

Historically, because of Singapore's heavy reliance on exporting as a primary vehicle of growth, the role and structure of Singapore's financial system had been geared toward financing foreign trade. However, reflecting a transition to rapid industrialization and diversification, since the late 1960s marked emphasis has been placed on structuring the financial system toward the development needs of the economy and the growth of a regional financial center.

In its initial stage, the Monetary Authority was largely concerned with the development of a statutory and institutional framework for central banking in Singapore. Consequently, monetary policy was relatively passive, and the development of monetary policy instruments relatively slow. Since 1973, with the emergence of inflation and recession, monetary policy has assumed an active role through the use of moral suasion, changes in requirements on minimum cash balances and on liquidity ratio, special deposit requirements, overall as well as selective credit control, and money market operations.

## Structure of Financial System

### Official institutions

*Board of Commissioners of Currency.*—In the early period (1826–1903) when Singapore was part of the Straits Settlements (Penang, Malacca, and Singapore), various silver dollars (such as the Mexican dollar, the British trade dollar, the Hong Kong dollar, the Spanish dollar, and the American trade dollar) were in circulation, each of which was introduced at a different period of time. During that period, the Currency Ordinance of 1899 established a Board of Commissioners of Currency, made the issuance of notes the exclusive responsibility of the Straits Settlements Government, and replaced all banknotes with Currency Board notes. In 1903, the new silver Straits dollar was introduced. Currency Ordinance No. 23 of 1938 established the new Currency Commission with Singapore as the head office, and the currency issue was changed from the Straits Settlements basis to the Pan-Malayan basis. Consequently, the Straits dollar was changed to the Malayan dollar, and Singapore emerged as the political and economic center of the region. The Currency Act of 1950 extended the Malayan currency area to include Sarawak and North Borneo, and led to the issuance of new currency notes in 1954. The advent of Malaysian independence in 1957 and the declaration of self-government by Singapore in 1959 necessitated a revision of the currency agreement and, accordingly, a new agreement was concluded in 1960.

When Singapore left Malaysia (August 1965), the Singapore Government decided to establish its own currency rather than to share a common currency with Malaysia. The Government also decided that the new monetary authority should take the form of a currency board rather than a central bank, as the former was considered better suited to inspire confidence in the new currency. The Board of Commissioners of Currency, Singapore, established by the Currency Act, 1967, assumed the note-issuing function for Singapore, effective June 12, 1967.[1]

The two most important features of the currency board system in Singapore are that (a) the issunce of notes and coins is entrusted to the Board of Commissioners of Currency, Singapore (Currency Act, sec. 14), and (b) the Board is required to maintain a minimum of 100 per cent external assets cover (valued at current market prices) for currency issued (sec. 23). The currency board system is "automatic" in relation to the issuance of legal tender currency, and this, together with the 100 per cent foreign assets cover, ensures that there is no scope for "fiduciary" or discretionary creation of currency. The currency board system in Singapore has proved to be simple to operate and has prevented any overissue of currency. The system has been able to maintain public confidence in the stability of the value of the Singapore dollar, thus contributing to the steady growth of foreign trade and inflows of foreign investment, which are so essential to the development of the economy. Although the 100 per cent external cover requirement could lead to rigidity in the system, the continuing balance of payments surpluses have provided sufficient external reserves, while budgetary policy and the Government's debt management have yielded appropriate variations in money supply. The system, however, could cause an unnecessary locking up of external reserves, some of which might otherwise be used for financing domestic investment should the need arise. Moreover, as the system lacked a lender-of-last-resort facility before December 1972, it tended to induce commercial banks, particularly domestic banks, to hold larger liquid and cash reserves than they would otherwise do if there had been a central bank.

[1] The Malaysian dollar ceased to be legal tender in Singapore from January 16, 1969. However, even after the currency split, the three Governments (Malaysia, Singapore, and Brunei) agreed on an arrangement by which their currencies would be freely interchangeable at par. The currency interchangeability between Malaysia and Singapore lasted until May 8, 1973.

*Monetary Authority of Singapore.*—Before the establishment of of the Monetary Authority of Singapore, the functions of a central bank were divided among the Singapore Board of Commissioners of Currency, which is entrusted with the issuance and management of currency, the Accountant-General, who functioned as the Government's banker and accountant, and the Office of the Commissioner of Banking, which dealt with the inspection and supervision of commercial banks. The Accountant-General managed the clearinghouse and was authorized to deal in Singapore Government securities as a means of maintaining and developing the securities market, rather than as an instrument of monetary policy. Two other agencies in the Ministry of Finance, which also performed central bank functions, were the Foreign Exchange Control Department and the Commissioner for Finance Companies. The former operated the existing exchange controls and the latter regulated the working of finance companies.

As these units developed separately over time in response to emerging requirements, it became evident that the centralization of them within a single organization was urgently needed to enhance the effectiveness of monetary management and to ensure a coordinated approach to financial policy and development. Apart from administrative tidiness, the amalgamation of these various units into a coherent structure was also expected to give the organization a sense of purpose and direction, which was then lacking. The experience of the past years indicated that a new organization should possess adequate means to moderate the impact of external fluctuations upon the domestic economy. Furthermore, it might be expected more actively to promote economic development in Singapore than the separate agencies had been able to do.

The Monetary Authority, which was established on January 1, 1971 under the Monetary Authority of Singapore Act, 1970, assumed unified control of all central banking functions, except the issue of legal tender currency which continued to be vested with the Currency Board. Although currency issue is a normal function of a central bank, the authorities had concluded, after discussions with the banking and business communities, in view of the historical background and needs of Singapore's economy, that an autonomous Currency Board would be better suited to the task of maintaining public confidence in the Singapore dollar.

The Monetary Authority was established as a corporation wholly owned and controlled by the Government. The principal objectives of the Authority are (a) to act as a banker for the Government, (b) to promote monetary and exchange conditions that are conducive to the growth of the economy, and (c) to exercise the combined functions of the Commissioner of Banking, the Commissioner for Finance Companies, the Accountant-General, and the Controller of Foreign Exchange, with respect to the monetary and banking matters that are normally performed by a central bank (the Monetary Authority of Singapore Act, secs. 4 and 21). It is authorized to accept reserve deposits from banks, enforce liquid assets and cash reserve ratios, issue and manage public debt, discount treasury bills, underwrite approved loans, promote the development of money and capital markets, and finance economic development in Singapore (sec. 22). It is empowered to invest its funds in gold and foreign exchange (sec. 23) and government and other appropriate securities (sec. 22). An amendment to the Monetary Authority of Singapore Act in November 1972 further strengthened the functions of the Monetary Authority by allowing it to purchase, sell, discount, and rediscount bills of exchange and promissory notes, and to grant advances to banks and other institutions against specified collateral; thus, the amendment explicitly empowered the Monetary Authority to act as a lender of last resort. The Monetary Authority has also been empowered to issue directives to financial institutions. Since April 1, 1977, the Authority is also responsible for the supervision and development of the insurance industry.

***Economic Development Board.***—The Economic Development Board was established in 1961 (the Economic Development Board Act, August 1, 1961) as an autonomous statutory agency with wide powers to attract and promote new industries in Singapore and to act as an industrial development bank. An initial capital of S$100 million was provided by the Government, but the Board's resources may be augmented by borrowings from the Government and the public. In its industrial financing, the Development Board was initially authorized to grant long- and short-term loans to industrial enterprises, subscribe to stocks and bonds, underwrite shares and bonds, and guarantee loans raised by industrial enterprises (the Economic Development Board Act, sec. 16, subsec. 1). The Board was also allowed to participate in equity capital of private enterprises. However, the industrial financing function was subsequently transferred to the Development Bank of Singapore, which was established in 1968.

***Development Bank of Singapore.***—The Development Bank of

Singapore was incorporated as a public limited company on July 16, 1968 with an authorized capital of S$200 million, of which S$100 million has been subscribed and paid by the Government (49 per cent), private financial institutions, such as commercial banks and insurance companies (25 per cent), and the general public (26 per cent). The Development Bank is also empowered to raise additional funds from domestic, foreign, and international institutions.

The Development Bank took over the industrial financing function of the Economic Development Board with the primary object of providing long- and medium-term loans, equity participation, and guarantees to manufacturing and processing industries. It also provides financial assistance to approved development projects of the Singapore Government in tourism, shipping, transportation, and other service industries, and the urban renewal program. The Development Bank also functions as a commercial bank and is licensed under the Banking Act.

***Central Provident Fund.***—The Central Provident Fund absorbs savings from the public, as both employees and employers contribute to pension funds for employees when they retire. Before January 1971, employees had to contribute 8 per cent of their gross monthly wage up to a maximum of S$150 and employers contributed an equal sum. Thereafter, the contributions were progressively increased to 16.5 per cent from July 1978 for both employees and employers, to 20.5 per cent for employers, and to 18.0 per cent for employees from July 1980. Since 1975 the Government has allowed contributors to the Provident Fund to withdraw a part or all of their contributions for hire purchase of public housing or apartments to encourage private ownership of homes. Most of the public savings collected by the Fund have been invested in government securities which are held until maturity. As a result, the Fund has been the largest holder of medium- and long-term government bonds, absorbing the bulk of new issues.

***Post Office Savings Bank.***—The Post Office Savings Bank was first established in 1877 and became an independent statutory corporation under the Post Office Savings Bank of Singapore Act, 1971. It is the only bank in Singapore which is exempted from all the provisions of the Banking Act and the Finance Companies Act. The basic objectives of the Savings Bank are to mobilize domestic savings for public development projects and to encourage thrift by providing a safe place for funds with an assured rate of return. The Savings Bank operates through 106 post offices and branches throughout the island. It accepts deposits from individuals and public organizations but not from companies. Repayment of deposits is guaranteed by the Government and the interest paid thereon is exempted from income tax. During the 1960s, while the total number of depositors had increased considerably, the amount of deposits remained relatively stagnant and even declined in some years (1964–66). This was in part due to competition from commercial banks. These provided comparable security, liquidity, and rates of interest, and generally better services. The Post Office Savings Bank therefore raised its deposit rate of interest and provided other incentives, such as abolishing the limit on individual accounts and increasing the limits on demand withdrawals. Cumbersome operating procedures were also simplified. As a result of these measures, the amount of deposits increased rapidly during the 1970s. In addition, to enable the Bank to play a more dynamic role as a financial intermediary, a subsidiary company called the Credit Post Office Savings Bank was established in 1974 to extend housing loans to depositors at interest rates lower than prevailing market rates; previously, the Bank had not made loans to individuals. Finally, its investment policy was modified in 1972 to include not only investment in government securities but also in banks and other financial institutions approved by the Ministry of Finance.

### Private financial institutions

*Commercial banks.*[2]—The driving forces behind the rapid development of commercial banking in Singapore have been foreign trade, foreign investments, and economic development. A commercial bank was first established in Singapore in 1840, with the setting-up of a branch office of the Union Bank of Calcutta. The banks that followed were generally foreign, mostly British, French, Dutch, German, U.S., and Indian. In 1903 the first domestic bank was incorporated with the establishment of a domestic Chinese bank. It was set up to meet the banking requirements of the growing local Chinese business community in connection with the rubber boom that took place just before World War I. The banking system that developed was largely complementary to that of the foreign banks; the Chinese relied on foreign banks for foreign exchange transactions, while the foreign banks in

[2] In addition to the regular commercial banks, the Development Bank of Singapore has also been allowed since 1968 to engage in some commercial banking functions, including acceptance of deposits. Also, there are 49 (as of March 1981) representative offices in Singapore—all branches or offices of foreign banking institutions.

turn received surplus deposits from the domestic banks, collected from the Chinese community.

The number of commercial banks has increased rapidly since 1970, from 37 in that year to 100 at the end of March 1981. Of these, 13 were domestically owned and 87 were foreign owned, primarily by banks in the United States, Japan, Hong Kong, the United Kingdom, and other European countries. This rapid increase in the number of foreign banks reflected the growing realization on the part of foreign banking interests that Singapore would attract business from international companies and could serve as a base for their regional operations, particularly through the Asian Dollar Market. The existence of a large number of foreign banks has also contributed to a high degree of competition among banks and to banking efficiency in general.[3]

Commercial banking operations in Singapore are governed by the Banking Act, 1970, regulations and guidelines issued from time to time by the Monetary Authority, and other relevant laws of Singapore. The main provisions of the Banking Act include the required minimum capital of banks (sec. 9); the maintenance of reserve funds (sec. 18); prohibited businesses (secs. 25–29); minimum liquid assets and cash reserve requirements (secs. 34–35); purposes and types of loans (sec. 38); inspection of bank books, accounts, and transactions (secs. 39–41); and numbered accounts (secs. 50–52).

The provisions for restrictions on the business of banks include the maximum limit of credit that may be granted to any one customer, the prohibiting of advances against the security of the bank's own shares, and the prohibition of trading activity. Excessive direct investment in any financial, commercial, agricultural, industrial, or other undertaking is also prohibited, and acquisition of immovable property and loans secured by such security are subject to restrictions. The provision for numbered accounts has not yet been implemented, pending a review of its legal and practical implications.

The Monetary Authority controls the scope and activities of all banks through the terms of its licenses and through its supervisory and regulatory powers over the banks. Pursuant to this control, the Monetary Authority has developed various categories of banks and bank licenses. At present, the commercial banks in Singapore comprise three categories, namely, full-license banks, restricted banks, and offshore

[3] Although their number is small, domestic banks, with their extensive network of branches, have access to about half the total nonbank deposits in Singapore.

banks. The full-license banks, which total 37, may engage in the entire range of domestic and foreign banking transactions. All domestically incorporated banks (13) and older established foreign banks (24) are in this category. The authorities devised the "restricted" bank and "offshore" bank concepts to allow foreign banks access to Singapore, while protecting the domestic market for local or existing foreign banks. Accordingly, in 1971, the Monetary Authority offered restricted licenses to a selected number of international banks whose countries of origin had not been or were not well represented in Singapore. With few exceptions, banks under the restricted category are primarily wholesale rather than retail oriented. The 13 banks that had been granted restricted banking licenses may engage in most of the activities permitted to the full-license banks. They are free to extend loans in the domestic sector and to participate in foreign exchange and Asian dollar activities; however, they may not operate savings accounts, nor accept total deposits of less than S$250,000 per deposit. A restricted bank is generally limited to one branch. The offshore banks (50) deal mainly in the offshore market. These banks are permitted to deal in foreign exchange and offshore lending, but may not accept deposits from or extend loans to Singaporean residents exceeding a limit of S$30 million per offshore bank, except with the approval of the Monetary Authority.

*Asian Currency Units.*—From 1968 the Government authorized certain banks to establish a separate accounting unit, called the Asian Currency Unit (ACU), the sole function of which would be to accept nonresident currency deposits and to utilize the resources in funding Asian corporate financing activities. The field of operation became known as the Asian Dollar Market. As of March 1981, there were 120 ACUs: 8 operated by local commercial banks, 77 by foreign commercial banks, 34 by merchant banks, and 1 by a foreign-owned investment company (for further details, see subsection on Asian Currency Market).

*Merchant banks.*—Merchant banks in Singapore are not governed by either the Banking Act or the Finance Companies Act. They are incorporated and regulated under the Companies Act, 1967, but unlike regular companies they come under the supervision of the Monetary Authority. Since 1972, merchant banks have grown rapidly in Singapore in response to the rising demand for industrial finance and the need for new issues and for amalgamation of companies. They deal in corporate finance, investment portfolio management, medium- and long-term finance, new issues of capital, merger and acquisitions of companies, management advice, underwriting and flotation of shares and stocks, and leasing facilities. In their early stages of development, most of the merchant banks in Singapore participated in the discount house or short-term money market businesses. But, since the establishment of discount houses in November 1972, the discount business has been separated from the merchant banks. Merchant banks cannot accept deposits from individuals or institutions other than banks and finance companies; they cannot engage in foreign exchange transactions or operate ACUs without prior approval from the Monetary Authority. The merchant banks are predominantly multinational in ownership, and their activities are supervised by the Monetary Authority through the broad guidelines drawn up for these operations.

*Discount houses.*—The development of the money market accelerated and the scope of the market considerably widened following the establishment of four discount houses along the lines of the London discount house system. The first three were established in November 1972 and the fourth in 1974. Local banks, foreign banks, other financial institutions, and foreign discount houses were invited to participate in the discount houses. Initially, the discount houses were managed by persons seconded from discount houses in the United Kingdom and Australia. At present they are run by local managers. The four discount houses collectively form the discount market, which is part of the wider money market.

Discount houses operate under guidelines laid down by the Monetary Authority. The size of their borrowings is limited to 30 times their paid-up capital and reserves. Discount houses must also maintain an asset ratio whereby at least 70 per cent of their total assets are in the form of short-term government paper, with the remaining assets comprising private securities. They accept short-term deposits and invest in treasury bills and short-term government and commercial paper. Discount houses have recourse to the Monetary Authority on the collateral of treasury bills and government securities.

## Nonbank financial institutions

*Finance companies.*—The development of finance companies has been closely related to the activities of banks. At the end of March 1981, there were 34 finance companies in operation, of which 16 were affiliated with commercial banks. Finance companies may accept fixed and savings deposits but are prohibited from providing checking facilities. Apart from the provision of hire-purchase finance of motor vehicles and other consumer durable goods, house mortgages and the financing of such sectors as building and construction, manufacturing, shipping, and general commerce, some finance companies also provide equipment leasing and accounts receivable financing.

The operations of finance companies are regulated by the Finance Companies Act (January 10, 1968), which is administered by the Monetary Authority of Singapore. The Act sets out provisions governing the establishment and operations of finance companies. These relate, among other things, to the maximum amount of loans to one customer as a percentage of paid-up share capital (sec. 18), minimum downpayments and maximum maturity periods for different types of loans and the maximum rate of interest for deposits and for loans (sec. 24), the minimum required reserve fund (sec. 13), the minimum holdings of liquid assets as a percentage of deposit liabilities (sec. 25), and the minimum capital requirements (sec. 7). In 1978, the minimum cash reserve ratio was 6 per cent and the minimum liquid assets ratio 10 per cent, with the ratio being varied by the Monetary Authority from time to time in response to monetary and economic conditions. The Finance Companies Act also lays down regulations on loans and advances, trade, investments, and holdings of immovable property by finance companies (secs. 20–22). Dealings in foreign exchange and gold are prohibited (sec. 18). At the end of March 1981, finance companies accepted S$2,399 million in deposits, of which 90 per cent, or S$2,181 million, was in fixed deposits. Their total deposits were about 14 per cent of commercial banks' deposits.

***Insurance companies.***—Insurance companies are covered by the Insurance Act, 1966, and supplementary regulations administered by the Insurance Commissioner's Department of the Monetary Authority of Singapore. The Insurance Act was modified by the Insurance Funds (Life Business) Order 1968 and the Insurance Funds (General Business) Order 1968. Insurance companies accept insurance premiums and use their funds to advance loans to clients for building houses and other purposes, and to invest in real estate, shares, debentures, and government securities. The Insurance Act stipulates that with respect to life insurance business, insurance companies are required to invest not less than 75 per cent of their Singaporean insurance funds in assets specified in the

Second Schedule[4] to the Insurance Act, including a minimum of 20 per cent in Singapore Government securities. General insurance companies are required to invest not less than 55 per cent of their Singaporean insurance funds in assets specified in the Second Schedule, of which no less than 15 per cent should be in Singapore Government securities. To increase the overall acceptance capacity of the local insurance market, a reinsurance company, the Singapore Reinsurance Corporation, was incorporated in September 1973. As of March 1981 there were 74 insurance companies in Singapore, of which 9 transact reinsurance business only.

*Money brokers.*—The first international money broker started operations in Singapore in mid-1972. Until then, the market was very basic, with local brokers performing the simple function of consummating deals between banks in the local Singapore dollar deposit market. As of March 1981, there were seven international money brokers and one local money broker in Singapore, all members of international brokerage groups with a substantial number of branches in the major financial centers abroad. The brokers deal only in currencies and only with banks and approved financial institutions.[5]

## Singapore's Financial Markets

Since its inception in 1971, the Monetary Authority has developed a modest market for government securities, widened and activated the money market, and generally brought confidence and greater stability to the company share market. The international monetary crisis of 1971–73 (which induced significant flows of foreign funds into Singapore) and the establishment and operation of new merchant banks, discount houses, and money brokers also contributed to the rapid growth of Singapore's money and capital markets. The liberal banking and exchange regulations, on the other hand, were important factors responsible for making the markets more internationally oriented. These improvements in the scope and structure of the money and capital markets, in turn, increased the volume and range of local financial assets and

[4] The Second Schedule refers to the authorized local assets comprising primarily government securities, approved shares and debentures, real estate and land in Singapore, loans secured on real estate, land, and insurance policies in Singapore, cash balances and demand deposits with commercial banks, and other approved investments.

[5] Mention should also be made of another nonbank financial institution. This is the money-loan association that is found in a number of countries of Southeast Asia. It is variously known as "hwei," "kutu," "tontine," or "chit fund." In Singapore, such institutions are subject to licensing and regulation under the Chit Funds Act, 1971.

widened the scope of monetary control, allowing the Monetary Authority to use traditional central banking instruments in the money market to make direct liquidity control more effective.

## Money market

The money market in Singapore consists of the Singapore dollar deposit market and the foreign exchange market.

The Singapore dollar deposit market comprises both overnight funds and term deposits. These are mainly for 1-month or 3-month periods, but may extend up to 6 and 12 months. The market is used mainly by the banks to meet their liquidity requirements and commercial loan portfolios. In addition, there is a secondary market, consisting mainly of bills of exchange, treasury bills, and the Singapore dollar negotiable certificate of deposits, which was first issued in May 1975.[6] The rapid growth of these financial assets has been due largely to official measures taken to provide banks with short-term earning assets through a substantial expansion in the issue of treasury bills, provision for discounting facilities, and approval for the operation of money dealers and discount houses.[7] Generally, local banks are net lenders of interbank funds, while foreign banks are net borrowers, largely for the purpose of maintaining liquidity. The freeing of interest rate quotation by banks in July 1975, which hitherto was determined by the Association of Banks under a cartel arrangement, made interest rates more sensitive to changes in domestic and international market conditions and contributed to the growth of the money market.

The foreign exchange market consists of both Singapore dollar-based foreign exchange, mainly against U.S. dollars, and the "third currency" exchange not involving Singapore dollars. There are 85 authorized banks and 29 merchant banks licensed to deal in foreign exchange and 7 brokers who are allowed to operate only on an agency basis. Market forces determine the foreign exchange rates. The forward market is still small but growing. Commercial banks have been making available, on a

[6] Issuance of negotiable certificates of deposit is limited to banks that are specifically approved by the Monetary Authority. They are issued in multiples of S$50,000 subject to a minimum of S$100,000 and a maximum of S$1 million, except for restricted banks, when the minimum is S$250,000. There is no restriction on the purchase and sales of these negotiable certificates of deposit by nonresidents.

[7] The Monetary Authority conducts operations in treasury bills on behalf of the Government, and is ready to buy back treasury bills through the discount houses; the rediscount rate of the Monetary Authority is a "penalty rate," i.e., it is slightly higher than the discount rate quoted by the houses.

daily basis, forward rates for periods up to one year. Most forward transactions are between the Singapore dollar and the U.S. dollar. The nonbanking sector is permitted to deal in forward exchange to cover forward transactions, including borrowing for business purposes. The Monetary Authority does not intervene in the forward market, but enters, infrequently, into swap transactions with banks. The "third currency" market is fast becoming important, with deutsche mark, Japanese yen, Swiss francs, and sterling the principal currencies.

The concept of a foreign currency deposit market housed in the banking system in Singapore was in many ways a logical progression from Singapore's historic role as one of Asia's key entrepôt trade centers to a regional financial center. Singapore-based banks have been assuming risks for the rest of the region, squaring their own books in the afternoon when London and European markets open. Thus, Singapore provides a vital link with the European market.

### Capital market

The Stock Exchange of Singapore[8] is the chief organized capital market, where bonds and shares are issued, purchased, and sold. The securities industry and listed companies are regulated by the Securities Industry Act, 1973. The Act stipulates that stockbrokers and dealers in securities are required to be licensed and to maintain trust accounts subject to audit. In March 1973, the Securities Industry Act was introduced in order to control speculative manipulation of the stock market, takeovers, or mergers. The Securities Industry Council was also formed in February 1973 to act as an advisory council and a watchdog over the market; new issues of shares through public subscription must be approved by the Council.

Various steps have been taken to develop the domestic capital market. Government bonds with varied maturities have been issued at frequent intervals. The brokerage fee was lowered in 1975 in order to stimulate activities in government bonds through the Exchange. The Monetary Authority has relaxed exchange control regulations and nonresidents are now allowed to buy and sell securities listed on the Exchange. There is no restriction on the remittance of money out of

[8] Until 1973, Singapore and Kuala Lumpur shared a single market for bonds and shares with the two trading rooms linked by direct telephone lines. However, the termination of the currency interchangeability in May 1973 brought about the split of the joint stock exchange, and this resulted in the incorporation of the Stock Exchange of Singapore. Full operation at a separate exchange commenced on July 4, 1973.

Singapore on the sale of securities and no taxation of capital gains. Underwriting facilities have been provided in the capital market by the various commercial and merchant banks. Turnover at the Stock Exchange in 1981 amounted to S$13.5 billion, representing a sharp increase from the generally depressed level at around S$1–2 billion during 1974–77.

### *Asian Currency Market*

The Asian Currency Market, popularly known as the Asian Dollar Market, is an international money and capital market located in Singapore, which began operations in October 1968. The size of the market has expanded rapidly since its inception, both in terms of resources as well as in the number of financial institutions; as measured by the total liabilities of the banks in the market, resources rose from US$31 million in 1968 to almost US$65.1 billion in March 1981.

The rapid growth of the market can be attributed to several factors. First, the accelerated economic growth of the region generated a growing regional demand for an international financial center that could cater to regional needs. The termination of the preferential exchange control arrangements among sterling area countries in June 1972 also contributed to the growth of demand for regional funds. Second, Singapore's traditional role as the major entrepôt trading center in the region and its overlapping working hours with the major financial centers in Europe provided a distinct advantage over competing regional financial centers. Third, the Singapore Government has introduced a series of measures designed to promote the growth of the market. These included the provision of fiscal incentives such as the removal in 1969 of the 40 per cent withholding tax on interest paid on deposits; the reduction in 1973 of the corporate income tax on interest receipts derived from offshore loans from 40 per cent to 10 per cent; the waiver of the stamp duties on negotiable certificates of deposit, bills of exchange in 1970, and on bond certificates issued in the Asian Currency Market in 1973. Since 1978, the concessionary tax rate of 10 per cent was extended to cover all offshore income derived by the ACU from its offshore operations.

To facilitate operations in the market, an interbank market was inaugurated, and negotiable certificates of deposit denominated in U.S. dollars were issued in 1970. In November 1977 floating rate U.S. dollar negotiable certificates of deposit were introduced, shortly after they were first issued in the Eurocurrency market. To encourage lending operations, the liquidity requirement (20 per cent of deposit liabilities) was eliminated in 1972, thereby making the participants in the market more competitive in their operations vis-à-vis the Eurocurrency market. Initially, participation by Singaporean nonbank residents in the market was subject to various restrictions. Over the years, however, these have been progressively lifted and since June 1978 with the liberalization of exchange control, the restrictions have been completely eliminated. Residents can now invest or borrow from the Asian Dollar Market without any limit or restrictions.

To operate in the market, banks must obtain licenses from the Monetary Authority and are required to maintain a bookkeeping unit called the Asian Currency Unit (ACU) to distinguish between records of transactions in the market and those of domestic banking business. ACUs are authorized to accept deposits in all currencies other than Singapore dollars and to lend to both nonresidents and residents.[9] While transactions in the Asian Currency Market can occur in all foreign currencies, in June 1979 about 90 per cent of deposits were in U.S. dollars.

The financial resources of ACUs consist of inter-ACU funds, funds from the Eurocurrency market, and deposits by nonbanking sectors mainly comprising the regional multinational corporations and private individuals. During 1970–81, as a result of the rapid expansion of the regional activities of the international corporations and the transfer of deposits by private individuals from the Eurocurrency market to the Asian Currency Market, primary deposits increased rapidly at an annual rate of over 60 per cent, reaching US$9.5 billion at the end of March 1981. However, the share of these nonbank deposits in total deposits declined during the period as bank deposits grew even more rapidly, due primarily to an expansion of interbank transactions within ACUs and with the Eurocurrency market. Since 1971, there has been a net inflow of funds to the Asian Currency Market from the Eurocurrency market reversing a previous trend of funds flowing from the Asian Currency Market to the Eurocurrency market. This reflects the changing character of the market from a marginal supplier of idle local funds for the Eurocurrency market to a channel for investment finance to the

[9] Previously, exchange control approval was required for accepting deposits from Singaporean residents above a specified limit and lending to Singaporean residents for other than specified purposes. Since the complete liberalization of exchange control in June 1978, these restrictions no longer apply. ACUs may deal in all foreign currencies with Singaporean residents. If a loan is made to a nonresident, exchange control approval may be required from the country in which the nonresident resides.

region.[10] *Pari passu* with this shift, deposit interest rates have become increasingly competitive vis-à-vis Eurocurrency rates.

In the past, because of the absence of suitable investment outlets in southeast Asia, most ACU funds were invested either in the Eurocurrency market or in companies in Europe. However, the rapid growth of economic activities in this region in the early 1970s generated a need for greater financial resources. As a result, about US$29 billion, or about 73 per cent of the market's resources at the end of 1979, has been absorbed by Asian countries. It is estimated that the bulk of such loans to Asian countries was accounted for by Hong Kong, Japan, and countries of the Association of South East Asian Nations,[11] all of which have been net borrowers from ACUs. Some of these placements have taken the form of large syndicated loans for financing development projects, with maturities ranging from three to ten years. Interest rates on most of these loans were floating rates based on the Singapore Inter-Bank Offered Rate (SIBOR). The maturity structure of total assets and liabilities of the ACUs, however, indicates that it is still basically a short-term market where the bulk of transactions do not exceed one year.[12]

The Asian Currency Market has also been active in floating long-term bonds. From 1971, when the first bond was issued, to the early part of 1975, there were only 4 issues totaling US$70 million, the amount of each issue ranging from US$10 million to US$30 million. Since 1976, however, activities in the bond market picked up rapidly owing partly to a number of changes in taxation and exchange control regulations introduced in that year; in 1980, 18 bond issues totaling US$659 million were floated in the market.

The Asian Currency Market has benefited the Singaporean economy directly by providing employment, tax, and other revenues, as well as indirectly by upgrading skills and expertise in offshore banking operations. Rough estimates indicate that income and profits derived from the

[10] At the end of 1979, net claims of the ACUs on Asian countries totaled US$8 billion, an increase of US$7 billion from the end of 1973, while net liabilities to European countries amounted to US$6 billion, an increase of US$5 billion from the end of 1973.

[11] The Association of South East Asian Nations consists of Indonesia, Malaysia, the Philippines, Singapore, and Thailand.

[12] At the end of March 1981, loans with maturities of up to three months accounted for 62 per cent of total assets, and deposits of the same category accounted for 74 per cent of total liabilities, while loans and deposits of more than one-year maturity constituted 17 per cent of total assets and 5 per cent of total liabilities.

market amounted to about 3 per cent of national income in 1975. The authorities have introduced a series of measures designed to minimize any adverse effects of the market on domestic monetary management. In 1973, when Singapore experienced unprecedented inflation, the authorities introduced a special reserve requirement against domestic banks' net foreign interbank liabilities, in order to restrain the expansion of domestic bank credit. This requirement was abolished in March 1974, as the inflow of speculative foreign funds began to slow down following the flotation of the Singapore dollar on June 21, 1973. As a result of these measures, the presence of the market has not so far posed any important difficulties to domestic monetary management.

## Monetary Policy Instruments and Their Effectiveness

Prior to the establishment of the Monetary Authority, the authorities preferred to keep official control over banking activities to a minimum. The Singapore Board of Commissioners of Currency had the automatic function of issuing currency against prescribed assets and no policy functions. The Commissioner of Banking had the supervisory function of ensuring that banks observed sound banking practices mainly to protect depositors' interests.

Since its establishment on January 1, 1971, and until about the latter part of 1972, the Monetary Authority was concerned largely with the development of the statutory and institutional framework of central banking in Singapore. Consequently, monetary policy was relatively passive and the development of monetary policy instruments relatively slow. With emergence of inflationary pressures in 1973, and the development of recessionary tendencies in subsequent years, monetary policy has assumed a more active role. The Monetary Authority is authorized to set the statutory required minimum cash balance and liquidity ratio for commercial banks and finance companies, to engage in money market operations, and to provide general instructions and guidance to the banks regarding the volume and direction of their advances.

Commercial banks in Singapore are required to maintain a minimum cash balance with the Monetary Authority of 6 per cent of their deposit and other liabilities, and a minimum liquid assets ratio of 20 per cent of deposit and other liabilities, out of which a minimum of 10 per cent has to be held in primary liquid assets,[13] while finance companies have to

[13] As from August 16, 1973, the definition and computation of the liquid

maintain 6 per cent of their total deposit liabilities in minimum cash balances and a minimum of 10 per cent in liquid assets. The Monetary Authority has used the statutory required minimum cash balance and the liquidity ratio flexibly in the past, raising them late in 1972 to curb the expansion of bank credit and lowering them in the middle of 1974 to stimulate the growth of bank credit in the light of the recessionary condition in the economy. In January 1973, the Monetary Authority also introduced a special reserve requirement on net foreign interbank liabilities in order to discourage the inflow of short-term capital during the inflationary period. This requirement was gradually reduced to zero in March 1974, when the speculative foreign capital inflow largely subsided, following the floating of the Singapore dollar on June 21, 1973. However, in March 1974, the Monetary Authority imposed a ceiling on total bank credit to limit the expansion of bank credit, and it exercised selective control to restrain the growth of credit for speculative purposes; the credit ceiling was lifted in January 1975.

The money market operations of the Monetary Authority consist primarily of issuing and rediscounting treasury bills, rediscounting trade bills, making overnight loans to the commercial banks, and carrying on operations in the foreign exchange market. The Monetary Authority uses the discount houses as its agents for purchases and sales of commercial and treasury bills. Following the 1972 amendment to the Monetary Authority of Singapore Act, the discount houses were allowed to borrow from the Monetary Authority on the collateral of treasury bills and other government securities; the lender-of-last-resort facility to commercial banks has not been operative. The market for government securities has been relatively narrow and dominated by medium-term securities, which are mostly held to maturity by the Central Provident Fund. The most important operation in terms of the value of paper involved is the export rediscounting facility. Begun in May 1975 in conjunction with the export drive, it was initially confined to certain kinds of export transactions and only to selected types of paper, but its coverage has gradually been extended, so that it embraces most of the

assets ratio have undergone some important changes. The definition of deposit liabilities was extended to include net borrowing from banks, and the definition of liquid assets and primary liquid assets was altered to exclude net bank balances from liquid assets and to allow short-term government securities with a maturity of less than one year to be regarded as primary liquid assets. The excess balances at the Monetary Authority are not a good indicator of bank liquidity, for banks normally place their excess balances with discount houses or in treasury bills in order to earn interest. A better indicator of bank liquidity is the total liquidity ratio.

important bills of exchange and other documents used in export finance. The duration of this credit facility is limited to 90 days. Overnight loans to banks have been extended only in limited cases to relieve banks of temporary shortages of funds. Foreign exchange operations have also been limited to the extent that they do not disrupt the orderliness of the exchange market; the Monetary Authority engages in swap operations with the commercial banks, but not on a large scale.

In Singapore there have been no official regulations governing commercial banks on interest rates payable on deposits or loans to customers. Even after the establishment of the Monetary Authority, interest rates were controlled by the Association of Banks in consultation with the Monetary Authority. As from July 1975 each bank has been free to quote its own rates, thus allowing more competition among financial institutions in Singapore. This measure reflects the prevailing official thinking that in a small and open economy such as Singapore's, the effectiveness of an "independent" bank rate would be very limited, for any divergence between domestic interest rates and external rates by more than 1 or 2 percentage points would induce capital flows. The difficulty is further accentuated by the fact that the Monetary Authority cannot engage in effective open market operations to supplement the bank rate policy.

# Currency Act[1]

An Act to establish the Board of Commissioners of Currency, Singapore, and the national currency of Singapore, and to provide for matters connected therewith.

[7th April, 1967 [2]]

## PART I. PRELIMINARY

1. This Act may be cited as the Currency Act. Short title.

2. In this Act, unless the context otherwise requires— Interpretation.

"Board" means the Board of Commissioners of Currency, Singapore, established by section 3 of this Act;

"Commissioners" means the Board of Commissioners of Currency, Malaya and British Borneo, reconstituted in accordance with the terms of the 1960 Currency Agreement;

"foreign" means pertaining to a country other than Singapore;

"foreign exchange" means foreign currencies and claims in and to foreign currencies;

"issue" includes reissue;

"the 1960 Currency Agreement" means the Malaya British Borneo Currency Agreement, 1960.

## PART II. ESTABLISHMENT, CONSTITUTION AND OBJECTIVES AND ADMINISTRATION OF BOARD

3. (1) There shall be established a Board to be known as the "Board of Commissioners of Currency, Singapore". Establishment and purpose of Board.

(2) The Board shall issue currency notes and coins in Singapore in accordance with section 14 of this Act.

4. (1) The Board shall be a body corporate with perpetual succession and a common seal with power, subject to the provisions of this Incorporation, etc.

[1] *Singapore Statutes,* Cap. 64 (1970). Originally Act No. 5 of 1967. Relevant citations: Acts Nos. 35 of 1967; 3 of 1968; and 2 of 1969.

[2] Parts I and II, secs. 19 and 22, Part IV and sec. 32 of the Act came into operation on April 7, 1967 and secs. 11 to 18, 20, 21, 23 to 27 and 33 to 35 on June 12, 1967.

Act, to acquire and dispose of property, both movable and immovable, and may sue and be sued in its corporate name and perform such other acts as bodies corporate may by law perform.

(2) The Board shall have its head office in Singapore.

(3) The Board may appoint a person or persons or corporation to be its agents or correspondents for the purposes of this Act.

(4) No resolution or decision taken by the Board and no other act or thing made or done by the Board or any officer or servant of the Board in the exercise of any right or power or in the performance of any duty conferred or imposed upon the Board, or upon such officer or servant, under or by virtue of the provisions of this Act shall be invalid by reason only that the same was not taken, made or done within Singapore.

(5) The Board shall not be subject to any tax, fee or levy whatsoever.

Employment of officers, etc.

5. (1) The Board may appoint such officers and employees as it considers to be necessary for the efficient conduct of the business of the Board upon such terms and conditions as may be determined by the Board.

(2) The Board and its officers and servants shall be deemed to be public servants within the meaning of the Penal Code.

Composition of the Board.

6. (1) The Board shall consist of—

(*a*) the Chairman, who shall be the Minister responsible for finance;

(*b*) the Deputy Chairman, who shall be appointed by the President for a specific period and shall vacate his office without prejudice to his eligibility for reappointment at the expiration of that period; and

(*c*) four other members possessing recognised banking, financial or business experience who shall be appointed by the President from time to time for such periods as the President may decide.

(2) The Deputy Chairman shall act for the Chairman whenever he is absent.

(3) If the Deputy Chairman is temporarily absent from Singapore or temporarily incapacitated through illness or any other sufficient reason from the performance of his duties, another person may be appointed by the President during such temporary absence or incapacity.

(4) If a member appointed under paragraph *(c)* of subsection (1) of this section suffers an incapacity which is likely to be prolonged, the

President may appoint a temporary substitute to act with the full powers of that member until such time as the President determines that the incapacity has ceased.

7. (1) The Board shall meet at least once in each calendar year and at such times or places as may be deemed necessary by the Chairman:

Meetings of the Board.

Provided that the Chairman shall call a meeting as soon as practicable after receiving a request from at least two members.

(2) A quorum for any meeting of the Board shall be three members.

(3) No meeting of the Board, as provided for in this section, shall be held unless the Chairman or the Deputy Chairman is present.

(4) The Chairman and the Deputy Chairman shall each have two votes and the members appointed under paragraph *(c)* of subsection (1) of section 6 of this Act shall each have one vote.

(5) Any question arising at a meeting of the Board shall be decided by a majority of votes.

(6) In the event of an equality of votes the Chairman presiding at the meeting shall have a casting vote.

8. (1) The Deputy Chairman or a member shall be relieved of his office if he—

General disqualifications for Deputy Chairman and other members.

*(a)* becomes bankrupt or insolvent, applies for any benefits under the law for the relief of bankrupt or insolvent debtors, compounds with his creditors or makes any assignment in whole or in part of his income from the Board for the benefit of such creditors;

*(b)* is convicted of an offence involving dishonesty or fraud or moral turpitude;

*(c)* becomes totally or permanently incapable of performing his duties; or

*(d)* is guilty of misbehaviour that would bring his office into disrepute.

(2) The President shall terminate the appointment of a member who absents himself from three consecutive meetings of the Board without leave.

9. (1) A member who is directly or indirectly interested in a contract made, or proposed to be made, by the Board shall disclose the nature of his interest at the first meeting of the Board at which he is present after the relevant facts have come to his knowledge.

Member's interest in contract to be made known.

(2) A disclosure under subsection (1) of this section shall be recorded in the minutes of the Board and, after the disclosure, such member—

(*a*) shall not take part in any deliberation or decision of the Board with respect to that contract; and

(*b*) shall be disregarded for the purpose of constituting a quorum of the Board for any such deliberation or decision.

(3) No act or proceeding of the Board shall be questioned on the ground of the contravention by a member of the Board of the provisions of this section.

Preservation of secrecy.

10. Except for the purposes of the performance of his duties or the exercise of his functions or when lawfully required to do so by any court or under the provisions of any law, no member, officer or employee of the Board shall disclose to any person any information which he has acquired in the performance of his duties or the exercise of his functions.

## PART III. CURRENCY

Currency of Singapore.

11. (1) The unit of currency of Singapore shall be the Singapore dollar, which shall be divided into one hundred cents.

(2) The abbreviated form of the Singapore dollar shall be "S$".

Par value.

12. The par value of the Singapore dollar shall be 0.290299 grammes of fine gold which shall not be varied except by the President in accordance with the Articles of Agreement of the International Monetary Fund.[3]

Use of Singapore dollar.

13. All monetary obligations or transactions in Singapore shall be deemed to be expressed and recorded, and shall be settled in the Singapore dollar unless otherwise provided for by law or validly agreed upon between the parties.

---

[3] The Second Amendment to the Articles of Agreement of the International Monetary Fund, effective April 1, 1978, abrogated par values under the Articles. Provision is made for a new par value system if the Fund decides in its favor by 85 per cent of the total voting power. Should such a decision be taken, each member would be able to decide whether to propose a par value for its currency. Under such a regime the margins around parity within which exchange transactions involving currencies with par values would have to be confined would be wider than those consistent with the original Articles of Agreement.

**14.** (1) The Board shall have the sole right to issue currency notes and coins in Singapore and, subject to subsection (3) of this section, only such notes and coins issued by the Board shall be legal tender in Singapore.

**Board to have sole right to issue currency legal tender.**

(2) *(a)* Notes issued by the Board shall be legal tender up to their face value for the payment of any amount.

*(b)* Coins issued by the Board, if the coins have not been illegally dealt with, shall be legal tender up to their face value in Singapore as follows:

(i) in the case of coins of a denomination exceeding one dollar —for the payment of any amount;

(ii) in the case of coins of the denomination of fifty cents and one dollar—for the payment of an amount not exceeding ten dollars; and

(iii) in the case of coins of a denomination lower than fifty cents—for the payment of an amount not exceeding two dollars.

(3) Notwithstanding the provisions of subsection (1) of this section—

*(a)* the notes and coins of any series or denominations issued by the Board of Commissioners of Currency, Malaya and British Borneo, which were legal tender in Singapore immediately prior to the date of the coming into operation of this Act; and

*(b)* coins made available by the Commissioners to the Board under the provisions of paragraph *(b)* of clause 18 of the 1960 Currency Agreement,

shall continue to be legal tender in Singapore for such time as the President may, on the recommendation of the Board, by notification in the *Gazette* determine.

(4) *(a)* Notes issued by the Commissioners which were legal tender in Singapore immediately prior to the date of the coming into operation of this Act shall be legal tender in Singapore as follows:

(i) currency notes of denominations of one dollar and above— for the payment of any amount; and

(ii) currency notes of denominations of less than one dollar— for the payment of any amount not exceeding two dollars.

*(b)* Coins issued by the Commissioners which were legal tender in Singapore immediately prior to the date of the coming into operation of this Act and coins made available by the Commissioners to the Board under the provisions of paragraph *(b)*

of clause 18 of the 1960 Currency Agreement, if the coins have not been illegally dealt with, and if of silver have not become diminished in weight by wear or otherwise, so as to be of less weight than the weight in that behalf specified in the First Schedule to the 1960 Currency Agreement as the least current weight, shall be legal tender in Singapore as follows:

(i) up to an amount not exceeding ten dollars in the case of coins of the denomination of fifty cents and above; and

(ii) up to an amount not exceeding two dollars in the case of coins of a lower denomination.

(5) For the purposes of this Act, a coin shall be deemed to have been illegally dealt with where the coin has been impaired, diminished, or lightened otherwise than by fair wear and tear, or has been defaced by having any name, word, device, or number stamped or engraved thereon, whether the coin has or has not been thereby diminished or lightened.

(6) In any criminal proceedings in which the genuineness of any currency note or coin may be in question, a certificate signed by the Deputy Chairman of the Board that he is satisfied by personal examination that such note or coin is or is not forged shall be held to be conclusive evidence of the same and neither the Deputy Chairman nor any officer of the Board shall be cross-examined with regard to the contents of such certificate unless the court otherwise orders.

Bills and notes payable to bearer on demand.

**15.** (1) No person shall draw, accept, make or issue any bill of exchange, promissory note or engagement for the payment of money payable to bearer on demand or borrow, owe or take up any sum or sums of money on bills or notes payable to bearer on demand.

(2) Cheques or drafts payable to bearer on demand may be drawn on bankers or agents by their customers or constituents in respect of moneys in the hands of these bankers or agents held by them at the disposal of the persons drawing such cheques or drafts.

(3) Any person who contravenes the provisions of this section shall, notwithstanding anything to the contrary in the Criminal Procedure Code, on conviction by a Magistrate's Court be liable to a fine equal to the amount of the bill, note or engagement in respect whereof the offence is committed notwithstanding that the amount of such fine may be in excess of the original jurisdiction of such court.

(4) No prosecution under this section shall be instituted without the sanction of the Public Prosecutor.

16. (1) The Board shall issue, on demand by any person at any of its offices, currency notes to the equivalent value of sums in sterling lodged by that person with the Board's agent in London for its account; and shall pay, on demand by any person, sterling in London to the equivalent value of currency notes lodged with it by that person: Conversion of currency notes and coins into sterling and vice versa.

Provided that such notes have been issued by the Board.

(2) The Board may, at its option, issue coins in the same manner and subject to the same conditions as are prescribed in subsection (1) of this section for the issue of currency notes.

(3) Coins issued shall, subject to any regulations made under section 31 of this Act, be redeemed by the Board in the same manner and subject to the same conditions as are prescribed in subsection (1) of this section for the redemption of currency notes.

17. Notwithstanding the provisions of section 16 of this Act, the Board may issue and redeem in its absolute discretion, currency notes and coins against gold and other currencies eligible for inclusion in the reserve of external assets specified under section 24 of this Act. Conversion of currency notes and coins into gold and other foreign currencies and vice versa.

18. (1) All issues and redemptions of currency notes and coins by the Board shall be effected at the parity specified in section 12 of this Act. Exchange rate.

(2) The Board shall be entitled—

*(a)* to charge and levy from any person obtaining currency notes and coins or sterling, or gold or other currencies, a commission at such rate or rates as may, from time to time, be determined:

Provided that the commission charged shall be consistent with the Articles of Agreement of the International Monetary Fund;[4]

*(b)* to determine, from time to time, the minimum sum or sums which a person shall be entitled to lodge with the Board or its agents, as the case may be, for the purpose of obtaining currency notes and coins or sterling or gold or other currencies;

*(c)* to prescribe the hours of the day during which the Board will issue and redeem currency.

(3) The amounts of such rate or rates and minimum sum or sums shall be notified in the *Gazette* by the Board.

---

[4] The Second Amendment to the Articles of Agreement of the International Monetary Fund, effective April 1, 1978, abolished the official price of gold under the Articles. See footnote 3 to section 12 of this Act.

Form and design of currency notes and coins.

19. (1) Currency notes issued by the Board shall be of such denomination and of such form and design and printed from such plates and on such paper and may be authenticated in such manner as the Board may, from time to time, decide.

(2) The plates shall be prepared and kept and the notes printed, issued and cancelled in accordance with any directions of the Board for the prevention of fraud and improper use.

(3) Coins issued by the Board shall be of such denominations and of such weight, form and design, and made of such metal or metals as the Board may, from time to time, decide.

(4) The Board shall publish in the *Gazette* the denominations and other characteristics of notes and coins issued by it.

Demonetisation of currency notes and coins.

20. (1) The Board may declare by notification published in the *Gazette* the withdrawal of any particular issue or denomination of notes and coins issued by the Board.

(2) Any such notification shall give holders of the notes and coins to be withdrawn a reasonable period, in any event not less than six months, within which such notes or coins shall be exchanged at their face value for other legal tender issued by the Board.

Imperfect notes or coins.

21. (1) No person shall be entitled to recover from the Board the value of any mutilated or imperfect note or coin or any coin which has been illegally dealt with.

(2) The circumstances in which, and the conditions and limitations subject to which the value of mutilated or imperfect notes or coins, or coins which have been illegally dealt with, may be refunded as an act of grace shall be within the absolute discretion of the Board.

Restriction on the use of photographs, drawing or design of notes in advertisements, etc.

22. Except with the permission of the Board, no person shall, in any size, scale or colour, use any photograph of or any drawing or design resembling any notes or part thereof, in any advertisement or on any merchandise or products which that person manufactures, sells, circulates or otherwise distributes.

Currency Fund.

23. (1) The Board shall establish a Currency Fund (hereinafter in this Act referred to as "the Fund") which shall be maintained and managed exclusively by the Board in the manner prescribed in this Act.

(2) There shall be paid into the Fund—

*(a)* all gold, sterling and other foreign currencies received in exchange for currency notes or coins; and

(*b*) the proceeds of any transactions under paragraph (*c*) of subsection (6) of this section, less all expenses incurred in connection therewith.

(3) Save as otherwise provided in this Act the Fund shall be applied for meeting the redemption of currency and for no other purpose.

(4) A portion of the Fund shall be held in liquid form and such portion may be determined and varied from time to time by the Board, except that at no time shall less than thirty per cent of the Fund be so retained without the unanimous approval of all members of the Board.

(5) The liquid portion of the Fund held in accordance with the provisions of subsection (4) of this section shall be held in any or all of the following forms:

(*a*) gold in any form;

(*b*) sterling and other foreign exchange in the form of—

(i) demand or time deposits, maturing within two years, with the Board's agents or correspondents abroad;

(ii) bank balances and money at call;

(iii) Treasury Bills;

(iv) notes or coins;

(*c*) securities, maturing within two years, of or guaranteed by foreign Governments or international financial institutions.

(6) Notwithstanding anything contained in the preceding subsections, the Board may—

(*a*) use any coin held for the account of the Fund for the purpose of having it reminted into current coin;

(*b*) pay from the Fund the cost of the purchase of metal to be minted into current coin; and

(*c*) sell any coin held for the account of the Fund.

(7) The value of the Fund for any of the purposes of this Act shall be the current realisable value of the whole of the assets held in the Fund, investments of the Fund being valued at their current market price at the time of valuation; and for the purposes of valuation, the assets shall be converted into dollars at the rate of exchange specified in section 12 of this Act.

**External assets of Fund.**

24. The Fund shall consist of all or any of the following external assets:

(*a*) gold in any form;

(*b*) sterling and other foreign exchange in the form of—

(i) demand or time deposits with the Board's agents or correspondents abroad;
(ii) documents and instruments customarily used for the making of payments or transfers in international transactions;
(iii) bank balances and money at call;
(iv) Treasury Bills;
(v) notes or coins;

*(c)* securities of or guaranteed by foreign Governments or international financial institutions;

*(d)* any readily available international drawing facility which the Board, after consultation with the International Monetary Fund and with the approval of the President, deems suitable for inclusion; and

*(e)* any other asset which the Board, with the approval of the President, deems suitable for inclusion.

Currency Fund Income Account.

25. (1) All dividends, interest or other revenue derived from investments or from the utilisation in any other manner of the moneys of the Fund and all commissions paid to the Board in connection with the issue or redemption of currency notes or coins shall be paid into an account to be called "the Currency Fund Income Account" (hereinafter in this Act referred to as "the Income Account").

(2) There shall be charged upon the Income Account—

*(a)* all expenses incurred by or on behalf of the Board in the preparation, transport, issue, redemption and demonetisation of currency notes and coins, and in the transaction of any business relating to such currency authorised by law, other than the expenses referred to in subsection (6) of section 23 of this Act;

*(b)* any expenses incurred by or on behalf of the Board in connection with the protection of the currency against forgery or counterfeiting of currency notes or coins; and

*(c)* all other expenses properly incurred by the Board in the execution of its functions under this Act:

Provided that the Board may charge upon the Fund and not upon the Income Account any expenditure of an exceptional nature.

(3) At the end of each financial year, any surplus in the Income Account shall be paid into the Consolidated Fund but if on the last day in any financial year there is a deficiency in the Income Account, it shall be charged upon and paid out of the Consolidated Fund:

Provided that if on the last day in any financial year, the face value of the Board's currency notes and coins in circulation exceeds the value of the Fund calculated in accordance with subsection (7) of section 23 of this Act, there shall be paid into the Fund the whole of the said surplus in the Income Account or such part thereof as shall make up the moneys of the Fund as aforesaid to an amount equal to the face value of the currency notes and coins then in circulation; but if the said surplus in the Income Account is insufficient to make up the deficiency in the Fund, the balance of such deficiency shall be charged upon and paid out of the Consolidated Fund.

(4) If on the last day in any financial year, the value of the Fund so calculated exceeds one hundred per cent of the face value of the Board's currency notes and coins then in circulation, the Board may direct that the whole or part of such excess be transferred from the Fund to the Income Account.

Meeting of deficiencies in the Fund.

26. If the assets of the Fund should at any time prove insufficient to meet legal demands upon the Board, such deficiencies shall be charged upon and paid out of the Consolidated Fund.

Board of Survey.

27. Unissued stocks of currency notes and coins held by the Board shall on the first business day of each year and at such other times as may be decided by the Board, be verified by a Board of Survey to be constituted under regulations made by the Board.

## PART IV. MISCELLANEOUS

Board's financial year.

28. The financial year of the Board shall begin on the 1st day of January and end on the 31st day of December of each year.

Audit.

29. The accounts of the Board shall be audited by the Auditor-General.

Annual accounts and report.

30. (1) The Board shall, as soon as practicable, after the close of its financial year, transmit to the President a copy of its annual accounts and report and the accounts shall then be published in the *Gazette.*

(2) The annual accounts and report shall be presented to Parliament as soon as may be after such publication.

(3) The Board shall, as soon as may be, after the end of every third month, make up and publish in the *Gazette* an abstract showing the whole amount of currency notes and coins in circulation on that day.

(4) The Board shall also publish at half yearly intervals in the *Gazette* an abstract showing—

(*a*) the amount of the liquid portion of the Fund; and

(*b*) the nominal value and price paid for and, where appropriate, the latest known market price, of the securities belonging to the Fund.

Regulations.

31. The Board may make such regulations as may be required from time to time for carrying into effect the provisions of this Act.

PART V. TRANSITIONAL AND REPEAL

Preliminary acts and expenses.

32. Upon the coming into operation of this Act, any act done and preliminary expenses incurred by the Government in connection with the establishment of the Board, including the printing of notes and minting of coins to be issued by the Board, shall have the same effect and validity as if such acts had been validly done and such expenses validly incurred by the Board; and the Board may continue any act so commenced but remaining unfinished at the date of the coming into operation of this Act as if such act had been initiated by the Board.

Continued issue of the Commissioners' coins.

33. Notwithstanding the provisions of section 14 of this Act the Board may for such period or periods as the Board may determine after the day on which the said section comes into operation, abstain from issuing its own coins or particular denominations thereof, and may enter into agreement with the Commissioners for the continued supply in Singapore of coins of the Commissioners in such denominations as may be required.

Rates of exchange between notes and coins of the Commissioners and of the Board.

34. (1) The notes and coins of the Commissioners which continue to be legal tender under subsection (3) of section 14 of this Act shall be exchanged for the notes and coins of the Board at the rates set out in the Schedule [5] to this Act.

(2) The President may, by order published in the *Gazette,* add to, amend or vary the rates of exchange set out in the Schedule to this Act.

Protection of the Board, the Commissioners and the employees thereof and of the Government and public officers.

35. No action, suit or other proceeding shall be brought or instituted in any court against, and no liability, claim or demand whatsoever shall lie against, the Board or any officer, servant or employee thereof, the Commissioners or any officer, servant or employee thereof, or the Government or any public officer in respect of any matter or thing authorised or permitted by the Currency (Amendment) Act, 1967, or any matter or thing arising under, resulting from or consequent on the passing or operation of the said Act.

[5] The Schedule is omitted from this volume.

36. The Currency Ordinance, 1960, is hereby repealed, save that the provisions of the 1960 Currency Agreement, relating to the establishment of separate currency authorities shall continue to have the force of law in Singapore. Repeal and saving.

*{The Schedule is omitted from this volume.}*

## Coin Act[1]

An Act to regulate the import and export of coin.

[9th October, 1903]

1. This Act may be cited as the Coin Act. Short title.

2. In this Act— Interpretation.

"banker" means any corporation carrying on the business of bankers or financial agents in Singapore;

"money-changer" means a person who carries on the business of money-changing as his chief business.

3. (1) The Minister may by order— Prohibition by Minister of importation, exportation and circulation of coin.

(*a*) prohibit the importation into Singapore of such coins, whether legal tender within Singapore or not, as are in such order specified;

(*b*) prohibit the exportation from Singapore of such coins, being legal tender within Singapore, as are in such order specified.

[1] *Singapore Statutes*, Cap. 62 (1955). Originally Ord. No. 24 of 1903. Relevant citations: Ords. Nos. 37 of 1952; 71 of 1959; G.N. S 223/59; G.N. S (N.S.) 177/59; and G.N. S (N.S.) 179/59.

(2) The Minister may by order—

(*a*) prohibit the circulation in Singapore of such foreign coins, not being legal tender within Singapore, as are in such order specified;

(*b*) exempt any country or state from the operation of any order prohibiting the import into or export from Singapore of such coins as are in such order specified.

Publication of order.

(3) Every order made under this section shall be published in the *Gazette,* and shall not come into force until so published.

Penalty for importing or exporting coin in contravention of order.

4. (1) Any person who, in contravention of any such order, imports or exports or attempts to import or export any coin in such order specified to the amount of five dollars in nominal value or upwards in the case of copper or bronze coin, or of twenty-five dollars in nominal value or upwards in the case of silver coin, shall be liable to a fine not exceeding two thousand dollars.

(2) Any coin so imported or exported or attempted to be imported or exported in contravention of any such order shall be forfeited.

(3) In any case in which it has been proved, to the satisfaction of a court, that coin has been exported in contravention of any such order, it may impose, in addition to the fine authorized by this section, a further penalty not exceeding the amount or value of the coin so found to have been exported.

(4) This section shall not apply to any coin imported or exported with the permission in writing under the hand of the Minister or of any officer appointed in that behalf by the President; such permission shall specify the terms on which such coin may be imported or exported, as the case may be.

(5) Any person importing or exporting coin in contravention of the terms of such permission shall be liable to a fine not exceeding two thousand dollars, and any coin so imported or exported shall be forfeited. The provision contained in subsection (3) shall apply in the case of any coin exported in contravention of the terms of any such permission.

Penalty for circulating prohibited coin.

(6) Any person who, in contravention of any such order, circulates or attempts to circulate any coin in such order specified shall be liable to a fine not exceeding fifty dollars, and the coin shall be forfeited.

(7) For the purposes of this section, a person is not deemed to circulate coin who gives such coin to a banker or money-changer in exchange for other coins or for notes.

5. Any coin, the circulation of which in Singapore is for the time being prohibited by any such order as aforesaid, found within Singapore otherwise than in the possession of a banker or money-changer, after the expiration of thirty days from the publication in the *Gazette* of such order, may, if it amounts to the nominal value of five dollars or upwards in the case of copper or bronze coin, or twenty-five dollars or upwards in the case of silver coin, be forfeited, and may be seized without warrant by any police officer and detained pending adjudication.

Forfeiture of prohibited coin.

6. A Justice of the Peace, if satisfied by sworn information in writing that there is good cause to believe that any coin which has been imported, or is in the act of being imported or exported, in contravention of any such order, is likely to be found in any place to the nominal value of fifty dollars or upwards, may by warrant under his hand direct any police officer, named or specified therein, to enter such place and search the same and seize all coin or coins found therein, the import or export of which is for the time being prohibited, and detain the same pending adjudication.

Search under warrant of Justice of the Peace for coin imported or exported in contravention of order.

7. Any person found offending against this Act may be arrested by any police officer without warrant.

Police may arrest without warrant.

8. Forfeitures of coin may be declared under this Act—

(*a*) by the High Court in proceedings instituted by the Attorney-General under the Government Proceedings Act;

(*b*) by the convicting court in all cases where a person is convicted of an offence under this Act in respect of such coin;

(*c*) by a Magistrate's Court where no person is convicted and the nominal value of the coin does not exceed five hundred dollars.

Forfeiture of coin by whom declared.

9. The court may direct any fine or portion of a fine imposed and levied under this Act to be paid to the informer.

Fine paid to informer.

# Monetary Authority of Singapore Act[1]

An Act to establish a corporation to be known as the Monetary Authority of Singapore and to provide for the transfer to the corporation of certain functions and assets of the Government and for matters incidental thereto and connected therewith.

[Parts I, II, V and VI: 26th December, 1970;
Parts III and IV: 1st January, 1971]

## PART I. PRELIMINARY

Short title.

1. This Act may be cited as the Monetary Authority of Singapore Act.

Interpretation.

2. In this Act, unless the context otherwise requires—

"Authority" means the Monetary Authority of Singapore established under section 3 of this Act;

"bank" means a bank licensed under the Banking Act;

"board" means the board of directors of the Authority;

"director" means a director appointed under subsection (1) of section 8 of this Act and the chairman of the board, the deputy chairman and the Accountant-General;

"managing director" means a director appointed under subsection (1) of section 9 of this Act;

"Minister" means the Minister charged with the responsibility for finance.

## PART II. ESTABLISHMENT, CAPITAL AND ADMINISTRATION OF THE AUTHORITY

Establishment of the Authority.

3.—(1) There shall be established an Authority to be called "the Monetary Authority of Singapore" which shall be a body corporate and shall have perpetual succession and may sue and be sued in its own name.

---

[1] Act No. 42 of 1970 was amended by the Monetary Authority of Singapore (Amendment) Act, 1972 (Law No. 31 of 1972). The latter, "An Act to amend the Monetary Authority of Singapore Act (Chapter 195 of the Revised Edition)," became law on December 22, 1972.

(2) The Authority shall have a common seal and such seal may, from time to time, be broken, changed, altered and made anew as to the Authority seems fit, and, until a seal is provided under this section, a stamp bearing the inscription "The Monetary Authority of Singapore" may be used as the common seal.

(3) All deeds, documents and other instruments requiring the seal of the Authority shall be sealed with the common seal of the Authority by the authority of the Authority in the presence of the managing director and of some other person duly authorised by the Authority to act in that behalf and shall be signed by the managing director and by such duly authorised person, and such signing shall be sufficient evidence that the common seal of the Authority has been duly and properly affixed and that the said seal is the lawful common seal of the Authority.

(4) The Authority may by resolution or otherwise appoint an officer of the Authority or any other agent either generally or in a particular case to execute or sign on behalf of the Authority any agreement or other instrument not under seal in relation to any matter coming within the powers of the Authority.

Principal objects of the Authority.

4. The principal objects of the Authority shall be—

*(a)* to act as banker to, and financial agent of, the Government;
*(b)* to promote, within the context of the general economic policy of the Government, monetary stability and credit and exchange conditions conducive to the growth of the economy; and
*(c)* to exercise the powers and to perform the duties and functions that are transferred to the Authority under section 21 of this Act.

Authorised capital.

5.—(1) The authorised capital of the Authority shall be one hundred million dollars.

(2) On the establishment of the Authority such portion of the authorised capital as the Government may decide shall be subscribed and paid up by the Government.

(3) The paid-up portion of the authorised capital may be increased from time to time by such amount as the Government may approve.

(4) The payment of such increase in the authorised capital may be made by way of such transfers from the General Reserve Fund as the Government, in consultation with the board, may from time to time approve.

General Reserve Fund.

6.—(1) There shall be a General Reserve Fund of the Authority.

(2) At the end of each financial year, the net profit of the Authority for that year shall be determined after allowing for the expenses of operation and after provision has been made for bad and doubtful debts, depreciation in assets, contributions to staff and pension funds and such other contingencies as are usually provided for by banks.

(3) Subject to subsection (4) of this section, such part of the net profit of the Authority, as the board determines, shall be placed to the credit of the General Reserve Fund and the remainder shall be paid to the Government.

(4) Where at the end of a year the General Reserve Fund is—

*(a)* less than half the paid-up capital of the Authority, the whole of the net profit shall be credited to the General Reserve Fund; and

*(b)* not less than half the paid-up capital of the Authority but less than twice the paid-up capital of the Authority, not less than thirty per cent of the net profit shall be credited to the General Reserve Fund.

Board of directors.

7.—(1) There shall be a board of directors of the Authority which shall be responsible for the policy and general administration of the affairs and business of the Authority.

(2) The board shall, from time to time, inform the Government of the banking and credit policy of the Authority.

(3) The board shall consist of—

*(a)* the Minister responsible for finance who shall be the chairman;

*(b)* the Permanent Secretary (Economic Development), Ministry of Finance who shall be the deputy chairman;

*(c)* the Accountant-General; and

*(d)* four other directors appointed in accordance with sections 8 and 9 of this Act.

Appointment of directors.

8.—(1) The directors referred to in paragraph *(d)* of subsection (3) of section 7 of this Act shall be appointed by the President.

(2) The directors so appointed—

*(a)* shall not act as delegates on the board from any commercial, financial, agricultural, industrial or other interests with which they may be connected;

*(b)* shall hold office for a term not exceeding three years and shall be eligible for reappointment; and

*(c)* may be paid by the Authority out of the funds of the Authority such remuneration and allowances as may be determined by the President.

(3) The provisions of paragraphs *(b)* and *(c)* of subsection (2) of this section do not apply to a director who is appointed managing director under section 9 of this Act.

Appointment of managing director.

9.—(1) The President shall, with the approval of the Public Service Commission, appoint one of the directors appointed under section 8 of this Act to be the managing director.

(2) The managing director shall be an employee of the Authority on such terms and conditions of service as the President may decide.

(3) The managing director shall be entrusted with the day-to-day administration of the Authority, and may, subject to this Act, make decisions and exercise all powers and do all acts which may be exercised or done by the Authority.

(4) The managing director shall be answerable to the board for his acts and decisions.

(5) In the event of the absence or inability to act of the managing director, the Minister may appoint a director to discharge his duties during the period of such absence or inability.

Disqualification of directors.

10.—(1) No person may be appointed as or remain a director of the Authority who is a director or salaried official of any bank licensed under the provisions of the Banking Act.

(2) The disqualification referred to in subsection (1) of this section does not apply to the directors referred to in paragraphs *(b)* and *(c)* of subsection (3) of section 7 of this Act.

(3) The President may terminate the appointment of any director appointed under subsection (1) of section 8 of this Act if he—

*(a)* resigns his office;
*(b)* becomes of unsound mind or incapable of carrying out his duties;
*(c)* becomes bankrupt or suspends payment to or compounds with his creditors;
*(d)* is convicted of an offence involving dishonesty or fraud or moral turpitude;
*(e)* is guilty of serious misconduct in relation to his duties;

(f) is absent, without leave, from three consecutive meetings of the board; or

(g) fails to comply with his obligations under section 13 of this Act.

Vacancies in the office of director.

11. If any director appointed under subsection (1) of section 8 of this Act dies or resigns or otherwise vacates his office before the expiry of the term for which he has been appointed another person may be appointed by the President for the unexpired period of the term of office of the director in whose place he is appointed.

Meetings and decisions of the board.

12.—(1) The chairman of the board shall summon meetings as often as may be required but not less frequently than once in three months.

(2) At every meeting of the board a quorum shall consist of four directors, and decisions shall be adopted by a simple majority of the votes of the directors present and voting except that in the case of an equality of votes the chairman shall have a casting vote.

Director's interest in contract to be made known.

13.—(1) A director who is directly or indirectly interested in a contract made, or proposed to be made, by the Authority shall disclose the nature of his interest at the first meeting of the board at which he is present after the relevant facts have come to his knowledge.

(2) A disclosure under subsection (1) of this section shall be recorded in the minutes of the board and, after the disclosure, the director—

(a) shall not take part in any deliberation or decision of the board with respect to that contract; and

(b) shall be disregarded for the purpose of constituting a quorum of the board for any such deliberation or decision.

(3) No act or proceeding of the board shall be questioned on the ground that a director has contravened the provisions of this section.

Preservation of secrecy.

14.—(1) Except for the purpose of the performance of his duties or the exercise of his functions or when lawfully required to do so by any court or under the provisions of any written law, no director, officer or employee of the Authority shall disclose to any person any information relating to the affairs of the Authority or of any person which he has acquired in the performance of his duties or the exercise of his functions.

(2) Any person who contravenes the provisions of subsection (1) of this section shall be guilty of an offence under this Act and shall be liable on conviction to imprisonment for a term not exceeding three

years or to a fine not exceeding five thousand dollars or to both such imprisonment and fine.

Remuneration not to be related to profits.

15. No salary, fee, wage or other remuneration or allowance paid by the Authority shall be computed by reference to the profits of the Authority.

Public servants.

16. The directors, including the managing director, and the officers and employees of the Authority of every description shall be deemed to be public servants within the meaning of the Penal Code.

## PART III. PROVISIONS RELATING TO STAFF, TRANSFER OF FUNCTIONS, EMPLOYEES AND ASSETS, ETC.

List of posts and appointment of employees.

17.—(1) The Authority may from time to time approve a list of posts which it thinks necessary for the purposes of this Act and may add to or amend that list. The first such list of posts shall contain posts for all the persons transferred to the service of the Authority under section 18 of this Act.

(2) No person may be employed by the Authority unless he holds a post appearing in the list of posts for the time being in force.

(2A) The Authority may, by notification in the *Gazette,* declare that appointments and promotions to such posts or classes of posts as it thinks fit, and the termination of appointment, dismissal, and disciplinary control of persons appointed to such posts, shall be vested in the Authority and, upon such notification, the Authority shall exercise such functions on the advice of the Public Service Commission.

(3) Subject to the provisions of this section—

*(a)* appointments and promotions to all posts shall be made by the Authority; and

*(b)* the termination of appointment, dismissal and disciplinary control of the employees of the Authority shall be vested in the Authority.

(4) [Repealed] [2]

(5) Notwithstanding the provisions of this section, the Authority may appoint persons temporarily for a period not exceeding two months to posts in the list of posts for the time being in force.

---

[2] Repealed by Law No. 31 of 1972, Monetary Authority of Singapore (Amendment) Act, 1972.

(6) The Authority may make rules, not inconsistent with the provisions of this Act or of any other written law, for the appointment, promotion, disciplinary control and terms and conditions of service of all persons employed by the Authority.

(7) Without prejudice to the generality of subsection (6) of this section, the Authority shall prescribe the rates of remuneration payable to persons employed by the Authority, and no person so employed shall be paid otherwise than in accordance with such rates.

Transfer of employees.

18. Upon the coming into operation of this Act, such persons, as the Minister may decide, who were employed by the Government immediately prior to the date of the coming into operation of this Act and were exercising any of the powers or were discharging any of the functions or duties vested in the Authority by this Act, shall be deemed to be transferred to the service of the Authority on terms not less favourable than those they enjoyed immediately prior to their transfer and such terms (which shall be determined by the Authority) shall take into account the salaries and conditions of service including any accrued rights to leave, enjoyed by them while in the employment of the Government.

Pension schemes, provident fund, etc.

19.—(1) The Authority may, with the approval of the President, make rules for the establishment of a scheme or schemes for the payment of pensions, gratuities, provident fund or other superannuation benefits to such employees or classes of employees of the Authority as it may determine, or to their legal personal representatives or dependants, on the death or retirement of such employees from the service of the Authority or on their otherwise leaving the service of the Authority.

(2) The Authority in making under subsection (1) of this section any pension, provident fund or other superannuation rules which affect any persons transferred to the service of the Authority under section 18 of this Act shall in such rules provide for the payment to such persons or their dependants of benefits not less in value than the amount of any pension, provident fund, gratuity or allowance for which such persons would have been eligible under the Pensions Act had they continued in the service of the Government and any such pension, provident fund or superannuation rules relating to length of service of persons shall provide for the recognition as service under the Authority by persons so transferred of service by them under the Government.

(3) Nothing in the rules to be made under subsection (1) of this section shall adversely affect any conditions that would have been applicable to persons transferred to the service of the Authority from

their service with the Government as regards any pension, gratuity or allowance under the Pensions Act.

(4) Where any person in the service of the Authority whose case does not come within the scope and effect of any pension or other schemes established under this section retires or dies in the service of the Authority or is discharged from such service, the Authority may grant to him or to such other person or persons wholly or partly dependent on him, as the Authority may think fit, such allowance or gratuity as the Authority may determine.

**No entitlement in respect of abolition or reorganization of office.**

**20.** Notwithstanding the provisions of the Pensions Act, no person who is transferred to the service of the Authority under section 18 of this Act shall be entitled to claim any benefits under this Act on the ground that he has been retired from the service of the Government on account of abolition or reorganization of office.

**Transfer of functions, powers, duties, assets and liabilities, etc., to the Authority.**

21.—(1) Upon the coming into operation of this Act, there shall be transferred to the Authority—

*(a)* all the functions, duties and powers of the Minister for Finance, the Commissioner of Banking and the Accountant-General under the Banking Act;

*(b)* all the functions, duties and powers of the Minister for Finance, the Commissioner for Finance Companies and the Accountant-General under the Finance Companies Act; and

*(c)* the functions, duties and powers of the Minister for Finance and the Controller of Foreign Exchange under the Exchange Control Act.

(2) After the coming into operation of this Act, there shall be transferred to the Authority such other functions, duties and powers as are conferred by or in pursuance of any written law upon the Minister or any public officer as the President may, from time to time, by notification in the *Gazette,* specify.

(3) Upon or after the coming into operation of this Act, such movable property, assets, rights, interests and privileges as well as such debts, liabilities and obligations connected therewith or appertaining thereto which are related to finance and are vested in or conferred upon the Minister pursuant to any written law, as the President may by notification in the *Gazette* specify, shall be deemed to have been transferred to and vested in the Authority without further assurance.

(4) Where in any written law or any document whatsoever there is a reference to the Minister for Finance, the Commissioner of Banking,

the Commissioner for Finance Companies, Commissioner of Chit Funds, the Accountant-General or the Controller of Foreign Exchange in connection with or related to the performance of any of the functions, duties and powers that are transferred to the Authority under subsection (1) or (2) of this section the written law or document shall have effect as if the Authority had originally been referred to in the written law or document instead of the Minister for Finance, the Commissioner of Banking, the Commissioner for Finance Companies, Commissioner of Chit Funds, the Accountant-General or the Controller of Foreign Exchange, as the case may be.

(5) The Minister shall have power to do all acts or things that he considers necessary or expedient to give effect to the provisions of subsections (1), (2) and (3) of this section.

(6) If any question arises as to whether—

*(a)* any of the functions, duties and powers; or

*(b)* any movable property, assets, rights, interests, privileges, debts, liabilities and obligations,

have been transferred to or vested in the Authority under subsections (1), (2) and (3) of this section, a certificate under the hand of the President shall be conclusive evidence of such transfer or vesting.

## PART IV. POWERS, DUTIES AND FUNCTIONS OF THE AUTHORITY

Powers, duties and functions of the Authority.

22. The Authority may, in addition to the powers, duties and functions transferred to it by virtue of section 21 of this Act, exercise and discharge the following powers, duties and functions, that is to say, it may—

*(a)* accept deposits of money;

*(b)* issue demand drafts and other kinds of remittances made payable at its own office or the offices of agencies or correspondents;

*(c)* purchase, accept on deposit and sell gold coin or bullion;

*(d)* purchase, sell, discount and rediscount Treasury bills of the Government;

*(e)* purchase and sell securities of the Government or of any public authority which have been publicly offered for sale or form part of an issue which is being made to the public at the time of acquisition;

*(f)* purchase, sell, discount and rediscount bills of exchange and promissory notes arising out of bona fide commercial transactions bearing two or more good signatures and maturing within three

months (exclusive of days of grace) from the date of acquisition;

*(g)* grant advances to such financial institutions or class of financial institutions as the Authority may from time to time approve for periods not exceeding three months against—

(i) Treasury bills of the Government and securities of the Government;

(ii) gold coin or bullion;

(iii) such bills of exchange and promissory notes as are eligible for purchase, discount or rediscount by the Authority up to seventy-five per cent of their nominal value;

(iv) warehouse warrants or their equivalent (securing possession of goods), in respect of goods duly insured and with a letter of hypothecation from the owner:

Provided that no such advance shall exceed sixty per cent of the current market value of the goods in question;

*(h)* invest in securities of the Government or of any public authority for any amount, and to mature at any time on behalf of staff and pension funds and other internal funds of the Authority;

*(i)* acquire, hold and sell shares of any corporation set up with the approval of, or under the authority of, the Government for the purpose of promoting the development of a money market or securities market in Singapore or for the financing of economic development in Singapore;

*(j)* purchase and sell currency, and purchase, sell, discount and rediscount bills of exchange and Treasury bills drawn in or on places outside Singapore;

*(k)* borrow money, establish credits and give guarantees in any currency, inside and outside Singapore, on such terms and conditions as it may deem fit;

*(l)* maintain accounts with central banks outside Singapore and with other banks inside and outside Singapore;

*(m)* purchase and sell securities of, or guaranteed by, such guarantor, governments or international financial institutions as may be approved by the board, or purchase and sell securities and investments authorised by the President on the recommendation of the board;

*(n)* act as correspondent, banker or agent for any central bank or other monetary authority and for any international bank or international monetary authority established under governmental auspices;

*(o)* open accounts for, and accept deposits from, the Government,

public authorities, banks and other credit institutions in Singapore;

(*p*) underwrite loans in which it may invest;

(*q*) undertake the issue and management of loans publicly issued by the Government or by any public authority; and

(*r*) do generally all such things as may be commonly done by bankers and are not inconsistent with the exercise of its powers or the discharge of its duties under this Act.

Investment of funds.

23. The funds of the Authority may be invested in all or any of the following:—

(*a*) gold coin or bullion;

(*b*) notes, coin, bank balances and money at call in such country or countries as may be approved by the board;

(*c*) Treasury bills of such government or governments as may be approved by the board;

(*d*) securities of, or guaranteed by, such government or governments or international financial institutions as may be approved by the board;

(*e*) such securities and investments as may be authorised by the President on the recommendation of the board.

Authority as a banker to, and financial agent of, the Government and manager of its external assets.

24.—(1) The Authority shall act as a banker to, and a financial agent of, the Government.

(2) Whenever the Authority receives and disburses Government moneys it shall keep account thereof and may be paid an agency fee for its services.

(3) The Authority may act generally as agent for the Government on such terms and conditions as may be agreed between the Authority and the Government, where the Authority can do so appropriately and consistently with the provisions of this Act and with its duties and functions as a monetary authority.

(4) The Authority shall, subject to the provisions of the Financial Procedure Act and any other written law, manage the external assets of the Government.

Special loans to banks and financial institutions.

**24A.** The Authority may, if it thinks such action is necessary to safeguard monetary stability, make a loan or advance to a bank carrying on business under the Banking Act or to such financial institutions or class of financial institutions as the Authority may from time to time approve against such form of security as the Authority may consider sufficient.

**24B.**—(1) The Authority may, if it thinks it necessary in the public interest, request information from and make recommendations to such financial institutions as the Authority may from time to time approve and may issue directions for the purpose of securing that effect is given to any such request or recommendation. Power to issue directions to financial institutions.

(2) Before issuing any direction under subsection (1) of this section the financial institution or financial institutions concerned shall, unless the Authority in respect of any particular direction decides that it is not practicable or desirable, be given an opportunity to make representations with regard to the proposed direction within such time as the Authority shall specify.

(3) Upon receipt of any representations referred to in subsection (2) of this section the Authority shall consider them and, may—

*(a)* reject such representations; or

*(b)* amend or modify the proposed direction in accordance with the representations, or otherwise,

and in either event, it shall thereupon issue a direction in writing, to such financial institution or financial institutions, as the case may be, requiring that effect be given to the proposed direction or to the proposed direction as subsequently amended or modified by it within a reasonable time, and the financial institution or financial institutions, as the case may be, shall comply with such direction.

(4) Any financial institution that fails or refuses to comply with a direction given under this section shall be guilty of an offence under this Act and shall be liable on conviction to a fine not exceeding five thousand dollars.

**25.** In the exercise of its powers and the performance of its functions under this Act the Authority may— Agents.

*(a)* establish agencies at such places outside Singapore as it thinks fit;

*(b)* arrange with and authorise a person to act as agent of the Authority outside Singapore;

*(c)* act as agent of a bank carrying on business inside or outside Singapore; and

*(d)* act as agent of any public authority either generally or for a particular purpose inside or outside Singapore.

## PART V. MISCELLANEOUS

**26.**—(1) The Authority may at any time for the purpose of carrying out its functions under this Act request such persons or classes of per- Statistics.

sons as it may decide to collect and furnish such statistical information as the Authority may specify and those persons or classes of persons shall comply with that request.

(2) Statistical information received from the persons or classes of persons referred to in subsection (1) of this section shall be regarded as secret between them and the Authority.

(3) Any person who fails to comply with a request of the Authority under subsection (1) of this section shall be guilty of an offence under this Act and shall be liable on conviction to a fine not exceeding five hundred dollars.

Authority's financial year.

27. The financial year of the Authority shall begin on the 1st day of April and end on the 31st day of March of each year, except that for the year 1970 the financial year shall begin on the date of the establishment of the Authority and shall end on the 31st day of March 1971.

Audit.

28. The accounts of the Authority shall be audited by the Auditor-General.

Preparation and publication of annual accounts and annual report.

29.—(1) The Authority shall within six months from the close of its financial year—

(a) transmit to the President a copy of the annual accounts certified by the Auditor-General, and those accounts shall then be published in the *Gazette*; and
(b) transmit to the President a report by the board on the working of the Authority throughout the year and that report shall be published by the Authority.

(2) The Authority shall cause the annual accounts and the annual report to be presented as soon as may be to Parliament.

Borrowing from Authority by officers and employees.

30. The Authority shall not lend money to an officer or employee of the Authority, except—

(a) for the purchase, erection, alteration, renovation or enlargement of a house in which he resides or intends to reside;
(b) to discharge a mortgage or encumbrance on such a house; or
(c) for the purchase of a vehicle.

Power to appoint attorney.

31. The Authority may, by instrument under its common seal, appoint a person (whether in Singapore or in a place outside Singapore) to be its attorney, and the person so appointed may, subject to the instrument, do any act or execute any power or function which he is authorised by the instrument to do or execute.

32. The Authority shall not be subject to any tax, fee or levy whatsoever. Exemption from taxes, fees and levies.

33. The validity of an act or transaction of the Authority shall not be called in question in any court on the ground that any provision of this Act has not been complied with. Validity of acts and transactions of Authority.

34. The Government shall be responsible for the payment of all moneys due by the Authority but nothing in this section authorises a creditor or other person claiming against the Authority to sue the Government in respect of his claim. Guarantee by Government.

35. No prosecution in respect of any offence under this Act shall be instituted without the consent in writing of the Attorney-General. Fiat of Attorney-General.

36. Notwithstanding the provisions of any other written law, a District Court has jurisdiction to try all offences under this Act and to impose the full penalty prescribed therefor. Jurisdiction.

37. The Authority may, with the approval of the President, make regulations for the better carrying out of the objects and purposes of this Act. Power of Authority to make regulations.

38. Notwithstanding the provisions of section 1 of this Act, the Minister may at any time before the date of the coming into operation of Part II of this Act do all such acts and incur all such expenses as he may consider necessary in connection with the establishment of the Authority; and upon that date all such acts and expenses shall be deemed to have been done and incurred by the board. Preliminary acts and expenses.

39. Nothing in this Act affects the operation of the Currency Act. Operation of Act not to affect the Currency Act.

## PART VI. TRANSITIONAL

40.—(1) Any fund, scheme, contract, document, licence, permission or resolution constituted, prepared, made, granted or approved under the Exchange Control Act, the Finance Companies Act, the Banking Act or any other written law relating to such functions, powers and duties as are transferred to the Authority under this Act, shall, except where otherwise expressly provided in this Act or in any other written law, continue and be deemed to have been constituted, prepared, made, granted or approved, as the case may be, under this Act. Transitional provisions.

(2) Any legal proceeding or cause of action pending or existing immediately before the commencement of this Act by or against the Government in respect of any functions or assets which under and by virtue of this Act are transferred to, or vested in, the Authority, may be continued and enforced by or against the Authority as it might have been by or against the Government, as the case may be, had this Act not come into operation.

## Banking Act[1]

An Act to provide for the licensing and regulation of the business of banking.

[1st January, 1971]

### PART I. PRELIMINARY

Short title.

1. This Act may be cited as the Banking Act.

Interpretation.

2.—(1) In this Act, unless the context otherwise requires—

"the Authority" means the Monetary Authority of Singapore as established under section 3 of the Monetary Authority of Singapore Act; [2]

"bank" means any company which carries on banking business and holds a valid licence granted under section 7 or 72 of this Act. All branches and offices in Singapore of such a company shall be deemed to be one bank for the purposes of this Act;

"banking business" means the business of receiving money on current or deposit account, paying and collecting cheques drawn by or paid in by customers, the making of advances to customers, and includes such

[1] Act No. 41 of 1970 was published in the *Government Gazette Acts Supplement*, No. 56, October 30, 1970. The Four Schedules to this Act are not published in this volume.

[2] In accordance with the version published in the *Government Gazette Acts Supplement*, No. 56, October 30, 1970, references formerly in this Act to the Minister, the Commissioner of Banking and the Accountant-General have, in accordance with sec. 21 (4) of the Monetary Authority of Singapore Act (Cap. 195), been replaced by references to the Authority, and various consequential alterations have been made.

other business as the Authority may prescribe for the purposes of this Act;

"company" means any company defined in any written law for the time being in force relating to companies, any company formed in pursuance of any Royal Charter or Letters Patent, and any company incorporated or registered under any written law in force in Singapore and includes any company incorporated outside Singapore which has complied with the provisions of any written law for the time being in force relating to companies;

"director" includes any person occupying the position of director of a corporation by whatever name called and includes a person in accordance with whose directions or instructions the directors of a corporation are accustomed to act and an alternate or substitute director;

"licence" means a licence granted under section 7 or 72 of this Act;

"place of business" in relation to a bank includes a mobile branch of the bank and a branch established and maintained for a limited period only;

"published reserves" means reserves which appear in the accounts of the bank but does not include any reserves which are represented by the writing down of the value of assets or by provision for the depreciation of fixed assets or which are maintained for any specific purposes;

"savings account liabilities" in relation to a bank means the total deposits at that bank which normally require the presentation of passbooks for the deposit or withdrawal of moneys;

"sight liabilities" in relation to a bank means the total deposits at that bank which are repayable on demand, but does not include savings account liabilities or the deposits of any other bank at that bank;

"time liabilities" in relation to a bank means the total deposits at that bank which are repayable otherwise than on demand, but does not include savings account liabilities or the deposits of any other bank at that bank.

(2) Without prejudice to any other meaning which the word "insolvent" may have, a bank shall, for the purposes of this Act, be deemed to be insolvent if either it has ceased to pay its debts in the ordinary course of business or is unable to pay its debts as they become due.

(3) For the purposes of sections 10, 25, 27 and 28 of this Act "capital funds" means—

*(a)* in the case of a bank whose head office is situated in Singapore—the paid-up capital and published reserves of that bank; and

*(b)* in the case of a bank whose head office is situated outside Singapore—the net head office funds and such other liabilities as the Authority may decide.

## PART II. APPOINTMENT OF ASSISTANTS

Appointment of assistants.

3.—(1) The Authority may authorize or appoint any person to assist it in the exercise of its functions and duties under this Act, either generally or in any particular case.

(2) The members of the Authority and any person appointed by it pursuant to subsection (1) of this section shall be deemed to be public servants within the meaning of the Penal Code.

## PART III. LICENSING OF BANKS

Licensing of banks.

4.—(1) No banking business shall be transacted in Singapore except by a company which is in possession of a valid licence granted under this Act by the Authority authorizing it to conduct banking business in Singapore.

(2) Any person who contravenes the provisions of subsection (1) of this section shall be guilty of an offence under this Act and shall be liable on conviction to imprisonment for a term not exceeding three years or to a fine not exceeding five thousand dollars or to both such imprisonment and fine and in the case of a continuing offence to a further fine of one thousand dollars for every day during which the offence continues after conviction.

Use of word "bank".

5.—(1) No person or body of persons, whether incorporated or not, other than a bank shall, without the written consent of the Authority, use the word "bank" or any of its derivatives in any language, or any other word indicating it transacts banking business, in the name, description or title under which the person or body of persons is transacting business in Singapore or make or continue to make any representation to such effect in any bill head, letter paper, notice, advertisement or in any other manner whatsoever:

Provided that nothing in this section prohibits an association of banks formed for the protection of common interests from using the word "bank" or any of its derivatives in any language as a part of its name or description of its activities.

(2) Any person or body of persons whether incorporated or not who contravenes the provisions of subsection (1) of this section shall be guilty of an offence under this Act and shall be liable on conviction to imprisonment for a term not exceeding one year or to a fine not exceeding one thousand dollars or to both such imprisonment and fine and in the case of a continuing offence to a further fine of two hundred and

fifty dollars for every day during which the offence continues after conviction.

Examination of persons suspected of transacting banking business.

6. Whenever the Authority has reason to believe that a person is transacting banking business without a licence, it shall have the power to examine the books, accounts and records of that person in order to ascertain whether or not that person has violated or is violating any provisions of this Act, and any refusal to submit such books, accounts and records shall be prima facie evidence of the fact of operation without a licence.

Application for licence.

7.—(1) A company which desires authority to carry on banking business in Singapore shall apply in writing to the Authority for a licence under this section and shall supply—

(*a*) a copy of the memorandum of association and articles of association or other instrument under which the company is incorporated, duly verified by a statutory declaration made by a senior officer of the company;

(*b*) a copy of the latest balance-sheet of the company; and

(*c*) such other information as may be called for by the Authority.

(2) Upon receiving an application under subsection (1) of this section, the Authority shall consider the application and may, subject to the provisions of section 9 of this Act, grant a licence, with or without conditions, or refuse a licence.

(3) The Authority may at any time vary or revoke any existing conditions of a licence or impose conditions or additional conditions thereto.

(4) The Authority shall, prior to any action under subsection (3) of this section, notify its intention to take such action to the bank concerned and shall give the bank an opportunity to submit reasons why the conditions of its licence should not be so varied or revoked.

(5) Where a licence is subject to conditions the bank shall comply with those conditions.

(6) Any bank which fails to comply with any of the conditions of its licence shall be guilty of an offence under this Act and shall be liable on conviction to a fine not exceeding five thousand dollars and in the case of a continuing offence to a further fine of one thousand dollars for every day during which the offence continues after conviction.

Licence fees.

8.—(1) Every bank in Singapore shall pay such annual licence fee as the Authority may by notification in the *Gazette* prescribe.

(2) The Authority may prescribe different licence fees in respect of different classes or categories of banks and such fees shall apply uniformly to such classes or categories.

(3) The manner of payment of the licence fee shall be as specified by the Authority.

Minimum capital requirements.

9.—(1) Subject to the provisions of this Act, a bank shall not be granted or hold a licence unless—

*(a)* in the case of a bank whose head office is situated in Singapore, its capital issued and paid up is not less than three million Singapore dollars deduction having been made in respect of a debit balance, if any, appearing in the profit and loss account of the bank; and

*(b)* in the case of a bank whose head office is situated outside Singapore—

(i) its capital issued and paid up is not less than the equivalent of six million Singapore dollars deduction having been made in respect of a debit balance, if any, appearing in the profit and loss account of the bank; and

(ii) it holds net head office funds of not less than three million Singapore dollars in Singapore in respect of its business in Singapore, at all times, in the form of assets approved by the Authority.

(2) A bank incorporated in Singapore shall not reduce its paid-up capital during the currency of its licence without the approval of the Authority.

Capital funds.

10.—(1) The Authority may require banks to maintain capital funds in Singapore in proportion to their total assets or to every category of assets at such ratio or ratios as may from time to time be prescribed.

(2) Any bank which fails to comply with the requirements of the Authority under the provisions of subsection (1) of this section shall be guilty of an offence under this Act and shall be liable on conviction to a fine not exceeding five thousand dollars and in the case of a continuing offence to a further fine of one thousand dollars for every day during which the offence continues after conviction.

Foreign government-owned banks.

11. A bank shall not be granted or hold a licence if the Authority is satisfied that fifty per cent or more of its capital issued and paid up is owned by or on behalf of the government of any country other than Singapore or of an agency of any such government, or that all or a

majority of the persons having the direction, control or management of the bank are appointed by or on behalf of any such government or agency:

Provided that the Authority may, in its absolute discretion, grant a licence to any such bank for such period or periods not exceeding one year at any one time as it may think fit.

Branches.

12.—(1) No bank shall open a new place of business or change the location of an existing place of business in Singapore without submitting a written application in respect thereof to the Authority, which may—

(*a*) give its approval; or

(*b*) without assigning any reason therefor, refuse to give its approval.

(2) No bank incorporated in Singapore shall open a new branch, agency or office in any place outside Singapore without submitting a written application in respect thereof to the Authority, which shall approve or reject the application.

(3) Any bank which contravenes the provisions of subsection (1) or (3) [3] of this section shall be guilty of an offence under this Act and shall be liable on conviction to a fine not exceeding five hundred dollars and in the case of a continuing offence to a further fine of one hundred dollars for every day during which the offence continues after conviction.

Fees to be paid in respect of branches of banks.

13.—(1) The Authority may from time to time by notification in the *Gazette* specify the annual licence fees which banks in Singapore shall pay for each of their branches.

(2) The manner of payment shall be as specified by the Authority.

Mergers.

14.—(1) A bank incorporated in Singapore shall not after the coming into operation of this Act be merged or consolidated with or be taken over by any other bank or banks or their subsidiaries or related companies as described in section 6 of the Companies Act or acquire an interest exceeding twenty per cent of the voting share capital of any other bank without application to, and approval by, the Authority.

(2) In considering such an application the Authority shall have power to call for such information as it may require.

[3] The editor notes that this reference should probably read "(2)."

Amendment of bank's constitution.

15.—(1) Every bank incorporated in Singapore shall, prior to the making of any amendment or alteration in the memorandum of association and articles of association or other instrument under which it is incorporated, furnish to the Authority particulars in writing of the proposed amendment.

(2) Every bank whether incorporated inside or outside Singapore shall within three months after the making of any alteration in the memorandum of association and articles of association or other instrument under which it is incorporated furnish to the Authority particulars in writing (verified by a statutory declaration made by a senior officer of the bank) of the alteration.

(3) Any bank which contravenes the provisions of subsection (1) or (2) of this section shall be guilty of an offence under this Act and shall be liable on conviction to a fine not exceeding five hundred dollars.

Revocation of licence.

16.—(1) The Authority may by order revoke a licence issued under this Act—

*(a)* if it is satisfied that the bank holding that licence—

(i) has ceased to transact banking business in Singapore;

(ii) proposes to make, or has made, any composition or arrangement with its creditors or has gone into liquidation or has been wound up or otherwise dissolved;

(iii) is carrying on its business in a manner likely to be detrimental to the interests of the depositors of the bank or has insufficient assets to cover its liabilities to its depositors or the public;

(iv) is contravening the provisions of this Act; or

(v) has been convicted of any offence under this Act or any of its officers holding a managerial or executive position has been convicted of any offence under this Act; or

*(b)* if, upon taking action under subsection (2) of section 44 of this Act, it considers that it is in the public interest to revoke the licence.

(2) The Authority shall before revoking any licence under the provisions of subsection (1) of this section cause to be given to the bank concerned notice in writing of its intention to do so, specifying a date, not less than twenty-one days after the date of the notice, upon which the revocation will take effect and calling upon the bank to show cause to the Authority why the licence should not be revoked.

(3) When the Authority has revoked a licence under the provisions of subsection (1) of this section it shall forthwith inform the bank of the revocation.

(4) Any bank whose licence has been revoked pursuant to the provisions of this section shall have a right of appeal to the High Court against the order of revocation.

(5) An order of revocation made by the Minister shall not take effect until the expiration of a period of twenty-one days after the Commissioner has informed the bank of such order.

(6) If within such period the bank concerned gives due notice of appeal to the High Court such order shall not take effect unless the order is confirmed by the Court or the appeal is for any reason dismissed by that Court.

(7) The making of an appeal by a bank under this section shall in no way affect the exercise of the powers of the Minister and the Commissioner in relation to that bank under sections 44, 45, 46, 47 and 48 of this Act.

Effect of revocation of licence.

17.—(1) Where an order of revocation becomes effective under section 16 of this Act—

*(a)* notice of such revocation shall be published in the *Gazette;* and

*(b)* the bank shall, as from the date of such notice, cease to transact any banking business in Singapore except as may be approved by the Commissioner for the purpose of winding up its banking business.

(2) The provisions of paragraph *(b)* of subsection (1) of this section shall not prejudice the enforcement by any person of any right or claim against the bank or by the bank of any right or claim against any person.

## PART IV. RESERVE FUNDS, DIVIDENDS, BALANCE-SHEETS AND INFORMATION

Maintenance of reserve fund.

18.—(1) Every licensed bank—

*(a)* shall maintain a reserve fund; and

*(b)* shall transfer to such reserve fund out of the net profits of each year, after due provision has been made for taxation—

(i) so long as the amount of the reserve fund is less than fifty per centum of the paid-up capital, a sum not less than fifty per centum of such net profits;

(ii) so long as the amount of the reserve fund is fifty per cent but less than one hundred per cent of the paid-up capital, a sum not less than twenty-five per cent of those net profits; and

(iii) so long as the amount of the reserve fund is one hundred per cent or more of the paid-up capital, a sum not less than five per cent of those net profits.

(2) If the Authority is satisfied that the aggregate reserve fund of a licensed bank whose head office is situated outside Singapore is adequate for its business, it may, by order in writing, exempt that bank from the provisions of subsection (1) of this section.

(3) Any bank which fails to comply with the provisions of subsection (1) of this section shall be guilty of an offence under this Act and shall be liable on conviction to a fine not exceeding ten thousand dollars.

Maintenance of adequate provision for bad and doubtful debts.

**19.** Every bank shall make provision for bad and doubtful debts and before any profit or loss is declared ensure that that provision is adequate.

Dividends.

**20.** A bank shall not pay any dividend on its shares until all its capitalized expenditure (including preliminary expenses, organization expenses, share selling commission, brokerage, amount of losses and any item of expenditure not represented by tangible assets) has been completely written off.

Publication and exhibition of audited balance-sheet.

**21.**—(1) Every bank shall, within six months after the close of each financial year or within such period as the Authority may approve, publish in at least four local daily newspapers, one each published in the Malay, Chinese, Tamil and English languages, and exhibit thereafter throughout the year in a conspicuous position in each of its offices and branches in Singapore—

(*a*) a copy of its latest audited annual balance-sheet, and a copy of the profit and loss account, together with any notes thereon, and a copy of the report of the auditors:

Provided that in the case of a bank incorporated outside Singapore, the abovementioned statements may be made in a manner that complies with the law for the time being applicable in the place of its incorporation or origin;

(*b*) the full and correct names of all persons who are directors for the time being of the bank; and

(*c*) the names of all subsidiary companies for the time being of the bank.

(2) A copy of each of the documents referred to in subsection (1) of this section shall be sent to the Authority by the bank, prior to the

first publication thereof under that subsection, together with a copy of the directors' report.

(3) In addition to the balance-sheet and other documents required to be lodged with the Authority under subsection (2) of this section, every bank shall lodge with the Authority with that balance-sheet and other documents a duly audited balance-sheet showing its assets used in, and liabilities arising out of its operation in, Singapore as at the date to which its balance-sheet was made up and a duly audited profit and loss account which gives a true and fair view of the profit or loss arising out of the bank's operation in Singapore for the last preceding financial year of the bank:

Provided that the bank shall be entitled to make such apportionments of expenses incurred in connection with operations or administration affecting both Singapore and elsewhere and to add such notes and explanations as in its opinion are necessary or desirable in order to give a true and fair view of the profit or loss of its operations in Singapore.

(4) The Authority may, in its absolute discretion, regard the balance-sheet and profit and loss account as having been duly audited for the purpose of subsection (3) of this section if the balance-sheet and profit and loss account are accompanied by a report by an approved auditor which complies, insofar as it is practicable, with the provisions of section 174 of the Companies Act.

(5) In the case of a bank incorporated in Singapore the annual balance-sheet and profit and loss account of the bank referred to in subsection (1) of this section and the balance-sheet and profit and loss account referred to in subsection (3) of this section shall be in such form as the Authority may approve; in the case of a bank incorporated outside Singapore only the balance-sheet and profit and loss account referred to in subsection (3) of this section shall be in such form as the Authority may approve.

(6) The Authority may require any bank to submit such further or additional information as it may deem necessary either by way of explanation, amplification or otherwise with regard to the balance-sheets and profit and loss accounts sent by that bank under subsections (2) and (3) of this section and that information shall be submitted within such period and in such manner as the Authority may require.

(7) Any bank which fails to comply with the provisions of this section shall be guilty of an offence under this Act and shall be liable on conviction to a fine not exceeding five hundred dollars and in the case of a continuing offence to a further fine of one hundred dollars for every day during which the offence continues after conviction.

Information to be furnished by banks.

22.—(1) Every bank shall furnish to the Authority at such time and in such manner as the Authority may prescribe, all such information as the Authority may reasonably require for the proper discharge of its functions.

(2) Every bank shall send to the Authority and the Chief Statistician—

(a) not later than fifteen days after the last day of each month a statement in the form set out in the First Schedule[4] to this Act showing the assets and liabilities of its banking offices and branches in Singapore at the close of business on the last business day of the preceding month;

(b) not later than one month after the last day of each quarter of a calendar year, a statement in the form set out in the Second Schedule[4] to this Act giving an analysis of loans and advances of its banking offices and branches in Singapore as at the 31st day of March, 30th day of June, 30th day of September and the 31st day of December, respectively; and

(c) not later than six months after the close of its financial year a statement in the form set out in the Third Schedule[4] to this Act showing the income and expenditure in respect of its banking business in Singapore.

(3) The Authority may vary or amend the forms set out in the First, Second and Third Schedules to this Act.

(4) The Authority may require any statement submitted to it pursuant to subsections (1) and (2) of this section to be accompanied by a certificate—

(a) of the auditor appointed by the bank pursuant to subsection (1) of section 53 of this Act; or

(b) of any other auditor appointed by the Authority pursuant to subsection (2) of section 53 of this Act,

as to whether in the opinion of the auditor, the statement or information is correct.

(5) Any information received from a bank under this section shall be regarded as secret between that bank, the Authority and the Chief Statistician.

(6) Nothing in this section shall prevent the Chief Statistician or the Authority from preparing and publishing consolidated statements aggregating such information as may be furnished under this section.

[4] Not published in this volume.

(7) Any bank which fails or neglects to furnish any information required by the Authority or the Chief Statistician under the provisions of this section shall be guilty of an offence under this Act and shall be liable on conviction to a fine not exceeding five thousand dollars and in the case of a continuing offence to a further fine of one thousand dollars for every day during which the offence continues after conviction.

23.—(1) Every bank shall send to the Authority not later than fifteen days after the last day of each month a statement in the form to be prescribed by the Authority showing particulars of all advances, loans or credit facilities granted by it to— Action to be taken if advances are against the interests of depositors.

*(a)* any of its directors;

*(b)* any firm in which it or any of its directors is a partner, manager or agent, or to any individual or firm of whom or of which any of its directors is a guarantor;

*(c)* any corporation that is deemed to be related to the bank as described in section 6 of the Companies Act;

*(d)* any of its officers, employees or other persons being persons receiving remuneration from it in excess of one year's remuneration of the officer, employee or person;

*(e)* any private or public company in which it or any of its directors, officers, employees or other persons who receive remuneration from the company has an interest as a director, manager, agent or guarantor; or

*(f)* any individual in whom, and any firm or company in which, any of its directors has an interest, directly or indirectly, as declared under the provisions of section 24 of this Act other than such advances, loans and credit facilities, particulars of which have already been supplied pursuant to paragraphs *(a)* to *(e)* of this subsection.

(2) If on examination of the particulars supplied by a bank under subsection (1) of this section it appears to the Authority that any such advances, loans or credit facilities are being granted to the detriment of the interests of the depositors of that bank, the Authority may by order in writing prohibit that bank from granting any further advances, loans or credit facilities or impose such restrictions on the grant thereof as the Authority thinks fit, and may further direct that bank to secure repayment of any such first-mentioned advances, loans or credit facilities within such time and to such extent as may be specified in the order.

24.—(1) Every director of a bank who has in any manner whatsoever, whether directly or indirectly, an interest in an advance, loan or credit facility or proposed advance, loan or credit facility from that Disclosure of interest by directors.

bank shall as soon as practicable declare the nature of his interest to the board of directors of that bank and the secretary of that bank shall cause such declaration to be circulated forthwith to all the directors.

(2) The requirements of subsection (1) of this section do not apply in any case where the interest of the director consists only of being a member or creditor of a company which is interested in an advance, loan or credit facility or proposed advance, loan or credit facility from that bank if the interest of the director may properly be regarded as of a trivial nature.

(3) For the purposes of subsection (1) of this section, a general notice given to the board of directors of a bank by a director to the effect that he is an officer or member of a specified company or a member of a specified firm and he is to be regarded as having an interest in any advance, loan or credit facility which may, after the date of the notice, be made to that company or firm shall be deemed to be a sufficient declaration of interest in relation to any advance, loan or credit facility so made if—

*(a)* it specifies the nature and extent of his interest in the particular company or firm;

*(b)* his interest is not different in nature or greater in extent than the nature and extent so specified in the notice at the time any advance, loan or credit facility is made; and

*(c)* it is given at the meeting of the directors or the director takes reasonable steps to ensure that it is brought up and read at the next meeting of the directors after it is given.

(4) Every director of a bank who holds any office or possesses any property whereby, whether directly or indirectly, duties or interest might be created in conflict with his duties or interest as director shall declare at a meeting of the directors of that bank the fact and the nature, character and extent of the conflict.

(5) The declaration referred to in subsection (4) of this section shall be made at the first meeting of the directors held—

*(a)* after he becomes a director of the bank; or

*(b)* if already a director, after he commences to hold the office or to possess the property, as the case may be.

(6) The secretary of that bank shall cause to be brought up and read any declaration made under subsection (1) or (4) of this section at the next meeting of the directors after it is given, and shall record any declaration made under this section in the minutes of the meeting at which it was made or at which it was brought up and read.

(7) Any director who acts in contravention of subsection (1) or (4) of this section shall be guilty of an offence under this Act and shall be liable on conviction to imprisonment for a term not exceeding three years or to a fine not exceeding five thousand dollars or to both such imprisonment and fine.

## PART V. PROHIBITED BUSINESS

Advances, credits and guarantees.

25.—(1) A bank shall not—

*(a)* grant or permit to be outstanding to any customer any advances, loans or credit facilities or give any financial guarantees or incur any other liabilities on his behalf to an aggregate amount of such advances, loans, facilities, guarantees or liabilities in excess of sixty per cent of the capital funds or, with the approval of the Authority, up to but not in excess of one hundred per cent of the capital funds of the bank:

Provided that the provisions of this paragraph do not apply to—

(i) transactions with the Government;

(ii) transactions between banks;

(iii) the purchase of telegraphic transfers or loans or advances made against telegraphic transfers;

(iv) any facilities granted against letters of credit or bills or guarantees or documents in respect of imports into or exports from Singapore; or

(v) any other type of transactions which the Authority may from time to time approve;

*(b)* grant any advance or credit facility against the security of its own shares;

*(c)* grant unsecured advances, unsecured loans or unsecured credit facilities which in the aggregate and outstanding at any one time exceed the sum of five thousand Singapore dollars—

(i) to any of its directors, whether those advances, loans or credit facilities are obtained by its directors jointly or severally;

(ii) to a firm in which it or any of its directors has an interest as a partner, manager or agent, or to any individual or firm of whom or of which any of its directors is a guarantor; or

(iii) to any corporation, other than a bank, that is deemed to be related to the bank as described in section 6 of the Companies Act; or (*d*) grant to any of its officers, other than a director, or its employees or other persons, being persons receiving remuneration from a bank (other than public, registered or licensed accountants, advocates and solicitors, architects, estate agents, doctors and any other persons receiving remuneration from a bank in respect of their professional services) unsecured advances, unsecured loans or unsecured credit facilities which in the aggregate and outstanding at any one time exceed one year's emolument of that officer or employee or person.

(2) In paragraphs *(c)* and *(d)* of subsection (1) of this section, the expression "unsecured advances, unsecured loans or unsecured credit facilities" means advances, loans or credit facilities made without security, or in respect of any advance, loan or credit facility made with security, any part thereof which at any time exceeds the market value of the assets constituting that security, or where the Authority is satisfied that there is no established market value, on the basis of a valuation approved by it.

(3) In paragraph *(c)* of subsection (1) of this section, the expression "director" includes the wife, husband, father, mother, son or daughter of a director.

(4) All the directors of the bank shall be liable jointly and severally to indemnify the bank against any loss arising from the making of any unsecured advance, unsecured loan or unsecured credit facility under sub-paragraphs (i), (ii) and (iii) of paragraph *(c)* of subsection (1) of this section.

(5) Any bank which contravenes any of the provisions of this section shall be guilty of an offence under this Act.

Trade.

26.—(1) A bank shall not engage, whether on its own account or on a commission basis, and whether alone or with others, in the wholesale or retail trade, including the import or export trade, except in the course of the satisfaction of debts due to it for the purpose of carrying on its banking business.

(2) Any bank which contravenes the provisions of subsection (1) of this section shall be guilty of an offence under this Act.

Investments.

27.—(1) A bank shall not acquire or hold any part of the share capital of, or otherwise have an interest in, any financial, commercial, agricultural, industrial or other undertaking exceeding in the aggregate forty per cent of that bank's capital funds except such shareholding as the bank may acquire in the course of the satisfaction of debts due to it, which shareholding shall, however, be disposed of at the earliest suitable opportunity.

(2) This section does not apply in respect of—

*(a)* any shareholding approved in writing by the Authority in another bank or in a subsidiary company formed by the bank concerned for the carrying out of nominee, executor or trustee functions or other functions incidental to banking business; or

*(b)* any shareholding approved by the Authority in any corporation set up for the purpose of promoting development in Singapore.

(3) The provisions of subsection (1) of this section do not apply to the Development Bank of Singapore, Limited.

(4) Any bank which contravenes the provisions of subsection (1) of this section shall be guilty of an offence under this Act.

Immovable property.

28.—(1) A bank shall not purchase or acquire any immovable property or any right therein exceeding in the aggregate forty per cent of that bank's capital funds except as may be reasonably necessary for the purpose of conducting its business or of housing or providing amenities for its staff:

Provided that this does not prevent a bank—

*(a)* from letting part of any building which is used for the purpose of conducting its business; or

*(b)* from securing a debt on any immovable property and, in the event of default in payment of the debt, from holding that immovable property for realisation by sale or auction at the earliest suitable opportunity.

(2) The provisions of this section do not apply to the Development Bank of Singapore, Limited.

(3) Any bank which contravenes the provisions of subsection (1) of this section shall be guilty of an offence under this Act.

Loans secured by immovable property.

29.—(1) A bank shall not make any loans or advances exceeding in the aggregate thirty per cent of the amount of its deposits in Singapore (including the deposits and borrowings from any other bank at that bank) on the security of immovable property for the purpose of purchasing, improving or altering the immovable property:

Provided that any bank whose business is principally in such loans or advances may, with the prior written consent of the Authority, make such loans or advances in an aggregate amount up to, but not in excess of sixty per cent of the amount of its deposits in Singapore (including the deposits and borrowings from any other bank at that bank).

(2) A loan or advance secured solely by a mortgage, deed of trust, or other such instrument upon immovable property or by notes or other obligations which are so secured, is, for the purpose of subsection (1) of this section, a loan or advance secured by immovable property; a loan or advance secured in part by mortgage, deed of trust, or other instrument upon immovable property, or by notes or other obligations which are so secured, or by any other form of security, is, for the purposes of this subsection, a loan or advance secured by immovable property to the extent, but only to the extent, of the value of that immovable property as a security as determined by the Authority.

(3) Nothing in this section shall be construed to prohibit any bank from accepting as security for a loan or advance made in good faith without security or upon security subsequently found to be inadequate, a mortgage, deed of trust, or other instrument upon immovable property, or notes or other obligations which are so secured.

(4) The provisions of this section do not apply to the Development Bank of Singapore, Limited.

(5) Any bank which contravenes the provisions of subsection (1) of this section shall be guilty of an offence under this Act.

Liquidation of prohibited transactions.

**30.**—(1) Subject to this Act any bank which, before the date of the coming into operation of this Act, has entered into any transaction contrary to any of the provisions of sections 25, 26, 27, 28 and 29 of this Act shall, within six months of that date, submit a statement of the transaction to the Authority and shall furthermore, within that time or such further time as the Authority may specify, liquidate the transaction or come within the limitations prescribed by those sections and dispose of any property or right that may have been acquired thereby.

(2) Any bank which fails to comply with the provisions of subsection (1) of this section shall be guilty of an offence under this Act.

Deductions for purposes of sections 25, 27 and 28.

**31.** For the purposes of sections 25, 27 and 28 of this Act there shall be deducted from the capital funds of the bank any debit balance appearing in the profit and loss account of the bank.

Proof of compliance with section 25, 27, 28 or 29.

**32.** Any bank, if at any time called upon in writing by the Authority so to do, shall satisfy the Authority by the production of such evidence or information as it may require, that the bank is not in contravention of any of the provisions of section 25, 27, 28 or 29 of this Act.

33.—(1) Any bank whose head office is situated outside Singapore may apply in writing to the Authority for an order relieving that bank from the restrictions or limitations imposed by sections 25, 27 and 28 of this Act in relation to any transactions referred to in those sections and the Authority may make such an order subject to such conditions as it thinks fit.

Relief from limitations imposed by sections 25, 27 and 28.

(2) The Authority shall make an order under subsection (1) of this section only if it is satisfied that the making of the order is in the interests of the creditors and depositors of the bank.

(3) An order made by the Authority under subsection (1) of this section shall be effective for such period as the Authority may decide and shall cease to have effect on such date as may be specified in the order except that no order may be made which is expressed to have effect for a period longer than two years from the date of the coming into operation of this Act.

(4) The Authority may make an order under subsection (1) of this section in respect of transactions entered into by the bank before or after the commencement of this Act.

## PART VI. MINIMUM ASSET REQUIREMENTS

34.—(1) The Authority may, from time to time, prescribe by notice in writing a minimum amount or amounts of liquid assets to be held by banks.

Minimum liquid assets.

(2) The minimum amount or amounts of the assets so prescribed to be held shall be expressed in the form of a percentage or percentages which those assets shall bear to the sight, savings account, time and other liabilities of each bank, either jointly or separately, and the percentage or percentages may be varied by the Authority by notice in writing.

(3) Whenever the Authority issues a notice under subsection (1) of this section, each bank shall be allowed such uniform period of grace, being not less than one month, as may be specified in the notice, in which to comply with its provisions.

(4) A bank shall not, during any period in which it has failed to comply with any notice under subsection (1) of this section, without the approval of the Authority, grant further advances to any person.

(5) For the purpose of computing the minimum amount or amounts of liquid assets under this section and specified assets under section 36

of this Act, and the sight, savings account, time and other liabilities of a bank carrying on business in Singapore and elsewhere, the offices and branches of the bank in Singapore shall be deemed to constitute a separate bank carrying on business in Singapore.

(6) For the purposes of this section liquid assets are—

*(a)* notes and coin which are legal tender in Singapore;
*(b)* balances with the Authority;
*(c)* balances with banks in Singapore, after deducting therefrom balances held for banks in Singapore;
*(d)* net money at call in Singapore;
*(e)* Treasury bills issued by the Government and maturing within three months (exclusive of days of grace); and
*(f)* such other assets as the Authority may from time to time approve.

(7) The Authority may by notice in writing require each bank to render such returns as the Authority deems necessary for the implementation of this section.

(8) Any bank that fails to comply with any of the provisions of this section shall be liable to pay, on being called upon to do so by the Authority, a penalty interest charge of not more than one-tenth of one per cent of the amount of the deficiency for every day during which the deficiency continues.

(9) Any bank that fails or refuses to pay a penalty interest charge under subsection (8) of this section shall be guilty of an offence under this Act.

Minimum cash balances.

35.—(1) The Authority may from time to time require banks to maintain minimum cash balances, not exceeding thirty per cent of each bank's deposit and other liabilities, on deposit with the Authority as reserves against their deposit and other liabilities.

(2) Subject to the limit specified in subsection (1) of this section, the Authority may prescribe different ratios for different types of liabilities and may further prescribe the method of computing the amount of the required reserves, but the ratios shall be uniform for all banks.

(3) Any prescription of, or change in, the minimum reserve requirements under subsection (1) or (2) of this section shall take effect only after the expiration of thirty days' notice to the banks of the Authority's intention to take such action.

(4) Where a bank (in this section referred to as "the defaulting bank") has failed to maintain sufficient minimum cash balances required

under subsection (1) of this section the Authority may by order in writing direct the defaulting bank to make good the deficiency within the period specified in the order and the defaulting bank shall comply with the requirements of the order.

(5) If the defaulting bank fails to make good the deficiency within the period specified in the order referred to in subsection (4) of this section it shall be lawful, notwithstanding the provisions of any other written law, for the Authority to serve a notice in writing upon any other bank with which the defaulting bank has a credit balance, whether in current or deposit account, directing that bank to transfer to the Authority such amount as is specified in the notice as being equivalent to the amount of the deficiency in the minimum cash balances of the defaulting bank required under subsection (1) of this section and the other bank shall immediately comply with the requirements of that notice.

(6) No action shall lie against, and no liability shall attach to, any bank that complies with the requirements of a notice referred to in subsection (5) of this section for any loss or damage suffered by the defaulting bank as a result of the other bank taking action in compliance with the requirements of that notice.

(7) The Authority may, in addition to any action taken under subsections (4) and (5) of this section, impose on any bank that fails to maintain sufficient minimum cash balances required under subsection (1) of this section a penalty interest charge of not more than one-tenth of one per cent per day of the amount of the deficiency for every day during which the deficiency continues.

(8) Any bank that fails or refuses to pay a penalty interest charge under subsection (7) of this section shall be guilty of an offence under this Act.

Minimum asset requirement.

36.—(1) The Authority may require banks to maintain a minimum amount or amounts of assets specified in subsection (2) of this section to be held by banks in Singapore expressed as a percentage or percentages which such assets shall bear to the sight, savings account, time and other liabilities of each bank either jointly or separately.

(2) For the purposes of subsection (1) of this section, the specified assets are—

*(a)* the assets specified in paragraphs *(a)* to *(f)* of subsection (6) of section 34 of this Act;

*(b)* loans or advances made to persons in Singapore;

*(c)* securities issued by the Government, or by any public authority established by any law, and any other securities issued in Singapore and approved for the purposes of this section by the Authority; and

*(d)* other assets in Singapore which may be approved by the Authority for the purposes of this section.

(3) Any bank which fails to comply with any of the requirements of the Authority under the provisions of subsection (1) of this section shall be guilty of an offence under this Act and shall be liable on conviction to a fine not exceeding five thousand dollars and in the case of a continuing offence to a further fine of one thousand dollars for every day during which the offence continues after conviction.

## PART VII. POWERS OF CONTROL OVER BANKS

Regulation of interest rates of banks.

37.—(1) The Authority may from time to time determine and announce the rates of interest payable to or by banks, the rates of discount chargeable by banks, or the rates of commission and other charges payable to banks.

(2) The provisions of subsection (1) of this section do not apply to transactions between banks in Singapore.

Recommendations to banks concerning credits and investments.

38.—(1) The Authority may, in respect of loans and advances or investments of banks, make recommendations to the banks in respect of the following:—

*(a)* the purposes for which they may or may not be granted or made;

*(b)* the maximum maturities or, in the case of loans and advances, the type and minimum amount of security which shall be required and, in the case of letters of credit, the minimum or margin deposit; or

*(c)* the limits for any particular category of loans, advances or investments or for the total amount outstanding in respect of such loans, advances or investments.

(2) Any recommendation made under subsection (1) of this section shall apply uniformly to all banks engaging in the transactions covered by the recommendation.

(3) Where the Authority has made a recommendation under subsection (1) of this section and the banks have accepted it without objections, or have failed to notify the Authority of their objections or

have failed to forward their representations to it within the time specified in subsection (4) of this section, it may issue a direction in writing to each bank on any of the matters referred to in subsection (1) of this section requiring that effect be given to the recommendation within a reasonable time, and the banks shall comply with that direction.

(4) Where the Authority has made a recommendation and the banks have, or any bank has, notified the Authority within fourteen days of the receipt of the recommendation that the banks, or any bank, objects to the recommendation, it shall call upon the banks or bank, as the case may be, to make representations in writing within one month of the notification concerning those objections.

(5) Upon receipt of such representations the Authority shall consider them and may—

*(a)* reject the representations; or

*(b)* amend or modify the recommendation in accordance with the representations, or otherwise,

and in either event, it shall thereupon issue a direction in writing to the banks or bank, as the case may be, requiring that effect be given to the original recommendation or to the recommendation as subsequently amended or modified by the Authority within a reasonable time, and the banks or any bank, as the case may be, shall comply with that direction.

(6) The provisions of this section do not apply to the Development Bank of Singapore, Limited.

Inspection of banks.

39. The Authority shall, from time to time, inspect under conditions of secrecy, the books, accounts and transactions of each bank and of any branch, agency or office outside Singapore opened by a bank incorporated in Singapore.

Special investigation of banks.

40.—(1) The Authority may at any time make an investigation, under conditions of secrecy, of the books, accounts and transactions of any bank, if it has reason to believe that any bank is carrying on its business in a manner likely to be detrimental to the interest of its depositors and other creditors, or has insufficient assets to cover its liabilities to the public, or is contravening the provisions of this Act.

(2) The Authority may appoint an auditor, other than the auditor appointed by the bank or the Authority under section 53 of this Act, to exercise the powers of the Authority under section 39 of this Act and subsection (1) of this section.

Production of bank's books, accounts and documents.

41.—(1) For the purposes of an inspection or investigation under section 39 or 40 of this Act, the bank under inspection or investigation shall afford the Authority access to and shall produce its books, accounts and documents and shall give such information and facilities as may be required to conduct the investigation:

Provided that those books, accounts and documents shall not be required to be produced at such times or at such places as would interfere with the proper conduct of the normal daily business of that bank.

(2) If any book, account or document or information is not produced in accordance with subsection (1) of this section, it shall be presumed subject to satisfactory evidence being furnished by the bank justifying such a refusal to produce that book, account or document or information, that the bank concerned has been carrying on business in contravention of the terms of its licence with effect from that day and shall be liable on conviction to a fine not exceeding five thousand dollars and in the case of a continuing offence to a further fine of one thousand dollars for every day during which the offence continues after conviction.

Banking secrecy.

42.—(1) Except as provided in sections 40 and 41 of this Act, nothing in this Act authorizes the Authority to inquire specifically into the affairs of any individual customer of any bank and any incidental information relating to the affairs of an individual customer obtained by the Authority in the course of an inspection or investigation made by it under the provisions of this Act shall be secret between the Authority and that bank:

Provided that nothing in this section shall be deemed to limit any powers conferred upon the High Court or a Judge thereof by Part IV of the Evidence Act or to prohibit obedience to an order made under that Part.

(2) No official of any bank and no person who by reason of his capacity or office has by any means access to the records of the bank registers or any correspondence or material with regard to the account of any individual customer of that bank shall give, divulge or reveal any information whatsoever regarding the moneys or other relevant particulars of the account of that customer to—

(*a*) any person who, or any bank, corporation or body of persons which, is not resident in Singapore; or

(*b*) any foreign government or organization, unless—

(i) the customer or his personal representatives gives or give his or their permission so to do;

(ii) the customer is declared bankrupt; or

(iii) the information is required to assess the creditworthiness of the customer in connection with or relating to a bona fide commercial transaction or a prospective commercial transaction.

(3) For the purposes of paragraph *(a)* of subsection (2) of this section a bank, corporation or body of persons shall be regarded as not residing in Singapore if the control and management of the business thereof is exercised outside Singapore.

(4) Any person who contravenes the provisions of this section shall be guilty of an offence under this Act and shall be liable on conviction to a fine of ten thousand dollars or to imprisonment for a term not exceeding three years or to both such fine and imprisonment.

Information of insolvency, etc.

43. Any bank which considers that it is, or is likely to become, unable to meet its obligations, or is insolvent, or is about to suspend payments, shall forthwith inform the Authority of that fact.

Action by Authority if bank is unable to meet obligations, etc., or is conducting business to the detriment of depositors.

44.—(1) Where—

*(a)* a bank informs the Authority that it is likely to become unable to meet its obligations, or that it is insolvent, or about to suspend payments;

*(b)* a bank becomes unable to meet its obligations, or is insolvent, or suspends payments;

*(c)* after an inspection or investigation is made under section 39 or 40 of this Act, the Authority is of the opinion that the bank—

(i) is carrying on its business in a manner likely to be detrimental to the interest of its depositors or its creditors;

(ii) is insolvent or is likely to become unable to meet its obligations or is about to suspend payment;

(iii) has contravened or failed to comply with any of the provisions of this Act; or

(iv) has contravened or failed to comply with any condition attached to its licence; or

*(d)* the Authority considers it in the public interest to do so,

the Authority may exercise such one or more of the powers specified in subsection (2) of this section as appears to it to be necessary.

(2) Subject to subsection (1) of this section, the Authority may—

*(a)* require the bank concerned forthwith to take any action or to do or not to do any act or thing whatsoever in relation to its business as the Authority may consider necessary;

(*b*) appoint a person to advise that bank in the proper conduct of its business; or

(*c*) assume control of and carry on the business of that bank or direct some other person to assume control of and carry on the business of that bank.

(3) The Authority may, upon representation made to it or on its own motion, modify or cancel any action taken by it under subsection (2) of this section, and in so modifying or cancelling any action may impose such conditions as it thinks fit, subject to which the modification or cancellation shall have effect.

Powers of Authority.

45. Where the Authority has taken action under subsection (2) of section 44 of this Act, it may, without prejudice to the powers conferred by paragraph *(b)* of subsection (1) of section 16 of this Act, exercise one or more of the following powers, that is to say:—

(*a*) confirm, vary or reverse any requirement, appointment or direction made by it;

(*b*) make such order as it may think fit in relation to the affairs of the bank and exercise any power which it may exercise under subsection (2) of section 44 of this Act;

(*c*) present a petition to the High Court for the winding up of the bank by the High Court.

Duration of control.

46.—(1) Where the Authority has assumed control of the business of a bank in pursuance of section 44 of this Act it shall remain in control of, and continue to carry on, the business of that bank in the name and on behalf of the bank until such time as it is satisfied that the reasons for which it assumed control of the business have ceased to exist, or that it is no longer necessary for the protection of the depositors of the bank that it should remain in control of the business.

(2) Where the Authority has assumed control of the business of a bank in pursuance of section 44 of this Act or ceased to control the business of a bank in pursuance of this section, it shall notify that fact in the *Gazette.*

Bank under control of Authority to co-operate with Authority.

47.—(1) Where the Authority has assumed control of the business of a bank in pursuance of section 44 of this Act the bank shall submit its business to the control of the Authority and shall provide the Authority with such facilities as it may require to carry on the business of that bank.

(2) Any bank which fails to comply with subsection (1) of this section or with any requirement of the Authority thereunder shall be

guilty of an offence under this Act and shall be liable on conviction to a fine not exceeding five thousand dollars and in the case of a continuing offence to a further fine of one thousand dollars for every day during which the offence continues after conviction.

Remuneration and expenses of Authority and others in certain cases.

48.—(1) The Authority may at any time (whether or not the appointment of such person has terminated) fix the remuneration and expenses to be paid by a bank to any person appointed by the Authority under subsection (2) of section 44 or section 45 of this Act to advise the bank in the proper conduct of its business.

(2) Where, under paragraph *(c)* of subsection (2) of section 44 or paragraph *(b)* of section 45 of this Act, the Authority has assumed control of the business of a bank or some other person has assumed control of the business of a bank pursuant to a direction or order of the Authority, the Authority may, at any time, whether or not it or that other person has ceased to be in control of the business of the bank, fix the remuneration and expenses to be paid by the bank to the Authority and to any person employed or authorized by it under section 3 of this Act to assist it in the control of and the carrying on of the business of the bank, or to that other person, as the case may be.

Moratorium.

49.—(1) The Authority may, if it considers it to be in the interests of the depositors of a bank make an order prohibiting that bank from carrying on banking business or from doing or performing any act or function connected with banking business or any aspect thereof that may be specified in the order.

(2) The Authority may, if it considers it to be in the interests of the depositors of a bank, apply to the High Court for an order staying the commencement or continuance of any proceedings by or against the bank in regard to any business of the bank. Such an order shall be valid for a period not exceeding six months.

(3) So long as an order under subsection (1) of this section remains in force the licence granted to that bank under this Act shall be suspended.

## Part VIII. Numbered Accounts

Banks may with the approval of the Authority open numbered accounts.

50.—(1) For the purposes of this Part, the expression "numbered accounts" means accounts opened with banks in Singapore that are identifiable only by a number or code word or by such other means as the Authority may determine.

(2) No bank in Singapore shall open numbered accounts for its customers except with the prior approval in writing of the Authority which may attach such limitations, conditions, qualifications and exceptions thereto as it thinks fit.

(3) Any bank which contravenes the provisions of subsection (2) of this section shall be guilty of an offence under this Act and shall be liable on conviction to a fine not exceeding ten thousand dollars.

Types of numbered accounts.

51.—(1) Numbered accounts facilities offered by banks to their customers may extend to current accounts, deposit accounts, securities deposit accounts and safes, but shall not extend to credit facilities.

(2) The owners of the numbered accounts shall only be known to such senior officers of the bank as the bank may decide.

Secrecy of numbered accounts.

52.—(1) The officials of any bank operating numbered accounts on behalf of its customers or any person who by reason of his capacity or office has by any means access to the records of the bank, registers, correspondence or any other material with regard to numbered accounts shall keep absolute secrecy thereof in the interests of the bank's customers.

(2) The officials of any bank and other persons mentioned in subsection (1) of this section shall not give, divulge or reveal any information whatsoever regarding the name or identity of the owner of a numbered account to any individual, corporation, bank, public administration, judicial or military authorities unless—

(*a*) the owner of the numbered account or his personal representatives gives or give his or their permission so to do;
(*b*) the owner is declared bankrupt;
(*c*) a suit arises between the bank and the owner relating to a banking transaction; or
(*d*) the owner is required so to do by order of a Judge of the Supreme Court made for special cause for the purposes of any civil or criminal proceedings.

(3) Part IV of the Evidence Act does not apply to numbered accounts.

(4) Any person who contravenes the provisions of this section shall be guilty of an offence under this Act and shall be liable on conviction to a fine of ten thousand dollars or to imprisonment for a term not exceeding three years or to both such fine and imprisonment.

## PART IX. MISCELLANEOUS

53.—(1) Notwithstanding the provisions of the Companies Act, every bank shall appoint annually an auditor approved by the Authority. Auditing.

(2) The Authority may appoint an auditor—

*(a)* if the bank fails to appoint an auditor; or
*(b)* if it considers it desirable that another auditor should act with the auditor appointed under subsection (1) of this section,

and may, at any time, fix the remuneration to be paid by the bank to that auditor.

(3) The duties of an auditor appointed under subsections (1) and (2) of this section shall be—

*(a)* to carry out, for the year in respect of which he is appointed, an audit of the accounts of the bank; and
*(b)* to make a report in accordance with section 174 of the Companies Act—
  (i) in the case of a bank incorporated in Singapore—upon the annual balance-sheets and profit and loss accounts that are referred to in subsections (1) and (3) of section 21 of this Act; and
  (ii) in the case of a bank incorporated outside Singapore—upon the annual balance-sheet and profit and loss account that are referred to in subsection (3) of section 21 of this Act.

(4) The auditor's report shall be attached to the balance-sheet and the profit and loss account and a copy thereof shall be sent to the Authority.

54. In order to facilitate the clearing of cheques and other credit instruments for banks carrying on business in Singapore, the Authority shall, in conjunction with banks operating in Singapore, by regulations, establish a Clearing House. Clearing House and settlement of balances between banks.

55.—(1) The Authority may, at any time by notice in the *Gazette,* declare any day or days to be a bank holiday or holidays. Declaration of holidays.

(2) No bank shall do any business with the public on any day declared a bank holiday under the provisions of subsection (1) of this section.

(3) A bank holiday declared under the provisions of subsection (1) of this section shall not necessarily be a public holiday and nothing in

this section shall be deemed to affect the provisions of any written law which may from time to time be in force in Singapore relating to public holidays.

(4) Any reference to a bank holiday in any written law which may from time to time be in force in Singapore shall include any day declared to be a bank holiday under the provisions of this section and any day which is a public holiday within the meaning of any written law which may be in force in Singapore relating to public holidays.

Priority of deposit liabilities.

56. Where a bank becomes unable to meet its obligations or becomes insolvent or suspends payment, the assets of that bank in Singapore shall be available to meet all deposit liabilities of the bank in Singapore; and such deposit liabilities shall have priority over all other liabilities of the bank.

Execution of instruments under seal.

57. Notwithstanding anything contained in the articles of association or regulations of any bank incorporated in Singapore with respect to the execution of instruments under its seal, but without prejudice to anything in such articles or regulations not inconsistent herewith, the seal of the bank shall not be affixed to any instrument except in the presence of a director of the bank and of one other person being either a director or an officer of the bank duly authorized in that behalf, and the director and that other person as aforesaid shall sign every instrument to which the seal of the company is so affixed in their presence.

Disqualification of directors and employees of banks.

58. Notwithstanding the provisions of any other written law, any person—

*(a)* who is or becomes bankrupt, suspends payments or compounds with his creditors; or

*(b)* who is or has been convicted in any country of an offence involving dishonesty or fraud and has not received a free pardon for the offence for which he was convicted; or

*(c)* who has been a director of, or directly concerned in the management of, a bank licensed under this Act or which was licensed under the Banking Ordinance, 1958, (repealed by this Act) which is being or has been wound up by a court or the licence of which has been revoked,

shall not, without the consent in writing of the Authority, act or continue to act as the director, manager, secretary or other officer in any bank.

Offences by directors or managers.

59.—(1) Any person being a director, managing director or manager of a bank who—

(*a*) fails to take all reasonable steps to secure compliance by a bank with the provisions of this Act or any other written law applicable to banks in Singapore; or

(*b*) fails to take all reasonable steps to secure the accuracy and correctness of any statement submitted under this Act or of any other written law applicable to banks in Singapore,

shall be guilty of an offence under this Act and shall, in respect of each offence, be liable on conviction to imprisonment for a term not exceeding two years or to a fine not exceeding three thousand dollars or to both such imprisonment and fine.

(2) In any proceedings against a person under subsection (1) of this section it shall be a defence to prove that he had reasonable grounds for believing that another person was charged with the duty of securing compliance with the requirements of those laws or with the duty of ensuring that those statements were accurate and that that person was competent and in a position to discharge that duty.

(3) A person shall not be sentenced to imprisonment for any offence under subsection (1) of this section unless, in the opinion of the court, he committed the offence wilfully.

Offences by directors, employees and agents.

60. Any director, manager, trustee, auditor, employee or agent of any bank who—

(*a*) wilfully makes or causes to be made, a false entry in any book of record or in any report, slip, document or statement of the business, affairs, transactions, conditions, assets or accounts of that bank;

(*b*) wilfully omits to make an entry in any book of record or in any report, slip, document or statement of the business, affairs, transactions, conditions, assets or accounts of that bank, or wilfully causes any such entry to be omitted; or

(*c*) wilfully alters, abstracts, conceals or destroys an entry in any book of record or in any report, slip, document or statement of the business, affairs, transactions, conditions, assets or accounts of that bank, or wilfully causes any such entry to be altered, abstracted, concealed or destroyed,

shall be guilty of an offence under this Act and shall be liable on conviction to a fine not exceeding ten thousand dollars or to imprisonment for a term not exceeding three years or to both such fine and imprisonment.

Indemnity.

61. No liability is incurred by—

(*a*) any public officer;

(*b*) any person authorized or employed by the Authority under section 3 of this Act;

(*c*) any person appointed under paragraph (*b*) of subsection (2) of section 44 of this Act to advise a bank in the proper conduct of its business;

(*d*) any person who has assumed control of the business of a bank pursuant to a direction or order of the Authority under paragraph (*c*) of subsection (2) of section 44 or paragraph (*b*) of section 45 of this Act; or

(*e*) any person appointed under subsection (2) of section 40 of this Act,

as a result of anything done by him bona fide in the exercise of any power, or the performance of any function or duty, conferred or imposed by or under this Act.

Power to compound.

62. The Authority may, without instituting proceedings against any person for any offence under this Act, or any regulations made thereunder, which is punishable only by a fine or a default penalty, demand and receive the amount of the fine or default penalty or such reduced amount as it thinks fit from that person, whereupon—

(*a*) if the person pays that amount to the Authority within fourteen days after the demand, no proceedings shall be taken against him in relation to the offence; or

(*b*) if the person does not so pay the amount so demanded, the Authority may cause proceedings to be instituted in relation to the offence.

Publication of list of banks.

63. The Authority shall cause to be published in the *Gazette* in the month of April in each year a list of all banks to which licences have been issued under this Act and if any licence is issued, revoked or surrendered during the interval between the publication of two such lists, notice thereof shall also be caused to be published in the *Gazette*.

General penalty.

64. Any bank which contravenes or fails to comply with any provisions of this Act for which no penalty is expressly provided shall be guilty of an offence under this Act and shall be liable on conviction to a fine not exceeding fifty thousand dollars.

Offences triable in District Court.

65. Notwithstanding the provisions of any other written law, offences under this Act may be tried in a District Court, which shall have

the power to impose the maximum penalty prescribed for any offence under this Act.

**66.** No prosecution in respect of any offence under this Act shall be instituted except with the consent of the Attorney-General.

Consent of Attorney-General.

**67.** There shall be recoverable as a civil debt due to the Authority from the bank concerned—

Recovery of fees, expenses, etc.

*(a)* the amount of any fees payable under sections 8 and 13 of this Act;

*(b)* any remuneration and expenses payable by the bank to any person appointed under paragraph *(b)* of subsection (2) of section 44 of this Act; and

*(c)* any remuneration and expenses payable by the bank to the Authority or to any person employed or authorized by the Authority under section 3 of this Act to assist it in the control of and the carrying on of the business of the bank or to any other person who has assumed control of the business of the bank pursuant to a direction or order of the Authority under paragraph *(c)* of subsection (2) of section 44 or paragraph *(b)* of section 45 of this Act or to any person appointed under subsection (2) of section 40 of this Act.

**68.** Nothing in this Act affects the operation of the Companies Act, and any bank that is liable to be incorporated under that Act continues to be so liable as if this Act had not been passed but in case of conflict between that Act and this Act the provisions of this Act prevail unless otherwise provided in this Act.

Operation of Act not to affect the Companies Act.

**69.** This Act does not apply to the Post Office Savings Bank established under the Post Office Savings Bank Act or to any co-operative society registered under the Co-operative Societies Act or to any business of pawnbroking carried on by a person licensed under the Pawnbrokers Act or to finance companies licensed under the Finance Companies Act.

Exemption.

**70.** The Authority may make such regulations from time to time as it may deem necessary for carrying into effect the provisions of this Act.

Regulations.

**71.** All regulations, instructions, orders and decisions made under or in accordance with the Banking Ordinance, 1958, as amended and extended by the Banking (Amendment and Extension) Act, 1965, re-

Saving.

main valid and binding and shall be deemed to have been made under the provisions of this Act until they are amended or repealed.

## PART X. TRANSITIONAL

Transitional licensing provisions.

72.—(1) Notwithstanding the provisions of sections 4 and 9 of this Act, any bank specified in the Fourth Schedule [5] to this Act which on 1st January 1970 was carrying on banking business in Singapore shall, upon the date of the coming into operation of this Act, be granted a licence under this Act, which may be made subject to such conditions, if any, as are contained in any licence under which the bank was carrying on banking business in Singapore immediately before that date.

(2) Any bank which is granted a licence under the provisions of this section shall comply with the provisions of section 9 of this Act within a period of two years from the date of the coming into operation of this Act.

(3) If any bank licensed under the provisions of this section fails to comply with the provisions of section 9 of this Act in accordance with subsection (2) of this section, the licence granted to it under this section shall become null and void except insofar as may be necessary for the purpose of winding up its banking business.

(4) The Authority may, in any particular case, extend the period provided by subsection (2) of this section and the period of validity of the licence concerned.

*{The four Schedules are omitted from this volume.}*

[5] Not published in this volume.

# Finance Companies Act[1]

An Act to license and control finance companies and for matters connected therewith.

[10th January, 1968]

## PART I. PRELIMINARY

1. This Act may be cited as the Finance Companies Act. Short title.

2. In this Act, unless the context otherwise requires— Interpretation.

"auditor" means any person approved by the Authority as a finance company auditor for the purposes of this Act;

"the Authority" means the Monetary Authority of Singapore established under section 3 of the Monetary Authority of Singapore Act[2];

"company" means a company incorporated or registered under the Companies Act or pursuant to any corresponding previous written law;

"deposit" means a loan of money at interest or repayable at a premium but does not include a loan to a company or other body corporate upon terms involving the issue of debentures or other securities;

"depositor" means a person entitled, or prospectively entitled, to repayment of a deposit whether made by him or not;

"director" includes any person occupying the position of director of a finance company by whatever name called and includes a person in accordance with whose directions or instructions the directors of a finance company are accustomed to act and an alternate or substitute director;

"finance company" means any company licensed under this Act to carry on financing business, and all branches and offices in Singapore of such a company shall be deemed to be one finance company for the purposes of this Act;

"financing business" means the business of—

---

[1] *Singapore Statutes,* Cap. 191 (1970). Originally Act No. 43 of 1967. Relevant citation: No. 21 of 1969.

[2] In accordance with the version published in *Singapore Statutes,* Cap. 191 (1970), references formerly in this Act to the Minister, the Commissioner for Finance Companies, and the Accountant-General have, in accordance with sec. 21 (4) of the Monetary Authority of Singapore Act (Cap. 195), been replaced by references to the Authority, and various consequential alterations have been made.

(*a*) borrowing money from the public, by acceptance of deposits and issuing certificates or other documents acknowledging or evidencing indebtedness to the public and undertaking to repay the money on call or after an agreed maturity period; and

(*b*) lending money to the public or to a company deemed to be related to the finance company by virtue of section 6 of the Companies Act (in this Act referred to as the "related company") on the basis that the public or the related company undertakes to repay the money, whether within an agreed period of time or not, or by instalments,

and includes the business of financing hire-purchase transactions arising out of hire-purchase agreements, as defined in the Hire-Purchase Act, where the money used, or to be used, for such business is borrowed from the public;

"public company" means a company incorporated in Singapore other than a private company.

## PART II. LICENSING OF FINANCE COMPANIES

Licensing of finance companies.

3. (1) No financing business shall be transacted in Singapore except by a public company that is in possession of a valid licence granted by the Authority authorising it to conduct financing business in accordance with the provisions of this Act.

(2) Any person who contravenes the provisions of subsection (1) of this section shall be guilty of an offence under this Act and shall be liable on conviction to imprisonment for a term not exceeding three years or to a fine not exceeding five thousand dollars or to both such imprisonment and fine.

Use of words "finance company".

4. No person or body of persons, whether incorporated or not, other than a finance company licensed under this Act shall, without the consent of the Authority, use the words "finance company" or any of its derivatives in any language, or any other words indicating that it transacts financing business, in the name, description or title under which such person or body of persons is transacting business in Singapore or make or continue to make any representations to such effect in any bill-head, letter paper, notice, advertisement or in any other manner whatsoever:

Provided that nothing in this section shall prohibit an association of finance companies formed for the protection of common interests from using the words "finance company" or any of its derivatives in any language as part of its name or description of its activities.

Examination of persons suspected of transacting financing business.

5. (1) Whenever the Authority has reason to believe that a person is conducting financing business without a licence, it may call for the books, accounts and records of such person in order to ascertain whether or not such person has violated or is violating any provisions of this Act, and any person wilfully refusing to submit such books, accounts and records shall be guilty of an offence under this Act and shall be liable on conviction to imprisonment for a term not exceeding one year or to a fine not exceeding one thousand dollars or to both such imprisonment and fine.

(2) Upon the conviction of any person under subsection (1) of this section a District Court shall have power to order the production of any books, accounts and records to the Authority and any person failing to comply with such order shall be guilty of an offence under this Act and shall be liable on conviction to imprisonment for a term not exceeding one year or to a fine not exceeding one thousand dollars or to both such imprisonment and fine and, in the case of a continuing offence, to a fine not exceeding one hundred dollars for each day during which the offence continues.

Application for licence.

6. (1) As from the date of the coming into operation of this Act, any public company proposing to conduct financing business in Singapore shall, before commencing any such business, apply in writing to the Authority for a licence under this Act.

(2) In considering any application by a public company for a licence the Authority may require to be satisfied as to—

(*a*) the financial condition of the company;

(*b*) the character of the management of the company;

(*c*) the adequacy of the capital structure and earning prospects of the company;

(*d*) the objects of the company as disclosed in its memorandum of association;

(*e*) the convenience and needs of the community to be served; and

(*f*) whether the public interest will be served by the granting of a licence.

(3) The Authority may grant a licence with or without conditions, or refuse to grant a licence.

(4) The Authority may at any time vary or revoke any existing conditions of a licence or impose additional conditions.

(5) Where a licence is granted subject to conditions the finance company shall comply with those conditions and any finance company that fails to comply with any conditions of its licence shall be guilty of an offence under this Act and shall be liable on conviction to a fine not exceeding five thousand dollars.

Minimum capital requirements of a finance company.

7. Subject to the provisions of this Act, no finance company shall be granted or shall hold a licence unless its capital, issued and paid up in cash, and unimpaired by losses or otherwise, is not less than five hundred thousand dollars.

Restriction on opening of branches of a finance company.

8. (1) No finance company shall open any new branch, agency or office, whether inside or outside Singapore, without submitting an application in writing to the Authority.

(2) In considering such application, the Authority may require to be satisfied by an inspection under section 26 of this Act or otherwise, as to—

*(a)* the financial condition of the company;
*(b)* the general character of the management of the company;
*(c)* the adequacy of the capital structure and earning prospects of the company;
*(d)* the convenience and needs of the community to be served; and
*(e)* whether the public interest will be served by the opening or, as the case may be, change of location of the place of business.

(3) Upon being so satisfied as to the matters referred to in subsection (2) of this section, the Authority may—

*(a)* grant the application; or
*(b)* without assigning any reason therefor, refuse to grant the application,

and its decision thereon shall be final.

(4) Any finance company that fails to comply with subsection (1) of this section shall be guilty of an offence under this Act and shall be liable on conviction to a fine not exceeding five hundred dollars for every day during which the default continues.

Mergers, etc., of a finance company.

9. (1) No finance company carrying on business in Singapore shall be merged or consolidated with or acquire a majority interest in any other finance company without the prior approval of the Authority.

(2) In considering such an application, the Authority shall have power to call for such information as it may require.

(3) The Authority may—

(*a*) approve the application; or

(*b*) refuse the application.

Amendment of constitution of a finance company.

**10.** (1) Every finance company that intends to alter its memorandum of association or articles of association shall, before proposing any resolution in this regard, furnish to the Authority for its approval particulars in writing (verified by a statutory declaration made by the secretary of the finance company) of the proposed alteration.

(2) The Authority may thereupon—

(*a*) approve the proposed alteration without modification;

(*b*) approve the proposed alteration with modification; or

(*c*) refuse to approve the proposed alteration.

(3) If the Authority approves the proposed alteration with modification, the finance company shall adopt the proposed alteration as so modified or not proceed with the proposed alteration and if the Authority refuses to approve the proposed alteration it may request the finance company to withdraw the proposed alteration and the finance company shall comply with the Authority's request.

(4) Any finance company which fails to comply with the requirements of subsection (1) of this section or with any request by the Authority made under subsection (3) of this section shall be guilty of an offence under this Act and shall be liable on conviction to a fine not exceeding three hundred dollars for every day during which the default continues.

Revocation of licence.

**11.** (1) The Authority—

(*a*) shall, by order, revoke the licence of a finance company if the company ceases to carry on the business for which it has been licensed in Singapore or goes into liquidation or is wound up or otherwise dissolved;

(*b*) may, in its discretion, by order, revoke the licence of a finance company if, in its opinion, the finance company—

(i) is carrying on its business in a manner likely to be detrimental to the interests of its depositors;

(ii) has insufficient assets to cover its liabilities to its depositors;

(iii) carries on business while its paid-up capital (unimpaired by losses or otherwise) is less than five hundred thousand dollars; or

(iv) is contravening or has contravened the provisions of this Act; and

(*c*) may, also in its discretion, by order, revoke the licence of a finance company—

(i) if the finance company or any person who is in a managerial or executive position in that finance company has been convicted of any offence under this Act; or

(ii) if it considers it in the public interest to do so:

Provided that before revoking any licence, the Authority shall give the finance company notice in writing of its intention to do so, specifying a date, not less than twenty-one days after the date of the notice, upon which such revocation will take effect and calling upon the finance company to show cause to the Authority why such licence should not be revoked.

(2) Where the Authority has revoked a licence under the provisions of subsection (1) of this section, it shall forthwith inform the finance company by notice in writing of such revocation.

Publication of list of finance companies.

12. The Authority shall cause to be published in the *Gazette* in the month of April in each year a list of all finance companies to which licences have been issued under this Act and if any licence is issued or revoked during the interval between the publication of two such lists, notice thereof shall also be caused to be published in the *Gazette*.

## PART III. RESERVE FUNDS, DIVIDENDS, BALANCE SHEETS AND INFORMATION

Maintenance of reserve fund by finance companies.

13. Every finance company shall—

(*a*) maintain a reserve fund;

(*b*) if the paid-up capital of the finance company is not less than two million dollars, transfer to such reserve fund out of the net profits of each year after due provision has been made for taxation—

(i) so long as the amount of the reserve fund is less than fifty per cent of the paid-up capital, a sum equal to not less than thirty per cent of the net profits;

(ii) so long as the amount of the reserve fund is not less than fifty per cent but less than one hundred per cent of the paid-up capital, a sum equal to not less than fifteen per cent of the net profits;

(iii) so long as the amount of the reserve fund is not less than one hundred per cent of the paid-up capital, a sum equal to not less than five per cent of the net profits; and

(c) if the paid-up capital of the finance company is less than two million dollars, transfer to such reserve fund out of the net profits of each year after due provision has been made for taxation—

(i) so long as the amount of the reserve fund is less than fifty per cent of the paid-up capital, a sum equal to not less than fifty per cent of the net profits;

(ii) so long as the amount of the reserve fund is not less than fifty per cent but less than one hundred per cent of the paid-up capital, a sum equal to not less than twenty-five per cent of the net profits;

(iii) so long as the amount of the reserve fund is not less than one hundred per cent of the paid-up capital, a sum equal to not less than ten per cent of the net profits.

Restriction on payment of dividends by finance companies.

14. No finance company shall pay any dividend on its shares until all its capitalized expenditure (including preliminary expenses, organisation expenses, share selling commission, brokerage, amount of losses incurred and any item of expenditure not represented by tangible assets) has been completely written off.

Exhibition of balance-sheet by finance companies.

15. Every finance company shall exhibit throughout the year, in a conspicuous position in every office and branch of that finance company, a copy of its last audited balance-sheet together with the full and correct names of all persons who are directors of the finance company, as soon as such balance-sheet is audited. A copy of such balance-sheet shall be published in at least each of four local daily newspapers, printed in the Malay, Tamil, Chinese and English languages not later than six months after the end of each financial year.

In this section, the expression "financial year" shall have the same meaning as is assigned to that expression in section 4 of the Companies Act, except that for the word "corporation" therein there shall be substituted the words "finance company".

Information and statistics to be furnished by finance companies.

16. (1) Every finance company shall furnish to the Authority at such time and in such manner as the Authority may prescribe, all such information and data as it may reasonably require for the proper discharge of the Authority's functions under the provisions of this Act.

(2) Nothing in this Act shall authorise the Authority to enquire specifically into the affairs of an individual depositor of a finance company and any information relating to the affairs of such individual depositor obtained by it in the course of an inspection or investigation

made under this Act shall be secret between it and that finance company:

Provided that nothing in this section shall be deemed to limit any powers conferred upon the High Court or a Judge by Part IV of the Evidence Act or to prohibit obedience to an order made under that Part or any such law.

(3) Every finance company that fails or neglects to furnish any information required by the Authority under subsection (1) of this section and within the time specified by the Authority shall be guilty of an offence under this Act and shall be liable on conviction to a fine not exceeding one thousand dollars for every day during which the default continues.

## PART IV. REGULATION OF BUSINESS

Acknowledgment of indebtedness.

**17.** Where a finance company has accepted money from any person as a deposit the company shall within two months after the acceptance of the money issue to that person a document which acknowledges or evidences or constitutes an acknowledgment of the indebtedness of the company in respect of that deposit.

Demand deposits, dealings in foreign exchange, etc., by finance companies.

**18.** (1) No finance company shall—

*(a)* accept any deposit which is repayable on demand by cheque, draft or order drawn by a depositor on the finance company;

*(b)* deal in gold or foreign exchange of whatever kind;

*(c)* grant unsecured advances, unsecured loans or unsecured credit facilities which in the aggregate and outstanding at any one time exceed ten per cent of the paid-up share capital and published reserves of the finance company and which as regards—

(i) any individual director whether borrowing on his own account or jointly with another director;

(ii) a firm in which it or any of its directors has an interest as a partner, manager or agent, or any individual or firm of whom or of which any of its directors is a guarantor;

(iii) a corporation that is deemed to be related to the finance company as described in section 6 of the Companies Act; or

(iv) any other person or body of persons whether incorporated or not,

exceed at any time the sum of five thousand dollars; or

*(d)* grant or permit to be outstanding to any customer any advances, loans or credit facilities, or give financial guarantees or incur any

other liabilities on his behalf to an aggregate amount of such advances, loans or credit facilities, guarantees or liabilities in excess of sixty per cent of the paid-up share capital and published reserves of the finance company:

Provided that, with the approval of the Authority, the percentage referred to in this paragraph may be increased to one hundred per cent of the paid-up share capital and published reserves of the finance company.

(2) In paragraph *(c)* of subsection (1) of this section, the expressions "unsecured advances", "unsecured loans" or "unsecured credit facilities" mean advances, loans or credit facilities made without security or, in respect of any advance, loan or credit facility made with security, any part thereof which at any time exceeds the market value of the assets constituting that security, or where the Authority is satisfied that there is no established market value, on the basis of a valuation approved by the Authority.

(3) In paragraph *(c)* of subsection (1) of this section, the word "directors" includes the wife, husband, father, mother, son or daughter of a director.

(4) All the directors of a finance company shall be liable jointly and severally to indemnify a finance company against any loss arising from the making of any unsecured advance, loan or credit facility under subparagraph (i), (ii) or (iii) of paragraph *(c)* of subsection (1) of this section.

Dealing by a finance company in its own shares, etc.

**19.** (1) Except as is otherwise expressly provided by this Act, no finance company shall give, whether directly or indirectly and whether by means of a loan guarantee or the provision of security or otherwise, any financial assistance for the purpose of or in connection with a purchase or subscription made or to be made by any person of, or for, any shares in the finance company or, where such company is a subsidiary, in its holding company, or in any way purchase, deal in or lend money on its own shares.

(2) Nothing in subsection (1) of this section shall prohibit—

*(a)* the provision by a finance company, in accordance with any scheme for the time being in force, of money for the purchase of or subscription for fully-paid shares in the finance company or its holding company, being a purchase or subscription by trustees of or for shares to be held by or for the benefit of employees of such company, including any director holding a salaried employment or office in such company; or

(*b*) the giving of financial assistance by a finance company to persons, other than directors, bona fide in the employment of that company or of a subsidiary of that company with a view to enabling those persons to purchase fully-paid shares in the finance company to be held by themselves by way of beneficial ownership.

(3) If there is any contravention of this section, the finance company and every officer of such company who is in default shall be guilty of an offence under this Act and shall be liable on conviction to imprisonment for a term not exceeding one year or to a fine not exceeding two thousand dollars.

(4) Nothing in this section shall operate to prevent the finance company from recovering the amount of any loan made in contravention of this section or any amount for which it becomes liable on account of any financial assistance given in contravention of the provisions of this section.

Restrictions on trade by finance companies.

20. (1) No finance company shall engage, whether on its own account or on a commission basis, and whether alone or with others, in the wholesale or retail trade, including the import or export trade, except for the purpose of carrying on its financing business.

(2) Except as provided in this Act a finance company shall not carry on any kind of business other than financing business.

Restrictions on investments by finance companies.

21. (1) No finance company shall acquire or hold any part of the share capital of, or otherwise have a direct interest in, any financial, commercial, agricultural, industrial or other undertaking exceeding in the aggregate twenty-five per cent of the paid-up share capital and published reserves of that finance company except such shareholding as the finance company may acquire in the course of realising debts due to it, which shareholding shall, however, be disposed of at the earliest suitable moment.

(2) Notwithstanding the provisions of subsection (1) of this section, the percentage holding or interest referred to in that subsection may upon the application of a finance company to the Authority, and with the consent of the Authority, be increased to not more than fifty per cent of the paid-up share capital and published reserves of that finance company.

Restrictions on holding immovable property by finance companies.

22. (1) No finance company shall purchase or acquire any immovable property, or any right, title or interest therein exceeding in the aggregate at any one time twenty-five per cent of the finance company's paid-up share capital and published reserves, except as may be reasonably necessary for the purpose of conducting its business or of housing or providing amenities for its staff, but this shall not prevent a finance company—

(*a*) from letting part of any building which is used for the purpose of conducting its business; or

(*b*) from securing a debt on any immovable property and in the event of default in payment of such debt, from holding that immovable property for realisation by sale or auction at the earliest suitable moment.

(2) This section shall not apply to such property as may from time to time be approved by the Authority.

(3) The Registrar of Titles in issuing any certificate of title or registering any assurance in the Registry of Titles and Deeds or any purchaser shall be exonerated from enquiring as to any matter or fact relating to the title of a finance company to, or to the power of a finance company in dealing with, any immovable property, or any right, title and interest therein, which has been purchased or acquired in contravention of the prohibition contained in this section and shall be protected from the effect of notice of any such matter or fact.

Liquidation of prohibited transactions by finance companies.

23. Any company which, before the date of the coming into operation of this Act, had entered into any transaction prohibited by the provisions of sections 18, 19, 20, 21 and 22 of this Act shall, if it is licensed under this Act, within six months of that date, submit a statement of those transactions to the Authority and shall, furthermore, within the said time, or such further time as the Authority may specify, liquidate those transactions or failing liquidation of those transactions be subject to the restrictions specified in sections 18, 19, 20, 21 and 22 of this Act and be bound accordingly to dispose of any movable or immovable property, or any right, title or interest therein as may have been acquired as a result of those prohibited transactions.

Orders by the Authority.

24. (1) The Authority may, by order, prescribe—

(*a*) the maximum rates of interest that finance companies shall pay on different types or classes of deposits;

(*b*) the maximum amount or amounts, expressed as a percentage or percentages, of total assets that finance companies may hold in one or more types or classes of loans, or advances;

(*c*) the minimum down payments and maximum maturity periods for different types or classes of loans, or advances granted by finance companies;

(*d*) the maximum rates of interest or commission and other charges and the methods of computing such interest or commission and other charges that finance companies may impose on different types or classes of loans, or advances granted by them;

(*e*) the maximum amount of loans or advances which finance companies may grant to any person or class of persons; and

(*f*) the reserves to be maintained with the Authority.

(2) Any order made under subsection (1) of this section shall apply uniformly to all finance companies, or to any class or classes of finance companies, and shall, together with its effective date, be published in the *Gazette.*

## PART V. MINIMUM LIQUID ASSETS

Minimum holdings of liquid assets by finance companies.

25. (1) Every finance company shall maintain a minimum holding of liquid assets, as defined in subsection (4) of this section, but a period of six months after the date of the coming into operation of this Act shall be allowed for compliance with this requirement.

(2) The minimum amount of liquid assets to be maintained by finance companies shall be determined from time to time by the Authority and shall be expressed as a percentage of the liabilities of each finance company on account of deposits.

(3) The Authority shall prescribe the method of computing the amount of liquid assets to be held by finance companies.

(4) For the purposes of this section "liquid assets" means all or any of the following:

(*a*) notes and coins that are legal tender in Singapore;

(*b*) net balances at banks in Singapore;

(*c*) net money at call in Singapore;

(*d*) Singapore Treasury bills;

(*e*) other assets that the Authority may prescribe.

(5) Any finance company that fails to comply with any requirement of this section shall be liable, on being called upon to do so by the Authority (in addition to any other penalty that may be imposed under this Act) to pay a penalty interest charge of not less than one-fifteenth of one per cent of the amount of the deficiency for every day during which the default continues and shall not while the default

continues accept any deposits or enter into new commitments without the approval of the Authority.

## PART VI. INSPECTION OF FINANCE COMPANIES

Inspection and investigation of finance companies and production of books, etc.

**26.** (1) The Authority may, from time to time, inspect or cause to be inspected under conditions of secrecy, the books, accounts and transactions of any finance company and of any branch, agency or office outside Singapore opened by a finance company incorporated in Singapore.

(2) The Authority may at any time make an investigation, under conditions of secrecy, of the books, accounts and transactions of a finance company, if the Authority has reason to believe that such finance company is carrying on its business in a manner detrimental to the interests of its depositors and other creditors or has insufficient assets to cover its liabilities to the public, or is contravening the provisions of this Act.

(3) The Authority may appoint any auditor, other than the auditor appointed by the finance company under the provisions of section 172 of the Companies Act, to exercise the powers of the Authority under subsections (1) and (2) of this section.

(4) For the purpose of an inspection or investigation under this section, a finance company shall afford the Authority access to its books, accounts and documents and shall give such information and facilities as may be required to conduct the investigation:

Provided that such books, accounts and documents shall not be required to be produced at such times and at such places as would interfere with the proper conduct of the normal daily business of that finance company.

(5) If any book, account or document or information is not supplied in accordance with subsection (4) of this section, the finance company concerned shall be guilty of an offence under this Act and shall be liable on conviction to a fine not exceeding two thousand dollars and to a further fine of two hundred and fifty dollars in respect of every day during which the default continues after conviction.

Powers of the Authority to issue orders after an inspection.

**27.** (1) If the Authority finds upon an inspection under section 26 of this Act that the affairs of a finance company are being conducted in a manner likely to be detrimental to the interests of the depositors or prejudicial to the interests of the finance company, the Authority may by order require the finance company to take such corrective action as the Authority considers to be necessary or require the finance company to discontinue such practices or procedures.

(2) No order shall be issued under subsection (1) of this section unless the finance company has been given a reasonable opportunity to present its views to the Authority.

(3) The Authority may, upon representation being made to it, or on its own motion, modify or cancel any order issued under subsection (1) of this section, and, in so modifying or cancelling any order, may impose such conditions as it thinks fit.

## PART VII. SUBMISSION OF ACCOUNTS AND AUDITOR'S REPORT

Directors to submit copy of profit and loss account and auditor to submit copy of his report to Authority.

28. (1) The directors of a finance company shall submit to the Authority a copy of the profit and loss account and balance-sheet made out pursuant to subsections (1) and (3) of section 169 of the Companies Act.

(2) Every auditor of a finance company shall submit to the Authority a copy of his report as to every balance-sheet and profit and loss account (including every consolidated balance-sheet and consolidated profit and loss account) that he is required under section 174 of the Companies Act to make to members of the finance company.

## PART VIII. MISCELLANEOUS

The Authority to administer the Act.

29. (1) The Authority shall be charged with the general administration of this Act and the exercise of the functions imposed on it by this Act.

(2) The Authority may authorise or appoint any person to assist it in the exercise of its functions and duties under this Act, either generally or in a particular case.

(3) The members of the Authority shall be deemed to be public servants within the meaning of the Penal Code.

Prohibition against transacting of financing business on public holidays.

30. No finance company shall transact any business with the public on any day that is a public holiday under the provisions of the Holidays Act, or on any day declared to be a bank holiday under any written law relating to banking.

Indemnity.

31. The Authority shall not be subject to any action, claim or demand by or liability to any person in respect of anything done or omitted to be done in good faith in pursuance or in execution or intended execution or in connection with the execution or intended execution of any power conferred upon the Authority by this Act.

Finance company unable to meet obligations to inform Authority.

32. Any finance company that considers that it is likely to become unable to meet its obligations or is about to suspend payments shall forthwith inform the Authority of such fact.

Moratorium.

33. (1) The Authority may, if it considers it to be in the interests of the depositors of a finance company, by order—

*(a)* prohibit a finance company from carrying on its business; and

*(b)* stay the commencement or continuance of any actions or proceedings against a finance company in regard to its business for a specified period of time on such terms and conditions as the Authority deems reasonable, and may from time to time extend the period up to a total period of moratorium of not more than six months.

(2) So long as an order under subsection (1) of this section remains in force, any licence granted to such finance company under this Act shall be suspended.

Memorandum and articles of association of a finance company.

34. (1) Every company that was not carrying on financing business in Singapore before the date of the coming into operation of this Act shall, before it is granted a licence by the Authority to carry on financing business under this Act, include in its memorandum of association or articles of association the restrictions, limitations and prohibitions contained in sections 18, 19, 20, 21 and 22 of this Act.

(2) Every company that—

*(a)* has carried on financing business in Singapore before the date of the coming into operation of this Act; and

*(b)* is licensed under this Act,

but whose memorandum of association or articles of association do not include all or any of the restrictions, limitations or prohibitions contained in sections 18, 19, 20, 21 and 22 of this Act, shall be deemed to have included in its memorandum of association or articles of association all or any of such restrictions, limitations or prohibitions as are not so included.

(3) To the extent that any such restriction, limitation or prohibition so deemed to have been included in those memorandum of association

or articles of association under subsection (2) of this section, is inconsistent with any provision already included in the memorandum of association or articles of association that restriction, limitation or prohibition shall prevail over such provision.

Disqualification of directors of a finance company.

35. (1) Without prejudice to anything contained in the Companies Act, any person who is a director, manager or other officer concerned with the management of a finance company shall cease to hold office—

*(a)* if he becomes bankrupt, suspends payments or compounds with his creditors; or

*(b)* if he is convicted of an offence involving dishonesty or fraud.

(2) No person who has been a director of, or directly concerned in the management of, a finance company licensed under this Act which has been wound up by a court shall without the express authority of the Authority, act, or continue to act, as director of, or be directly concerned in, the management of any finance company.

(3) Any person acting in contravention of subsection (1) or (2) of this section shall be guilty of an offence under this Act and shall be liable on conviction to imprisonment for a term not exceeding three years or to a fine not exceeding five thousand dollars or to both such imprisonment and fine.

Penalty for offences not otherwise provided for.

36. (1) Any finance company which, or person who, contravenes or fails to comply with any provisions of this Act or any order made under this Act for which no penalty is expressly provided shall be guilty of an offence under this Act and shall be liable on conviction to imprisonment for a term not exceeding three years or to a fine not exceeding five thousand dollars or to both such imprisonment and fine.

(2) The Authority may, without instituting proceedings against any person for any offence under this Act, or any regulations made thereunder, which is punishable only by a fine or a default penalty, demand and receive the amount of such fine or default penalty or such reduced amount as he thinks fit from such person, whereupon—

*(a)* if such person pays such amount to the Authority within fourteen days after the demand, no proceedings shall be taken against him in relation to the offence; and

*(b)* if such person does not so pay the amount so demanded, the Authority may cause proceedings to be instituted in relation to the offence.

37. (1) Any person who, being a director, managing director or manager of a finance company— Offences by directors or managers.

(*a*) fails to comply, or to take all reasonable steps to secure compliance by the finance company, with the provisions of this Act or any order made under this Act or any other law relating to finance companies in force in Singapore; or

(*b*) fails to ensure or to take all reasonable steps to ensure the accuracy and correctness of any statement or information submitted under this Act or of any other law relating to finance companies in force in Singapore,

shall be guilty of an offence under this Act and shall be liable on conviction by a District Court to imprisonment for a term not exceeding three years or to a fine not exceeding five thousand dollars or to both such imprisonment and fine.

(2) In any proceedings against a person under subsection (1) of this section it shall be a defence to prove that he had reasonable grounds to believe and did believe that a competent and reliable person was charged with the duty of securing compliance with the provisions of this Act or any order made under this Act or any other written law relating to finance companies in Singapore or with the duty of securing that those statements were accurate and correct and that the person was in a position to discharge that duty.

(3) A person shall not be sentenced to imprisonment for any offence under subsection (1) of this section unless in the opinion of the court the offence was committed wilfully.

38. Where any public or private company or firm holds itself out to be a licensed finance company when it is not licensed under this Act, such company or firm shall be guilty of an offence under this Act and every director, manager or every officer of such company and the proprietor or every partner or officer of such firm shall, unless he proves that such holding out by the company or firm was made without his knowledge or consent, be guilty of an offence under this Act and shall be liable on conviction to imprisonment for a term not exceeding two years or to a fine not exceeding four thousand dollars or to both such imprisonment and fine. Holding out as finance company.

39. No prosecution in respect of any offence under this Act shall be instituted except by, or under the direction of, the Attorney-General acting upon a complaint made by the Authority. Fiat of Attorney-General.

Exemptions

**40.** (1) This Act shall not apply to—

(*a*) any bank licensed under the Banking Act;

(*b*) the Post Office Savings Bank established under the Post Office Savings Bank Act;

(*c*) any co-operative society registered under the Co-operative Societies Act; or

(*d*) any business of pawnbroking carried on by a person licensed under the Pawnbrokers Act.

(2) Notwithstanding any provisions in this Act, the Authority may exempt any finance company from any or all of the provisions of this Act.

Winding up provisions.

41. (1) Without prejudice to the provisions of the Companies Act—

(*a*) a company (whether or not it is being wound up voluntarily) may be wound up under an order of the Court on the petition of the Authority; and

(*b*) the Court may order the winding up of a company if—

(i) the company has held a licence under this Act and that licence has expired or has been revoked; or

(ii) the company has carried on financing business in Singapore in contravention of the provisions of this Act.

(2) In the winding up of a company that has been carrying on financing business, the depositors shall be deemed to be holders of debentures issued to them by the company and secured by a floating charge over all the property and undertaking of the company.

Redemption of securities held by finance company.

42. (1) As soon as practicable after the making of an order for the winding up of a finance company, the liquidator of the company shall publish in the *Gazette* a notice requiring every debtor of the finance company to redeem any property he has deposited with the company as security for any loan that he has obtained from the finance company, and shall also send by registered post such notice to every debtor whose security is held by the finance company and whose name is mentioned in the statement of affairs made out under section 234 of the Companies Act.

(2) The notice shall specify the latest date up to which any security may be redeemed, which date shall not be less than three months from the date of the notice.

(3) After the latest date for redeeming any security held by the finance company specified in the notice, the liquidator may proceed to

realise any security held by the finance company forthwith, notwithstanding any agreement setting out any other period of redemption previously entered into between the finance company and the debtor.

Operation of Act not to affect the Companies Act.

43. Nothing in this Act shall affect the operation of the Companies Act, and any company that is liable to be incorporated under that Act shall continue to be so liable as if this Act had not been passed but in case of conflict between that Act and this Act the provisions of this Act shall prevail unless otherwise provided in this Act.

Regulations.

44. (1) The Authority may, from time to time, make such regulations for, or in respect of, every purpose which is deemed by it necessary for carrying out the provisions of this Act and for the prescribing of any matter which is authorised or required under this Act to be so prescribed.

(2) Without prejudice to the generality of subsection (1) of this section, the Authority may by such regulations—

*(a)* prescribe fees to be charged under this Act; and

*(b)* regulate advertisements of finance companies.

## PART IX. TRANSITIONAL

Transitional licensing provisions.

45. (1) Notwithstanding the provisions of section 7 of this Act, any company which on 5th December 1967 was carrying on financing business in Singapore may, within one month after the date of the coming into operation of this Act, apply for a licence and shall be granted a licence by the Authority which shall be valid up to and including 30th June 1968.

(2) Thereafter, such licence may be renewed for such further period, or periods, as the Authority may decide and be subject to such conditions as it may impose.

(3) A private company which has been granted a licence under subsection (1) of this section shall not be entitled to claim to be an exempt private company under the Companies Act.

Firms that have been carrying on financing business.

46. (1) Notwithstanding section 7 of this Act, any firm that had been carrying on financing business in Singapore before 5th December 1967 may apply for and may be granted a licence if such firm incorporates itself as a public company within three months of the date of the coming into operation of this Act.

(2) A licence granted under subsection (1) of this section may be valid for such period as the Authority may decide and be subject to such conditions as the Authority may impose.

## Money-Changing and Remittance Businesses Act, 1979[1]

An Act to provide for the licensing of persons who carry on money-changing or remittance business and for matters connected therewith.

Be it enacted by the President, with the advice and consent of the Parliament of Singapore, as follows:

[28th September, 1979]

Short title and commencement.

1. This Act may be cited as the Money-changing and Remittance Businesses Act, 1979, and shall come into operation on such date as the Minister may, by notification in the *Gazette,* appoint.

Interpretation.

2. (1) In this Act, unless the context otherwise requires—

"Authority" means the Monetary Authority of Singapore established under section 3 of the Monetary Authority of Singapore Act;

"licence" means a money-changer's licence or a remittance licence, as the case may be, issued under this Act;

"money-changer's licence" means a licence issued under this Act authorising the holder thereof to carry on money-changing business;

"money-changing business" means the business of buying or selling foreign currency notes;

"remittance business" means the business of accepting monies for the purpose of transmitting them to persons resident in another country;

"remittance licence" means a licence issued under this Act authorising the holder thereof to carry on remittance business.

---

[1] *Singapore Government Gazette Acts Supplement,* No. 25, October 5, 1979, Act No. 20 of 1979.

(2) For the purposes of this Act, a person shall be deemed to be carrying on money-changing business if he—

*(a)* advertises that he is ready to buy or sell foreign currency notes; or

*(b)* offers to buy or sell foreign currency notes.

Scope of Act to persons.

3. This Act shall not be construed as requiring any person who accepts foreign currency notes from a customer or client in payment for goods sold or services rendered by him to obtain a money-changer's licence.

Authority responsible for administration of Act.

4. The Authority shall be responsible for the administration of this Act and may authorise any of its officers to exercise any powers and perform any duties or functions of the Authority under this Act.

Persons carrying on money-changing business to be licensed.

5. (1) No person shall carry on any money-changing business unless he is in possession of a valid money-changer's licence.

(2) A person who contravenes or fails to comply with the provisions of subsection (1) shall be guilty of an offence and shall be liable on conviction to a fine not exceeding five thousand dollars or to imprisonment for a term not exceeding six months or to both such fine and imprisonment.

Persons carrying on remittance business to be licensed.

6. (1) No person shall carry on any remittance business unless he is in possession of a valid remittance licence.

(2) A person who contravenes or fails to comply with the provisions of subsection (1) shall be guilty of an offence and shall be liable on conviction to a fine not exceeding five thousand dollars or to imprisonment for a term not exceeding six months or to both such fine and imprisonment.

Application for licence.

7. (1) Any person who desires to obtain a licence shall make an application to the Authority in such form as the Authority may require.

(2) Upon receiving an application under subsection (1), the Authority shall consider the application and may grant a licence with or without conditions or refuse to grant a licence without assigning any reason therefor.

(3) In considering any application by a person for a licence the Authority may require to be satisfied as to—

(a) the good character of the applicant or, if the applicant is a company, the general character of the management of the company;
(b) the financial condition of the applicant; and
(c) whether the public interest will be served by the granting of a licence.

(4) The Authority may at any time vary or revoke any of the existing conditions of a licence or impose new conditions.

License fee.

8. Every licensee shall pay such licence fee as may be prescribed.

Period for which licence is in force.

9. A licence shall be in force for such period as the Authority may determine and may be renewed at the discretion of the Authority on its expiry.

Revocation of a licence.

10. (1) The Authority may, by order, revoke a licence if it is satisfied that the licensee—

(a) has ceased to carry on the business for which he has been licensed or, if the licensee is a company, goes into liquidation or is wound up or otherwise dissolved; or
(b) is contravening or has contravened the provisions of this Act; or
(c) has failed to comply with or observe any of the conditions of his licence; or
(d) has made a false or incorrect statement in his application for a licence; or
(e) has carried on or is carrying on business in a manner likely to be detrimental to the interests of the public or his customers; or
(f) has been convicted of any offence involving dishonesty or moral turpitude or, if the licensee is a company, any of its officers holding a managerial or an executive position has been convicted of any offence involving fraud or moral turpitude.

(2) The Authority shall, before revoking any licence under the provisions of subsection (1), give the licensee notice in writing of its intention to do so, specifying a date, not less than thirty days after the date of the notice, upon which such revocation shall take effect and calling upon the person concerned to show cause to the Authority why such licence should not be revoked.

(3) When the Authority has revoked a licence under the provisions of subsection (1), it shall forthwith inform the person concerned by notice in writing of such revocation.

(4) The person whose licence has been revoked may, within twenty-

one days of the receipt of the notice referred to in subsection (3), or within such extended period of time as the Minister may allow, appeal in writing against such revocation to the Minister whose decision shall be final.

(5) An order of revocation shall not take effect until the expiration of a period of thirty days after the order has been served on the licensee.

(6) If within that period the licensee concerned gives due notice of appeal to the Minister the order shall not take effect unless the order is confirmed by or is for any reason dismissed by the Minister or the appeal is withdrawn.

**Effect of revocation.**

11. (1) Where an order of revocation becomes effective under section 10, the licensee concerned shall cease to carry on money-changing or remittance business, as the case may be.

(2) The provisions of subsection (1) shall not prejudice the enforcement by any person of any right or claim against the licensee concerned or by the licensee concerned of any right or claim against any person arising out of or concerning any matter or thing done prior to the revocation of the licence.

**Powers to investigate.**

12. (1) Any person duly authorised by the Authority to act on its behalf may at any reasonable time enter any premises where a licensee is carrying on business, or any premises where he reasonably suspects any business is being carried on in contravention of this Act, and may inspect the premises and any book or document on those premises which he reasonably requires to inspect for the purpose of ascertaining whether a contravention of this Act or any regulations made thereunder is being or has been committed.

(2) Any person who—

*(a)* fails without reasonable excuse to admit any person who demands admission to the premises in pursuance of subsection (1); or

*(b)* on being required by a person referred to in subsection (1) to do so, fails without reasonable excuse to permit the person to inspect the premises; or

*(c)* on being required by a person referred to in subsection (1) to produce any book or document in his possession or under his control and which that person reasonably requires to inspect for the purpose specified in subsection (1), fails without reasonable excuse to produce it to him and to permit him to take copies of it or of any entry in it,

shall be guilty of an offence and shall be liable on conviction to a fine not exceeding two thousand dollars.

(3) A person who is carrying out an investigation for the purpose of ascertaining whether an offence under this Act has been committed may exercise all or any of the powers conferred upon a police officer by the Criminal Procedure Code in relation to the investigation of a seizable offence.

Power to arrest.

13. Any person duly authorised to act on behalf of the Authority may, without warrant, arrest any person reasonably suspected of having committed an offence under this Act, if the accused person refuses to give his name and address or gives a name and address which the first mentioned person has reason to believe is false.

Liability of directors, partners, etc.

14. (1) Where an offence under this Act has been committed by a body corporate, any person, who at the time of the commission of such offence was a director, secretary, manager or other officer of the company or who was purporting to act in any such capacity, shall be liable to be proceeded against and punished accordingly unless he proves that the offence was committed without his consent or connivance and that he exercised such diligence to prevent the commission of the offence as he ought to have exercised having regard to the nature of his function in that capacity and to all the circumstances.

(2) Any person who would have been guilty of an offence if anything had been done or omitted to be done by him personally shall be guilty of such offence and shall be liable to the same penalty if such thing had been done or omitted to be done by his partner, agent or servant in the course of his partnership business or in the course of his employment, as the case may be, unless he proves that the offence was committed without his knowledge or consent and that he took all reasonable precautions to prevent the doing of or omission to do such thing.

(3) Nothing in subsection (2) shall relieve any partner, agent or servant from any liability for an offence.

Service of order, etc.

15. An order or a notice required or authorised by this Act to be given to any person may be—

(*a*) delivered to that person; or
(*b*) left at the place of abode or the place of business of that person; or

(*c*) sent by registered post to the last known address of that person.

**Conduct of proceedings.**

16. Proceedings in respect of any offence under this Act or any regulations made thereunder may be conducted by any officer of the Authority authorised in writing in that behalf by the Authority.

**Indemnity.**

17. Neither the Authority nor any person authorised by the Authority shall be subject to any action, claim or demand by or liability to any person in respect of any thing done or omitted to be done in good faith in pursuance or in execution or intended execution or in connection with the execution or intended execution of any power conferred upon the Authority by this Act.

**Regulations.**

18. (1) The Authority may, from time to time, make such regulations for, or in respect of, every purpose which is deemed necessary for carrying out the provisions of this Act and for the prescribing of any matter which is authorised or required under this Act to be so prescribed.

(2) Without prejudice to the generality of subsection (1), the Authority may by such regulations—

(*a*) prescribe fees to be charged under this Act; and

(*b*) regulate the conduct of money-changing and remittance business by persons holding licences issued under this Act.

**Exemptions.**

19. (1) This Act shall not apply to any company which has a valid licence granted under the Banking Act authorising it to conduct banking business in Singapore.

(2) The Authority may, by notification published in the *Gazette,* exempt any person or categories of persons from the provisions of this Act.

**Transitional provisions.**

20. Notwithstanding the provisions of this Act, a person who, immediately before the commencement of this Act, was carrying on money-changing or remittance business shall be entitled to do the same without a licence for a period of three months beginning from the commencement of this Act, and if before the expiration of that period he applies for a licence then he may continue to do the same until the licence is granted or finally refused or the application for a licence is withdrawn.

# Moneylenders Act[1]

An Act to make provision for the regulation of moneylending.

[11th September, 1959]

Short title. **1.** This Act may be cited as the Moneylenders Act.

Interpretation. **2.** In this Act unless the context otherwise requires—

"authorized name" and "authorized address" mean respectively the name under which and the address at which a moneylender is authorized by a licence granted under this Act to carry on business as a moneylender;

"company" means any body corporate being a moneylender;

"firm" means an unincorporated body of two or more individuals or one or more individuals and one or more corporations or two or more corporations who have entered into partnership with one another with a view to carrying on business for profit;

"interest" does not include any sum lawfully charged in accordance with the provisions of this Act by a moneylender for or on account of stamp duties, fees payable by law and legal costs but, save as aforesaid, includes any amount by whatsoever name called in excess of the principal paid or payable to a moneylender in consideration of or otherwise in respect of a loan;

"licence" means a moneylender's licence issued under this Act;

"moneylender" includes every person whose business is that of moneylending or who carries on or advertises or announces himself or holds himself out in any way as carrying on that business whether or not that person also possesses or earns property or money derived from sources other than the lending of money and whether or not that person carries on the business as a principal or as an agent but does not include—

*(a)* any body corporate, incorporated or empowered by a special Act of Parliament or by any other Act to lend money in accordance with that Act;

*(b)* any society registered under the Co-operative Societies Act;

*(c)* any person bona fide carrying on the business of banking or insurance or bona fide carrying on any business not hav-

[1] *Singapore Statutes,* Cap. 220 (1970). Originally Ord. No. 58 of 1959. Relevant citations: Ord. No. 6 of 1960; Acts Nos. 19 of 1967; 13 of 1969; 48 of 1970; and 22 of 1975.

ing for its primary object the lending of money in the course of which and for the purposes whereof he lends money;

*(d)* any pawnbroker licensed under the provisions of any written law in force in Singapore relating to the licensing of pawnbrokers;

*(e)* any finance company licensed under the Finance Companies Act.

"principal" means, in relation to a loan, the amount actually lent to and received by the borrower;

"Registrar" means the Registrar of Moneylenders appointed under this Act and includes an Assistant Registrar.

Certain persons and firms presumed to be moneylenders.

3. Save as excepted in paragraphs *(a)*, *(b)*, *(c)*, *(d)* and *(e)* of the definition of "moneylender" in section 2 of this Act, any person who lends a sum of money in consideration of a larger sum being repaid shall be presumed until the contrary is proved to be a moneylender.

Appointment of Registrars.

4. The Minister may appoint any public officer to be Registrar of Moneylenders under this Act and may also appoint as many public officers as he may think fit to be Assistant Registrars of Moneylenders.

Licences to be taken out by moneylenders.

5. (1) Every moneylender residing and carrying on the business of moneylending in Singapore whether as principal or as agent, shall take out a licence annually.

(2) A licence shall be taken out in respect of each name under which moneylending business is conducted. No licence shall be issued to a person not ordinarily resident in Singapore or to a firm where the person proposed to be responsible for the management of the firm is not ordinarily resident in Singapore.

(3) A licence taken out by a person as a partner in a firm shall be deemed to be a licence to the firm, and every other partner actively conducting in Singapore the moneylending business of that firm shall be subject to the provisions of this Act in like manner as if he had himself taken out the licence and shall be deemed to hold a licence.

(4) Licences shall be substantially in such form as the Minister may direct and shall be granted, on payment of the prescribed fee, by the Registrar or an Assistant Registrar or by officers authorized by either of them.

(5) Every licence shall come into operation on the date specified therein and shall be valid for a period of twelve months.

Particulars to be shown on licences.

6. (1) Every licence granted to a moneylender shall show his true name and the name under which, and the address at which, he is authorized by the licence to carry on business as such, and in the case of an agent in addition the true name of the principal, whether an individual or a firm, on whose behalf such business is carried on. A licence shall not authorize a moneylender to carry on business at more than one address or under more than one name or under any name which includes the word "bank" or otherwise implies that he carries on the business of banking, and no licence shall authorize a moneylender to carry on business under any name except—

(*a*) his true name or in the case of an agent the true name of the principal on whose behalf the agent carries on business; or
(*b*) the name of a firm in which he is a partner or of which he is an agent; or
(*c*) a business name, whether of an individual or of a firm in which he is a partner or of which he is an agent, under which he or the firm or in the case of an agent his principal has been registered under the Business Names Act.

(2) Any licence taken out in a name other than the moneylender's true name shall be void.

List to be published.

7. (1) The Registrar shall from time to time cause to be published in the *Gazette* a list of all persons licensed under this Act, and shall also cause to be so published any addition to or alteration in the list.

(2) Every such printed list purporting to be published as aforesaid shall be evidence in all courts that the persons therein specified are licensed according to the provisions of this Act; and the absence of the name of any person from such printed list shall be evidence, unless the contrary is shown, that that person is not licensed according to the provisions of this Act.

Offences.

8. If any person—

(*a*) takes out a licence in any name other than his true name; or
(*b*) carries on business as a moneylender without holding a licence or, being licensed as a moneylender, carries on business as such in any name other than his authorized name or at any place other than his authorized address or addresses; or
(*c*) in the course of business as a moneylender enters as principal or agent into any agreement with respect to any advance or repayment of money or takes any security for money otherwise than in his authorized name,

he shall be guilty of an offence under this Act and on conviction shall be liable to a fine not exceeding five thousand dollars and for a second or subsequent offence shall be liable to a fine not exceeding five thousand dollars or to imprisonment for a term not exceeding twelve months or to both such fine and imprisonment and an offender being a company shall for a second or subsequent offence be liable to a fine not exceeding ten thousand dollars:

Provided that a moneylender who is not, or in the case of a firm none of the partners of which are, ordinarily resident in Singapore may without being guilty thereby of an offence carry on business in Singapore without holding a licence if he carries on such business solely through an agent duly licensed under this Act to carry on such business in Singapore under the name of that moneylender.

Grounds for refusing licence.

9. (1) A licence shall not be refused except on one or more of the following grounds:

(*a*) that satisfactory evidence has not been produced of the good character of the applicant and, in the case of a company or of a firm, of the persons responsible for the management thereof;

(*b*) that satisfactory evidence has been produced that the applicant or any person responsible or proposed to be responsible for the management of his business as a moneylender is not a fit and proper person to hold a licence;

(*c*) that the applicant or any person responsible or proposed to be responsible for the management of his business as a moneylender is by order of a court disqualified from holding a licence;

(*d*) that the applicant has not complied with the provisions of section 5 of this Act with respect to applications for licences;

(*e*) that the applicant or his firm has after the coming into operation of this Act knowingly lent money to a person under the age of twenty-one years;

(*f*) that the applicant, or any partner, director or other person who is or will be responsible for the management of the firm, is below the age of twenty-one years:

Provided that where an application is made by any person for a licence to carry on business as an agent for a principal such licence may also be refused on one or more of the following grounds:

(i) that satisfactory evidence has not been produced of the good character of the principal and, where the principal is a firm, of the persons responsible for the management thereof;

(ii) that satisfactory evidence has been produced that the principal is not a fit and proper person to carry on the business of moneylending;

(iii) that the principal or any present or former agent of the principal is by an order of a court disqualified from holding a licence;

(iv) that the principal or any present or former agent of the principal has after the coming into operation of this Act knowingly lent money to a person under the age of twenty-one years.

(2) Any person aggrieved by the refusal of a licensing officer to grant a licence may appeal to the Minister in such manner as the Minister may, by rules, prescribe and the decision of the Minister shall be final.

Revocation of licence.

**10.** (1) The Registrar may by order revoke a licence if he is satisfied—

*(a)* that the holder of the licence—

(i) has ceased to carry on the business of a moneylender or, if the licensee being a company, goes into liquidation or is wound up or otherwise dissolved; or

(ii) is no longer a fit and proper person to continue to hold the licence; or

*(b)* that the holder of the licence, or if he is a partner of a firm or is a company, any person responsible for the management of the firm or company—

(i) has been convicted of any offence involving dishonesty or moral turpitude; or

(ii) is carrying on or has carried on the business of a moneylender in such a manner as renders him unfit to continue to hold the licence; or

(iii) is contravening or has contravened the provisions of this Act; or

(iv) has been convicted of any offence under this Act or the rules made thereunder.

(2) The Registrar shall, before revoking any licence under the provisions of subsection (1) of this section, give the person concerned notice in writing of his intention to do so, specifying a date, not less than twenty-one days after the date of the notice, upon which such revocation shall take effect and calling upon the person concerned to show cause to the Registrar why such licence should not be revoked.

(3) When the Registrar has revoked a licence under the provisions

of subsection (1) of this section he shall forthwith inform the person concerned by notice in writing of such revocation.

(4) The person whose licence has been revoked may, within fourteen days after the date of the notice referred to in subsection (3) of this section, or such extended period of time as the Minister may allow, appeal in writing against such revocation to the Minister whose decision thereon shall be final.

(5) An order of revocation shall not take effect until the expiration of a period of fourteen days after the Registrar has informed the licensee concerned of the order.

(6) If within that period the licensee concerned gives due notice of appeal to the Minister the order shall not take effect unless the order is confirmed by the Minister or the appeal is for any reason dismissed by the Minister or is withdrawn.

(7) An order of revocation made under this section shall not affect any moneylending transaction entered into before the order is made.

Names to be stated on documents issued by moneylenders.

11. A moneylender shall not for the purpose of the business carried on by him as such issue or publish or cause to be issued or published any advertisement, circular, business letter or other document which does not show in such manner as to be not less conspicuous than any other name, the authorized name of the moneylender, and any moneylender who acts in contravention of this section shall be guilty of an offence and shall be liable on conviction to a fine not exceeding five hundred dollars in respect of the offence.

No circular implying a banking business to be issued.

12. If a moneylender for the purpose of the business carried on by him as such issues or publishes or causes to be issued or published any advertisement, circular or document of any kind whatsoever containing expressions which might reasonably be held to imply that he carries on the business of banking he shall on conviction be liable to a fine not exceeding one thousand dollars and on a second or subsequent offence shall be liable to a fine not exceeding one thousand dollars or to imprisonment for a term not exceeding twelve months or to both such fine and imprisonment and an offender being a company shall for a second or subsequent offence be liable to a fine not exceeding five thousand dollars.

Restriction on moneylenders' advertisements.

13. (1) No person shall knowingly send or deliver or cause to be sent or delivered, to any person, except in response to his written request any circular or other document advertising the name, address or telephone number of a moneylender or containing an invitation—

(*a*) to borrow money from a moneylender;
(*b*) to enter into any transaction involving the borrowing of money from a moneylender; or
(*c*) to apply to any place with a view to obtaining information or advice as to borrowing any money from a moneylender.

(2) Subject as hereunder provided, no person shall publish, or cause to be published, in any newspaper or other printed paper issued periodically for public circulation or by means of any poster or placard, an advertisement advertising any such particulars or containing any such invitation as aforesaid:

Provided that an advertisement in conformity with the requirements of this Act relating to the use of names on moneylenders' documents may be published by or on behalf of a moneylender in any newspaper or in any such paper as aforesaid or by means of a poster or placard exhibited at any authorized address of the moneylender if it contains no addition to the particulars necessary to comply with the said requirements except any of the following particulars, that is to say—

(*a*) any authorized address at which he carries on business as a moneylender and the telegraphic address and telephone number thereof;
(*b*) any address at which he formerly carried on business;
(*c*) a statement that he lends money with or without security and of the highest and lowest sums that he is prepared to lend; and
(*d*) a statement of the date on which the business carried on by him was first established.

(3) No moneylender or any person on his behalf shall employ any agent or canvasser for the purpose of inviting any person to borrow money or to enter into any transaction involving the borrowing of money from a moneylender and no person shall act as such agent or canvasser or demand or receive, directly or indirectly, any sum or other valuable consideration by way of commission or otherwise for introducing or undertaking to introduce to a moneylender any person desiring to borrow money.

(4) Where any document issued or published by or on behalf of a moneylender purports to indicate the terms of interest upon which he is willing to make loans or any particular loan, the document shall either express the interest proposed in terms of a rate per cent per annum or per month.

(5) Any person acting in contravention of any of the provisions of this section shall be guilty of an offence against this Act and shall in respect of each offence be liable on conviction to imprisonment for a

term not exceeding six months or to a fine not exceeding five hundred dollars or to both such imprisonment and fine.

Boards to be affixed at place of business of moneylenders.

14. (1) Every person licensed as a moneylender under the provisions of this Act shall affix in a conspicuous position outside his authorized address a board bearing the authorized name and the authorized address of the business and the words "Licensed Moneylender" in Malay, English, Chinese and Tamil distinctly printed in letters not less than two inches high.

(2) Any person who fails to comply with the provisions of subsection (1) of this section shall be liable on conviction to a fine not exceeding fifty dollars.

Contract by unlicensed moneylender unenforceable.

15. No contract for the repayment of money lent after the coming into operation of this Act by an unlicensed moneylender shall be enforceable:

Provided that money lent on behalf of a principal through an agent who is licensed under the provisions of this Act to carry on the business of moneylending on behalf of that principal shall be deemed to have been lent by a licensed moneylender.

Note or memorandum of moneylender's contract to be given to the borrower.

16. (1) No contract for the repayment by a borrower or his agent of money lent to him or to any agent on his behalf by a moneylender or his agent after the coming into operation of this Act or for the payment by him of interest on money so lent, and no security given by the borrower or by any such agent as aforesaid in respect of any such contract, shall be enforceable unless a note or memorandum in writing of the contract in the English language and in the prescribed form is signed by the parties to the contract or their respective agents or, in the case of a loan to a partnership firm, by a partner in or agent of the firm, and unless a copy thereof authenticated by the lender or his agent is delivered to the borrower or his agent or, in the case of a loan to a partnership firm, to a partner in or agent of the firm, before the money is lent, and no such contract or security shall be enforceable if it is proved that the note or memorandum aforesaid was not so signed before the money was lent or before the security was given, as the case may be:

Provided always that where a security is given to secure an immediate loan and subsequent loans, the security shall be enforceable in respect of any subsequent loan thereby secured if the note or memorandum in respect of the subsequent loan is signed and delivered to the borrower before the money is lent.

(2) No contract made after the date of the coming into operation of the Moneylenders (Amendment) Act, 1975 for the repayment by a borrower or his agent of money lent to him or to any agent on his behalf by a moneylender or his agent, or for the payment by him of interest on the money so lent, and no security given by the borrower or any such agent as aforesaid in respect of any such contract shall be enforceable unless the money lent was given to the borrower or his agent in the form of an account payee crossed cheque with the words "licensed moneylender" endorsed legibly below the signature of the moneylender or his agent on the cheque made payable to the borrower or his agent; [2]

(3) No moneylender or his agent shall present to any bank any crossed cheque drawn by another moneylender or his agent and made payable to a borrower or his agent and any moneylender or his agent who acts in contravention of this subsection shall be guilty of an offence under this Act and shall be liable on conviction to a fine not exceeding two thousand dollars or to imprisonment for a term not exceeding twelve months or to both such fine and imprisonment.

(4) Any person, not being a moneylender, who presents to any bank more than two crossed cheques in any one month drawn by any moneylender or his agent and made payable to a borrower or his agent shall be guilty of an offence under this Act and shall be liable on conviction to a fine not exceeding two thousand dollars or to imprisonment for a term not exceeding twelve months or to both such fine and imprisonment.

(5) In the course of any investigation or proceedings into or relating to an offence by any person under subsection (3) or (4) of this section, the Public Prosecutor may, notwithstanding anything in any other written law to the contrary, by notice in writing, require the man-

---

[2] The Moneylenders (Amendment) Act, 1975, provides in sec. 14 that "notwithstanding the repeal of subsection (2) of section 16 of the Moneylenders Act, that repealed subsection shall be of full force and effect with regard to those contracts made before the date of the commencement of the Moneylenders (Amendment) Act, 1975." The repealed subsec. (2) of sec. 16 of the Moneylenders Act read:

"No contract for the repayment by a borrower or his agent of money lent to him or to any agent on his behalf by a moneylender or his agent after the coming into operation of this Act or for the payment by him of interest on money so lent, and no security given by the borrower or by any such agent as aforesaid in respect of any such contract shall if the amount of the loan is one hundred dollars or above be enforceable unless the money lent was given to the borrower or his agent in the form of a crossed cheque with the words 'licensed moneylender' endorsed legibly below the signature of the moneylender or his agent on the cheque, made payable to the borrower or his agent."

ager of any bank to furnish him with such information as he may require to enable him to identify any person having an account at that bank and the manager of any bank who wilfully neglects or fails to comply with the terms of that notice and within such time as may be specified in that notice shall be guilty of an offence under this Act and shall be liable on conviction to a fine not exceeding one thousand dollars or to imprisonment for a term not exceeding six months or to both such fine and imprisonment.

(6) In this section the expression "borrower" includes a surety.

(7) Any moneylender or his agent who makes a loan in the form other than that prescribed by subsection (2) of this section shall be guilty of an offence under this Act and shall be liable on conviction to a fine not exceeding two thousand dollars or to imprisonment for a term not exceeding six months or to both such fine and imprisonment.

(8) The provisions of subsections (1) and (2) of this section shall not apply to loans or advances by a moneylender on current account where interest is payable on the daily balances with monthly or more extended rests at a rate not exceeding fifteen per cent per annum.

Stamping of note or memorandum.

**17.** Notwithstanding the provisions of the Stamp Act, any note or memorandum, including a promissory note, setting out the contract for the repayment by a borrower of money lent to him by a registered moneylender, shall not be stamped unless—

*(a)* the licence number of the moneylender is stated in the note or memorandum;

*(b)* a copy of the note or memorandum is handed to the Commissioner of Stamps who shall forward such copy to the Comptroller of Income Tax; and

*(c)* the note or memorandum is presented for stamping within seven days after its execution.

Prohibition of compound interest.

**18.** (1) Any contract made whether before or after the coming into operation of this Act, for the loan of money by a moneylender shall be illegal in so far as it provides, directly or indirectly, for the payment of compound interest, or for the rate or amount of interest to be increased by reason of any default in the payment of sums due under the contract:

Provided that provision may be made by any such contract that if default is made in the payment upon the due date of any sum payable to the moneylender under the contract, whether in respect of principal or interest, the moneylender shall be entitled to charge simple interest on that sum from the date of the default until the sum is paid, at a rate not exceeding the rate payable in respect of the principal apart from any default and any interest so charged shall not be reckoned for the purposes of this Act as part of the interest charged in respect of the loan.

(2) The provisions of subsection (1) of this section shall not apply to transactions known as thavannai transactions, between one moneylender and another moneylender, provided that any such transaction is evidenced by a written document duly stamped.

(3) The provisions of subsection (1) of this section shall not apply to loans or advances by a moneylender on current account where interest is payable on the daily balances with monthly or more extended rests at a rate not exceeding fifteen per cent per annum.

Accounts to be kept in permanent books.

**19.** (1) Every moneylender shall keep or cause to be kept a regular account of each loan made whether before or after the coming into operation of this Act clearly stating in plain words and in English numerals with or without the numerals of the script otherwise used the terms and transactions incidental to the account entered in a book paged and bound in such manner as not to facilitate the elimination of pages or the interpolation or substitution of pages.

(2) Every moneylender shall keep or cause to be kept such books of accounts relating to his business as are prescribed so as to exhibit and explain the financial position in his business, including a book or books containing entries from day to day in sufficient detail of all cash received and paid.

(3) Every moneylender shall submit to the Registrar a statement in such form as the Registrar may require showing his cash and loan position for each quarter of the year not later than the end of the second week of the next ensuing quarter.

(3A) Every moneylender shall, when so required by the Registrar, account for or explain any item or particulars appearing in the statement submitted to the Registrar under subsection (3) of this section.

(4) The Registrar may from time to time inspect, under conditions of secrecy, the books of accounts of a moneylender and a moneylender shall, when so required by the Registrar afford the Registrar access to his books of accounts and to any cheque drawn by the moneylender or his agent that has been cleared by any bank and to any note or memorandum setting out a contract for the repayment of money lent in which he is or has been concerned.

(5) If any person subject to the obligations of this section fails to comply with any of the requirements of subsection (1) of this section, he shall not be entitled to enforce any claim in respect of any transaction in relation to which default has been made.

(6) Any person who fails to comply with the requirements of this section or any requisition made by the Registrar under subsection (3A) of this section shall be guilty of an offence under this Act and shall be liable on conviction to a fine not exceeding one thousand dollars and in the case of a continuing offence to a further fine not exceeding one hundred dollars for each day or part thereof during which the offence is continued after conviction.

Obligation to supply information as to state of loan and copies of documents relating thereto.

**20.** (1) In respect of every contract for the repayment of money lent by a moneylender whether made before or after the coming into operation of this Act the moneylender shall, on any reasonable demand in writing being made by the borrower at any time during the continuance of the contract and on tender by the borrower of the sum of fifty cents for expenses, supply to the borrower or, if the borrower so requires, to any person specified in that behalf in the demand, a statement of account in English figures signed by the moneylender or his agent showing—

(*a*) the date on which the loan was made, the amount of the principal of the loan and the rate per cent per annum or the amount of interest charged; and

(*b*) the amount of any payment already received by the moneylender in respect of the loan and the date on which it was made; and

(*c*) the amount of all sums due to the moneylender for principal but unpaid and the dates upon which they became due and the amount of interest due and unpaid in respect of each such sum; and

(*d*) the amount of every sum not yet due which remains outstanding and the date upon which it will become due.

A statement of account given in the form in the First Schedule [3] to this Act shall be deemed to comply with the requirements of this subsection.

(2) A moneylender shall, on any reasonable demand in writing by the borrower and on tender of the sum of one dollar, supply a copy of any document relating to a loan made by him or any security therefor to the borrower or, if the borrower so requires, to any person specified in that behalf in the demand.

[3] The First Schedule is omitted from this volume.

(3) If a moneylender to whom a demand has been made under this section fails without reasonable excuse to comply therewith within one month after the demand has been made he shall not, so long as the default continues, be entitled to sue for or recover any sum due under the contract on account either of principal or interest, and interest shall not be chargeable in respect of the period of the default and, if such default is made or continued after proceedings have ceased to lie in respect of the loan, the moneylender shall be liable on conviction to a fine not exceeding fifty dollars for every day on which the default continues.

(4) A moneylender, receiving any payment of money under a contract for the repayment of money lent, shall immediately thereafter endorse on the stamped note or memorandum setting out that contract the amount of money received and the date it was received by him and shall forthwith issue to the payer a duly stamped receipt therefor and any moneylender who contravenes the provisions of this subsection shall be guilty of an offence under this Act and shall be liable on conviction to a fine not exceeding two thousand dollars.

(5) Where a moneylender has been convicted of an offence under subsection (4) of this section and the borrower has not repaid in full the amount due and payable under the contract for repayment of money lent, the contract shall not be enforceable in respect of any moneys still unpaid under that contract.

(6) If a moneylender is convicted of an offence under subsection (4) of this section the court shall cause particulars of the conviction to be endorsed on the note or memorandum of the contract for repayment of money lent.

Provisions as to bankruptcy proceedings for moneylenders' loans.

21. (1) Where a debt due to a moneylender in respect of a loan made by him whether before or after the coming into operation of this Act includes interest, that interest shall, for the purposes of the provisions of the Bankruptcy Act, be calculated at a rate not exceeding four per cent per annum, but nothing in the foregoing provision shall prejudice the right of the moneylender to receive out of the estate, after all the debts proved in the estate have been paid in full, any higher rate of interest to which he may be entitled.

(2) No proof of a debt due to a moneylender in respect of a loan made by him shall be admitted for any of the purposes of the Bankruptcy Act unless the affidavit verifying the debt has exhibited thereto a statement which complies with the provisions of section 20 of this Act and shows, where the amount of interest included in the unpaid balance represents a rate per cent per annum exceeding four per cent,

the amount of interest which would be so included if it were calculated at the rate of eight per cent per annum.

(3) Where on the date of the coming into operation of this Act property is vested in the Official Assignee by reason of any adjudication or vesting order or other order having the like effect, made under the provisions of the Bankruptcy Act or which is the subject of a composition or scheme of arrangement approved thereunder, but where no dividend has been declared or payment by way of dividend has been made, the provisions of subsections (1) and (2) of this section shall apply notwithstanding that the order vesting the property or a receiving order made in respect of it was made or the composition or scheme of arrangement was approved or any debt provable or payable in respect of it was incurred before the date of the coming into operation of this Act.

(4) General rules may be made under the Bankruptcy Act for the purpose of carrying into effect the objects of this section.

Accounts under section 20 to be produced when suing in court.

22. (1) Where proceedings are taken in any court by a moneylender for the recovery of any money lent whether before or after the coming into operation of this Act or the enforcement of any agreement or security made or taken in respect of money lent either before or after the coming into operation of this Act, he shall produce a statement of his account as prescribed in section 20 of this Act.

(2) Where there is evidence which satisfies the court that the interest charged in respect of the sum actually lent is excessive and that the transaction is harsh and unconscionable or substantially unfair, the court shall reopen the transaction and take an account between the moneylender and the person sued and shall, notwithstanding any statement or settlement of account or any agreement purporting to close previous dealings and create a new obligation, reopen any account already taken between them and relieve the person sued from payment of any sum in excess of the sum adjudged by the court to be fairly due in respect of such principal, interest and legal costs as the court, having regard to the risk and all the facts and circumstances (including facts and circumstances arising or coming to the knowledge of the parties after the date of the transaction) may adjudge to be reasonable, and, if any such excess has been paid or allowed in account by the borrower or other person sued may order the moneylender to repay it and may set aside either wholly or in part or revise or alter any security given or agreement made in respect of money lent by the moneylender and, if the moneylender has parted with the security, may order him to indemnify the borrower or other person sued:

Provided that nothing in this subsection shall prevent any further or other relief being given in circumstances in which a court of equity would give such relief.

(3) Any court in which proceedings might be taken for the recovery of money lent by a moneylender shall have and may, at the instance of the borrower or surety or other person liable or of the trustee in bankruptcy, exercise the like powers as may be exercised under this section where proceedings are taken for the recovery of money lent, and the court shall have power, notwithstanding any provision or agreement to the contrary, to entertain any application under this Act by the borrower or surety or other person liable notwithstanding that the time for repayment of the loan or any instalment thereof may not have arrived.

(4) On any application relating to the admission or amount of a proof by a moneylender in any bankruptcy proceedings the Official Assignee shall exercise the like powers as may be exercised by the court under this section when proceedings are taken for the recovery of money:

Provided that if the moneylender is dissatisfied with the decision of the Official Assignee the court may, on the application of the moneylender made under the Bankruptcy Act reverse or vary that decision.

(5) The foregoing provisions of this section shall apply to any transaction whatever its form may be that is substantially one of moneylending by a moneylender.

(6) Nothing in the foregoing provisions of this section shall affect the rights of any bona fide assignee or holder for value without notice.

(7) Nothing in this section shall be construed as derogating from the existing powers or jurisdiction of any court.

Interest above 12 per cent per annum for a secured loan or 18 per cent per annum for an unsecured loan presumed excessive.

23. (1) Where in any proceedings taken in any court by a moneylender in respect of any money lent whether before or after the coming into operation of this Act or in respect of any agreement or security in respect of money lent either before or after the coming into operation of this Act it is found that the interest charged exceeds the prescribed maximum rate of interest for such loan, the court shall, unless the contrary is proved, presume for the purposes of section 22 of this Act that the interest charged is excessive and that the transaction is harsh and unconscionable or substantially unfair, but this provision shall be without prejudice to the powers of the court under that section where the court is satisfied that the interest charged, although not exceeding twelve per cent per annum, or eighteen per cent per annum as the case

may be is excessive or that the transaction is harsh or unconscionable or substantially unfair.

(2) Where a court reopens a transaction of a moneylender under section 22 of this Act the court may require the moneylender to produce any licence granted to him in accordance with the provisions of this Act and may cause such particulars as the court thinks desirable to be endorsed on any such licence and a copy of the particulars to be sent to the Registrar.

(3) The powers of a court under subsection (3) of section 22 of this Act may be exercised notwithstanding that the moneylender's right of action for the recovery of the money lent is barred.

(4) In no case shall interest at any time be recoverable by a moneylender of an amount in excess of the sum then due as principal unless a court, having regard to all circumstances, otherwise decrees.

(5) No person who is neither a moneylender nor one of the persons referred to in paragraphs *(a)* to *(e)* inclusive of the definition of "moneylender" contained in section 2 of this Act shall, in respect of money lent by him, in any case recover in excess of the money actually lent by him (whether the excess is claimed by way of interest or otherwise) any sum greater than an amount equal to simple interest at the rate of twenty per cent per annum on the money actually lent by him.

(6) A moneylender who charges interest for a loan at a rate exceeding the maximum rate of interest prescribed for such a loan shall be guilty of an offence under this Act and shall be liable on conviction to a fine not exceeding two thousand dollars and for a second or subsequent offence—

*(a)* to a fine not exceeding five thousand dollars or to imprisonment for a term not exceeding one year or to both such fine and imprisonment; or

*(b)* where the moneylender is a company, to a fine not exceeding ten thousand dollars.

Burden of proof of amount lent.

24. (1) Where in any proceedings taken in any court by a moneylender for the recovery of any money lent whether before or after the coming into operation of this Act or the enforcement of any agreement or security made or taken in respect of money lent either before or after the coming into operation of this Act any dispute arises as to the amount of the money lent to and received by the borrower the burden of proving such amount shall be on the moneylender.

(2) The fact that the borrower has signed a note or memorandum

which complies with the provisions of section 16 of this Act and in which the amount of the money lent to and received by the borrower is set out shall not of itself raise any presumption that the amount of money so set out was actually lent to or received by the borrower.

Repayment of loan.

25. (1) The borrower shall be entitled to repay any money lent or interest thereon by cheque, money order or postal order and where in any proceedings taken in any court by a moneylender for the recovery of any money lent whether before or after the coming into operation of this Act or the enforcement of any agreement or security made or taken in respect of money lent either before or after the coming into operation of this Act, the borrower gives evidence that he has posted a cheque, money order or postal order to the moneylender at his authorized address in payment of the money lent or any part thereof or of interest thereon, it shall be presumed that the amount stated in the cheque, money order or postal order has been paid to the moneylender towards payment of the money lent or interest thereon, as the case may be.

(2) A moneylender shall not accept in repayment of an amount exceeding ten dollars from a borrower in respect of the principal sum of or interest due for any loan given unless such repayment is made by cheque, money order or postal order.

(3) A moneylender who contravenes the provisions of subsection (2) of this section shall be guilty of an offence under this Act and shall be liable on conviction to a fine not exceeding five hundred dollars.

Prohibition of charge for expenses on loans by moneylender.

26. Any agreement between a moneylender and a borrower or intending borrower for the payment by the borrower or intending borrower to the moneylender of any sum on account of costs, charges or expenses other than stamp duties, fees payable by law and legal costs incidental to or relating to the negotiations for or the granting of the loan or proposed loan shall be illegal, and if any sum is paid to a moneylender by a borrower or intending borrower as, for or on account of any such costs, charges or expenses other than as aforesaid, that sum shall be recoverable as a debt due to the borrower or intending borrower, or in the event of the loan being completed, shall, if not so recovered, be set off against the amount actually lent and that amount shall be deemed to be reduced accordingly.

Calculation of interest.

27. Where the interest charged on a loan is not expressed in terms of a rate per cent per annum, the rate of interest per cent per annum charged on the loan shall be calculated in accordance with the Second

Schedule [4] to this Act or, where the contract provides for the payment of equal instalments of principal and interest at equal intervals of time, in accordance with the formula given in the Third Schedule [5] to this Act.

Notice and information to be given on assignment of moneylender's debts.

28. (1) Where any debt in respect of money lent by a moneylender, whether before or after the coming into operation of this Act, or in respect of interest on any such debt, or the benefit of any agreement made or security taken in respect of any such debt or interest, is assigned to any assignee, the assignor (whether he is the moneylender by whom the money was lent or any person to whom the debt has been previously assigned) shall, before the assignment is made—

*(a)* give to the assignee notice in writing that the debt, agreement or security is affected by the operation of this Act; and

*(b)* supply to the assignee all information necessary to enable him to comply with the provisions of this Act relating to the obligation to supply information as to the state of loans and copies of documents relating thereto,

and any person acting in contravention of any of the provisions of this section shall be liable to indemnify any other person who is prejudiced by the contravention and shall also be guilty of an offence against this Act and shall in respect of each offence be liable on conviction to imprisonment for a term not exceeding one year or to a fine not exceeding one thousand dollars or to both such imprisonment and fine:

Provided that an offender being a company shall be liable to a fine of five thousand dollars.

(2) In this section the expression "assigned" means assigned by any assignment inter vivos other than an assignment by operation of law, and the expressions "assignee" and "assignor" have corresponding meanings.

Application of Act as respects assignees.

29. (1) Subject as hereinafter provided the provisions of this Act shall continue to apply as respects any debt to a moneylender in respect of money lent by him whether before or after the coming into operation of this Act or in respect of interest on money so lent or of the benefit of any agreement made or security taken in respect of any such debt or interest notwithstanding that the debts or the benefit of the agreement or security may have been assigned to any assignee and, except where the context otherwise requires, references in this Act to a moneylender shall accordingly be construed as including any such assignee as aforesaid.

[4] The Second Schedule is omitted from this volume.

[5] The Third Schedule is omitted from this volume.

(2) No assignment of any debt in respect of money lent by a moneylender whether before or after the coming into operation of this Act shall be valid unless the moneylender is licensed under this Act.

(3) Notwithstanding anything in this Act—

*(a)* any agreement with or security taken by a licensed moneylender in respect of money lent by him after the coming into operation of this Act shall be valid in favour of any bona fide assignee or holder for value without notice of any defect due to the operation of this Act and of any person deriving title under him; and

*(b)* any payment or transfer of money or property made bona fide by any person, whether acting in a fiduciary capacity or otherwise, on the faith of the validity of any such agreement or security without notice of any such defect shall, in favour of that person, be as valid as it would have been if the agreement or security had been valid:

Provided that in every such case the moneylender shall be liable to indemnify the borrower or any other person who is prejudiced by virtue of this section and nothing in this subsection shall render valid an agreement or security in favour of or apply to proceedings commenced by an assignee or holder for value who is himself a moneylender.

(4) Notwithstanding anything contained in this Act, for the purposes of this section an assignee or holder for value or person making any such payment or transfer as aforesaid shall not be prejudicially affected by notice of any such defect as aforesaid unless—

*(a)* it is within his own knowledge, or would have come to his knowledge if such inquiries and inspections had been made as ought reasonably to have been made by him; or

*(b)* in the same transaction, with respect to which a question of notice to such assignee, holder for value or person arises, it has come to the knowledge of his counsel as such or of his solicitor or other agent as such, or would have come to the knowledge of his solicitor or other agent as such if such inquiries and inspections had been made as ought reasonably to have been made by the solicitor or other agent.

(5) Nothing in this section shall render valid for any purpose any agreement, security or other transaction which would, apart from the provisions of this Act, have been void or unenforceable.

Attestation of certain promissory notes.

**30.** (1) Whenever a promissory note is taken as security for any loan and the borrower is a person who does not understand the written language on the note the note shall be attested by an advocate and solicitor, a Magistrate, Justice of the Peace, commissioner for oaths or such other person as may be appointed by the Minister generally for that purpose. The attestor shall explain the terms of the promissory note to the borrower, and shall certify thereon that the borrower appeared to understand the meaning of the note. The money borrowed shall be paid over by the lender to the borrower in the presence of the attestor who shall certify the fact upon the promissory note.

(2) Any promissory note required to be attested under this section and not so attested shall be void and the lender shall not be entitled to recover any loan for which the note is taken as security.

Penalty for taking promissory note in which amount left blank or not truly stated.

31. Any moneylender who makes any note or memorandum under section 16 of this Act or who takes as security for any loan a promissory note or other contract for the repayment of money lent in which the principal or rate of interest is, to the knowledge of the moneylender, not truly stated or is left blank shall be guilty of an offence and shall be liable on conviction to a fine not exceeding two thousand dollars or, in the event of a second or subsequent offence, to imprisonment for a term not exceeding six months or to a fine not exceeding five thousand dollars or to both such imprisonment and fine.

False statements or representations to induce borrowing an offence.

32. If any moneylender or any manager, agent or clerk of a moneylender or if any person being a director, manager or other officer of any company, by any false, misleading or deceptive statement, representation or promise or by any dishonest concealment of material facts fraudulently induces or attempts to induce any person to borrow money or to agree to the terms on which money is or is to be borrowed, he shall be guilty of an offence and shall be liable on conviction to imprisonment for a term not exceeding two years or to a fine not exceeding five thousand dollars or to both such imprisonment and fine.

Harassing debtor, besetting his residence, etc.

33. (1) Any moneylender, who, either personally or by any person acting on his behalf, harasses or intimidates his debtor or any member of the debtor's family at, or watches or besets, the residence or place of business or employment of the debtor, or any place at which the debtor receives his wages or any other sum periodically due to him, shall be guilty of an offence, and shall be liable on conviction to a fine not exceeding two thousand dollars, or to imprisonment for a term not exceeding three months or to both such fine and imprisonment:

Provided that an offender being a company shall be liable to a fine of five thousand dollars.

(2) Any person reasonably suspected of having committed an offence under subsection (1) of this section who refuses or fails to

accompany a police officer when required to do so for the purposes of any investigation under this Act may be arrested without warrant.

Special provisions relating to non-resident principal.

34. (1) When any fine is imposed on an agent who is or has been licensed under this Act to carry on a moneylending business on behalf of a principal not resident in Singapore, the fine, if it has been imposed in respect of an offence under this Act committed by the agent in the course of carrying on such business shall, unless the court imposing the fine otherwise directs, be recoverable out of the property situate in Singapore belonging to the principal as well as out of the property belonging to the agent and any such property of the principal may be taken in execution and sold under any warrant issued against the agent for the levy of the amount of the fine.

(2) When it is made to appear to any court by any person entitled to make an application under section 22 of this Act that any transaction entered into with a moneylender not resident in Singapore prima facie ought to be reopened the court may—

(*a*) issue an order of attachment attaching any property of the moneylender situate within Singapore until such time as the moneylender submits to the jurisdiction of the court and gives security to the satisfaction of the court that any order made against him for repayment of any sum or for an indemnity will be duly satisfied; and

(*b*) authorize the service out of the jurisdiction of any summons or other process applying for the reopening of the transaction under section 22 of this Act.

Powers of police officer.

34A. Any police officer not below the rank of sergeant who is authorized in writing by the Registrar, or by a police officer not below the rank of Assistant Superintendent of Police, may at all times enter into the premises of any licensed moneylender or any person who is suspected of carrying on the business of moneylending to inspect or seize any book or document relating to any moneylending transaction without a warrant being issued by a Magistrate for that purpose.

Power of Minister to grant exemptions.

35. (1) The Minister may, upon payment of the prescribed fee, exempt, with or without conditions, any body corporate or society from all or any of the provisions of this Act, and may revoke any exemption granted by him at any time by the service of a notice of revocation in writing on the body corporate or society.

(2) Every exemption under subsection (1) of this section shall in the first instance be valid for a period of three years or less from the

date of the granting thereof but may, upon payment of the prescribed fee, be extended thereafter, with or without additional conditions, for further periods not exceeding three years at a time.

(3) Any body corporate or society which immediately before 1st December 1967 had been previously exempted from the provisions of this Act by the Minister, by notification published in the *Gazette,* shall be deemed to have been exempted under this section from that date until 31st December 1967.

36. The Minister may make rules generally to give effect to the provisions of this Act and, in particular, may by such rules provide for— Rules.

(*a*) the forms to be used for the purposes of this Act;
(*b*) the fees to be charged under this Act;
(*c*) the books of account to be kept by a moneylender;
(*d*) the manner in which accounts and files relating to loans by moneylenders are to be kept and the particulars to be entered therein; and
(*e*) the maximum rate of interest to be charged for any loan or class of loans.

*{The three Schedules are omitted from this volume.}*

## Pawnbrokers Act[1]

An Act to consolidate the law relating to pawnbrokers.

[1st January, 1899]

1. This Act may be cited as the Pawnbrokers Act. Short title.

[1] *Singapore Statutes,* Cap. 195 (1955); Cap. 222 (1970). Originally Ord. No. 4 of 1898. Relevant citations: Ords. Nos. 1 of 1903; 11 of 1912; 26 of 1921; 45 of 1934; 63 of 1935; 41 of 1936; 15 of 1939; 37 of 1952; 12 of 1957; 71 of 1959; 38 of 1960; Acts Nos. 23 of 1966; and 7 of 1977.

Interpretation.

2. In this Act—

"pawnbroker" includes every person who carries on the business of taking goods and chattels in pawn;

"pawner" means a person delivering an article for pawn to a pawnbroker;

"pledge" means an article pawned with a pawnbroker;

"Registrar" means the Registrar of Pawnbrokers appointed under the provisions of section 7 of this Act;

"shop" includes a dwelling-house and warehouse or other place of business or place where business is transacted;

"unfinished goods or materials" includes any goods of any manufacture or of any part or branch of any manufacture, either mixed or separate, or any materials whatever plainly intended for the composing or manufacturing of any goods, after such goods or materials are put into a state or course of manufacture or into a state for any process or operation to be performed thereupon or therewith, and before the same are completed or finished for the purpose of wear or consumption.

## PAWNBROKERS

Persons to be deemed pawnbrokers.

3. (1) Any person who—

*(a)* receives or takes of or from any person whomsoever any goods or chattels by way of security for the repayment of any sum or sums of money, not exceeding one thousand dollars advanced, thereon; or

*(b)* purchases or receives or takes in goods or chattels and pays or advances or lends thereon any sum or sums of money, not exceeding one thousand dollars, with or under an agreement or understanding expressed or implied or to be from the nature and character of the dealing reasonably inferred that those goods or chattels may be afterwards redeemed or repurchased on any terms,

shall be deemed to be a person carrying on the business of taking goods and chattels in pawn, and every such transaction, article, payment, advance and loan shall be deemed a pawning, pledge or loan respectively within this Act.

(2) Nothing in this Act shall extend to any loan of money exceeding one hundred dollars and secured by a pawn or pledge, if the rate of interest does not exceed ten per cent per annum and if no further or other profit or advantage is taken or agreed for on the loan, or shall

extend to prevent a pawnbroker under this Act from taking in pawn goods or chattels exceeding in value the sum of one thousand dollars or lending thereon a sum exceeding that amount.

4. The provisions of this Act relating to pawnbrokers shall extend to and include the executors or administrators of deceased pawnbrokers, except that an executor or administrator shall not be answerable for any penalty or forfeiture personally or out of his own estate, unless the same is incurred by his own act or neglect.

Application of the Act to executors, etc., of pawnbrokers.

5. (1) For the purposes of this Act anything done or omitted to be done by the servant or agent of a pawnbroker, in the course of or in relation to the business of the pawnbroker, shall be deemed to be done or omitted, as the case may be, by the pawnbroker.

Act done by servant to be deemed the act of the pawnbroker.

(2) Anything by this Act authorized to be done by a pawnbroker may be done by his servant or agent.

6. The rights, powers and benefits by this Act reserved to and conferred on pawners shall extend to, and be deemed to be reserved to, and conferred on, the assignees of pawners, and to and on the executors or administrators of deceased pawners; but any person representing himself to a pawnbroker to be the assign, executor or administrator of a pawner shall, if required by the pawnbroker, produce to the pawnbroker the assignment, probate, letters of administration or other instrument under which he claims.

Extension of rights, etc., of pawners to their assigns, executors, etc.

## LICENCES

7. (1) The Minister may appoint a Registrar of Pawnbrokers and such number of Assistant Registrars of Pawnbrokers and other officers as he may consider necessary or expedient for the purposes of this Act.

Appointment of Registrar and Assistant Registrars.

(2) An Assistant Registrar shall have and may exercise all the powers conferred on the Registrar by this Act subject to such limitations as the Registrar sees fit to impose.

8. (1) Every pawnbroker shall annually take out from the Registrar a licence for carrying on his business for which there shall be charged and paid before the issue of the licence such fee as the Minister may prescribe. Application for such a licence shall be made in accordance with such rules as may be made under the provisions of section 45 of this Act.

Issue of licences by the Board.

(2) Licences shall be subject to such conditions, if any, as may be imposed by the Registrar in addition to those prescribed in section 9 of this Act.

(3) A separate licence shall be taken out and paid for by a pawnbroker for each pawnbroker's shop kept by him.

(4) Every licence shall be dated on the day on which it is issued and shall determine on the thirty-first day of December.

(5) Any person who acts as a pawnbroker without having in force a valid licence issued by the Registrar shall be guilty of an offence and shall be liable on conviction to a fine not exceeding two thousand dollars and in the case of a second or subsequent conviction shall in addition be liable to imprisonment for a term not exceeding six months.

Conditions subject to which licences may be issued.

**9.** (1) No licence shall be issued by the Registrar to a pawnbroker in respect of any premises unless the Registrar is satisfied—

*(a)* that the applicant is of good character and is a fit and proper person to carry on the business of pawnbroking;
*(b)* that the premises to be licensed are structurally adapted for use as a pawnbroker's shop and are in all other respects suitable for that purpose;
*(c)* that the premises will not be used for the conduct or transaction of any business other than that of pawnbroking; and
*(d)* that the applicant has deposited with the Accountant-General a sum of five thousand dollars as security for the proper conduct of his business under the licence.

(2) The Registrar may in his discretion refuse to issue or renew a license in respect of any applicant or any premises without assigning any reason therefor.

Power of Registrar to cancel licence.

**9A.** (1) The Registrar may cancel a licence and forfeit the whole or such part of the money deposited with the Accountant-General under paragraph *(d)* of subsection (1) of section 9 of this Act as the Registrar may think fit if he is satisfied that—

*(a)* the licensed pawnbroker's shop is being conducted in an improper or unsatisfactory manner; or
*(b)* the licensee has been convicted of an offence under this Act; or
*(c)* the licensee has failed to comply with any of the conditions upon which the licence was issued; or
*(d)* since the issue of the licence, the licensee or the premises has ceased to comply with any of the requirements set out in subsection (1) of section 9 of this Act.

(2) The Registrar shall, before cancelling a licence and forfeiting any money under the provisions of subsection (1) of this section, give the licensee concerned notice in writing of his intention to do so specifying a date, not less than fourteen days after the date of the notice, upon which such cancellation and forfeiture shall be made and calling upon the licensee to show cause to the Registrar why his licence should not be cancelled and why his money should not be forfeited.

(3) The Registrar, on receiving any representation from a licensee, may, instead of cancelling a licence and forfeiting any money under the provisions of subsection (1) of this section, impose a penalty not exceeding five thousand dollars on the licensee and may recover the penalty from any cash deposit or other form of security given by the licensee to the Registrar.

(4) Any cancellation of a licence shall not affect the duties and liabilities of the licensee as a pawnbroker under this Act.

Appeal to the Minister.

**9B.** Any person aggrieved by the refusal of the Registrar to issue or renew a licence or the decision of the Registrar to cancel a licence and forfeit any money belonging to the licensee or to impose a penalty may, within ten days of the written notification to him of the refusal, cancellation, forfeiture or imposition of the penalty, appeal in writing to the Minister whose decision thereon shall be final and conclusive.

Pawnshop to keep open after expiration of licence for redemption of articles.

**10.** Upon the expiration or sooner determination of any licence the pawnbroker shall keep open the licensed premises daily from 8 a.m. to 6 p.m. for the redemption of articles pawned with him; and, for all purposes of this Act, except the receiving of articles in pawn, shall continue to exercise the rights and privileges and be subject to the duties and liabilities of a licensed pawnbroker until the whole of the articles held by him in pawn have been redeemed or the latest period of redemption for any of such articles has expired.

## General Obligations of Pawnbroker

Description of articles pawned, etc., to be entered in a book.

**11.** (1) Every pawnbroker shall—

*(a)* keep and use in his business such books and documents as are prescribed, and shall enter therein in a clear and legible hand, in such style of character, language or dialect as the Minister directs, the particulars required by rules, and shall make all inquiries necessary for that purpose;

Signboards.

*(b)* keep always exhibited at or over the outer door of his shop a

signboard of such size and in such position as the Registrar directs having printed thereon, in the English, Malay, Chinese and Tamil languages, the words "Pawnbroker's Shop"; and

Copy of rates to be exposed.

(*c*) keep exposed in some convenient place in the shop, so as to be near to and visible to all comers, a legible copy of the rates of profit he may lawfully take under this Act, and also the same information in the English, Malay, Chinese and Tamil languages as is by rules required to be printed on pawn tickets.

(2) Every pawnbroker shall make such monthly returns as may be prescribed by rules made under the provisions of section 45 of this Act.

Penalty.

(3) Any pawnbroker who fails in any respect to comply with this section shall be guilty of an offence under this Act.

## PAWNING, REDEMPTION AND SALE

Pawnbroker to grant a pawn ticket.

**12.** A pawnbroker shall on taking a pledge in pawn give to the pawner a pawn ticket, and shall not take a pledge in pawn unless the pawner takes the pawn ticket.

Profit and charges allowed to pawnbroker.

**13.** (1) A pawnbroker may take profit on a loan on a pledge at a rate not exceeding that specified in Schedule B.[2]

(2) A pawnbroker may demand and take the charges specified in the said Schedule.

(3) A pawnbroker shall not in respect of a loan on a pledge take any profit or demand or take any charge or sum whatever other than those specified in the Schedule.

(4) A pawnbroker shall, if required at the time of redemption, give a receipt for the amount of loan and profit paid to him.

(5) The Minister may by order amend the rate of profits and charges specified in Schedule B to this Act.

(6) All orders made under subsection (5) of this section shall be published in the *Gazette* and shall be presented to Parliament as soon as may be after publication and if a resolution is passed pursuant to a motion notice whereof has been given for a sitting day not later than the first available sitting day of Parliament next after the expiry of three months from the date when orders are so presented annulling the

[2] Schedule B is omitted from this volume.

orders or any part thereof as from a specified date, the orders or that part thereof as the case may be shall thereupon become void as from that date but without prejudice to the validity of anything previously done thereunder or to the making of new orders.

Period of redemption of pledge.

14. Every pledge shall be redeemable within six months from the day of pawning, exclusive of that day, or in the case of a pledge for a sum exceeding fifty dollars within such longer term as may have been specially agreed upon at the time of pawning.

Forfeiture of pledge for $50 and under if not redeemed.

15. A pledge pawned for fifty dollars or under, if not redeemed within the time allowed by this Act, shall at the end of the time of redemption become and be the pawnbroker's absolute property.

Pledges exceeding $50 redeemable until sale.

16. A pledge pawned for any sum exceeding fifty dollars shall further continue redeemable until it is disposed of as in this Act provided, although the time of redemption has expired.

Sale by auction of pledge for a sum exceeding $50.

17. (1) A pledge pawned for any sum exceeding fifty dollars shall, when disposed of by the pawnbroker, be disposed of by sale by an auctioneer licensed in that behalf and not otherwise.

(2) The regulations contained in Schedule C shall be observed with reference to the sale.

(3) A pawnbroker may bid for and purchase at a sale by auction made under this Act a pledge pawned with him; and on such purchase he shall be deemed the absolute owner of the pledge purchased.

(4) The Minister may, by writing under his hand, license fit persons to conduct sales of forfeited pledges for such periods as in the licence are specified, and may revoke any such licence without assigning any reason.

Offences by auctioneer.

18. Any auctioneer who does anything in contravention of this Act relating to auctioneers, or fails to do anything which he is required by this Act to do, shall be guilty of an offence under this Act.

Right of holder of pawn ticket to inspect sale book.

19. At any time within four months after the auction at which a pledge pawned for above fifty dollars is sold, the holder of the pawn ticket may inspect the entry of the sale in the pawnbroker's book and in the filled-up catalogue of the auction, authenticated by the signature of the auctioneer, or in either of them.

Obligation on pawnbroker to account for surplus within four months subject to set-off.

**20.** (1) Where a pledge pawned for above fifty dollars is sold, and appears from the pawnbroker's book to have been sold for more than the amount of the loan and profit due at the time of sale, the pawnbroker shall on demand pay the surplus to the holder of the pawn ticket in case the demand is made within four months after the sale, the necessary costs and charges of the sale being first deducted.

(2) The pawnbroker shall send to the Registrar, on the first day of every calendar month, a list, written in the English language, showing the result of the sales of such pledges during the preceding calendar month, in Form 3 in Schedule A[3] or in such other form as is prescribed, and the Registrar shall keep such list for three months in a place easily accessible to the public.

(3) If on the demand mentioned in subsection (1) it appears from the pawnbroker's book that the sale of a pledge or pledges has resulted in a surplus and that, within four months before or after sale, the sale of another pledge or other pledges of the same person has resulted in a deficit, the pawnbroker may set off the deficit against the surplus, and shall be liable to pay the balance only after the set-off.

Offences as to a pledge for a sum exceeding $50.

**21.** Any pawnbroker who with respect to pledges for loans of above fifty dollars—

*(a)* does not bona fide, according to the directions of this Act, sell a pledge pawned with him; or

*(b)* enters in his book a pledge as sold for less than the sum for which it was sold, or fails duly to enter the same; or

*(c)* refuses to permit any person entitled under this Act to inspection of an entry of sale in the pawnbroker's book or of a filled-up catalogue of the auction, authenticated by the auctioneer's signature, to inspect the same; or

*(d)* fails without lawful excuse, the proof whereof shall lie on him, to produce such a catalogue on lawful demand; or

*(e)* refuses to pay on demand the surplus to the person entitled to receive the same,

shall in every such case be guilty of an offence under this Act.

## Delivery Up of Pledge

Right of holder of pawn ticket to redeem pledge.

**22.** The holder for the time being of a pawn ticket shall be presumed to be the person entitled to redeem the pledge, and, subject to this Act, the pawnbroker shall accordingly, on payment of the loan and

[3] Schedule A, containing Form 3, is omitted from this volume.

profit, deliver the pledge to the person producing the pawn ticket, and he is hereby indemnified for so doing.

23. A pawnbroker shall not, except as in this Act provided, be bound to deliver back a pledge unless the pawn ticket for it is delivered to him.

**Production of pawn ticket on redemption.**

24. (1) Where a pledge is destroyed or damaged by or in consequence of fire or lost, the pawnbroker shall nevertheless be liable, on application within the period during which the pledge would have been redeemable, to pay the value of the pledge after deducting the amount of the loan and profit, such value to be assumed to be one quarter more than the amount of the loan.

**Liability of pawnbroker in case of fire or loss.**

(2) A pawnbroker shall be entitled to insure to the extent of the value so estimated.

25. (1) If a person entitled and offering to redeem a pledge shows, to the satisfaction of a Magistrate's Court, that the pledge has become or has been rendered of less value than it was at the time of the pawning thereof by or through the default or neglect or wilful misbehaviour of the pawnbroker, the Court may, if it thinks fit, award a reasonable compensation to the owner of the pledge in respect of the damage, and the amount awarded shall be deducted from the amount payable to the pawnbroker or shall be paid by the pawnbroker, as the case may require, in such manner as the Court directs, provided that no suit shall thereafter be brought by the owner in any civil court in respect of the same matter.

Compensation for loss or depreciation of pledge.

(2) When a pawnbroker has been directed to pay a sum of money to the owner of a pledge under this section, the sum so directed to be paid shall be recoverable as a fine.

26. (1) The following provisions shall have effect for the protection of owners of articles pawned and of pawners not having their pawn tickets to produce.

Protection of owner and of pawner not having pawn ticket.

(2) Any person claiming to be the owner of a pledge but not holding the pawn ticket, or any person claiming to be entitled to hold a pawn ticket but alleging that the same has been lost, mislaid, destroyed or stolen or fraudulently obtained from him, may apply to the pawnbroker for a printed form of declaration, which the pawnbroker shall deliver to him.

(3) If the applicant delivers back to the pawnbroker the declaration

duly made before a Magistrate or a notary public by the applicant and by a person identifying him, the applicant shall thereupon have as between him and the pawnbroker all the same rights and remedies as if he produced the pawn ticket:

Provided that such a declaration shall not be effectual for that purpose unless it is duly made and delivered back to the pawnbroker not later than on the third day after the day on which the form is delivered to the applicant by the pawnbroker.

(4) The pawnbroker is hereby indemnified for not delivering the pledge to any person until the expiration of the period aforesaid.

(5) The pawnbroker is hereby further indemnified for delivering the pledge or otherwise acting in conformity with the declaration, unless he has actual or constructive notice that the declaration is fraudulent or is false in any material particular.

(6) Declarations under this section may be in Form 1 or 2 of Schedule A,[4] as the nature of the case requires.

(7) Every declaration under this section shall be deemed to be a declaration within the meaning of sections 199 and 200 of the Penal Code.

Delivery to owner of property unlawfully pawned.

27. (1) In each of the following cases:

(*a*) if any person is convicted under this Act before a Magistrate's Court of knowingly and designedly pawning with a pawnbroker anything being the property of another person, the pawner not being employed or authorized by the owner thereof to pawn the same;

(*b*) if any person is convicted in any court of any offence against property which offence is defined or dealt with by any provision of sections 378 to 420 both inclusive of the Penal Code, and it appears to the Magistrate's Court or other court that such property has been pawned with a pawnbroker; or

(*c*) if in any proceedings before a Magistrate's Court or other court it appears to the court that any goods and chattels brought before the court have been unlawfully pawned with a pawnbroker,

the court, on proof of the ownership of the goods and chattels, may, if it thinks fit, order the delivery thereof to the owner, either on payment to the pawnbroker of the amount of the loan or any part thereof, or without payment thereof or of any part thereof, as to the court, accord-

[4] Schedule A is omitted from this volume.

ing to the conduct of the owner and the other circumstances of the case, seems just and fitting.

(2) The court may also adjourn the proceedings for the attendance of the pawnbroker, and may summon the pawnbroker to attend at the adjourned hearing, and if, after hearing the pawnbroker, the court is of opinion that the pawnbroker has not exercised due care in taking in pawn any stolen property, the court may order the pawnbroker to pay a fine not exceeding two thousand dollars.

Liability of pawnbroker for taking stolen goods in pawn without due care.

**28.** Any pawnbroker who without reasonable excuse, the proof whereof shall lie on him, refuses or neglects to deliver a pledge to the person entitled to have delivery thereof under this Act shall be liable to a fine not exceeding five thousand dollars, and the court may, with or without imposing a fine, order the delivery of the pledge on payment of the amount of the loan and profit.

Summary order for delivery of pledge to person entitled.

## General Restrictions on Pawnbroker

**29.** Any pawnbroker who—

Prohibition as to taking or purchasing of pledge in certain circumstances.

(*a*) takes an article in pawn from any person who appears to be intoxicated, or from a person apparently under the age of sixteen years;

(*b*) purchases or takes in pawn or exchanges a pawn ticket issued by another pawnbroker;

(*c*) employs any servant or other person under the age of sixteen years to take pledges in pawn;

(*d*) under any pretence purchases, except at public auction, any pledge while in pawn or with him;

(*e*) suffers any pledge while in pawn with him to be redeemed with a view to his purchasing it;

(*f*) makes any contract or agreement with any person pawning or offering to pawn any article or with the owner thereof for the purchase, sale or disposition thereof within the time of redemption;

(*g*) sells, pawns or otherwise disposes of any pledge pawned with him, except at such time and in such manner as are authorized by this Act;

(*h*) makes an advance upon any article pledged with him otherwise than in money which is legal tender in Singapore; or

(*i*) takes any goods or chattels in pawn from any person before 8 a.m. or after 8 p.m.,

shall be liable to a fine not exceeding five thousand dollars.

## UNLAWFUL PAWNING AND TAKING IN PAWN

Penalty for wrongfully pawning the property of another.

**30.** (1) Any person who knowingly and designedly pawns with a pawnbroker anything being the property of another person, the pawner not being employed or authorized by the owner thereof to pawn the same, shall be liable to a fine not exceeding two thousand dollars.

(2) In addition to any fine imposed under subsection (1), the court may order the accused to pay by way of compensation to the owner any sum not exceeding the full value of the pledge as ascertained by the court, such sum to be levied and taken in the same manner as a fine.

Proceedings where person offering article in pawn does not give a good account of himself;

**31.** (1) Any person who—

*(a)* offers to a pawnbroker an article by way of pawn, being unable or refusing to give a satisfactory account of the means by which he became possessed of the article; or

or gives false information;

*(b)* wilfully gives false information to a pawnbroker as to whether an article offered by him in pawn to the pawnbroker is his own property or not, or as to his name and address or as to the name and address of the owner of the article; or

or attempts without title to redeem a pledge.

*(c)* not being entitled to redeem and not having any colour of title by law to redeem a pledge, attempts or endeavours to redeem the same,

shall be guilty of an offence under this Act.

(2) In every such case, and also in any case where, on an article being offered in pawn to a pawnbroker he reasonably suspects that it has been stolen or otherwise illegally or clandestinely obtained, the pawnbroker may seize and detain the person and the article, or either of them, and shall deliver the person and the article or either of them (as the case may be) as soon as may be into the custody of a police officer, who shall as soon as may be convey the person, if so detained, before a magistrate, to be dealt with according to law.

Person in possession of pawn ticket presumed to have been in possession of the article pawned.

**32.** Any person found in possession of a pawn ticket shall, until he satisfies the court to the contrary, be presumed to have been in possession of the pawned article to which the pawn ticket refers.

33. (1) If any person, under suspicious circumstances, offers any articles in pawn to a pawnbroker, or, without having any colour of title by law to redeem a pledge, attempts to redeem it, and the pawnbroker has reason to suspect such want of title, the pawnbroker shall inquire of the person how he came by the articles or the pawn ticket, as the case may be.

Duty of pawnbroker on offer of pledges or redemption under suspicious circumstances.

(2) If the person is not able or refuses to give a satisfactory account of himself or of the means by which he became possessed of the articles or pawn ticket, or wilfully gives any false information concerning the articles or pawn ticket, or as to his name or address, or as to the name or place of abode of the owner of the articles, or if there is any other reason to suspect that the articles or pawn ticket have been stolen or otherwise illegally or clandestinely obtained, the pawnbroker may seize and detain the person offering the articles or pawn ticket, and shall deliver him with the articles or pawn ticket into the custody of a police officer.

34. Any pawnbroker who knowingly takes in pawn any linen or apparel or unfinished goods or materials entrusted to any person to wash, scour, iron, mend, manufacture, work up, finish or make up, shall be liable to a fine not exceeding two thousand dollars; and shall likewise restore the pledge to the owner thereof in the presence of the court or as the court directs.

Prohibition as to taking in pawn linen, apparel, unfinished goods, etc., in certain cases.

35. (1) If the owner of any linen or apparel or unfinished goods or materials entrusted to any person as aforesaid and unlawfully pawned with a pawnbroker, or the owner of any other article unlawfully pawned with the pawnbroker, the last-mentioned owner having on oath satisfied a Magistrate's Court that his goods have been unlawfully obtained, taken or withheld from him, makes out on oath before a Magistrate's Court that there is a good cause to suspect that a pawnbroker has taken in pawn the linen, apparel, goods, materials or articles aforesaid without the privity or authority of the owner, and makes appear to the satisfaction of the Magistrate's Court probable grounds for such suspicion, the Magistrate's Court may issue a warrant for searching, within the hours of business, the shop of the pawnbroker.

Search warrant for linen, etc., unlawfully pawned.

(2) If the pawnbroker, on request by a police officer authorized by the warrant to make the search, refuses to open the shop or permit it to be searched, a police officer may break it open within the hours of business and search as he thinks fit therein for the linen, apparel, goods, materials or articles aforesaid, doing no wilful damage, and if any pawnbroker or other person oppose or hinders the search he shall be guilty of an offence under this Act.

(3) If on the search any linen, apparel, goods, materials or articles aforesaid is or are found and the property of the owner thereof is made out to the satisfaction of a Magistrate's Court, the Court shall cause the same forthwith to be restored to the owner thereof.

## Penalties and Police Regulations

General penalty.

36. Any pawnbroker or other person who is guilty of an offence under this Act, in respect whereof a specific forfeiture or penalty is not prescribed by this Act, or of any breach of this Act, shall be liable to a penalty not exceeding two thousand dollars.

Application of penalty.

37. Any penalty recovered under this Act, not directed to be otherwise applied, may be applied under the direction of the Magistrate's Court in which it is recovered as follows:

(*a*) where the complainant is the party aggrieved, a sum not exceeding one-half of the penalty may be paid to him;

(*b*) where the complainant is not the party aggrieved, there shall be paid to him no part or such part only of the penalty as the Court thinks fit.

Penalty on common informer compounding information.

38. Any person who lays an information for an offence alleged to have been committed under this Act by which he was not personally aggrieved, and afterwards, directly or indirectly, receives, without the permission of the court, any sum of money or other reward for compounding, delaying or withdrawing the information, shall be guilty of an offence under this Act.

Detention of person offering forged pawn ticket, etc.

39. If any person utters, produces, shows or offers to a pawnbroker a pawn ticket which the pawnbroker reasonably suspects to have been counterfeited, forged or altered, the pawnbroker may seize and detain the person and the ticket or either of them, and shall deliver the person and the ticket or either of them, as the case may be, into the custody of a police officer.

Pawnbroker's books subject to examination by police.

40. (1) The books required by this Act to be kept by a pawnbroker shall be produced by him for examination at any time during business hours on demand by any Justice of the Peace or by any police officer not under the rank of corporal, who are hereby severally authorized to enter at any time during business hours any pawnbroker's shop without warrant to search for and examine the said books and to take extracts and copies therefrom.

(2) Any pawnbroker who fails to comply with this section shall be guilty of an offence under this Act.

41. (1) Information as to property lost, stolen or otherwise fraudulently disposed of shall be given by the police, as soon as possible after such loss or fraud, to all pawnbrokers, with lists and descriptions of the same.

Information to be given by police to pawnbrokers of lost and stolen property.

(2) If any property answering such lists and descriptions is in the possession of any pawnbroker or is thereafter offered to or shown to any pawnbroker he shall, without unnecessary delay, give information to that effect at the nearest police station or to any police officer, with the name, address and identity card number of the person in whose possession the property was seen, and in default thereof he shall be liable to a fine not exceeding two thousand dollars.

(3) The pawnbroker in such a case may also detain the person offering or showing the property until the arrival of the police.

42. Any police officer not under the rank of corporal may enter any pawnbroker's shop at any time during business hours, and may search without warrant the house, shop or premises of the pawnbroker for any articles that he may have reason to suspect to be therein and to have been dishonestly obtained or dishonestly placed there.

Police officers may enter pawnshops, etc.

43. (1) Any police officer having reason to believe that a person in or loitering about a pawnbroker's shop under suspicious circumstances has with him any article dishonestly obtained may detain that person and require him to produce any articles he may have with him.

Police officers may arrest persons loitering about pawnshops under suspicious circumstances.

(2) If any articles are produced which the police officer has reason to suspect to have been unlawfully obtained, he may take or cause to be taken the person and the articles to the nearest police station.

(3) If any person so required to produce such articles refuses to be searched, the police officer may take him or cause him to be taken before a Justice of the Peace, who if he sees fit may search the person or order him to be searched, and if any such articles are found may detain him with the articles so found to be dealt with according to law.

44. All offences under this Act or any rules made thereunder shall be tried before a Magistrate's Court or District Court.

Jurisdiction.

## Rules

Rules.

45. (1) The Minister may make rules prescribing—

(*a*) the form of the books to be kept by pawnbrokers and the particulars to be entered therein;
(*b*) the form of the note or pawn ticket to be issued by pawnbrokers and the particulars to be entered therein;
(*c*) generally the manner and conditions in and under which the business of pawnbroking shall be conducted;
(*d*) the fees to be paid for licences by pawnbrokers and by auctioneers under this Act, and the manner in which sales under this Act shall be held;
(*e*) the procedure to be followed by applicants for licences as pawnbrokers and the procedure and proceedings of the Board; [5]
(*f*) the form of the monthly returns to be made by pawnbrokers;
(*g*) all matters stated or required in this Act to be prescribed; and
(*h*) generally to give effect to the provisions of this Act.

(2) Any person contravening any rule made under this Act shall be liable to a fine not exceeding one thousand dollars.

*{Schedules A and B are omitted from this volume.}*

## Schedule C

### Regulations as to auction of pledges above fifty dollars

1. Auctions shall be held within the first seven days of each month at times and places approved by the Registrar. At least seven days' notice in writing of

[5] Section 23 (1) and (3) of An Act to amend the Pawnbrokers Act. No. 7 of 1977 (Cap. 222 of the Revised Edition) provides:

"(1) Upon the date of the commencement of this Act, the Pawnbrokers Licensing Board established under section 7 of the Pawnbrokers Act prior to the date of the commencement of this Act shall cease to exist and all rights, obligations and liabilities of the Board which may have existed immediately prior to the date of the commencement of this Act shall be transferred to and shall vest in the Registrar.

..............................................................................................................

"(3) In any written law and in any document whatsoever, unless the context otherwise requires, any reference to the Board shall be construed as a reference to the Registrar."

all sales shall be given by the auctioneer to the Registrar, and to the public by means of an advertisement in a public newspaper and by notices, in the various vernacular languages and in English, to be posted in sufficient number and in conspicuous places to the satisfaction of the Registrar, stating—

(*a*) the pawnbroker's name and place of business;
(*b*) the month in which the pledges were pawned; and
(*c*) the place where the auction is to be held.

2. The advertisement shall be inserted on two several days in the same newspaper, and the second insertion shall be at least three clear days before the first day of sale.

3. Pawnbrokers shall send all forfeited pledges to a licensed auctioneer at least three days before the sale, duly ticketed and numbered, and they shall be fully exposed for sale to public view by the auctioneer for at least two days before the day of sale.

4. All sales shall be held in places quite open to the general public and large enough for the accommodation of intending purchasers.

5. The auctioneer shall publish in English catalogues of the pledges, stating—

(*a*) the pawnbroker's name and place of business;
(*b*) the month in which each pledge was pawned; and
(*c*) the number of each pledge as entered at the time of pawning in the pledge book.

6. The pledges of each pawnbroker in the catalogue shall be separate from any pledges of any other pawnbroker.

7. Where a pawnbroker bids at a sale, the auctioneer shall not take the bidding in any other form than that in which he takes the biddings of other persons at the same sale; and the auctioneer, on knocking down any article to a pawnbroker, shall forthwith declare audibly the name of the pawnbroker as purchaser.

8. The auctioneer shall, within fourteen days after the sale, deliver to the pawnbroker a copy of the catalogue or of so much thereof as relates to the pledges of that pawnbroker, filled up with the amounts for which the several pledges of that pawnbroker were sold and authenticated by the signature of the auctioneer.

9. The pawnbroker shall preserve a copy of every such catalogue for three years at least after the auction.

# Chit Funds Act, 1971[1]

An Act to provide for the licensing and regulation of chit funds.

Be it enacted by the President with the advice and consent of the Parliament of Singapore, as follows:

[21st December, 1971]

[1] *Singapore Government Gazette Acts Supplement,* No. 2, January 7, 1972, Act No. 28 of 1971.

## Part I. Preliminary

Short title and commencement.

1. (1) This Act may be cited as the Chit Funds Act, 1971, and shall come into operation on such date as the Minister may, by notification in the *Gazette,* appoint.

(2) The Minister may appoint different dates for the coming into operation of the different Parts or provisions of this Act.

Interpretation.

2. In this Act, unless the context otherwise requires—

"agreement" means the document which contains the terms and conditions agreed to and adopted by the subscribers and the chit fund company;

"chit fund" means a scheme or arrangement based wholly on the terms and conditions set out in section 24 of this Act or the regulations made thereunder or any scheme or arrangement that is deemed to be a chit fund under section 19 of this Act but does not include any scheme or arrangement which only partakes of the nature of a chit fund within the meaning of section 20 of this Act;

"chit fund amount" means the pool or the aggregate of the contributions payable on any specified day or in respect of any specified interval;

"chit fund business" means the business of carrying on chit funds;

"chit fund company" means a company which carries on chit fund business and holds a valid licence granted under section 7 of this Act. All branches and offices in Singapore of such company shall be deemed to be one chit fund company for the purposes of this Act;

"Commissioner" means the person appointed under section 3 of this Act to hold office of Commissioner of Chit Funds;

"contribution" means the sum of money payable periodically by each subscriber under the agreement;

"essential terms and conditions" means the terms and conditions specified in section 24 of this Act;

"interest" means that amount of money which the subscriber agrees to forego in order to purchase the chit fund amount;

"Minister" means the Minister charged with the responsibility for finance;

"prize" or "prize amount" means the difference between the chit fund amount and the interest;

"public company" means a company limited by shares incorporated in Singapore other than a private company;

"rebate" means the share of the interest payable to each subscriber;

"subscriber" includes any person who has agreed to participate in a chit fund or has signed the agreement in token thereof.

## PART II. APPOINTMENT OF COMMISSIONER OF CHIT FUNDS

Commissioner of Chit Funds.

3. (1) For the purposes of this Act there shall be a Commissioner of Chit Funds who shall be appointed by the Minister.[2]

(2) The Commissioner shall be charged with the general administration of this Act and the exercise of the functions imposed upon him by this Act.

(3) The Commissioner may authorise or appoint any person to assist him in the exercise of his functions and duties under this Act, either generally or in any particular way.

(4) The Commissioner and any person authorised or appointed by him pursuant to subsection (3) of this section shall be deemed to be public servants within the meaning of the Penal Code.

## PART III. LICENSING OF CHIT FUND COMPANIES

Licensing of Chit Funds.

4. (1) No chit fund business shall be transacted in Singapore except by a public company which is in possession of a valid licence granted under this Act by the Commissioner with the approval of the Minister authorising it to conduct chit fund business in accordance with the provisions of this Act.

(2) Any person who contravenes the provisions of subsection (1) of this section shall be guilty of an offence under this Act and shall be liable on conviction to imprisonment for a term not exceeding three years or to a fine not exceeding five thousand dollars or to both such imprisonment and fine and in the case of a continuing offence to a further fine of one thousand dollars for every day during which the offence continues after conviction.

Use of words "chit" and "chit fund".

5. (1) No person or body of persons, whether incorporated or not, other than a chit fund company licensed under this Act shall, without the written consent of the Commissioner, use the word "chit" or the words "chit fund" or any of its or their derivatives in any language, or any other word indicating it transacts chit fund business, in the name, description or title under which such person or body of persons is transacting business in Singapore or make or continue to make any

[2] The functions, duties, and powers of the Commissioner of Chit Funds under this Act were transferred to the Monetary Authority of Singapore in accordance with the Monetary Authority of Singapore (Transfer of Functions) Notification, 1973.

representation to such effect in any bill head, letter paper, notice, advertisement or in any other manner whatsoever.

(2) For the purposes of subsection (1) of this section the words "hwei", "kutu" and "tontine" or any other word in any other language having the same meaning or being to the like intent shall be deemed to be derivatives of the word "chit".

(3) Nothing in this section shall prohibit an association of chit fund companies formed for the protection of common interests from using the word "chit" or the words "chit fund" or any of its or their derivatives in any language as a part of its name or description of its activities.

(4) Any person who contravenes the provisions of subsection (1) of this section shall be guilty of an offence under this Act and shall be liable on conviction to imprisonment for a term not exceeding one year or to a fine not exceeding one thousand dollars or to both such imprisonment and fine and in the case of a continuing offence to a further fine not exceeding one hundred dollars for every day during which the offence continues after conviction.

Examination of persons suspected of transacting chit fund business.

6. Whenever the Commissioner has reason to believe that a person is transacting chit fund business without a licence, he shall have the power to examine the books, accounts and records of such person in order to ascertain whether or not such person has violated or is violating any provisions of this Act, and any refusal to submit such books, accounts and records shall be *prima facie* evidence of the fact of operation without a licence.

Application for licence.

7. (1) A public company which desires authority to carry on chit fund business in Singapore shall apply in writing to the Commissioner for a licence under this section and shall supply—

*(a)* a copy of the memorandum of association and articles of association or other instrument under which the company is incorporated, duly verified by a statutory declaration made by a senior officer of the company;

*(b)* a copy of the latest balance-sheet of the company; and

*(c)* such other information as may be called for by the Commissioner.

(2) In considering any application by a public company for a licence the Commissioner may require to be satisfied as to—

*(a)* the financial character of the company;

*(b)* the character of the management of the company;

(*c*) the adequacy of the capital structure of the company and earning prospects of the company;

(*d*) the objects of the company as disclosed in its memorandum of association;

(*e*) the convenience and needs of the community to be served;

(*f*) whether the public interest will be served by granting of a licence.

(3) The Commissioner, with the approval of the Minister, may grant a licence with or without conditions, or refuse to grant a licence.

(4) The Commissioner may at any time vary or revoke any existing conditions of a licence or impose conditions or additional conditions thereto.

(5) Where a licence is subject to conditions the chit fund company shall comply with those conditions.

(6) Any chit fund company which fails to comply with any of the conditions of its licence shall be guilty of an offence under this Act and shall be liable on conviction to a fine not exceeding five thousand dollars and, in the case of a continuing offence, to a further fine of one thousand dollars for every day during which the offence continues after conviction.

Licence fees.

**8.** (1) Every chit fund company in Singapore shall pay such annual licence fee as the Commissioner may by notification in the *Gazette* prescribe.

(2) The Commissioner may prescribe different licence fees in respect of different classes or categories of chit fund companies and such fees shall apply uniformly to such classes or categories.

(3) The manner of payment of the licence fee shall be as specified by the Commissioner.

Minimum capital requirements.

**9.** (1) Subject to the provisions of this Act, no chit fund company shall be granted or shall hold a licence unless its capital, issued and paid up in cash, and unimpaired by losses or otherwise, is not less than two hundred thousand dollars.

(2) The Commissioner may require such percentage of the issued and paid-up capital as may be prescribed in regulations made under this Act to be deposited in such manner as may be prescribed.

(3) No chit fund company incorporated in Singapore shall reduce its paid-up capital during the currency of its licence without the approval of the Commissioner.

Restriction of opening of branches of chit fund companies.

**10.** (1) No chit fund company shall open a new place of business or change the location of an existing place of business in Singapore without submitting a written application in respect thereof to the Commissioner.

(2) Upon receipt of an application under subsection (1) of this section, the Commissioner may—

*(a)* give his approval; or

*(b)* without assigning any reason therefor, refuse to give his approval,

and his decision thereon shall be final.

(3) No chit fund company incorporated in Singapore shall open a new branch, agency or office in any place outside Singapore.

(4) Any chit fund company which contravenes the provisions of subsection (1) or (3) of this section shall be guilty of an offence under this Act and shall be liable on conviction to a fine not exceeding five hundred dollars and in the case of a continuing offence to a further fine of one hundred dollars for every day during which the offence continues after conviction.

Fees to be paid in respect of branches of chit fund companies.

**11.** (1) The Commissioner may from time to time by notification in the *Gazette* specify the annual licence fees which chit fund companies in Singapore shall pay for each of their branches.

(2) The manner of payment shall be as specified by the Commissioner.

Limitation on mergers, etc., of a chit fund company.

**12.** (1) No chit fund company incorporated in Singapore shall be merged or consolidated with or be taken over by another company or companies or their subsidiaries or related companies as described in section 6 of the Companies Act (whether such company is or companies are incorporated in Singapore or outside Singapore) nor shall such company or companies acquire an interest exceeding twenty per cent of the voting share capital of a chit fund company without application to, and approval by, the Commissioner.

(2) In considering such an application, the Commissioner shall have power to call for such information as he may require.

(3) The Commissioner may—

*(a)* approve the application; or

*(b)* refuse the application.

(4) Any chit fund company whose application has been refused by the Commissioner may within one month of being notified of the

refusal by the Commissioner appeal against his refusal to the Minister whose decision thereon shall be final.

13. (1) Every chit fund company in Singapore shall, prior to the making of any amendment or alteration in its memorandum of association or articles of association, or other instrument under which it is incorporated, furnish to the Commissioner for his approval particulars in writing (verified by a statutory declaration made by a senior officer of the chit fund company) of such proposed amendment or alteration.

Amendment of constitution of a chit fund company.

(2) The Commissioner may thereupon—

*(a)* approve the proposed alteration without modification;
*(b)* approve the proposed alteration with modification; or
*(c)* refuse to approve the proposed alteration.

(3) If the Commissioner approves the proposed alteration with modification, the chit fund company shall adopt the proposed alteration as so modified or not proceed with the proposed alteration and if the Commissioner refuses to approve the proposed alteration he may request the chit fund company to withdraw the proposed alteration and the chit fund company shall comply with the Commissioner's request.

(4) Any chit fund company which fails to comply with the requirements of subsection (1) of this section or with any request by the Commissioner made under subsection (3) of this section shall be guilty of an offence under this Act and shall be liable on conviction to a fine not exceeding three hundred dollars for every day during which the default continues.

14. (1) The Commissioner may by order revoke a licence issued under this Act—

Revocation of licence.

*(a)* if he is satisfied that the chit fund company holding that licence—
  (i) has ceased to transact chit fund business in Singapore or is carrying on any other business other than chit fund business;
  (ii) proposes to make, or has made, any composition or arrangement with its creditors or has gone into liquidation or has been wound up, whether voluntary or involuntary, or otherwise dissolved;
  (iii) is carrying on its business in a manner likely to be detrimental to the interests of the subscribers of its chit funds or has insufficient assets to cover its liabilities to its subscribers or the public;

(iv) is contravening the provisions of this Act or the regulations made thereunder; or

(v) has been convicted of any offence under this Act or the regulations made thereunder or if any of its officers holding a managerial or executive position has been convicted of any offence under this Act or the regulations made thereunder; or

*(b)* if he considers it in the public interest to do so.

(2) The Commissioner shall, before revoking any licence under the provisions of subsection (1) of this section, give the chit fund company concerned notice in writing of his intention to do so, specifying a date, not less than twenty-one days after the date of the notice upon which such revocation shall take effect and calling upon the chit fund company to show cause to the Commissioner why such licence should not be revoked.

(3) When the Commissioner has revoked a licence under the provisions of subsection (1) of this section, he shall forthwith inform the chit fund company by notice in writing of such revocation.

(4) The chit fund company may, within fourteen days of the receipt of the notice referred to in subsection (3) of this section, or such extended period of time as the Minister may allow, appeal in writing against such revocation to the Minister whose decision thereon shall be final.

Effect of revocation of licence.

15. (1) Where an order of revocation becomes effective under section 14 of this Act—

*(a)* notice of such revocation shall be published in the *Gazette;* and

*(b)* the chit fund company shall, as from the date of such notice, cease to transact any chit fund business in Singapore except as may be approved by the Commissioner for the purpose of winding up its chit fund business.

(2) The provisions of paragraph *(b)* of subsection (1) of this section shall not prejudice the enforcement by any person of any right or claim against the chit fund company or by the chit fund company of any right or claim against any person.

Exhibition of licence.

16. (1) The licence issued under subsection (3) of section 7 of this Act, or a certified copy thereof, shall, so long as it remains valid, be exhibited in a conspicuous position at the principal place of business of the chit fund company and in the event of revocation under sec-

tion 14 of this Act, the licence and all certified copies thereof shall be surrendered forthwith to the Commissioner.

17. The Commissioner shall cause to be published in the *Gazette* in the month of April in each year a list of all chit fund companies to which licences have been issued under this Act. Publication of list of companies.

## PART IV
### CHIT FUNDS—GENERAL PROVISIONS

18. Any person who promotes or conducts, or aids, assists, or takes any part in the promotion or conduct of any chit fund otherwise than in accordance with the provisions of this Act shall be guilty of an offence under this Act and shall be liable on conviction to imprisonment for a term not exceeding three years or to a fine not exceeding five thousand dollars or to both such imprisonment and fine. Prohibition of chit funds conducted in contravention of this Act.

19. Any scheme or arrangement which is based wholly on the essential terms and conditions set out in section 24 of this Act or has all the attributes and incidents of a chit fund within the scope and intent of that section shall, notwithstanding that it is called by any other name, be deemed to be a chit fund for the purposes of this Act. When scheme or arrangement deemed to be a chit fund.

20. (1) Every scheme or arrangement by whatever name called which is not based wholly on the essential terms and conditions set out in section 24 of this Act or which is based on terms and conditions inconsistent wholly or in part with those essential terms and conditions, shall for the purposes of this Act be deemed only to partake of the nature of a chit fund. A scheme or arrangement which is deemed only to partake of the nature of a chit fund prohibited.

(2) Regulations made under this Act may describe or define what schemes or arrangements shall be deemed only to partake of the nature of a chit fund for the purposes of this section.

(3) Any person who promotes or conducts, or aids, assists, or takes any part in the promotion or conduct of any scheme or arrangement which only partakes of the nature of a chit fund within the meaning of this Act shall be guilty of an offence under this Act and shall be liable on conviction to imprisonment for a term not exceeding three years or to a fine not exceeding five thousand dollars or to both such imprisonment and fine.

(4) No right or claim under any scheme or arrangement which only partakes of the nature of a chit fund within the meaning of this

Act or regulations made thereunder shall, without prejudice to the provisions of subsection (1) of this section, be enforceable by action in any court.

Security.

**21.** The licensing of any company under this Act shall not be regarded as authorising the promotion or formation of any chit fund or the acceptance by that company of any instalment or interest from any subscriber until such security as is provided in regulations made under this Act in respect of that chit fund has been deposited by the chit fund company in accordance with those regulations.

Receipt of contributions.

**22.** A chit fund company may receive contributions due from intending subscribers at the time of the signing of the agreement pursuant to subsection (3) of section 24 of this Act but if within fourteen days after the expiration of one month of the signing of the agreement the chit fund does not commence, the contributions received shall be returned to the subscribers.

## FORMATION AND ESSENTIAL TERMS AND CONDITIONS

Formation of chit funds.

**23.** Every chit fund shall be formed by the execution of a written agreement between the chit fund company on the one part and the intending subscribers severally on the other part.

Essential terms and conditions of a chit fund.

**24.** (1) Every agreement made under section 23 of this Act shall contain all the following terms and conditions with the actual amounts, dates and other particulars necessary in each case, namely—

*(a)* that the chit fund is to be for a specific amount and for a specified number of subscribers only;

*(b)* that the subscribers are to contribute equal portions of the amount;

*(c)* that the contribution of each subscriber is to be paid to the chit fund company in money in equal amounts of a specified value during a specified period;

*(d)* that each contribution is to be payable on a date specified therefor or within such number of days of grace after that date as may be specified;

*(e)* that on or after each date on which the contributions are payable, the chit fund amount is to be put up for sale by the chit fund company among the subscribers either by auction or by way of sealed tenders;

*(f)* that each of the subscribers is to be entitled to purchase the chit fund amount once and not oftener during the period of that chit

fund, and that no subscriber who has been declared the purchaser at any such sale is to be entitled or permitted to bid or tender at any subsequent sale;

(*g*) that every bid or tender of a subscriber at a sale is to indicate the sum which he is willing to forego as interest for the privilege of obtaining the prize on that occasion;

(*h*) that of the subscribers entitled to bid at any sale, the subscriber who offers the highest interest is to be declared the purchaser;

(*i*) that the purchaser is to be entitled to receive the prize consisting of the chit fund amount less the interest offered by him, on producing guarantors to stand surety for the due payment of his future contributions in respect of that chit fund;

(*j*) that the chit fund company is to deduct for commission and working expenses a specified sum or a sum bearing a specified proportion to the prize amount or to the chit fund amount;

(*k*) that the interest is to be distributed in equal proportion among all the subscribers;

(*l*) that a subscriber, who has not yet purchased a chit fund amount and who defaults in either the payment of a contribution or the production of guarantors shall be entitled to a refund of actual contributions already paid by him in accordance with subsection (2) of section 31 of this Act or subsection (1) of section 32 of this Act, as the case may be.

(2) The agreement mentioned in subsection (1) of this section shall also contain—

(*a*) the full name and address of the chit fund company and of each of the subscribers;

(*b*) the business address of the chit fund company or the exact location of the place where the records of the chit fund are to be kept and where its business is to be transacted;

(*c*) the number of the subscriber's identity card issued by the Government of Singapore or in the case of a subscriber who has not been issued with a Singapore identity card such other record of identification as may be prescribed; and

(*d*) such other terms and conditions not inconsistent with this Act, or with the essential terms and conditions referred to in subsection (1) of this section, as are considered necessary for the better management and control of the chit fund.

(3) In respect of every chit fund, the agreement shall be signed in original and duplicate by the chit fund company and each intending subscriber, either in person or by duly authorised agent, and each signature shall be attested by a witness present at the time of signing.

Duty of chit fund company to acknowledge subscriber's rights.

**25.** As soon as may be after the agreement has been signed by each intending subscriber, the chit fund company shall give him a written acknowledgement that the subscriber is entitled to participate in the chit fund.

CONDUCT OF A CHIT FUND

Meetings of subscribers.

**26.** (1) Where the provisions of this Act or the regulations made thereunder or the terms and conditions of the agreement require any matter to be decided by a meeting of the subscribers, the chit fund company shall convene a meeting for the purpose within seven days of its becoming aware of the event requiring a meeting and shall serve written notice on each of the subscribers not less than five days before the date selected by the chit fund company for the meeting.

(2) Every such notice shall state the time, date and place at which the meeting is to be held, and the business to be transacted at the meeting.

(3) The notice may either be served personally on each subscriber or sent to him by registered or certified post; and any notice sent to a subscriber by registered post shall be deemed to have been duly served if it was addressed to the registered address of that subscriber or to any other address notified by him in writing to the chit fund company.

Minutes of meeting.

**27.** The chit fund company shall enter in a book to be kept for that purpose the minutes of the proceedings of every meeting of the subscribers. The minutes shall in every case contain the following particulars—

(*a*) the place, date, time, and duration of the meeting;
(*b*) the names of the subscribers who were present;
(*c*) the items of business transacted at the meeting,

and in the case of a meeting at which a chit fund amount is auctioned, the following additional particulars:

(*d*) the serial number of the auction;
(*e*) the name of each bidder and the amount of each bid;
(*f*) the name of the purchaser; and
(*g*) the amount of the interest.

Alteration of the agreement.

**28.** Subject to the provisions of this Act and the regulations made thereunder and subject also to any terms or conditions contained in the agreement as to the matters or the mode in which alterations of the agreement may be made, any alteration of the figures, amounts, dates or other particulars which are not likely to affect the intention or the legal effect of the essential terms and conditions, or any alteration of the additional terms and conditions contained in any agreement, shall be made only at any meeting of the subscribers, duly convened for the purpose, by the votes of a majority, the aggregate of whose contributions is not less than three-fourths of the chit fund amount.

Receipts for contributions paid and entry of payments in pass-book.

29. (1) Every subscriber shall receive a receipt issued by or on behalf of the chit fund company for each contribution paid by him.

(2) Every subscriber shall be issued with a pass-book into which each payment made by him shall be entered by the chit fund company.

Production of guarantors by purchaser of chit fund amount.

30. Every subscriber who is declared the purchaser of a chit fund amount shall, as a condition precedent to the payment of the prize amount to him by the chit fund company, produce at least two guarantors to stand surety for the payment of the contributions due from him for the remainder of the chit fund period.

Effect of failing to produce guarantors.

31. (1) If a subscriber purchasing the chit fund amount fails to produce the guarantors required under section 30 of this Act within two weeks of the auction, the chit fund company shall either—

(*a*) within seven days of the expiration of the said two weeks declare the next highest bidder, who has not purchased the chit fund amount, to be purchaser of the chit fund amount according to his bid on his producing the guarantors as required under section 30 of this Act; or

(*b*) within two weeks after the expiration of the said two weeks conduct a fresh sale of that chit fund amount and give not less than seven days' notice of the date to each of the subscribers then entitled to bid at the sale.

(2) Where a subscriber is unable to produce the guarantors as required under section 30 of this Act, the subscriber shall have the right to a refund of the actual amount of the earlier contributions paid by him to the chit fund company, without any deduction whatsoever. The refund shall be paid by the chit fund company within three weeks from the date of the auction.

(3) In the event of a refund to a subscriber under subsection (2) of this section by a chit fund company, the chit fund company shall be entitled to remove the name of that subscriber from the register of subscribers kept under section 37 of this Act and to substitute therefor the name of the new subscriber.

Substitution of new subscriber for defaulting subscriber who has not purchased any chit fund amount.

32. (1) Where default in the payment of any contribution is made by any subscriber who has not purchased a chit fund amount, the chit fund company shall be entitled to remove the name of the defaulting subscriber from the register of subscribers kept under section 37 of this Act and to substitute therein the name of a new subscriber except that the removal of his name from the register shall not be deemed to prejudice the right of the defaulting subscriber to a refund of the actual amount of any earlier contributions paid to him, at such time and with such deductions by way of penalty as may be prescribed by regulations made under this Act.

(2) All the rights and liabilities that would under the agreement have accrued to or been incurred by the defaulting subscriber after the date of such substitution if he had not made default, shall be deemed to be transferred to the new subscriber.

(3) No collateral undertaking, as to mutual rights and obligations entered into by the chit fund company and the new subscriber for the purposes of the substitution of the new subscriber, shall be deemed to affect in any respect the duties and liabilities of the new subscriber under the terms and conditions of the agreement.

Voluntary reduction of membership in lieu of substitution of new subscriber.

33. (1) In any case referred to in section 32 of this Act the chit fund company may, before substituting a new subscriber in place of the defaulting subscriber whose name is removed from the register under that section, convene a meeting of the remaining subscribers for the purpose of obtaining their consent to a reduction of the number of subscribers and of the chit fund amount by refraining from substituting a new subscriber in place of the defaulting subscriber.

(2) If at the meeting so convened, the subscribers by a majority representing not less than two-thirds of the chit fund amount consent to such reduction and to the necessary alteration of the agreement, the chit fund company shall record the same in the minute book kept under section 27 of this Act.

(3) Upon the recording of the alteration made for the purposes of a voluntary reduction under this section, every subscriber who was the purchaser of a chit fund amount sold at any auction prior to the date of the reduction, shall be liable to continue the payment of the contributions specified in the agreement until the aggregate amount so contributed by him becomes equal to the chit fund amount at the time of the sale at which he was declared the purchaser.

Liability of defaulting subscriber who has already purchased chit fund amount.

34. (1) Where default in the payment of any contribution is made by a subscriber who has already purchased a chit fund amount, that subscriber and his guarantors shall be liable to make immediate payment to the chit fund company of the aggregate of all the contributions payable by him to the end of the chit fund period.

(2) Upon receiving the contributions pursuant to subsection (1) of this section, the chit fund company shall immediately deposit those contributions in any bank that is approved by the Commissioner.

(3) Any money received under subsection (1) of this section exceeding the amount required to cover the contribution of the defaulting subscriber shall be returned forthwith by the chit fund company to the defaulting subscriber or his guarantors, as the case may be.

(4) A chit fund company may charge interest on any money due under subsection (1) of this section at the rate and by the method prescribed in regulations made under this Act.

Transfer of subscriber's rights.

35. (1) Any subscriber who has not purchased a chit fund amount may make over his rights in the chit fund by a transfer in writing to any person approved by the chit fund company.

(2) Notice of every transfer made under subsection (1) of this section shall be given forthwith to the chit fund company, in writing signed by the transferor and the transferee.

(3) On receipt of the notice of any transfer made under subsection (1) of this section, the chit fund company shall make the appropriate entries in the register of subscribers kept under section 37 of this Act.

(4) Where the transfer of the rights of any subscriber under subsection (1) of this section is proved to have been made to any person who was insolvent at the time of the transfer or to have been made with the intention of defeating the provisions of any written law in force in Singapore, the transfer shall not be deemed to operate as a discharge to that subscriber from his duties and liabilities under the terms and conditions of the agreement.

(5) Notwithstanding anything contained in any other written law to the contrary, the stamp duty payable on any transfer under this section shall be in accordance with the provisions of the Stamp Act.

Transfer of right of chit fund company to recover contributions to be voidable.

36. Any transfer made by the chit fund company of its right to recover the contributions payable by subscribers, who have purchased chit fund amounts, shall not defeat or delay the rights of any subscriber who has not purchased a chit fund amount and shall be voidable at the instance of such subscriber if such transfer is likely to defeat or delay

the rights of that subscriber under the terms and conditions of the agreement.

Books to be kept by chit fund company.

**37.** The chit fund company shall keep and from day to day regularly post up the following books:

(*a*) a register of subscribers containing—

(i) the names and full addresses of all subscribers with the respective dates on which the subscribers signed the agreement, and the date on which any subscriber ceased to be a subscriber by reason of a transfer of rights or of a substitution in case of default;

(ii) in the case of any transfer of rights by a subscriber, the name and full address of the person to whom the rights are transferred with the date of such transfer and the date on which notice thereof is given to the chit fund company; and

(iii) the name and full address of any person substituted in place of a defaulting subscriber, with the date on which he is so substituted;

(*b*) the minute book required under section 27 of this Act;

(*c*) an account book containing separate accounts of the following:

(i) the contributions paid by each subscriber and the respective dates of such payments;

(ii) the prize amounts paid to purchasers of the chit fund amount and the respective dates of such payments;

(iii) the amount of the commission or remuneration received by the chit fund company and the registration fees paid by it; and

(iv) the amount of the rebate paid to each subscriber on each occasion and the date of such payment.

Liability of chit fund company to subscribers.

**38.** (1) The chit fund company shall be liable to each subscriber for any amount due to that subscriber in respect of the chit fund.

(2) The chit fund company shall not be entitled to withdraw from the management of the chit fund without the written consent of all the subscribers.

(3) Where the chit fund company is in liquidation or is being wound up, whether voluntarily or otherwise, any debt owing by the company to any subscriber under the terms and conditions of the agreement relating to the chit fund shall, notwithstanding anything contained in any other written law to the contrary, be a first charge

upon any property acquired or held by it for the purposes of that chit fund, including property held by the Commissioner as security pursuant to regulations made under this Act.

**Prohibition of bid or tender by chit fund company.**

39. (1) No chit fund company licensed under section 7 of this Act shall be entitled to bid or submit a tender or shall bid or submit a tender either directly or indirectly, at any sale of a chit fund amount held by auction or by tenders in connection with any chit fund formed or conducted by that company.

(2) Any chit fund company licensed under section 7 of this Act may, in lieu of substituting a new subscriber in the place of each defaulting subscriber, take up the share of one or more defaulting subscribers, and in every such case the chit fund company shall be entitled to take, without an auction or other sale and without any interest, the successive chit fund amounts available after the last of the continuing eligible subscribers has purchased his prize amount.

**Termination of a chit fund.**

40. (1) A chit fund shall be deemed to terminate upon the occurrence of any of the following events:

*(a)* on the expiry of the chit fund period as specified in the agreement or where it is curtailed by reason of any voluntary reduction of membership duly effected under section 33 of this Act;

*(b)* on the failure of the chit fund company to conduct the chit fund in accordance with the provisions of this Act, the regulations made thereunder or the terms and conditions of the agreement;

*(c)* on the chit fund company going into liquidation or being wound up, whether voluntarily or involuntarily, or otherwise being dissolved;

*(d)* on steps being taken for the winding up of the company either voluntarily or by order of the Commissioner or the Minister;

*(e)* on the licence being revoked by the Commissioner under section 14 of this Act.

(2) Upon the termination of a chit fund otherwise than by the expiry of the chit fund period as specified in the agreement or by a voluntary reduction of a chit fund under section 33 of this Act every subscriber who has not purchased a chit fund amount shall be entitled either—

*(a)* to recover from the chit fund company the aggregate of the actual amounts contributed by each subscriber as contributions under the agreement prior to the termination of the chit fund; or

*(b)* to apply to a court of competent jurisdiction for an order—

(i) directing each subscriber who has drawn a prize amount in that chit fund to deposit in court upon the due dates the several contributions, which, if the chit fund had not terminated, would have been payable by such subscriber to the chit fund company, until the aggregate of the amounts paid to the chit fund company by that subscriber before the termination of the chit fund and of the amounts so deposited in court become equal to the chit fund amount at the time of the sale at which that subscriber was declared the purchaser; and

(ii) declaring that all amounts so deposited in court shall be divided rateably among the subscribers who have not drawn a prize amount in that chit fund, and setting out for that purpose any scheme of distribution that may be necessary.

(3) Where any action is instituted by a subscriber for the enforcement of a claim under paragraph *(a)* of subsection (2) of this section, the chit fund company may apply for an order of court under paragraph *(b)* of subsection (2) of this section in like manner as a subscriber and any sum of money that may be received under such an order by such subscriber instituting the action, shall be set off against the amount claimed in the action.

**Sale by sealed tender as alternative to auction.**

41. The sale of the chit fund amounts may, if the terms and conditions of the agreement provided therefor, be effected by way of sealed tenders as an alternative to an auction if, at a duly convened meeting of the subscribers held before the sale of the first chit fund amount, the subscribers by a majority representing three-fourths of the chit fund amount resolve to adopt the method of sealed tenders; and the method adopted for the sale of the first chit fund amount shall be followed at each subsequent sale in connection with that chit fund:

Provided that in every case where the tenders of two or more subscribers are of the same value, the chit fund amount shall be put up for sale by auction among those subscribers, and the initial bid at every such auction shall be the amount set out in the tenders of those subscribers.

**Financial limits to be observed by chit funds.**

42. (1) The total value of the chit fund to be conducted at any one time by a chit fund company shall be as prescribed by regulations made under this Act.

(2) For the purposes of this section, the "total value of the chit fund" means the aggregate of the chit fund amounts that are to be collected and put up for sale during the period of that chit fund.

43. (1) No chit fund company shall lend to any person other than to a subscriber who has not purchased the chit fund amount.

Limits on lending powers of chit fund company.

(2) A chit fund company may lend to a subscriber who has not purchased the chit fund amount but the amount so lent shall not exceed seventy-five per cent of the aggregate contributions already paid by that subscriber or such other percentage as may be specified in regulations made under this Act.

(3) A chit fund company that lends to a subscriber under subsection (2) of this section shall not be deemed to be a moneylender under the Moneylenders Act and that Act shall not accordingly apply to any transaction under this section.

## PART V. RESERVE FUND, DIVIDENDS, BALANCE SHEET, INFORMATION AND REGULATION OF BUSINESS

44. (1) Every chit fund company shall maintain a reserve fund.

Maintenance of reserve funds.

(2) At the end of each financial year the net profit of each chit fund company shall be determined after allowing for taxation, and after making provision for bad or doubtful debts.

(3) Such part of the net profits as is specified in this subsection shall be transferred to the reserve fund at the end of each financial year, as follows:

*(a)* where the reserve fund is two hundred per centum or more of the paid-up capital, a sum of not less than five per centum of such net profits;

*(b)* where the reserve fund is not less than one hundred per centum but less than two hundred per centum of the paid-up capital, a sum of not less than fifteen per centum of such net profits;

*(c)* where the reserve fund is less than one hundred per centum of the paid-up capital, a sum of not less than thirty per centum of such net profits.

45. Every chit fund company shall, before the profit and loss account and balance sheet are made out, take steps to ensure that all bad debts have been written off and make adequate provision for doubtful debts.

Bad and doubtful debts.

46. No chit fund company shall pay any dividend on shares, until all its capitalized expenditure (including preliminary expenses, organisation expenses, share selling, commission, brokerage, amount of losses incurred and any item of expenditure not represented by tangible assets) has been completely written off.

Restriction on payment of dividends by chit fund companies.

Exhibition of audited balance-sheet.

47. Every chit fund company shall exhibit throughout the year in a conspicuous position in every office and branch of that chit fund company, a copy of its last audited balance-sheet and profit and loss account together with the full and correct names of all persons who are directors of the chit fund company, as soon as such balance-sheet is audited.

Information and statistics to be furnished by chit fund companies.

48. (1) Every chit fund company shall furnish to the Commissioner, at such time and in such manner as the Commissioner may prescribe, all such information and data as he may reasonably require for the proper discharge of his functions under the provisions of this Act.

(2) Every chit fund company that fails or neglects to furnish any information required by the Commissioner under subsection (1) of this section, and within the time specified by the Commissioner, shall be guilty of an offence under this Act and shall be liable on conviction to a fine not exceeding one thousand dollars for every day during which the default continues.

## PART VI. INSPECTION OF CHIT FUND COMPANIES

Inspection and investigation of chit fund companies and production of books, etc.

49. (1) The Commissioner may, from time to time, inspect or cause to be inspected under conditions of secrecy, the books, accounts and transactions of any chit fund company.

(2) The Minister may at any time direct the Commissioner to make an investigation, under conditions of secrecy, of the books, accounts and transactions of a chit fund company, if he has reason to believe that such chit fund company is carrying on its business in a manner detrimental to the interests of its subscribers and other creditors or has insufficient assets to cover its liabilities to the public, or is contravening the provisions of this Act or the regulations made thereunder.

(3) The Commissioner may appoint any auditor, other than the auditor appointed by the chit fund company under the provisions of section 172 of the Companies Act, to exercise the powers of the Commissioner under subsections (1) and (2) of this section.

(4) For the purpose of an inspection or investigation under this section, a chit fund company shall afford the Commissioner access to its books, accounts and documents and shall give such information and facilities as may be required to conduct the investigation:

Provided that such books, accounts and documents shall not be required to be produced at such times and at such places as shall interfere with the proper conduct of the normal daily business of that chit fund company.

(5) If any book, account or document or information is not supplied in accordance with subsection (4) of this section, the chit fund company concerned shall be guilty of an offence under this Act and shall be liable on conviction to a fine not exceeding two thousand dollars and to a further fine of two hundred and fifty dollars for every day during which the default continues after conviction.

**Powers of the Commissioner to issue orders after an inspection.**

**50.** (1) If the Commissioner finds upon an inspection under section 49 of this Act that the affairs of a chit fund company are being conducted in a manner likely to be detrimental to the interests of the subscribers or prejudicial to the interests of the chit fund company, the Commissioner may by order require the chit fund company to take such corrective action as the Commissioner considers to be necessary or require the chit fund company to discontinue such practices or procedures.

(2) No order shall be issued under subsection (1) of this section unless the chit fund company has been given a reasonable opportunity to present its views to the Commissioner.

(3) The Commissioner may, upon representation being made to him, or on his own motion, modify or cancel any order issued under subsection (1) of this section and, in so modifying or cancelling any order, may impose such conditions as he thinks fit.

## PART VII. MISCELLANEOUS PROVISIONS

Recovery of fees, expenses, etc.

51. There shall be recoverable as a civil debt due to the Government from the chit fund company concerned the amount of any fees payable under this Act or any regulations made thereunder.

Exemption.

52. Notwithstanding any of the provisions of this Act, the Commissioner may, with the approval of the Minister, exempt any chit fund company from any or all of the provisions of this Act.

Winding up provisions.

53. (1) Without prejudice to the provisions of the Companies Act—

*(a)* a chit fund company (whether or not it is being wound up voluntarily) may be wound up under an order of the court on the petition of the Minister; and

*(b)* the court may order the winding up of a chit fund company if—

(i) that company has held a licence under this Act and that licence has expired or has been revoked;

(ii) that company has been declared insolvent;

(iii) that company has carried on chit fund business in Singapore in contravention of the provisions of this Act.

(2) In the winding up of a chit fund company that has been carrying on chit fund business, every subscriber who has not purchased a chit fund amount shall be entitled to recover his contribution in the manner set out in subsection (2) of section 40 of this Act.

Redemption of securities held by chit fund company.

54. (1) As soon as practicable after the making of an order for the winding up of a chit fund company, the liquidator of such company shall publish in the *Gazette* a notice requiring every debtor of the chit fund company to redeem any property he has deposited with the company as security for any loan that he has obtained from the chit fund company, and shall also send by registered post such notice to every debtor whose security is held by the chit fund company and whose name is mentioned in the statement of affairs made out under section 234 of the Companies Act.

(2) The notice shall specify the latest date up to which any security may be redeemed, which date shall not be less than three months from the date of the notice.

(3) After the latest date for redeeming any security held by the chit fund company specified in the notice, the liquidator may proceed to realise any security held by the chit fund company forthwith, notwithstanding any agreement setting out any other period of redemption previously entered into between the chit fund company and the debtor.

Operation of Act not to affect certain Acts.

55. (1) Nothing in this Act shall affect the operation of the Companies Act, and any company that is liable to be incorporated under that Act shall continue to be so liable as if this Act had not been passed but in case of conflict between that Act and this Act the provisions of this Act shall prevail, unless otherwise provided in this Act.

(2) Nothing in this Act shall, unless it is expressly provided to the contrary, affect the operation of any written law relating to moneylending, finance companies, banking or insurance or the liability of any chit fund company under any such law.

General penalty.

56. Any chit fund company which, or any person who being a director, officer, employee or agent of a chit fund company, contravenes or fails to comply with any of the provisions of this Act for which no

penalty is expressly provided shall be guilty of an offence under this Act and shall be liable on conviction to a fine not exceeding five thousand dollars.

Offences triable in District Court.

57. Notwithstanding the provisions of any other written law, offences under this Act or any regulations made thereunder may be tried in a District Court which shall have the power to impose the maximum penalty prescribed for any offence under this Act.

Consent of the Attorney-General.

58. No prosecution in respect of any offence under this Act or the regulations made thereunder shall be instituted except with the consent of the Attorney-General.

Offences by directors, managing directors or managers.

59. (1) Any person who, being a director, managing director or manager of a chit fund company—

(*a*) fails to comply or take all reasonable steps to secure compliance by the chit fund company with the provisions of this Act or any other written law relating to chit fund companies in Singapore; or

(*b*) fails to ensure or to take all reasonable steps to ensure the accuracy and correctness of any statement or information submitted under this Act or of any other written law relating to chit fund companies in force in Singapore,

shall be guilty of an offence under this Act and shall, in respect of each offence, be liable on conviction to imprisonment for a term not exceeding three years or to a fine not exceeding five thousand dollars or to both such imprisonment and fine.

(2) In any proceedings against a person under subsection (1) of this section it shall be a defence to prove that he had reasonable grounds to believe and did in fact believe that a competent and reliable person was charged with the duty of securing compliance with the provisions of those laws or with the duty of ensuring that those statements were accurate and that that person was in a position to discharge that duty.

(3) A person shall not be sentenced to imprisonment for any offence under subsection (1) of this section unless, in the opinion of the court, he committed the offence wilfully.

Holding out as chit fund company.

60. Where any public or private company or firm holds itself out to be a licensed chit fund company when it is not licensed under this Act, such company or firm shall be guilty of an offence under this Act, and every director, manager or every officer of such company or the

proprietor, partner or officer of such firm shall, unless he proves that such holding out by the company or firm was made without his knowledge or consent, be guilty of an offence under this Act and shall be liable on conviction to imprisonment for a term not exceeding two years or to a fine not exceeding four thousand dollars or to both such imprisonment and fine.

**Regulations.**

61. (1) The Commissioner may, with the approval of the Minister, from time to time make all such regulations for, or in respect of, every purpose which is deemed to him necessary for carrying out the provisions of this Act and for the prescribing of any matter which is authorised or required under this Act to be so prescribed.

(2) In particular and without prejudice to the generality of the powers conferred by subsection (1) of this section, the Commissioner may, with the approval of the Minister, by such regulations—

*(a)* prescribe fees to be charged under this Act;

*(b)* prescribe the procedure to be adopted in registering the agreement or any other document or filing any document;

*(c)* prescribe the accounts or books to be kept and the forms to be used by the chit fund company in any case where express provision is not made by this Act; and for providing for the periodical inspection of such accounts or books by the Commissioner or by an officer authorised by the Commissioner;

*(d)* prescribe the periods during which the several documents registered or filed in the office of the Commissioner shall be preserved, and the method of disposal of such documents at the end of those periods;

*(e)* prescribe in the agreement the duration of a chit fund, the highest rebate to be offered, the latest date on which contributions are to be paid and the nature of the security to be given to the chit fund company by the purchaser of the prize and the amount of the commission that may be charged by a chit fund company;

*(f)* prescribe the security to be given by the chit fund company for the discharge of its liabilities under the agreement and the place where such security shall be lodged;

*(g)* prescribe the total value of chit funds to be conducted at any one time by a chit fund company in relation to the paid-up capital of that company;

*(h)* prescribe additional essential terms and conditions or modify or amend existing terms and conditions under section 24 of this Act;

*(i)* regulate advertisements of chit fund companies;

(*j*) vary the security to be furnished by the chit fund company or the subscriber, as the case may be;

(*k*) prescribe the rights, obligations, duties and liabilities of subscribers and the chit fund company.

(3) Every chit fund company which contravenes the regulations made pursuant to subsection (1) of this section shall be guilty of an offence under this Act and shall be liable on conviction to a fine not exceeding two thousand dollars.

## PART VIII. TRANSITIONAL PROVISIONS

Transitional licensing provisions.

62. (1) Notwithstanding the provisions of section 4 of this Act, any public or private company which on the 1st day of October, 1971, was carrying on chit fund business in Singapore may, within one month after the date of the coming into operation of this Act, apply for a licence and shall be granted a licence by the Commissioner which shall be valid up to and including the 30th day of June, 1972.

(2) Thereafter, such licence may be renewed for such further period, or periods, as the Commissioner may decide and be subject to such conditions as he may impose.

(3) A private company which has been granted a licence under subsection (1) of this section shall not be entitled to claim to be an exempt private company under the Companies Act.

Firms or associations that have been carrying on chit fund business.

63. (1) Notwithstanding section 4 of this Act, any firm, association or body of persons that has been carrying on chit fund business in Singapore before the 1st day of October, 1971, may apply for and may be granted a licence if such firm, association or body of persons, as the case may be, incorporates itself as a public company within three months of the date of the coming into operation of this Act.

(2) A licence granted under subsection (1) of this section shall be valid for such period as the Commissioner may decide and be subject to such conditions as the Commissioner may impose.

# Economic Development Board Act[1]

An Act to establish the Economic Development Board Act.

[1st August, 1961]

Short title. 1. This Act may be cited as the Economic Development Board Act.

Interpretation. 2. In this Act, unless the context otherwise requires—

"Board" means the Economic Development Board established under section 3 of this Act;

"goods, materials or things" includes capital or consumer goods of every description, including aircraft, ships, machinery, food and drugs;

"industrial enterprise" means any sole proprietorship, partnership, company or co-operative society wherever registered or incorporated under any law for the time being in force relating to companies, co-operative societies or businesses and engaged in or proposing to engage in any one or more of the following purposes or functions:

(*a*) manufacture and sale of goods, materials or things or the subjection of goods, materials or things to any process, including that of repairs, breaking-up, reconditioning or maintenance;

(*b*) the exploration for, and exploitation of, natural resources, including—

(i) the working of a mine, quarry or any other source of mineral deposits; or

(ii) the treatment or preparation for sale, consumption or use, and the storage or removal, of any substance from any mine, quarry or other source of mineral deposits;

(*c*) transport, dock, water or electricity undertaking, including the business of wharfingers and stevedores;

(*d*) the storage of goods, materials or things;

(*e*) the working of a plantation;

(*f*) fishing;

---

[1] *Singapore Statutes,* Cap. 189 (1970). Originally Ord. No. 21 of 1961. Relevant citations: Acts Nos. 9 of 1966; 4 of 1969; 3 of 1972; 38 of 1973; and 17 of 1975.

(*g*) the business of a tourist enterprise as defined in the Tourist Promotion Board Act;

"underwrite" means to contract, with or without conditions, to subscribe for stocks, shares, bonds or debentures of an industrial enterprise with a view to the resale of the whole or part of it.

Establishment of Economic Development Board.

3. (1) There shall be established in accordance with the provisions of this Act a body to be called the "Economic Development Board".

(2) The Board when established shall be a body corporate with perpetual succession and a common seal with power, subject to the provisions of this Act, to acquire and dispose of property, both movable and immovable, and may sue and be sued in its corporate name and perform such other acts as bodies corporate may by law perform.

Chairman of the Board.

4. The Minister shall appoint a Chairman of the Board who shall, subject to the provisions of this Act, hold office for such period and on such terms as the Minister may determine.

Constitution of the Board.

5. (1) The Board shall consist of—

(*a*) the Chairman of the Board appointed under section 4 of this Act;

(*b*) the Director of the Board appointed under section 7 of this Act; and

(*c*) not less than four and not more than ten other members who shall be appointed by the Minister.

(2) The quorum of the Board shall be four.

(3) The Board shall meet together once at least in every month.

(4) The members of the Board appointed by the Minister under the provisions of paragraph (*c*) of subsection (1) of this section shall, unless their appointment is revoked by the Minister under the provisions of subsection (9) of this section, or unless they resign during their period of office, hold office for a term of three years or for such shorter period as the Minister may in any case determine.

(5) The Minister may appoint not more than two members of the Board to be Deputy Chairmen of the Board.

(6) The Chairman or the person lawfully acting as Chairman at any meeting of the Board shall have an original as well as a casting vote.

(7) A member of the Board shall not, in any meeting of the Board, participate in any discussion relating to, and shall not vote in respect of,

any application to the Board for a loan in which he is interested or in respect of any business or management in which he is interested, and if he does so his vote shall not be counted, nor shall he be counted in the quorum present at that meeting.

(8) The members of the Board shall be paid out of the funds of the Board such salaries, fees or allowances as the President may determine.

(9) The Minister may at any time revoke the appointment of the Chairman or of any other member of the Board.

**5A.** At any time when the Chairman is absent or otherwise incapable of acting, or there is a vacancy in the office of Chairman—

*(a)* such one of the Deputy Chairmen as the Minister may direct, or in default of any such direction such one of them as they may agree; or

*(b)* if there is only one Deputy Chairman, that Deputy Chairman,

may exercise any of the functions of the Chairman.

**5B.** At any time when every person who is Chairman or Deputy Chairman is absent or otherwise incapable of acting, or there is no such person, such member of the Board as the Minister may direct, or in default of any such direction such member as the Board may agree, may perform any of the functions of the Chairman.

Directions by the Minister.

**6.** (1) The Minister may, after consultation with the Board or otherwise, give to the Board such directions, not inconsistent with the provisions of this Act, as he deems fit, as to the exercise and performance by the Board of its powers, duties and functions under this Act, and the Board shall give effect to all such directions.

(2) The Board shall furnish the Minister with such information with respect to its property and activities as he may from time to time require.

Director of the Board.

**7.** (1) The Board shall, with the approval of the Minister, appoint a Director of the Economic Development Board who shall perform such duties as the Board may entrust or delegate to him:

Provided that the first Director of the Board shall be appointed by the Minister.

(2) If the Director of the Board is temporarily absent from Singapore or temporarily incapacitated through illness or for any other sufficient reason from the performance of his duties, another person

may be appointed in the manner provided by subsection (1) of this section to be the Director of the Board during such temporary absence or other incapacity.

Appointment of officers and servants.

**8.** (1) The Board may from time to time appoint and employ such officers and servants as may be necessary for the purposes of this Act and may from time to time dismiss them.

(2) All officers and servants of the Board shall be under the administrative control of the Board.

Ineligibility for employment as officers of the Board.

**9.** (1) No person shall be eligible for employment as an officer or servant of the Board who has, directly or indirectly, by himself or his partner, any share or interest in any contract with, for or on behalf of the Board.

(2) Any officer or servant of the Board who has or acquires any such share or interest shall be liable in the discretion of the Board to summary dismissal without notice.

(3) No officer or servant shall be deemed to have or acquire any such share or interest by reason only that—

*(a)* he is or becomes a member of an incorporated company which owns land situated in Singapore or has a contract with or executes work for the Board, unless he has a beneficial interest in shares of that company and the total nominal value of these shares exceeds ten thousand dollars or one-tenth of the total nominal value of the issued share capital of the company whichever is the less; or

*(b)* he has or acquires a share in any loan issued by the Board or in any security for the same.

Rules for establishment of pension or provident fund scheme.

**10.** (1) Subject to the approval of the Minister, the Board may make rules for the establishment of a scheme or schemes for the payment of pensions, gratuities, provident fund or other superannuation benefits to such officers or classes of officers of the Board, as it may determine, on their death or retirement from the service of the Board or on their otherwise leaving the service of the Board.

(2) The following provisions shall apply to any scheme established under this section:

*(a)* no assurance on the life of any contributor under any such scheme, and no moneys or other benefits payable under any such assurance, and no payment made under any such scheme

to any person who has been employed by the Board, shall be assignable or transferable, or liable to be garnished, attached, sequestered or levied upon for or in respect of any debt or claim whatsoever other than a debt due to the Board or to the Government;

*(b)* no donation by the Board or contribution by its officers made under any such scheme and no interest thereon shall be assignable or transferable or liable to be garnished, attached, sequestered or levied upon for or in respect of any debt or claim whatsoever other than a debt due to the Board or to the Government;

*(c)* no such donation, contribution or interest shall be subject to the debts of the contributor, nor shall such donation, contribution or interest pass to the Official Assignee on the bankruptcy of such contributor, but, if such contributor is adjudicated a bankrupt or is declared insolvent by a court, such donation, contribution or interest shall, subject to the provisions of this Act, be deemed to be subject to a trust in favour of the persons entitled thereto on the death of the contributor;

*(d)* the bankruptcy of a contributor shall not affect the making of deductions from the salary of the contributor in accordance with any such scheme, but such deductions shall continue to be made notwithstanding the provisions of any written law, and the portion of salary so deducted shall not be deemed to form part of his after-acquired property;

*(e)* subject to the provisions of any such scheme, all moneys paid or payable under any such scheme on the death of a contributor shall be deemed to be subject to a trust in favour of the persons entitled thereto under the will or intestacy of such deceased contributor, or under a nomination in such form as may be prescribed in such scheme, and shall not be deemed to form part of his estate or be subject to the payment of his debts but shall be deemed to be property passing on his death for the purposes of the Estate Duty Act;

*(f)* any contributor may, by a memorandum under his hand, appoint a trustee or trustees of the moneys payable on his death out of any such scheme and may make provision for the appointment of a new trustee or new trustees of such moneys and for the investment thereof: such memorandum shall be in the form prescribed in such scheme and shall be deposited with the Board;

*(g)* if at the time of the death of any contributor or at any time afterwards, there is no trustee of such moneys or it is expedient

to appoint a new trustee or new trustees, then and in any such case a trustee or trustees or a new trustee or trustees may be appointed by the High Court or a Judge thereof; and

*(h)* the receipt of a trustee or trustees duly appointed, or in default of any such appointment and of written notice thereof to the Board, the receipt of the legal personal representative of a deceased contributor shall be a discharge to the Board for any moneys payable on his death out of any such scheme.

Appointment of committees and delegation of powers.

**11.** (1) The Board may, in its discretion, appoint from among its own members or other persons who are not members of the Board such number of committees consisting of members or other persons or members and other persons for purposes which, in the opinion of the Board, would be better regulated and managed by means of such committees.

(2) The Board may, subject to such conditions or restrictions as it thinks fit, delegate to any such committee or the Chairman or the Director all or any of the powers, functions and duties by this Act vested in the Board, except the power to borrow money or to raise loans by the issue of bonds and debentures; and any power, function or duty so delegated may be exercised or performed by such committee or the Chairman or the Director, as the case may be, in the name and on behalf of the Board.

(3) The Board may, subject to such conditions or restrictions as it thinks fit, delegate to any employee thereof all or any of the Board's functions and duties by this Act vested in the Board, except the power to borrow money or to raise or grant loans or advances to or subscribe to or underwrite the issue of stocks, shares, bonds or debentures of industrial enterprises; and any power, function or duty so delegated may be exercised or performed by such employee in the name and on behalf of the Board.

(4) The Board may continue to exercise any power conferred upon it, or perform any function or duty under this Act, notwithstanding the delegation of such power, function or duty under the provisions of this section.

Appointment of member to act on behalf of Chairman outside Singapore.

**11A.** The Chairman of the Board may, with the approval of the Minister, appoint a member of the Board to perform the functions of the Chairman outside Singapore in relation to such matters or class of matters as the Chairman may specify.

Protection from personal liability.

**12.** (1) No matter or thing done and no contract of any kind entered into by the Board and no matter or thing done by any member of the Board or by any employee thereof or any other person whomsoever acting under the direction of the Board shall, if the matter or thing was done or the contract was entered into bona fide for the purpose of executing the provisions of this Act, subject any such member or employee or any person acting under the direction of the Board personally to any action, liability, claim or demand whatsoever in respect thereof.

(2) Any expense incurred by the Board or any member, employee or other person so acting under the direction of the Board shall be borne by and repaid out of the funds of the Board.

Members and officers of the Board deemed to be public servants.

13. The members of the Board and the employees thereof, of every description, shall be deemed to be public servants within the meaning of the Penal Code.

Provision of working capital.

14. For the purpose of enabling the Board to carry out its objects and to defray expenditure properly chargeable to capital account, including defraying initial expenses, and for the provision of working capital, the Minister may authorize payment to the Board of such sums as he may determine.

Borrowing powers.

15. (1) The Board may, from time to time, for the purposes of this Act raise loans—

(*a*) from the Government; or

(*b*) with the consent of the Minister and subject to the provisions of any written law, within or otherwise than within Singapore, by the creation and issue of debentures, stocks or bonds or otherwise.

(2) The Board shall pay interest on such loans at such rate and at such times, and shall make such provision for the mode and time or times of repayment of principal, as may be approved by the Minister:

Provided that approval of the Minister shall not be required, under the provisions of this subsection, for the rate of interest to be paid on a loan by means of a financial agreement whereby credit facilities are granted for the purchase of goods, materials or things.

(3) The Board may, from time to time, borrow by way of temporary loan or overdraft from a bank or otherwise, any sum which it may temporarily require—

(*a*) for the purpose of defraying expenses pending the receipt of revenues receivable by it in respect of the period of account in which those expenses are chargeable; or (*b*) for the purpose of defraying, pending the receipt of money due in respect of any loan authorised to be raised under the provisions of subsection (1) of this section, expenses intended to be defrayed by any such loan.

(4) Bonds and debentures of the Board shall be guaranteed by the Government as to the repayment of principal and the payment of interest at such rate as may be approved by the Minister under the provisions of subsection (2) of this section.

(5) For the purposes of subsection (1) of this section, the power to raise loans shall include the power to make any financial agreement whereby credit facilities are granted to the Board for the purchase of goods, materials or things.

Powers of the Board.

**16.** (1) The Board shall have power—

(*a*) with the written approval of the Minister, to underwrite the issue of stocks, shares, bonds or debentures by industrial enterprises;

(*b*) with the written approval of the Minister, to guarantee on such terms and conditions as may be agreed upon, loans raised by industrial enterprises which—

(i) are repayable within a period not exceeding twenty-five years; or

(ii) are floated in the public market;

(*c*) to grant loans or advances to, or subscribe to stocks, shares, bonds or debentures of industrial enterprises;

(*d*) to manage, control or supervise industrial enterprises by nominating directors or advisers or otherwise collaborating with them or entering into partnerships or any other arrangement for jointly working with them;

(*e*) with the written approval of the Minister, to establish, sell shares of, invest in and manage industrial enterprises;

(*f*) to act as agent for the Government or, with its approval, for any other person in the transaction of any business with an industrial enterprise in respect of loans or advances granted or debentures subscribed by the Government or such other person;

(*g*) to acquire, sell or lease land for the purposes of industrial sites, for the housing of employees or for general economic development;

(*h*) to lay out industrial estates for sale or lease;

(*i*) to provide technical advice and assistance to industrial enterprises and to build up a corps of engineering and managerial staff to provide such assistance;

(*j*) to exercise all functions and powers and perform all duties which, under or by virtue of any other written law, are or may be or become vested or delegated to it;

(*k*) to receive in consideration of the services rendered by it such commission as may be agreed upon;

(*l*) to provide and maintain, either within Singapore or otherwise, housing accommodation, including convalescent or holiday houses for employees of the Board; to provide and maintain for such employees clubs and playing fields and to provide educational facilities for them; to grant loans to such employees, or to act as guarantor for loans taken by them, to enable them to purchase their own houses and vehicles; and to award scholarships or to give loans to such employees to obtain professional, technical or other training;

(*m*) with the written approval of the Minister, to award compensation to any person sustaining any damage by reason of the exercise of any of the powers, under this Act, by the Board or by any employee thereof;

(*n*) to act as agents for any industrial enterprise;

(*o*) to carry out experimental work and to conduct, promote and encourage the study of, and research in, matters connected with any of the Board's purposes and functions;

(*p*) from time to time to invest any of the funds of the Board in securities authorised for the investment of trust funds by any written law for the time being in force, and, with the approval of the Minister, in other securities, within or otherwise than within Singapore;

(*q*) with the concurrence of the Housing and Development Board, to finance or carry out or assist in carrying out any scheme in connection with urban redevelopment; and

(*r*) generally to do all such matters and things as may be incidental to or consequential upon the exercise of its powers or the discharge of its duties under this Act.

(2) The Board may, in addition to the powers vested in it by subsection (1) of this section, exercise such other powers as the Minister may authorise the Board in writing to exercise.

(3) The Board shall, when it is exercising powers authorised by the Minister under subsection (2) of this section, be deemed to be exercising powers vested in it by subsection (1) of this section.

Rights of the Board in case of default.

**17.** (1) Where any industrial enterprise which is under a liability to the Board under an agreement makes any default in repayment or otherwise fails to comply with the terms of its agreement with the

Board, the Board shall, without prejudice to any other rights or remedies which it may possess under the law, have the right to take over the management of such industrial enterprise, as well as the right to sell and realise the property pledged, mortgaged, hypothecated or assigned to the Board.

(2) Any transfer of property made by the Board in exercise of its powers of sale and realisation under subsection (1) of this section shall vest in the transferee all rights in or to the property transferred as if the sale had been made by the owner of the property.

(3) The Board shall have the same rights and powers with respect to goods manufactured or produced wholly or partly from goods forming part of security held by it, as it had with respect to the original goods.

(4) Where the Board takes over the management of an industrial enterprise under the provisions of subsection (1) of this section, it shall be deemed to be the owner of such industrial enterprise for purposes of suits by or against such industrial enterprise and shall sue and be sued in the name of the owner of such industrial enterprise.

Power to call for repayment before agreed period.

**18.** Notwithstanding any agreement to the contrary, and without prejudice to any other rights or remedies which it may possess under the law, the Board may by notice require any industrial enterprise, to which it has granted any loan or advance, forthwith to discharge in full its liabilities to the Board—

*(a)* if it appears to the Board that false or misleading information in any material particular was given in the application for the loan or advance; or

*(b)* if the industrial enterprise has failed to comply with the terms of its contract with the Board in the matter of the loan or advance; or

*(c)* if there is a reasonable apprehension that the industrial enterprise is unable to pay its debts or that proceedings for liquidation may be commenced in respect thereof; or

*(d)* if the property pledged, mortgaged, hypothecated or assigned to the Board as security for the loan or advance is not insured and kept insured by the industrial enterprise to the satisfaction of the Board, or depreciates in value, in the opinion of the Board, by more than twenty per cent and further security to the satisfaction of the Board is not given; or

*(e)* if, without the permission of the Board, machinery and other equipment, whether forming part of the security or otherwise,

is removed from the premises of the industrial enterprise without being replaced; or

(*f*) if for any reason it is necessary in the opinion of the Board to protect the interests of the Board.

Special provisions for enforcement of claims by the Board.

19. (1) Where by reason of the breach of any condition of an agreement between the Board and an industrial enterprise, the Board becomes entitled to call for the immediate payment of any loan or advance granted by it before the due date or where the due date has expired, and the industrial enterprise fails to repay such loan or advance, any officer of the Board generally or especially authorised by the Board in that behalf may apply to the High Court for one or more of the following reliefs, namely:

(*a*) for an order for the sale of the property pledged, mortgaged, hypothecated or assigned to the Board as security for the loan or advance; or

(*b*) for transferring the management of the industrial enterprise to the Board; or

(*c*) for an interim injunction where there is apprehension of the machinery or the equipment being removed from the premises of the industrial enterprise without the permission of the Board.

(2) An application under subsection (1) of this section shall state the nature and extent of the liability of the industrial enterprise to the Board, the ground on which it is made and such other particulars as may be prescribed.

(3) Where the application is for the reliefs mentioned in paragraphs (*a*) and (*c*) of subsection (1) of this section, the judge shall make an interim order attaching the security or so much of the property of the industrial enterprise as would on being sold realise in his estimation an amount equivalent in value to the outstanding liability of the industrial enterprise to the Board, together with the costs of the proceedings taken under this section with or without an interim injunction restraining the industrial enterprise from transferring or removing its machinery or equipment.

(4) Where the application is for the relief mentioned in paragraph (*b*) of subsection (1) of this section, the judge shall grant an interim injunction restraining the industrial enterprise from transferring or removing its machinery or equipment and issue a notice calling upon the industrial enterprise to show cause on a date to be specified in the notice as to why the management of the industrial enterprise should not be transferred to the Board.

(5) Before making any order under subsection (3) or subsection (4) of this section, the judge may, if he thinks fit, examine the officer making the application.

(6) At the same time as he makes an order under subsection (3) of this section, the judge shall issue to the industrial enterprise a notice accompanied by copies of the order, the application and the evidence, if any, recorded by him, calling upon it to show cause on a date to be specified in the notice as to why the interim order of attachment should not be made absolute or the injunction confirmed.

(7) If no cause is shown on or before the date specified in the notice under subsections (4) and (6) of this section, the judge shall forthwith make the interim order absolute and direct the sale of the attached property or transfer the management of the industrial enterprise to the Board or confirm the injunction.

(8) If cause is shown, the judge shall proceed to investigate the claim of the Board and the provisions of the Rules of the Supreme Court, 1934, shall as far as practicable apply to such proceedings.

(9) On an investigation made under subsection (8) of this section, the judge shall make an order—

*(a)* confirming the order of attachment and directing the sale of the attached property; or

*(b)* varying the order of attachment so as to release a portion of the property from attachment and directing the sale of the remainder of the attached property; or

*(c)* releasing the property from attachment, if he is satisfied that it is not necessary in the interests of the Board; or

*(d)* confirming or dissolving the injunction; or

*(e)* transferring the management of the industrial enterprise to the Board or rejecting the claim made in this behalf:

Provided that when making any order under paragraph *(c)* of this subsection, the judge may make such further orders as he thinks necessary to protect the interests of the Board, and may apportion the costs of the proceedings in such manner as he thinks fit:

Provided further that unless the Board intimates to the judge that it will not appeal against any order releasing any property from attachment, such order shall not be given effect to until the expiry of the period fixed under subsection (11) of this section within which an appeal may be lodged, or if an appeal is lodged unless the Court of Appeal otherwise directs, until the appeal is disposed of.

(10) An order of attachment or sale of property under this section shall be carried into effect as far as may be practicable in the manner

provided in the Rules of the Supreme Court, 1934, for the seizure and sale of property in execution of a judgment or order, as if the Board were the judgment creditor.

(11) Any party aggrieved by an order under subsection (7) or subsection (9) of this section may, within thirty days from the date of the order, appeal to the Court of Appeal, and upon the appeal, that Court may after hearing the parties make such orders as it thinks proper.

Compulsory acquisition of land.

20. Where any immovable property, not being State land, is needed for the purposes of the Board and cannot be acquired by agreement, the Board may request and the President may, if he thinks fit, direct the acquisition of that property and in that case, the property may be acquired in accordance with the provisions of any written law relating to the acquisition of land for a public purpose and any declaration required under any such law that the land is so needed may be made notwithstanding that compensation is to be paid out of the funds of the Board, and the declaration shall have effect as if it were a declaration that the land is needed for a public purpose made in accordance with that written law.

Accounts of the Board.

21. (1) The Board shall prepare in respect of each financial year ending on the 31st day of March a statement of account in a form approved by the Minister.

(2) For the purposes of this Act, "financial year" means a period of twelve months ending on the 31st day of March in any year:

Provided that for the year 1969 the financial year shall be deemed to mean the period of fifteen months commencing on the 1st day of January, 1969 and ending on the 31st day of March, 1970.

(3) The statement of account referred to in subsection (1) of this section shall be audited by a qualified auditor to be appointed in respect of each financial year by the Minister, and the auditor shall make a report on the accounts examined by him.

(4) The remuneration of the auditor appointed by the Minister under subsection (3) of this section shall be fixed by the Minister and shall be paid out of the funds of the Board.

(5) So soon as the accounts have been audited, the Board shall send the Minister a copy of the statement of account and the report thereon by the auditor referred to in subsection (3) of this section, and the Minister shall present a copy of every such statement and report to Parliament.

**22.** So soon as may be after the 1st day of April in each year but not later than the 30th day of September in each year unless expressly authorised in writing by the Minister, the Board shall prepare a report of its operations in the preceding financial year and shall send a copy of such report to the Minister who shall present a copy of every such report to Parliament. Annual report.

**23.** The Board shall obtain in advance the approval of the Minister for its annual estimates of expenditure in respect of office administration and for any supplementary estimates of such expenditure. Annual estimates.

**24.** For the purpose of the registration of any assurance pertaining to the sale or the purchase by the Board of any land, the mortgage of such land or the reconveyance or discharge of such mortgage— Special provisions as to sale or purchase by the Board of land, etc.

(*a*) in the case of land registered under the provisions of the Registration of Deeds Act, the provisions of section 12 of that Act shall not apply; and

(*b*) in the case of land registered under the provisions of the Land Titles Act, where a solicitor is not employed by the Board, a certificate of an officer of the Board shall be sufficient for the purposes of subsection (4) of section 50 of the Land Titles Act.

**24A.** (1) The fixing of the common seal of the Board shall be authenticated by the signature of—

(*a*) the Chairman or a Deputy Chairman; and

(*b*) an officer of the Board authorised by the Board, either generally or specially, to act for that purpose.

(2) Any document purporting to be a document duly executed under the seal of the Board shall be admissible in evidence and shall, unless the contrary is proved, be deemed to be a document so executed.

**25.** (1) The Minister may, after consulting with the Board, make such regulations as he may consider necessary or desirable for the proper conduct of the business of the Board including, without prejudice to the generality of the foregoing, regulations with regard to any of the following matters: Regulations.

(*a*) the convening of meetings of the Board and the procedure to be followed thereat;

(*b*) the appointment or establishment of committees of the members of the Board, and the co-opting of persons other than members of the Board to such committees;

(*c*) the provision of a common seal and the custody and use thereof;

*(d)* the manner in which documents, cheques and instruments of any description shall be signed or executed on behalf of the Board;

*(e)* the manner and terms of issue and redemption of bonds and debentures by the Board; and

*(f)* generally for the exercise of the Board's powers under the provisions of this Act.

(2) All regulations made under this Act shall be published in the *Gazette* and shall be presented to Parliament as soon as may be after publication and, if a resolution is passed pursuant to a motion notice whereof has been given for a sitting day not later than the first available sitting day of Parliament next after the expiry of three months from the date when such regulations are so presented annulling the regulations or any part thereof as from a specified date, the regulations or that part thereof, as the case may be, shall thereupon become void as from that date but without prejudice to the validity of anything previously done thereunder or to the making of new regulations.

Winding up.

26. The Board shall not be wound up except by or under the authority of an Act.

Vesting of the Singapore Industrial Promotion Board's assets and liabilities in the Board.

27. Upon the coming into operation of this Act—

*(a)* the Singapore Industrial Promotion Board shall cease to exist as a body corporate;

*(b)* all the assets and movable and immovable property of every description and all the powers, rights and privileges in connection therewith or appertaining thereto which immediately before the coming into operation of this Act were vested in the Singapore Industrial Promotion Board shall forthwith vest in the Board freed and discharged from any trust whatsoever, but subject nevertheless to the provisions of this Act; and

*(c)* all liabilities and obligations of the Singapore Industrial Promotion Board which may have existed immediately before the coming into operation of this Act shall be transferred to and vest in the Board.

# Post Office Savings Bank of Singapore Act, 1971 [1]

An Act to establish a corporation to be known as the Post Office Savings Bank of Singapore and to provide for the transfer to, and for the vesting in, the corporation of the functions, assets and liabilities of the Post Office Savings Bank established under the Post Office Savings Bank Act (Chapter 198 of the 1970 Revised Edition) and to repeal the said Act.

Be it enacted by the President with the advice and consent of the Parliament of Singapore, as follows:

[10th November, 1971]

## PART I. PRELIMINARY

Short title and commencement.

1. This Act may be cited as the Post Office Savings Bank of Singapore Act, 1971, and shall come into operation on such date as the Minister may, by notification in the *Gazette,* appoint.

Interpretation.

2. In this Act, unless the context otherwise requires—

"Bank" means the Post Office Savings Bank of Singapore established under section 3 of this Act;

"Board" means the Board of Directors referred to in section 7 of this Act;

"Chairman" means the Chairman appointed by the Minister under section 8 of this Act;

"director" means a director appointed under subsection (1) of section 7 of this Act and includes the Chairman;

"General Manager" means the General Manager appointed under section 17 of this Act and includes any person appointed to act as General Manager;

"guardian" means the father of a minor, or if the father is dead, the mother, or if both parents are dead or absent from Singapore or are incapable of acting owing to disability or other cause and no guardian of the minor has been appointed by will or deed or under any other written law for the time being in force or by

[1] *Singapore Government Gazette Acts Supplement,* No. 29, November 19, 1971, Act No. 13 of 1971.

any competent court, any adult person with whom the minor is residing and by whom he is being maintained;

"minor" means a person who has not attained the age of eighteen years.

## PART II. ESTABLISHMENT, INCORPORATION, FUNCTION, POWERS AND CONSTITUTION OF THE BANK

Establishment and incorporation of the Bank.

3. There is hereby established a body to be known as the "Post Office Savings Bank of Singapore" which shall be a body corporate with perpetual succession, and with power to sue and be sued in its corporate name and to perform such other acts as bodies corporate may by law perform, and to exercise such other powers as are conferred under or by virtue of this Act.

Objects of the Bank.

4. The principal objects of the Bank shall be—

(*a*) to provide means for the deposit of savings and to encourage thrift;

(*b*) to mobilise domestic savings for the purpose of public development; and

(*c*) to take over the functions and duties of the Post Office Savings Bank established under the Post Office Savings Bank Act and to continue to carry on its business in Singapore and elsewhere.

Powers of the Bank.

5. For the purpose of carrying out the objects set out in section 4 of this Act, the Bank may—

(*a*) receive deposits that are repayable either on demand or otherwise;

(*b*) advance and lend money to, or give a guarantee for the benefit of, any person having an account with the Bank;

(*c*) construct, manufacture, produce, purchase, take on hire or hire-purchase, install, maintain and repair anything required for the purposes of its business;

(*d*) enter into and carry out agreements with any person (including the Government) for the carrying on by him, whether as agent or otherwise, of any of the activities which the Bank may carry on or for the carrying on jointly by him and the Bank of any of those activities;

(*e*) acquire land which is required by it for, or in connection with, the exercise of its powers or as to which it can reasonably be foreseen that it will be so required;

(*f*) dispose (whether absolutely or for a term of years) of any part of its undertaking or any property which in its opinion is not required by it for or in connection with the exercise of its powers, and in particular, to dispose of an interest in, or right over, any property which, subject to that interest or right, is retained by it;

*(g)* for the purposes of its business subscribe for or acquire any of the securities of an incorporated company or other body corporate, procure its admission to membership of an incorporated company limited by guarantee and not having a share capital, promote the formation of an incorporated company or participate in the promotion of such a company or acquire in[2] an undertaking or part of an undertaking;

*(h)* do anything for the purpose of advancing the skill of persons employed by it or that of persons who, though not so employed are engaging themselves, or have it in contemplation to engage themselves, in work of a kind in the case of which it has or may have a direct or indirect concern in the products thereof;

*(i)* provide houses, hostels and other like accommodation for persons engaged in its business;

*(j)* make loans to persons employed by it (including, in particular, loans to assist them to acquire housing accommodation), and guarantee loans made to persons so employed (including, in particular, loans made by building societies and other bodies for housing purposes);

*(k)* promote recreational activities for, and activities conducive to the welfare of, persons who are, or have been, engaged in its business and the families of such persons and assist the promotion by others of such activities; and

*(l)* do all such other things as are incidental or conducive to the attainment of its object.

6. (1) The Bank shall have a common seal and such seal may, from time to time, be broken, changed, altered and made anew as to the Bank seems fit,[3] and, until a seal is provided under this section, a stamp bearing the inscription "Post Office Savings Bank of Singapore" may be used as the common seal.

Common seal.

(2) All deeds, documents and other instruments requiring the seal of the Bank shall be sealed with the common seal of the Bank by authority of the directors in the presence of the General Manager and of some other person duly authorised by the directors to act in that behalf and shall be signed by the General Manager and by such duly authorised person, and such signing shall be sufficient evidence that the common

[2] Editor queries whether "in" is necessary.

[3] Editor queries whether this phrase should read "as the Bank sees fit."

seal of the Bank has been duly and properly affixed and that the said seal is the lawful common seal of the Bank.

(3) The directors may by resolution or otherwise appoint an officer of the Bank or any other agent either generally or in a particular case to execute or sign on behalf of the Bank any agreement or other instrument not under seal in relation to any matter coming within the powers of the Bank.

(4) The provisions of section 12 of the Registration of Deeds Act shall not apply to any instrument purporting to have been executed under the provisions of subsection (2) of this section.

Board of Directors.

7. (1) The management of the Bank and of its properties and its business shall be vested in a Board of Directors consisting of not less than five and not more than eight directors who shall be appointed by the Minister.

(2) The directors shall hold office for a term not exceeding three years and shall be eligible for re-appointment.

(3) The Minister may at any time revoke the appointment of any director.

(4) Any director may, with the approval of the Minister, resign from his office.

Chairman.

8. (1) The Minister shall appoint one of the directors to be Chairman of the Board.

(2) The Minister may appoint any director to act as temporary Chairman during the temporary absence from Singapore, or during the temporary incapacity owing to illness or otherwise, of the Chairman.

Salaries, fees and allowances payable to directors.

9. There shall be paid to the Chairman and other directors, out of the funds of the Bank, such salaries, fees and allowances as the Minister may, from time to time, determine.

Vacation of office of director.

10. The office of director shall be vacated if the director—

*(a)* becomes of unsound mind;

*(b)* becomes a bankrupt or suspends payment to, or makes any arrangement or composition with, his creditors;

*(c)* has been absent for more than three consecutive meetings of the directors without permission of the directors;

*(d)* resigns from his office; or

(*e*) is convicted of an offence involving dishonesty or fraud or moral turpitude.

Filling of vacancies in the office of director.

11. If any director dies or has his appointment revoked or otherwise vacates his office before the expiry of the term for which he has been appointed, another person may be appointed by the Minister for the unexpired period of the term of office of the director in whose place he is appointed.

Meetings of directors.

12. (1) The Chairman shall summon meetings as often as may be required but not less frequently than once in three months.

(2) At every meeting of the Board, a quorum shall consist of four directors, and decisions shall be adopted by a simple majority of the votes of the directors present and voting except in the case of an equality of votes the Chairman shall have a casting vote.[4]

(3) The Chairman, or in his absence such director as the directors present shall select, shall preside at meetings of the Board.

(4) Subject to the provisions of subsection (2) of this section, the Board shall not be precluded from holding any meeting or acting in any matter merely by reason of any vacancy in its membership.

(5) Subject to the provisions of this Act, the Board may make standing orders to regulate its own procedure, and in particular, the holding of meetings, the notice to be given of such meetings, the proceedings thereat, the keeping of minutes and the custody, production and inspection of such minutes.

Director's interest in contract to be made known.

13. (1) A director who is directly or indirectly interested in a contract made, or proposed to be made, by the Bank shall disclose the nature of his interest at the first meeting of the Board at which he is present after the relevant facts have come to his knowledge.

(2) A disclosure under subsection (1) of this section shall be recorded in the minutes of the Board and, after the disclosure, the director—

(*a*) shall not take part in any deliberation or decision of the Board with respect to that contract; and
(*b*) shall be disregarded for the purpose of constituting a quorum of the Board for any such deliberation or decision.

(3) No act or proceeding of the Board shall be questioned on the ground that a director has contravened the provisions of this section.

[4] Editor queries whether there has been an omission here.

Validity of acts of directors.

**14.** The acts of a director shall be valid notwithstanding any defect that may afterwards be discovered in his appointment or qualifications.

Secrecy.

**15.** (1) No director, officer, employee or agent of the Bank shall disclose to any person any information relating to the affairs of the Bank or of any person or customer of the Bank which he has acquired in the performance of his duties or the exercise of his functions:

Provided that nothing in this section shall be deemed to limit any power conferred upon the Supreme Court or a Judge thereof by the Evidence Act or to prohibit obedience to an order made under that Act or any such law.

(2) Any person who contravenes the provisions of subsection (1) of this section shall be guilty of an offence under this Act and shall be liable on conviction to imprisonment for a term not exceeding three years or to a fine not exceeding five thousand dollars, or to both such imprisonment and fine.

Directions by the Minister.

**16.** (1) The Minister may, after consultation with the Bank, give such general directions, not inconsistent with the provisions of this Act, as to the policy to be followed by the Bank in the exercise and performance of its powers, functions and duties under this Act as appear to the Minister to be necessary and the Bank shall, as soon as possible, give effect to any such direction.

(2) The Bank shall furnish the Minister with information with respect to its properties and activities in such manner and at such times as he may require.

## PART III. PROVISIONS RELATING TO STAFF, TRANSFER OF EMPLOYEES, ETC.

Appointment of General Manager.

**17.** (1) The Bank shall, with the approval of the Minister, appoint a General Manager on such terms and conditions as the Bank may think fit.

(2) The General Manager shall—

*(a)* be the chief executive officer of the Bank;

*(b)* be responsible to the Board for the proper administration and management of the Bank in accordance with the policy laid down by the Board; and

*(c)* not be removed from office without the consent of the Minister.

(3) The Minister shall consult the Public Service Commission be-

fore granting his approval under subsection (1) of this section or before giving his consent under paragraph *(c)* of subsection (2) of this section.

(4) If the General Manager is temporarily absent from Singapore or temporarily incapacitated by reason of illness or for other reasons temporarily unable to perform his duties, another person may be appointed by the Bank to act in the place of the General Manager during any such period of absence from duty.

**18.** (1) The Bank may from time to time approve a list of posts which it thinks necessary for the purposes of this Act and may add to or amend that list. The first such list of posts shall contain posts for all the persons transferred to the service of the Bank under section 19 of this Act.

List of posts and appointment of employees.

(2) No person may be employed by the Bank unless he holds a post appearing in the list of posts for the time being in force.

(3) Subject to the provisions of this section—

*(a)* appointments and promotions to all posts shall be made by the Bank; and

*(b)* the termination of appointment, dismissal, and disciplinary control of the employees of the Bank shall be vested in the Bank.

(4) Notwithstanding the provisions of this section, the Bank may appoint persons temporarily to posts in the list of posts for the time being in force.

(5) The Bank may make rules, not inconsistent with the provisions of this Act or of any other written law, for the appointment, promotion, disciplinary control and terms and conditions of service of all persons employed by the Bank.

(6) Without prejudice to the generality of subsection (5) of this section, the Bank shall prescribe the rates of remuneration payable to persons employed by the Bank, and no person so employed shall be paid otherwise than in accordance with such rates.

**19.** (1) Upon the date of the coming into operation of this Act, such persons as the Minister may decide who were employed by the Government immediately prior to the date of the coming into operation of this Act and were exercising any of the powers or were discharging any of the functions or duties vested in the Bank by this Act, shall be deemed to be transferred to the service of the Bank on terms not less favourable than those they enjoyed immediately prior to their transfer

Transfer of employees.

and such terms (which shall be determined by the Bank) shall take into account the salaries and conditions of service including accrued rights to leave, enjoyed by them while in the employment of the Government.

(2) Notwithstanding the provisions of subsection (1) of this section, the persons who are to be transferred to the service of the Bank, with the exception of persons holding such grades as the Minister may determine, shall as soon as practicable be given the option of remaining in the service of the Government.

Pension schemes, provident fund, etc.

**20.** (1) The Bank may, with the approval of the Minister, make rules for the establishment of a scheme or schemes for the payment of pensions, gratuities, provident fund or other superannuation benefits to such employees or classes of employees of the Bank as it may determine, or to their legal personal representatives or dependents, on the death or retirement of such employees from the service of the Bank or on their otherwise leaving the service of the Bank.

(2) The following provisions shall apply to any scheme established under subsection (1) of this section:

(*a*) no assurance on the life of any contributor under any such scheme, and no moneys or other benefits payable under any such assurance, and no payment made under any such scheme to any person who has been employed by the Bank, shall be assignable or transferable, or liable to be garnished, attached, sequestered or levied upon for or in respect of any debt or claim whatsoever, other than a debt due to the Bank or to the Government;

(*b*) no donation by the Bank or contribution by its officers made under any such scheme and no interest thereon shall be assignable or transferable or liable to be attached, sequestered or levied upon for or in respect of any debt or claim whatsoever other than a debt due to the Bank or to the Government;

(*c*) no such donation, contribution or interest shall be subject to the debts of the contributor, nor shall such donation, contribution or interest pass to the Official Assignee on the bankruptcy of such contributor, but, if such contributor is adjudicated a bankrupt or is declared insolvent by a court, such donation, contribution or interest shall, subject to the provisions of this Act, be deemed to be subject to a trust in favour of the persons entitled thereto on the death of the contributor;

(*d*) the bankruptcy of a contributor shall not affect the making of deductions from the salary of the contributor in accordance with any such scheme, but such deductions shall continue to be made notwithstanding the provisions of any written law, and the portion of salary so deducted shall not be deemed to form part of his after-acquired property;

(*e*) subject to the provisions of any such scheme, all moneys paid or payable under any such scheme on the death of a contributor shall be deemed to be subject to a trust in favour of the persons entitled thereto under the will or intestacy of such deceased contributor, or under a nomination in such form as may be prescribed in such scheme, and shall not be deemed to form part of his estate or be subject to the payment of his debts but shall be deemed to be property passing on his death for the purposes of the Estate Duty Act;

(*f*) any contributor may by a memorandum under his hand appoint a trustee or trustees of the moneys payable on his death out of any such scheme and may make provision for the appointment of a new trustee or new trustees of such moneys and for the investment thereof; such memorandum shall be in the form prescribed in such scheme and shall be deposited with the Bank;

(*g*) if at the time of the death of any contributor or at any time afterwards, there is no trustee of such moneys or it is expedient to appoint a new trustee or new trustees, then and in any such case a trustee or trustees or a new trustee or trustees may be appointed by the Supreme Court or a Judge thereof; and

(*h*) the receipt of a trustee or trustees duly appointed, or in default of any such appointment and of written notice thereof to the Bank, the receipt of the legal personal representative of a deceased contributor shall be a discharge to the Bank for any moneys payable on his death out of any such scheme.

(3) The Bank in making rules under subsection (1) of this section relating to any pension, provident fund or other superannuation benefits which affect any person transferred to the service of the Bank under section 19 of this Act shall in such rules provide for the payment to such persons or their dependants of benefits not less in value than the amount of any pension, provident fund, gratuity or allowance for which such persons would have been eligible under the Pensions Act, had they continued in the service of the Government and any such rule relating to length of service of persons shall provide for the recognition as service under the Bank by persons so transferred of service by them under the Government.

(4) Nothing in the rules to be made under subsection (1) of this section shall adversely affect the conditions that would have been appli-

cable to persons transferred to the service of the Bank from their service with the Government as regards any pension, gratuity or allowance payable under the Pensions Act.

(5) Where any person in the service of the Bank, who does not come within the scope and effect of any pension or other schemes established under this section, retires or dies in the service of the Bank or is discharged from such service, the Bank may grant to him or to such other person or persons wholly or partly dependent on him, as the Bank may think fit, such allowance or gratuity as the Bank may determine.

No entitlement in respect of abolition or re-organisation of office.

21. Notwithstanding the provisions of the Pensions Act, no person who is transferred to the service of the Bank under section 19 of this Act shall be entitled to claim any benefit under this Act on the ground that he has been retired from the service of the Government on account of abolition or re-organisation of office.

Remuneration not to be related to profits.

22. No salary, fee, wage or other remuneration or allowance paid by the Bank to any director, officer, employee or agent shall be computed by reference to the profits of the Bank.

Public servants.

23. The directors and the officers and employees of the Bank of every description shall be deemed to be public servants within the meaning of the Penal Code.

## PART IV. PROVISIONS RELATING TO THE CARRYING ON OF THE BUSINESS OF THE BANK

Transfer of the business, etc., of the Post Office Savings Bank.

24. Upon the date of the coming into operation of this Act, all movable properties, assets, privileges, debts, liabilities and obligations vested in or belonging to, and all other business transacted by, the Post Office Savings Bank established under the Post Office Savings Bank Act shall be transferred to and vest in the Bank without further assurance and its business shall be carried on by the Bank.

Deposits and repayment.

25. Deposits of money to be paid into the Bank shall be received and repaid under such conditions as may be prescribed by the Bank.

Security of Government.

26. The repayment of all moneys deposited in the Bank together with interest thereon is guaranteed by the Government and accordingly, if at any time the assets of the Bank shall be insufficient to pay the lawful claims of every depositor, such deficiency shall be charged

and paid out of the Consolidated Fund and the Minister for Finance shall certify such deficiency to Parliament without delay.

27. Interest on savings and time deposit accounts shall be payable at such rate or rates as may from time to time be prescribed by the Bank with the approval of the Minister. Interest rates.

28. The Bank may levy a charge for any service rendered to its customers. Service charge.

29. The Bank may charge interest on loans given to persons having an account at the Bank at such rate or rates as may from time to time be prescribed by the Bank with the approval of the Minister. Interest on loans.

30. No deposit in the Bank, and no interest on any such deposit, shall be attached, sequestered or levied upon for or in respect of any debt or claim whatsoever: Attachment of deposits.

Provided that—

*(a)* upon notice of a claim under a judgment of any court, it shall be lawful for the General Manager in his discretion to retain in the account a sum sufficient to answer such claim and to pay into the court on its order the amount of such claim or the total amount of the deposits and interest in the account if the claim be for a greater sum; and

*(b)* a court shall only make an order under this section if it is satisfied that the judgment debtor has an account for his own sole benefit with the Bank.

31. (1) For the purpose of obtaining proof of the death of a customer of the Bank or of ascertaining the proper person to receive moneys standing in the name of a minor, person of unsound mind or deceased person, the General Manager, or such other officer as the General Manager shall appoint for that purpose, may take evidence on oath or affirmation according to law. Power to administer oath.

(2) Any person who upon such oath or affirmation makes any statement that is false, and which he either knows or believes to be false, or does not know to be true, shall be deemed to be guilty of an offence under section 193 of the Penal Code.

32. The Bank may, by instrument under its common seal, appoint a person (whether in Singapore or in a place outside Singapore) to be its attorney, and the person so appointed may, subject to the provisions Power to appoint attorney.

of the instrument, do any act or execute any power or function which he is authorised by the instrument to do or execute.

Settlement of disputes.

33. (1) If a dispute arises between the Bank and—

(*a*) any customer of the Bank;

(*b*) a person who claims to be the legal personal representative or next of kin or creditor of a customer of the Bank, or the assignee of a customer who is bankrupt or insolvent; or

(*c*) a person who claims to be entitled to money deposited in the Bank,

the matter shall be referred to an arbitrator to be appointed by the Minister, and whatever award, order or determination made by such arbitrator shall be binding and conclusive on all parties and shall be final to all intents and purposes without any appeal.

(2) Upon a reference under this section, an arbitrator may inspect any book belonging to the Bank, relating to the matter in dispute, and may administer an oath or affirmation to any witness appearing before him.

## PART V. FINANCIAL PROVISIONS

Bank's financial year.

34. The financial year of the Bank shall begin on the 1st day of January and end on the 31st day of December of each year:

Provided that for the years 1971 and 1972 the financial year shall begin on the date of the establishment of the Bank and shall end on the 31st day of December, 1972.

Expenses.

35. All expenses incurred for carrying out the purposes of this Act shall be met from the funds of the Bank.

Estimates.

36. (1) The Bank shall in every year cause to be prepared and adopt annual estimates of income and expenditure of the Bank for the ensuing year.

(2) Supplementary estimates may be adopted by the Bank.

(3) A copy of all annual and supplementary estimates shall, upon their adoption by the Bank, be sent forthwith to the Minister who may approve or disallow any item or portion of any item shown in the estimates, and shall return the estimates as amended by him to the Bank and the Bank shall be bound thereby.

(4) The estimates as approved by the Minister shall be published in the *Gazette*.

**37.** The balance of the revenue of the Bank in any financial year after deducting the expenses incurred for carrying out the purposes of this Act and such sums as the Bank may think fit in respect of bad debts, depreciation of assets and other contingencies shall be applied for the creation of a general reserve fund or such other reserves or other capital fund as the Bank may deem appropriate. General reserve fund.

**38.** The Bank may, from time to time, for the purposes of this Act, raise loans from the Government or with the consent of the Minister, from any source either by the creation and issue of debentures, stocks or bonds, or otherwise, as the Minister may direct. Loans.

**39.** (1) Subject to the provisions of this Act, moneys in the Bank shall, as far as practicable and except for such sums as may be assigned to be kept in hand for the general purposes of the Bank, be invested in such stocks, funds and securities or such other investments as the Minister for Finance may from time to time approve. Investment of funds.

(2) Any sum of money that may from time to time be required for the repayment of deposits in the Bank or for the payment of interest thereon or expenses incurred in the execution of this Act, may be raised by the sale of the whole or a part of such securities:

Provided that any sum of money which may be required for the purposes aforesaid may, with the approval of the Minister for Finance, be advanced to the Bank by the Accountant-General out of the Consolidated Fund until they can be raised by the sale of such securities, and the Bank shall pay all interest due on such advances.

**40.** (1) The Bank shall cause proper accounts and other records in relation thereto to be kept, and an annual statement of accounts to be prepared in respect of each financial year. Accounts.

(2) The annual statement of accounts of the Bank shall present a true and fair view of the financial position of the Bank and of the results, for the year to which it relates, and the operations of the Bank.

(3) All such accounts shall be submitted for audit not later than the 30th day of April in every year.

**41.** (1) The Minister shall nominate in each year the Auditor-General or a company auditor (hereinafter in this Act referred to as "the Auditor") to audit the accounts of the Bank. Audit.

(2) The Auditor shall be paid out of the revenue of the Bank such remuneration, expenses or fees as the Minister, after consultation with the Bank, shall direct.

(3) For the purpose of any audit of accounts under this Act, the Auditor may by notice in writing require the production before him of any book, deed, contract, account, voucher or other document which he may deem necessary, and may require any person holding or accountable for any such document to appear before him and make and sign a declaration with respect thereto and may require from any person such information or explanation as he deems necessary.

(4) Any person who, being required by the Auditor under subsection (3) of this section to produce any document or to appear before him and make and sign a declaration or to furnish information or explanation, fails without reasonable excuse to comply with such requisition, shall be guilty of an offence under this Act and shall be liable on conviction to a fine not exceeding two hundred dollars, and in the case of continuing failure to a fine not exceeding one hundred dollars for each day after the first day during which such failure continues.

Auditor's report.

42. The Auditor shall, as soon as practicable and not later than three months after the accounts have been submitted for audit, send an annual report of his audit to the Bank. He shall also submit such periodical and special reports to the Minister and to the Bank as may appear to him to be necessary.

Annual statement of accounts.

43. (1) The Bank shall, within two months of the Auditor's annual report, send to the Minister a statement of accounts and the balance-sheet in respect of the year for which the accounts were audited, signed by the Chairman and certified by the Auditor, together with a copy of the Auditor's report of such annual accounts.

(2) The Minister shall cause a copy of the annual statement of accounts, balance-sheet and the Auditor's annual report referred to in subsection (1) of this section to be presented to Parliament.

Annual report.

44. (1) The Bank shall, as soon as practicable after the end of each year, cause to be prepared and transmitted to the Minister a report dealing generally with the activities of the Bank during the preceding year and containing such information relating to the proceedings and policy of the Bank as the Minister may, from time to time, direct.

(2) The Minister shall cause a copy of every such report to be presented to Parliament.

Publication of annual report, etc.

45. The annual report, the annual statement of accounts and balance-sheet, together with the Auditor's annual report, of the Bank shall be published in the *Gazette*.

## PART VI. MISCELLANEOUS

Exemption from stamp duty.

46. No power or letter of attorney or other such document given by a customer of the Bank authorising any person to make deposits in the Bank on behalf of the customer, or to sign any agreement or instrument required by the rules made under this Act to be signed on making such deposit, or to receive back any sum of money deposited in the Bank, or the interest arising therefrom, nor any bond, statutory declaration, or other instrument or document whatsoever required or authorised to be given, signed, made or produced in pursuance of this Act or the rules made thereunder, shall be subjected to or be charged with any stamp duty whatsoever.

Exemption.

47. The Bank shall be exempted from the provisions of the Banking Act and the Finance Companies Act.

Validity of acts and transactions of Bank.

48. The validity of an act or transaction of the Bank shall not be called in question in any court on the ground that any provision of this Act has not been complied with.

Power to make rules.

49. (1) The Bank may, with the approval of the Minister, make rules for the management and regulation of its business.

(2) In particular and without prejudice to the generality of the foregoing powers such rules may—

(*a*) prescribe limits of deposits;
(*b*) prescribe the modes of making deposits;
(*c*) prescribe the modes of withdrawing deposits;
(*d*) prescribe the amount of interest payable, and modes of calculating interest, on deposits;
(*e*) prescribe the times at which deposit books shall be returned to the Bank by customers;
(*f*) regulate deposits by minors, guardians, trustees, societies, bodies corporate, firms and bodies of persons acting collectively;
(*g*) prescribe conditions for the withdrawal of moneys by minors, guardians, trustees, societies, bodies corporate, firms and bodies of persons acting collectively;
(*h*) prescribe the modes of dealing with the accounts of deceased persons or of persons of unsound mind;
(*i*) prescribe the conditions governing the sale of and repayment of gift vouchers;
(*j*) prescribe the conditions upon which gift vouchers may be used for making deposits of money in the Bank;

(*k*) prescribe the conditions governing the acceptance or rejection of gift vouchers for the purpose of making deposits in the Bank;

(*l*) prescribe the conditions governing the operation of time deposit accounts;

(*m*) prescribe the conditions upon which loans may be made to customers; and

(*n*) prescribe the mode of calculating interest payable in respect of loans.

**Repeal.**

**50.** The Post Office Savings Bank Act is hereby repealed.

**Transitional provisions.**

**51.** (1) Any scheme, contract, document or arrangement constituted, prepared, made, granted or approved under the Post Office Savings Bank Act shall, except where otherwise expressly provided in this Act or in any other written law, continue and be deemed to have been constituted, prepared, made, granted or approved, as the case may be, under this Act.

(2) Any subsidiary legislation made under the Post Office Savings Bank Act, so far as such subsidiary legislation relates to matters falling within the scope of this Act, shall remain in force and have the force of rules made under this Act until it has been revoked or replaced by subsidiary legislation issued or made under this Act.

(3) Any proceeding, matter or cause of action pending or existing immediately prior to the date of the coming into operation of this Act by or against the Government in respect of any of the functions, assets, privileges, rights, obligations and liabilities transferred to, or vested in, the Bank under this Act, may be continued and enforced by or against the Bank in the name of the Government in accordance with the provisions of any written law and the practice and procedure in force relating to proceedings by or against the Government.

# Securities Industry Act, 1973[1]

An Act to consolidate and amend the law with respect to the securities industry and trading in securities and for purposes connected therewith and to repeal the Securities Industry Act, 1970 (No. 61 of 1970).

Be it enacted by the President with the advice and consent of the Parliament of Singapore, as follows:

[28th March, 1973]

## PART I. PRELIMINARY

1. (1) This Act may be cited as the Securities Industry Act, 1973, and shall come into operation on such date as the Minister may, by notification in the *Gazette,* appoint. **Short title and commencement.**

(2) The Minister may appoint different dates for the coming into operation of the different Parts or provisions of this Act.

2. (1) In this Act, unless the context otherwise requires— **Interpretation.**

"agent", in relation to a dealer, includes a person who is or has at any time been a banker of the dealer;

"auditor" means an approved company auditor within the meaning of the Companies Act;

"business", in relation to a dealer, means a business of dealing in securities;

"committee", in relation to a stock exchange, means the persons for the time being in whom the management of the stock exchange is vested;

"company" has the same meaning as is assigned to that expression in the Companies Act;

"corporation" has the same meaning as is assigned to that expression in the Companies Act;

"dealer" means a person who carries on a business of dealing in securities as a corporation whether or not he carries on any other business, but does not include an exempt dealer;

---

[1] *Singapore Government Gazette Acts Supplement,* No. 20, April 13, 1973, Act No. 17 of 1973. Additional citations: Acts Nos. 51 of 1973; and 6 of 1974.

"dealer's representative" means a person, by whatever name described, in the direct employment of, or acting for, or by arrangement with, a dealer, not being an exempt dealer, who performs for that dealer any of the functions of a dealer (other than work ordinarily performed by accountants, clerks or cashiers) whether his remuneration is by way of salary, wages, commission or otherwise; and includes any director or officer of a corporation who performs for the corporation any of the said functions (whether or not his remuneration is as aforesaid);

"dealing in securities" means (whether as principal or agent) making or offering to make with any person, or inducing or attempting to induce any person to enter into or to offer to enter into—

*(a)* any agreement for or with a view to acquiring, disposing of, subscribing for, or underwriting securities; or

*(b)* any agreement the purpose or pretended purposes of which is to secure a profit to any of the parties from the yield of securities or by reference to fluctuations in the price of securities;

"director" has the same meaning as is assigned to that expression in the Companies Act;

"exempt dealer" means—

*(a)* a person who carries on a business of dealing in securities only through the holder of a dealer's licence for his own account;

*(b)* any person acting in the capacity of manager or trustee under a unit trust scheme a deed in respect of which is approved by the Registrar or the Minister under Division 5 of Part IV of the Companies Act;

*(c)* a corporation that is authorised under any written law to be a dealer in the short term money market;

*(d)* any public statutory corporation constituted under any written law in Singapore; or

*(e)* such other person or class of persons as the Minister may by order declare to be an exempt dealer if the main business carried on by such person or class of persons is a business other than the dealing in securities, and if the dealing in securities is by way of—

(i) making or offering to make with any person an agreement for or with a view to the underwriting of securities;

(ii) making an invitation to persons to subscribe for securities or to purchase securities on the first sale thereof;

(iii) issuing any document which is or is deemed to be a prospectus within the meaning of the Companies Act; or

(iv) acquiring or disposing of securities only through the holder of a dealer's licence;

"investment adviser" means a person who carries on a business of advising others concerning securities or who as part of a regular business issues or promulgates analyses or reports concerning securities but that expression does not include—

*(a)* a bank as defined in section 2 of the Banking Act;

*(b)* a company or society registered under the Insurance Act;

*(c)* an advocate and solicitor or accountant in practice whose carrying on of that business is solely incidental to the practice of his profession;

*(d)* a company registered under the Trust Companies Act;

*(e)* a dealer or his employee or a dealer's representative or exempt dealer whose carrying on of that business is solely incidental to the conduct of his business of dealing in securities; or

*(f)* a person who is the proprietor of a newspaper and holder of a permit issued under the Printing Presses Act where—

(i) insofar as the newspaper is distributed generally to the public it is distributed only to subscribers to, and purchasers of, the newspaper for value;

(ii) the advice is given or the analyses or reports are issued or promulgated only through that newspaper;

(iii) that person receives no commission or other consideration for giving the advice or for issuing or promulgating the analyses or reports; and

(iv) the advice is given and the analyses and reports are issued or promulgated solely as incidental to the conduct of that person's business as a newspaper proprietor.

"investment representative" means a person in the direct employment of or acting for or by arrangement with an investment adviser who performs for such investment adviser any of the functions of an investment adviser (other than work ordinarily performed by accountants, clerks or cashiers) whether his remuneration is by way of salary, wages, commission or otherwise; and includes any director or officer of a corporation who performs for such corporation any of the said functions (whether or not his remuneration is as aforesaid);

"licence" means—

(*a*) a dealer's licence;

(*b*) an investment adviser's licence; or

(*c*) a representative's licence,

under Part IV;

"member company" means a company which carries on a business of dealing in securities and is recognized as a member company by a stock exchange;

"Minister" means the Minister for Finance;

"Registrar" means the Registrar of Companies under the Companies Act, and includes any Deputy or Assistant Registrar of Companies;

"relevant authority" means—

(*a*) [2]

(*b*) in relation to a member company, the stock exchange by which the company is recognized; and

(*c*) in relation to any other person, the Registrar;

"representative" means a dealer's representative or an investment adviser's representative;

"rules", in relation to a stock exchange, means the rules governing the conduct of the stock exchange or the members thereof by whatever name called and wherever contained and includes rules contained in the memorandum of association and the articles of association of the stock exchange;

"securities" means debentures, stocks and shares in a public company or corporation, funds or bonds of any government or of any body, corporate or unincorporate, and includes any right or option in respect thereof and any interest as defined in section 84 of the Companies Act;

"stockbroker" means a person who is a member of a stock exchange and a director of a member company;

"stock exchange" means any body corporate which has been approved by the Minister under subsection (2) of section 6;

"stock market" means a market, exchange or other place at which securities are regularly offered for sale, purchase or exchange;

"trust account" means a trust account established under section 37;

"unit trust scheme" means any arrangement made for the purpose, or having the effect of providing facilities for the participation by persons as beneficiaries under a trust, or profits or income

[2] Deleted by sec. 2(*b*) of Act No. 6 of 1974, the Securities Industry (Amendment) Act, 1974.

arising from the acquisition, holding, management or disposal of securities or any other property.

(2) Regulations may provide that, subject to any terms and conditions prescribed, all or any of the provisions of this Act—

*(a)* shall not have effect in relation to any specified person or to any person who is a member of a specified class of persons—

(i) who is or may be a dealer or investment adviser by reason only of his doing anything which is merely incidental to another business;

(ii) who does not deal in securities for or on behalf of any other person; or

(iii) who is a dealer or investment adviser by reason only of the entering into by him of any specified transaction or class of transactions; or

*(b)* shall not have effect in relation to the representative of any person referred to in paragraph *(a)*; or

*(c)* shall have effect in relation to any person referred to in paragraph *(a)* or *(b)* to such extent as is prescribed.

## PART II. ADMINISTRATION

**Consultative or advisory body.**

3. (1) The Minister may establish from time to time such consultative or advisory body, as he thinks fit, consisting of such representatives of business, government and the Monetary Authority of Singapore as he may appoint, to advise him on matters relating to the securities industry.

(2) Any consultative or advisory body established under subsection (1) shall have the power in the exercise of its functions to enquire into any matter or thing related to the securities industry and for this purpose may summon any person to give evidence on oath or affirmation or produce any document or material necessary for the purpose of the enquiry.

**Registrar may consult advisory body.**

4. The Registrar may from time to time and shall, if so directed by the Minister, consult the opinion of the body referred to in section 3 for the proper and effective implementation of this Act.

## PART III. STOCK EXCHANGES

**Establishment, etc., of stock markets.**

5. (1) No person shall establish or maintain or assist in establishing or maintaining or hold himself out as providing or maintaining a stock market that is not the stock market of a stock exchange.

(2) Any person who contravenes the provisions of subsection (1) shall be guilty of an offence under this Act and shall be liable on conviction to a fine not exceeding three thousand dollars and in the case of a second or subsequent conviction to a fine not exceeding fifteen thousand dollars.

Power of Minister to approve a stock exchange.

6. (1) Application for approval as a stock exchange may be made to the Minister in the prescribed form and manner.

(2) The Minister may in writing approve a body corporate as a stock exchange if he is satisfied—

*(a)* that at least ten members of the body will carry on business dealing in securities independently of and in competition with each other;

*(b)* that the rules of the body make satisfactory provision—

(i) for the exclusion from membership of persons who are not of good character and high business integrity;

(ii) for the expulsion, suspension or disciplining of members for conduct inconsistent with just and equitable principles in the transaction of business or for a contravention of or failure to comply with the rules of the stock exchange or the provisions of this Act;

(iii) with respect to the conditions under which securities may be listed for trading in the market proposed to be conducted by the body;

(iv) with respect to the conditions governing dealings in securities by members;

(v) with respect to the class or classes of securities that may be dealt in by members; and

(vi) generally for the carrying on of the business of the stock exchange with due regard to the interests of the public; and

*(c)* that the interests of the public will be served by the granting of his approval.

Minister to approve amendments to rules.

7. (1) Where an amendment is made, whether by way of rescission, alteration or addition, to the rules of a stock exchange the committee of the stock exchange shall forward a written notice thereof to the Minister for approval.

(2) [3]

[3] Deleted by sec. 3*(b)* of Act No. 6 of 1974, the Securities Industry (Amendment) Act, 1974.

(3) The Minister may give notice to the stock exchange concerned that he approves the amendment or that he disapproves the whole or any specified part of the amendment in question and until such notice is given the amendment shall not have force and effect.

(4) Any notice under this section may be served personally or by post.

## PART IV. LICENCES

8. Where a person would, but for this section, be liable to a penalty for not being the holder of a particular type of licence, he shall not be so liable— Application of this Part.

*(a)* until the expiration of the period of six months (or such further period as the Minister may specify) next succeeding the date of the coming into operation of this Part; or

*(b)* where, before the expiration of that period, he applies for that type of licence, until—

(i) he is issued with such a licence; or

(ii) his application is refused.

9. (1) No person shall carry on a business of dealing in securities or hold himself out as carrying on such a business unless he is the holder of a dealer's licence under this Part. Dealer's licence.

(2) Subsection (1) shall not apply to an exempt dealer.

10. No person shall act as a dealer's representative unless he is the holder of a dealer's representative's licence under this Part. Dealer's representative's licence.

11. (1) A person shall not act as an investment adviser or hold himself out to be an investment adviser unless he is the holder of an investment adviser's licence under this Part. Investment adviser's licence.

(2) [4]

12. A person shall not act as an investment representative unless he is the holder of an investment representative's licence under this Part. Investment representative's licence.

13. (1) An application for a licence or for the renewal of a licence shall be made to the Registrar in the prescribed form and manner and Applications for licence or renewal.

[4] Deleted by sec. 4 of Act No. 6 of 1974, the Securities Industry (Amendment) Act, 1974.

shall be accompanied by the prescribed fee and, in the case of an application for renewal of a licence, shall be made within one month before the expiry of the licence.

(2) The Registrar may require an applicant to supply him with such further information as he considers necessary in relation to the application.

(3) The Registrar shall not refuse to grant or renew a licence without first giving the applicant an opportunity of being heard.

Registrar to grant or renew dealer's licence to a corporation or investment adviser's licence to an individual or corporation in certain circumstances.

14. (1) A dealer's licence shall only be granted to a corporation.

(2) The Registrar shall grant or renew a dealer's licence if—

(*a*) after consideration of the character of the directors and secretary of the corporation and of the corporation's financial position; and

(*b*) after consideration of the interests of the public,

he is of the opinion that the applicant corporation is a fit and proper person to hold the licence applied for.

(3) The Registrar shall grant or renew an investment adviser's licence if—

(*a*) after consideration—

(i) where the applicant is an individual—of the character and financial position of the applicant;

(ii) where the applicant is a corporation—of the character of the directors and secretary of the corporation and of the corporation's financial position; and

(*b*) after consideration of the interests of the public,

he is of the opinion that the applicant is a fit and proper person to hold the licence applied for.

Registrar to grant or renew representative's licence in certain circumstances.

15. The Registrar shall grant or renew a representative's licence if after consideration of the application he is of the opinion that the applicant is a fit and proper person to hold the licence applied for.

False statements.

16. A person who in connection with an application for a licence or for the renewal of a licence wilfully makes a statement false or misleading in a material particular knowing it to be false or misleading or wilfully omits to state any matter or thing without which the application is misleading in a material respect shall be guilty of an offence under this Act and shall be liable on conviction to a fine of three thou-

sand dollars or to imprisonment for a term of one year or to both such fine and imprisonment.

Power of the Registrar to enquire into share transactions.

17. (1) In deciding whether a dealer or his representative or an investment adviser or his representative is a fit and proper person to hold a licence under this Act the Registrar may enquire into any transactions involving the purchase or sale of securities entered into by that person, whether directly or indirectly, during any period of twelve months preceding the application for a licence or renewal of a licence, as the case may be (referred to in this section as "the relevant period") to ascertain if that person has in such transaction or series of transactions used dishonest, unfair or unethical devices or trading practices, whether such devices or trading practices constitute an offence under this Act or otherwise.

(2) For the purposes of subsection (1) the Registrar may, in such form and within such time as he may specify by notice in writing, require a dealer or his representative or an investment adviser or his representative to submit detailed information of all or any transactions involving the purchase or sale of securities, whether such transactions were completed—during the relevant period—before or after the date of the coming into operation of this Act.

(3) Any person who fails or refuses to submit information to the Registrar within the time specified in the notice referred to in subsection (2) or who gives false or misleading information shall, in addition to any other penalty that may be imposed under this Act, be liable in the case of an application for renewal of a licence to have his licence cancelled under section 23 and in the case of first application for a licence to have his application rejected.

Power of Registrar to impose conditions or restrictions.

18. (1) The Registrar may grant or renew a licence subject to such conditions or restrictions as he thinks fit.

(2) A person who contravenes or fails to comply with any condition of, or restriction in, his licence shall be guilty of an offence under this Act.

Security to be lodged in respect of dealer's licence.

19. (1) Except in the case of a dealer who is a member company, the Registrar shall not grant or renew a dealer's licence unless there is lodged with the Accountant-General a security in the sum of one hundred thousand dollars (or such greater sum as the Minister may by order determine) in respect of the licence.

(2) A security required by subsection (1) shall be by cash deposit

or by such other method as the Accountant-General may in any particular case allow.

(3) A security lodged under subsection (1) shall be applied by the Accountant-General subject to and in accordance with the regulations made under this Act.

Period of licence.

**20.** (1) Subject to subsection (2), a licence shall expire one year after the date of issue thereof.

(2) A licence that has been renewed in accordance with the provisions of this Part shall continue in force for a period of twelve months next succeeding the date upon which but for its renewal it would have expired.

Change of address.

**21.** (1) The holder of a dealer's licence or investment adviser's licence shall, upon any change in the address of the principal place of business at which he carries on the business in respect of which the licence is held, forthwith notify the Registrar of the new address in the prescribed form and, upon ceasing to carry on that business, shall forthwith so notify the Registrar in writing.

(2) The holder of a representative's licence who ceases to be a representative of the dealer or investment adviser in relation to whom the representative's licence was issued shall forthwith so notify the Registrar in writing.

(3) No holder of a representative's licence shall work for or have an arrangement with a dealer or investment adviser who is not the dealer or investment adviser in relation to which his licence was issued unless he has lodged a notice in the prescribed form with the Registrar.

Register of licence holders.

**22.** (1) The Registrar shall keep in such form as he thinks fit a register of the holders of current licences, specifying—

*(a)* in relation to each holder of a dealer's or investment adviser's licence—

(i) his name;

(ii) the address of the principal place of business at which he carries on the business in respect of which the licence is held; and

(iii) where the business is carried on under a name or style other than the name of the holder of the licence, the name or style under which the business is carried on; and

*(b)* in relation to each holder of a representative's licence—

(i) his name;

(ii) the name of the dealer or investment adviser in relation to whom the licence was issued; and

(iii) where the business of that dealer or investment adviser is carried on under a name or style other than the name of the dealer or investment adviser, the name or style under which that business is carried on.

(2) Any person may, upon payment of the prescribed fee, inspect and take extracts from the register kept under subsection (1).

(3) Except as provided in subsection (2), the power of inspection conferred by paragraph *(a)* of subsection (2) of section 11 of the Companies Act, shall not apply in respect of a document filed or lodged with the Registrar under this Act.

Power of Registrar to cancel licence, etc.

23. (1) The holder of a licence may be required to appear before the Registrar to show cause why his licence should not be cancelled and why he should not be disqualified either permanently or temporarily from holding such a licence—

*(a)* in the case of an individual—on the ground that he is not a fit and proper person to hold the licence; or

*(b)* in the case of a corporation—on the ground that the corporation is not a fit and proper person to hold the licence or that any director or secretary of the corporation is not a fit and proper person to be a director or secretary (as the case may be) of a corporation holding such a licence.

(2) On being satisfied that the relevant ground referred to in subsection (1) has been established the Registrar may order that the licence of the person concerned be cancelled and that that person be disqualified, either permanently or for such period as the Registrar may specify, from holding another such licence.

Appeals.

24. (1) Any person who is aggrieved by any decision of the Registrar under this Part, other than a decision under section 23, may appeal to the Minister and any person who is aggrieved by the decision of the Registrar under section 23 may appeal to the High Court so long as the appeal in each case is made within thirty days of the decision of the Registrar.

(2) In any appeal under this section the decision of the Minister or the Court, as the case may be, shall be final and shall be given effect to by the Registrar.

## PART V. RECORDS

Application of this Part.

**25.** (1) This Part applies to a person who is—

(*a*) a dealer;
(*b*) a dealer's representative;
(*c*) an investment adviser;
(*d*) an investment representative; or
(*e*) [5]
(*f*) a financial journalist.

(2) In this Part "financial journalist" means a person who contributes advice concerning securities or prepares analyses or reports concerning securities for publication in a *bona fide* newspaper or periodical.

(3) In this Part a reference to securities is a reference to securities which are quoted on a stock exchange in Singapore.

Register of securities.

**26.** (1) A person to whom this Part applies shall maintain a register in the prescribed form of the securities in which he has an interest.

(2) [6]

(3) Particulars of the securities in which a person to whom this Part applies has an interest and particulars of his interest in those securities shall be entered in the register within seven days of the acquisition of the interest or of the date of the coming into operation of this Act.

(4) For the purposes of this section—

(*a*) where a person has an interest under a trust and the property subject to the trust consists of or includes securities and a person knows or has reasonable grounds for believing that he has an interest under the trust and that the property subject to the trust consists of or includes those securities that person shall be deemed to have an interest in those securities;

(*b*) where a body corporate has an interest in securities and—

(i) the body corporate is or its directors are accustomed or under an obligation whether formal or informal to act in accordance with the directions, instructions or wishes of a person in relation to those securities; or

---

[5] Deleted by sec. 8(*b*) of Act No. 6 of 1974, the Securities Industry (Amendment) Act, 1974.

[6] Deleted by sec. 9 of Act No. 6 of 1974, the Securities Industry (Amendment) Act, 1974.

(ii) a person has, the associates of a person have, or a person and his associate have, a controlling interest in the body corporate,

that person shall be deemed to have an interest in those securities; and

*(c)* where a body corporate that has not more than twenty members has an interest in securities a person who is a member of the body corporate and an associate of such a person shall be deemed to have an interest in those securities.

(5) *(a)* Where there is a change (not being a prescribed change) in the interest or interests of a person to whom this Part applies in securities he shall enter in the register full particulars of the change including the date of the change and the circumstances by reason of which that change has occurred.

*(b)* The entry shall be made within seven days after the date of the change.

*(c)* For the purposes of this subsection where a person acquires or disposes of securities there shall be deemed to be a change in the interest or interests of that person.

(6) For the purposes of paragraphs *(b)* and *(c)* of subsection (4) a person is an associate of another person if the first-mentioned person would be an associate of another person for the purposes of paragraph *(c)* of subsection (4) of section 6A of the Companies Act.

(7) In determining for the purposes of this section whether a person has an interest in a security the provisions of subsection (3) and subsections (6) to (10) both inclusive of section 6A of the Companies Act shall have effect and in applying those provisions a reference to a share shall be read as a reference to a security.

Notice of particulars to Registrar.

27. (1) A person to whom this Part applies shall give notice to the Registrar in the prescribed form containing such particulars as are prescribed including the place at which he will keep the register of his interests in securities.

(2) The notice shall be given—

*(a)* in the case of a person who is required by this Act to hold a licence—as part of his application for the licence; or

*(b)* in the case of any other person—

(i) if the person is a person to whom this Part applies at the commencement of this Act—within one month after that date; or

(ii) if the person becomes a person to whom this Part applies after that date—within fourteen days after becoming such a person.

(3) The notice shall be so given notwithstanding that the person has ceased to be a person to whom this Part applies before the expiration of the period referred to in subsection (2).

(4) A person who ceases to be a person to whom this Part applies shall, within fourteen days of his so ceasing, give notice of the fact in the prescribed form to the Registrar.

(5) A person who fails or neglects to give notice as required by this section shall be guilty of an offence under this Act and shall be liable on conviction to a fine of one thousand dollars.

Reference to prosecution.

**28.** (1) It is a defence to a prosecution for failing to comply with section 26 or 27 if the defendant proves that his failure was due to his not being aware of a fact or occurrence the existence of which was necessary to constitute the offence and that—

(*a*) he was not so aware on the date of the summons;

(*b*) he became so aware less than fourteen days before the date of the summons; or

(*c*) he became so aware not less than fourteen days before the date of the summons and complied with the relevant section within fourteen days after becoming so aware.

(2) For the purposes of subsection (1), a person shall conclusively be presumed to have been aware of a fact or occurrence at a particular time of which a servant or agent of the person being a servant or agent having duties or acting in relation to his master's or principal's interest or interests in the securities concerned, was aware at that time.

Production of register.

**29.** (1) The Registrar or any person authorised by him in that behalf may require any person to whom this Part applies to produce for inspection the register required to be kept pursuant to section 26 and the Registrar or any person so authorised may make extracts from the register.

(2) Any person who fails to produce a register for inspection or fails to allow any person authorised by or under subsection (1) to make a copy of or make extracts from the register shall be guilty of an offence under this Act.

**30.** (1) The Registrar or any person authorised by him in that behalf may by notice in writing require the proprietor or publisher of a newspaper or periodical to supply him with the name and address of the financial journalist who has contributed any advice or prepared any analysis or report that has been published in a newspaper or periodical owned or published by that proprietor or publisher or with the names and addresses of all the financial journalists who have contributed any such advice or prepared any such analysis or report within a period specified in the notice.

Particulars of financial journalists.

(2) A proprietor or publisher of a newspaper or periodical who wilfully fails to comply with a notice under subsection (1) shall be guilty of an offence under this Act.

31. The Registrar may supply a copy of the extract of a register obtained pursuant to section 29 to any person who in the opinion of the Registrar should in the public interest be informed of the dealing in securities disclosed in the register.

Extract of register.

## PART VI. CONDUCT OF SECURITIES BUSINESS

32. (1) No person who is the holder of a licence shall represent or imply or knowingly permit to be represented or implied in any manner to any person that his abilities or qualifications have in any respect been approved by the Registrar.

Certain representations prohibited.

(2) The statement that a person is the holder of a licence under this Act is not a contravention of this section.

33. Where, in a letter, circular or other communication issued by any person [that person] [7] refers to any securities issued by a corporation or other person, he shall cause to be included in the letter, circular or other communication, in type not less legible than that used in the body thereof, a concise statement of the nature and extent of his interest, if any, in the securities.

Disclosure of certain interest.

34. (1) A dealer shall not, as principal, deal in any securities with a person who is not the holder of a dealer's licence unless he first informs the person with whom he is dealing that he is acting in the transaction as principal and not as agent.

Dealings as principal.

(2) For the purposes of subsection (1) dealings as principal include dealings on behalf of a corporation in which the dealer or its directors have a controlling interest.

[7] Editor's insertion. Cf. sec. 10 of Act No. 6 of 1974, the Securities Industry (Amendment) Act, 1974.

(3) Where a dealer has failed to comply with subsection (1) in respect of a contract for the sale of securities by him, the purchaser of the securities may, if he has not disposed of them, rescind the contract by a notice of rescission, in writing, given to the dealer within seven days after the receipt of the contract note and, where a dealer has failed to comply with that subsection in respect of a contract for the purchase of securities by him, the vendor of the securities may, in the like manner, rescind the contract.

## PART VII. ACCOUNTS AND AUDIT

Application of this Part.

35. This Part applies to and in relation to the business of a dealer within the meaning of this Act, whether that business is carried on in Singapore or elsewhere.

Accounts to be kept by dealers.

36. (1) A dealer shall keep or cause to be kept in the English language such accounting and other records as will sufficiently explain the transactions and financial position of his business and enable true and fair profit and loss accounts and balance-sheets to be prepared from time to time and shall cause those records to be kept in such a manner as to enable them to be conveniently and properly audited.

(2) If accounting and other records are kept by a dealer at a place outside Singapore the dealer shall cause to be sent to and kept at a place in Singapore such statements and returns with respect to the business dealt with in those records as will enable to be prepared true and fair profit and loss accounts and balance-sheets.

(3) Without affecting the generality of subsection (1) a dealer shall keep or cause to be kept the following accounts and records:

*(a)* a Bought and Sold Book recording the name of the buyer and the seller respectively of every security bought or sold by the dealer in the course of his business;

*(b)* a Scrip Receipt Book containing copies of acknowledgments of receipt of securities received by the dealer from clients for sale or safe custody and clearly showing the name or names in which the particular securities are registered;

*(c)* a Cash Book containing entries of all amounts paid or received by the dealer in the course of his business;

*(d)* a Journal;

*(e)* a Ledger or Ledgers showing all transactions—

(i) with clients of the dealer;

(ii) with other dealers; and

(iii) in respect of nominal or private accounts;

(*f*) a General Scrip Register recording the receipt and disposal by the dealer of all securities other than those dealt with in the Safe Custody Scrip Register;

(*g*) a Safe Custody Scrip Register recording all securities held by the dealer for safe custody; and

(*h*) an Underwriting Register recording all underwriting and sub-underwriting transactions entered into by the dealer.

(4) Every entry in a Safe Custody Scrip Register and in an Underwriting Register kept by a dealer shall be dated and initialled by the person making the entry.

(5) For the purposes of this section any account or record required to be kept by a dealer may be kept either by making entries in a bound book or by recording the matters in question in any other manner, as approved by the Registrar.

(6) Where any account or record required by this section to be kept is not kept by making entries in a bound book but by some other means the dealer concerned shall take reasonable precautions for guarding against falsification and for facilitating discovery of any falsification.

**Certain moneys received by dealers to be paid into a trust account.**

37. (1) A dealer shall establish and keep in a bank or banks in Singapore one or more trust accounts designated or evidenced as such into which he shall pay—

(*a*) all amounts (less any brokerage and other proper charges) that are received from or on account of any person (other than a dealer) for the purchase of securities and that are not attributable to securities delivered to the dealer before or within five bank trading days after receipt of those amounts; and

(*b*) all amounts (less any brokerage and other proper charges) that are received for or on account of any person (other than a dealer) from the sale of securities and that are not paid to that person or as that person directs within five bank trading days after receipt of such amounts.

(2) A person who—

(*a*) contravenes or fails to comply with any provision of this section shall be guilty of an offence under this Act and shall be liable on conviction to a fine not exceeding two thousand dollars; or

(*b*) with intent to defraud contravenes or fails to comply with any provision of this section shall be guilty of an offence under this Act and shall be liable on conviction to a fine not exceeding three thousand dollars or to imprisonment for a term not exceeding two years or to both such fine and imprisonment.

Purposes for which money may be withdrawn from trust account.

**38.** A dealer shall not withdraw any moneys from a trust account except for the purpose of making a payment—

(*a*) to the person entitled thereto; or

(*b*) [8]

(*c*) that is otherwise authorized by law.

Moneys in trust accounts not available for payment of debts, etc.

**39.** Save as otherwise provided in this Part, moneys held in a trust account shall not be available for payment of the debts of a dealer or be liable to be paid or taken in execution under an order or process of any court.

Claims and liens not affected.

**40.** Nothing in this Part shall be construed as taking away or affecting any lawful claim or lien which any person has against or upon any moneys held in a trust account or against or upon any moneys received for the purchase of securities or from the sale of securities before such moneys are paid into a trust account.

Dealer to appoint auditor.

**41.** A dealer shall appoint an auditor to audit his accounts and where for any reason the auditor ceases to hold that office the dealer shall within fourteen days appoint another auditor.

Dealer to lodge auditor's report.

**42.** (1) A dealer shall within six months of the end of the financial year lodge with the relevant authority an auditor's report containing information on such matters as are prescribed.

(2) If a dealer fails to comply with the provisions of subsection (1) the relevant authority shall forthwith report the matter to the Minister.

(3) For the purposes of subsection (1) "financial year" has the meaning assigned to that expression in the Companies Act.

Auditor to send report to relevant authority in certain cases.

**43.** Where in the performance of his duties as auditor for a dealer an auditor becomes aware of any matter which in his opinion may adversely affect the financial position of the dealer to a material extent or may constitute a breach of section 36, 37 or 38 he shall within seven

[8] Deleted by sec. 13 (*b*) of Act No. 6 of 1974, the Securities Industry (Amendment) Act, 1974.

days send a report in writing on such matter to the relevant authority and a copy thereof to the dealer.

Report of auditor to be forwarded to Minister in certain cases.

44. (1) If after consideration of an auditor's report furnished under section 43 the relevant authority is not satisfied—

*(a)* that the financial position of the dealer in respect of whom the report is made is such as to enable him to meet all his commitments as a dealer; and

*(b)* that the dealer has complied with the requirements of this Act,

the relevant authority shall, and for any other reason which it thinks proper, the relevant authority may, forward the said report to the Minister with any further report thereon which it thinks proper to make.

(2) It shall be a defence to any proceedings in defamation in respect of any statement made in any such report of an auditor or in any such further report of the relevant authority if the defendant satisfies the court that the statement was made *bona fide* and without malice.

Power of Minister to appoint independent auditor, etc.

45. (1) Where the Minister has received—

*(a)* a report under subsection (2) of section 42 from the relevant authority; or

*(b)* an auditor's report forwarded to him pursuant to section 44 by a relevant authority,

he may, if he is satisfied that it is in the interests of the dealer concerned, the dealer's clients or the public generally to do so, appoint in writing an independent auditor or such other person or body of persons as he may decide to examine, audit and report either generally or in relation to any particular matter upon the books, accounts and records of and securities held by the dealer.

(2) Where the Minister is of opinion that the whole or any part of the costs and expenses of an auditor appointed by him under this section and section 46 should be borne by the dealer or relevant authority concerned, he may, by order in writing, direct such dealer or relevant authority to pay a specified amount, being the whole or part of such costs and expenses, within the time and in the manner specified.

(3) Where a dealer or relevant authority has failed to comply with an order of the Minister under subsection (2) proceedings may be taken by the Minister in any court of competent jurisdiction to recover the amount in question as a civil debt recoverable summarily.

Power of Minister to appoint independent auditor, etc., upon application of client.

46. (1) Upon receipt of an application in writing from a person who alleges that a dealer has failed to account to him in respect of any moneys or securities held or received by that dealer for or on his behalf, the Minister may appoint in writing an independent auditor or such other person or body of persons as he may decide to examine, audit and report either generally or in relation to any particular matter upon the books, accounts and records of and securities held by that dealer.

(2) Every application under subsection (1) shall state—

(*a*) the particulars of the circumstances under which the dealer received the moneys or securities in respect of which he is alleged to have failed to account;

(*b*) the particulars of those moneys or securities and of the transactions of the applicant and the dealer relating thereto; and

(*c*) such other particulars as are prescribed.

(3) Every statement in any such application shall be verified by a statutory declaration made by the applicant and shall, if made *bona fide* and without malice, be privileged.

(4) The Minister shall not appoint an independent auditor, person or body of persons under subsection (1) unless he is satisfied—

(*a*) that the applicant has good reason for making the application; and

(*b*) that it is expedient in the interests of the dealer or the applicant or the public generally that the books, accounts and records of and securities held by the dealer should be examined, audited and reported upon.

Auditor, etc., to report to Minister.

47. An independent auditor, a person or body of persons, as the case may be, appointed by the Minister under section 45 or 46 shall, upon the conclusion of the examination and audit in respect of which he was appointed, make a report thereon to the Minister.

Powers of auditor, etc.

48. An independent auditor, a person or body of persons, as the case may be, appointed by the Minister to examine and audit the books, accounts and records of and securities held by a dealer may for the purpose of carrying out such examination and audit—

(*a*) examine on oath any director, manager or secretary of that dealer and any of the dealer's servants and agents and any other auditor appointed under this Act in relation to those books, accounts, records and securities;

(*b*) employ such persons as he considers necessary; and

(*c*) by instrument in writing under his hand authorize any person employed by him to do, in relation to such examination and audit, any act or thing that he could himself do in his capacity as auditor, except to examine any person on oath or to exercise the powers conferred by this paragraph.

**Prohibition against communication of certain matters by auditor, etc., and employees.**

49. Except for the purpose of carrying into effect the provisions of this Act, or so far as may be required for the purpose of any proceedings, civil or criminal, an independent auditor, a person or body of persons, as the case may be, appointed by the Minister under section 45 or 46 and an employee of any such auditor shall not communicate any matter which may come to his knowledge in the performance of his duties as such auditor or employee, to any person other than the Minister, or to the relevant authority in relation to the dealer concerned, or to any other person specified by the Minister or such relevant authority or, in the case of an employee, to any person other than the auditor by whom he is employed.

**Books, accounts and records to be produced upon demand.**

50. (1) Upon request by an independent auditor, a person or body of persons, as the case may be, appointed by the Minister under section 45 or 46 or by a person who produces a written authority in that behalf given under paragraph (*c*) of section 48—

(*a*) a director, manager or secretary of a dealer and the dealer's servants and agents shall produce any books, accounts, records and securities held by the dealer relating to his business; and

(*b*) an auditor appointed by a dealer shall produce any books, accounts and records held by him relating to the business of the dealer.

(2) A director, manager or secretary of a dealer and the dealer's servants and agents and any auditor appointed by the dealer, shall answer all questions relevant to an examination and audit which are put to him by an independent auditor, a person or body of persons, as the case may be, appointed by the Minister under section 45 or 46 or by a person who produces a written authority in that behalf given under paragraph (*c*) of section 48.

(3) Any person who contravenes or fails to comply with the provisions of subsection (1) or (2) shall be guilty of an offence under this Act and shall be liable on conviction to a fine not exceeding three thousand dollars or to imprisonment for a term not exceeding two years or to both such fine and imprisonment.

Penalty for destroying, concealing or altering records or sending records or other property out of Singapore.

**51.** (1) A person who, with intent to defeat the purposes of this Part or with intent to prevent, delay or obstruct the carrying out of any examination and audit under this Part—

*(a)* destroys, conceals or alters any book, account, record or document relating to the business of a dealer; or

*(b)* sends or attempts to send or conspires with any other person to send out of Singapore any such book, account, record or document or any property of any description belonging to or in the disposition of or under the control of a dealer,

shall be guilty of an offence under this Act and shall be liable on conviction to a fine not exceeding three thousand dollars or to imprisonment for a term not exceeding two years or to both such fine and imprisonment.

(2) If in a prosecution for an offence under subsection (1) it is proved that the person charged—

*(a)* destroyed, concealed or altered any book, account, record or document referred to in subsection (1); or

*(b)* sent or attempted to send or conspired to send out of Singapore any such book, account, record or document or any property referred to in subsection (1),

the onus of proving that in so doing he did not act with intent to defeat the purposes of this Part or with intent to prevent delay or obstruct the carrying out of an examination and audit under this Part shall lie on him.

Right of committee to impose obligations, etc., on member companies not affected by this Part.

**52.** Nothing contained in this Part shall prevent the committee of a stock exchange from imposing on the member companies any further obligations or requirements which the committee thinks fit with respect to—

*(a)* the audit of accounts;

*(b)* the information to be furnished in reports from auditors; or

*(c)* the keeping of accounts, books and records.

## PART VIII [9]

## PART IX. FIDELITY FUNDS

Interpretation.

**60.** In this Part, unless inconsistent with the context or subject-matter—

---

[9] Repealed by sec. 19 of Act No. 6 of 1974, the Securities Industry (Amendment) Act, 1974.

"committee", in relation to a fidelity fund of a stock exchange, means the committee of that stock exchange;

"Court" means the High Court;

"fidelity fund" or "fund" means a fidelity fund established under section 61;

"stock exchange" means, in relation to a fidelity fund, the stock exchange which established the fidelity fund.

**Establishment of fidelity funds.**

61. (1) A stock exchange shall establish and keep a fidelity fund which shall be administered by the committee on behalf of the stock exchange.

(2) The assets of a fidelity fund shall be the property of the stock exchange but shall be kept separate from all other property and shall be held in trust for the purposes set out in this Part.

**Moneys constituting fidelity fund.**

62. The fidelity fund of a stock exchange shall consist of—

*(a)* all moneys paid to the stock exchange by member companies in accordance with the provisions of this Part;

*(b)* [10]

*(c)* the interest and profits from time to time accruing from the investment of the fund;

*(d)* all moneys paid to the fund by the stock exchange;

*(e)* all moneys recovered by or on behalf of the stock exchange in the exercise of any right of action conferred by this Part;

*(f)* all moneys paid by an insurer pursuant to a contract of insurance or indemnity entered into by the committee of the stock exchange under section 82; and

*(g)* all other moneys lawfully paid into the fund.

**Fund to be kept in separate bank account.**

63. All moneys forming part of a fidelity fund shall, pending the investment or application thereof in accordance with this Part, be paid or transferred into a bank in Singapore.

**Payments out of fund.**

64. Subject to this Part, there shall from time to time be paid out of the fidelity fund of a stock exchange as required and in such order as the committee deems proper—

*(a)* the amount of all claims, including costs, allowed by the committee or established against the stock exchange under this Part;

*(b)* all legal and other expenses incurred in investigating or defending claims made under this Part or incurred in relation to the

[10] Deleted by sec. 20 *(b)* of Act No. 6 of 1974, the Securities Industry (Amendment) Act, 1974.

fund or in the exercise by the committee of the rights, powers and authorities vested in it by this Part in relation to the fund;

(*c*) all premiums payable in respect of contracts of insurance or indemnity entered into by the committee under section 82;

(*d*) the expenses incurred or involved in the administration of the fund including the salaries and wages of persons employed by the committee in relation thereto; and

(*e*) all other moneys payable out of the fund in accordance with the provisions of this Act.

Accounts of fund.

**65.** (1) A stock exchange shall establish and keep proper accounts of its fidelity fund and shall before the 31st day of March in each year cause a balance-sheet in respect of such accounts to be made out as at the preceding 30th day of June.

(2) The committee of the stock exchange shall appoint an auditor to audit the accounts of the fidelity fund.

(3) The auditor appointed by the committee shall regularly and fully audit the accounts of the fidelity fund and shall audit each balance-sheet and cause it to be laid before the committee not later than three months after the balance-sheet was made out.

Management sub-committee.

**66.** (1) The committee of a stock exchange may appoint a management sub-committee of not less than three and not more than five persons being members of the stock exchange, at least one of whom is also a member of the committee.

(2) The committee of a stock exchange may by resolution delegate to a sub-committee appointed by it under this section all or any of its powers, authorities and discretions under this Part (other than those under this section, section 69, subsections (3), (4) and (5) of section 72).

(3) Any power, authority or discretion so delegated may be exercised by members forming a majority of the sub-committee as if by this Part that power, authority or discretion had been conferred on a majority of the members of the sub-committee.

(4) Any such delegation may at any time in like manner be rescinded or varied.

(5) The committee of a stock exchange may at any time remove any member of a sub-committee appointed by it under this section and may fill any vacancy in the sub-committee howsoever arising.

67. (1) The fidelity fund of a stock exchange shall consist of an amount of not less than two million dollars, or such other sum as may by order be determined by the Minister from time to time, to be paid to the credit of the fund on the establishment of a stock exchange under this Act.

Fidelity fund to consist of an amount of two million dollars.

(2) The fidelity fund shall be increased by an annual payment into the fund of a sum that is equal to ten per cent or more of the net income of a stock exchange for any one financial year.

68. If the fidelity fund is reduced below the sum of two million dollars or such other sum as the Minister may, by order, determine, the committee shall take steps to make up the deficiency—

Provisions if fund is reduced below two million dollars.

*(a)* by transferring an amount that is equal to the deficiency from other funds of a stock exchange to the fidelity fund; or

*(b)* in the event that there are insufficient funds to transfer under paragraph *(a)*, by determining the amount which each member company shall contribute to the fund.

69. (1) If at any time a fidelity fund is not sufficient to satisfy the liabilities that are then ascertained of the stock exchange in relation thereto, the committee may impose on every member company a levy of such amount as it thinks fit.

Levy to meet liabilities.

(2) The amount of such levy shall be paid within the time and in the manner specified by the committee either generally or in relation to any particular case.

(3) No member company shall be required to pay by way of levy under this section more than one hundred thousand dollars in the aggregate.

70. (1) A stock exchange may from time to time from its general funds give or advance on such terms as the committee thinks fit any sums of money to its fidelity fund.

Power of stock exchange to make advances to fund.

(2) Any moneys advanced under subsection (1) may from time to time be repaid from the fidelity fund to the general funds of the stock exchange.

71. Any moneys in a fidelity fund that are not immediately required for its purposes may be invested by the committee in any manner in which trustees are for the time being authorized by law to invest trust funds.

Investment of fund.

Application of fund.

72. (1) Subject to this Part, a fidelity fund shall be held and applied for the purpose of compensating persons who suffer pecuniary loss from any defalcation committed by a member company or any of its directors or by any of the clerks or servants of such a member company in relation to any money or other property which, whether before or after the date of the coming into operation of this Act, in the course of or in connection with the business of that company—

*(a)* was entrusted to or received by a member company or any of its directors or any of the company's clerks or servants for or on behalf of any other person; or

*(b)* (the member company being in respect of the money or other property either the sole trustee or trustees or trustee or trustees with any other person or persons) was entrusted to or received by the member company or any of its directors or any of the company's clerks or servants as trustee or trustees or for or on behalf of the trustees of that money or property.

(2) Save as otherwise provided in this section, the total amount that may be paid under this Part to all persons who suffer loss through defalcations by a member company or any of its directors or through defalcations by any of the company's clerks or servants shall not, in any event, exceed in respect of that member company the sum of one hundred thousand dollars, but for the purposes of this subsection any amount paid from a fidelity fund shall to the extent to which the fund is subsequently reimbursed therefor be disregarded.

(3) *(a)* If, after taking into account all ascertained or contingent liabilities of a fidelity fund, the committee considers that the assets of the fund so permit, the committee may decide to increase the total amount which may be applied from that fund pursuant to the provisions of subsection (2) and shall inform the Registrar accordingly who shall then cause notice of such decision to be published in the *Gazette.*

*(b)* From the date of the publication until the notice is revoked or varied the amount specified in the notice shall be the total amount which may be applied as aforesaid.

(4) Where the committee decides to revoke or vary the notice under subsection (3), the committee shall inform the Registrar accordingly, who shall then cause notice of such revocation or variation to be published in the *Gazette*; and a notice which is so varied shall have effect accordingly.

(5) If, in any particular case after taking into account all ascertained or contingent liabilities of a fidelity fund, the committee considers that

the assets of the fund so permit the committee may apply out of the fund such sum in excess of the total amount limited by or under this section as the committee in its absolute discretion thinks fit in or towards the compensation of persons who have suffered pecuniary loss as provided in subsection (1).

(6) For the purposes of this section "director of a member company" includes a person who has been, but at the time of any defalcation in question has ceased to be a director of a member company if, at the time of the defalcation, the person claiming compensation has reasonable grounds for believing that person to be a director of a member company.

**As to claims against fund.**

73. (1) Subject to this Part, every person who suffers pecuniary loss as provided in subsection (1) of section 72 shall be entitled to claim compensation from the fidelity fund and to take proceedings in the Court as provided in this Act against the stock exchange to establish such claim.

(2) Subject to subsection (3), a person shall in no case have any claim against the fidelity fund in respect of—

(*a*) a defalcation committed before the date of the coming into operation of this Act; or

(*b*) a defalcation in respect of money or other property which prior to the commission of the defalcation had in the due course of the administration of a trust ceased to be under the sole control of the director or directors of the member company concerned.

(3) Upon the dissolution of the Stock Exchange of Malaysia Members' Fidelity Guarantee Fund (in this section referred to as "the Fund") maintained pursuant to the articles of association of a stock exchange, known as the Stock Exchange of Malaysia and Singapore, the amount in the Fund that, under the terms of the dissolution, is paid to the Singapore members of the Fund shall be transferred to and become part of the fidelity fund of a stock exchange established under section 61.

(4) Nothing in this section shall affect the liability of the Fund to meet, in the manner and to the extent provided by the articles of association of the Stock Exchange of Malaysia and Singapore, claims against the Fund arising before the date of dissolution.

(5) Subject to this Part, the amount which any claimant shall be entitled to claim as compensation from a fidelity fund shall be the

amount of the actual pecuniary loss suffered by him (including the reasonable costs of and disbursements incidental to the making and proof of his claim) less the amount or value of all moneys or other benefits received or receivable by him from any source other than the fund in reduction of the loss.

(6) In addition to any compensation payable under this Part interest shall be payable out of the fidelity fund concerned on the amount of the compensation, less any amount attributable to costs and disbursements, at the rate of five per centum per annum calculated from the day upon which the defalcation was committed and continuing until the day upon which the claim is satisfied.

Rights of innocent partner in relation to fund.

74.[11]

Notice calling for claims against fund.

75. (1) The committee of a stock exchange may cause to be published in a daily newspaper published and circulating generally in Singapore a notice, in or to the effect of the form prescribed, specifying a date, not being earlier than three months after the said publication, on or before which claims for compensation from the fidelity fund, in relation to the person specified in the notice, may be made.

(2) A claim for compensation from a fidelity fund in respect of a defalcation shall be made in writing to the committee—

*(a)* where a notice under subsection (1) has been published on or before the date specified in the said notice; or

*(b)* where no such notice has been published within six months after the claimant became aware of the defalcation,

and any claim which is not so made shall be barred unless the committee otherwise determines.

(3) No action for damages shall lie against a stock exchange or against any member or employee of a stock exchange or of a committee or management sub-committee by reason of any notice published in good faith and without malice for the purposes of this section.

Power of committee to settle claims.

76. (1) The committee may, subject to this Part, allow and settle any proper claim for compensation from a fidelity fund at any time after the commission of the defalcation in respect of which the claim arose.

[11] Repealed by sec. 27 of Act No. 6 of 1974, the Securities Industry (Amendment) Act, 1974.

(2) Subject to subsection (3), a person shall not commence proceedings under this Part against a stock exchange without leave of the committee unless—

*(a)* the committee has disallowed his claim; and

*(b)* the claimant has exhausted all relevant rights of action and other legal remedies for recovery of the money or other property in respect of which the defalcation was committed available against the member company in relation to whom or to which the claim arose and all other persons liable in respect of the loss suffered by the claimant.

(3) A person who has been refused leave by a committee may apply for leave to a judge of the Court in chambers who may make such order in the matter as he thinks fit.

(4) The committee after disallowing (whether wholly or partly) any claim for compensation from a fidelity fund shall serve notice of such disallowance in the prescribed form on the claimant or his solicitor.

(5) No proceedings against a stock exchange in respect of a claim which has been disallowed by the committee shall be commenced after the expiration of three months after service of notice of disallowance under subsection (4).

(6) In any proceedings brought to establish a claim evidence of any admission or confession by or other evidence which would be admissible against the member company or other person by whom it is alleged a defalcation was committed shall be admissible to prove the commission of the defalcation notwithstanding that the member company or other person is not the defendant in or a party to those proceedings, and all defences which would have been available to that member company or person shall be available to the stock exchange.

(7) The committee or, where proceedings are brought to establish a claim, the Court, if satisfied that the defalcation on which the claim is founded was actually committed, may allow the claim and act accordingly, notwithstanding that the person who committed the defalcation has not been convicted or prosecuted therefor or that the evidence on which the committee or Court (as the case may be) acts would not be sufficient to establish the guilt of that person upon a criminal trial in respect of the defalcation.

Form of order of Court establishing claim.

77. (1) Where in any proceedings brought to establish a claim the Court is satisfied that the defalcation on which the claim is founded was actually committed and that otherwise the claimant has a valid claim the Court shall by order—

(*a*) declare the fact and the date of the defalcation and the amount of the claim; and

(*b*) direct that the committee concerned allow the claim as so declared and deal with the same in accordance with the provisions of this Part.

(2) The Rules Committee may make rules for or with respect to practice and procedure generally upon proceedings under this Part.

(3) In any such proceedings all questions of costs shall be in the discretion of the Court.

Power of committee to require production of securities, etc.

78. The committee may at any time and from time to time require any person to produce and deliver any securities, documents or statements of evidence necessary to support any claim made or necessary for the purpose either of exercising its rights against a member company or the directors thereof or any other person concerned or of enabling criminal proceedings to be taken against any person in respect of a defalcation, and in default of delivery of any such securities, documents or statements of evidence by such first-mentioned person, the committee may disallow any claim by him under this Part.

Subrogation of stock exchange to rights, etc., of claimant upon payment from fund.

79. On payment out of a fidelity fund of any moneys in respect of any claim under this Part the stock exchange shall be subrogated to the extent of such payment to all the rights and remedies of the claimant in relation to the loss suffered by him from the defalcation.

Payment of claims only from fund.

80. No moneys or other property belonging to a stock exchange other than the fidelity fund shall be available for the payment of any claim under this Part whether the claim is allowed by the committee or is made the subject of an order of the Court.

Provision where fund insufficient to meet claims or where claims exceed total amount payable.

81. (1) Where the amount at credit in a fidelity fund is insufficient to pay the whole amount of all claims against it which have been allowed or in respect of which orders of the Court have been made as aforesaid, then the amount at credit in the fund shall, subject to the provisions of subsection (2) be apportioned between the claimants in such manner as the committee thinks equitable, and any such claim so far as it then remains unpaid shall be charged against future receipts of the fund and paid out of the fund when moneys are available therein.

(2) Where the aggregate of all claims which have been allowed or in respect of which orders of the Court have been made (as aforesaid)

in relation to defalcations by or in connection with a member company exceeds the total amount which may pursuant to subsection (2) of section 72 be paid under this Part in respect of that member company then the said total amount shall be apportioned between the claimants in such manner as the committee thinks equitable, and upon payment out of the fund of the said total amount in accordance with such apportionment of all such claims and any orders relating thereto and all other claims against the fund which may thereafter arise or be made in respect of defalcations by or in connection with the said company shall be absolutely discharged.

Power of committee to enter into contracts of insurance.

82. (1) A stock exchange may in its discretion enter into any contract with any person or body of persons, corporate or unincorporate, carrying on fidelity insurance business in Singapore whereby the stock exchange will be insured or indemnified to the extent and in the manner provided by such contract against liability in respect of claims under this Part.

(2) Any such contract may be entered into in relation to member companies generally, or in relation to any particular member company or member companies named therein, or in relation to member companies generally with the exclusion of any particular member company or member companies named therein.

(3) No action shall lie against a stock exchange or against any member or servant of a stock exchange or the committee or against any member of a management sub-committee for injury alleged to have been suffered by any member company by reason of the publication in good faith of a statement that any contract entered into under this section does or does not apply with respect to it.

Application of insurance moneys.

83. No claimant against a fidelity fund shall have any right of action against any person or body of persons with whom a contract of insurance or indemnity is made under this Part in respect of such contract, or have any right or claim with respect to any moneys paid by the insurer in accordance with any such contract.

## PART X. TRADING IN SECURITIES

False trading and markets.

84. (1) It shall be unlawful for any person directly or indirectly for the purpose of creating a false or misleading appearance of active trading in any securities on any stock market in Singapore or a false or misleading appearance with respect to the market for any such securities—

(*a*) to effect any transaction in such securities which involves no change in the beneficial ownership thereof;

(*b*) to enter an order or orders for the purchase of such securities with the knowledge that an order or orders of substantially the same size, at substantially the same time and at substantially the same price, for the sale of any securities, has or have been or will be entered by or for the same or different parties; or

(*c*) to enter any order or orders for the sale of such securities with the knowledge that an order or orders of substantially the same size, at substantially the same time and at substantially the same price, for the purchase of such securities, has or have been or will be entered by or for the same or different parties.

(2) A transaction in securities involves no change in the beneficial ownership thereof within the meaning of paragraph *(a)* of subsection (1) if a person who held an interest in the securities before the transaction or a person associated with the first-mentioned person in relation to the securities holds an interest in the securities after the transaction.

(3) In determining whether a person held or holds an interest within the meaning of subsection (2), the provisions of section 6A of the Companies Act shall have effect and in applying those provisions any reference to shares shall be read as a reference to securities.

(4) For the purposes of subsection (2) a person is associated with another person in relation to securities if the first-mentioned person is—

(*a*) a corporation that by virtue of section 6 of the Companies Act is deemed to be related to that other person;

(*b*) a person in accordance with whose directions, instructions or wishes that other person is accustomed or likely to act in relation to the securities;

(*c*) a person who is accustomed or likely to act in accordance with the directions, instructions or wishes of that other person in relation to the securities;

(*d*) a body corporate that is or the directors of which are accustomed or likely to act in accordance with the directions, instructions or wishes of that other person in relation to the securities; or

(*e*) a body corporate in accordance with the directions, instructions or wishes of which or of the directors of which that other person is accustomed or likely to act in relation to the securities.

**Market rigging transactions.**

85. (1) It shall be unlawful for any person directly or indirectly to effect a series of transactions in any securities on a stock market in Singapore creating actual or apparent active trading in such securities for the purpose of inducing the purchase or sale of such securities by others.

(2) It shall be a defence to a prosecution under subsection (1) if the defendant satisfies the Court that he acted without malice and solely to further or protect his own lawful interests.

**Inducement to purchase or sell securities by dissemination of information.**

86. It shall be unlawful for a dealer, stockbroker or other person who is selling or offering for sale, or purchasing or offering to purchase any securities, whether in consideration or anticipation of a reward or benefit, or otherwise to induce a purchase or sale of such securities on a stock market in Singapore by the circulation or dissemination in the ordinary course of business of information to the effect that the price of any such securities will or is likely to rise or fall because of market operations by any one or more persons, conducted for the purpose of raising or depressing the price of such securities.

**Employment of manipulative and deceptive devices.**

87. It shall be unlawful for any person directly or indirectly in connection with the purchase or sale of any securities—

*(a)* to employ any device, scheme or artifice to defraud;

*(b)* to engage in any act, practice or course of business which operates or would operate as a fraud or deceit upon any person; or

*(c)* to make any untrue statement of a material fact or to omit to state a material fact necessary in order to make the statements made in the light of the circumstances under which they were made, not misleading.

**Penalty.**

88. Any person who contravenes any provision of this Part shall be guilty of an offence under this Act and shall be liable on conviction to a fine not exceeding thirty thousand dollars or to imprisonment for a term not exceeding five years or to both such fine and imprisonment.

## PART XI. GENERAL

**Restrictions on use of title "stockbroker".**

89. A person who is not a stockbroker within the meaning of this Act shall not take or use or, by inference, adopt the name or title of stockbroker or take or use or have attached to or exhibited at any place any name, title or description implying or tending to the belief that he is a stockbroker.

Inspection of books and records of licence holder and others.

**90.** (1) For the purpose of ascertaining whether the holder of a licence has complied with the provisions of this Act applicable to him in that capacity, and any conditions or restrictions subject to which the licence was granted or renewed, the Registrar may inspect and make copies of or take extracts from—

*(a)* any document, record or matter required by or under this Act or the conditions of the licence to be kept by the holder of that licence; and

*(b)* the books of a person, in so far as they relate to the business of the holder of that licence.

(2) The Registrar may, where he considers it necessary for the protection of investors, require any person to disclose to him in relation to any purchase or sale of securities the name of the person from or to or through whom the securities were bought or sold and the nature of the instructions given to the person in respect of that purchase or sale.

(3) The holder of a licence under this Act, and the servants and agents of that person shall, on being required by the Registrar so to do, produce any document, record or matter referred to in subsection (1) or disclose the information required under subsection (2).

(4) No person shall obstruct or hinder the Registrar in the exercise of any of his powers under this section or obstruct any person in the exercise of any of those powers that he is duly authorised to exercise.

(5) Where the Registrar has reason to suspect that any person has contravened any of the provisions of this Act or has been guilty of any fraud or offence under this or any other Act or law with respect to trading or dealing in securities, the Registrar may make such investigation as he thinks expedient for the due administration of this Act.

(6) Notwithstanding anything in this section, the Minister may, where it appears to him in the public interest so to do, appoint any person as an inspector to investigate any matter concerning trading or dealing in securities.

(7) Except where otherwise expressly provided by or under this or any other Act, any power, authority, duty or function conferred or imposed by or under this or any other Act on the Registrar may be exercised or performed by any person authorised by the Registrar to exercise or perform that power, authority, duty or function.

Court may make certain orders.

**91.** (1) Where, on the application of the Registrar, it appears to the High Court that a person has contravened this Act or any conditions of a licence he holds or is about to do an act with respect to dealing or trading in securities that, if done, would be such a contravention, the Court may, without prejudice to any orders it would be entitled to make otherwise than pursuant to this section, make one or more of the following orders:

(*a*) in the case of persistent or continuing breaches of this Act or of the conditions of a licence he holds, an order restraining a person from carrying on a business as a dealer in securities, or as a dealer's representative or from holding himself out as so carrying on business or acting;

(*b*) an order restraining a person from acquiring, disposing of or otherwise dealing with any securities specified in the order;

(*c*) an order appointing a receiver of the property of a dealer;

(*d*) an order declaring a contract relating to securities to be void or voidable;

(*e*) for the purpose of securing compliance with any other order under this section, an order directing a person to do or refrain from doing a specified act; or

(*f*) any ancillary order deemed to be desirable in consequence of the making of an order under paragraph (*a*), (*b*), (*c*), (*d*) or (*e*).

(2) The Court shall, before making an order under subsection (1), satisfy itself, so far as it can reasonably do so, that the order would not unfairly prejudice any person.

(3) The Court may, before making an order under subsection (1), direct that notice of the application be given to such persons as it thinks fit or direct that notice of the application be published in such manner as it thinks fit, or both.

(4) Any person who contravenes or fails to comply with an order under subsection (1) that is applicable to him shall be guilty of an offence under this Act and shall be liable on conviction to a fine of three thousand dollars or to imprisonment for a term not exceeding one year or to both such fine and imprisonment.

(5) Subsection (4) does not affect the powers of the Court in relation to the punishment of contempts of the Court.

(6) The Court may rescind, vary or discharge an order made by it under this section or suspend the operation of such an order.

Production and inspection of books where offence suspected.

92. (1) If, on an application made to a judge of the High Court in chambers by the Registrar, there is shown to be reasonable cause to believe that any person has committed an offence in connection with trading or dealing in securities and that evidence of the commission

of the offence is to be found in any books or papers of or under the control of a dealer an order may be made—

(*a*) authorizing the Registrar to inspect those books or papers or any of them and make copies thereof or take extracts therefrom for the purpose of investigating and obtaining evidence of the offence; or

(*b*) requiring the dealer or such other person as is named in the order to produce those books or papers or any of them to a person named in the order at a place so named.

(2) An order under this section shall not require books or papers to be produced at a place other than the place of business of the person named in the order unless the Court is satisfied that the books or papers are not required in the conduct of the business or that there are special reasons requiring the books or papers to be produced at some other place.

General penalty.

93. (1) A person who contravenes or fails to comply with any provision of this Act shall be guilty of an offence under this Act and, where no penalty is expressly provided, shall be liable on conviction to a fine not exceeding two thousand dollars.

(2) Where a person, being a corporation, is guilty of an offence under this Act any director, manager, secretary or other officer of the corporation who was knowingly a party to the offence shall also be guilty of that offence.

Convicted persons liable to pay compensation.

94. A person who is convicted of an offence under Part X shall be liable to pay compensation to any person who has purchased or sold any securities at a price affected by the act or transaction, the subject of the offence, for the damage suffered by him as a result of that purchase or sale.

Proceedings by whom and when to be taken.

95. (1) Proceedings for an offence—

(*a*) against any provision of Part X may be taken only with the consent of the Attorney-General; and

(*b*) against any other provision of this Act may be taken by the Registrar or, with the consent of the Attorney-General, by any other person.

(2) The Registrar may, without instituting proceedings against any person for an offence under this Act or the regulations made thereunder which is punishable only by a fine, demand and receive the amount of such fine or such reduced amount as he thinks fit from such person, whereupon—

(a) if such person pays such amount to the Registrar within fourteen days after the demand no proceedings shall be taken against him in relation to the offence;

(b) if such person does not pay the amount so demanded, the Registrar may cause proceedings to be instituted in relation to the offence.

96. (1) The Minister may make regulations for or with respect to— **Regulations.**

(a) prescribing forms for the purposes of this Act;

(b) prescribing fees to be paid in respect of any matter or thing required for the purposes of this Act;

(c) the issue of and contents of contract notes;

(d) the preparation by dealers of balance-sheets and profit and loss accounts and the form and contents thereof;

(e) the specification of manipulative and deceptive devices and contrivances in connection with the purchase or sale of securities that are prohibited;

(f) the regulation or prohibition of the sale of securities by a person who is not and is not entitled to become the holder of those securities;

(g) the regulation or prohibition of trading on the floor of a stock exchange by stockbrokers or their representatives directly or indirectly for their own accounts or for discretionary accounts and the prevention of such excessive trading on a stock exchange but off the floor of a stock exchange by stockbrokers or their representatives directly or indirectly for their own accounts as the Minister may consider is detrimental to the maintenance of a fair and orderly market. Regulations under this paragraph may provide for the exemption of such transactions as the Minister may decide to be necessary in the public interest or for the protection of investors;

(h) the regulation of borrowing in the ordinary course of business by dealers and stockbrokers as the Minister may consider necessary or appropriate in the public interest or for the protection of investors;

(i) regulating the publication of advertisements offering the services of dealers or offering securities for purchase or sale and the form and content of such advertisements; and

(j) all matters or things which by this Act are required or permitted to be prescribed or which are necessary or expedient to be prescribed to give effect to this Act.

(2) Save as otherwise expressly provided in this Act, the regulations—

(a) may be of general or specifically limited application; and

(b) may impose a fine of not more than two thousand dollars or imprisonment for a term not exceeding one year or both such fine and imprisonment for any contravention thereof.

97. The Securities Industry Act, 1970 is hereby repealed.

98.[12]

[12] Repealed by sec. 11 of Act No. 51 of 1973, the Securities Industry (Amendment) Act, 1973.